The Illustrated Encyclopedia of
BIRDS

The
Illustrated
Encyclopedia
of
BIRDS

THE DEFINITIVE REFERENCE
TO BIRDS OF THE WORLD

Consultant-in-Chief Dr. CHRISTOPHER M. PERRINS

In association with

INTERNATIONAL COUNCIL FOR BIRD PRESERVATION

PRENTICE
HALL
EDITIONS

New York · London · Toronto · Sydney · Tokyo · Singapore

PRENTICE HALL PRESS
15 Columbus Circle
New York, NY 10023

List of species derived from *A Complete Checklist of Birds of the World* by Richard Howard and Alick Moore, © Richard Howard and Alick Moore 1980, 1984, 1990

Migration diagram on pp. 30–31
© Harrow House Editions, a division of Time Life International Limited, London.

Originally published in Great Britain.

This book was conceived, edited and designed by Marshall Editions
170 Piccadilly, London W1V 9DD

PRENTICE HALL EDITIONS is an imprint of Prentice Hall Press.

PRENTICE HALL PRESS and colophons are registered trademarks of Simon & Schuster Inc.

Library of Congress Cataloging-in-Publication Data

The Illustrated encyclopedia of birds: The definitive reference to birds of the world / consultant-in-chief, Christopher M. Perrins.
    p.   cm.
  ISBN 0-13-083635-4
  1. Birds.   I. Perrins, Christopher M.
QL673.I45 1991
598—dc20

Typeset by MS Filmsetting Limited, Frome, Somerset

Originated and printed by Arnoldo Mondadori, Vicenza, Italy

10 9 8 7 6 5 4 3 2 1

First Prentice Hall Press Edition

Consultant-in Chief
Dr. Christopher M. Perrins
Director, The Edward Grey Institute for Ornithology,
University of Oxford

U.S. Consultant
Dr. Jerome A. Jackson
Professor of Biological Sciences and Curator of Mammals,
Mississippi State University

Australian Consultant
Dr. Hugh Ford
Senior Lecturer, Department of Zoology,
University of New England, Armidale, New South Wales

EDITOR	**Jonathan Elphick**
MANAGING DIRECTOR	**Ruth Binney**
EDITORIAL COORDINATORS	**Lindsay McTeague**
	Corinne Wilson
EDITORIAL ASSISTANTS	**Roger Few**
	John Woodward
	Rick Morris
	Barbara Fuller
	Fred Gill
	Carol Hupping
ART DIRECTOR	**John Bigg**
ART EDITOR	**Daphne Mattingly**
DESIGN ASSISTANT	**Jonathan Bigg**
PICTURE COORDINATOR	**Zilda Tandy**
ILLUSTRATION AUTHENTICATOR	**Alan Greensmith**
RESEARCH	**Jazz Wilson**
INDEX	**Kathie Gill**
PRODUCTION	**Barry Baker**
	Janice Storr
	Nikki Ingram

CONTENTS

From the earliest times, birds have captured the imagination of people the world over. Their flight, songs, colors, displays and migrations are among the world's most compelling natural wonders. Sadly though, of the 9,300 species listed in this fine book, over one thousand are now under sentence of death as a result of habitat loss, human exploitation and greed.

In the last four hundred years, our planet has lost about one hundred bird species. Many of these occurred in isolated ecosystems where they could not cope with feral animals introduced there. Some were hunted out of existence. A few were lost because of the destruction of rain forest. But in recent decades an escalating rate of destruction of bird habitat, especially of tropical forest and wetlands, has threatened massive extinction of bird species. Exponential growth in human population, in the consumption of resources, and in the degradation of the environment is the cause. Although the world has both the knowledge and the resources to reverse today's threatening trends, the will to do so has been lacking. Each of us can make a difference.

As President of the International Council for Bird Preservation (ICBP), I would like you to ask yourself this question as you read through these pages: what would our world be like if we were to lose a thousand of the bird species listed in this volume? At present we can only guess at what the total long-term biological cost of this tragedy might be. For example, for each bird species, we are also likely to lose around 35 species of plants and 90 species of insects, some of which may contain genetic material from which new pharmaceuticals or crop strains could be synthesized. What this may mean for the biosphere is largely unknown. One thing is certain though. We humans are the cause of this problem, and only we can provide the solution.

ICBP currently has more than 60 field and research projects under way, and is providing solutions to the most pressing of the world's bird conservation problems. ICBP's field program is managed by a team of professional conservationists working around the world. Our projects include species rescue missions, habitat management plans, education programs and scientific surveys. ICBP also supports the development of nature conservation groups, publishes conservation manuals, conducts media campaigns to highlight problems of critical importance, and advises governments and agencies on development policy and practice. The protection of key tropical forest areas, wetlands and oceanic islands are central elements of ICBP's program, always with an emphasis on the sustainable development of natural resources.

For the one thousand bird species currently under threat, ICBP, its constituent organizations and its individual members around the world provide hope of survival. To preserve the quality of all life on earth, these birds must be saved. There could be no better advocate for such a message than this book.

Russ Peterson

Dr. Russell W. Peterson
President
International Council for Bird Preservation

The world is inhabited by more than nine thousand species of birds, and no group of animals – even the mammals such as ourselves – arouses our interest so much. Their colors, songs and conspicuousness combine to make birds the ideal objects for study and aesthetic appreciation. The way in which many of them come to feeding tables put out for them in winter makes it easy for us to observe their antics. But their attractive nature does not merely make them fun to watch. The ways in which they have been observed have meant that professional zoologists have also turned to them for study, and this study has, in turn, led the way to our understanding of many aspects of the natural world, including taxonomy, behavior and ecology.

Sadly, with the increasing changes that humans are bringing to our environment, some of these studies have taken on a new urgency. Pollution, the introduction of pests, overhunting and, above all, habitat destruction, have had a serious effect on the populations of many bird species. Currently, about one thousand – more than one in ten of the world's bird species – are considered by the International Council for Bird Preservation (ICBP) to be threatened or endangered.

Probably more than a hundred bird species have been exterminated since the early days of recorded exploration of the globe in the seventeenth century. And there is growing evidence to suggest that the spread of peoples around the world even earlier than this, especially the spread through the Pacific islands, may have wiped out many more before written records were kept. For example the ancestors of the Maoris exterminated all the moas in New Zealand – at least 12 species.

We urgently need to know more about birds and their habitat requirements in order to be able to afford them the protection they need. Habitat protection is particularly imperative because many species have very special requirements as far as their living conditions are concerned. If we can protect the habitats essential to the survival of these birds, not only may we save for future generations many of the currently threatened species, but we will also save countless thousands of other animals and plants which live in and comprise these same habitats.

We hope that this book will increase our understanding of this irreplaceable part of our natural heritage. It is not possible, of course, to describe and illustrate every one of the 9,300 species, but every family of living birds is represented and we have endeavored to describe a variety of species from each. Birds have been selected to provide typical examples from throughout each family's range and to cover some of the more unusual or endangered species. More than 40 experts and 15 artists were commissioned to help with this major task. If this book's publication contributes in any way to the growing awareness of the need for greater environmental responsibility on the part of humans, then all concerned will feel that their efforts have been worthwhile.

Dr. Christopher M. Perrins
Director
Edward Grey Institute for Ornithology, University of Oxford

Birds, for all their wonderful diversity, are animals that are remarkably similar in basic body plan and biology. Essentially, they are creatures built for flight, and the way that their bodies are constructed and operate reflects this outstanding unifying feature.

The skeleton

Although the skeletons of birds are constructed on the same general lines as those of most other vertebrates, there are a number of significant differences, which are particularly associated with flight. The avian skeleton consists of a strong central "box" of bones, with attachments: the head and the neck, and the wings, legs and feet. The central box is similar in concept to the structural engineer's box girder. At the upper surface is the lumbar or thoracic part of the backbone, short compared with that of most mammals and often with the stout vertebrae almost fused into a solid rod. Toward the rear, it becomes part of an elongated and strong pelvic girdle. The lower surface of the box girder is formed by the massive sternum or breastbone which, except in flightless birds, is deeply keeled or ridged to support the huge flight muscles.

The lumbar backbone and sternum are joined by a series of flattened ribs, which are fixed at both ends and form the sides of the box girder. For extra strength, the avian rib possesses a special feature, an uncinate process, which protrudes rearward like a spur from each rib, and overlaps the rib or ribs behind it. Within this robust box, the bulk of the bird's vital organs are well protected. And so long and strong is the bird's sternum, that the abdominal area vulnerable to damage in an accident, a heavy fall or a fight is minimal.

In predominantly aquatic diving birds, such as the auks, the bone structure may be heavier to offset buoyancy that would make diving difficult. The box girder is so rigid that it protects the internal organs during dives to depths of 160 feet (50 meters) below the ocean.

The muscles of flight

The most conspicuous and characteristic muscles attached to a bird's skeleton are the massive ones that power its flight. These are located on each side of the keel of the breastbone and there are two muscles on each side.

The large outer muscle, the pectoralis, is attached via strong ligaments to the innermost long bone of the wing, the humerus, and provides the pull for the propulsive downbeat of the wing. To raise the wing for the next flap demands less energy, because the feathers twist and flex. Thus the raising muscle, the supracoracoideus, is smaller. The main lifting tendon operates through a "pulley" system, running behind the coracoid bone and then up and over the front of the shoulder blade, or scapula, and back down onto the humerus.

The power of flight

Birds are not the only creatures that can fly, but they are unique in being clad with feathers – no bird is devoid of a feather covering. Feathers are formed in special cells in a bird's skin from the protein keratin which also makes up the body scales on reptiles.

Feathers serve a variety of purposes. The smooth outline of the bodies of almost all birds is due to the structure and arrangement of the body, or contour, feathers. These provide efficient streamlining while being windproof and, sometimes, waterproof. Beneath this sleek exterior are the down feathers which help to maintain the body temperature. The tail feathers (rectrices) are normally comparatively long and strong. In flight they provide stability and assistance to the wings in steering; they also help in braking during landing.

Most of a bird's feathers can be moved to some degree by muscles in the skin: those of the tail are particularly mobile. It is the various wing feathers of a bird that have the greatest influence on flight. There are two essential components to flight: propulsion and lift. Propulsion is provided by the "primary" feathers, usually from 9 to 11 in number, and the outermost feathers in the wing. These are normally long and strong, firm yet flexible, since they must push air back and down to provide forward motion on the downbeat, yet allow air to pass easily between them on the upbeat. Each overlaps the next in a venetian-blind arrangement, with the narrower leading edge vane of each feather overlying the broad rear vane of the next feather out in the wing.

Much of the lift, the force counteracting gravity and keeping the bird airborne, is produced by the innermost section of the wing, carrying the large secondary and tertial feathers and their much smaller coverts. As in an aircraft wing, these feathers form an airfoil in cross-section, with a convex upper surface and a concave lower one. As this section of wing moves through the air, propelled by the thrust from the primary feathers, air moves faster over the longer upper surface than the shorter lower one. This creates a pressure difference between the two surfaces – the high-speed air being at lower pressure – and this, in turn, produces an upward force, lift.

This simple principle is complicated by the fact that the wing also provides resistance to the air, causing "drag" which slows the bird down. The propulsive force of the wing beat must overcome both drag and gravity if the bird is to move forward and stay aloft. Both lift and drag are increased by changing the "angle of attack" (the angle of the wing to the air). At very low speeds or high angles of attack, the air can become turbulent and lift is lost.

How a bird's wing works

The wing of a hummingbird, set in a socket allowing movement in almost any direction, is one of the most efficient organs of flight in the animal kingdom. It enables the bird to fly forward, sideways, up and down, to hover

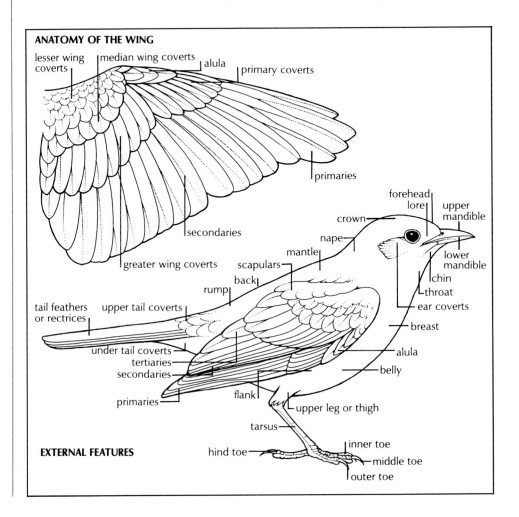

ANATOMY OF THE WING

lesser wing coverts | median wing coverts | alula | primary coverts | primaries | secondaries | greater wing coverts

EXTERNAL FEATURES

forehead | lore | upper mandible | crown | nape | mantle | lower mandible | chin | throat | ear coverts | breast | alula | belly | scapulars | back | rump | tail feathers or rectrices | upper tail coverts | under tail coverts | tertiaries | secondaries | primaries | flank | upper leg or thigh | tarsus | hind toe | inner toe | middle toe | outer toe stationary, and even to fly backward. At the other extreme, the wing of the flightless Ostrich *Struthio camelus*, though much reduced, is used in display, as a cooling fan, and in helping balance during fast running.

Between these extremes are numerous other wing designs, evolved and adapted to the lifestyle of the bird – and often critical to the way in which a bird is classified. Many small and medium-sized passerines have medium-length wings with the primaries set in a triangle – a "general purpose" layout. Obviously evolved to a more specialized life are the slim, sickle-shaped wings of the swallows and swifts, fast-flying, highly aerial birds. The broad, long wings of eagles and vultures, often with deeply slotted tips, allow these birds to soar with minimum energy expenditure on rising hot air currents. The long, slim wings of the albatrosses and shearwaters perform a similar function in the very different wind conditions that prevail over the stormy open oceans. Short, rounded wings, often deeply slotted at the tips, facilitate speedy take-off and high maneuverability. They are characteristic of the gamebirds and the forest-dwelling hawks.

Like the rest of a bird's skeleton, the wing bones must not only be lightweight but must also be strong enough to take the considerable stresses produced by flight. In some larger birds, such as albatrosses and vultures, the long bones are hollow, but with bony cross-struts of a "Warren girder" pattern familiar to structural engineers. The wings are anchored to the body through a complex pectoral (shoulder) girdle, considerably different in layout and appreciably stronger than in most mammals. Slim shoulder blades lie alongside the backbone and are bound to this and the ribs by short, strong ligaments. They meet the coracoids to form the socket where the wing is attached, and are braced together across the front of the breast by the two collar bones, which are fused together at their other ends to form the *V*-shaped "wishbone."

The layout of bones in the wing resembles that of a mammal arm. The humerus, or upper arm bone, attached via a ball-and-socket joint to the pectoral girdle, is long and strong. At its outer end (but often concealed by the covering layer of body feathers) is the "elbow," where the humerus joins the radius and ulna. To this section are attached the lift-producing secondaries. The outermost section of the wing is a condensed assortment of wrist and hand bones. The alula is mounted on a vestigial thumb, movable for low-speed flight control. The primaries, responsible for flight propulsion, are set on a group of flattened bones derived from the "palm of the hand" and the second digit.

Walking and running

Because flight is such a dominant feature of bird life, other forms of locomotion may seem to be secondary in importance. For some groups this is far from true – especially in the various flightless orders. Some, such as the Ostrich, Emu and rheas, have evolved as specialist runners, with modifications to the

standard pattern of the avian leg very similar to those seen in fast-running mammals such as the horse. In the penguins, the legs are much reduced, minimizing heat loss to their extremely cold environment. The wings provide the birds' propulsive power, but in much modified form as stiff paddles, which are used on and – more effectively – under the water.

In the vast majority of birds, an appreciable proportion of their total weight (sometimes as much as 25 percent) is accounted for by the massive pectoral flight muscles located on the sternum. As a result, the center of gravity lies well in front of the hip joint, where the leg is attached to the body. In order to walk or run well, or to perch without undue effort, this imbalance has to be overcome, partly by a stout, elongated pelvic girdle and a strong and effective arrangement of muscles, and partly by adaptations of the anatomy of the leg itself.

Although the components are similar to those in any mammal hind limb, the proportionate lengths of the various bones in the bird limb differ significantly. The avian thigh (femur) is normally short and stout and runs forward from the hip almost horizontal to the ground. This means that the knee of a bird is usually concealed within the body feathers and located just below the center of gravity.

What emerges from the feathers, looking like the thigh, is actually the shin (the tibio-fibula). Thus the joint visible in the middle of the avian leg, looking like a knee but acting the wrong way around, is the ankle. The section between this and the clearly identifiable toes is usually slender and covered in scales (occasionally it is feathered). This is the tarsus – a single bone consisting of the fused tarsus and metatarsus. At the end of the tarsus are the toes, normally three pointing forward and one pointing back. This arrangement may differ between orders, but there are never more than four toes.

In the typical avian arrangement, the knee and ankle are at a distance both from the hip and from contact with the ground. In concert with the elastic ligaments around them, they operate in opposite directions. This produces a limb which provides both an efficient shock absorber on landing and an effective "catapult" to launch the bird on take-off.

Food and feeding

The power of flight has allowed a great diversification in feeding, but this has been achieved only at a cost. In being able to fly, the birds have, metaphorically speaking, sacrificed their "hands," making them unavailable for functions such as gathering and eating food. So no matter what their food may be, it is only by adaptations of legs and feet, and bills, and of feeding techniques, that birds can cope with it. These collective adaptations to securing food are enormously diverse and provide valuable clues to the identification of birds.

A bird's skull is composed of an almost spherical, thin-walled cranium, with relatively large orbits to hold the eyes. Beneath the cranium is the lower jaw (mandible), hinged, as in the reptiles, by means of movable bones

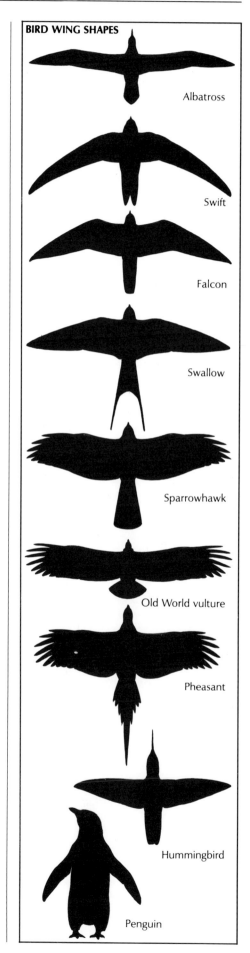

BIRD WING SHAPES

Albatross

Swift

Falcon

Swallow

Sparrowhawk

Old World vulture

Pheasant

Hummingbird

Penguin

called quadrates. Instead of a simple joint (like a door hinge) as in mammals, the birds have a double-jointed, wide-gaping articulation which helps a cormorant to swallow a large flatfish, or a puffin to hold several small fish in its bill and still catch more.

The upper mandible is not firmly anchored to the skull, but hinged on the forehead: the flexibility this confers is best seen in action in a parrot tackling tough seed. Also, the skull is joined to the topmost neck vertebra in a simple (and very maneuverable) ball-and-socket joint. Coupled with the large number of neck vertebrae, this provides the birds with a head that is far more mobile than that of mammals.

Bills and bill shapes

The two bony mandibles, upper and lower, carry the outwardly visible parts of the bill as horny sheaths. These, and the bones beneath, vary in size and shape depending on the food and feeding techniques of the bird. Good examples are the powerfully hooked bills of birds of prey; the long, slender, probing bills of many waders; the complex banana-shaped filter of the flamingos; and the strong pyramidal, or wedge-shaped, bills of the seed-eaters.

Irrespective of the size of its prey, or the volume of carrion present in its diet, the "basic equipment" of a bird of prey is the same – a powerful hooked bill and an equally powerful set of talons. Although the bill may, on occasion, deliver the coup de grâce, it is the talons that are the main feeding aids, normally immobilizing or killing the prey. The ferocious-looking bill is primarily a feeding aid: birds lack teeth and thus have no ability to chew, so a bird of prey tears chunks of flesh from a carcass and bolts them down. When it comes to feeding newly hatched nestlings, however, even the largest eagle can tear off morsels of flesh little bigger than a match and feed them with great delicacy to its eaglet.

Not all flesh-eaters have hooked bills, nor do they all rely on talons for the kill. Herons, egrets and storks, for example, specialize in eating fish and other aquatic or waterside animals. Long-legged and long-necked, they rely on a swift, stabbing strike with a large, daggerlike bill to transfix their prey.

Wetland feeders

The wide range of wading birds that visit coasts and estuaries often secure their prey from deep in the most glutinous mud. Here, the bill's nerve-rich tip provides a sensor for identifying prey, and its flexibility allows a worm, crustacean or mollusk to be grasped and withdrawn without an accompanying mouthful of mud. At the top of the shore and on drier sandbanks, plovers hunt for food. These short-billed birds locate much of their prey by sight and rarely probe. Sometimes they employ "foot pattering" to lure hidden prey to the surface.

Lower on the shore, in muddier surroundings, live probing birds with bills of medium length. The Redshank *Tringa totanus* is typical. It can penetrate up to $1\frac{1}{4}$–$1\frac{3}{4}$ in (3–4 cm) into soft mud, but can also use its finely pointed

1 Common Raven; 2 Icterine Warbler; 3 Channel-billed Toucan; 4 Green Woodpecker; 5 Northern Cardinal; 6 Blue-and-yellow Macaw; 7 Golden Eagle; 8 Common Redshank; 9 Giant Hummingbird; 10 Mallard; 11 Red-breasted Merganser; 12 Anhinga.

bill to pick small animals off the mud or water surface. One stage more advanced are shorebirds such as the godwits, which can plunge their much stouter bills into mud to depths of more than 5 in (12 cm), and the various curlews, whose downcurved bills may well exceed 6 in (15 cm) in length. The curlews are typical of many shorebirds in breeding on wet moorland or tundra, where they can probe in the moist soil for worms and other invertebrates.

The other larger group of birds whose specialist habitats are water and wetlands are the wildfowl. Those such as the geese, which favor drier habitats, have long, flexible necks and tough, sharp-edged, wedge-shaped bills suitable for cropping grass. Many ducks graze the vegetation at the water's edge but also dabble in the soft mud for plant seeds and stems. The prime example of a dabbler is the Northern Shoveler *Anas clypeata*, whose huge spoon-shaped bill has an edging of fine projections or lamellae. As a beakful of mud is forced out over them, these trap food particles. In deeper waters, both fresh and saline, are a range of diving ducks seeking both plant and animal foods, often at considerable depths. The mergansers, known as sawbills because of the toothlike edges to their slim bills, are specialist and adept fish-catchers.

Land feeders

Most small birds eat one or more types of food, namely insects, fruits and seeds. Typical of insect-eaters are the warblers, with small, needle-sharp bills ideal for extracting insects, their eggs, or larvae from cracks in tree bark. Despite this typically insectivorous bill structure, warblers regularly eat fruit at times of the year when there is a need to accumulate stored fats prior to migration. In a similar way, many birds with bills adapted for a diet of fruit are really omnivores. For instance, many of the thrushes feed with equal enthusiasm, depending on season and on food availability, on fruits and on various invertebrates, their moderately stout yet pointed bills allowing them such diversity of behavior.

Although many seed-eaters may feed insects to their young to provide growing birds with sufficient proteins, birds such as finches do have a chiefly vegetarian diet. This is one of the best groups in which to observe adaptive diversity and its benefits. Most important of these is the reduction of potentially harmful competition for scarce resources by partitioning available food supplies on the basis of the ability of the bill to deal with the seed.

In the simplest examples, size alone determines the way the bill is used. At one end of the scale are the tiny bills of the seed-eating Redpoll *Acanthis flammea*, while at the other are the hawfinches with their massive nut-crushing bills. More subtle are the differences between different finches. The rounded bill and peglike tongue of bullfinches are well adapted to "handle" dormant buds and remove the protective scales so that the nutritious developing flower within can be easily consumed. By contrast, the long, slim, tweezerlike bill of

1 Common Pheasant; 2 Carrion Crow; 3 Northern Jacana; 4 Green Woodpecker; 5 Great Cormorant; 6 Rock Ptarmigan; 7 Eurasian Coot; 8 House Sparrow; 9 American Harpy Eagle; 10 Gray Heron; 11 Ostrich.

goldfinches can extract seeds from the prickly seed heads of thistles, which other finches are unable to penetrate. The ultimate in seed-eating is the bill of the aptly named crossbills, adapted to extract the seeds from conifer cones.

Male and female

In some bird families it is usual for males and females to have similar plumage; in others the sexes differ in appearance to varying degrees. As a rule, when the sexes differ the male bird is the larger and more colorfully feathered, while the female has duller plumage, which may help to conceal her on the nest.

For most, but not all birds, there is a single breeding season in any year. Typically, in this period, cock birds find and protect nesting territories, and may sing or display to intimidate rival males and attract mates. Songs vary from the sweet, melodious phrases of the Nightingale *Luscinia megarhynchos* to the mechanical laugh of the Laughing Kookaburra *Dacelo novaeguineae*.

Courtship rituals are as varied as birds' voices. Among the most spectacular are the displays of birds of paradise and some of the pheasants. Such birds tend to be polygamous – the males attract and mate with many females on their display grounds, or "leks." Such behavior is not the norm, however, since most birds are monogamous and many mate for life. Fertilization is internal but, apart from a few species, the male bird does not possess a penis. Instead most males have a small erectile protuberance at the base of the cloaca (the reproductive opening) through which sperm pass into the cloaca of the female.

Eggs and egg-laying

The ability to fly so effectively, and the ample scope for diversity of lifestyle that this has allowed, has inevitably brought with it some anatomical constraints. The need for lightness and strength is obvious, not just for adult birds but also for developing young. A slowly maturing group of fetuses of mammalian type, steadily increasing in weight inside the female until birth, would impose a number of impossible physical demands. These would not merely overstrain the female's physique in terms of muscle power and oxygen supply but would put an unacceptable strain on the box girder skeletal structure which, although extremely strong, is ill adapted to carrying an increasing load of this magnitude.

In most birds, a series of eggs is rapidly produced, each within a protective shell. Each is quickly laid before the next has grown to burdensome proportions. The egg is normally laid into a nest, where it can be incubated at will by parents which remain free to fly to save their own lives if danger threatens. In addition, the female can live a normal daily life, unrestricted and able to flee from predators unencumbered, in contrast to the heavily gravid females of many mammals. There are, however, some problems with this system: levels of egg losses to adverse climatic conditions and to nest predators can be very high. Often more

TYPES OF NEST

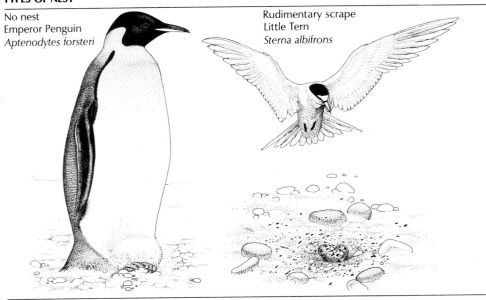

No nest
Emperor Penguin
Aptenodytes forsteri

Rudimentary scrape
Little Tern
Sterna albifrons

Nest camouflaged
in vegetation
Sky Lark
Alauda arvensis

Waterborne nest
Great Crested Grebe
Podiceps cristatus

Excavated burrow
River Kingfisher
Alcedo atthis

Disused rabbit burrow
Manx Shearwater
Puffinus puffinus

Bare rock ledge
Common Murre
Uria aalge

Cave wall saliva nest
Edible-nest Swiftlet
Aerodramus fuciphagus

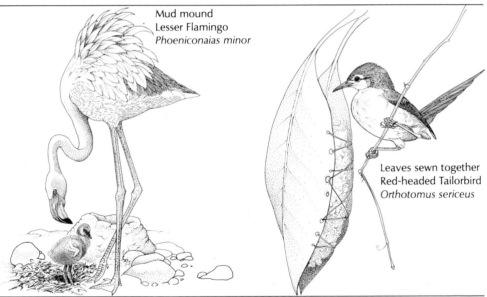

Mud mound
Lesser Flamingo
Phoeniconaias minor

Leaves sewn together
Red-headed Tailorbird
Orthotomus sericeus

Excavated tree hole
Pileated Woodpecker
Dryocopus pileatus

Walled-up tree hole
Great Indian Hornbill *Buceros bicornis*

than half of a bird's nesting attempts may fail in this way, but usually replacement clutches are quickly produced.

The relationship between the size of the egg and the size of the bird is complex. One reason for this is that some birds lay just one egg in their clutch, while others may lay 15 or more, or produce several clutches of 4 or 5 eggs during a season. Generally, the smaller birds lay proportionately larger eggs. In small birds such as the tits, a single egg may amount to 8 or 10 percent of the female's body weight. Some birds, such as the smaller storm-petrels and plovers, lay eggs that are 25 percent of their body weight. In Ostriches, however, the gigantic egg, with a volume of over $4\frac{1}{4}$ pints (2 liters) and a weight of around 3 lb (1,400 grams), represents only 1 percent of her body weight.

The egg is initially formed by the ovary. The fertilized ovum starts its journey to the outside world on the surface of a spherical yolk sac down a tube known as the oviduct. En route it receives first a coating of the protein albumen (the egg white) and then a calcareous protective shell, each secreted by cells in the oviduct wall.

As the shelled egg nears the end of the oviduct, variously colored pigments are added, mostly derived from bodily waste, for example, broken down, spent red blood corpuscles, which are usefully excreted in this way. Common ground colors include pastel grays, blues and greens, the most common applied markings being shades of lavender, brown and black. The tadpolelike nature of many of these superficial markings is caused by movements of the egg within the oviduct as the dark pigments are being squeezed onto the shell.

Often, the colors and patterns offer clear benefits in camouflaging the egg against its background (the sandy, dark-flecked eggs of many beach-nesting terns and shorebirds are excellent examples). In the crowded circumstances of colonial nesting, individual pattern variations may help the returning parent identify its own egg. In contrast, unmarked white eggs tend to characterize hole-nesting birds – presumably such eggs are easier to see as the bird settles to incubate in the darkness.

The range of nests

Nest types relate broadly to groups of birds and their habitats. The simplest of "nests" are those in which the eggs are laid directly on the ground. The apparent vulnerability of such a site to predators is often offset by the physical protection offered by the surroundings. Murres, for example, lay their eggs on exposed cliff ledges accessible only to birds. In other cases, protection is derived from the concealment offered by the colors and patterns of the eggshell (and later the down of the chick), which provide extremely effective camouflage. Shorebird nests of this type often appear as simple "scrapes" in the ground, but closer inspection reveals hundreds of fragments of seaweed, shell and twig brought by the nesting birds to ornament the nest margin.

This simple nest pattern is developed further by other shorebirds, and by many wildfowl

13

and gulls. Dead vegetation, and all types of flotsam and jetsam, are gathered into a mound, with a shallow depression at its summit containing the clutch of eggs. The structure is often bulky but low in cliff-nesting birds such as gannets and cormorants but, in the case of wildfowl and gulls nesting in areas vulnerable to flooding, may be built up into a sizable pyramid, as in cranes and swans. A floating nest is a logical evolutionary development from this and achieves extra protection from flooding. Several grebes and the marsh terns build nests in this way.

Various other forms of protection are afforded by the cup-shaped nests made by the majority of birds and, in particular, by the small and medium-sized song birds. The eggs cluster naturally at the base of the cup, where they (and subsequently the nestlings) are sheltered from the wind and from the eyes of predators. Such nests usually have a framework of twigs and are lodged firmly in a cluster of twigs or a forked branch. Finer materials, grass and rootlets are woven into this structure, which may also be reinforced with mud. The cup is lined with other fine materials such as hair which further improve the insulation.

Domed nests are yet another logical evolutionary development. They offer improved insulation and greater concealment of the nest contents from prying eyes. The nest of the Long-tailed Tit *Aegithalos caudatus*, built of spiders' webs, hair and feathers, with an outer camouflage coat of fragments of lichen, is also flexible and can stretch to accommodate the growing brood. Similar in their protective concept, but markedly different in structure, are the mud nests of many swallows and martins, built up with small pellets of mud gathered from beside nearby pools. Often hemispherical and fixed to a natural rock face or man-made alternative, some also have an entrance tunnel which provides even greater protection.

Birds as diverse as various tits, doves, owls and crows use the natural protection of holes in old trees, banks, cliffs and buildings to shelter their nests. Others excavate their own holes. The woodpeckers are supremely well adapted for this, as are the barbets, and their disused nests (often hacked into living hardwood) quickly find alternative occupants. Kingfishers, bee-eaters and sand martins are examples of birds that excavate their own nest-burrow in sandy soils, often in exposed banks.

The most elaborate nest structures tend to be found among tropical birds, and all are a tribute to the ability and agility of the birds that weave them, using only their beaks and feet to do so. Again, a major purpose of such nests seems to be added protection from predators, including snakes and lizards. The caciques and oropendolas of South America weave flask-shaped nests high in the trees, with pendant, trumpet-shaped entrance funnels. Some African sunbirds suspend their nests from a slender woven thread. The widest variety of such nests is made by members of the weaver family living in the tropics of Africa and Asia.

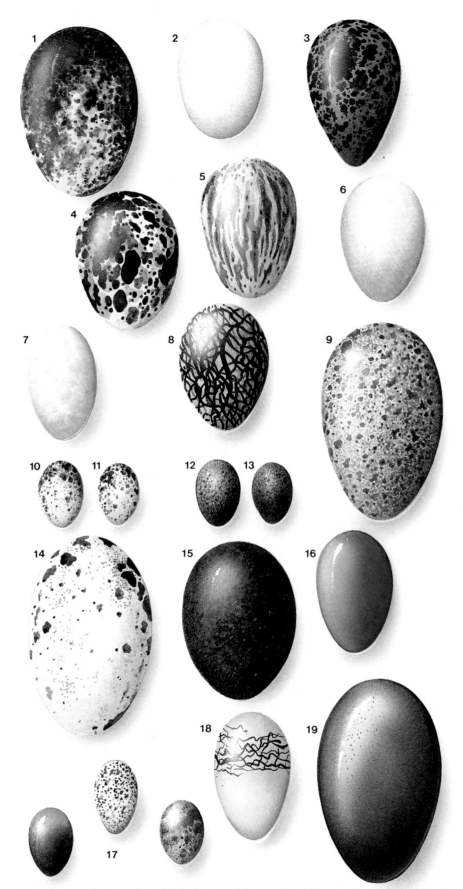

1 Osprey; 2 Common Barn-Owl; 3 Black-bellied Plover; 4 Bronze-winged Courser; 5 Lesser Bird of Paradise; 6 Stripe-backed Bittern; 7 Eared Grebe; 8 African Jacana; 9 Black Crow; 10 Eurasian Cuckoo (in nest of 11); 11 Great Reed Warbler; 12 Eurasian Cuckoo (in nest of 13); 13 Meadow Pipit; 14 Black Vulture; 15 Peregrine Falcon; 16 White-throated Laughing-Thrush; 17 Winding Cisticola; 18 Grayish Saltator; 19 Chilean Tinamou.

Incubating the eggs

The incubation period – the time taken for the fertilized embryo to develop into a chick and break out of the eggshell – varies considerably. As a rule, the smaller the bird, the shorter the incubation period. The range is from about 10 to 12 days in small song birds to as many as 84 days in the great albatrosses and the kiwis. Most birds start to incubate only when their clutch of eggs is complete, but some, notably many predatory birds, start to incubate with the laying of the first egg. Small birds normally lay one egg a day: larger ones may lay at two, three or four-day intervals.

The females of most species – and the males of those in which both sexes share the incubation – have a "brood patch." This is a patch of wrinkled skin on the breast and belly, rich in superficial blood vessels, which supplies bodily warmth to the developing eggs. Some seabirds, such as gannets and boobies, lack a brood patch. Instead, the lobes of the webbed feet are used to overlap and warm the eggs. Living in extreme cold, Emperor Penguins *Aptenodytes forsteri* and King Penguins *A. patagonicus* incubate with their single egg resting across their feet (thus insulated from the ice beneath), enveloping it in a mufflerlike fold of skin that is rich in both blood vessels and insulating blubber.

Most clutches of eggs of smaller birds all hatch within about 24 hours, but in those species which start incubation before all the eggs are laid, the eggs hatch at intervals.

Life of the young

In the passerines, and some other types of bird, the young that hatch from the eggs are naked, blind and helpless. They remain dependent on their parents for food and protection until they are fully feathered and able to leave the nest. The nestling period following hatching, in which young birds are confined to the nest, ranges from 14 days in smaller birds to several months for the larger raptors and up to a year for the great albatrosses. Such young are described as nidicolous and even after fledging may remain under parental care for days, weeks or even months.

In the wildfowl, shorebirds and gulls, and some other groups, the nestling hatches covered in insulating and camouflaging down. Within a few hours it is dry, and able to walk or swim from the nest on its disproportionately well-developed legs. Its eyes are open and it may immediately range far from the nest, largely feeding for itself but usually under the protective eyes of one of its parents until, and often after, it is able to fly. Such young are known as nidifugous. In some such species, the fledged young of an early brood may assist in feeding their siblings from later broods. Co-operative breeding strategies have long been known to involve helpers at the nest, but it seems that also included may be aid with nest-building, the attraction of mates, and courtship.

Northern Sparrowhawk: chicks have down and open eyes on hatching, but remain in the nest for several weeks, being fed and brooded by their parents.

Dunnock: chicks blind, naked and virtually immobile on hatching, but grow very quickly – a typical nidicolous bird.

Greater Honeyguide: chick kills host chick (Red-throated Bee-eater) in its nest burrow using its hook-tipped bill. Several other groups of birds, including some cuckoos, have independently evolved the strategy of brood parasitism.

Wood Duck: soon after hatching, chicks leap from their tree hole nest and can run around and feed, though their parents protect them and help them find food – a nidifugous bird.

Birds evolved, so the fossil record suggests, from a branch of the great reptiles, the dinosaurs. Indeed, the earliest known bird, *Archaeopteryx lithographica*, is so like a reptile that some of its fossils were long mistaken for those of true reptiles. The forerunners of the birds were active, lizardlike animals which probably ran rapidly on their large hind legs. Smaller forelegs were held off the ground and long tails used for balance.

Archaeopteryx lived about 140 million years ago, in the Jurassic period, and was the size of a long-tailed pigeon. All of the few known specimens come from slate quarries in southern Germany and show impressions of feathers clearly outlined around the skeleton. Even the long tail has a large pair of feathers on each of its sections. This tail suggests that early flight may have been rather clumsy: in modern birds the tail is "telescoped" into a short pygostyle from which the tail feathers emerge at more or less the same position, providing a much more rigid surface for the control of flight.

By contrast, the number and shape of the large wing feathers, and the way in which they were positioned on the forelimb of *Archaeopteryx*, are all very similar to those seen in birds today and suggest that this bird was capable of powered flight.

Exactly how *Archaeopteryx* evolved is still a matter of dispute, but a reasonable explanation is that its lizardlike ancestors lived in trees. *Archaeopteryx* seems to have had an opposable hind claw on its hind legs, like modern birds but unlike lizards, which might have evolved to help its ancestors hold onto branches in the trees. Once in the trees, there was an advantage in evolving longer forelimbs for grasping branches, another characteristic of *Archaeopteryx*. Its simple teeth (a feature shared with lizards) suggest that it was an insect-eater.

Also unknown is how the feathers evolved. Reptile scales and feathers are both made of the substance keratin, so feathers are almost certainly derivatives of scales. Possibly the scales along the rear edge of the forelimbs were first modified to help the animal glide between branches. As birds became warm blooded – an evolutionary benefit to very active animals – these scales or early feathers were also modified to provide an insulating cover to the body.

Because forest-dwelling animals, especially small, hollow-boned ones, do not fossilize well, the early fossil record of birds is very poor. Indeed we know as little about the immediate descendants of *Archaeopteryx* as we know about its ancestors. There are very few fossil birds within the next 50 million years of evolution. The exceptions include *Enaliornis*, a flightless, toothed, loonlike bird, its relation *Hesperornis*, and *Ichthyornis*. From the extent of the fossil record, these three were clearly important members of the fauna for a long period. *Ichthyornis* was a flying bird, showing almost no lizardlike characteristics, except for teeth. By the late Eocene epoch, some 55 to 50 million years ago, birds had become more numerous. Fossils from this era can be placed in the bird families that exist today.

How birds are classified

Classifying animals is useful for a number of reasons. It provides a means of putting some pattern into the enormous variation that exists in nature and helps in understanding the relationships that exist between different individuals. A full classification also gives each species of animal and plant a name; these internationally accepted scientific names create a universal scientific language that everyone can understand.

When a species is first described, it must be given a scientific name. For instance, the Common Barn-Owl is *Tyto alba* Scopoli 1769. The first of these Latin names, which always starts with a capital letter, refers to the genus, a name which is common to a number of closely related species; for example, many species of gull are in the genus *Larus*, many thrushes in the genus *Turdus*. The second name, *alba*, which should always start with a lower-case letter, is the specific name and is unique to that species. This second part of the name, which is often descriptive of the creature (*alba* is the Latin for "white"), may be given to a species in another genus, for example *Calidris alba* and *Platalea alba*, but obviously cannot be used for another species of *Tyto*. These two names are together known as the binomial.

The third name, Scopoli, and the date, 1769, refer to the person who named the bird and the date when this description was published. In this case, Scopoli originally put the Common Barn-Owl in another genus of owls, *Strix*, and only later was it classified in the genus *Tyto*. It is technically correct to signify this in the name by putting the generic name in brackets, hence (*Tyto*) *alba* Scopoli 1769.

Strictly speaking, all four parts of the name form the scientific name but, in practice, the amount of information given varies with the purpose of the text. Sometimes yet more information may be given, such as in the scientific journal or book in which the description was published, but most standard texts, such as this one, give only the generic and specific names; these are all that is necessary to identify each species uniquely. As well as its scientific name, a bird or any other animal or plant may also be called by its common, or English, name. Such names are much less accurate and often vary from country to country.

Once species have been named, it is necessary to find some way of showing their relationships. The species within a genus are, by definition, more closely related to each other than birds in different genera. Above the genus, there is a hierarchy of different groupings which are used to classify animals further. A sample classification is illustrated (*right*).

Such a hierarchical structure provides a sort of family tree of relationships and makes it possible to see how closely or distantly species are related. This classification also gives a little information about a bird. Even if one knows nothing about a certain species except that it is an owl, it is possible to make a cautious guess about some of its attributes from that information alone: in the case of *Tyto alba* it is safe enough to assume that it will look much like other owls and is likely to be a nocturnal bird and to lay white eggs in a hole in a tree. Among owls, there are exceptions to both the last two characteristics, but they are few.

Species and subspecies

The species is the single most important taxonomic level, and we all intuitively know what a species is. A Golden Eagle *Aquila chrysaetos* is a species and is separate from a Common Barn-Owl *Tyto alba*, which is different from a Herring Gull *Larus argentatus*. However, it is exceedingly difficult to define a species in a completely watertight way. The simplest definition is that a species is "a group of actually or potentially interbreeding natural populations which is reproductively isolated from other such populations." What this means is, that, for example, while all Golden Eagles, will breed with other Golden Eagles, they do not normally interbreed with any other species of eagle.

In practice this is usually fairly straightforward, but it is the geographical separation between Golden Eagles in Europe and in North America that prevents them from interbreeding. This explains the necessity of the qualifying phrase "or potentially interbreeding."

Almost certainly, if these birds were put together they would interbreed. Short of trying to breed endless combinations of bird populations artificially in captivity, there is no way in which taxonomists can be absolutely sure – they have to use their judgement. This is why different books often list families as having different numbers of species.

Many species with wide distributions have populations which differ slightly from one another in appearance. Individuals in these adjacent populations interbreed, and so it would be against our definition to call them different species. Such varying populations are called subspecies, or races, and are given a subspecific name which is added to the end of the normal binomial scientific name.

For example, the European and North American races of the Barn Swallow both belong to the same species, *Hirundo rustica*, but the European race is paler underneath. It is called *Hirundo rustica rustica*, while the American subspecies, with more rufous underparts, is called *Hirundo rustica erythrogaster*. Provided that it is clear which species is being talked about, such names are often shortened, for example to *H. r. rustica* and *H. r. erythrogaster*, or even to race *rustica* and race *erythrogaster*.

KINGDOM:	Animalia (animals)
PHYLUM:	Chordata (animals with spinal cords)
SUBPHYLUM:	Vertebrata (animals with backbones)
CLASS:	Aves (birds)
SUBCLASS:	Neornithes (modern birds)
ORDER:	Strigiformes (all owls)
FAMILY:	Tytonidae (barn owls)
GENUS:	*Tyto*
SPECIES:	*alba*

The process of speciation

It is a fact of ecology that no two species of bird can coexist if they have identical ecological requirements. This has had a significant effect on the evolution of birds because it has resulted in the formation of new species. Over the course of time, the individuals of a species may become separated into two or more groups. This can happen, for example, when some individuals get blown off course on migration and arrive on an island where that species has not previously existed.

In an alternative scenario, the separation may happen slowly over longer periods of time: the gradual drying out of the centre of a land mass may cause the vegetation that was there to die out, leaving two discrete blocks of vegetation on either side. As a result, the birds that live in these habitats would themselves become separated.

A common way in which such subdivision occurred in North America and Europe was for the habitats (and hence the birds in them) to be forced southward during ice ages and to become subdivided either on to the east and west coats or on to promontories of land in the south such as Spain, Italy and Greece.

Eventually, such climatic changes reversed, as has happened since the ice ages. Then, gradually, the habitats spread northward again, together with their bird populations, and the subgroups of birds of each species met up

again. What happened then was crucial. Almost inevitably, the two groups would have evolved small differences from each other as they adapted to their new habitats. If they interbred, they would have gradually merged into a single population and there would be no visible signs of the differences today.

If they did not interbreed, is it correct to assume that they competed with one another? Almost certainly they would have done so. If one subgroup was much more successful than the other, this one would have out-competed the other, which would have become extinct, and again there would be no signs of this today. But if they both had slightly different advantages under different conditions, they might have developed separate ecological niches and have come to coexist. In these circumstances, there would now be two species where there was formerly only one.

This separation and rejoining, plus the development of ecological differences, is thought to be the main way in which new species of bird have evolved. When the two potential species were living alongside each other once more, the processes of natural selection would tend to favour those individuals that mated with their own kind rather than interbred. However, if interbreeding were equally successful, then the two subgroups would mix up again and two species would not form.

In this situation, there would be a distinct

advantage accorded to individuals that evolved ways of recognizing their "own" species and avoided mating with closely related, similar-looking but incompatible species. Distinctive plumages or distinctive songs, often known as isolating mechanisms, evolved as well as ecological differences. This explains why closely related species often have either some distinctive plumage or distinctive songs.

The Hawaiian finches

Islands such as Hawaii are ideal places in which to observe the process of speciation. The first birds to reach Hawaii, some 15 to 20 million years ago, were probably like a modern finch. In the absence of competition, these birds have gradually evolved into more than 40 distinct species, in a process known as adaptive radiation.

The ancestral bird probably visited flowers and fed there on insects and nectar. Some then became specialized to feed almost exclusively on nectar, with only a few insects in the diet, while others became exclusively insect-eaters. One species, *Hemignathus munroi*, has a bill with an elongated upper mandible which it uses to probe crevices for insects.

The fruit and seed-eaters probably arose from the early insect-eaters. As heavier beaks gradually evolved they allowed birds to crack open nuts and seeds or enabled them to eat the soft flesh of fruits.

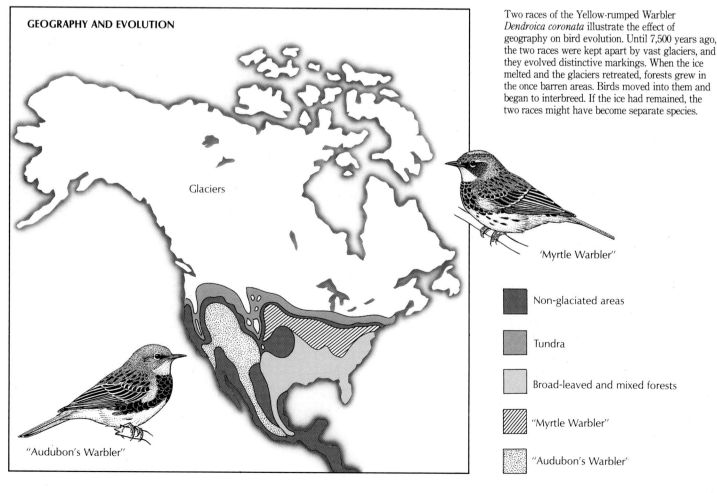

GEOGRAPHY AND EVOLUTION

Glaciers

'Myrtle Warbler'

"Audubon's Warbler"

Two races of the Yellow-rumped Warbler *Dendroica coronata* illustrate the effect of geography on bird evolution. Until 7,500 years ago, the two races were kept apart by vast glaciers, and they evolved distinctive markings. When the ice melted and the glaciers retreated, forests grew in the once barren areas. Birds moved into them and began to interbreed. If the ice had remained, the two races might have become separate species.

■ Non-glaciated areas

■ Tundra

□ Broad-leaved and mixed forests

▨ "Myrtle Warbler"

▨ "Audubon's Warbler'

HAWAIIAN FINCHES

FRUIT

Each Hawaiian finch lives in a distinct niche and is adapted to a different way of life, feeding on insects, insect larvae, fruits, seeds and nectar.

FRUIT AND SEEDS

INSECTS

INSECTS AND SOME NECTAR

NECTAR AND SOME INSECTS

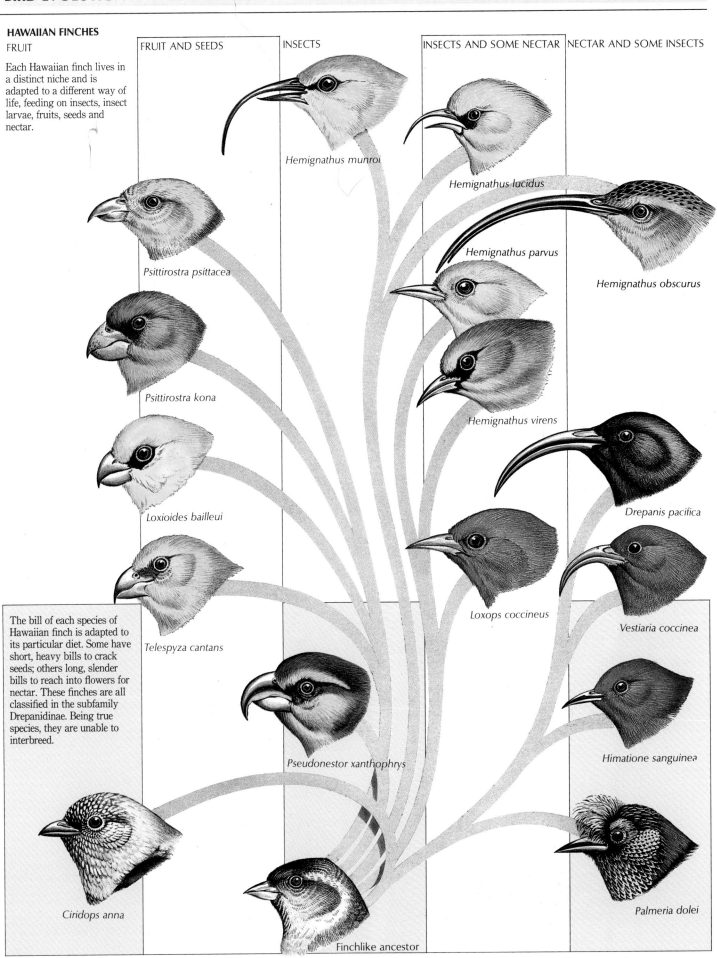

Hemignathus munroi

Hemignathus lucidus

Psittirostra psittacea

Hemignathus parvus

Hemignathus obscurus

Psittirostra kona

Hemignathus virens

Loxioides bailleui

Drepanis pacifica

Telespyza cantans

Loxops coccineus

Vestiaria coccinea

The bill of each species of Hawaiian finch is adapted to its particular diet. Some have short, heavy bills to crack seeds; others long, slender bills to reach into flowers for nectar. These finches are all classified in the subfamily Drepanidinae. Being true species, they are unable to interbreed.

Pseudonestor xanthophrys

Himatione sanguinea

Ciridops anna

Finchlike ancestor

Palmeria dolei

CLASSIFICATION OF BIRDS

Currently, the classification of birds is in a state of flux: new scientific techniques, especially those examining the similarity of the DNA between different families and even species of birds, are indicating that important changes to the traditional classification may be necessary. As yet, many of these exciting issues are not fully resolved, so in this book we have erred on the side of tradition and caution.

As discussed on pages 16–18, it is not always possible to be certain whether two groups of birds – for example, ones living on different islands – belong to the same species or to two different ones. In the same way, there is no final, objective measure of whether certain groups of species should all belong to one family or order or be divided into two. One can aim for consistency, but in the end it is a matter of opinion. As a result, no two books on the subject of birds of the world will necessarily contain the same number of species or families or even orders.

Birds form the Class Aves of the Phylum Chordata (animals with a spinal chord). Within this class, birds have been divided into two subclasses – the Archaeornithes, containing only *Archaeopteryx* and the fossil toothed birds such as *Hesperornis*, and the Neornithes, containing all other birds. The latter group has been subdivided into two superorders, the Palaeognathae and the Neognathae. The former contains the large flightless birds such as the Ostrich and Emu and some primitive flying birds, while the latter contains all the other birds that are alive today. This main subdivision of the birds is made primarily on the basis of their palate structure.

There are slightly more than 9,000 species of birds alive in the world today. These are divided into some 28–30 orders of birds. Within the superorder Neognathae, there is a major division. A single order, the Passeriformes, contains well over half of all the species of living birds. This order, which contains many of the common small birds such as thrushes and tits, has no popular English name. Although it is often referred to as the perching birds, because of the design of the foot, this name is hardly helpful when one thinks of how many other birds perch perfectly well. In this book this great group of birds is referred to as the passerines. By contrast, all the other orders of birds are often referred to as the nonpasserines.

The following text lists all the orders of birds with a brief summary of each order and its supposed relationships with other groups of birds. The number immediately following the name of each order indicates the total number of species within it, as recognized in this book. It should be noted that not only do different authorities list different numbers of species in families, but there also is a wide divergence on whether the subdivisions within an order are families, subfamilies and so on.

SUPERORDER PALAEOGNATHAE

The first four orders listed here are often collectively referred to as the Ratites (from the Latin *rata*, a raft), a reference to their large, flat sternum which lacks a keel. The keel is an important area of attachment for the major flight muscles, but since, in flightless birds, the flight muscles are not needed and so are greatly reduced, the keel has also disappeared.

1 Struthioniformes: 1
Ostrich. Large, flightless African bird. Foot reduced to only two toes, one of these quite small.

2 Rheiformes: 2
Rheas. Large, flightless South American birds. Foot reduced to three toes.

3 Casuariiformes: 4
This order contains two families: Dromaiidae (Emu) and Casuariidae (cassowaries). Large, flightless Australasian birds. Foot reduced to three toes.

4 Apterygiformes: 3
Kiwis. Medium-sized, flightless birds from New Zealand. Nocturnal. Kiwis have nostrils at the tip of their bill and a good sense of smell. They are probably related to the extinct moas of the Order Dinornithiformes; some ornithologists put both the kiwis and moas in the Order Apterygiformes.

5 Tinamiformes: 46
Tinamous. Gamebirdlike species from Central and South America. Thought to be a primitive group unrelated to the true gamebirds, which they superficially resemble. They have a number of primitive features which link them to the Ratites. Unlike the latter, however, the tinamous still fly, but they do not fly long distances and their keels are reduced. Their most likely relations are the rheas of the Rheiformes (2), which makes sense since they are also South American.

SUPERORDER NEOGNATHAE

6 Sphenisciformes: 18
Penguins. A highly specialized Southern Hemisphere marine group, with wings modified into powerful flippers for swimming. Once thought to be so different from other birds that they were put in a separate superorder (Impennes); more recent studies suggest that they may be distantly related to the Procellariiformes (9), with which they share some characteristics: in particular, some fossil penguins have tubed nostrils, like many members of the Order Procellariiformes.

7 Gaviiformes: 5
Loons. Aquatic birds, occurring at high latitudes in the Northern Hemisphere. Usually breed on fresh water, but spend the winter on the sea. Traditionally grouped with the grebes of the Podicipediformes (8), but now thought not to be closely related. They show a number of morphological differences, the most obvious being their webbed feet, compared with the lobed feet of grebes. Recent research suggests that they may share a common ancestry with the gulls: see Charadriiformes (16).

8 Podicipediformes: 21
Grebes. Small to medium-sized diving birds. All breed on fresh water, but many winter at sea. Relationships with other orders obscure: see Gaviiformes (7).

9 Procellariiformes: 110
A large group of seabirds, including four families: Diomedeidae (albatrosses), Procellariidae (fulmars, petrels and shearwaters), Hydrobatidae (storm-petrels) and Pelecanoididae (diving-petrels). They have a very long upper arm (humerus); the resulting long wings give the albatrosses and shearwaters their characteristic gliding ability. A number of species have distinctive tubed nostrils (hence the name tubenoses sometimes used for the group). All four families have very similar breeding biology: all species lay only a single egg and have slow rates of development.

10 Pelecaniformes: 62
Another major order of seabirds, encompassing six families in three suborders: the Phaethontes, containing a single family, the Phaethontidae (tropicbirds); the Pelecani, containing four families, the Sulidae (gannets and boobies), Pelecanidae (pelicans), Phalacrocoracidae (cormorants and shags), Anhingidae (anhingas, darters or snakebirds); and the Fregatae, containing a single family Fregatidae (frigatebirds). All but the cormorants are very small families. All are fish-eating birds, most of them marine. A distinguishing feature is that all species in this order are totipalmate – they have three webs linking the four toes. The frigatebirds and albatrosses share some skeletal characteristics, suggesting a link between these two orders. A link between this order and the next order, the Ciconiiformes, has also been suggested.

11 Ciconiiformes: 117
A big order of large, long-legged wading birds, which prey mainly on fish and amphibians, but also on large insects such as locusts. Includes three major families: Ardeidae (herons and bitterns), Ciconiidae (storks) and Threskiornithidae (ibises and spoonbills); two families containing only one aberrant species each, Scopidae (Hammerkop) and Balaenicipitidae (Whale-headed Stork); and the small family Phoenicopteridae (flamingos). The origins of this order have been much debated and possibly the birds currently placed here are not all closely related: links with the Pelecaniformes (10) and the Gruiformes (15) have been suggested and, in addition, the storks may share a common ancestry with the New World vultures, more conventionally placed in this book in the Falconiformes (13). The flamingos are a highly distinctive group of filter-feeding birds. Their relationships to other birds have been a matter of considerable debate. They are often thought to form a link between the herons and the wildfowl of the Anseriformes (12). There is now evidence that their closest ancestor may be a fossil bird *Presbyornis*, a primitive shorebird, and that they should be thought of as an early offshoot of the birds that gave rise to the stilts and avocets in the Family Recurvirostridae of the Charadriiformes (16).

12 Anseriformes: 150

A large group, including the ducks, geese and swans of the Family Anatidae. Also included in this order is a small family, the Anhimidae (screamers), containing species which are not at first sight very similar to the other wildfowl, but seem to be an early offshoot of this order. The order as a whole may share ancestry with the Charadriiformes (16).

13 Falconiformes: 290

A very large order containing five families. The New World vultures (Cathartidae) are sometimes placed in a separate order and are now thought by some to be a specialized derivative of the storks of the Ciconiiformes (11). The largest family (sometimes considered as a separate order) is the Accipitridae, which includes the kites and their relatives, sea and fish eagles, Old World vultures, snake eagles, harriers, sparrowhawks and relatives, buteos and relatives, and eagles. Two unusual families contain only one species each: the Pandionidae (Osprey), highly specialized for diving into water to catch fish, and the Sagittariidae (Secretary Bird), highly specialized for catching snakes. The Falconidae is a rather uniform family (thought by some to constitute a separate order). It consists mostly of the true falcons, birds which take mammals and, especially, other birds as prey, usually killing them in midair. It also contains the few species of caracara: these are primarily insect-eaters and scavengers but, unusually for birds of prey, most of them eat some fruit seeds or other plant material.

14 Galliformes: 274

Gamebirds. This large order contains the families Megapodiidae (mound-builders), Cracidae (curassows and guans), Meleagridae (turkeys), Tetraonidae (grouse), Phasianidae (New World quails, partridges and peafowl) and Numididae (guineafowl). Most are ground-dwelling vegetarians and all have nidifugous young – chicks that leave the nest within a few hours of hatching. The Hoatzin was once thought to be an aberrant gamebird, but is now classified as a cuckoo in the Cuculiformes (20).

15 Gruiformes: 190

This is a complex order, containing no fewer than 12 families, many of which are small (eight of the families contain fewer than ten species and four of them contain only a single species) and poorly known. At first glance, they do not all look particularly closely related; all live on the ground rather than in trees, many of them, such as the rails and cranes, in wet habitats – indeed, some of the rails are largely aquatic. Although a few nest above ground level, most nest on the ground or make floating nests among aquatic vegetation. The families are: Mesitornithidae (mesites), Turnicidae (buttonquails and Quail Plover), Pedionomidae (Plains-wanderer), Gruidae (cranes), Aramidae (Limpkin), Psophiidae (trumpeters), Rallidae (rails and coots), Heliornithidae (finfoots), Rhynochetidae (Kagu), Eurypygidae (Sunbittern), Cariamidae (seriemas) and Otididae (bustards). The relationship of this order to others is not clear. However, the rail-like jacanas – see Charadriiformes (16) – seem to form a link between this order and the Gruiformes, and it has been suggested that the Plains-wanderer is not a member of the Gruiformes, but is more closely related to the plovers and seedsnipe and should be placed in the Charadriiformes (16).

16 Charadriiformes: 337

This large and widespread group is split into three distinct suborders. The first is the Charadrii. This contains all the shorebirds, of which there are up to 13 families (some ornithologists split this large assemblage into two suborders). The families are: Jacanidae (jacanas, or lily-trotters), Rostratulidae (painted-snipes), Dromadidae (Crab Plover), Haematopodidae (oystercatchers), Ibidorhynchidae (Ibisbill), Recurvirostridae (avocets and stilts), Burhinidae (thick-knees), Glareolidae (coursers and pratincoles), Charadriidae (plovers and lapwings), Pluvianellidae (Magellanic Plover, sometimes included within the Charadriidae), Scolopacidae (sandpipers, phalaropes and snipes), Thinocoridae (seedsnipes) and Chionididae (sheathbills); the latter forms a link between this suborder and the next one, the Lari. The Lari contains four families: the Stercorariidae (skuas and jaegers), Laridae (gulls), Sternidae (terns) and Rynchopidae (skimmers). The third suborder contains just one distinctive marine family, the Alcidae (auks). These three groups are clearly different in a number of ways, including their general appearance and feeding ecology. The most closely related order to the Charadriiformes seems to be the Gruiformes (15) but the flamingos of the Ciconiiformes (11) may also be close relatives.

17 Pteroclidiformes: 16

Sandgrouse. Restricted to dry areas of the Old World (though absent from Australasia). The sandgrouse have certain characteristics in common with the next order, the Columbiformes, and some ornithologists put them in the same order. The sandgrouse may form a link between the pigeons and plovers.

18 Columbiformes: 300

Pigeons and doves. There is no ornithological distinction between the names "pigeon" and "dove," although pigeon is generally used for the larger species. This is a large group with a worldwide distribution, though absent from high latitudes. The extinct Dodo from Mauritius and the Rodriguez Solitaire and Réunion Solitaire, from nearby Indian Ocean islands, were large, flightless members of this order, but are classified in a family (Raphidae) of their own. All the pigeons and doves are placed in the Family Columbidae. The Columbiformes may also be related to the Charadriiformes (16).

19 Psittaciformes: 342

Parrots, including lories and lorikeets, cockatoos, typical parrots and parakeets, and macaws. A larger order of colorful birds, almost all of which are inhabitants of the tropics. A characteristically shaped bill, which is used for seed- and fruit-eating, is found in all species. Their distinctive, highly specialized nature obscures any relationships with other orders.

20 Cuculiformes: 159

This order contains two main families, the Musophagidae (turacos, or plantain-eaters), which inhabit African forests and woodlands, and the Cuculidae (cuckoos), which have a worldwide distribution: they are famed for their parasitic habits, but by no means all of them are parasitic. Some ornithologists now think that the two families are not closely related and put the turacos in an order of their own, Musophagiformes. In addition to these two families, the Opisthocomidae, a family containing only the remarkable Hoatzin, is nowadays included in this order. It was formerly thought to be a very aberrant gamebird.

21 Strigiformes: 174

Owls. A distinctive order of mostly nocturnal or crepuscular predatory birds. The barn owls are considered to be sufficiently different from other owls, Strigidae, to merit a separate family, Tytonidae. Indeed, some recent research suggests that these two families may not be very closely related, but share similar characteristics as a result of convergent evolution. Links with the Falconiformes (13) and Caprimulgiformes (22) have been suggested.

22 Caprimulgiformes: 109

A distinctive order of birds which are mainly nocturnal or crepuscular and which feed mainly on insects. All have bills with very broad gapes for snapping up their prey. There are five families: Steatornithidae (the Oilbird), Podargidae (frogmouths), Nyctibiidae (potoos), Aegothelidae (owlet-nightjars) and Caprimulgidae (nightjars and nighthawks). The Oilbird is the only member of its family and is an aberrant member of the order; it feeds on large, oily, strongly aromatic fruits which it finds at night by using its well-developed sense of smell. All members of the other four families rely wholly or partly on insect food, hence they are largely confined to the warmer areas of the world. Links with the Strigiformes (21) have been suggested.

23 Apodiformes: 429

This large order contains three families: the Apodidae (swifts) and the closely related Hemiprocnidae (tree swifts), and the Trochilidae (hummingbirds). At first sight, the hummingbirds appear very different from the other two families: their affinity is not accepted by all ornithologists. However, they all share some characteristics of wing structure; in particular, they have a very short upper arm (humerus), though from this design they have evolved different ways of flying. Links with the Caprimulgiformes (22) have been suggested.

24 Coliiformes: 6

Mousebirds. An order containing only a very small family (Coliidae) of rather unusual species. Confined to Africa, they have clearly been distinct from other groups for a long time. Affinities are uncertain, but links with the Psittaciformes (19) have been suggested.

25 Trogoniformes: 39

A smallish order containing only the single family Trogonidae (trogons). Many are brilliantly colored birds, featuring metallic greens. They inhabit forests in Central and

South America and are largely fruit-eating. Their relationships with other orders of birds are uncertain.

26 Coraciiformes: 204

A large order containing some nine or ten families: Alcedinidae (kingfishers), Todidae (todies), Momotidae (motmots), Meropidae (bee-eaters), Coraciidae (rollers), Leptosomatidae (the Cuckoo-Roller, or Courol), Upupidae (the Hoopoe), Phoeniculidae (wood-hoopoes) and Bucerotidae (hornbills). Some ornithologists put the five species of ground-roller, all found only in Madagascar, into a separate family of their own, the Brachypteraciidae; here they are included in the Coraciidae. It is not entirely clear that this diverse group should be placed in a single order, since it is by no means certain that they share a common ancestry. Links between some of them and the Piciformes (27) and Passeriformes (28) have been suggested.

27 Piciformes: 381

An order containing one large family, the Picidae (woodpeckers), one medium-sized family, the Capitonidae (barbets), and four smaller ones, the Galbulidae (jacamars), Bucconidae (puffbirds), Indicatoridae (honeyguides) and Ramphastidae (toucans). There seem to be some strong links between some of these families and some of those in the Coraciiformes (26); indeed, it has been suggested that the Galbulidae and Bucconidae should be placed in that order. Toucans seem to be specialized descendants of the barbets.

28 Passeriformes: 5,414

By far the largest order of birds, containing some 60 percent of all bird species. As a group, they share a large number of characteristics, strongly suggesting that they have descended from a common ancestor and hence should be treated as a single group. The order has traditionally been divided into four suborders, two of which are very small: the Eurylaimi contains only the single family Eurylaimidae (broadbills, with 14 species) and the Menurae contains just two families Menuridae (lyrebirds) and Atrichornithidae (scrub-birds), each of which contains only two species. However, recent research suggests that the Menurae may not in fact be primitive members of the order, but should be placed alongside a number of predominantly Australian families, including the Paradisaeidae (birds of paradise) and Ptilonorhynchidae (bowerbirds). This makes sense since all four species in the Menurae are Australian.

The other two suborders are much larger. The Tyranni contains some 12 families and 1,108 species. It is predominantly a group of the New World, with the great majority of species being found in Central and South America. Within it, two major groups can be distinguished: one contains the Tyrannidae (tyrant flycatchers), Cotingidae (cotingas) and Pipridae (manakins). The cotingas and tyrant flycatchers overlap in character to a considerable degree: several genera of birds formerly held to be cotingas have, in recent years, been moved to the Tyrannidae. The second main group contains the families Formicariidae (antbirds and gnateaters), Dendrocolaptidae (woodcreepers), Furnariidae (ovenbirds) and Rhinocryptidae (tapaculos). All these families, in both major groups, are found only in the New World. While some members of the suborder are clearly related to each other, there are a few which have traditionally been put in the Tyranni where the situation looks less certain. These include Pittidae (pittas), found throughout the Old World tropics, Philepittidae (asities, or false sunbirds), found only in Madagascar, and Xenicidae (New Zealand wrens). Not only are they less clearly similar to the main Tyrannid stock on morphological grounds, but their distributions also suggest that they may not belong to this primarily South American group.

The final suborder is the Oscines and this is the largest, containing some 57 families and 4,288 species. It includes many major families such as Alaudidae (larks), Hirundinidae (swallows), Laniidae (shrikes), Troglodytidae (wrens), Turdidae (thrushes), Muscicapidae (Old World flycatchers), Sylviidae (Old World warblers), Paridae (tits), Nectariniidae (sunbirds), Meliphagidae (honeyeaters), Vireonidae (vireos), Parulidae (wood warblers), Emberizidae (buntings, New World sparrows, tanagers and relatives), Icteridae (American blackbirds, orioles and relatives), Fringillidae (finches), Ploceidae (weavers and relatives), Passeridae (sparrows and relatives, or passerine finches), Sturnidae (starlings), Paradisaeidae (birds of paradise) and Corvidae (crows).

Special mention must be made of two families, the Muscicapidae and Emberizidae. Traditionally, these names are applied to two families containing about 147 and 284 species, respectively. However, recent research has suggested that the relationships of several of the old families related to these two families are complex and they may be very close, perhaps too close to merit full family status.

In the first case, the result has been that some ornithologists now lump a great number of species together in a single enlarged family Muscicapidae, containing the former families Turdidae (thrushes), Orthonychidae (logrunners and relatives), Timaliidae (babblers, including the two African rockfowl *Picathartes*, sometimes given a family, Picathartidae, of their own), Paradoxornithidae (parrotbills, sometimes included in the Timaliidae), Sylviidae (Old World warblers, including the gnatcatchers, sometimes given a family, Polioptilidae, of their own), Muscicapidae (Old World flycatchers), Monarchidae (monarch flycatchers, which includes the African wattle-eyes and puff-back flycatchers, sometimes given a family, Platysteiridae, of their own, and fantails, sometimes given a family, Rhipiduridae, of their own), Maluridae (fairy-wrens), Acanthizidae (Australasian warblers) and Pachycephalidae (thickheads, or whistlers). These families are then regarded as subfamilies. Notwithstanding this, the old families are homogeneous groups and easier to work with than the very large grouping above, so many ornithologists retain them – as we do in this book.

Similarly, many ornithologists regard the family Emberizidae as including not only the old family Emberizidae (buntings and New World sparrows), now demoted to subfamily status, but also the odd Plush-capped Finch, in a subfamily of its own, the Catamblyrhynchinae, the Cardinalinae (cardinal grosbeaks, formerly a subfamily of the Fringillidae) and the Thraupinae (tanagers). In this book these families are combined in this way. Sometimes, the Emberizidae is also regarded as including the Drepanidinae (Hawaiian finches, or Hawaiian honeycreepers), which we regard in this book as being a subfamily of the family Fringillidae (finches), the Parulidae (wood warblers) and Icteridae (American blackbirds, orioles and relatives).

There are no good English names for the four suborders of the Passerines, but the Tyranni and the Oscines are separated on the basis of the structure of their syrinx ("songbox"), with the Oscines being thought to be the more advanced. Hence the Tyranni are often referred to as the sub-Oscines. The Oscines are often referred to as the songbirds, because of their vocal abilities. However, in view of the fact that many other birds can sing quite well, this is about as appropriate as referring to the whole of the Passeriformes as the perching birds.

The study of bird geography concerns the broad patterns in which bird species are found throughout the world. The world is divided into a series of regions, as shown on the map. Each region has its own distinctive assemblage of birds (avifauna).

The area of the world in which a species may naturally be found is called its range. For migrants, there will be a winter, or non-breeding range, and a summer, or breeding range. A species or family of birds found exclusively in a region is described as endemic.

Bird distribution

The way in which birds are spread across the globe depends largely on physical geography – especially habitat and climate – and the ecology of the species, including food, nest-site requirements, competitors and predators.

In many parts of the world, the impact of human activity may influence distribution. Thus a bird's range may become restricted through local extermination or by the destruction of its habitat. Humans may also extend a species' range, either deliberately, by introducing favorite birds to new areas (such as the House Sparrow *Passer domesticus* to North America), or incidentally, by creating suitable conditions where none existed before (in the case of the House Sparrow, by building settlements in deserts, for example).

However, basic questions remain about the way in which bird families are distributed over the Earth, and why some are spread very widely and others are very restricted.

Shifting continents

The world's major avifaunal regions reflect the past history of planet Earth and its landmasses and, although there is much overlap, each is distinguished by a characteristic set of species. About 300 million years ago, the world was essentially one huge landmass, Gondwanaland. Over the millennia, this gradually split

THE MAJOR ZOOGEOGRAPHICAL REGIONS

NEARCTIC

NEOTROPICAL

NEARCTIC REGION

Like the Palearctic region (with which it is sometimes combined as the Holarctic), the Nearctic has a cold climate in the north and is relatively poor in bird diversity. A significant difference affecting bird distribution is the north–south arrangement of major mountain ranges in this region compared with the east–west pattern in the Palearctic. Many species are migratory, wintering in Central and South America.

Of the region's 61 families, none is endemic, though the turkey family is almost so. Typical birds include cranes, cuckoos, wrens, tyrant flycatchers, mockingbirds, wood warblers and New World sparrows. Four families are endemic to the Holarctic region: the loons, grouse, auks and waxwings.

NEOTROPICAL REGION

This is the richest of all regions in bird life, with over one-third of all known bird species breeding in it and containing almost half the world total if winter visitors are included. A striking difference from other regions is that some 70 percent of its land area is low-lying, well watered and tropical. As much as 32 percent of the South American region is covered by tropical rain forest (compared with about 9 percent of Africa and 4.5 percent of Australia), and almost 40 percent by savanna.

There are more than twice as many endemic families in the Neotropical as in any other region – 31 of its 95 families are endemic, including the rheas, screamers, trumpeters, Hoatzin, Sunbittern, seedsnipe, potoos, Oilbird, woodcreepers, ovenbirds, antbirds and tapaculos.

ETHIOPIAN REGION

This region (sometimes called the Afrotropical region) lacks the climatic variety of other regions and large areas receive relatively little rain: thus there is a high proportion of desert, grassland and savanna habitats. Accordingly, there are many terrestrial and seed-eating birds and relatively few waterbirds. Seventy-three families breed in the region, of which seven are endemic (Ostrich, Hammerkop, Secretary Bird, turacos, mousebirds, woodhoopoes, helmet shrikes). Other typical birds include francolins, guineafowl, bustards, coursers, sandgrouse, bee-eaters, barbets, honeyguides, larks, grass warblers, shrikes, waxbills, weavers and starlings.

up, eventually forming the continents as we know them today.

The Australasian region separated from the rest of the southern landmass 50 million years ago. The area that is now Australia drifted toward Southeast Asia, but was probably not close enough for many birds to cross to it until some 10 million years ago, by which time its original avifauna had been isolated for long enough to develop along unique lines.

The first birds to reach Australasia probably came from South America, some of them perhaps via Africa. Studies of the flightless species, including penguins, and probably the parrots, pigeons and other groups certainly indicate affinities between birds of these regions. Among the songbirds it seems that a few ancient forms evolved and diversified to exploit the variety of habitats available. In doing so they became much like northern bird families, such as the warblers, in a process known as convergent evolution.

The birds of the Ethiopian, or Afrotropical, region largely evolved in isolation, but some forest species, such as the hornbills, show close links with their Oriental counterparts and reflect the fact that Africa and India were once joined. The indigenous avifauna of the Neotropical region, by far the richest in the world, includes such varied families as the rheas, the screamers, the Hoatzin *Opisthocomus hoazin*, the seedsnipes and the potoos. Other characteristic groups, which have far more species here than in the Nearctic, include the hummingbirds, tinamous, puffbirds, jacamars and toucans. The avifauna of the Neotropical region bears the hallmarks of geographical isolation. Only in the last 3 million years or so has it been joined to the Nearctic via the isthmus of Panama.

The Nearctic region was once connected with Europe through Greenland, and at various times the Bering Strait was bridged to form a link with Asia – indeed, the Nearctic and

PALEARCTIC

ORIENTAL

HIOPIAN
TROPICAL)

AUSTRALASIAN

Palearctic are sometimes combined as the Holarctic region. The Nearctic contains ancient bird forms, such as the wrens, mockingbirds and thrashers, which show its early isolation; later ones such as the cranes, cuckoos and kingfishers that arrived from Europe; and yet more recent ones, such as trogons, that may have come from Asia. The newest arrivals in the Nearctic include the hummingbirds, which have penetrated north from South America.

The Palearctic region, now effectively isolated by the Atlantic and Pacific oceans, has rather blurred boundaries in the south where the region merges with the Oriental and Ethiopian regions. Because the Sahara Desert has been a far greater barrier to bird movement than the Mediterranean Sea, the birds of North Africa rightly belong in the Palearctic region.

The Oriental or southern Asian region has a distinctive population of birds. But on the chains of islands that include Borneo, Sulawesi, the Moluccas, the Philippines and Indonesia, there exists a strange mixture of Oriental, Australasian and intermixed bird groups.

Within many of these five avifaunal regions, subregions can be distinguished (*see map, p. 366*). They contain distinctive endemic genera and species of birds and even endemic families. Examples include the mesites, asities and cuckoo rollers of some Indian Ocean islands, and the New Zealand wrens and wattlebirds.

A changing scene

The distribution of birds is not fixed in time: it has changed much in the past and remains ever-changing today. Many apparent anomalies in bird distribution are explained by past events, such as the effects of the last Ice Age.

Refuge areas in southern Europe, which remained free from glaciation, provided havens for some species that were forced out of northern Europe by the ice sheets. Instead of a single, uniform race across northern Europe, there were now isolated groups in southwest and southeast Europe.

When the ice retreated north, these groups of birds also moved back north and often met again. By then they might have evolved into recognizable races. Alternatively they may have remained the same but retained different "traditions" during migration. The White Storks *Ciconia ciconia* of western Europe still migrate south over Gibraltar; those of the east still migrate southeast over the Bosphorus. The dividing line remains sharp and easily mapped.

More recent changes in bird populations include the increase and westward spread of several Eurasian species, including the Syrian Woodpecker *Picoides syriacus*, while species such as Cetti's Warbler *Cettia cetti* have made a northward expansion in western Europe. Climatic changes seem only partly the reason for this. It may be that the species have changed genetically and can thus tolerate a greater variety of habitats or withstand greater climatic extremes. By contrast, the ranges of birds such as the White Stork have contracted. This can be partly explained by human change of land use, but may have a natural element.

Changes of range

When a species has had several years of high breeding success but suddenly faces a year of very poor food supply, the birds have to move out in search of food elsewhere. This is an "eruption" from the breeding range and an "irruption" into the new winter range. Bearded Reedlings *Panurus biarmicus* and Red Crossbills *Loxia curvirostra* have extended their range in Europe as a result of such movements.

1900   1950

1972

Red-backed Shrike
Lanius collurio

The Red-backed Shrike (*above*) has declined dramatically as a breeding bird in Britain, perhaps chiefly because of a gradual change to cooler, wetter summers over the past century, which has reduced the abundance of flying insects, the bird's main food. By contrast, the Collared Dove (*below*) has undergone a remarkable expansion of its range across Europe from its homeland in south-central Asia.

SPREAD OF COLLARED DOVE

Collared Dove
Streptopelia decaocto

Limit of range in
- 1930
- 1945
- 1955
- 1965
- 1975

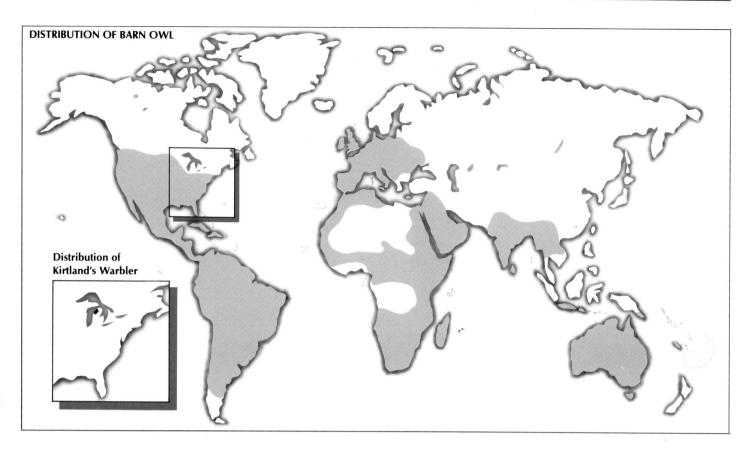

DISTRIBUTION OF BARN OWL

Distribution of
Kirtland's Warbler

Cattle Egrets *Bubulcus ibis* crossed the Atlantic in about 1930, reaching South America from Africa. This may have been due to something as simple as a flock of egrets being caught up in an exceptional easterly gale and swept far off course. But once this major barrier had been overcome, range extension became dramatic. Cattle Egrets rapidly spread north and south in the Americas and are now very widely distributed. At the same time, the species spread southeastward, via New Guinea, to Australia and New Zealand.

Range expansion by "leaps" from Australia to New Zealand has provided the most numerous examples of such dramatic changes. The Gray-backed White-eye *Zosterops lateralis* crossed to New Zealand in 1856, followed in the next 120 years by ten other species, including such diverse birds as herons, shorebirds and swallows.

The Northern Fulmar *Fulmarus glacialis* is a species that has spread its range through indirect human assistance. Increased fish and whale offal from trawlers helped it increase in numbers and subsequently spread around the coasts of western Europe through the twentieth century. Lesser Black-backed Gulls *Larus fuscus* have made incursions into new territory by adopting the habit of nesting on roofs of city and dockside buildings, instead of their normal island and clifftop sites.

The influence of climate

The ranges of other seabirds have changed as a result of variations in climate. In a warmer phase during the 1920s and 1940s, the breeding areas of the Thick-billed Murre *Uria lomvia*,

the Dovekie *Alle alle* and the Ivory Gull *Pagophila eburnea* all retreated northward.

Climate is still affecting many kinds of bird in Africa and Europe. As reduced rainfall (made worse by human exploitation of the forests and savanna) has increased the aridity in the Sahel region south of the Sahara, species such as the Ostrich *Struthio camelus* that once bred there have died out, while others that winter there have suffered population crashes. In 1969 numbers of Whitethroats *Sylvia communis* in western Europe dropped catastrophically. This species, and other species that depend on rich feeding late in winter in the Sahel to fuel them for their migrations back across the Sahara, have been badly hit. Sand Martins *Riparia riparia*, Common Redstarts *Phoenicurus phoenicurus* and several warblers have also similarly declined.

Within its range, a species may vary considerably. This may be due to past isolation or expansions into new habitats, which have encouraged the development of new races, or it may be a response to climatic change.

In cold areas, birds tend to be rather larger than in warmer parts of their range since this reduces the surface area of the body relative to bulk and helps minimize heat loss. The Herring Gulls *Larus argentatus* of northern Norway are often nearly twice the weight of those of Britain and France. In the cold parts of a species' range, bills and legs are smaller than average. This also reduces heat loss.

Birds tend to be darker in wet parts of their range than in drier areas. This is partly a response to the ability of darker pigment to absorb heat from the sun, which may result in a

The map (*above*) contrasts the very wide distribution of the Common Barn-Owl with the extremely limited distribution of Kirtland's Warbler, which breeds only in one very small area of specialized forest habitat in northern Michigan, USA.

20 percent saving in energy over the paler forms, while lighter colors reflect the heat in hot, arid regions.

Other geographical variations, for example in bird size and behavior, reflect adaptations to climate and availability of food. The race of the Northern Wheatear *Oenanthe oenanthe* that breeds in Greenland is larger than the races found farther south. Its much longer wings reflect its longer migratory flights. The number of eggs laid in a clutch may also change with latitude. Snow Buntings *Plectrophenax nivalis*, for instance, lay larger clutches the farther north they nest. This is probably so that they can take advantage of increased availability of food, especially in early summer in the Arctic, when there is a sudden superabundance of insects for small birds to eat.

A gradual change observed from one part of a bird's geographical range to another is called a cline. Birds from the extremities of the range may be so different that they can appear to be different species, but the gradations between them are so gradual that it is difficult to separate them, and two species are not usually recognized. Many European bird species, such as the European Robin *Erithacus rubecula* and the Song Thrush *Turdus philomelos* are darker in plumage in the westerly part of their range than in the east, but otherwise show very little difference in appearance.

No animal lives in isolation – every species interacts with its neighbors. Birds, for example, eat vegetation, fruits, insects, fish, mammals or even other birds, and usually have to avoid being eaten by some other creature, in turn. And birds may compete with each other, or indeed with other animals, for both food and nest sites.

As a result of these activities, each species has a wide range of interactions with other species within the community in which it lives. Ecology is the study of the particular ways in which individual species live. However, it is through evolution by natural selection that the great range of adaptations exhibited by birds, and other animals, has come about.

Ecology and evolution

The resources that are available to birds are often limited. There are a finite number of territories available in suitable habitats, nest sites may be scarce or food may be in short supply. When a resource such as food is plentiful, individuals will find it easy to survive, and the population will increase in numbers. As a result of this, there will be less food available for each individual.

At this point, there will be competition for resources. The individuals that will win through and survive will be those that are strongest and fittest. This is the underlying principle of natural selection, Darwin's theory which forms the basis for our understanding of evolution. Because offspring tend to inherit the characteristics of their parents, this means that the young born to successful birds will themselves be likely to show those characteristics that made their parents successful. Through natural selection, the numbers of individuals showing those characteristics that have proved most successful will increase.

An example of how this works can be seen in the Blackbird *Turdus merula* of Europe. Over much of its range this species is a partial migrant, which means that some individuals migrate in winter while others remain where they were born. In cold winters, more of those that do not migrate die, but in mild winters the migrants suffer more losses than those that stay at home.

The balance of advantage between being a resident and being a migrant is a fine one, and depends on the weather, which the birds are unable to forecast. In addition, the tendency to

Emerald Dove

Golden Heart

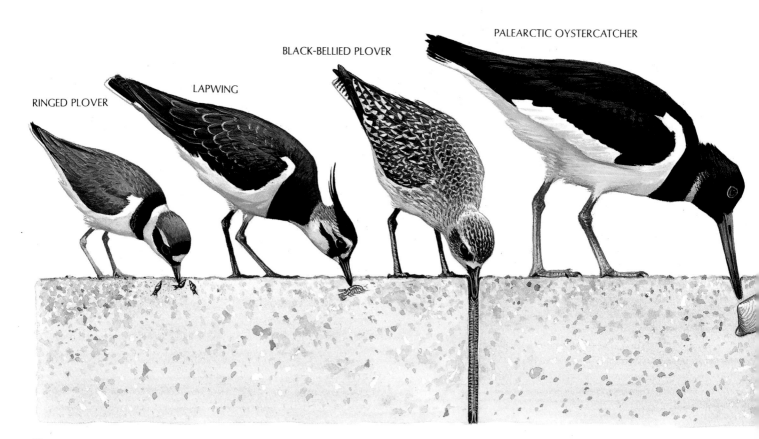

RINGED PLOVER

LAPWING

BLACK-BELLIED PLOVER

PALEARCTIC OYSTERCATCHER

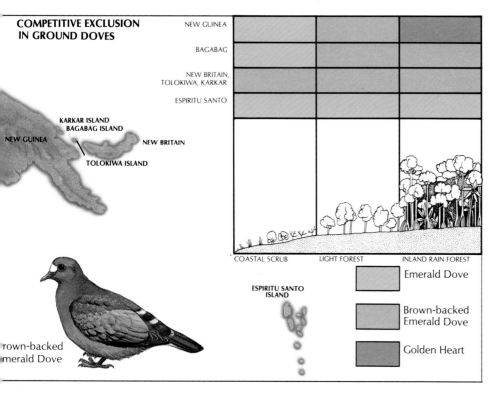

COMPETITIVE EXCLUSION IN GROUND DOVES

NEW GUINEA
BAGABAG
NEW BRITAIN, TOLOKIWA, KARKAR
ESPIRITU SANTO

COASTAL SCRUB · LIGHT FOREST · INLAND RAIN FOREST

KARKAR ISLAND
BAGABAG ISLAND
NEW GUINEA
NEW BRITAIN
TOLOKIWA ISLAND

ESPIRITU SANTO ISLAND

Emerald Dove

Brown-backed Emerald Dove

Golden Heart

Brown-backed Emerald Dove

There are three similar species of ground-dove in the New Guinea region (*left*). Where all three occur together, they occupy different habitats, but where only two species are found, one dominates by moving into the "spare" habitat. On islands where only one species occurs, it occupies all three habitats. This lends evidence to the theory that the choice of habitat for a species is determined by competition.

Shorebirds have bills of various lengths that enable them to probe to different depths in mud and sand in search of food (*below left*). They range from short-billed plovers that feed at or near the surface to long-billed godwits and curlews that can reach deep-burrowing prey such as lugworms. Each species thus avoids competition for limited resources by being adapted to take a particular range of prey.

Although the Shag and the Great Cormorant hunt for food in the same habitat in the breeding season, they specialize in taking different kinds of fish (*below*) and hence do not compete with one another.

WESTERN CURLEW

BAR-TAILED GODWIT

Shag

Great Cormorant

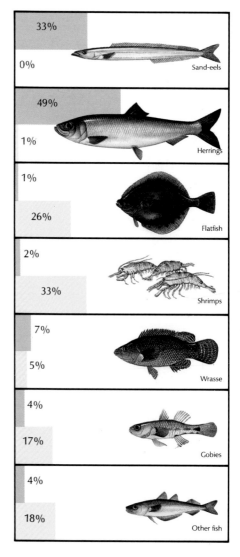

Shag	Great Cormorant	
33%	0%	Sand-eels
49%	1%	Herrings
1%	26%	Flatfish
2%	33%	Shrimps
7%	5%	Wrasse
4%	17%	Gobies
4%	18%	Other fish

migrate or stay at home tends to be inherited: the young are likely to do what their parents did. As a result, ecologists find that following hard winters, a high proportion of the Blackbird population are migrants, many of the residents having been eliminated, whereas after a series of mild winters the stay-at-homes are more numerous. In the final analysis, it is natural selection that determines the balance, and it can quickly alter the equilibrium through a change in migratory behavior that matches the ecological conditions.

Rapid environmental change – to which birds must adapt or die – is sometimes brought about through human activity. Evolution can be observed in action in the case of the Black-tailed Godwit *Limosa limosa* in the Netherlands. These wading birds breed on wet, grassy meadows, but increasingly over the past half-century these areas have been subject to mechanized mowing, which kills the young birds if they cannot fly. Hence, it confers an important advantage if the parent godwits breed early so that their young have reached the flying stage by the time the meadows are cut. As a direct result of survival of the fittest, favoring the early breeders, the birds now breed, on average, about two weeks earlier than they did 50 years ago.

The elements of selection
The forces of natural selection can be considered to have two separate elements. First, natural selection favors the survivors, those that compete successfully with others of their species, find the most food, survive the longest or breed most productively, and thus leave most offspring to future generations.

The second element is competition between species. Because no species lives in isolation, individuals of one species may have to compete for resources, such as food or nest sites, with those of another species. Of two species of flycatcher, for instance, one may take some food which would otherwise have been available to the other.

The evolutionary result of this competitive situation is that in all communities of birds each individual species has an ecology that differs to some degree from that of any other. The reason for this diversification is simple: no two species that lived in exactly the same way would ever be equally good at doing so – one must, inevitably, be slightly better than the other. And the one that was more successful would prosper at the other's expense. Eventually, unless the less successful species could evolve different habits, it would become extinct.

The ecological niche
Because of the way the forces of evolution operate, every species can indeed be found to differ in a crucial way from all the others. Each species is said to have a different, and exclusive, ecological niche. Birds of the genus *Phalacrocorax* amply illustrate this.

In Europe there are two species of this genus, the Shag *P. aristotelis* and the Great Cormorant *P. carbo*. Both birds live in the same general areas, often nesting on the same cliffs. But while the Shag fishes in the open sea, the Great Cormorant feeds on the bottom in shallow waters. This means that the two birds take prey of different types, are not in competition with each other, and occupy separate niches. Another example of this phenomenon of niche separation is provided by the closely related and very similar Common Tern *Sterna hirundo* and Arctic Tern *S. arctica*. These two species reduce or avoid competition by being adapted to feeding in different conditions: the Common Tern is more successful at fishing on cloudy days, while the Arctic Tern hunts better during windy weather.

A much more complex situation can be seen among shorebirds when, as happens in many parts of the world, a large number of species feed together on the tideline. Close examination shows that these birds are not all feeding in exactly the same place or in the same way. For example, the Ringed Plover *Charadrius hiaticula* "patters" on the surface with its feet, apparently to cause small worms to move and be more easily found, caught and eaten. Conversely, the Pied Avocet *Recurvirostra avosetta* "scythes" through the mud with its bill in search of small animals, but it can only do this if the mud is very soft.

In situations such as this, or in mixed flocks of birds foraging in woodland, it is easy to see that individuals are competing for resources, not only with their own species, but also with individuals of other species. The adaptations that prevent direct competition reflect the birds' evolution. In fact, the degree to which species differ in their diets is thought to be a reflection of the history of competition between the species.

Range and competition
Ecologists still do not understand many elements of the way that species interact with one another, and how this affects the distribution or range of a bird. Usually, related species either overlap within their range or they have quite separate ranges, but on rare occasions the ranges of two closely related species may abut each other. For example the Common Loon *Gavia immer* and the Yellow-billed Loon *G. adamsii* occur in immediately adjacent ranges. Ranges are not necessarily limited by apparent natural barriers such as deserts or, for land birds, the ocean.

Another example of how range can vary occurs when a species fades out in the middle of a large landmass for no obvious reason, as with the Green Woodpecker *Picus viridis*. One possible explanation for this is that in the "bare" areas the bird has been unable to compete with not one, but many other species. Such a situation is known as diffuse competition.

Evidence for competition between species can be deduced from what happens to one species in the presence and absence of another closely related one. Among the European tits there are two very similar species, the Marsh Tit *Parus palustris* and the Willow Tit *P. montanus*. In most regions, these two species tend to feed in different areas, the Marsh Tit in deciduous woodland, the Willow Tit in coniferous woods. However, on the Aland Islands which lie between Sweden and Finland, only the Willow Tit is present, and here it forages equally in both types of woodland. It is logical to suppose that on the mainland the Willow Tit does not occupy deciduous woodland because it is less efficient at foraging in such a habitat than the Marsh Tit.

Island ecology
The ecology of bird populations on islands has attracted a great deal of interest, not least because they can be thought of as "living laboratories." Islands tend to have far fewer species than comparable areas of mainland. And the farther they are from the mainland, the fewer the species.

It is thought that the small populations of island species may die out from time to time and have to be repopulated by a new wave of immigrants. So the low number of species found on islands is probably a reflection of a high rate of extinction and a low rate of recolonization. The greater the distance from the mainland, the more difficult such recolonization becomes.

Islands also demonstrate other aspects of bird ecology. It is not uncommon to find that, in a group of islands, certain species are present on some islands but missing from others. As a rule, there tend to be fewer closely related species on islands than there are on adjacent areas of mainland. This suggests that co-existence between such species may be difficult, and that competing species may limit each other's distributions.

Around the islands of New Guinea there are many smaller islands, but by no means all the same species occur on each one. On New Guinea itself, there are three species of ground-dove, the Emerald Dove *Chalcophaps indica*, the Brown-backed Emerald Dove *C. stephani* and the Golden Heart *Gallicolumba rufigula*. Each bird occupies a different habitat, and the three are found, respectively, in coastal scrub, light forests and rain forest.

On one smaller island, the Golden Heart is absent and the Brown-backed Emerald Dove occupies both light and rain forests. On several other islands, both the Emerald Dove and Golden Heart are absent, but the Brown-backed Emerald Dove occupies all three habitats. The conclusion would seem to be that the different species can use a range of habitats but only in the absence of the competing species. Why one species should be dominant in any situation is not clear. Possibly the species that arrived first became established and adapted to the local environment and was later able to out-compete other arrivals.

Vacant niches
When birds of a community have adapted to the local competition of other species, does this imply that they have filled the environment? Would it be possible for more species to arrive,

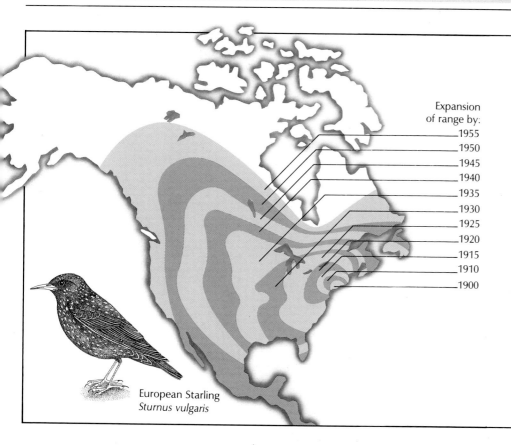

European Starling
Sturnus vulgaris

Expansion of range by:
1955
1950
1945
1940
1935
1930
1925
1920
1915
1910
1900

THE SUCCESSFUL STARLING
Until relatively recently, the range of the European Starling was Europe and western Asia, but it now occupies more than twice the area of its natural range, having been introduced to four other continents. Its most spectacular spread was in North America. In 1890 some 120 individuals were introduced to Central Park, New York City. Within a mere 60 years, the species had colonized the entire USA and much of Canada and Mexico, as shown on the map. The fact that it achieved this remarkable colonization in so short a time is chiefly a reflection of the European Starling's ability to exploit artificial environments such as towns and cities. It is also an aggressive breeder, ousting other birds from their nest-holes.

find niches in which to survive, and fit themselves into the community?

Little is known about this question of vacant niches. Under natural conditions, the spread of species from one area to another is presumably very gradual, but it is possible to gain insights by studying what has happened when humans have introduced species to an area. Sometimes the introduced birds have spread rapidly and increased enormously in numbers. For example, the European Starling *Sturnus vulgaris* was introduced to the USA in 1890 when about 120 individuals were released in New York. By 1950 the bird could be found throughout almost the whole of the USA and much of southern Canada, by which time it had possibly increased a millionfold.

The problem with this example is that it tells us little about the ecology of the natural environment. The starling is a bird that can take advantage of man-made habitats and, almost without exception, has not spread into the natural habitats of the areas into which it has been introduced.

Changing environments
Each individual bird species has evolved its own ecology over a long period of time, during which it can become finely tuned to its environment. But life is dynamic and ever-changing. This means that adaptation cannot be perfect because the environments themselves change. In the relatively recent past, most temperate areas have altered markedly as ice ages have come and gone, while in the more immediate past, and in the present, human activity has wrought widespread and rapid changes to many parts of the globe.

These recent changes have caused great concern for the future of bird populations. Because the environmental changes brought about by humans are so rapid, birds have little chance of adapting through natural selection which requires the passing on of "successful" traits from one generation to the next.

Nowhere is the situation more striking than in the tropical rain forest, habitat of a large proportion of the world's bird fauna. Many of the birds that live in these forests are highly specialized for survival in their various niches and almost certainly are unable to adapt to the changes caused by forest destruction.

Other species that merit concern are those confined to very small areas, especially islands. For example, there are no fewer than four threatened species of parrot in the Caribbean islands: the St Lucia Amazon *Amazona versicolor*, the Red-necked Amazon *A. arausiaca*, the St Vincent Amazon *A. guildingii* and the Imperial Amazon *A. imperialis*. Not only are these birds suffering from loss of their habitats, but their populations are also very small and are so much more vulnerable to extermination by natural disasters such as hurricanes. A further measure of the threat to island birds is the statistic that no fewer than ten species of parrot from islands are known to have become extinct in the last three centuries, including another from the Caribbean, the Red Macaw *Ara tricolor* from Cuba.

The annual cycle of resources
Although many birds have evolved characteristics that enable them to compete with other species for limited resources, this is not necessarily the case all year round. For example,

in most temperate areas food is plentiful in summer but scarce in winter.

Birds breed in summer because this is when food is most abundant. Laying females need plentiful supplies of food if they are to be able to form eggs, and parent birds need plenty of nourishment for themselves and their brood. Furthermore, the inexperienced young birds must leave the nest when food is fairly plentiful if they are to have a chance of learning how to collect food efficiently before the lean times of winter arrive.

In winter, when no new food is being produced, resources become scarcer with each day's consumption. This, coupled with short day length and the need for extra food intake to keep up the body temperature in cold weather, means that late winter can be a difficult time indeed for birds.

Shortage of food outside the summer period is one of the reasons that so many species must migrate. They simply would not be able to survive on the food available at this time of year. Nevertheless, migration, too, has its problems. Migrants must have good food supplies if they are to lay down the fat reserves necessary for their long journeys, and when they arrive at their winter quarters they have to compete for resources with a whole new ecological community. In addition, migrants may face huge problems of climatic changes in their wintering grounds. For instance, the numbers of an Old World warbler, the Whitethroat *Sylvia communis*, that survived to breed in Britain were reduced by as much as 77 percent in one year because of a serious drought in the Sahel region to the south of the Sahara, where the species winters.

Compared with the sedentary human lifestyle, the strategy of migration might seem both costly and hazardous, but in fact this is far from the case. In temperate and boreal parts of the world, the majority of the breeding birds are migrants which spend their winter in more hospitable areas. To be a successful migrant, a bird must have somewhere suitable to go to, must know how to navigate, and must be physically capable of making the journey there and back again.

For most species migration is a twice-yearly journey made from a summer breeding area in which food is plentiful to a more clement wintering place and back again, but a few nonbreeding birds migrate during the summer to molt. Migration does not necessarily have to be undertaken by all the birds of a species, or even all the birds of a particular population of a species. It all depends on where birds are living and often there are considerable differences between populations from the north and south of a bird's range and between old and young birds from the same area.

Patterns in space and time

The pattern of bird migration varies hugely between species. In summer, the most important factor is the nest, so the bird's home must be in a definite locality. For instance, many migrant seabirds fly thousands of miles between breeding seasons, but will return not just to the same colony but to exactly the same nest site, on the same ledge.

In the winter, following migration, the birds are not constrained by the needs of breeding and many roam over large areas seeking good feeding conditions. By contrast, others defend a well-defined winter territory and may be as localized as in the summer. Among land birds

The map shows a selection of long-distance migrants. The Arctic Tern makes the longest journey of all, a total of up to 22,400 mls (36,000 km) for the round trip. The Short-tailed Shearwater flies a total of up to 19,900 mls (32,000 km). The little Willow Warbler is the most numerous of all long-distance Old World migrants. Eleonora's Falcon migrates very late in the year, since its breeding season is timed to coincide with the main migration of small birds on which it feeds its young. Although the Northern Wheatear has a huge breeding range, all populations winter in Africa. Unlike Eleonora's Falcon, Swainson's Hawk relies on updraughts of warm air over land to soar, so it migrates via the land bridge of Central America rather than across the sea.

MIGRATION ROUTES

Arctic Tern
Sterna paradisaea

Short-tailed Shearwater
Puffinus tenuirostris

Willow Warbler
Phylloscopus trochilus

Eleonora's Falcon
Falco eleonorae

Northern Wheatear
Oenanthe oenanthe

Swainson's Hawk
Buteo swainsonii

this second pattern of behavior has been proved for the Reed Warbler *Acrocephalus scirpaceus* in Africa and for several shorebirds, including the Black-bellied Plover *Pluvialis squatarola* in Europe and America. Such territorial birds must be able to insinuate themselves into the local bird populations that are exploiting the food supply that they also need. The more widespread migrants are often generalist feeders, able to take advantage of locally abundant foods.

In birds that breed in the Northern Hemisphere most migrations are orientated north-south. Birds such as the warblers, swallows and martins winter in Central and South America, in Africa or in southern Asia, then stream northward in April and May to occupy breeding grounds right up to the Arctic Circle.

In the relatively recent past their migratory movements have been shaped by the enormous changes in climate that followed the last glaciation. Over the past ten thousand years, as the ice has retreated and the climate improved, many of these species have expanded northward by some 2,000 mls (3,000 km) or more. Others have spread laterally. For instance, the tiny Willow Warbler *Phylloscopus trochilus* now breeds through Siberia almost into Alaska; its ancestors were confined to Africa and, possibly, adjacent parts of Europe and Asia at the height of the last glaciation.

Similarly, the arctic-breeding ducks, geese and swans, shorebirds, loons and terns have all gradually migrated farther north with the warming of the polar regions. The northernmost regions in which snow and ice melt in summer have the advantage of being predator-free, but are inhospitable to birds during the long, cold winter. Such regions are, however, very productive during the short summer and provide a safe place in which to raise chicks.

Other migrations include bird populations that simply move down from high breeding areas on mountains to warmer areas closer to sea level. There are also many species that breed in continental areas, such as central Europe, where climatic conditions, though extreme, are favorable in summer but not in winter, then migrate to coastal regions to take advantage of the milder winter weather.

Finding the way

Accurate navigation is essential for any migrant bird. Even if there is a large, suitable reception area, the smallest mistake can mean that individual birds perish through missing their targets. Scientists now realize that birds have evolved a wide range of navigational systems. Most species are able to make use of several, and particularly of the internal clock, the 24-hour rhythm which many animals possess. This enables daytime migrants to compensate for the movement of the sun across the sky and to use it to work out direction.

Experiments carried out in a planetarium with the American migrant Indigo Bunting *Passerina cyanea* have shown that this bird can navigate accurately using the stars. The young bird watches them to determine, in the pattern of the night sky, the location of the center of rotation – that is, North. Because of the wobbling of the Earth on its axis, this is an essential safeguard to ensure accurate direction-finding.

Experiments with European Robins *Erithacus rubecula* have shown that they can determine direction from the Earth's magnetic field. But they can detect this planetary magnetism only if they are on the move, not when sedentary or restrained. The birds' internal sensor is thought to have something to do with the tiny nodules of the iron-containing mineral magnetite found in the heads of some species.

As with navigation by the stars, this mechanism takes account of the long-term changes in the guiding phenomenon. The Earth's magnetic field reverses at regular intervals which may be as long as a few hundred thousand years – a short time compared with the evolutionary history of birds. Because they detect direction by "measuring" the acute angle the lines of force make with the Earth's surface, not by reacting to the polarity of the lines of force, migrants can accommodate such changes.

Making the journey

The ability to find its way is of no use to a bird if it is physically incapable of making the journey. Migrant birds normally fly, but there are many flightless species, such as penguins, which migrate by swimming and walking – and some seabirds capable of flight also swim on their migratory treks. During their journey

---

NAVIGATION BY THE STARS AND SUN

1. Many birds migrate at night and have been shown to be capable of navigating by the stars. Garden Warblers placed in cages in a planetarium were shown an artificial night sky. When exposed to the star pattern they normally encountered during their southerly fall migration, most of the birds made migratory movements in the "correct" direction (*top*), but when the star map was "switched off" they became disoriented and made random movements (*bottom*).

2. Birds are also capable of navigating by the sun. European Starlings placed in an experimental aviary were able to maintain the same angle with respect to the sun whether receiving its rays directly (*top*) or reflected by mirrors (*bottom*). As long as the birds could see the sun, they could use their "sun compass" to orient themselves in the "correct" migratory direction. However, when the sun was obscured on overcast days or by covering the aviary windows with translucent paper, the birds became totally disoriented.

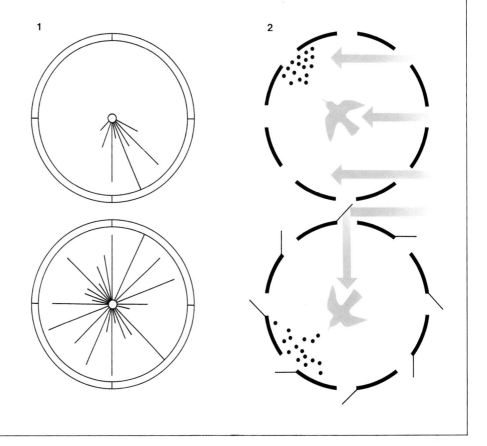

birds need energy. Some, such as swallows and swifts, are able to feed on the wing while migrating, but others need to lay up a preparatory store of energy.

Although the energy needed for continuous flapping flight is considerable, many birds can lay down stores of fat large enough to keep them flying nonstop for four days. In the case of a small bird such as the Blackpoll Warbler *Dendroica striata*, this can take it from the Massachusetts coast in a long curve out across the Atlantic, to make landfall in the southern West Indies or even South America – a flight of more than 2,000 mls (3,000 km). Such birds may double their weight just before migration. Some slightly bigger birds are more efficient in flight: fat stores enable the American Golden Plover *Pluvialis dominica* to make regular flights direct from Alaska to Hawaii – a distance of 2,500 mls (4,000 km).

Birds such as these, which are active fliers, must store and use vast amounts of energy for migration. Others are able to take advantage of energy within the atmosphere. The two major ways of doing this are practiced by large land birds, which soar between thermals, and seabirds, which use the wind over the waves. The energy needed for a bird to hold its wings out and make just the minimal adjustments to control its flight, is only 3 to 5 percent of the energy required for flapping flight. However, if the thermals fail or the wind drops over the ocean, all the bird can do is land on the ground or water and wait for conditions to improve.

The migrants that soar over land use traditional migration routes. These take them to areas where thermals can be guaranteed and which avoid all but the shortest ocean crossings. The route around the Texan coast or the one through Hawk Mountain are classic North American examples, while in Europe the two major crossing points are at the Strait of Gibraltar and the Bosphorus. Each autumn several hundred thousand large birds, mainly birds of prey and White Storks *Ciconia ciconia*, pass through them.

Migration and bird physiology

The adoption of a migratory lifestyle has many consequences for a bird. The creature's whole physiology is adapted to ensure that the migrations can be successfully accomplished, for if they are not, the bird will die. As well as their internal 24-hour clock, birds have a second clock tuned to a yearly cycle (the circannual rhythm). This second clock appears to trigger a variety of physiological processes throughout the year, including the onset of breeding, the annual molt and so on.

For a migrant, fat deposition and migratory activity must be fitted in at the correct time of year, which inevitably reduces the time available for other activities. Comparison of two European chats, the Stonechat *Saxicola torquata* and the Whinchat *Saxicola rubetra*, highlight this situation. Using data gathered in Britain by hundreds of amateur birdwatchers for the British Trust for Ornithology it has been possible to work out that the long-distance

The Willow Warbler has longer, more pointed wings than its otherwise very similar close relative the Chiffchaff. This seems to be related to its need to carry more "fuel," in the form of fat, on its much longer migration which takes it as far as central Africa.

Willow Warbler
Phylloscopus trochilus

pointed wing

Chiffchaff
Phylloscopus collybita

rounded wing

migrant, the Whinchat, generally has time to lay only one (or occasionally two) clutches of eggs each summer, whereas the more sedentary Stonechat usually fits in three.

Whinchats nest in grassy areas and have a more vulnerable nest so, despite having a slightly larger clutch of eggs, each pair has a potential productivity every year of fewer than 2.5 young. Conversely, each Stonechat pair produces an average of 5.5 fledged young. However, the stay-at-home Stonechat is much more vulnerable to cold winter weather than the Whinchat is to hazards during migration. The result is that Stonechat populations tend to fluctuate between low numbers following cold winters, and high numbers after a succession of mild years. Whinchat populations are much more stable.

Many species use special stopover areas where they land, recuperate, and feed during migration. Detailed studies at such sites have shown that a small bird can, in the course of a single day, lay down up to 5 percent of its body weight in the form of fat for use as fuel in flight. Many migrant species also show physical adaptations to their chosen way of life. Most insectivorous species tend to have rounded wings to make for more agility in chasing their prey. However, a long-distance migrant is much more efficient in flight if it has longer, pointed wings. Hence this characteristic is dominant in a long-distance migrant compared with a close relative that stays at home.

The extent of migration

The record-breaker among migrants is undoubtedly the Arctic Tern *Sterna paradisaea*. Some birds breed far to the north of the Arctic Circle and winter in the southern oceans. Indeed, some spend the northern summer in continuous daylight and then, at the other end of the world, experience continuous daylight for the other half of the year.

Most migrants are not as extreme as this: while many species migrate thousands of miles, others undertake much more modest movements. In the Palearctic-African regions, a member of a northern population of a migrant species might migrate 3,000 mls (5,000 km) for winter. A member of a southern population of the species might move a mere 60 mls (100 km), or even stay put. In the south of its range, this species might start breeding as early as late February, while in the north breeding may not start until late May.

Many species are partial migrants in part of their range. In this case, the adult males tend to stay and defend their territories in the breeding areas throughout the winter. However, young birds, and often all females, may migrate to milder sites to winter. The early possession of a good territory is so important to the male's chances of breeding successfully that it is worth the risk for him to remain in his winter territory. If he is alive and in good condition the following spring he will be the first choice as a mate when the females return.

Although they are a very well-defined group of animals, with a distinctive body plan, birds show considerable variation in relation to the demands imposed by their varied habitats and ways of life. These variations include overall size, the shape and size of the bill, legs, nest and eggs, flying ability, longevity and so on.

Some birds soar with hardly a flap of their wings for hours on end, while others beat their wings so fast that they become a blur. There are birds that swim in the roughest of seas and dive to great depths and there are those that have forsaken flight altogether to run across the land faster than most mammals.

On these pages we present a survey of the extremes of the bird world to give an idea of the impressive range of adaptations evolved by these amazing creatures.

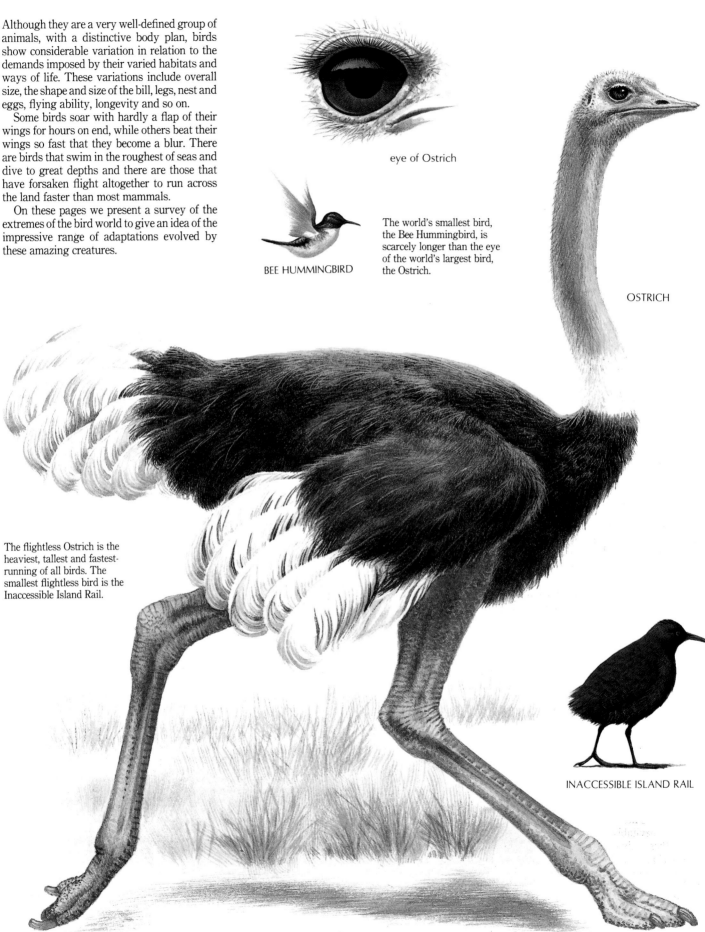

eye of Ostrich

BEE HUMMINGBIRD

The world's smallest bird, the Bee Hummingbird, is scarcely longer than the eye of the world's largest bird, the Ostrich.

OSTRICH

The flightless Ostrich is the heaviest, tallest and fastest-running of all birds. The smallest flightless bird is the Inaccessible Island Rail.

INACCESSIBLE ISLAND RAIL

The Andean Condor is the heaviest of all birds of prey, while the smallest bird of prey is the Bornean Falconet.

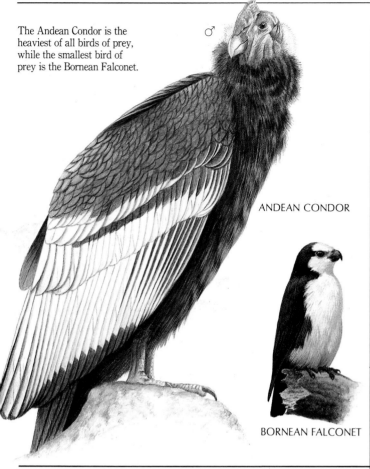

ANDEAN CONDOR

BORNEAN FALCONET

Among seabirds, the Emperor Penguin is the world's heaviest and tallest species, and the Least Storm-Petrel is the smallest.

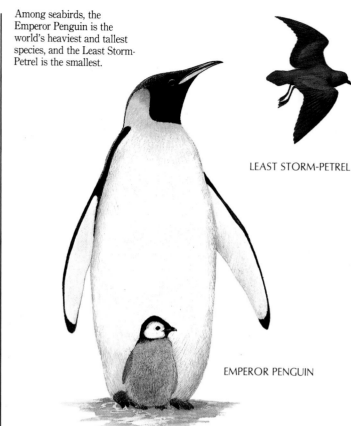

LEAST STORM-PETREL

EMPEROR PENGUIN

The Peregrine Falcon is the fastest-moving bird when diving on its prey; among the fastest in level flight is the Red-breasted Merganser. The bird with the slowest powered flight is the American Woodcock.

PEREGRINE FALCON

AMERICAN WOODCOCK

RED-BREASTED MERGANSER

The fastest swimmer of all birds is the Gentoo Penguin. The fastest-running flying bird is the Greater Roadrunner.

GENTOO PENGUIN

GREATER ROADRUNNER

VITAL STATISTICS

Heaviest and tallest flightless bird	Ostrich (*Struthio camelus*)	Weight: up to 156.5 kg (345 lb) in male Height: up to 2.74 m (9 ft) in male (to top of head)
Heaviest flying birds other contenders:	Great Bustard (*Otis tarda*) Kori Bustard (*Ardeotis kori*) Trumpeter Swan (*Cygnus buccinator*) Whooper Swan (*Cygnus cygnus*) Mute Swan (*Cygnus olor*)	Weight: up to 18 kg (40 lb) in male Up to 16 kg (35¼ lb) in male
Heaviest bird of prey	Andean Condor (*Vultur gryphus*)	Weight: up to 14 kg (31 lb) in male
Heaviest and tallest seabird	Emperor Penguin (*Aptenodytes forsteri*)	Weight: up to 40 kg (88 lb) Height: up to 1.2 m (4 ft)
Largest wingspan	Wandering Albatross (*Diomedea exulans*)	Up to 3.63 m (12 ft)
Largest wingspan of any land bird	Andean Condor (*Vultur gryphus*) Marabou Stork (*Leptoptilos crumeniferus*)	Up to 3.2 m (10½ ft)
Smallest bird	Bee Hummingbird (*Calypte helenae*)	Weight: 1.6 g ($\frac{1}{20}$ oz) Length: 5.7 cm (2¼ in)
Smallest bird of prey	Bornean Falconet (*Microhierax latifrons*)	Weight: 35 g (1¼ oz) Length: 15 cm (6 in)
Smallest flightless bird	Inaccessible Island Rail (*Atlantisia rogersi*)	Weight: 34.7 g (1⅕ oz) Length: 12.5 cm (5 in)
Smallest seabird	Least Storm-Petrel (*Halocyptena microsoma*)	Weight: 28 g (1 oz) Length: 14 cm (5½ in)
Fastest-moving bird	Peregrine Falcon (*Falco peregrinus*)	In a dive, or stoop, may reach 180 km/h (112 mph)
Fastest flier in level flight	Common Eider (*Somateria mollissima*)	Can probably exceed an air speed of 76 km/h (47 mph)
Slowest-powered bird flight	American Woodcock (*Scolopax minor*)	8 km/h (5 mph)
Fastest wing beat	Horned Sungem (*Heliactin cornuta*)	90 beats per second; probably faster (possibly up to 200 beats per second) in display flight of some hummingbirds
Highest-flying bird	Rüppell's Griffon (*Gyps rueppelli*)	11,274 m (37,000 ft or 7 miles)
Fastest-running bird	Ostrich (*Struthio camelus*)	At least 72 km/h (45 mph), possibly up to 96.5 km/h (60 mph) in short bursts
Fastest-running flying bird	Greater Roadrunner (*Geococcyx californianus*)	42 km/h (26 mph)
Longest migration	Arctic Tern (*Sterna paradisaea*)	Up to 36,000 km (22,400 miles) round trip between Arctic and Antarctic
Most aerial bird	Sooty Tern (*Sterna fuscata*)	3 years (perhaps 8–10 years) permanently in air
Most aerial land bird	Eurasian Swift (*Apus apus*)	Up to 3 years permanently in air, before breeding
Fastest swimmer	Gentoo Penguin (*Pygoscelis papua*)	Up to 27.4 km/h (17 mph) in short bursts
Deepest and longest dive	Emperor Penguin (*Aptenodytes forsteri*)	265 m (869 ft); submerged for 18 minutes
Deepest-diving flying bird	Common Loon (*Gavia immer*)	Up to 81 m (265 ft)
Longest legs relative to body length	Black-winged Stilt (*Himantopus himantopus*)	60% of body length
Shortest legs	Swifts (Family Apodidae)	Tarsus 10–12 mm ($\frac{1}{3}$–$\frac{1}{2}$ in)
Longest bill	Australian Pelican (*Pelecanus conspicillatus*)	34–47 cm (13¼–18½ in)
Longest bill in relation to body length	Sword-billed Hummingbird (*Ensifera ensifera*)	The 10.5 cm (4$\frac{1}{10}$ in) bill is longer than the rest of the body
Shortest bills	Nightjars (Family Caprimulgidae) Swifts (Family Apodidae)	8–10 mm ($\frac{1}{4}$–$\frac{1}{3}$ in) 10–11.5 mm ($\frac{1}{3}$–$\frac{1}{2}$ in)
Only sideways-curving bill	Wrybill (*Anarhynchus frontalis*)	
Longest and largest tail	Crested Argus Pheasant (*Rheinartia ocellata*)	Length: up to 1.73 m (5 ft 8 in) Width: 13 cm (5 in)
Most and least feathers counted	Whistling Swan (*Cygnus columbianus columbianus*) Ruby-throated Hummingbird (*Archilochus colubris*)	25,216 feathers 940 feathers
Largest eyes (largest of any land vertebrate)	Ostrich (*Struthio camelus*)	Diameter: 5 cm (2 in)

NESTS

Largest tree nest	Bald Eagle (*Haliaeetus leucocephalus*)	Width: up to 2.9 m (9½ ft) Depth: 6 m (19½ ft)
Largest nest-mounds (built for incubation of eggs by heat they generate)	Dusky Scrub Fowl (*Megapodius freycinet*)	Height: up to 5 m (16½ ft) Width: 11 m (36 ft)
Largest communal nests	Sociable Weaver (*Philetairus socius*)	Up to 300 nest chambers
Largest roofed nest	Hammerkop (*Scopus umbretta*)	Width: up to 2 m (6 ft) Depth: up to 2 m (6 ft)
Largest nest of a small bird	White-throated Cachalote (*Pseudoseisura gutturalis*)	Bird length 21 cm (8¼ in); nest diameter up to 1.5 m (5 ft)
Longest nest-burrow	Rhinoceros Auklet (*Cerorhinca monocerata*)	Length: 8 m (26 ft)
Smallest nests	Vervain Hummingbird (*Mellisuga minima*) Bee Hummingbird (*Calpyte helenae*)	About half the size of a walnut shell Thimble-sized

EGGS AND YOUNG

Largest egg	Ostrich (*Struthio camelus*)	Up to 17.8 cm (7 in) long by 14 cm (5½ in) across Weight up to 1.78 kg ($3\frac{9}{10}$ lb)
Smallest egg	Bee Hummingbird (*Calypte helenae*)	Length: as little as 6.35 mm ($\frac{1}{4}$ in) Weight: as little as 0.25 g ($\frac{1}{100}$ oz)
Largest egg proportionate to the weight of the layer	Little Spotted Kiwi (*Apteryx owenii*) Ringed Plover (*Charadrius hiaticula*) Storm-petrels (Family Hydrobatidae)	About 25% of the body weight
Largest clutch (nidifugous bird) (nidicolous bird)	Grey Partridge (*Perdix perdix*) Blue Tit (*Parus caeruleus*)	Average 15–19 eggs Average 10–11 eggs
Longest incubation	Brown Kiwi (*Apteryx australis*) Wandering Albatross (*Diomedea exulans*)	74–84 days, exceptionally 85 days 75–82 days, exceptionally 85 days
Shortest incubation	Great Spotted Woodpecker (*Picoides major*) and various small passerines (Order Passeriformes)	As short as 10 days
Quickest birds to fledge	Megapodes (Family Megapodiidae) Cabot's Tragopan (*Tragopan caboti*)	Almost immediately Within 24 hours of hatching
Slowest birds to fledge	Royal Albatross (*Diomedea epomophora*) Wandering Albatross (*Diomedea exulans*)	9–12 months
Fastest to breeding maturity	Old World quails (Family Phasianidae), including the Common Quail (*Coturnix coturnix*)	From 10 weeks
Slowest to breeding maturity	Sooty Albatross (*Phoebetria fusca*) Royal Albatross (*Diomedea epomophora*) Wandering Albatross (*Diomedea exulans*)	13 years 6–10 years
Most northerly breeding bird	Ivory Gull (*Pagophila eburnea*)	Above 79°N on floating ice in Arctic Canadian waters
Most southerly breeding bird	Antarctic Petrel (*Thalassoica antarctica*) Snow Petrel (*Pagodroma nivea*)	Thiel Mountains, Antarctica, 80° 30′S, 25° 00′W Mt. Provender in the Shackleton Range, Antarctica, 80° 23′S, 29° 55′W

NUMBERS

Most abundant wild bird (and world's worst avian agricultural pest)	Red-billed Quelea (*Quelea quelea*)	Estimated adult breeding population of 1,500,000,000
Most abundant seabird	Probably Wilson's Storm-Petrel (*Oceanites oceanicus*)	Estimated adult breeding population of hundreds of millions

RANGE

Most widespread species	Osprey (*Pandion haliaetus*) Peregrine Falcon (*Falco peregrinus*) Common Barn-Owl (*Tyto alba*) Snowy Plover (*Charadrius alexandrinus*)	
Most widespread passerine	Barn Swallow (*Hirundo rustica*)	
Most widespread introduced bird	House Sparrow (*Passer domesticus*)	

LONGEVITY – NON-PASSERINES	Years	LONGEVITY – PASSERINES	Years
Royal Albatross (*Diomedea epomophora*)	58.0	Blackbird (*Turdus merula*)	20.3
Palearctic Oystercatcher (*Haematopus ostralegus*)	36.0	Eurasian Starling (*Sturnus vulgaris*)	20.0
Arctic Tern (*Sterna paradisaea*)	33.9	Rook (*Corvus frugilegus*)	19.9
Osprey (*Pandion haliaetus*)	31.2	Northern Bullfinch (*Pyrrhula pyrrhula*)	17.5
Mallard (*Anas platyrhynchos*)	29.0	Barn Swallow (*Hirundo rustica*)	16.0
Long-eared Owl (*Asio otus*)	27.7	Great Tit (*Parus major*)	15.0
White Stork (*Ciconia ciconia*)	26.2	Red-winged Blackbird (*Agelaius phoeniceus*)	14.2
Purple Heron (*Ardea purpurea*)	25.5	Common Cardinal (*Cardinalis cardinalis*)	13.5
Blue-faced Booby (*Sula dactylatra*)	22.9	European Robin (*Erithacus rubecula*)	12.9
Mute Swan (*Cygnus olor*)	21.7	White-crowned Sparrow (*Zonotrichia leucophrys*)	12.8
Eurasian Swift (*Apus apus*)	21.1	Bohemian Waxwing (*Bombycilla garrulus*)	12.6
Red-bellied Woodpecker (*Melanerpes carolinus*)	20.4	White-browed Babbler (*Pomatostomus superciliosus*)	12.1
Little Penguin (*Eudyptula minor*)	18.9	House Sparrow (*Passer domesticus*)	12.0
Black Coot (*Fulica atra*)	18.3	Plain-throated Sunbird (*Anthreptes malacensis*)	11.7
Mourning Dove (*Zenaida macroura*)	17.1	Black-and-White Warbler (*Mniotilta varia*)	11.1
Common Kestrel (*Falco tinnunculus*)	16.2	Reed Warbler (*Acrocephalus scirpaceus*)	11.0
Kea (*Nestor notabilis*)	14.1	Grey-backed White-eye (*Zosterops lateralis*)	10.7
Eurasian Cuckoo (*Cuculus canorus*)	12.9	Sky Lark (*Alauda arvensis*)	10.1
Laughing Kookaburra (*Dacelo novaeguineae*)	12.3	White-breasted Nuthatch (*Sitta carolinensis*)	9.4
Common Quail (*Coturnix coturnix*)	7.6	Bay-backed Shrike (*Lanius vittatus*)	7.9
Ruby-throated Hummingbird (*Archilochus colubris*)	5.0	House Wren (*Troglodytes aedon*)	6.2

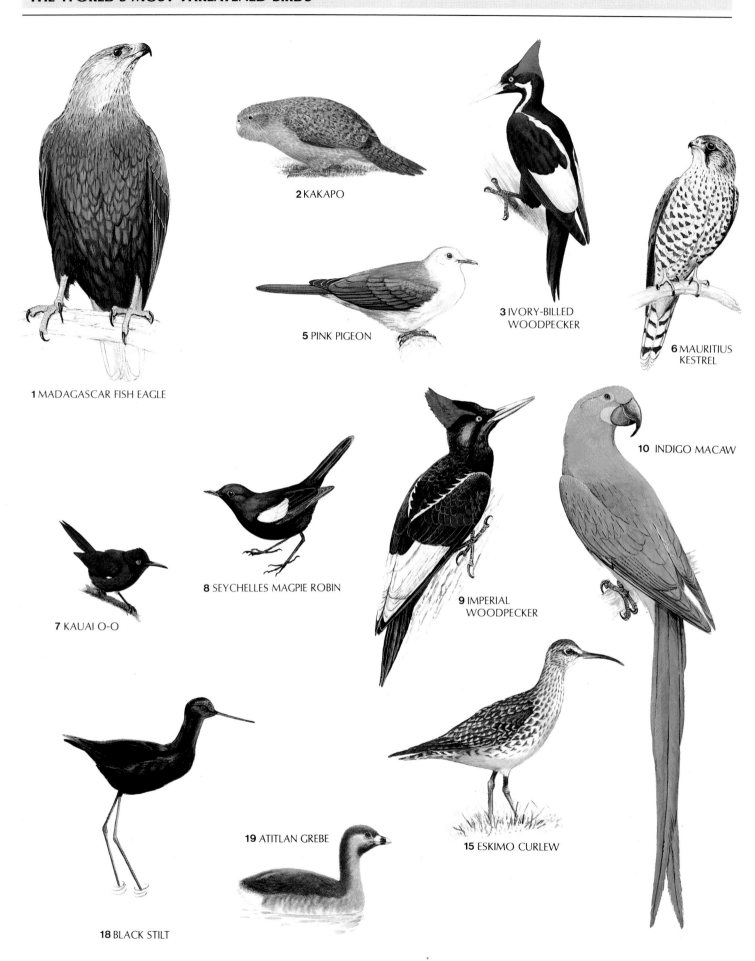

2 KAKAPO

5 PINK PIGEON

3 IVORY-BILLED
WOODPECKER

6 MAURITIUS
KESTREL

1 MADAGASCAR FISH EAGLE

10 INDIGO MACAW

8 SEYCHELLES MAGPIE ROBIN

9 IMPERIAL
WOODPECKER

7 KAUAI O-O

19 ATITLAN GREBE

15 ESKIMO CURLEW

18 BLACK STILT

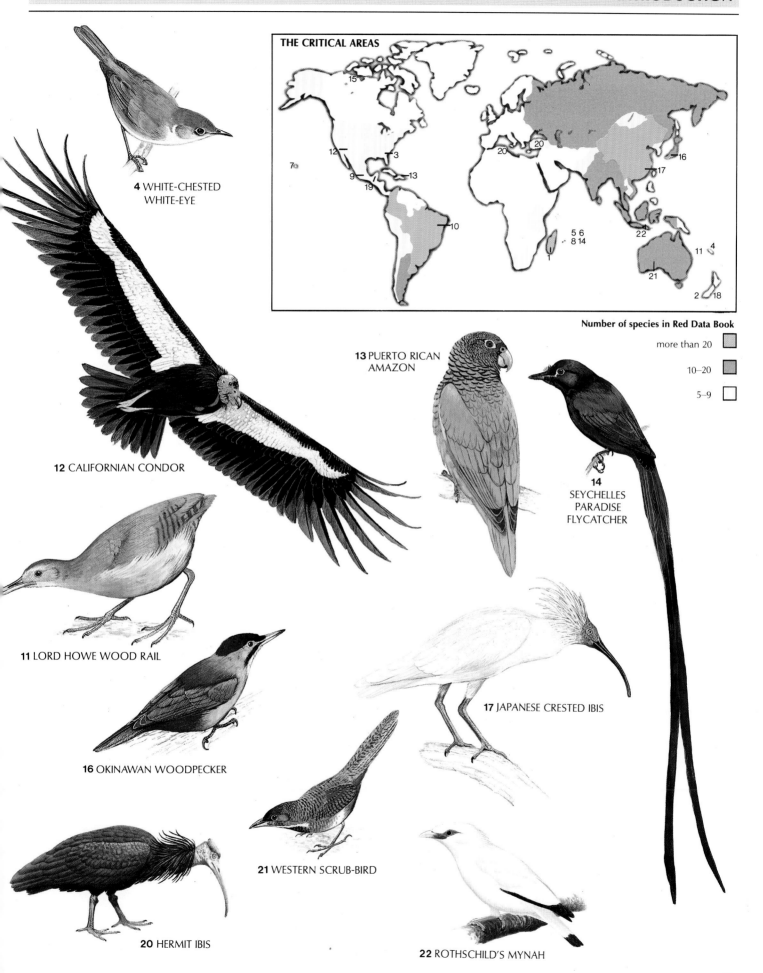

THE CRITICAL AREAS

Number of species in Red Data Book

more than 20

10–20

5–9

4 WHITE-CHESTED WHITE-EYE

12 CALIFORNIAN CONDOR

13 PUERTO RICAN AMAZON

14 SEYCHELLES PARADISE FLYCATCHER

11 LORD HOWE WOOD RAIL

16 OKINAWAN WOODPECKER

17 JAPANESE CRESTED IBIS

21 WESTERN SCRUB-BIRD

20 HERMIT IBIS

22 ROTHSCHILD'S MYNAH

All over the world, birds are in danger. However, this threat is not evenly distributed across the globe. The reasons for this relate to the differences in degrees of diversity in the regions and the varied threats to which birds are exposed. As a general rule, the more specialized a bird in terms of its habitat and food requirements, the less flexibility it will have to adapt to new conditions if its livelihood is under threat.

Bird conservation

The bird kingdom is under great threat. For a variety of reasons, some 1,000 birds – more than 10 percent of all bird species – are in danger of extinction. Quite apart from the moral issues involved in the tragic loss of so many beautiful and unique creatures, birds are sensitive indicators of the health of our environment, so such an accelerated loss must be of concern to anyone who cares about the future life of our planet.

The forces of destruction

During the twentieth century, the industrial and technological advances achieved by humankind have been greater than in any other period in our history and have allowed some of the world's inhabitants, especially of Europe and North America, to attain unprecedented levels of material prosperity. But any sense of achievement must be balanced by a recognition that this "progress" has involved a huge expenditure of natural resources, which has brought our planet to a point of ecological crisis and resulted in the demise of huge numbers of plants and animals, including many birds.

Every creature on planet Earth needs a place to live. For many this place, or habitat, is not only highly specialized and restricted in its area, but is also being systematically destroyed. As habitats are obliterated, so bird species are threatened with extinction.

One of the principal habitat problems concerning birds has been the clearance of forest for agriculture, or for timber and pulp to make paper. Tropical rain forest – a habitat that supports the greatest diversity of the Earth's wildlife – is being lost at a rate of up to 25 million acres (10 million hectares) a year, which is equivalent to an area the size of Austria. Little more than half of the world's original rain forest still stands, and it is predicted that 12 percent of this will be lost by the year 2000.

Inevitably this scale of destruction now threatens hundreds of bird species. Typical groups that are at serious risk are pheasants, birds of prey, hornbills, parrots and pigeons. In Brazil alone, the country with the largest areas of remaining forest, there are 121 species of bird now threatened with extinction. Indonesia, another nation in which huge areas of tropical rain forest are being destroyed, has 126 endangered species, the highest total for any country in the world.

Forests are not the only important wildlife areas to have experienced a serious reduction over the last century. Almost all of the major habitat types have been similarly affected.

Steppe and grasslands have been widely plowed for arable purposes or subjected to intensive overgrazing by livestock. On the Indian subcontinent, the Great Indian Bustard *Choriotis nigriceps* is seriously threatened because its grassland home is being reduced to desert by the excessive grazing action of domestic animals.

Wetland habitats – large, inaccessible areas, sometimes with a climate and conditions hostile to the presence of humans – have long been considered "wastelands" to be conquered and reclaimed. Their widespread drainage and conversion to farmland have brought about a serious decline in many species of waterbird. Cranes, such as the Whooping Crane *Grus americana* of North America, are typical victims of this habitat loss, with almost half the world's total of 15 species now threatened with extinction.

A war on birds

Loss of habitat is the single most important factor in the decline of many bird species. However, direct exploitation, either in the form of hunting or collection of eggs, can have a profound impact on the status of some birds.

There is no more glaring example of the human capacity for senseless slaughter than the story of the Passenger Pigeon *Ectopistes migratorius*. This bird once moved across North America in flocks numbering millions and was possibly the most abundant bird on Earth. Taking advantage of this free and seemingly inexhaustible supply of food, people shot the pigeons with abandon and in 1878 a single dealer handled as many as three million birds in the course of the year. Small wonder, perhaps, that within 35 years this carnage had reduced the population to a single individual in Cincinnati Zoo and that now the bird is extinct.

Such a tragic episode, far from proving to be a high-water mark in human exploitation of birds as a food resource, has been followed by yet more examples of unreasoned decimation. For instance, megapodes, found largely in Indonesia, New Guinea and Australia, are a primitive group of turkeylike birds which lay their eggs in the ground. Here, they are incubated by heat conducted from the soil surface. Since the eggs are so large and highly nutritious, they are widely collected by local people. However, the egg harvest has now reached levels that are unsustainable and, largely as a consequence, 8 of the world's 19 megapode species are now endangered, including the Nicobar Scrub Fowl *Megapodius nicobariensis* and the Moluccas Scrub Fowl *M. wallacei*.

Higher levels of national prosperity have been no guarantee of humane attitudes toward birds. In the countries bordering the Mediterranean and on islands such as Cyprus and Malta, millions of hunters go out each spring and autumn to wage war on passing migrants, some of which are no heavier than a few grams. By dint of the gun and an array of traps and snares, the most efficient of which is a stick smeared with adhesive lime, the hunters take

an annual bag of 900 million birds. It is estimated that one in seven of all the migrants passing through the Mediterranean falls victim to their ravages.

The reason for this assault on birds was once a matter of survival, since they provided an essential supply of food for local populations. Today, this is not so, yet the hunt continues, largely as a sporting activity with a high machismo rating.

A cruel trade

A human passion for keeping cage birds and an attendant international trade in brightly colored species from Africa, Asia and South America, are the major causes of a decline in numbers, particularly for the world's parrots. Of this highly diverse and beautiful family, 78 species are in danger of extinction – a figure that constitutes 1 in 13 of the world's total of endangered bird species.

Yet again, the sustainability of the harvest does not appear to concern the trappers or the dealers – a fact well illustrated by the case of Spix's Macaw *Cyanopsitta spixii* and the Indigo Macaw *Anodorhynchus leari* from South America. The former is probably already extinct, the final handful of young having been taken and sold for $50,000 each. The population of the Indigo Macaw has crashed to only about 60 individuals, but even these few continue to be pursued by poachers.

A further aspect of this trade that must concern conservationists is the method of transportation. Large numbers of birds are often crammed into boxes without food or water. This means that millions of them will arrive at their destination as corpses. It is estimated that for every bird that reaches the petshop alive, another four have died.

The innocent invaders

During the course of their unceasing wanderings around the globe, humans have taken with them, either deliberately or inadvertently, an array of other animals. Because the wildlife of many remote places, especially islands, has evolved in complete isolation, often in the absence of predators, it is highly vulnerable to the introduction of alien species of animal.

On tiny Stephens Island off New Zealand, a lighthouse keeper's cat made ornithological history in 1874 when it carried in to its owner a new species of bird, the Stephens Island Wren *Xenicus lyalli*. This single cat then capped its achievement by bringing home the island's entire population of wrens, thus exterminating the species in only six months.

The island of Mauritius in the Indian Ocean, once the home of the Dodo *Raphus cucullatus*, holds a number of species of bird found nowhere else in the world. The arrival of humans, complete with domestic livestock, pets and scavengers, including a number of Indian birds, monkeys, pigs, mongooses and rats, soon began to take a toll of the indigenous inhabitants.

In addition to eating the Mauritian birds and their eggs, the "invading" species have competed for food and nest sites with the native avian population and have destroyed the island habitats. The Mauritius Kestrel *Falco punctatus* is a typical victim, hovering on the brink of extinction with a wild population of fewer than 50 adult birds. The Mauritius Parakeet *Psittacula echo* is in an even more precarious position, with a total in 1990 of only some 15 individuals.

The tell-tale signs

The decline of bird populations as a consequence of human-created changes in the environment often has implications for more than just the birds themselves. Deforestation in Nepal is a classic example. This small Himalayan country has lost 30 percent of its forest cover in the last 25 years. Inevitably, such habitat destruction has had an adverse effect on many of the country's birds, such as the Cheer Pheasant *Catreus wallichii*.

There have also been serious consequences for the Nepalese people, since the roots of the millions of trees acted as a huge sponge, retaining the heavy monsoon rains and also holding in place the soil on the steep mountain slopes. Now that the trees have been felled, 2,800 million cubic feet (80 million cubic meters) of once cultivable soil are lost every year through erosion and landslides.

Monitoring the response of a bird such as the Cheer Pheasant to our disruption of the environment could serve, in effect, as a warning sign for impending ecological problems. Equally, measures that serve to restore a bird's numbers are often beneficial to every other inhabitant in an area, including the human population. A more sustainable system of tree-felling, for example, accompanied by the replanting of native trees, would benefit the Nepalese people as well as the threatened Cheer Pheasants.

Conservation in action

The need for effective measures on behalf of the world's birds has never been more urgent. There are many local and national conservation bodies, particularly in the developed world, helping to safeguard our wildlife. However, the International Council for Bird Preservation (ICBP) is the only worldwide conservation body working solely on behalf of birds. Established in 1922, it is also the oldest international conservation organization.

One of the ICBP's first objectives was to fight for the protection of migratory birds as they passed through North America – an early expression of a commitment to issues that transcended national boundaries. Today the ICBP maintains this international character, with representatives and active sections in more than 100 countries. It also continues to campaign for migrants – to stop the annual massacre of birds as they pass through the Mediterranean region.

Another important aspect of its work is to raise finance and manage over 60 field and research projects. In Mauritius, for instance, the ICBP, in conjunction with other conservation bodies, has organized a captive-breeding program for the Mauritius Kestrel *Falco punctatus* and for another of the island's threatened endemics, the Pink Pigeon *Columba mayeri*. In Sulawesi in Indonesia, the ICBP employs field staff to study and protect the Maleo Fowl *Macrocephalon maleo*, one of the threatened species of megapode.

A key element in the work of the ICBP is an attempt to promote a heightened awareness of birds and the dangers they face, both in the political sphere, such as at the European parliament in Strasbourg, and in the wider community. Representative of this effort is the publication of educational books in Morocco, Greece, Portugal, Turkey and Lebanon – a measure that aims to encourage a more caring attitude toward wildlife, and to end the slaughter of migrants in the Mediterranean.

Perhaps more so than other animals, birds are colorful, numerous and readily visible. Their accessibility and vitality make them an excellent vehicle for encouraging interest in nature generally. In effect, this popularity makes them emblems, or flagships, helping to focus concern not only for themselves, but for a whole array of other animals and even for whole ecosystems. For example, efforts to conserve the Great Indian Bustard *Choriotis nigriceps* in the desert regions of western India have resulted in the establishment of national parks where a whole community of plants, insects, reptiles, mammals and birds can thrive.

The role of research

All the work of the ICBP is based on hard facts. The organization compiles up-to-date information on more than a thousand threatened birds and coproduces, with the International Union for the Conservation of Nature and Natural Resources (IUCN), the most authoritative reference available on these species, the *Bird Red Data Book*. In addition, it has computerized data on the areas of the globe holding the greatest diversity of wildlife. These areas are "hot spots" that require immediate attention if the greatest number of the Earth's species are to be safeguarded.

Many of the techniques necessary to safeguard endangered birds are generally known. The requirements now are political will and financial support. Failure to mobilize these resources in the face of this crisis will result in a tragic impoverishment of the world's wildlife heritage.

ILLUSTRATED CATALOG OF BIRDS
The pages that follow contain full-color illustrations of some 1,200 species of bird. Selected species are arranged on a series of double page plates each of which is followed overleaf by descriptions of the birds, numerically keyed to a miniature of the illustration.

To give an idea of the variation that can exist between birds of the same species, illustrations may show significant differences between male ($\male$) and female ($\female$), juvenile (juv) and immature (imm) birds, and between breeding and nonbreeding plumage. Except where otherwise indicated, adult breeding plumage is assumed. A selection of distinctive races (subspecies) has also been illustrated. The birds are not drawn exactly to scale, but the biggest and smallest birds in each plate are usually depicted as such.

Except in a few cases, where the arrangement of birds on the color plate necessitated a departure from this sequence, the birds are arranged taxonomically by order and family according to the Howard and Moore world checklist, printed in full at the end of the book. Descriptions of the orders of birds can be found on pages 19–21.

The families of birds are briefly described preceding the examples of representative species. Every species description includes basic information relating to typical range and habitat, and size. The size is the measurement from bill tip to tail tip of a living or freshly dead individual straightened out.

Where appropriate, the conservation status given to birds by the ICBP according to the *Bird Red Data Book* is designated in both species accounts and in the world checklist by a key letter:

E Endangered. Known to be in danger of extinction and unlikely to survive if factors causing the threat continue to operate.

V Vulnerable. Less threatened than birds Endangered, but likely to become Endangered.

I Indeterminate. Thought to be Endangered, Vulnerable or Rare, but insufficiently known.

K Insufficiently known, but suspected to be at risk.

R Rare. Small but stable population which may be at risk and requires careful monitoring.

S Of special concern. Safe at present, but of conservation interest.

? Candidate *Bird Red Data Book*. Under consideration for inclusion in *Bird Red Data Book*.

X Probably extinct.

OSTRICH, RHEAS, CASSOWARIES, EMU, KIWIS, TINAMOUS

race *massaicus*
"Masai Ostrich" ♂

OSTRICH

♂

race *molybdophanes*
"Somali Ostrich"

juv

race *massaicus*
♀ with eggs
and chick

♀

EMU

♂ turning eggs

♂

GREATER RHEA

42

DWARF CASSOWARY

chick

imm

DOUBLE-WATTLED CASSOWARY

ANDEAN TINAMOU

GREAT TINAMOU

LITTLE TINAMOU

BROWN KIWI

LITTLE SPOTTED KIWI

THICKET TINAMOU

eggs

ELEGANT CRESTED TINAMOU

43

OSTRICH, RHEAS, CASSOWARIES, EMU, KIWIS, TINAMOUS

FAMILY STRUTHIONIDAE
Ostrich
There is only one species in this family.

1/ OSTRICH
Struthio camelus

RANGE: **Africa: formerly widespread throughout and into Middle East; now fragmented, with main populations in W and E Africa and South Africa**
HABITAT: **dry savanna**
SIZE: $78\frac{3}{4}$–$98\frac{1}{2}$ in (200–250 cm) high to top of head

Both the numbers and range of the world's largest and heaviest bird have been reduced dramatically in the last 100 years by hunting and habitat destruction. Today the Ostrich survives chiefly in the protected game parks of East Africa. There are 4 races: of the 2 illustrated here, the Masai Ostrich *S. c. massaicus* occurs in southern Kenya and Tanzania, while the Somali Ostrich *S. c. molybdophanes* occurs mainly in the Horn of Africa.

Adapted to survive in dry and seasonal conditions, the Ostrich can withstand a 25 percent loss in body weight through dehydration. With its strong legs and toes, it can run swiftly over open terrain, compensating for its inability to fly.

The taller male chooses a breeding site and 3 or more females may mate with him, each laying her clutch of 2–11 creamy white eggs in a communal nest that is a mere scrape on the ground. In all, 10–40 or more (record is 78) eggs are laid but no more than 19–25 can be incubated. Incubation takes 42 days, the dominant female sitting on the eggs during the daytime and the male taking his turn at night. Chicks leave the nest soon after hatching.

FAMILY RHEIDAE
Rheas
Large flightless birds. Powerful legs. Plumage gray or brown, with some white. Sexes similar. Nest in scrapes on ground. Eggs 10–50, golden-yellow, fading to off-white in Greater Rhea, green in Lesser Rhea. Incubation 35–40 days, chicks leave nest soon after hatching. 2 species.

2/ GREATER RHEA
Rhea americana

RANGE: **S Brazil to Patagonia**
HABITAT: **grassland**
SIZE: $51\frac{1}{4}$ in (130 cm) high to top of head

The range of this, the largest bird in the Americas, has contracted enormously in recent years because of hunting and the spread of agriculture. Its stronghold is the Argentinian pampas, where flocks of more than 100 birds may still be found during the dry winters.

During the spring, the males become solitary and much more aggressive, fighting to win harems of 2–15 females. Each successful male constructs a nest scrape, about 3 ft (1 m) in diameter, in which the females lay their eggs. The male assumes sole responsibility for incubation, taking just an hour's feeding and watering break each midday. All the eggs in the clutch tend to hatch on the same day, and the male continues to cover his brood for warmth during the cold nights.

FAMILY DROMAIIDAE
Emu
There is only one species in this family.

3/ EMU
Dromaius novaehollandiae

RANGE: **Australia**
HABITAT: **open and semiarid bush**
SIZE: **71 in (180 cm) high to top of head**

Second only to the Ostrich in size, the Emu is unique among all birds in the form of its feathering, with 2 quills of equal size sprouting from each growing point. Though it feeds on coarse grasses, it prefers succulent plants and also eats fruit, flowers, seeds and insects. It is a nomadic species, some individuals ranging as far as 620 mls (1,000 km) in a single year as they follow the pattern of rainfall. Males feed intensively in the fall, building up large reserves of body fat for the breeding season. Each mates with 1–3 females, and a total of 8–20 blue-green eggs are laid in the nest depression. The male incubates these for 56 days. Chicks leave the nest when 2–7 days old, but the male must care for them for up to 18 months before they are fully independent.

The Emu is the only large flightless species that has maintained much of its former range. It may even have become more numerous with the spread of farmland—it learned to exploit grain crops to such effect that the Australian army was enlisted to shoot the birds in the "Emu Wars" of 1932. Despite the slaughter of many birds, the Emus won.

FAMILY CASUARIIDAE
Cassowaries
Large, flightless. Powerful legs. Plumage black. Blue and red skin on head and neck. Prominent horny "casque" on the top of the head, which may help clear the way through dense vegetation. Sexes similar. Nest on ground. Eggs 4–8, pale to dark green. Incubation 50 days, chicks leave nest soon after hatching. 3 species.

4/ DOUBLE-WATTLED CASSOWARY
Casuarius casuarius

RANGE: **New Guinea, N Australia**
HABITAT: **moist forest**
SIZE: **63 in (160 cm) high to top of head**

Formerly common and widespread in New Guinea, the Double-wattled Cassowary is now rare due to hunting pressure and the destruction of its forest habitat. It is solitary for much of the year, wandering large territories in search of fallen fruit, insects and small vertebrates on the forest floor. It makes contact with other individuals only when breeding.

Courtship is initiated by the male, as he circles the considerably larger and brighter female, uttering booming notes from his inflated throat pouch. After laying her eggs, the female departs. In the next few weeks she will wander through the territories of several successive males, mating with each one and laying batches of eggs in each of their nests. The males incubate the eggs and care for the young alone.

5/ DWARF CASSOWARY
Casuarius bennetti

RANGE: **New Guinea, New Britain**
HABITAT: **forest up to 10,000 ft (3,000 m)**
SIZE: $43\frac{1}{4}$ in (110 cm) high to top of head

The Dwarf Cassowary, or Moruk, is widely regarded as the world's most dangerous bird. Prior to nesting, the females may become exceedingly aggressive, attacking any nearby creature by slashing with a lethally sharp, enlarged claw, 4 in (10 cm) in length. Such attacks have been known to cause fatal injuries among the New Guinea highlanders.

This species ranges higher than the other cassowaries, reaching bushy mountainous terrain, where it can pluck fruit from shrubs and heathy plants. The horny head casque may be used to turn over leaf litter to reveal food.

FAMILY APTERYGIDAE
Kiwis
Flightless ground-dwellers. Long, downcurved bill, rounded body. Acute sense of smell; nostrils at tip of long bill rather than at base as in other birds. Plumage brown or gray, hairlike. Sexes similar, though females larger. Nest on ground. Eggs 1–2, white. Incubation 65–85 days, chicks leave nest within 7 days of hatching. 3 species.

6/ BROWN KIWI
Apteryx australis
RANGE: **New Zealand**
HABITAT: **native forest, pine plantations**
SIZE: **$27\frac{1}{2}$ in (70 cm)**

The Brown Kiwi is widespread in New Zealand, although it has disappeared due to human settlement and forest destruction in many parts of its range. Flightless and nocturnal, it spends most of its time in dense undergrowth. It has no visible wings or tail but it has strong, stout legs for running. Its plumage of coarse body feathers gives the bird a shabby appearance but protects it when moving through dense, thorny thickets.

Kiwis were once thought to subsist primarily on earthworms. Recent studies of their stomach contents have shown that they have a much more catholic diet including beetles, cicadas, grubs, spiders, pond-life and fallen berries. They can detect items of food under several inches of soil, using the nostrils at the tip of the long bill.

7/ LITTLE SPOTTED KIWI
Apteryx owenii [?]
RANGE: **South Island of New Zealand**
HABITAT: **dry, open forest, woodland, meadows**
SIZE: **$19\frac{3}{4}$ in (50 cm)**

This, the smallest of the kiwis, is the most furtive and shy of the 3 species, although it was the most familiar to the early aboriginal settlers of New Zealand. It has suffered since that time, partly because the Maoris slaughtered thousands of the birds to make ceremonial feather cloaks, but also because they were killed for their meat. After the arrival of European settlers, the introduction of cats, rats and pigs accelerated their decline, causing them to disappear entirely from North Island.

Relative to its body size, the Little Spotted Kiwi lays the largest egg of any bird. The egg is 4–5 times heavier than those of other, similar-sized birds, and the female requires a 24-day laying cycle to produce it. The yolk makes up over 60 percent of the weight of the egg (twice as much as in a normal egg), and the young take a lengthy 70 days to hatch. The chicks can feed themselves within a week of hatching.

FAMILY TINAMIDAE
Tinamous
Plump body, short tail. Flight clumsy. Plumage mainly brown or gray with bars, streaks and spots. Coloration bolder in females. Ground-nesters. Eggs 1–12, glossy, variable in color, including green, yellow, blue and nearly black. Incubation by male for 16–20 days, chicks leave nest soon after hatching. 46 species.

8/ GREAT TINAMOU
Tinamus major
RANGE: **SE Mexico to E Bolivia and Brazil**
HABITAT: **tropical and subtropical rain forest**
SIZE: **$17\frac{3}{4}$ in (45 cm)**

The Great Tinamou dwells deep in the rain forests of Central and South America, preferring areas where there is a distinct layer of understory vegetation beneath the forest canopy. It is heard much more often than it is seen, uttering a long trill that rises and then declines in pitch. Like all tinamous, it spends most of its time on the ground but, if disturbed, it will burst from the floor with a loud roar of wings and fly a short distance through the forest.

In Brazil it nests during May and June, the male clearing a slight depression in the forest floor, where the female lays her glossy violet eggs. It is likely that the female lays more than one clutch, each with a different male, but detailed information on their breeding habits is lacking. Many tinamous have highly prized flesh, and this species is avidly hunted both by indigenous forest people and by settlers. The birds are also threatened by the exploitation and destruction of their habitat.

9/ LITTLE TINAMOU
Crypturellus soui
RANGE: **S Mexico to E Bolivia and SC Brazil**
HABITAT: **scrubby forest edge, secondary forest, overgrown clearings**
SIZE: **$9\frac{1}{2}$ in (24 cm)**

The classification of this widespread species is extremely complicated, involving at least 14 races with no clear division from one form to the next. It may be quite common in some areas, although its timidity and small size cause it to be easily overlooked. Only its tremulous whistled call – one of the most haunting sounds of the American tropical forests – yields any clue as to its presence.

The Little Tinamou nests in June and July, laying 2 eggs the color of terracotta clay. These are incubated by the male alone. Outside the breeding season, the birds often gather in small foraging parties. Unlike many species (though like the Thicket Tinamou), its flesh is not highly regarded, and hunting seems to impose few risks on its future.

10/ THICKET TINAMOU
Crypturellus cinnamomeus
RANGE: **Mexico, Costa Rica, Colombia, Venezuela**
HABITAT: **semiarid regions in scrubby woodland and forest edge**
SIZE: **12 in (30 cm)**

Though the Thicket Tinamou can fly nimbly with a rapid, quail-like flutter, it prefers to hide rather than escape from danger, remaining absolutely motionless on the forest floor. It often occurs in areas where people have disturbed the natural vegetation, and it feeds on small insects, berries and other items of vegetation that it finds on the ground. The bird's song consists of a mournful and pure trio of fluty whistles, the second higher in pitch than the others. It is a frequent sound during the early morning and the late evening.

The Thicket Tinamou is a solitary bird for much of the year, keeping within a small home range. The breeding season is from March to July, when the females each lay 3–7 lustrous purple eggs. The newly hatched young are soon able to find their own food and become independent after approximately 20 days, when they are still only half-grown.

11/ ANDEAN TINAMOU
Nothoprocta pentlandii
RANGE: **Andes from S Ecuador to N Chile and N Argentina**
HABITAT: **puna meadows above 10,000 ft (3,000 m)**
SIZE: **11 in (28 cm)**

There are some 7 races of this small tinamou along the spine of the Andes Mountains. They are typical inhabitants of the short-grass meadows of the puna zone, habitats that can become mercilessly cold at night. In the southern part of the species' range in Chile, the birds frequently enter the terraced alfalfa fields of the Aymara Indians.

The Andean Tinamou's mellow whistles are easy to hear but, with its cryptic coloration, alert senses and rather shy disposition, it is extremely difficult to spot. When disturbed, it will fly off strongly with intermittent wing beats, rather like a partridge or grouse, and if pressed will fly distances of several hundred yards. The male incubates the glossy, chocolate-colored eggs alone and cares for the young after hatching.

12/ ELEGANT CRESTED TINAMOU
Eudromia elegans
RANGE: **Argentina, Paraguay, Bolivia, N Chile**
HABITAT: **arid and semiarid steppe, scrub and woodland**
SIZE: **$15\frac{3}{4}$ in (40 cm)**

Named for its long, forward-curving black crest, this species is widespread across southern South America. It occupies a variety of open habitats up to about 11,500 ft (3,500 m) in altitude. Unusually among the tinamous, it has only 3 toes on each foot, lacking the short, backward-pointing fourth toe. This adaptation may allow it to run more efficiently across the open terrain.

Elegant Crested Tinamous are fairly gregarious. Up to 100 adults may gather in a single flock, although smaller groups are the norm. Like many other tinamous, they are fond of "dustbathing," rubbing their feathers vigorously in the dry earth. This may help keep their plumage in good condition, including ridding it of parasites.

The classification of the genus *Eudromia* is still under debate but there appear to be 2 distinct, although closely related, species. The second species is the more northerly Quebracho Crested Tinamou *E. formosa*.

GENTOO PENGUIN

fully grown chick

KING PENGUIN

juv

juv

young chick

EMPEROR PENGUIN

FJORDLAND
CRESTED PENGUIN

well-grown chick

ADÉLIE PENGUIN

CHINSTRAP PENGUIN

ROCKHOPPER
PENGUIN

ROYAL PENGUIN

MACARONI PENGUIN

YELLOW-EYED PENGUIN

LITTLE PENGUIN

juv

JACKASS PENGUIN

juv

HUMBOLDT PENGUIN

chick in
nesting burrow

MAGELLANIC PENGUIN

juv

GALAPAGOS PENGUIN

PENGUINS

FAMILY SPHENISCIDAE
Penguins
Medium to large flightless marine birds; wings modified to form flat paddles. Plumage blue-black or blue-gray above, white below. Sexes similar. Eggs 1–2, whitish. Incubation 33–62 days. Chicks remain with parents, or in nurseries without them, for up to 10 weeks, or over 13 months in King Penguin. 18 species.

1/ KING PENGUIN
Aptenodytes patagonicus
RANGE: **subantarctic, Falkland Islands**
HABITAT: **oceanic; breeds on coasts**
SIZE: **37½ in (95 cm)**

The King Penguin has a most unusual breeding cycle, for each pair raises only 2 chicks every 3 years. In the first year the single egg is laid in November (early summer in the Southern Hemisphere) and incubated by both parents alternately until it hatches after 55 days. By June the chick has reached 80 percent of its adult weight. The parents virtually stop feeding it in winter and it has to survive until spring on very little food, banded together with other chicks in nurseries to resist the cold. Regular feeding starts again in September and the chick fledges 2–3 months later, ready to spend the summer hunting at sea.

Meanwhile, the parent birds have to molt, and cannot lay again until February (late summer). By winter the chicks are still very small and many die during the next few months. Those that survive fledge the following January. Parents following this timetable cannot breed again until the following summer. In some colonies it seems that most adults breed only once every 2 years.

2/ EMPEROR PENGUIN
Aptenodytes forsteri
RANGE: **Antarctic**
HABITAT: **oceanic; breeds on pack ice**
SIZE: **45¼ in (115 cm)**

Standing some 110 cm (43 in) high to the top of its head, the Emperor is the largest of the penguins. It also has the most southerly distribution, for it breeds around the Antarctic coasts in huge colonies on the sea ice that surrounds the continent in winter. It is rarely seen north of the ice.

Each pair produces an egg in May or June (early winter). The female then goes to sea to feed, leaving the male to incubate the egg on his feet beneath a fold of skin for some 60 days, during which time temperatures plummet to as low as −75°F (−60°C). His body warmth is vital to the unhatched chick, so the male cannot leave the egg for a moment and cannot feed. During his 110-day fast, which begins during courtship, the male loses 45 percent of his initial body weight. He survives the intense winter cold and blizzards by huddling together with the other brooding males.

The female returns at about the time of hatching and feeds the chick, freeing the male to make a long journey across the ice to feed in open water. Later, the chicks gather into nurseries, freeing both parents to go to sea to gather food. The chicks make their way to the sea in midsummer before it becomes frozen over.

3/ GENTOO PENGUIN
Pygoscelis papua
RANGE: **Antarctic, subantarctic, S South America**
HABITAT: **oceanic; breeds on coasts**
SIZE: **31¾ in (81 cm)**

Gentoo Penguins found in the northern parts of their range tend to be more sedentary, often remaining at their colonies throughout the year, while those that breed on the Antarctic continent disappear from the land for the winter.

The breeding colonies are small and are often sited on headlands or behind beaches. Breeding starts as the snow clears in spring: the 2 eggs are laid in a saucer of vegetation and pebbles and are incubated by both parents. About a month after hatching, the chicks gather into nurseries, while the parents make short daily trips to gather food. Krill is a very important part of the diet, and breeding fails in years when the krill do not appear close to the shore.

4/ ADÉLIE PENGUIN
Pygoscelis adeliae
RANGE: **Antarctic**
HABITAT: **oceanic; breeds on rocky coasts**
SIZE: **28 in (71 cm)**

The most southerly of the penguins, apart from the Emperor, the Adélie nests in large colonies on islands and headlands around much of the Antarctic coast. Suitable breeding sites are limited by the availability of ground that becomes bare of snow in summer, near water that becomes free of ice; the breeding adults must have ready access to open water to provide food for their chicks. Experienced breeders return to the same sites year after year and usually to the same mates. The Antarctic summer is very short, so they have little time to breed. The eggs are laid in late November (midsummer) and incubated first by the male and then by the female for a total of 35 days. After 3–4 weeks in the nest, the dark, woolly chicks band together in nurseries while the adults gather food. In another 4 weeks the chicks are fledged, going to sea in February (late summer) when they are only three-fourths of the adult weight.

5/ CHINSTRAP PENGUIN
Pygoscelis antarctica
RANGE: **Antarctic**
HABITAT: **oceanic; breeds on rocky coasts**
SIZE: **26¾ in (68 cm)**

The most numerous penguin, with several million in the South American sector of the Antarctic alone, the population of the Chinstrap, or Bearded, Penguin seems to be increasing because of the extra food made available by the great reduction in numbers of krill-eating whales as a result of the whaling industry.

Chinstraps are the most aggressive of Antarctic penguins and, where they breed alongside Gentoos or Adélies, male Chinstraps may attack their larger neighbors and oust them from their nests. Generally, though, they prefer better drained sites, often nesting on sloping, rocky ground that the other 2 species avoid. They lay later than the others and, unusually, the female takes the first shift of incubation, so she must fast for up to 30 days as well as expending energy in producing the 2 eggs.

6/ FJORDLAND CRESTED PENGUIN
Eudyptes pachyrhynchus
RANGE: **New Zealand, on SW of South Island (Fjordland) and Stewart Island**
HABITAT: **rocky shores; breeds in coastal forest or small caves**
SIZE: **28 in (71 cm)**

Also known as the Victoria Penguin, the Fjordland Crested Penguin is a relatively rare species, with a population in the region of 5,000 birds. It feeds on squid, krill and fish.

It usually nests in small groups, beneath rocky overhangs or in dense vegetation, and defends its territory with harsh cries. As with other crested penguins, the female lays 2 eggs, but the second egg is considerably larger than the first. Both eggs hatch, but only one chick is reared – usually from the second egg. The smaller first egg appears to be an insurance against the second being infertile; when both hatch, the larger chick monopolizes the food supply and the other starves and dies.

7/ ROCKHOPPER PENGUIN
Eudyptes chrysocome
RANGE: **subantarctic islands, S South America**
HABITAT: **oceanic; breeds on island cliffs**
SIZE: **$21\frac{1}{2}$ in (55 cm)**

The Rockhopper is the smallest of the polar penguins, and one of the most quarrelsome. It is named for its skill at scaling steep rock faces to reach its clifftop nest sites. Instead of waddling along like most penguins, it hops from boulder to boulder with its feet together, head thrust forward and flippers held back. The birds generally come ashore at a particular landing place, move onto special drying areas to dry and preen their feathers, then ascend to the colony along customary, well-worn paths. Rockhopper Penguins in the northern part of the range lay their eggs earlier than those in the south, the timing being related to the ocean temperature.

8/ ROYAL PENGUIN
Eudyptes schlegeli
RANGE: **Macquarie Island, S of New Zealand**
HABITAT: **oceanic; breeds on coasts**
SIZE: **30 in (76 cm)**

The Royal Penguin may be only a race or a color phase of the Macaroni Penguin; it differs from that species in its larger size, stouter bill and the gray and white sides to its face, chin and throat. Royal Penguins are generally thought to be restricted to Macquarie Island, but birds with features characteristic of the species have been seen with Macaroni Penguins at other southern ocean island breeding colonies. Intermediates between Royal and Macaroni Penguins have turned up at Macquarie Island and at Marion Island, in the southern Indian Ocean. Although well known by early explorers and sealers, the Royal Penguin was not described scientifically until 1876.

As with other species of penguin, Royal Penguins were killed for the oil that could be gained by boiling their bodies. Between 1894 and 1914 some 150,000 birds were taken every season, although this does not seem to have had major long-term effects on the population. Today, there is probably a total population of over 1 million on Macquarie Island, and the largest single colony contains up to half a million birds and covers more than 15 acres (6 hectares) of coastal terraces.

9/ MACARONI PENGUIN
Eudyptes chrysolophus
RANGE: **subantarctic, South America**
HABITAT: **oceanic; breeds on coasts**
SIZE: **$27\frac{1}{2}$ in (70 cm)**

The Macaroni Penguin is typical of the crested penguins, with long, slender yellow plumes flowing back on each side of its head and a large, deeply sculptured bill. It moves on land by hopping, a remarkably efficient technique that enables it to climb rapidly from sea level up to its nesting colonies, which are usually located on steep terrain such as scree slopes and glacial moraines. These colonies can be immense: one on South Georgia numbers some 5 million pairs.

Like the Rockhopper Penguin, the Macaroni

Penguin is unusual in that, although 2 eggs are laid, the first is much smaller than the second and either fails to hatch or produces a weak chick that soon dies. The 36-day incubation is carried out in 2 long shifts, 1 by each parent, during which each loses up to 30 percent of its body weight. After breeding, the parents spend 2 weeks fattening up on krill caught on long offshore foraging trips before molting.

10/ YELLOW-EYED PENGUIN
Megadyptes antipodes [?]
RANGE: **New Zealand, on SE South Island, Stewart, Auckland and Campbell islands**
HABITAT: **inshore waters; breeds in scrub or low forest**
SIZE: **30 in (76 cm)**

This large penguin with its bright yellow eye is one of the rarest of all penguins, partly because agricultural land reclamation has destroyed its breeding habitat in several areas. However, the population may also be limited as a result of the birds' unusual nesting habits, for the pairs breed in isolation.

Yellow-eyed Penguins feed mainly on fish and squid, coming ashore every night to roost on sandy beaches. Each bird is a resident of a particular area and they form strong, long-lasting pair-bonds.

11/ LITTLE PENGUIN
Eudyptula minor
RANGE: **New Zealand, Chatham Island, S Australia, Tasmania**
HABITAT: **inshore; roosts and breeds on coast**
SIZE: **$15\frac{3}{4}$ in (40 cm)**

The Little Penguin (also called the Little Blue, or Fairy, Penguin) is the smallest of the penguins. It lives on cool temperate coasts, feeding mainly on fish in shallow inshore waters. The bird spends each night ashore, favoring rocky beaches.

Little Penguins are monogamous and they generally return to the same mate each year. They will also return to the same nest site – in a cave, burrow, or beneath vegetation, often some distance inland. The pair may breed in isolation or as part of a colony, but among individual populations breeding times are well synchronized. Two broods can be raised in a season.

12/ JACKASS PENGUIN
Spheniscus demersus [S]
RANGE: **coasts of S Africa**
HABITAT: **cool coastal oceans; breeds on coast**
SIZE: **$27\frac{1}{2}$ in (70 cm)**

There were once a million or more Jackass Penguins, but the population has dropped to 150,000 in the last 20 years. The birds were badly affected by the oil pollution that first hit their breeding and feeding areas in 1967, when the Suez Canal was closed and oil tankers were diverted around southern Africa. Today they are under threat from increased commercial fishing for the pilchards that once made up half their diet.

Although it feeds in the cool Benguela Current,

the Jackass Penguin breeds on dry land under the hot African sun. It avoids overheating by nesting in burrows or under rocks, and by being active on land only at night.

13/ HUMBOLDT PENGUIN
Spheniscus humboldti [?]
RANGE: **coastal Peru and Chile to 40° S**
HABITAT: **shores, offshore islands and offshore waters**
SIZE: **$26\frac{3}{4}$ in (68 cm)**

Penguins are all cold-adapted birds but some species occur in tropical areas where the water is cooled by cold currents sweeping up from Antarctica. The Humboldt, or Peruvian, Penguin is one of these, occurring on coasts washed by the cold Humboldt Current. It feeds largely on fish such as anchovies, cooperating to herd them into compact shoals which can be preyed on at will.

At one time the Humboldt Penguin nested in burrows excavated in deep guano (accumulated, dried bird droppings) on offshore islands, but since the removal of much of the guano they have nested in caves on the shoreline. They nest at any time of year and new eggs, hatchlings and large chicks may appear side by side in a cave.

14/ MAGELLANIC PENGUIN
Spheniscus magellanicus
RANGE: **S coast of South America from Chile to Brazil**
HABITAT: **coasts and offshore islands**
SIZE: **$27\frac{1}{2}$ in (70 cm)**

Magellanic Penguins are noisy birds when ashore, producing a loud, staccato braying which is answered by neighboring birds, building up until the whole colony is in uproar. They use their feet to dig holes in grassy slopes or beneath forest trees, often high above the water. The holes are big enough to accommodate both adults, which retire to them at night.

The adult penguins prey mainly on fish and cuttlefish, returning to their burrows and feeding their brood by regurgitation. Groups of older chicks often leave the burrows and congregate on the beach, where they are more conveniently fed by their parents. At the end of the breeding season they migrate to more northerly waters.

15/ GALAPAGOS PENGUIN
Spheniscus mendiculus
RANGE: **Galapagos Islands**
HABITAT: **coasts and offshore waters**
SIZE: **$19\frac{1}{2}$ in (50 cm)**

Like the Humboldt Penguin, the Galapagos Penguin owes its distribution to the cold Humboldt Current, which flows up the west coast of South America to the Galapagos island group, a volcanic archipelago astride the Equator.

It feeds on small fish, often in the company of boobies, terns and shearwaters. Between sorties, the birds rest on sandy shores and rocky beaches. The birds generally nest in small groups on sheltered coasts and, since soft soil for burrowing is rare on the islands, the 2 eggs are generally laid in caves or holes in the volcanic rock.

LOONS, GREBES

non-breeding

RED-THROATED LOON

ARCTIC LOON

non-breeding

race *viridigularis*

COMMON LOON

non-breeding

non-breeding

YELLOW-BILLED LOON

non-breeding

LITTLE GREBE

non-breeding

PIED-BILLED GREBE

ATITLAN GREBE

non-breeding

SHORT-WINGED GREBE

non-breeding

GREAT CRESTED GREBE

non-breeding

HOARY-HEADED GREBE

n-breeding

CLARK'S GREBE

HORNED GREBE

HOODED GREBE

WESTERN GREBE

51

LOONS, GREBES

FAMILY GAVIIDAE
Divers

Large diving waterbirds. Breeding plumage white below, variable above but always with vertical white stripes on neck; winter plumage grayish, paler above than below. Sexes similar. Nest in mound of vegetation. Eggs usually 2, dark brown to olive, spotted or blotched in black. Incubation 24–29 days. Chicks leave nest within 1 day of hatching but are brooded on parents' backs or under a wing for warmth and protection. 4 species.

1/ RED-THROATED LOON
Gavia stellata

RANGE: circumpolar Arctic S to temperate latitudes
HABITAT: breeds on freshwater lakes and pools; winters mainly on coastal waters
SIZE: $20\frac{3}{4}$–27 in (53–69 cm)

The Red-throated Loon is a slender, graceful bird, with a slightly upturned bill and a rusty-red throat patch. Unlike other members of its family, which require a long run across the water to become airborne, the Red-throated Loon can take off easily from small bodies of water. This allows it to nest beside pools only 33 ft (10 m) across in its breeding grounds on the Arctic tundra and on temperate moorland. Such pools seldom contain enough fish and the birds fly several miles to larger lakes or to the ocean to obtain food for their young.

The female usually lays 2 eggs and they are incubated by both parents for about 28 days. After hatching, competition between the young for the food brought by the parents frequently leads to the death of the weaker chick.

2/ ARCTIC LOON
Gavia arctica

RANGE: circumpolar Arctic and N temperate latitudes; winters to S
HABITAT: breeds on large, deep lakes; winters on coastal waters
SIZE: $22\frac{3}{4}$–$28\frac{3}{4}$ in (58–73 cm)

In its handsome breeding plumage, the Arctic Loon has a glossy black throat patch that shimmers with color in strong sunlight. In the Siberian race *G. a. viridigularis*, the throat patch has a green sheen, while the northern European race *G. a. arctica*, which is illustrated, and the race *G. a. pacifica* from North America and coastal northeast Siberia, both have a purple gloss to the throat. However, some ornithologists consider the latter to be a separate species entirely, named the Pacific Loon, *G. pacifica*.

Arctic Loons prefer to breed alongside large lakes, where they find most of their food, though they will fly up to 7 mls (10 km) to other waters if necessary. When feeding, they dive for about 45 seconds, probably reaching depths of 10–20 ft (3–6 m). They occasionally use their wings under water to assist their webbed feet.

The nest is a low mound of aquatic vegetation next to the water. The normal clutch is 2 and incubation lasts for about 28 days. Fledging takes another 12–13 weeks, by which time the young birds are beginning to catch their own fish.

3/ COMMON LOON
Gavia immer

RANGE: N North America, Greenland and Iceland; winters to S
HABITAT: breeds on large, deep lakes; winters on coastal waters
SIZE: 27–$35\frac{3}{4}$ in (69–91 cm)

With its greater size, thick neck and strong spear-shaped bill, the Common Loon is a much heavier bird than the Red-throated and Arctic loons. In the breeding season, its upperparts are patterned all over with bold white barring, and 2 white necklaces mark its black head and neck. Its calls, used to advertise and defend the breeding territory, are among the loudest of any bird and consist of a variety of yodeling, howling and wailing cries that can carry for long distances across the water. At their most intense, these sound like manic laughter.

It has been suggested that "loon," came originally from the old Norse name *lomr*. *Lomr* may mean to moan, in which case it refers to the birds' wailing calls, but some sources suggest it means lame or clumsy and refers to the birds' awkward gait on land. A loon's feet are set far back on its body, so it usually humps itself along on its breast and belly. It builds its nest close to the water's edge so that it has the minimum distance to move on land.

4/ YELLOW-BILLED LOON
Gavia adamsii

RANGE: circumpolar high Arctic
HABITAT: breeds beside freshwater pools and rivers; winters on coastal waters
SIZE: 30–$35\frac{3}{4}$ in (76–91 cm)

The Yellow-billed Loon is the largest of the 4 species. It is very similar in plumage at all times of the year to the Common Loon, though in summer the white pattern on the upperparts is more bold and the slightly upturned bill is a conspicuous pale cream.

The Yellow-billed Loon's habit of nesting at the edge of running water is unique among the divers and appears to occur only in the Russian part of the bird's range; such behavior has not been

recorded in North America. It is essential that the river is not subject to dramatic fluctuations in level, which could either flood the nest or leave it stranded so far from the water that the parents would have great difficulty shuffling across land to reach their young.

FAMILY PODICIPEDIDAE
Grebes

Medium to large diving waterbirds. Usually brown or gray underparts, whitish beneath; head, throat and neck often brightly colored in breeding season. Sexes similar. Nest on floating decaying vegetation. Eggs 2–6, white or cream. Incubation 20–30 days. Chicks leave nest soon after hatching but are brooded on parents' backs or go to a nursery nest for warmth and protection. 20 species.

5/ LITTLE GREBE
Tachybaptus ruficollis

RANGE: S Eurasia, Africa and Indonesia; northerly breeders migrate S for winter
HABITAT: shallow fresh water; winter habitat includes sheltered estuaries and coastal waters
SIZE: $9\frac{3}{4}$–$11\frac{1}{2}$ in (25–29 cm)

The Little Grebe is a dumpy, short-necked waterbird lacking any kind of a tail and with a short, slightly upturned bill. During the breeding season, this species becomes much more vocal than most other grebes, uttering a distinctive and penetrating trill. A bird attempting to chase a rival from its territory will call vigorously, rush low over the water at its opponent and indulge in violent splashing and diving. During courtship, both sexes will often trill together in duet. The birds' nest is a floating platform of waterweed anchored to vegetation or sometimes to a bush growing in the water. The 4–6 eggs are incubated by both sexes for about 20 days.

6/ PIED-BILLED GREBE
Podilymbus podiceps
RANGE: S South America N to S Canada
HABITAT: shallow standing or slow-moving
fresh water
SIZE: $12\frac{1}{4}$–15 in (31–38 cm)

The short, stocky body of the Pied-billed Grebe contrasts markedly with the bird's large head and prominent bill. The bill is not unlike a chicken's, nearly half as deep as it is long. It is whitish in color with a black band at the midpoint, making it the most conspicuous feature on this otherwise rather dull dark gray-brown bird.

Many Pied-billed Grebes are sedentary, spending summer and winter on the same stretch of water. They sometimes form loose flocks in winter but break up into breeding pairs and establish territories in the spring. In the northern parts of the range, the lakes and pools freeze over in winter. Birds that breed there either migrate south to find suitable winter quarters or move to brackish, ice-free lagoons on the coast.

7/ ATITLAN GREBE
Podilymbus gigas   X
RANGE: confined to Lake Atitlan,
Guatemala
HABITAT: reedy margins of a large lake
SIZE: $18\frac{3}{4}$ in (48 cm)

The Atitlan Grebe is a close relative of the Pied-billed Grebe, though it is half as large again in size. Its wings are very short and the bird is practically flightless. The species' home, Lake Atitlan, lies at an altitude of over 6,000 ft (nearly 2,000 m) in the Guatemalan highlands.

Since it is confined to this single body of water, the Atitlan Grebe is vulnerable to any adverse changes that may occur in the lake. It has probably never been very numerous, but its numbers dropped dramatically after the introduction into the lake of alien fish that competed for food with the grebes and preyed on their chicks. In 1965 there were only 80 grebes left. Later the population started to recover, but subsequent destruction of the reedbeds around the lake, pollution and a drop in water level prompted numbers to fall again. Since the 1970s, the population has steadily declined and the bird is now apparently extinct.

8/ SHORT-WINGED GREBE
Rollandia micropterum
RANGE: confined to Lakes Titicaca, Umayo
and Poopo in Peru and Bolivia
HABITAT: large mountain lakes
SIZE: 11 in (28 cm)

Like other grebes of Central and South American lakes, the Short-winged Grebe is incapable of flight. It lives on a series of lakes 10,000 ft (over 3,000 m) high in the central Andes. At such altitudes the nights are bitterly cold. Like a number of other small grebes, it therefore indulges in "sun-basking" to offset the loss of heat from its body.

Early in the morning, and again in the late afternoon, Short-winged Grebes rest on the water, with their backs to the sun. They raise their wings slightly and lift the feathers on their backs and sides to allow the sunshine to penetrate to the skin. By soaking up warmth in this way, they reduce the amount of energy they need from their food just to keep warm.

9/ HOARY-HEADED GREBE
Podiceps poliocephalus
RANGE: W and SE Australia and New
Zealand
HABITAT: large open waters, including
swamps, lakes and estuaries
SIZE: $9\frac{3}{4}$–$11\frac{1}{2}$ in (25–29 cm)

The Hoary-headed Grebe takes its name from the fine white streaking running from front to back across its brown forehead and cheeks. It is a short, stubby bird, lacking all but a rudimentary tail. Unlike most other grebes, the species is highly colonial when breeding. Colonies can consist of several hundred pairs with each nest only 3 ft (1 m) apart from the next. This species also differs from most other grebes in that it rarely calls. With no territory to defend, there is little need for loud cries or trills.

Hoary-headed Grebes site their nests in vegetation in shallow water. As with other Australian waterbirds, nesting takes place when floods appear after heavy rain; the timing of breeding can therefore differ from one year to the next.

10/ GREAT CRESTED GREBE
Podiceps cristatus
RANGE: temperate Eurasia, E and South
Africa, Australia and New Zealand
HABITAT: shallow, standing or slow-
moving fresh water with emergent
vegetation; moves to estuaries and coastal
lagoons in winter
SIZE: 18–20 in (46–51 cm)

The Great Crested Grebe is renowned for its elaborate courtship rituals. Both sexes have a double black head crest and chestnut and black tippets (ear ruffs) and, during courtship, they erect these feathers, which gives their heads a markedly triangular outline. The pair indulge in a "weed-dance," during which pieces of waterweed are held in the bill as the 2 birds come together, breast to breast, and rear up out of the water, swinging their heads from side to side. The dance is both elegant and stately.

Like other grebes, the Great Crested Grebe feeds on fish, insects, crustaceans and mollusks. When the young hatch, the parents feed them small fish and also a supply of small feathers. Adults, too, will regularly swallow feathers molted from their belly and flanks. It is believed that the feathers bind material together in the gut, helping the birds regurgitate waste pellets. Regular regurgitation probably helps to clear the gut of harmful parasites.

11/ HORNED GREBE
Podiceps auritus
RANGE: circumpolar N North America and
Eurasia
HABITAT: breeds on both small and large
waters; winters on large lakes and
sheltered coasts
SIZE: $12\frac{1}{4}$–15 in (31–38 cm)

The courtship behavior of the Horned Grebe, like that of the Great Crested Grebe, is dramatic and elaborate. To enhance their appearance, the birds erect the golden-chestnut crests running back and upward from each eye and the black tippets, or ear ruffs, under their eyes.

In one ritual, however, the display feathers are smoothed down as one bird rears up out of the water and bends its head and neck downward. As it does so, it bears a striking resemblance to a penguin and this particular display has been called the "ghostly penguin dance."

Horned Grebes gather a pile of aquatic vegetation for their nest. Sometimes they anchor the pile to plants in the water, but often it rests on a small rock at or just below the water level.

12/ HOODED GREBE
Podiceps gallardoi   R
RANGE: S Patagonia
HABITAT: large freshwater lakes
SIZE: 14 in (36 cm)

The Hooded Grebe was recognized as a new species only in 1974 and was at first believed to be confined to a single lake in Santa Cruz province, southwest Argentina. Subsequent investigations have revealed that it is widely, but thinly, distributed over a considerable area, inhabiting a number of large, basaltic lakes scattered throughout the region. The population of Hooded Grebes is quite small, though not as tiny as was once thought. Two estimates made in 1986 put the number at 3,000–5,000 individuals.

13/ WESTERN GREBE, CLARK'S GREBE
Aechmophorus occidentalis, A. clarkii
RANGE: W North America, from S Canada
to Mexico
HABITAT: breeds on freshwater lakes;
winters mainly on the ocean
SIZE: 22–29 in (56–74 cm)

Until recently, Clark's Grebe (also known as the Mexican Grebe) was considered a race of the Western Grebe but it is now regarded as a separate species. The birds share the same general range and habitat, although Clark's Grebe is much less common to the north. Hybrids between the 2 species are occasionally reported.

Western Grebes perform a series of elaborate courtship rituals. During their "rushing" ceremony, for example, male and female rise up out of the water together. Holding themselves erect, with only their legs under the surface, they rush along side by side for about 22–33 yd (20–30 m) before sinking back into the water.

Western Grebes are fairly gregarious, with several birds breeding on the same water. Flocks of many hundreds or even thousands gather at migration stopovers and in the wintering areas.

ALBATROSSES, SHEARWATERS AND PETRELS, STORM-PETRELS, DIVING-PETRELS

juv

adult + egg at nest

WAVED ALBATROSS

adult feeding
chick at nest

BLACK-BROWED ALBATROSS

WANDERING ALBATROSS

juv

white phase

SOOTY ALBATROSS

imm

SOUTHERN GIANT PETREL

at nest

NORTHERN FULMAR

PINTADO PETREL

CAHOW
at nest burrow

BROAD-BILLED PRION

SHORT-TAILED SHEARWATER

MANX SHEARWATER

CORY'S SHEARWATER

race *mauretanicus*
"Balearic Shearwater"

LEACH'S STORM-PETREL

WILSON'S STORM-PETREL

COMMON DIVING-PETREL

LITTLE SHEARWATER

ALBATROSSES, SHEARWATERS AND PETRELS, STORM-PETRELS, DIVING-PETRELS

FAMILY DIOMEDEIDAE
Albatrosses

Large, open ocean birds. Long, narrow wings and long, hooked bill. White with dark upperparts, wing tips, brow or tail; 2 species all dark. Sexes similar. Nest usually on pile of soil and vegetation. 1 egg, white. Incubation 65–79 days, chicks remain in nest 4–12 months. 14 species.

1/ WANDERING ALBATROSS
Diomedea exulans

RANGE: **S oceans, N of 60° S; breeds on several islands across S oceans**
HABITAT: **oceanic**
SIZE: **42–53 in (107–135 cm)**

Together with the Royal Albatross *D. epomophora* and the Amsterdam Island Albatross *D. amsterdamensis*, this species is one of the "great albatrosses." These 3 are the largest of all seabirds and have the greatest wingspans of any bird species, with a spread of 8–11 ft (2.5–3.3 m). The birds spend most of their time out over the open ocean, soaring with the help of the thermal currents, sometimes covering up to 300 mls (500 km) a day. It lands on the ocean only in calm weather or to feed on squid, fish and food refuse from ships. It comes to land on subantarctic islands only to nest and rear its young.

Wandering Albatrosses are slow-breeding but long-lived, with an average lifespan of 30 years. Although capable of breeding when 3–4 years old, they do not start doing so until they are 7–8. Since incubation takes 11 weeks, and fledging 40 weeks, breeding is possible only in alternate years.

2/ WAVED ALBATROSS
Diomedea irrorata

RANGE: **SE Pacific Ocean; breeds on Hood Island, (Galapagos) and Isla de la Plata (W of Ecuador)**
HABITAT: **waters of Humboldt Current**
SIZE: **33–37 in (84–94 cm)**

This exclusively tropical albatross numbers some 6,000–12,000 individuals. It feeds on fish, squid and other invertebrates. Its long, narrow wings make it an efficient glider but give it poor braking power and a high stalling speed. This makes land arrivals and departures difficult, especially on its nesting islands which are strewn with boulders and cacti. Successful breeding is preceded by an elaborate courtship dance called the "ecstatic ritual." Calls noted during courtship include *ha-ha-ha* noises and a drawn out *whoo-oo*.

3/ BLACK-BROWED ALBATROSS
Diomedea melanophris

RANGE: **S oceans, from 65° to 10° S; breeds on several islands across S oceans**
HABITAT: **oceanic**
SIZE: **32½–36½ in (83–93 cm)**

One of the most numerous of the albatrosses, this species nests alongside the similar Gray-headed Albatross *D. chrysostoma*, often gathering in great colonies. The nest is a barrel-shaped pile of mud and grass, about 24 in (60 cm) high. The male arrives at the colony a week before the female, who stays for 1 day for mating, goes to sea for

another 10 days and finally returns 2 days before laying. The species' main food is krill, which may explain why it can nest every year, while the Gray-headed Albatross, which feeds on nutritionally poor squid, breeds only in alternate years.

4/ SOOTY ALBATROSS
Phoebetria fusca

RANGE: **Atlantic and Indian oceans; breeds on several islands in this region**
HABITAT: **oceanic**
SIZE: **33–35 in (84–89 cm)**

The Sooty Albatross and its close relative, the Light-mantled Sooty Albatross *P. palpebrata*, differ from other members of their family in their proportionally longer, narrower wings and tapering tail and more solitary nesting habits. Their flight is graceful and agile and their displays include synchronized flights up and down in front of the colony by courting and established pairs. They breed on cliffs or at sites inland where there is sufficient slope in front of the nests to enable them to take off easily. They start breeding when they are 11–13 years old, after a 3–4 year courtship, and young are reared only in alternate years.

FAMILY PROCELLARIIDAE
Shearwaters and petrels

Small, medium or large short-tailed, slender-winged, open ocean birds. Plumage usually black, gray or brown, with white. Sexes similar. Nest in burrows or crevices; sometimes on ledges or open ground. Eggs 1, white. Incubation 43–60 days, chicks remain in nest 2–5 months. 72 species.

5/ SOUTHERN GIANT PETREL
Macronectes giganteus

RANGE: **S oceans, N to 10° S; breeds on various islands and on Antarctic coasts**
HABITAT: **oceanic**
SIZE: **33¾–39 in (86–99 cm)**

Popularly called Stinkers because of their rank smell and their habit of feeding on carrion, the 2 species of giant petrel (the other is the Northern

Giant Petrel *M. halli*) were separated only recently on the basis of slight physical but marked ecological differences. The largest of the petrels, these birds rival some of the albatrosses in size. They are agile on land and feed on land as well as at sea. They use their massive bills to rip into the flesh of dead animals such as seals and whales.

The nest is a low saucer of pebbles or soil and vegetation. Both sitting adults and nestlings defend themselves with the common petrel habit of spitting oil. The white phase of this species is spread through the breeding population, accounting for 15 percent of birds in places.

6/ NORTHERN FULMAR
Fulmarus glacialis

RANGE: **North Pacific and Atlantic oceans**
HABITAT: **oceanic; breeds on coasts**
SIZE: **17¾–19½ in (45–50 cm)**

The Northern Fulmar has grown in numbers over the last 100 years, either because of the increased quantities of offal discarded first by whalers and now by fishing boats, or through changes in ocean water temperatures. St Kilda once had the only colony in the British Isles, but colonies are now found on all cliff coasts and the total British and Irish population is now over 350,000 pairs.

The nests are sited on sea cliffs but sometimes farther inland on cliffs, walls and buildings. The birds visit the sites for most of the year, performing soaring displays and uttering cackling calls. Of the 2 plumage forms, the pale phase is the more numerous in the Arctic, the dark phase at lower latitudes, although the detailed picture is complex and a range of intermediates also occurs.

7/ PINTADO PETREL
Daption capense

RANGE: **S oceans and W coast of South America; breeds on islands in S oceans**
HABITAT: **oceanic**
SIZE: **15¾–16 in (38–40 cm)**

A regular follower of ships, this petrel, also known as the Cape Petrel or Cape Pigeon, gathers in large flocks where surface currents cause a concentration of krill and other crustaceans. Pintado Petrels breed in colonies on cliff faces, making pebble nests on open ledges. The males clear snow from the ledges and guard the sites, while the females spend 2–3 weeks feeding at sea, returning 1 day before laying.

8/ CAHOW
Pterodroma cahow   E

RANGE: **nonbreeding range unknown; breeds on 5 small islets off E Bermuda**
HABITAT: **open seas; breeds on rocky islets**
SIZE: **16 in (41 cm)**

Before the arrival of settlers, hundreds of thousands of Cahows may have bred in Bermuda. Hunters, domestic animals and accompanying rats soon forced the birds from the mainland onto rocky islets. Even there, they declined through competition for nest sites with tropicbirds, predation by rats and poisoning by DDT. Their numbers are now extremely low. The Cahow takes its name from its eerie mating call, heard in late autumn. The birds used to dig burrows on their former nesting grounds, but now lay their single egg in a rocky burrow formed by water erosion. An alternative name is Bermuda Petrel.

9/ BROAD-BILLED PRION
Pachyptila vittata

RANGE: **S oceans; breeds on various islands in S oceans, also on coasts of South Island (New Zealand)**
HABITAT: **oceanic**
SIZE: **9¾–11¾ in (25–30 cm)**

The shape of the bill, with its wide base, gives the Broad-billed Prion an almost froglike appearance. The edges of the bill are fringed with comblike plates that act as filters in the same manner as the baleen plates of whales. The bird scoops a mouthful of water and squeezes it back out through the plates, leaving the prey behind. Pinhead-sized crustaceans called copepods provide most of its food. The Broad-billed Prion breeds in colonies in summer. It usually visits its nest at night, to avoid predation by marauding skuas.

10/ CORY'S SHEARWATER
Calonectris diomedea

RANGE: **breeds Mediterranean and Atlantic islands; winters E coast North America, S to Uruguay and into W Indian Ocean**
HABITAT: **warm seas**
SIZE: **18–20¾ in (46–53 cm)**

Cory's Shearwaters take most of their food from the water's surface, eating fish, squid and other crustaceans. They sometimes gather in such huge concentrations on the ocean that they have been mistaken for land.

The birds breed on uninhabited islands, where their colonies are so dense that the nest-burrows are almost touching. The incubation period for the single egg is about 54 days, and the young fledge 14 weeks later. Young and, latterly, adults and eggs have been cropped for food on the Selvagens and other island groups, and they have even been "farmed" by the provision of artificial burrows.

11/ SHORT-TAILED SHEARWATER
Puffinus tenuirostris

RANGE: **breeds S Australia, Tasmania; migrates to N Pacific after breeding**
HABITAT: **coasts and offshore waters in breeding season; open ocean otherwise**
SIZE: **16–17 in (41–43 cm)**

This species lives in flocks, diving from the ocean surface or from the air 3 ft or more beneath the waves to catch krill and sometimes small squid and fish. At times, the ocean may become churned white with plunging birds. They nest in burrows under tussocks in vast colonies. The chicks are deserted by the parents in late April or early May (or at 13 weeks old) and swim out to sea.

This species is known in Australia as the Muttonbird because of its tasty flesh. Some fat nestlings are still killed, for their meat and for their oily stomach contents which are used in pharmaceuticals. The harvest is strictly controlled and poses no threat to the species' survival.

12/ MANX SHEARWATER
Puffinus puffinus

RANGE: **breeds N Atlantic and Mediterranean islands; migrates S as far as South America after breeding**
HABITAT: **offshore oceans above continental shelf**
SIZE: **11¾–15 in (30–38 cm)**

The contrast between the dark upperparts and light underparts of the Manx Shearwater is much less distinct in the browner Balearic Shearwater *P. p. mauretanicus*, a race which breeds in the western Mediterranean.

Manx Shearwaters nest in colonies, usually on isolated islands. They arrive at the colonies as early as February and choose mainly the darkest nights to visit their burrows as a defence against attacks from Great Black-backed Gulls *Larus marinus*. The pairs call to one another with a variety of loud, raucous screams and howls. The chicks fledge at 70 days, but are deserted by their parents 1–2 weeks earlier.

13/ LITTLE SHEARWATER
Puffinus assimilis

RANGE: **N and S Atlantic, S Pacific and Indian oceans; breeds on Atlantic islands and the Antipodes Islands**
HABITAT: **coastal waters**
SIZE: **9¾–11¾ in (25–30 cm)**

Unlike most shearwaters, Little Shearwaters do not gather in large groups on the ocean but are solitary. These birds occupy the nest area for up to 4 months before the eggs are laid, defending the site against other shearwaters. This is probably because they nest in crevices, which are in short supply, instead of digging their own burrows.

FAMILY HYDROBATIDAE
Storm-petrels

Small, open ocean birds. Plumage black, or black and brown with white rump feathers. Sexes similar. Nest in crevices and burrows. Eggs 1, white, may be speckled. Incubation 40–50 days, chicks remain in nest 2–2½ months. 20 species.

14/ WILSON'S STORM-PETREL
Oceanites oceanicus

RANGE: **breeds from Tierra del Fuego and the Falkland Islands to the coasts of Antarctica; migrates to N Indian Ocean and N Atlantic Ocean after breeding season**
HABITAT: **oceanic**
SIZE: **6–7½ in (15–19 cm)**

Arguably the most abundant seabird in the world, Wilson's Storm-Petrel regularly gathers in large flocks to feed and follows in the wake of ships. This small bird's diet consists largely of crustaceans, which it catches by plucking them from the surface, pattering its feet on the water to "anchor" itself against the breeze. The egg, laid in a burrow, is one-quarter of the adult's weight. At its peak, the nestling reaches twice the adult weight; it fledges at 1½ times the adult weight.

15/ LEACH'S STORM-PETREL
Oceanodroma leucorhoa

RANGE: **breeds from Japan NE to Alaska, then S to Mexico; winters S to C Pacific and S Atlantic**
HABITAT: **oceanic**
SIZE: **7½–8½ in (19–22 cm)**

This species feeds mainly on crustaceans, fish and squid, although it also follows whales and seals to feed on their feces. Generally solitary at sea, it breeds in colonies under banks and boulders. The concentration of birds flying around over the colony may become so dense that midair collisions take place. The bird excavates nest-burrows up to 6 ft (1.8 m) long, digging with its bill and feet. The birds return to their burrow at night and there is some evidence that they locate their individual tunnels by smell.

FAMILY PELECANOIDIDAE
Diving-petrels

Compact, small to medium, short-necked, auklike birds. Plumage black above, white below. Sexes similar. Nest in burrows. Eggs 1, white. Incubation 45–53 days, chicks remain in nest 1½–2 months. 4 species.

16/ COMMON DIVING-PETREL
Pelecanoides urinatrix

RANGE: **breeds on many S ocean islands, coasts of S Australia, Tasmania, New Zealand**
HABITAT: **oceanic**
SIZE: **7¾–9¾ in (20–25 cm)**

The diving-petrels of the southern oceans are, in some respects, the ecological counterpart of the smaller species of northern auks. Their wings are small, which gives them a whirring, auklike flight, and they use them to "fly" underwater. Diving-petrels are best known for their habit of flying into one side of a steep wave and out of the other.

The Common, or Subantarctic, Diving-Petrel is known in New Zealand by the Maori name of "Kuaka," which describes its call. It is especially vocal at night, when it moves to and from its nest burrows under the cover of darkness to avoid attacks by skuas.

TROPICBIRDS, PELICANS, GANNETS AND BOOBIES

RED-BILLED TROPICBIRD

juv

race *fulvus*

race *lepturus*
with chick at nest

WHITE-TAILED TROPICBIRD

GREAT WHITE PELICAN

juv

AUSTRALIAN PELICAN

BROWN PELICAN

AMERICAN WHITE PELICAN

non-breeding

non-breeding

white phase

white phase
Galapagos form

brown phase

juv

NORTHERN GANNET

MASKED BOOBY

white-tailed
brown phase

RED-FOOTED BOOBY

juv

BROWN BOOBY

white-tailed and
white-headed brown phase

♂

race *brewsteri*

race *plotus*

juv

PERUVIAN BOOBY

♀ with chick at nest

ABBOTT'S BOOBY

♂

TROPICBIRDS, PELICANS, GANNETS AND BOOBIES

FAMILY PHAETHONTIDAE
Tropicbirds

Elegant, highly aerial seabirds with 2 elongated central tail feathers, longer in the male; juveniles lack these. Plumage white, marked with black and sometimes tinged pink or gold. Bills stout and curved, serrated on the cutting edge to hold prey. Legs very short. Nest in holes or on bare ground. Eggs 1, blotched red-brown. Incubation 40–46 days. Chicks left alone at nest while parents forage; leave nest at 11–15 weeks. 3 species.

1/ RED-BILLED TROPICBIRD
Phaethon aethereus
RANGE: **tropical Atlantic, E Pacific, NW Indian oceans**
HABITAT: **open sea; breeds on islands**
SIZE: **35½–39½ in (90–100 cm)**

These attractive seabirds wander far over the tropical oceans, singly or in pairs. Although they dive into the ocean to catch fish and squid, they spend most of their time in flight and seldom land on the surface. Their narrow tail streamers are the same length as their bodies. These may help to stabilize the birds both underwater and when they are twisting through the air in pursuit of flying fish. Courtship takes place mainly in the air, with several birds screaming shrilly as they fly close together with rapid wing beats and make long glides with downward-curving streamers. Adults often bear scars on their heads and necks from fierce fights over mates and nest sites.

Breeding colonies on islands contain hundreds of pairs, the birds usually nesting on rock ledges or in crevices. They may lay in any month of the year. The single chick is fed on average twice every 3 days until it flies off alone 12–13 weeks after hatching.

2/ WHITE-TAILED TROPICBIRD
Phaethon lepturus
RANGE: **all tropical and subtropical oceans**
HABITAT: **open sea; breeds on islands**
SIZE: **28–31½ in (71–80 cm)**

The White-tailed Tropicbird has 13–16 in (33–40 cm) long tail streamers. It competes for nest sites with the larger Red-billed and Red-tailed Tropicbirds. Such competition may have forced the golden race *P. l. fulvus*, which breeds only on Christmas Island, to nest in tree holes in the dense jungle. Elsewhere, the species nests in crevices, beneath rocky overhangs or on the bare ground – as is the case with the other race illustrated, *P. l. lepturus*, which breeds on several islands in the Indian Ocean.

Both parents incubate the single egg, which hatches after about 40 days. The chick is ready to fly some 11 weeks later. White-tailed Tropicbirds do not have an annual breeding cycle. Instead, the average interval between successful egg-laying is about 40 weeks.

FAMILY PELECANIDAE
Pelicans

Large waterbirds, with long, straight bills and extensible throat pouches. Plumage usually gray or white. Sexes similar. Nest on the ground or in trees. Eggs 1–4, white. Chicks remain in nest for about 5 weeks (tree-nesting species) or 3 weeks (ground-nesters); chicks of ground-nesters then collect in nurseries, or "pods." Incubation 28–31 days. 7 species.

3/ GREAT WHITE PELICAN
Pelecanus onocrotalus
RANGE: **S Europe, Africa, Asia**
HABITAT: **lakes and inland seas**
SIZE: **55–69 in (140–175 cm)**

This large white pelican is intensely gregarious, roosting and resting in great flocks. It normally fishes in groups, forming a circle of birds which swim forward, periodically jerking their wings open and plunging their bills toward the center of the circle. In this way they "herd" schools of fish and scoop them up in their huge throat pouches. This pelican's daily food intake of about 2½ lb (1.2 kg) may comprise either a few large fish or hundreds of small ones.

Adult birds develop a crest, a yellow patch on the foreneck and a pinkish bloom to the plumage during the breeding season. The males display in groups to attract receptive females. Mated pairs display further and the female selects a nest site. Breeding colonies of up to 30,000 pairs may occur, sometimes far from water.

4/ AUSTRALIAN PELICAN
Pelecanus conspicillatus
RANGE: **Australia and Tasmania**
HABITAT: **shallow marine and inland waters**
SIZE: **59–71 in (150–180 cm)**

The Australian Pelican is a highly sociable bird, feeding, roosting and nesting in large flocks. Adults have a short gray crest and a yellowish or pinkish throat pouch, which becomes scarlet during courtship. Males display communally,

with rituals that include swinging the head and clapping the mandibles of the bill together. After they have paired up, a male and female parade to the nest site.

They breed on small islands, often making their nests in bushes, and may lay their eggs at any time of the year. Two weeks after hatching, the young may climb into the adult's pouch to feed on regurgitated food. Pelicans feed predominantly on fish but also catch crustaceans and other aquatic animals.

5/ AMERICAN WHITE PELICAN
Pelecanus erythrorhynchos
RANGE: **North America**
HABITAT: **freshwater lakes and shallow coastal waters**
SIZE: **50–70 in (127–178 cm)**

The American White Pelican occurs in flocks at all times. The birds arrive in their breeding colonies, which are often far from their feeding areas, in April or May. By this time the males have developed a horny knob on the upper mandible which they lose after the breeding season. Courtship is communal, and after a male and female have paired up the female leads the male away in a ritual parade.

The birds build a nest of stones, sticks and weeds on the ground, which may form a substantial mound. They avoid perching on trees at all times of the year, preferring to rest on the ground, often on islands and sand-spits; they roost near the water's edge.

6/ BROWN PELICAN
Pelecanus occidentalis
RANGE: **Pacific and Atlantic coasts of North and South America; Galapagos Islands**
HABITAT: **shallow coastal waters and islands**
SIZE: **$43\frac{1}{4}$–54 in (110–137 cm)**

Unlike the other pelicans, this species feeds by diving for fish, making spectacular plunges into the water from heights of 10–33 ft (3–10 m) above the surface. As it enters the water, it opens its bill and traps the prey in its expanded pouch.

Brown Pelicans nest in colonies on the ground or in trees. The male occupies a potential nest site from which he displays, leaving the spot only for brief flights until he attracts a mate. Mating takes place on the site and the male then collects branches and other nesting material to present ritually to his partner. The sexes share in incubation of the 2–3 eggs for 30 days. During the first week after hatching, the adults provide the young with well-digested fish which they regurgitate into the nest. The young finally fly from the nest after 11–12 weeks.

Brown Pelicans have a variety of calls, including grunts and "pops" in the adults and screams and groans uttered by the chicks.

FAMILY SULIDAE
Gannets and boobies
Plunge-diving seabirds, with torpedo-shaped bodies. Long, stout bills with serrated cutting edges and closed nostrils. Long, pointed wings and short legs. Plumage white below, variable above. Feet and facial skin often brightly colored and variable between sexes. Nest on ground, on cliffs or in trees. Eggs 1–4, whitish. Incubation 42–55 days, chicks remain at or near nest for 14–22 weeks. 9 species.

7/ NORTHERN GANNET
Sula bassana
RANGE: **E and W coasts of North Atlantic**
HABITAT: **marine offshore**
SIZE: **$35\frac{1}{2}$ in (90 cm)**

This conspicuous white bird is renowned for its spectacular plunging dives from heights of up to 100 ft (30 m), with its wings half-folded and its body dropping vertically into the water. Shoals of mackerel and herring attract great flocks which appear to be in a feeding frenzy as they alternately rise and plummet into the ocean.

Northern Gannets nest in huge colonies, of which there are about 37 in the world, containing a total of more than 200,000 pairs. The birds remain largely faithful to their mate and their nest site, and indulge in complex displays concerned with pair-bonding and with site ownership. Their colonies are intensely active and noisy. Because the peak food supply is both seasonal and dependable, egg-laying takes place on a consistently similar date every year. With an assured food supply, the single chick has a high chance of survival, but large numbers of the white-spotted brown juveniles die on migration to the south of their breeding range, before they reach maturity.

8/ PERUVIAN BOOBY
Sula variegata
RANGE: **coastal Peru and N Chile**
HABITAT: **offshore waters**
SIZE: **29 in (74 cm)**

One of the 3 abundant seabirds of the famous guano islands of Peru (together with the Guanay Cormorant and the Chilean Pelican), the Peruvian Booby relies on the shoals of anchovettas in the cold Humboldt Current to sustain its immense local concentrations. The population is numbered in millions and the mass diving of huge flocks of these birds is an unforgettable experience. Guano consists of the rocklike dried droppings of the birds, built up over many years to depths of up to 300 ft (90 m).

Overexploitation of the anchovetta stocks by fishing fleets has led to a catastrophic decline in the numbers of Peruvian seabirds. In some years, the natural oceanographic phenomenon El Niño brings warm water into the fishing grounds, which also causes severe reductions in food supply and results in colossal seabird mortality. Formerly, the birds could rapidly recover their numbers after the event but since overfishing, the rate of recovery has been much slower.

9/ ABBOTT'S BOOBY
Sula abbotti　　　　　　　　　　　E
RANGE: **E Indian Ocean**
HABITAT: **open sea**
SIZE: **31 in (79 cm)**

Abbott's Booby is a beautiful and highly unusual member of its family; it is also the most scarce. The species nests only on Christmas Island, beneath the rain forest canopy, and there are fewer than 2,000 pairs. About 30 percent of the rain forest, including significant sections of the bird's habitat, has been destroyed by phosphate mining operations. Today, most of the island is a national park.

The survival of the species is hampered by a low rate of breeding. After an extremely prolonged growing period of 22 weeks in the nest, the single offspring is fed for another 33 weeks in the nesting tree. This means that it is confined to the island during the monsoon (from November to March), when it is at risk from high winds and starvation. The long breeding cycle prevents the birds from nesting every year and most pairs lay at 2-year intervals. Breeding rates are further reduced by the adults' habit of taking "rest" years. The juvenile birds that are reared are unique among the gannets and boobies in that their plumage closely resembles that of the adult males.

10/ MASKED BOOBY
Sula dactylatra
RANGE: **all tropical oceans**
HABITAT: **open sea**
SIZE: **30–33 in (76–84 cm)**

Also known as the Blue-faced Booby, this mainly dazzling white booby fishes over the open ocean and tends to nest on arid islands. Despite the low density and patchy distribution of prey far out at sea, its breeding colonies may contain thousands of pairs.

Breeding Masked Boobies have a number of ritual displays and their pair-bonding behavior includes the symbolic building of a nest, using mere fragments of no structural value. The usual clutch is 2 eggs, although the first-hatched chick invariably kills its sibling early in life. This prevents competition for the often scarce food. The laying of a second egg is an insurance policy against breeding failure. Should the first egg fail to hatch, or the oldest chick quickly perish, the second chick will take its place.

11/ RED-FOOTED BOOBY
Sula sula
RANGE: **all tropical oceans**
HABITAT: **open sea**
SIZE: **28–31 in (71–79 cm)**

The Red-footed Booby is probably the most numerous member of its family. There are several color phases across its huge range, but all have conspicuous red feet. Unlike most other members of the family, the species nests in trees. This habit may have partly protected it from human disturbance, helping to account for its comparative abundance today.

In their relatively nonseasonal environment, the birds breed opportunistically, waiting until there is an ample food supply. However, it is common for the supply to fail at a later stage, causing heavy mortality among the young. The surviving juveniles disperse widely and may travel thousands of miles from their birthplace. They can be distinguished from the adults by their blackish-brown bills, purplish facial skin and yellowish legs.

12/ BROWN BOOBY
Sula leucogaster
RANGE: **all tropical oceans**
HABITAT: **open sea**
SIZE: **$29\frac{1}{2}$–$31\frac{1}{2}$ in (75–80 cm)**

The Brown Booby breeds mainly on islands, often on cliffs or steep slopes. On well-vegetated slopes, the birds will perch freely in trees. They frequently share the islands with Red-footed or Masked Boobies, but avoid competition by hunting farther inshore, specializing in low, slanting dives to catch fish and squid. The birds spend much time in the air and perform some of their courtship rituals in flight.

The breeding colonies tend to be smaller and more scattered than those of the Red-footed and Masked Boobies. As with the Masked Booby, older chicks kill their siblings. On many islands the birds breed annually, but on Ascension Island in the Atlantic they tend to breed at less than yearly intervals, triggered by favorable changes in the food supply. Of the two races illustrated, *S. l. plotus* breeds in and around the Indian Ocean, Australia and some Pacific islands, while *S. l. brewsteri* nests in the eastern Pacific and along the western coast of Mexico.

CORMORANTS, ANHINGAS, FRIGATEBIRDS

race *lucidus*
"White-breasted Cormorant"

race *carbo*

race *sinensis*

juv

DOUBLE-CRESTED
CORMORANT

GREAT CORMORANT

SHAG

non-breeding

non-breeding

race *hypoleucos*

CAPE CORMORANT

non-breeding

PIED CORMORANT

feeding chicks
at nest

juv

RED-LEGGED CORMORANT

GUANAY CORMORANT

race *varius*

race *albiventor*
"Falkland Islands Shag"

non-breeding

race *atriceps*
"Blue-eyed
Cormorant"

♂

ANHINGA

IMPERIAL SHAG

♀

non-breeding

PYGMY CORMORANT

juv

FLIGHTLESS CORMORANT

GREAT FRIGATEBIRD

♂

♀

♂

chick at nest

CHRISTMAS ISLAND FRIGATEBIRD

CORMORANTS, ANHINGAS, FRIGATEBIRDS

FAMILY PHALACROCORACIDAE
Cormorants

Medium to large fish-eaters; dive underwater. Long neck and long, laterally flattened, hooked bill, large feet set far back on body. Plumage dark, white head and underparts in some species. Sexes similar. Nest on cliffs, on ground or in trees. Eggs 1–6, pale blue. Incubation 22–26 days, chicks remain in nest for about 28 days. 32 species.

1/ DOUBLE-CRESTED CORMORANT
Phalacrocorax auritus

RANGE: **North America**
HABITAT: **marine and inland waters**
SIZE: **29–36 in (74–91 cm)**

This medium-sized, gregarious cormorant breeds in colonies containing up to 3,000 pairs, both on the coast and inland close to dependable supplies of food. The male's courtship display includes dances in the water, during which he presents the female with nesting material, and ritualized displays on the nest site. The birds lose the double crest on the crown after pairing. The crests of eastern races such as *P. a. auritus* are dark, while those of western races such as *P. a. albociliatus* are mainly white.

Young birds are fed by their parents about 6 times per day, a rate typical of inshore birds. After about a month the young leave the individual nest sites and start to wander around the colony in groups. At 5–6 weeks they start to fly.

2/ GREAT CORMORANT
Phalacrocorax carbo

RANGE: **N Atlantic, Africa, Eurasia, Australasia**
HABITAT: **coastal and fresh water**
SIZE: **31½–39½ in (80–100 cm)**

There are several races of the Great Cormorant, showing varying amounts of white in the plumage. They include *P. c. carbo*, which breeds around the North Atlantic, *P. c. sinensis*, which breeds from southern Europe to central Asia, and *P. c. lucidus* of sub-Saharan Africa.

In some places, this species is persecuted because of its appetite for fish. Its daily intake of food averages 14–25 oz (400–700 g), equivalent to some 15 percent of its body weight. The birds catch their prey during underwater dives that may last for over a minute.

The breeding colonies may number up to 2,000 pairs, although they are usually smaller and often fragmented. They may be located on the coast or inland, on cliffs, slopes or in trees. The courtship display includes wing-flicking, covering and uncovering the conspicuous white flank patch, and a throwing back of the head.

3/ CAPE CORMORANT
Phalacrocorax capensis

RANGE: **South Africa, Namibia**
HABITAT: **coasts**
SIZE: **24–25¼ in (61–64 cm)**

The Cape Cormorant is abundant in southwestern Africa, with more than 1 million birds benefiting from the nutrient-rich Benguela Current that

flows past the coast. It is a highly gregarious species and can be seen feeding with other types of bird, often well offshore. Valued for its guano (rocklike, dried droppings used as a fertilizer), it is encouraged to roost and nest on artificial "guano platforms."

In its huge breeding colonies, which may contain 100,000 birds, the nests are placed on cliffs, on the ground or in bushes. The female usually lays 2–3 eggs and breeding is timed to coincide with periods when pilchards are especially abundant. Like the Guanay Cormorants of Peru, however, the birds may desert their breeding colonies en masse if food suddenly becomes scarce. Outside the breeding season, the Cape Cormorant disperses widely along the coast.

4/ SHAG
Phalacrocorax aristotelis

RANGE: **coastal W and S Europe and N Africa**
HABITAT: **marine coasts**
SIZE: **25½–31½ in (65–80 cm)**

The adult Shag is an attractive bird with blackish-green plumage, green eyes and a long, wispy, forward-curving crest in the breeding season. Although usually a quiet bird like other cormorants, it has a sonorous grunting call, often accompanied by throat-clicking. It prefers clear, cold oceans, avoiding estuaries and inland waters, and will travel up to 7 mls (11 km) from its colony in order to feed.

Typically, Shag colonies are neither large nor dense, although some reach a total of more than 1,000 pairs. After breeding, the birds tend to disperse along the coast, but northern populations, such as those from northern Norway, may migrate more than 600 mls (1,000 km) south. There is evidence that some breeding colonies have their own specific wintering areas.

5/ GUANAY CORMORANT
Phalacrocorax bougainvillei

RANGE: **coastal Peru and Chile**
HABITAT: **marine coasts**
SIZE: **30 in (76 cm)**

Once called the most valuable fowl in the world because of its guano (accumulated dried droppings used as a fertilizer), the Guanay Cormorant used to breed in colonies of hundreds of thousands, or even millions per island, on islands off Peru. The birds still breed at densities of about 3 nests per yard and when the 2–3 young are present with their parents, the huddle is exceedingly dense.

As a denizen of the cold Humboldt Current, the bird relies on the abundant shoals of anchovettas to sustain its numbers. Overfishing has caused a dramatic decline in the numbers of these cormorants. In the past, the population regularly suffered from a loss of food with the periodic incursion of warm water into the region (a phenomenon called El Niño).

However, mass mortality was quickly followed by an exponential increase in the surviving population once the cold up-welling current returned. Now, the stock of anchovettas has been so reduced by the fishermen that the birds can no longer make good their numbers following the periodic crashes.

6/ PIED CORMORANT
Phalacrocorax varius

RANGE: **Australia and New Zealand**
HABITAT: **coasts; also estuaries and inland waters**
SIZE: **26–33 in (66–84 cm)**

This striking cormorant, although patchily distributed, sometimes congregates in groups of many thousands. It nests in colonies on islands, either on the ground or in low shrubs and trees, sometimes using the same trees as other species. Although eggs may be laid in autumn and spring, individual birds probably nest once a year.

Throwing back the head is a typical part of the courtship ritual in cormorants, and in the Pied Cormorant the display is greatly enhanced by the bird's bright facial pattern. Of the two races illustrated, *P. v. hypoleucos* breeds along the coast of Western Australia and locally inland, while *P. v. varius* occurs in New Zealand. Adults of the latter race have yellow rather than orange facial skin.

7/ RED-LEGGED CORMORANT
Phalacrocorax gaimardi

RANGE: SW South America
HABITAT: marine coasts
SIZE: 28–30 in (71–76 cm)

This strikingly handsome bird is unusual among the cormorants for its relatively solitary habits, unexpectedly chirpy voice and its restricted distribution on the Pacific coast of South America. It occurs on almost all of the Peruvian guano islands, but often sparsely, nesting alone or in small groups in cavities on ocean cliffs. Only occasionally do the birds cluster densely enough to be termed colonial.

Similarly, when foraging, the Red-legged Cormorant often flies singly for long distances and hunts alone or in pairs, although feeding groups sometimes occur. The birds build large nests which include items such as the cases of tube-dwelling worms and fronds of gelatinous seaweed that glue the structure to the rock.

8/ IMPERIAL SHAG
Phalacrocorax atriceps

RANGE: S South America, subantarctic islands, Antarctic peninsula
HABITAT: marine coasts
SIZE: $28\frac{1}{4}$ in (72 cm)

Several races of the Imperial Shag are recognized with a distribution that stretches across the southern latitudes. They have varying amounts of white in their plumage and differently colored caruncles (swollen outgrowths at the base of the upper mandible of the bill), but all have distinctive blue rings around the eyes throughout the year and a forward-curving, wispy crest in the breeding season. Two races are illustrated: the Falkland Islands Shag or King Cormorant *P. a. albiventor* and the Blue-eyed Cormorant *P. a. atriceps* of mainland South America.

The Falkland Islands Shag is an isolated race and the only cormorant that occurs on these South Atlantic islands. It forms huge colonies on flattish rocks and may also nest among penguins and albatrosses. The Blue-eyed Cormorant, by contrast, is widespread along the coast of southern Chile and Argentina.

9/ PYGMY CORMORANT
Phalacrocorax pygmeus   ?

RANGE: Eurasia
HABITAT: inland waters
SIZE: $17\frac{3}{4}$–$21\frac{3}{4}$ in (45–55 cm)

The smallest of the cormorants, the Pygmy Cormorant differs from most members of its family in its preference for densely vegetated lowland freshwater habitats in warm latitudes. It nests in trees or among reeds, most colonies numbering tens or hundreds of birds. Where it nests in waterside trees, it often shares the branches with herons, egrets and ibises. Young

birds leave the nest before they can fly; they fledge after about 10 weeks.

Outside the breeding season, many Pygmy Cormorants migrate south, and it is in the wintering areas that larger flocks of the birds may gather. At this time of the year they may also visit brackish and saltwater habitats.

10/ FLIGHTLESS CORMORANT
Nannopterum harrisi   R

RANGE: Galapagos Islands
HABITAT: marine, close to breeding islands
SIZE: 35 in (89 cm)

The Flightless Cormorant occurs only on the islands of Fernandina and Isabela in the Galapagos archipelago, where it numbers about 800 pairs. It is highly sedentary and, as its name suggests, it is unable to fly, having only vestigial wings. It feeds by diving into the ocean from the shore; octopuses form a large part of its diet.

In its relatively seasonless tropical environment, the Flightless Cormorant can breed at any time of the year, although the peak nesting period is from March to September. A single bird may breed several times in 12 months. Although it may readily shift nest site and change its mate for successive breeding attempts, it frequently retains both. A bird taking over from its mate at the nest will ritually present its partner with seaweed as a way of maintaining the pair-bond.

FAMILY ANHINGIDAE
Anhingas

Large, freshwater fish-eaters. Extremely long, slender neck. Small head and long, thin, dagger-shaped bill with serrated cutting edges. Very long tail with corrugated outer feathers. Plumage black, brown, gray and white. Females paler than males. Nest in trees or reeds near water. Eggs 2–6, pale green. Incubation 26–30 days, chicks leave nest after about 5 weeks. 4 species.

11/ ANHINGA
Anhinga anhinga

RANGE: SE USA to N South America
HABITAT: inland and brackish waters; can occur on coasts
SIZE: 34 in (86 cm)

The Anhinga, like the other members of its family, is much more slender than the cormorants, with an elongated neck and a thin, straight bill. Often it swims with only the head and neck above the surface, the neck held in a sinuous *S*-shape resembling the curve of a snake. Indeed, Snake Bird is an alternative name for this species. It occurs in rivers, lakes and lagoons, where it hunts for fish by stealth, spearing them underwater with its sharp bill. Like other darters, it has a hinge mechanism in its neck, enabling it to snap its head forward suddenly to seize prey.

Darters have large, broad wings which are excellent for soaring, and in level flight they alternate flaps with glides. Their courtship ritual includes an aerial display, in which they plane down to the nesting area from great heights. They are gregarious birds at all times, sometimes breeding in groups of several hundred, along with cormorants and herons.

FAMILY FREGATIDAE
Frigatebirds

Large aerial seabirds. Long wings, deeply forked tail. Long, hooked bill. Breeding males black with varying amounts of white beneath and with a scarlet throat pouch. Females and immatures mostly dark brown with white on underparts. Nest in trees or on ground. Eggs 1, white. Incubation 44–55 days, chicks remain in nest for 5–6 months. Young fed for up to 1 year. 5 species.

12/ CHRISTMAS ISLAND FRIGATEBIRD
Fregata andrewsi   V

RANGE: Christmas Island and surrounding oceans
HABITAT: oceanic
SIZE: 35–40 in (89–102 cm)

This species breeds only on Christmas Island in the eastern Indian Ocean, where fewer than 1,000 pairs remain. The frigatebirds have suffered from years of human persecution, but they are now fully protected in their island home. Ironically, the Christmas Island Frigatebird occasionally causes the death of another rare endemic bird, Abbott's Booby *Sula abbotti*, by hounding it for fish and forcing it to crash down into the jungle canopy.

Like other frigatebirds, the males display in small groups to passing females by presenting their inflated scarlet throat pouch, trembling their outspread wings and producing a distinctive warbling call. If a female is attracted by a male's courtship display, she descends alongside him. After mating, the pair build a flimsy nest of twigs on the display site.

13/ GREAT FRIGATEBIRD
Fregata minor

RANGE: tropical and subtropical Indian and Pacific oceans, and off Brazil
HABITAT: open sea
SIZE: 34–$39\frac{1}{2}$ in (86–100 cm)

With a maximum wingspan of over 6 ft (2 m), but weighing a mere $2\frac{1}{2}$ lb (1.2 kg), the frigatebirds have a far greater wing area than any seabirds of comparable weight. They spend most of their lives in the air and seldom land on the water. Instead they feed on the wing by snatching surface prey. Some individuals, particularly younger adults, practice "piracy", harrying other seabirds until they drop their meals. Although they lack waterproof plumage and cannot swim, the frigatebirds range hundreds of miles from dry land.

The Great Frigatebird is probably the most numerous of the frigatebirds. Thousands of pairs may gather in breeding colonies in trees and bushes on oceanic islands, often in company with Lesser Frigatebirds.

The breeding cycle of the Great Frigatebird is one of the longest in the seabird world, with the single young requiring 6 months to fledge and at least another 6 months of support from its parents. Adults can therefore breed only once in 2 years. The breeding rate is further reduced by the adults' habit of taking "rest" years and by the heavy loss of eggs and young through interference from nonbreeding males that attack nesters and steal nest material.

HERONS AND BITTERNS

BLACK-CROWNED NIGHT HERON

juv

AMERICAN BITTERN

WHITE-CRESTED
TIGER HERON

LITTLE BITTERN

♂

BOAT-BILLED
HERON

SQUACCO HERON

juv

CATTLE EGRET

race *rogersi*

race *virescens*

race *sundevalli*

winter

GREEN-BACKED HERON

LITTLE EGRET

winter

BLACK HERON

juv

PURPLE HERON

winter

GREAT EGRET

GRAY HERON

juv

GOLIATH HERON

white phase
"Great White
Heron"

GREAT BLUE HERON

HERONS AND BITTERNS

FAMILY ARDEIDAE
Herons and bitterns
Small to large. Long-legged, most with long neck and powerful, stabbing bill. Some males larger or more colorful than females. Nest in trees, bushes, reedbeds. Eggs 1–7, variable. Incubation 14–30 days, chicks remain in nest 28–55 days. 60 species.

1/ GRAY HERON
Ardea cinerea

RANGE: **widespread in Eurasia and Africa**
HABITAT: **shallow freshwaters of all types; also coasts, especially in winter**
SIZE: **$35\frac{1}{2}$–$38\frac{1}{2}$ in (90–98 cm)**

This species haunts a variety of waterside habitats, where it catches fish, frogs and small mammals in its long, daggerlike bill. It breeds farther north than any other heron, and some populations suffer high rates of mortality in severe weather. However, the birds have a marked capacity for recovering their numbers after such losses.

Gray Herons usually build their nests in tall trees up to 80 ft (25 m) above the ground. Colony size is variable, with about 200 being the maximum in most areas, although concentrations of over 1,000 breeding birds have been recorded. A pair readily lays another clutch of eggs if their first is destroyed; they can repeat this 2–3 times.

2/ GREAT BLUE HERON
Ardea herodias

RANGE: **S Canada to Central America, Caribbean, Galapagos Islands; winters S USA to N South America**
HABITAT: **river edges, marshes, swamps, mudflats**
SIZE: **40–50 in (102–127 cm)**

This species is the largest of the North American herons. Although most populations have blue-gray plumage, a white color phase – the Great White Heron – occurs in marine habitats in southern Florida and Cuba.

Great Blue Herons forage largely in water, walking slowly or standing and waiting for prey to draw near. Occasionally they hunt more actively, running, hopping and flicking their wings. They feed mostly on fish, aquatic invertebrates, frogs and small mammals. Breeding adults have plumes on their backs and perform elaborate courtship displays which include feather-fluffing, stereotyped postures, twig-shaking and display flights. They nest in colonies, usually in remote areas, with nests in trees up to 130 ft (40 m) above the ground.

3/ GOLIATH HERON
Ardea goliath

RANGE: **S and E Africa, Madagascar, S Iraq**
HABITAT: **coastal and inland wetlands with extensive shallows**
SIZE: **53–59 in (135–150 cm)**

The largest of the heron family, this huge bird can wade through much deeper water than related species. Although it eats some amphibians, it feeds chiefly on fish, including specimens up to

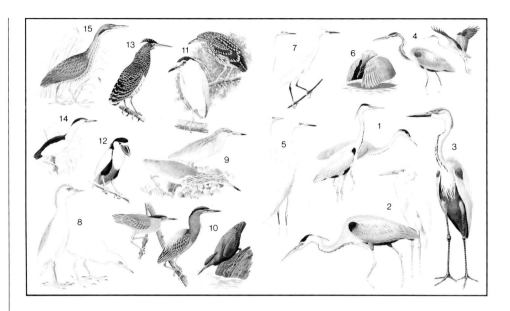

$4\frac{1}{2}$–$6\frac{1}{2}$ lb (2–3 kg) in weight. It typically occurs alone or as a single pair.

The Goliath Heron nests on the ground in reeds or on a low bush standing in the water. The nest itself is built from reed stems or twigs and is up to 3 ft (1 m) across. The 2–3 pale blue eggs are incubated by both parents for about 4 weeks, and the young take another 6 weeks to fledge.

4/ PURPLE HERON
Ardea purpurea

RANGE: **S Eurasia, Africa**
HABITAT: **freshwater wetlands with extensive emergent vegetation**
SIZE: **$30\frac{3}{4}$–$35\frac{1}{2}$ in (78–90 cm)**

The Purple Heron has longer toes than other, similar-sized species. These enable the bird to walk over floating vegetation without sinking and to stride over thick bushes without having to grasp individual twigs. The large feet are clearly visible in flight and form a useful clue to identification.

Most Purple Herons nest in small colonies of up to 20 pairs in dense stands of reeds or rushes growing in shallow water. Occasionally, they choose low trees. The nest is a platform of reeds or twigs and extra platforms are often constructed nearby. These are used by the nonincubating bird and, later, by the developing young.

5/ GREAT EGRET
Egretta alba

RANGE: **worldwide, especially widespread in S hemisphere**
HABITAT: **freshwater wetlands of all kinds; also coasts in winter**
SIZE: **$33\frac{1}{2}$–40 in (85–102 cm)**

This extremely widespread heron suffered greatly in the late 19th century from the demands of the millinery trade. It is estimated that over 200,000 of these birds were killed for their plumage in a single year. The Royal Society for the Protection of Birds (RSPB) in Britain and the Audubon Society in America were originally formed in response to the outcry caused by the carnage of

this bird and other birds for their plumage. Today, land drainage and habitat destruction are the chief threats to the bird's wellbeing.

Great Egrets breed in low trees or reedbeds, usually in small colonies. Each male establishes a small territory around his chosen nest site and begins the construction of the nest, building a platform of twigs or reeds on which he displays to the female. Both sexes then finish the nest ready for laying, although some building work will continue until the young have fledged.

6/ BLACK HERON
Egretta ardesiaca

RANGE: **sub-Saharan Africa and Madagascar**
HABITAT: **shallow freshwater wetlands and coastal swamps**
SIZE: **$17\frac{1}{4}$–$18\frac{1}{2}$ in (44–47 cm)**

The uniform, dark, slate-gray plumage of the Black Heron is common to both sexes. This is a widespread bird occurring in shallow waters across much of tropical Africa. Its nests are normally found scattered throughout large colonies of other herons and egrets.

The Black Heron is renowned for its special hunting posture. Moving slowly across shallow water, it lowers its head and long neck and half raises its wings, bringing them forward until the edges meet over the top of its head. It is as if a small, black umbrella is drifting across the water's surface. The function of this odd behavior may be to shade the water from the sun, in this way greatly increasing the heron's chances of spotting the movement of fish or other prey beneath the surface.

7/ LITTLE EGRET
Egretta garzetta
RANGE: S Eurasia, Africa and Australasia
HABITAT: shallow fresh and brackish
water, also estuaries and coasts
SIZE: $21\frac{3}{4}$–$25\frac{1}{2}$ in (55–65 cm)

A century ago, this species was nearly exterminated from parts of its range to satisfy the hat trade, eager for the 10 in (25 cm) long plumes which form part of the bird's breeding plumage. These feathers are silky in appearance and soft to the touch. However, changing fashions and active campaigning by bodies such as the RSPB and Audubon Society have removed this threat.

Little Egret colonies can contain many hundreds or even thousands of pairs. They are remarkably agile when climbing over thin twigs and build their nests in trees. The young leave the nest before fledging to perch on nearby branches.

8/ CATTLE EGRET
Bubulcus ibis
RANGE: S Eurasia, Africa, Australasia, S
USA and northern S America
HABITAT: freshwater wetlands, farmland
and open country
SIZE: 19–21 in (48–53 cm)

The Cattle Egret has an enormous range that spans 6 continents. In the past 50 years, it has successfully colonized North and South America, Australia and New Zealand. In Australia, there have also been deliberate introductions of this beneficial species.

Cattle Egrets commonly feed around grazing cattle and wild game herds, which flush prey such as grasshoppers, beetles and lizards from cover as they move. The birds' food includes many invertebrates that are serious parasites of cattle, such as ticks and blood-sucking flies.

During the breeding season, Cattle Egrets sport long, buff feathers on their heads, backs and chests, and their bills and legs assume a bright pinkish-red color. They nest in dense colonies, often in company with other species. The nests can be virtually touching, with as many as 100 in a single tree.

9/ SQUACCO HERON
Ardeola ralloides
RANGE: S Europe, SW Asia, Africa
HABITAT: freshwater marshes, swamps
and lakes
SIZE: $17\frac{1}{4}$–$18\frac{1}{2}$ in (44–47 cm)

As a result of its overall buff plumage and retiring habits, the Squacco Heron is a difficult species to spot among marsh vegetation. As it takes flight, however, there is a startling change in appearance, with the white wings, rump and tail becoming clearly visible.

Like many herons and egrets, the Squacco Heron gains an elegant crest and ornamental back plumes for the breeding season. In addition, its bill and legs, which are yellowish-green in winter, change to blue and pink respectively. Breeding takes place in mixed colonies with related species, the nests being built in low trees, bushes or reeds. Each clutch contains 3–6 eggs laid on a platform of twigs or reeds.

10/ GREEN-BACKED HERON
Butorides striatus
RANGE: worldwide tropics and subtropics
HABITAT: freshwater and coastal wetlands
SIZE: $15\frac{3}{4}$–19 in (40–48 cm)

The Green-backed, or Striated, Heron shows great differences in plumage across its vast geographical range, with races that include *B. s. sundevalli* of the Galapagos Islands, *B. s. rogersi* of northwest Australia and the American race *B. s. virescens*. It is usually a secretive species, feeding mainly at night and creeping among dense marsh vegetation. However, it sometimes feeds by day at urban ponds, stalking around the edges or perching on jetties and boats.

Colonial breeding is rare and restricted to small, loose groups. Most nests are solitary and placed in low bushes or trees, often overhanging water. The nest itself is built of twigs, but is so flimsy that the 2–4 eggs may be visible from below.

11/ BLACK-CROWNED NIGHT HERON
Nycticorax nycticorax
RANGE: worldwide except N temperate
regions and Australia
HABITAT: salt, brackish and freshwater
wetlands
SIZE: $22\frac{3}{4}$–$25\frac{1}{2}$ in (58–65 cm)

The Black-crowned Night Heron is an extremely widespread species. It lives up to its name in being active mainly in the evening and through the night, hunting for frogs and toads, small fish and crustaceans.

Breeding takes place in colonies in trees, with up to 30 nests crowded into a single tree. Although they sometimes nest with other heron species, Black-crowned Night Herons are usually segregated in their own part of the colony. Each nest is an untidy platform of twigs, initiated by the male and completed by the female while the male continues to supply the twigs. When feeding their young, the birds hunt more frequently during the daytime.

12/ BOAT-BILLED HERON
Cochlearius cochlearius
RANGE: Mexico S to Bolivia, N Argentina
HABITAT: edges of lakes and rivers,
mangroves and other wooded swamps
SIZE: $17\frac{3}{4}$–$19\frac{3}{4}$ in (45–50 cm)

Perhaps the most bizarre of the herons in appearance, this species features a wide, flattened bill and a prominent black crest. The sexes have similar plumage, but juvenile birds are buffy below, and their crests are not as pronounced as those of the adults.

Generally, Boat-billed Herons are sedentary and gregarious in habit. They roost during the day in mangroves or other shady trees and emerge to feed at night, standing crouched and waiting for prey, or walking slowly through the shallows. Occasionally they feed more actively, darting around and sometimes using their broad bills as scoops with which to capture stationary prey. They eat mainly fish, shrimp and other aquatic invertebrates, and often utter froglike croaks when feeding.

13/ WHITE-CRESTED TIGER HERON
Tigriornis leucolophus
RANGE: tropical W Africa
HABITAT: riverine forest
SIZE: $23\frac{1}{2}$–$31\frac{1}{2}$ in (60–80 cm)

Little is known about this highly secretive bird. It lives in dense tropical forests, apparently breeds in solitary pairs, and feeds mainly at night. The "Tiger" part of its common name comes from the pronounced bars or stripes on its plumage. The alternative name of tiger bittern has been used for this and several related species because of their bitternlike booming call and their adoption of an upright posture typical of the bitterns.

The few nests that have been found were placed in trees beside rivers. The timing of egglaying is probably related to rainfall patterns and changes in water level. The normal clutch appears to consist of 1–2 whitish, red-blotched eggs.

14/ LITTLE BITTERN
Ixobrychus minutus
RANGE: parts of Europe, W Asia, sub-
Saharan Africa, Australia; European
population winters in tropical Africa
HABITAT: freshwater marshes, peat bogs,
disused clay pits and similar habitats,
with dense vegetation and tall reeds
SIZE: $10\frac{1}{2}$–14 in (27–36 cm)

This shy, tiny bittern is generally reluctant to fly and is not easily flushed from cover. If startled, it will often "freeze," beak pointing skyward, the delicately streaked plumage of its breast camouflaging it against the reeds among which it lives. When it does take to the air, it reveals a surprisingly bold pattern of greenish-black head, back, tail and flight feathers contrasting sharply with the creamy-buff neck and wing patches.

Little Bitterns are active chiefly at dusk or at night. They stalk their prey by walking slowly in a crouched position among the reeds. Sometimes they simply stand and wait for their food to come to them. They eat mostly small fish, frogs, insects, spiders and shrimp.

15/ AMERICAN BITTERN
Botaurus lentiginosus
RANGE: C Canada to C USA; winters S USA,
Caribbean, Mexico, Central America
HABITAT: fresh and saltwater marshes,
swamps and bogs
SIZE: $25\frac{1}{4}$ in (64 cm)

The American Bittern is a stocky brown heron with a black and brown wing pattern in flight. Juvenile birds have more streaking on the back and breast, but closely resemble adults. Like other bitterns, these birds often point their bills to the sky when threatened and even sway back and forth like reeds in the wind.

The male American Bittern's 3-syllable pumping or booming call probably serves to advertise territory as well as to attract females. The nest is a platform woven of plant material on a mound of vegetation or on the ground among cats'-tails or other emergent plants. The population of this species is declining all over its range because of marsh drainage and other habitat changes.

WHALE-HEADED STORK, HAMMERKOP, STORKS, SPOONBILLS AND IBISES, FLAMINGOS

WHITE STORK

BLACK STORK

at nest

juv

WOOD STORK

WHALE-HEADED STORK

MARABOU STORK

juv

AFRICAN OPEN-BILL STORK

HAMMERKOP

SACRED IBIS

HERMIT IBIS

winter

GLOSSY IBIS

juv

SCARLET IBIS

ROSEATE SPOONBILL

juv

race *roseus*

juv

GREATER FLAMINGO

WHITE SPOONBILL

ANDEAN FLAMINGO

feeding chick on nest

WHALE-HEADED STORK, HAMMERKOP, STORKS, SPOONBILLS AND IBISES, FLAMINGOS

FAMILY SCOPIDAE
Hammerkop
There is only one species in this family.

1/ HAMMERKOP
Scopus umbretta
RANGE: **S and C Africa, Madagascar**
HABITAT: **shallow fresh water**
SIZE: **$19\frac{1}{2}$ in (50 cm)**

The erected crest on the back of this bird's head mirrors the stout beak and produces the distinctive, hammerhead shape from which the species takes its name. Hammerkops feed on frogs, fish and invertebrates and build huge, domed nests which are among the most extraordinary constructions in the bird world. Up to 6 ft (2 m) high and across and weighing 55–110 lb (25–50 kg), it is made of sticks, reeds, grass and dead plant stems placed in a tree fork, on a cliff or on the ground. The actual nest chamber lies inside and the entrance hole is reduced in size with mud. Finally the nest itself is lined with waterweed and dry grass. The whole structure may take 6 weeks to build.

The 3–7 whitish eggs are incubated for about 30 days. The young make their first flight at about 7 weeks but may return nightly for up to a month thereafter to roost in the nest.

FAMILY BALAENICIPITIDAE
Whale-headed Stork
There is only one species in this family.

2/ WHALE-HEADED STORK
Balaeniceps rex [S]
RANGE: **Sudan, Uganda, Zaire to Zambia**
HABITAT: **swamps**
SIZE: **$39\frac{1}{4}$–$47\frac{1}{4}$ in (100–120 cm)**

This species takes its name (and its alternative name of Shoebill) from its huge, clog-shaped bill which it carries pointing downward, even resting it on its neck. Its eyes are also exceptionally large and set forward, giving it binocular vision.

The large bill is probably an adaptation for catching and holding the large, slippery lungfish which form one of its main sources of food. It also eats young crocodiles, turtles and smaller fish. Like other storks, this species claps the mandibles of its bill together in display and threat, producing in this case a loud, hollow sound. The Whale-headed Stork usually nests on floating vegetation, laying a clutch of 1–3 white eggs, which are incubated for about 30 days. The young leave the nest when 13–14 weeks old, returning to roost there for a week or so.

FAMILY CICONIIDAE
Storks
Large, long-legged and long-necked wading birds; long, heavy bill. Plumage mainly black, gray and white. Sexes similar. Nest in trees, on cliffs or (White Stork) buildings. Eggs 3–5 (1 in Saddle-bill Stork), white. Incubation 30–50 days. Nestling period 7–18 weeks. 19 species.

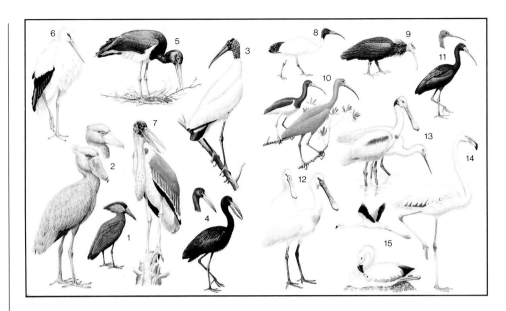

3/ WOOD STORK
Mycteria americana
RANGE: **SE USA, Mexico, Central America, W South America to N Argentina**
HABITAT: **ponds, marshes, swamps, lagoons**
SIZE: **$33\frac{3}{4}$–40 in (86–102 cm)**

Wood Storks are gregarious birds and sometimes flocks of 100 or more soar high above the ground on thermals, flying with their heads and necks extended. Wood Storks feed mostly on fish, but also take reptiles, frogs and aquatic invertebrates. They forage in water up to their bellies, moving their open bill from side to side. When it encounters prey, the bird snaps it shut. They nest colonially, with up to 25 nests per tree, placed up to 100 ft (30 m) above the ground.

4/ AFRICAN OPEN-BILL STORK
Anastomus lamelligerus
RANGE: **sub-Saharan Africa, Madagascar**
HABITAT: **swamps, marshes, flooded areas and margins of large rivers**
SIZE: **$35\frac{1}{2}$ in (90 cm)**

When this species closes its bill, only the tips of the mandibles meet. Behind them, the 2 halves of the bill curve away from each other to leave a wide gap – hence the common name. This is an adaptation for dealing with the bird's principal food, large water snails: by inserting the tip of its bill into the snail, the stork can snip through the muscle and withdraw the snail from its shell. As well as wading through shallows seeking snails, African Open-bill Storks have been seen riding on the backs of Hippopotamuses.

5/ BLACK STORK
Ciconia nigra
RANGE: **temperate and S Eurasia, S Africa**
HABITAT: **forest swamps; also open, drier country**
SIZE: **$37\frac{1}{2}$–$39\frac{1}{4}$ in (95–100 cm)**

There is an interesting dichotomy in the habitat and nest sites of the Black Stork. Some, perhaps the majority, inhabit wet places, particularly well-wooded areas with plentiful streams and pools in extensive clearings. Here, the birds breed in large trees, building nests of sticks reinforced with earth and grass.

The other habitat type is much drier, more open country, where the birds nest on cliff ledges or even in caves, at altitudes of up to 6,500 ft (2,000 m). In both cases, however, the birds shun contact with people, in contrast to their close relative, the White Stork.

6/ WHITE STORK
Ciconia ciconia [?]
RANGE: **temperate and S Europe, N Africa, S and E Asia; winters in Africa, India and S Asia**
HABITAT: **open, moist lowlands and wetlands, generally close to human habitation**
SIZE: **$39\frac{1}{4}$–$45\frac{1}{4}$ in (100–115 cm)**

The natural nest sites of the White Stork are trees and cliff ledges, but a great many pairs, certainly the majority in Europe, nest on buildings. Despite much human affection for the species, its population has declined in many areas because of the drainage of marshy feeding areas and the use of pesticides on farmland where many also feed.

The main display of the White Stork involves bill-clappering, in which the mandibles are clapped rapidly together. This persists as a form of greeting between the pair throughout the nesting period.

7/ MARABOU STORK
Leptoptilos crumeniferus
RANGE: **tropical and subtropical Africa**
HABITAT: **large wetlands and open country**
SIZE: **59 in (150 cm)**

An adult Marabou Stork has a large throat pouch that hangs down in front of its neck. The pouch contains a system of air sacs that can be inflated and deflated through a connection with the nostrils. The pouch certainly is not a food-storing crop, as has sometimes been assumed, but it seems likely that it has a role in courtship display.

Marabou Storks obtain much of their food from scavenging and they are often attracted to lion kills and human rubbish tips. They are also regular intruders at flamingo colonies, where they prey on both eggs and chicks.

FAMILY THRESKIORNITHIDAE
Spoonbills and ibises
Large, long-legged. Bills thin, downcurved (ibises) or long, spatulate (spoonbills). Plumage mainly black, brown or white, but also red and pink. Sexes similar. Nest of sticks in trees, reeds or on cliffs. Eggs 2–5, white or blue. Incubation about 21 days, nestling period 14–21 days; young return to be fed until 5–11 weeks old. 31 species.

8/ SACRED IBIS
Threskiornis aethiopica
RANGE: sub-Saharan Africa, Madagascar, Iraq
HABITAT: inland and coastal shallow wetlands
SIZE: 25½–29½ in (65–75 cm)

This species is now extinct in Egypt where it was venerated in ancient times. It is depicted in many murals and in hieroglyphics and mummified specimens are common in burial places; over 1.5 million birds were found in one group of tombs.

When the Sacred Ibis flies, bare patches of skin under the wings and at the sides of the breast show as scarlet, contrasting with the black and white body and wings. The black head and neck are naked, lacking feathers, but they do not become so until the bird is about 2 years old. Until then they are feathered white, mottled with black.

9/ HERMIT IBIS
Geronticus eremita   E
RANGE: NW Africa and Turkey
HABITAT: mountainous and semiarid deserts; also upland wetlands, farmland
SIZE: 28–31 in (71–79 cm)

Sadly, this is a seriously threatened species that now breeds only in Morocco and Turkey, although it formerly bred in southern Europe and in the Middle East. The reasons for the decline are unclear, but the bird seems unable to adapt to changes in food supply and, perhaps, climate. Dry seasons are known to cause considerable mortality among the young. The few remaining colonies of the Hermit Ibis (also known as the Northern Bald Ibis or Waldrapp) are on cliffs in steep valleys. Here, nests of twigs, grass and straw are built, often decorated with bits of paper.

10/ SCARLET IBIS
Eudocimus ruber
RANGE: Venezuela, Colombia, coastal Guianas and Brazil; Trinidad
HABITAT: coastal swamps, mangroves, lagoons, estuaries, mudflats
SIZE: 24 in (61 cm)

This species is gregarious, foraging and roosting communally, often with several heron and egret species. A sunset flight of Scarlet Ibises to their roost in a mangrove thicket is a magnificent sight. Their range overlaps in several places with the White Ibis *E. albus* and hybridization occurs.

Scarlet Ibises feed mainly on crabs, mollusks and other invertebrates, probing for them on mudflats with their curved bills. They will also take fish, frogs and insects. They breed colonially, constructing nests of twigs and sticks.

11/ GLOSSY IBIS
Plegadis falcinellus
RANGE: widespread but scattered in Central America, Africa, S Eurasia and Australasia
HABITAT: shallow freshwater and coastal wetlands
SIZE: 22–26 in (56–66 cm)

The overall dark chestnut and black plumage of this bird has a purple and green iridescence that gives the species its name. Glossy Ibises breed in colonies, sometimes of thousands of pairs, almost always in association with herons and egrets. However, they are clearly less tolerant of disturbance than these other species and have declined in many areas. Outside the breeding season, flocks of Glossy Ibises feed in shallow wetlands and open fields. They roost communally, often sharing waterside trees with herons.

12/ WHITE SPOONBILL
Platalea leucorodia
RANGE: temperate and S Eurasia, India, tropical W and NE Africa
HABITAT: shallow fresh, brackish and saltwater wetlands
SIZE: 31–35 in (79–89 cm)

This bird feeds with the mandibles of its bill held slightly open and the spoon-shaped tip immersed in shallow water. As the bird swings its head from side to side, the bill makes scything movements below the surface in search of shrimp and other aquatic life. Feeding usually takes place with small groups of birds wading in lines, which may increase efficiency if one bird is able to catch prey disturbed by the next one.

White Spoonbills are sensitive to disturbance, and this, as well as the drainage and pollution of their marshland habitats, has caused the population to decline in many areas.

13/ ROSEATE SPOONBILL
Ajaia ajaja
RANGE: SE USA, Central America, Colombia, Ecuador, E Peru, Bolivia, N Argentina
HABITAT: marshes, lagoons, mangroves, mudflats
SIZE: 31¾ in (81 cm)

These spectacular pink and white spoonbills are gregarious birds, often seen foraging or flying in small flocks. They sweep their bills through shallow water to catch small fish, crustaceans and other aquatic invertebrates, and also eat some plant material. In the USA, they were persecuted by plume-hunters for the millinery trade. Although they suffer locally from habitat destruction, their numbers and range in south-central USA have recently increased.

Roseate Spoonbills nest in small colonies, often with a variety of heron species. They are monogamous and have elaborate courtship behavior that includes the presentation of twigs, flight displays and bill-clappering. Their nests of sticks and twigs are constructed in bushes, trees or reeds or, occasionally, on the ground.

FAMILY PHOENICOPTERIDAE
Flamingos
Large, very long-legged and long-necked wading birds. Plumage red, pink and white. Sexes similar. Nest a mound of mud. Eggs 1–2, white. Incubation about 28 days, nestling period 5–8 days; chicks dependent on adults for food for another 4 weeks. 5 species.

14/ GREATER FLAMINGO
Phoenicopterus ruber
RANGE: S Europe, SW Asia, E, W and N Africa, West Indies, Central America, Galapagos Islands
HABITAT: saline or alkaline lakes, lagoons and deltas
SIZE: 49¼–57 in (125–145 cm)

The extraordinary slender build and the curious bill of a flamingo are both adaptations for feeding. Small shrimp and other crustaceans are sifted from the bottom mud by a pumping action of the tongue which forces mud and water through the comblike lamellae on either side of the bill. The head is held upside down at the end of the very long neck and swung to and fro as the bird walks slowly forward. The great length of the legs and the neck allows the birds to feed in much deeper water than other species, so avoiding competition.

There are 2 races of the Greater Flamingo. *P. r. ruber* breeds on the Caribbean Islands and surrounding mainland coasts, with an outpost in the Galapagos Islands. It has much redder plumage than the other race and its bill is orange-pink and black with a yellowish base. The second race *P. r. roseus*, with paler plumage and a pink and black bill, is restricted to the Old World.

15/ ANDEAN FLAMINGO
Phoenicoparrus andinus   ?
RANGE: Andes of Peru, Bolivia, Chile, Argentina above 8,000 ft (2,500 m)
HABITAT: salt lakes
SIZE: 40 in (102 cm)

Andean Flamingos are spectacular in flight. Like other flamingos, they fly with their neck extended and their legs trailing behind, uttering gooselike "honking" calls. Their numbers have declined recently and they may now be the scarcest flamingos, probably with fewer than 50,000 birds.

As with other flamingos, both sexes constantly repair their mud nest mound while incubating the single egg. The downy white chicks have straight bills at first and are fed liquid secretions from the adults' crops until their bills are fully developed. This avian "milk" contains fat, protein, some carbohydrates and blood cells. It is also rich in red pigment, obtained by the birds from their food, which gives flamingos' feathers their pink and red coloring. Mobile young gather into a common flock, or nursery, guarded by the adults in turn.

SCREAMERS, SWANS, GEESE AND RELATIVES

CRESTED SCREAMER

WHITE-FACED WHISTLING DUCK

GRAYLAG GOOSE

race *rubrirostris*

race *anser*

race *flavirostris*

race *albifrons*
juv

race *albifrons*

WHITE-FRONTED GOOSE

BLACK SWAN

juv

race *columbianus*
"Whistling Swan"

♂   ♂ winter   ♀

FRECKLED DUCK

♂

race *bewickii*
"Bewick's Swan"

juv

race *bew...*
"Bewick's
variations
p...

MUTE SWAN

TUNDRA SWAN

race *leucoptera*
"Greater Magellan Goose"

MAGELLAN GOOSE

♀

race *picta*
"Lesser Magellan Goose"
white phase

♂

race *picta*
♂ barred phase

MAGPIE GOOSE ♀feeding chick

race *atlanticus*
"Greater Snow Goose"
snow phase

ce *caerulescens*
esser Snow Goose"
ue phase

SNOW GOOSE

HAWAIIAN GOOSE

RED-BREASTED GOOSE

race *minima*

EGYPTIAN GOOSE

race *canadensis*

CANADA GOOSE

SCREAMERS, SWANS, GEESE AND RELATIVES

FAMILY ANHIMIDAE
Screamers

Large, gooselike waterbirds. Long, partially webbed toes and short, hooked bill. Mainly black, gray and brown. Sexes similar. Nest on ground close to water. Eggs 2–7, whitish. Incubation 40–45 days, chicks leave nest and feed themselves soon after hatching. 3 species.

1/ CRESTED SCREAMER
Chauna torquata

RANGE: S Brazil, Uruguay and N Argentina
HABITAT: marshes in open grassland and woodland
SIZE: $33\frac{1}{2}$–$37\frac{1}{2}$ in (85–95 cm)

Screamers take their name from their loud, far-carrying calls, though these are more a harsh honking than a true scream. They can be heard up to nearly 2 mls (3 km) away.

The Crested Screamer has a short, downcurved bill, long, thick legs and only a trace of webbing between the long toes. Two sharp, bony spurs project from the bend of each wing. The spurs are used in fighting, either between rival screamers or to drive off enemies, including hunting dogs and other predators. Screamers often fly to great heights, sailing in wide circles until almost out of sight.

The large nest, a mound of vegetation, is built close to shallow water. When they hatch, the young already have a covering of down feathers and they leave the nest within a few hours. They fledge when about 60–75 days old.

FAMILY ANATIDAE
Swans, geese and ducks

Medium to large waterbirds. Most thickset, with webbed feet and flattened bills. Plumage variable, often bright. Sexes different in many species. Nests usually platform of vegetation; some hole-nesters. Eggs 4–14, pale, unmarked. Incubation 18–39 days, young leave nest and (except Magpie Goose) feed themselves soon after hatching. 147 species.

2/ MAGPIE GOOSE
Anseranas semipalmata

RANGE: N Australia and S New Guinea
HABITAT: overgrown swamps and lagoons and adjacent farmland
SIZE: $29\frac{1}{2}$–$33\frac{1}{2}$ in (75–85 cm)

With its long neck, long legs and bold pied plumage, the Magpie Goose is one of the most distinctive of all wildfowl. It has only partial webbing between the toes and the male has a pronounced dome to the top of the head.

The natural food of the Magpie Goose includes aquatic plants and seeds. In northern Australia the birds have damaged rice crops, both by grazing and trampling, but careful adjustment of water levels in the rice paddies has helped to reduce the problem.

The nest is a large platform of vegetation, plucked off and trampled in shallow water, before being built up into a mound. Uniquely among wildfowl, the parents feed their young bill to bill.

3/ WHITE-FACED WHISTLING DUCK
Dendrocygna viduata

RANGE: tropical South America, sub-Saharan Africa, Madagascar and the Comoro Islands
HABITAT: rivers, lakes, swamps, marshes
SIZE: 17–$18\frac{3}{4}$ in (43–48 cm)

The White-faced Whistling Duck has the upright stance, long neck and long legs typical of the whistling ducks. It has broad wings and powerful flight and can also swim buoyantly, upending to feed on seeds and invertebrates.

A pair of White-faced Whistling Ducks will indulge in mutual preening. The 2 birds stand facing one another and nibble gently at each other's head and neck feathers. This may have a useful function in ridding these relatively inaccessible areas of parasites, but it is likely that such intimate actions help to reinforce the pair bond. The birds usually nest in tall vegetation, but occasionally choose the fork of a low tree.

4/ MUTE SWAN
Cygnus olor

RANGE: temperate Eurasia; introduced to parts of North America, South Africa and Australia
HABITAT: lowland freshwater lakes and marshes; coastal lagoons and estuaries
SIZE: $49\frac{1}{4}$–61 in (125–155 cm)

The Mute Swan is a familiar sight in town parks in Britain where it has long been protected. Much wilder populations occur in continental Europe and Asia, forming flocks on lakes and estuaries. The species is misnamed, since it utters a variety of snoring, snorting and hissing calls and its wings produce a loud throbbing sound in flight.

Males (called cobs) have larger knobs on their bills than females (pens), especially in the breeding season. A pair of Mute Swans will vigorously defend a territory around the mound of vegetation that forms their nest. However, the birds breed colonially in a few places and there the strong territorial instinct is reduced so much that their nests are only about 3 ft (1 m) apart.

5/ BLACK SWAN
Cygnus atratus

RANGE: Australia; introduced into New Zealand
HABITAT: large freshwater and brackish marshes and lagoons; also estuaries and coastal bays
SIZE: $45\frac{1}{4}$–55 in (115–140 cm)

The Black Swan is a highly gregarious species, occurring in enormous flocks, up to 50,000 strong. It breeds in colonies of hundreds of pairs, the nests placed just beyond pecking distance from one another. Like many Australian waterbirds, the Black Swan can delay breeding in times of drought but can quickly take advantage of sudden rains and flood conditions. Long-distance movements have also been recorded in response to such extremes of climate.

The nest is typically a pile of vegetation, up to 3 ft (1 m) across at the base, built in shallow water. The 5–6 pale green eggs are incubated for up to 40 days by both parents. In most other wildfowl, the female carries out the incubation alone.

6/ TUNDRA SWAN
Cygnus columbianus

RANGE: breeds Arctic North America and USSR; winters S to temperate latitudes
HABITAT: breeds on marshy tundra; winters on freshwater marshes and estuaries
SIZE: $47\frac{1}{4}$–59 in (120–150 cm)

Three races of the all-white Tundra Swan are recognized: these include the Whistling Swan *C. c. columbianus* of North America and the Bewick's Swan *C. c. bewickii* of Eurasia, both illustrated. The amount of yellow on the bill of the Bewick's Swan is extremely variable and can in fact be used to identify individual birds.

Most swans return each winter to the same locality and there is great faithfulness between pairs. The birds build their nest on marshy ground and lay a clutch of 3–5 eggs. The young swans migrate with their parents and they spend their first winter together as a family.

7/ WHITE-FRONTED GOOSE
Anser albifrons

RANGE: **circumpolar Arctic; winters S to temperate latitudes**
HABITAT: **breeds in tundra; winters on open marshes and on agricultural land**
SIZE: **26–33$\frac{3}{4}$ in (66–86 cm)**

White-fronted Geese have a high-pitched, laughing call and are actually named "laughing geese" in more than one European language. They are gregarious birds, occurring in winter flocks of many tens of thousands. When nesting, however, they scatter widely across the tundra. There are 4 or 5 races, distinguished by bill color and plumage: those illustrated are *A.a. albifrons*, breeding in Arctic Siberia, and *A.a. flavirostris*, breeding in western Greenland.

The nest is a shallow hollow, lined with down from the female's breast. The down both insulates and helps to conceal the 4–7 eggs. The goslings quickly learn to peck at grass and other surrounding vegetation. This, together with the underground parts of marsh plants and several different agricultural crops, provides most of their food.

8/ GRAYLAG GOOSE
Anser anser

RANGE: **mainly temperate latitudes of Eurasia**
HABITAT: **freshwater marshes and open water; often winters on farmland**
SIZE: **29$\frac{1}{2}$–35$\frac{1}{2}$ in (75–90 cm)**

The Graylag Goose once bred widely throughout western Europe, but the drainage of marshes and deliberate persecution caused a dramatic reduction in its breeding range. However, it is now expanding again and some wintering flocks contain tens of thousands of geese. There are 2 races: *A.a. anser* breeds in Europe, while the pink-billed *A.a. rubrirostris* breeds in Asia. They overlap in eastern Europe and western USSR.

Large winter flocks on farmland may damage crops and pasture. The bill of the Graylag Goose is adapted for probing in marshy ground and pulling up roots; it is also ideal for grazing and for slicing pieces off turnips and potatoes.

9/ SNOW GOOSE
Anser caerulescens

RANGE: **Arctic North America; winters on both seaboards and S to Gulf of Mexico**
HABITAT: **breeds on Arctic tundra; winters on freshwater and salt marshes farmland**
SIZE: **25$\frac{1}{2}$–33 in (65–84 cm)**

There are few more magnificent sights than a flock of tens of thousands of Snow Geese. Glistening white, the birds descend like snowflakes, their black wing tips seeming to flicker as they turn before landing. The 2 races, the Greater and the Lesser, are distinguished mainly by size. While the adult Greater Snow Goose is always white, the Lesser Snow Goose shows both the white "snow" phase and a dark gray "blue" phase.

Snow Geese nest in colonies of many thousands of pairs on the Arctic tundra. In winter, they journey south, some flying non-stop for 2,000 mls (3,500 km) or more to reach the Gulf of Mexico, where harvested rice fields provide ample food.

10/ HAWAIIAN GOOSE
Branta sandvicensis $\boxed{V}$

RANGE: **confined to the Hawaiian Islands**
HABITAT: **sparsely vegetated slopes of volcanoes**
SIZE: **22–28 in (56–71 cm)**

By 1952, extensive hunting and introduced predators had reduced the once numerous population of the Hawaiian Goose, estimated at 25,000 birds at the end of the 19th century, to as few as 30 individuals. Since then, captive breeding in both Hawaii and England has enabled well over 1,000 birds to be released back into the wild. By 1976, the total population in the wild was around 750.

The Hawaiian Goose has only partial webbing on its feet, reflecting its largely terrestrial habits. In its home on the Hawaiian Islands, there is little standing water. The nest is a simple scrape in the ground, usually in the shelter of a rock or a clump of vegetation.

11/ CANADA GOOSE
Branta canadensis

RANGE: **Arctic and temperate North America; introduced into Europe and New Zealand**
HABITAT: **lowland wetlands**
SIZE: **21$\frac{1}{2}$–43$\frac{1}{4}$ in (55–110 cm)**

The Canada Goose has been divided into 10–12 races, based on distribution, size and coloring. The smallest races (such as *B.c. minima* from west Alaska) breed in the Arctic; the larger races (such as *B.c. canadensis* from eastern Canada) breed farther south. In recent decades, the large birds have successfully moved into town parks and many are tame. Introduced birds in Britain (of the race *B.c. canadensis*) have colonized gravel workings and are now common throughout the lowland parts of the country.

The bird's nest is usually placed on the ground, often sheltered by vegetation, but tree and even cliff-ledge nest sites have been reported, and rafts and other artificial platforms are readily adopted.

12/ RED-BREASTED GOOSE
Branta ruficollis

RANGE: **breeds in the Siberian Arctic; winters close to the Black, Caspian and Aral seas**
HABITAT: **breeds on tundra; winters on open farmland close to major wetlands**
SIZE: **20$\frac{3}{4}$–21$\frac{1}{2}$ in (53–55 cm)**

A remarkable association exists between this scarce, strikingly plumaged goose and various birds of prey. Red-breasted Geese nest on the Arctic tundra, concentrating in small groups of up to 5 pairs around the nests of Peregrines, Rough-legged Hawks and, sometimes, large gulls. In defending their own nests against predators, these aggressive birds keep intruders, such as gulls and Arctic Foxes, away from the nests of the surrounding geese.

The geese may site their nests within 33 ft (10 m) of birds of prey, apparently without risk of attack from their "protectors." The nest is usually placed on a steep bank or on the top of a low cliff. The total world population is probably fewer than 25,000 individuals.

13/ FRECKLED DUCK
Stictonetta naevosa $\boxed{?}$

RANGE: **Australia**
HABITAT: **open freshwater and brackish lakes and swamps**
SIZE: **19$\frac{1}{2}$–21$\frac{1}{2}$ in (50–55 cm)**

This duck takes its name from the fine, buff or whitish speckles on its plumage. Like many Australian waterfowl, it is highly responsive to the vagaries of the climate. Prolonged drought in the areas where it is most numerous, in the southwest and southeast of the country, sends birds wandering over great distances. Where they find water, pairs quickly settle down to breed and rear young. Later, if conditions permit, there will be a return to their normal distribution until the next drought again disperses the birds. Freckled Ducks always place their nests close to water, often supported by the twigs or branches of flooded bushes.

14/ MAGELLAN GOOSE
Chloephaga picta

RANGE: **S South America and the Falkland Islands**
HABITAT: **grassland and marshes**
SIZE: **23$\frac{1}{2}$–25$\frac{1}{2}$ in (60–65 cm)**

As grazing birds, Magellan Geese have come into conflict with sheep farmers in South America. Bounties have been offered for both birds and eggs, but although large numbers are killed and eggs are systematically removed, the species is not under serious threat. Its habitats are extensive and the human population is sparse. Although pressure on the birds is severe in some areas, in others the geese are unmolested.

The white and gray male has a whistling call used in display, to which the rufous and gray-brown female responds with a lower cackling. The illustration shows the 2 races of the Magellan Goose: the Lesser *C.p. picta*, with its white and barred phases, and the Greater *C.p. leucoptera*.

15/ EGYPTIAN GOOSE
Alopochen aegyptiacus

RANGE: **Nile valley and sub-Saharan Africa**
HABITAT: **tropical and subtropical wetlands**
SIZE: **24$\frac{3}{4}$–28$\frac{3}{4}$ in (63–73 cm)**

A large, upright bird, the Egyptian Goose has 2 color phases, one gray-brown on the upperparts, the other red-brown. The species is remarkable for the great variety of nest sites that it uses. Some birds nest on the ground, like most other geese and sheldgeese, often choosing the shelter of bushes or clumps of grass. Other pairs prefer to nest off the ground, using ledges on cliffs or old buildings. Some select the abandoned nests of other birds, often high in the crowns of trees.

A typical clutch consists of 5–8 eggs, which are incubated by the female for about 28 days. The downy young that hatch out on ledges or in trees face a perilous tumble to the ground as they leave the nest. The parents do not assist the chicks, but call to them from below until they pluck up courage to step into space.

SHELDUCKS, STEAMER DUCKS, PERCHING DUCKS AND DABBLING DUCKS

WOOD DUCK ♀ ♂

GREEN-WINGED TEAL
race *crecca* ♀
race *carolinensis* ♂
race *crecca* ♂

MUSCOVY DUCK

COMB DUCK race *melanotos* ♀
race *melanotos* ♂

MALLARD ♂ ♀

race *chlorotis* ♂
NEW ZEALAND TEAL
race *chlorotis* ♀

race *armata*
"Chilean Torrent Duck" ♂

TORRENT DUCK

race *armata* ♀

NORTHERN SHOVELER ♀ ♂

AMERICAN WIGEON

AFRICAN PYGMY GOOSE

AMERICAN BLACK DUCK

NORTHERN PINTAIL

race *gambensis*

SPUR-WINGED GOOSE

NORTHERN SHELDUCK

juv

MAGELLANIC FLIGHTLESS
STEAMER DUCK

juv

SHELDUCKS, STEAMER DUCKS, PERCHING DUCKS AND DABBLING DUCKS

1/ NORTHERN SHELDUCK
Tadorna tadorna

RANGE: temperate Eurasia; winters S to N
Africa, India, China and Japan
HABITAT: estuaries, shallow seas
SIZE: 23–26 in (58–67 cm)

These large, gooselike birds feed with a scything
action of the bill through soft mud and sand,
picking up mollusks, crustaceans and other invertebrates. In early spring, they gather in groups in
which the males court the females with melodious
whistling calls, rearing up and throwing back
their heads. Arguments with neighbors often
develop into furious aerial chases.

Most Northern Shelducks nest in holes, either
underground or in hollow trees. They will also
nest under buildings and in straw stacks. The
young of several broods often combine into large
"nurseries," under the care of just a few of the
parents. The rest of the adults depart for their
molting grounds. Much of the population of
northwestern Europe, numbering some 100,000
birds, migrates to molt in the Waddenzee on the
north German coast.

2/ MAGELLANIC FLIGHTLESS STEAMER DUCK
Tachyeres pteneres

RANGE: extreme S South America
HABITAT: marine, especially rocky or
gravelly coasts with offshore kelp beds
SIZE: 24–33 in (61–84 cm)

The heavy, bulky build of the Magellanic Flightless Steamer Duck is enhanced by the large head
and strong bill. It is incapable of flight, though it
can escape predators by furiously threshing and
paddling over the water with its stubby wings. It
is this action, once described as "steaming," that
earned these ducks their name. The males, in
particular, also use their wings to strike one
another in combat. The blows are reinforced by
large bony knobs on the carpal joints at the bends
of the wings.

Magellanic Flightless Steamer Ducks feed exclusively on marine invertebrates, especially mussels and crabs. They dive for their food among
forests of kelp fronds and also dabble in gravel
under shallow water.

The nest is usually among grass tussocks near
water, but is occasionally in a deserted penguin
burrow. Although generally sited close to water,
nests of this species have been found up to half a
mile (1 km) inland.

3/ SPUR-WINGED GOOSE
Plectropterus gambensis

RANGE: most of sub-Saharan Africa
HABITAT: fresh waters in open grassland
SIZE: 29½–39 in (75–100 cm)

With its long legs and neck, this large goose
appears rather ungainly. It uses its long bill for
grazing on waterside vegetation or for pulling up
aquatic plants, and it also feeds on floating seeds.

Spur-winged Geese have a hidden weapon, a
spur 1 in (2.5 cm) long on the carpal joint at the
bend of each wing. It is used in disputes when
competing birds strike each other with opened
wings. The nest is usually a mound of vegetation

built among tall plants and up to 14 eggs are laid.
The goslings develop their wing spurs when only
a few weeks old. There are 2 races: *P. g. gambensis*, which occurs over most of the species' range,
and *P. g. niger* found south of 15°S, which has the
white on the underparts restricted to the center of
the chest and lower belly.

4/ MUSCOVY DUCK
Cairina moschata

RANGE: Central and South America
HABITAT: freshwater marshes and pools in
wooded areas; brackish coastal lagoons
SIZE: 26–33 in (66–84 cm)

The Muscovy Duck has been widely introduced
outside its native lands as a domestic fowl. Unlike
the glossy greenish-black wild birds, the domestic
birds may be green-black, gray or white or a
mixture of colors. The knob at the base of a
domestic male's bill is red and surrounded by bare
red skin. Muscovy Ducks are omnivorous, feeding
on the leaves and seeds of marsh plants, as well as
small reptiles, fish, crabs and insects.

In the wild, these shy birds roost in small
groups in trees, safe from ground predators. The
only time they leave the shelter of the forest is
when the savannas are flooded. Both wild and
domestic Muscovy Ducks prefer to nest in holes in
trees, and they take readily to nest-boxes.

5/ COMB DUCK
Sarkidiornis melanotos

RANGE: sub-Saharan Africa, India,
Southeast Asia and tropical South
America
HABITAT: rivers, swamps, lakes
SIZE: 22–30 in (56–76 cm)

This bird takes its name from the fleshy blackish
knob at the base of the male's bill: this knob has a
crenellated edge rather like a comb. Comb Ducks
are highly mobile, with flocks of 50 or more birds
moving to take advantage of flooded conditions in
different areas.

Outside the breeding season, flocks of Comb
Ducks often consist entirely of males or of

females. During the breeding season, each male
may have 2 mates and several nesting "pairs" can
form small breeding colonies. The nest is usually
in a hole in a tree, in an old wall or on the ground,
well concealed in tall vegetation.

6/ AFRICAN PYGMY GOOSE
Nettapus auritus

RANGE: sub-Saharan Africa, Madagascar
HABITAT: freshwater pools, large lakes;
less often coastal lagoons and estuaries
SIZE: 12–13 in (30–33 cm)

The drake African Pygmy Goose is among the
most attractive of the smaller wildfowl. Although
the bird is really a duck, the rounded head and
short, stubby bill are gooselike, hence the name.

African Pygmy Geese spend much of their time
perching in trees, on branches overhanging the
water, usually in pairs or small groups but
sometimes in groups of up to 200 birds. They peck
seeds and small leaves from the surface, dive to
reach underwater plants, or pluck seeds, leaves
and buds from emergent vegetation. They are
especially fond of water lily seeds. The bird's
nest is usually placed in a hole, normally in a
tree, cliff or termite mound, but frequently in the
thatched roof of a hut.

7/ WOOD DUCK
Aix sponsa

RANGE: North America: E population
breeds S Canada to Florida, W population
breeds British Columbia to California;
winters in S of breeding range
HABITAT: fresh waters in wooded areas;
more open flooded areas in winter
SIZE: 17–20 in (43–51 cm)

The remarkable coloration of the male Wood
Duck greatly contrasts with the mottled gray-
brown of the female. It was the drake's superb
plumage which nearly led to the species' extinction. In the 19th century the feathers were in great
demand for ornament and for fishing flies.

However, because protection measures were
taken in time, and since the Wood Duck's habit of

nesting in tree holes meant that it took readily to nest-boxes, it was possible to restore the species to many areas of eastern North America in which tree clearance and drainage, as well as shooting, had led to its serious decline.

8/ TORRENT DUCK
Merganetta armata

RANGE: **Andes**
HABITAT: **fast-flowing streams**
SIZE: **17–18 in (43–46 cm)**

The Torrent Duck is perfectly adapted to life in fast-flowing water. It has a streamlined shape, powerful legs, a broad, stiff tail used for steering, and sharp claws to enable it to cling to slippery rocks. It feeds by making frequent underwater forays from its perch on a boulder. It forages for caddis fly and other larvae on the river bottom, catches small fish, and picks various food items from the surface. Although few nests have been found, they are always near water in a crevice or hollow of some kind, between rocks or under overhangs. The ducklings are able to tackle the most turbulent water as soon as they hatch.

Several races have been described, separated geographically along the 5,000-ml (8,000-km) length of the Andes. The one illustrated is the Chilean Torrent Duck *M. a. armata* of central Chile and western Argentina.

9/ AMERICAN WIGEON
Anas americana

RANGE: **breeds N and C North America; winters S to Gulf of Mexico**
HABITAT: **freshwater marshes, ponds; winters on marshes, coastal lagoons**
SIZE: **18–22 in (45–56 cm)**

American Wigeons are highly gregarious in winter, occurring in flocks of many tens of thousands. In summer the breeding pairs disperse, spreading throughout the pothole country of the North American prairies and northward into the wooded muskeg of Canada and Alaska.

Although classed as a dabbling duck, the American Wigeon obtains only some of its plant food by dabbling in shallow water. More often, tightly packed flocks of birds graze on marshes and pastures. The nest is a shallow cup of grasses in concealing vegetation near water.

10/ GREEN-WINGED TEAL
Anas crecca

RANGE: **breeds North America, N Eurasia; winters S USA, Central America, Caribbean, temperate Eurasia, tropical Asia**
HABITAT: **freshwater pools, marshes; in winter also on estuaries, coastal lagoons**
SIZE: **13–15 in (34–38 cm)**

This abundant small duck has 2 distinct races, the European *A. c. crecca*, with a horizontal white flank stripe, and the North American *A. c. carolinensis*, with a vertical white chest stripe. These are male characteristics; females are indistinguishable.

Green-winged Teals can launch themselves almost vertically into the air when disturbed,

"springing" off the water, whence comes an old collective noun for a group of these agile and beautiful little ducks – a "spring" of teal. Once in flight, dense flocks will wheel and turn in perfect unison. The male has a characteristic, far-carrying, liquid *preep preep* call. The diet consists of small invertebrates and some seeds, most of which the birds find by dabbling in the shallows.

11/ NEW ZEALAND TEAL
Anas aucklandica   V

RANGE: **isolated sites in New Zealand**
HABITAT: **freshwater swamps and streams among trees; estuaries and ocean bays**
SIZE: **14–18 in (34–46 cm)**

The entire population of these secretive, night-time feeding birds may now number fewer than 2,000. Estimates suggest that there are about 1,000 of the race *A. a. chlorotis*, once widespread throughout New Zealand, but now found only in small isolated populations in areas relatively free of predators, notably on Great Barrier Island. Some 500 of the race *A. a. aucklandica* survive on several islands near Auckland Island, and about 30 of the race *A. a. nesiotis* remain on Dent Island, an islet off Campbell Island.

Habitat destruction and introduced predators seem to have been the main causes of the bird's severe decline. However, captive breeding programs are proving successful and several hundred birds have been released back into the wild in recent years.

Both of the island races are flightless: presumably, flightlessness was an adaptation to life on small islands where there were originally no ground predators. When cats were introduced, they soon took their toll of this easy prey.

12/ MALLARD
Anas platyrhynchos

RANGE: **N hemisphere, N of the tropics; introduced to Australia and New Zealand**
HABITAT: **wide range of fresh and coastal waters**
SIZE: **20–25½ in (50–65 cm)**

The success of the Mallard, ancestor of most domestic ducks, reflects its supreme adaptability. It can become completely tame in urban areas, relying on human handouts for food, although it is as wild as any wildfowl in other habitats.

Mallards feed by dabbling in shallows, or upending to reach greater depths. They are omnivorous, eating both invertebrates and plant matter. Natural nest sites are in thick vegetation close to water, but in towns the birds use holes in trees and buildings and even window ledges.

13/ AMERICAN BLACK DUCK
Anas rubripes

RANGE: **NE North America; winters S to Gulf of Mexico**
HABITAT: **freshwater marshes in woods; winters on estuaries, coastal marshes**
SIZE: **21–24 in (53–61 cm)**

American Black Ducks feed on plants and invertebrates and nest in dense vegetation close to water. As with some other close relatives of the Mallard,

but unlike nearly all other northern hemisphere dabbling ducks, the male lacks any bright nuptial plumage. The species may now be under threat because females are more attracted by brightly colored male Mallards than by their own kind. Since the recent expansion of the Mallard's range in eastern North America, hybridization has become more common and widespread. Habitat degradation and overhunting pose further threats to the bird's population.

14/ NORTHERN PINTAIL
Anas acuta

RANGE: **Eurasia and North America; winters S to Panama, C Africa, India, Philippines**
HABITAT: **open marshes; winters on estuaries and coastal lagoons**
SIZE: **male 25–29 in (63–74 cm) including 4 in (10 cm) central tail feathers; female 17–25 in (43–63 cm)**

The handsome drake Northern Pintail has long tail streamers which he cocks out of the water as he swims. This species is strongly attracted to fall stubblefields; a single site may hold more than 500,000 birds. In some parts of North America, wheat and corn is grown specially for them. It is left unharvested in the fall to attract the vast hordes and keep them from damaging more vulnerable crops.

Apart from pecking at grain, Northern Pintails feed mainly in the water. They upend, using their long necks to reach deeper than other ducks sharing their range. They scour the bottom of pools and marshes for plant roots and leaves, as well as aquatic invertebrates.

15/ NORTHERN SHOVELER
Anas clypeata

RANGE: **Eurasia and North America S of the Arctic Circle; winters S to the subtropics**
HABITAT: **freshwater pools and marshes; also on estuaries and coastal lagoons in winter**
SIZE: **17–20 in (44–52 cm)**

This bird's distinctive bill acts as a superb filter for food. As the duck swims along with the front half of the bill submerged, it creates a stream of water that flows in at the bill's tip. Rapid tongue action aids the flow and directs it out at each side, any particles being strained from the water by intermeshing projections on the upper and lower mandibles.

Groups of Northern Shovelers often circle slowly as they feed. Their combined paddling action brings food items – tiny seeds and floating animals – to the surface in deep water. Northern Shovelers will also dabble in shallows, selecting larger food items. Here, however, they come into competition with other ducks, something their sieving method normally avoids.

DIVING DUCKS, SEA DUCKS, SAWBILLS AND STIFFTAILS

TUFTED DUCK

COMMON EIDER

RED-CRESTED POCHARD

CANVASBACK

BLACK SCOTER

HARLEQUIN DUCK

WHITE-BACKED DUCK

MARBLED TEAL

race *jamaicensis* ♀

♂ race *ferruginea* "Peruvian Ruddy Duck"

jamaicensis ♂

♀ winter

♀ summer

RUDDY DUCK

♂ summer

♂ winter

OLDSQUAW

♀

COMMON GOLDENEYE

♀

♂

RED-BREASTED MERGANSER

♂

♀

♂

MUSK DUCK

HOODED MERGANSER

DIVING DUCKS, SEA DUCKS, SAWBILLS AND STIFFTAILS

1/ MARBLED TEAL
Marmaronetta angustirostris [?]

RANGE: **Mediterranean region E to Pakistan and NW India**
HABITAT: **shallow freshwater and brackish lakes, lagoons and marshes**
SIZE: **$15\frac{1}{4}$–$16\frac{1}{2}$ in (39–42 cm)**

The Marbled Teal takes its name from the whitish blotches that liberally mark its sandy-gray plumage. Although it resembles the teals, which are dabbling ducks, this species is now generally regarded as more closely related to the pochards, or diving ducks, and is increasingly known as the Marbled Duck. In particular, its courtship displays and other behavior patterns are more similar to the diving ducks.

Breeding usually takes place in small colonies, sometimes with the nests no more than 3 ft (1 m) apart. The normal nest site is on the ground, concealed under low bushes or in thick vegetation close to the water. However, in southern Spain nests have been found concealed in the roofs of grass- and reed-thatched huts. The birds do not excavate holes in the thatch but make use of natural cavities.

Populations of this duck have declined over most of its range as shallow wetlands have been drained. However, there have been recent increases in numbers reported from Spain and North Africa.

2/ RED-CRESTED POCHARD
Netta rufina

RANGE: **E Europe and SC Asia**
HABITAT: **freshwater lakes, rivers, deltas and coastal lagoons**
SIZE: **$20\frac{3}{4}$–$22\frac{1}{2}$ in (53–57 cm)**

Red-crested Pochards have been spreading slowly north in Europe in the last 50 years. Their principal range is in the Mediterranean basin, but there are small pockets of breeding birds farther north in France, the Netherlands and Denmark. Birds from these countries began to appear regularly in eastern England in the 1950s and 1960s, but the picture has become confused since then by escapes from captivity. This colorful species is popular with waterfowl keepers.

The birds lay a clutch of up to 10 pale green or olive eggs in a well-concealed nest of aquatic vegetation, often built on a base of twigs. The female incubates alone, while the male moves away and joins other males for the annual molt.

3/ CANVASBACK
Aythya valisineria

RANGE: **S Canada to Mexico**
HABITAT: **breeds on prairie marshes; winters on lakes, lagoons and estuaries**
SIZE: **$18\frac{3}{4}$–24 in (48–61 cm)**

The Canvasback is the largest of the pochards, or diving ducks. Both male and female have a relatively long sloping forehead, high, peaked crown, long bill and long neck giving them a distinctive silhouette. The Canvasback is one of the typical breeding species of the prairie pothole country of southern Canada and northern USA – a vast area of rolling farmland with numerous small ponds (potholes) and marshes.

The ducks feed mainly on aquatic vegetation, diving to depths of 30 ft (9 m). Often, they are closely followed by American Coots and American Wigeons. As soon as the Canvasbacks surface with a beakful of food, the other birds give chase and try to steal it.

4/ TUFTED DUCK
Aythya fuligula

RANGE: **Eurasia**
HABITAT: **lakes and ponds, sometimes in towns; winters on larger waters, estuaries, lagoons**
SIZE: **$15\frac{3}{4}$–$18\frac{1}{2}$ in (40–47 cm)**

Tufted Ducks are gregarious birds that gather in large winter flocks and breed in loose colonies, with their nests only a few yards apart. They have successfully moved into towns and cities, colonizing park lakes and relying on people for scraps of food.

Tufted Ducks are expert divers, able to reach depths of 16–20 ft (5–6 m) and remain underwater for 20–30 seconds. Their natural diet includes a wide variety of small mollusks and other aquatic invertebrates. The birds' nests are rarely far from water, concealed in tussocks of grass or under bushes. There the females incubate the clutches of 7–12 eggs for about 24 days.

5/ COMMON EIDER
Somateria mollissima

RANGE: **Arctic and N temperate Eurasia and North America**
HABITAT: **coastal waters, estuaries**
SIZE: **$19\frac{1}{2}$–28 in (50–71 cm)**

The down feathers that the female Common Eider plucks from her breast to line the nest have long been valued by people for their insulating properties. In Iceland and Norway, breeding colonies of Common Eiders have been protected in order to maximize the production of eider down. Artificial nesting sites, the control of predators and freedom from disturbance have enabled colonies of up to 10,000 pairs to become established and to be maintained over many years. The down is care-

fully collected and cleaned, and then sold to manufacturers of sleeping bags and quilts. Pure eider down is still considered superior to any man-made substitute and commands a high price.

With heat loss delayed by the insulating feathers around the nest, the female Common Eider incubates her clutch of 4–6 olive-green eggs for 28 days. After hatching, the young from several broods may come together to form a "nursery."

6/ HARLEQUIN DUCK
Histrionicus histrionicus

RANGE: **Iceland, Greenland, Labrador, NW North America, NE Siberia and Japan**
HABITAT: **fast-flowing rivers and streams and inshore coastal waters**
SIZE: **$13\frac{1}{4}$–$17\frac{3}{4}$ in (34–45 cm)**

The strikingly marked Harlequin Duck is most at home in fast-flowing water, in which it is an expert swimmer. It can maneuver upstream with great skill, using eddies and slack water close to the bank, and sometimes rushes over the surface of the water, half-flying, half-swimming. Swimming with the current, it can shoot rapids and pass through turbulent water without difficulty. When on the ocean, which it mainly frequents in winter, it seems to spend most of the time just where the surf is breaking most vigorously.

In flight, the Harlequin Duck passes fast and low over the water, precisely following each bend in a stream. Its nest, like that of most other ducks, is well concealed in vegetation, often overhanging a river bank.

7/ OLDSQUAW
Clangula hyemalis

RANGE: **Arctic Eurasia and North America; winters S to cool temperate regions**
HABITAT: **breeds on tundra pools and by the coast; winters in ocean bays**
SIZE: **14–$18\frac{1}{2}$ in (36–47 cm)**

Oldsquaw have no fewer than 4 plumage changes during the course of a year: both sexes have distinct summer, fall, winter and eclipse plumages, the last one after breeding. They are sea ducks, spending nearly all their time on salt water, although some birds breed beside fresh water. The courtship display of the male includes a far-carrying yodeling call that is wonderfully evocative of wild places.

This duck is among the most accomplished divers of all wildfowl. It can remain underwater for as long as a minute and reach depths of 180 ft (55 m), a feat proven by individuals becoming entangled in fishing nets. It pursues and catches fish during dives, while in shallower water it plucks mollusks and crustaceans from the bottom.

8/ BLACK SCOTER
Melanitta nigra

RANGE: **Arctic and N temperate Eurasia and North America; winters to the S**
HABITAT: **breeds on freshwater lakes and marshes; winters in ocean bays and estuaries**
SIZE: **$17\frac{3}{4}$–$21\frac{1}{4}$ in (44–54 cm)**

The only relief from the all-black plumage of the male Black Scoter is a patch of yellow on the bill. In the Eurasian race *M. n. nigra* the yellow covers only a small area halfway along the upper mandible, but in the North American race *M. n. americana* the yellow covers most of the upper mandible and a prominent knob at the base of the bill. The latter is sometimes regarded as a separate species.

During courtship, rival males rush at each other, seemingly skating over the surface, with their heads outstretched, before coming to an abrupt halt in a flurry of spray. The females, too, will indulge in short rushes, usually at males they are rejecting. Another display given by the male involves raising the head and tail out of the water and producing a surprisingly pure and musical whistle. On a still day the sound can carry for many hundreds of yards.

Black Scoters nest beside large lakes as well as tiny moorland pools. If possible, they take their young to the ocean soon after hatching.

9/ COMMON GOLDENEYE
Bucephala clangula

RANGE: **N Eurasia and North America; winters to S**
HABITAT: **breeds on lakes and pools in forests; winters on lakes, estuaries, ocean bays**
SIZE: **$16\frac{1}{2}$–$19\frac{1}{2}$ in (42–50 cm)**

The Common Goldeneye's head is distinctively rounded and its steep forehead and short bill help in identification at long range. The bird's natural breeding site is a cavity in a tree or a dead stump. Inside the nest-hole, the only lining materials for the 8–12 eggs are a few chips of rotten wood and down feathers plucked from the female's breast.

With forest clearance, tree holes have become rarer and the Common Goldeneye has declined in many areas. However, the species takes readily to nest-boxes and programs involving several hundreds or even thousands of boxes are in operation. A nest-box program played a vital role in persuading the species to colonize Scotland in recent years.

10/ HOODED MERGANSER
Mergus cucullatus

RANGE: **2 populations. W population breeds S Alaska to NW USA; winters S Alaska to California. E population breeds S Canada, N and C USA; winters Florida, N Mexico**
HABITAT: **breeds and winters by rivers and lakes in forests; also winters on estuaries, coasts**
SIZE: **$16\frac{1}{2}$–$19\frac{1}{2}$ in (42–50 cm)**

The male Hooded Merganser has a pronounced black and white crest on his head. When raised, the crest forms a quarter-circle of white outlined in black, greatly enlarging the appearance of the head. The bird's bill is long and thin and is used for grasping fish.

The Hooded Merganser places its nest in a hole in a tree up to 52 ft (16 m) above the ground. Here the female lays and incubates 6–12 white eggs. It was once thought that the female brought the newly hatched young down to the ground in her bill. In fact, it has since been discovered that all she does is to call encouragingly from the base of the tree and wait for the young to tumble down to her. Being so light and covered in soft down, they rarely come to much harm.

11/ RED-BREASTED MERGANSER
Mergus serrator

RANGE: **N Eurasia and North America; winters S to Mediterranean, E China, Gulf of Mexico**
HABITAT: **breeds by rivers, estuaries and coasts; winters on estuaries and coastal bays**
SIZE: **$20\frac{1}{2}$–$22\frac{3}{4}$ in (52–58 cm)**

The Red-breasted Merganser is just as much at home on the ocean as it is on fresh water. It is a long-necked, long-bodied duck, whose bill is also long and thin with a hooked tip. Serrations along the sides of the mandibles help the bird grasp fish.

The Red-breasted Merganser's appetite for fish has brought it into conflict with fishing interests, particularly on rivers with trout and salmon. The true effect of the bird on fish stocks is mostly rather slight but, as is often the case with wild predators, the bird is accused of causing more damage than it actually carries out. In some places it is ruthlessly hunted.

12/ RUDDY DUCK
Oxyura jamaicensis

RANGE: **North and South America; introduced into Britain**
HABITAT: **breeds and winters on well-vegetated lakes; also winters on coastal lagoons and bays**
SIZE: **$13\frac{3}{4}$–17 in (35–43 cm)**

The male Ruddy Duck has white cheeks, a black cap and a remarkable large blue bill, which gives every appearance of having just been painted. The tail consists of short stiff feathers that can be held up at a jaunty angle or kept flat along the water, contributing to the bird's dumpy appearance. The race *O. j. jamaicensis* occurs in the West Indies, while *O. j. ferruginea*, the Peruvian Ruddy Duck, is found in Peru and Bolivia.

The male Ruddy Duck's display has been compared to the movements of a toy boat. He rushes over the water, paddling furiously, with his tail and lower body submerged, chest lifted out of the water, shoulders hunched, head down and bill pressed down onto his raised chest. In another sequence, the male beats his bill rapidly on his chest before jerking his head forward and calling. Although the male does not help the female with incubation of the eggs, he often stays close by and then accompanies his mate and his growing brood.

13/ MUSK DUCK
Biziura lobata

RANGE: **S Australia and Tasmania**
HABITAT: **breeds by freshwater and brackish lakes and marshes; winters on lakes, estuaries and coastal bays**
SIZE: **male 24–$28\frac{3}{4}$ in (61–73 cm);
female $18\frac{1}{2}$–$23\frac{1}{2}$ in (47–60 cm)**

Both sexes of the Musk Duck have dark oily-looking plumage, but the male alone has a flat lobe of skin hanging down below the lower mandible. The male is also nearly one-third larger than the female – an unusual size difference in any kind of bird.

The male Musk Duck has a particularly vigorous display, throwing his head back over his body, fanning his tail back till it almost meets his head, and splashing noisily with both feet together. At the same time, he utters a loud grunt followed immediately by a piercing whistle.

The male is strongly territorial, defending an area of fresh water against other males and attempting to attract several females to his territory. The bird's nest is concealed in vegetation at the water's edge or occasionally in a hollow of a tree stump or root.

14/ WHITE-BACKED DUCK
Thalassornis leuconotos

RANGE: **sub-Saharan Africa**
HABITAT: **freshwater lakes, pools and marshes**
SIZE: **15–$15\frac{3}{4}$ in (38–40 cm)**

The White-backed Duck is a stubby bird, with no more than a rudimentary tail. Its overall shape, with its low sloping back and long neck, gives the bird more the appearance of a grebe than a duck. The race, *T. l. insularis* that occurs on Madagascar is a little smaller and darker than the more widespread African race.

The White-backed Duck lives exclusively in freshwater habitats, particularly those with plenty of emergent vegetation. It is perfectly adapted to an aquatic life, being an accomplished diver, and comes onto dry land only to breed. Its feet are placed so far to the rear of its body that it can barely walk. It either builds its nest right on the edge of the water or uses the old, floating nests of coots and grebes. The 4–6 eggs are large for the size of the bird and are a glossy brown, quite unlike those of any other wildfowl.

NEW WORLD VULTURES, OSPREY, KITES, HONEY BUZZARDS AND FISH EAGLES

♂

ANDEAN CONDOR

♂

KING VULTURE

TURKEY VULTURE

CRESTED BAZA
race *subcristata*

dark phase

pale phase

OSPREY
race *carolinensis*

♂

AMERICAN SWALLOW-TAILED KITE

WESTERN HONEY
BUZZARD

BRAHMINY KITE

juv

juv

BALD EAGLE

juv

BLACK KITE
race *migrans*

SNAIL KITE
♂

♀

WHITE-TAILED SEA EAGLE

juv

BAT HAWK
race *alcinus*

juv

AFRICAN FISH EAGLE

NEW WORLD VULTURES, OSPREY, KITES, HONEY BUZZARDS AND FISH EAGLES

FAMILY CATHARTIDAE
New World vultures

Large carrion-feeders. Broad wings, powerful bill. Plumage mostly brownish black. Naked head or face. Sexes alike. Nest in hollows in trees or rocks. Eggs 1–2, white, cream, pale green, some blotched brown. Incubation 32–41 days; 54–58 days in King Vulture and condors. Chicks remain in nest 10–25 weeks. 7 species.

1/ TURKEY VULTURE
Cathartes aura

RANGE: S Canada to Tierra del Fuego, Caribbean, Falkland Islands
HABITAT: variable, including desert, grassland, farmland, forest
SIZE: $25\frac{1}{2}$–$31\frac{1}{2}$ in (65–80 cm)

The Turkey Vulture, or "buzzard" as it is popularly known, is a common and conspicuous bird over large parts of its range. A carrion-feeder and general scavenger, it is adaptable enough to thrive in an extraordinarily wide range of habitats and climatic zones, from the cold deserts of Patagonia to the tropical forests of Amazonia. Most populations are more or less resident in one area, but those of western USA are migratory, wintering in South America.

Turkey Vultures are easy to recognize in gliding flight by the distinctive raised angle of their wings and by their habit of continually tilting from one side to the other as they fly.

2/ KING VULTURE
Sarcorhamphus papa

RANGE: C Mexico to N Argentina; Trinidad
HABITAT: tropical forest
SIZE: 30 in (76 cm)

With its striking plumage and the ornate pattern of bare skin and wattles on its head, the King Vulture is one of the most colorful of all the birds of prey. The immature birds are almost all black at first but become increasingly white as they grow older.

Although they are quite common, King Vultures are often difficult to spot when flying high over the dense forest they usually frequent. Unlike the other New World vultures, they seldom occur in groups. Their strong bills enable them to tackle a wide variety of carrion, and they can locate animal remains even in dense cover using their well-developed sense of smell. They often take advantage of dying fish stranded on river banks.

3/ ANDEAN CONDOR
Vultur gryphus

RANGE: Andes, from W Venezuela to Tierra del Fuego
HABITAT: high mountains; down to the coast in Peru and S Chile
SIZE: $43\frac{1}{4}$ in (110 cm)

With a weight of up to 25 lb (12 kg) and a wingspan of over 10 ft (3 m), this immense high-mountain vulture is the largest of all the world's birds of prey. Soaring majestically for hours on outstretched wings, it can withstand most of the buffeting winds that howl around the Andean summits and rake the tip of South America.

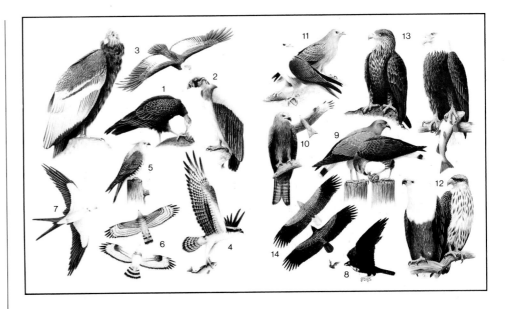

Although Andean Condors have become scarce in many parts of their range, in others they remain fairly numerous and groups of them may gather at large carcasses. They feed extensively on carrion, sometimes also attacking and killing sickly or dying animals. They are regular visitors to the vast seabird colonies along the Peruvian coast where they prey heavily on eggs.

FAMILY PANDIONIDAE
Osprey

There is only one species in this family.

4/ OSPREY
Pandion haliaetus

RANGE: breeds North America, Eurasia (mainly migrants), NE Africa, Australia; winter visitor and nonbreeding migrant elsewhere
HABITAT: coasts, rivers, lakes, wetlands
SIZE: $21\frac{3}{4}$–$23\frac{3}{4}$ in (55–58 cm)

The Osprey has an almost worldwide distribution. Several races are recognized, differing slightly in size and in the plumage on the breast. The one illustrated is the North American race *P. h. carolinensis*, with a pale breast band (especially females) and a dark crown. The sexes sometimes differ in darkness of breast and crown, and females are larger than males, as in most birds of prey. Many Ospreys are coastal birds, but others breed around inland lakes and rivers.

They feed almost exclusively on fish, soaring or circling up to 100 ft (30 m) above the water and often hovering briefly. When they catch sight of prey near the surface, they make a spectacular headlong plunge, throwing their feet forward at the last moment. The soles of the feet have sharp spines that help the birds grasp slippery fish.

The large nest is built on a cliff, in a tree or even on the ground in some habitats. Incubation of the 2–4 red-blotched creamy-white eggs takes about 38 days. Ospreys suffered decades of poisoning in the USA from the pesticide DDT, but the population is now recovering its numbers.

FAMILY ACCIPITRIDAE/1
Honey buzzards and kites

Medium to large birds of prey. Plumage highly variable, but usually darker above than below. Sexes similar. Nest of sticks in tree, often mixed with rubbish (kites). Eggs white, spotted reddish, 1–3 (honey buzzards); 2–7 (kites). Incubation 30–35 days (honey buzzards); 28–38 days (kites). Chicks remain in nest 40–45 days (honey buzzards); 25–60 days (kites). 32 species.

5/ CRESTED BAZA
Aviceda subcristata

RANGE: N and E Australia, New Guinea, Moluccas, Bismarck Archipelago, Solomon Islands
HABITAT: forest and woodland, particularly rain forest edge; also clearings and gardens
SIZE: $13\frac{3}{4}$–18 in (35–46 cm)

The Crested, or Pacific, Baza is a medium-sized attractively plumaged bird of prey, with a short crest that can be raised or lowered. Its prominent eyes, barred plumage and short legs combine to give it a pigeonlike or cuckoolike appearance. The northeastern and eastern Australian race *A. s. subcristata* is illustrated; there is a total of 15 other races, which tend to be darker in the east and paler in the west.

The bird hunts either from a perch in the tree canopy or by flying slowly over the treetops. When it spots prey such as large insects and tree frogs, it may snatch them with a fast dive or reach them by hovering into the foliage, clambering among the branches or even hanging from twigs with beating wings. Occasionally, lizards and small birds provide prey; the Crested Baza is also partial to fruit such as figs.

Breeding birds perform undulating display flights, climbing with deep, labored flaps and then diving while uttering a reedy 2-note whistle. The fragile nest is built high in the tree canopy, and the 2–3 (rarely up to 5) eggs are incubated by both sexes.

6/ WESTERN HONEY BUZZARD
Pernis apivorus
RANGE: **Europe E to Central Asia; winters sub-Saharan Africa**
HABITAT: **mature woodland**
SIZE: **$20\frac{1}{2}$–$23\frac{1}{2}$ in (52–60 cm)**

The underparts of the Western Honey Buzzard vary greatly in color, from almost white to almost black, with various intermediate forms. All forms, however, have a characteristic pattern of bars on the underside of the wings and tail. Other distinctive features are the small, cuckoolike head, the long, rather narrow tail and the flat angle of the wings when the bird is gliding.

This species is a highly specialized feeder, relying almost entirely on bees, wasps and hornets. It eats the larvae, the pupae and even the nests, as well as the adult insects, carefully breaking off the stings before swallowing them. Birds from the northern part of the range migrate to Africa for the winter.

7/ AMERICAN SWALLOW-TAILED KITE
Elanoides forficatus
RANGE: **SE USA, Mexico S to N Argentina**
HABITAT: **woodland and forest**
SIZE: **$23\frac{1}{2}$ in (60 cm)**

With its distinctive black and white plumage and long, deeply forked tail, this beautiful bird is unlikely to be mistaken for any other species. Few birds of prey can match the sheer gracefulness of its flight.

The American Swallow-tailed Kite feeds entirely on the wing, capturing aerial insects and eating them as it flies along. It will also pluck small lizards and snakes from trees and bushes and snatch eggs and nestlings of small birds, eating all of these morsels without landing on the ground. It can even swoop down to the surface of water and take a drink in flight, rather like a giant swallow.

8/ BAT HAWK
Machaerhamphus alcinus
RANGE: **Southeast Asia, tropical Africa**
HABITAT: **forested and well-wooded country; also towns with plentiful trees**
SIZE: **$18\frac{1}{2}$ in (47 cm)**

Although the Bat Hawk resembles a large falcon in general shape, its leisurely flight action is more like that of a kite. When hunting, however, it breaks into a fast pursuit with rapid wing beats.

It is largely inactive during the day, hunting over open areas or around the mouths of bat caves at dusk. As well as catching and eating small bats in flight, it also preys on swallows and swiftlets. Immature birds are browner than the adults above and show more white plumage below. The largest and darkest of the 3 races is the one illustrated: *M.a. alcinus* from Malaysia, Sumatra and Borneo. A wholly dark adult form of the Bat Hawk occurs in tropical Africa.

9/ SNAIL KITE
Rostrhamus sociabilis
RANGE: **Florida, Cuba, E Mexico S to Argentina**
HABITAT: **freshwater marshes with open water**
SIZE: **17 in (43 cm)**

The Snail Kite has large, fairly broad wings in relation to its smallish body. Although it is not particularly graceful in the air, it is perfectly equipped for slow, flapping flight as it quarters marshland vegetation in search of its principal prey – aquatic apple snails of the genus *Pomacea*.

When it locates a snail, this bird swoops down to the water, snatches the shell with one foot and takes it to a perch, where it uses its long, finely hook-tipped bill to extract the flesh from within. The Florida population of this species, known as the Everglade Kite, came close to extinction but its numbers have increased dramatically due to legal protection and habitat management.

10/ BLACK KITE
Milvus migrans
RANGE: **S Europe, much of Africa and Asia, Australia**
HABITAT: **open or semiopen lowlands, often wetlands; human settlements**
SIZE: **$21\frac{3}{4}$–$23\frac{1}{2}$ in (55–60 cm)**

This widespread and common bird is poorly named, for its plumage is really dark brown. Birds from the western part of the range, such as *M. m. migrans* of most of Europe, the Middle East and northwest Africa, tend to have pale heads. The eastern races are darker with whitish patches at the base of the outer wing feathers. African races are distinctive for their all-yellow bills.

The versatile Black Kite can kill small prey on the ground and snatch fish from the surface of water, but it also feeds widely on carrion. It is a bold scavenger and thief, entering villages to steal food and visiting refuse tips in and around towns.

11/ BRAHMINY KITE
Haliastur indus
RANGE: **S and Southeast Asia, N Australia**
HABITAT: **coastal and inland waters**
SIZE: **19 in (48 cm)**

The distinctive Brahminy Kite hunts rather like a harrier. It quarters at low altitude before dropping down to take live prey such as frogs, small reptiles and insects from the ground and fish from the water. It also feeds on carrion and is a common scavenger around human habitations and harbors in some regions, including India.

The nest is a pile of sticks lined with leaves, usually placed in a tree or among mangroves. The female lays and incubates up to 4 eggs, the male providing her with food while she is on the nest.

FAMILY ACCIPITRIDAE/2
Sea and fish eagles
Large birds of prey. Broad wings, soaring flight. Massive bill. Plumage usually brown and white. Sexes similar. Nest of sticks on cliff or in tree. Eggs 1–2, white. Incubation 40–45 days, chicks remain in nest for about 10 weeks. 10 species.

12/ AFRICAN FISH EAGLE
Haliaeetus vocifer
RANGE: **sub-Saharan Africa**
HABITAT: **coastal and inland waters**
SIZE: **29–33 in (74–84 cm)**

With its unique combination of white, chestnut and black plumage, this handsome fish eagle is unmistakable. It usually occurs close to water and is common over much of its range. It is a wonderfully agile flier, and although it can lift fish straight from the surface while still in flight, it usually makes a spectacular plunge into the water with its feet stretched forward.

The African Fish Eagle spends much of its time perching in an upright pose on a favorite lookout post. It is a vocal bird, both on its perch and while in flight. Its far-carrying, almost gull-like call is one of the best-known wild sounds of Africa.

13/ BALD EAGLE
Haliaeetus leucocephalus
RANGE: **North America**
HABITAT: **usually near lakes, rivers, coasts**
SIZE: **31–37 in (79–94 cm)**

This, the national bird of the USA, is common today only in Alaska and parts of the northwestern states. Persecution and pesticide contamination have caused it to become a rarity in much of eastern USA, although long-term recovery programs have helped to bring about a gradual increase in its population.

Versatile predators, Bald Eagles catch a variety of live prey including birds, small mammals and, especially, fish. Groups of them congregate at salmon spawning grounds in Alaska where the mass of exhausted fish provide rich pickings. Bald Eagles also scavenge widely and will rob other birds, such as Ospreys, of their catches. Pairs remain faithful and maintain their bond each year with spectacular aerial displays in which the 2 birds lock talons and tumble downward through the air.

14/ WHITE-TAILED SEA EAGLE
Haliaeetus albicilla
RANGE: **W Greenland, Iceland, N, C and SE Europe (recently reintroduced to Britain, to Rhum in the Inner Hebrides), N Asia**
HABITAT: **coasts, lakes, rivers, wetlands**
SIZE: **$27\frac{1}{2}$–$35\frac{1}{2}$ in (70–90 cm)**

White-tailed Sea Eagles are more bulky and have heavier bills than most other eagles likely to be seen in the same northerly areas. Their immense, broad wings give them a vulturelike appearance in flight.

Magnificent soarers, White-tailed Sea Eagles can also perform deft aerial maneuvers if the occasion demands. They are skilled hunters of waterfowl, seabirds and small mammals, and expertly snatch fish from the surface of water with their talons, usually after a shallow diving approach. They will rob birds, and perhaps even otters, of their prey and readily feed on carrion. The huge nest of sticks may be built in the top of a tree, on a crag or on the ground on a small island if it is free of terrestrial predators.

OLD WORLD VULTURES, SNAKE EAGLES, HARRIER-HAWKS AND HARRIERS

RÜPPELL'S GRIFFON

LAMMERGEIER

LAPPET-FACED VULTURE

race *melanotis*

EUROPEAN BLACK VULTURE

CRESTED SERPENT-EAGLE

juv

juv

PALM-NUT VULTURE

EGYPTIAN VULTURE

MARSH HARRIER
race *aeruginosus*

♂ ♀

race *cyaneus*

HEN HARRIER

♀

♂

AFRICAN
HARRIER-HAWK

race
caerulescens

♂ ♀

PIED
HARRIER

CRANE HAWK

dark phase

pale phase

♀

BATELEUR

juv

SHORT-TOED EAGLE

OLD WORLD VULTURES, SNAKE EAGLES, HARRIER-HAWKS AND HARRIERS

FAMILY ACCIPITRIDAE/3
Old World vultures

Large, soaring birds. Carrion-feeders. Broad wings. Bare head or face. Plumage variable, mainly dark. Sexes similar. Nest of sticks, in trees or on cliff ledges. Eggs 1–2, white or pale brown, sometimes with darker markings. Incubation 42–60 days, chicks remain in nest for 10–18 weeks. 15 species.

1/ EUROPEAN BLACK VULTURE
Aegypius monachus   [?]
RANGE: S Europe, Turkey E to China
HABITAT: **mainly open country, including mountains**
SIZE: $39\frac{1}{2}$–$43\frac{1}{4}$ in (100–110 cm)

Weighing up to 25 lb (12 kg) and with a wingspan of over 9 ft (2.75 m) on large individuals, this is the biggest of all the Old World vultures. Although its plumage is in fact dark sooty-brown, it appears black from a distance. Even at long range, the pale feet are conspicuous in flying birds. Immatures are slightly paler in plumage.

The European Black, or Cinereous, Vulture is almost extinct over most of its range in Europe, but some 400 pairs still survive in the sierras of south-central Spain. A powerful bird, it is generally, but not always, able to dominate griffon vultures at carcasses. Unlike them, it readily descends into vegetation cover to feed on carrion. Each pair returns annually to the same treetop nest, adding new material to the already huge platform of sticks.

2/ LAPPET-FACED VULTURE
Aegypius tracheliotus
RANGE: **sub-Saharan Africa, Middle East, S Arabia**
HABITAT: **arid open country, extending into mountains and semidesert**
SIZE: $39\frac{1}{2}$–$41\frac{1}{4}$ in (100–105 cm)

A massive, dark bird, this is the most powerful of the African vultures. It usually dominates and often robs other species at carcasses, where it is often the last to arrive. It can break easily through flesh with its huge beak and, since there are no feathers on its neck, it can probe deep inside a carcass without fouling its plumage with blood.

The Lappet-faced Vulture is normally a solitary bird but may occur in small groups at times. However, each pair usually nests alone, building a flat structure of sticks, up to 10 ft (3 m) wide and 3 ft (1 m) deep, at the top of a thorny tree. A single egg is laid in a depression in the middle of the nest lined with dry grass. Both sexes take turns to incubate the egg over a 7-week period.

3/ RÜPPELL'S GRIFFON
Gyps rueppellii
RANGE: **Senegal to N Nigeria, Sudan, W Ethiopia, Uganda, Kenya, N Tanzania**
HABITAT: **wild, open country, in both mountains and lowlands**
SIZE: 35–37 in (89–94 cm)

The basically dark adult plumage of Rüppell's Griffon is patterned with extensive pale scalloping, especially on the underparts. The underwing

pattern is very distinctive – a bold white bar near the inner leading edge and 2 rows of white spots across the entire wing.

Rüppell's Griffon is a powerful species usually capable of dominating all but the larger Lappet-faced Vulture when feeding on carrion. It is the central African representative of the small group of griffon vultures. All are large, gregarious birds and superb long-distance foragers which gather in dense flocks at carcasses.

4/ EGYPTIAN VULTURE
Neophron percnopterus
RANGE: **N, C and E Africa, S Europe, Middle East, SW Asia, India**
HABITAT: **open country; cliffs and crags preferred for breeding**
SIZE: 21–26 in (53–66 cm)

This largely whitish bird is widespread over Africa and the warm, drier regions of Europe and Asia. It feeds largely on carrion but, being small and weak-billed, it generally waits its turn at a carcass to pick up minor scraps left behind by larger vultures. Otherwise, it is a versatile scavenger on all sorts of food. In some parts of Africa, Egyptian Vultures are among the few true tool-users in the bird world. They have been seen picking up stones in their bills and hurling them onto Ostrich eggs to break open the thick shells.

Egyptian Vultures prefer to breed in rocky terrain, where they build their nests on crags and in caves. Their aerial display flights involve dives and swoops, with the birds rolling over and presenting their talons to each other in midair.

5/ LAMMERGEIER
Gypaetus barbatus
RANGE: **Africa, S Europe E to C Asia**
HABITAT: **mainly mountains and high plateaus**
SIZE: $39\frac{1}{2}$–$45\frac{1}{4}$ in (100–115 cm)

This huge, distinctively colored bird is scarce over most of its range and particularly favors wild, remote, mountain regions. The prominent bristles that extend from its black mask have earned it the alternative name of Bearded Vulture. Young Lammergeiers are generally brownish, with more uniform plumage than their parents.

Lammergeiers are quite unlike other large vultures in shape. In flight, their long, narrow wings and longish tails make them look almost like gigantic falcons. Their seemingly effortless gliding ability is unequaled, and they spend most of the day on the wing. At carcasses, they specialize in feeding on tough hide and bones. These birds are well known for their habit of dropping bones from a height on to rocky sites, or "ossuaries," smashing them open so that the marrow is accessible. The same sites are used for many years in succession.

6/ PALM-NUT VULTURE
Gypohierax angolensis
RANGE: **tropical Africa**
HABITAT: **mainly woodland and cultivated land; also mangroves, harbors**
SIZE: 22–$24\frac{1}{2}$ in (56–62 cm)

Although it starts life with the dark brown coloration common to many Old World vultures, this curious bird becomes increasingly mottled during the immature stage until it eventually takes on the striking white adult plumage.

Its diet is also remarkable. Although it feeds to some extent on crabs, small fish, amphibians and various invertebrates, it is largely vegetarian – a most unusual feature for a bird of prey. Its principal food is the husk of the oil palm fruit, and it tends to be rare in places where oil palms are not found. The Palm-nut Vulture remains in the same area for much of the year. It often lives close to water.

FAMILY ACCIPITRIDAE/4
Snake eagles

Large, mainly specialist feeders on reptiles. Short, powerful toes. Plumage usually gray or brown. Sexes similar. Nest small, built of sticks, in tree. Eggs 1, usually white. Incubation 35–55 days, chick leaves nest at 10–15 weeks. 12 species.

7/ SHORT-TOED EAGLE
Circaetus gallicus

RANGE: **S and E Europe, NW Africa, Middle East, SW Asia, India**
HABITAT: **mixed open country, including mountains**
SIZE: **24½–26½ in (62–67 cm)**

Short-toed Eagles show marked variation in plumage. Basically brown above and white below, they usually, but by no means always, have dark heads and the underparts and underwings have a variable amount of dark speckles and bars.

Short-toed Eagles are accomplished fliers, often foraging at low altitude and frequently hovering. Their short, powerful toes are adapted for dealing with their main prey, the snakes and lizards that they find on open hillsides and other suitable terrain. In parts of southern Europe, the birds follow the plow to snatch prey disturbed from the ground. Large snakes are torn apart and eaten on the ground, but the birds will take off with small snakes and swallow them whole.

8/ BATELEUR
Terathopius ecaudatus

RANGE: **sub-Saharan Africa, SW Arabia**
HABITAT: **savanna, open woodland, plains, semidesert**
SIZE: **22–24 in (56–61 cm)**

Long-winged, almost tail-less and colorful, the Bateleur is quite unlike any other bird of prey. The bird's common name is French for "tightrope-walker," an apt allusion to its fast, gliding flight in which it continually tilts from side to side. It is often on the wing for most of the day. During the breeding season it performs spectacular courtship flights, with fast pursuits, dives and even the occasional 360-degree lateral roll.

Bateleurs are typical birds of the African savanna. They take a wide range of animal prey, including small mammals, snakes, lizards and some invertebrates, but many are primarily hunters of birds. They also feed readily on carrion and are bold and aggressive pirates of other predators and scavengers.

9/ CRESTED SERPENT-EAGLE
Spilornis cheela

RANGE: **India, China, Southeast Asia, Indonesia, Philippines**
HABITAT: **mainly forest or woodland; some races in open savanna**
SIZE: **11–21 in (28–53 cm)**

With over 20 geographical races, many of them island forms, this is an extremely variable species both in terms of size and, to a lesser extent, plumage. Most races have dark brown plumage in the adult with a prominent blackish crest or "hood." The race illustrated, *S.c. melanotis*, is from the southern part of the Indian peninsula.

Except when they are soaring above the canopy, Crested Serpent-Eagles can be very difficult to spot in their forest habitat. They hunt largely in tree cover, usually watching from a perch and swooping to the ground to catch reptiles such as tree snakes. They also eat dead snakes. This species also preys occasionally on small mammals and birds.

FAMILY ACCIPITRIDAE/5
Harrier-hawks and the Crane Hawk

Medium-sized, long-legged, long-tailed birds of prey. Plumage mainly gray. Sexes similar. Nest of twigs, in tree or rock crevice. Eggs 1–3, white. Incubation 35–40 days (?), chicks remain in nest about 7 weeks (?). 3 species.

10/ AFRICAN HARRIER-HAWK
Polyboroides typus

RANGE: **sub-Saharan Africa**
HABITAT: **forest, woodland, savanna, bush, cultivated land**
SIZE: **24–26¾ in (61–68 cm)**

The African Harrier-Hawk, or Gymnogene, does much of its hunting in bushes and trees rather than in flight. The small size of its head and its slender, double-jointed legs enable it to search for prey in all kinds of holes, hollows and crevices. It feeds on a range of small prey including insects and other invertebrates, mammals, birds and eggs. It frequently raids the nests of colonial weavers. The fruit of the oil palm is a favored food in West Africa.

The nest of twigs lined with green leaves is built in the tree canopy or low down in a rock crevice under cover. Both sexes share in incubating the 1–2 eggs and in feeding the young, although the female takes the major role. The immature birds are mainly brown, paler on the belly with barred tails.

11/ CRANE HAWK
Geranospiza caerulescens

RANGE: **Mexico S to Argentina**
HABITAT: **tropical lowlands, usually with trees, often near water**
SIZE: **16–20 in (41–51 cm)**

There is considerable variation among the 6 races of this bird, ranging from the black race *G.c. nigra* found in most of Mexico to others in South America, such as *G.c. caerulescens* of eastern Ecuador and Colombia to the Guianas and northern Brazil, which are pale gray above and usually finely barred darker gray below. All, though, show the characteristically banded black and whitish tails. Immatures are generally more yellow-brown below.

Whether this bird is closely related to the 2 species of harrier-hawk is unclear, but it, too, forages slowly and methodically, searching in a variety of holes and cavities for a broadly similar range of prey. It also has extremely flexible leg joints. It usually occurs near water and often inhabits forested swamps, or woodland with pools and streams.

FAMILY ACCIPITRIDAE/6
Harriers

Slender, long-winged, long-legged birds of prey. Plumage usually grayish or black and white in males, brownish in females. Nest on ground or in bush. Eggs 3–6, occasionally up to 8 or more, usually plain white. Incubation 28–31 days, chicks leave nest after 36–60 days. 10 species.

12/ HEN HARRIER
Circus cyaneus

RANGE: **North and South America, N Europe, N Asia; migrates to S**
HABITAT: **largely open country, dry or wet**
SIZE: **17¼–20½ in (44–52 cm)**

Like the Marsh Harrier, this is a widespread species. Whereas the lower underparts of the male in the European race *C.c. cyaneus* are plain whitish, those of the American race *C.c. hudsonius* are marked with reddish-brown spots. Immatures, like the females, are browner, streaked dark below, and show a white rump above a clearly barred tail.

In many areas, the fortunes of Hen Harriers are closely tied to the population cycles of small mammals such as voles. They hunt for these with a low, quartering flight, during which the wings show the characteristic *V* posture common to all harriers. Although they usually roost singly on the ground, Hen Harriers sometimes congregate on winter nights in groups of about 10.

13/ PIED HARRIER
Circus melanoleucos

RANGE: **E Siberia S to Mongolia, N Korea, N Burma; winters to the S**
HABITAT: **open country, including steppe and wetlands**
SIZE: **18–20 in (46–51 cm)**

The handsome male Pied Harrier is unmistakable. The females, however, are rather similar to those of Pallid and Montagu's Harriers, but they are much paler and only sparsely streaked below. The immature birds are brown above and dark chestnut below.

Pied Harriers are frequent visitors to rice paddies in their winter quarters, where they feed largely on frogs. In the breeding season they are, like other harriers, birds of open country, including steppe, bogs with scattered birches and lowland meadows. Here, they feed mainly on small mammals and birds but also catch frogs, lizards and some invertebrates.

14/ MARSH HARRIER
Circus aeruginosus

RANGE: **W Europe E across Asia, Madagascar, Borneo, Australia**
HABITAT: **usually lowland wetlands, especially with reedbeds**
SIZE: **19–22¾ in (48–58 cm)**

The sexes show markedly different plumage among the harriers, and this species is no exception. A widespread bird, it also shows marked variation across its geographical range. The race *C.a. aeruginosus*, illustrated, is from Europe, Israel, and Central Asia. Immatures are dark brownish in color.

The Marsh Harrier generally nests in thick marsh vegetation, but it forages widely over nearby lowland habitats. The prey ranges from small mammals and birds to amphibians, small fish and large invertebrates. Carrion is sometimes eaten. When the female is incubating and tending the young, the male hunts for them both, calling his mate off the nest when he returns with food and dropping it for her to catch in midair.

GOSHAWKS, SPARROWHAWKS AND BUTEONINES

juv

GABAR GOSHAWK

pale phase

dark phase

♀

DARK CHANTING-GOSHAWK

NORTHERN GOSHAWK

♀

NORTHERN
SPARROWHAWK

white phase
"White Goshawk"

gray phase
"Gray Goshawk"

♂

♂

♂

BESRA SPARROWHAWK

juv

SHARP-SHINNED HAWK

race *novaehollandiae*

VARIABLE GOSHAWK

COOPER'S HAWK

juv

LIZARD BUZZARD

SLATE-COLORED HAWK

GRASSHOPPER
BUZZARD-EAGLE

juv

COMMON BLACK HAWK

SAVANNA HAWK

CROWNED SOLITARY EAGLE

GOSHAWKS, SPARROWHAWKS AND BUTEONINES

FAMILY ACCIPITRIDAE/7
Goshawks, sparrowhawks and relatives

Small to large birds of prey, many feeding mainly or entirely on birds. Broad wings and long tails. Plumage mainly gray, brown or blackish, often barred below. Sexes may differ in size (females larger) and plumage. Nest very varied, usually of sticks in tree. Eggs usually 1–6, white often blotched brown. Incubation 28–50 days, chicks remain in nest 25–110 days. 53 species.

1/ DARK CHANTING-GOSHAWK
Melierax metabates

RANGE: **sub-Saharan Africa, SW Morocco, SW Arabia**
HABITAT: **open woodland, bush, savanna**
SIZE: **16–19 in (41–48 cm)**

The Dark Chanting-Goshawk is a medium-sized, rather long-legged hawk, likely to be confused only with the slightly larger Pale Chanting-Goshawk *M. canorus*. The 2 species are largely separated geographically and by habitat. They take their name from the males' tuneful, whistling "chants," delivered from the tops of trees early in the breeding season.

Dark Chanting-Goshawks keep a lookout for prey from the tops of bushes, trees, termite mounds or similar vantage points, swooping down swiftly to seize lizards, small mammals, small birds and insects. They will also pursue flying birds and regularly forage on the ground.

2/ GABAR GOSHAWK
Micronisus gabar

RANGE: **sub-Saharan Africa, SW Arabia**
HABITAT: **woodland and scrub**
SIZE: **11–14 in (28–36 cm)**

Gabar Goshawks resemble true sparrowhawks in general appearance, although some all-black, melanistic forms occur. Immature birds have browner upperparts than the adults and streaked plumage on the throat and breast.

Gabar Goshawks are bold and active hunters, both chasing birds in the air and seizing them, as well as lizards, on the ground. At the start of the breeding season, the males perch high in trees, uttering piping display calls, and a pair will often display by chasing each other in and out of the trees. The female generally builds the nest, lining the center with soil, matted spiders' webs and even pieces of rag. She also incubates the eggs and brings most of the food to the young.

3/ LIZARD BUZZARD
Kaupifalco monogrammicus

RANGE: **sub-Saharan Africa**
HABITAT: **savanna and bush**
SIZE: **13¾–15 in (35–38 cm)**

Lizard Buzzards are smallish, long-legged but rather heavily built hawks found in the tropical grasslands and wooded savanna of Africa. Although they resemble the adults, the immature birds are somewhat duller and browner in their overall plumage.

Unlike most birds of prey, this species catches much of its prey in tall grass or other dense ground vegetation. It hunts from a series of perches either in cover or on exposed branches. Large insects, lizards and small snakes form the bulk of its food, along with frogs and small rodents. Although it eats some of its larger victims on the ground, it carries most of its prey back to the perch.

4/ VARIABLE GOSHAWK
Accipiter novaehollandiae

RANGE: **coastal N and E Australia, Tasmania, New Guinea, E Indonesia, Solomon Islands**
HABITAT: **forest and forest edge, riverine forest**
SIZE: **13–21¾ in (33–55 cm)**

This striking bird has some 20 races. Plumage and size vary greatly, as the species' name suggests. The Australian and Tasmanian birds of the race *A. n. novaehollandiae* are larger, and may be gray above and white beneath, or all white. Birds of the race *A. n. leucosomus* from New Guinea and nearby islands may be gray above and rufous beneath, dark gray and chestnut, or all white. Many of the other island races are small and brightly colored.

The Variable Goshawk feeds on birds, reptiles and mammals up to the size of rabbits, as well as some insects and carrion. It searches for most of its prey from a concealed perch, even the white forms remaining remarkably inconspicuous in the forest canopy. The birds often attack after a stealthy glide and display great agility when pursuing prey through the trees.

5/ BESRA SPARROWHAWK
Accipiter virgatus

RANGE: **W Himalayas E to S China, Southeast Asia, Indonesia, Philippines**
HABITAT: **evergreen forest or other well-timbered areas**
SIZE: **11–14 in (28–36 cm)**

The barring on the underparts of the Besra Sparrowhawk is obscured to varying degrees by a chestnut coloration, which is most heavy on the race of *A. v. vanbemmeli* from Sumatra. The race illustrated, with pale underparts and strong barrings, is *A. v. besra*, found in India south of Bombay and on Sri Lanka and the Andaman Islands. Immature Besra Sparrowhawks are generally browner above than the adults.

This species is common over much of the forested country from southern Asia to Indonesia. Like most sparrowhawks, it is a fast and agile bird-catcher, taking prey both on the wing and from the ground. It also eats some large insects and lizards. Courtship involves chasing and soaring displays during which the birds frequently call. The nest of sticks is placed in a tree and is often built on top of an old crow's nest or even a squirrel's drey.

6/ NORTHERN SPARROWHAWK
Accipiter nisus

RANGE: **Europe and NW Africa E to Bering Sea and Himalayas**
HABITAT: **chiefly woodland or forest**
SIZE: **11–15 in (28–38 cm)**

Widespread over much of Eurasia, Northern Sparrowhawks are almost entirely hunters of birds, with small mammals usually forming less than 3 percent of their diet. Although they sometimes pursue and fly down prey in the open, they more often hunt in cover, systematically moving from one perch to the next and taking prey in a short, swift attack. They are supremely agile in the air, able to twist and turn rapidly around obstacles and maneuver to surprise their victims. Bird prey varies considerably in size, from Great Tits *Parus major* to Common Pheasants *Phasianus colchicus*, with females generally taking larger species than the males.

Both sexes build the nest, usually close to the tree trunk, some 20–50 ft (6–15 m) above the ground. The 4–5 eggs are laid at intervals of 2 or more days and are incubated solely by the female. The European race *A. n. nisus* is illustrated; there are 5 other races, of which *A. n. wolterstorffi* from Corsica and Sardinia is the most distinct, being smaller and much darker. Some northerly populations migrate south for the winter to Africa and parts of southern Asia.

7/ SHARP-SHINNED HAWK
Accipiter striatus

RANGE: **North, Central and South America, Caribbean**
HABITAT: **woods, forests and other well-timbered areas**
SIZE: **9¾–13 in (25–33 cm)**

This species shows considerable geographical variation across its range. In North America, males are slate-gray above and closely barred rufous below, while the large females are brown above and barred brown below. The race *A.s. velox*, found over much of the species' North American range, is typical of this type. In stark contrast, the race *A.s. chionogaster*, found in Guatemala, Honduras, El Salvador and Nicaragua, is very dark above and white below. There is also some size variation. Races from the West Indies, for instance, are all rather small.

In its general behavior, the Sharp-shinned Hawk is similar to most small members of the genus *Accipter*. It is principally a bird-catcher, surprising its prey with a sudden dash from cover. Populations that breed in northern North America spend the winter from central USA south to Costa Rica.

8/ COOPER'S HAWK
Accipiter cooperii

RANGE: **S Canada S to NW Mexico**
HABITAT: **woodland, riverside belts of trees**
SIZE: **14–20 in (36–51 cm)**

Cooper's Hawk is midway in size between the Sharp-shinned Hawk and Northern Goshawk. Principally a woodland bird, it rarely strays from cover except when hunting. It is an active bird-catcher, using both pursuit and snatch-and-grab tactics. It snatches mammals such as squirrels and chipmunks during sallies from a lookout perch and skilfully pursues bats emerging from their roosts. The female is much larger than the male and can tackle prey up to the size of the Ruffed Grouse *Bonasa umbellus*.

The male builds the nest using sticks that he breaks from trees in flight, grasping them with his talons as he passes. The nest is usually placed at least 33 ft (10 m) up in the branches of a conifer.

9/ NORTHERN GOSHAWK
Accipiter gentilis

RANGE: **circumpolar N**
HABITAT: **temperate and boreal woods and forests**
SIZE: **19–26 in (48–66 cm)**

The Northern Goshawk occurs across Eurasia and North America, with considerable geographical variation. Siberian races are much paler than the race *A.g. gentilis* of Europe, southwest Asia and Morocco, while North American birds (of 3 races) have noticeably dark crowns and a prominent white stripe above the eye. Juveniles are brown above, with pronounced dark drop-shaped markings below. There is a marked size difference between the sexes, with females up to 50 percent heavier than the males.

Northern Goshawks are powerful, fast-moving hunters, with females fully capable of subduing full-grown cock pheasants or hares. They prey on a wide variety of bird and mammal species, depending on which are available in each locality. Some reports suggest that the birds store items of prey that are too large to consume in one meal.

FAMILY ACCIPITRIDAE/8
Buzzards and other buteonines, harpy eagles

Large birds of prey, feeding mainly on mammals and reptiles caught on the ground. Long, broad wings adapted for soaring. Females usually only slightly larger than males. Sexes usually similar in plumage: brown, rufous, black and white in various combinations. Nest usually of sticks in tree. Eggs 1–4, white or cream, often with brown or reddish markings. Incubation 21–60 days, nestling period 45–100 days. 55 species.

10/ GRASSHOPPER BUZZARD-EAGLE
Butastur rufipennis

RANGE: **W, C and E Africa**
HABITAT: **mainly savanna, bush and semidesert**
SIZE: **15¾–17 in (40–43 cm)**

Kestrel-like at rest, and reminiscent of a harrier in flight, the Grasshopper Buzzard-Eagle is nevertheless a distinctive bird when seen at close range. It is primarily insectivorous, catching large numbers of grasshoppers and mantises, although it also takes some small birds, mammals and snakes. It is well known for its habit of hunting around grass fires and over burnt ground to take advantage of fleeing and exposed prey.

The Grasshopper Buzzard-Eagle is migratory, moving from its drier breeding grounds, where it spends the rainy season, to more wooded habitats in the dry season. It usually nests in a low tree, building a deep structure of sticks and lining it with leaves.

11/ SLATE-COLORED HAWK
Leucopternis schistacea

RANGE: **Amazonia, S Venezuela, E Colombia, Ecuador, Peru and Bolivia**
HABITAT: **forests**
SIZE: **17–18 in (43–46 cm)**

The hawks in the Central and South American genus *Leucopternis* are small to medium birds of prey. They are similar to buzzards, except that their wings are short and rounded – a typical adaptation for hunting and maneuvering in forests. Immature birds show much irregular white barring on both the lower underparts and leg feathers.

The Slate-colored Hawk usually occurs along forest streams, flooded stretches and swamps. It hunts from a series of perches, waiting quietly for prey to appear below and dropping down to seize its victims at the water's edge. Its prey includes frogs and snakes. Little else is known of this bird's behavior.

12/ COMMON BLACK HAWK
Buteogallus anthracinus

RANGE: **S USA to coastal South America, Caribbean**
HABITAT: **coastal lowlands, including wetlands; inland streams**
SIZE: **18–22¾ in (46–58 cm)**

This distinctly broad-winged, short-tailed bird is most common in low-lying coastal savanna, although it also occurs along wooded streams farther inland. It tends to be a rather sluggish hunter, using low, concealed perches or foraging on the wing at low altitude. It does little soaring, except during the breeding season.

Coastal populations feed extensively on crabs but also take other shore invertebrates and stranded fish. To expose the flesh of a crab, the bird hooks its bill under the front of the shell and tears it off backward. Other prey includes insects, frogs, snakes and small rodents, but rarely birds.

13/ SAVANNA HAWK
Buteogallus meridionalis

RANGE: **E Panama to C Argentina**
HABITAT: **open grassland, including wet areas**
SIZE: **20–24 in (51–61 cm)**

Adult Savanna Hawks are strikingly rufous birds, especially in flight, when they also show dark wing edges and a broad white band and white tip to the otherwise black tail. Immatures are a duller, darker brown above and buffish-white below, with thickly streaked dark sides to the breast.

Rather long-legged birds, Savanna Hawks spend much of their time sitting in a characteristically upright pose on exposed perches. They hunt from these, preying on insects, amphibians, snakes, fish, small mammals and small birds. Occasionally, the hawks drop onto prey from flight, and groups of them may be attracted to grass fires or may follow the plow to snatch creatures disturbed from hiding.

14/ CROWNED SOLITARY EAGLE
Harpyhaliaetus coronatus [?]

RANGE: **E Bolivia to N Patagonia**
HABITAT: **sparse woodland and savanna**
SIZE: **29–32 in (74–81 cm)**

This South American species is a large, robust bird of prey with longish legs and a short tail that gives it a distinctive silhouette in flight. Immatures are browner above than the adults and buffish-white with dark streaking on their underparts. Crowned Solitary Eagles occur mainly in dry, open country with scattered trees.

Described as ponderous and rather sluggish, and frequently as very tame, the Crowned Solitary Eagle perches freely on fenceposts, utility poles and bare trees. It hunts either from its perch or by sailing low over the ground, catching small to medium-sized mammals and birds and, probably, also snakes.

BUTEOS AND OTHER BUTEONINES, HARPY EAGLES

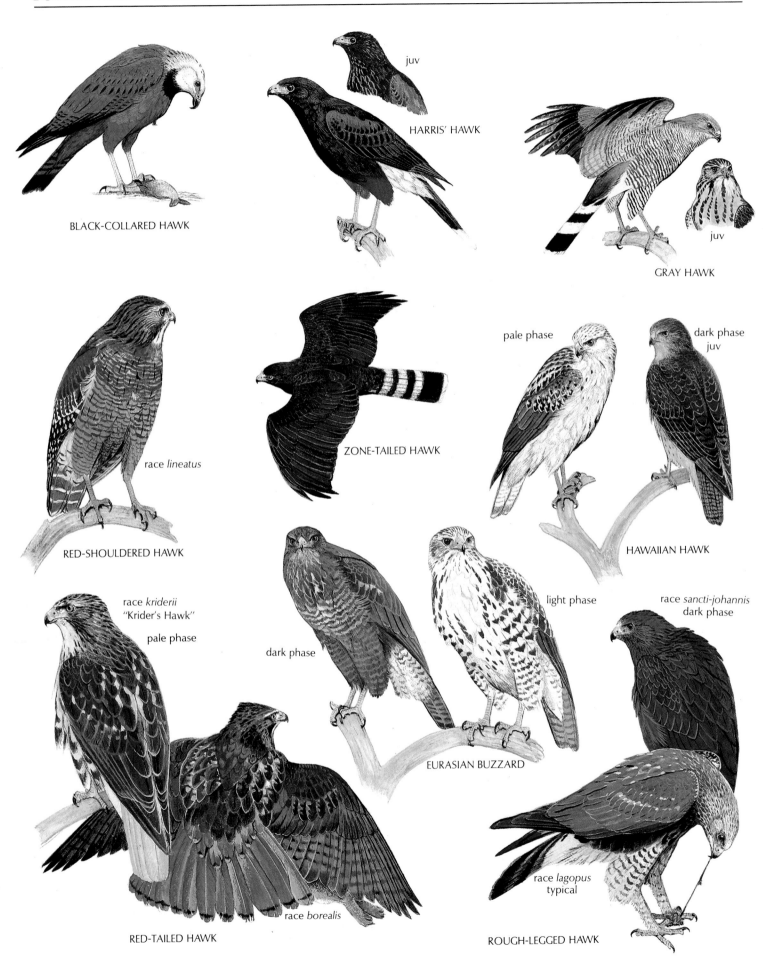

BLACK-COLLARED HAWK

juv

HARRIS' HAWK

GRAY HAWK

juv

race *lineatus*

RED-SHOULDERED HAWK

ZONE-TAILED HAWK

pale phase

dark phase
juv

light phase

race *sancti-johannis*
dark phase

HAWAIIAN HAWK

race *kriderii*
"Krider's Hawk"

pale phase

dark phase

EURASIAN BUZZARD

race *borealis*

RED-TAILED HAWK

race *lagopus*
typical

ROUGH-LEGGED HAWK

LONG-LEGGED BUZZARD

typical

race *augur* "Augur Buzzard"

typical

dark phase

typical

typical

race *rufofuscus*

JACKAL BUZZARD

GUIANA CRESTED EAGLE

juv

NEW GUINEA HARPY EAGLE

AMERICAN HARPY EAGLE

PHILIPPINE EAGLE

BUTEOS AND OTHER BUTEONINES, HARPY EAGLES

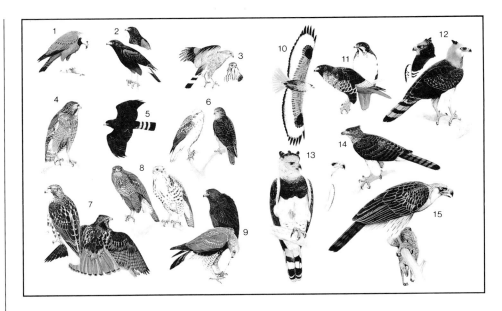

1/ BLACK-COLLARED HAWK
Busarellus nigricollis

RANGE: **Mexico S to Argentina**
HABITAT: **tropical lowlands, open or semi-open country near water**
SIZE: **19–20 in (48–51 cm)**

At rest, this is a bulky but rather small-headed hawk; in flight, it shows its broad, blunt wings and very short tail. Immature birds are duller than the distinctive adults, with dark streaking. Its principal food is fish, which it snatches either from the surface in swooping flight or by plunging into shallow water, usually from a low perch. Small spines on the undersides of its feet help the bird grasp and hold its prey. An alternative common name for this species is Fishing Buzzard.

Common in some parts of its extensive range, the Black-collared Hawk breeds around swamps and marshes or occasionally in plantations. Its nest is a large platform of sticks, sometimes decorated with leaves, placed up to 50 ft (15 m) high in a mangrove or other tree.

2/ HARRIS' HAWK
Parabuteo unicinctus

RANGE: **SW USA, Central and South America**
HABITAT: **lowlands, with or without scattered trees, semideserts**
SIZE: **19–22 in (48–56 cm)**

Harris' Hawk is primarily a bird of dry, open habitats. It is an accomplished hunter, taking a wide variety of small to medium-sized birds, including ducks, as well as small rodents, other mammals up to the size of full-grown rabbits, and lizards. It hunts by gliding at low levels or by swooping suddenly onto prey from a low perch. It sometimes perches on the ground.

The nest is a relatively neat structure of twigs, sticks and roots, lined with grass, leaves and pieces of bark. This is usually built up to 33 ft (10 m) from the ground in a tree or cactus. The 2–4 eggs are incubated for some 30 days and the young leave the nest after about 6 weeks.

3/ GRAY HAWK
Buteo nitidus

RANGE: **SW USA, Central and South America**
HABITAT: **tropical and subtropical woodland and forest**
SIZE: **15–17 in (38–43 cm)**

Despite its common name, the Gray Hawk is a small member of the genus *Buteo*. It is typically broad-winged, but fast-moving and agile when hunting. A woodland bird, its short wings and long tail allow it to steer skilfully around trees in pursuit of prey. It takes some birds, but over most of its range it preys mainly on lizards, snatching them by gliding down from a lookout perch.

The usual call of the Gray Hawk is a high-pitched *cree-ee-ee*, but it also utters flutelike cries in flight, apparently during courtship. The bird's nest is often well hidden by foliage, and placed 33–40 ft (10–12 m) up in a large tree. Populations of this species from southwestern USA and northern Mexico are migratory.

4/ RED-SHOULDERED HAWK
Buteo lineatus

RANGE: **North America, S to C Mexico**
HABITAT: **mixed or deciduous woodland and nearby open country**
SIZE: **16–20 in (41–51 cm)**

This widespread, handsomely proportioned buteo often occurs in damp woodland. A generally secretive bird, it keeps to cover for most of the time, although it is sometimes seen around open areas in winter. It takes a wide variety of prey, including birds, small mammals, lizards, snakes, frogs and toads. Its flight is active, with rapid wing beats followed by periods of gliding. It often calls while in the air.

There are 5 races of the Red-shouldered Hawk. The races *B.l. texanus* and *B.l. elegans* from southwestern USA and Mexico are much darker and more rufous below than those of the eastern race *B.l. lineatus*. Two isolated races, *B.l. alleni*, and *B.l. extimus* in Florida are typically much paler on the head and underparts, often showing little or no rufous barring below.

5/ ZONE-TAILED HAWK
Buteo albonotatus

RANGE: **SW USA, Central and South America**
HABITAT: **wooded and semiopen country**
SIZE: **18–21 in (46–53 cm)**

The Zone-tailed Hawk is a slim, rather rakish buteo that takes its name from the gray bands on its tail. The sexes are similar in plumage, although, as in many birds of prey, females are noticeably larger and immatures show copious white spotting below.

These birds are found in a variety of semiopen landscapes, usually with at least some trees, and in broken ground on the middle and lower slopes of mountains. In some parts of their range, especially in tropical America, they occur in more wooded country. They usually hunt for prey in flight, sometimes flying with Turkey Vultures *Cathartes aura*, which have a similar silhouette. It has been suggested that this resemblance allows them to approach closer to prey that would not normally flee from a nonpredatory passing vulture. Their victims include rodents, lizards, amphibians and birds, which they catch with a rapid swoop. Zone-tailed Hawks are courageous defenders of nests and will swoop at, or even strike, people who come too close.

6/ HAWAIIAN HAWK
Buteo solitarius ⓡ

RANGE: **island of Hawaii; has also wandered to Maui and Oahu**
HABITAT: **varied; especially in light woodland and edges of fields, generally from 2,000–5,000 ft (600–1,500 m), but usually with trees**
SIZE: **16–18 in (41–46 cm)**

One of Hawaii's many endemic breeding birds, the Hawaiian Hawk is among the smallest of the buteos. Rats are its main prey, but these were introduced to the islands by settlers. Previously the Hawaiian Hawk must have eaten mainly large insects and birds. It is an adaptable species and usually occurs alone or in pairs.

There are 2 color phases in this species. In the light phase, adults are basically dark brown above, with somewhat paler heads, and whitish below with rusty markings. Immatures are generally paler, except on the wings. Dark phase adult birds are blackish-brown below, but with some pale feathering on the throat. The immature birds are similar but with irregularly mottled and barred underparts.

7/ RED-TAILED HAWK
Buteo jamaicensis

RANGE: **North and Central America, Caribbean**
HABITAT: **extremely varied, but usually with some tree cover**
SIZE: **20–24¾ in (51–63 cm)**

This large, handsome buteo is widespread throughout its range and tolerant of a great variety of habitats, from woodland to prairies and alpine meadows. Highly versatile in its hunting methods, the Red-tailed Hawk catches a wide range of prey, including mammals, birds, reptiles and insects. Although it often swoops from a high perch or utility pole, it can also quarter the ground in flight before stopping, and hover in one spot by flapping against a moderate wind.

There are about 14 races of the Red-tailed Hawk, varying considerably in plumage and, to a certain extent, in size. Most, such as *B.j. borealis* of eastern North America, are basically dark brown above and pale below, show some degree of dark marking across the belly and have chestnut tails. Some of the birds in Alaska and Canada are uniformly dark above and below, with a dusky tail. The distinctive Krider's Hawk *B.j. kriderii* occurs mainly in the Great Plains region.

8/ EURASIAN BUZZARD
Buteo buteo

RANGE: **Europe E across Asia to the Bering Sea**
HABITAT: **varied, but usually with some tree cover**
SIZE: **20–22½ in (51–57 cm)**

The Eurasian Buzzard is a fairly thickset, medium to large hawk, with broad wings and a rather short, but ample, tail. It shows more variation in plumage than any other European bird of prey. Pale forms are present in many populations and very frequent in some, resulting in a bewildering range of plumage. Many of these have white heads, underparts and underwings. The Steppe Buzzard *B.b. vulpinus*, from the north and east of the range, is characterized by dark red to gray-brown underparts and an orange-gray tail.

The Eurasian Buzzard spends much of its time in the air, soaring over open terrain and woodland edges, with its wings raised in a shallow V. Rodents and other small mammals form the bulk of its prey, and it frequently feeds on carrion during the winter. It often calls in flight, uttering a far-carrying, plaintive cry. In many places, this is one of the most common birds of prey, although it has declined dramatically in parts.

9/ ROUGH-LEGGED HAWK
Buteo lagopus

RANGE: **N Europe E across Asia, North America**
HABITAT: **mainly Arctic or subarctic open terrain**
SIZE: **20–24 in (51–61 cm)**

The Rough-legged Hawk is slightly larger than the Eurasian Buzzard, but is noticeably bulkier, with longer wings and a longer tail. Like the Eurasian Buzzard, it is variable in plumage, with several races across its circumpolar range. The 2 races illustrated, *B.l. lagopus* of northern Europe and northwestern USSR and *B.l. sancti-johannis* of North America, both occur in pale and dark phases and a wide range of intermediates.

This species often hovers when hunting. Its numbers are closely governed by the abundance of small rodents, its main prey. In its Arctic breeding grounds in Scandinavia, lemmings are its principal source of food, and their population cycles markedly affect the bird's breeding success. Like northerly Eurasian Buzzards, Rough-legged Hawks are highly migratory, wintering far to the south of their breeding range.

10/ LONG-LEGGED BUZZARD
Buteo rufinus

RANGE: **C and SE Europe E to C Asia, N Africa**
HABITAT: **mainly lowland, open country, often arid or semiarid**
SIZE: **20–26 in (51–66 cm)**

This species is similar to the Rough-legged Hawk in general outline, and almost suggests a small eagle in flight. Its plumage is very variable, with both dark and pale phases and intermediates. At close quarters, juvenile birds show pale margins to the feathers on their dark upperparts and are less uniform in appearance than the adults.

Long-legged Buzzards are birds of dry steppe, semidesert and mountainous habitats, reaching altitudes of 13,000 ft (4,000 m). Lizards and small mammals provide the bulk of their prey. Populations from the northern part of the range migrate south for the winter, occurring in a belt from northern Africa east to northern India.

11/ JACKAL BUZZARD
Buteo rufofuscus

RANGE: **E and S Africa**
HABITAT: **varied; mainly hilly country**
SIZE: **18–21 in (46–53 cm)**

This is a very common and widespread bird in Africa, with 2 principal races, differing in the color of their underparts. The Jackal Buzzard *B.r. rufofuscus* occurs in southern Africa, while the Augur Buzzard *B.r. augur* ranges from Zimbabwe to the Ethiopian highlands. The species takes its name from its high-pitched, yelping call.

Jackal Buzzards fly with markedly raised wings and a rocking, side-to-side action. They hunt both on the wing and from perches, swooping to seize rodents, lizards, snakes, birds and insects. Often seen perching on telegraph poles and fenceposts, these birds frequently fly down to feed on carrion by the roadside, even darting between speeding cars. They breed either on cliffs or in trees, using their large stick nests for several years in succession.

12/ GUIANA CRESTED EAGLE
Morphnus guianensis   R

RANGE: **Honduras S to N Argentina**
HABITAT: **tropical lowland forest**
SIZE: **31–35 in (79–89 cm)**

This very large, handsome bird of prey occurs in 2 forms, the less common dark phase having once been regarded as a separate species. The broad, rounded wings and long tail equip the bird for maneuvering around forest trees in pursuit of prey. Although it may regularly soar above the forest canopy, it spends most of its time perched in tall trees. It preys on small monkeys, opossums, birds and reptiles.

The Guiana Crested Eagle is uncommon throughout its range, and, like most lowland rain forest birds, it faces the threat of deforestation. Although it is known to build a bulky nest high in the tallest forest trees, there are few details of its breeding habits.

13/ AMERICAN HARPY EAGLE
Harpia harpyja   R

RANGE: **S Mexico S to N Argentina**
HABITAT: **lowland tropical forest**
SIZE: **36–43¼ in (91–110 cm)**

A huge forest eagle, this species has immense feet and talons that make it one of the most powerful birds of prey in the world. A mighty predator, it can tackle large monkeys, sloths and porcupines, as well as eat some birds and reptiles.

The American Harpy Eagle picks most of its prey from the trees, plunging through the canopy and maneuvering with great skill between the branches. Its nest is composed of thick sticks and is about 5 ft (1.5 m) across. It is often built in the crown of a giant silk-cotton tree up to 165 ft (50 m) from the ground.

14/ NEW GUINEA HARPY EAGLE
Harpyopsis novaeguineae   ?

RANGE: **New Guinea**
HABITAT: **rain forest and gallery forest; visits clearings and gardens**
SIZE: **29½–35½ in (75–90 cm)**

The New Guinea Harpy Eagle is a very large eagle, with an erectile crest, a facial ruff, short wings, a long tail and bare legs. With a naturally low population density and probably also a low reproductive rate, it is threatened by hunting for its wing and tail feathers by New Guinea highlanders, equipped today with firearms, which has exterminated it in some areas. It is also threatened by habitat destruction.

This enigmatic species hunts in the style of a goshawk, perching inconspicuously inside the forest and changing perches by flying through or below the canopy. It feeds on mammals up to the size of wallabies and piglets, as well as on birds and reptiles. It may locate its prey by sound, dropping from its perch into the undergrowth, the erected ruff of feathers on its face possibly helping it to concentrate the sound as the facial disks of owls do. It is agile on the ground, where it will pursue prey on foot. Pairs of these birds advertise their presence and maintain contact by dueting with loud, resonant calls at dawn and dusk.

15/ PHILIPPINE EAGLE
Pithecophaga jefferyi   E

RANGE: **Philippines**
HABITAT: **rain forest**
SIZE: **34–40 in (86–102 cm)**

Now restricted to a few patches of forest on some of the Philippine islands, this magnificent eagle is one of the rarest and most endangered birds of prey in the world, with an estimated population of only 200 birds. It is threatened with extinction principally by severe losses of its forest habitat.

The Philippine Eagle is a huge, powerful and distinctive bird, short-winged and long-tailed, with a remarkably deep, laterally compressed bill. Sometimes known as the Monkey-eating Eagle, it is a fearsome hunter both of monkeys and flying lemurs (colugos). It is also big enough to tackle small deer and large birds such as hornbills. It hunts either from a perch in the trees, or ·by gliding low over the canopy, watching for any movement below.

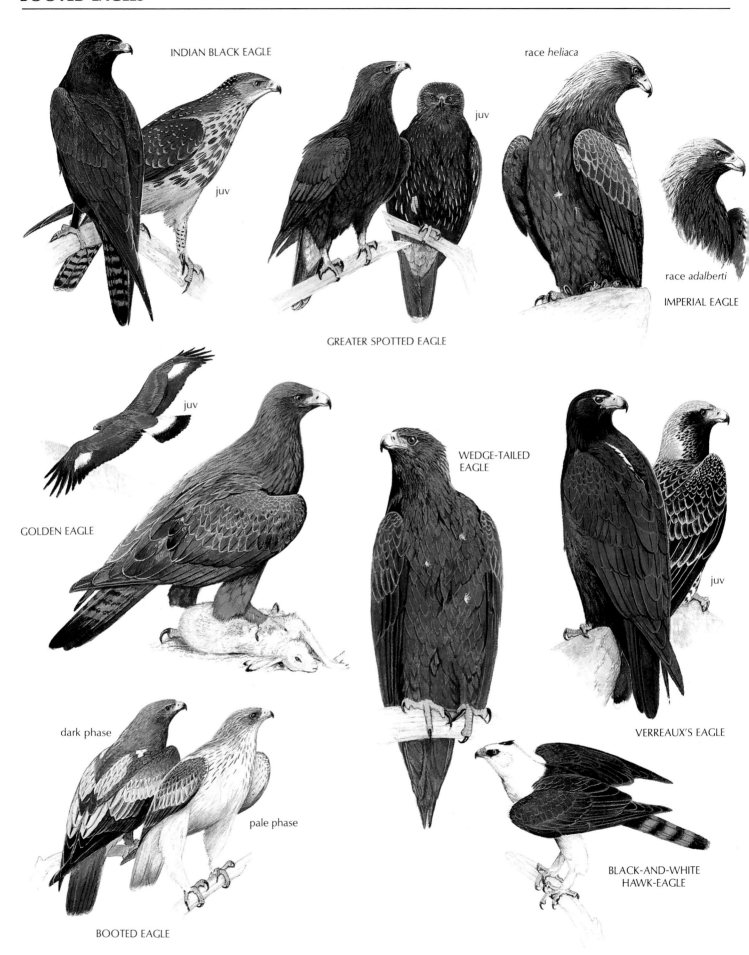

INDIAN BLACK EAGLE

juv

race *heliaca*

juv

race *adalberti*

IMPERIAL EAGLE

GREATER SPOTTED EAGLE

juv

GOLDEN EAGLE

WEDGE-TAILED EAGLE

juv

VERREAUX'S EAGLE

dark phase

pale phase

BLACK-AND-WHITE HAWK-EAGLE

BOOTED EAGLE

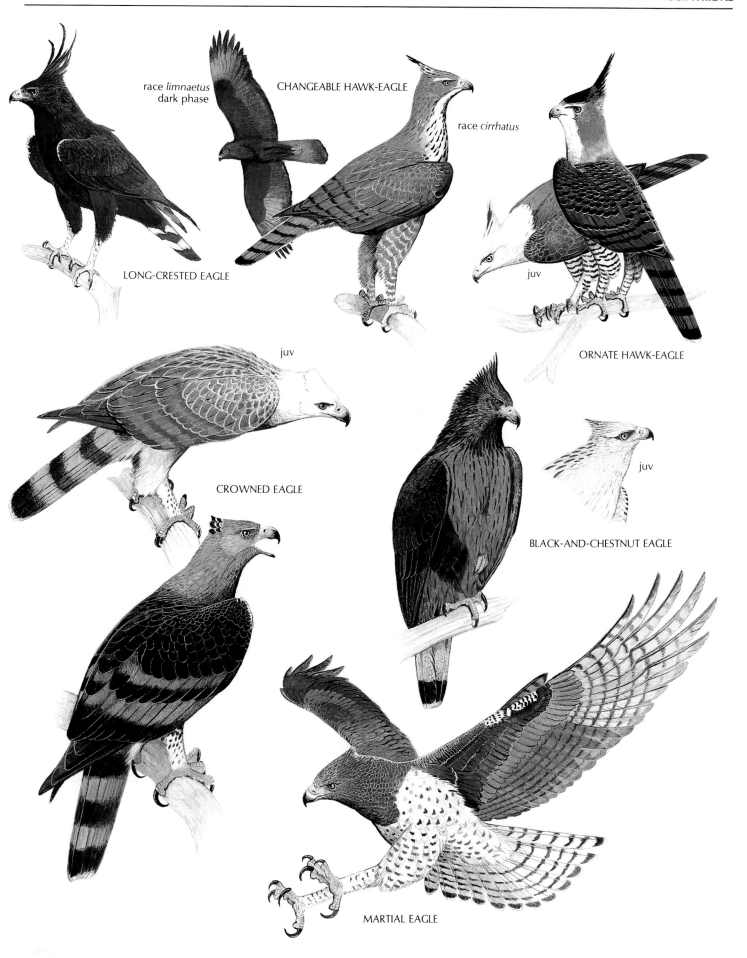

race *limnaetus* dark phase

CHANGEABLE HAWK-EAGLE

race *cirrhatus*

LONG-CRESTED EAGLE

juv

ORNATE HAWK-EAGLE

juv

CROWNED EAGLE

juv

BLACK-AND-CHESTNUT EAGLE

MARTIAL EAGLE

BOOTED EAGLES

FAMILY ACCIPITRIDAE/9
Booted eagles

Large birds of prey with feathered legs. Feed mainly on live prey. Sexes similar in plumage, females usually larger. Plumage usually brown, some forest-dwelling species with black and white, a few also with chestnut, one all black. Large stick nest usually in trees or on cliff ledges; sometimes use abandoned nest of another bird of prey. Eggs usually 1–2, white with brown or reddish markings. Incubation 40–50 days, nestling period 50–120 days. 31 species.

1/ INDIAN BLACK EAGLE
Ictinaetus malayensis

RANGE: **India, Sri Lanka, Burma, Malaysia SE to Sulawesi, Moluccas**
HABITAT: **mainly hill forests**
SIZE: **27–31¾ in (69–81 cm)**

The Indian Black Eagle has a relatively lightweight body and very long wings with long primary feathers which it spreads wide like outstretched fingers: these features enable this unusual eagle to fly remarkably slowly over or through the forest canopy in its search for prey.

Although it takes a wide range of prey, including lizards, small mammals and birds, it is best known for its habit of snatching up eggs or nestlings, sometimes tearing the whole nest from among the branches and carrying it off to devour the contents at leisure. Its highly specialized feet, with the outer toe and talon very short but the others equipped with very long, straight talons, doubtless help it to achieve this.

The Indian Black Eagle also occurs in more open terrain, quartering the ground like a giant harrier. It may seize small mammals on the ground and can put on a surprising burst of speed when it snatches bats and swiftlets from around the mouths of caves.

2/ GREATER SPOTTED EAGLE
Aquila clanga

RANGE: **breeds extreme E Europe E across N Asia; some birds resident, others winter in S of range, many winter as far S as NE Africa, Middle East, N India and China**
HABITAT: **mainly woodland or forest, usually near water or wetlands**
SIZE: **26–29 in (66–74 cm)**

This thickset eagle's wings usually appear remarkably broad and blunt-ended in flight. Apart from a whitish crescent across the rump, adults are dark brown, although an uncommon pale phase is light buffish-brown. The prominent white spots on the juveniles give the species its name. Juvenile pale phase birds are strikingly pale sandy-buff with blackish flight feathers.

The Greater Spotted Eagle scavenges widely, readily visiting carrion, but also hunts a wide variety of live prey, including small mammals, birds, reptiles, amphibians and insects. Bird prey includes waterbirds, from young herons snatched from their nests to ducks and coots; in dealing with the latter, the eagle may separate one bird from a flock and then repeatedly stoop at it, forcing it to dive until it becomes exhausted and can easily be seized when at the surface.

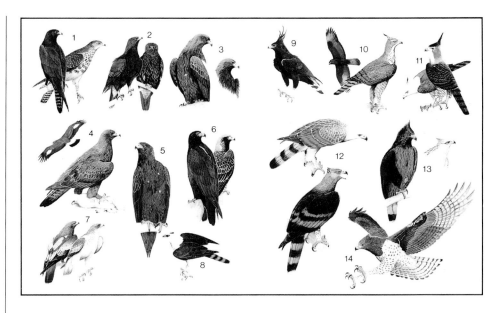

3/ IMPERIAL EAGLE
Aquila heliaca [?]

RANGE: **breeds E Europe to C Asia, Spain; some populations migratory, especially in C Asia (winter S to N India)**
HABITAT: **mainly lowland areas, usually with trees**
SIZE: **31–33 in (79–84 cm)**

This imposing eagle is only slightly smaller than the Golden Eagle; its crown and neck feathers are even more striking, being yellowish-white rather than gold. Although it is still widespread in parts of central Asia, numbers of European birds have decreased greatly.

The Spanish race of this bird, *A. h. adalberti*, is geographically isolated from its much more widespread eastern European and Asian counterpart *A. h. heliaca*. It differs principally in having a much more extensive area of white plumage on the leading edge of the wings, and is often regarded as a separate species. The Spanish Imperial Eagle is now an extremely rare and endangered bird.

4/ GOLDEN EAGLE
Aquila chrysaetos

RANGE: **Europe, N Asia, North America, parts of N Africa and Middle East**
HABITAT: **mountains, plains, sea coasts**
SIZE: **30–39 in (76–99 cm)**

A consummate flier, even in the strongest winds, this is generally regarded as the most impressive of the *Aquila* eagles. Contrary to popular belief, it is not normally a spectacular hunter, relying instead on patient quartering at low altitude and a sudden rush-and-pounce attack. Medium-sized mammals and birds usually form its main prey, but it will also feed on carrion.

Although it is the most widespread and numerous large eagle in the northern hemisphere, the Golden Eagle has declined in numbers in some parts of its range. This is as a result of human disturbance and habitat modification as well as direct persecution, including poisoning and shooting, because of the bird's allegedly serious depredations of game and lambs.

Golden Eagles usually build their nest of branches on cliffs or crags, or in trees. Most pairs have several nests, which they use roughly in rotation. If it is re-used over many successive seasons a nest can grow to a huge size: up to 6 ft (2 m) high and up to 5 ft (1.5 m) across.

5/ WEDGE-TAILED EAGLE
Aquila audax

RANGE: **Australia, Tasmania, S New Guinea**
HABITAT: **varied, but avoids intensively settled and cultivated areas**
SIZE: **33¾–41 in (86–104 cm)**

This is a huge, dark eagle with a long, wedge-shaped tail. Young birds are brown with a pale nape and shoulders, and gradually darken until they are almost black in their seventh year. The small Tasmanian population is threatened by habitat destruction and direct persecution.

Wedge-tailed Eagles search for food by soaring, quartering the ground or by sitting on a high perch. They take live mammals, birds and reptiles up to the size of a young kangaroo or ibis. Their main prey in pastoral areas consists of rabbits and hares, although they sometimes kill lambs and young goats. Juvenile eagles often eat carrion, gathering like vultures at animals killed on roads. Pairs perform soaring and undulating or rolling and foot-clasping displays. The huge stick nest is built in a substantial tree fork or, occasionally, on a cliff ledge and the 1–2 (rarely 3) eggs are incubated mainly by the female.

6/ VERREAUX'S EAGLE
Aquila verreauxii

RANGE: **sub-Saharan Africa, Sinai, S Arabia**
HABITAT: **rocky mountains, cliffs and gorges; also dry savanna**
SIZE: **31¾–37¾ in (81–96 cm)**

Also widely known as the Black Eagle, this is the African counterpart of the Golden Eagle. It has a marked preference for medium-sized mammals, and in many parts of its range it feeds chiefly on hyraxes. Its narrow wing bases and broad primary feathers give this elegant, well-proportioned eagle a unique outline in flight.

Verreaux's Eagle is a superb flier, and it indulges in spectacular display flights, alternating breathtakingly steep dives with great upward swoops, often followed by a roll or a somersault. Males perform a remarkable pendulum-like series of gyrations. Although 2 eggs are usually laid and hatched, it is extremely rare for more than 1 chick to survive: the older chick kills its weaker, younger sibling. This "Cain and Abel" rivalry is found in other birds of prey, but is virtually invariable in this species.

7/ BOOTED EAGLE
Hieraaetus pennatus
RANGE: **breeds NW Africa, SW Europe, SE Europe E into Asia; most European birds winter in Africa S of Sahara, most Asian birds in India**
HABITAT: **forest and woodland and adjacent open country, especially in hilly and upland areas**
SIZE: **18–20¾ in (46–53 cm)**

This eagle is a dashing hunter. It feeds on a variety of birds and small mammals, perching high in a tree or soaring above the forest canopy to spot its prey, then diving or stooping after it from heights of 330–800 ft (100–250 m) or more.

The Booted Eagle takes its common name from its heavily feathered legs. It occurs in a pale phase and a dark phase. Pale phase birds outnumber dark phase birds in most of Europe by about 7 to 3, but in Asia the proportions seem more equal. Pale phase juveniles have much gingery smudging and streaking on the underparts, while those of the dark phase are similar to the adults.

8/ BLACK-AND-WHITE HAWK-EAGLE
Spizastur melanoleucus
RANGE: **Central and South America**
HABITAT: **forests, adjacent open country**
SIZE: **20¾–24 in (53–61 cm)**

The prey of the Black-and-white Hawk-Eagle is believed to consist largely of small to medium-sized mammals and birds. In some parts of the bird's range in South America, it occurs along rivers, perhaps because these often provide the only open spaces in forests. In such habitats, it is known to take birds up to the size of cormorants and mergansers.

Although it is such a conspicuous bird, it is rarely seen and seems to be a relatively scarce and local species. Immatures are rather similar to the adults, but with whitish edges to the wing coverts.

9/ LONG-CRESTED EAGLE
Spizaetus occipitalis
RANGE: **sub-Saharan Africa**
HABITAT: **woodland, cultivated land, open country with trees**
SIZE: **20–22 in (51–56 cm)**

The Long-crested Eagle preys mainly on small rodents, catching them by dropping down from a prominent perch. Over much of Africa, this bird is well known through its habit of hunting from fenceposts, utility poles and roadside trees. It hunts chiefly in the early morning and toward evening and often rests in the shade of a large tree during the heat of midday.

They are noisy birds, especially at the onset of the breeding season, uttering loud, high-pitched screaming cries and a harsh *kik-kik-kik-kik-kee-eh* call, both from perches and on the wing. Immatures are similar to the adults, but are rather browner and show white tips to the neck and upper wing covert feathers.

10/ CHANGEABLE HAWK-EAGLE
Spizaetus cirrhatus
RANGE: **India, Sri Lanka, Southeast Asia**
HABITAT: **savanna, open country, forests in some areas**
SIZE: **22–31¾ in (56–81 cm)**

Different races of this species vary considerably in plumage and size, and while most have a prominent crest (hence the alternative name for the species, Crested Eagle) some have only a vestigial crest, and others are completely crestless. Generally, adults are like the race *S. c. cirrhatus*, from India south of the Ganges Plain and West Bangladesh. The almost crestless race, *S. c. limnaetus*, from the Himalayas to the Philippines, Borneo and Java, is unusual in having a dark phase as well as the normal form.

This eagle hunts mainly from a perch and seizes most of its prey – mainly small mammals and lizards, along with a few birds – on the ground. It builds its large nest of sticks lined with leaves high in a big tree.

11/ ORNATE HAWK-EAGLE
Spizaetus ornatus
RANGE: **Central and South America; Trinidad and Tobago**
HABITAT: **tropical forest and adjacent open country**
SIZE: **24–26 in (61–66 cm)**

Like most forest birds of prey, the Ornate Hawk-Eagle carries out most of its hunting from a perch. Its prey includes a variey of small mammals and birds up to the size of chachalacas, the smaller herons, quails and parrots. These birds are most easily seen when soaring, wheeling in leisurely circles, usually fairly low above the forest canopy, holding their wings horizontal but angled slightly forward. During the breeding season, pairs take part in aerial displays, soaring together. The male may perform aerial loops and undulating displays. At this time, these handsome birds are very noisy, calling with high-pitched screams and whistling notes.

12/ CROWNED EAGLE
Spizaetus coronatus
RANGE: **sub-Saharan Africa**
HABITAT: **mainly forests, sometimes hillsides and more open areas**
SIZE: **31¾–35¾ in (81–91 cm)**

Named for its short crest, this large, powerful and impressive eagle is a formidable predator, feeding almost entirely on mammals. In dense forest, monkeys are the main prey. Here, its short, broad wings and long tail give the Crowned Eagle great maneuverability in flight. In more open areas, it takes such animals as small antelopes, hyraxes, mongooses and rats, and occasionally even domestic cats. Females are larger than males and usually have more heavily barred underparts and a shorter crest.

In contrast to many eagles, a pair of Crowned Eagles usually builds only one nest, which may be used over a long period of time. It is constructed from sticks, with a lining of green branches, and sited high in a forest tree, at a height of 40–150 ft (12–45 m). Just before mating, the male displays to his mate by running around her with wings raised to show off their striking, rich chestnut linings. Usually, both parents share the duties of incubation and care of the young.

13/ BLACK-AND-CHESTNUT EAGLE
Spizaetus isidori
RANGE: **Andes from Venezuela to Argentina**
HABITAT: **mainly mountain forest, usually at 5,300–9,200 ft (1,600–2,800 m)**
SIZE: **24¾–29 in (63–74 cm)**

This thickset, rather powerful bird is sometimes known as Isidor's Eagle. It probably carries out most of its hunting by soaring around the treetops and swooping down on its prey. It takes many medium-sized tree-dwelling mammals, such as monkeys, sloths and squirrels, and also quite large birds such as guans and curassows. Some prey is caught on the ground.

The Black-and-chestnut Eagle builds a large nest, which may measure more than 3 ft (1 m) deep and 6 ft (2 m) or more across. This is constructed almost entirely from live branches, which the bird collects by plunging down and breaking off the branch with its momentum as it passes it.

Like so many eagles, this species is sparsely distributed, even in the most suitable habitats, and is threatened by deforestation.

14/ MARTIAL EAGLE
Polemaetus bellicosus
RANGE: **sub-Saharan Africa**
HABITAT: **mainly savanna; also some cultivated areas**
SIZE: **31¾–37¾ in (81–96 cm)**

This is the largest and most powerful African eagle. It also spends much more time on the wing than most other species, except for the Bateleur, and often soars at great heights. Hunting both from perches and on the wing, it kills a wide range of birds, small to medium-sized mammals and lizards. The birds can spot prey from a considerable distance and usually attack it by a long, slanting stoop at high speed.

The female is usually more heavily spotted than the male and is larger; a large female may have a wingspan of 8½ ft (2.6 m). Immatures are paler above than the adults and have clear white plumage from the throat to the under tail coverts.

Breeding success is variable, with some pairs rearing only 1 young bird in 3 years. The birds are vulnerable to persecution, chiefly by farmers who often unfairly accuse them of taking livestock.

SECRETARY BIRD, CARACARAS AND FALCONS

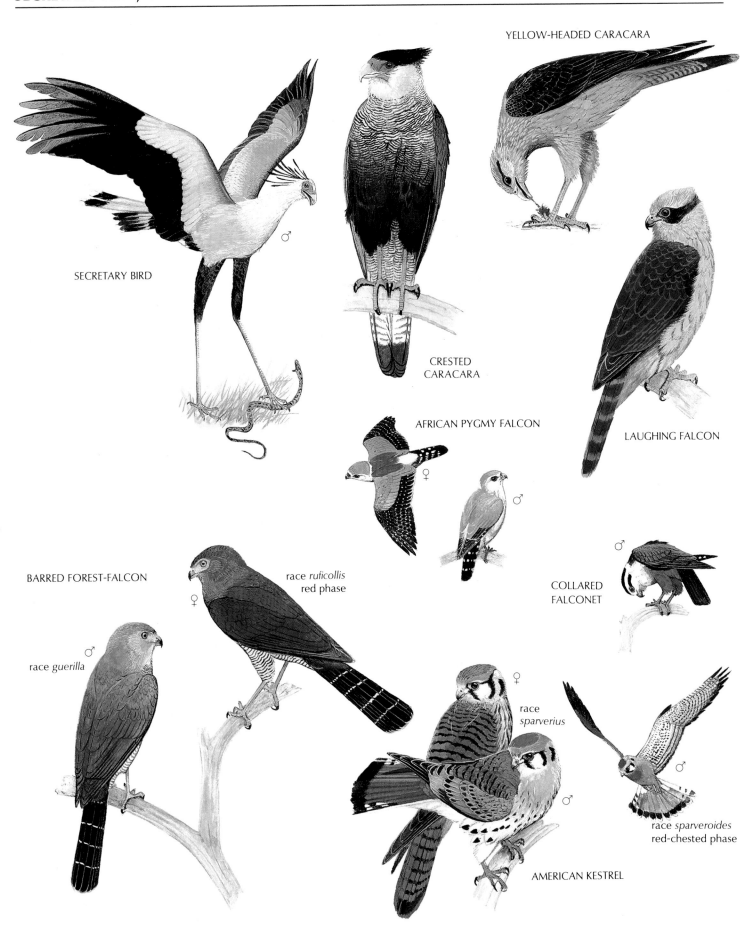

YELLOW-HEADED CARACARA

SECRETARY BIRD

CRESTED
CARACARA

AFRICAN PYGMY FALCON

LAUGHING FALCON

BARRED FOREST-FALCON

race *ruficollis*
red phase

race *guerilla*

COLLARED
FALCONET

race
sparverius

race *sparveroides*
red-chested phase

AMERICAN KESTREL

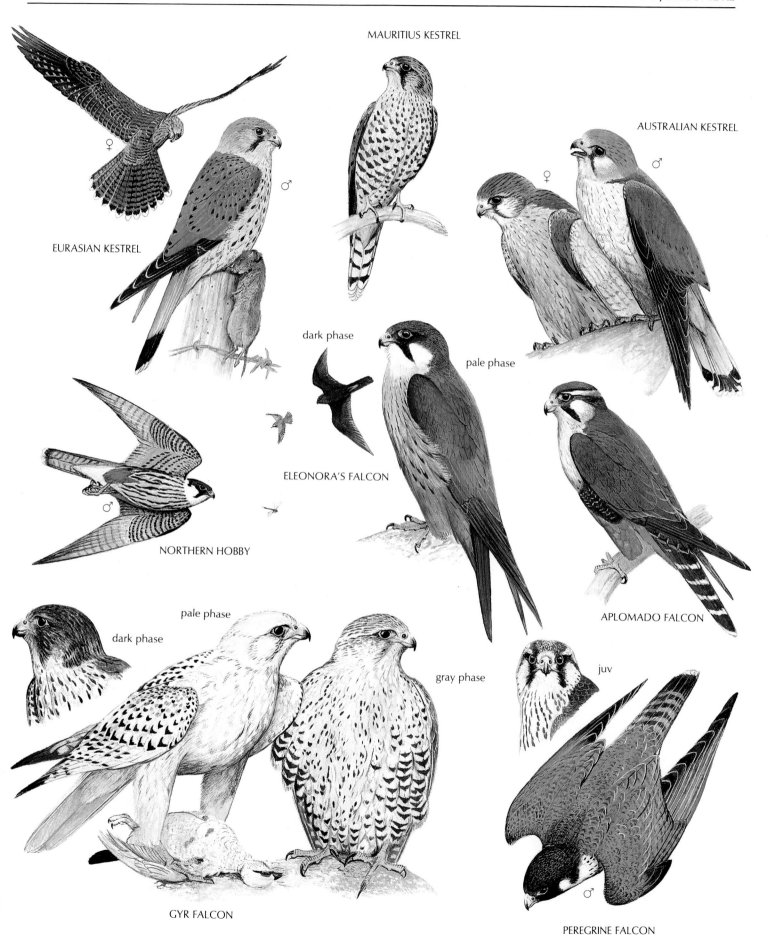

MAURITIUS KESTREL

AUSTRALIAN KESTREL

♀

♂

EURASIAN KESTREL

♀

♂

dark phase

pale phase

ELEONORA'S FALCON

NORTHERN HOBBY

♂

APLOMADO FALCON

pale phase

dark phase

gray phase

juv

GYR FALCON

♂

PEREGRINE FALCON

SECRETARY BIRD, CARACARAS AND FALCONS

FAMILY SAGITTARIIDAE
Secretary Bird
There is only one species in this family.

1/ SECRETARY BIRD
Sagittarius serpentarius
RANGE: **sub-Saharan Africa**
HABITAT: **open savanna and grassland**
SIZE: **$49\frac{1}{4}$–59 in (125–150 cm)**

The Secretary Bird takes its name from the fancied resemblance of its distinctively ornamented head to an old-fashioned clerk or secretary, with a quill pen stuck behind his ear.

Secretary Birds forage for prey on the ground, striding along with a deliberate, measured tread, and are famous for their ability to immobilize and kill snakes. They also feed widely on other reptiles, as well as small mammals, the eggs and young of ground-nesting birds and large insects.

During courtship displays, the birds soar high above the ground, their long legs and tail projecting behind them, and utter weird groaning calls. The nest is a great flat platform of sticks up to 8 ft (2.4 m) across. The 2–4 greenish-white eggs are incubated by the female for about 45 days. The young leave the nest at 10–11 weeks.

FAMILY FALCONIDAE/1
Caracaras
Large birds with naked faces and deep, powerful bills. Mainly omnivorous carrion-eaters, with long legs and flat claws. Plumage mainly dark, some white or pale below or on head, some finely barred. Sexes alike. Nest of sticks usually in trees or on cliffs. Eggs 2–3, whitish, buff or pinkish, marked red-brown. Incubation about 32 days, nestling period about 42 days. 9 species.

2/ CRESTED CARACARA
Polyborus plancus
RANGE: **Florida and SW USA, Central and South America**
HABITAT: **open or semiopen country**
SIZE: **20–24 in (51–61 cm)**

The Crested Caracara is capable of killing a wide variety of prey, including small mammals, young or disabled birds, fish, frogs, insects and other invertebrates, as well as being a scavenger and carrion-eater. Unlike the vultures with which they often associate at a carcass, Crested Caracaras do not soar, but have a direct, purposeful flight with noisy wing beats. They patrol highways early in the morning in search of animals killed during the night, often finding them before the vultures, which depend on warm thermal air currents later in the day for soaring.

3/ YELLOW-HEADED CARACARA
Milvago chimachima
RANGE: **Panama S to N Argentina**
HABITAT: **savanna, scrub, semiopen country**
SIZE: **$15\frac{1}{4}$–18 in (39–46 cm)**

This caracara is a fairly small, lightly built species, but, like its larger and more robust relatives, it is a scavenger and carrion-eater,

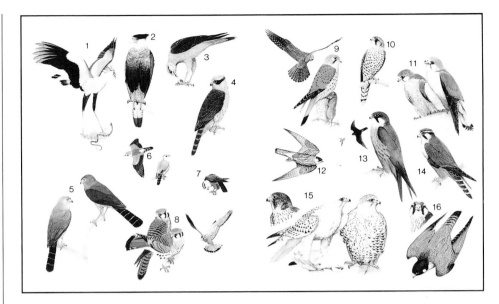

as well as a predator of various insects and assorted small birds and mammals. It is particularly well known for its habit of perching on livestock to feed on the ticks on their skin.

Yellow-headed Caracaras spend much of their time in small groups, and often perch high in trees. They have a buoyant flight with even wing beats and occasional sweeping glides. They build large stick nests, usually in a tree.

FAMILY FALCONIDAE/2
Falcons
Small to medium birds of prey, compact, most with long, pointed wings. Typically highly aerial, many catching prey in midair. Toothed and notched bills for killing prey with bite to the neck. Sexes usually similar in plumage (except most kestrels); females larger. Plumage varied, but most darker above than below; many with brown, chestnut and blue-gray. No nest; use scrape on cliff ledge or in tree cavity, or take over old nests of other birds. Eggs 2–6, usually buff, heavily speckled with red-brown. Incubation 28–36 days, nestling period 25–49 days. 48 species.

4/ LAUGHING FALCON
Herpetotheres cachinnans
RANGE: **Central and South America**
HABITAT: **tropical lowlands, in both semiopen and wooded country**
SIZE: **17–20 in (43–51 cm)**

This unique bird takes its name from its cackling alarm call. More frequently heard, however, especially at dawn and dusk, is a distinctive, 2-note call, typically *gua-co*, with the first note higher, repeated continuously. The Laughing Falcon likes to perch on an exposed branch in the topmost layer of the forest, where it can watch for prey – chiefly snakes – without being seen. Once it sights a snake, the bird drops on it like a stone and seizes the reptile just behind the head with its bill. It usually kills it swiftly with a powerful bite that may sever the snake's head. It then carries its prey to a perch – in its bill if it is a small snake and in its feet if it is a large one. It swallows small snakes whole, but has to tear larger ones to pieces.

5/ BARRED FOREST-FALCON
Micrastur ruficollis
RANGE: **Central and South America**
HABITAT: **tropical and subtropical forest**
SIZE: **$12\frac{1}{4}$–15 in (31–38 cm)**

The forest-falcons form a distinctive group of long-tailed birds with short, rounded wings, adapted for hunting birds in woodland. The Barred Forest-Falcon forages on the wing or sallies out from a perch to catch prey. It eats a variety of small birds, as well as some lizards and small rodents. It takes advantage of birds following army ants in search of food, dashing out from cover to snatch them by surprise.

This species shows considerable variation in plumage across its wide range. The races illustrated are *M. r. guerilla* from Mexico to Nicaragua and *M. r. ruficollis* from Brazil and Paraguay.

6/ AFRICAN PYGMY FALCON
Polihierax semitorquatus
RANGE: **E and S Africa**
HABITAT: **arid thornbush and scrub**
SIZE: **$7\frac{1}{2}$–$9\frac{1}{2}$ in (19–24 cm)**

This tiny African falcon is almost shrikelike, with its habit of sitting on exposed perches and diving swiftly on to its prey. It eats small lizards, small birds and small rodents, seized on the ground, as well as many large insects, which are often caught in midair. This is usually a solitary species, found in pairs or groups of up to 4 birds, which generally remain in the same area day after day and year after year. It uses the abandoned nests of other birds, especially weavers and starlings, for roosting, sheltering from rainstorms and nesting.

7/ COLLARED FALCONET
Microhierax caerulescens
RANGE: **India SE to Malaysia**
HABITAT: **forests with open clearings**
SIZE: **$5\frac{1}{2}$–$7\frac{1}{2}$ in (14–19 cm)**

This tiny falcon uses exposed perches for hunting. Insects are its main prey, and it frequently catches them in flight by darting out from the perch and returning to eat them on its perch. It may also take a few small birds. The Collared Falconet is often known as the Red-legged Falconet, but this is an inappropriate name, as the bird has only some chestnut feathering on its black legs.

8/ AMERICAN KESTREL
Falco sparverius

RANGE: **breeds SE Alaska and Canada S to extreme S South America; N birds winter S to Panama**
HABITAT: **open country: mountain meadows, grassland, deserts, open woodland, agricultural land and urban areas**
SIZE: **9–12¼ in (23–31 cm)**

The American Kestrel feeds on insects and other invertebrates and on small snakes, lizards, birds and small mammals, including bats, catching its prey either by swooping down on it from a perch or after hovering overhead.

One of the brightest-plumaged of all the kestrels, the American Kestrel is unusual in that, even as juveniles, the sexes have distinct plumages. There is considerable geographical variation in size and in plumage, particularly in that of the male. The 2 races illustrated are *F. s. sparverius*, from much of North America, and the red-chested phase of *F. s. sparveroides* from Cuba and the Isle of Pines.

9/ EURASIAN KESTREL
Falco tinnunculus

RANGE: **breeds most of Europe, Africa, Asia; N and E birds winter from Britain S to S Africa and N India S to Sri Lanka**
HABITAT: **diverse, from moors to tropical savanna and urban areas; avoids tundra, dense forest, deserts**
SIZE: **12¼–13¾ in (31–35 cm)**

The Eurasian Kestrel is one of the world's most abundant birds of prey, with a very wide distribution and the ability to adapt well to a range of artificial habitats.

Although it is a competent bird-catcher, and feeds widely on insects and other invertebrates, the Eurasian Kestrel is best-known as a hunter of small mammals. It frequently hovers for prolonged periods on fast-beating wings as it scans the ground. When prey is spotted, the bird descends in a series of swoops and hoverings, before finally dropping to snatch it in its feet. It also hunts from a high perch and will sometimes snatch birds in midair. Most of the 10 or 11 races are similar to the race illustrated, *F. t. tinnunculus* from Europe, northwest Africa and Asia South to Arabia, Tibet and extreme southeastern USSR.

10/ MAURITIUS KESTREL
Falco punctatus   E

RANGE: **SW corner of Mauritius**
HABITAT: **a few areas of dense evergreen forest in rugged gorges and escarpments**
SIZE: **11–13 in (28–33 cm)**

Although it never seems to have been very abundant, the Mauritius Kestrel was once widespread in the dense forest that used to clothe much of the island of Mauritius. Today, it is restricted to the few areas of forest that remain. By 1974 only 6 individuals were believed to be left. The numbers improved slightly in the 1980s and have been supplemented by a captive breeding and release program. But total numbers are probably still below 50, making this one of the most endangered birds in the world.

Its rather short, rounded wings do not equip the Mauritius Kestrel well for hovering, but give it great maneuverability in the forest canopy. Lizards, especially iridescent green tree geckos, small birds and large insects, seem to be its major food.

11/ AUSTRALIAN KESTREL
Falco cenchroides

RANGE: **Australia, Tasmania, New Guinea**
HABITAT: **open and lightly wooded country, farmland, urban areas**
SIZE: **11¾–13¾ in (30–35 cm)**

Like some of its relatives, this kestrel, which is also known as the Nankeen Kestrel, has adapted well to artificial landscapes. It hunts in the usual kestrel fashion, including hovering, and preys mainly on large insects, small mammals and reptiles. Mouse and locust plagues may attract large concentrations of these birds.

Courting Australian Kestrels perform aerial maneuvers in mock aggression, and the male may ritually feed the female before mating. No nest is built. Instead, the 3–7 eggs are laid in a tree hollow or sometimes on a cliff ledge or city building or in the old stick nests of other birds.

12/ NORTHERN HOBBY
Falco subbuteo

RANGE: **breeds Europe, NW Africa, Asia; winters in E and S Africa S to Cape Province, and S to N India and S China**
HABITAT: **mainly semiopen country with some tree cover**
SIZE: **12¼–14 in (31–36 cm)**

The Northern Hobby is a long-winged, aerial hunter, swift and extremely agile in the air. It feeds mainly on flying insects, such as dragonflies, and on birds, and is even capable of catching fast-flying, agile swifts and swallows, although it probably takes far more immatures than adults. It often eats insects on the wing, holding them in its feet, but usually takes birds back to a perch to deal with. It often hunts in the evening, taking birds flocking together at roosts and sometimes bats.

13/ ELEONORA'S FALCON
Falco eleonorae

RANGE: **breeds Canary Islands, Morocco and Mediterranean islands; winters chiefly in Madagascar**
HABITAT: **breeds on sea cliffs and adjacent rocky tablelands; outside breeding season in wider range of habitats**
SIZE: **14–15¾ in (36–40 cm)**

Named after a medieval Sardinian princess, this large, rakish falcon has even longer wings than the Northern Hobby. It occurs in 2 main color phases, a pale phase and a dark phase. Eleonora's Falcon breeds in colonies, usually of 5–20 birds, but sometimes up to 200, timing the rearing of its young to coincide with a superabundant food supply – the millions of small birds crossing the Mediterranean on their autumn migration. In winter it feeds mainly on flying insects.

14/ APLOMADO FALCON
Falco femoralis

RANGE: **breeds Mexico to extreme S South America; birds from extreme N and S winter to S and N respectively**
HABITAT: **open or lightly wooded country**
SIZE: **14½–17¾ in (37–45 cm)**

This falcon feeds mainly on birds and insects taken in flight. It is sufficiently swift and agile to catch such fast-flying birds as pigeons and parrots. Until the beginning of the 20th century, the Aplomado Falcon bred regularly in southwestern USA, but it became increasingly rare and was last known to nest in Texas and New Mexico in the 1950s, although single birds have been seen occasionally since then. The reasons for this decline are unknown, but a significant factor may have been the development of the species' habitat for agriculture. It is now scarce in northern Mexico, where the use of pesticides poses a serious threat.

15/ GYR FALCON
Falco rusticolus

RANGE: **Greenland, Iceland and Arctic Europe, Asia and North America**
HABITAT: **sea cliffs, uplands, other open country**
SIZE: **20–22¾ in (51–58 cm)**

This is the largest and most powerful of the falcons, fully capable of taking prey the size of grouse and ducks, or sometimes even larger, more formidable birds, including buzzards and owls. The Gyr Falcon will also catch small rodents and occasionally kills mammals as large as hares. It generally catches its prey after a long, level chase low over the ground, in which it demonstrates its speed and stamina.

16/ PEREGRINE FALCON
Falco peregrinus   V

RANGE: **almost cosmopolitan; absent from Sahara, C Asia, most of South America**
HABITAT: **mountains, uplands, sea cliffs**
SIZE: **14–18¾ in (36–48 cm)**

To many, the Peregrine Falcon is the ultimate predatory bird – a robustly built, fast-flying falcon which typically kills its prey in a spectacular diving stoop, often from a great height. Most of the prey comprises medium-sized birds, almost all of which are caught or killed on the wing. Pigeons and doves are the preferred prey wherever they occur in the bird's range.

Long persecuted by egg-collectors, gamekeepers and pigeon fanciers, the Peregrine Falcon faced a new threat from the effects of pesticides in the 1950s and 1960s and many populations in Europe and North America declined alarmingly. More recently, there has been a recovery in some areas including Britain, but in parts of Europe numbers are still low.

MEGAPODES, GUANS AND CURASSOWS, TURKEYS, GROUSE, NEW WORLD QUAILS

chick emerging from nest mound

AUSTRALIAN BRUSH-TURKEY

MALLEE FOWL

CRESTED GUAN

PLAIN CHACHALACA

♀

♂

red phase
♀

dark phase
♀

NOCTURNAL CURASSOW

♂

GREAT CURASSOW

SPRUCE GROUSE

race *scoticus*
"Red Grouse"

♂

♂ summer ♂ winter

WILLOW PTARMIGAN

♀ summer

♀

WILD TURKEY

WESTERN CAPERCAILLIE

♂

♀

GREATER PRAIRIE CHICKEN

gray phase

♀

♂

race *virginianus*

♂ ♀

RUFFED GROUSE

gray phase

♂

race *ridgwayi*
"Masked Bobwhite"

♂

♀

♂

CALIFORNIA QUAIL

MONTEZUMA QUAIL

NORTHERN BOBWHITE

MEGAPODES, GUANS AND CURASSOWS, TURKEYS, GROUSE, NEW WORLD QUAILS

FAMILY MEGAPODIIDAE
Megapodes

Large, robust ground birds with sturdy legs. Sexes similar. Eggs white to brown with chalky covering. Clutch size for individual female known only for Mallee Fowl (5–33 eggs, usually 15–24) and Orange-footed Scrub Fowl *Megapodius reinwardt* (3–13 eggs). Eggs laid in mounds of decaying vegetation or sand which provide heat for incubation (about 50 days for Australian Brush-Turkey and Mallee Fowl). Young independent upon hatching. 19 species.

1/ AUSTRALIAN BRUSH-TURKEY
Alectura lathami

RANGE: **coastal and subcoastal E Australia from Cape York to mid-New South Wales**
HABITAT: **rain forest, thick scrub, well-vegetated urban areas**
SIZE: **27½ in (70 cm)**

The powerful legs and feet of the Australian Brush-Turkey are typical of the ground-feeding megapodes. It uses its feet to rake up a variety of animal and vegetable foods from the forest floor, including insects and other invertebrates, fruits and seeds. Powerful runners, Australian Brush-Turkeys fly only to escape danger or to roost in trees at night.

Like most megapodes, it lays its eggs in a mound which acts as an incubator. Built of leaf litter and soil raked together by the male, the mound heats up as the organic matter decays. The male maintains the correct temperature of about 33°C (91.4°F) by adding material or opening up the mound to ventilate it and advertises his handiwork with loud booming calls. These can attract several females, which between them lay a total of 18–24 eggs in separate hollows excavated by the male. When the young hatch they dig their way out of the mound and immediately run off to live a solitary and independent life. They can fly within hours of leaving the nest mound.

2/ MALLEE FOWL
Leipoa ocellata   [V]

RANGE: **inland S Australia, extending to coast in some areas**
HABITAT: **eucalyptus scrub and woodland (mallee)**
SIZE: **23½ in (60 cm)**

The Mallee Fowl is a denizen of the low, multi-stemmed eucalyptus woodland known as mallee. Most of this unique habitat has been cleared for cereal cultivation and the few nature reserves may be too small to maintain viable populations of the species. The Mallee Fowl feeds by using its large feet to rake through leaf litter in search of seeds, buds, insects and other small animals.

In late winter and spring, the male and female build the nest mound, using moist leaf litter and sand, with an egg chamber of wet, rotting litter. The male maintains a constant temperature of 91.4°F (33°C) in the mound by testing it with the sensitive inside of his bill. When he has assessed the temperature, he opens or closes the mound to release or retain the heat produced by fermentation or, later in the season, to expose or protect it from the fierce sun. The female lays her eggs from spring to fall.

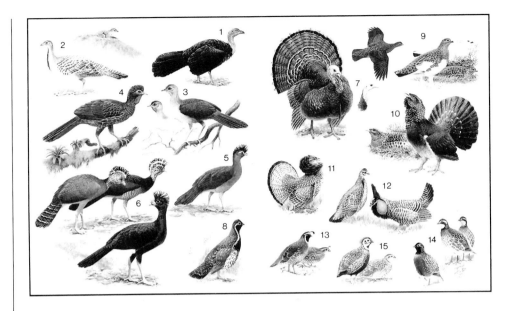

FAMILY CRACIDAE
Guans and curassows

Large, often tree-dwelling forest birds with blunt wings and long, broad tails. Plumage generally dark with white patches; many species with crests or casques. Males often larger. Nests of twigs and rotting foliage, low in trees or on ground. Eggs 2–4, white or cream. Incubation 22–34 days. Chicks leave nest at 1 day old; in some species can fly at 3–4 days, but are cared for by females or both parents for some time. 45 species.

3/ PLAIN CHACHALACA
Ortalis vetula

RANGE: **S Texas to W Nicaragua and NW Costa Rica; introduced to islands off Georgia**
HABITAT: **lowland semiarid scrub forest, thickets, forests**
SIZE: **18 in (46 cm)**

The Plain Chachalaca is generally a shy bird in the wild and is usually located by its call – a raucous repetition of its name which is taken up by others in a harsh, rhythmic chorus, most often during the twilight of dawn and dusk. Like other members of its family, it walks along branches to feed on berries, buds and tender young leaves. In the breeding season – from early March to September in Texas – the pinkish-gray bare skin on each side of the male's chin turns bright red.

4/ CRESTED GUAN
Penelope purpurascens

RANGE: **Mexico to W Ecuador and N Venezuela**
HABITAT: **humid forest, scrub, hilly areas up to 3,300 ft (1,000 m)**
SIZE: **35¾ in (91 cm)**

This bird has disappeared from many areas as a result of forest clearance and uncontrolled hunting and now has a rather patchy distribution. Most active at dawn and dusk, they are often seen in pairs, walking or running along branches to feed on wild figs, berries and succulent foliage. Although primarily tree-dwelling, they sometimes descend to the ground to eat fallen fruit. In the dry season the males perform a display in which they fly slowly with wings beating rapidly to produce a loud drumming rattle.

5/ NOCTURNAL CURASSOW
Nothocrax urumutum

RANGE: **NW South America to E Peru**
HABITAT: **forests**
SIZE: **26 in (66 cm)**

As its name suggests, this species is most active at night. It sings on both moonlit and dark nights from high in the forest with a soft dovelike cooing, followed by a pause and a guttural hoot. Its odd specific name, *urumutum*, is derived from a Brazilian Indian name based on its song.

The Nocturnal Curassow is a secretive bird, and is said to spend the day concealed in a tree cavity or a hole in the ground. It will descend to the forest floor to feed on ripe fallen fruit, but always retreats to the trees for safety. The 2 white eggs are laid in a large nest of sticks, built in a tree and usually well concealed by vegetation.

6/ GREAT CURASSOW
Crax rubra

RANGE: **Mexico to W Ecuador and W Colombia**
HABITAT: **humid to semiarid, undisturbed mature forest; also scrub**
SIZE: **38 in (97 cm)**

The Great Curassow is sensitive to disturbance, and is one of the first birds to disappear when a forest is exploited by man. It is also hunted throughout its range; its populations have become increasingly fragmented and it is now rare.

It normally feeds on the forest floor on a variety of leaves and fruit, but retires to the upper canopy for cover. Usually seen in pairs, it forages in small family groups after breeding. The song of the male is a long, low, booming sound with a ventriloquial quality. The female is variable in color, the red phase and dark phase being most common; there is also a rare barred phase.

FAMILY MELEAGRIDIDAE
Turkeys
Large ground birds with strong legs and bare skin on head and neck. Plumage dark with metallic highlights; males brighter and usually much bigger than females. Ground-nesters. Eggs 8–15, cream speckled brown. Incubation 28 days. Chicks usually leave nest after 1 night, but are cared for by female for first 2 weeks. 2 species.

7/ WILD TURKEY
Meleagris gallopavo
RANGE: USA, Mexico
HABITAT: forests, clearings, brushland
SIZE: male 48 in (122 cm); female $33\frac{3}{4}$ in (86 cm)

Wild Turkeys are opportunists with broad tastes; they will eat seeds, nuts, berries, green foliage and small animals, such as grasshoppers and other invertebrates and even lizards and salamanders. The birds generally forage on the ground, although they are strong fliers over short distances and roost in trees at night.

The polygamous males attract hens during the breeding season by elaborate displays, strutting and gobbling with fanned tails and swollen wattles. The hens incubate the eggs and tend their broods alone.

FAMILY TETRAONIDAE
Grouse
Medium to large, plump birds with short, rounded wings. Males generally larger, with darker, ornamented plumage. Females cryptic. Ground-nesters. Eggs 5–12, white to brown with dark blotches. Incubation 21–27 days. Chicks leave nest within a few hours of hatching; many can fly short distances within 5–8 days. 17 species.

8/ SPRUCE GROUSE
Dendragapus canadensis
RANGE: W Alaska to E Canada and N USA
HABITAT: boggy areas in conifer forest with carpets of moss
SIZE: 15–17 in (38–43 cm)

The Spruce Grouse is a typical forest grouse, feeding on the buds, twigs and needles of coniferous trees during the winter but switching to berries and other fruits in summer.

Although solitary and largely silent for much of the year, the male displays energetically and noisily in the mating season. Inflating the red skin above his eyes and uttering low-pitched hoots, he struts and whirrs his wings in a forest clearing to attract a female.

9/ WILLOW PTARMIGAN
Lagopus lagopus
RANGE: N hemisphere at latitudes above 50° N
HABITAT: treeless tundra, moors, heaths, Arctic willow bogs
SIZE: $14\frac{1}{2}$–$16\frac{1}{2}$ in (37–42 cm)

Populations of the Willow Ptarmigan undergo regular 3–10 year cycles, depending on locality. The increases may be related to nutrient cycles

in the soil that affect the birds' food plants. Although the chicks are fed on insects as well as plant food, adults often feed mainly on the catkins, twigs and buds of willow and birch, and the shoots and berries of bilberries and other plants. Birds of the British and Irish race *L.l. scoticus*, known as the Red Grouse, live largely on the young shoots of heather. Red Grouse, formerly considered a separate species, do not molt into white plumage like other races.

10/ WESTERN CAPERCAILLIE
Tetrao urogallus
RANGE: N Europe, including Scotland
HABITAT: mature conifer forest
SIZE: male $34\frac{1}{4}$ in (87 cm); female $23\frac{1}{2}$ in (60 cm)

This magnificent, turkeylike bird is the biggest of the grouse and the species most intimately associated with forests. It feeds largely on pine seeds and pine needles in winter, but switches in summer to a diet of leaves, stems and berries of bilberries, cranberries and bog whortleberries, together with other sedges and plants. The chicks are fed on insects at first.

In spring, the males gather together at traditional sites, or "courts," in forest clearings, to perform a dramatic courtship ritual. With tail fanned out and throat feathers puffed up, a male challenges rival males with a song consisting of a series of clicking notes, rather like water dripping into a bucket, which accelerate until they run together into a soft drum-roll sound and end in a noise like the popping of a cork from a wine bottle.

11/ RUFFED GROUSE
Bonasa umbellus
RANGE: Alaska, Canada, N USA
HABITAT: deciduous and conifer forest, abandoned farmland
SIZE: 17 in (43 cm)

This highly prized gamebird, which occurs in distinct gray and red phases, is notable for its courtship display. The monogamous male lays claim to a thick stand of aspens and attracts a mate by beating his wings to produce a hollow, accelerating drumming. At the same time, he raises his head crest, extends his neck ruff and fans his tail to its full extent. After mating, the female usually selects a nest site among male aspen trees where she can feed on the catkins during incubation of her 11–12 eggs.

12/ GREATER PRAIRIE CHICKEN
Tympanuchus cupido
RANGE: SC Canada to Gulf of Mexico
HABITAT: grassland
SIZE: 17–$18\frac{3}{4}$ in (43–48 cm)

Once common on the American prairies, this large grouse has become increasingly rare as its habitat has dwindled. It feeds on leaves, buds, fruits and seeds, as well as on insects such as grasshoppers in summer. In spring the males gather at traditional "booming grounds" – communal courtship arenas – where they inflate their orange neck pouches and perform spectacular stamping dances, accompanied by loud booming cries.

FAMILY PHASIANIDAE/1
New World quails
Small to medium, rounded birds, with strong serrated bills. Plumage brighter than on Old World quails, males with distinctive markings. Ground-nesters. Eggs 6–16, white, sometimes marked. Incubation 18–23 days. Chicks leave nest within a few hours in some species and can fly when only 1 week old. 31 species.

13/ CALIFORNIA QUAIL
Lophortyx californica
RANGE: British Columbia S to Baja California
HABITAT: brush and grassland, irrigated and fallow arable land
SIZE: $9\frac{1}{2}$–11 in (24–28 cm)

The California Quail is an attractive, very gregarious bird which forms winter flocks, or coveys, of 200–300 birds. These usually forage together on foot for seeds, especially those of vetches and other legumes. The birds rarely fly unless alarmed but, unlike other quails, they roost in dense trees or shrubs rather than on the ground.

California Quails nest among low herbage, carefully concealing their eggs in shallow scrapes lined with dead leaves and grasses.

14/ NORTHERN BOBWHITE
Colinus virginianus
RANGE: E USA to SW USA and Mexico
HABITAT: open pine forests, clearings
SIZE: $7\frac{3}{4}$–11 in (20–28 cm)

Named in imitation of its cheerful mating call, this is a social species which forms flocks, or coveys, of 15–30 birds in fall. The birds feed together on the seeds and fruits of grasses, shrubs and crops such as sorghum and soybeans. Each covey roosts on the ground in a tight bunch with heads pointing out, and explodes into the air if flushed.

The race *C. v. virginianus* occurs in central and eastern USA. The Masked Bobwhite *C. v. ridgwayi* is a distinctive southern race, with a small, endangered population, which has been reintroduced from Mexico to its former range in southeastern Arizona.

15/ MONTEZUMA QUAIL
Cyrtonyx montezumae
RANGE: S Arizona, New Mexico, Texas, N Mexico
HABITAT: open, grassy, pine, juniper and oak woodland
SIZE: 7 in (18 cm)

The handsome Montezuma Quail is a bird of the mountainous, arid southwest of America and is able to tolerate long periods without rain. Its stout legs are well adapted for digging up moisture-rich bulbs and the tubers of nut grasses; it also eats a variety of seeds and insects.

Its call is a gentle whistle. The birds usually nest in the late summer rainy season. After the chicks are fledged, they form flocks, or coveys, of 8–10 birds which feed on the ground and hide in the grass if disturbed.

PARTRIDGES AND OLD WORLD QUAILS

♂

SEE-SEE PARTRIDGE

♀

race
castaneiventer

HIMALAYAN SNOWCOCK

race cranchii

race
melanogaster

ROCK PARTRIDGE

RED-NECKED FRANCOLIN

"Montana" phase
♂

♂

GRAY PARTRIDGE

INDIAN GRAY FRANCOLIN

MADAGASCAR PARTRIDGE

LONG-BILLED WOOD PARTRIDGE

COMMON HILL-PARTRIDGE

STONE PARTRIDGE

CRESTED WOOD-PARTRIDGE

CEYLON SPURFOWL

COMMON QUAIL

ASIAN BLUE QUAIL

115

PARTRIDGES AND OLD WORLD QUAILS

FAMILY PHASIANIDAE/2
Partridges and francolins

Stout, rounded, medium-sized gamebirds, with short, powerful wings and strong legs. Sexes distinct, with males brighter. Mostly ground-feeding seed-eaters. Nest usually open scrape on ground. Eggs usually 2–19, whitish to dark olive. Incubation 16–25 days, chicks leave nest soon after hatching. 98 species.

1/ SEE-SEE PARTRIDGE
Ammoperdix griseogularis

RANGE: S USSR, Iran to NW India
HABITAT: **arid foothills and semidesert**
SIZE: **9½ in (24 cm)**

The See-see Partridge is typical of the rough, broken, treeless terrain found on the rocky hillsides of central and southern Asia. It forages in flocks of up to 20 individuals, picking through the rocks and vegetation for seeds and other morsels.

Single birds are very rarely seen except during the mating season, when each male establishes and defends his own breeding territory. The mating system is basically monogamous, but several females may lay their eggs in the same nest, which is usually sited in a sheltered position near a tuft of grass.

2/ HIMALAYAN SNOWCOCK
Tetraogallus himalayensis

RANGE: E Afghanistan E to W Nepal, NW China
HABITAT: **high-altitude mountain slopes**
SIZE: **20–22 in (51–56 cm)**

Found high up on some of the highest mountains in the world, the large Himalayan Snowcock is well adapted to its harsh environment. Its predominantly gray and white plumage blends in with the landscape of gray rock and snow, and its broad diet includes the seeds, leaves, shoots and roots of a variety of plants, particularly sedges. It often has to cover a lot of ground to find enough to eat and may range over an area of up to 250 acres (1 square kilometer) each day.

In autumn and winter it often associates in larger flocks of 15–20 birds, but in the breeding season the flocks break up as the males court the females with loud 5-note whistles. The nests, which are simple hollows lined with dry grass and feathers, are often made in caves.

3/ ROCK PARTRIDGE
Alectoris graeca

RANGE: European Alps, SE Yugoslavia, Greece, Bulgaria
HABITAT: **rocky heaths, pastures, grassland**
SIZE: **13½–15 in (34–38 cm)**

The Rock Partridge is a common sight in the grasslands and among the vineyards of the eastern Mediterranean area, where flocks of up to 100 birds may work their way between the vines in search of seeds, fruits and shoots. Like many partridges, it has a variable diet, for although it is essentially vegetarian in adulthood, the breeding females and chicks eat quantities of insects, spiders and other small animals.

Rock Partridges are monogamous and often pair for life. As with other partridges in the genus *Alectoris*, the female may lay 2 clutches of up to 14 eggs each season, incubating 1 clutch herself while the male incubates the other.

4/ RED-NECKED FRANCOLIN
Francolinus afer

RANGE: C and S Africa
HABITAT: **forest clearings with brushwood**
SIZE: **11¾–16 in (30–41 cm)**

The francolins are a group of fairly large, powerful gamebirds distinguished by the patches of bare skin on their heads or necks. The Red-necked Francolin is a very variable species with as many as 18 races, found throughout much of Africa south of the Equator. The races illustrated are *F. a. cranchii* from northern Angola, northern Zambia and western Tanzania; *F. a. melanogaster* from Mozambique and eastern Tanzania; and *F. a. castaneiventer* from southern and eastern Cape Province to northern Transvaal.

It often feeds in mixed groups with other francolins, searching for food among the low vegetation of forest edges and clearings. Much of its diet consists of tubers, bulbs, shoots, berries, roots and seeds, but it will also eat insects and other invertebrates.

The mated pairs tend to remain within their breeding territories throughout the year, suggesting that the pairs mate for life. The clutch of 3–9 eggs is laid in a scrape under a shrub and incubated by the female alone. As with many gamebirds, the chicks develop fast and are able to fly 10 days after hatching.

5/ INDIAN GRAY FRANCOLIN
Francolinus pondicerianus

RANGE: E Iran, India, Sri Lanka
HABITAT: **dry plains, thorny scrub**
SIZE: **13 in (33 cm)**

Its ability to tolerate dry conditions has made the Indian Gray Francolin one of the most common resident gamebirds in southern Asia. Recognized by its distinctive yellow throat markings, it lives in grasslands and semiarid thorny scrub, often near crops or villages. The birds usually occur in small family groups, roosting together in small trees or shrubs. They feed on weed seeds and cultivated grain, as well as large numbers of insects during the summer.

The breeding season in India is prolonged and nests containing eggs have been recorded in every month of the year. The brood of 6–9 chicks is generally reared by both parents.

6/ GRAY PARTRIDGE
Perdix perdix

RANGE: W and C Europe
HABITAT: **open country, farmland**
SIZE: **11¾ in (30 cm)**

Originally a bird of open grassland and steppe, the Gray Partridge has adapted well to farmland. It is a common sight in arable fields in many parts of Europe, although in some areas, such as Britain, it has been badly hit by the widespread use of farm pesticides, which destroy the insects that form the main food supply for the chicks during the first 2 weeks after hatching. Herbicides have also had a serious effect, since these kill the "weeds" that the insects live on.

Outside the breeding season the birds associate in family flocks, or coveys, but in late winter the breeding adults form monogamous pairs. Each male defends a territory which, on farmland, includes a hedgerow to provide cover for the nest. The female lays the largest clutch of any bird, up to 25 eggs, or even more, and an average of 19 in some areas.

The "Montana" variety, illustrated along with a more typical adult male, has far more chestnut on its breast and belly.

7/ LONG-BILLED WOOD PARTRIDGE
Rhizothera longirostris
RANGE: **Malaysia, Sumatra, W Borneo**
HABITAT: **dry forest, especially bamboo**
SIZE: **14 in (36 cm)**

This large tropical partridge lives at altitudes of up to 4,000 ft (1,200 m) in dense upland forest, particularly in areas of thick bamboo. This preference for remote, inaccessible country, coupled with its extreme wariness, means that it is rarely seen – although it will occasionally give away its location by calling loudly at night.

In Malaya the local people are said to catch the birds by luring them into traps with imitations of their calls, which suggests that they are territorial. Apart from this, little is known about their breeding behavior. Only one nest has been found, located in a bamboo thicket; in captivity the female lays 2–5 eggs, incubating them for 18–19 days.

8/ MADAGASCAR PARTRIDGE
Margaroperdix madagarensis
RANGE: **Madagascar**
HABITAT: **secondary scrub and grassland**
SIZE: **12 in (30 cm)**

Many partridges breed as monogamous pairs, and the males and females are similar in appearance. The male Madagascar Partridge, by contrast, is much brighter than the female, indicating an emphasis on courtship that is typical of polygamous species, in which the male courts and mates with many females. The birds nest from March to June and a large clutch of up to 20 eggs has been reported.

The Madagascar Partridge is a medium-sized grassland bird that lives in heathy, mountainous areas. It often forages on cultivated ground, particularly where it is overrun with weeds and secondary scrub. It also occurs in rice fields, where it probably eats rice grain as well as weed seeds and insects.

9/ COMMON HILL-PARTRIDGE
Arborophila torqueola
RANGE: **N and E India, S Tibet**
HABITAT: **evergreen forest and scrub**
SIZE: **10 in (25 cm)**

The Common Hill-Partridge is a denizen of thick undergrowth in the upland forests of India and south China. It is usually found at altitudes of 5,000–9,000 ft (1,500–2,700 m), in pairs or groups of up to 10 birds.

The male has a distinctive black throat pattern that is echoed in reduced form in the plumage of the female. The birds pair off in April to July throughout most of their range, laying 4–5 eggs in a scrape beneath a bush or near the base of a tree.

10/ CRESTED WOOD-PARTRIDGE
Rollulus roulroul
RANGE: **S Burma, Thailand, Malaysia, Sumatra and Borneo**
HABITAT: **tropical forest**
SIZE: **10 in (25 cm)**

Partridges in general are open country birds, but the wood-partridges of Southeast Asia are found in thick tropical rain forest, where they are rarely seen and difficult to study. The Crested Wood-Partridge is the most spectacular of these species, with richly colored plumage and, in the male, a red, brushlike crest. It feeds on seeds, fruit, insects and small mollusks and appears to eat more animal material than most partridges.

Its nesting habits are also atypical. Instead of the usual scrape, it builds a large domed nest with a small entrance and, in one case, a captive female was seen to lead her brood back to the nest each evening and close the entrance with twigs – a routine that continued until the chicks were 25 days old.

11/ STONE PARTRIDGE
Ptilopachus petrosus
RANGE: **Africa, Senegal to Kenya**
HABITAT: **rocky hills**
SIZE: **10 in (25 cm)**

This bantamlike African species is well adapted to the arid conditions of areas such as the sub-Saharan Sahel region, where pairs or small family groups can be seen combing the sandy landscape for seeds, insects and some green plants. For preference, however, it frequents areas of dense vegetation among boulder-strewn rocky hills.

The breeding period is very variable, owing to the erratic nature of the food supply in the arid habitat. The birds form monogamous pairs which appear to be permanent, but outside the breeding period the family groups may gather together to feed in larger flocks.

12/ CEYLON SPURFOWL
Galloperdix bicalcarata
RANGE: **Sri Lanka**
HABITAT: **moist upland forest to 5,000 ft (1,500 m)**
SIZE: **13–14 in (33–36 cm)**

The Ceylon Spurfowl lives in the dense tropical forests that mantle the foothills and mountains of Sri Lanka, feeding on a variety of seeds, tubers and berries. The birds prefer jungle-covered hillsides with river valleys, where they establish well-defined breeding territories which they defend vigorously against intruders. Because of this, they are easily caught by the local people, who use captive decoy birds to lure them to traps.

The breeding adults may form permanent pair-bonds. They lay a clutch of 2 eggs during the monsoon period from November to March.

As with other members of the family, the young forage with their parents in small family groups, or coveys, and rapidly learn to find their own food.

FAMILY PHASIANIDAE/3
Old World quails
Small, compact, like miniature partridges. Ground birds of open grassland and swamp. Adults seed-eaters, chicks eat insects. Mainly monogamous, but males often brighter. Some breed on migration. Nest a scrape on the ground. Eggs 4–15, white to olive. Incubation 14–22 days, chicks leave nest soon after hatching. 9 species.

13/ COMMON QUAIL
Coturnix coturnix
RANGE: **Eurasia**
HABITAT: **open grassland**
SIZE: **7 in (18 cm)**

The Common Quail is rarely seen in the wild, but is well known from its distinctive, loud, ventriloquial, trisyllabic call, often rendered as *wet-my-lips*. It usually forages close to the ground beneath the cover of vegetation, and will run when it is alarmed rather than take flight. Despite this, it will fly long distances to reach its breeding grounds; those that breed in Europe migrate from Africa each year. The males arrive first and call to attract the females when they appear. The normal clutch is 7–12 eggs and the chicks are cared for by the female alone.

In Europe the Common Quail has adapted well to agricultural landscapes, particularly cereal crops, but, like the Gray Partridge, its breeding success is limited by the lack of insect food for its chicks in areas where pesticides and herbicides are in common use.

14/ ASIAN BLUE QUAIL
Coturnix chinensis
RANGE: **W India, Southeast Asia, Philippines, Indonesia, New Guinea, NE Australia**
HABITAT: **open grassland**
SIZE: **5½ in (14 cm)**

One of the smallest of all gamebirds, this boldly marked quail is found over a wide range throughout much of eastern Asia and Australasia. It favors dense grassland, swamp edge and cultivated ground, where it feeds mainly on grass seeds and some insects. It generally forages in family coveys of 6–7 individuals.

In many areas it is nomadic, moving into an area to breed after rainfall. The 4–7 eggs are incubated by the female alone for about 16 days – the shortest incubation period of any gamebird.

PHEASANTS, GUINEAFOWL

BLOOD PHEASANT

BLYTH'S TRAGOPAN

HIMALAYAN
MONAL PHEASANT

RED JUNGLEFOWL

race *nycthemera*

SILVER PHEASANT

CHEER PHEASANT

typical hybrid ♂

race *colchicus*
♂

melanistic hybri
♂

typical h

COMMON PHEASANT

LADY AMHERST'S PHEASANT

GREAT ARGUS PHEASANT

COMMON PEAFOWL

CONGO PEAFOWL

HELMETED GUINEAFOWL

VULTURINE GUINEAFOWL

PHEASANTS, GUINEAFOWL

FAMILY PHASIANIDAE/4
Pheasants

Medium to large, often colorful, long-tailed birds. Sexes distinct, with males often spectacular in polygamous species. Generally vegetarian ground-feeders found in tropical and subtropical forest. Nest usually a scrape on ground. Eggs 2–12, whitish to olive. Incubation 18–28 days, chicks leave nest soon after hatching. 48 species.

1/ BLOOD PHEASANT
Ithaginis cruentus

RANGE: **Himalayas, Nepal, Tibet, China, Burma**
HABITAT: **high-altitude coniferous forest**
SIZE: **$17\frac{3}{4}$ in (45 cm)**

Like all pheasants, the Blood Pheasant is at risk from habitat destruction and human exploitation for food, but it is less vulnerable than most because of its preference for remote places. There is extensive geographical variation in the plumage, with 2 main types; the illustration shows the type found in races in the north of the species' range.

This is a gregarious bird and flocks of 10–30 individuals may be seen working their way through the forest, feeding on fir and juniper sprouts, berries, mosses and bamboo shoots. Blood Pheasants also eat insects during the breeding season in April and May.

2/ BLYTH'S TRAGOPAN
Tragopan blythii ⬛R

RANGE: **Assam, Burma, Tibet**
HABITAT: **densely wooded valleys at high altitude**
SIZE: **$24\frac{3}{4}$–$27\frac{1}{4}$ in (63–69 cm)**

This is one of 5 species of tragopan which live in the forests of Asia. The males all have striking plumage which plays an important part in courtship. They are unusual among pheasants because they nest in trees, often using old nests built by other species.

Blyth's Tragopan has a preference for the thick undergrowth of dense evergreen mountain forest. It feeds mainly on seeds, berries and buds, although it will also take insects and other small animals. In hard winters when food is scarce it tends to move down to lower altitudes, but not as much as other mountain-dwelling pheasants. At night it roosts in trees, which are often some distance from the feeding areas.

3/ HIMALAYAN MONAL PHEASANT
Lophophorus impejanus

RANGE: **E Afghanistan, NW Pakistan, S Tibet, Burma**
HABITAT: **open mixed forest on rocky slopes**
SIZE: **22–$25\frac{1}{4}$ in (56–64 cm)**

The glorious iridescent metallic plumage of the male Himalayan Monal Pheasant is one of the most spectacular sights of the Asian forests, particularly during courtship when the bird indulges in dramatic display flights over the cliffs and crags of its mountain home. The female is dull

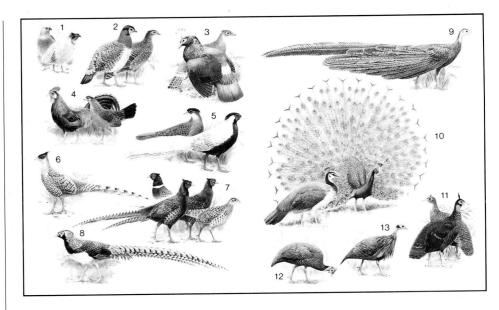

by comparison, to provide camouflage while she incubates her clutch of 4–5 eggs.

For much of the year these birds prefer to live in oak and mixed forest, feeding on ground-living insects and tubers, but in autumn they often move up into the mountain grasslands above the tree line to forage for insect larvae. They will dig through the snow with their bills to reach food, excavating holes up to 12 in (30 cm) deep. Like other pheasants, they are threatened by hunting throughout their range.

4/ RED JUNGLEFOWL
Gallus gallus

RANGE: **Southeast Asia**
HABITAT: **forests and open country**
SIZE: **male $23\frac{1}{2}$–$31\frac{1}{2}$ in (60–80 cm); female 17–18 in (43–46 cm)**

This bird, the wild ancestor of the domestic fowl, is an opportunist feeder which is at home in a variety of habitats. Normally found in forest with fairly dense undergrowth, frequently with bamboo, it often emerges into clearings and scrubland at the forest edge, where flocks of up to 50 birds forage for a variety of foods, including grain, seeds and insects.

The birds appear to feed in the same area throughout the year. They breed in the dry season from March to May, the polygamous males courting several females with displays of their superb plumage. The 5–6 eggs are laid in a hollow scraped in the ground near a bush.

5/ SILVER PHEASANT
Lophura nycthemera

RANGE: **S China, E Burma, Indochina, Hainan**
HABITAT: **broad areas of grassland bordered by forest**
SIZE: **male $35\frac{1}{2}$–50 in (90–127 cm); female $21\frac{3}{4}$–$26\frac{3}{4}$ in (55–68 cm)**

The Silver Pheasant is essentially a grassland bird and rarely penetrates into dense forest. Like the Red Junglefowl, it has a broad diet, feeding on a wide range of animal and vegetable matter

including beetles, flower petals, grass and leaves. Its plumage is variable throughout its range and there are about 14 races. The one shown, *L. n. nycthemera* from South China and northeast Vietnam, is the largest and whitest.

Like most grassland pheasants, it has a polygamous mating system, with dominant males courting many females and defending their territory with loud whistling calls.

6/ CHEER PHEASANT
Catreus wallichii ⬛E

RANGE: **Himalayas**
HABITAT: **steep, grassy hillsides**
SIZE: **male $35\frac{1}{2}$–$46\frac{1}{2}$ in (90–118 cm); female 24–30 in (61–76 cm)**

Many of the pheasants of Asia are threatened with extinction as a result of habitat destruction and hunting, and the Cheer Pheasant is no exception. It is now extinct in many areas of Pakistan but attempts are being made to reintroduce it, using birds bred in captivity.

In the wild the Cheer Pheasant has a preference for grass-covered hillsides with scattered trees and will often forage around human settlements. The adults are largely vegetarian, but the young appear to feed on insects during the first 2 weeks after hatching.

Cheer Pheasants are territorial but the territories are quite small, with up to 6 breeding pairs occupying 250 acres (1 square kilometer). The 9–10 eggs are laid in a nest built on the ground, usually in the lee of a large boulder.

7/ COMMON PHEASANT
Phasianus colchicus

RANGE: **Asia; introduced to Europe, Australia and North America**
HABITAT: **lowland farmland, woodland, upland scrub**
SIZE: **male $29\frac{1}{2}$–$35\frac{1}{2}$ in (75–90 cm); female $20\frac{1}{2}$–$25\frac{1}{4}$ in (52–64 cm)**

Introduced to many areas of the world for shooting, the Common Pheasant is the most widely distributed of all the gamebirds. The well-camouflaged females can be hard to spot, but the colorful males are a frequent and conspicuous sight on open farmland. In Europe there are now a variety of races, including *P. c. torquatus*, from eastern China, and *P. c. colchicus*, from Transcaucasia and the eastern and southeastern Black Sea region, plus a bewildering variety of typical and dark (melanistic) forms. The melanistic form and some others result partly from interbreeding with the Green Pheasant *Phasianus versicolor*, from Japan.

In its native range (chiefly in India, Southeast Asia and China) the Common Pheasant lives on open forest-grassland. It is an opportunist feeder, taking a variety of seeds, grain, fruit, insects and other small animals, and this is one reason why it has adapted so well to other habitats such as agricultural land.

The male is polygamous, gathering a harem of females on his display territory and defending them against rival males. In autumn the birds are gregarious, but in winter the sexes tend to segregate. Common Pheasants roost in trees at night.

8/ LADY AMHERST'S PHEASANT
Chrysolophus amherstiae [?]

RANGE: **China, NE Burma; introduced to Britain**
HABITAT: **high bamboo-covered mountain slopes**
SIZE: **male $45\frac{1}{4}$–59 in (115–150 cm); female $22\frac{3}{4}$–$26\frac{3}{4}$ in (58–68 cm)**

One of the most spectacular of the true pheasants, this is also one of the most elusive: a secretive bird which rarely emerges from the thorny thickets and bamboo scrub of its remote mountain habitat. Even those introduced to Britain are not often seen, for the wild population breeds in dense woodland with thick undergrowth, and little is known about its breeding biology.

Bamboo shoots form an important part of its diet in its native range, but it will also eat small animals, including spiders, earwigs and beetles. Lady Amherst's Pheasants have even been seen feeding in shallow flowing water, turning over stones in search of aquatic animals.

9/ GREAT ARGUS PHEASANT
Argusianus argus

RANGE: **Borneo, Sumatra, Malaya and Thailand**
HABITAT: **lowland and hill forest**
SIZE: **male up to 80 in (203 cm); female up to 30 in (76 cm)**

Male pheasants of polygamous species are generally much more ornate than the females. The Great Argus Pheasant of Southeast Asia is an extreme example of this rule, for the adult male has very large secondary wing feathers, decorated with golden eyespots, which he uses to dazzling effect in courtship.

Each male clears a display site in the forest a considerable distance from that of his nearest rival. Having attracted a female with loud calls, he dances before her. At the climax of the dance he spreads his wing feathers in 2 great, glittering fans and if the female is sufficiently impressed, she will consent to mating. She then leaves to lay her eggs and rear the chicks alone, while the male courts other females. The normal clutch consists of only 2 eggs.

Birds of both sexes tend to be solitary by habit. They eat a wide range of foods, including fallen fruits, ants, slugs and snails.

10/ COMMON PEAFOWL
Pavo cristatus

RANGE: **Sri Lanka, India, Pakistan, Himalayas; introduced worldwide**
HABITAT: **forests and semiopen country with streams**
SIZE: **male $78\frac{3}{4}$–90 in (200–229 cm); female 34 in (86 cm)**

The dramatic display of the male Common Peafowl (often known as the Peacock) is a familiar sight in parks and gardens throughout the world, where it has been widely introduced as an ornamental bird.

In its native Asia it favors deciduous forests flanking hillside streams, with thick undergrowth and thorny creepers. It will also forage over farmland, particularly among dense, tall crops such as sugar cane. It has a broad diet, which includes grain, berries, green crops, insects, small reptiles and mammals.

The long train of the male consists of greatly elongated upper tail coverts, which can be thrown up and spread out into a spectacular fan by raising the tail beneath. Thus glorified, the male will back slowly toward a potential mate before swiveling around to dazzle her with the full radiance of his display. Compliant females are gathered into a harem and jealously guarded.

11/ CONGO PEAFOWL
Afropavo congensis [S]

RANGE: **Congo and associated river systems**
HABITAT: **tropical rain forest**
SIZE: **$22\frac{3}{4}$–28 in (58–71 cm)**

The 49 species of pheasant are all natives of Asia, with one exception – the Congo Peafowl. This exquisite bird is a denizen of the dense tropical rain forests of central Africa, which effectively concealed it from western scientists until its "discovery" in 1936.

Although it resembles the Common Peafowl in build and diet – eating a wide variety of fruits and insects, including termites which it digs from their mounds – the Congo Peafowl has a quite different breeding system. Both sexes have superb iridescent plumage, and they are believed to form monogamous pairs. In captivity the hen bird lays 3 eggs which are incubated by both parents. An undisputed nest has never been found in the wild, but it is possible that the birds nest in trees.

FAMILY NUMIDIDAE
Guineafowl

Large ground-feeding birds with strong bills and long legs. Plumage typically black, spotted with white; sexes similar. Gregarious, roost in trees. Nest simple scrape on the ground. Eggs 6–22, cream to light brown. Incubation 23–30 days, chicks leave the nest 1–2 days after hatching. 6 species.

12/ HELMETED GUINEAFOWL
Numida meleagris

RANGE: **E Chad to Ethiopia, E to Rift Valley, S to borders of N Zaire, N Kenya and Uganda**
HABITAT: **open grassland**
SIZE: **21–$22\frac{3}{4}$ in (53–58 cm)**

Distinguished by the conspicuous horny casque on top of its naked, richly pigmented head, the Helmeted Guineafowl has been domesticated all over the world as a food species. In the wild it is a common resident throughout its range.

Outside the breeding season, Helmeted Guineafowl may forage in flocks consisting of several hundred birds, searching for bulbs, tubers, berries, insects and snails on savanna, farmland and scrub edge. Working together in a large flock may help the birds to locate scattered food resources, as well as providing some form of defence against predators, but during the breeding season the flock splits up into monogamous pairs. The clutch, consisting of 6–19 eggs, is laid in a scrape on the ground and is incubated by the female alone.

13/ VULTURINE GUINEAFOWL
Acryllium vulturinum

RANGE: **sub-Saharan Africa**
HABITAT: **edges of evergreen forest**
SIZE: **$19\frac{3}{4}$ in (50 cm)**

The largest and most impressive of the guineafowl, this species has a distinctive red eye and a flamboyant hackle of elongated, iridescent feathers striped in black, white and blue. Locally common throughout its range, it lives in matted thickets and tangled scrub at the margins of lowland forest, forming flocks of 20–30 birds which often follow troops of monkeys to feast on fallen fruit.

The flocks break up in the breeding season, as with other guineafowl, and the breeding adults form pairs. The clutch of 4–6 eggs is laid in a scrape on the ground, and incubated by the female for 24–30 days.

MESITES, BUTTONQUAILS, PLAINS-WANDERER, CRANES, LIMPKIN, TRUMPETERS

♀

PLAINS-WANDERER

race *sylvatica*
LITTLE BUTTONQUAIL

♀
QUAIL PLOVER

GRAY-WINGED
TRUMPETER

BLACK CROWNED
CRANE

race *pavonina*

juv

LIMPKIN

WHITE-BREASTED MESITE

race *tabida*
"Greater Sandhill Crane"

rust-stained

juv

juv

SANDHILL CRANE

DEMOISELLE CRANE

SARUS CRANE

race *antigone*

juv

BROLGA

juv

WHOOPING CRANE

juv

juv

SIBERIAN WHITE CRANE

juv

chick

COMMON CRANE

MESITES, BUTTONQUAILS, PLAINS-WANDERER, CRANES, LIMPKIN, TRUMPETERS

FAMILY MESITORNITHIDAE
Mesites

Medium-sized ground-dwellers. Seldom fly. Plumage brown or gray above, paler or spotted below. Sexes alike or different. Twig nests in bushes. Eggs 1–3, whitish, with brown spots. Incubation unknown, chicks leave nest soon after hatching. 3 species.

1/ WHITE-BREASTED MESITE
Mesitornis variegata R

RANGE: **3 tiny areas in W Madagascar**
HABITAT: **undisturbed dry forest**
SIZE: **9¾ in (25 cm)**

All 3 species of mesite are found only in Madagascar and all are endangered. This thrush-sized bird scratches about for insects among the dead leaves that carpet the forest floor. It has been seen only in 3 isolated pockets of remote forest; in 1986 it was rediscovered in one of these, in the Ankara nature reserve, having last been seen there in 1931. The main threat to this species is tree-felling, but if feral rats, cats or dogs become established in its last refuge, it will be even more at risk.

FAMILY TURNICIDAE
Buttonquails

Small to medium ground-dwelling quail-like birds, with only 3 toes. Plumage buff with brown, gray and cream markings; females brighter. Nest in ground hollow. Eggs 3–7, pale gray to buff, heavily marked with chestnut, gray or other colors. Incubation 12–14 days, chicks leave nest almost immediately after hatching. 15 species.

2/ LITTLE BUTTONQUAIL
Turnix sylvatica

RANGE: **S Spain, Africa, S and Southeast Asia, Indonesia, Philippines**
HABITAT: **dry grassland, scrub; sometimes crops**
SIZE: **5–6 in (13–15 cm)**

Buttonquails are similar in general appearance to quails (pp. 114–17), although they are not related to them. They have the peculiar habit of slinking low on the ground and rocking backward and forward on their feet.

Shy and secretive, the Little Buttonquail keeps to the undergrowth, where it feeds on grass seeds and some insects. The larger female advertises with a low, cooing call, dominates courtship and mates with several males in succession. Each male must incubate his clutch – for a period of 13 days – and rear the chicks alone.

3/ QUAIL PLOVER
Ortyxelos meiffrenii

RANGE: **a narrow band S of Sahara**
HABITAT: **very dry, sandy bush**
SIZE: **6 in (15 cm)**

Restricted to arid areas, the Quail Plover inhabits regions with enough rough, dry grasses to make it very difficult to see as it skulks secretively on the ground. If it is flushed from its hiding place, it takes to the air with a strange, jerky, butterfly-like flight, resembling the flight of a bush-lark –

hence its alternative common name of Lark Quail. When it flies, it reveals a distinctive black and white pattern on its wings.

The common names of this odd little bird, which is classified in a different genus from the rest of the buttonquails, reflect its puzzling appearance: it looks like a cross between a small, dumpy plover, a typical buttonquail and a lark. When it runs it looks rather like a miniature courser.

The Quail Plover has a very patchy distribution, although it is locally quite common, especially where the grass *Cenchurus catharticus* grows. Its nest is a shallow scrape lined with grass and often edged with small pebbles. The male incubates the 2 eggs alone.

FAMILY PEDIONOMIDAE
Plains-wanderer

There is only one species in this family.

4/ PLAINS-WANDERER
Pedionomus torquatus ?

RANGE: **inland SE Australia**
HABITAT: **sparse native grassland**
SIZE: **6–6¾ in (15–17 cm)**

The Plains-wanderer feeds during the day (not by night as was once believed), foraging for seeds and some insects. It walks furtively through the grass, sometimes stopping to bob its head like a wader or to stand on tiptoe and crane its neck to check for any trouble. When danger threatens, it prefers to freeze in a squatting position rather than take to the air.

The nest is a grass-lined scrape made under a clump of grass. The female, dominant in courtship, calls with a mournful booming and may mate with several males. The clutch of 2–5 yellowish eggs with gray markings is incubated mainly by the male for about 23 days. The chicks soon leave the nest and are reared by the male.

The Plains-wanderer has declined in numbers, due to conversion of much of its habitat to cropland and dense pasture. It is a sedentary bird, abandoning an area only when forced to do so by fire, cultivation or overgrazing.

FAMILY GRUIDAE
Cranes

Large, long-legged, long-necked birds. Plumage mainly white or gray, with colored plumes or bare skin. Males usually larger. Platform nest of vegetation on ground or in shallow water. Eggs 1–3 (up to 4 in Gray Crowned Crane), white or various colors. Incubation 28–36 days. Chicks leave nest soon after hatching; remain with parents until fledged at 2–4 months. 15 species.

5/ COMMON CRANE
Grus grus

RANGE: **N temperate Eurasia; winters S to N Africa, India and Southeast Asia**
HABITAT: **breeds in open forest swamps and moorland bogs; winters in shallow wetlands**
SIZE: **43¼–47¼ in (110–120 cm)**

Like the other members of the crane family, the Common Crane is famous for its dancing display. This is performed not only during courtship, but also by small groups of birds. The birds walk around in circles, bowing, bobbing, pirouetting and stopping, bending to pick up small objects and toss them over their heads. These rituals are interspersed with graceful jumps high into the air.

The species' main call is a loud trumpeting, which is uttered by courting pairs as they stand facing each other with outspread wings, necks stretched and bills pointing skyward. It is also heard from the *V*-formations of migrating flocks.

6/ SANDHILL CRANE
Grus canadensis

RANGE: **breeds NE Siberia, Alaska, Canada, N USA; winters S USA to C Mexico; small resident populations in Florida and Mississippi, Cuba**
HABITAT: **tundra, marshes, grassland, fields**
SIZE: **42 in (107 cm)**

Sandhill Cranes may congregate at migration stopovers or on the wintering grounds in flocks of hundreds, creating an extraordinary din with their grating, rattling, trumpetlike calls. They are ground-gleaners, foraging for a wide variety of plants, aquatic invertebrates, insects, worms, frogs and small mammals.

There are 5 races, varying in size. The race illustrated, the Greater Sandhill Crane *G. c. tabida*, breeds from southwest British Columbia to northern California and Nevada. The rusty-brown color of adults in some areas is due to their habit of probing with their bills into mud and soil containing reddish iron oxide. When they preen, they transfer the stain to their plumage.

7/ WHOOPING CRANE
Grus americana   E

RANGE: **breeds C Canada; winters coastal Texas**
HABITAT: **breeds on muskeg and prairie pools; prairie and stubble fields on migration; winters on coastal marshes**
SIZE: **51 in (130 cm)**

In flight, adult Whooping Cranes show black outer flight feathers that contrast with their otherwise white plumage. Like all cranes, they fly with their heads and necks extended. With a total population of fewer than 200 individuals, it is one of the world's most endangered birds. Attempts are being made to start new populations by using Sandhill Cranes as foster parents.

Whooping Cranes are opportunist feeders, taking a wide variety of plant and animal food from dry land and shallow water. The courtship ceremony involves elaborate dances, and the bird's most common call is a whooping or trumpeting *ker-loo*.

8/ SARUS CRANE
Grus antigone

RANGE: **India, Southeast Asia, N Australia**
HABITAT: **cultivated plains, marshes, river banks**
SIZE: **47¼–55 in (120–140 cm)**

One of the larger members of its family, the Sarus Crane has recently extended its range to Australia, a jump of nearly 3,000 mls (5,000 km) from its range in Southeast Asia. It was first identified there in 1964 in northeast Queensland. Over the next 10 years, it was reported from more than 30 localities and it now seems to be well established and more than holding its own in competition with the smaller, native Brolga.

9/ BROLGA
Grus rubicundus

RANGE: **N and E Australia S to Victoria**
HABITAT: **shallow, open swampland and wet grassland**
SIZE: **37½–49¼ in (95–125 cm)**

The Brolga is a large, gray crane native to damp habitats in parts of Australia. It has declined in abundance in the southeastern section of its range because of the drainage of shallow wetlands. It feeds mainly on tubers, which it digs up from the mud with its bill, but will also eat grain, insects, mollusks and small vertebrates.

Brolgas perform elaborate dancing displays, bowing and stretching, advancing and retiring,

with much wing-flapping and trumpeting. They also leap high and plane down again, and hurl pieces of grass or twigs. Elements of their display have been incorporated into Aboriginal dances.

10/ SIBERIAN WHITE CRANE
Grus leucogeranus   E

RANGE: **breeds in 2 areas in N Siberia; winters around Caspian Sea, India and perhaps China**
HABITAT: **breeds on marshy tundra and forest tundra; winters in shallow freshwater wetlands**
SIZE: **47¼–55 in (120–140 cm)**

Formerly more widespread and fairly common, this is now one of the rarest cranes, probably numbering no more than a few hundred breeding individuals. It seems to be intolerant of disturbance and unable to adapt to change.

The principal known wintering site of the Siberian White Crane is at the Bharatpur nature reserve in northern India. Here, a mere 30–40 birds arrive each autumn, having run the gauntlet of a long migration, hunters and the Himalayas.

In a truly international conservation initiative, Siberian White Crane eggs are taken from nests in the Siberian tundra and flown to the International Crane Foundation in the USA. The chicks are reared by hand, to produce eggs when they are 6 or more years old. These eggs are then flown back to the USSR, where they are placed in the nests of Common Cranes. The aim of this captive breeding program is to establish a viable population in European Russia.

11/ DEMOISELLE CRANE
Anthropoides virgo

RANGE: **breeds SE Europe and C Asia; winters NE Africa, India E to Burma**
HABITAT: **breeds on marshes and drier steppes; winters on open wetlands and agricultural land**
SIZE: **35½–39½ in (90–100 cm)**

On migration, large numbers of these cranes regularly cross high mountain ranges, including the Himalayas. At one pass, over 60,000 were counted in a 12-day period in autumn, most flying at altitudes of 16,500–26,000 ft (5,000–8,000 m).

Wintering flocks of Demoiselle Cranes can number many thousands and may cause damage to arable crops before the harvest. After the harvest, the birds clean up the spilt grain and take many invertebrates from the ground.

12/ BLACK CROWNED CRANE
Balearica pavonina

RANGE: **Africa, from Senegal to C Ethiopia, N Uganda and NW Kenya**
HABITAT: **open swamps, marshes, grassland**
SIZE: **43¼–51 in (110–130 cm)**

This crane is a widespread and familiar bird in some parts of its range and is well regarded by local people. A closely related species, the Gray Crowned Crane *B. regulorum*, sometimes regarded as merely a race of this species, occurs in southern Africa.

A pair or small group of Crowned Cranes begin their display by bowing several times toward one another. Then, spreading their wings, they proceed to hop and prance, jumping 3–6 ft (1–2 m) into the air and landing gently on dangling feet.

FAMILY ARAMIDAE
Limpkin
There is only one species in this family.

13/ LIMPKIN
Aramus guarauna

RANGE: **SE USA, Antilles, S Mexico E of Andes to N Argentina**
HABITAT: **marshes, open or wooded swamps, mangroves**
SIZE: **23–28 in (58–71 cm)**

The Limpkin is a long-legged wading bird which flies with its neck and head extended. It is largely terrestrial, has rounded wings and makes only short, low flights. The call, often given at night, consists of a variety of shrieks and screams, or melancholy wails and cries. Limpkins walk with an undulating tread so that they appear to be limping – hence their common name.

Limpkins probe and grasp with their laterally compressed bill, which is well adapted for removing freshwater snails from their shells. The birds also feed on mussels, and occasionally on seeds, small reptiles and frogs, insects, worms and crayfish. Although usually solitary, they sometimes hunt in small groups. The nest is a woven mat of reeds and sticks built in or under shrubs and trees near water. The normal clutch contains 6–7 brown-spotted buff eggs, which are incubated for about 20 days. The chicks leave the nest the day they hatch but remain with their parents.

FAMILY PSOPHIIDAE
Trumpeters
Ground-dwellers. Thickset body, small head. Weak, rounded wings. Plumage mainly black. Sexes alike. Nest in tree holes or palms. Eggs 6–10, white or green. Incubation period unknown, chicks leave nest soon after hatching. 3 species.

14/ GRAY-WINGED TRUMPETER
Psophia crepitans

RANGE: **Guianas, E Venezuela to W Ecuador, N Peru, Brazil N of the Amazon**
HABITAT: **tropical rain forest**
SIZE: **18–21 in (46–53 cm)**

This bird is sometimes known as the Common Trumpeter. A gregarious species, it feeds on the rain forest floor and roosts in flocks of up to 20 individuals. It is largely terrestrial and a poor flier, although it roosts in trees up to 33 ft (10 m) above the ground. Like the other members of the family, it is a noisy bird, uttering a variety of booming and trumpeting calls – hence the common name for this group of birds.

Trumpeters eat mainly fallen fruits, nuts and insects, and have been known to follow along beneath foraging arboreal animals, pecking at the debris dropped to the ground. Their courtship displays are noisy affairs, often conducted by groups; birds strut, dance and even somersault.

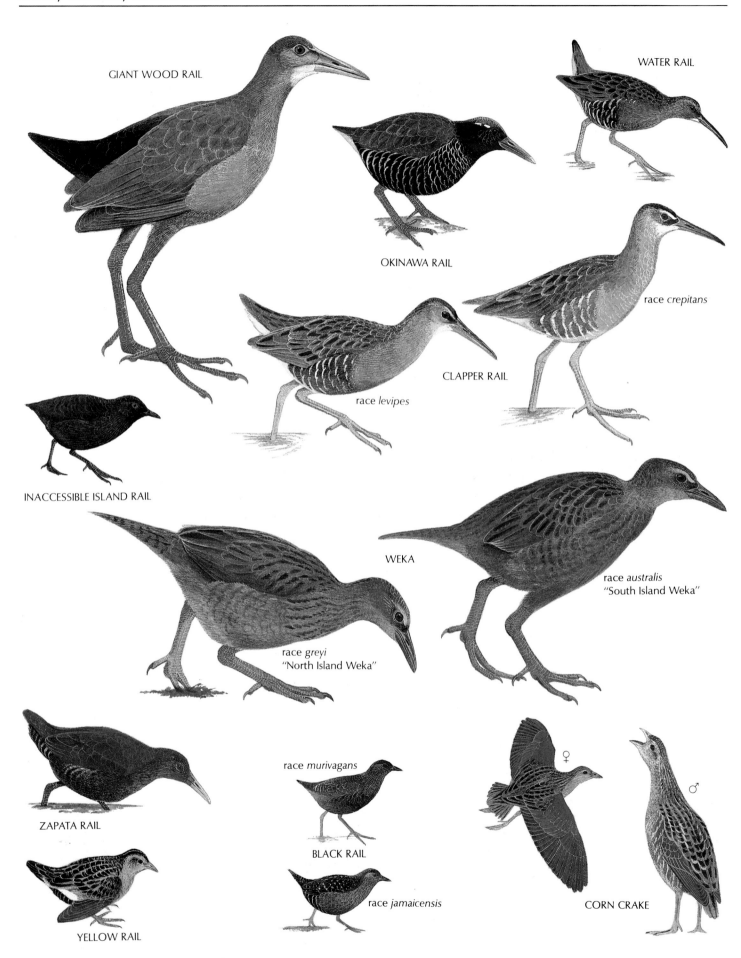

GIANT WOOD RAIL

WATER RAIL

OKINAWA RAIL

race *crepitans*

INACCESSIBLE ISLAND RAIL

CLAPPER RAIL

race *levipes*

WEKA

race *australis*
"South Island Weka"

race *greyi*
"North Island Weka"

ZAPATA RAIL

race *murivagans*

♀

♂

BLACK RAIL

race *jamaicensis*

CORN CRAKE

YELLOW RAIL

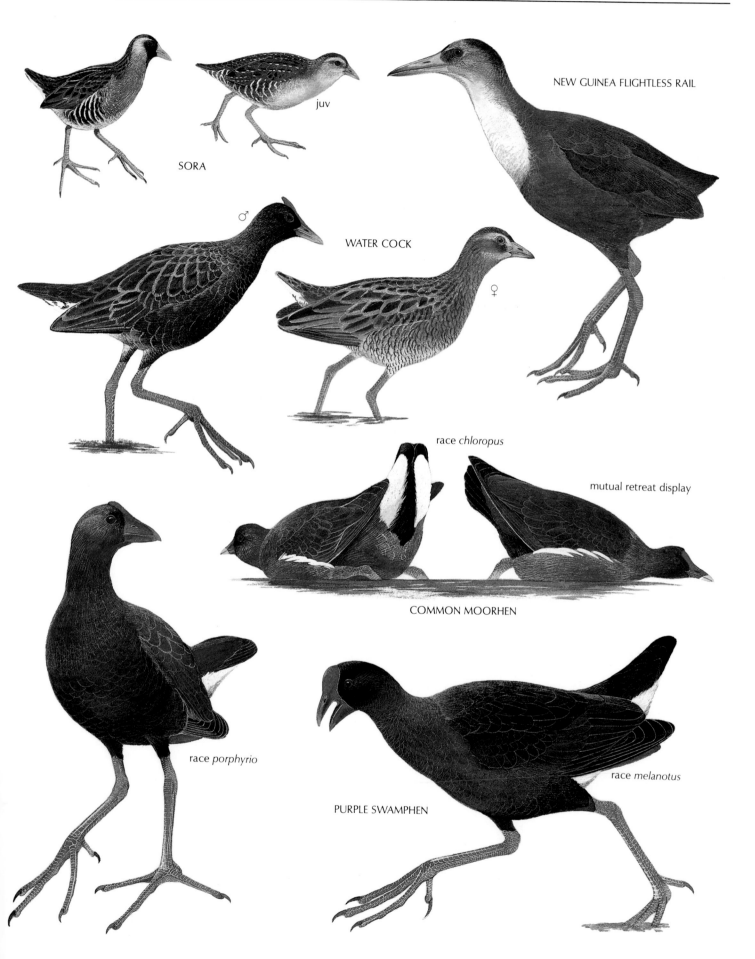

NEW GUINEA FLIGHTLESS RAIL

juv

SORA

♂

WATER COCK

♀

race *chloropus*

mutual retreat display

COMMON MOORHEN

race *porphyrio*

race *melanotus*

PURPLE SWAMPHEN

RAILS, CRAKES, GALLINULES

FAMILY RALLIDAE
Rails

Small to medium ground-dwelling birds with long legs and short, rounded wings. Uniform in structure, but family splits naturally into 3 groups: the rails; the crakes and gallinules; and the more aquatic coots. Mostly drab brown, reddish-brown or gray, with pale spots or flashes in some species; some more brightly colored. Sexes generally similar. Nest on ground or in bushes. Eggs 2–16, whitish, yellowish or brownish, often with reddish, gray, brown or black spots or blotches. Incubation 20–30 days. Chicks leave nest soon after hatching to be cared for by both parents; independent in up to 8 weeks. 124 species.

1/ GIANT WOOD RAIL
Eulabeornis ypecaha
RANGE: Brazil, Paraguay, Uruguay, Argentina
HABITAT: wet river valleys with good cover
SIZE: 21 in (53 cm)

Like most rails, this species is a secretive, cautious bird. It usually stays well concealed, but if there is no obvious danger it will display an engaging curiosity. It feeds alone during the day, using its long bill to probe the soft soil and plant debris for small animals; but at night the birds often gather in small groups just before roosting and join in a chorus of loud wails and screams.

These rails appear to breed in isolated pairs, nesting about 3 ft (1 m) above the ground in the branches of shrubs or small trees. The 5 or so glossy eggs vary in color between different nests from a clear white to pastel yellow or even pink.

2/ OKINAWA RAIL
Rallus okinawae   ?
RANGE: N Okinawa Island, S Japan
HABITAT: dense upland evergreen forest, near swampy or grassy areas
SIZE: 11 in (28 cm)

Short-winged and effectively flightless, the Okinawa Rail is typical of many species of rail that have evolved on islands. With no native predators to escape from, flight was unnecessary, so the birds abandoned it as a waste of energy.

Although this particular rail had been seen alive a few times over the previous 3 years, it was not described scientifically until 1981, when a roadside carcass was found and examined. The Okinawa Rail's population of some 500 birds is threatened by deforestation. It is closely related to the more widespread Barred Rail *R. torquatus* found on islands in the west Pacific. Like the Barred Rail, it roosts in trees, eats large insects and other invertebrates, and lays 4 eggs.

3/ WATER RAIL
Rallus aquaticus
RANGE: Eurasia, from Iceland to Japan; N Africa
HABITAT: marshes, swamps, wet meadows
SIZE: 11 in (28 cm)

With its very narrow body, the Water Rail has the ideal build for slipping noiselessly, in a rather rat-like fashion, through the reed stems of its habitat.

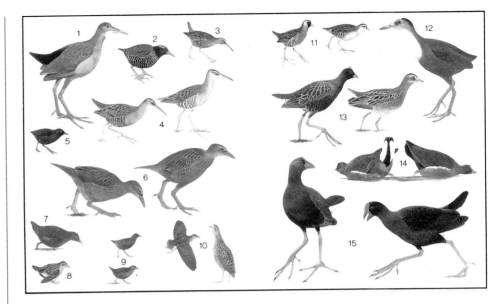

Although one of the most widespread and common rails, it is a shy, skulking bird, particularly in summer, but when the marshes freeze in winter it often emerges to forage across open ground.

The Water Rail will tackle a wide variety of prey, from insects to amphibians and nestling birds, and may leap up to 3 ft (1 m) to snatch a dragonfly from its perch above the water. Like almost all rails, it can swim well when necessary. Although rarely seen during the breeding season, it is often heard then and at other times as it utters a wide range of loud, blood-curdling groans and piglike grunts and squeals, a process known as "sharming." The nest is well hidden, often in a tussock of rushes, and the 5 or more highly mobile chicks, covered in black down, are soon able to race around the marsh after their parents.

4/ CLAPPER RAIL
Rallus longirostris
RANGE: S Canada to N Peru; Caribbean islands
HABITAT: brackish estuaries and salt marsh, especially with glasswort plants
SIZE: 12½–18 in (32–46 cm)

The species takes its common name from the loud clattering, cackling calls that sound like an old-fashioned clapper or rattle. These birds characteristically respond to thunder with a chorus of vocal response. Once a common sight on salt marshes throughout much of America, the Clapper Rail has suffered badly from habitat loss and hunting over the last 50 years. Even without these pressures, it leads a precarious existence, nesting among salt marsh grasses where it is liable to lose whole clutches of eggs to a single high spring tide. When the eggs do survive to hatch, however, the downy, black chicks, like the adults, can swim well and even submerge by grasping underwater plants with their feet when threatened.

Clapper Rails feed mainly on crabs and smaller crustaceans, supplemented by seeds and tubers. In severe winters the northern birds move south, but most are resident.

5/ INACCESSIBLE ISLAND RAIL
Atlantisia rogersi   R
RANGE: Inaccessible Island (S Atlantic)
HABITAT: tussock grass
SIZE: 5 in (12.5 cm)

This rail, which weighs a mere 1⅕ oz (34.7 g) is the world's smallest flightless bird. Discovered as late as 1923, it lives rather like a small mammal, constructing runs and burrows through the roots of windy and exposed tussock grass meadows. Almost 2,000 mls (3,200 km) from land both to east and west, Inaccessible Island is uninhabited and very small, with a total area of only 4½ sq mls (12 sq km). There are an estimated 4,000 Inaccessible Island Rails but, like almost all flightless rails, they would be easy meat for ground predators and their continued survival will be at risk should cats, rats or other predators be introduced to the island.

6/ WEKA
Gallirallus australis
RANGE: New Zealand
HABITAT: scrubland, forest edge
SIZE: 21 in (53 cm)

Wekas are very large, flightless rails with powerful bills and feet. They are inquisitive and omnivorous birds, with a diet that includes grass, seeds, fruit, mice, birds, eggs, beetles and snails. They frequently raid garbage pails and even enter fowl runs to eat the chicks. They can be voracious predators of other ground-dwelling birds and have upset the natural population balance on some of the islands to which they have been introduced. Conversely, Wekas kill many rats.

There are 4 races, distinguished by details of plumage and slight differences in size. The North Island race *G. a. greyi*, with grayer underparts, was once more widespread, but is now found only in the Gisborne district in the west, where it thrives in both rural and urban habitats; it has also been reintroduced to other parts of North Island, sometimes with success. The pale-colored Buff Weka *G. a. hectori* was once found in the east of South Island, but was extinct there by the early 1920s. Fortunately, it had been introduced to Chatham Island in 1905 and the population there is thriving. The race *G. a. australis*, which is quite common in parts of the western side of South Island, has a streaked red-brown and black breast; there is also a dark phase in the southwest. The Stewart Island race *G. g. scotti* also has a dark phase.

7/ ZAPATA RAIL
Cyanolimnas cerverai   R

RANGE: **Cuba**
HABITAT: **dense, scrubby marshland**
SIZE: **11¾ in (30 cm)**

This little-known rail inhabits only one part of its Caribbean island home – the Zapata Swamp, southeast of Havana. It is a noisy bird with a loud, croaking alarm note, making it surprisingly easy to locate among the thick marshland plants.

It often has a trusting and inquisitive nature and, owing to its unusually short wings, is a poor flier. This makes it vulnerable to attack, but so far the remoteness of its swampland habitat has guaranteed its survival. It is distributed over a larger area of the Zapata Swamp than was previously thought and should be in no immediate danger, unless there is a severe drought, fire or some other such catastrophe.

8/ YELLOW RAIL
Coturnicops noveboracensis

RANGE: **E Canada to Mexico; also Siberia, China, Japan**
HABITAT: **hay meadows and tussock grass near fresh running water**
SIZE: **7 in (18 cm)**

With its short bill and compact form, this bird is more of a crake than the rail its name suggests. It is one of the few members of its family to occur in both the Old and New Worlds. In North America it is most familiar as a winter migrant, and many birds are shot as they fly south.

In summer it has very precise habitat requirements, which include plenty of clear running water and a good supply of snails. It finds both of these in remote, sheltered hay meadows, where it often gives itself away by a call that sounds like stones being clacked together.

The nest is superbly concealed in the grass. The nestlings are very mobile by 2 days after hatching and are able to haul themselves through the vegetation, using the well-developed claw on each wing. They are fed by the parents at first, but gradually become independent when they are about 3 weeks old.

9/ BLACK RAIL
Laterallus jamaicensis

RANGE: **S North America, Caribbean, Central and South America to N Chile**
HABITAT: **marshes, among reeds and sedges**
SIZE: **6¾ in (17 cm)**

Timid and unpredictable, this tiny bird is extremely hard to follow. At the slightest alarm it will leave its feeding area or nest and vanish noiselessly into the dense vegetation. If it has to flee, it never attempts a long run across open

ground, but darts like lightning from one tussock to the next.

There are 4 races, 2 of which are illustrated: *L. j. murivagans* from coastal Peru and *L. j. jamaicensis* of central and eastern USA, Cuba and Jamaica. The Black Rail's semiroofed nest of fine grasses might be mistaken for that of a finch in the absence of the 4–7 pale cream eggs with reddish spots, which are typical of the rails.

10/ CORN CRAKE
Crex crex   ?

RANGE: **Europe, W Asia, N Africa; winters in sub-Saharan Africa**
HABITAT: **coarse grassland, hay meadows**
SIZE: **9¾ in (25 cm)**

The Corn Crake has suffered a dramatic decline over the last century – probably as a result of changing agricultural techniques and the increased use of pesticides.

The males are very vocal just before the eggs are laid, pointing their heads up and producing a sound like a splinter drawn across a comb. Advertising their ownership of territory to the females and challenging rival males, they utter their craking call both day and night. Once incubation is underway, however, they fall silent.

In flight, they can be recognized by their rich chestnut wing patches. Although their flight appears weak, fluttering and brief, with dangling legs, they can fly fast and strongly when they migrate by night, traveling long distances to their winter quarters as far away as South Africa.

11/ SORA
Porzana carolina

RANGE: **Canada to Venezuela and Peru, including Caribbean islands**
HABITAT: **freshwater marshes, also wet meadows in prairie regions; winters by salt and brackish waters**
SIZE: **9 in (23 cm)**

Many thousands of these birds fell to the shot-guns of American hunters each year as they migrated to their coastal wintering grounds; now the birds face a threat from the destruction of their breeding marshes. Although they are still among the most abundant and widespread of American rails, the days are gone when dense flocks of Soras were to be found huddled on salt marshes, islands and even seagoing vessels.

In its summer haunts the Sora is a shy bird, rarely seen, and usually detected by its call: a loud, staccato *cuck* accompanied by sneezing and whinnying sounds. It lays a large clutch – usually 8–12 eggs – which is incubated by both sexes.

12/ NEW GUINEA FLIGHTLESS RAIL
Amaurornis ineptus

RANGE: **N and S New Guinea**
HABITAT: **mangrove swamps, bamboo thickets at edges of rivers**
SIZE: **14–15 in (36–38 cm)**

This little-known flightless rail is so large, powerful and stout-limbed that it resembles a miniature cassowary (pp. 42–45). It has a heavy, hatchet-

like bill and strong feet with which it can defend itself against most predators, including the dogs introduced to New Guinea. It also uses its powerful bill to dispatch and devour rats. A wary bird, the New Guinea Flightless Rail can run swiftly and may also take to the branches of shrubs or trees to escape danger. It roosts in trees, usually more than 24 in (60 cm) above the ground. Like many other rails, it has a harsh voice, uttering an *aaah-aaah* call rather like the squealing of a pig.

13/ WATER COCK
Gallicrex cinerea

RANGE: **India to Japan, Philippines, Sulawesi (Celebes)**
HABITAT: **reedy swamps, paddy fields, sugar cane, brackish marshes**
SIZE: **17 in (43 cm)**

Sometimes known by its Hindi name, Kora, this largely vegetarian species is a twilight feeder, which eats shoots, tubers and seeds, as well as the odd insect. In the breeding season the males can be aggressively territorial, but during the rest of the year it is a cautious, retiring bird, scuttling for cover at the first hint of danger.

During the breeding season, the male can be distinguished from his mate by his almost black plumage and a vivid, blood-red frontal shield. In winter he loses this head ornamentation and becomes brown and gray like the female. The pair builds a cootlike nest of aquatic vegetation and raises 2 broods of 3–6 chicks each year.

14/ COMMON MOORHEN
Gallinula chloropus

RANGE: **throughout temperate and tropical Eurasia, Africa, North and South America; but not Australasia**
HABITAT: **small ponds, rivers, wet marshes**
SIZE: **13¾ in (35 cm)**

Possibly the most abundant species of rail in the world, the Common Moorhen is an unlikely candidate for success, for it is a poor flier and a barely adequate swimmer, preferring to search for food on foot with a delicate, high-stepping gait. Males are highly territorial and will fight with their large feet; many are badly injured in the process. The chicks become independent very quickly and often help their parents feed a second brood.

15/ PURPLE SWAMPHEN
Porphyrio porphyrio

RANGE: **Europe, Africa, S Asia, Southeast Asia to Australasia**
HABITAT: **reedbeds, scrubby marsh margins, tussock swamps**
SIZE: **17¾ in (45 cm)**

The Purple Swamphen has earned itself a bad reputation in some areas owing to its habit of feeding on the tender shoots of cultivated rice. Largely vegetarian, it may become extremely numerous where food is plentiful; scores of birds can often be seen in the early morning, when they climb the marsh vegetation to sunbathe as the first rays of dawn penetrate the mist. Usually, a single pair seems to do all the nesting; occasionally, a second female may lay in the nest.

GALLINULES AND COOTS, FINFOOTS, KAGU, SUNBITTERN, SERIEMAS, BUSTARDS

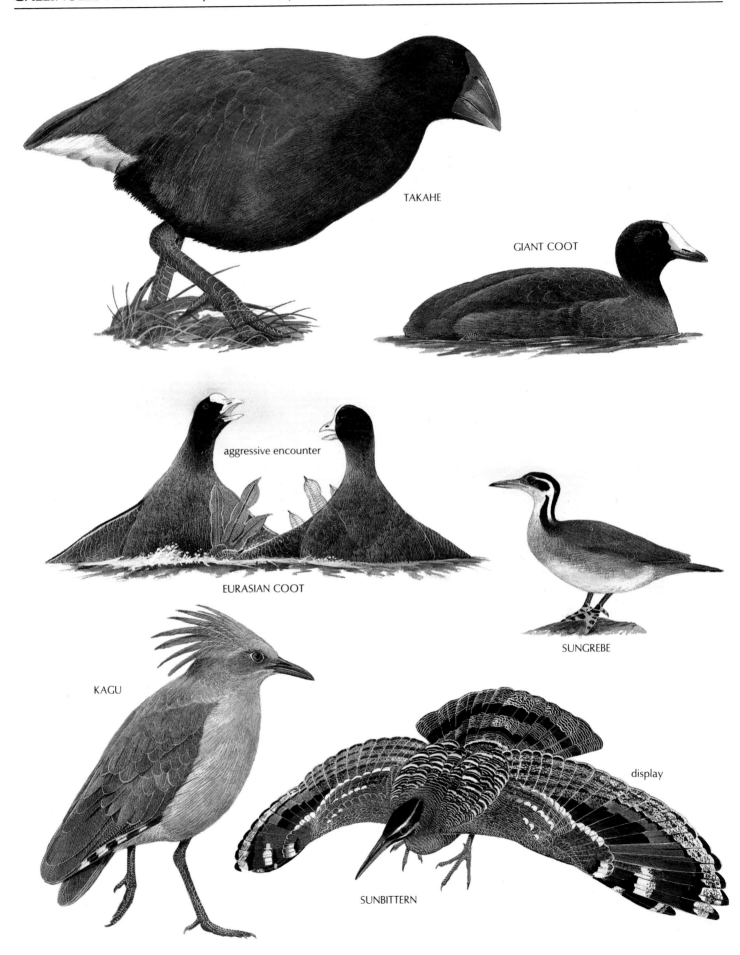

TAKAHE

GIANT COOT

aggressive encounter

EURASIAN COOT

SUNGREBE

KAGU

display

SUNBITTERN

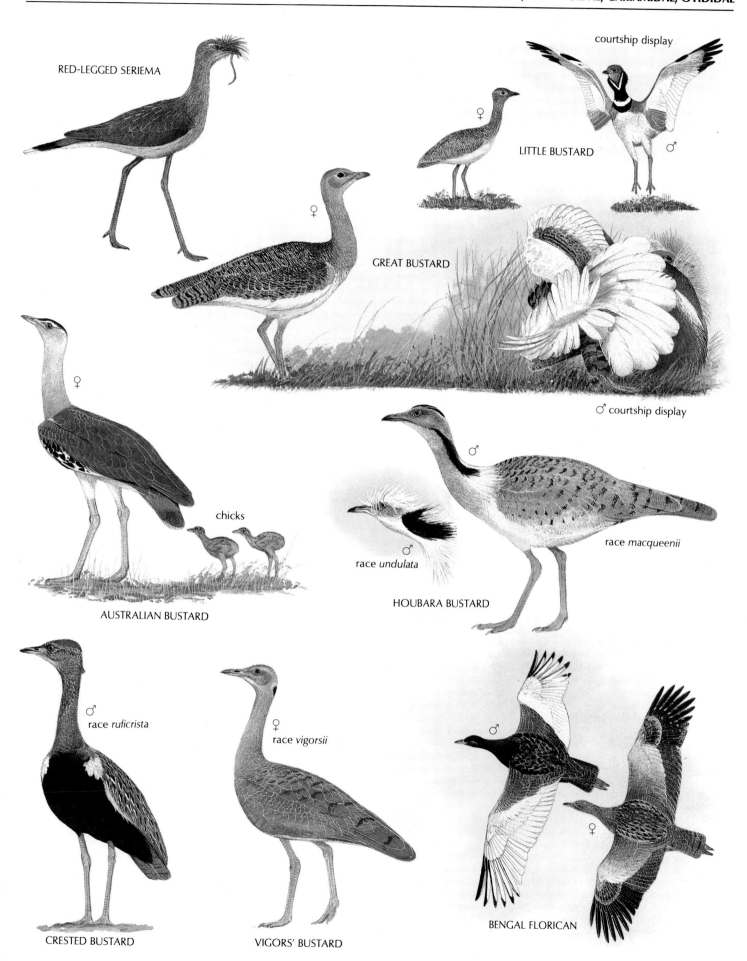

RED-LEGGED SERIEMA

courtship display

♀ LITTLE BUSTARD ♂

♀ GREAT BUSTARD

♂ courtship display

♀

chicks

♂ race *undulata*

♂

race *macqueenii*

AUSTRALIAN BUSTARD

HOUBARA BUSTARD

♂ race *ruficrista*

♀ race *vigorsii*

♂

♀

CRESTED BUSTARD

VIGORS' BUSTARD

BENGAL FLORICAN

GALLINULES AND COOTS, FINFOOTS, KAGU, SUNBITTERN, SERIEMAS, BUSTARDS

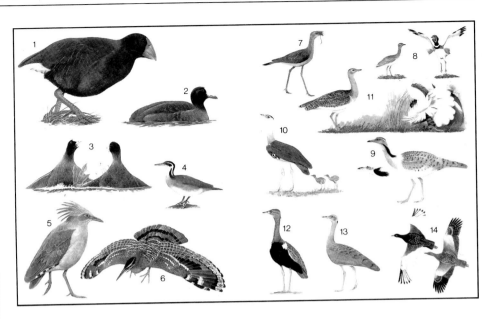

1/ TAKAHE
Porphyrio mantelli　　E

RANGE: **New Zealand, now restricted to Murchison and Kepler ranges in SW South Island; introduced to Mana Island**
HABITAT: **mountain tussock grassland and (rarely) adjacent woodland**
SIZE: **24¾ in (63 cm)**

Like many other flightless island birds, this large rail has suffered a catastrophic decline in the face of competition and predation by introduced animals. It was first described scientifically in 1849. Its numbers dwindled rapidly until, by 1900, it was believed to be extinct.

In 1948 it was rediscovered living in remote alpine and subalpine tussock grassland in southwest South Island. Here it feeds on the seed heads and tender bases of the grasses. Today it has to compete for the grass with introduced deer and generally loses the contest.

Takahes mate for life, nesting on the ground among tussocks. Introduced predators, such as stoats, take a heavy toll of the eggs and young, and the breeding success rate is low. Captive breeding, conservation and predator control have helped to preserve the species, but the Takahe remains endangered.

2/ GIANT COOT
Fulica gigantea

RANGE: **Peru, Chile, Bolivia and Argentina**
HABITAT: **mountain lakes, usually above 11,500 ft (3,500 m) in puna**
SIZE: **23½ in (60 cm)**

Life at high altitudes is especially harsh in winter, but instead of migrating to lower altitudes, the Giant Coots congregate in small flocks around the widely scattered volcanic springs of the region. There they find pools that are kept clear of ice by the warm water and enough food to see them through until spring. This bird builds a large floating nest, up to 10 ft (3 m) in diameter, anchored to emergent weed in shallow water.

3/ EURASIAN COOT
Fulica atra

RANGE: **widespread through Europe, Asia, Japan and Australasia**
HABITAT: **large ponds, lakes and marshes, usually at low altitude**
SIZE: **17 in (43 cm)**

The most widespread and common of all the coots, the species is a bold and familiar bird in Europe. It feeds mainly on aquatic plants, but it also eats aquatic insects.

During the spring breeding season both sexes are extremely territorial, and the slightest violation of a boundary by another coot will provoke a tremendous show of strength as the intruder is attacked with both claws and bill.

In winter coots become very sociable, flocking together in hundreds or even thousands on food-rich lakes and rivers. Juvenile birds are much paler than the adults, with lighter, duller legs, a grayish bill and brown eyes, and lack the adults' white frontal shield.

FAMILY HELIORNITHIDAE
Finfoots

Medium to large, elongated, grebelike, aquatic birds. Long head and neck, broadly lobed toes and long, graduated, stiff tail. Plumage brown and gray with white markings. Females smaller. Nest a shallowly indented platform of twigs lined with leaves, on low branches or flood debris. Eggs 2–4, cream, with reddish-brown or purple markings. Incubation 11 days (Sungrebe); naked helpless chicks are carried from nest by parent even before their eyes have opened (Sungrebe). 3 species.

4/ SUNGREBE
Heliornis fulica

RANGE: **Mexico to Bolivia and Argentina**
HABITAT: **heavily forested lowland streams, freshwater ponds and lagoons**
SIZE: **11–11¾ in (28–30 cm)**

Named for their cootlike lobed feet, the finfoots appear to be close relatives of the rails, although superficially they resemble grebes. The Sungrebe, or American Finfoot, frequents the slower backwaters of large streams where it rarely emerges from the shade of bankside vegetation. It eats mollusks, insects and other small animals, as well as some seeds. It often swims half submerged.

The nest is built in a bush over water. When the 2 chicks hatch, they are removed and carried by the male, both on the water and in the air, clamped tightly into pouches beneath each wing.

FAMILY RHYNOCHETIDAE
Kagu

There is only one species in this family.

5/ KAGU
Rhynochetos jubatus　　E

RANGE: **New Caledonia**
HABITAT: **dense forest**
SIZE: **23½ in (60 cm)**

One of the most endangered birds in the world, the Kagu is another example of a ground-dwelling island bird that has been virtually wiped out by introduced predators and habitat loss. Effectively flightless, it feeds on the ground, stalking over the forest floor with a curiously upright stance and probing in the soil with its large bill for grubs, worms and snails.

Both sexes have the flamboyant crest, and during courtship they dance around each other with wings spread to display the black, red and white bars on the slate-gray plumage. They nest on the ground, both parents taking turns to incubate the single cream or yellowish egg with red-brown and gray blotches for 36 days. The young bird becomes independent some 14 weeks after hatching.

FAMILY EURYPYGIDAE

There is only one species in this family.

6/ SUNBITTERN
Eurypyga helias

RANGE: **S Mexico to Bolivia and C Brazil**
HABITAT: **forested streams, rivers, lakes**
SIZE: **18 in (46 cm)**

This bird forages with slow, sedate steps and occasionally wades through shallow water, but will fly across deeper pools. It feeds mainly on insects, spiders, small crustaceans, frogs and small fish, seizing them from the mud and rocks, from beneath the water or among damp litter on the forest floor, with heronlike jabs of its long, straight bill.

Although the Sunbittern spends most of its time in the shade, it is sometimes found in sunny clearings, when its spectacular display is seen to best advantage. The bird lowers its neck, spreads its wings and raises and fans its tail, suddenly revealing the striking areas of orange-chestnut surrounded by pale orange-buff on its primary wing feathers. These resemble a sunset – hence the bird's common name.

The Sunbittern lays its 2 whitish or buff dark-blotched eggs in a bulky, globular nest of stems and leaves in a tree some 10–20 ft (3–6 m) above the ground. Both sexes incubate the eggs for about 27 days; the nestling period is some 21 days.

FAMILY CARIAMIDAE
Seriemas
Large, terrestrial birds with long necks, long legs and elongated bodies. Plumage gray-brown and white, with black and white on wings and black or black and white at end of tail. Nest of sticks in bush or low tree. Eggs 2, whitish to buff with brown, gray or purple markings. Incubation 25–26 days; chicks, though covered in down on hatching, remain in nest until they are well grown. 2 species.

7/ RED-LEGGED SERIEMA
Cariama cristata
RANGE: C and E Brazil S through Paraguay to N Argentina
HABITAT: mixed grassland and open scrub
SIZE: $27\frac{1}{2}$ in (70 cm)

The Red-legged, or Crested, Seriema rarely flies, usually escaping danger by running rapidly with its head lowered. It spends all its time on the ground except for roosting and nesting low in trees and bushes. It has an omnivorous diet, which regularly includes small snakes.

Seriemas are hunted for their meat and are shy and wary of humans. Red-legged Seriemas are often taken from the nest and reared among domestic chickens where they make excellent "watchdogs," warning farmers of approaching predators or other intruders with their noisy yelping or screaming calls.

FAMILY OTIDIDAE
Bustards
Medium to large terrestrial birds with long legs, long necks and sturdy tapering bodies. Feet with 3 toes. Sexes usually differ in size and/or plumage. Plumage cryptic combinations of brown, buff, chestnut, gray, black and white. Nest a bare scrape in the ground. Eggs 1–6, olive, olive-brown, reddish. Incubation 20–25 days. Chicks leave nest soon after hatching, fledge at about 5 weeks. 22 species.

8/ LITTLE BUSTARD
Tetrax tetrax ?
RANGE: S Europe, NW Africa E to C Asia
HABITAT: open areas with tall grasses, open scrubland, farmland
SIZE: $15\frac{3}{4}$–$17\frac{3}{4}$ in (40–45 cm)

Short, stocky birds, these are among the lightweights of the bustard family, weighing less than $2\frac{1}{4}$ lb (1 kg). Outside the breeding season, the male's striking slate-gray chin and throat and black and white neck pattern are replaced by buff feathers with dark markings.

Little Bustards are gregarious birds, forming flocks of up to a thousand or more outside the breeding season at favored feeding grounds, including fields of crops. The displays of breeding males, both to advertise ownership of their territories to nearby males and to attract females, are comical to watch. They include surprisingly loud foot stamps, nasal *prrt* calls and a hissing sound produced by the short, seventh primary feather when the bird flaps its wings and leaps 3–6 ft (1–2 m) vertically into the air, revealing his white breast and underwings.

9/ HOUBARA BUSTARD
Chlamydotis undulata ?
RANGE: breeds Canary Islands, N Africa, Middle East, SW and C Asia; Asian breeders winter S to Arabia, Pakistan, Iran and NW India
HABITAT: semidesert, arid plains and steppes
SIZE: $21\frac{1}{2}$–$25\frac{1}{2}$ in (55–65 cm)

Outside the breeding season, the Houbara Bustard lives in small flocks of 4–10 birds, occasionally more, which feed and roost together. It is omnivorous, feeding on fruit, seeds, shoots, leaves and flowers as well as large insects, spiders, centipedes, small lizards and snakes.

The greatest threat to the Houbara Bustard is from excessive hunting, particularly in its winter quarters. As with other bustards, habitat destruction is also playing a part in its decline. The North African race *C. u. undulata* and the larger, paler race *C. u. macqueenii* from Egypt east to Central Asia are illustrated.

10/ AUSTRALIAN BUSTARD
Choriotis australis
RANGE: N and inland Australia
HABITAT: open woodland, grassland and shrub steppe
SIZE: $31\frac{1}{2}$–$47\frac{1}{4}$ in (80–120 cm)

This species was once quite common, but has declined greatly since the European settlement of Australia, due to heavy hunting, agriculture and the depredations of introduced mammals.

The male Australian Bustard displays by inflating his neck with air, so that the long neck feathers spread out into a great fan or apron, drooping his wings and raising his tail. He struts about in this posture with his head thrown back, uttering loud booming and roaring noises. He mates with any females attracted to his small display mound.

11/ GREAT BUSTARD
Otis tarda ?
RANGE: Morocco, Iberia, parts of N and C Europe, Turkey, parts of S USSR
HABITAT: extensive gently undulating grassy plains and steppes, lightly wooded areas, farmland
SIZE: $29\frac{1}{2}$–$41\frac{1}{4}$ in (75–105 cm)

This imposing bird is the world's heaviest flying bird: a particularly large male can weigh as much as 40 lb (18 kg). Females are much lighter, at up to 11 lb (5 kg). Great Bustards are sociable outside the breeding season, forming large flocks that move around in search of seasonally available plant and invertebrate food. Many flocks contain only one sex, especially immature males.

At the onset of the breeding season, mature males leave the flock and make their way to the traditional display grounds. Several males display together, each raising and spreading his tail so that it lies flat along his back, retracting his neck and inflating his throat pouch with air. This exposes the white neck and undertail feathers. At the same time, the bird twists his partially opened wings to reveal white "rosettes" of feathers on either side of his body.

12/ CRESTED BUSTARD
Eupodotis ruficrista
RANGE: just S of Sahara, from N Senegal locally to W and E Sudan; E Africa, from Ethiopia to EC Tanzania; S Africa S to N South Africa
HABITAT: arid or semiarid savanna
SIZE: $19\frac{1}{2}$ in (50 cm)

This small, rather stocky bustard is found in 3 widely separated areas of Africa. Two of its 3 races, the small, scarce northern race *E. r. savilei* and the eastern race *E. r. gindiana* are sometimes regarded as separate species, Savile's Bustard and the Buff-crested Bustard. The southern race *E. r. ruficrista* is illustrated.

The Crested Bustard is usually encountered singly or in pairs. A secretive bird, it often avoids detection by hiding motionless in thick cover. Males perform dramatic "rocket flights," in which they call with increasing volume, then run forward and fly up vertically to about 100 ft (30 m), throw themselves upside-down, puff out their breast feathers and then drop vertically, flapping their wings to halt their fall at the last moment, then gliding down to land.

13/ VIGORS' BUSTARD
Eupodotis vigorsii
RANGE: W South Africa, S Namibia
HABITAT: dry, open, stony Karoo, semi-desert and desert edge with scattered shrubs and short grass
SIZE: 22–$23\frac{1}{2}$ in (56–60 cm)

Also known as the Black-throated Bustard or Karoo Korhaan, Vigors' Bustard is very variable in plumage, particularly in the redness of the upperparts, grayness of the underparts and overall intensity of color.

Vigors' Bustard lives in groups of up to 8 individuals, and each group defends a small territory of a few hundred yards radius for a month or more during the breeding season. It is a noisy bird, especially in the morning and sometimes at night, its calls carrying long distances. Pairs perform croaking duets, the female replying with a *kok* note to the male's *squark*.

14/ BENGAL FLORICAN
Houbaropsis bengalensis ?
RANGE: NE India, Nepal, Kampuchea, S Vietnam
HABITAT: plains with tall grasses interspersed with scattered shrubs
SIZE: 26–$26\frac{3}{4}$ in (66–68 cm)

All bustards are threatened by habitat destruction and hunting, but none more than the Bengal Florican, which is rare, patchily distributed and seriously at risk. There are probably only a few hundred birds left in India and Nepal, and the tiny populations in Indochina are unknown.

Unusually for a bustard, the female is slightly larger than the male and differs greatly in her plumage from the striking black and white male. The sexes remain more or less separate apart from the brief mating period. Males perform courtship displays in which they leap 25–30 ft (8–10 m) into the air, emitting a strange, deep humming sound and uttering loud croaks.

non-breeding

PHEASANT-TAILED JACANA

CRAB PLOVER

race *jacana* juv

race *hypomelaena*

WATTLED JACANA

race *jacana*

PALEARCTIC OYSTERCATCHER

♂

♀

GREATER PAINTED-SNIPE

AMERICAN BLACK OYSTERCATCHER

FAMILIES JACANIDAE, ROSTRATULIDAE, DROMADIDAE, HAEMATOPODIDAE, IBIDORHYNCHIDAE, RECURVIROSTRIDAE, BURHINIDAE

IBISBILL

PIED AVOCET

RED-NECKED AVOCET

chick

race *mexicanus*
"Black-necked Stilt"

race *knudseni*
"Hawaiian Stilt"

race *himantopus*
juv

race *himantopus*
BLACK-WINGED STILT

STONE-CURLEW

CAPE DIKKOP

BANDED STILT

BEACH THICK-KNEE

SHOREBIRDS: JACANAS, OYSTERCATCHERS, STILTS AND AVOCETS, THICK-KNEES AND OTHERS

FAMILY JACANIDAE
Jacanas

Medium, long-legged waterbirds. Extremely elongated toes and claws for walking on floating vegetation. Plumage mostly brown, with black and white on head. Females larger. Nest on floating leaves or platforms. Eggs 4, heavily marked and shiny. Incubation 22–24 days. Chicks leave nest soon after hatching, but depend on male for protection for some time. 8 species.

1/ PHEASANT-TAILED JACANA
Hydrophasianus chirurgus

RANGE: India to S China, Southeast Asia, Indonesia; N population winters in S Asia
HABITAT: well-vegetated fresh water
SIZE: 12¼ in (31 cm); up to 22¾ in (58 cm) in breeding plumage

The striking Pheasant-tailed Jacana's long, drooping tail, present only in the breeding season, is unique among the Charadriiformes. Each female mates with 7–10 males in a season and it is the males' responsibility to incubate the eggs. If disturbed, a male may remove the eggs to a safer spot by pressing each one between his throat and breast and walking backward over the vegetation. The young can run, swim and dive as soon as they leave the nest. When danger threatens, they may submerge themselves almost completely beneath a floating leaf at a command from their father.

2/ WATTLED JACANA
Jacana jacana

RANGE: Panama S to C Argentina; Trinidad
HABITAT: tropical freshwater ponds, marshes, streams with emergent vegetation
SIZE: 8–9 in (20–23 cm)

The Wattled Jacana runs across the surface of floating leaves, searching for snails and other invertebrates and pecking pieces of vegetation. It also frequents damp pastures. Its flight is straight, swift and close to the water and is interspersed with periods of gliding. The race *J.j. jacana* is found over most of the species' South American range, and the dark race *J.j. hypomelaena* occurs from western Panama to northern Colombia.

Females mate with more than one male in each season and compete vigorously with one another for the opportunity to mate. Since the males incubate and care for the young, one female may even destroy the eggs of a successful rival in order to gain access to a male. Studies in Panama showed that each female's territory overlapped with the territories of up to 3 males.

FAMILY ROSTRATULIDAE
Painted-snipes

Small, dumpy wading birds. Broad, rounded wings. Plumage brown and chestnut, marked with black, buff, white and yellow. Sexes differ. Nest on ground among vegetation. Eggs 2–4, white or yellowish, blotched black and purple. Incubation 20–22 days. Chicks leave nest soon after hatching, but depend on male for protection for some time. 2 species.

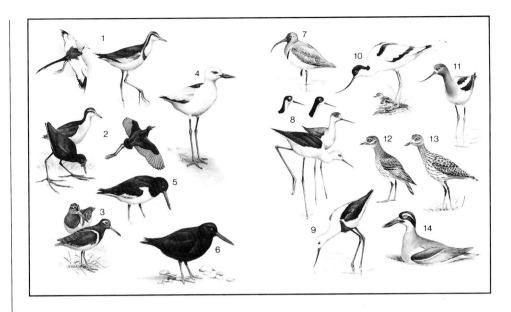

3/ GREATER PAINTED-SNIPE
Rostratula benghalensis

RANGE: Africa, Asia and Australia
HABITAT: well-vegetated freshwater wetlands, including marshes, paddy fields
SIZE: 6½–9 in (17–23 cm)

When feeding out in the open, this wading bird will freeze motionless if danger threatens, holding its position until the threat has passed. The female is both larger and more brightly colored than the male. She calls, a soft *koht-koht-koht*, at dusk and at night, often while in flight.

Males and females face each other in the courtship display, spreading their wings outward and forward until the tips are in front of their heads, at the same time fanning their tails. Each female may lay several clutches, each incubated by different males. The nest is a mound of waterweeds among vegetation in shallow water.

FAMILY DROMADIDAE
Crab Plover

There is only one species in this family.

4/ CRAB PLOVER
Dromas ardeola

RANGE: coasts of Indian Ocean; breeds Gulf of Oman, Gulf of Aden and Red Sea
HABITAT: sandy beaches and coastal dunes
SIZE: 15–16 in (38–41 cm)

In its typical pose, with the head hunched between the shoulders, the body of the Crab Plover appears gull-like, but the bird's long legs clearly indicate that it is a wader. It uses its thick bill to capture and crack open the shells of crabs. Both sexes have the same bold black and white plumage.

The birds breed in dense colonies. Unlike other members of the Order Charadriiformes, this species excavates nesting tunnels up to 5 ft (1.5 m) long, and the sandy ground of a breeding colony becomes honeycombed with holes. A single, large, pure white egg is laid in a chamber at the end of each tunnel. The chick remains in the nest tunnel after hatching and is fed by the parents which bring live crabs from the shore.

FAMILY HAEMATOPODIDAE
Oystercatchers

Large, thickset waders. Long, stout bill. Plumage black or black and white, with orange-red bill and pink legs. Sexes similar. Nest in scrapes, sometimes colonially. Eggs 3–4, brown or gray, spotted and streaked. Incubation 24–29 days. Chicks leave nest soon after hatching, but are fed by parents for at least 6 weeks. 11 species.

5/ PALEARCTIC OYSTERCATCHER
Haematopus ostralegus

RANGE: breeds Eurasia; winters S to Africa and Indian Ocean
HABITAT: breeds on coasts and near inland fresh waters; winters only on coasts
SIZE: 15¾–18 in (40–46 cm)

Like that of other oystercatchers, the stout orange bill of the Palearctic Oystercatcher is triangular in cross-section and reinforced so that it does not bend easily. Birds that feed mainly on cockles and mussels have a bladelike tip suited to hammering open the shells and severing the muscle within. Those that feed on invertebrates in sand and mud have finer, more pointed bills for probing.

Territories are advertised and boundaries disputed by noisy displays involving loud, piping calls, which take place among groups of these birds all year round. The nest is a mere scrape on the ground, sometimes decorated with stones or pieces of shell. Outside the breeding season the adults develop a white neck collar, making them similar to an immature bird in its first winter.

6/ AMERICAN BLACK OYSTERCATCHER
Haematopus bachmani

RANGE: Pacific coast of North America, from Alaska to Baja California
HABITAT: rocky coasts and islands, occasionally sandy beaches
SIZE: 15 in (38 cm)

Oystercatchers have loud, piercing calls which can be heard above the sound of crashing surf, facilitating communication between individuals.

They are noisy birds, frequently calling at night. The downy, highly mobile chicks follow their parents, which first present food to them and then train them to find and procure food for themselves. Opening mollusks and crab shells is a very difficult task; it can be accomplished in less than a minute by an experienced bird but many months are required to master the technique. Young birds are able to fly in about 35 days but associate with their parents for up to a year, learning feeding techniques.

FAMILY IBIDORHYNCHIDAE
Ibisbill

There is only one species in this family.

7/ IBISBILL
Ibidorhyncha struthersii

RANGE: **Central S Asia**
HABITAT: **stony, upland river valleys**
SIZE: **15–16 in (38–41 cm)**

This rare, little-known species takes its name from its distinctive, downcurved red bill which superficially resembles that of an ibis. The bold plumage is common to both sexes. It haunts remote mountain regions, where it uses its bill to probe among stones of riverbeds and rake through gravel to find small fish and invertebrates.

During courtship, the rear of the black cap is raised in display to form a slight crest. Aerial displays are used to defend breeding territories. The nest is a shallow scrape on a patch of shingle containing up to 4 pale, spotted eggs. The incubation period is thought to be about 30 days.

FAMILY RECURVIROSTRIDAE
Stilts and avocets

Large, long-legged, long-billed waders. Plumage mostly black and white. Sexes similar. Nest in scrapes. Eggs 3–4, buff-brown, dark markings. Incubation 22–26 days. Chicks leave nest soon after hatching, but depend on parents for protection often until well after fledging. 7 species.

8/ BLACK-WINGED STILT
Himantopus himantopus

RANGE: **worldwide in tropics, subtropics and warm temperate latitudes**
HABITAT: **coastal and inland wetlands**
SIZE: **13¾–15¾ in (35–40 cm)**

The extraordinarily long, bright pink legs of this slender shorebird extend 7 in (18 cm) beyond the tail when the bird takes to the wing. The length of the legs allows the Black-winged Stilt to feed in deeper water than other shorebirds, but when feeding on dry terrain, it has to bend its legs awkwardly so that its bill can reach the ground.

The birds breed in loose colonies in marshy ground or on the bare mud of salt pans. When incubating the eggs, the adults have problems with their long legs. In the sitting posture, each folded leg projects behind in a prominent *V* shape. The race *H. h. himantopus* is from Eurasia, India and Africa; the race *H. h. knudseni* is restricted to Hawaii, where it is rare and endangered; and the race *H. h. mexicanus* occurs from North America south to northern South America.

9/ BANDED STILT
Cladorhynchus leucocephalus

RANGE: **S Australia**
HABITAT: **inland salt lakes, estuaries and lagoons**
SIZE: **15–16 in (38–41 cm)**

The Banded Stilt eats brine shrimp and other crustaceans, wading, and sometimes swimming, to probe and peck in the water. It feeds in flocks, the members of the group sometimes converging to herd their prey.

Although it can occur in flocks of several thousand, the Banded Stilt has seldom been found breeding. It nests erratically in huge, massed colonies, where occasional heavy rains fill desert salt pans. The eggs are laid in a scrape on flat nesting islands left by the receding water. The downy chicks may swim several miles to shore, in groups with adults.

10/ PIED AVOCET
Recurvirostra avosetta

RANGE: **breeds W and C Eurasia; winters mainly in Africa and the Middle East**
HABITAT: **saline or brackish wetlands, coastal and inland**
SIZE: **16½–17¾ in (42–45 cm)**

The delicately pointed, upturned bill of the Pied Avocet is a highly specialized feeding tool. It is held slightly open just below the surface of shallow water or very soft mud and swept from side to side as the bird walks slowly forward. Small invertebrates and larger worms are located by touch. The species can also upend in deeper water and sweep its bill to and fro through the mud on the bottom. Pied Avocets nest on muddy islets, forming dense colonies usually containing some 10–200 pairs. Each pair defends the few yards around the nest against rivals, but all the pairs cooperate in driving away intruders.

11/ RED-NECKED AVOCET
Recurvirostra novaehollandiae

RANGE: **S and inland Australia**
HABITAT: **lagoons, lakes, marshes, estuaries**
SIZE: **15¾–17¾ in (40–45 cm)**

The Red-necked Avocet haunts shallow waters inland and on the coast. It is a sociable species, feeding and roosting in flocks and nesting in loose colonies. They feed on small crustaceans, aquatic insects, worms, mollusks and some seeds. Like Pied Avocets, they forage by sweeping their upturned bills from side to side through shallow water or mud and sometimes stir the water up with their bills to reveal more food. Their partially webbed feet enable them to swim.

FAMILY BURHINIDAE
Thick-knees (stone-curlews)

Large, thickset, terrestrial birds. Stout bill, large eyes. Plumage mainly brown. Sexes alike. Nests on ground. Eggs 2–3, white to brownish-gray, spotted and blotched. Incubation 25–27 days. Chicks can stand and walk by 2 days old and leave nest soon after, but fed by parents for first few days. 9 species.

12/ STONE-CURLEW
Burhinus oedicnemus

RANGE: **W and S Europe, SW Asia, N Africa, Middle East, Indian subcontinent**
HABITAT: **open farmland, heaths, semi-desert**
SIZE: **15¾–17¼ in (40–44 cm)**

The Stone-Curlew lives mainly in dry, open terrain. It can run swiftly across the ground, and is partly nocturnal in habits. In spring, each pair establishes a territory that may be many acres in extent. They indulge in circling display flights and call frequently at dusk, often continuing through the night. The far-carrying call is similar to a call of the curlew, hence the species' name.

The nest is a shallow scrape on the ground, almost always placed to give a good all-around view. Some pairs decorate their nests with small stones and even pellets of rabbit dung. The incubating bird is well camouflaged and slips quietly away in times of danger, long before an intruder has approached the nest.

13/ CAPE DIKKOP
Burhinus capensis

RANGE: **sub-Saharan Africa**
HABITAT: **open or scrub country**
SIZE: **17 in (43 cm)**

Unlike other thick-knees, the Cape, or Spotted, Dikkop is not particularly shy and will nest close to towns and villages. It has even been found in large suburban gardens. It is most active at dusk and during the night, resting in the shade of bushes, such as acacias, during the heat of the day. Its nest is a bare scrape.

This species often appears along roads at night, on the lookout for snails and other invertebrates on the open ground. Unfortunately, this habit makes it a frequent casualty of speeding traffic.

14/ BEACH THICK-KNEE
Esacus magnirostris

RANGE: **coasts of N Australia, New Guinea, New Caledonia, Solomon Islands, Philippines, Indonesia, Andaman Islands**
HABITAT: **sandy beaches and inshore reefs**
SIZE: **20¾–22¾ in (53–58 cm)**

Also known as the Beach Stone-Curlew, this species is a plain-colored, large and heavily built thick-knee that wails mournfully at night. It is almost exclusively a ground-dweller, running to escape danger, and only taking to the air when hard pressed.

The Beach Thick-knee feeds on crabs and other hard-shelled marine animals by seizing them as it walks along the tideline with its characteristic dawdling gait. It uses its heavy bill to crack and smash them open. Feeding takes place mostly at night; the bird rests during the day by squatting on its long legs. Its nest is a scrape in shingle or sand just above the high water mark, placed among beach debris or, on occasion, under a sheltering bush.

EGYPTIAN PLOVER

non-breeding

NORTHERN LAPWING

♂

CREAM-COLORED COURSER

SOUTHERN LAPWING

AUSTRALIAN PRATINCOLE

COMMON PRATINCOLE

BLACKSMITH PLOVER

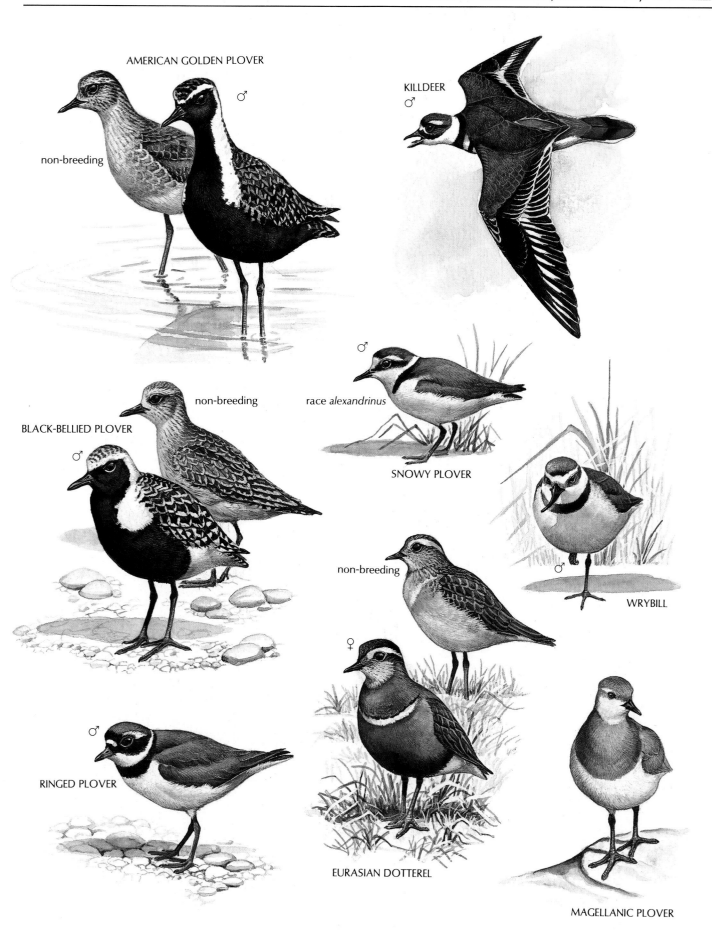

AMERICAN GOLDEN PLOVER

non-breeding

♂

KILLDEER
♂

BLACK-BELLIED PLOVER

non-breeding

♂

race *alexandrinus*

SNOWY PLOVER

non-breeding

♀

WRYBILL
♂

RINGED PLOVER
♂

EURASIAN DOTTEREL

MAGELLANIC PLOVER

SHOREBIRDS: COURSERS AND PRATINCOLES, PLOVERS, MAGELLANIC PLOVER

FAMILY GLAREOLIDAE
Coursers and pratincoles

Small, long-legged (coursers) or long-winged and short-legged (pratincoles) birds. Plumage mainly brown, buff, white. Bolder markings on head and breast. Sexes alike. Nest in scrapes. Eggs 2–4, buff or brown, variably marked. Incubation 17–31 days. Chicks leave nest soon after hatching; fed by parents for first few days. 17 species.

1/ EGYPTIAN PLOVER
Pluvianus aegyptius
RANGE: W, C and NE Africa
HABITAT: river valleys and marshes
SIZE: $7\frac{1}{2}$–$8\frac{1}{4}$ in (19–21 cm)

The Egyptian Plover's breeding habits are unique among shorebirds. The adults bury their 2–3 eggs under a thin layer of sand, about $\frac{1}{8}$ in (3 mm) thick. Warmed by the sun, the sand helps to incubate the clutch. Should the weather become cooler, the parents incubate the eggs by sitting on them in the normal way, and they also do so at night. Conversely, if the daytime temperature becomes very high, the male or female will cool the eggs by shading them with its body or by wetting the sand with water carried in its belly feathers.

The young hatch in the sand and quickly leave the "nest" area. Until the chicks are about 3 weeks old, they crouch whenever danger threatens and the adults quickly cover them with sand.

2/ CREAM-COLORED COURSER
Cursorius cursor
RANGE: N and E Africa, Middle East to W Pakistan; N African birds winter just S of Sahara, Middle Eastern birds in Arabia, SW Asian birds in NW India
HABITAT: open arid plains with sparse vegetation; margins of cultivated land
SIZE: $8\frac{1}{4}$–$9\frac{1}{2}$ in (21–24 cm)

The pale sandy-brown plumage of this species provides perfect camouflage in its desert habitat. It is much more conspicuous in flight, however, when it reveals the striking black and white pattern on the underside of its wings.

The Cream-colored Courser feeds by running about vigorously and grabbing beetles, grasshoppers and other invertebrates in its bill and also by digging for concealed prey with its bill. When disturbed, it will run swiftly, stopping at intervals to rise onto tiptoe and stretch its neck to check for danger. Northern (especially northeastern) populations are the most migratory, whereas island races are year-round residents.

3/ AUSTRALIAN PRATINCOLE
Stiltia isabella
RANGE: breeds N and inland Australia; most populations winter N to extreme N Australia, New Guinea and other Papuan islands, Indonesia
HABITAT: bare, open plains, fields, edges of lagoons
SIZE: $7\frac{3}{4}$–9 in (20–23 cm)

The graceful Australian Pratincole feeds both in the air and by running about on the ground, snapping up insects in its wide gape. It needs to

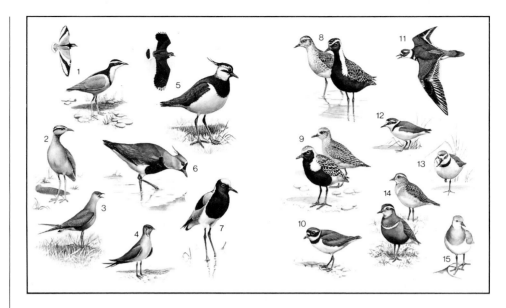

drink frequently at its hot, dry breeding grounds and can tolerate brackish water by excreting excess salt through special nasal glands.

They breed in loose colonies on stony plains, usually near water. The courtship display involves both male and female running, head down, toward or parallel to one another; they also pump their heads up and down, touch heads with their bills pointing to the ground, and half open their upwardly pointing wings. The clutch of 2 eggs is laid on the bare ground and incubated by both sexes. The incubating bird remains in the hot sunshine, raising its feathers and panting to lose heat. Soon after hatching, the chicks are led to the shade of vegetation or burrows.

4/ COMMON PRATINCOLE
Glareola pratincola
RANGE: S Eurasia, N Africa; winters S Africa
HABITAT: flood plains, deltas, steppes
SIZE: $9\frac{1}{4}$–$10\frac{1}{2}$ in (23.5–26.5 cm)

As with other pratincoles, the long-winged, fork-tailed appearance of the Common, or Collared, Pratincole in flight is reminiscent of a tern or even a large swallow. Large flocks gather to feed on flying ants and other insects and will follow swarms of locusts over long distances in Africa.

Common Pratincoles have rather ternlike breeding habits. Large colonies nest on bare or sparsely vegetated ground, the 2–3 eggs in each clutch laid in a slight scrape. When a predatory bird appears over the colony, all the adults in the area will fly up and mob it, giving harsh *kirrik* calls until the intruder moves away.

FAMILY CHARADRIIDAE
Plovers

Small to medium, short-billed waders. Plumage mainly black, brown and white. Sexes similar, or males slightly larger. Ground-nesters. Eggs 2–4, cryptically patterned in most species. Incubation 18–38 days, chicks leave nest and can feed themselves soon after hatching. 65 species.

5/ NORTHERN LAPWING
Vanellus vanellus
RANGE: breeds temperate Eurasia; most populations migrate S in winter to Mediterranean, India, China
HABITAT: breeds on open ground, including farmland, freshwater marshes, saltmarshes; also visits estuarine mud flats
SIZE: 11–$12\frac{1}{4}$ in (28–31 cm)

The Northern Lapwing is a common and familiar bird over much of Europe. Its broad, rounded wings produce a distinctive creaking sound during the wheeling, rolling and tumbling display flight. The sounds are accompanied by a characteristic plaintive cry, from which the bird takes its alternative English name, Peewit.

The female carries out most of the incubation of the 4 eggs. The young are perfectly camouflaged, and crouch down the instant they hear their parents' alarm calls. Modern intensive farming and land drainage have drastically reduced the Northern Lapwing's habitat in many areas and the species is also vulnerable to severe winters.

6/ SOUTHERN LAPWING
Vanellus chilensis
RANGE: South America, mainly E of Andes
HABITAT: savanna, wet grassland, farmland
SIZE: $14\frac{1}{2}$–15 in (37–38 cm)

This plover readily adapts to feeding on cultivated land, taking earthworms, grubs and insects. The slightest intrusion, day or night, causes it to utter its loud, strident alarm calls. For this reason, it is often regarded as a semidomesticated "watchdog" at farmsteads and suburban homes. It is a gregarious bird, found in small flocks at any time of the year.

When approached, an incubating bird will slip away some distance from the nest before taking flight. It will then make sweeping passes at the intruder while emitting loud cries of protest.

7/ BLACKSMITH PLOVER
Anitibyx armatus

RANGE: Kenya to South Africa
HABITAT: margins of fresh and saline wetlands and adjacent open ground
SIZE: $11-12\frac{1}{4}$ in (28–31 cm)

The bold plumage of the adult Blacksmith Plover becomes even more striking when the bird takes flight, enhanced by the contrast between the black and gray upperwings and the black and white underwings. The bird's nest is no more than a shallow depression in the ground, often merely the hoofprint of a grazing mammal. This species takes its name from its harsh and metallic call – a *chink-chink* just like the sound of a blacksmith's hammer striking the anvil.

8/ AMERICAN GOLDEN PLOVER
Pluvialis dominica

RANGE: breeds Arctic North America; winters C South America
HABITAT: breeds on tundra; otherwise coastal mud flats, inland marshes and grassland
SIZE: $9\frac{1}{2}-11$ in (24–28 cm)

There is a striking difference in this bird between the breeding and nonbreeding plumage. However, the upperparts of adult and immature have a golden hue all year. The speckling on the back camouflages the incubating bird. This species undertakes a long seasonal migration apparently accomplished nonstop by many birds. Eastern Canadian breeders take the shortest "Great Circle" route over the western Atlantic, but other populations take inland routes across the USA.

9/ BLACK-BELLIED PLOVER
Pluvialis squatarola

RANGE: breeds circumpolar Arctic; winters worldwide on coasts to S
HABITAT: breeds on lowland tundra; winters on coastal mud flats and lagoons
SIZE: $10\frac{1}{2}-11\frac{3}{4}$ in (27–30 cm)

Although the black axilliary feathers, or "armpits," of this bird are seen only in flight, they form a unique and distinctive field character. They are especially useful in winter when the overall gray plumage of the standing bird lacks any obvious distinguishing marks. The Black-bellied Plover is highly migratory, reaching the southern shores of Australia and South Africa from its breeding grounds in the high Arctic. Adults share incubation of the 4 eggs, but the male takes more responsibility for rearing the chicks.

10/ RINGED PLOVER
Charadrius hiaticula

RANGE: breeds Arctic E Canada and Eurasia; winters Europe and Africa
HABITAT: breeds on shingle beaches and tundra; winters along coasts and some inland wetlands
SIZE: $7-7\frac{3}{4}$ in (18–20 cm)

The white collar and broad black breast band of the adult Ringed Plover gives the species its name. The breast band is blacker and deeper in the adult male than in the female. This species' wistful *too-li* call is used by the off-duty bird to call its mate from the nest when danger threatens. Later, when the chicks have hatched, Ringed Plovers are experts at the broken-wing display, in which they pretend to be injured. They flutter with drooped wings and spread tail while calling loudly and plaintively, in an effort to distract a potential predator away from the vulnerable young in the nest.

11/ KILLDEER
Charadrius vociferus

RANGE: breeds S Canada to SC Mexico, West Indies, coastal Peru and extreme N Chile; winters N South America
HABITAT: open expanses near wet areas, ponds, rivers
SIZE: $8\frac{1}{4}-9\frac{3}{4}$ in (21–25 cm)

This plover takes its name from its *killdee-killdee* calls. Widespread through the Americas, it is a rare visitor to Europe and Hawaii.

Killdeers make their nest scrapes in an area with short, sparse vegetation or none at all. Bits of grass, pebbles and other loose material end up in the scrape as a result of a ritual ceremony in which the birds slowly walk away from the nest while tossing the material over their shoulders. The birds often nest on gravel roads where their eggs are crushed by cars. They may also nest on flat gravel rooftops, although the chicks are sometimes trapped by parapets or perish when they leap to the ground. However, they often survive leaps from buildings 3–4 stories high.

12/ SNOWY PLOVER
Charadrius alexandrinus

RANGE: temperate and S Eurasia and North America, South America, Africa
HABITAT: coastal and inland brackish or saline wetlands
SIZE: $6-6\frac{3}{4}$ in (15–17.5 cm)

The worldwide range of this bird is belied by its British name, Kentish Plover, which merely relates to the place where it was first discovered in England in 1787. The species formerly bred in small numbers in the county of Kent, but it died out there early this century through egg collecting and habitat destruction. The Eurasian and North African race *C. a. alexandrinus* is illustrated.

The 3–4 eggs are laid in a shallow scrape in the sand. Their buff color with fine black marks acts as excellent camouflage. The young, too, are cryptically patterned. When their parents give the alarm call, they flatten themselves to the ground and become indistinguishable from small irregularities in the surface of the sand.

13/ WRYBILL
Anarhynchus frontalis

RANGE: New Zealand
HABITAT: breeds along shallow, stony rivers; winters on estuaries, in harbors
SIZE: $7\frac{3}{4}$ in (20 cm)

This small plover is unique in that the tip of its bill bends to the right. It feeds by walking in clockwise circles, probing over mud and under pebbles. The bird's winter migration from South Island to North Island takes place in January and it returns to its southern breeding grounds in August. Its total world population numbers some 4,000–5,000 birds.

Wrybills nest in small scrapes among pebbles and near water. Sadly, spring floods now often wipe out breeding populations. Introduced plant species have colonized many braided rivers, stabilizing sand and pebble banks and influencing flow patterns, possibly forcing the birds to breed in less favorable locations.

14/ EURASIAN DOTTEREL
Eudromias morinellus

RANGE: breeds Arctic and mountainous Eurasia; winters N Africa and Middle East
HABITAT: breeds on tundra and mountain plateaus; winters on open, often stony ground
SIZE: $7\frac{3}{4}-8\frac{1}{2}$ in (20–22 cm)

Although the bright white eye stripes and white chest band of this bird are very distinctive, they act to break up its outline when it is nesting among the short tundra or mountain vegetation of its breeding grounds.

The male Eurasian Dotterel is solely responsible for incubation and the rearing of young. Each female often lays 2 or more clutches of 3 eggs for different males. The birds are extremely tame, allowing people to approach them closely at all times of the year. There are many recorded cases of incubating males being touched while on the nest, or even returning to sit on eggs or young held on the ground in a person's hand.

FAMILY PLUVIANELLIDAE
Magellanic Plover
There is only one species in this family.

15/ MAGELLANIC PLOVER
Pluvianellus socialis

RANGE: breeds Tierra del Fuego N through S Patagonia; winters N on the coast of Argentina
HABITAT: shores of lakes, ponds, lagoons; winters by river mouths and bays
SIZE: $7\frac{3}{4}$ in (20 cm)

This enigmatic shorebird's entire population may number fewer than 1,000 individuals. Few ornithologists have seen it, and it may be more closely related to turnstones (pp. 142–45) or sheathbills (pp. 146–49) than to plovers. It forages by pecking, turning stones and digging.

Magellanic Plovers nest near shallow fresh or brackish water where each pair defends a strip of shoreline about 1,000–1,500 ft (300–500 m) long. The nest scrape, which is lined with gravel, is usually placed in an area of shingle, small rocks or gravel mixed with sand. The sexes share incubation of the 2 dark-streaked grayish eggs. Usually, only a single chick survives. Uniquely among shorebirds, it is fed partly by regurgitation from the parents' bills; they continue to feed it for at least 12 days after it has fledged at about 28 days.

SHOREBIRDS: SANDPIPERS AND SNIPES

GREATER YELLOWLEGS

non-breeding

BAR-TAILED GODWIT

♂

SPOTTED SANDPIPER

WANDERING TATTLER

ESKIMO CURLEW

RUDDY TURNSTONE

♂

non-breeding

♀

WESTERN CURLEW

RED-NECKED PHALAROPE

♂

non-breeding

♀

non-breeding

RED KNOT

♂

non-breeding

DUNLIN

chick

SPOON-BILLED
SANDPIPER

EURASIAN WOODCOCK

♂ variants

♂

♂

♀

COMMON SNIPE

SHORT-BILLED DOWITCHER

RUFF

143

SHOREBIRDS: SANDPIPERS AND SNIPES

FAMILY SCOLOPACIDAE
Sandpipers and snipes
Small to large, mainly long-billed, often long-legged shorebirds. Plumage patterned brown, black and white, some with reddish breeding plumage. Sexes similar. Ground-nesters. Eggs 2–4, buff or green, variably marked. Incubation period 18–30 days. Chicks leave nest within 1 day of hatching and may travel up to $1\frac{1}{4}$ mls (2 km) to feeding areas; cared for by parents until they fledge. 86 species.

1/ BAR-TAILED GODWIT
Limosa lapponica

RANGE: **breeds Eurasian Arctic; winters S to S Africa and Australasia**
HABITAT: **breeds on marshy and scrubby tundra; winters on estuaries**
SIZE: **$14\frac{1}{2}$–16 in (37–41 cm)**

The rich mahogany-chestnut summer plumage of this species provides good camouflage for nesting birds against the colored mosses and low scrub of the Arctic tundra. The thin, slightly upturned bill is approximately 20 percent longer in the female than in the male. In a typical flock feeding along the edge of the tide, the females wade and probe in deeper water than the males.

The nest is usually placed on a drier raised hummock above the damp ground. Both sexes incubate the 4 eggs and rear the young, the off-duty bird often perching, incongruously, on top of a bush or low tree.

2/ ESKIMO CURLEW
Numenius borealis [E]

RANGE: **formerly bred (still breeds?) NW Territories, Canada and Alaska; wintered (still winters?) mainly from S Brazil to C Argentina**
HABITAT: **Arctic tundra in breeding season; prairies and coastal grassland on migration; pampas grassland in winter**
SIZE: **$11\frac{1}{2}$–$13\frac{1}{4}$ in (29–34 cm)**

This diminutive curlew is one of the world's rarest birds, with a total population of perhaps fewer than 20 individuals. Once it was an abundant species: until the end of the last century, the Eskimo Curlew was seen in huge flocks on migration, when it was shot by the thousands during its long journey across southern Labrador, Nova Scotia, New England and the Mississippi valley en route to its South American winter quarters.

This relentless, wholesale slaughter by hunters, especially between 1850 and 1890, was the main reason for its catastrophic decline, but the large-scale conversion of grasslands for agriculture has almost certainly contributed to its demise. Adverse climatic changes may also have played a part.

Although no breeding or wintering sites are currently known, it is still seen occasionally in tiny numbers on migration: there were at least 4 reliable reports of the species in 1987. Today, it is fully protected by law in Canada and the United States, but, sadly, this protection may have come too late.

3/ WESTERN CURLEW
Numenius arquata

RANGE: **breeds temperate and N Eurasia; winters S to Africa, India, Southeast Asia**
HABITAT: **breeds on open vegetated land; winters mainly on coastal wetlands**
SIZE: **$19\frac{1}{2}$–$23\frac{1}{2}$ in (50–60 cm)**

The distinctive, long, decurved bill of the Western Curlew is perfectly adapted for the bird's main feeding technique of probing deeply into soft mud. The movement of invertebrate prey is detected by the sensitive tips of the mandibles. Food items are also picked from the surface, including mollusks, worms and, while inland, even berries.

During courtship, the male Western Curlew indulges in a shallow, gliding flight accompanied by a rich, bubbling and trilling song, which can also be heard outside the breeding season. It is one of the most evocative spring sounds of upland moorland areas. The nest is a shallow hollow among grass tussocks, lined with grass stems.

4/ GREATER YELLOWLEGS
Tringa melanoleuca

RANGE: **breeds N North America, non-breeders S along coasts; winters SW Canada to extreme S South America; vagrant elsewhere**
HABITAT: **breeds on tundra; otherwise coastal mudflats and marshes, shores of inland lakes**
SIZE: **14 in (36 cm)**

The Greater Yellowlegs is usually seen alone or in small flocks. It nests in muskeg country, along the tundra-forest edge and on the high tundra of North America, migrating south for the winter to warmer regions. It feeds mainly in shallow waters, wading in to sweep its bill with a sideways motion or dash about after visible prey. Its diet consists largely of small fish, insects and their larvae, snails, worms and tadpoles.

This species sometimes associates with the Lesser Yellowlegs *F. flavipes*, especially during migration. When it does, its greater size and its longer, stouter bill make it easy to distinguish.

5/ SPOTTED SANDPIPER
Actitis macularia

RANGE: **breeds North America; winters S from Mexico to S Brazil**
HABITAT: **open and wooded areas, usually near water**
SIZE: **$7\frac{1}{2}$ in (19 cm)**

The Spotted Sandpiper occupies varied habitats from sea level to the tree line. Tipping up its tail at nearly every step, it teeters along the water margins, stalking diverse aquatic and terrestrial insects. Its main call is a clear, whistled *peet-weet*, and it utters a repetitious *weet* during the breeding season. Its curious, jerky flight, with short glides on down-bowed wings alternating with groups of shallow, flickering wing beats, is shared only by its close relative in the Old World, the Common Sandpiper *A. hypoleucos*. Like a number of other American shorebirds, including the Greater and Lesser Yellowlegs, the Spotted Sandpiper is a rare wanderer to Europe; in 1975, a pair nested in Scotland, but deserted their 4 eggs.

Certain females of this species may be polyandrous, mating with 2 or more males. Females may or may not help with incubation.

6/ WANDERING TATTLER
Heteroscelus incanus

RANGE: **breeds Alaska; winters from Pacific coast of Central America to Australia**
HABITAT: **breeds by mountain streams; winters on rocky coasts and reefs**
SIZE: **$10\frac{1}{4}$–$11\frac{1}{2}$ in (26–29 cm)**

This species is well named for its extraordinary transoceanic migration. From a restricted breeding area in Alaska, it flies to wintering grounds scattered over numerous Pacific islands as far west as the Great Barrier Reef in Australia.

The nest is placed on bare shingle beside a mountain stream and is sometimes just a bare scrape among the stones. In other cases, it is lined with rootlets, grass and small twigs. Little is known about the bird's breeding details, as few nests have been found. It seems likely that both parents incubate the 4 eggs and rear the young.

7/ RUDDY TURNSTONE
Arenaria interpres

RANGE: **breeds circumpolar Arctic, and N temperate region in Scandinavia; winters S worldwide to C Argentina, South Africa and Australia**
HABITAT: **breeds on tundra and coastal plains; winters on coasts**
SIZE: **$8\frac{1}{4}$–$10\frac{1}{4}$ in (21–26 cm)**

Flocks of these birds walk busily over heaps of seaweed on the shore, flicking pieces with the bill, quickly grabbing any morsel of food that appears. Invertebrates and their larvae make up the main part of their diet, but the birds also feed on other items, including dead animals and human waste. Males are duller than females. During the breeding season, each pair defends a small territory around the nest site. Both adults share in incubating the 3–4 eggs and in rearing the young.

8/ RED-NECKED PHALAROPE
Phalaropus lobatus

RANGE: **breeds circumpolar Arctic and N temperate regions; winters in the tropics**
HABITAT: **breeds on freshwater marshes, including uplands; marine in winter**
SIZE: **7–$7\frac{1}{2}$ in (18–19 cm)**

Like the other 2 species of phalarope, Red-necked Phalaropes are adapted for swimming, rather than merely wading, with lobed toes to propel them through water. They feed daintily while swimming, spinning around to stir up the water and picking small creatures from the surface.

As with the other phalaropes, the female Red-necked Phalarope is more brightly colored than the male and takes the dominant role in courtship. After she has laid her clutch of 4 eggs in a shallow cup among moss, the male carries out all the incubation and rearing of the young – hence the adaptive significance of his duller plumage, since it is an advantage for him to be better camouflaged than the female. A proportion of females lay more clutches for other males, but still take no part in tending the young.

9/ EURASIAN WOODCOCK
Scolopax rusticola

RANGE: **breeds temperate Eurasia; many winter S to Mediterranean, India and Southeast Asia**
HABITAT: **broad-leaved or coniferous woodland; feeds more in the open in winter**
SIZE: **13–$13\frac{3}{4}$ in (33–35 cm)**

This shorebird is unusual in that it inhabits woodland, where its cryptic coloration provides excellent camouflage. During the breeding season the male performs "roding" flights at dusk and dawn, flying very slowly with irregular, flickering wing beats just above the tops of the trees and seeking females on the ground. As he does so, he utters several very quiet, deep, grunting notes followed by a thin, wheezy, high-pitched *tsiwick*.

After mating, the male Eurasian Woodcock may stay with the female until the clutch is laid, but he then leaves the incubation and rearing of the chicks entirely to her. The female can fly short distances carrying her chicks between her legs.

10/ COMMON SNIPE
Gallinago gallinago

RANGE: **breeds N temperate North America and Eurasia; many winter widely to S**
HABITAT: **freshwater and coastal wetlands**
SIZE: **$9\frac{3}{4}$–$10\frac{1}{2}$ in (25–27 cm)**

The Common Snipe pushes its long, straight bill vertically into water and soft mud in search of invertebrates. The rhythmic upward and downward pumping action of its bill as it feeds is reminiscent of a sewing machine at work.

When displaying over the breeding territory, the male Common Snipe circles high in the air and then dives groundward. As he does so, he holds out his outer tail feathers at a sharp angle to the rest of his tail. The air rushing past makes them vibrate and give out a bleating sound, often known as "winnowing." Other species of snipe make a similar noise with their tails. The nest is a scrape, often placed near a grassy tussock.

11/ SHORT-BILLED DOWITCHER
Limnodromus griseus

RANGE: **breeds N North America; winters North America S to Brazil**
HABITAT: **breeds muskeg, ponds, marshes; winters chiefly on coastal mudflats**
SIZE: **$10\frac{1}{2}$–$12\frac{1}{4}$ in (27–31 cm)**

The Short-billed Dowitcher is a medium-sized, short-legged, dumpy shorebird, showing a white wedge-shaped patch from the tail to the middle of the back in flight. In winter plumage it is difficult to distinguish this bird from its close relative, the Long-billed Dowitcher *L. scolopaceus*. The 2 species often occur together on migration.

However, whereas Long-billed Dowitchers generally prefer freshwater pools on migration and in their wintering quarters, Short-billed Dowitchers favor saltwater and brackish habitats outside the breeding season. Here they feed in mud and shallow water, often in large flocks. They often submerge their heads entirely in water as they probe for aquatic insects, other marine life and plant food.

12/ RED KNOT
Calidris canutus

RANGE: **breeds Arctic Canada and Siberia; winters South America, S Africa and Australia**
HABITAT: **breeds on tundra; winters on estuaries and beaches**
SIZE: **9–$9\frac{3}{4}$ in (23–25 cm)**

The Red Knot undergoes a marked change in plumage through the year, from its rich chestnut-orange breeding dress to the pale gray of winter. Flocks that form in fall and winter can be tens of thousands strong and will perform rapid aerial maneuvers in which the entire flock twists and turns with great synchrony. At a distance, the flock can give the appearance of a writhing mass of smoke.

Although the rather duller, white-bellied female helps with incubation, she departs soon after, leaving the male to rear the brood. This means that more invertebrate food is available for the chicks than if a second adult were present.

13/ DUNLIN
Calidris alpina

RANGE: **circumpolar Arctic and N temperate regions; winters S to subtropics**
HABITAT: **breeds on tundra, moorland, marshes; winters on estuaries or inland wetlands**
SIZE: **$6\frac{1}{4}$–$8\frac{1}{2}$ in (16–22 cm)**

The Dunlin is the most common small shorebird of the Northern Hemisphere. It may occur in passage and winter flocks of tens of thousands in favored estuaries, but also appears in tiny groups in small coastal creeks. Extensive banding has shown that wintering birds return year after year not just to the same estuary, but to the same part of the estuary, with almost no mixing between flocks only a few miles apart. This species is very variable in size, birds of southern and western races being far smaller than those of some of the east Siberian and New World races.

Dunlins nest in shallow depressions among short vegetation. Both sexes share in the incubation of the 4 eggs, but the female leaves soon after the young have hatched.

14/ SPOON-BILLED SANDPIPER
Eurynorhynchus pygmeus [?]

RANGE: **breeds NE Siberia; winters coasts of SE India to Burma, coastal SE China**
HABITAT: **breeds on coastal marshy tundra; winters on muddy coasts and brackish lagoons**
SIZE: **$5\frac{1}{2}$–$6\frac{1}{4}$ in (14–16 cm)**

The spoon-shaped bill of this species is an adaptation for feeding. The bird forages in soft mud or shallow water, sweeping its bill from side to side as it walks. The broadened bill tip is already obvious in the newly hatched young.

The Spoon-billed Sandpiper's total population is small, with a best estimate of no more than 2,800 pairs; the true figure may well be considerably lower. However, accurate censuses are extremely difficult to carry out. The male apparently carries out most of the incubation of the 4 eggs as well as rearing the young.

15/ RUFF
Philomachus pugnax

RANGE: **breeds N Eurasia; winters Mediterranean, S Africa, India and Australia**
HABITAT: **lowland freshwater wetlands, marshes and wet pastures**
SIZE: **$7\frac{3}{4}$–$12\frac{1}{2}$ in (20–32 cm)**

In the breeding season, the male Ruff develops remarkable plumes, variable in both color and pattern, around his head and neck. Groups of rival males form "leks" at which they display to one another and advertise to visiting females. Some hold small territories within the lek, while others move from one position to another.

Each female may mate with one or more males, before moving away up to 1,600 ft (500 m) from the lek area. There she makes a shallow scrape, lays a clutch of 4 eggs, incubates them and rears the young. The males, in all their finery, take no part in nesting.

SEEDSNIPES, SHEATHBILLS, SKUAS AND JAEGERS, GULLS

WHITE-BELLIED SEEDSNIPE

SNOWY SHEATHBILL

GREAT SKUA

non-breeding

LONG-TAILED JAEGER

typical

IVORY GULL

juv

non-breeding

GRAY GULL

race *argenteus*
non-breeding

non-breeding

MEW GULL

race *michahellis*

race *argenteus*

HERRING GULL

non-breeding

FRANKLIN'S GULL

GREAT BLACK-BACKED GULL

first winter

race *scopulinus*
"Red-billed Gull"

race *hartlaubii*
"Hartlaub's Gull"

juv

non-breeding

SILVER GULL

ROSS'S GULL

BLACK-LEGGED KITTIWAKE

first winter

juv

non-breeding

non-breeding

SABINE'S GULL

SWALLOW-TAILED GULL

147

SEEDSNIPES, SHEATHBILLS, SKUAS AND JAEGERS, GULLS

FAMILY THINOCORIDAE
Seedsnipes

Small, dumpy partridgelike. Plumage cryptic, males more strongly marked. Nest in scrapes. Eggs 4, buff or cream, speckled and blotched. Incubation 25 days, nestling period 49–55 days. 4 species.

1/ WHITE-BELLIED SEEDSNIPE
Attagis malouinus

RANGE: Tierra del Fuego N to S Chile and Argentina
HABITAT: sparsely vegetated hillsides above the treeline
SIZE: 10–11½ in (26–29 cm)

The bright white underparts and underwings of the White-bellied Seedsnipe contrast markedly with its patterned pale brown upperparts, particularly when the bird is in flight. Apart from its main diet of seeds, it also consumes green leaves and cactus buds. Succulent plant parts appear to be the only source of water for the bird, since it has never been seen to drink.

The female lays her eggs in a scrape on the ground lined with pieces of vegetation. She carries out incubation while the male acts as a lookout, perching near the nest and warning of approaching danger. The young are led away from the nest by both parents within a few hours of hatching.

FAMILY CHIONIDIDAE
Sheathbills

White, pigeonlike with horny bill sheath. Sexes alike. Crevice-nesters. Eggs 2 (sometimes 3 or 4), white or grayish, blotched. Incubation 28–32 days, nestling period 50–60 days. 2 species.

2/ SNOWY SHEATHBILL
Chionis alba

RANGE: breeds Antarctic peninsula and islands N to South Georgia; winters N to Patagonia and the Falkland Islands
HABITAT: marine coasts
SIZE: 15¾ in (40 cm)

The pure white Snowy Sheathbill is a versatile scavenger that haunts seabird colonies, especially those of penguins, and visits the garbage tips of Antarctic scientific bases. It feeds on carcasses, feces and offal of every description and also snatches eggs and chicks from the breeding penguins. Outside the breeding season, its diet consists of intertidal beach animals and algae.

The nest is placed in a rock crevice or under a boulder. Both parents take turns to incubate the 2–4 eggs, but it is rare for more than 2 young to be reared. The young take up to 9 weeks to fledge.

FAMILY STERCORARIIDAE
Skuas and jaegers

Large seabirds, some with elongated central tail feathers. Plumage all brown, or brown above, creamy white below. Sexes alike. Nest in scrapes. Eggs usually 2, olive, brown blotches. Incubation 23–30 days, nestling period 24–55 days. 7 species.

3/ GREAT SKUA
Catharacta skua

RANGE: temperate and Arctic North Atlantic
HABITAT: breeds on open ground, usually near the coast; winters at sea, though probably within 30 mls (50 km) of the coast
SIZE: 20–26 in (51–66 cm)

Great Skuas obtain much of their food by chasing other seabirds and forcing them to disgorge whatever they are carrying. In the case of the Gannet, which is significantly larger than the Great Skua, the attacker seizes hold of a wing tip or the bird's tail and forces it down onto the ocean. It continues to hold on fast until the Gannet disgorges.

Breeding takes place in loose colonies, each pair vigorously defending its own territory. Encroaching animals, or humans, are repeatedly dive-bombed and struck on the head until they retreat. The nest is a shallow scrape on the ground.

4/ LONG-TAILED JAEGER
Stercorarius longicaudus

RANGE: breeds circumpolar high Arctic; winters in S hemisphere
HABITAT: breeds on Arctic tundra and marshes; winters at sea
SIZE: 19½–22¾ in (50–58 cm)

The Long-tailed Jaeger is the most slender and elegant member of its family, with a central pair of tail feathers that extend about 7 in (18 cm) beyond the remainder. During the breeding season, this species concentrates on hunting lemmings, rather than parasitizing other seabirds. The breeding performance of the jaegers is closely linked to the abundance of lemmings. In years when lemmings are scarce, the jaegers may not breed at all, or will fail to rear any young, but they breed very successfully in good lemming years.

The nest is a shallow, lined scrape on the ground, and both parents incubate the 2 eggs. When food is short, the first chick to hatch may kill the second chick so that it does not have to share the limited food supply.

FAMILY LARIDAE
Gulls

Heavy-bodied, long-winged seabirds. Plumage mainly white, gray and black in adults, brown markings in juveniles. Sexes similar. Nest sites variable. Eggs usually 2–3, greenish or brownish, mottled. Incubation 21–35 days, nestling period 21–49 days. 47 species.

5/ IVORY GULL
Pagophila eburnea

RANGE: high Arctic islands and coasts
HABITAT: breeds on cliffs; winters among or on the edge of pack-ice
SIZE: 15¾–18 in (40–46 cm)

The Ivory Gull is a dumpy, almost pigeon-shaped, all-white bird. When it walks, its short legs give it a rolling gait. It obtains much of its food by scavenging among the channels in pack-ice, following Polar Bears and picking up the remnants of their meals, as well as their feces.

The Ivory Gull nests on cliff ledges on remote Arctic islands in colonies varying in size from a handful to several hundred pairs. It also breeds on nunataks, rocky peaks projecting from the icecaps of Greenland and Spitsbergen.

6/ GRAY GULL
Larus modestus

RANGE: breeds N Chile; winters Chile, Peru and Ecuador
HABITAT: breeds on coastal deserts, coasts
SIZE: 18 in (46 cm)

This abundant gull of the Pacific coast of South America is remarkable for breeding in the barren deserts that extend 50 mls (80 km) inland from the coast of northern Chile. The birds nest in loose colonies of several thousand pairs on the dry, boulder-strewn ground. Cooling onshore breezes prevent temperatures rising too high but, even so, the incubating birds stand over the clutch of 1–2 eggs to shade them from the heat of the day. The desert provides no food, but the Gray Gulls find all they need to eat on the coast, by foraging along the tideline or following trawlers.

7/ MEW GULL
Larus canus

RANGE: **temperate and N Eurasia and NW North America**
HABITAT: **breeds in marshes and wet scrubland; winters on the shores of oceans and large lakes**
SIZE: **15¾–18 in (40–46 cm)**

Mew Gulls nest in colonies, sometimes on the ground, but often in the tops of bushes or scrub. In parts of Norway the birds are encouraged to nest in open boxes on poles because their eggs provide food for the local inhabitants. The usual clutch contains 3 eggs, which are incubated by both parents for about 3 weeks. The young take another 4–5 weeks to fledge.

In winter, the birds gather in large roosts on estuarine mudflats or large fresh waters. They may feed along the shore or fly well inland to forage for invertebrates in pastures, returning to the roosting site in the evening.

8/ HERRING GULL
Larus argentatus

RANGE: **circumpolar N, temperate and Mediterranean**
HABITAT: **varied; coastal and inland, including urban areas**
SIZE: **22–26 in (56–66 cm)**

The Herring Gull is one of the most successful of all seabirds, having adapted in recent decades to living on human refuse and nesting on roofs in many areas. It is now commonplace in towns, some well inland, and strenuous efforts have been made to prevent the gulls from nesting on, and fouling, important buildings.

The Herring Gull's nest is an untidy gathering of vegetation and scraps of garbage. Soon after they have hatched in the nest, the young peck instinctively at the prominent red spot on the lower mandible of their parents' bills. The action induces an adult bird to regurgitate the food in its crop. The race *L. a. argenteus* breeds in northwest Europe, while the yellow-legged *L. a. michahellis* breeds in the Mediterranean region, though it is expanding northward.

9/ GREAT BLACK-BACKED GULL
Larus marinus

RANGE: **coastal NE North America, SW Greenland and NW Europe**
HABITAT: **coasts, locally inland waters and moors**
SIZE: **28–31 in (71–79 cm)**

The Great Black-backed Gull takes its name from its large size and black back and wings. It is a highly predatory gull, especially in the breeding season when it may live almost exclusively on seabirds and, if they are available, rabbits. At other times of the year, it often obtains food by scavenging at garbage tips, around fishing ports and along the shore.

Breeding may take place in loose colonies or the birds may build solitary nests, usually on a rock promontory or on a ridge with a good view all around. The nest is a bulky pile of vegetation.

10/ FRANKLIN'S GULL
Larus pipixcan

RANGE: **breeds on North American prairies; winters on coasts of Central and South America**
HABITAT: **breeds in freshwater marshes; winters on coasts**
SIZE: **13–15 in (33–38 cm)**

The soft gray upperparts and white underparts of this gull have earned it the local name of Prairie Dove. Within its restricted breeding range, the species is abundant, nesting in colonies of several thousand pairs in marshes or beside lakes. The birds feed on surrounding farmland, eating a variety of agricultural pests such as wireworms and cutworms.

The nests are built of vegetation close to or in shallow water. The females lay 3 eggs and the young hatch with either a gray or a brown downy coat, although these two color phases do not persist in the adult plumage.

11/ SILVER GULL
Larus novaehollandiae

RANGE: **S Africa, Australia, New Zealand**
HABITAT: **coasts, inland lakes and rivers**
SIZE: **15–17 in (38–43 cm)**

There are several races of the Silver Gull, including *L. n. novaehollandiae* of southern Australia and Tasmania, *L. n. forsteri* of northern Australia and New Caledonia, the Red-billed Gull *L. n. scopulinus* of New Zealand, and Hartlaub's Gull *L. n. hartlaubii* of southern Africa. All are common and adaptable birds, which have successfully exploited urban habitats. They often feed around harbors and garbage tips, and forage widely over farmland.

The Red-billed Gull breeds in huge colonies numbering as many as 100,000 birds. Some of the largest colonies occur on offshore islands. At least one breeding site, however, is located well inland, in an area of thermal springs.

12/ ROSS'S GULL
Rhodostethia rosea

RANGE: **Arctic Siberia, Canada and Greenland**
HABITAT: **breeds on Arctic tundra and scrub; winters at sea**
SIZE: **11¾–12½ in (30–32 cm)**

Perhaps the most beautiful of all the gulls, Ross's Gull in its breeding plumage has white underparts suffused with pink. For a long time the breeding grounds of this small gull were quite unknown, though they were obviously in northern latitudes. They were finally discovered in northern Siberia in 1905, where the birds were found nesting among low scrub in river valleys. More recently, breeding has been confirmed in northern Canada and in Greenland. The birds build a nest of vegetation that may stand 8 in (20 cm) above the damp, swampy ground.

13/ BLACK-LEGGED KITTIWAKE
Rissa tridactyla

RANGE: **circumpolar Arctic and temperate coasts**
HABITAT: **coastal and open sea**
SIZE: **15¼–18 in (39–46 cm)**

This widespread species is often known simply as the Kittiwake: the other species, the Red-legged Kittiwake, is restricted to the Bering Sea region of the North Pacific. Kittiwakes traditionally nest in large colonies on narrow cliff ledges, building a nest of seaweed, lined with grass. As the seaweed dries, it cements itself to the rock. In recent years, ledges on buildings have proved attractive to Black-legged Kittiwakes, and there are now many nesting colonies around harbors and fishing ports.

The 2–3 eggs are incubated by both parents for about 27 days. The young, when they hatch, have strong claws on their toes, enabling them to cling to their precarious home.

14/ SWALLOW-TAILED GULL
Creagrus furcatus

RANGE: **breeds Galapagos Islands and Colombia; winters off NW South America**
HABITAT: **breeds on coasts; winters on open sea**
SIZE: **21½–23½ in (55–60 cm)**

With its dark gray head, boldly patterned wings and deeply forked tail, the Swallow-tailed Gull has a particularly striking appearance. Its eyes are much larger than those of most gulls and are more forward-facing, giving the bird binocular vision. These are adaptions that help the birds find food at night. Swallow-tailed Gulls range several hundred miles from their breeding grounds out over the ocean and take squid and other sea creatures that come to the surface after dark.

The bird's nest is a cup of small stones among rocks in which it lays a single egg. The incubation period is 34 days and the young chick is then brooded and guarded by one parent throughout the day.

15/ SABINE'S GULL
Xema sabini

RANGE: **circumpolar Arctic**
HABITAT: **breeds Arctic coasts and islands; winters on the open sea**
SIZE: **13–14 in (33–36 cm)**

Small invertebrates form the principal food for the elegant Sabine's Gull and the bird uses various methods to pursue its prey. These include pecking daintily along the water's edge, running over mud like a shorebird, swimming and spinning around on the water like a phalarope, and diving into the ocean from above.

Presumably as a defense against predators, parents lead their young away from the nest as soon as they hatch. The adults also perform a distraction display if danger threatens their chicks. Both these types of behavior are more typical of shorebirds than of gulls.

TERNS, SKIMMERS, AUKS

BLACK TERN

non-breeding

CASPIAN TERN

ARCTIC TERN

ROYAL TERN

SOOTY TERN

COMMON NODDY

WHITE TERN

juv

juv

INCA TERN

bridled form

BLACK SKIMMER

COMMON MURRE

non-breeding

non-breeding

DOVEKIE

BLACK GUILLEMOT

ATLANTIC PUFFIN

n-breeding

chick

ANCIENT MURRELET

MARBLED MURRELET

FAMILY STERNIDAE
Terns

Slender seabirds, with long, pointed wings and forked tails. Plumage mainly white, gray, brown and black. Sexes alike. Nest sites variable. Eggs 1–3, cream, greenish or brownish, blotched. Incubation 13–30 days, chicks leave nest soon after hatching but remain near parents. 41 species.

1/ BLACK TERN
Chlidonias nigra

RANGE: **breeds central S Eurasia and North America; winters in tropics mainly N of Equator**
HABITAT: **breeds on marshes and pools; winters on coasts**
SIZE: $8\frac{1}{2}$–$9\frac{1}{2}$ in (22–24 cm)

The Black Tern feeds mainly on aquatic insects and their larvae and obtains almost all its prey in flight. Instead of hovering above the water and then diving into it, like many other species of tern, the Black Tern and the other "marsh terns" of the genus *Chlidonias* hover and then swoop down to peck from the water's surface in mid-flight. Black Terns also hawk for insects in midair and even follow the plow on farmland, darting down to snatch small worms and other invertebrates exposed on the soil.

The bird's nest is composed of aquatic vegetation and is often floating, anchored to growing plants. The usual clutch is 3 eggs. The young leave the nest when they are a few days old and hide in nearby vegetation.

2/ CASPIAN TERN
Hydroprogne caspia

RANGE: **worldwide, but breeding range is fragmentary**
HABITAT: **breeds on coastal and inland marshes; winters on coasts**
SIZE: $18\frac{3}{4}$–$23\frac{1}{4}$ in (48–59 cm)

The Caspian Tern is the largest of the terns, with an orange-red, daggerlike bill. It breeds in large colonies or in solitary pairs, its nests merely scrapes in the ground, sometimes with a little vegetation.

The Caspian Tern's range is remarkable in covering all 5 continents, but the breeding areas are hundreds of miles apart. This is probably because the species requires remote coastal and marshland nesting sites with rich feeding areas close by. Such places are naturally scarce and some potential sites may have become unsuitable due to human activity.

3/ ARCTIC TERN
Sterna paradisaea

RANGE: **breeds circumpolar Arctic and sub-Arctic; winters S to Antarctic Ocean**
HABITAT: **breeds on coasts; winters at sea**
SIZE: 13–15 in (33–38 cm)

The annual migration of the Arctic Tern is probably the longest of any bird. From their breeding grounds in the Arctic, the birds fly south to winter in the oceans just north of the Antarctic pack-ice, a round trip of more than 20,000 mls (32,000 km) every year. Because they breed in the

northern summer and visit the Antarctic Ocean during the southern summer, they experience more daylight hours in the course of a year than any other living animal.

Arctic Terns breed in colonies on shingle beaches and among rocks. Like some other terns, they vigorously defend their nests against predators, or even approaching humans, by dive-bombing and actually striking the intruders around the head with their beaks.

4/ SOOTY TERN
Sterna fuscata

RANGE: **tropical and subtropical latitudes**
HABITAT: **breeds on coasts and islands; winters on the open sea**
SIZE: 17–$17\frac{3}{4}$ in (43–45 cm)

The Sooty Tern is mainly black above and white beneath, with a long, forked tail. It takes its alternative name, Wideawake Tern, from its loud, repeated call of *ker-wacky-wack*, and perhaps also from its nocturnal feeding habits. The bird hardly ever seems to land on the water, but obtains its food by swooping down and pecking from the surface. It seems likely that it actually sleeps on the wing.

Nesting takes place in enormous colonies, numbering tens or even hundreds of thousands of birds. However, egg-collecting by humans has been a serious problem in some areas, and variations in food supply can also cause significant fluctuations in breeding success.

5/ ROYAL TERN
Thalasseus maximus

RANGE: **breeds on coasts of Central America and W Africa; winters on coasts to S**
HABITAT: **coastal and marine**
SIZE: 18–$20\frac{3}{4}$ in (46–53 cm)

In the past, Royal Terns were commonly observed on the west coast of Africa but it was thought that they were migrants from the American breeding range. Then a large colony was discovered about 30 years ago in Mauritania, and smaller ones

subsequently in Senegal and Gambia. It is still not known whether the species undergoes any transatlantic migration or whether the colonies are entirely separate.

Colonies are often large, with up to several thousand pairs. The young are looked after by their parents for an unusually long time. Adults have been observed still feeding chicks that are 5 months old.

6/ INCA TERN
Larosterna inca

RANGE: **Ecuador to Chile**
HABITAT: **coastal and marine**
SIZE: $15\frac{3}{4}$–$16\frac{1}{2}$ in (40–42 cm)

The dapper blue-gray plumage of the Inca Tern is adorned with an extraordinary white moustachial plume that extends back below the eye and then curls around and down toward the breast. This is a gregarious species, roosting in flocks of many thousands on sandy beaches, along with flocks of gulls.

Inca Terns are graceful flyers, often hovering over the water before dipping down with rapid movements to snatch a food item from the surface. They also follow feeding whales and seals to seize scraps of food.

7/ COMMON NODDY
Anous stolidus

RANGE: **equatorial**
HABITAT: **breeds on cliffs and wooded islands; winters on the open sea**
SIZE: $15\frac{3}{4}$–$17\frac{3}{4}$ in (40–45 cm)

The Common Noddy's pale lavender-gray forehead and crown give the bird a white-capped appearance when seen in the distance. The name "noddy" refers to the bird's habit of bowing and nodding its head during courtship. The pair indulge in prolonged displays, with the male ritually presenting food to his mate.

The Common Noddy's choice of nest site varies greatly over its wide range. In many places colonies nest in the open on the ground, others use broad cliff ledges, while some build nests of twigs and plant stems in the branches of trees and scrub. The female lays only 1 egg and the combined incubation and fledging periods total over 11 weeks.

8/ WHITE TERN
Gygis alba

RANGE: **equatorial**
HABITAT: **open sea; nests on wooded islands**
SIZE: **11–13 in (28–33 cm)**

The White Tern has pure white plumage, large black eyes and a slightly upturned black bill. In flight, the wings appear almost translucent against the sky and this, together with its buoyant and graceful flight, has led to the species also being called the Fairy Tern (although there is another species, *Sterna nereis*, in Australia, New Zealand and New Caledonia that is more properly known by this name).

Unlike most terns, with their colonial habits, this species is a solitary breeder. It does not build a nest, but lays its single egg on a tiny cliff ledge, or on a horizontal tree branch supported by a small fork or even just a knot or slight unevenness on the branch. There is often barely room for the incubating bird. The chick hatches after about 5 weeks, complete with strong feet and claws with which it clings to its tiny nest site.

FAMILY RYNCHOPIDAE
Skimmers

Medium waterbirds. Extended, flattened lower bill. Black or brown, white or pale gray underparts. Sexes similar. Nest in scrapes. Eggs 2–5, white-beige, blotched. Incubation 22–24 days, nestling period 25–30 days. 3 species.

9/ BLACK SKIMMER
Rynchops niger

RANGE: **S North America, Caribbean and South America**
HABITAT: **coastal and riverine marshes**
SIZE: **15¾–19½ in (40–50 cm)**

Like the 2 other species of skimmer, the Black Skimmer has an extraordinary bill in which the lower mandible is flattened and is a third as long again as the rounded upper mandible. When feeding, the bird flies close to the surface of the water, with only the tip of the lower mandible submerged. As soon as this encounters prey, such as small fish and shrimp, the bird throws its head downward and snaps its bill shut.

Much feeding takes place at dawn and dusk, and also by moonlight. Uniquely among birds, skimmers have vertical pupils in their eyes that can be closed to slits in bright sunshine, or opened to full circles in poor light.

FAMILY ALCIDAE
Auks

Small to medium short-tailed, short-necked marine divers. Flightless following annual molt. Dark brown or black, underparts white. Sexes similar. Nest ashore on ledges or in crevices. Eggs 1–2, variable. Incubation 29–42 days, nestling period 2–50 days. 22 species.

10/ DOVEKIE
Alle alle

RANGE: **North Atlantic and adjacent Arctic**
HABITAT: **breeds on coastal scree and in rock crevices; otherwise on open sea**
SIZE: **7¾–9¾ in (20–25 cm)**

The Dovekie is a small, stubby seabird, with little or no neck and short wings. Its principal food is plankton, small crustaceans and other marine animals. During the breeding season it brings food back to the nest in its crop, which, when full, produces a distinct bulge in the throat.

Breeding colonies may contain several million pairs of Dovekies, their nests placed deep among the fallen rocks of coastal scree. Colonies are constantly patrolled by the species' main predators, Glaucous Gulls, which wait their chance to snatch unwary birds as they enter or leave their nest-holes.

11/ COMMON MURRE
Uria aalge

RANGE: **circumpolar Eurasia and North America**
HABITAT: **open sea; breeds on coastal cliffs**
SIZE: **15¾–17 in (40–43 cm)**

On land, the upright stance of the Common Murre, combined with its dark head and upperparts and white underparts, give the bird the appearance of a small penguin. The bridled form is a genetic variation that occurs only in the North Atlantic, more often in northern populations.

Common Murres breed in large colonies on narrow cliff ledges. Each pair's single egg is markedly pointed so that it will roll in a circle if pushed and not fall off the ledge. The chicks leave the nest site when they are only about 3 weeks old. Their wing covert feathers grow first, giving them just enough power to half-glide, half-fly from the ledge down to the water. The chicks then swim away out to sea, usually with the male parents. This early departure from the ledges means that the parents can take their young to the food supply instead of continuing to bring the food to them from as far as 50 mls (80 km) away.

12/ BLACK GUILLEMOT
Cepphus grylle

RANGE: **North Atlantic and adjacent Arctic**
HABITAT: **breeds on coasts; winters mainly in coastal waters**
SIZE: **11¼–14 in (30–36 cm)**

In contrast to its pale, mottled winter plumage, the breeding dress of the Black Guillemot is a bold jet-black, except for a broad white patch on the upper side of the wing and white on the inner half of the underwing. The bird also has bright red legs and feet that show up distinctly in clear water and on land. It utters a loud and melodious whistling call, both in flight and on the water, and as it calls, it reveals the bright red lining of its mouth. During courtship, one bird circles closely around its mate, producing a softer version of the whistle at frequent intervals.

Black Guillemots breed alone or in small colonies of up to 100 pairs. They may nest under boulders, in rock crevices or in caves, laying their eggs on the bare earth or rock.

13/ MARBLED MURRELET
Brachyramphus marmoratus

RANGE: **N Pacific, S to Japan and California**
HABITAT: **inshore marine; breeds in woodland and tundra near the coast**
SIZE: **9½–9¾ in (24–25 cm)**

The Marbled Murrelet takes its name from the pale edgings to its feathers that give the bird a mottled appearance, especially in the breeding season. Although it is an abundant species, with hundreds of thousands occurring off the coasts of Alaska, its breeding habits are virtually unknown. Only a few solitary nests have ever been found. Two of these were several miles inland in forested areas, placed in the fork of a large branch and in a tree hollow about 100 ft (30 m) above the ground. Two other nests were in hollows in the open tundra of small subarctic islands.

14/ ANCIENT MURRELET
Synthliboramphus antiquus

RANGE: **N Pacific and Bering Sea, S to Japan and Mexico**
HABITAT: **coastal and open sea; breeds on coasts**
SIZE: **9½–10½ in (24–27 cm)**

Large breeding colonies of Ancient Murrelets, containing up to 40,000 pairs, occur in coastal forests. The birds make their nests in burrows up to 3 ft (1 m) deep among rocks, grass or even tree roots. The eggs are incubated by both parents. The incubating bird calls from the burrow to help its mate find the correct nest entrance within the colony. The young leave the nest within 2–3 days of hatching and scramble down the slopes and cliffs from the nest site to join their parents on the open ocean.

This species' curious name comes from the fine, hairlike white feathers on its head that develop during the breeding season, resembling the white hairs of an old person.

15/ ATLANTIC PUFFIN
Fratercula arctica

RANGE: **N Atlantic and adjacent Arctic**
HABITAT: **open sea; breeds on coasts**
SIZE: **11–11¾ in (28–30 cm)**

The most distinctive feature of the Atlantic Puffin is its large red, yellow and gray-blue bill, shaped rather like the bill of a parrot. The coloring of this extraordinary appendage is particularly bright during the breeding season and helps to attract mates.

The depth of the bill, and especially its sharp edges, enable the bird to catch and hold fish. A dozen or more can be held at one time and, as each fish is caught, it is held between the tongue and the upper mandible, freeing the lower mandible for more catches. Atlantic Puffins also use their beaks to excavate nesting burrows, which can be several yards long, in grassy clifftops.

SANDGROUSE, DOVES AND PIGEONS

BLACK-BELLIED SANDGROUSE

♂

♀

PALLAS' SANDGROUSE

♂

chicks

FERAL PIGEON
checkered type

FERAL PIGEON
red type

WOOD PIGEON

ROCK DOVE

SNOW PIGEON

LAUREL PIGEON

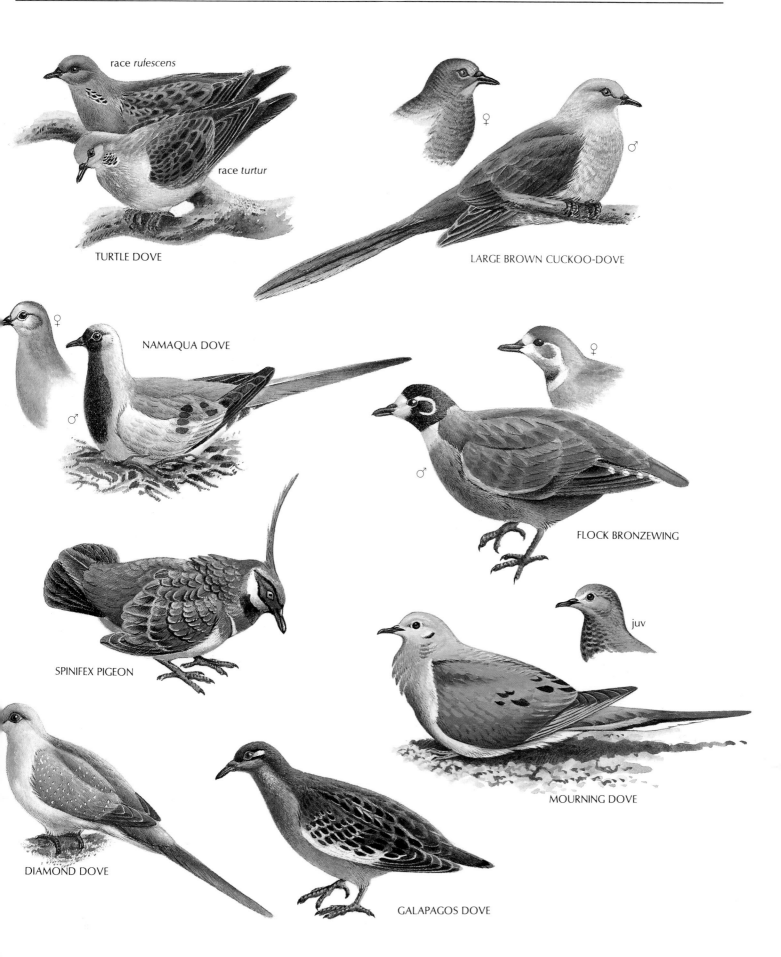

race *rufescens*

race *turtur*

TURTLE DOVE

♀

♂

LARGE BROWN CUCKOO-DOVE

♀

♂

NAMAQUA DOVE

♀

♂

♂

FLOCK BRONZEWING

SPINIFEX PIGEON

juv

MOURNING DOVE

DIAMOND DOVE

GALAPAGOS DOVE

SANDGROUSE, DOVES AND PIGEONS

FAMILY PTEROCLIDIDAE
Sandgrouse

Dumpy, medium, seed-eating ground birds. Usually long-tailed. Cryptic plumage. Sexes differ. Nest in scrape on ground. Eggs 3 (rarely 2), dull pinkish, greenish or cream with brown or olive spots or blotches. Incubation 21–31 days, chicks leave nest soon after hatching. 16 species.

1/ PALLAS' SANDGROUSE
Syrrhaptes paradoxus

RANGE: **SW USSR to China and Mongolia**
HABITAT: **arid open plains and valleys**
SIZE: **$11\frac{3}{4}$–16 in (30–41 cm)**

Uniquely in its family, Pallas' Sandgrouse has a lengthened tip to the longest wing feather. Like most sandgrouse, and as an adaptation to its arid habitat, the male has highly absorbent belly feathers which enable him to store water after immersing his underparts in a water hole and carry it back to his chicks. They drink it eagerly as he stands erect, allowing the water to run down a central groove in his belly feathers.

In the last century and early in this one, thousands of these birds would, from time to time, spread west across Europe. These events occurred mainly in the spring and early summer, probably triggered by unseasonal cold weather and food shortages. After such irregular irruptions, breeding often took place far to the west of the normal range, even in Britain. The last large irruption took place in 1908, although there have been a few smaller ones since then, involving only a few birds. It is not clear why these dramatic movements have apparently ceased, but it is probably due to a contraction in the range of the species in western Siberia since the early 1900s.

2/ BLACK-BELLIED SANDGROUSE
Pterocles orientalis

RANGE: **S to SE Europe, N Africa, SW Asia**
HABITAT: **flat and upland plains, saltflats**
SIZE: **13–$13\frac{3}{4}$ in (33–35 cm)**

As with other sandgrouse and all birds of arid areas, water plays a vital role in the daily regime of the Black-bellied Sandgrouse. Flocks of up to 50 birds forage during the day for tiny seeds. They roost in the open, then just before dawn fly to the nearest source of fresh water, natural or artificial. In regions with little water, flocks may come from a wide area until several hundred or even thousand may have gathered. Much jostling and squabbling takes place as each bird drinks its fill, before finally departing for another day's feeding.

In flight, flocks of Black-bellied Sandgrouse utter a soft gurgling or bubbling call, helping to keep the birds in contact with one another.

FAMILY COLUMBIDAE
Doves and pigeons

Small to large, dumpy, mainly tree-dwelling birds. Plumage variable. Sexes usually similar. Simple twig nest; a few nest on the ground or in holes. Both sexes produce a curdlike substance, "pigeon's milk," from their crop to feed the young. It resembles mammalian milk in composition. Eggs 1–2, white. Incubation 13–28 days, nestling period 12–36 days. 300 species.

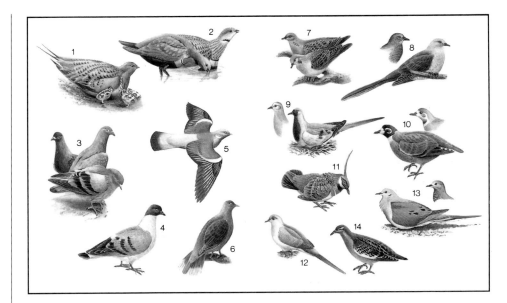

3/ ROCK DOVE & FERAL PIGEON
Columba livia

RANGE: **native to S Eurasia and N Africa; domesticated worldwide**
HABITAT: **cliffs and gorges, close to open country; domestic form mainly urban**
SIZE: **$12\frac{1}{4}$–$13\frac{1}{2}$ in (31–34 cm)**

The wild Rock Dove is a bird of cliffs and rocky terrain, but its feral descendants thrive in towns and cities throughout the world. Originally, wild-caught Rock Doves were reared for food and, later, for producing fancy breeds and racing pigeons. Escapes, which still continue, soon led to feral populations gathering in urban areas, using building ledges for nest sites and gleaning scraps of food from the streets and surrounding fields. These Feral Pigeons vary greatly in plumage. While some are similar to Rock Doves in coloration, others are rusty red or checkered.

The remarkable homing ability exploited in racing pigeons is at odds with the almost entirely sedentary habits of both wild and feral birds. In the wild, movements of more than a few miles are rare, yet racing pigeons can find their way home from distances of hundreds or even thousands of miles without difficulty.

4/ SNOW PIGEON
Columba leuconota

RANGE: **Himalayas, NW Burma, W China and SW Turkestan**
HABITAT: **mountainous areas with high rainfall, above 6,500–10,000 ft (2,000–3,000 m)**
SIZE: **$12\frac{1}{4}$–$13\frac{1}{2}$ in (31–34 cm)**

As well as having white plumage, the Snow Pigeon lives up to its name by inhabiting areas close to or even above the snow line. It nests in cliff caves, sometimes forming small colonies.

Outside the breeding season, Snow Pigeons roost on cliff ledges well up the mountainsides, flying down into the nearby valleys for food as soon as the sun rises high enough. Birds foraging for seeds in a field still partly covered by melting snow are quite difficult to see, as the patterned plumage provides effective camouflage.

5/ WOOD PIGEON
Columba palumbus

RANGE: **Europe, N Africa, SW Asia, Iran and India; also Azores**
HABITAT: **woodland and adjacent farmland**
SIZE: **$15\frac{3}{4}$–$16\frac{1}{2}$ in (40–42 cm)**

Wood Pigeons are serious pests of agricultural crops in some areas, with flocks sometimes numbering thousands or even tens of thousands. These birds frequently raid fields planted with cereals, brassicas (cabbages, kale and brussels sprouts), clover and peas.

The distinctive display flight of the male Wood Pigeon (also rarely performed by the female) consists of a towering flight with several slow wing beats toward the top, when the wings produce 2–3 very loud claps. These sounds may come either from direct contact between the wings or by a whip-crack effect of the feather tips. The bird then glides downward and flies up again to repeat the process.

6/ LAUREL PIGEON
Columba junoniae　　　　　　　R

RANGE: **Canary Islands (Las Palmas, Gomera and Tenerife)**
HABITAT: **mountainous, scrub-covered slopes and adjacent cultivated areas**
SIZE: **$14\frac{1}{2}$–15 in (37–38 cm)**

Hunting and habitat destruction have contributed to the scarcity of this species, restricted as it is to just one group of islands. Laurels form part of the scrub vegetation in which it lives, hence its name.

The natural food of the Laurel Pigeon is chiefly fruit, berries and seeds obtained from trees in mountainous areas. Much feeding also takes place on harvested flax and cereal crops farther down the slopes. The Laurel Pigeon can run quickly, rather like a partridge. At other times, it walks with a long, swinging gait, accompanied by bowing of the head and raising of the tail.

7/ TURTLE DOVE
Streptopelia turtur
RANGE: **Europe, N Africa, SW Asia; winters in Africa S of the Sahara but N of the Equator**
HABITAT: **open woodland and cultivated land with trees in sheltered lowlands**
SIZE: **10¼–11 in (26–28 cm)**

The soft, purring *turr-turr* call, from which the Turtle Dove takes its name, is a familiar sound of summer days in Europe. The notes are repeated several times as a territorial advertisement song lasting about 15 seconds. Another call, given in moments of excitement and, perhaps, anger, is a short, explosive popping sound just like the pulling of a cork from a bottle.

Although it is protected through most of its European breeding range, the Turtle Dove is shot and netted in huge numbers for sport and for food while on migration, particularly in countries bordering the Mediterranean. The 2 races illustrated are *S. t. turtur* of Europe, the Canary Islands and Asia Minor and *S. t. rufescens* of Egypt and northern Sudan.

8/ LARGE BROWN CUCKOO-DOVE
Macropygia amboinensis
RANGE: **E coast of Australia, New Guinea, Indonesia, Philippines**
HABITAT: **rain forest shrubbery and forest edge**
SIZE: **11¾–17¾ in (30–45 cm)**

This bird spends much of its time in the tops of trees or shrubs, making short flights from one perch to another on its rounded wings. Its penetrating, high-pitched *coo* carries well through the dense rain forest vegetation.

Large Brown Cuckoo-Doves feed on a variety of fruits from the forest canopy and understory and are particularly fond of introduced weeds and shrubs on the forest edge. They are agile climbers and can reach berries on thin branches. Sometimes, the birds will pick grit from the ground to aid digestion. Their nest is a platform of twigs and vines built in a low fork, in a vine tangle or on the top of a tree fern. The single white egg is incubated by both sexes.

9/ NAMAQUA DOVE
Oena capensis
RANGE: **sub-Saharan Africa, Arabia, S Israel**
HABITAT: **open semidesert and arid scrub**
SIZE: **10¼–11 in (26–28 cm)**

Almost half the total length of this small dove is taken up by its extraordinarily long, diamond-shaped tail. Each time the bird lands, the tail is raised and fanned. The male also fans his tail during his courtship display while he indulges in a hovering, butterflylike flight, descending close to the female.

Although they are brightly patterned, Namaqua Doves are difficult to see on the ground, as they blend perfectly with the background of dry soil and stones. The birds walk with a peculiar mincing gait, often appearing rather hunch-backed, as they peck here and there for tiny seeds and the occasional insect.

10/ FLOCK BRONZEWING
Phaps histrionica
RANGE: **inland N Australia**
HABITAT: **native grassland**
SIZE: **10½–11½ in (27–29 cm)**

The Flock Bronzewing, or Flock Pigeon, has long wings that enable it to cover great distances in its search for food and water in a dry environment. Once observed in immense flocks, it has declined severely through the overgrazing of its habitat by domestic livestock.

Flock Bronzewings feed on the ground, foraging for the seeds of grass and other plants. They also pick up the undigested seeds from cattle dung. They rest and feed in the blazing sun and must fly to water holes twice daily, in the morning and evening, to replenish their water reserves. During the breeding period, courting males bow and partly open their wings to show the bronze panels. The loosely colonial nests are grass-lined scrapes under tussocks or bushes. Both sexes incubate the eggs, the male sitting by day and the female by night.

11/ SPINIFEX PIGEON
Petrophassa plumifera
RANGE: **inland N Australia**
HABITAT: **hummock grassland in arid, rocky terrain**
SIZE: **7½–9 in (19–23 cm)**

Small flocks of this desert-dwelling bird scurry along the ground, often for long distances, or make short, low flights with bursts of flapping followed by glides. At night, they huddle together to roost on the ground. They feed on the seeds of grasses and other plants of the dry interior of Australia and drink frequently.

Male Spinifex Pigeons perform bowing displays in courtship and rivals fight by chasing, circling and buffeting each other with their wings. The birds may breed throughout the year but do so mostly in spring or after rain has fallen.

12/ DIAMOND DOVE
Geopelia cuneata
RANGE: **northern and inland Australia; usually absent from coastal E and S**
HABITAT: **dry woodland and scrub**
SIZE: **7½–8¾ in (19–22 cm)**

The tiny Diamond Dove is widespread across the drier parts of Australia and is seen in the extreme east and south only after irregular coastward movements during dry periods. It feeds on the ground, eating the small seeds of grasses, herbs and other plants, as well as some green vegetation and insects. It walks along slowly when feeding but can also scurry with its tail held clear of the ground. In arid regions, it must drink daily, in the morning and in the afternoon; it wanders nomadically in search of food and water.

In courtship, the male performs a bowing display with his tail raised and fanned. The frail nest of twigs or grass stems is built in a low tree fork and the 2 white eggs are incubated by both male and female.

13/ MOURNING DOVE
Zenaida macroura
RANGE: **SE Alaska, S Canada to C Panama, Caribbean**
HABITAT: **farms, open woods, towns, gardens**
SIZE: **11¾ in (30 cm)**

This long-tailed sandy dove shows white outer tail feathers in flight. The sexes appear similar but juvenile birds have heavy spotting on their wings. Outside the breeding season, Mourning Doves are generally found in flocks and they roost communally. They are mostly ground feeders, taking a variety of grain and seeds and, occasionally, small invertebrates. The advertising call is a series of 3–4 mournful coos, from which the birds take their common name.

Mourning Doves are widely hunted gamebirds, but their populations remain large. They produce 2 or 3 broods each season and have benefited from the conversion of forests to farmland. In the deep South, for example Mississippi, they begin nesting in February and continue until the end of October, sometimes having as many as 6 nesting attempts in a season.

They are monogamous and have elaborate courtship displays, with the male strutting before the female or chasing her, while puffing his feathers and cooing. The males also perform display flights, with periods of noisy flapping and gliding. They are solitary nesters, building a flimsy platform in shrubs or trees at heights of up to 50 ft (15 m).

14/ GALAPAGOS DOVE
Zenaida galapagoensis
RANGE: **Galapagos Islands**
HABITAT: **dry, rocky, low-lying areas with some scrub or cactus**
SIZE: **8 in (20 cm)**

Like many Galapagos birds, this dove is very tame. It spends much of its time on the ground, and is an accomplished walker and runner. Although it occasionally eats cactus pulp, it feeds mostly on seeds. It sometimes scratches for food, flicking dirt toward its body. Although usually silent, its occasional calls consist of long, rolling cooing notes.

The male's courtship display includes strutting, tail-spreading, bowing, wing-drooping and feather-puffing. The male and female also run around each other. The simple nest is made of grass and often placed on the ground under a sheltering rock. The birds have also been known to use an old nest of the Galapagos Mockingbird *Nesomimus trifasciatus* for a foundation. Like many other doves, the Galapagos Dove may perform distraction displays to lure intruders away from its nest.

DOVES AND PIGEONS

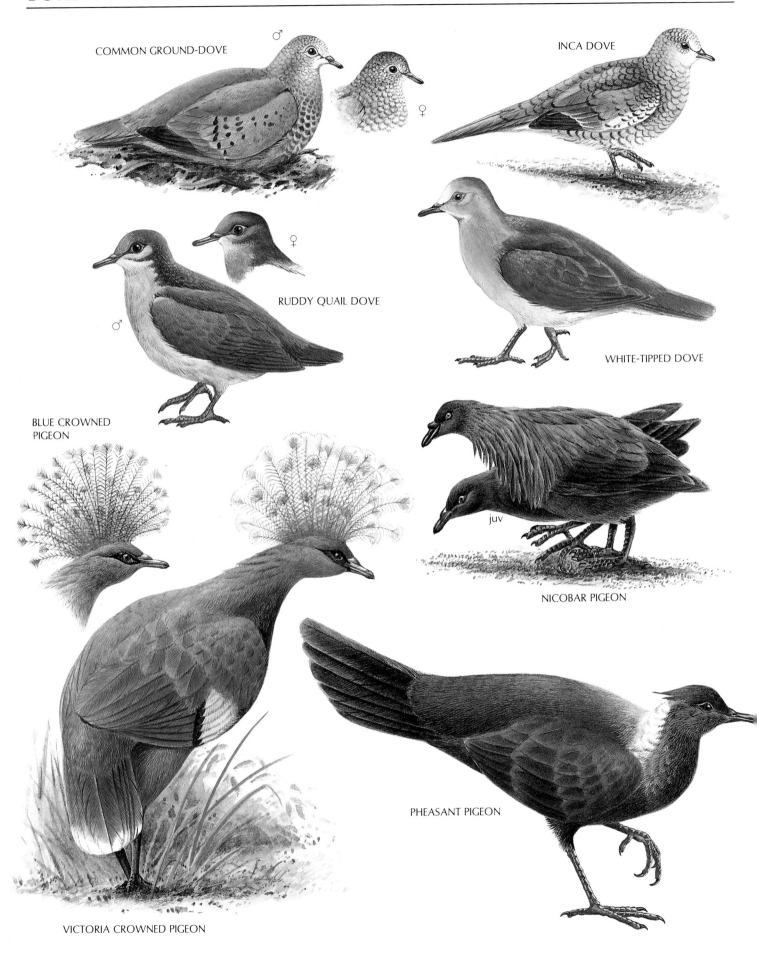

COMMON GROUND-DOVE ♂ ♀

INCA DOVE

RUDDY QUAIL DOVE ♀

♂

WHITE-TIPPED DOVE

BLUE CROWNED PIGEON

juv

NICOBAR PIGEON

PHEASANT PIGEON

VICTORIA CROWNED PIGEON

TOOTH-BILLED PIGEON

juv

AFRICAN GREEN PIGEON

GREEN IMPERIAL PIGEON

race *magnificus*

race *puella*

WOMPOO FRUIT-DOVE

MADAGASCAR BLUE PIGEON

juv

TOP-KNOT PIGEON

LUZON BLEEDING HEART

NEW ZEALAND PIGEON

DOVES AND PIGEONS

1/ COMMON GROUND-DOVE
Columbina passerina

RANGE: S USA and Caribbean to Ecuador and Brazil; Bahamas
HABITAT: open country, roadsides, farms, grassland
SIZE: 6½ in (16.5 cm)

Common Ground-Doves are tiny birds, little larger than sparrows. They usually occur in pairs, although they will often gather in flocks in winter. Largely terrestrial, they forage on the ground, bobbing their heads as they walk. Small seeds and berries make up the bulk of their diet, along with the occasional insect. Their usual call is a soft, cooing whistle. When they do fly, their bright chestnut primary wing feathers are apparent. The female is generally duller than the male.

Courtship displays are elaborate, with the male strutting about before the female or chasing her, cooing as he does so and puffing his feathers out. The birds nest mostly on the ground, but will also use bushes, palm fronds, vines and low shrubs. The flimsy cup is made from grasses and plant fibers. The pair sometimes re-use the nest for a second brood and occasionally use the old nest of another species as a platform for their own.

2/ INCA DOVE
Scardafella inca

RANGE: locally from SW USA to N Costa Rica
HABITAT: towns, open areas, farms, riverside scrub, cactus, mesquite
SIZE: 8 in (20 cm)

This tiny dove reveals the rich chestnut color of its primary wing feathers when it takes flight. Its usual call is a series of 2-note coos, but it also utters a variety of soft or throaty display, threat and alarm calls. Inca Doves form flocks in winter and roost communally. On cold nights, they are known to huddle together in groups, with some birds on top of the others forming "pyramids." They are largely terrestrial feeders, foraging mainly for seeds and cultivated grain. As with all pigeons, the young are fed on crop "milk" – a liquid food secreted in the esophagus of the adults.

Inca Doves are monogamous, with an elaborate courtship display in which the male struts, head-bobs, fans his tail and utters cooing notes. They nest in bushes or shady trees, 3–23 ft (1–7 m) above the ground.

3/ WHITE-TIPPED DOVE
Leptotila verreauxi

RANGE: S Texas and Mexico S to W Peru, C Argentina and Uruguay; Trinidad and Tobago, Aruba
HABITAT: arid to semiarid environments; open woodland, plantations
SIZE: 11 in (28 cm)

This solitary, terrestrial dove, also known as the White-fronted Dove, feeds mostly on seeds it finds on the ground, but it also eats some insects. Although often hidden among trees, shrubs or other cover, it emerges into the open to feed. If disturbed, it will frequently fly up to perch in a tree. Its voice has been likened to the sound

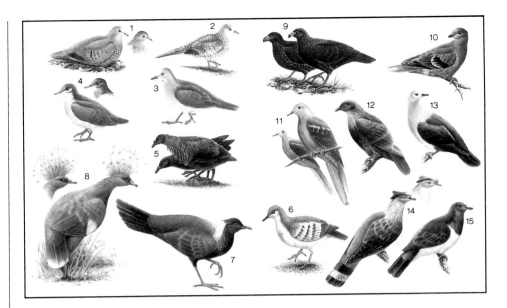

produced when a person blows across the top of a narrow-mouthed bottle. White-tipped Doves build a flimsy platform nest of small twigs, in which they lay a clutch of 2 white eggs. Over much of this bird's extensive range, nesting occurs in all months of the year, but breeding is seasonal in some localities.

4/ RUDDY QUAIL DOVE
Geotrygon montana

RANGE: Mexico, Central America S to Bolivia and Brazil; Caribbean
HABITAT: humid lowland forest
SIZE: 9 in (23 cm)

This dove is especially adapted for life in the shadows of tropical forests. Although it appears as a beautifully colored bird in good light, the colors blend into the shadows of the forest floor, allowing the Ruddy Quail Dove to remain undetected from only a few yards away. Its diet includes seeds and small fruit found on the forest floor. The repetitive call is a deep, booming *coo*.

The flimsy twig nest is lined with leaves and placed on a stump, a low branch, or a tangle of vegetation less than 6 ft (2 m) above the forest floor. The parents share the incubation duties, with the incoming parent often bringing a leaf to add to the nest.

5/ NICOBAR PIGEON
Caloenas nicobarica

RANGE: Nicobar and Andaman islands, E through Indonesia and the Philippines to New Guinea and the Solomon Islands
HABITAT: forested islands
SIZE: 13 in (33 cm)

The Nicobar Pigeon is a ground pigeon, with a knob on its bill, a cape of long, hacklelike plumes and a white tail. It occurs only on small islands over its extensive range. This is perhaps because competitors or predators exclude the species from breeding on large islands and continental areas. It has declined markedly in abundance through heavy hunting pressure and clearance of habitat.

The Nicobar Pigeon forages alone on the ground for fallen fruits, seeds and nuts. It can even eat hard nuts that humans can open only with a hammer. This is made possible by the bird's muscular gizzard. Nicobar Pigeons commute in large flocks between their foraging and breeding islands.

6/ LUZON BLEEDING HEART
Gallicolumba luzonica

RANGE: Luzon and Polillo islands (Philippines)
HABITAT: forests
SIZE: 11–12 in (28–30 cm)

Of all the 5 species of bleeding heart dove, this bird most lives up to its name. The bright red oval patch on its breast forms a groove between surrounding pink "blood-stained" feathers and has misled many people into believing the bird is seriously injured. It is an important element in the bird's courtship displays.

Although it lives exclusively in forests, the Luzon Bleeding Heart obtains all its food on the ground, where it forages for fallen seeds and berries. Unusually for a bird in the pigeon family, it also takes some grubs and other invertebrates. When danger threatens, it usually flies only a short distance before it lands and scuttles off into thick vegetation.

7/ PHEASANT PIGEON
Otidiphaps nobilis

RANGE: New Guinea and offshore islands, Aru Islands
HABITAT: foothill and mountain rain forest
SIZE: 18 in (46 cm)

The Pheasant Pigeon is a large, fowl-like, ground-dwelling pigeon. In many respects, it resembles a megapode (pp. 110–13) rather than other pigeons. It keeps to the undergrowth, walking with its bantamlike tail pumping up and down, but it can run fast and will fly heavily and noisily to escape danger. It feeds on fallen fruits, berries, seeds, insects and mollusks.

In courtship, the male performs a bowing display with his tail raised and gives a loud, growling call. The female responds by preening his head. The nest of sticks is placed in a tree, in the undergrowth or on the ground between the buttressed roots of a tree. The male supplies the material for the nest and the female works it into a platform. Both parents incubate the single white egg and rear the young.

8/ VICTORIA CROWNED PIGEON
Goura victoria [?]
RANGE: N New Guinea, Biak and Yapen islands
HABITAT: lowland rain forest
SIZE: 26 in (66 cm)

There are 3 species of crowned pigeon in New Guinea: the Victoria Crowned Pigeon, the Blue Crowned Pigeon *G. cristata* and the Maroon-breasted Crowned Pigeon *G. scheepmakeri*. They are the world's largest pigeons, but have sadly declined in abundance as a result of heavy hunting pressure.

Victoria Crowned Pigeons forage on the ground in small flocks, searching for fallen fruit, berries and seeds. If disturbed, they fly off noisily to perch on a tree branch. A male defends his territory by opening one wing, ready to strike buffeting blows on any intruder, while fanning and tilting his tail. In courtship he performs a bowing display, nodding his lowered head and fanning his tail up and down while giving a booming call. Male and female then preen each other.

9/ TOOTH-BILLED PIGEON
Didunculus strigirostris [V]
RANGE: Upolu and Savaii islands (Samoa)
HABITAT: wooded mountainsides at altitudes of 1,000–4,500 ft (300–1,400 m)
SIZE: 13 in (33 cm)

The massive hooked bill of this pigeon is reminiscent of the bill of that symbol of extinction the Dodo *Raphus cucullatus*, which was a distant relative. It is itself now vulnerable, having significantly declined since its discovery in 1845, through persecution by people and also through the introduction of cats, rats and, especially, pigs to its island homes. Its total world population is estimated at between 5,000 and 7,000 individuals.

Formerly believed to be strictly a ground feeder, the Tooth-billed Pigeon has recently been found to feed frequently on fruits in trees. It can fly strongly and roosts in trees. It probably also breeds in trees, although no nest has been found.

10/ AFRICAN GREEN PIGEON
Treron calva
RANGE: sub-Saharan Africa
HABITAT: forests, riverine woods, savanna
SIZE: 11 in (28 cm)

The overall dark olive-green plumage of this small pigeon provides perfect camouflage in its typical forest habitat. A feeding flock moving through the foliage will freeze on the approach of danger and become almost impossible to spot until it starts to move again. This is an agile species, capable of climbing through foliage and clinging to twigs in its search for fruit and seeds. It can even hang upside-down while feeding.

There are some 18 races of this species. Plumage color varies from darker green in more forested areas to a paler, yellowish green in drier regions. The race illustrated, *T. c. calva*, occurs in Guinea, northern Angola and western Congo.

11/ WOMPOO FRUIT-DOVE
Ptilinopus magnificus
RANGE: E coast of Australia, from Cape York to N New South Wales, lowland New Guinea
HABITAT: rain forest
SIZE: 13¾–17¾ in (35–45 cm)

Despite its striking and beautiful coloration (it is also known as the Magnificent Fruit-Dove), this pigeon is difficult to locate in the forest canopy, unless it calls with the deep double coo that gives it its common name. It has declined in abundance in the south of its range through habitat destruction, and has also suffered from heavy hunting.

Wompoo Fruit-Doves feed in the canopy, eating a variety of fruits. They clamber about in the foliage and often reveal their presence by the sound of falling fruit. They make seasonal movements in search of food, mostly keeping to rain forest canopy. Their frail stick nests are built on leafy branches and they lay a single white egg.

No other pigeons – indeed, few birds – show such a great difference in size between races as this species. The race *P. m. puella* from New Guinea is one of the smallest – scarcely larger than a Turtle Dove *Streptopelia turtur* – while the race *P. m. magnificus* from southeastern Australia is the size of a Wood Pigeon *Columba palumbus*.

12/ MADAGASCAR BLUE PIGEON
Alectroenas madagascariensis
RANGE: Madagascar
HABITAT: evergreen forest
SIZE: 10¼ in (26 cm)

Parties of up to 12 or more of these pigeons move through the forests of Madagascar, keeping mainly to the treetops and feeding exclusively on fruit. They would be extremely difficult to see at all, if it were not for their habit of perching on dead trees projecting above the level of the forest canopy or, occasionally, on the forest edge. These birds are thought to undertake migratory movements within Madagascar, possibly related to dry and wet seasons, but the details are not clear.

Few, if any, nests of this species have been found. However, judging by the spread of dates when adults in breeding condition and juvenile birds have been collected, the breeding season is a prolonged one, lasting at least from July to March.

13/ GREEN IMPERIAL PIGEON
Ducula aenea
RANGE: India, Southeast Asia, Philippines, Indonesia, New Guinea
HABITAT: evergreen forest, mangrove swamps; also more open country with scattered woods
SIZE: 17–18 in (43–46 cm)

The principal food of this large, handsome pigeon is soft fruits, often those varieties containing hard stones. This species does not have the muscular

gizzard for grinding up hard objects and the long gut of most members of its family. Instead, it has a relatively soft stomach and short, wide gut, through which the fruit stones pass intact. The seed within is able to germinate and form new trees in the course of time.

Flocks of Green Imperial Pigeons forage through forest trees, searching for any that are in fruit. They return each night to communal roosts. If the day's food tree is not exhausted, they will return to it the next day until they have eaten the entire crop.

14/ TOP-KNOT PIGEON
Lopholaimus antarcticus
RANGE: E coast of Australia
HABITAT: rain forest
SIZE: 16½–17¾ in (42–45 cm)

The Top-knot Pigeon is named for the remarkable double crest it sports on its head. It feeds on a variety of rain forest fruits, including those of palms, and has taken readily to the introduced Camphor Laurel planted in towns and farmland. This large pigeon feeds only in the tree canopy, where it scrambles about among the foliage. Although still seen in large flocks, it has declined in abundance through habitat destruction. Its flocks fly strongly and purposefully on long, pointed wings, either above the canopy or over open country. They are nomadic birds, making long seasonal movements in search of food.

In the breeding season, the male Top-knot Pigeon performs a unique bowing display, quite unlike that of other pigeons. He erects his crest and presses his bill on his breast, his body held erect. Then he makes a deep bow, uttering a squeak at its lowest point before raising his body again. The nest is a platform of sticks built high in the outer branches of a tree, and the single white egg is incubated by both sexes.

15/ NEW ZEALAND PIGEON
Hemiphaga novaeseelandiae
RANGE: New Zealand
HABITAT: forests; also woodland patches in farmland
SIZE: 20 in (51 cm)

This is a large, colorful pigeon, with back and neck plumage that may appear gray, bronze-purple or green, depending on the light. It is a heavy bird that lands noisily in trees and crashes about while feeding. It eats a range of fruits, flowers and green vegetation, including leaves and grass. It tends to perch quietly when people approach, often allowing them to come within 3–6 ft (1–2 m).

In spring, the New Zealand Pigeon regularly performs a flight display, involving loops and stalls. Breeding takes place predominantly in summer. The nest is an open bowl of interlacing twigs, placed in the forest canopy or at a branching point well off the ground. The large Chatham Island race *H. n. chathamensis* of this species is currently endangered, with a population of no more than about 50 birds.

KEA, KAKAPO, VULTURINE PARROT, COCKATOOS, LORIES AND LORIKEETS

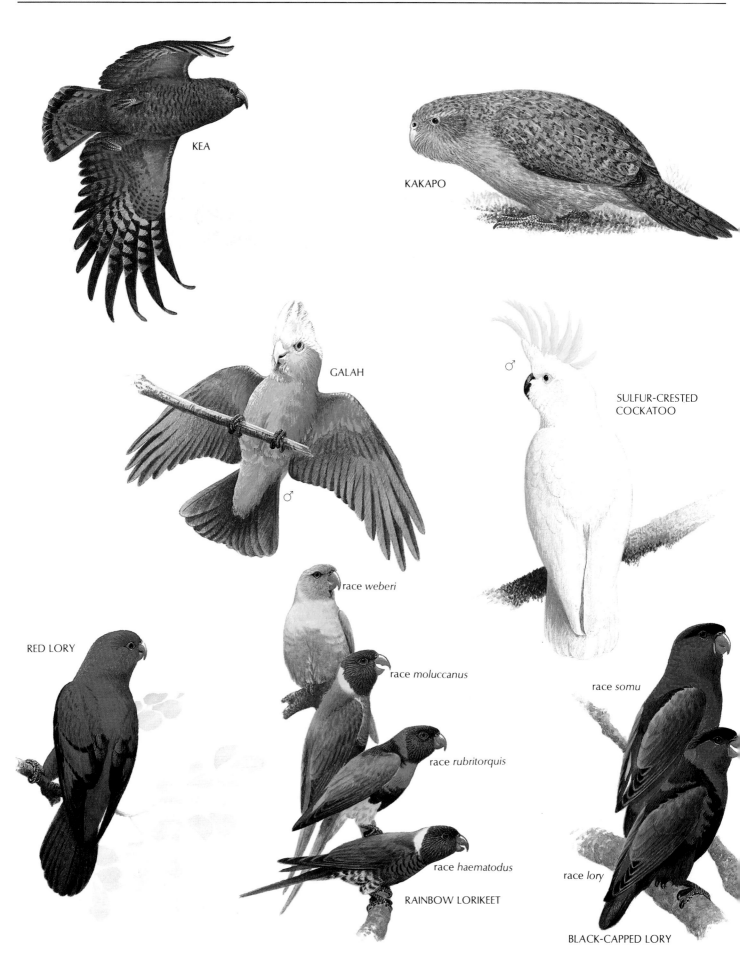

KEA

KAKAPO

GALAH

♂

SULFUR-CRESTED COCKATOO

♂

RED LORY

race *weberi*

race *moluccanus*

race *somu*

race *rubritorquis*

race *haematodus*

RAINBOW LORIKEET

race *lory*

BLACK-CAPPED LORY

VULTURINE PARROT

♀

RED-TAILED
BLACK COCKATOO

♂

PALM COCKATOO

BUFF-FACED
PYGMY PARROT

♂

race *insignis*
"Rajah Lory"

♂

♀

COCKATIEL

BLACK LORY

race *atra*

COLLARED LORY

PURPLE-CROWNED LORIKEET

163

KEA, KAKAPO, VULTURINE PARROT, COCKATOOS, LORIES AND LORIKEETS

FAMILY PSITTACIDAE
Parrots

Small to large fruit, seed and nectar-eaters. Tree, shrub and ground-dwellers. Distinctive, down-curved, hooked bills. Contains several distinct subgroups, including the lories and lorikeets, which feed on pollen and nectar using brush-tipped tongues; the cockatoos, with their movable crests and narrow, stubby tongues; and the typical parrots and parakeets, which have broad, fleshy tongues with spoon-shaped tips. Plumage very variable: mostly greenish, but some brilliantly colored. Sexes generally similar. Nest typically in tree cavities. Eggs 1–8, white. Incubation 17–35 days, nestling period 21–70 days. 340 species.

1/ KEA
Nestor notabilis

RANGE: **South Island (New Zealand)**
HABITAT: **mountain forest and ridges often above snow line; coastal forest in winter**
SIZE: **18 in (46 cm)**

Of the 6 parrot species native to New Zealand, the Kea, its close relative the Kaka *N. meridionalis*, and the Kakapo are all very unusual. The Kea uses its elongated upper bill (longer in the male) to tear into carrion, fruit, leaves and insects. It has been accused of killing sheep, and many Keas have been shot, but the accusations are probably unfounded, and it is now protected by law.

The Kea's name reflects its call, which is unforgettable when heard echoing among the mist-veiled mountain tops. The male is polygamous and will often breed with several females at the same time. The nests are built on the ground, on rock ledges or in hollow logs.

2/ KAKAPO
Strigops habroptilus   [E]

RANGE: **New Zealand, originally widespread, now reduced to 2 introduced populations on Little Barrier Island and Codfish Island**
HABITAT: **forest and scrub; may depend on fruiting yellow-wood trees for breeding**
SIZE: **24¾ in (63 cm)**

The Kakapo is quite unlike other parrots, for it is a nocturnal, ground-dwelling bird that is the only parrot to have become completely flightless. It is the heaviest of all parrots. The Kakapo evolved at a time when there were no ground predators to attack it or devour its eggs; the introduction of stoats, rats and other predators by European settlers proved disastrous, and it has now virtually disappeared from the mainland. The last breeding population on Stewart Island declined dramatically in recent years, and in the mid-1980s nearly all the remaining birds were transferred to predator-free Codfish Island.

Another unique feature of the Kakapo is its mating system. Normally solitary, the males gather at traditional mating grounds, or "leks," in late summer and advertise for mates with loud booming calls which may be heard over ½ ml (1 km) away. The females visit the leks and mate with the males of their choice. The nest is built in a burrow or among dense vegetation, and the female incubates and rears the 1–2 chicks alone.

3/ VULTURINE PARROT
Gypopsitta vulturina

RANGE: **NE Brazil**
HABITAT: **dry and periodically flooded forest**
SIZE: **9 in (23 cm)**

This odd-looking parrot owes its name to its distinctive bare forehead. It is possible that, as in vultures, this enables the bird to feed without matting its head plumage – except that in the parrot's case the food is fruit pulp and not bloody carcasses. There is another parrot sometimes called the Vulturine Parrot, but better known as Pesquet's Parrot *Psittrichas fulgidus*, from New Guinea, that also feeds on soft fruit and has a similarly bare forehead.

The Vulturine Parrot is an inconspicuous bird, normally seen feeding quietly on fruits, seeds and berries in the upper forest canopy. The details of its way of life and nesting habits are still unknown and may remain so, for it is rapidly declining as its native forests fall to the chainsaw.

4/ PALM COCKATOO
Probosciger aterrimus

RANGE: **New Guinea, including some smaller islands, NE Australia**
HABITAT: **edges of rain forest bordering on savanna, in lowlands up to 2,500 ft (750 m)**
SIZE: **19½–24¾ in (50–63 cm)**

This magnificent bird with its splendid crest is the largest of all cockatoos and the largest Australian parrot. It is also notable for its dramatic displays, given as pairs establish their territories before the beginning of the breeding season, which ranges from August to February. The male – slightly larger than the female – grips a stick with his foot and pounds a tree trunk to produce a loud drumming. As with all parrots, the bird's feet have 2 forward-pointing and 2 backward-pointing toes, which give it a strong, dexterous grip.

The nest is built in a steeply sloping tree cavity, usually in open woodland on the edge of the rain forest, and the female incubates the single egg alone. The pair may use the same cavity for several years in succession. Outside the breeding season the birds often forage in small groups.

Although not yet endangered, the Palm Cockatoo is threatened by the illegal cage-bird trade, by hunting and by destruction of its habitat.

5/ RED-TAILED BLACK COCKATOO
Calyptorhynchus magnificus

RANGE: **N and W Australia, with isolated inland populations**
HABITAT: **scrub, open woods, river forest**
SIZE: **19½–24 in (50–61 cm)**

Like the 2 other species of black cockatoo, this species is a seed-eater. A feeding group of Red-tailed Black Cockatoos will often make themselves obvious by audibly snapping their bills as they split nuts to eat the seeds and scatter the husks on the ground beneath the trees. In savanna they forage in large nomadic flocks of up to 100 birds, but in forested country they tend to be less gregarious, often occurring in pairs or small family groups. In some parts of their range, the species has declined since forestry work has resulted in a scarcity of nest-hollows. The distinctive helmetlike crest of both sexes is raised when they are landing and when they are alarmed or excited.

6/ GALAH
Eolophus roseicapillus

RANGE: **most of Australia**
HABITAT: **eucalyptus woodland, watercourse vegetation and grassland**
SIZE: **13¾ in (35 cm)**

This is the most common cockatoo – indeed, one of the most common of all parrots – in Australia. It is one of the few species to have benefited from the European settlement, having increased its range and numbers in response to forest clearance, crop planting and the provision of water points. It is considered a pest by cereal growers, for it takes grain as well as grass seeds, fruits, green shoots and insects. The Galah is sometimes known as the Roseate Cockatoo.

The nest is usually in a vertical tree hollow, though holes in cliffs are sometimes used. The pairs bond for life and defend the nest-hollow against intruders. Both male and female share the incubation and feeding of the 2–6 young. The newly fledged birds gather into treetop nurseries of up to 100 birds, which eagerly await the return of their parents with food. After 6–8 weeks, the young are left to fend for themselves while their parents go away to molt. Young Galahs spend their first 2 or 3 years among large wandering flocks of nonbreeding birds.

7/ SULFUR-CRESTED COCKATOO
Cacatua galerita
RANGE: **Melanesia, New Guinea, N and E Australia**
HABITAT: **lowland forest, savanna and partly cleared land up to 5,000 ft (1,500 m)**
SIZE: **15–19½ in (38–50 cm)**

Common throughout most of its range, this handsome, noisy parrot often associates in large flocks outside the breeding season, descending on grasses, shrubs and trees to feed on seeds, fruits, palm hearts and insects. It can even be seen in urban areas. It is an occasional pest in crops and is sometimes shot for this reason. Sulfur-crested Cockatoos also suffer as a result of hunting in New Guinea. While the flock is feeding on the ground, a few birds stand sentinel in nearby trees and warn of danger with loud, raucous cries. At dusk the flock returns to a habitual roost.

During the breeding season the flocks break up. Breeding pairs nest in vertical cavities in eucalyptus trees, usually near water, and both parents incubate the 2–3 eggs.

8/ COCKATIEL
Nymphicus hollandicus
RANGE: **Australia, throughout interior**
HABITAT: **open scrub, woods, near water**
SIZE: **12½ in (32 cm)**

This slender cockatoo, which is sometimes called the Quarrion, usually forages for fruits and seeds in pairs or small groups, but occasionally these groups gather into great flocks that can cause extensive damage to crops, especially sunflower, sorghum and millet. Northern birds are nomadic, but in the south they are seasonal migrants.

Both sexes are crested, but the male's facial markings are brighter. They usually breed after rainfall, at any time of year. The 5 eggs are laid on a bed of wood-dust in any suitable tree cavity close to water and are incubated by both birds.

9/ BUFF-FACED PYGMY PARROT
Micropsitta pusio
RANGE: **N and E New Guinea lowlands and offshore islands, Bismarck Archipelago**
HABITAT: **lowland forest, regrowth and remnant trees**
SIZE: **3 in (8 cm)**

One of 6 very similar pygmy parrots found on New Guinea and neighboring islands, the Buff-faced Pygmy Parrot is a tiny bird, with short, stiff, spiny tail feathers like those of woodpeckers

(pp. 214–21). The stiffened feathers are used for the same purpose – to support the parrot as it forages for food on tree trunks.

It is exceptional among birds in feeding on lichen and fungi, but it will also eat fruits, seeds and insects, picking them out of the bark as it works its way smoothly and acrobatically over the trunk and branches. The birds travel in groups and roost together in holes made in the nests of tree-dwelling termites. The nest-holes, too, are excavated in termites' nests that are still occupied by the insects.

10/ BLACK LORY
Chalcopsitta atra
RANGE: **W New Guinea and adjacent islands**
HABITAT: **forest edge, groups of trees in savanna, coastal plantations**
SIZE: **11¾ in (30 cm)**

The Black Lory is a medium-sized parrot with a long, rounded tail. The northwestern race *C. a. atra*, which is all black except for a purple rump, is typical of western races, whereas the eastern race *C. a. insignis*, which is sometimes known as the Rajah Lory, has red markings on the face, under the wings and on the belly.

Large flocks of Black Lories have been seen foraging along the forest edges and descending upon coconut palms and flowering trees in clearings, calling with shrill screeches that sound as if they are made by much smaller birds. Details of their lifestyle are obscure

11/ RED LORY
Eos bornea
RANGE: **Moluccas**
HABITAT: **coastal and mountain forest up to 4,000 ft (1,250 m), mangroves**
SIZE: **12¼ in (31 cm)**

On moonlit nights, flocks of 20 or more Red Lories will often fly to and fro over the coastal forests of Seram, screeching loudly. At rich feeding sites, such as flowering *Eugenia* trees, many more will gather to feast on the nectar, mopping it up with the brush-tipped tongues typical of lories and lorikeets. They also eat pollen and small insects.

These birds appear to nest in cavities high up in mature trees. From the successful breeding of a pair of Red Lories in captivity, 2 eggs were produced, and the young birds left the nest at 7 and 9 weeks after hatching. They had still not acquired the adult plumage at 7 months.

12/ RAINBOW LORIKEET
Trichoglossus haematodus
RANGE: **SW Pacific including Indonesia, New Guinea, N and E Australia**
HABITAT: **rain forest, eucalyptus forest and coconut groves up to 6,500 ft (2,000 m)**
SIZE: **11–12½ in (28–32 cm)**

This is one of the most widespread, spectacular and variable of the lories, with 21 races scattered over the southwest Pacific. The illustration shows *T. h. weberi* of Flores Island, *T. h. haematodus* of the southern Moluccas and western New Guinea, *T. h. moluccanus* of eastern Australia and Tas-

mania and *T. h. rubritorquis* of northern Australia.

Rainbow Lorikeets normally feed in the upper canopy in screeching, chattering flocks of 5–20 birds, eating fruits, insects, pollen and nectar; they are important pollinators of coconut flowers. They spend the night in great communal roosts, sometimes with several thousand birds.

13/ BLACK-CAPPED LORY
Lorius lory
RANGE: **lowland New Guinea and offshore islands**
HABITAT: **undisturbed rain forest, swamp forest**
SIZE: **11 in (28 cm)**

This stocky, rather shy bird has a ringing, melodious cry, quite unlike the usual screeching of parrots. It is usually seen in pairs or small groups flying just above the treetops, but larger flocks gather at flowering or fruiting trees where they feed on nectar, pollen, flowers, fruit and insects.

During the courtship display, the perching male faces his mate in an upright posture with his wings open and head turned to one side, and bobs his body up and down. The 1–2 white eggs are incubated by the female – though the male roosts in the nest at night – and take 24 days to hatch.

There are 7 races, including *L. l. lory*, from northwestern New Guinea and nearby islands, and *L. l. somu*, from southern New Guinea.

14/ COLLARED LORY
Phigys solitarius
RANGE: **Fiji Islands**
HABITAT: **rain forest, disturbed forest, plantations, coconut palms, urban trees**
SIZE: **8 in (20 cm)**

Feeding flocks of these small lories often congregate around coconut palms, landing on the fronds and working their way down to the nectar-rich flowers in short, fluttering leaps, displacing other birds, such as honeyeaters, which may already be feeding. The nest is sometimes made in a rotting coconut still on the tree, but usually the birds make use of a cavity in a tree trunk or stump. The 2 young are fed by both parents for about 8 weeks.

15/ PURPLE-CROWNED LORIKEET
Glossopsitta porphyrocephala
RANGE: **SW and S Australia (not Tasmania)**
HABITAT: **dry open woods, mallee scrub**
SIZE: **6¼ in (16 cm)**

Small nomadic flocks of Purple-crowned Lorikeets are a common sight in dry eucalyptus woodland from December to August, outside the breeding season. The flocks visit flowering and fruiting trees to feed on fruits; they also harvest pollen and nectar from the blossoms, using comb-like fringes on their tongues. Rich food sources will attract many flocks which feed together, but they split up again to move on.

The nests of Purple-crowned Lorikeets are usually in unlined hollows in eucalyptus trees, with knot-hole entrances, often in loose colonies. Both birds may roost in the hollow, but only the female incubates the 2–3 eggs.

LORIES AND LORIKEETS, PARROTS AND PARAKEETS

JOSEPHINE'S LORY

WHISKERED LORIKEET

race marshalli

race coxe

DOUBLE-EYED FIG PARROT

ECLECTUS PARROT

AUSTRALIAN
KING PARROT

imm

BUDGERIGAR

SWIFT PARROT

RED-CHEEKED PARROT

♀

imm

imm

race *platenae* ♂

race *discurus* ♀

BLUE-CROWNED RACKET-TAILED PARROT

RED-FRONTED PARAKEET

CRIMSON ROSELLA

VASA PARROT

GRAY PARROT

NIGHT PARROT

LORIES AND LORIKEETS, PARROTS AND PARAKEETS

1/ JOSEPHINE'S LORY

Charmosyna josefinae

RANGE: **W and C New Guinea**
HABITAT: **mountain forest, at
2,500–6,500 ft (800–2,000 m)**
SIZE: **$9\frac{1}{2}$ in (24 cm)**

This slender, long-tailed parrot is quiet and unobtrusive in its habits and easily overlooked as it forages through the forest canopy in the mountains of New Guinea. It flies in pairs or small groups, sometimes with Fairy Lorikeets *C. pulchella*, landing to gather pollen and nectar from tree blossom, or climbing slowly through the tendrils of a clinging vine to feed at the large white flowers. Occasionally it gives a soft squeaking call, but most of the time it searches in silence.

2/ WHISKERED LORIKEET

Oreopsittacus arfaki

RANGE: **W, C and NE New Guinea**
HABITAT: **mountain forest, at
6,500–12,300 ft (2,000–3,750 m)**
SIZE: **6 in (15 cm)**

Rarely seen beyond the mist forests of the New Guinea mountains, this slim, active bird, which is also known as the Plum-faced Lorikeet, often forages in small, mixed flocks in the company of flowerpeckers, honeyeaters and other lorikeets. Gathering in flowering trees, the birds search busily among the foliage for nectar, pollen, fruits and flowers, clambering out onto the thin outer twigs and often hanging upside-down to reach tempting blossoms.

In display the male struts back and forth along a branch, calling excitedly, then bobs and thrusts his head toward the female. Details of the nest and eggs are unknown.

3/ DOUBLE-EYED FIG PARROT

Opopsitta diophthalma

RANGE: **New Guinea, W Papuan islands
and NE Australia**
HABITAT: **subtropical and tropical rain
forest up to 5,300 ft (1,600 m)**
SIZE: **6 in (15 cm)**

A rain of chewed debris drifting down from a fig tree will often betray a party of Double-eyed Fig Parrots feeding high in the canopy. True to their name, these small green parrots feed mainly on the seeds of figs, although they also eat other fruits, as well as nectar and insects. They feed quietly, but the parties often call noisily when moving between the trees, or home to their communal roosts at night.

The males are more colorful than the females and their head color varies among the 8 races. Of these, *O. d. coxeni* from southeast Queensland and northeast New South Wales is now threatened as a result of habitat loss. Other races include *O. d. marshalli* from the Cape York Peninsula in northern Queensland.

Both sexes prepare the nest, excavating a short tunnel in soft timber, usually near the rain forest edge. There are 2 eggs.

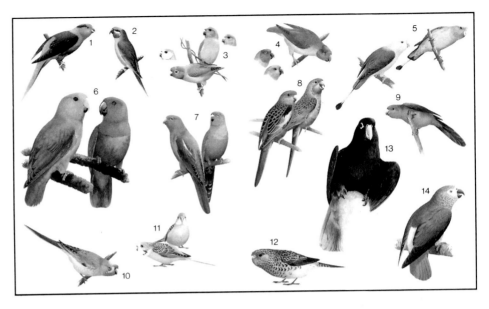

4/ RED-CHEEKED PARROT

Geoffroyus geoffroyi

RANGE: **Lesser Sundas, Moluccas, New
Guinea, NE Australia**
HABITAT: **wide range of lowland forest,
including secondary forest, rain forest,
mangroves, savanna, up to 2,500 ft
(800 m)**
SIZE: **$7\frac{3}{4}$–$9\frac{3}{4}$ in (20–25 cm)**

Red-cheeked Parrots are more often heard than seen as they feed on fruits, seeds, nectar and flower buds in the upper forest canopy. They usually forage in pairs or groups of up to 30, but sometimes gather in great feeding aggregations around rich food sources such as concentrations of fruiting trees. After feeding all day, the big flock splits up into smaller groups which spend the night in communal roosts.

Both the male, with his brightly coloured face and bill, and the duller female are involved in drilling the nest-hole in a dead tree at the forest edge, but the female incubates the 2–4 eggs alone.

5/ BLUE-CROWNED RACKET-TAILED PARROT

Prioniturus discurus ?

RANGE: **Philippines, Jolo Island (Sulus)**
HABITAT: **forests, clearings, banana groves**
SIZE: **$10\frac{1}{2}$ in (27 cm)**

The 9 species of racket-tailed parrot owe their name to their curious, elongated central tail feathers, which extend into bare shafts with disk-shaped "rackets" on the ends. These appear on both sexes as they mature, but those of the female are shorter than the male's.

The Blue-crowned Racket-tailed Parrot is widely distributed through the Philippines, with 5 races showing color variations. The most distinctive are the widespread race *P. d. discurus*, which is largely green with a blue crown, and *P. d. platenae* found on Palawan and its adjacent islands, which has a completely blue head and blue-green underparts.

These birds are most commonly seen in undisturbed forest, flying high above the canopy in small, noisy flocks. Uttering shrill screeches, the whole flock will descend to strip a fruiting tree, and in newly cleared land near forest they can cause considerable damage in banana plantations as they feed on the green maturing fruit. They often forage in the company of cockatoos, Bald Starlings *Sarcops calvus* and pigeons, eating fruits, nuts and seeds. Their breeding behavior has not been studied, but they appear to nest colonially in tall dead trees.

6/ ECLECTUS PARROT

Eclectus roratus

RANGE: **Lesser Sundas, Solomon Islands,
New Guinea, NE Australia**
HABITAT: **lowland rain forest and dense
savanna up to 3,300 ft (1,000 m)**
SIZE: **15–$17\frac{3}{4}$ in (38–45 cm)**

Plumage differences between the sexes are not unusual among parrots, but few differ so dramatically as the male and female Eclectus Parrot. Both are glossy, brilliant birds, but whereas the male is bright green with blue and red patches, the female is crimson with a blue belly. When they are feeding among the green foliage, this makes her more conspicuous than her mate, something which is unique among parrots.

Calling loudly, pairs or small parties travel widely through the upper canopy in search of fruits, nuts, nectar and leaf buds. In the evening they engage in display flights before gathering in large groups of up to 80 birds to roost for the night. The nest is built in a large vertical hollow in a rain forest tree near a stream. It is possible that the birds breed communally, with other adults helping the pair rear their brood of 2 chicks.

7/ AUSTRALIAN KING PARROT
Alisterus scapularis
RANGE: **E Australia except Tasmania**
HABITAT: **dense forest; visits open woodland and parkland outside breeding season**
SIZE: **17 in (43 cm)**

Although vividly colored, the Australian King Parrot is a subdued bird compared to other parrots. It tends to feed quietly and unobtrusively in the forest canopy, taking tree seeds – especially those of eucalyptus and acacias – as well as fruits, nuts and nectar. When the family groups disperse after breeding, the immature birds often gather into large flocks and cause severe damage to orchard crops.

Males and females are dramatically different in appearance, the males having brilliant scarlet plumage, whereas females are largely green. They breed in dense forest, frequently nesting in trees with very deep cavities; the entrance may be over 33 ft (10 m) up the tree, but the 3–6 eggs are often laid close to ground level.

8/ CRIMSON ROSELLA
Platycercus elegans
RANGE: **E Australia except Tasmania**
HABITAT: **eucalyptus forest, woods and gardens up to 6,000 ft (1,900 m); in N restricted to mountain forests above 1,500 ft (450 m)**
SIZE: **14 in (36 cm)**

There are 2 very closely related rosellas – the Yellow Rosella *P. flaveolus* and the Adelaide Rosella *P. adelaidae* – which are considered by some ornithologists to belong to the same species as the Crimson Rosella. However, their coloration is so different that they are frequently classified as separate species. The Crimson Rosella is the most striking, both sexes having the same rich red and blue plumage; in immature birds much of the red is replaced by green.

The adults occur in pairs or small groups and stay in the same area throughout the year, but the immature birds are nomadic, wandering in flocks of up to 30. They feed mainly on the seeds of grasses, shrubs and trees such as eucalyptus and acacias, but will also eat fruits, nectar and insects. They nest in tree cavities.

9/ RED-FRONTED PARAKEET
Cyanoramphus novaezelandiae
RANGE: **New Zealand, New Caledonia**
HABITAT: **mature forest, tall scrub on treeless islands**
SIZE: **9¾–11 in (25–28 cm)**

Once widespread in New Zealand and nearby islands, this long-tailed parrot has declined to the point where 2 island races are now extinct and another is likely to follow them. Fortunately it breeds well in captivity, and captive-bred birds have been released at various island and mainland sites. This species is also known as the Red-crowned Parakeet.

It eats a variety of fruits, seeds, flowers, leaves and buds, working its way through the lower and middle branches of trees and often coming down to ground level to feed on any fallen items as well

as grass shoots. The pair breeds in a cavity such as a rock crevice, a tree hole, a burrow or a hole at the base of a grass tussock. The female alone incubates the eggs, but the male helps feed the 5–9 young.

10/ SWIFT PARROT
Lathamus discolor
RANGE: **breeds Tasmania; winters SE Australia**
HABITAT: **eucalyptus woodland, parkland**
SIZE: **9¾ in (25 cm)**

The Swift Parrot is named for its fast, direct flight, a valuable asset to a bird which migrates long distances each year. It breeds only in Tasmania and the adjacent islands, crossing the 125 ml (200 km) Bass Strait in March to spend the southern winter on the Australian mainland.

It usually forages in small parties, which gather into large flocks for migration and to take advantage of particularly rich food sources. The birds feed in the canopy on nectar, pollen, fruit, seeds and insects.

In Tasmania the pairs often breed in loose colonies, each nesting in an unlined tree cavity high above the ground. As with most parrots, the female alone incubates the 3–5 eggs.

11/ BUDGERIGAR
Melopsittacus undulatus
RANGE: **throughout inland Australia**
HABITAT: **tussock grassland, arid and semiarid scrub and woodland close to water**
SIZE: **6½ in (17 cm)**

This small parrot is best known as a solitary cage bird, but in the wild it is a gregarious, wide-ranging nomad which often travels in large flocks. The flocks occur throughout the year in the Australian heartland, but their size varies with the food supply; in years of relatively high rainfall and abundant food the Budgerigar is one of the most numerous of all Australian parrots. Wild birds are always green.

Budgerigars are agile, swift-flying birds, and the flocks rarely stay in one place for long. They feed mainly in the early morning and late afternoon, avoiding the hottest part of the day, and spend much of their time collecting seeds from ground vegetation including grasses and weeds.

They breed at any time of year when food is abundant, usually after rains. The pairs nest in colonies, using small tree cavities such as eucalyptus knot-holes, and may raise several broods each season.

12/ NIGHT PARROT
Geopsittacus occidentalis   I
RANGE: **arid and semiarid regions of central Australia**
HABITAT: **low succulent vegetation bordering salt lakes; tussock grasses when in seed**
SIZE: **9 in (23 cm)**

For many years the Night Parrot was thought to be extinct, but recent sightings show that it still exists, albeit in very reduced numbers. Its decline

has probably been accelerated by overgrazing of its habitat by sheep and rabbits and by its vulnerability, as a ground-nester, to predators such as foxes and cats.

Rarely seen, it remains a mystery in many respects. It may be nocturnal, as its name implies, but there is little evidence for this. It spends most of its time on the ground, feeding singly or in pairs on the seeds of grasses and shrubs.

The 2–4 eggs are laid on a rough stick platform placed under spinifex tussocks or low shrubs and reached by a tunnel through the foliage.

13/ VASA PARROT
Coracopsis vasa
RANGE: **Madagascar, Comoro Islands**
HABITAT: **forest and savanna below 3,300 ft (1,000 m)**
SIZE: **19½ in (50 cm)**

These noisy, conspicuous parrots are usually seen in small flocks, although larger groups may gather at favorite feeding or roosting sites. They feed on fruits, nuts, berries and seeds up in the treetops and are fond of resting on the branches of dead trees. Their flight, often high above the forest canopy, is distinctive and rather crowlike, with slow, flapping wing beats. Little is known of the species' breeding habits, although it is thought that the breeding season lasts from at least October to December, and the birds nest in sites such as the hollow limbs of trees.

Like its only close relative, the Black Parrot *C. nigra* of Madagascar, the Comoro Islands and Praslin Island in the Seychelles, the Vasa Parrot is hunted for food; habitat destruction is an even greater threat to these birds.

14/ GRAY PARROT
Psittacus erithacus
RANGE: **C Africa, Sierra Leone E to Kenya and NW Tanzania**
HABITAT: **lowland forest, wooded savanna, mangroves**
SIZE: **13 in (33 cm)**

In eastern Gabon vast flocks of over 5,000 Gray Parrots gather at traditional roosting sites each night, perching on the fronds of oil palms. Elsewhere the roosts are smaller, but it is common to find more than 100 birds in a single tree. In the morning they leave in small groups, often following regular routes, to feed in the rain forest or feast on palm nuts in plantations. On their return in the evening, they call with loud, rhythmic whistles and raucous shrieks before settling down.

They breed in loose colonies, each pair occupying its own tree. The 2–4 eggs are laid in a cavity and incubated by the female, but the chicks are fed by both birds.

The Gray Parrot is renowned the world over as a cage bird and has remarkable powers of vocal mimicry. There is evidence of a reduction in numbers due to trapping near towns, but in many places this is an abundant species, with regular roosts of 5,000–10,000 birds occurring in 2 places in Gabon.

PARROTS AND PARAKEETS, MACAWS, HANGING PARROTS

PEACH-FACED LOVEBIRD

♂

HYACINTH MACAW

ROSE-RINGED PARAKEET

race *luchsi*

SUN CONURE

MONK PARAKEET

race *monachus*

♀

race *ochrocephala*

race *tresmariae*

♂

YELLOW-CROWNED AMAZON

SPECTACLED PARROTLET

SCARLET MACAW

BLUE-AND-YELLOW MACAW

HAWK-HEADED PARROT

ST VINCENT AMAZON

BLUE-CROWNED HANGING PARROT

1/ PEACH-FACED LOVEBIRD
Agapornis roseicollis

RANGE: SW Angola, Namibia (not NE), N Cape Province
HABITAT: dry wooded steppe, usually in belts of trees along watercourses
SIZE: 6 in (15 cm)

Abundant ripening seeds in the dry steppe of southwest Africa may attract flocks of up to 200 Peach-faced Lovebirds. Small, noisy and agile, they climb through the vegetation using their bills for support, gathering the seeds of trees and grasses, as well as grain crops and sunflowers.

As with other lovebirds, pairs of Peach-faced Lovebirds preen each other attentively – hence their name – and nest in colonies, either in rock crevices, under eaves, or by moving into the many-chambered nests of communal weaver birds. The male feeds his mate as she broods the eggs and young.

2/ BLUE-CROWNED HANGING PARROT
Loriculus galgulus

RANGE: Malaya, Singapore, Sumatra, Borneo and some adjacent islands
HABITAT: light woodland in lowlands, plantations, orchards, gardens
SIZE: 4¾ in (12 cm)

Like the other 10 species of hanging parrot, the Blue-crowned Hanging Parrot takes its name from its extraordinary habit of roosting at night or resting during the day by hanging upside-down from a branch. The bird holds its feet together and arches its body so far back that its head may be behind its feet.

These little parrots are most commonly seen flying above the treetops on fast-whirring wings, or feeding in flowering shrubs and trees. Their diet consists of nectar, flowers, fruits, seeds and possibly also small insects. When feeding on sticky food such as nectar, the birds constantly brush their fine, pointed bills on leaves and twigs.

When they climb, Blue-crowned Hanging Parrots take extremely long strides, turning the whole body as they stretch each leg forward. They may also hold their tails stiffly against a branch as a prop, like woodpeckers, and grasp twigs with their bills.

Blue-crowned Hanging Parrots nest between January and July, choosing a hollow in a dead or living tree. This is lined with a very thick layer of leaves, which are carried to the nest-hole by the female in her rump feathers. Like some other hanging parrots, this species is very popular as a cage bird in its native range.

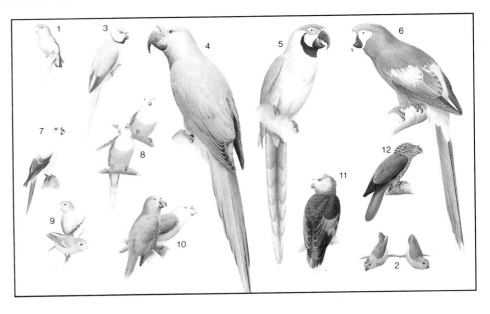

3/ ROSE-RINGED PARAKEET
Psittacula krameri

RANGE: C Africa E to Uganda, India, Sri Lanka; introduced to Middle and Far East, North America, England, Netherlands, Belgium, West Germany
HABITAT: woodland, farmland
SIZE: 16 in (41 cm)

Bold, gregarious opportunists, Rose-ringed Parakeets will often associate in flocks of a thousand or more to feast on crops of grain or ripening fruit. They will even invade grainstores, ripping open the sacks with their hooked bills and squabbling over the spoils.

During the breeding season the flocks split up; each pair nests in a tree cavity after an elaborate courtship ritual in which the female twitters and rolls her eyes at the strutting male, rubs bills with him and accepts gifts of food.

4/ HYACINTH MACAW
Anodorhynchus hyacinthinus [?]

RANGE: C Brazil, E Bolivia, NE Paraguay
HABITAT: dry forest along watercourses, wet forest edges, among palms
SIZE: 37½–39½ in (95–100 cm)

Easily recognized by its cobalt-blue plumage and gray-black bill, the Hyacinth Macaw is the largest of all the parrots. It feeds mainly on palm fruits and nuts, and small flocks of 3–6 birds are often sighted foraging among palm trees in swampy places, or on the edge of the forest. When disturbed, these majestic macaws screech loudly, circle overhead with their long tails streaming, then settle in the tops of tall trees.

Little is known about the breeding habits of the Hyacinth Macaw in the wild, although pairs have been seen nesting in the hollow trunks of palms and large deciduous trees. These birds laid clutches of 2–3 eggs, and the young flew from the nest some 4 months after egg-laying.

Like many parrots, the Hyacinth Macaw is endangered by hunting and trapping for the pet trade, and only 2,500–5,000 remain in the wild, mostly in Brazil.

5/ BLUE-AND-YELLOW MACAW
Ara ararauna

RANGE: E Panama to N Bolivia and SE Brazil
HABITAT: forests along watercourses and swampy regions up to 1,500 ft (500 m)
SIZE: 86 cm (34 in)

Although the large Blue-and-yellow Macaw is threatened by habitat destruction and large-scale trapping for the cage-bird trade, it is still common in the more remote parts of its range and can often be seen flying over the treetops in pairs, screeching raucously.

It feeds on a variety of leaves, seeds, fruits and nuts. In Manu National Park, Peru, Blue-and-yellow Macaws have been seen eating at least 20 species of plant, many containing substances that are distasteful or toxic to humans, but apparently not to them. These macaws, and others, are often attracted to mineral licks where they eat clay, and this may help detoxify the noxious compounds in their diet.

Blue-and-yellow Macaws nest in tree cavities and usually lay a clutch of 2 white eggs.

6/ SCARLET MACAW
Ara macao

RANGE: S Mexico, Central America to N Bolivia and C Brazil
HABITAT: lowland forest, to 1,300 ft (400 m)
SIZE: 33½ in (85 cm)

Probably the best known of all the New World parrots, these spectacular macaws are generally seen in pairs, family groups or flocks of up to 20 birds. At sunrise they fly from their communal roosting sites to scattered feeding grounds in the forest, where they eat a variety of leaves, fruits and seeds taken from high in the trees. They are noisy in flight, uttering loud metallic screeches, but they always feed in silence. At dusk they return to their roosts, flying wing tip to wing tip through the thickening twilight.

They nest in cavities in large trees, and the availability of sites appears to limit the number of breeding pairs in any population. The chicks fledge at 3 months, but remain with their parents for some time thereafter.

Scarlet Macaws are adaptable birds which thrive in a variety of habitats, and they are more widely distributed than any other macaw species. Despite this, they are now under threat and several local populations have become extinct through deforestation and trapping.

7/ SUN CONURE
Aratinga solstitialis

RANGE: **NE South America**
HABITAT: **savanna**
SIZE: **11¾ in (30 cm)**

A series of shrill, 2-note screeches will often draw attention to this brilliantly colored, gregarious parrot, which frequently gathers in large noisy flocks to feed on blossoms, fruits, seeds and nuts in the treetops.

It uses cavities in palm trees as nesting sites, but the details of its breeding behavior in the wild are still unknown. In captivity the female alone incubates the clutch of 4 eggs for a month and the young fledge some 8 weeks after they have hatched.

The Sun Conure is very similar to the Jandaya Conure *A. jandaya* and the Golden-capped Conure *A. auricapilla*; indeed, some ornithologists consider them all to be races of the same species.

8/ MONK PARAKEET
Myiopsitta monachus

RANGE: **C Bolivia, Paraguay and S Brazil to C Argentina; introduced to USA, Puerto Rico**
HABITAT: **open woods, savanna, arid acacia scrub, cultivated land**
SIZE: **11½ in (29 cm)**

This common parrot is an extremely social bird, gathering in well-organized flocks of 100 or more to feed on seeds, fruits, flowers and insects while sentinels keep watch for predators from nearby vantage points. On farmland the Monk Parakeet can become a pest, frequently raiding citrus orchards and cereal crops.

Uniquely among parrots, it builds a bulky nest of dry, often thorny twigs in the upper branches of a tree. Some pairs nest in isolation, but others build their nests alongside or on top of existing nests to form a massive structure with up to 20 separate compartments. They use the nests throughout the year for roosting as well as breeding, each pair incubating a clutch of 5–8 eggs on a bed of twigs. Birds that have escaped from captivity have nested in the wild in several areas of North America.

Primarily a lowland species, the Monk Parakeet is abundant throughout most of its range. Four races are usually recognized, of which 2 are similar to *M. m. monachus* from southern Brazil, Uruguay and northeastern Argentina. The fourth race is the distinctive *M. m. luchsi*, known only from one area of central Bolivia.

9/ SPECTACLED PARROTLET
Forpus conspicillatus

RANGE: **E Panama, Colombia, W Venezuela**
HABITAT: **open woods, forest edges and clearings, savanna**
SIZE: **4¾ in (12 cm)**

Most South American parrots are being badly hit by deforestation, but the little Spectacled Parrotlet prefers open country and is actually increasing its range as the forests come down. Small flocks are often to be seen over clear-felled areas, busily foraging among the scrub and undergrowth for leaf buds, fruits, berries, and the seeds of grasses and herbaceous plants. As they feed, they keep up a constant chatter and twitter of soft, finchlike calls, quite unlike the raucous screeches of larger parrots. The flight of the Spectacled Parrotlet is swift but erratic.

Males are brighter than females, with blue markings on the wing, rump, lower back, and behind the eye. Immatures resemble females. The clutch of 4 white eggs is laid in a cavity in a tree or fencepost, or sometimes even in a termite nest.

10/ YELLOW-CROWNED AMAZON
Amazona ochrocephala

RANGE: **C Mexico, Trinidad, S to Amazon basin and E Peru; introduced to S California and S Florida**
HABITAT: **deciduous and humid lowland forest, open woods, savanna, pine ridges**
SIZE: **13¾ in (35 cm)**

The Yellow-crowned Amazon has suffered badly in some localities from deforestation and, because of its high reputation as a mimic of human speech, from the activities of the trappers who supply the pet trade. Despite this reputation, it does not seem to mimic other birds or animals in the wild, confining itself to a variety of metallic shrieks, whistling contacts, and repeated, screeching *kurrowk* squawks.

It is a very variable species, with 9 races, including *A. o. ochrocephala* of western Colombia, northern Brazil and Trinidad and *A. o. tresmariae*, found on the Tres Marias Islands off western Mexico. The race *A. o. oratrix*, from Mexico, has an entirely yellow head; it is in great demand as a cage bird and is now regarded as rare and in need of immediate protection. Like the race *A. o. auropalliata* from the Pacific slope of Central America, it is often regarded as a separate species.

Yellow-crowned Amazons are opportunist feeders which gather in small groups in the treetops to forage for a wide variety of seeds, berries, fruits and flowers. At dusk they return to their habitual roosts, flying with characteristic shallow wing beats below body level, rather like those of a duck.

11/ ST VINCENT AMAZON
Amazona guildingii   E

RANGE: **St Vincent (Lesser Antilles)**
HABITAT: **humid forest at 1,150–2,000 ft (350–600 m)**
SIZE: **15¾–18 in (40–46 cm)**

This large, picturesque, and colorful amazon parrot is found only in the forests of the island of St Vincent, where it has suffered badly from habitat loss due to agricultural development, and from hunting. Once in imminent danger of extinction, it has been saved – for the present – by protective legislation and captive breeding initiated in 1988, and the population now numbers some 450–500 individuals.

The adult plumage is variable and virtually no 2 birds are exactly alike, but there are 2 basic color phases: the yellow-brown phase, illustrated, and the green phase, which has the upper parts mainly dusky green, the base of the primaries green, and the underwing coverts and undersides of the flight feathers green.

Noisy and gregarious, these parrots often forage in flocks of up to 20, gathering fruits, seeds, and flowers from the upper canopy. The flocks break up into pairs at the onset of the dry season in January or February, but the number of breeding pairs in any area is limited by the number of suitable nest-holes in large, mature trees. The 2 eggs are incubated by the female alone. Juveniles leave the nest as duller versions of the adults and do not progress from green juveniles to yellow-brown adults as has sometimes been suggested.

12/ HAWK-HEADED PARROT
Deroptyus accipitrinus

RANGE: **South America N of the Amazon, W to SE Colombia and NE Peru**
HABITAT: **mixed forest and savanna**
SIZE: **13¾ in (35 cm)**

This handsome parrot, which is sometimes known as the Red-fan Parrot, has long red and blue feathers on its nape which can be raised to form a ruff, giving it a uniquely hawklike appearance. This bird is also distinctive in flight, for it normally flies low through the forest, skimming the treetops, giving a few shallow flaps followed by a short glide, with its wings held angled slightly downward, its rounded gray-black tail feathers spread and its head raised. It sometimes calls with a variety of chattering notes and soft whistles.

Hawk-headed Parrots have been seen in pairs and in small flocks of up to 10 birds, which spend much of the day feeding or resting in the treetops. Their diet consists of the fruits, seeds and nuts of various palms and other plants.

The Hawk-headed Parrot nests in old woodpecker holes in trees, but little else is known about its breeding behavior. Like many parrots, it is under threat from deforestation and is declining in numbers in the southern part of its range.

TURACOS, CUCKOOS, HOATZIN

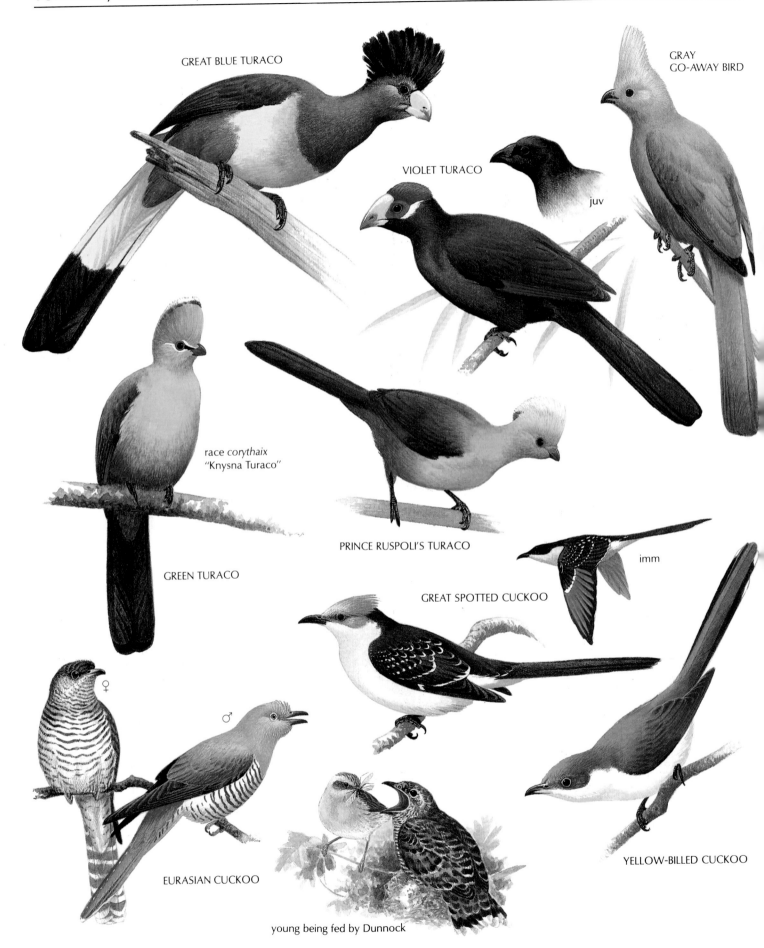

GREAT BLUE TURACO

GRAY
GO-AWAY BIRD

VIOLET TURACO

juv

race *corythaix*
"Knysna Turaco"

PRINCE RUSPOLI'S TURACO

GREEN TURACO

GREAT SPOTTED CUCKOO

imm

♀

♂

EURASIAN CUCKOO

young being fed by Dunnock

YELLOW-BILLED CUCKOO

174

race *scolopacea* ♂

♀

race *cyanocephala* ♀

COMMON KOEL

PHEASANT COUCAL

CHANNEL-BILLED CUCKOO

GROOVE-BILLED ANI

♂

imm rufous-backed phase

DIDRIC CUCKOO

chick

HOATZIN

GREATER ROADRUNNER

TURACOS, CUCKOOS, HOATZIN

FAMILY MUSOPHAGIDAE
Turacos

Medium to large woodland birds. Plumage gray, green, blue or purple, with silky, hairlike feathers on head and breast of most species and unique green and red pigments in plumage of *Musophaga* and *Tauraco* species. Sexes alike. Nests in trees, usually flimsy platform of twigs. Eggs 2, whitish. Incubation 21–24 days. Silky nestlings use tiny claws on wing joints to scramble to edge of nest at 10–12 days; at about 4 weeks, leave nest for good, several days before they can fly. 20 species.

1/ GREAT BLUE TURACO
Corythaeola cristata

RANGE: **W Africa from Guinea to Nigeria, Congo Basin to Kenya and Tanzania**
HABITAT: **lowland rain forest, patches of forest in savanna, mountain forest**
SIZE: **29½ in (75 cm)**

This beautiful bird is by far the largest of the turacos: its alternative name is the Giant Turaco. It is adept at running along branches but is a poor flier. Most flights are merely glides from tall trees, and they often end abruptly in low vegetation; the bird then climbs quickly back to the treetops.

Great Blue Turacos usually move around in small parties, several of which may congregate at large fruit-bearing trees near the borders of their territories. The birds start feeding soon after dawn and continue to feed for much of the day, except when it is very hot. At dusk each party flies noisily toward a traditional roosting tree. The nest is built in a tall tree.

2/ GRAY GO-AWAY BIRD
Corythaixoides concolor

RANGE: **S Africa, N to Angola and Zaire**
HABITAT: **dry, open woodland, parks, gardens**
SIZE: **19 in (48 cm)**

A loud, nasal, descending *g'wa-ay g'wa-ay* is often the first indication that this bird is about. It is also known as the Gray Lourie. A sociable species, it travels in parties of up to 20 birds, hopping busily about the trees. It is a greedy, untidy feeder, dropping many fruits, pods and flowers of the figs and acacias that make up much of its diet. It sometimes eats crops of vegetables in gardens.

A clutch of 3, or rarely 4, eggs is laid in a loose nest of sticks, usually built in a thorny acacia tree.

3/ VIOLET TURACO
Musophaga violacea

RANGE: **W Africa, Senegal to Cameroon**
HABITAT: **tall forest, riverside forest**
SIZE: **17 in (43 cm)**

The Violet Turaco, or Violet Plantain-eater, prefers to stay well out of sight in the dense canopy of tall trees, where it searches for fruits, especially figs, by running along branches or bounding from bough to bough. If disturbed, it will keep still but when approached too closely it flies away with powerful flaps and long glides, which show off its crimson wings. The red in the plumage of this and other turacos is produced by a copper-based pigment called turacin. The Violet Turaco's

main call is a long series of deep, gargling *cou-cou-vhou* notes that run into each other, producing a pulsing roar when, as is nearly always the case, 2 birds call in a slightly asynchronous duet.

4/ GREEN TURACO
Tauraco persa

RANGE: **patchy from Senegal E to Zaire, Tanzania and S to South Africa**
HABITAT: **evergreen forest, forested savanna, abandoned cultivation, gardens**
SIZE: **16½ in (42 cm)**

There are several races of this widespread turaco. The race illustrated is the typical South African race *T. p. corythaix*, known as the Knysna Turaco or Knysna Lourie. Two northern races have rounded, plain green crests, while others have pointed crests tipped with white or blue. The brilliant green plumage in this and other *Tauraco* species is not due to iridescence, as in other birds, but to a unique green pigment, turacoverdin, which contains copper.

Green Turacos feed in groups in the treetops, gorging themselves on fruit. If one begins to call, the rest will follow, producing a chorus of growling, guttural cries. In the nesting season the birds pair off and become very territorial. The male courts his mate by displaying his wings and feeding her with regurgitated food.

5/ PRINCE RUSPOLI'S TURACO
Tauraco ruspolii   R

RANGE: **2 locations in Ethiopia**
HABITAT: **juniper forest with dense undergrowth, scrub, acacia**
SIZE: **16 in (41 cm)**

This elusive turaco has been found only within 2 small areas in Ethiopia – one 45 by 20 mls (70 by 30 km) and the other a mere 10 mls (25 km) square. It has typical cackling, growling and gobbling calls, but very little is known about its way of life. As it is secretive and difficult to find, its population is hard to estimate, and it may be at risk both from loss of habitat and from competition with the White-cheeked Turaco *T. leucotis*.

FAMILY OPISTHOCOMIDAE
Hoatzin

There is only one species in this family.

6/ HOATZIN
Opisthocomus hoazin

RANGE: **Amazon and Orinoco river basins and rivers of the Guianas, from Guyana and Brazil to Ecuador and Bolivia**
HABITAT: **flooded and riverside forest**
SIZE: **23¾ in (60 cm)**

This odd bird is a poor flier which usually glides from tree to tree, clumsily flapping up to reach its goal and clambering through the foliage, using its large but weak wings for support. The adults gather in groups of 10–50 to loaf in the trees and feed on the leaves of arum and other marsh plants, communicating with harsh croaking calls.

They are cooperative breeders, and 2–6 adults may help build the nest and care for the eggs and young. They lay 2–3 yellow-buff eggs, dappled with blue or brown spots. The Hoatzin is the only tree-dwelling bird in which the chicks habitually leave the nest soon after hatching. The nestlings have 2 hooked claws on the first and second digits at the bend of each wing, which they use to grip twigs as they explore around the nest. These claws reminded ornithologists of the 3-clawed wings of the earliest known bird, *Archaeopteryx* (p. 16), and it was suggested that the Hoatzin was a "living fossil." Today it is sometimes classified with the gamebirds (pp. 110–21) but is probably most closely related to the cuckoos.

FAMILY CUCULIDAE
Cuckoos and coucals

Medium to large, mainly scrub and woodland birds. Size and weight unusually variable in both sexes. Plumage generally browns, grays, often with barred or streaked underparts and spots or flashes in open tail. Eggs 10–15 per season in parasitic species (more if losses high), variable in color to mimic hosts' eggs; 2–5, usually bluish or whitish, in nonparasitic species. Incubation period 11–16 days, nestling period 16–24 days. 138 species.

7/ GREAT SPOTTED CUCKOO
Clamator glandarius

RANGE: **breeds SW Europe to Asia Minor, Africa; N populations winter in N Africa and S of Sahara, S populations winter in C Africa**
HABITAT: **open woods, bushy heath, scrub**
SIZE: **15¾ in (40 cm)**

The generic name of this bird, *Clamator* from the Latin for a noisy speaker, gives a clue to one of its most prominent characteristics – a rasping, chattering call, with a gobbling quality, often given from a hidden perch. The Great Spotted Cuckoo is often seen hopping about on the ground or in bushes, searching for caterpillars. It is fond of the large, hairy kinds, although it may remove most of the hairs before swallowing the insects.

This cuckoo lays its eggs in the nests of various species of crow. Unlike that of the Eurasian Cuckoo, the nestling does not throw the eggs or chicks of its foster parent out of the nest, but usually successfully competes for food with the chicks or smothers them.

8/ EURASIAN CUCKOO
Cuculus canorus

RANGE: **breeds Europe, Asia S to Nepal, China, Japan; winters in Africa**
HABITAT: **farmland with hedgerows, woods, heaths and moors**
SIZE: **13 in (33 cm)**

The monotonous but attractive 2-note call of the male Eurasian Cuckoo is a welcome symbol of spring in many parts of its breeding range. Most females resemble the males, but in addition to the common gray phase, females also have a rare rufous phase. Juvenile birds also show a similar variation, with the rufous phase more common than in the female.

The Eurasian Cuckoo lays its eggs in the nests of other birds: over 100 host species have been recorded in Europe. The female cuckoo finds the nests of host birds when fresh eggs have been laid; an egg is removed from each and a cuckoo's egg laid in its place, often closely resembling the existing eggs. When the chick hatches after 12 days, it throws the other eggs and chicks out of the nest to monopolize the food brought by its foster parents. After 17 days it leaves, eventually flying south for the winter – 1 or 2 months after the adult cuckoos have departed.

9/ DIDRIC CUCKOO
Chrysococcyx caprius

RANGE: **sub-Saharan Africa**
HABITAT: **savanna woodland, farmland, plantations**
SIZE: **7–8 in (18–20 cm)**

Although present all year near the Equator, this small, colorful cuckoo is a migrant in both the north and south of its range. Males are brighter than females and are fond of high, open perches from which they can pounce on their insect prey.

The eggs are laid in the nests of a variety of birds, including bishops, weavers and sparrows, or occasionally wagtails and flycatchers. The female sometimes removes one of the host's eggs immediately, and when the cuckoo chick hatches,

it usually ejects any remaining eggs and nestlings, and is reared alone. It is fledged at about 21 days. Immature birds have 2 color phases: a rufous-backed phase and a green-backed phase.

10/ COMMON KOEL
Eudynamys scolopacea

RANGE: **N and E Australia, India, Southeast Asia to New Guinea and Solomon Islands**
HABITAT: **forests with fruiting trees**
SIZE: **15½–18 in (39–46 cm)**

In the breeding season this cuckoo can often be heard calling – the male uttering loud, shrill whistles and the characteristic *ko-el* call, while the female responds with short, piercing whistles.

Like most cuckoos, they lay their eggs in the nests of other birds: in India, the hosts are crows, while in Australia they include large honeyeaters and orioles. The chick takes all the food and either starves out or ejects the other nestlings. The adults forage for fruits in the forest canopy and often visit gardens to steal cultivated fruits.

There are 15 or more races of the Common Koel, including the race *E. s. scolopacea* from India, Sri Lanka and the Nicobar Islands and *E. s. cyanocephala* from eastern Australia, which is sometimes considered to be a separate species.

11/ CHANNEL-BILLED CUCKOO
Scythrops novaehollandiae

RANGE: **breeds N and E Australia; winters New Guinea to Sulawesi (Celebes)**
HABITAT: **open forest, swamp woodland**
SIZE: **23–25½ in (58–65 cm)**

With its heavy curved bill, this bulky bird looks more like a toucan than a cuckoo. It usually feeds singly or in small groups in the tops of large trees, eating ripe figs and other fruits, as well as large insects. It is most active at dawn and dusk, but it also feeds at night, when it can be located by its raucous, repetitive cries.

It generally lays its eggs in the nests of crows and butcherbirds such as the Pied Currawong *Strepera graculina*, often laying 2 or more eggs in one nest. When the young hatch they do not throw out the other nestlings but simply take most of their food.

12/ YELLOW-BILLED CUCKOO
Coccyzus americanus

RANGE: **S Canada, USA S to Central America; winters in South America**
HABITAT: **open woods, streamside thickets**
SIZE: **12¼ in (31 cm)**

The handsome Yellow-billed Cuckoo is usually seen as it makes a dash across a forest clearing or flies swiftly from tree to tree. It is surprisingly agile among the trees as it forages for fruit and insects; it has a taste for hairy tent caterpillars and when these are abundant the Yellow-billed Cuckoos are often not far behind.

Unlike Old World cuckoos, these birds build their own nests: small flimsy affairs placed in bushes or trees. They rarely lay their eggs in the nests of other species, but a female will sometimes lay in the nest of another Yellow-billed Cuckoo.

13/ GROOVE-BILLED ANI
Crotophaga sulcirostris

RANGE: **SW USA to N South America**
HABITAT: **open brushy areas, pastures, orchards, secondary woodland, thickets**
SIZE: **13½ in (34 cm)**

This rather unkempt-looking bird, with its large, parrotlike bill and floppy tail, is usually seen in small, loose flocks, foraging for grasshoppers and other insects in the wake of grazing cattle (or, in the tropics, in the wake of army ants).

It is a sociable bird, roosting in groups of 30–40. It also breeds communally, with up to 4 pairs building a bulky cup nest in a thorn bush or tree. All the birds share the duties of incubation and feeding the chicks, and young birds of previous broods may help to feed later broods.

14/ GREATER ROADRUNNER
Geococcyx californianus

RANGE: **W USA, E to Louisiana, S to S Mexico**
HABITAT: **semidesert, chaparral, grassland, farmland, occasionally moist woodland**
SIZE: **20–24 in (51–61 cm)**

This slender, ground-dwelling bird has earned a place in popular mythology, partly on account of its athleticism – it can run at 12 mls (20 km) per hour or more – and partly because it occasionally kills and eats small rattlesnakes. Normally it takes less challenging prey, including gophers, mice, lizards, scorpions, tarantulas and centipedes, as well as large insects and various fruits.

The Great Roadrunner has evolved unusual ways of surviving in its hostile environment. On cold desert nights, it allows its body temperature to fall slightly, saving energy, and becomes slightly torpid. When day breaks, the bird warms itself up by exposing patches of dark skin on its back to the heat of the sun. Roadrunners live in permanent pairs, staying in their breeding territory throughout the year. The compact cup nest is built in a low tree or shrub, or on a clump of cactus, and the young are tended by both parents.

15/ PHEASANT COUCAL
Centropus phasianinus

RANGE: **N and E Australia, New Guinea, Timor**
HABITAT: **tall, dense ground cover including long grass, swamp vegetation and cane fields**
SIZE: **19¾–27½ in (50–70 cm)**

Coucals are giant, ungainly ground cuckoos, with long tails, which spend much of their time stalking through dense undergrowth in search of small animals such as insects, crabs, frogs, lizards, mice and nestlings.

The mottled and barred brown plumage of the Pheasant Coucal makes it difficult to see in thick cover, but it often gives itself away by rapid hooting calls. It flies heavily on short, rounded wings. The females are larger than the males.

The nest is a platform of sticks, usually sited on trampled ground or in a low bush and hooded by pieces of surrounding vegetation pulled over it. Both adults incubate the 2–5 eggs.

BARN AND BAY OWLS, TYPICAL OWLS

COMMON
BARN-OWL

race *alba*

EASTERN SCREECH OWL

rufous phase

gray phase

brown
individual

BAY OWL

CRESTED OWL

EURASIAN
SCOPS OWL

gray individual

PEL'S FISHING OWL

juv

SPECTACLED OWL

GREAT HORNED OWL

juv

race *pallescens*

race *virginianus*

BROWN FISH
OWL

NORTHERN
HAWK OWL

race *bubo*

♂

SNOWY OWL

♀

NORTHERN EAGLE OWL

FAMILY TYTONIDAE
Barn and bay owls

Medium, nocturnal predators. Soft, dense plumage, heart-shaped facial disk, relatively small eyes and long, slender, feathered legs and feathered toes. Large ears, sense of hearing exceptional. Sexes alike in plumage but females mostly slightly larger than males. Orange-buff to blackish-brown upperparts, white, rufous or blackish-brown underparts. Nest in barns, holes in trees or among rocks, or on ground (Grass Owl *Tyto capensis*). Eggs usually 2–6 (sometimes up to 11), white. Incubation 27–34 days, nestling period 49–56 days. 14 species.

1/ COMMON BARN-OWL
Tyto alba

RANGE: **Americas, Europe, Africa, Arabia, India, Southeast Asia, Australia**
HABITAT: **mainly open or semiopen lowlands, including farmland**
SIZE: **13–13¾ in (33–35 cm)**

In many areas, these beautiful birds nest in barns, outbuildings, ruins and the like, but in others they prefer holes in trees. Common Barn-Owls hunt mostly on the wing, low down, with a characteristic light, buoyant action, frequent changes of direction and, sometimes, periods of hovering. They can locate and capture their prey solely by using their phenomenal sense of hearing. Small rodents are normally the main prey, and cyclic fluctuations in their numbers partly govern the numbers and breeding success of the owls.

Most Common Barn-Owls, such as the race *T. a. alba* from Britain, France, southern Europe and Tenerife and Gran Canaria in the Canary Islands, are strikingly white below and pale sandy-gold and gray above. By contrast, other races, such as *T. a. guttata* from central and eastern Europe, have a dark buffish breast.

2/ BAY OWL
Phodilus badius

RANGE: **N India, Southeast Asia**
HABITAT: **mainly tropical forest**
SIZE: **9–13 in (23–33 cm)**

Although this is apparently a fairly common and widespread species, relatively little is known about its ecology. Its short wings and long tail are typical of an owl which hunts in thick cover, and it is known to prey on small mammals, birds, lizards, amphibians and insects. The fact that hunting birds have often been seen around water also suggests that they may eat fish. Typical nesting and roosting sites of this species are in holes or crevices in trees. This was the only known bay owl until 1951 when the Congo, or Itombwe, Bay Owl was first described: it is still known only from a single specimen.

FAMILY STRIGIDAE
Typical owls

Small to large predators, great majority wholly or partly nocturnal. Soft, dense plumage. Large head with saucer-shaped facial disk and very large eyes and ears, with exceptional night vision and very senstive hearing. Feathered legs and toes (except fishing owls and fish owls). Sexes generally alike

in plumage, but females usually larger. Usually cryptically patterned brown or gray. Nest mainly in holes or in abandoned nests of other species; a few nest on ground or in burrows. Eggs 1–14, (usually 2–7), white. Incubation 15–35 days, nestling period 24–52 days; young may leave nest before they can fly, 15–35 days after hatching. 160 species.

3/ EURASIAN SCOPS OWL
Otus scops

RANGE: **breeds S Europe, N Africa, E to SW Siberia; N populations and some S ones, winter in tropical Africa**
HABITAT: **open woodland, parks, orchards, gardens, roadside trees, town squares**
SIZE: **7½–7¾ in (19–20 cm)**

This small, superbly camouflaged owl (which may be either gray-brown or red-brown in basic color) is particularly hard to detect at its daytime roost. Indeed, it is far more often heard than seen, its song – a monotonously repeated single, plaintive, whistling, note – being one of the most characteristic sounds of the Mediterranean night. The Scops Owl is unusual among European owls in being largely a true summer migrant. Large insects such a crickets, cicadas, cockchafers and moths are its main prey, with moths frequently taken in flight and often attracting the owls to hunt around streetlights.

4/ EASTERN SCREECH OWL
Otus asio

RANGE: **E North America from extreme S Quebec and Ontario to E Montana and C Texas and from S Canada to the tip of Florida and NE Mexico**
HABITAT: **open forest, riverside woodland, orchards and other cultivated land, parks and gardens with large trees**
SIZE: **7½–9 in (19–23 cm)**

There are 2 color phases of this small owl: a rust-red rufous phase and a gray phase. The ear tufts are conspicuous when erect, but may be held against the head where they are nearly invisible.

Like many nocturnal owls, Eastern Screech Owls are more often heard than seen. Their primary song is a tremulous, descending whinny. They also utter a quickly repeated, monotonous *who-who-who* all on one pitch. Twitters and barks are given in agitation and in response to predators around the nest. A very close relative (formerly regarded as belonging to the same species), the Western Screech Owl *O. kennicottii*, found to the west of the Rockies, is very similar in appearance but can be distinguished by its different songs – a series of short whistles accelerating in tempo and a brief trill followed by a longer one.

This species has a varied diet, eating large invertebrates, fish, amphibians, reptiles, birds and mammals. Small mammals and birds and large insects form their chief prey, but these owls sometimes kill birds larger than themselves.

5/ CRESTED OWL
Lophostrix cristata

RANGE: **S Mexico to Bolivia, E Ecuador, Amazonian Brazil E of Andes**
HABITAT: **forest, tall, second growth and patches of woodland bordering streams and rivers, chiefly in tropical lowlands**
SIZE: **15–15¾ in (38–40 cm)**

These distinctive owls are sometimes considered to form a link between the small *Otus* owls and the large *Bubo* owls, and recent evidence also suggests a relationship with the spectacled owls *Pulsatrix* of Central and South America. The Crested Owl is somewhat rare and local in distribution over its large range, but its perceived rarity could be due to its strictly nocturnal habits. During the day it roosts in thick cover, usually only 10–30 ft (3–9 m) up, and often near a stream. Although the sexes are alike, this owl has 2 color phases, one uniform dark brown, the other pale buff. Its diet is known to include large cockroaches, beetles, caterpillars and other insects, but may also incorporate other small animals.

The voice of this enigmatic owl has only recently been recorded. Its calls are brief, beginning with 3–4 low stuttering notes followed by a deep-throated growl that has a somewhat resonant quality.

6/ SPECTACLED OWL
Pulsatrix perspicillata

RANGE: S Mexico to NW Argentina and S Brazil
HABITAT: lowland forest, savanna, plantations
SIZE: 17–18 in (43–46 cm)

As with some other species of owl, the Spectacled Owl shows some evidence of 2 color phases: one dark on the upperparts, one lighter. Birds from Central America tend to be darker than those from South America. As with most owls, females are, on average, larger than males. The Spectacled Owl has a voice that includes a gruff *bu-hu-hu*, a descending whistled call and a series of 6–8 low resonant hoots with a slight popping quality – sometimes likened to the resonant tapping of a woodpecker. At times 2 of these birds will duet, each calling with a slightly different tone.

During the day, the Spectacled Owl usually perches hidden just below the forest canopy, but on rare occasions it has been seen hunting on overcast or foggy days. Its diet includes a diversity of small mammals (including rodents and bats), birds, lizards, land crabs and large insects.

The 2 eggs are laid in tree hollows and cavities. The chicks leave the nest before they can fly well and are tended by their parents for some time. In contrast to their parents, the young are white with brown wings and have brown spectacles.

7/ GREAT HORNED OWL
Bubo virginianus

RANGE: North America, except tundra regions of Alaska and Canada, S to Tierra del Fuego
HABITAT: lowlands to tree line in deciduous or coniferous boreal, temperate and tropical forests, prairies, deserts, farmland and occasionally suburban areas
SIZE: 17–20¾ in (43–53 cm)

Because of its large size and huge range, this is one of the most commonly observed owls. The Great Horned Owl is closely related to its Eurasian counterpart, the Northern Eagle Owl. Like that species, it has been separated into many races, which vary both in size and color.

The largest races are found at high latitudes and altitudes and the smallest in tropical lowland forests and deserts. The birds in humid forests are darkest, while those from deserts or areas with snow for much of the year are much paler. There are also orange-breasted and white-breasted color phases. The race *B. v. virginianus* is a dark form from eastern North America, while the race *B. v. pallescens* is a pale desert race from Arizona and northwestern Mexico. The song of the Great Horned Owl consists of a series of booming hoots, and it has a range of calls including barks, growls and screams.

Great Horned Owls lay their eggs in a variety of sites, often taking over abandoned stick nests of hawks, crows and magpies. They also nest in large cavities in trees and cliffs. Occasionally they will nest in open farm buildings and other man-made structures or even on the ground. The usual clutch is 2–3 white eggs. The female is responsible for the incubation, which requires about 32 days. The young leave the nest when they are

about 5–6 weeks old but do not fly well until they are 9–10 weeks old.

Great Horned Owls prey predominantly upon small mammals and birds but have a very wide diet that includes invertebrates, fish, amphibians, reptiles, mammals and birds. Their prey ranges in size from large insects to jack rabbits, skunks and grouse.

8/ NORTHERN EAGLE OWL
Bubo bubo

RANGE: N Africa, Eurasia (not British Isles)
HABITAT: mainly wild, broken country, often in hills with tree cover, but not dense forests; also desert edge
SIZE: 23½–29½ in (60–75 cm)

Northern Eagle Owls are very large, powerful nocturnal predators, able to take mammals up to the size of young Roe Deer and birds as big as cock Capercaillies *Tetrao urogallus*. It is also known to prey on other owls and on raptors as large as buzzards. Mostly though, they feed on a wide variety of very much smaller prey. The male's song is a deep double hoot, perfectly described in the species' German name *Uhu*, and audible over half a mile (1 km) or more away in still conditions. The largest, darkest and most heavily streaked Northern Eagle Owls tend to be those from northern populations such as the race *B. b. bubo* from Europe to France, Greece and northern Ukraine, while the smallest and palest are the desert forms from north Africa and the Middle East.

9/ BROWN FISH OWL
Bubo zeylonensis

RANGE: Middle East (rare); India and Southeast Asia
HABITAT: forest and woodland along streams and lakes
SIZE: 21¼–22½ in (54–57 cm)

This is the most widespread of the 4 Asian fish owls. They are all large birds, specially adapted to their way of life in having bare legs and feet, with many tiny, sharp spines on the soles of their toes which enable them to grasp wet and slippery prey. The Brown Fish Owl's feet are bare because feathers would soon become soiled with fish scales and slime and are not needed for protection against the bites of prey, as may be their function in other owls. One fish owl, Blakiston's Fish Owl *B. blakistoni* does have feathered legs, doubtless to protect it from the extreme cold it experiences in the rivers of eastern Siberia, northeastern China and northern Japan in winter.

Although the Brown Fish Owl is fairly well known, much of its ecology has never been studied. The birds are known to hunt from trees overhanging the water, from rocks or by wading in the shallows, but have also been seen flying over the surface and taking fish from the water. Fish and freshwater crabs dominate their diet, plus some reptiles, amphibians, insects, small mammals and birds.

Brown Fish Owls lay their 1–2 eggs on a ledge or cleft in a cliff, in a tree hole or in the deserted nest of a bird of prey; in India, they have been known to use abandoned buildings.

10/ PEL'S FISHING OWL
Scotopelia peli

RANGE: sub-Saharan Africa, excluding SW
HABITAT: forested river banks, wetlands
SIZE: 20–24 in (51–61 cm)

This is the most widely distributed and best known of the 3 African fishing owls, as well as the largest. Its calls, usually heard soon after dark and before dawn, are a series of resounding hoots, repeated at 10-second intervals for several minutes at a time and audible up to 2 mls (3 km) away. It occasionally catches frogs, crabs and mussels but its main food is fish weighing 3½–9 oz (100–250 g). The bird makes a shallow dive from a low perch above the water, catching the fish in its feet. Sandbanks are also used as fishing places. Its legs and feet are unfeathered, as are those of the other fishing owls.

11/ SNOWY OWL
Nyctea scandiaca

RANGE: circumpolar Arctic
HABITAT: mainly on tundra; also in other wild habitats, from coastal islands to moorland
SIZE: 20¾–26 in (53–66 cm)

The Snowy Owl has a rounded head with a curiously catlike expression. There is a particularly great difference in size between the sexes, females being up to 20 percent larger than males. Also unusual is the marked difference in plumage between the almost all-white male and the strongly barred and chevroned female.

This species is a sufficiently large and versatile predator to be able to take a wide range of small to medium-sized bird and mammal prey, but over much of its breeding range it feeds largely on lemmings. Its distribution, numbers and breeding performances are closely tied to the regular population cycles of lemmings, so it is a nomadic and opportunist bird. Many wander far south in winter, and numbers can be large and reach "invasion" proportions when food shortages follow a bumper breeding year. Although most hunting is done at dawn and dusk, Snowy Owls also hunt in broad daylight.

12/ NORTHERN HAWK OWL
Surnia ulula

RANGE: N Eurasia, North America, mainly subarctic
HABITAT: boreal and mountain forest with easy access to clearings and forest edge
SIZE: 14–15¼ in (36–39 cm)

This distinctive species is one of a relatively small number of owls which are habitually active during the daytime. Superficially, it resembles a small hawk, with its short, rounded wings and long tail, and its occasional aerial hunting forays, when it dashes through the trees in pursuit of a bird, can be reminiscent of the Sparrowhawk *Accipter nisus*. Mainly, though, it hunts from a prominent perch. In summer, the prey consists almost entirely of small voles, plus some other mammals and small birds, but in winter the Northern Hawk Owl may take a greater proportion of birds. Like other northern owls, its numbers can vary dramatically in relation to the availability of its prey.

NORTHERN PYGMY OWL

gray phase

rufous phase

PEARL-SPOTTED OWLET

PAPUAN HAWK-OWL

race *ocellata*

ELF OWL
young in nest-hole

race *leucopsis*

BOOBOOK OWL

race *vidalii*

LITTLE OWL

race *hypugaea*

race *lilith*

juv at nest-burrow entra

BURROWING OWL

race *sylvatica*
rufous phase

chick

race *aluco*
gray phase

GREAT GRAY OWL

EURASIAN TAWNY OWL

LONG-EARED OWL

race *otus*
cryptic posture

race *nebulosa*

AFRICAN WOOD OWL

SHORT-EARED OWL

NORTHERN
SAW-WHET OWL

juv

JAMAICAN OWL

TYPICAL OWLS

1/ AFRICAN WOOD OWL
Strix woodfordi
RANGE: **sub-Saharan Africa, except extreme S**
HABITAT: **forests, plantations**
SIZE: **11¾–13¾ in (30–35 cm)**

The African Wood Owl is a big-headed, cryptically colored, highly nocturnal wood owl. It generally hunts from a low perch, taking most of its prey from the ground, but also picks insects off vegetation while in flight and is surprisingly agile at hawking for flying insects. Insects of many kinds form its main prey, but a few frogs, small snakes, birds and small mammals are also eaten.

This species was, until recently, placed in the genus *Ciccaba*, along with 4 species found in Central and South America. Although these species are similar in appearance to the African Wood Owl and share features such as the relatively simple structure of their inner ears, many ornithologists now believe that the similarities are due to convergent evolution in similar habitats, rather than to a true relationship, and classify the African Wood Owl in the genus *Strix*, along with Eurasian wood owls such as the Eurasian Tawny Owl and Great Gray Owl.

2/ EURASIAN TAWNY OWL
Strix aluco
RANGE: **Europe, N Africa, parts of W Asia, China, Korea, Taiwan**
HABITAT: **chiefly woodland or areas with some trees, including urban areas**
SIZE: **14½–15¼ in (37–39 cm)**

Seldom seen, due to its strictly nocturnal habits, the Eurasian Tawny Owl is nevertheless better known than other European owls through its familiar song – a long, quavering hooting, used to proclaim territorial ownership, advertise its presence to a mate, and during courtship. The male's hoot is slightly lower pitched and more clearly phrased than that of the female; sometimes they perform a duet to strengthen the pair-bond. More often, however, the female replies with a *kewick* call, a variant of which is used by both sexes as a contact call. This combination is popularly represented as *tu-whit, to-woo* and wrongly ascribed to a single bird.

The Eurasian Tawny Owl is primarily a hole-nester, most often in trees and, like other owls, has a breeding regime in which the female remains with the young until they are well grown, while the male hunts for the whole family. The birds feed mainly on small mammals, but they are very adaptable and will readily switch to other prey, such as small birds. It is this versatility which lies behind their wide distribution and their ability to colonize villages, towns and large cities.

Between 10 and 15 races of the Eurasian Tawny Owl are recognized, with distinct reddish-brown and gray color phases in most regions. The reddish-brown phase is more common in the race *S. a. sylvatica* of western Europe (and predominates in Britain), and the gray phase is more common in the northern and eastern European race *S. a. aluco*.

3/ GREAT GRAY OWL
Strix nebulosa
RANGE: **N Europe, N America, N Asia**
HABITAT: **dense, mature boreal forest**
SIZE: **25½–27½ in (65–70 cm)**

Despite its size – it has a wingspan of over 5 ft (1.5 m) – this magnificent northern forest owl feeds largely on voles. It is often active in daylight and is also capable of finding and capturing its prey in deep snow, apparently by hearing alone. In northern Europe, most Great Gray Owls breed in the old nests of other birds of prey, but some nest on tree stumps and broken-off trunks or on the ground, while a few use artificially built nests and nest-boxes. This is one of a number of owls which is exceptionally bold in defense of its nest: it will launch determined attacks on and even strike humans, occasionally causing injuries.

There are 2 races: *S. n. nebulosa* of North America and *S. n. lapponica* of Eurasia. The North American race has more barred and mottled underparts, with fewer streaks.

4/ PEARL-SPOTTED OWLET
Glaucidium perlatum
RANGE: **sub-Saharan Africa**
HABITAT: **woodland and savanna**
SIZE: **6½–7 in (17–18 cm)**

As it is often active by day, the Pearl-spotted Owlet is often the most readily seen owl in woodland and savanna in Africa. Prominent "false eyes" on the rear of its head are a useful identification feature. It shows a decided preference for open bush-type savanna and shuns areas where the ground cover is other than sparse.

A vigorous and active hunter, this little owl operates from a perch, striking in a rapid dive and taking insects, small reptiles and small mammals. It also chases and catches flying insects and bats, and some birds. The Pearl-spotted Owlet is the most diurnal of the African owls, regularly hunting during the day, especially during the breeding season, although it also hunts at night. It usually nests in the abandoned tree hole of a barbet or woodpecker, but sometimes chooses a natural hole or an artificial nest-box.

5/ NORTHERN PYGMY OWL
Glaucidium gnoma
RANGE: **W North America (N to Alaska, E to Rocky Mountains) S to Guatemala**
HABITAT: **dense woodland in mountains and foothills**
SIZE: **6½ in (17 cm)**

Small, earless owls with long tails and shrikelike flight, this species and the Ferruginous Pygmy Owl *G. brasilianum*, from the extreme southwestern USA, look much alike, but occupy different habitats. Both these species and many of their relatives have a pair of prominent, white-edged black patches at the back of their heads; these markings, which resemble eyes, may help the owls to survive by confusing predators and prey.

The tiny Northern Pygmy Owl is strong and ferocious out of all proportion to its size. It sometimes takes prey much larger than itself. It feeds on mice, large insects, ground squirrels, gophers, chipmunks and small birds. It is active during the daytime, hunting mainly in the early morning and late afternoon.

This species nests in natural cavities or old woodpecker excavations in trees, mostly in coniferous woods. There are 2 color phases, a gray one and reddish-brown one.

6/ ELF OWL
Micrathene whitneyi
RANGE: **SW USA S to Baja California and N Mexico; winters in Mexico**
HABITAT: **deserts, riparian areas, mountain oak and mixed pine and oak forests**
SIZE: **5¼–5¾ in (13.5–14.5 cm)**

The Elf Owl is the world's smallest owl. Within its range, its short tail and less robust shape distinguish it from other Lilliputian, "earless" owls, the Northern Pygmy Owl and the Ferruginous Pygmy Owl.

Unlike the pygmy owls, the Elf Owl is strictly nocturnal. Hiding in daylight – often in plain sight, but motionless – it becomes active as night falls, using its feet to catch prey, often hovering over the ground and above trees and flowers, or darting after insects from a perch, much like a flycatcher. Its diet consists mainly of sphinx moths, grasshoppers, beetles, crickets and scorpions. It sometimes hawks for insects around campfires and streetlamps. Noisy chirps and puppylike yips, often in a series, are its most common calls.

The Elf Owl uses holes excavated by woodpeckers as roosting and nesting cavities. It has to dispute ownership of the holes with the woodpeckers or, when appropriating those abandoned by them, with other hole-nesting birds, from other owls to flycatchers and Cactus Wrens.

7/ LITTLE OWL
Athene noctua

RANGE: **Europe, N Africa, Middle East, Asia**
HABITAT: **varied open or semi-open areas**
SIZE: **$8\frac{1}{4}$–9 in (21–23 cm)**

The Little Owl shows considerable variation in color, ranging from extremes such as the dark, strongly marked race *A. n. vidalii* from western Europe, to the very pale desert races, such as the Middle Eastern race *A. n. lilith*.

This is a relatively easily seen owl, as it is quite active during the day and also often roosts in open and rather obvious situations, frequently in traditional sites. It is much more terrestrial than most owls, often foraging on foot and also sometimes nesting in holes in the ground, including rabbit burrows. Like the Burrowing Owl, the Little Owl has the comical-looking habit of bobbing its head up and down when agitated. Although hunting may commence before dusk, it is mainly done after dark. A wide variety of small mammals and birds, reptiles, amphibians and invertebrates from insects to earthworms, are eaten, the last predominating in most areas.

8/ BURROWING OWL
Athene cunicularia

RANGE: **extreme SW Canada, W USA, Florida, Central America and South America (except the Amazon Basin)**
HABITAT: **grassland, deserts, farmlands with low-growing or sparse vegetation, airports, golf courses**
SIZE: **7–$9\frac{3}{4}$ in (18–25 cm)**

The Burrowing Owl is often active in daylight. This, coupled with its open land habitat, make it more visible than most owls. It can easily be distinguished from other small owls in its range by its long, sparsely feathered legs.

Burrowing Owls feed largely on insects and small mammals. They lay their eggs in a burrow in the ground, often one excavated by a small mammal. Where there are no burrowing animals, they excavate their own burrows in sandy soil, using their bills as well as their long legs.

The owls spend much of their time perched at the entrance to their burrows or on a hummock or fencepost, blinking in the sunlight and bobbing their bodies up and down dramatically when disturbed. They have a mellow *toot tooo* territorial song and adults utter a harsh rattle if a predator approaches the nest. The young make a sound like a rattlesnake when cornered.

9/ NORTHERN SAW-WHET OWL
Aegolius acadicus

RANGE: **E and C North America from Nova Scotia S to N Midwest USA; W North America from S Alaska to S California; also extends S in E and W mountain ranges, in W as far as S Mexico**
HABITAT: **coniferous, deciduous and mixed deciduous and coniferous forests and woods, riverside thickets**
SIZE: **$6\frac{1}{2}$–$7\frac{1}{2}$ in (17–19 cm)**

This relatively tame little owl is a smaller version of the more widespread Tengmalm's, or Boreal, Owl of northern Europe, Siberia, Alaska and Canada. The 2 species overlap in a 125 ml (200 km) wide zone in southern Canada and the northern Midwest USA, and it is still not completely understood how they can coexist.

The odd name refers to the bird's song, which resembles the sound of a saw-blade being sharpened. Northern Saw-whet Owls also utter a variety of whistles, single notes and rasping sounds. They eat mainly mice and voles, supplemented with the occasional small bird, and lay their eggs in abandoned woodpecker holes.

10/ PAPUAN HAWK-OWL
Uroglaux dimorpha

RANGE: **sparsely distributed throughout New Guinea; Yapen Island**
HABITAT: **lowland rain forest, rarely reaching as high as 5,000 ft (1,500 m)**
SIZE: **$11\frac{3}{4}$–13 in (30–33 cm)**

As its name suggests, the Papuan Hawk-Owl is more hawklike than other owls, with a slim build, small head and a very long tail for an owl, which accounts for half its total length. Although they share the same rather hawklike appearance, the southern hawk-owls of the genera *Uroglaux* and *Ninox* are very different in other ways and are not closely related.

The Papuan Hawk-Owl is a rare and little-known species, whose calls and nesting habits still remain to be discovered. It feeds on insects, rodents and birds up to the size of pigeons.

11/ BOOBOOK OWL
Ninox novaeseelandiae

RANGE: **Australia, Tasmania, Lesser Sundas, Moluccas, S New Guinea, Norfolk Island, New Zealand**
HABITAT: **forest, woodland, scrub, urban trees**
SIZE: **$9\frac{3}{4}$–$13\frac{3}{4}$ in (25–35 cm)**

This common small brown owl's familiar double hoot, from which it takes its name, is reminiscent of the call of the European Cuckoo *Cuculus canorus*. Some of the 14 or so races have been regarded as separate species. There are 4 Australian races, including the pale rufous or sandy-brown *N. n. ocellata* from northern, inland and much of western Australia and the darker, heavily spotted *N. n. leucopsis* from Tasmania.

Boobook Owls feed mainly on insects, sometimes caught around town lights, and also on small mammals, birds and geckos. By day they roost in thick foliage or sometimes in tree hollows, caves or buildings.

12/ LONG-EARED OWL
Asio otus

RANGE: **breeds Europe, parts of N Africa, N Asia, N America; birds from extreme N migrate S, some beyond breeding range in America and Far East**
HABITAT: **woods, forests, copses, shelterbelts, mature scrub**
SIZE: **$13\frac{3}{4}$–$14\frac{1}{2}$ in (35–37 cm)**

Like the Short-eared Owl, the Long-eared Owl is a long-winged bird which hunts over open country, specializing largely in taking small mammal prey, such as voles, and fluctuating widely in numbers and distribution in response to a cyclic food supply. Long-eared Owls nest in dense woods, plantations, stands of trees and tall, thick scrub, almost always using the old nests of birds such as crows or raptors, or sometimes squirrel's dreys.

Long-eared Owls are strictly nocturnal. Like Scops Owls and Screech Owls, they often adopt an extraordinary elongated, cryptic posture when perched in trees during the daytime and look exactly like broken branches. Compared with the Eurasian race *A. o. otus*, most North American Long-eared Owls of the race *A. o. wilsonianus* are more barred than streaked below, have a more golden-red facial disk and yellow rather than orange-red eyes.

13/ SHORT-EARED OWL
Asio flammeus

RANGE: **N Europe, N Asia, North and South America; N populations migrate E, W or S, some far to S of breeding range**
HABITAT: **moors, heath, grassland, marshes and other open habitats**
SIZE: **$14\frac{1}{2}$–$15\frac{1}{4}$ in (37–39 cm)**

In contrast to the Long-eared Owl, this species nests on the ground in open country, including the edges of wetlands, coastal dunes and small islands. Both species are partial migrants, with Short-eared Owls commonly frequenting coastal marshes and even farmland in winter.

Often hunting by day (especially in winter), Short-eared Owls can be very conspicuous and easily seen – unlike most owls. The male's song is a series of low, muted hoots, often uttered during aerial display flights. Like the Long-eared Owl, this species displays in flight by clapping its wing tips rapidly beneath its body; the sound thus produced carries a surprisingly far.

14/ JAMAICAN OWL
Pseudoscops grammicus

RANGE: **Jamaica**
HABITAT: **woodland, parklike areas**
SIZE: **$11\frac{3}{4}$–14 in (30–36 cm)**

As with some of the other "unique" owls that are placed in a genus of their own, this one's affinities are uncertain. Whatever its ancestry, its population is limited since it is found only on the island of Jamaica. Very little is known of its biology. This strictly nocturnal owl hunts in both open country and woodland. The voice of the Jamaican Owl is a guttural growl, sometimes interpreted as a *wow*, and an occasional high-pitched, tremulous *whoooo*. It nests in a tree cavity or in a protected fork between branches hidden by vegetation.

OILBIRD, FROGMOUTHS, POTOOS, OWLET-NIGHTJARS, NIGHTHAWKS AND NIGHTJARS, SWIFTS

OILBIRD

nestling

race *brachyurus* ♂

race *phalaenoides* ♂

dark brown phase

COMMON POTOO

gray phase

TAWNY FROGMOUTH

AUSTRALIAN OWLET-NIGHTJAR

gray phase

race *sennetti* ♂

rufous phase
roost hole

COMMON NIGHTHAWK

race *minor* ♀

♂

COMMON POORWILL

♀

WHIP-POOR-WILL

♂

♀

EUROPEAN NIGHTJAR

♂

courtship display flight

SCISSOR-TAILED NIGHTJAR

♂

♀

STANDARD-WINGED NIGHTJAR

courtship display flight

nest site

BLACK SWIFT

EDIBLE-NEST SWIFTLET

BROWN SPINETAILED SWIFT

CHIMNEY SWIFT

nest

WHITE-THROATED SWIFT

OILBIRD, FROGMOUTHS, POTOOS, OWLET-NIGHTJARS, NIGHTHAWKS AND NIGHTJARS, SWIFTS

FAMILY STEATORNITHIDAE
Oilbird
There is only one species in this family.

1/ OILBIRD
Steatornis caripensis

RANGE: **Panama to N South America, Trinidad**
HABITAT: **humid forest, caves**
SIZE: **19 in (48 cm)**

Flocks of these large, social birds feed together at night, often traveling long distances from the caves where they roost and nest colonially to find the oily fruits of laurels, palms and incense trees. Many of these fruits are aromatic and it is likely that the Oilbirds find them using their excellent sense of smell. They do not settle on the trees, but gather the fruit in flight with their long hooked bills and store it in their stomachs, digesting it during the day when they are back in the caves.

In the pitch darkness of the cave they find their way by echolocation. The 2–4 white eggs are incubated in a nest of regurgitated fruit, seeds and the birds' own droppings by both parents for 32–35 days. The chicks remain in the nest for 90–120 days. Fed on a similar diet to the parents they put on a lot of fat and in the late nestling period may weigh half as much again as an adult. Local people sometimes kill them for their oil. The birds are now widely protected by law.

FAMILY PODARGIDAE
Frogmouths
Medium to large with short, rounded wings and cryptic plumage. Flat bills with huge gape. Nocturnal, mainly insect-eaters; large eyes. Sexes usually similar. Nest built of twigs or down, spiders' webs and lichens in tree. Eggs 1–3, white. Incubation 30 days, nestling period 30 days. 13 species.

2/ TAWNY FROGMOUTH
Podargus strigoides

RANGE: **Australia and Tasmania**
HABITAT: **open forest, rain forest edge, urban trees**
SIZE: **13¾–21 in (35–53 cm)**

A master of camouflage, the Tawny Frogmouth roosts by day on the branch of a tree, where its cryptic, mottled gray plumage looks like bark.

It varies geographically in size and color; the northern race *P. s. phalaenoides*, for example, is smaller and paler than the southern race *P. s. brachyurus*. Females of some races have an uncommon rufous phase. The Tawny Frogmouth feeds at night on small ground animals such as beetles, centipedes, frogs and mice, which it catches by planing down from a perch.

FAMILY NYCTIBIIDAE
Potoos
Medium to large with soft, cryptic plumage. Nocturnal insect-eaters; small bills with huge gape; very large eyes. Sexes alike. Eggs 1–2, white, spotted, laid in small depression on tree stump or branch with no nest. Incubation at least 33 days, nestling period 44–50 days. 5 species.

3/ COMMON POTOO
Nyctibius griseus

RANGE: **W Mexico to Uruguay, West Indies**
HABITAT: **lowland tropical forest, forest edge, open woods along streams, mangroves**
SIZE: **14–16 in (36–41 cm)**

Named for its melancholy 2-note call, the Common Potoo feeds by night, flying up from a favored perch to capture in its large mouth insects on the wing. By day it normally perches motionless on a branch, stiffening to resemble a snag of splintered wood if it is alarmed. Its intricately patterned cryptic plumage varies from grayish to dark brown. It nests in a tree, usually laying a single egg which is placed in an unlined depression in a tree branch.

FAMILY AEGOTHELIDAE
Owlet-nightjars
Small, dumpy, with large-eyed, owl-like faces and strong legs. Also known as owlet-frogmouths. Bill with huge gape. Insect-eaters. Plumage cryptic gray, brown, rufous, black and white; sexes similar. Nest in a tree or rock cavity. Eggs 2–5, white. Incubation and nestling period unknown for most species. 8 species.

4/ AUSTRALIAN OWLET-NIGHTJAR
Aegotheles cristatus

RANGE: **Australia, Tasmania, S New Guinea**
HABITAT: **open forest and woodland**
SIZE: **8¼–9¾ in (21–25 cm)**

The Australian Owlet-Nightjar is a delicate, mottled gray or rufous bird, with short wings, large eyes, very soft plumage and a mothlike flight. The race *A. c. cristatus* from southern Australia is gray-bellied, whereas *A. c. leucogaster* from northern Australia has a white belly.

It feeds by night, hunting for insects on the wing, pouncing from a perch or chasing them on the ground. By day it roosts alone in a crevice or hole, but will sometimes sun itself at the entrance and often utters its churring call in daylight.

Both male and female build the nest — a bed of fresh acacia and eucalyptus leaves at the base of a tree hollow or cliff crevice. They also probably share the incubation of the 2–5 (usually 3) eggs for about 26 days. Both sexes feed the young, which leave the nest on fledging at about 20–30 days, but they stay with their parents for several months thereafter.

FAMILY CAPRIMULGIDAE
Nighthawks and nightjars
Short-legged, long-tailed, hawklike insect-eaters, with large eyes and small bills with huge gape. Cryptic gray, brown, rufous and black plumage, often with white patches on head, wings and tail, most prominent in males. Active mainly at twilight. Nest a shallow scrape on ground. Eggs 1–2, white or pale brown, usually blotched, cryptic. Incubation 16–20 days, nestling period 16–20 days. 82 species.

5/ COMMON NIGHTHAWK
Chordeiles minor

RANGE: **breeds in North America (except extreme N) and West Indies; winters in South America S to Argentina**
HABITAT: **open fields, gravelly areas, grassland, savanna, semidesert, towns**
SIZE: **9½ in (24 cm)**

The white patches on the sharply pointed wings of the Common Nighthawk are often its most conspicuous feature as it swoops and wheels through the twilight in pursuit of flying insects. It will eat moths, flies, grasshoppers, beetles, mosquitoes and ants; indeed, one bird was found to have the remains of 2,175 ants in its stomach.

The male performs a dramatic courtship ritual, swooping down with booming wings onto a perch near a potential mate, then displaying on the ground. The bird's color varies from dark brown in the eastern North American race *C. m. minor* to paler grayish brown in the Great Plains race *C. m. sennetti*: these color differences are subtle in adults but striking in juveniles.

6/ COMMON POORWILL
Phalaenoptilus nuttallii

RANGE: **breeds in W USA and Mexico; winters S to C Mexico**
HABITAT: **arid and semiarid country, prairie, scrub woodland, pine forest**
SIZE: **8 in (20 cm)**

The smallest of the North American nightjars, the Common Poorwill is usually seen as it flies up from roadsides at night. In flight it resembles a large moth. The male has bolder white tips to his tail than the female. The name "poorwill" is derived from its simple 2-note whistle.

It usually catches its insect prey by aerial pursuit, flying up to take moths, grasshoppers and beetles, but it will also snap up insects from the ground. In desert areas during winter the Common Poorwill becomes torpid and enters a state resembling hibernation. This is most unusual among birds.

7/ WHIP-POOR-WILL
Caprimulgus vociferus

RANGE: **breeds in E USA and S Canada, also SW USA and Mexico; winters from Mexico through Central America to Panama**
HABITAT: **deciduous, mountain and mixed pine-oak forests and woods**
SIZE: **9¾ in (25 cm)**

The Whip-poor-will takes its name from its distinctive call, which may be repeated 100 times or more without interruption. Like all nightjars, it feeds at night and by twilight, pursuing insects on the wing. The hunting bird flies close to the ground, its wide mouth gaping to scoop up prey.

Whip-poor-wills tend to synchronize their breeding with the full moon, presumably to make hunting easier when they are feeding the young. The eggs are laid directly on the ground, after a courtship in which both birds display on the ground, strutting with their differently patterned tails spread while the male purrs to his mate and she "chuckles" in return.

8/ EUROPEAN NIGHTJAR
Caprimulgus europaeus

RANGE: **breeds in Europe, E to C Asia and N to S Scandinavia; winters in Africa**
HABITAT: **scrub, heathland, recently felled woodland**
SIZE: **11 in (28 cm)**

This bird, like other members of its family, is usually located by its song — a persistent, monotonous churring, accompanied by wing claps during the male's evening display flights in the breeding season. He has white spots on his wings and tail which are prominent during various displays.

The tiny bill of the nightjar gives little indication of the huge gape, which is fringed with stiff bristles to improve its efficiency as a snare. The bird always hunts on the wing, wheeling and darting through the gloom as it chases moths and other night-flying insects.

By day it rests, perched horizontally along a branch or on the ground, relying on its superb camouflage for concealment.

9/ STANDARD-WINGED NIGHTJAR
Macrodipteryx longipennis

RANGE: **tropical Africa**
HABITAT: **open forest**
SIZE: **11 in (28 cm)**

The Standard-winged Nightjar is named for the flaglike "standards" of the male's wings: these are the second primary flight feathers which become elongated to 18–21 in (45–53 cm) in the breeding season. The male uses them in his courtship display. He circles slowly around a potential mate, with his wings vibrating rapidly and the standards blowing up over his back. The effect is spectacular, but the standards must hamper flight and make the male more vulnerable to predators. Once they have done their job, they usually break off, allowing the bird to fly normally again.

10/ SCISSOR-TAILED NIGHTJAR
Hydropsalis brasiliana

RANGE: **E Peru, Brazil S of Amazon, Paraguay, Uruguay, N and C Argentina**
HABITAT: **lowland forest, dry woods, clearings**
SIZE: **male 20 in (51 cm); female 11¾ in (30 cm)**

Like the Standard-winged Nightjar, this species has elongated feathers, in this case the central and outermost feathers of the tail. Both sexes have them, but they are much longer in the male. They are probably important in the bird's courtship display, but little is known about its breeding behavior. The Scissor-tailed Nightjar hunts by night, capturing its prey by aerial pursuit. It usually flies close to the ground, mouth open, ensnaring large moths and smaller insects.

FAMILY APODIDAE
Swifts

Small to medium, long-winged, highly aerial insect-eaters; short beaks with huge gape; very short legs and strong feet for clinging to vertical surfaces. Generally dull brown or black with white markings, sexes alike. Nest a cup of saliva-cemented material attached to a crevice, or on a branch or leaf. Eggs 1–6, white. Incubation 17–28 days, nestling period 34–72 days. 92 species.

11/ BLACK SWIFT
Nephoecetes niger

RANGE: **W North America from Alaska to California and Central America S to Costa Rica, West Indies; winters in tropical America**
HABITAT: **mountains**
SIZE: **7 in (18 cm)**

This is the largest and rarest North American breeding swift. Like all swifts, it hawks for insects on the wing. In bad weather the insects tend to fly low, so the swift hunts near the ground. In good weather the hunting is better high above the ground, and the swift will often ascend so high that it fades from sight.

It nests on cliffs and in canyons and often chooses a site behind a waterfall, so that it has to fly in and out through the cascading water. This provides excellent defense against predators.

12/ EDIBLE-NEST SWIFTLET
Aerodramus fuciphagus

RANGE: **Malaysia, Indonesia**
HABITAT: **tropical forest with caves, limestone areas, sandstone sea cliffs**
SIZE: **4 in (10 cm)**

All swifts use dried saliva to cement their nesting materials together, but the cave swiftlets use more than most. The nests of this species are cups of almost pure saliva and are collected in great quantities for use in Chinese bird's-nest soup.

The birds breed in vast colonies in the high recesses of large caves. The adults use echo-location to navigate in the dark and so find their way to the nest.

13/ BROWN SPINETAILED SWIFT
Hirundapus gigantea

RANGE: **India, Southeast Asia, Indonesia**
HABITAT: **forested valleys, grassy hilltops**
SIZE: **8¼ in (21 cm)**

Despite its heavy-bodied appearance, this bird is a spectacularly fast and acrobatic performer in the air. It uses its speed and agility to catch flying insects such as bees, wasps, flies and beetles and, like many other swifts, it spends much of its life on the wing. A courting pair will even mate in flight, falling down through the air as they press their bodies together. The nest is built in a rock crevice or hollow tree. It is made of leaves, feathers and other material gathered in flight and is glued together with saliva.

14/ CHIMNEY SWIFT
Chaetura pelagica

RANGE: **breeds E USA and S Canada; winters in Central and NE South America**
HABITAT: **open and wooded areas, often in towns**
SIZE: **5 in (13 cm)**

This small, dark swift is an extremely gregarious bird which nests and roosts in huge colonies, sometimes numbering several thousand birds, which may overlap like shingles on a roof. Originally the nest sites and roosting sites were hollow trees, but today the colonies take over air shafts or large chimneys.

The nest is made of thin twigs which the bird snatches in its feet while in flight. There is some evidence of cooperative breeding, with "helpers" assisting the pair with rearing the young.

15/ WHITE-THROATED SWIFT
Aeronautes saxatilis

RANGE: **N Central America and W USA**
HABITAT: **mountains and ocean cliffs**
SIZE: **6¾ in (17 cm)**

This is a common and conspicuous bird in areas where there are plenty of suitable nest sites, such as crevices in cliffs. Their penetrating, screaming calls are freely uttered as the birds wheel over the crags and cliffs. This species is only a summer visitor to much of its range in the USA. It often breeds high in the mountains, and has been recorded nesting at 13,000 ft (4,000 m). The clutch size is large for a swift, with as many as 6 eggs.

SWIFTS, TREE SWIFTS, HUMMINGBIRDS

nest

LESSER SWALLOW-
TAILED SWIFT

nest

AFRICAN
PALM SWIFT

EURASIAN SWIFT

ALPINE SWIFT

♀   ♂

CRESTED TREE SWIFT

nest

♂

REDDISH
HERMIT

WHITE-TIPPED SICKLEBILL

LONG-TAILED HERMIT

♂

VIOLET SABREWING

♀

♀

at nest

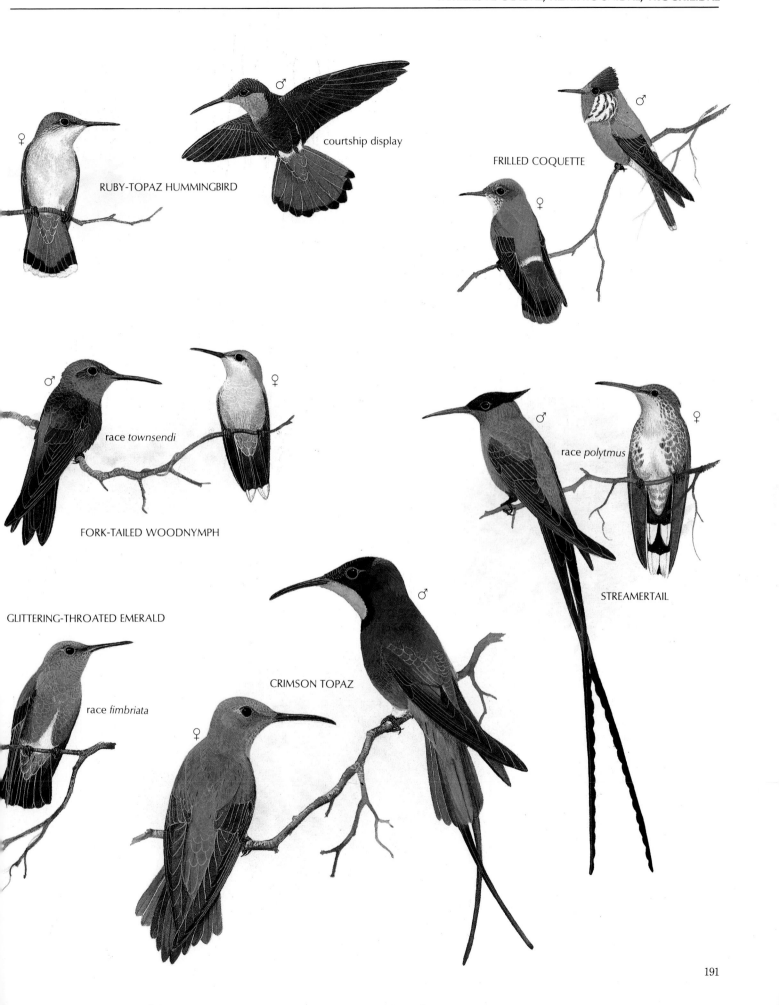

RUBY-TOPAZ HUMMINGBIRD

courtship display

FRILLED COQUETTE

race *townsendi*

FORK-TAILED WOODNYMPH

race *polytmus*

STREAMERTAIL

GLITTERING-THROATED EMERALD

CRIMSON TOPAZ

race *fimbriata*

191

SWIFTS, TREE SWIFTS, HUMMINGBIRDS

1/ LESSER SWALLOW-TAILED SWIFT
Panyptila cayennensis

RANGE: S Mexico to Peru and Brazil
HABITAT: aerial, over many types of terrain
SIZE: 5 in (13 cm)

With its deeply forked tail, this is the most swallowlike of all the true swifts, although in the air it usually holds its tail closed in a single point. Its flight is fast and agile, if slightly erratic, as it coasts and then accelerates with rapid wing beats. It is normally seen alone or in pairs, flying very high, but it sometimes joins other swifts as they wheel through the sky hawking for flying insects.

The nest is a large, conical tube of felted plant down and feathers, gummed together with saliva and attached to a tree trunk, wall or rock face. The nest is used for roosting as well as breeding.

2/ AFRICAN PALM SWIFT
Cypsiurus parvus

RANGE: sub-Saharan Africa, except much of Ethiopia, Somalia and S Africa
HABITAT: aerial, near palms
SIZE: 6 in (15 cm)

This slender, pale brown swift is always found in association with palms and may gather in huge flocks at favorite trees. Even in the middle of urban areas it may be very common indeed. It usually forages in groups at treetop height, circling and jinking on its long, narrow wings and occasionally spreading its deeply forked tail as it banks into a steep turn.

Its nest is little more than a pad of feathers and plant down, glued to the vertical underside of a palm frond with saliva. The 2 eggs are also glued to the nest, and the parents incubate them by turns, clinging vertically to the nest. The nestlings have long curved claws, enabling them to cling on tightly as the palm fronds are whipped about violently during windy weather.

3/ ALPINE SWIFT
Tachymarptis melba

RANGE: Mediterranean and S Asia to India, also S and E Africa; N birds winter in Africa S to South Africa and in India
HABITAT: aerial over hilly country
SIZE: 8¾ in (22 cm)

More than twice the size of the Eurasian Swift, this powerful swift may even resemble a small falcon in silhouette. It is usually seen hunting high over the rocky terrain which, at one time, provided its only nest sites, on cliffs. Today it often nests and roosts in tall buildings, and this has enabled it to expand northward, over less rugged terrain. The birds build the nest from straw and feathers gathered in flight. Most clutches contain 3 eggs. A Swiss study has shown that the adults return to the same site year after year and have a high survival rate – 2 lived to 19 years.

Alpine Swifts are monogamous, retaining the same mate for several years, but they breed in colonies of up to 170 pairs. They rarely fly in bad weather, preferring to roost in the colony; at such times nonbreeding adults will roost in the open nearby, clustering together for warmth.

4/ EURASIAN SWIFT
Apus apus

RANGE: most of Europe, parts of N Africa and C Asia and E almost to Pacific; winters in tropical Africa
HABITAT: aerial; breeds in buildings and rock crevices
SIZE: 5½ in (14 cm)

No land bird is more aerial than the Eurasian Swift. It feeds, drinks, sleeps and mates on the wing, returning to earth only to lay its eggs and feed its chicks. A young bird may spend up to 4 years in the air, from the moment it leaves the nest to the day it returns to the colony to rear its own family. Not surprisingly, it is a superb flier: wheeling, climbing and diving as it scoops flying insects from the air, or engages in excited chases, uttering its characteristic shrill, screaming calls.

These swifts nest in colonies, mostly in roof spaces. The adults feed their young on insects carried back in their throat pouches. When insects are scarce during cold or adverse weather, the young will survive for several days without food by becoming torpid, so reducing energy loss.

FAMILY HEMIPROCNIDAE
Tree swifts
Medium swifts with crests and long, forked tails. Able to perch (unlike true swifts). Plumage brighter than true swifts, males with chestnut cheeks. Nest a tiny basket of plant fragments glued to side of a branch with saliva. Eggs 1, white. Incubation and nestling period unknown. 3 species.

5/ CRESTED TREE SWIFT
Hemiprocne longipennis

RANGE: India, Southeast Asia
HABITAT: open woods, clearings, gardens
SIZE: 6 in (15 cm)

True swifts spend nearly all their time in the air, but the Crested Tree Swift is well able to perch and often lands on treetops to rest and preen, sitting bolt upright with its crest raised. Refreshed, it swoops away in graceful arcs to gather

insects on the wing, or dive down to a forest pool to scoop up a billful of water. It is most active at dawn and dusk and can often be seen hunting in loose flocks. The Latin names for the genus and family mean "half-swallow": indeed, these birds have evolved several swallowlike characteristics, including their shape and plumage and the habit of hawking for insects from a perch.

Unlike true swifts, these birds breed as isolated pairs and vigorously defend their territories. The single egg fills the tiny nest like an acorn in its cup. The nest is a fragile basket made of bark and leaf fragments glued together with saliva and similarly cemented to the side of a branch. Both parents take turns to incubate the egg, their weight supported by the branch.

FAMILY TROCHILIDAE
Hummingbirds
Small, slender-billed nectar-eaters. Agile in the air, can hover and fly backward. Brilliant, often iridescent plumage; males often brighter, some with ornate tail feathers. Eggs 1–2, white. Cup nest, usually on horizontal twig. Incubation 14–23 days, nestling period 18–38 days. 334 species.

6/ LONG-TAILED HERMIT
Phaethornis superciliosus

RANGE: E Mexico to Bolivia and C Brazil
HABITAT: lowland forest understory and tall secondary growth
SIZE: 6 in (15 cm)

Hermits are so-called because they keep to the dark understory of tropical forests, especially along streams and edges where they forage along regular routes. The very long, downcurved bill of the Long-tailed Hermit equips it for extracting nectar from large flowers such as heliconias and passion flowers, but it also gleans insects and spiders from leaves and cobwebs.

The males form singing assemblies, or "leks," and compete with each other to attract mates. The best singers usually mate with all the available females. The nest is a deep cup of plant fibers and spiders' silk attached beneath the drooping tip of a large leaf or palm frond.

7/ REDDISH HERMIT
Phaethornis ruber

RANGE: Colombia and Venezuela to N Bolivia and S Brazil
HABITAT: humid forest undergrowth, forest edge, secondary woodland, scrub
SIZE: $3\frac{1}{2}$ in (9 cm)

Like other hermits, this small hummingbird prefers to fly along a circuit of food sources instead of establishing a feeding territory, picking insects from beneath large leaves between visits to nectar-bearing flowers. It has an insectlike, weaving flight that generates an audible humming – a common characteristic of hummingbirds and the origin of their name.

For courtship, the males sing competitively in a group, called a lek. Their shrill, repetitive calls attract females, which mate with the males of their choice, then leave to build cone-shaped nests on palm-frond tips close to the ground.

8/ WHITE-TIPPED SICKLEBILL
Eutoxeres aquila

RANGE: Costa Rica to W Ecuador and NE Peru
HABITAT: forest understory, forest edge, secondary growth
SIZE: 5 in (13 cm)

This highly specialized hummingbird has a strongly downcurved bill for probing the curved blooms of plants such as certain heliconias. It prefers to feed at hanging bunches of flowers, clinging to them with its powerful feet as it sips the nectar. In the process it becomes well dusted with pollen and unwittingly carries it to other heliconia flowers to bring about cross-pollination.

Many tropical plants rely on hummingbirds as pollinators. In this case, the precise fit of the bird's bill in the flower suggests that both have evolved together, providing the plant with a reliable pollinator and the White-tipped Sicklebill with an exclusive source of nectar.

9/ VIOLET SABREWING
Campylopterus hemileucurus

RANGE: S Mexico to W Panama
HABITAT: mountain forest, in understory and at edges, especially near streams
SIZE: 6 in (15 cm)

This large, elegant hummingbird is named for the glittering violet plumage of the male and the thickened and flattened shafts of the outer 2 primary feathers. The female is mainly gray and, unusually for a hummingbird, smaller.

Less aggressive than other hummingbirds of its size, the Violet Sabrewing rarely maintains feeding territories. It often takes nectar from banana flowers and is common in banana plantations. It can often be located while feeding by its explosive twittering.

During the 6-month breeding season, the males associate in leks to sing for mates, each perching on a sapling and calling with evenly spaced, piercing notes. The female builds the cup-shaped nest alone.

10/ RUBY-TOPAZ HUMMINGBIRD
Chrysolampis mosquitus

RANGE: Trinidad and Tobago, N and C South America
HABITAT: arid open country, gardens, lowlands up to 5,750 ft (1,750 m)
SIZE: $3\frac{1}{2}$ in (9 cm)

Common in the lowlands of Trinidad and Tobago during much of the year, the striking Ruby-topaz Hummingbird was collected by the thousands during the last century when many species of hummingbird were sold as ornaments for the parlor and for dressing ladies' hats. The females escaped this fate, having relatively drab greenish-gray plumage.

The glittering male courts his mate alone, putting on a spectacularly beautiful display in which he circles rapidly around her with widely fanned tail and raised crown feathers. He is very aggressive at this time and will even attack birds of prey. The nest is a tiny lichen-covered cup lined with plant down.

11/ FRILLED COQUETTE
Lophornis magnifica

RANGE: E and C Brazil
HABITAT: forest, scrub, parkland
SIZE: $2\frac{3}{4}$ in (7 cm)

All the hummingbirds of the genus *Lophornis* are adorned with crests, but the male Frilled Coquette is one of the most spectacular. His fanlike ruffs of white feathers tipped with iridescent green form a dramatic contrast with the rich chestnut crown feathers, and in flight he looks more like a butterfly than a bird, as he hovers to feed from a flower.

During courtship the male and female hover together, dancing up and down in the air. After mating, the female builds a simple cup-shaped nest in low vegetation, fastening it down by working the fibers of the bottom and one side around the supporting twig.

12/ FORK-TAILED WOODNYMPH
Thalurania furcata

RANGE: NW and C South America from W Ecuador to E Bolivia and Paraguay
HABITAT: humid forest and forest edge in lowlands and foothills
SIZE: male 4 in (10 cm); female 3 in (8 cm)

Although solitary by nature, the Fork-tailed Woodnymph is a bold, inquisitive bird that shows very little fear of man. It will often approach passers-by and hover in front of them in a blur of wings before returning to its feeding routine. There are some 23 races; the race *T. f. townsendi* (illustrated) occurs from eastern Guatemala to southwestern Honduras.

Unusually for a hummingbird, the female is considerably smaller than her mate. Being so small has its drawbacks: small hummingbirds need to absorb a great deal of energy to maintain their body heat and may have to eat up to half their body weight in food every day. At night hummingbirds often become torpid, regaining their normal temperature when the sun raises the air temperature the following day.

13/ STREAMERTAIL
Trochilus polytmus

RANGE: Jamaica
HABITAT: semiarid lowlands to high mountains, including man-made habitats
SIZE: $9\frac{3}{4}$ in (25 cm)

Many hummingbirds are threatened by the destruction of their native forests, but the Streamertail thrives in open country, and its numbers have actually increased as the Jamaican forests have been felled. Known locally as the Doctor Bird, it is a common sight throughout the island and a frequent visitor to suburban flower gardens.

The male is the most spectacular of all Jamaican hummingbirds. He has glittering green plumage with two 6 in (15 cm) long, black tail feathers. During the mating display he will fly before a perched female in short pendulums, chirping rhythmically, or perch near her and wave his fluttering streamers from side to side.

The race *T. p. polytmus*, from most of Jamaica, has a red bill tipped with black in the male; dull red-brown with a black tip in the female. The other race, *T. p. scitulus*, is restricted to the extreme eastern part of the island and has an entirely black bill.

14/ GLITTERING-THROATED EMERALD
Amazilia fimbriata

RANGE: N South America, E of Andes to S Bolivia and S Brazil
HABITAT: shrubby secondary growth, forest edge, up to 1,650 ft (500 m)
SIZE: 3 in (8 cm)

This tiny hummingbird feeds mainly on nectar, taking it from blossoms in low shrubbery or at midheight in the forest. It often perches on bare, exposed twigs, calling with a soft tapping note like 2 small pebbles being struck together. Like many other hummingbirds, it will defend its feeding territory vigorously against intruders.

It nearly always nests low down, often less than 3 ft (1 m) from the ground, attaching its nest to a fork in a bush or the tip of a low tree branch. In Surinam it seems to nest at any time of year, but elsewhere its breeding may be more seasonal.

The race illustrated is *A. f. fimbriata*, from French Guiana, southern Venezuela and eastern Brazil.

15/ CRIMSON TOPAZ
Topaza pella

RANGE: Guianas, SE Venezuela, NE Brazil, E Ecuador
HABITAT: rain forest
SIZE: male 8 in (20 cm); female 7 in (18 cm)

The Crimson Topaz is a relatively large hummingbird, but over a third of the male's length is accounted for by 2 long, slender, inward-curving tail feathers. They are the finishing touch to a plumage which is quite breathtaking in its beauty.

With their relatively short bills, these birds are less specialized than long-billed hummingbirds and will take nectar from a wide variety of flowers, as well as catching insects. Their calls have been described as a chicklike *peep peep*.

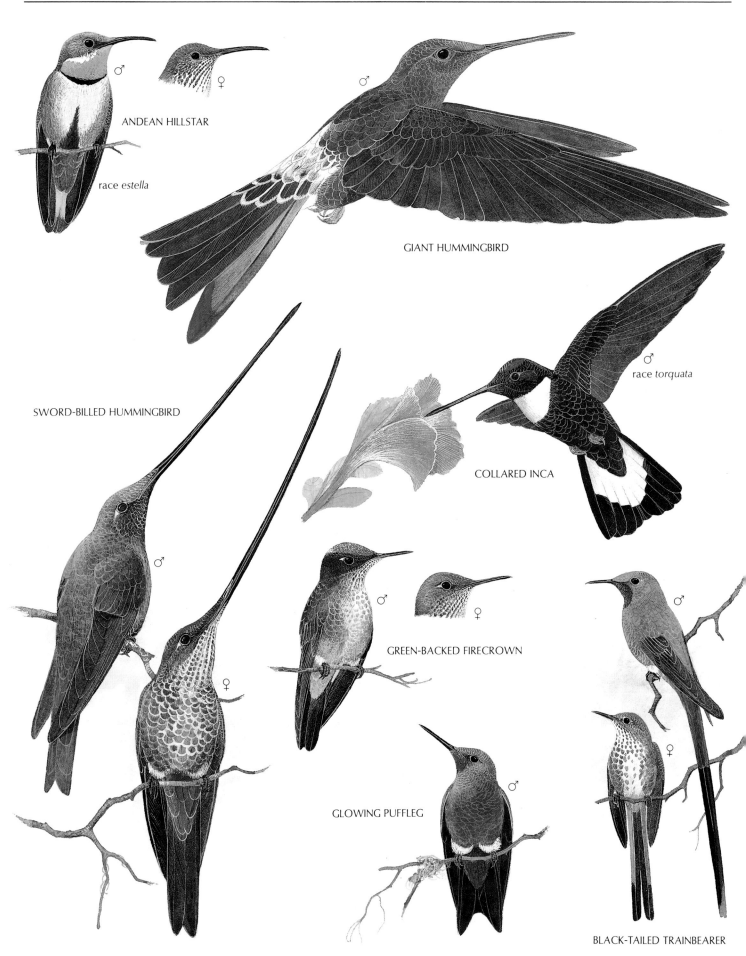

ANDEAN HILLSTAR

race *estella*

GIANT HUMMINGBIRD

SWORD-BILLED HUMMINGBIRD

race *torquata*

COLLARED INCA

GREEN-BACKED FIRECROWN

GLOWING PUFFLEG

BLACK-TAILED TRAINBEARER

RED-TAILED COMET

BEARDED HELMETCREST

race *guerinii*

LONG-TAILED SYLPH

MARVELOUS SPATULETAIL

RUBY-THROATED HUMMINGBIRD

♀ feeding chicks

BEE HUMMINGBIRD

at nest

AMETHYST WOODSTAR

CALLIOPE HUMMINGBIRD

HUMMINGBIRDS

1/ ANDEAN HILLSTAR
Oreotrochilus estella

RANGE: **Andes from Ecuador to Argentina, Chile and N Peru**
HABITAT: **rocky gorges, grassy low scrubby growth with grasses, high plateaus**
SIZE: **5 in (13 cm)**

The Andean Hillstar lives in the harsh climate and sparse vegetation above 13,000 ft (4,000 m). The race *O. e. estella* is from southern Peru to northern Chile and northwestern Argentina; the males of some other races, isolated on high mountains, such as *O. e. chimborazo* from Mount Chimborazo, Ecuador, have a different pattern of colors on the head. Like some other hummingbirds, the Andean Hillstar can become torpid to cope with periods of extreme stress in its tough environment.

This species uses its disproportionately large feet to perch rather than hover when it is feeding on nectar. Females feed in abundant gorges containing high concentrations of blooms close to nest sites, whereas males tend to feed in open areas where the flowers are more dispersed. Courtship thus brings the male into the female's territory, which is the reverse of the situation in most hummingbirds.

Nests are well protected from the weather as a result of their hammocklike structure and thick insulation of mosses, lichens and plant down. The 2 white eggs are incubated for 20 days. The young fledge in 22–38 days and often continue to use the nest as a roost.

2/ GIANT HUMMINGBIRD
Patagona gigas

RANGE: **Andes from Ecuador to Chile and Argentina**
HABITAT: **mountain scrub and river bank forest, cultivated land**
SIZE: **7½–7¾ in (19–20 cm)**

This is the largest of all hummingbirds. In flight, it resembles a large swift with a long bill. Its long, pointed wings occasionally perform a flap-sail flight pattern, and its wing beats are noticeably slower than those of other hummingbirds when hovering before flowers to glean food.

When incubating the 2 eggs, the adult birds seem to overflow the tiny nest, which is constructed of mosses and lichens on top of a large branch. Young birds are fed regurgitated nectar and insects.

3/ COLLARED INCA
Coeligena torquata

RANGE: **NW Venezuela to N Bolivia**
HABITAT: **wet, humid mountain forest, shrubby forest edge**
SIZE: **6 in (15 cm)**

One of the more common hummingbirds in its preferred habitat, the Collared Inca feeds low at forest shrubbery and forest edges. It hovers for long periods at pendant flowers on shrubs and vines, and also takes flying insects that have been stirred up by mixed flocks of forest birds. The race *C. t. torquata* from Colombia and eastern Ecuador is illustrated; other races have differently

colored plumage on their crowns, lower back and underparts.

These silent birds dart about actively, following their chosen circuits, or "trap-lines," of flowers rather than defending a feeding territory. The breeding season is variable; it is generally in spring and summer, although a nest has been found in November.

4/ SWORD-BILLED HUMMINGBIRD
Ensifera ensifera

RANGE: **Venezuela to N Bolivia**
HABITAT: **humid mountain forest, forest edge, shrubby hillside**
SIZE: **9¾ in (25 cm)**

Seldom seen at ground level, the Sword-billed Hummingbird habitually stays in the middle and upper levels of trees. Its uniquely long bill, which is nearly the length of its body, enables it to reach nectar deep inside the longest flower corollas. It particularly favors *Datura* and *Passiflora* flowers, which it finds along regular routes through the forest, and also hawks the occasional insect in midair.

When it is perched, the Sword-billed Hummingbird holds its bill upward, presumably because its neck and body would otherwise be unable to bear the strain. The call of this unusual species is a low, guttural *trrr*. Breeding begins in early spring. The mossy cup nest is built among the roots of epiphytic plants, such as bromeliads, growing on trees high above the ground.

5/ GREEN-BACKED FIRECROWN
Sephanoides sephanoides

RANGE: **breeds Chile and W Argentina; winters to E Argentina**
HABITAT: **scrub and gardens**
SIZE: **4¼ in (11 cm)**

This common hummingbird is known to feed on the nectar of *Escallonia serrata* and the waxy-white flowers of *Pernettya mucronata*. It also searches old yucca heads for insects and seizes tiny flying insects. The male Green-backed Firecrown has a twittering song and a high-pitched

tsee, often followed by a metallic rattling call.

The flight of this species is rather slow for a hummingbird, and at intervals the bird may fold its wings and drop down 12 in (30 cm) or so before beating its wings again.

6/ GLOWING PUFFLEG
Eriocnemis vestitus

RANGE: **NW Venezuela to E Ecuador and N Peru**
HABITAT: **high mountain forest edge, scrub**
SIZE: **3½ in (9 cm)**

In good light this bird's brilliant colors, particularly its upper tail coverts, really do glow, while its spectacular white leg muffs make it look as though each leg is wrapped in fresh cotton. All pufflegs have these leg muffs, which vary in color between the different species.

The Glowing Puffleg is both solitary and pugnacious, chasing potential competitors from the flowering shrubs at which it hovers or briefly clings to sip nectar.

7/ BLACK-TAILED TRAINBEARER
Lesbia victoriae

RANGE: **Colombia and Ecuador S to S Peru**
HABITAT: **grassy slopes and shrubby areas, upper subtropical and temperate zones of the Andes**
SIZE: **male up to 9¾ in (25 cm), female up to 5½ in (14 cm)**

This species favors the drier highlands and is replaced by the Green-tailed Trainbearer *L. nuna* at lower elevations. The Black-tailed Trainbearer sips nectar from the flowers of tall shrubs and trees at all levels. The male's song is a rattling trill that descends at the end; it changes to simple, high-pitched chip notes while he is foraging.

The deeply forked tail is much longer in the male than in the female, measuring up to over half his total length. During courtship displays he spreads his magnificent tail wide as he chases and dives near his potential mate, producing a sound like the ripping of a piece of cloth. The nest is a wide, open cup.

8/ RED-TAILED COMET
Sappho sparganura

RANGE: Andes of Bolivia, Chile and W Argentina
HABITAT: high Andean scrub, brush and plateau
SIZE: $7\frac{3}{4}$ in (20 cm)

All comet hummingbirds have long, iridescent red tails tipped with velvety black, although the different species vary in the shades of red.

The Red-tailed Comet is often seen feeding at flowering bushes with other hummingbirds. A red-flowered plant, *Psitacanthus cuneifolius*, parasitic on the creosote bush, is a particular favorite of this species. In between feeding bouts, the bird perches to conserve energy in sunny sheltered areas, but may give chase after giving *chit-it* calls if another male appears. In flight both sexes fan their forked tails, and at rest they nervously bob their tails up and down.

The nest is woven out of plant fibers and moss, often lined with hair, and is sited in a sheltered spot on a wall, tree or rock ledge.

9/ BEARDED HELMETCREST
Oxypogon guerinii

RANGE: NW Venezuela, N and C Colombia
HABITAT: bushy or grassy slopes above 10,000 ft (3,000 m)
SIZE: $4\frac{1}{4}$ in (11 cm)

The female Bearded Helmetcrest lacks the unique crest and white beard of the male, but both are well camouflaged to blend into their open environment. The race shown, *O.g. guerinii*, is found in eastern Colombia and has a white beard with a black central stripe and glittering green borders in the male.

Bearded Helmetcrests forage at low flowering shrubs by hovering or clinging briefly to sip nectar from the blossoms or capture visiting insects. Outside the main flowering season, the Bearded Helmetcrest is often found between scrub and open grasslands, sometimes walking across the matted grass or making short, hovering leaps in search of insects.

The deep, thick, cup nests, which are attached to rocky cliffs, steep banks or branches of the shrub *Espeletia*, have been spotted in July and September, and a young fledgling was once found in December.

10/ LONG-TAILED SYLPH
Aglaiocercus kingi

RANGE: Venezuela, Colombia, Ecuador, Peru and Bolivia
HABITAT: from 3,000–10,000 ft (900–3,000 m) in tropical and subtropical humid forest and scrub, gardens, plantations
SIZE: male 7 in (18 cm); female 4 in (10 cm)

The Long-tailed Sylph feeds at almost any level in forest edge and open areas. It forages by "traplining" – making a regular circuit of flowers within a territory – and sometimes joins other hummingbirds in the forest canopy. It also takes nectar or insects while hovering or briefly perching, and will dart out to capture tiny insects. It can reach speeds of 30–47 mph (50–75 km/h).

The domed moss and plant fiber nest with a side entrance is fastened to a leafy twig. Nesting occurs between February and October.

11/ MARVELOUS SPATULETAIL
Loddigesia mirabilis ?

RANGE: N Peru
HABITAT: subtropical forest and scrub
SIZE: male $11\frac{1}{2}$ in (29 cm); female 4 in (10 cm)

The Marvelous Spatuletail has only 4 fully developed tail feathers, compared with the 10 typical of other hummingbirds. Particularly marvelous are the 2 outermost tail feathers of the male, each of which has a long, bare shaft ending in a broad spatule, or racket, and curve inward to cross over one another.

During his courtship display the male frames his iridescent throat plumage with his decorative tail feathers, flying back and forth in front of his prospective mate.

Little is known about this very localized species, recorded only from the Chachapoyas region of Peru, east of the Rio Utcubamba between 7,500 and 8,500 ft (2,300 and 2,600 m).

12/ RUBY-THROATED HUMMINGBIRD
Archilochus colubris

RANGE: breeds E North America; winters coastal SE USA to NW Costa Rica
HABITAT: woodland and swamp
SIZE: $3\frac{1}{2}$ in (9 cm)

These tiny migratory birds generally reach wintering grounds in south Mexico and Central America after achieving the remarkable feat of crossing the Gulf of Mexico. Males leave their breeding territories immediately after the nesting season, and females follow soon after the young have fledged. The young migrate alone.

Male Ruby-throated Hummingbirds defend nectar resources as breeding territories with highly stylized pendulum displays; females defend the nest area. Outside the breeding season, both sexes defend nectar sources vigorously. Red tubular flowers are a favored food source; tiny flying insects and small spiders are also eaten.

Antisocial at all times, these birds do not form a pair-bond. The female builds the tiny nest of spiders' webs and plant down, often near water, where she incubates the 2 white eggs and rears the young alone.

13/ AMETHYST WOODSTAR
Calliphlox amethystina

RANGE: South America E of Andes to S Peru, N Bolivia, Paraguay, NE Argentina
HABITAT: tropical forest, scrub, savanna, grassland
SIZE: $2\frac{1}{4}$–3 in (6–8 cm)

The Amethyst Woodstar is one of the smallest of all hummingbirds, and females are smaller than males. It is found in almost any habitat within its range except rain forest, but populations can be quite local.

This is a solitary species, which makes its rounds of flowering shrubs and small trees in search of nectar and tiny insects. It forages well into the canopy and often perches high. Its hovering wings, beating at up to 80 times per second, make a distinctive insectlike buzz. The male arcs back and forth like a pendulum when displaying to the female. The nest is a tiny cup of plant fiber and down, which generally straddles a small branch.

14/ BEE HUMMINGBIRD
Calypte helenae ?

RANGE: Cuba and Isle of Pines
HABITAT: forest and forest edge, gardens; occasionally in fairly open country
SIZE: $2\frac{1}{4}$ in (6 cm)

The Bee Hummingbird is the smallest bird in the world, the male being slightly smaller than the female. Its body measures only $\frac{1}{2}$ in (1.25 cm), the bill and tail making up the total length. It weighs no more than $\frac{1}{15}$ oz (2 g) – even some large beetles weigh 20 times as much.

Uncommon and local in distribution, the Bee Hummingbird can be found in many areas from the coast to the mountain. It feeds from near ground level into the canopy of open forest on any plant which blooms and produces nectar.

When feeding from flowers, the Bee Hummingbird holds its body horizontal, unlike the common hummingbird of Cuba, the Cuban Emerald *Chlorostilbon ricordii* and many other hummingbirds, which feed vertically. Its tiny wings beat 50–80 times a second as it hovers.

It is sometimes hard to distinguish these tiny birds from insects, and their voices are also insectlike. When at rest, the Bee Hummingbird perches on small, exposed branches high off the ground. Its eggs, too, are minuscule, varying from $\frac{1}{4}$ in (6.35 mm) to less than $\frac{1}{2}$ in (11.4 mm) long.

15/ CALLIOPE HUMMINGBIRD
Stellula calliope

RANGE: breeds W North America; winters SW Mexico
HABITAT: mountain meadows, edges of coniferous forest
SIZE: 3 in (8 cm)

The Calliope Hummingbird is the smallest bird breeding in the North American continent north of Mexico. Juveniles resemble females, lacking the male's magenta-striped gorget and possessing cinnamon underparts.

Northward migration in early spring usually follows the Pacific coast, since snow on high mountains restricts the availability of nectar and insect foods. Southward migration in late summer follows mountain ridges, and late wildflowers are the main food source during this time.

Male birds form territories around favored food plants and repel interlopers with wide U-shaped aggressive displays, using the sun's brilliant reflection from the metallic purple feathers on their chins for added effect.

Female territories center on the tiny plant down and spiders' web nest, typically built in a tree near the edge of the forest. The 2 eggs hatch after 15 days' incubation, and the chicks fledge after 20 days' care, exclusively by the female. Once the young are able to feed themselves, she chases them away from her own food source.

race *striatus*

SPECKLED MOUSEBIRD

RESPLENDENT
QUETZAL

♀

♂

♀

LESSER PIED
KINGFISHER

♂

GREEN KINGFISHER

♂

SHOVEL-BILLED KINGFISHER

STORK-BILLED KINGFISHER

race *novaeguineae*

♂

LAUGHING KOOKABURRA

♂ ♀

COLLARED TROGON

BAR-TAILED
TROGON

♂

♂

ORANGE-BREASTED
TROGON

♀

BELTED KINGFISHER

♂

♀

race *ispida*

♂

AFRICAN PYGMY
KINGFISHER

race *hispidoides*
in nest–burrow

RIVER KINGFISHER

♂

nest in termite colony

SACRED KINGFISHER

race *doris*

COMMON PARADISE KINGFISHER

race *galatea*

BLUE-BREASTED KINGFISHER

MOUSEBIRDS, TROGONS, KINGFISHERS

FAMILY COLIIDAE
Mousebirds

Small, gregarious birds. Long, spikily pointed tails. Short, rounded wings. Outer toes very mobile. Soft plumage brown or gray, with loose crest. Some have bright red or blue face or neck markings. Sexes similar. Untidy cup nest in bushes. Eggs 1–8, whitish or speckled. Incubation 11–14 days, nestling period about 17 days. 6 species.

1/ SPECKLED MOUSEBIRD
Colius striatus

RANGE: C, E and S Africa
HABITAT: woodland, scrub, gardens, hedges
SIZE: $11\frac{3}{4}$–14 in (30–36 cm)

Mousebirds take their name from their striking, rodentlike appearance as they creep and scramble through vegetation. Members of family groups follow each other with alternate whirring and gliding flight, their extremely long tails, up to $8\frac{1}{2}$ in (22 cm) long, projecting stiffly behind them. They often perch in clusters and more than 20 birds may roost together in a tight bunch. There are some 17 races: *C. s. striatus* from southwestern South Africa is illustrated.

Speckled Mousebirds use their robust, arched, hooked bills to feed on all kinds of vegetable matter. Flocks of them can cause much damage in gardens and orchards.

FAMILY TROGONIDAE
Trogons

Medium forest birds. Bill wide, hooked, with stiff bristles around gape. Feet small and weak. Tail long, often square-ended and broad. Plumage soft, dense and colorful; males with upperparts often brilliant metallic green, breast and belly bright red, pink, orange or yellow. Sexes fairly similar, but females duller. Unlined nest in cavity. Eggs 2–4, buffish or whitish. Incubation (known only for few American species) 17–19 days, nestling periods about 17–18 days. 39 species.

2/ RESPLENDENT QUETZAL
Pharomachrus mocinno [V]

RANGE: S Mexico to W Panama
HABITAT: humid cloud forest, usually at 4,000–10,000 ft (1,200–3,000 m)
SIZE: $13\frac{3}{4}$–15 in (35–38 cm)

The male Resplendent Quetzal's middle wing coverts are very long and the upper tail coverts form a train of filmy streamers, up to 3 ft (1 m) long. These undulate and flutter during normal flight, as well as in aerial courtship displays. Where areas of undisturbed cloud forest still exist, Resplendent Quetzals can still be fairly common, but their numbers have decreased due to the destruction of forest. The birds have also suffered from persistent trapping for the cage-bird trade, despite legal protection.

Resplendent Quetzals are mainly fruit-eaters, although they will also take some invertebrates, and even small vertebrates, when feeding their young. They generally keep to the canopy, where their green upperparts provide surprisingly effective camouflage in the leafy shade.

3/ COLLARED TROGON
Trogon collaris

RANGE: tropical Mexico S to W Ecuador, N Bolivia and E Brazil; Trinidad
HABITAT: humid and wet forest and forest edges; also riverine forest in Amazonia
SIZE: $9\frac{3}{4}$ in (25 cm)

The most widespread of the New World trogons, this species is typical of the family both in color and pattern. Collared Trogons are usually solitary or travel in pairs. They often sit motionless for extended periods, but will sally out from perches to snatch insects or pluck hanging fruit.

Collared Trogons nest in unlined cavities, usually enlarging existing holes in rotting wood or breaking into arboreal termite nests. Both sexes share the incubation and care of the young.

4/ BAR-TAILED TROGON
Apaloderma vittatum

RANGE: mountains of C Africa, from Nigeria to Mozambique
HABITAT: forest
SIZE: 11 in (28 cm)

Usually found alone or in pairs, the Bar-tailed Trogon is a somewhat sluggish African bird. It often sits for long periods on a favorite perch in the midlevels of the forest and is inconspicuous there until it swoops out after a flying insect. Although silent for much of the time, the Bar-tailed Trogon has a characteristic sharp *wup* note that it repeats with increasing volume about 12 times. It is a sedentary, territorial species, but the size of individual territories varies considerably.

5/ ORANGE-BREASTED TROGON
Harpactes oreskios

RANGE: Burma to Vietnam, Java, Borneo
HABITAT: evergreen forest, bamboo; also sparse woodland
SIZE: $11\frac{3}{4}$ in (30 cm)

The plumage of the male Orange-breasted Trogon is not as resplendent as that of many other species but it is, perhaps, more subtly beautiful. This species sometimes takes insects from the ground; it also flutters to snatch prey from twigs and can catch winged insects in flight. Across its range, this species is less confined to wet evergreen forest than most other Southeast Asian trogons.

FAMILY ALCEDINIDAE
Kingfishers

Small to medium, long-billed, large-headed. Plumage variable, bright. Sexes alike or differ. Nest in holes they excavate in earth banks, rotting trees or termite mounds, or in existing holes in trees. Eggs usually 2–3 in tropics, up to 10 at higher latitudes, white. Incubation 17–27 days, nestling period 22–37 days. 92 species.

6/ BELTED KINGFISHER
Megaceryle alcyon

RANGE: breeds through most of North America; winters in ice-free areas S to West Indies and N Colombia
HABITAT: streams, rivers, ponds, marshes
SIZE: $11\frac{3}{4}$ in (30 cm)

This solitary kingfisher prefers clear waters with overhanging trees, wires or other perches. It usually hovers and dives for fish, but will also prey on insects, crayfish, frogs, snakes and even the occasional mouse. A loud, dry, rattling call often announces the presence of this bird.

The breeding distribution of the Belted Kingfisher seems to be limited only by the availability of foraging sites and earth banks in which it can excavate its nest chamber. This lies at the end of an upward-sloping tunnel 3–16 ft (1–5 m) long.

7/ LESSER PIED KINGFISHER
Ceryle rudis

RANGE: Africa, Middle East, S Asia
HABITAT: lakes, broad rivers, estuaries
SIZE: $9\frac{3}{4}$ in (25 cm)

By hovering rather than perching as it watches for fish, the Lesser Pied Kingfisher can hunt over broad stretches of water. It is the only kingfisher species that regularly fishes far offshore.

Studies of breeding colonies in Uganda show that the Lesser Pied Kingfisher leads a complex social life. As in many tropical birds, the breeding pair receive help with the nesting chores from up to 4 full-grown, nonbreeding adults. Sometimes these are the offspring from the previous year, but often the helpers are quite unrelated. The system allows a colony to raise the greatest number of young under the prevailing conditions.

8/ GREEN KINGFISHER
Chloroceryle americana

RANGE: **extreme S USA S to W Peru, C Argentina, and Uruguay; Trinidad, Tobago**
HABITAT: **streams bordered by shrubby habitat or forest, some mountain streams**
SIZE: **7½ in (19 cm)**

Generally solitary, the Green Kingfisher would easily go unnoticed as it watches for prey were it not for its characteristic habit of frequently raising its head and bobbing its tail. More than one Green Kingfisher may be seen in a suitable site, but they jealously guard their favorite hunting perches and are rarely seen together. Clarity of the water is important for hunting success. This species dives mainly for small fish, 1–2 in (3–5 cm) in length. Its flight is straight and low over the water, the white on the wings and sides of the tail flashing conspicuously as it passes.

This species utters a low, but distinctive *choot* or *chew* call and a descending series of *tew-tew-tew* notes. Its alarm call is a soft, ticking rattle.

9/ RIVER KINGFISHER
Alcedo atthis

RANGE: **breeds Europe, NW Africa, Asia, Indonesia to Solomon Islands; winters in S of range**
HABITAT: **clear, slow-moving streams and small rivers, canals, ditches, reeds, marshes; coasts in winter**
SIZE: **6¼ in (16 cm)**

This bird and the Belted Kingfisher are the most northerly breeding species of kingfisher. Along with the European race *A. a. ispida*, the illustration shows *A. a. hispidoides*, which ranges from northern Sulawesi to the Bismarck Archipelago off Papua New Guinea.

The River Kingfisher is aggressively territorial, defending a ½–3 ml (1–5 km) stretch of stream in winter, even from its mate. In spring it will drive away both rivals and small songbirds. It excavates its burrow in the bank of a stream, river or gravel pit, usually above water; most nest-burrows are 18–36 in (45–90 cm) long. It rarely feeds away from water and is an expert fisher.

10/ AFRICAN PYGMY KINGFISHER
Ceyx picta

RANGE: **tropical Africa**
HABITAT: **grassy glades near forest edge, streams, lakeshores, dry woodland**
SIZE: **4¾ in (12 cm)**

This bird is one of the world's smallest kingfishers. Although it takes some of its prey from water, it feeds mainly on dry land, where it catches

insects, millipedes, spiders and, occasionally, even small frogs. At higher latitudes, from Senegal to Eritrea and from Zambia to Natal, this species is a breeding visitor, arriving for the summer rainy season. It migrates at night, and many birds are killed when, attracted by the light, they collide with windows and buildings.

11/ LAUGHING KOOKABURRA
Dacelo novaeguineae

RANGE: **E and SE Australia; introduced to Tasmania and SW Australia**
HABITAT: **open forest, urban trees**
SIZE: **15¾–17¾ in (40–45 cm)**

This giant kingfisher has a loud, rollocking, territorial call that sounds like maniacal human laughter. It also utters softer chuckles. There are just 2 races: *D. n. novaeguineae*, is the widespread and well-known bird of the eastern half of Australia, while the other, smaller race *D. n. minor* is confined to the Cape York Peninsula.

Laughing Kookaburras feed by pouncing on a variety of terrestrial invertebrates, reptiles, small mammals, birds and nestlings. They can even devour snakes up to 3 ft (1 m) in length. Although they are not closely associated with water, they will sometimes catch fish with plunging dives and, on occasion, raid suburban goldfish ponds. They live in family groups that defend the same territories year round.

12/ SHOVEL-BILLED KINGFISHER
Clytoceyx rex

RANGE: **mainland New Guinea**
HABITAT: **forest**
SIZE: **12½ in (32 cm)**

The forests of New Guinea have the greatest diversity of kingfishers in the world. This large, brown bird is one of the more unusual species, with a massive, stubby bill that is often caked in mud. The tail, which is brown in females and blue in males, is often cocked when the bird is perched.

The Shovel-billed Kingfisher is often seen on the ground, foraging on exposed mud banks. It digs for insects, snails, earthworms and small vertebrates and forages in mangroves for crabs.

13/ STORK-BILLED KINGFISHER
Halcyon capensis

RANGE: **Southeast Asia, E Pakistan, India, Nepal, Sri Lanka**
HABITAT: **rivers and streams in wooded lowlands, paddy fields; sometimes at wooded lakes or on the coast, especially among mangroves**
SIZE: **13–14 in (33–36 cm)**

This is one of 3 species of stork-bill in Southeast Asia. They are among the biggest of the world's many kingfisher species, exceeded in size only by the kookaburras, the Shovel-billed Kingfisher and 3 giant *Megaceryle* species.

All species of stork-bill are vocal, but shy, birds. They are rather sluggish in habit, hunting from a branch overhanging water and plunging down vertically for fish, frogs, crustaceans, insects and small land vertebrates such as lizards and nestling birds.

14/ BLUE-BREASTED KINGFISHER
Halcyon malimbica

RANGE: **tropical W Africa**
HABITAT: **rain forest, gallery forest, mangroves**
SIZE: **9¾ in (25 cm)**

This large kingfisher is the forest-dwelling counterpart of the better-known Woodland Kingfisher *H. senegalensis* of Africa's savanna woodlands. The latter has a loud, trilling "laughing" song lasting about 3 seconds. The Blue-breasted Kingfisher has a similar song, but it is greatly slowed down, with 7–10 long, plaintive whistles. It is usually unseen as it sings, perched in the dark undergrowth.

The breeding site of this species is an unlined cavity that the birds excavate in the nest of a termite colony. This is usually located in a tree some 33 ft (10 m) above the forest floor.

15/ SACRED KINGFISHER
Halcyon sancta

RANGE: **Australia, Tasmania, Indonesia, New Guinea, Solomon Islands, some SW Pacific islands, New Zealand**
HABITAT: **open forest and woodland**
SIZE: **7½–9 in (19–23 cm)**

This kingfisher is a land-dweller that often occurs far from water. Although its population is widely distributed, most of its 6 or so races are very similar in plumage. However, the color of the bird's breast can vary considerably from season to season. The female is similar to the male, but with a duller, greener crown, back, wings and tail and usually with paler underparts.

Sacred Kingfishers feed on a variety of ground-dwelling insects and small reptiles, catching their prey by pouncing from perches. Those living near water also catch small fish and crustaceans. This is a migrant bird in southern Australia, arriving to breed in spring and wintering on the Indonesian islands to the north. The nest is a hole excavated in a rotting tree or termite nest. The birds open up an initial cavity by flying at the nest site and striking it with their bills.

16/ COMMON PARADISE KINGFISHER
Tanysiptera galatea

RANGE: **New Guinea, offshore islands, Moluccas**
HABITAT: **lowland rain forest, swamp forest, gallery forest, patches of scrub, plantations**
SIZE: **13–17 in (33–43 cm)**

The Common Paradise Kingfisher perches inconspicuously, low in the forest understory, slowly pumping its tail, which is two-thirds the length of its body. It feeds on insects, worms and lizards, which it catches with a pounce to the ground or a sallying flight to nearby foliage. Adults are highly sedentary, maintaining small territories that they strongly defend. The 3–5 white eggs are laid in a tunnel, excavated by both sexes in a termite nest. The races illustrated are *T. g. galatea* of northwest New Guinea, the western Papuan islands and Morotai, and *T. g. doris* of the northern Moluccas.

201

TODIES, MOTMOTS, BEE-EATERS, ROLLERS AND GROUND-ROLLERS, CUCKOO-ROLLER, HOOPOE, WOOD-HOOPOES, HORNBILLS

juv

CUBAN TODY

juv

EUROPEAN BEE-EATER

race *nubicus*
"Northern Carmine
Bee-eater"

BLUE-CROWNED MOTMOT

AUSTRALIAN BEE-EATER

juv

CARMINE BEE-EATER

juv

EASTERN BROAD-
BILLED ROLLER

juv

EUROPEAN ROLLER

♂

race *epops*

SCALY GROUND-ROLLER

CUCKOO-ROLLER

HOOPOE

FAMILIES TODIDAE, MOMOTIDAE, MEROPIDAE, CORACIIDAE, LEPTOSOMATIDAE, UPUPIDAE, PHOENICULIDAE, BUCEROTIDAE

♀

♂

GREEN WOOD-HOOPOE

EASTERN YELLOW-
BILLED HORNBILL

race *bicornis*

GREAT INDIAN HORNBILL

race *coronatus*

MALABAR PIED HORNBILL

♀

♂

SOUTHERN GROUND HORNBILL

203

TODIES, MOTMOTS, BEE-EATERS, ROLLERS AND GROUND-ROLLERS, CUCKOO-ROLLER, HOOPOE, WOOD-HOOPOES, HORNBILLS

FAMILY TODIDAE
Todies

Small, large-headed, long-billed. Plumage mainly bright green above, throat red, underparts white or with pastel tints. Sexes alike. Nest in excavated earthen burrows. Eggs 2–5, white. Incubation 21–22 days, nestling period 19–20 days. 5 species.

1/ CUBAN TODY
Todus multicolor

RANGE: **Cuba and Isle of Pines**
HABITAT: **bushy ravines, thickets on mountain slopes, grazed open woodland**
SIZE: **$4\frac{1}{4}$ in (11 cm)**

This tody feeds mainly on flying insects, darting out from a favorite perch to capture them with an audible snap of its bill. Occasionally, it will prey on small lizards. Sedentary, and occurring either alone or in pairs, this species defends its territory against other todies. The call of the Cuban Tody is a rapid, staccato rattle. A whirring sound made by the wings is most often heard during the breeding season. As a group, todies are renowned for their voracious appetites and for the rapid rate at which they feed their young.

FAMILY MOMOTIDAE
Motmots

Small to medium, heavy-billed. Long, usually racket-tipped tail. Plumage usually brown or rufous, with blues and greens, boldly marked face and crown. Sexes similar. Nest in crevices or burrows. Eggs 3–4, white. Incubation 15–22 days, nestling period 24–38 days. 9 species.

2/ BLUE-CROWNED MOTMOT
Momotus momota

RANGE: **E Mexico to NW Peru, NW Argentina and SE Brazil; Trinidad, Tobago**
HABITAT: **rain forest, deciduous forest, coffee and cocoa plantations, semiopen habitats**
SIZE: **16 in (41 cm)**

Alone or in pairs, this motmot perches with an upright stance, swinging its racket-tipped tail from side to side like a pendulum. The racket shape results from the preening of segments of the inherently weak vane from the long central tail feathers. This species' diet includes insects and spiders, as well as some fruit. Prey items are characteristically held in the serrated bill and thrashed against a branch before they are swallowed. The call of the Blue-crowned Motmot is a fairly loud double note of low frequency, sometimes uttered in a long sequence *hudu … hudu, du, du, du*.

FAMILY MEROPIDAE
Bee-eaters

Small, large-headed, graceful birds. Long, slightly downcurved bills. Central tail feathers usually long. Plumage mainly green with rufous, buff, yellow, red, carmine, blue or black. Sexes similar. Nest in burrows. Eggs 2–4 in tropics, up to 10 in Eurasia, white. Incubation 18–22 days, nestling period 22–31 days. 23 species.

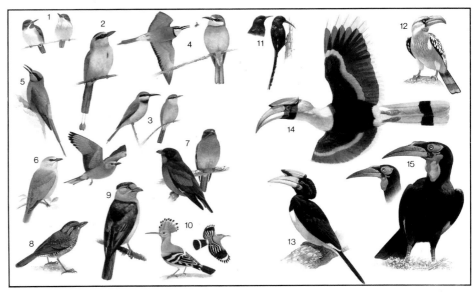

3/ AUSTRALIAN BEE-EATER
Merops ornatus

RANGE: **Australia, New Guinea, Lesser Sundas**
HABITAT: **light woodland, scrub, grassland, sandy pasture, arable land**
SIZE: **$8\frac{1}{4}$–11 in (21–28 cm)**

Also known as the Rainbow Bird, this is the only bee-eater that occurs in Australia. Its winter range extends across the islands to the north, and some birds migrate up to 2,500 mls (4,000 km).

Australian Bee-eaters feed on a variety of large insects, catching their prey in flight. They are gregarious birds throughout the year, and groups of 30–40 may breed cooperatively.

4/ EUROPEAN BEE-EATER
Merops apiaster

RANGE: **breeds NW Africa, Europe, SW Asia, S Africa; winters W and SE Africa**
HABITAT: **warm, wooded and cultivated lowland**
SIZE: **$9\frac{3}{4}$–$10\frac{1}{2}$ in (25–27 cm)**

Banding has shown that some individuals migrate 10,000 mls (16,000 km) between their summer and winter quarters. In Europe, their principal food is bumblebees, but the birds feed largely on honeybees and dragonflies in Africa. Thousands of European Bee-eaters are killed each year by beekeepers. Migrants crossing the Red Sea also run the gauntlet of attacks by Sooty Falcons, but on the whole the species is not endangered.

5/ CARMINE BEE-EATER
Merops nubicus

RANGE: **breeds N and S tropics of Africa; winters nearer the Equator**
HABITAT: **open bushy savanna, river plains, open pastures, tilled fields with trees or hedges, marshes, mangroves**
SIZE: **14–$15\frac{1}{4}$ in (36–39 cm)**

Carmine Bee-eaters are gregarious birds, nesting in colonies of 100–1,000 pairs, and, in some cases, 10,000 pairs. Their tail streamers measure up to 5 in (12 cm). Northern birds such as *M. n. nubicus* have blue-green throats, while their southern counterparts *M. n. nubicoides* have vivid pink throats. These 2 populations breed 1,250 mls (2,000 km) apart, at opposite times of the year, and are sometimes regarded as separate species.

Carmine Bee-eaters hunt on the wing, flying far to find swarms of locusts, bees, ants and cicadas. They are strongly attracted to bush fires, where they can readily catch fleeing grasshoppers. They also hunt by riding on the backs of ostriches, bustards, storks, cranes, antelopes, camels, goats and cattle, snatching prey that the animals disturb from the grass.

FAMILY CORACIIDAE
Rollers and ground-rollers

Medium, stout birds. Short-necked, large-headed. Plumage mainly blue and rufous, with lilac, olive and brilliant azure. Sexes similar. Nest in holes. Eggs 2–6, white. Incubation 17–19 days, nestling period 25–30 days. 12 species.

6/ EUROPEAN ROLLER
Coracias garrulus

RANGE: **breeds Mediterranean, E Europe to W Siberia; winters tropical Africa**
HABITAT: **open forest, especially with clearings and patches of heathland; also parks, well-wooded farmland**
SIZE: **$11\frac{3}{4}$–$12\frac{1}{2}$ in (30–32 cm)**

During this century, European Rollers have dwindled in number in northwestern parts of their range because of changes in land management. But in eastern Europe and Asia they remain common as breeding birds, and in parts of Africa they winter in abundance.

European Rollers feed principally on insects, although they have also been known to eat snails and frogs. They normally hunt from a low perch, swooping down to seize their prey on the ground or, sometimes, catching insects in midair. Rollers take their name from their aerobatic, rolling display flights, and this species is no exception, rocking from side to side as it dives steeply down and even performing aerial somersaults.

7/ EASTERN BROAD-BILLED ROLLER
Eurystomus orientalis
RANGE: N and E Australia, New Guinea, Southeast Asia, India, China
HABITAT: woodland
SIZE: 11½ in (29 cm)

This species is often known as the Dollarbird in the Far East and Australia, owing to the large, coinlike, whitish mark on each wing, which is conspicuous when the bird takes flight.

Eastern Broad-billed Rollers sally out from treetop perches to catch large beetles and other flying insects, often with aerobatic maneuvers. If they cannot swallow their victims in flight, they will take them back to the perch and batter their bodies against the wood to soften them. Usually seen alone or in pairs, these birds have a harsh, chattering call.

8/ SCALY GROUND-ROLLER
Brachypteracias squamigera   R
RANGE: NE and C Madagascar
HABITAT: deep rain forest with scant undergrowth
SIZE: 11¾ in (30 cm)

This species dwells in the shade of the forest floor, where it feeds mainly on insects and small lizards. It is a rather heavy, slow bird that moves only a few steps between lengthy pauses or uses its short, rounded wings to make whirring flights to low perches. This bird is perhaps less rare than was once thought, for its silent and secretive habits make it extremely difficult to locate. However, its habitat continues to disappear, and the loss is threatening the population of this and many other forest animals.

FAMILY LEPTOSOMATIDAE
Cuckoo-Roller
There is only one species in this family.

9/ CUCKOO-ROLLER
Leptosomus discolor
RANGE: Madagascar and Comoro Islands
HABITAT: forest and scrub
SIZE: 16½ in (42 cm)

Pairs of these birds are relatively common in savanna with scattered tall trees from sea level up to 6,500 ft (2,000 m). But the birds cannot survive in newly cleared areas which are gradually eroding their natural range. They are usually seen in the high canopy, flying slowly from tree to tree or feeding from the highest branches. They take locusts, stick insects, beetles and larvae, along with larger prey such as chameleons. The male Cuckoo-Roller has an undulating display flight. Distinctive calls may be given from a conspicuous perch, and pairs keep in close contact with soft, bubbling calls. Nesting takes place in a tree hole, where the 2 cream-buff eggs are laid in an unlined chamber.

FAMILY UPUPIDAE
Hoopoe
There is only one species in this family.

10/ HOOPOE
Upupa epops
RANGE: Europe, Asia, Africa, Madagascar; N birds winter in the tropics
HABITAT: woodland, savanna, parks, lawns, orchards, farmland
SIZE: 11 in (28 cm)

The Hoopoe's striking plumage, its mobile crest, its far-carrying *hoo-poo-poo* call, and its association with human settlement make it a familiar bird. Daytime migrants are so conspicuous that, despite pungent, defensive secretions, they are a favorite prey of Eleonora's and Sooty Falcons. The nest is a thinly lined cavity in a tree or wall or in the ground. The eggs vary in color from gray to pale yellow or olive and become heavily stained in the nest. The clutch size varies from 2–9, and incubation takes 15–16 days. The nestling period lasts about 4 weeks.

FAMILY PHOENICULIDAE
Wood-hoopoes
Long-tailed, short-legged. Long, downcurved bill. Plumage black, glossy blue or green; white spots in the wings and tail. Sexes similar. Nest in tree holes. Eggs 2–5, pale blue. Incubation 16–18 days, nestling period 27–30 days. 8 species.

11/ GREEN WOOD-HOOPOE
Phoeniculus purpureus
RANGE: sub-Saharan Africa
HABITAT: woodland, thorn bushes
SIZE: 15–16 in (38–41 cm)

This is the most widespread and best known of Africa's 8 species of wood-hoopoe. It feeds by gleaning caterpillars, insect eggs and grubs, spiders and other food items from tree trunks, branches and foliage.

Green Wood-Hoopoes are noisy, gregarious birds that indulge in remarkable social territorial displays. Several times each hour, they will cackle loudly, rock back and forth in an exaggerated manner, preen and pass pieces of bark from one to another. Each breeding pair is helped at the tree-hole nest by up to 10 birds.

FAMILY BUCEROTIDAE
Hornbills
Medium to large. Long bill, often with large casque. Long tail, broad wings. Plumage black, white, brown or gray. Bill, facial skin, eyes and feet often brightly colored. Sexes alike or differ. Nest in holes in trees or rocks, entrance usually sealed. Eggs 1–7, white. Incubation 25–40 days, nestling period 45–86 days. 48 species.

12/ EASTERN YELLOW-BILLED HORNBILL
Tockus flavirostris
RANGE: NE Africa
HABITAT: dry woodland savanna
SIZE: 19½–23½ in (50–60 cm)

This hornbill has a rare mutual association with the dwarf mongoose, in which each helps the other locate food and watch for predators. It displays in pairs, holding its wings fanned and head bowed, and uttering hoarse clucking calls.

The eggs are laid in a natural tree hole, the entrance to which is then reduced to a narrow, vertical slit by the female, using mud and droppings. Safely enclosed within the hole, she incubates the eggs and receives insects and fruit through the slit from the male. Feeding continues in this way until the chicks are half-grown. The female then breaks free, and the chicks reseal the nest until they have fledged.

13/ MALABAR PIED HORNBILL
Anthracoceros coronatus
RANGE: India
HABITAT: monsoon forest
SIZE: 29½–31½ in (75–80 cm)

This occurs in small flocks that move about together to feed on fruit and small creatures gleaned from foliage. The race *A. c. coronatus* is found in southern India and Sri Lanka.

Flocks of Malabar Pied Hornbills congregate at regular roost sites within which mated pairs remain close together throughout the year. In summer, they move off to nest alone. The eggs are incubated by the female in a natural tree hole. The male carries fruit to his incarcerated mate, storing them in his crop and regurgitating them one at a time through the narrow slit in the nest wall.

14/ GREAT INDIAN HORNBILL
Buceros bicornis
RANGE: India E to Thailand, S to Sumatra
HABITAT: tropical rain forest
SIZE: 39¼–47¼ in (100–120 cm)

This large hornbill lives high in the forest canopy, feeding mainly on fruit, such as figs, and some small animals. In flight, its "whooshing" wing beats can be heard over half a mile (1 km) away. Its loud, honking calls are also obvious. The race *B. b. bicornis* occurs in western India and from the Himalayas to Indochina and Malaysia.

Great Indian Hornbills nest in tree cavities, both sexes helping to seal the entrance. After the nesting cycle of 4–5 months, the families may form into small flocks that range widely in search of food. Much of the rain forest habitat in western India and mainland Asia has been felled, making this spectacular bird a vulnerable species.

15/ SOUTHERN GROUND HORNBILL
Bucorvus cafer
RANGE: Africa S of the Equator
HABITAT: open savanna and grassland
SIZE: 35½–51 in (90–130 cm)

This, the largest of the hornbills, differs from most other species in being carnivorous and largely terrestrial and in not sealing the entrance to its nest. Groups of up to 11 birds occupy territories of about 40 square miles (100 square kilometers) and proclaim their presence at dawn with booming calls. They catch small animals while patrolling their territories on foot.

Only the dominant pair breeds, but the other group members help in territorial defense, in lining the nest with dry leaves, and in feeding the breeding female and single chick.

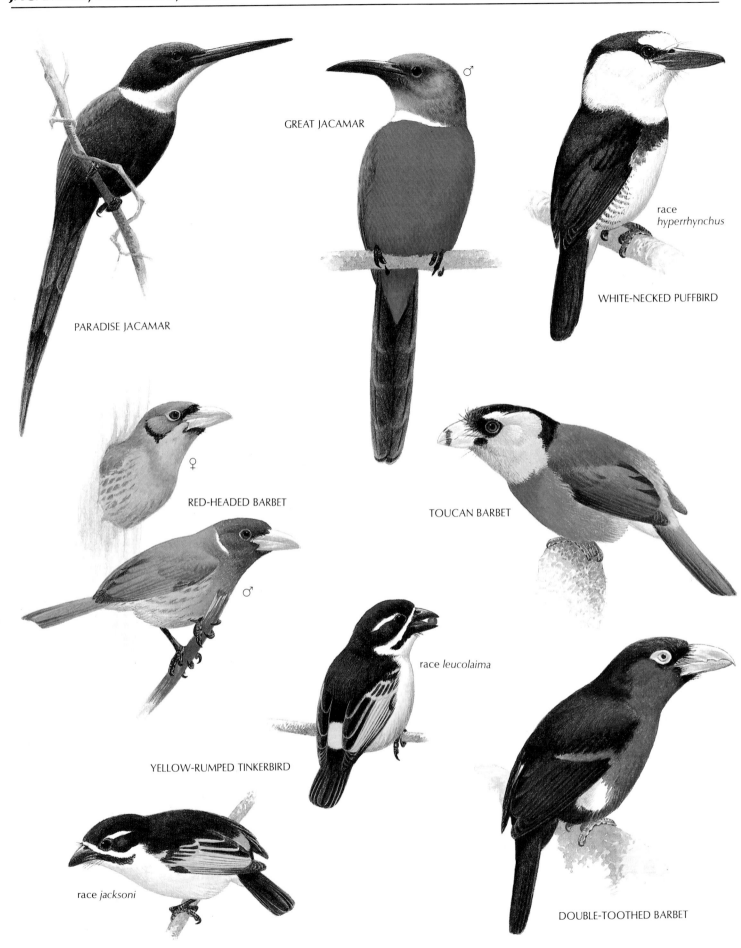

GREAT JACAMAR

race
hyperrhynchus

PARADISE JACAMAR

WHITE-NECKED PUFFBIRD

♀

RED-HEADED BARBET

TOUCAN BARBET

♂

race *leucolaima*

YELLOW-RUMPED TINKERBIRD

race *jacksoni*

DOUBLE-TOOTHED BARBET

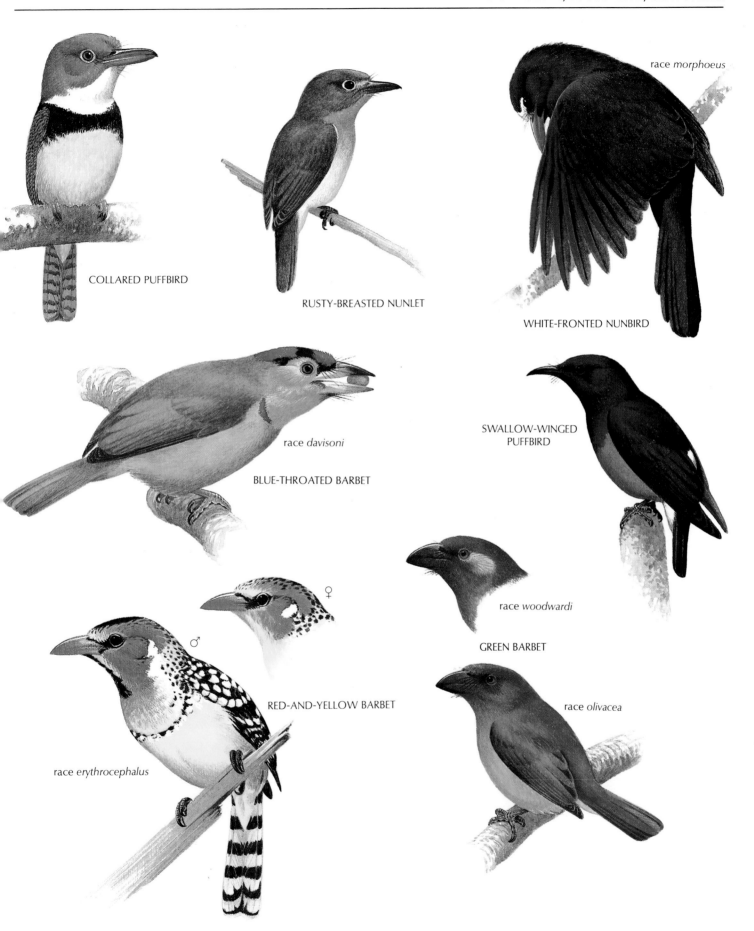

COLLARED PUFFBIRD

RUSTY-BREASTED NUNLET

race *morphoeus*

WHITE-FRONTED NUNBIRD

race *davisoni*

BLUE-THROATED BARBET

SWALLOW-WINGED
PUFFBIRD

race *woodwardi*

GREEN BARBET

♂

♀

RED-AND-YELLOW BARBET

race *erythrocephalus*

race *olivacea*

JACAMARS, PUFFBIRDS, BARBETS

FAMILY GALBULIDAE
Jacamars

Small to medium, with long, pointed bills. Plumage iridescent golden-green and purple above and mainly chestnut and white below, or dark chestnut, brown or blackish, often with white on the underparts. Sexes differ slightly. Nest in burrows. Eggs 2–4, white. Incubation 20–23 days, nestling period 19–26 days (Rufous-tailed Jacamar *Galbula ruficauda*). 17 species.

1/ PARADISE JACAMAR
Galbula dea

RANGE: S Venezuela and Guianas S to N Bolivia
HABITAT: humid tropical forest and forest edge, savanna, margins of watercourses
SIZE: 11¾ in (30 cm)

This striking jacamar has central tail feathers up to 7 in (18 cm) in length, making the tail longer than the bird's body. Its sleek, black, iridescent plumage flashes copper, bronze and blue as the bird darts about in the sunlight after insects. The sexes have similar plumage. This species excavates nest cavities in termite mounds in trees. The song is a series of peeping notes.

Paradise Jacamars are usually seen alone, in pairs or in small groups. It perches quietly, its head moving from side to side as it scans the surroundings before sallying out in pursuit of its insect prey. Typically, a bird begins its attack with a dive from its perch, followed by a twisting pursuit, with sudden changes in direction. When successful, the bird returns with an undulating flight and bangs the prey, held in its bill, against the perch before eating it. It often accompanies mixed-species flocks.

2/ GREAT JACAMAR
Jacamerops aurea

RANGE: Costa Rica S through N South America to N Bolivia
HABITAT: humid tropical forest, secondary growth woodland, edges of water
SIZE: 11¾ in (30 cm)

This is the largest of the jacamar species. The heavy bill is nearly 2 in (5 cm) long. Immatures are similar to adults, but less iridescent.

Great Jacamars are usually solitary or found in pairs. Compared with smaller jacamars, they may appear sluggish in habit as they perch quietly on exposed limbs, usually just under the canopy or lower down. They catch most of their prey, including butterflies, beetles and dragonflies, with a sallying flight, but they will also dart forward to glean insects, spiders, lizards and other small vertebrates from vegetation. Their vocalizations include loud whistles and a variety of soft call notes. Pairs nest in termite mounds in trees, up to 50 ft (15 m) from the ground.

FAMILY BUCCONIDAE
Puffbirds

Small to medium. Large-headed, stout. Plumage black, brown, reddish-brown and white. Sexes differ slightly. Nest in burrows. Eggs 2–3 (occasionally 4), white. Incubation unknown. Nestling period 20–30 days. 32 species.

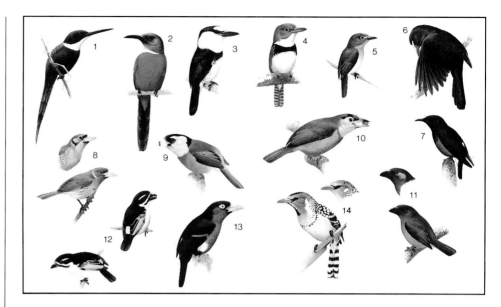

3/ WHITE-NECKED PUFFBIRD
Notharchus macrorhynchos

RANGE: S Mexico to N South America, N Bolivia, SE Brazil, Paraguay, N Argentina
HABITAT: humid tropical forest, open secondary growth, savanna
SIZE: 9¾ in (25 cm)

Both sexes share the contrasting black and white plumage, but immature birds have buff-gray on the forehead and underparts. The bill is heavy and hooked and this, together with the puffed-up feathers of the head, gives the bird a large-headed appearance. The race illustrated, *N. m. hyperrhynchus*, occurs in Mexico.

White-necked Puffbirds often sit quietly on their perches for extended periods. They feed by sallying out and hawking large insects in flight, or by taking them from foliage. Occasionally, these birds will drop down from the canopy and forage around army ant swarms. They also take lizards and small vertebrates. This species is usually quiet, but occasional calls include a series of weak twitters or purring notes. Both sexes help to excavate the nesting cavity in arboreal termite mounds.

4/ COLLARED PUFFBIRD
Bucco capensis

RANGE: N South America S to N Peru
HABITAT: humid tropical forest
SIZE: 7¾ in (20 cm)

This little-known puffbird has the large-headed appearance typical of its family. Its bill is stout and well adapted for dealing with large insects. Its song is a series of *ca-will* notes, rather like that of the nightjar called the Common Poorwill *Phalaenoptilus nuttallii*. There are few details of its nesting habits, but presumably it nests in the same way as other puffbirds.

Collared Puffbirds sit quietly on their perches from the middle layers of the forest up to the subcanopy, where they are easy to overlook. They are largely insectivorous, catching flying prey on the wing or gleaning insects from foliage, but they probably eat some small vertebrates as well. They are usually found alone or in pairs, but they sometimes accompany mixed-species flocks.

5/ RUSTY-BREASTED NUNLET
Nonnula rubecula

RANGE: S Venezuela, N Peru, N Brazil S to Paraguay and N Argentina
HABITAT: humid tropical forest; especially seasonally flooded forest
SIZE: 6 in (15 cm)

This small, inconspicuous member of the puffbird family is sleeker in appearance than most puffbirds. Like most of them, it typically sits quietly on a perch and sallies out to capture flying insect prey, or gleans insects and other items from vines or other vegetation. It may also take small lizards. Its perches are often in the midlevel to understory layers, where it sits upright and often allows people to approach closely.

Rusty-breasted Nunlets are generally quiet, unlike their noisy relatives, the nunbirds. Very little is known of their breeding biology, but they probably nest in burrows they dig in the ground or in termite nests, like other puffbirds.

6/ WHITE-FRONTED NUNBIRD
Monasa morphoeus

RANGE: Central America, W Venezuela S to N Bolivia, Amazonian Brazil
HABITAT: humid tropical forest, river edges, swamps, secondary growth forest
SIZE: 11¾ in (30 cm)

These birds change perches frequently, much more than most other members of the puffbird family. They fly directly, with rapid wing beats followed by short glides. They sit quietly on each perch and sally out to catch flying insects or glean prey from foliage on the ground. Sometimes groups of up to 6 birds will join mixed-species flocks. The race illustrated is *M. m. morphoeus* from southern and eastern Brazil.

White-fronted Nunbirds are more vocal than other puffbirds, uttering a wide variety of rolling, churring and whistling notes. Groups of 10 or more may sing in chorus. A few nesting records suggest that this species excavates a downward-sloping burrow, about 3 ft (1 m) long, in the ground. The eggs are laid in a chamber at the end. Up to 6 adults may help with the nesting duties.

7/ SWALLOW-WINGED PUFFBIRD
Chelidoptera tenebrosa

RANGE: **N South America E of the Andes S to N Bolivia and S Brazil**
HABITAT: **forest edge, savanna, scrub**
SIZE: **6 in (15 cm)**

This puffbird is common along waterways from sea level up to at least 3,300 ft (1,000 m). It occurs alone, in pairs or in small groups of 3–6. While other puffbirds forage within the forest, this species forages above it. It sallies from its perch in fast pursuit of flying insects, returning at a more leisurely pace with its prey.

The voice of the Swallow-winged Puffbird consists of weakly whistled *pi-pu* and *pit-wit-wit* calls. This species nests in sandy banks along streams and road cuttings, excavating a 3–6 ft (1–2 m) burrow that angles downward. It lays 2 eggs on bare dirt or pieces of grass. These hatch into naked, slaty black chicks which begin coming to the burrow entrance when their growing feathers are still surrounded by sheaths, but they quickly retreat when disturbed.

FAMILY CAPITONIDAE
Barbets

Small to medium, plump, large-headed arboreal birds. Stout, often notched bills. Facial bristles. Plumage colorful, with green, blue, red, yellow and black. Sexes usually similar. Nest in tree holes. Eggs 2–4, white. Incubation 12–19 days, nestling period 20–35 days. 81 species.

8/ RED-HEADED BARBET
Eubucco bourcierii

RANGE: **Costa Rica, Panama, Colombia, Ecuador, W Venezuela, N Peru**
HABITAT: **humid mountain forest**
SIZE: **6 in (15 cm)**

The Red-headed Barbet usually lives at altitudes of 4,000–8,000 ft (1,200–2,400 m), but on the western slopes of the Andes in Colombia it may be found at 1,300 ft (400 m). Often just one or a pair of these birds will accompany a mixed flock of forest species. As well as feeding on fruit and, occasionally, some small vertebrates, they spend much of their time foraging around clusters of dead leaves in search of invertebrates. Despite their small size, they are rather sluggish and heavy in their movements, often pausing to tug at a berry or probe into bark and foliage. They are often heard tearing into dried leaves well before they are seen.

Although usually silent, they are known to give low, cicadalike rattling calls and squirrel-like sputters and chatters. The males have been heard singing with a prolonged, toadlike trill.

9/ TOUCAN BARBET
Semnornis ramphastinus   [V]

RANGE: **W Colombia, W Ecuador**
HABITAT: **humid mountain forest and forest edge at, 3,300–8,000 ft (1,000–2,400 m)**
SIZE: **7¾ in (20 cm)**

This is the largest and most heavily built of the American barbets. It usually forages singly or in pairs, although it will also follow mixed-species flocks. It hops actively along branches, often cocking its tail and turning to and fro in sudden about-face movements. At other times, it sits quietly for lengthy spells. It eats mainly fruit and invertebrates, but it will occasionally take small vertebrates such as lizards.

The song of the Toucan Barbet is a rhythmic series of loud, resonant, almost honking notes that may continue for several minutes. A pair will duet, either in synchrony or out of time. If disturbed, this bird will snap its bill loudly. The Toucan Barbet is popular as a cage bird: this, and the loss of its forest habitat, has caused a marked decline in its numbers.

10/ BLUE-THROATED BARBET
Megalaima asiatica

RANGE: **N India, Southeast Asia**
HABITAT: **light mixed forest, gardens**
SIZE: **9 in (23 cm)**

The Blue-throated Barbet is common from the Himalayan foothills down to low level plains. It prefers groves of fig trees around villages and wooded slopes, where it searches for fruit. It also eats large insects, which it strikes against a branch before swallowing. The race illustrated is *M. a. davisoni*, which ranges from southern Burma to southern China and northern Indochina.

It is a noisy species, which often calls together with other barbets, making a confusion of sounds. Pairs may call in such rapid succession that their duets sound as if they are coming from a single bird. The nest-hole is excavated in a tree branch, and the cavity may be used for several years, although a fresh entrance is often cut each season.

11/ GREEN BARBET
Cryptolybia olivacea

RANGE: **E Kenya, Tanzania, Malawi, S Africa**
HABITAT: **mountain forest to coastal woods**
SIZE: **7¾ in (20 cm)**

The Green Barbet has a very scattered distribution, being found in just a few isolated areas. It often occurs in groups or in mixed-species flocks, foraging for fruit, including figs, as well as termites and beetles, and is active, restless and sociable. Roosting holes excavated in trees may accommodate 4–5 birds, and other adults may help breeding pairs excavate nest-holes.

Its song is a series of up to 29 notes, with both male and female singing together, either at the same tempo or with one at twice the speed of the other. Up to 5 races of this bird are recognized; these include *C. o. olivacea*, which is found in eastern Kenya and Tanzania, and *C. o. woodwardi* of northern Natal province.

12/ YELLOW-RUMPED TINKERBIRD
Pogoniulus bilineatus

RANGE: **sub-Saharan Africa**
HABITAT: **evergreen forest thickets**
SIZE: **4 in (10 cm)**

This widespread species, which is also known as the Golden-rumped Tinkerbird, has 10 races across tropical Africa. These include *P. b. jacksoni* of east Africa and *P. b. leucolaima*, which ranges from Senegal to southern Sudan and south to northern Angola. It prefers dense forest and riverside trees, where it eats a wide variety of berries and seeds. It usually pauses to feed between fluttery flights through tangled vines and dense foliage, but will cross open spaces to isolated trees with plentiful fruit.

The Yellow-rumped Tinkerbird's song consists of groups of 3–5 notes given in a series lasting several minutes. The tiny bird fluffs its throat, droops its wings and flicks its tail at each note, constantly looking from side to side as it sings. A solitary, aggressive species, it uses its songs and attacks on intruders to maintain a well-defined territory around its nest-hole.

13/ DOUBLE-TOOTHED BARBET
Lybius bidentatus

RANGE: **W Africa E to Ethiopia and Kenya; S as far as N Angola**
HABITAT: **clearings, forest edge, parkland**
SIZE: **9 in (23 cm)**

Despite its bright coloration, this bird is less conspicuous than might be expected, preferring to keep to the shade of trees and bushes. A frequent, short, sharp note may be the best clue to its whereabouts. It feeds by darting out to catch flying termites or by clambering about to reach figs, fruit and nuts. The Double-toothed Barbet is named for the 2 prominent sharp projections on the upper mandible of its bill.

When several Double-toothed Barbets gather together, they flick and droop their tails and call a variety of low, grating sounds. Their song is a prolonged, buzzing trill. The nesting territories of this species are large, and the pair may fly long distances to reach fruiting trees.

14/ RED-AND-YELLOW BARBET
Trachyphonus erythrocephalus

RANGE: **E Ethiopia, Kenya, N Tanzania**
HABITAT: **woods, bushy areas, grassland with scattered trees**
SIZE: **9 in (23 cm)**

This is a ground-loving barbet, often found under bushes or foraging around termite mounds and banks of bare earth. It even clears dead insects from the fronts of parked cars. It is tame and bold, readily entering houses in search of food. There are 3 races: the one shown is *T. e. erythrocephalus*, from southern Kenya and northern Tanzania, which has more red on the head than the others.

The Red-and-yellow Barbet is aggressive to any smaller birds, and fights between rivals are frequent. Nevertheless, it is a gregarious species and up to 10 may feed together or gather to mob a snake or some other predator. They will also roost together in a group of holes dug in a bank. Nesting territories are defended, but up to 4 adult and 5 younger birds may attend each nest as communal helpers. The dominant pair often duet, producing a babbling medley, which sounds rather like *red 'n' yellow, red 'n' yellow*, from the top of a bush.

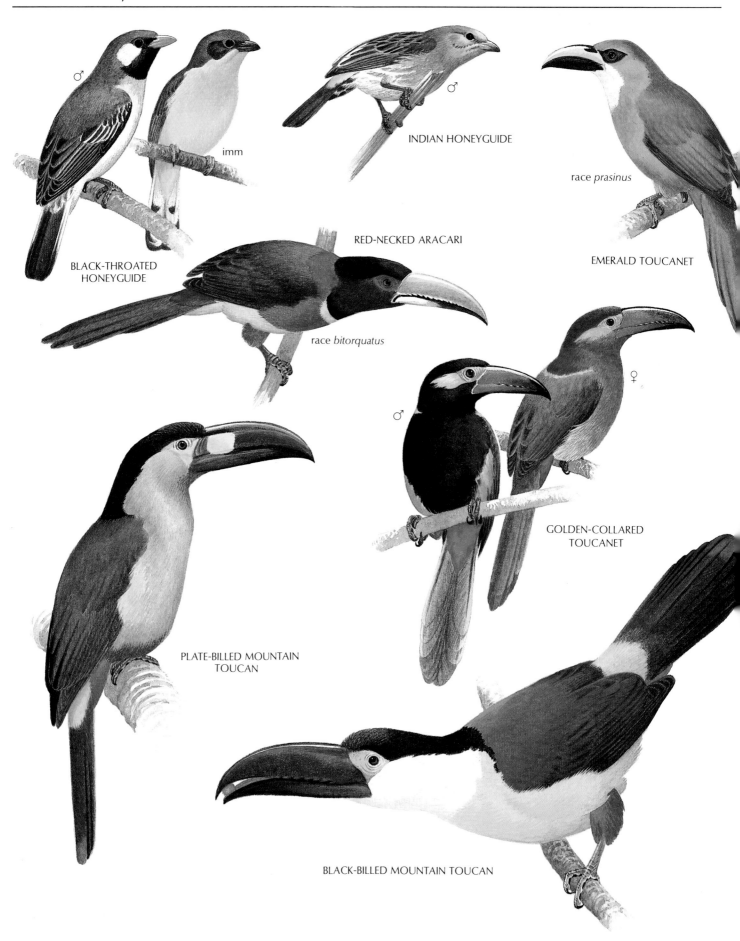

BLACK-THROATED
HONEYGUIDE

imm

INDIAN HONEYGUIDE

race *prasinus*

EMERALD TOUCANET

RED-NECKED ARACARI

race *bitorquatus*

GOLDEN-COLLARED
TOUCANET

PLATE-BILLED MOUNTAIN
TOUCAN

BLACK-BILLED MOUNTAIN TOUCAN

GROOVE-BILLED TOUCANET

GREEN ARACARI

♂

♀

GUIANAN TOUCANET

♀

KEEL-BILLED TOUCAN

TOCO TOUCAN

FAMILY INDICATORIDAE
Honeyguides
Small, gray-green birds with white tail markings. Sexes generally similar. Wax is a unique feature of their diet and 2 species guide mammal "helpers" to bee hives. Like cuckoos, most species rely on other species to raise their broods. Eggs 2–8, whitish, thick-shelled. Incubation 12–14 days, nestling period up to 30 days. 17 species.

1/ BLACK-THROATED HONEYGUIDE
Indicator indicator

RANGE: **Senegal to Ethiopia, and S to South Africa**
HABITAT: **woodland, open country with scattered trees, rarely dense forest**
SIZE: **8 in (20 cm)**

Honeyguides are often very difficult to see, for they tend to be solitary, inconspicuous birds that perch quietly in the forest, occasionally fluttering up to catch a fly on the wing or foraging in mixed-species flocks, and the Black-throated, or Greater, Honeyguide is no exception. The female of this species is browner and paler than the male.

When it locates a nest of bees, however, the Black-throated Honeyguide becomes very demonstrative, flicking its tail and chattering noisily to attract the attention of a human or a Honey Badger, or Ratel, and guide it to the hive. It falls silent while its "helper" breaks open the nest to get at the honey, then feeds on the bee grubs and wax, which it probably digests with the aid of bacteria in its gut. Other mammals that are possibly used as helpers are baboons, genets and mongooses. The Scaly-throated Honeyguide *I. variegatus* may also occasionally use helpers.

The male Black-throated Honeyguide advertises his readiness to mate by calling repeatedly from a favorite perch; he may use the same one for several years running. The eggs are laid among those of hole-nesting birds such as barbets, bee-eaters and woodpeckers, one to each nest. The naked, blind hatchling attacks the host's young with the hook on its bill, killing them so as to monopolize the food supply.

2/ INDIAN HONEYGUIDE
Indicator xanthonotus

RANGE: **Himalayas, from Pakistan to N Burma**
HABITAT: **forests, especially near cliffs and rock faces**
SIZE: **6 in (15 cm)**

This olive-brown, sparrow-sized bird is also known as the Yellow-rumped Honeyguide – a reference to the only bright feature of its plumage. This can make the bird quite conspicuous when it is perching with wings drooped, but usually it is hard to locate and observe, being a quiet denizen of thick woodland. As a result, many details of its behavior remain a mystery. The female is slightly smaller and duller than the male.

A study carried out in Nepal revealed that the males defend territories which are centered on the nests of giant honeybees. Wax is an important component of the species' diet, but it is not known whether the Indian Honeyguide guides mammals to hives. The nesting habits of this species are

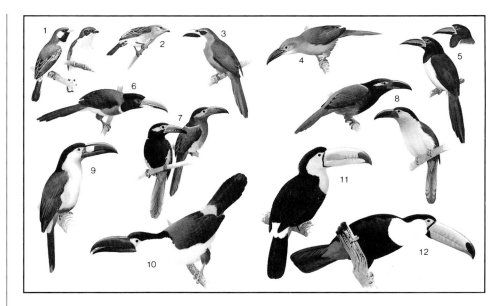

also uncertain, although it is possible that, like the African honeyguides, it parasitizes other birds. The males are polygamous, each mating with up to 18 females.

FAMILY RAMPHASTIDAE
Toucans
Medium, with very large, lightweight, brightly colored bills, strengthened by thin, bony, internal struts. Plumage black with red, yellow and white, olive and blue, or mainly green. Males and females generally alike but male's bill longer. Diet chiefly fruit and insects. Restricted to tropical American forests. Nest in tree holes usually with no lining except wood chips and a bed of regurgitated seeds. Eggs 2–4, white. Incubation 15–16 days, nestling period 43–51 days. 35 species.

3/ EMERALD TOUCANET
Aulacorhynchus prasinus

RANGE: **C Mexico through SE Peru to NW Venezuela**
HABITAT: **highland forest, highland and lowland forest edge, clearings**
SIZE: **11¾–13 in (30–33 cm)**

The brilliant green plumage of the Emerald Toucanet can make these birds very hard to see when they are sitting quietly among the foliage, but they are a glorious sight when they are feeding in the open. They usually forage in pairs or small flocks of 5–10 birds, seeking a wide range of food, including fruit, insects and the occasional lizard, as well as eggs and nestlings.

They are active, excitable birds, often cocking their tails and stretching their necks. They are also noisy, calling to each other with a variety of loud croaks, barks and rattles. The penetrating "song" of the Emerald Toucanet is said to resemble the sound of a crosscut saw.

The race *A. p. prasinus* is just one of many races and occurs in southeast Mexico; other races have the base of the lower mandible colored dark red instead of black.

4/ GROOVE-BILLED TOUCANET
Aulacorhynchus sulcatus

RANGE: **N Colombia, N Venezuela**
HABITAT: **humid forest, forest edge, secondary woodland**
SIZE: **14 in (36 cm)**

Similar to the Emerald Toucanet in both appearance and habits, the Groove-billed Toucanet is usually found at lower elevations, although it rarely descends into the warm lowlands. The 2 species occur together throughout the range of the Groove-billed Toucanet, especially at elevations of 5,000–6,500 ft (1,600–2,000 m).

Pairs or small flocks of these birds forage together in noisy, energetic fashion, feeding on fruit, insects or nestling birds anywhere from the high forest canopy to the smaller trees of the understory. Like the Emerald Toucanet, the Groove-billed Toucanet lays its eggs in a tree cavity, often in a hole that has been excavated by a woodpecker.

5/ GREEN ARACARI
Pteroglossus viridis

RANGE: **Colombia, N Bolivia, Venezuela, Guianas, Brazil**
HABITAT: **lowland rain forest**
SIZE: **11¾ in (30 cm)**

The aracaris are generally smaller and more lightly built than toucans and typically have red rumps and green wings and backs. There are 9 species found in Central America and Amazonia, but it is unusual to find more than 2 species in any one area. In some, the female differs slightly from the male: in the Green Aracari, the female's head and throat are chestnut, whereas the male's head and throat are black.

The Green Aracari is a lowland species, and rarely occurs higher than 2,000 ft (600 m), but it often ventures out of the forest interior to feed among the scattered trees and scrub of the forest edge. The birds forage through the canopy in small groups, actively seeking fruiting trees. They straggle through the foliage in single file, often leaping from branch to branch instead of flying, calling to one another with loud rattling cries. The birds lay their eggs in a tree cavity excavated by a woodpecker. These cavities are also used for roosting, and several birds may squeeze into the same hole each night.

6/ RED-NECKED ARACARI
Pteroglossus bitorquatus

RANGE: **lower Amazonia S of Amazon in Brazil**
HABITAT: **rain forest, forest edge, scrub**
SIZE: **15 in (38 cm)**

Also known as the Double-collared Aracari, this species is distinguished by its bright yellow breast band. It is very similar to the Ivory-billed Aracari *P. flavirostris*, however, this species does not have a breast band. The Amazon River separates the ranges of these 2 species, with the Ivory-billed Aracari to the north and the Red-necked Aracari to the south; the 2 have probably evolved from the same ancestor. There are 3 races, distinguished by the color of head, throat and bill: the one illustrated is *P. b. bitorquatus* from northeast Brazil.

Like other toucans, the Red-necked Aracari is an opportunist feeder. Loose bands consisting of 2–5 birds move through the forest in search of fruiting trees, picking up a variety of small animals, eggs and nestlings on the way. At night they roost in tree holes.

7/ GOLDEN-COLLARED TOUCANET
Selenidera reinwardtii

RANGE: **NW South America E of the Andes**
HABITAT: **lowland rain forest, forest edge**
SIZE: **13 in (33 cm)**

The toucanets of the genus *Aulacorhynchus* are upland birds but the 6 species in the genus *Selenidera* are restricted to lowland forests.

The Golden-collared Toucanet is generally uncommon throughout its range; it usually feeds in the rain forest interior. It rarely travels in flocks, preferring to forage alone or in pairs, high in the trees. Unusually for toucans, the sexes differ markedly in appearance.

Its normal call is a low, guttural, froglike croak, although one race is said to utter barking growls. Like other toucans, the Golden-collared Toucanet feeds mainly on berries and other fruits, generally swallowing them whole and disgorging the seeds and stones elsewhere at a later stage. In this way, toucans help to disperse the seeds of fruit-bearing plants throughout the forest.

8/ GUIANAN TOUCANET
Selenidera culik

RANGE: **NE Amazonia, Guianas and N Brazil S to lower reaches of Amazon**
HABITAT: **lowland rain forest, forest edge**
SIZE: **13¾ in (35 cm)**

The Guianan Toucanet has a longer bill than the other lowland toucanets and a shorter tail and wings. In other respects, however, it is typical of the genus *Selenidera*, with distinct sexual differences and conspicuous yellow tufts behind each eye, which may play an important role in the birds' courtship display.

Its behavior is also typical, since it is usually seen alone, in pairs or in small groups, searching for berries and small insects among the foliage at any level of the forest. The elusive nature of the Guianan Toucanet and its preference for remote habitats make it difficult to study and little is known about the nesting behavior of this or any other *Selenidera* species.

9/ PLATE-BILLED MOUNTAIN TOUCAN
Andigena laminirostris

RANGE: **NW South America, from SW Colombia through W Ecuador**
HABITAT: **humid and wet mountain forest and forest edge**
SIZE: **20 in (51 cm)**

This is one of 4 species of mountain toucan found in the forests of the Andes. It is unique in having an additional yellow plate on each side of its upper mandible. The function of this light, horny structure, if any, is not known.

The Plate-billed Mountain Toucan lives in humid mountain forests, from the subtropical zone at 1,000 ft (300 m) to the mid-altitude temperate zone at about 10,500 ft (3,200 m), but is generally uncommon throughout its range. It usually occurs in small groups, which join with other species in large feeding flocks that work their way through the forest. It has the typical broad diet of the toucans, taking insects and other small animals as well as fruit.

10/ BLACK-BILLED MOUNTAIN TOUCAN
Andigena nigrirostris

RANGE: **N South America, Colombia to NE Ecuador**
HABITAT: **mountain forest, cloud forest, forest edge, open areas with scattered trees**
SIZE: **20 in (51 cm)**

This is the most northerly of the mountain toucans and is considered to be comparatively common. However, this may be because it is a rather conspicuous bird, easily seen and recorded as it moves about the forest in search of fruit and animal prey. It is most often seen in wet mountain forest between 6,500 ft (2,000 m) and 10,000 ft (3,000 m). Above this altitude it becomes much less common and is replaced by the very similar Gray-breasted Mountain Toucan *A. hypoglauca*.

It normally associates in pairs or small groups, communicating with other birds with nasal yelping calls and hollow rattlings of its great black bill. Mountain toucans nest in tree cavities, like other toucans, but their nesting behavior has not been closely studied.

11/ KEEL-BILLED TOUCAN
Ramphastos sulfuratus

RANGE: **tropical Mexico to N Colombia and NW Venezuela**
HABITAT: **tropical lowland forest, forest edge, open areas with scattered trees, plantations**
SIZE: **17¾–22 in (45–56 cm)**

The 8 species of the genus *Ramphastos* are the largest and best known of the toucans. The Keel-billed Toucan is one of the most colorful of the group, with its bright yellow breast and multi-hued bill. Young birds are much duller than adults, and their bills continue to grow for some weeks after they fledge.

Normally seen in pairs or small flocks of 6–12 birds, Keel-billed Toucans feed on a wide variety of plant material, including catkins, berries and other fruits. A feeding bird will reach out and pluck a fruit with the tip of its long bill, then toss its head back to swallow its prize with a gulp. It also dines on insects and spiders, as well as occasional snakes, lizards, eggs and nestlings.

The Keel-billed Toucan has a distinctive, strongly undulating flight pattern, with intensive bursts of flapping alternating with short glides. Its voice is a series of mechanical clicks, like that of a tree frog, and it may also produce a harsh, dry rattle, like castanets.

12/ TOCO TOUCAN
Ramphastos toco

RANGE: **E South America, Guianas through Brazil to N Argentina**
HABITAT: **open woodland, river forest, forest edge, plantations, palm groves; avoids continuous lowland forest**
SIZE: **24 in (61 cm)**

The most familiar of all the toucans, the Toco Toucan is also the largest, with a massive bill which may be up to 7½ in (19 cm) long. Like that of other toucans, the bill is composed of lightweight horny material, braced internally by a system of struts, so it is not as heavy as it looks.

Toco Toucans are unusual in that they avoid dense rain forest, preferring more open habitats. They are often seen around human dwellings and are relatively common throughout their range. They generally forage in loose flocks, flying from site to site with the undulating flap-glide flight pattern characteristic of their genus, and communicating with toadlike croaks.

Like all toucans, the Toco Toucan nests in a tree cavity, favoring holes that are barely wide enough to permit entry and often using the same hole for several years in succession. The nest is lined with chips of wood and often covered with an accumulation of regurgitated seeds.

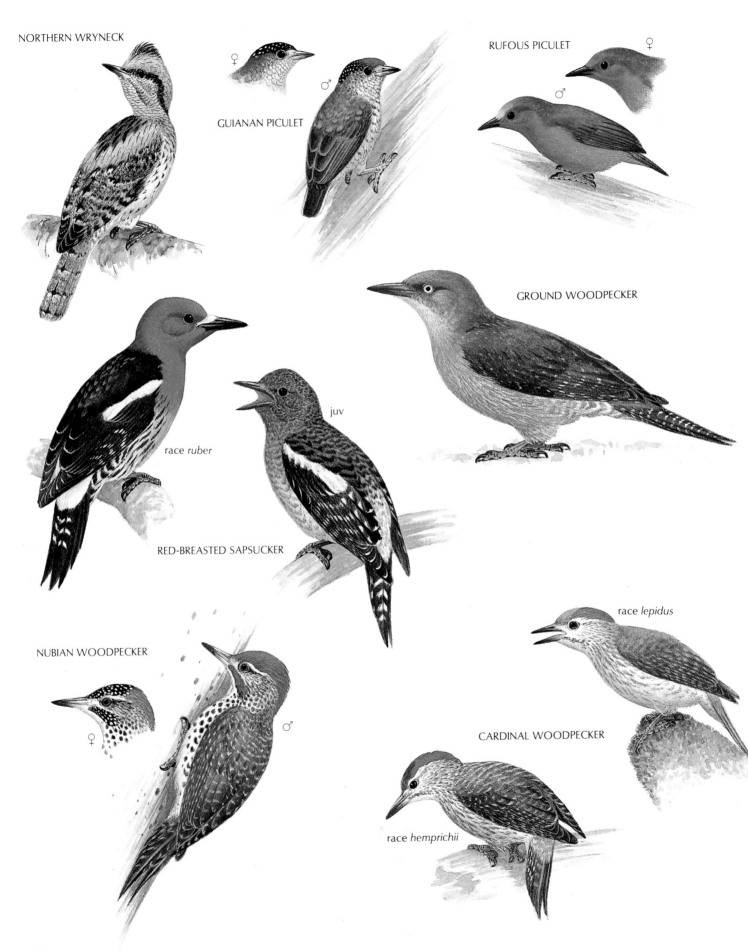

NORTHERN WRYNECK

GUIANAN PICULET

♀

♂

RUFOUS PICULET

♀

♂

GROUND WOODPECKER

race *ruber*

juv

RED-BREASTED SAPSUCKER

race *lepidus*

NUBIAN WOODPECKER

♀

♂

CARDINAL WOODPECKER

race *hemprichii*

♂ WHITE WOODPECKER

ACORN WOODPECKER

acorns wedged
in tree holes

♂

race *flavigula* ♂

♀

race *formicivorus*

juv

RED-HEADED WOODPECKER

♂ race *numidus*

race *pinetorum* ♀

GREAT SPOTTED WOODPECKER

juv

♂

race *septentrionalis* ♂

race *sanctorum* ♂

HAIRY WOODPECKER

FAMILY PICIDAE
Woodpeckers

Small to large, with stout, straight, pointed to chisel-tipped bills and strong, slender necks, and stiff tails used for support when climbing (except in wrynecks, subfamily Jynginae, and piculets, subfamily Picumninae). Most species (not wrynecks) habitually communicate by drumming with bills on trees. Most solitary, great majority tree-dwellers. Wrynecks blotched and peppered pattern of browns, sexes alike. Piculets brownish with red, orange or yellow marks and 3 white stripes on tail, females with white spots on black crown. Typical woodpeckers (subfamily Picinae) often black and white, some red, brown or green; usually with red or yellow on head, sexes differ in almost all species (females often lack colors on head). Nest an unlined, excavated cavity typically in tree, sometimes in termite nest, rarely in ground. Eggs 2–14, white. Incubation 11–21 days, nestling period 18–35 days. 199 species.

1/ NORTHERN WRYNECK
Jynx torquilla

RANGE: **breeds Eurasia to N Africa; winters C Africa and S Asia**
HABITAT: **open forest, parkland**
SIZE: **$6\frac{1}{4}$–$6\frac{1}{2}$ in (16–17 cm)**

When disturbed at its nest, the Northern Wryneck twists and writhes its neck into strange positions – hence its common name. These contortions resemble the movements of a snake and, when combined with snakelike hissing sounds, serve as an effective deterrent to small predators.

Northern Wrynecks feed predominantly on ants and other insects, taken from the ground or gleaned from vegetation on which they climb like other woodpeckers. However, they do not use their tail as a brace – it is soft-feathered, quite unlike the stiff prop of typical woodpeckers. Communication rarely includes the drumming characteristic of the piculets and true woodpeckers: instead, a repeated nasal *kwee*, a rattling call and brief *tuck* notes are heard. Tree-hole nest sites are usually usurped from other species, the birds often evicting the eggs and young of the legitimate occupiers in the process.

With their cryptic, nightjarlike plumage, these are unusual birds, classified in a subfamily of their own. They have only one close relative, the very similar Rufous-necked Wryneck *J. ruficollis* from southern Africa.

2/ GUIANAN PICULET
Picumnus minutissimus

RANGE: **Guianas**
HABITAT: **lowland forest edge, savanna, coffee plantations**
SIZE: **$3\frac{1}{2}$ in (9 cm)**

There are 27 species of piculet, which are, like the wrynecks, classified in a separate subfamily from the true woodpeckers. These tiny birds are all bewilderingly similar in appearance and all, like the wrynecks, lack the stiffened, proplike tail feathers of the true woodpeckers. The Guianan Piculet, which is also known as the Arrowhead Piculet, forages in pairs for small insects on twigs and branches of small trees and shrubs.

The nest cavity is excavated by male and female in soft wood, and both birds roost there during the breeding season. Nests are defended fiercely: a female feeding young has been seen to attack and chase off various species of bird that approached the nest site too closely.

3/ RUFOUS PICULET
Sasia abnormis

RANGE: **Burma, Thailand S through Malaya to Sumatra, Borneo, W Java and other Indonesian islands**
HABITAT: **lowland forest, dense second growth, bamboo thickets, river bank vegetation**
SIZE: **$3\frac{1}{2}$ in (9 cm)**

This restless little bird creeps and hops rapidly over the surfaces of low saplings, branches, vines, grasses and bamboo in search of food. It often forages among the vegetation in pairs or family groups for ants, their eggs, and the larvae of other insects. It also searches among the leaf litter of the woodland floor and investigates crevices for food. It is fond of habitats near water, and its toes have prominent ridges on their undersides that probably help it cling to smooth, wet branches. Unlike most members of the family, the Rufous Piculet has only 3 toes, not 4. The nest is a tiny hole about 1 in (2.5 cm) across, drilled in a decaying hollow bamboo or an old tree.

4/ WHITE WOODPECKER
Melanerpes candidus

RANGE: **S Surinam and Brazil to E Bolivia, Paraguay, W Uruguay, N Argentina**
HABITAT: **open woods, palm groves, savanna, chaco woodland**
SIZE: **$10\frac{1}{2}$ in (27 cm)**

The sociable White Woodpecker is often seen in small flocks. Its flight pattern is less undulating than that of other woodpeckers, and it will travel long distances to reach favored foraging sites. An omnivorous bird, the White Woodpecker eats some insects, but feeds mainly on plant matter. Its habit of eating oranges and other commercially grown fruit, which it may devour regularly in small flocks, has made it an unpopular species with orchard owners. The White Woodpecker also eats honey and grain.

During the breeding season, these woodpeckers indulge in communal bobbing and bowing displays. They nest in branch stubs, where the female typically lays 3–4 eggs, which are probably incubated by both parents.

5/ RED-HEADED WOODPECKER
Melanerpes erythrocephalus

RANGE: **E USA and S Canada**
HABITAT: **open woods, parks, scattered trees**
SIZE: **$7\frac{1}{2}$ in (19 cm)**

Both male and female of this handsome species have the completely red head that the juveniles lack until the spring following their year of hatching. They are highly aggressive birds whose red heads may help them when they are usurping nest-holes from other species of woodpecker (typically the Red-bellied Woodpecker *M. carolinus*); the striking head pattern seems to scare off the other birds.

Unusually for woodpeckers, the species catches flying insects in midair and swoops down to capture grasshoppers and other insects from the ground, rather than gleaning them from tree surfaces. The latter habit often exposes them to traffic dangers and many are killed on the roads.

In winter, migrant Red-headed Woodpeckers congregate in oak woodlands, where they feed on acorns. Nest sites, typically in isolated trees, but sometimes in utility poles or even in buildings, are often usurped from other species. If excavating a cavity themselves, the birds begin at a preexisting crack in soft wood. Clutches generally consist of 3–5 eggs, and the young are fed on insects and fruit by both parents.

6/ ACORN WOODPECKER
Melanerpes formicivorus

RANGE: NW Oregon S to Baja California, SW USA S to W Panama and N Colombia
HABITAT: oak savanna, parkland, mixed pine and oak woods
SIZE: 8 in (20 cm)

The Acorn Woodpecker's presence is easily detected by its characteristic food larders. Tree surfaces, utility poles, fenceposts and the sides of buildings are excavated and acorns firmly wedged in for future use. Its diet includes other nuts, insects and fruits, which are also stored. The 2 races illustrated are *M.f. formicivorus* from southwestern USA and northwestern Mexico and the isolated race *M.f. flavigula* from Colombia. Acorn Woodpeckers live in groups of 3–12 birds, which defend a communal territory of 10–15 acres (4–6 hectares) that comprises the group larder, foraging and nest sites.

7/ RED-BREASTED SAPSUCKER
Sphyrapicus ruber

RANGE: NW North America
HABITAT: coastal evergreen and some mountain coniferous forest, aspen and pine forest
SIZE: 7½ in (19 cm)

The male and female Red-breasted Sapsucker, unlike those of other sapsuckers, are indistinguishable in appearance. The race *S.r. ruber* from southeast Alaska to west Oregon is illustrated; the only other race, *S.r. daggetti*, found in northern coastal California and the mountains of central and southern California, is smaller, with a paler head, longer white "moustache" stripe, paler belly and more prominent white markings on the back. Unlike the related Yellow-bellied Sapsucker *S. varius* which migrates long distances, the Red-breasted Sapsucker is sedentary.

Sapsuckers excavate tiny holes in trees with a high sugar concentration, from which they can extract sugary sap. Exploratory holes are in horizontal rows, and when a good supply of sweet sap is found, vertical rows and even grid-shaped patterns are excavated. Insects, taken either from places where they are attracted to sap exuding from the tree or in midair, complete their diet.

The nest cavities generally have small entrance holes to deter competitors and are situated in trees with heart rot fungus. Clutches typically consist of 4–7 eggs, and the young are fed insects.

8/ NUBIAN WOODPECKER
Campethera nubica

RANGE: EC Africa
HABITAT: savanna
SIZE: 7 in (18 cm)

The Nubian Woodpecker's unforgettably loud, far-reaching series of metallic calls increases in tempo and ends with a squeaky trill. When one bird begins to call, its mate very often joins in as a duet, and their outburst may elicit vocal responses from neighboring pairs.

Nubian Woodpeckers glean insects mainly from the surface of trees, but also take some from within the bark. In addition, they sometimes drop to the ground to search for insect food. In Kenya, they have been reported as tapping the fruits of the baobab tree in order to induce ants to emerge, after which they snapped them up with the long, sticky tongue typical of woodpeckers.

Nests are either natural cavities or excavated holes in rotted wood. Nesting occurs before and during the main rains. Of a clutch of 2–5 eggs no more than 2 young fledge and they seem to acquire adult plumage rapidly.

9/ GROUND WOODPECKER
Geocolaptes olivaceus

RANGE: South Africa
HABITAT: upland grassland in rocky country
SIZE: 11 in (28 cm)

This unusual woodpecker has completely forsaken the trees. It forages alone or in small groups on the ground, pecking and probing to retrieve ants, their larvae and pupae, and hopping among rocks to probe crevices. On the rare occasions when it does take to the air, it flies heavily and for short distances, its red rump feathers showing conspicuously.

Ground Woodpeckers can be quite vocal, uttering a burst of up to 5 far-carrying *ree-chick, ree-chick* notes, both in territorial defense and as a location call for pair members. Other calls are a triple *tchew-kee* at the nest and harsh *peer* notes uttered in alarm. These woodpeckers mob terrestrial predators and hide from aerial ones. They drink regularly, and their distribution may be linked to the availability of water.

Breeding takes place from August to January. Nests, excavated primarily by the male, are sited at the end of a long tunnel in a dirt bank beside a stream or road cutting. A total of 4–5 eggs is laid and incubated, and the fledged young often remain with their parents for some time to forage as a family group.

10/ CARDINAL WOODPECKER
Dendropicos fuscescens

RANGE: sub-Saharan Africa
HABITAT: open forest, forest clearings and edges, savanna, brush
SIZE: 5–6 in (13–15 cm)

Also known as the Little Woodpecker, this is the most common woodpecker in sub-Saharan Africa. There are some 9 races, including the distinctive *D.f. lepidus* from parts of west and central Africa and *D.f. hemprichii* from Ethiopia, Somalia, and north and east Kenya.

The Cardinal Woodpecker probes and taps tree crevices to reveal subsurface insects; it also gleans moths, spiders and other insects from tree surfaces. It can excavate or snap off small twigs to reach beetle larvae inside, and also takes fruit in season. Foraging birds move rapidly over the branches and twigs of trees and bushes, often hanging upside-down, wings beating to maintain their position, as they investigate every nook and cranny. They call occasionally to maintain contact with their mate or other members of a family group. They may also join foraging parties of other bird species.

A sharp and tinny rattling call is used for territorial defense. Both sexes may also drum softly, ending with a sharp call.

11/ GREAT SPOTTED WOODPECKER
Picoides major

RANGE: N Eurasia to Middle East and N Africa
HABITAT: deciduous and coniferous forest from Arctic taiga to Mediterranean scrub
SIZE: 8½–9 in (22–23 cm)

The Great Spotted Woodpecker is widely distributed and, like its New World equivalent, the Hairy Woodpecker, shows considerable geographical variation. North African populations, such as the race *P.m. numidus* from northern Algeria and Tunisia, have a distinctive red and black checkered gorget extending right across the breast. Races found in northern Iran, the Caucasus and adjacent parts of southern USSR are smoky-breasted in contrast to the white of more northern populations, including the race *P.m. pinetorum* from Europe.

Most Great Spotted Woodpeckers are sedentary, but some northern populations may migrate south in winter to find food. Populations have declined as forests have been cleared, although the species is very adaptable and lives in all types of woodland, including parks and large gardens. Reforestation in Scotland has, in turn, led to the increase of the population there.

Although rather secretive at times, these birds often betray their presence with a loud *tchick* call, and on warm spring days the woods echo with the sound of their courtship and territorial drumming.

Their diet varies seasonally to include an abundance of insects in summer and vegetable material, including seeds, in winter. The birds use branches or stumps of trees as anvils to break open seeds in winter, and can wedge pine cones into crevices in order to peck out the kernels with their bills. Occasionally during the breeding season, Great Spotted Woodpeckers hack their way into nest-boxes or natural cavities and kill and eat the chicks of other hole-nesting birds, especially tits.

12/ HAIRY WOODPECKER
Picoides villosus

RANGE: Alaska and Canada, S to Central America, W Panama and Bahamas
HABITAT: coniferous and deciduous forest
SIZE: 7–9½ in (18–24 cm)

The Hairy Woodpecker is, in many respects, a New World counterpart of the Great Spotted Woodpecker. It is one of the most widely distributed and geographically variable of all woodpeckers. For instance, the race *P.v. septentrionalis*, from Alaska, Canada and parts of the central and western USA, has striking black and white plumage and may weigh up to 5 oz (135 g), whereas the race *P.v. sanctorum*, from southern Mexico and Central America, has black, white and chocolate-brown coloring and is much smaller, weighing only about 1½ oz (38 g). Northern populations may migrate south for food in winter, but most birds are sedentary.

Hairy Woodpeckers forage on trunks and major limbs of trees for surface and subsurface insects, berries, and seeds. Their calls include a loud *peek* location call and a rattling call.

race *crissoleucus*

RED-COCKADED
WOODPECKER

SCARLET-BACKED
WOODPECKER

GOLDEN-OLIVE
WOODPECKER

race *funebris*

THREE-TOED
WOODPECKER

PILEATED WOODPECKER

BLACK WOODPECKER

IVORY-BILLED WOODPECKER

CAMPO FLICKER

race *campestroides*

race *cafer*

NORTHERN
FLICKER

race *campestris*

♂

♀

♂

race *auratus*

♂

CHESTNUT-
COLORED
WOODPECKER

race *guttacristatus*

♂

GREATER FLAME-
BACKED WOODPECKER

GREAT SLATY WOODPECKER

♂

♂

OLIVE-BACKED
WOODPECKER

ORANGE-BACKED
WOODPECKER

♂

GREEN WOODPECKER

race *viridis*

♂

WOODPECKERS

1/ RED-COCKADED WOODPECKER
Picoides borealis [V]
RANGE: SE USA
HABITAT: mature open pine forest
SIZE: 7 in (18 cm)

This species has declined dramatically, largely because of human control of natural forest fires and the clear-cutting of forests in their early stages. Fire is an integral part of this bird's ecosystem, perpetuating pines while excluding hardwood trees, thus keeping the forests open. The bird's population is now fragmented, and the species is regarded as being at risk.

Red-cockaded Woodpeckers live in social groups called "clans." Each of these comprises one breeding pair, their fledglings, and male offspring from previous years (young females disperse in their first winter). The clans forage over home ranges that average about 200 acres (80 hectares) in size. This species nests and roosts in holes in the trunks of living pines. Even with the weakening effect of heart rot fungus, excavation may take several months. Small holes drilled above and below each cavity provide a continuous flow of gum that repels climbing rat snakes.

2/ THREE-TOED WOODPECKER
Picoides tridactylus
RANGE: N North America S to N USA, N Eurasia S to S Scandinavia, S Siberia, W China, N Japan; isolated mountain populations farther S
HABITAT: damp, dense coniferous forest
SIZE: 8½ in (22 cm)

Like its close relative, the Black-backed Woodpecker *P. arcticus*, this species is unusual in having only 3 toes on each foot, heavily barred flanks and yellow rather than red on the crown of the male. Its range is closely linked to the distribution of spruce trees and the bark beetles that infest them, although it will use other conifers and other food resources. These are 8 races: the 2 that are illustrated are *P. t. crissoleucus* of northern Siberia, which is a relatively white race, and *P. t. funebris* of southwest China and Tibet, which is the blackest of all the races.

The Three-toed Woodpecker carefully scours each tree on which it forages. It gleans insects from bark surfaces, scales bark from trees to obtain prey from beneath, and will also excavate insects from soft wood.

3/ SCARLET-BACKED WOODPECKER
Veniliornis callonotus
RANGE: SW Colombia, W Ecuador, NW Peru
HABITAT: arid scrub, dry forest
SIZE: 5½ in (14 cm)

Within its limited range, this stunning species shows considerable geographical variation in the amount of barring on the breast. Females lack the red tips on the black crown feathers, but are otherwise very similar to males. The Scarlet-backed Woodpecker occurs at elevations of up to 3,300 ft (1,000 m). Little else is known of its ecology or habits. Nesting appears to take place between May and October.

4/ GOLDEN-OLIVE WOODPECKER
Piculus rubiginosus
RANGE: Mexico to Argentina; Trinidad, Tobago
HABITAT: forest, forest edge, secondary growth
SIZE: 7½–9 in (19–23 cm)

This woodpecker is widely distributed and fairly common in some areas. In more northerly parts of its range, it occurs in pine-oak and oak forest; to the south it is found in oak and tropical deciduous forest and, at times, in tropical evergreen forest. There are about 20 races; *P. r. aeruginosus* is from northeastern Mexico.

A rather quiet, secretive bird, the Golden-olive Woodpecker feeds on tree-dwelling invertebrates, blackberries and other fruits. Its foraging includes much peering and poking into bark crevices and the excavation of sub-surface insects. Occasionally, it will feed on the ground. In Colombia, it is reported to join mixed-species foraging flocks.

5/ NORTHERN FLICKER
Colaptes auratus
RANGE: North America S to Nicaragua
HABITAT: open forest, savanna, open areas with widely scattered trees
SIZE: 10–14 in (25.5–36 cm)

Until recently, the Red-shafted Flicker (*C. a. cafer* and similar races) of western North America, the Yellow-shafted Flicker (*C. a. auratus* and the similar *C. a. luteus*) of eastern North America, and the Gilded Flicker (*C. a. chrysoides* and similar races) of southwestern USA and northern Mexico were considered to be separate species. Well-documented hybridization among these and other different forms has led to their present designation as a single species.

Although they occasionally take food from trees, Northern Flickers are perfectly at home on the ground, where they have become specialists in feeding on ants. They have a variety of calls, and both sexes produce the characteristic woodpecker drumming sound with their bills. In the absence of suitable trees for drumming, they often drum on buildings, television antennas and other artificial structures. Although they can excavate nest-holes in soft wood or cacti, they frequently use natural cavities or renovate old nests.

6/ CAMPO FLICKER
Colaptes campestris
RANGE: Surinam and lower Amazon Basin to E Bolivia, S Brazil, Paraguay, Uruguay, Argentina
HABITAT: grassland, savanna, forest edge
SIZE: 11¾ in (30 cm)

This species is an ant specialist and is not known to take other foods – it seems to be the most specialized of the flickers. Most food is taken from the ground, where the bird hops about in uneven terrain or walks on level turf. It often forages in small groups, sometimes in company with the Green-barred Flicker *C. melanochloros*. Foraging groups seem especially attracted to areas that have been recently burned. There are 2 races, often regarded as separate species: the northern *C. c. campestris* and the southern *C. c. campestroides*, often known as the Field Flicker.

Perhaps as a reflection of the scarcity of suitable nest sites, 2 or more pairs of Camp Flickers sometimes nest in close proximity. Nonbreeding adults may help out at some nests and, after fledging, family groups may remain together for some time.

7/ CHESTNUT-COLORED WOODPECKER
Celeus castaneus
RANGE: Mexico to Panama
HABITAT: dense, tropical evergreen forest and secondary growth
SIZE: 9–9¾ in (23–25 cm)

This is a fairly common woodpecker in many areas, but one that is difficult to see because of its dark plumage and shaded habitat. It is often easy to locate, however, because of its constant tapping as it forages on large branches and tree trunks in the middle to upper layers of the forest. The Chestnut-colored Woodpecker is often seen in pairs and may feed cooperatively to some extent.

This species is considered a pest in some cocoa plantations where it damages the fruit.

The call note of the Chestnut-colored Woodpecker is a low *kwar* or *keeyark*. This is sometimes followed by a lower, weaker *heh-heh-heh*. Other calls include a sharp, double squeak and a *howp* similar to that of a trogon.

8/ PILEATED WOODPECKER
Dryocopus pileatus
RANGE: **S Canada, E and NW USA**
HABITAT: **forest, especially moist forest**
SIZE: **15–18¾ in (38–48 cm)**

Unlike some other large species, the Pileated Woodpecker still thrives in many areas, partly because ants and termites, some of its staple prey, are always abundant. It forages for insects both in wood on the ground and in trees, and it also feeds readily on fruit in season. The female has a less extensive red cap than the male, the front of her crown being black, and she lacks the red on her "moustache" stripe.

The call of the Pileated Woodpecker is a loud series of *kuk-kuk-kuk* notes. The bird carefully selects a drumming surface that will resonate very loudly across the forest.

9/ BLACK WOODPECKER
Dryocopus martius
RANGE: **Eurasia except for SW China**
HABITAT: **northern to warm-temperate hardwood and coniferous forest**
SIZE: **17¾ in (45 cm)**

The Black Woodpecker, like its New World counterpart, the Pileated Woodpecker, has a large home range, estimated at 375–7,500 acres (150–3,000 hectares), depending on the quality of the habitat. Because of its large size, the boundaries are not clearly defined and several birds may have overlapping ranges.

This is a solitary species that is normally seen in pairs only during the breeding season. At other times, the sexes maintain separate territories or at least feed alone. The Black Woodpecker feeds primarily on ants, termites and the larvae of wood-boring beetles, but may occasionally eat the eggs and nestlings of other birds. It also eats some fruit in season.

10/ IVORY-BILLED WOODPECKER
Campephilus principalis   E
RANGE: **mountains of E Cuba (possibly also SE USA)**
HABITAT: **extensive, remote, mature forest**
SIZE: **19½ in (50 cm)**

This is the third largest woodpecker in the world, exceeded in size only by the closely related, and possibly extinct, Imperial Woodpecker *C. imperialis* of Mexico and the Great Slaty Woodpecker. It is one of the world's rarest birds. It is intimately associated with virgin forests, and its demise is tied to the loss of the forests and direct persecution by people. The felling of mature forests also cut back the bird's principal food supply of large beetle larvae. Since the early 1940s, records of Ivory-billed Woodpeckers in the USA have been treated with scepticism, but a slim hope remains

that some birds might have survived in remote forests in Louisiana, Mississippi or Florida.

The Cuban population of this bird declined at about the same time as the US population, but in recent years a few birds have been discovered in rugged, forested terrain in the island's eastern mountains. The Cuban government has set the area aside as a reserve.

11/ GREEN WOODPECKER
Picus viridis
RANGE: **W Eurasia from S Scandinavia, Europe to mountains of N Africa, Turkey, Iran, W Russia**
HABITAT: **deciduous and mixed forest edge, secondary growth, parklike habitats**
SIZE: **11¾ in (30 cm)**

This bird spends much of its time foraging on the gound for ants and grubs. When it finds an anthill, the Green Woodpecker tears into it with a vigorous twisting of the head and probing of the beak. It also gleans insects and spiders from tree surfaces, consumes fruits and seeds, and sometimes raids beehives. The female has an all-black "moustache," while juveniles have only a faint one and barred underparts. There are several races, including *P. v. viridis* of Europe and *P. v. vaillantii* of north Africa, which has strongly barred underparts and less red on the head in the female, whose "moustache" resembles that of the male.

The Green Woodpecker tends to be solitary outside the breeding season. Both sexes have similar calls, including a far-carrying laughing cry and a series of *kwit-up* notes with variations. This species rarely drums.

12/ OLIVE-BACKED WOODPECKER
Dinopium rafflesii
RANGE: **Southeast Asia from Tenasserim through Malay Peninsula to Sumatra, Borneo**
HABITAT: **dense lowland forest**
SIZE: **11 in (28 cm)**

This species is sometimes known as the Olive-backed Three-toed Woodpecker, a name which reveals both plumage and structural characteristics. It forages alone or in pairs in the forest understory by gleaning and probing for surface and sub-surface insects and spiders. Occasionally, it drops to the ground to investigate fallen logs.

The calls of the Olive-backed Woodpecker include a rapid, descending series of *kwee* notes. A slow tapping is used in communications between pair members at the nest site, but no drumming has been recorded.

13/ GREATER FLAME-BACKED WOODPECKER
Chrysocolaptes lucidus
RANGE: **S Asia from India to SW China, Greater Sundas and the Philippines**
HABITAT: **forest, forest edge, mangroves**
SIZE: **13 in (33 cm)**

This species is sometimes known as the Crimson-backed Woodpecker or Greater Golden-backed Woodpecker. Most of its food consists of insects.

It will tap along a branch to locate prey, and then dig into the wood to reach them. It has also been seen catching termites on the ground and even seizing winged termites in the air.

The Greater Flame-backed Woodpecker engages in distinctive and frequent bouts of drumming prior to nesting, often producing long, loud, rapid bursts that decrease in intensity. Vocalizations include a *keek* call note and a laughing series of *kow* notes that have been described as "harsh, loud, prolonged ... incessant and strident, such as might be made by a giant cicada." Many races have been described, most of them isolated geographically from one another. The race illustrated is *C. l. guttacristatus*, which ranges from northwest India to northern Vietnam.

14/ ORANGE-BACKED WOODPECKER
Reinwardtipicus validus
RANGE: **S Burma, S Thailand, Malaysia, Sumatra, Java, Borneo**
HABITAT: **lowland forest, secondary growth, partially cleared areas with large trees**
SIZE: **11¾ in (30 cm)**

This is a noisy woodpecker which taps loudly, calls frequently and forages from near ground level to the forest canopy. It forages by tapping to locate sub-surface insects and excavating to remove them. Occasionally, it scales bark from trees to reveal prey beneath. Its vocalizations all seem to be based on a metallic *pit* note. These notes are given singly, as a double note, or as a series of up to 9 notes. The Orange-backed Woodpecker excavates its nests in dead trees. The young remain with the parents and are fed large insect larvae for some time after fledging. They will also follow adults to excavations, where they retrieve food for themselves.

15/ GREAT SLATY WOODPECKER
Mulleripicus pulverulentus
RANGE: **N India to SW China, Thailand, Vietnam, Malaysia, Indonesia**
HABITAT: **lowland forest and swamp forest**
SIZE: **20 in (51 cm)**

Although a bird of the virgin forest, the Great Slaty Woodpecker will also live in partially cleared areas with large trees if there is undisturbed forest nearby. It is found in pairs or family groups that travel together to scattered feeding sites. These birds seem to use much of the range of foraging techniques used by other woodpeckers – gleaning, peering and poking, excavating and chasing insects on or near the ground. Their primary food seems to be ants, although they will also take termites and beetle larvae.

The loudest, most distinctive call of the Great Slaty Woodpecker is a braying cackle. Other vocalizations include a *dit* note, a rattling series of *dit*s and a flight call, rendered as *dwot*. Both sexes share in the nesting duties, and the young may remain with them for long periods, perhaps until the beginning of the next breeding season.

BROADBILLS, WOODCREEPERS, OVENBIRDS

LESSER GREEN BROADBILL

♂

AFRICAN BROADBILL

WEDGE-BILLED
WOODCREEPER

COMMON MINER

LONG-BILLED
WOODCREEPER

RED-BILLED SCYTHEBILL

race *nigrirostris*

BARRED WOODCREEPER

race
radiolatus

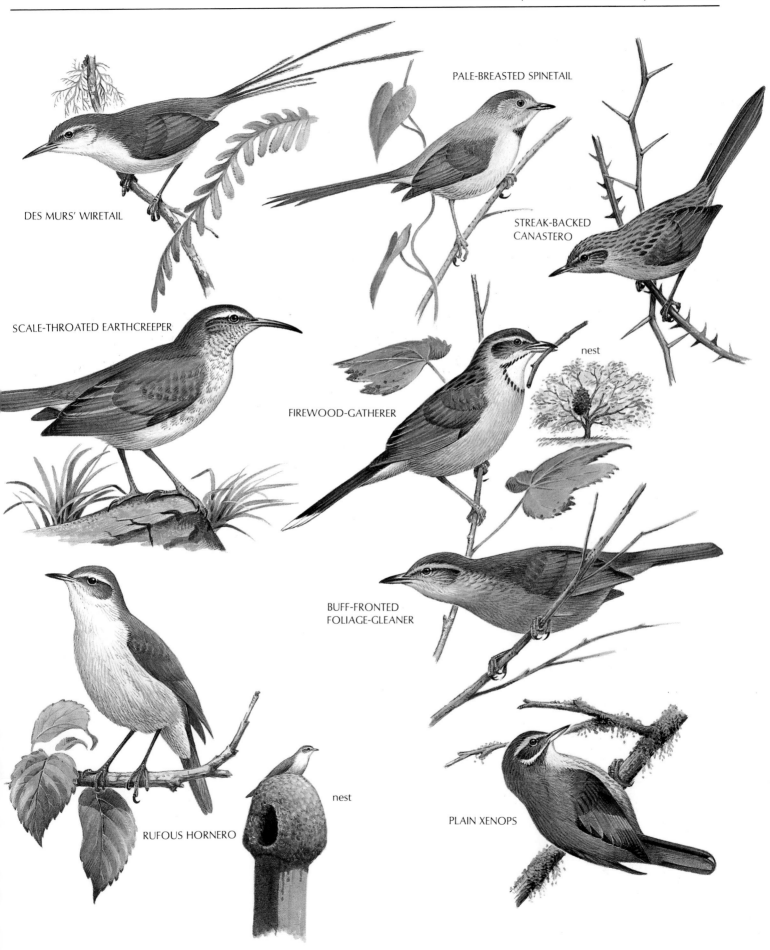

DES MURS' WIRETAIL

PALE-BREASTED SPINETAIL

STREAK-BACKED CANASTERO

SCALE-THROATED EARTHCREEPER

FIREWOOD-GATHERER

nest

BUFF-FRONTED FOLIAGE-GLEANER

RUFOUS HORNERO

nest

PLAIN XENOPS

BROADBILLS, WOODCREEPERS, OVENBIRDS

FAMILY EURYLAIMIDAE
Broadbills

Small to medium, stout birds, with large eyes and broad heads. Bill flattened with wide gape. Plumage loose, often colorful, especially in Asian species. Sexes differ in about half the species. Nest oval or purse-shaped, suspended. Eggs 2–8, white or pinkish, sometimes speckled. Incubation and nestling periods unknown. 14 species.

1/ AFRICAN BROADBILL
Smithornis capensis

RANGE: **Africa, from Ivory Coast and Kenya S to Natal and Angola**
HABITAT: **forest, secondary woodland, thickets**
SIZE: **5 in (13 cm)**

A dumpy, somewhat lethargic denizen of dense bush, the African Broadbill is a solitary, inconspicuous bird, which usually hunts from a perch low down among dimly lit vegetation. It feeds on flying insects, catching them in midair after short pursuit flights that may briefly show off its white rump patch.

It is heard more often than seen, particularly during the brief but remarkable display flight when, with wings vibrating rapidly, the bird flies in a tight circle around its perch. The vibration of its wings generates a distinctive rattling trill which can be heard from several yards away. The performance is often repeated over and over again, but since it usually occurs in a small clear space amid dense foliage, it is rarely seen.

2/ LESSER GREEN BROADBILL
Calyptomena viridis

RANGE: **Lower Burma and peninsular Thailand to Sumatra and Borneo**
HABITAT: **forest and secondary woodland, up to 5,500 ft (1,700 m) in Borneo**
SIZE: **8 in (20 cm)**

Although the bill of this Asian broadbill is higher and more arched than those of other species, it is almost concealed by the elongated feathers that surround it, giving the bird's head a rounded, almost froglike appearance.

The male looks as though he should be conspicuous, with his shining grass-green plumage, but he blends in well with the rich greens of the tropical forest and can be surprisingly hard to see. These birds move rather deliberately, although they are often livelier and noisier when foraging in small groups, calling with low whistles or the bubbling notes characteristic of the family.

The female is often larger than her mate and her plumage is a duller green. She lays 2 eggs in a pear-shaped nest, woven from plant fiber and suspended from low twigs just above the ground.

FAMILY DENDROCOLAPTIDAE
Woodcreepers

Medium, slender, insect-eating tree-climbers, with stiff, spiny tails. Bills very variable, from short and stout to long, thin and downcurved. Plumage brown to rufous, often streaked. Sexes alike. Nest built in tree cavities. Eggs 2–3, white or greenish-white. Incubation 15–20 days, nestling period unknown. 52 species.

3/ WEDGE-BILLED WOODCREEPER
Glyphorhynchus spirurus

RANGE: **S Mexico to N Bolivia, Amazonia**
HABITAT: **humid tropical forest, secondary woodland**
SIZE: **5½ in (14 cm)**

The cryptic coloration of the Wedge-billed Woodcreeper makes it hard to see when it clings motionless to a tree trunk. It hunts by hitching its way up trees and along branches, using its stiffened tail feathers as a prop in much the same way as a woodpecker. As it climbs, it taps at the bark with its short, slightly upturned bill, searching for small insects and spiders. Widespread and common, it is usually seen singly or in pairs, and it often occurs in mixed-species flocks.

4/ LONG-BILLED WOODCREEPER
Nasica longirostris

RANGE: **Venezuela to N Bolivia, Amazonia**
HABITAT: **humid tropical forest, seasonally flooded forest, swamps**
SIZE: **14 in (36 cm)**

The bill of this distinctive woodcreeper is ideally suited for probing the layered foliage of bromeliads and similar plants that grow on tropical forest trees. These plants often harbor a rich variety of insects, spiders and other small animals. The bird also searches for prey in the bark like its shorter-billed relatives. It is an agile climber which usually hunts alone or in pairs, communicating with eerie whistles.

5/ BARRED WOODCREEPER
Dendrocolaptes certhia

RANGE: **Mexico to N Bolivia, Amazonia**
HABITAT: **humid tropical forest, secondary woodland**
SIZE: **11 in (28 cm)**

The strongly built Barred Woodcreeper is noted for its habit of following columns of army ants as they swarm over the forest floor. It ignores the ants themselves, preying instead on the insects that try to escape them; woodcreepers have been seen flying back and forth from tree trunks, snatching the escapees from the ground or hawking them in midair. At other times it forages for prey much like other woodcreepers, working its way up one tree, then flying down to the foot of another to repeat the process.

The bill of the Costa Rican race *D.c.nigrirostris* is mainly black, whereas that of the upper Amazonian race *D.c.radiolatus* is red. More than 10 other races have been recognized, with a subtle variety of bill colors and plumage details: some Mexican populations have ivory-colored bills.

6/ RED-BILLED SCYTHEBILL
Campylorhamphus trochilirostris

RANGE: **Panama, through N South America to Bolivia, Paraguay, N Argentina**
HABITAT: **humid tropical forest, swamps**
SIZE: **11¾ in (30 cm)**

The spectacular downcurved red bill of this quite unmistakable woodcreeper is a superb adaptation for penetrating the convoluted foliage of tree ferns, bromeliads and other epiphytes (plants that grow on trees) in search of prey. This impressive bird feeds on spiders, insects and even the small frogs that live in the pools of water within the plants. It can also insert its long bill into the smallest bark crevice to pick out an insect that would be safe from almost any other bird. Like other woodcreepers and woodpeckers (pp. 214–21), Red-billed Scythebills use their stiffened tail feathers to support themselves on vertical tree trunks while clinging on with their strong feet.

FAMILY FURNARIIDAE
Ovenbirds

Medium, active, often ground-dwelling, extraordinarily diverse in form and habits. Plumage drab, sexes similar. True ovenbirds build domed mud nests; others build stick nests or use cavities. Eggs 2–5, white to blue. Incubation about 15 days, nestling period 13–18 days (known for only 6 species). 227 species.

7/ COMMON MINER
Geositta cunicularia
RANGE: S South America, from Peru and Brazil to Tierra del Fuego
HABITAT: arid sandy plains, dunes, grassland, from coasts to mountaintops
SIZE: 6¾–7½ in (17–19 cm)

The Common Miner takes its name from the long nest-burrow which it excavates in a slope, earth bank, cutting or sand dune. Up to 10 ft (3 m) long, the burrow ends in a roomy chamber which serves as a nest-hole during the breeding season and a roosting site for the rest of the year.

The birds forage for insects and seeds on the ground, running rapidly for short distances, then abruptly stopping to utter loud call-notes and peer about, frequently flicking up their tails and wing tips. After eating an insect, a Common Miner will often clean its bill by wiping both sides on a rock.

8/ SCALE-THROATED EARTHCREEPER
Upucerthia dumetaria
RANGE: S South America
HABITAT: arid slopes and thorny brush
SIZE: 9¾ in (25 cm)

The earthcreepers are all large, brown, ground-dwelling birds with downcurved bills. Normally silent and inconspicuous, the Scale-throated Earthcreeper often lives in arid terrain, where it searches for insects among the stones and boulders, or plunges its long bill into clumps of bunchgrass. If alarmed, it tends to run and hide rather than fly away; when it does fly, it rarely goes far.

The pair digs a nest-burrow up to 5 ft (1.5 m) deep in a sloping hillside or earth bank, lining the nest chamber with grasses and roots.

9/ RUFOUS HORNERO
Furnarius rufus
RANGE: E South America from Brazil to Argentina
HABITAT: groves of trees, open country
SIZE: 8 in (20 cm)

The word *hornero* is Spanish for "baker" – a reference to the bird's remarkable nest, which is made of mud reinforced with straw and shaped like a traditional baker's oven. Often built on top of a broad fencepost, or even on a house, the nest is a complex structure with a low entrance hole and a spiral, ascending passageway leading to the nesting chamber. It may take months to complete and is very durable, yet the birds build a new one each year. Abandoned nests are often adopted by other birds.

Rufous Horneros forage on the ground, using their strong, sharp bills to dig out earthworms and insect larvae. They move with a characteristic, high-stepping, deliberate gait, and the pairs will often sing together with loud ringing calls.

10/ DES MURS' WIRETAIL
Sylviorthorhynchus desmursii
RANGE: Chile and Argentina
HABITAT: humid forest, in thick understory, especially bamboo thickets
SIZE: 9½ in (24 cm)

A secretive, little-known denizen of dense forest, Des Murs' Wiretail, also known as Des Murs' Spinetail, is remarkable for its strange tail feathers. There are only 6 of them: the short outer pair is hidden among the tail coverts and the middle and inner pairs are very long – up to 3 times the length of the bird's body – but reduced to little more than fringed shafts. These often appear very worn, suggesting that they are used for some sort of abrasive purpose or for display.

Although they often show little fear of humans, Des Murs' Wiretails rarely emerge from the thick foliage where they find their food. However, they often reveal their presence by their persistent calls. They nest close to the ground amid dry vegetation, building a globular nest of plant fiber.

11/ PALE-BREASTED SPINETAIL
Synallaxis albescens
RANGE: SW Costa Rica to Argentina, E of Andes; Trinidad, Margarita Island
HABITAT: forest edge, plantations, mangroves, thickets, reedbeds, savanna, arid areas
SIZE: 6¼ in (16 cm)

The Pale-breasted Spinetail is usually seen foraging alone or with its mate, giving harsh chattering calls and bobbing its tail rapidly up and down as it picks its way over the ground in search of insect prey.

This bird has many races over its great range, but plumage differences are slight. Its choice of habitat is equally wide, ranging from sea level to at least 7,000 ft (2,100 m). It nests in trees or bushes, building a coarse, globe-shaped nest of small twigs with a narrow, tubular side entrance. Southern populations migrate northward outside the breeding season.

12/ STREAK-BACKED CANASTERO
Thripophaga wyatti
RANGE: NW Venezuela, NE Colombia, Ecuador to S Peru
HABITAT: mountain grassland with scattered bushes from the tree line to the snow line in the Andes
SIZE: 6 in (15 cm)

Although widespread and locally common, the Streak-backed Canastero has a patchy distribution on the open, rocky terrain just below the snow line on the Andes. It is occasionally found below the tree line in open terrain. The Streak-backed Canastero feeds on insects, hopping or running over the ground and frequently raising or flicking up its slightly cocked tail as it probes among the stones and grasses for its prey. When startled, it dives into thick vegetation.

In Spanish the word *canastero* means "basket maker," and refers to the large, domed basketlike nests of small twigs and grass built by this and the other 21 species of canastero.

13/ FIREWOOD-GATHERER
Anumbius annumbi
RANGE: Brazil, Uruguay, Paraguay, Argentina
HABITAT: open scrub and weedy areas
SIZE: 8¼ in (21 cm)

The nests of this common bird look like great piles of sticks ready for the fire, and are often built on conspicuous sites such as isolated trees or utility poles. The birds favor thorny twigs, lining them with wool and soft grass, and each nest may last for several years. The birds often incorporate brightly colored rags, bones, pieces of metal and other debris into the main structure of their remarkable nests, and may add snakeskin, crab shells, snail shells and fragments of bark to the lining of the neatly arched tunnel leading to the main section.

The Firewood-Gatherer generally hunts on the ground, searching out insects and other small animals among clumps of grass or weeds. Its call is a rapid *chick-chick-chee*, sung with such gusto that the bird's whole body shakes during the performance.

14/ BUFF-FRONTED FOLIAGE-GLEANER
Philydor rufus
RANGE: Costa Rica S to N Argentina
HABITAT: humid and wet mountain forest
SIZE: 7½ in (19 cm)

Sometimes foraging completely alone, but often as single birds in mixed flocks with other species, this bird lives up to its name by gleaning insects and spiders from tangled masses of vines growing up the trunks of forest trees, or by hopping rapidly along horizontal branches to search for prey among the foliage near their tips. The Buff-fronted Foliage-gleaner frequently twists its body and sweeps its tail when looking for insects, perhaps to dislodge or frighten them from their hiding places. Its curious calls have been described as froglike croaks and a snorting *churr*. It nests in a burrow excavated in an earth bank.

15/ PLAIN XENOPS
Xenops minutus
RANGE: SE Mexico to W Ecuador, and E of Andes S to N Argentina, Paraguay, S Brazil
HABITAT: humid forest and forest edge
SIZE: 4¾ in (12 cm)

There are several *Xenops* species and all but one have a distinctive white crescent on the cheek like that of the Plain Xenops. They also share a characteristic foraging habit, hopping and sidling along branches, peering from side to side in search of insects, spiders and other small creatures. Sometimes they hitch their way up tree trunks in the manner of woodcreepers, stopping to pry into small rotten twigs.

The Plain Xenops nests in a rotten stump, either excavating a cavity itself or taking over a hole dug by one of the small woodpeckers known as piculets. It roosts alone in a similar hole, usually choosing an old woodpecker nest.

ANTBIRDS AND GNATEATERS, TAPACULOS

BARRED ANTSHRIKE

race *intermedius*

♂

♀

BLUISH-SLATE
ANTSHRIKE

♂

♀

♀

BERTONI'S ANTWREN

♂

WHITE-FLANKED ANTWREN

♀

♂

GRAY ANTBIRD

♀

race *cinerascens*

♂

♀

CHESTNUT-TAILED ANTBIRD

♀

race *naevia*

♂

♂

SILVERED ANTBIRD

♂

WHITE-PLUMED ANTBIRD

♂ race *crissalis*

BLACK-FACED ANT-THRUSH

SCALED ANTPITTA

race *guatimalensis*

♂

♂

SLATE-CROWNED ANTPITTA

♂

RUFOUS GNATEATER

BLACK-THROATED
HUET-HUET

juv

♂

♂

♀

SLATY BRISTLEFRONT

UNICOLORED TAPACULO

ANTBIRDS AND GNATEATERS, TAPACULOS

FAMILY FORMICARIIDAE
Antbirds and gnateaters

Small to medium, generally long-legged birds forming a very diverse family, including ant-shrikes, antvireos, antwrens, ant-thrushes and antpittas, as well as species simply called ant-birds. Many (including gnateaters, sometimes classified in separate family) short-necked, round-bodied, almost tailless. Wings rounded for short flights in dense vegetation. Sexes usually differ. Males often dark gray or black, often with white spots and bars, sometimes with reddish-brown; females often brown. Gnateaters have pale brown upperparts, even paler below, with patterned heads, usually with tuft of long, silvery-white plumes behind each eye in males of most species and females of some. Most species suspend cup nests in forks of branches; some nest on top of fallen tree trunks or inside hollow stubs of palms; a few on the ground. Eggs 2, usually white or creamy (some pale blue or brown) with many dark (especially brown) markings. Incubation 14–16 days, nestling period 9–12 days. 246 species.

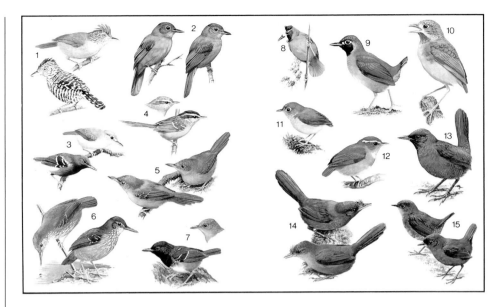

1/ BARRED ANTSHRIKE
Thamnophilus doliatus

RANGE: **Mexico to extreme N Argentina**
HABITAT: **lowland thickets and tangles**
SIZE: **5½–6¾ in (14–17 cm)**

This species is typically found in semiopen areas, such as dry forests or bushy savannas, but it is widespread where it has few competitors. In the heart of Amazonia where antbirds abound, however, it is confined to shrubby growth on river banks and islands.

The Barred Antshrike searches for insects primarily in the dim light of often impenetrable thickets. More often heard than seen, members of a pair keep in touch through a large repertoire of songs and calls. The song is a rolling rattle that ends in an emphatic nasal note. As it sings, the Barred Antshrike stretches its neck, raises its striking crest and vibrates its slightly fanned tail. The amount of black barring on the underparts of the male varies between races.

2/ BLUISH-SLATE ANTSHRIKE
Thamnomanes schistogynus

RANGE: **SW Amazonia**
HABITAT: **lowland forest**
SIZE: **5½ in (14 cm)**

In the permanent mixed-species flocks that sweep through the forest understory, this species serves as a sentinel guarding against hawks and other predators. As the advancing flock disturbs insects from their hiding places, the Bluish-slate Ant-shrike sallies out to capture them in the air or on foliage. Sometimes it gives false alarm calls to freeze its flock mates, which gives it an advantage in capturing fleeing insects. Occasionally the Bluish-slate Antshrike chases a small bird and forces it to disgorge an insect it has captured but not yet consumed. To construct its nest, the bird piles a huge ball of large dead leaves on a horizontal branch, which makes it appear like aerial leaf litter.

3/ WHITE-FLANKED ANTWREN
Myrmotherula axillaris

RANGE: **Central America to SE Brazil**
HABITAT: **humid lowland forest**
SIZE: **4 in (10 cm)**

White-flanked Antwrens are tiny dynamos that often flick their wings to flash white underneath. They almost always travel through the forest together with birds of one or more other species in mixed-species flocks.

White-flanked Antwrens are moderately specialized in foraging behavior, primarily finding insects on living leaves about 6–65 ft (2–20 m) off the ground. They typically move rapidly through branches, but also search by traveling up and down through the vines that encircle the tree trunks. In addition to simply picking insects off leaves, these antwrens are sometimes more acrobatic in their search for food, stretching, leaning, hanging and hovering to obtain prey.

4/ BERTONI'S ANTWREN
Drymophila rubricollis

RANGE: **SW Brazil, adjacent Paraguay and Argentina**
HABITAT: **bamboo thickets**
SIZE: **5½ in (14 cm)**

Bertoni's Antwren is associated with bamboo, an extremely important element in the South American landscape. Hopping and fluttering among the highly flexible bamboo stalks, this sprightly little bird uses its long tail to help it retain its balance. From its precarious perches, this bird reaches out in all directions to capture small insects, often knocking over dead leaves caught up in the bamboo in search of hidden prey. Pairs occupy a small territory within which they forage by themselves or temporarily associate with mixed flocks. Bertoni's Antwren has only recently been re-established as a species, distinct from the closely related Ferruginous Antwren *D. ferruginea*.

5/ GRAY ANTBIRD
Cercomacra cinerascens

RANGE: **Amazonia**
HABITAT: **forest**
SIZE: **6 in (15 cm)**

The Gray Antbird haunts the twisted masses of vines and lianas that are often found from mid-heights to the crowns of tall trees. It is very difficult to see, but it may be located by listening for its harsh, repeated *cruick-shank* song. This active forager often contorts its long tail up, down, or sideways as it stretches to pick off prey. In display, the long tail wags back and forth while the head moves in the opposite direction, giving the bird the grotesque shape of the letter *Z*.

Several races have been described: *C. c. cinerascens* from upper Amazonia has a small white patch between the "shoulders" and narrow white edges to its greater wing coverts.

6/ SILVERED ANTBIRD
Sclateria naevia

RANGE: **Amazonia**
HABITAT: **near water in wooded areas**
SIZE: **5½–6 in (14–15 cm)**

This bird is especially abundant where streams cut their way through areas of swampy forest. It works through the overhanging vegetation close to the water, picking insect prey from the surface of the water, from floating leaves and from twigs and branches. Less often, the Silvered Antbird hops on damp leaf litter or tree roots or through grass near the water's edge, but only if dense cover is nearby. Its distinctive song begins with a single emphatic note and continues with a long, rapidly delivered staccato series of notes that rises slightly and then softly trails off.

There are several races, including *S. n. naevia* of northeastern Venezuela, the Guianas and northern Brazil, which has gray and white scalloped underparts in the male and heavily brown-mottled white underparts in the female, and *S. n. argentata* of upper Amazonia, with only a few gray edges to the feathers of the male's underparts and the sides of the neck and body bright chestnut in the female.

7/ CHESTNUT-TAILED ANTBIRD
Myrmeciza hemimelaena
RANGE: Amazonia, mostly S of River Amazon
HABITAT: forest undergrowth
SIZE: $4\frac{3}{4}$ in (12 cm)

The Chestnut-tailed Antbird is found close to the forest floor, perching on branches, vertical stems and logs. It moves quickly through the undergrowth and picks prey off leaves, plant stems, or tops of fallen logs. It only occasionally jumps down to the leaf litter to capture insects or to use the ground as a perch from which to sally to the undersides of overhead leaves. The male utters a short series of loud, clear whistles that accelerate and fall in pitch; the female answers with a slower, more evenly paced, downward series.

8/ WHITE-PLUMED ANTBIRD
Pithys albifrons
RANGE: Amazonia, mostly N of River Amazon
HABITAT: forest undergrowth
SIZE: $4\frac{1}{4}$ in (11 cm)

The White-plumed Antbird feeds almost entirely by snapping up cockroaches, katydids and other insects fleeing formidable columns of army ants. To catch escaping insects, the White-plumed Antbird and other ant-following birds perch in the midst of the column of ants near the ground where the ants are thickest. The White-plumed Antbird moves from one vertical perch to another, apparently to avoid competitors as well as the ants. Competition is fierce for the best perches, and this small species is often relegated to the less desirable fringes of the ant swarm.

9/ BLACK-FACED ANT-THRUSH
Formicarius analis
RANGE: S Mexico to Amazonia
HABITAT: forest and woodland floor
SIZE: $6\frac{3}{4}$–$7\frac{1}{2}$ in (17–19 cm)

Pairs of Black-faced Ant-Thrushes forage apart but within easy calling distance of each other. Normally they strut about on the leaf litter, their tails cocked and their heads and tails bobbing slightly. They pick prey mostly off the ground, sometimes flicking leaves aside with their bills.

When it sings, the Black-faced Ant-Thrush stretches its head way up, dropping its tail slightly. The short song is distinctive but variable. There are many races, including *F. a. crissalis* from southeastern Venezuela, the Guianas and northern Brazil, which is typical of most, and *F. a. connectens* from eastern Colombia, which lacks the cinnamon color on the sides of the neck.

10/ SCALED ANTPITTA
Grallaria guatimalensis
RANGE: Mexico to Peru and Trinidad
HABITAT: mountains on damp ground near or in forest understory
SIZE: $6\frac{1}{4}$–$7\frac{1}{2}$ in (16–19 cm)

Very shy and difficult to see, the Scaled Antpitta travels alone, taking springing hops across the ground, searching for beetles and other insects, as well as other invertebrates, such as millipedes. In response to tape recordings of its song, the Scaled Antpitta hops up on a fallen log or tree stump or, if startled, flies rapidly for a short distance. Platform nests of Scaled Antpittas have been found mostly on top of fallen logs, but also inside lush plants growing against tree trunks and within the tangled branches of shrubs.

There are several races, including *G. g. guatimalensis*, found from southern Mexico to northern Nicaragua, and *G. g. regulus* from western Colombia, Ecuador and Peru, which differs from the rest in having a distinct white center line on its throat and a white crescent-shaped bar on its lower throat, bordered below by a black band.

11/ SLATE-CROWNED ANTPITTA
Grallaricula nana
RANGE: Andes and mountains of Colombia and Venezuela
HABITAT: thickets and understory
SIZE: $4\frac{1}{4}$ in (11 cm)

Extremely secretive birds, Slate-crowned Antpittas flick their wings constantly as they jump and scurry about on fallen logs and on branches very close to the ground. To capture small insects, they glean them from the branches and logs or make very short aerial sallies to foliage and stems, less often to the forest floor. Only occasionally do they move along the ground, rapidly attacking prey on the leaf litter. Upon hearing the songs of rivals, Slate-crowned Antpittas crouch down, puff out their feathers until they resemble fuzzy balls, and quietly stare out with their oversized eyes to locate the intruders.

12/ RUFOUS GNATEATER
Conopophaga lineata
RANGE: E and S Brazil, adjacent Paraguay and Argentina
HABITAT: forest understory
SIZE: 5 in (13 cm)

Gnateaters are extraordinarily shy of humans. Of the 8 species, the Rufous Gnateater is perhaps the most abundant and most easily observed. The characteristic white tuft of feathers behind the eye is normally folded into a thin line or obscured entirely. Females differ from males only in having this tuft of feathers gray rather than white.

Rufous Gnateaters move rapidly through stems, twigs and fallen limbs usually less than 3 ft (1 m) from the ground. From these low perches they obtain small insects by making short sallying flights, chiefly onto the ground, but also to nearby foliage and especially overhead leaves. Mostly solitary except while breeding, gnateaters deliver a peculiar call that sounds like a soft sneeze and that may serve to maintain territorial space between individuals.

FAMILY RHINOCRYPTIDAE
Tapaculos
Small to medium ground-dwellers, with short, rounded wings, often with very large, strong feet. Large movable flap covering nostril. Typically gray or brown, marked with black or rufous; long tail often held upright. Sexes mostly similar. Nest of grass, twigs and moss placed in earthen tunnels, rock crevices, hollow trees, thick plants and detritus on ground, or (as domed structure) in bushes. Eggs 2–3, typically white. Incubation and nestling periods unknown. 30 species.

13/ BLACK-THROATED HUET-HUET
Pteroptochos tarnii
RANGE: S Chile and adjacent Argentina
HABITAT: forest floor
SIZE: $9\frac{1}{2}$ in (24 cm)

Tapaculos of the genus *Pteroptochos* are the largest and strongest-legged of the family. The Black-throated Huet-huet (named for the sound of its call) lives in thickets and heavy undergrowth in wooded areas, primarily in the densest forests, but occasionally in deforested areas. It is a solitary bird, except when it forms breeding pairs during the season.

The Black-throated Huet-huet hunts for insects, especially beetles and their larvae, by moving rapidly across the ground or over mats of bamboo, and by exploring rotting fallen trees. It uncovers its prey by turning leaves and debris over with its bill. When pursued, it usually runs away but occasionally flies short distances before hiding in low trees.

14/ SLATY BRISTLEFRONT
Merulaxis ater
RANGE: SE Brazil
HABITAT: forest thickets
SIZE: $7\frac{1}{2}$ in (19 cm)

The Slaty Bristlefront lives on mountain slopes in tangled vegetation often containing bamboo, epiphytes or large vine-covered boulders. It works up and down steep banks, knocking over deposits of large dead leaves and creeping over and under boulders to search for insects. It walks with its body held horizontally and does not cock up its tail quite as much as other tapaculos.

When the Slaty Bristlefront pauses to sing, it lifts its body diagonally and points its bill skyward. The long, vibrant song consists of rapidly delivered clear metallic notes that fall in pitch and volume, ending with a faster series of soft guttural notes. The call is ringing and metallic.

15/ UNICOLORED TAPACULO
Scytalopus unicolor
RANGE: Andes S to N Bolivia
HABITAT: mountain forest thickets and undergrowth
SIZE: 5 in (13 cm)

The Unicolored Tapaculo inhabits high-altitude, humid and wet forest containing low tangles of vegetation, which in Peru often includes bamboo. Seeking insect prey, it hops on the ground or through fallen moss-covered limbs or bushy vegetation, often holding its tail upright. Members of this genus are very difficult to observe. At times these birds simply vanish underground, scurrying under piles of fallen leaves like rodents. Many a frustrated observer has stood "toe to bill" with a *Scytalopus* at his feet, singing but hidden under thick plants or tangles of roots.

COTINGAS, MANAKINS

KINGLET CALYPTURA

LOVELY COTINGA

SNOWY COTINGA

BARRED FRUITEATER

SCREAMING PIHA

AMAZONIAN UMBRELLABIRD

THREE-WATTLED BELLBIRD

♀

♂

♂

♀

courtship display

♂

♂

GUIANAN COCK OF THE ROCK

♂

WHITE-BEARDED MANAKIN

THRUSHLIKE MANAKIN

♂

LONG-TAILED MANAKIN

ce *chrysopterus*

♀

♂

RED-CAPPED MANAKIN

♂

courtship display

GOLDEN-WINGED MANAKIN

COTINGAS, MANAKINS

FAMILY COTINGIDAE
Cotingas

Small to large forest birds. Plumage variable. Males often brightly colored and ornamented, females duller. Nest usually in trees. Eggs 1–3, usually buff or olive, spotted and blotched with dark brown and gray. Incubation 19–28 days, nestling period 21–44 days. 65 species.

1/ BARRED FRUITEATER
Pipreola arcuata

RANGE: E and W slopes of the Andes, from W Venezuela and N Colombia to C Bolivia
HABITAT: cloud forest, generally above 6,500 ft (2,000 m)
SIZE: 8½ in (22 cm)

Fruiteaters forage singly or in pairs in the middle and upper layers of humid cloud forests, feeding on a variety of small fruits and small amounts of insect prey. Like other cotingas, they pluck fruit and snatch insects by sallying out in short flights from a perch. As they are quite heavy-bodied birds, they take fruit from a perched position or in a clumsy hover.

The Barred Fruiteater is the largest member of its genus and tends to occur at the highest altitudes, usually from 6,500 ft (2,000 m) up to the tree line at some 10,000–11,500 ft (3,000–3,500 m). Its song is an extremely high, thin, almost hissing *se-e-e-e-e-e-a-a-a-a*.

2/ KINGLET CALYPTURA
Calyptura cristata　　　　　　　　　　Ⅰ

RANGE: near Rio de Janeiro, Brazil
HABITAT: virgin forest, dense secondary growth
SIZE: 3 in (7.5 cm)

This is by far the smallest of the cotingas and, although externally similar to a manakin, aspects of its anatomy clearly show it to be a true cotinga. It has a very restricted range and no ornithologist has seen it this century.

Descriptions of foraging behavior indicate a diminutive opportunist, peering and poking into crevices for arthropods and snatching a ripe berry here and there. Its voice was reported to be loud for such a small bird and was described as brief, raucous and disagreeable.

3/ SCREAMING PIHA
Lipaugus vociferans

RANGE: Amazonian South America, S Venezuela, Guianas, SE coastal Brazil
HABITAT: lowland forest
SIZE: 9¾–11 in (25–28 cm)

The Screaming Piha lives among the trees, feeding primarily on fruit, as well as some insects and other arthropods. It is inconspicuous and often difficult to see, but the explosive, whistled song of the male is one of the characteristic sounds of the South American rain forest.

Male Screaming Pihas occupy large territories which they defend by their loud voices. These territories may be arranged in groups, with several birds adjacent to one another. The territorial call begins with a series of 3–5 accelerating, increasingly loud whistled *weeoo* notes, and

finishes with a piercing pair of *weeet weeoo* notes, dropping in pitch at the end. The males call frequently through the day, spending only a fraction of their time feeding.

4/ LOVELY COTINGA
Cotinga amabilis

RANGE: S Mexico to N Costa Rica
HABITAT: tropical forest
SIZE: 7¾ in (20 cm)

The Lovely Cotinga is one of the most striking of all Central American birds. The northernmost of the 7 species in the genus *Cotinga* occurs alone or in mixed-species flocks high in the forest canopy. Here, it feeds mostly on fruit. Like many Central American forest birds, it moves to higher ground to nest, dispersing to lower altitudes at other times. As with the males of the other *Cotinga* species, the intense blue of the male Lovely Cotinga's plumage results from the effect of light hitting the feathers, and is not a pigment as in cotingas of other genera.

The Lovely Cotinga has a strong, undulating flight. As they beat the air, the outer wing feathers of the male produce a rattling, tinkling sound, and this noise features in his courtship display flights above the canopy. The female uses strands of vegetation and fungus to construct the flimsy, shallow, cup nest. This is usually placed at least 100 ft (30 m) high in a large tree. As with some other cotingas, the female may destroy the nest after the young fledge, possibly to reduce the chance of a predator discovering the nest site, which may be used year after year.

5/ SNOWY COTINGA
Carpodectes nitidus

RANGE: Caribbean slopes of Honduras, Nicaragua, Costa Rica, W Panama
HABITAT: evergreen tropical forest
SIZE: 7½–8¼ in (19–21 cm)

The Snowy Cotinga is a rather tame bird, sometimes allowing people to approach close by. Much of the time it lives in the tree canopy, but it also frequents the forest edge and clearings that have

scattered trees. Its white color and pigeonlike flight have earned it the local name of *Paloma del espiritu santo* or "Dove of the holy spirit."

The Snowy Cotinga is primarily a fruit-eater but very little is known of its ecology. The few existing reports indicate that it may feed in flocks of 15 or more birds and that it may also take insects and spiders from the foliage.

6/ AMAZONIAN UMBRELLABIRD
Cephalopterus ornatus

RANGE: Amazonian South America, S Venezuela
HABITAT: open clearings, river edge or islands in lowland rain forest
SIZE: 20 in (51 cm)

This is the largest of all cotingas and one of the largest passerines. The 3 species of umbrellabird take their name from their fluffy, platformlike crests. The Amazonian Umbrellabird is entirely black, with a stout, crowlike bill and a long, feathered wattle hanging from its throat. The female is slightly smaller than the male and her crest and wattle are less well developed.

The most widespread of the umbrellabirds, the Amazonian Umbrellabird tends to haunt open patches in the rain forest and travelers occasionally glimpse it crossing over large rivers, with a deeply undulating flight, some 150 ft (50 m) above the water. The male's advertisement call is a long, booming *boooo* note, which he utters in an elaborate display, leaning forward and down with his crest spread and throat-wattle dangling.

7/ THREE-WATTLED BELLBIRD
Procnias tricarunculata

RANGE: Honduras to W Panama
HABITAT: breeds in forests above 5,000 ft (1,500 m); migrates to lower tropical forests
SIZE: male 11¾ in (30 cm); female 9¾ in (25 cm)

This is one of 4 species of bellbird, renowned for their extremely loud, explosive calls, the striking differences in plumage between the sexes, and the variety of bizarre wattles that adorn the heads of the males. In the Three-wattled Bellbird, one of the wattles hangs from the base of the upper mandible, while the other 2 hang from the edges of the bird's mouth. Bellbirds are difficult to observe because they restrict their activities to the crowns of large, fruiting trees. The huge gape of their bills allows them to eat large fruits whole and regurgitate the seeds later.

Male Three-wattled Bellbirds take no part in nesting, and try to mate with several females in each season. They defend large territories with their calls, which are some of the loudest sounds uttered by any bird. Each call consists of a deafening, explosive *bock* note, sounding more like a hammer hitting an anvil than the bell from which the bellbirds take their common name. This is followed by a sharp, ringing squeak. The female Three-wattled Bellbird builds the shallow cup nest of thin twigs, and must tend the single young in the nest for more than 30 days until it fledges – one of the longest nestling periods of any passerine.

8/ GUIANAN COCK OF THE ROCK
Rupicola rupicola
RANGE: **S Venezuela, Guianas, N Brazil, E Colombia**
HABITAT: **lowland tropical forest with rocky outcrops and boulders**
SIZE: **12½ in (32 cm)**

The brilliant-orange male Guianan Cock of the Rock and the equally handsome, blood-red or orange-red male Andean Cock of the Rock *R. peruviana* are among the most brightly colored of all tropical American birds. They are also remarkable for their group displays at traditional sites called "leks." Here, each male owns an area, or "court," of his own.

At a Guianan Cock of the Rock lek, 5–25 males occupy courts that may be adjacent or up to 33 ft (10 m) apart; each court is 3–6 ft (1–2 m) in diameter. Here they compete for the attention of the drabber, visiting females. The males are highly aggressive toward one another and perform ritualized threat displays, such as perching on vertical branches with the feathers of their wing and tail coverts fluffed up. They often utter a raucous *ka-rhaaow* call when flying into the lek and a variety of squawking and cawing notes during their aggressive encounters. They also make a low, whistling sound with their wings.

When a female visits the lek, the males fly down to the bare dirt patch in the center of each display court and "freeze" in a crouching posture. The female chooses a partner but is often interrupted by a neighboring, competing male as she tries to mate with her chosen male. She alone builds the nest, a large cup of mud and vegetation attached to a sheer rock face, cave or crevice. The same nest site may be used year after year.

FAMILY PIPRIDAE
Manakins
Small, forest birds. Large head, short bill. Males brightly colored, usually with much black. Females olive-green. Cup nest, low in cover. Eggs 2, whitish or buff, with brown markings. Incubation 17–21 days, nestling period 13–15 days. 51 species.

9/ THRUSHLIKE MANAKIN
Schiffornis turdinus
RANGE: **S Mexico to W Ecuador, Amazonia, Venezuela, Guianas**
HABITAT: **tropical forest**
SIZE: **6½ in (17 cm)**

The male Thrushlike Manakin has drab, brownish plumage, like the female. This is a marked contrast to that of most other males in its family, which are much brighter than the females, and there is now some uncertainty over the classification of this and the other 2 species of *Schiffornis*.

The song of the Thrushlike Manakin is a pure, syncopated, whistled series of 3–4 phrases, showing distinct variations across the bird's range.

As with the true manakins, the male may mate with several females, but he does not perform elaborate displays. Instead, he relies on persistent singing to defend his territory. The female alone builds the large cup nest composed of leaves, moss and twigs, placing it inconspicuously near the trunk or in the fork of a tree. The nestlings are notable for their long, copious black down.

10/ WHITE-BEARDED MANAKIN
Manacus manacus
RANGE: **tropical South America, NE Argentina; Trinidad**
HABITAT: **secondary growth woodland, riverside forest, forest edge**
SIZE: **4 in (10 cm)**

The White-bearded Manakin is one of the best-known species in the family, haunting a variety of wooded, lowland habitats, usually below 3,300 ft (1,000 m). The attractive white, black and gray plumage of the male contrasts with the dull olive-green of the female.

This is one of the few species of manakin that displays in a concentrated "lek" of small, adjacent courts. Each male creates his own display court, clearing leaves and vegetation from a patch of forest floor about 3 ft (1 m) wide. A large lek may host more than 50 males, and is usually first detected from many yards away by the birds' bright calls and the firecrackerlike snaps made by the males' specialized wing feathers. The display behavior includes a number of ritualized postures, movements and wing noises performed on the bare display court and on vertical and horizontal perches near the ground. Females visit one or more leks, choose a mate, and perform all the nesting duties alone.

11/ GOLDEN-WINGED MANAKIN
Masius chrysopterus
RANGE: **Andes from W Venezuela to Ecuador, E Andes in N Peru**
HABITAT: **humid cloud forest, from 4,000–7,500 ft (1,200–2,300 m); down to 2,000 ft (600 m) in W Colombia and Ecuador**
SIZE: **4 in (10 cm)**

The Golden-winged Manakin was until recently almost completely unknown in the wild. The male's combination of velvety-black and canary-yellow plumage, recumbent crest and black horns is unique in the family. The waxy, barbless feathers behind the crown vary in color according to race. The race *M. c. chrysopterus* of the eastern slopes of the Andes is illustrated.

The Golden-winged Manakin feeds on a variety of small fruits. It may forage alone or in mixed flocks of tanagers and other fruit-eating birds. The males defend large territories with froglike *nurrt* calls. Their complex displays include flying down on to a mossy fallen log, rebounding, and turning right around in midair. On the log, they adopt motionless, chin-down postures, with the tail pointed up, and side-to-side bowing displays, with the body plumage fluffed and the tail cocked at an angle.

12/ LONG-TAILED MANAKIN
Chiroxiphea linearis
RANGE: **W Central America, from S Mexico to N Costa Rica**
HABITAT: **dry woodland, open secondary growth**
SIZE: **male 7¾–8½ in (20–22 cm); female 4¼ in (11 cm)**

The male of this species is remarkable for the extremely elongated, wirelike, central tail feathers that are 4–5 in (10–12 cm) long and extend well beyond the rest of his tail. The females are dull olive-green, with only slightly elongated central tail feathers. As in most other manakins, immature males are similar in plumage to the females, but molt gradually over 3–4 years into the brilliant, full adult male regalia.

Male Long-tailed Manakins exhibit extraordinary courtship behavior, in which pairs or trios perform cooperative displays. In the main "cartwheel" display, the birds hop along a thin horizontal branch, each male, in turn, leaping up and fluttering over his companion or companions, when he reaches a special jumping off spot. The males within each group establish a dominance hierarchy, and if a visiting female remains at the display site to mate, the subordinate males fly off to leave her with the dominant male.

13/ RED-CAPPED MANAKIN
Pipra mentalis
RANGE: **S Mexico to W Colombia and W Ecuador**
HABITAT: **lowland tropical forest and secondary growth woodland**
SIZE: **4 in (10 cm)**

The male Red-capped Manakin defends a territory in the trees, advertising his presence with short *psit* calls and a longer, whistled *ptsweee* repeated frequently throughout the day. He can also produce a mechanical *snap* noise with his wing feathers in flight. The center of display activity is a main horizontal perch at least 13 ft (4 m) above the forest floor. The male performs flight displays to this perch from positions 16–32 ft (5–10 m) away, giving an excited, accelerating series of calls as he lands.

On the main perch, the male performs a variety of rituals, including the "backward slide," in which he lowers his foreparts, spreads his wings slightly, stretches his legs, exposing the yellow thighs, and slides backward along the perch with a series of extremely rapid steps. As in other manakins, the olive-green female carries out all the parental duties.

WHITE MONJITA

EASTERN PHOEBE

WHITE-FRONTED
GROUND TYRANT

race *pica*

♂

♀

race *nanus*

PIED WATER TYRANT

VERMILION FLYCATCHER

race *mexicanus*

SCISSOR-TAILED
FLYCATCHER

juv

EASTERN KINGBIRD

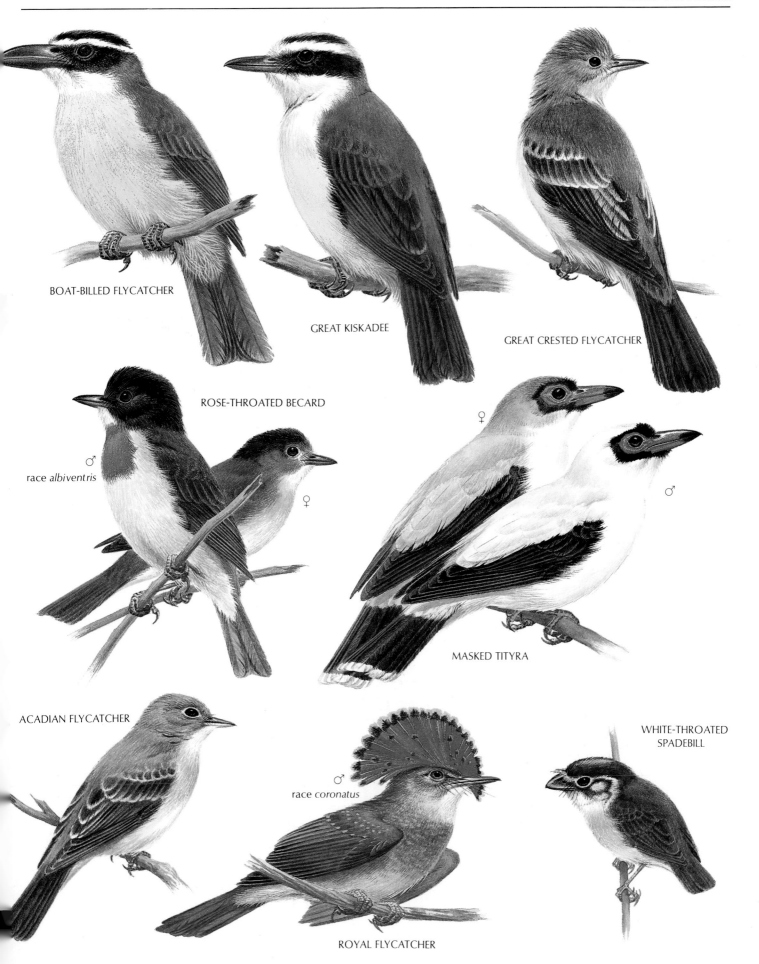

BOAT-BILLED FLYCATCHER

GREAT KISKADEE

GREAT CRESTED FLYCATCHER

ROSE-THROATED BECARD

race *albiventris* ♂

♀

♀ MASKED TITYRA ♂

ACADIAN FLYCATCHER

WHITE-THROATED SPADEBILL

race *coronatus* ♂

ROYAL FLYCATCHER

TYRANT FLYCATCHERS

FAMILY TYRANNIDAE
Tyrant flycatchers

Small to medium perching birds. Plumage generally dull olive above, yellowish or whitish below; some species with black, gray, brown, chestnut and white, some with red, orange, yellow or white crown stripes, many with crests (large and bright in 1 species). Sexes generally similar. Nests very variable, from woven cups in trees to globular nests with side entrances, hanging nests and excavated cavities. Eggs 2–8, whitish, sometimes mottled brown. Incubation 14–20 days, nestling period 14–23 days. 397 species.

1/ WHITE-THROATED SPADEBILL
Platyrinchus mystaceus

RANGE: **S Mexico to Argentina and Bolivia; Trinidad and Tobago**
HABITAT: **humid forest undergrowth, forest edge, second growth, open brush**
SIZE: **4 in (10 cm)**

This tiny, inconspicuous, stub-tailed flycatcher is usually found alone or in pairs, foraging somewhat nonchalantly for insects among the branches of the forest understory. It will perch silently for long periods, occasionally flitting its wings nervously, but when it spies an insect creeping along the underside of a nearby leaf it makes a quick dash and scoops it up with its broad, shovel-shaped bill. When it does call, it utters a short sharp *squeep*, and has a thin, high, buzzing song. The male usually has a concealed yellow crown stripe, which is much smaller or entirely lacking in the female.

In Mexico this species is found close to sea level, but in Bolivia it is most common at altitudes of 3,000–6,500 ft (900–2,000 m). It nests in trees, building a compact, cup nest of plant fibers.

2/ ROYAL FLYCATCHER
Pnychorhynchus coronatus

RANGE: **S Mexico to Guianas, Bolivia, Brazil**
HABITAT: **shaded lower levels of humid forest edge, often near streams**
SIZE: **6½ in (16.5 cm)**

The Royal Flycatcher is a rather nondescript-looking bird, but very occasionally, when aroused, it has been seen to erect its crest to form a spectacular fan. In males the crest feathers are vermilion tipped with blue, but in females the vermilion is replaced by orange in some races and yellow in others. Normally, the closed crest projecting backward, and its long broad bill give this species a hammer-headed appearance.

The birds are usually seen alone or in pairs in shady lowland forest, where they perch on low branches and sally out in pursuit of flying insects. Their broad bills make efficient insect-traps, and the long bristles on either side may help to catch prey and protect their eyes.

The nest is an elongated, loose, baglike structure up to 6 ft (1.8 m) long, attached to a slender branch or vine above a shaded stream.

3/ ACADIAN FLYCATCHER
Empidonax virescens

RANGE: **breeds USA from Great Lakes region S to E Texas, Gulf coast and C Florida; winters in Central and South America**
HABITAT: **moist, mature woodland**
SIZE: **5½–6½ in (14–16.5 cm)**

The flycatchers of the genus *Empidonax* are all very alike, being small, erect tail-flickers with similar habits, but their songs are distinctive. The song of the Acadian Flycatcher is particularly memorable, since the explosive *peet-sa*, with the accent on the first syllable, sounds like a demand for pizza.

Typically found in wet woodland, the Acadian Flycatcher hunts beneath the canopy of tall trees, darting after flying insects and catching them on the wing. Its nest is a frail, saucer-shaped basket suspended from horizontal forked twigs and lined with grasses, plant down, spiders' webs and, in the South, Spanish moss. From below, the nest is well camouflaged with long streamers.

4/ EASTERN PHOEBE
Sayornis phoebe

RANGE: **breeds N and E North America; winters SE and SC USA to Mexico**
HABITAT: **woods, farms, usually near water**
SIZE: **7 in (18 cm)**

Named for its pleasantly raspy *fee-bee* song, delivered incessantly during the breeding season, the Eastern Phoebe is a familiar sight on farmland and wooded roadsides throughout much of North America. It hunts in typical flycatcher fashion, sallying after insects from an exposed perch, and wagging its tail from side to side in a distinctive manner as it lands. When prospecting above a quiet pond surface for flies, it may hover briefly or flutter in pursuit like a butterfly, its bill clicking as it snaps up a meal.

An opportunist nester, it often uses man-made structures as breeding sites, favoring niches protected from the weather such as the rafters of farm outbuildings, porches and bridge supports.

5/ VERMILION FLYCATCHER
Pyrocephalus rubinus

RANGE: **breeds SW USA to S Argentina; a few birds wander to California and Gulf coast in winter**
HABITAT: **semiarid woodland near streams, ponds and rivers**
SIZE: **5½–6½ in (14–16.5 cm)**

Sallying out from a favored perch over a shallow pond or stream bed, a male Vermilion Flycatcher is a spectacular sight, with his brilliant plumage unique among tyrant flycatchers. By comparison, the female is undistinguished, with only a wash of salmon on her lower belly. Of the 12 or so races that have been described, those illustrated are *P. r. mexicanus*, found from southwestern USA to Mexico, and the race *P. r. nanus*, which occurs only in the Galapagos Islands, apart from San Cristobal (Chatham) Island. The Galapagos race has been isolated long enough to have developed distinct plumage – paler, duller red in males and plain yellowish underparts in females, rather than the streaked, creamy pink ones of mainland females. It has shorter wings and tail, longer legs and a different song.

As befits his dazzling coloration, the male is bold and aggressive in defense of the nest. He also puts on a fine courtship display, rising vertically in the air on vibrating wings with crest erect and tail lifted, singing his soft, tinkling song ecstatically, then hovering and slowly fluttering down to the female.

6/ WHITE-FRONTED GROUND TYRANT
Muscisaxicola albifrons

RANGE: **Peru to NW Bolivia and N Chile**
HABITAT: **rocky hillsides with bushes, at 13,000–16,500 ft (4,000–5,000 m)**
SIZE: **9 in (23 cm)**

The ground tyrants are long-legged mountain birds that hunt on the ground, rather like pipits. This is the largest and also the one found at the highest altitudes. The rocks and scattered bushes of its open habitat provide commanding perches for spotting its invertebrate prey, and when it does so it makes a quick flight or a dash across the ground to snatch it.

Most ground tyrants build open cup nests in crevices between rocks on the ground, but the details for this species are unknown.

7/ WHITE MONJITA
Xolmis irupero
RANGE: E Brazil, Uruguay, Paraguay, E Bolivia, N Argentina
HABITAT: open country, brush, savanna
SIZE: 6½ in (17 cm)

This relatively quiet, strikingly white and black flycatcher usually hunts from a perch. It will sit patiently on an exposed branch or fencepost, watching the ground intently. When the White Monjita spies an insect it flies down in graceful fashion to seize its meal. If a suitable perch is not available, it may hover briefly to search for prey. Its normal flight is swift and undulating, but the birds never seem to go far. White Monjitas nest in tree cavities and the abandoned nests of ovenbirds. They are often parasitized by the Shiny Cowbird *Molothrus bonariensis*.

8/ PIED WATER TYRANT
Fluvicola pica
RANGE: Panama, N and C South America E of the Andes; Trinidad
HABITAT: river banks, ponds and marshes
SIZE: 4¾–5½ in (12–14 cm)

Often seen in pairs around freshwater marshes and ponds in lowlands, these attractive and relatively tame flycatchers feed by gleaning insects from foliage on or near the ground, or over the water. While waiting for their next meal they frequently flick their tails downward, sometimes giving a distinctive nasal, buzzing *zhreeo* call.

In Trinidad they nest throughout the year, weaving a ball of dried grasses and leaves at the end of a small branch or in a bush, often over water, and lining the nest with feathers.

There are 2 races: *F. p. pica* is from Colombia, Venezuela, the Guianas, northern Brazil and Trinidad, while the southern race *F. p. albiventer*, sometimes considered a separate species, is from southern Brazil, eastern Bolivia, Paraguay, Uruguay and northern Argentina.

9/ GREAT CRESTED FLYCATCHER
Myiarchus crinitus
RANGE: breeds E North America from SC and E Canada to Texas and Gulf coast; winters S Florida to Mexico and South America
HABITAT: open woods, woodland edge
SIZE: 7–8 in (18–20 cm)

This noisy flycatcher is a familiar bird in settled areas, where its annual return to breed in specially provided nest-boxes is often eagerly awaited. If there are no nest-boxes, the birds will occupy deserted woodpecker holes, hollow posts and a variety of other cavities, natural and artificial, provided they are near open areas where they can pursue flying insects.

Great Crested Flycatchers and some other cavity-nesting flycatchers are well known for their habit of using cast snakeskins as nesting material. It was once thought that these somehow repelled marauding snakes on the prowl for eggs and nestlings, but the presence of various plastics in many nests suggests that the birds simply have a preference for such materials.

10/ GREAT KISKADEE
Pitangus sulphuratus
RANGE: S Texas to Argentina
HABITAT: semiopen areas, streamside thickets, woodland edge, orchards
SIZE: 9–9¾ in (23–25 cm)

One of the biggest and brightest of the tyrant flycatchers, the Great Kiskadee is a bold, noisy and aggressive opportunist. It dives for small fish or tadpoles from a perch, kingfisher-style, but after 3–4 such dives it has to dry out in the sun. At other times it will launch itself into the air to capture beetles, wasps and other flying insects, and may even forage for berries and seeds when insects are scarce. Its wide diet also includes the occasional small mammal, frog or lizard.

This bird is named for its bawling *kis-ka-dee* calls, usually heard in the morning or evening. It builds a bulky, domed nest of straw and weed stems, sometimes incorporating the smaller nest of another flycatcher in its own.

11/ BOAT-BILLED FLYCATCHER
Megarhynchus pitangua
RANGE: C Mexico to NW Peru, S Brazil and N Argentina
HABITAT: savanna, forest edge, clearings, plantations, usually near water
SIZE: 9 in (23 cm)

The massive, powerful bill of this large tyrant flycatcher reflects its varied diet which includes not only insects, but also berries, catkins and even the occasional frog or other small vertebrate. It can be found along almost any forest edge, but is most common along river banks where it often makes itself evident by its quarrelsome behavior and habit of mobbing passing hawks.

The nest is an open stick cup built high above the ground near the end of a bough. The female incubates the eggs alone, but the male stands guard in her absence.

12/ SCISSOR-TAILED FLYCATCHER
Tyrannus forficata
RANGE: breeds SW USA, uncommonly E to Mississippi; wanders N to Canada on migration; winters extreme S USA to Mexico and Central America
HABITAT: open country with scattered trees and brush
SIZE: 11¾–15 in (30–38 cm)

Spectacular behavior, delicate beauty and an exquisite forked tail place the scissor-tailed flycatcher in a class by itself. The courtship "sky dance" is famous, involving vertical and zigzag dives, tumbles and somersaults with the long tail feathers streaming and flicking like satin ribbons, all accented by rolling cackles that sound appropriately like applause.

In the true flycatcher manner it hunts from a perch, darting out after flying insects or dropping to the ground for grasshoppers or crickets. Between forays it will sit quietly on a fencepost, bare branch or treetop, sometimes for hours.

13/ EASTERN KINGBIRD
Tyrannus tyrannus
RANGE: breeds S Canada through USA to the Gulf coast; winters in Central and South America
HABITAT: open areas, woodland edge, streamsides, orchards
SIZE: 8¼–9 in (21–23 cm)

Celebrated for its dauntless defence of its breeding territory, the male Eastern Kingbird will attack anything that enters its airspace. Its main targets are larger birds, such as crows and hawks, which are chased relentlessly and rained with blows. At times this species will even land on its flying victim to knock it about more effectively. Its noisy, blustering calls typify its temperament.

Outside the breeding season it often forages in small, loose flocks. It feeds mainly on flying insects taken on the wing, but will also pluck berries from bushes while hovering. At dusk it retreats to a communal roost which may number hundreds or even thousands of birds.

14/ ROSE-THROATED BECARD
Pachyramphus aglaiae
RANGE: S Texas and S Arizona to Costa Rica
HABITAT: open woodland and dry scrub
SIZE: 6 in (15 cm)

Traditionally classified with the cotingas, the becards are now considered to be tyrant flycatchers. This species is the northernmost representative of the genus. Pairs are often seen perched conspicuously on the tops of trees on the edges of open areas, where they feed on insects, spiders and fruits seized during short flights.

The nest is a large, globular structure of sticks and other assorted vegetation, suspended from a branch some 20–70 ft (6–20 m) above a clearing. The clutch size of 5–6 eggs is large for a tropical bird and may be related to the protection provided by the walled hanging nest.

15/ MASKED TITYRA
Tityra semifasciata
RANGE: S Mexico to W Ecuador, Guianas and Amazonia
HABITAT: clearings in moist tropical forest, open woodland and second growth
SIZE: 8 in (20 cm)

Tityras are common birds of the forest edge throughout the American tropics. The Masked Tityra is the most wide-ranging species: a strong flier with a stout bill, it is frequently seen perched conspicuously in the top of a tree near a clearing and often draws attention to itself with noisy croaks and low grunts. The birds form monogamous pairs which stay together throughout the year and nest in cavities, sometimes driving off woodpeckers from choice sites. The female incubates the eggs, but both parents feed the young.

TYRANT FLYCATCHERS, SHARPBILL, PLANTCUTTERS, PITTAS, NEW ZEALAND WRENS, ASITIES, LYREBIRDS, SCRUB-BIRDS

SHORT-TAILED PYGMY TYRANT

race *rubrigastra*

race *wetmorei*

MANY-COLORED RUSH TYRANT

COMMON TODY FLYCATCHER

TORRENT TYRANNULET

SLENDER-FOOTED TYRANNULET

race *frater*

SHARPBILL

♂ courtship display

♂

RUFOUS SCRUB-BIRD

♀

SUPERB LYREBIRD

FAMILIES TYRANNIDAE, OXYRUNCIDAE, PHYTOTOMIDAE, PITTIDAE, XENICIDAE, PHILEPITTIDAE, MENURIDAE, ATRICHORNITHIDAE

race *granatina*

GARNET PITTA

race *ussheri*

♀

♂

RUFOUS-TAILED PLANTCUTTER

♂

GURNEY'S PITTA

AFRICAN PITTA

race *chloris*

♂

WATTLED FALSE SUNBIRD

RAINBOW PITTA

♀

RIFLEMAN

TYRANT FLYCATCHERS, SHARPBILL, PLANTCUTTERS, PITTAS, NEW ZEALAND WRENS, ASITIES, LYREBIRDS, SCRUB-BIRDS

1/ SLENDER-FOOTED TYRANNULET
Zimmerius gracilipes

RANGE: Guianas, S Venezuela, E Colombia, S to N Bolivia and E Brazil
HABITAT: forest, savanna, secondary growth
SIZE: $4\frac{1}{2}$ in (11.5 cm)

The Slender-footed Tyrannulet spends most of its time high in the outer canopy of tall trees, where its olive-green and yellow plumage and diminutive size make it very difficult to see against the foliage. Here it flutters about, gleaning insects from the leaves. Its diet also includes some berries. It often occurs singly or in pairs, but also joins mixed-species flocks. The Slender-footed Tyrannulet's call is a sharp, unmelodious *what*.

2/ TORRENT TYRANNULET
Serpophaga cinerea

RANGE: Costa Rica, W Panama, NW Venezuela, Colombia, N Bolivia
HABITAT: rocky streams in foothills and mountains
SIZE: 4 in (10 cm)

The Torrent Tyrannulet typically perches on a rock in midstream or on a bare branch hanging over water, where it nervously flicks its tail up and down as it watches for prey. Flying insects are caught after short pursuits and, at times, other insect food is picked from gravel bars. It usually occurs in pairs. The call note is a soft *tsip*, which is often repeated in a twittering manner, and which has a tonal quality that allows it to be heard above the sound of rushing water.

3/ MANY-COLORED RUSH TYRANT
Tachuris rubrigastra

RANGE: parts of Peru, Bolivia, Paraguay, S Brazil, Uruguay, E Argentina
HABITAT: tall cats'-tails and rushes of coastal and freshwater marshes
SIZE: $4\frac{1}{4}$ in (11 cm)

The Many-colored Rush Tyrant is local in distribution, scattered in small populations where suitably extensive habitat exists. Many seemingly suitable sites have not been colonized. It sometimes shows up in other habitats when on migration. This species has relatively long legs, which it uses to clamber about the stems of cats'-tails and rushes to glean insects in a wrenlike fashion. It also makes short sallying flights into the air to catch flying insects.

4/ SHORT-TAILED PYGMY TYRANT
Myiornis ecaudatus

RANGE: Costa Rica S to N Bolivia, Amazonian Brazil, Guianas, Trinidad
HABITAT: humid forest and forest edge
SIZE: $2\frac{3}{4}$ in (7 cm)

This elusive species of open wet and humid tropical forest is a tiny, virtually tailless bird that is the smallest of all the tyrant flycatchers. From its perch it flies up to snatch prey from foliage or

out to capture flying insects. It perches quietly for long periods and is easily overlooked. The voice of the Short-tailed Pygmy Tyrant befits its size – a repeated high-pitched *eek*, which sounds remarkably like a tree frog or a cricket.

5/ COMMON TODY FLYCATCHER
Todirostrum cinereum

RANGE: S Mexico to NW Peru, Bolivia, SE Brazil
HABITAT: bushy areas, secondary growth, thickets, gardens, overgrown clearings
SIZE: $3\frac{1}{2}$–4 in (9–10 cm)

This tiny flycatcher is a common bird, regularly seen in pairs. It forages by moving quickly among leaves to snatch insects, cocking its tail slightly and jerking it from side to side as it flutters and hops within the foliage. Its foraging actions are often more reminiscent of those of wrens than of other tyrant flycatchers. Sometimes it also sallies out after prey. The calls of this species include low, but sharp, chipping notes and a musical trill which members of a pair use to keep in contact with each other.

FAMILY OXYRUNCIDAE
Sharpbill
There is only one species in this family.

6/ SHARPBILL
Oxyruncus cristatus

RANGE: Costa Rica, Panama, SE Venezuela, Guyana, Surinam, E Peru, E and SE Brazil, Paraguay
HABITAT: rain and cloud forest from 1,300–6,000 ft (400–1,800 m), forest edge, secondary growth
SIZE: 6 in (15 cm)

The Sharpbill is a stocky bird which, true to its name, has a sharply pointed, conical bill. It moves rapidly through the forest canopy, alone or in mixed flocks. It gleans insects and spiders from the foliage at the tips of branches or from the bark of large limbs, and also eats ripe berries. To reach

its food, it often hangs upside-down like a tit. Its song is a rough, slightly descending trill.

The long crest of brightly colored, silky feathers on the bird's crown is usually concealed. This crest is crimson or scarlet in most races, including *O. c. frater* of Costa Rica and western Panama, but orange in the race *O. c. hypoglaucus* from Guyana and southeastern Venezuela.

The one nest that has been found was a shallow cup of loosely interwoven leaf stalks and a few dried leaves, with a thin coating of liverworts and spiders' webs. This was secured, with a dried salivalike substance, to a high branch.

FAMILY PHYTOTOMIDAE
Plantcutters
Small, long-tailed birds. Conical beak with serrated edges. Plumage streaked gray-brown above, rufous below in male; gray-brown above, pale ocher below in female. Nest in bushes and trees. Eggs 2–4, greenish-blue with dark spots. Incubation and nestling periods unknown. 3 species.

7/ RUFOUS-TAILED PLANTCUTTER
Phytotoma rara

RANGE: C and SC Chile, extreme W Argentina
HABITAT: open country with scattered bushes and thorn trees, wooded rivers, gardens, orchards
SIZE: $7\frac{1}{2}$–8 in (19–20 cm)

Although the 3 species of plantcutter are traditionally placed in a family of their own, recent data on their biochemistry and natural history suggest that they might be better incorporated in the cotinga family (pp. 230–33). As their name suggests, they use their thick, serrated bills for cutting or chewing off pieces of leaves, buds and fruits. Because of this behavior, the birds are sometimes regarded as pests. This species is also known as the Chilean Plantcutter.

During the breeding season, these birds remain in pairs, but at other times they may occur in groups of up to 6 individuals. The males sing with a rasping, metallic wheeze.

FAMILY PITTIDAE
Pittas
Small, very short-tailed, thrushlike birds of the forest floor. Plumage colorful. Sexes similar or different. Nest large, oval or domed, in fallen branches or bushes. Eggs 2–7 (usually 3–5), glossy white or pale buff, with reddish or purplish speckles or spots and fine lilac or gray markings. Incubation and nestling periods uncertain, probably 15–17 days and 14–21 days. 29 species.

8/ GARNET PITTA
Pitta granatina
RANGE: **peninsular Burma, Sumatra, Borneo**
HABITAT: **swampy forest**
SIZE: **6 in (15 cm)**

The bright colors of the Garnet Pitta conceal rather than draw attention to it in the contrasted shade of the forest floor. The race *P.g. ussheri* occupies northern Borneo, while *P.g. granatina* occurs in the south of the island.

The Garnet Pitta eats fruit, seeds and insects, foraging for them on the ground among leaf litter. It makes a prolonged whistling call that increases in volume and rises in pitch before stopping abruptly. The status of this rare bird is unclear, but it is certainly declining with the felling of its forest habitat.

9/ GURNEY'S PITTA
Pitta gurneyi E
RANGE: **peninsular Thailand and Burma**
HABITAT: **lowland forest**
SIZE: **8¼ in (21 cm)**

This colorful pitta was once described as not uncommon in the forests of Thailand, but so much of its habitat has been destroyed that it has become one of the world's most endangered birds. Indeed, it had not been seen for 34 years until its rediscovery in 1986. Even then, a nest was raided by bird trappers for the cage-bird trade. Gurney's Pitta is most noisy in the morning and evening, uttering a sharp double note accompanied by flapping wings and a jerk of the tail.

10/ AFRICAN PITTA
Pitta angolensis
RANGE: **W Africa from Sierra Leone to Cameroon, then S to N Angola; also Uganda, E Zaire, Tanzania, E Zimbabwe and Mozambique; nonbreeders sometimes seen S as far as Cape Province**
HABITAT: **thick evergreen forest**
SIZE: **8 in (20 cm)**

This bird is the only pitta that occurs in Africa. It prefers dense undergrowth, hopping along beneath the vegetation in search of slugs and insects, especially termites. It will scratch through the cover of leaf litter to the surface of anthills, flitting its tail up and down continually as it does so. If alarmed, the African Pitta utters a short, soft call and usually runs away rapidly, though it may sometimes fly into a tree to crouch out of sight behind a branch. It also has a threat display in which it crouches with feathers fluffed out, wings spread and bill pointing skyward.

11/ RAINBOW PITTA
Pitta iris
RANGE: **N Australia**
HABITAT: **thick bush, monsoon forest**
SIZE: **7 in (18 cm)**

Dense monsoon forest, mangrove swamps and bamboo thickets provide a home for this pitta. Uncommon and sedentary, it searches the forest floor for insects. It rarely flies, keeping to the ground, where it is well concealed and difficult to locate despite its bright coloration. A loud, clear, whistling call (often rendered as *want a whip*) may give it away. The call is often given from a tree in which the bird roosts.

FAMILY XENICIDAE
New Zealand wrens
Small, stocky birds, endemic to New Zealand. Poor fliers. Plumage greenish and whitish with some yellow. Females are generally duller than males. Nest in holes. Eggs 2–5, white. Incubation 19–21 days, nestling period 23–25 days (Rifleman); unknown for other 2 species. 3 species.

12/ RIFLEMAN
Acanthisitta chloris
RANGE: **New Zealand**
HABITAT: **forest, ranging from mature stands to secondary growth scrubland**
SIZE: **3 in (8 cm)**

The Rifleman has 3 races on North, South and Stewart islands, of which the southern race *A. c. chloris* is illustrated. It feeds by spiraling up tree trunks and probing for insects under the bark; its slightly upturned bill is well adapted for this task. It also gleans prey from foliage in the canopy. It remains in family groups for much of the year and is nonmigratory. Breeding takes place from October to January, with some nesting pairs assisted by unmated males.

FAMILY PHILEPITTIDAE
Asities
Plump tree-dwellers, endemic to Madagascar. Plumage black with yellow fringe to feathers in male, greenish in females; or metallic blue and yellow in males, dark green and yellowish in females. Partial breeding details known only for Velvet Asity *Philepitta castanea*: nest pear-shaped, suspended from branch and woven on to it at top, with projecting roof near side entrance at top. Eggs 3, white. 4 species.

13/ WATTLED FALSE SUNBIRD
Neodrepanis coruscans
RANGE: **Madagascar**
HABITAT: **thick forest**
SIZE: **4 in (10 cm)**

Locally common in the past in eastern Madagascar, the Wattled False Sunbird is threatened by habitat destruction. It occupies areas from sea level up to 6,000 ft (1,800 m), becoming increasingly common with higher altitude. In the forest, it may be found anywhere from the ground cover and leaf litter, through the middle layers to the high canopy. It also survives in undergrowth and in saplings in degraded forest, showing a degree of adaptability that may help it to survive in its rapidly changing environment.

The Wattled False Sunbird is solitary or found in small family groups, moving quietly through the foliage with soft, hissing contact calls. It visits long, showy flowers to feed, but, unlike the true sunbirds, its chief food is insects. The female lacks the blue wattle around the eye of the male and is duller and greener above.

FAMILY MENURIDAE
Lyrebirds
Large, long-legged, strong feet. Plumage brown above, buffish or gray-brown below. Males have very long, lyre-shaped tails. Nest bulky, domed. Eggs, usually 1, light gray to purplish-brown, with darker spots or streaks. Incubation about 50 days, nestling period about 47 days. 2 species.

14/ SUPERB LYREBIRD
Menura novaehollandiae
RANGE: **SE Australia, introduced to Tasmania**
HABITAT: **eucalyptus and rain forest**
SIZE: **male 31½–38½ in (80–98 cm); female 29–33 in (74–84 cm)**

The Superb Lyrebird is one of the largest and most remarkable of the passerines, renowned for the male's 20–24 in (50–60 cm) long lyre-shaped tail. It feeds mostly on the ground, scratching for insects and other large invertebrates.

From midwinter, male Superb Lyrebirds scratch up display mounds and sing. The song contains rich and powerful elements, along with a great variety of mimicked sounds from other birds. On still days, the song can be heard from some distance. When a female is present, the male's song becomes more frantic and he raises and vibrates his tail over his head and back. A successful male may mate with several females.

FAMILY ATRICHORNITHIDAE
Scrub-birds
Small, sturdy. Long tail, long legs, small wings. Plumage brown above, white and rufous-brown below. Males have black markings on breast. Nest domed. Eggs 1–2, buffish, brown blotches. Incubation 36–38 days, nestling period 21–28 days (Western Scrub-bird *A. clamosus* only). 2 species.

15/ RUFOUS SCRUB-BIRD
Atrichornis rufescens R
RANGE: **CE Australia**
HABITAT: **forest margins**
SIZE: **6½–7 in (16.5–18 cm)**

The Rufous Scrub-bird is restricted to 5 upland regions in northeastern New South Wales and extreme southeastern Queensland. It inhabits cool temperate rain forest where this adjoins eucalyptus forest, or subtropical rain forest where the canopy is fairly open. Both sites are moist and have dense ground cover. Rufous Scrub-birds can be extremely difficult to spot; usually they are detected only by the male's loud chipping song. Most of these birds are now in protected areas and their populations are being closely monitored.

LARKS, SWALLOWS AND MARTINS

dark phase

light phase

SINGING BUSH LARK

CLAPPER LARK

♂

♀

BLACK-CROWNED FINCH LARK

♂ fall

fall ♀

spring ♂

BLACK LARK

LESSER SHORT-TOED LARK

CRESTED LARK

HOOPOE LARK

♂

SKY LARK

HORNED LARK

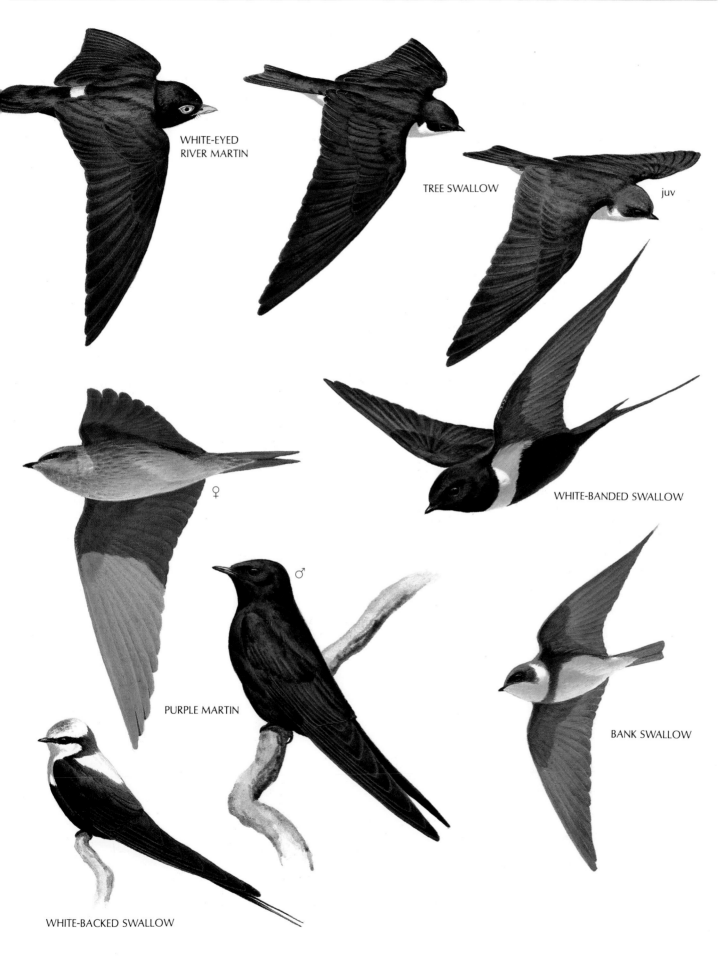

WHITE-EYED RIVER MARTIN

TREE SWALLOW

juv

WHITE-BANDED SWALLOW

♀

♂

PURPLE MARTIN

BANK SWALLOW

WHITE-BACKED SWALLOW

LARKS, SWALLOWS AND MARTINS

FAMILY ALAUDIDAE
Larks

Small ground dwellers, with elongated hind claws. Plumage mainly brown, cryptic, some with black and white markings; males of one species black. Sexes in most species similar. Nest on ground. Eggs 2–6, speckled, in most species. Incubation 10–16 days, nestling period about 10 days. 81 species.

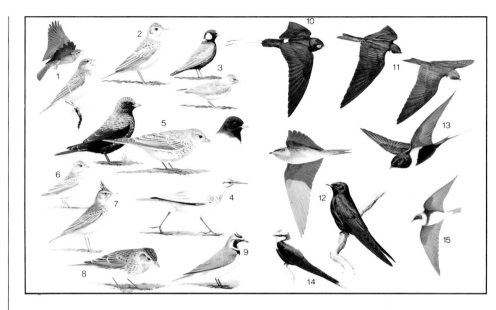

1/ SINGING BUSH LARK
Mirafra javanica

RANGE: **parts of Africa, Arabia, India, Malaysia, Indonesia, Australia**
HABITAT: **grassland, including crops**
SIZE: **5–5½ in (12.5–14 cm)**

This species has more than 20 races spread across its vast range. Its shade of plumage is variable, even within one race, the overall coloration generally matching that of the native habitat. The palest birds tend to occur in areas of bleached sand. It has been suggested that the fresh, darker plumage attained by many birds after the molt is timed to coincide with the rainy season, when the ground is darkest.

Singing Bush Larks feed on the ground, searching for invertebrates and seeds. They have a varied, melodious song, often with mimetic components, which is usually uttered in flight. Their nests are partly domed structures built under grassy tussocks.

2/ CLAPPER LARK
Mirafra apiata

RANGE: **S Africa**
HABITAT: **grassland of the highveld and dry Karoo**
SIZE: **6 in (15 cm)**

This solitary, medium-sized lark is easy to overlook as it forages across the ground for insects and seeds. It becomes conspicuous only when calling and displaying. It often imitates the calls of other birds, from plovers to waxbills, and performs a distinctive display flight consisting of a steep climb, a loud rattling of the wings and a downward dive. The descent is accompanied by a clear, whistling call. The Clapper Lark may repeat this display every 15–30 seconds.

Breeding takes place from October to February, timed to coincide with the ripening of seeds after the rainy period. The domed nest of fine grass and rootlets has a side entrance and is usually concealed at the base of a clump of vegetation.

3/ BLACK-CROWNED FINCH LARK
Eremopterix nigriceps

RANGE: **Cape Verde islands, S Sahara, E Africa, S Arabia, W Pakistan, NW India**
HABITAT: **grassy semidesert**
SIZE: **4 in (10.5 cm)**

These tiny larks are gregarious outside the breeding season and may form mixed foraging flocks in areas where several species occur. They feed on seeds and insects, taking them either from the ground or directly from low vegetation. They walk and run quickly across their dry, open habitat and typically crouch low against the

ground when they stop, although they will also stand more erect on occasion.

The Black-crowned Finch Lark makes a cup nest in bare ground and is one of several desert species that may build a windbreak of pebbles to protect the site.

4/ HOOPOE LARK
Alaemon alaudipes

RANGE: **N Africa, Sahara, Arabia E to Iran, Afghanistan**
HABITAT: **deserts**
SIZE: **7¾ in (20 cm)**

Seemingly well camouflaged on the ground, this lark is striking in flight when it reveals its black and white patterned wings. This wing pattern coloration and the long, downcurved bill are features shared by the much larger and completely unrelated Hoopoe *Upupa epops* (pp. 202–5) and give the bird its name. The Hoopoe Lark walks and runs across the ground, stopping suddenly to dig for food with its bill. Insect larvae provide much of its food, but it will also catch adult insects, snails and even small lizards. It breaks through to a snail's flesh by dropping or hammering the shell against a stone.

The Hoopoe Lark is not a sociable bird, although loose flocks may gather at garbage dumps. In the hottest areas, it avoids nesting on the baking surface, placing its nest several inches off the ground in vegetation.

5/ BLACK LARK
Melanocorypha yeltoniensis

RANGE: **S USSR, C Asia**
HABITAT: **steppe grassland**
SIZE: **7½ in (19 cm)**

The male of this thickset lark has unmistakable plumage – all black in the breeding season, but scalloped with the pale buff fringes of new feathers in the fall. The Black Lark's bill is small and conical, and the bird uses it to feed on seeds through most of the year. It remains on the bleak steppes through the winter, often digging through several inches of snow to reach its food.

It also catches a variety of invertebrates when these become available later in the year.

The song of the Black Lark consists of short phrases uttered from a perch. The nest is a shallow depression in the ground, sheltered by a tussock of plants.

6/ LESSER SHORT-TOED LARK
Calandrella rufescens

RANGE: **Canary Islands, N Africa E through Middle East, C Asia to N China**
HABITAT: **open grassland, semidesert, dry cultivated fields**
SIZE: **5 in (13 cm)**

The Lesser Short-toed Lark varies markedly in the color of its plumage, depending on the background color of its local habitat. The best distinguishing characteristic of this species is its *pritt* call, often uttered as a contact note. A close relative, the Short-toed Lark *C. cinerea*, overlaps with this species in range, and even in mixed flocks it is difficult to tell the 2 birds apart. The marginally larger Short-toed Lark, however, has a distinctly different 2-syllable call.

The Lesser Short-toed Lark feeds largely on insects through the winter. Gregarious outside the breeding season, it becomes territorial when nesting. Northern populations tend to migrate south for the winter.

7/ CRESTED LARK
Galerida cristata

RANGE: **N Africa, Europe, Middle East E to India, N China, Korea**
HABITAT: **open wasteland, arable fields, grassland, semidesert**
SIZE: **7½ in (19 cm)**

This species is remarkably similar to its close relative the Thekla Lark *G. theklae* and is best distinguished by its distinctive *whee, whee, whee, whee-ooo* call. In addition, the Crested Lark tends to breed at lower altitudes.

The Crested Lark spends most of its time on or near the ground, often perching on rocks and low vegetation. It has adapted to many artificial environments; indeed, it has been suggested that the species is steadily shifting its emphasis from steppe and semidesert habitats into areas where cultivation, deforestation and settlement have created open terrain.

8/ SKY LARK
Alauda arvensis

RANGE: **Europe, extreme N Africa, Middle East, NC and E Asia, Japan; introduced to Vancouver Island (Canada), Hawaii, Australia and New Zealand**
HABITAT: **open areas, arable fields**
SIZE: **7 in (18 cm)**

The Sky Lark is one of the best known species, renowned for its varied, prolonged song which is almost exclusively given in flight as the bird rapidly climbs, hovers and gradually descends.

This species has adapted well to cultivation and is now one of the most typical farmland birds in Europe. It feeds on the ground, taking seeds, grain and insects both from the surface and from low vegetation. The more northerly populations migrate southward for the winter.

9/ HORNED LARK
Eremophila alpestris

RANGE: **breeds high Arctic and mountains of Eurasia, SW and C Asia, Atlas Mts, most of North America; N races winter S of breeding range; isolated nonmigratory population in Andes**
HABITAT: **breeds Arctic, steppe and mountain plains in Old World, diverse habitats in North America; winters on beaches, coastal dunes, salt marshes and low-lying arable land**
SIZE: **6 in (15 cm)**

In Eurasia, the Horned Lark's distribution is discontinuous and widely separated by types of habitat in which different species of lark predominate. In North America, however, this species occurs in a variety of open habitats, including prairies, pastures, cultivated fields and deserts. There, the absence of competition from other lark species enables it to live much more widely. No fewer than 41 races have been described from its vast range, of which the northeastern North American race *E. a. alpestris* is shown here.

Northern populations of the Horned Lark tend to be highly migratory, wintering in flocks when they feed mainly on seeds. During the breeding season, the birds appear to be largely insectivorous. They feed on the ground and are almost constantly on the move as they forage.

FAMILY HIRUNDINIDAE
Swallows and martins
Small, streamlined, highly aerial birds, with wide gapes. Long, pointed wings. Tail usually forked. Plumage chiefly metallic blue-black, greenish black or brown above, pale or chestnut below. Sexes similar. Mud nests, holes or burrows. Eggs 1–8, white, some spotted red-brown. Incubation 13–16 days, nestling period 16–24 days (24–28 days in New World martins). 81 species.

10/ WHITE-EYED RIVER MARTIN
Pseudochelidon sirintarae   Ⅰ

RANGE: **C Thailand**
HABITAT: **river marshes in winter; summer habitat unknown**
SIZE: **6 in (15 cm)**

This species was discovered as recently as 1968, roosting in reedbeds in winter on the 62,000 acre (25,000 hectare) Lake Boraphet in Nakhon Sawan Province, central Thailand. In 1968, 10 birds were found, followed by 2 more in 1972. All that is known about the ecology of these birds is that they roost with thousands of swallows of other species.

The only other existing species in the genus *Pseudochelidon* is the African River Martin *P. eurystomina*, which occurs in Gabon and along the lower Congo and Ubangi rivers. Both these birds are unlike all other members of the family and probably diverged from the rest of the swallows and martins early in their evolution.

11/ TREE SWALLOW
Tachycineta bicolor

RANGE: **breeds C Alaska and Canada to CE USA; winters S USA, Caribbean, Central America**
HABITAT: **open areas near water, especially flooded areas with dead trees**
SIZE: **5–6 in (12.5–15 cm)**

During migration, this species forms huge flocks that often roost in the low vegetation of coastal marshes. Although it relies primarily on a diet of flying insects, in extreme cold it has been observed feeding on bayberries.

The Tree Swallow nests in ready-made holes, choosing old woodpecker cavities, crevices and nest-boxes in which to build its cup-shaped nest of dried grasses or pine needles. This is then lined with white feathers. The competition for feathers is keen and adults have been known to pluck feathers from the backs of domestic ducks. The usual clutch contains 4–6 white eggs and extra bird may occasionally assist the parents in caring for the brood.

12/ PURPLE MARTIN
Progne subis

RANGE: **breeds North America; winters in Amazon Basin, and sometimes as far N as Florida**
HABITAT: **open areas, often near water**
SIZE: **7 in (18 cm)**

This species has become intimately associated with human settlement in eastern North America. The Indians of southeastern USA provided calabash gourds for Purple Martins to use as nest sites. In return, the birds mobbed crows and other animals that fed on the Indians' crops or on meat hung out to dry. Early European settlers continued the tradition of providing homes for the birds. In western North America, the birds still nest in natural sites, usually dead trees with woodpecker holes.

Both parents feed the young which fledge within about 4 weeks of hatching. Young birds can catch flying insects within 5 days of fledging and are quickly independent of their parents.

13/ WHITE-BANDED SWALLOW
Atticora fasciata

RANGE: **S Venezuela, Guianas, Amazonian Brazil, NW Bolivia**
HABITAT: **rivers and small clearings, forest edge**
SIZE: **6 in (15 cm)**

Locally common along clear streams and less so along large, muddy rivers, this swallow seems to prefer areas with rocky, fast-flowing water fringed with forest. It usually occurs in small groups, and is both conspicuous and easily identified on the wing, although its deeply forked tail is often held closed in a point.

The White-banded Swallow flies somewhat erratically and close to vegetation and rocks as it pursues flying insects. At rest, it often perches on large rocks or other debris in the water. A whole group of birds may perch unnoticed until they suddenly take to the air.

14/ WHITE-BACKED SWALLOW
Cheramoeca leucosterna

RANGE: **S, E and W Australia**
HABITAT: **dry and sandy areas, forest edge**
SIZE: **6 in (15 cm)**

This somewhat nomadic swallow has recently expanded its range southward toward the coast. Usually seen in pairs or small groups, it favors areas near fresh water. Like others of its family, it feeds on flying insects, but its flight is more fluttering than that of many swallow species.

The White-backed Swallow is relatively quiet, but has a twittering song and gives a single *chip* or *chek* note in flight. It roosts and nests in holes about 30 in (75 cm) or more deep, excavated in sandy river banks, road cuttings and sand dunes. In cold weather, several roosting birds may use a single tunnel, and if the cold lasts for a prolonged period, the birds are able to enter a state of torpor to conserve energy.

15/ BANK SWALLOW
Riparia riparia

RANGE: **breeds North America and Eurasia; winters South America, Africa, Mediterranean, Near East, N India, E China, Southeast Asia**
HABITAT: **open and semi-open areas near water**
SIZE: **12–14 cm (5–5½ in)**

Also known as the Sand Martin outside of North America, this species is well known for its habit of excavating burrows in river banks. Other nest sites include cliffs formed by cuttings, gravel pits, and sawdust and coal dust piles. It typically digs its own burrow using its beak and feet, but it may also renovate old tunnels. The burrows are 1–4 ft (30–120 cm) long and are usually clustered near the top of a bank. Bank Swallows are highly gregarious and nest areas often contain several hundred pairs. The tunnels are so closely packed that they occasionally intersect one another.

Following the breeding season, Bank Swallows migrate south, often in company with other swallows. Together, they can form huge flocks, some containing 250,000 birds.

SWALLOWS AND MARTINS, WAGTAILS AND PIPITS, CUCKOO SHRIKES

BLUE SWALLOW

race *rustica*

race *erythrogaster*

HOUSE MARTIN

BARN SWALLOW

FANTEE SAW-WING

FOREST WAGTAIL

race *yarrellii* juv

race *yarrellii* ♂

race *alba*
"White Wagtail"

PIED WAGTAIL

race *flava*
"Blue-headed Wagtail"

race *feldegg*
"Black-headed Wagtail"

race *leucocephala*
"White-headed Wagtail"

race *flavissima*
♂

race *flavissima*
"Yellow Wagtail"
♀

GOLDEN PIPIT

YELLOW WAGTAIL

WATER PIPIT

♂

♂

ROCK PIPIT

BUFF-BELLIED PIPIT

CAPE LONGCLAW

eclipse plumage ♂

WHITE-WINGED
TRILLER

RICHARD'S PIPIT

♂

♀

LONG-TAILED MINIVET

BLUE CUCKOO-SHRIKE

BLACK-FACED CUCKOO-SHRIKE

SWALLOWS AND MARTINS, WAGTAILS AND PIPITS, CUCKOO SHRIKES

1/ BARN SWALLOW
Hirundo rustica
RANGE: breeds Europe and Asia, N Africa, North America; winters in S hemisphere
HABITAT: open areas, often near water
SIZE: 7 in (18 cm)

Although almost cosmopolitan, this species has only 6 races, including the widespread *H. r. rustica*, which breeds over much of Eurasia and north Africa, and *H. r. erythrogaster* of North America.

The Barn Swallow has benefited greatly from the destruction of forest habitats, the construction of buildings and bridges, and the provision of utility wires and fences. Over much of its nesting range, it attaches its mud nest to the rough walls of barns and other human structures and depends on wires for use as perches. Barn Swallows prey on small flying insects that they catch mainly during low flights over water or moist vegetation.

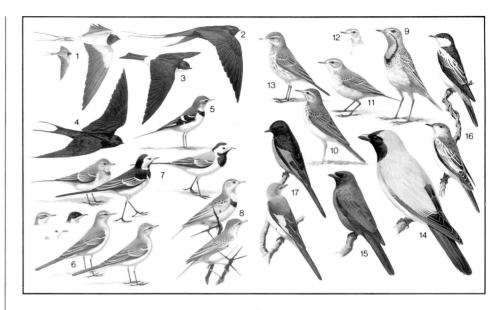

2/ BLUE SWALLOW
Hirundo atrocaerulea
RANGE: parts of E and S Africa
HABITAT: mountain grassland near streams
SIZE: 7¾ in (20 cm)

The Blue Swallow is the only member of its family that is listed in the African *Red Data Book*. Its population is regarded as vulnerable in Zimbabwe and endangered in South Africa because of widespread disturbance to its upland habitat. This species is unusual on several counts. It is migratory, but keeps within the tropics, breeding in the southern part of its range and wintering in Uganda. It shows marked sexual differences, in that the male has a long, forked tail while the female's tail is short. Lastly, it nests alone rather than in groups or colonies.

3/ HOUSE MARTIN
Delichon urbica
RANGE: breeds Europe, Asia (except far N, S), N Africa, irregularly S Africa; winters sub-Saharan Africa, Southeast Asia
HABITAT: open areas particularly near water and human habitations
SIZE: 5 in (13 cm)

House Martins are familiar birds in many areas, having adapted well to human settlement. They feed primarily on flying insects, especially flies and aphids. Outside the nesting season they feed and roost in very large flocks. They have a soft, twittering song, and their calls include shrill, high-pitched contact and alarm calls.

House Martins are often colonial, and their nests are sometimes so close that they are attached to one another. Their original breeding sites include sheltered cliffs, both inland and on the coast, and rock outcrops, but in many parts of their range, particularly in Europe, they have forsaken these sites for man-made ones, under the eaves of buildings, under bridges and in culverts.

4/ FANTEE SAW-WING
Psalidoprocne obscura
RANGE: Sierra Leone to Cameroon
HABITAT: savanna, forest edge, grassland, flooded areas
SIZE: 6½ in (17 cm)

This species occurs in a variety of open habitats, usually in small groups. It flies low, snatching flying insects such as small beetles. The name saw-wing (or rough-wing) used for this and the other 8 *Psalidoprocne* species of Africa and for the 2 American *Stelgidopteryx* species, refers to the series of barbs on the outer web of the outer primary wing feathers of the male. Their function is unknown, but they may produce the noise made by the bird's wings during courtship. Fantee Saw-wings excavate horizontal nest-burrows in road cuttings and earth banks.

FAMILY MOTACILLIDAE
Wagtails and pipits
Small, largely terrestrial, rather slender, long-tailed, long-toed birds. Plumage of wagtails either black and white or with gray, brown, bluish or greenish upperparts and whitish, yellowish or yellow underparts; Golden Pipit and longclaws mostly streaked brown above with yellow or reddish underparts; pipits mostly brown, streaked, paler below. Sexes differ slightly, alike in most pipits. Nest on ground; wagtails also nest in crevices in rocks and walls. Eggs 2–7, white, gray or brown, typically speckled brown. Incubation 12–20 days, nestling period 12–18 days. 58 species.

5/ FOREST WAGTAIL
Dendronanthus indicus
RANGE: breeds Manchuria, Korea, SE USSR; winters Southeast Asia, Indonesia
HABITAT: open areas in moist, often evergreen forest
SIZE: 6 in (15 cm)

This species belongs to a separate genus from most wagtails, and its tail-wagging action is unique in that the whole body sways from side to side, rather than up and down as in *Motacilla* species. The Forest Wagtail also differs from most members of its family in its preference for trees rather than open country and often occurs along wooded streams. Although most of its food is obtained at ground level, it will also run along branches to snatch insects.

6/ YELLOW WAGTAIL
Motacilla flava
RANGE: breeds Europe E across Asia to coastal Alaska; winters Africa, S Asia
HABITAT: marshes, lowland grassland, some arable crops
SIZE: 6½ in (17 cm)

Some 18 races of this bird have been described, in which the head pattern of the breeding male varies. The race *M. f. flavissima* of northwest Europe, Spain and north Africa has the most yellow head and is the race that best deserves the name Yellow Wagtail. Other races include: *M. f. leucocephala* of Mongolia, central Asia and northwest India; *M. f. flava* of northern Europe and southern Africa; and *M. f. feldegg* of southeast Europe, Asia Minor, Iraq and Iran. Females are generally indistinguishable racially.

The Yellow Wagtail occurs in flocks that run gracefully through the ground vegetation foraging for invertebrates.

7/ PIED WAGTAIL
Motacilla alba
RANGE: breeds most of Eurasia, except tropics; N birds winter S to Africa N of Equator, Arabia, India and Southeast Asia
HABITAT: open ground, often near water
SIZE: 7 in (18 cm)

This striking bird habitually bobs its tail. Its plumage varies across its extensive range. The wholly black-backed adult Pied Wagtail *M. a. yarrellii* of the British Isles, Spain and Morocco differs markedly from the gray-backed White Wagtail *M. a. alba* of the rest of Europe, north and east Africa, Iran, Arabia and Russia.

The Pied Wagtail is fond of water and often paddles into shallows and puddles as it searches for aquatic insects. It is also common in open ground away from water, and regularly occurs around farmyards, parks and buildings. It often uses communal roosts outside the breeding season. In some areas, these include artificially heated structures, such as power station cooling towers and heated greenhouses.

8/ GOLDEN PIPIT
Tmetothylacus tenellus
RANGE: **Horn of Africa S to Tanzania**
HABITAT: **dry open country**
SIZE: **5½ in (14 cm)**

The male Golden Pipit is a striking bird showing characteristics of both the wagtails and the pipits. A sedentary bird, this species is often very local in occurrence, even where apparently suitable habitat is extensive. It occurs in small flocks or family groups. The Golden Pipit performs its simple song during parachutelike glides from the tops of bushes to the ground, with its wings held in a *V* above its back.

9/ CAPE LONGCLAW
Macronyx capensis
RANGE: **South Africa, C Zimbabwe**
HABITAT: **open damp grassland**
SIZE: **7½ in (19 cm)**

This is a robustly built bird, generally seen doggedly foraging in small parties through short grassland. It quickly chases or pounces on any food item that is startled from cover and will often beat large insects on the ground before swallowing them. From time to time, it stands on a clump or mound to scan its surroundings.

The Cape Longclaw utters whistling and piping calls as well as a catlike *meeoo* of alarm. It frequently calls when perched on a fence or mound, as well as during its fluttering display flight, when it rises some 33 ft (10 m) into the air.

10/ RICHARD'S PIPIT
Anthus novaeseelandiae
RANGE: **sub-Saharan Africa, much of C, E and S Asia, New Guinea, Australia, New Zealand; N populations migrate to S of breeding range**
HABITAT: **open country**
SIZE: **7 in (18 cm)**

This large pipit has an upright stance and a long tail that it habitually wags up and down. It exhibits considerable variation in plumage, with the upperparts of many races quite darkly marked. The race illustrated is *A. n. novaeseelandiae* of South Island, New Zealand.

Richard's Pipit, sometimes called the New Zealand Pipit, hunts for invertebrates on the ground and will sometimes pursue insects in the air. It gives chirruping and trilling calls and sings in flight. The nest is placed in a slight depression on the ground. Its populations in warmer areas have a longer breeding season and may lay several small clutches.

11/ BUFF-BELLIED PIPIT
Anthus rubescens
RANGE: **breeds NE Siberia, N North America, W Greenland; winters S to Southeast Asia and Central America**
HABITAT: **breeds on mountains and tundra; winters on beaches, fields**
SIZE: **6½ in (17 cm)**

The Buff-bellied Pipit nests on the tundra in the north of its range but is a mountain bird farther south. It is both widespread and common in North America and is sometimes known as the American Pipit. Where this species' range meets that of the Water Pipit in Siberia, the 2 birds show differing habitat preferences. The Water Pipit tends to breed on open ground, while the Buff-bellied Pipit prefers more rocky areas.

12/ WATER PIPIT
Anthus spinoletta
RANGE: **S European mountains E across Asia to Lake Baikal; C and E Asian races winter S to Southeast Asia and Japan**
HABITAT: **breeds in mountains; winters in open country at lower elevations**
SIZE: **6½ in (17 cm)**

Formerly considered races of the same species, the Water Pipit, Rock Pipit and Buff-bellied Pipit have recently been separated on the basis of detailed studies. They are largely separate in geographical range and in habitat preferences.

The Water Pipit breeds above the tree line in high mountain areas, usually siting its nest close to rushing streams. In some regions it occurs close to glaciers and even nests above the snow line. In winter, however, it is driven by harsh conditions down to lower altitudes, to such habitats as flooded or damp meadows, watercress beds and other damp, arable land, and even to estuaries and coastal mudflats.

13/ ROCK PIPIT
Anthus petrosus
RANGE: **breeds NW France, British Isles, Scandinavia, Faroe Islands; some N populations winter in NW and S Europe**
HABITAT: **seashore**
SIZE: **6½ in (17 cm)**

The Rock Pipit gains most of its food by foraging among beach debris, searching for invertebrates such as insects and their larvae, mollusks and small crustaceans. In some regions, resident Rock Pipits defend feeding territories all year.

The birds nest either on sea cliffs or in a bank or under dense vegetation close to the shore. Seaweed is often incorporated into the cup nest. The normal clutch size is 4–5, but up to 9 eggs have been recorded in one nest.

FAMILY CAMPEPHAGIDAE
Cuckoo-shrikes
Small to medium, tree-dwellers. Most species grayish, black or pied, but one group with bright reds and yellows. Sexes differ in most species. Nest a shallow cup. Eggs 2–5, white or greenish, sometimes spotted. Incubation 14–23 days, nestling period 12–25 days. 70 species.

14/ BLACK-FACED CUCKOO-SHRIKE
Coracina novaehollandiae
RANGE: **breeds India, Southeast Asia, New Guinea, Australia; many SE Australian and Tasmanian birds winter in N Australia and New Guinea**
HABITAT: **woodland and forests**
SIZE: **13 in (33 cm)**

Black-faced Cuckoo-Shrikes have an undulating flight and when they land they shuffle their wings in a distinctive manner. The birds feed on larvae, beetles and other large insects that they snatch from leaves after scanning the foliage from below. The rather metallic voice of this bird includes a rolling *churrrink* contact call and a higher, trilling *chereer-chereer-chereer*, often given in display.

15/ BLUE CUCKOO-SHRIKE
Coracina azurea
RANGE: **Sierra Leone to Zaire**
HABITAT: **primary and secondary forest**
SIZE: **8½ in (22 cm)**

The Blue Cuckoo-Shrike is an unobtrusive bird that frequents the tops of tall trees. Although often solitary, it may be seen in small parties that hunt diligently through the foliage for beetles, grasshoppers and caterpillars. The calls of the Blue Cuckoo-Shrike range from grating noises to more pleasant musical notes.

16/ WHITE-WINGED TRILLER
Lalage sueurii
RANGE: **Sulawesi, Lesser Sundas, Java, SE New Guinea, Australia**
HABITAT: **open woodland and shrubland**
SIZE: **7 in (18 cm)**

Outside the breeding season, the male resembles the grayish-brown and buff female. An alternative name for the trillers is "caterpillar-eaters," and, indeed, they do take many larvae, which they glean or snatch from foliage. Nectar and fruit are also sometimes eaten.

White-winged Trillers are migrants, arriving as late as November in southern Australia. Males sing their vigorous trilling songs from the treetops, often pursuing one another.

17/ LONG-TAILED MINIVET
Pericrocotus ethologus
RANGE: **breeds E Afghanistan through Himalayas to Southeast Asia and China, N to Manchuria**
HABITAT: **open forest, sparsely wooded hills, mainly 3,300–8,000 ft (1,000–2,500 m)**
SIZE: **7 in (18 cm)**

A flock of these lively scarlet and black birds flying over the treetops against a snowy Himalayan backdrop is an unforgettable sight. Highly gregarious, Long-tailed Minivets are always on the move, hovering and fluttering in search of insects, buds and fruit. Individuals in a group keep in contact with sweet, twittering calls. This species is migratory in some areas, and many birds move to lower altitudes in winter.

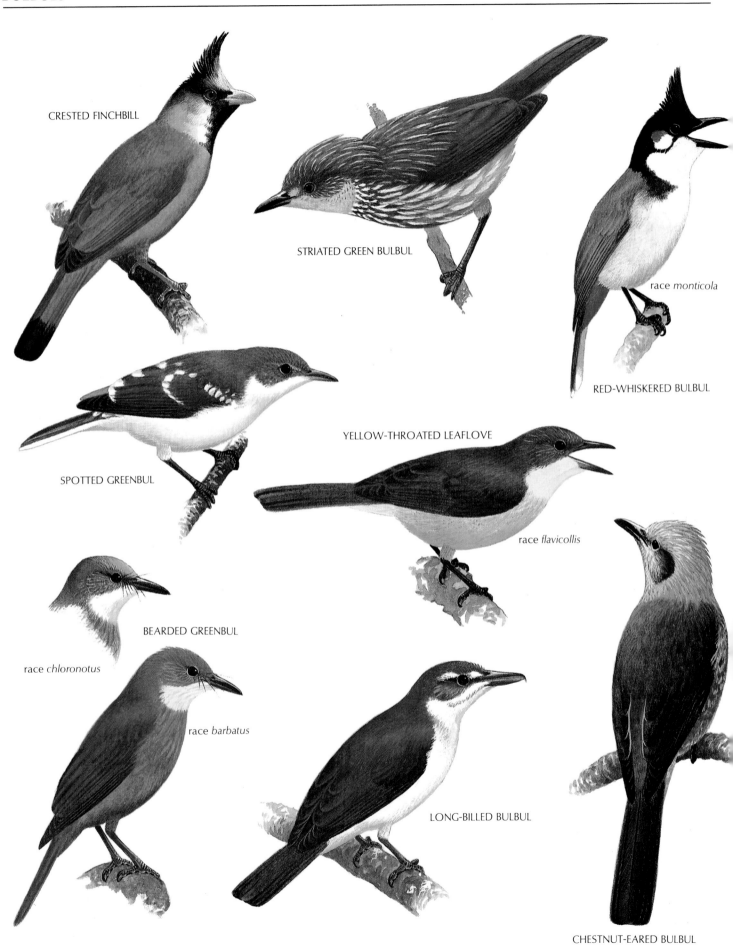

CRESTED FINCHBILL

STRIATED GREEN BULBUL

race *monticola*

RED-WHISKERED BULBUL

SPOTTED GREENBUL

YELLOW-THROATED LEAFLOVE

race *flavicollis*

BEARDED GREENBUL

race *chloronotus*

race *barbatus*

LONG-BILLED BULBUL

CHESTNUT-EARED BULBUL

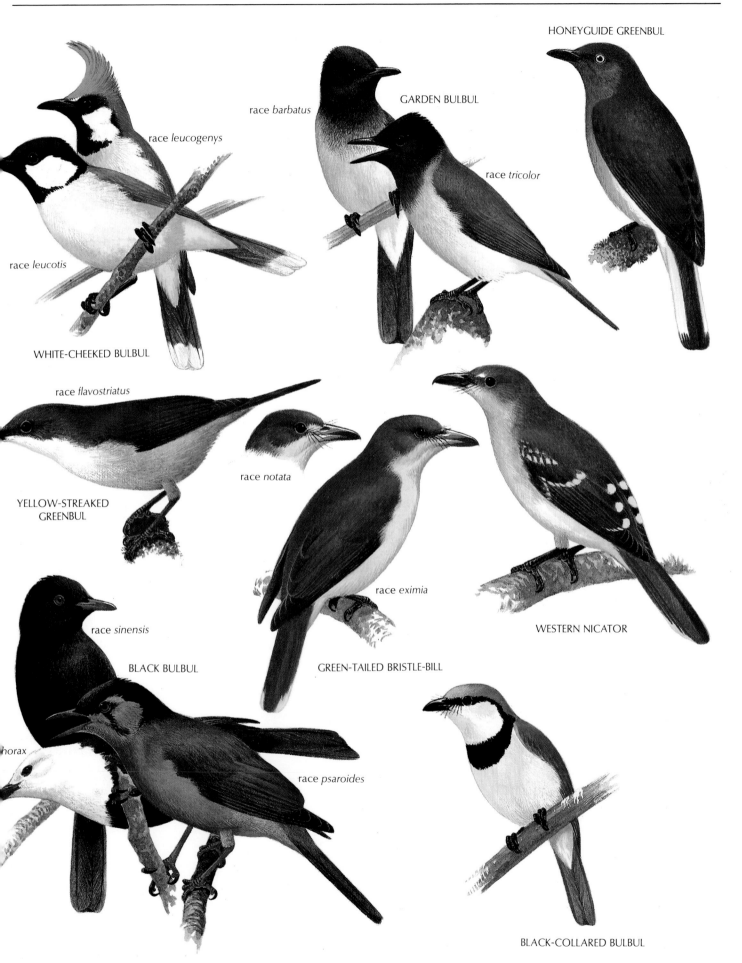

HONEYGUIDE GREENBUL

race *barbatus*

GARDEN BULBUL

race *leucogenys*

race *tricolor*

race *leucotis*

WHITE-CHEEKED BULBUL

race *flavostriatus*

race *notata*

YELLOW-STREAKED
GREENBUL

race *eximia*

WESTERN NICATOR

race *sinensis*

BLACK BULBUL

GREEN-TAILED BRISTLE-BILL

horax

race *psaroides*

BLACK-COLLARED BULBUL

251

FAMILY PYCNONOTIDAE
Bulbuls

Medium to small, drab, gregarious birds of trees and scrub. Often hooded or with pale eye ring. Short, slightly curved bills, stout legs. Generally melodious voices. Sexes similar. Nest cup-shaped, in tree. Eggs 2–5, purplish-pink. Incubation 12–14 days, nestling period 14–18 days. 124 species.

1/ CRESTED FINCHBILL
Spizixos canifrons

RANGE: **Assam, W Burma**
HABITAT: **forest, clearings, mountain scrub to 8,000 ft (2,500 m)**
SIZE: **8 in (20 cm)**

Most bulbuls have slender, medium-length bills, but the aptly named finchbills have short, stout bills which are like those of finches and used for the same purpose: cracking seeds. Adult Crested Finchbills have yellowish bills which look white in the field and are very distinctive.

Crested Finchbills are gregarious birds which often forage in flocks of 50 or more among bamboo, low, cut scrub and abandoned cultivation. Sometimes one will move to a high perch and use it as a base for catching flies on the wing, but they feed mainly on berries and seeds.

The 2-note alarm call is musical but strident, increasing to 5 syllables when the bird is really excited, with a rich, fluty quality typical of bulbuls.

2/ STRIATED GREEN BULBUL
Pycnonotus striatus

RANGE: **E Himalayas, W Burma**
HABITAT: **evergreen forest, rhododendron forest, bushes, to 10,000 ft (3,000 m)**
SIZE: **8 in (20 cm)**

This bulbul is a resident of hill forests but moves down to lower levels in winter. It prefers jungle and bushy forest that is not too dense or too high; flocks of up to 15 birds straggle loosely from bush to bush in search of fruit, each bird giving almost continuous sharp *tyiwut* calls. They will also join in a communal, full-throated but disjointed warbling song whenever they pause in their lively passage through the trees.

3/ RED-WHISKERED BULBUL
Pycnonotus jocosus

RANGE: **China, Assam, Nepal, India**
HABITAT: **open humid jungle, gardens**
SIZE: **8 in (20 cm)**

There are 6 races of this widespread and common species, each distinguished by the pattern of white on the tail feathers, the dark collar, the length of crest and bill, and the color of the back. The race shown is *P.j. monticola* of China and Assam, which has white tail tips and the darkest back.

Red-whiskered Bulbuls are familiar in gardens, even in the noisiest cities, where they live in pairs or gather in loose flocks. Each pair tends to remain in its territory all year, eating fruits and buds (often doing damage in gardens) or dropping to the ground to feed on ants. Their calls are typically noisy, full-throated and cheerful.

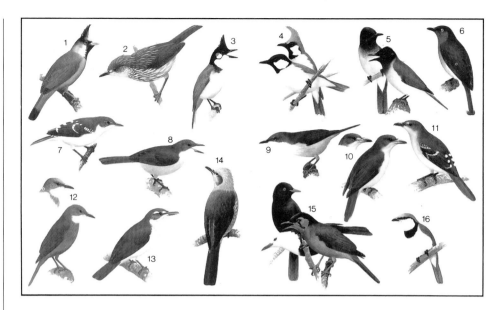

4/ WHITE-CHEEKED BULBUL
Pycnonotus leucogenys

RANGE: **Himalayas, NW India to S Iran**
HABITAT: **scrub jungle, bushy hillsides, villages**
SIZE: **8 in (20 cm)**

Sprightly and active, the White-cheeked Bulbul is common up to 7,000 ft (2,100 m) in the dry Himalayas, but in wetter east Nepal it occurs only in the lower, drier valleys.

It likes bushes of wild raspberry, berberis and roses, and small parties are often seen bustling noisily along hedgerows from village to village. In Kashmir it is a fearless, familiar bird, often entering houses to steal scraps from tables. It is a jaunty bird which perches on bush tops, bowing and flicking its wings and tail and keeping up a constant stream of calls.

The Himalayan race *P. l. leucogenys* is a long-crested form; *P. l. leucotis* is a crestless race with a much wider range farther west.

5/ GARDEN BULBUL
Pycnonotus barbatus

RANGE: **N Africa S to Tanzania**
HABITAT: **open forest, gardens, town parks**
SIZE: **7 in (18 cm)**

All over its large range the Garden, or Common, Bulbul announces its presence with the high, rich, fluty or bubbling calls typical of its family. It is an adaptable species which will thrive almost anywhere where there are fruits, buds and berries, although it does not like dense forest. In some areas, such as Egypt, it has extended its range to take advantage of the increase in irrigated orchards. It is often seen near houses and other buildings and can be very tame, but in more remote areas can be very inconspicuous.

The northern race *P. b. barbatus* is white under the tail but the southern race *P. b. tricolor* has a splash of yellow in the same place.

6/ HONEYGUIDE GREENBUL
Baeopogon indicator

RANGE: **W Africa from Sierra Leone to the Congo**
HABITAT: **forest clearings and secondary growth**
SIZE: **8 in (20 cm)**

This is a rather large, heavily built bulbul with conspicuous white outer tail feathers like those of a honeyguide (pp. 210–13). It also behaves a little like a honeyguide, keeping to the tops of tall trees, but its calls are quite distinctive, and its fluty, jumbled song resembles that of a thrush.

The Honeyguide Greenbul is a little-known species; its breeding behavior has not been studied in detail, although nests have been found placed far out on slender branches near the tops of forest trees.

7/ SPOTTED GREENBUL
Ixonotus guttatus

RANGE: **Ghana and Gabon to C Zaire**
HABITAT: **primary and secondary tropical forest**
SIZE: **6 in (15 cm)**

Easily recognized by the amount of white in its plumage, this is a common and fairly conspicuous bird. It lives in loose groups which draw attention to themselves by repeated cheerful calls and restless behavior in the treetops. Like some other bulbuls, it will often raise one wing over its back while it perches.

The nest of the Spotted Greenbul is built in a low tree beneath the high canopy of the forest and is a typical bulbul construction of thin rootlets and leaf stalks woven into the form of a shallow cup.

8/ YELLOW-THROATED LEAFLOVE
Chlorocichla flavicollis
RANGE: **W Africa from Senegal to Cameroon, Central African Republic and the Congo**
HABITAT: **forest edge and thorny thickets**
SIZE: **7 in (18 cm)**

The Yellow-throated Leaflove is a bird of the dense thickets where the savanna blends into the forest and is rarely seen among the tall forest trees. In some areas it is common, living in pairs or small parties which, although hidden by the dense foliage, are easily located by their loud, throaty, bubbling calls.

Some races, such as *C. f. flavicollis*, have the yellow throat referred to in the name, but others, such as *C. f. soror* of the Central African Republic, Congo and Sudan, are white-throated and duller.

9/ YELLOW-STREAKED GREENBUL
Phyllastrephus flavostriatus
RANGE: **Nigeria and Cameroon E and S to South Africa**
HABITAT: **mountain forest**
SIZE: **8 in (20 cm)**

This large bulbul is quite easily identified by its plumage and its liking for thick forests high in the mountains, where it keeps to trees and thick bush, often in the highest branches.

It creeps about close to the main trunks or in clustered creepers, searching for insects in the bundles of dead leaves that collect among the stems. Although rather sluggish, it will twist and stretch, or even hang upside-down, as it searches for food. This bird also has a habit of raising one wing over its back, lowering it and then raising the other.

Several races are distinguished on the basis of the color of the underparts and grayness of the head. The race shown is *P. f. flavostriatus* from eastern South Africa.

10/ GREEN-TAILED BRISTLE-BILL
Bleda eximia
RANGE: **W Africa, from Sierra Leone to Central African Republic and the Congo**
HABITAT: **tall tropical forest**
SIZE: **8 in (20 cm)**

Although this bulbul is always found among tall trees, it spends most of its time on or near the ground, often in the mixed-bird flocks that are so characteristic of African woodlands. It is frequently seen picking ants out of the huge columns of these insects that march across the leaf litter beneath the canopy.

It has a loud, explosive call, but its song is mellow, varied and thrushlike. The western race *B. e. notata* has a conspicuous yellow spot on its face, absent in the eastern race *B. e. eximia*.

11/ WESTERN NICATOR
Nicator chloris
RANGE: **Senegal to Gabon and the Congo, Zaire and Uganda**
HABITAT: **thick forest**
SIZE: **8¾ in (22 cm)**

In the color plate this looks like a conspicuous bird, but in the forest it can be very hard to see, for it rarely emerges from the dense foliage of tall trees. The Western Nicator lives in the tops of smaller trees or among the lower canopy of forest giants, and often the only clues to its presence are its harsh, wheezy or whistling calls and its beautiful, full-throated song.

The only time it comes close to the ground is when nesting, for it builds its frail, flat nest in a fork 3–6 ft (1–2 m) from the forest floor.

This species closely resembles some of the shrikes and was formerly classified with them in the family Laniidae (pp. 254–57).

12/ BEARDED GREENBUL
Criniger barbatus
RANGE: **Sierra Leone to Gabon and Central African Republic**
HABITAT: **rain forest**
SIZE: **8 in (20 cm)**

The most remarkable feature of the Bearded Greenbul is its beautiful, arresting whistle; it also sometimes utters a loud, throaty babbling. It is a gregarious bird which often joins mixed-species flocks roaming through the lower levels of the rain forest canopy.

The eastern race *C. b. chloronotus* has distinctive white throat feathers, whereas the race *C. b. barbatus*, found from Sierra Leone to Togo, has a yellow throat.

The nest, built on top of a shrub, is made of dead leaves, pieces of rotten wood and plant fiber, and is decorated with a few green sprays.

13/ LONG-BILLED BULBUL
Setornis criniger
RANGE: **Borneo, Sumatra, Bangka Islands**
HABITAT: **lowland primary forest**
SIZE: **7 in (18 cm)**

Although the striking Long-billed Bulbul is a common resident of the lowlands of Borneo, very little is recorded about its behavior or breeding biology.

Its white-tipped outer tail feathers help identify it in the dense woodland it prefers. Its varied diet is typical of bulbuls and includes dragonfly nymphs, beetles and other insects, and a wide range of fruits and berries.

14/ CHESTNUT-EARED BULBUL
Hypsipetes amaurotis
RANGE: **Japan, Taiwan, S China**
HABITAT: **forested slopes, gardens, parks**
SIZE: **10½ in (27 cm)**

Sociable and noisy, the Chestnut-eared Bulbul visits bird feeders in Japanese gardens and is a familiar sight in parks and wooded areas in towns. The birds that breed in the north move south in winter, often roaming in sizable flocks

that communicate with continual loud, fluty, rhythmic calls. In summer this species is very common in forests on lower mountain slopes.

For a bulbul it is a slim, long-tailed and slender-billed bird, with none of the stubby appearance of many of its African relatives. The race *H. a. amaurotis* is the Japanese form; *H. a. nagamichii* is the race found on Taiwan.

15/ BLACK BULBUL
Hypsipetes madagascariensis
RANGE: **SW India, Nepal E to Vietnam, Thailand, China**
HABITAT: **oak, pine, rhododendron forest**
SIZE: **9 in (23 cm)**

Several races have been described within the large range of the Black Bulbul. *H. m. sinensis* from southwest China, Thailand and Laos is a dark one, whereas *H. m. psaroides*, found along the Himalayas, is paler; the race *H. m. leucothorax* of western China and northern Vietnam has a white head.

The Black Bulbul is a summer visitor to the higher parts of its range, up to 10,000 ft (3,000 m) in the Himalayas, but elsewhere it is mainly resident. Common and very noisy, the birds may gather in boisterous bands of 100 or more individuals which stay a little while in one tree, fly up to catch insects or strip the twigs of berries, then swiftly stream out to the next.

The song is a series of clipped, single notes interspersed with a ringing bell-like tone, but other calls have been compared to a squealing pig and a creaky gate.

16/ BLACK-COLLARED BULBUL
Neolestes torquatus
RANGE: **Gabon, Congo, Zaire, Angola**
HABITAT: **grassy woodland, savanna**
SIZE: **6 in (15 cm)**

In many respects the small Black-collared Bulbul is an unusual member of its family. Indeed, its bright pigmentation, upright stance and arched bill misled early birdwatchers into the belief that it was a shrike. It keeps to more open areas than most bulbuls and has a unique display flight, ascending to 100 ft (30 m) or more and hovering in one spot for 2–3 minutes, emitting a continuous stream of twittering calls.

Despite all this, its feeding habits are typical of a bulbul, for it moves around in small parties and feeds on fruit.

LEAFBIRDS, FAIRY BLUEBIRDS, SHRIKES, BORNEAN BRISTLEHEAD

race *tiphia*

♂

COMMON IORA

♀

race *multicolor*

race *multicolor*

race *multicolor*

race *frontalis*

♂

race *aurifrons*

♂

GOLDEN-FRONTED LEAFBIRD

♀

courtship display

PUFFBACK

BLUE-BACKED FAIRY BLUEBIRD

♂

♂

BRUBRU SHRIKE

race *ludovicianus*

juv

♂

BLACK-HEADED TCHAGRA

♂

courtship display

LOGGERHEAD SHRIKE

COMMON GONOLEK

FIERY-BREASTED BUSH-SHRIKE

♂

♂

FISCAL SHRIKE

race *collaris*

♂

♀

race *subcoronatus*

♀

RED-BACKED SHRIKE

YELLOW-BILLED SHRIKE

race *tricolor*

♂

BORNEAN BRISTLEHEAD

♂

race *erythronotus*

LONG-TAILED SHRIKE

FOUR-COLORED BUSH-SHRIKE

LEAFBIRDS, FAIRY BLUEBIRDS, SHRIKES, BORNEAN BRISTLEHEAD

FAMILY CHLOROPSEIDAE
Leafbirds

Small to medium tree-dwellers. Plumage mostly green and yellow, males with black on face. Sexes differ. Cup-shaped nest. Eggs 2–3, pinkish or white with brown blotches. Incubation about 14 days, nestling period unknown. 12 species.

1/ COMMON IORA
Aegithina tiphia
RANGE: **India, Sri Lanka to Southeast Asia, Java, Borneo**
HABITAT: **forest, groves, cultivated land**
SIZE: **5½ in (14 cm)**

A small, active, insect-eating bird, the Common Iora is remarkable for its display. The courting male fluffs out his rump and his long white flank feathers and jumps into the air, gliding down again to his perch like a feathered ball. Often to be seen in pairs, the birds call constantly with a variety of sweet, sometimes mournful, whistles.

This species molts twice yearly; the male in his nonbreeding plumage resembles the duller female, except for his black tail. Of the races illustrated, *A. t. tiphia* ranges from the Himalayas to Burma, while *A. t. multicolor* occurs in southern India and Sri Lanka.

2/ GOLDEN-FRONTED LEAFBIRD
Chloropsis aurifrons
RANGE: **Sri Lanka, India, Himalayas to Southeast Asia, Sumatra**
HABITAT: **forest, open woodland, scrub**
SIZE: **7½ in (19 cm)**

There are several races of this widely distributed bird, differing both in size and in the color of the chin and throat. They include the blue-throated *C. a. aurifrons* of Bangladesh and India, and the black-throated *C. a. frontalis* of central and southern India. The blue shoulder patches, which are found in all races, are often concealed when the bird is at rest.

A great mimic, this leafbird is often to be seen foraging with almost titlike agility in flowering or fruiting trees; it is partial to both figs and mistletoe. As it spends much time exploring blossoms for nectar and insects, it is an important pollinator. It is a resident bird in most of its range, although it moves to lower zones in the Himalayas in winter.

FAMILY IRENIDAE
Fairy bluebirds

Medium-sized tree-dwellers. Very long upper and under tail coverts. Plumage brilliant blue and black. Females duller, greener. Eyes intensely red. Nest a twig platform in a tree fork. Eggs 2–3, glossy olive with brown blotching. Incubation and nestling period unknown. 2 species.

3/ BLUE-BACKED FAIRY BLUEBIRD
Irena puella
RANGE: **W India, Nepal to Southeast Asia, Philippines**
HABITAT: **heavy deciduous or evergreen forest**
SIZE: **10½ in (27 cm)**

A fruiting fig tree is a magnet for Blue-backed Fairy Bluebirds and their bustling activity, and incessant sharp, liquid calls add great charm to the forest scene. They are always on the move in the forest, usually working their way through the canopy or the middle layers of vegetation, and seldom descend to the ground.

When moving through the heavy shade of the foliage small groups of the birds can look dull black, until a shaft of sunlight suddenly illuminates the sapphire mantles of the males. In some races the upper tail coverts almost conceal the tail.

FAMILY LANIIDAE
Shrikes

Small to medium. Sharply hooked bill. Plumage variable, often bright. Sexes usually similar. Nest in trees and shrubs. Eggs 2–7, variable, streaked or blotched. Incubation 12–18 days, nestling period 12–20 days. 69 species.

4/ BRUBRU SHRIKE
Nilaus afer
RANGE: **tropical Africa**
HABITAT: **savanna woodland; occasionally forest edge**
SIZE: **6 in (15 cm)**

This bird is usually heard before it is seen. It takes its name from the male's repeated *bruuu-bruuu* call with which he proclaims his territory and keeps in close contact with the female. Like some other shrikes, when a pair are close together they often engage in "duetting," with the female answering the male's calls.

The Brubru Shrike occurs mainly in the tree canopy, where it gleans insects from the foliage, but it occasionally catches food on the wing.

5/ PUFFBACK
Dryoscopus gambensis
RANGE: **W, C and E Africa**
HABITAT: **savanna woodland; also thickets, forest clearings, mangroves and gardens**
SIZE: **7 in (18 cm)**

The species' name reflects the male's ability to fluff up the long, gray-white feathers of the lower back. During the courtship display, these feathers resemble a ball-shaped powder puff. This bird occurs singly or in pairs and spends most of its time in the tree canopy, rarely descending to ground level. It feeds mainly on insects but occasionally catches small lizards.

The Puffback is a vocal bird, with a wide variety of calls, including a chattering alarm note. In the breeding season, the male sings a melodious and warbling song and the female often joins in the singing during territorial disputes.

6/ BLACK-HEADED TCHAGRA
Tchagra senegala
RANGE: **sub-Saharan Africa, NW Africa, SW Arabia**
HABITAT: **open savanna woodland with bushes and long grass, margins of cultivated land**
SIZE: **8¾ in (22 cm)**

The Black-headed Tchagra feeds much like a thrush, hopping, running and creeping through the ground cover. It will also search for food among foliage and catches some of its prey in flight. Insects and their larvae make up the bulk of its diet but it also feeds on tadpoles, along with the occasional adult tree frog, and it often eats soft fruits.

Although this bird is secretive, its song-flight is conspicuous. Males defend territories throughout the year, singing a series of plaintive whistled notes from an exposed perch. During the courtship song-flights, they ascend noisily into the air and whistle as they glide back down to cover. Duetting is well developed, the female adding a drawn-out trill to the male's song; she often joins him in his song-flight.

7/ COMMON GONOLEK
Laniarius barbarus

RANGE: W Africa
HABITAT: **thorny acacia, dense shrub and woodland in savannas; also mangroves and riverside thickets**
SIZE: 8¾ in (22 cm)

A shy bird, the Common Gonolek is more often heard than seen. It hops nimbly through thickets and makes brief flights from cover to cover, using rapid, shallow wing beats followed by long glides. It preys on insects and other invertebrates, usually catching its food on the ground, but also foraging over tree trunks and branches and among foliage.

The male has a variety of calls, the most common being a repeated *whee-u* note. A pair will duet regularly, although the clicking notes contributed by the female are uttered so quickly that the performance sounds as if it is coming solely from the male. The birds are highly sensitive to disturbance and will readily abandon, or even destroy, their nests.

8/ FOUR-COLORED BUSH-SHRIKE
Telophorus quadricolor

RANGE: **coastal regions of E and S Africa**
HABITAT: **dense tangled bush; also forest edge**
SIZE: 8 in (20.5 cm)

Although their plumage is bright, these birds are difficult to observe in the wild. Usually it is the male's bell-like whistle that reveals their presence. The female shares the multihued appearance of the male but her tail is a lighter green, her throat is more orange-yellow and there are no red tinges on her underparts. An alternative name is Gorgeous Bush-Shrike.

The flimsy, shallow nest is placed in the fork of a shrub about 3 ft (1 m) above the ground. It is built from twigs, grass and rootlets and is lined with leaf stalks. The female bird carries out most of the incubation.

9/ FIERY-BREASTED BUSH-SHRIKE
Malaconotus cruentus

RANGE: **W and C Africa**
HABITAT: **lowland rain forest**
SIZE: 10 in (25 cm)

This beautiful bush-shrike usually occurs in pairs, although sometimes in groups of up to 6, in the tangled foliage of the rain forest canopy and middle layer. It searches among the leaves for beetles, grasshoppers, caterpillars and other invertebrates. Seeds and the remains of frogs have also been found in its stomach.

The large shallow cup nest of vine stems, leaf stalks and small twigs lined with black rootlets is loosely bound to branches. The 3 eggs are pinkish-white, spotted and blotched with maroon and pale purple. Like many other rain forest creatures, the Fiery-breasted Bush-Shrike is threatened by habitat destruction.

10/ YELLOW-BILLED SHRIKE
Corvinella corvina

RANGE: **W and C Africa, E to W Kenya**
HABITAT: **savanna woodland, suburban gardens**
SIZE: 12 in (30 cm)

Although its plumage is fairly drab, this shrike is conspicuous because of its noisy habits, its large size and its tapering, 7 in (18 cm) long tail. An alternative name is Western Long-tailed Shrike. The sexes differ in the central flank feathers that are exposed when the birds preen or display. These are rufous in the male but cinnamon or maroon in the female.

This is a noisy, gregarious species, occurring in groups of some 6–15 birds. All the members of a group help to defend the communal territory as well as feed the incubating female, the nestlings and the dependent juveniles. They catch insects, spiders, slugs and lizards, either by swooping from a perch or by pouncing on them after quartering a feeding site from the air.

11/ RED-BACKED SHRIKE
Lanius collurio

RANGE: **Europe, W Siberia, W Asia; winters mainly E and S Africa**
HABITAT: **breeds in bushes, thickets and hedgerows; winters in savanna woodland**
SIZE: 6¾ in (17 cm)

The Red-backed Shrike usually hunts by swooping from a perch to catch insects and small vertebrates such as frogs, birds and bats. Like many other northern shrikes, it has the habit of impaling its prey on thorns or barbed wire fences and keeping "larders" of stored food.

The species is widespread across western Eurasia, where it prefers to breed in lightly wooded areas with a rich undergrowth of thorn bushes. It winters in Africa, taking a southward route several hundred miles to the west of its return journey. Individual birds faithfully return to the same breeding and wintering areas. Both sexes build a deep cup nest, usually placed low in a thorn bush and lined with rootlets and wool.

12/ LONG-TAILED SHRIKE
Lanius schach

RANGE: **Iran and C Asia to China, Southeast Asia, Philippines, Indonesia, New Guinea**
HABITAT: **open country, scrub, farmland**
SIZE: 10 in (25 cm)

This species, which is named for its long tail, shows marked variation in plumage across its vast geographical range. The Rufous-backed Shrike *L. s. erythronotus* of central Asia and western India has a gray head, for instance, while the Black-headed Shrike *L. s. tricolor* of the Himalayas, Burma and northern Indochina has a black head.

Only the northerly populations migrate to lower latitudes after the breeding season; other populations are sedentary. The birds eat a wide variety of insects and small vertebrates, impaling and storing some in "larders." Their calls are harsh and discordant but the subdued song is melodious, with many mimicked components.

13/ LOGGERHEAD SHRIKE
Lanius ludovicianus

RANGE: **S Canada to Mexico and Florida**
HABITAT: **open country with thickets, hedgerows and farmland**
SIZE: 8¼–9 in (21–23 cm)

The Loggerhead Shrike occurs over much of North America, with the more northerly populations retreating southward in winter. It prefers open, thinly wooded country, where it feeds largely on insects, often impaling its prey on thorns. Habitat destruction and pesticides have caused its numbers to decline steadily.

The northern populations tend to lay more eggs than their southern counterparts. Studies of breeding birds in northern Colorado and Florida revealed average clutch sizes of 6.39 and 4.33 respectively. The southern races, including *L. l. ludovicianus* of southeastern USA, also tend to have lighter plumage.

14/ FISCAL SHRIKE
Lanius collaris

RANGE: **sub-Saharan Africa**
HABITAT: **open woodland savanna; also parks and forest clearings**
SIZE: 8¾ in (22 cm)

This widespread shrike has several races. Some, such as *L. c. subcoronatus* of southwest Africa, have a white eyebrow, while others, such as *L. c. collaris* of southern Africa, lack this. In all but one race, the females differ from the males in having chestnut flanks.

It is an aggressive, solitary species that readily attacks and kills other birds. Its "larders" of impaled prey may include grasshoppers, beetles, moths, butterflies, frogs and lizards. It maintains its territorial boundaries with both visual and vocal displays, although its song of tuneful whistles and mimicked sounds is reserved for courtship and nest displays. Both sexes build the deep cup nest of grass and twigs, often in the fork of a thorn tree up to 20 ft (6 m) above the ground.

FAMILY PITYRIASIDIDAE
Bornean Bristlehead
There is only one species in this family.

15/ BORNEAN BRISTLEHEAD
Pityriasis gymnocephala

RANGE: **Borneo**
HABITAT: **lowland forest**
SIZE: 10 in (25 cm)

This rare, rain forest bird takes its name from the short, bristlelike feathers that cover the top and sides of its head. The female shares the heavy build, massive hooked beak and general coloration of the male but differs in having red spots on the flanks.

The Bornean Bristlehead spends most of its time in the forest canopy, where it hunts for a variety of insects and their larvae. It is a sociable bird and often forms mixed foraging parties with other species. It utters both a harsh, crowlike call and a high-pitched whining, sometimes in chorus with others in the group. Little is known of its nesting habits.

HELMET SHRIKES, VANGA SHRIKES, WAXWINGS, PALMCHAT, DIPPERS, WRENS

HELMET BIRD

CORAL-BILLED NUTHATCH

♂

LONG-CRESTED
HELMET SHRIKE

BOHEMIAN
WAXWING

juv

GRAY HYPOCOLIUS

juv

♂

PALMCHAT

♀

PHAINOPEPLA

juv

juv

NORTH AMERICAN DIPPER

WHITE-THROATED DIPPER

race *gularis*

SEDGE WREN

race *zetlandicus*

WINTER WREN

BICOLORED WREN

ROCK WREN

race *indigenus*

ZAPATA WREN

FLUTIST WREN

BLACK-CAPPED DONACOBIUS

259

HELMET SHRIKES, VANGA SHRIKES, WAXWINGS, PALMCHAT, DIPPERS, WRENS

FAMILY PRIONOPIDAE
Helmet shrikes

Medium, highly sociable, tree-dwelling insect-eaters. Rather titlike when feeding. Sexes alike. Plumage in various combinations of black, brown and white, with patches of yellow, gray or chestnut in some species. Many with brightly colored bills and irises; *Prionops* species with colored eye wattles. Neat, compact nest built in forks or on horizontal boughs of trees high above ground. Eggs 2–6, white, pale blue, olive-green, or other colors, blotched or spotted with chestnut, brown or violet-brown. Incubation and nestling periods unknown. 9 species.

1/ LONG-CRESTED HELMET SHRIKE
Prionops plumata

RANGE: sub-Saharan Africa, except arid areas and S South Africa and Namibia
HABITAT: open deciduous woodland, orchard bush and cultivated areas with scattered trees
SIZE: $8\frac{1}{4}$ in (21 cm)

The conspicuous and gregarious Long-crested Helmet Shrike, like the other members of its family, invariably occurs in groups of up to 10 or more: these are smaller in this species in the breeding season (averaging 7 birds) than at other times. The group members chatter noisily as they leapfrog along the same foraging route in their territory each day. A wide range of loud, rolling, ringing calls is used to maintain contact and structure, and duetting probably reinforces the pair-bond. This species is also known as the Straight-crested Helmet Shrike, White Helmet Shrike or Common Helmet Shrike.

FAMILY VANGIDAE
Vanga shrikes

Small to medium, tree-dwelling, chiefly insect-eaters. Huge variations in bill shape and color of plumage. Sexes differ in some species. Many metallic black above, white beneath; some also with gray and chestnut; 2 species mainly blue. Breeding details known for only 8 species. Nest of twigs in trees. Eggs 3–4, white, cream, pink, greenish-blue, heavily blotched with gray or brown. Incubation and nestling periods unknown. 13 species.

2/ HELMET BIRD
Euryceros prevostii

RANGE: NE Madagascar
HABITAT: primary, dense evergreen forest from sea level to 6,000 ft (1,800 m)
SIZE: $10\frac{1}{2}$–$12\frac{1}{4}$ in (27–31 cm)

Its large, heavy bill distinguishes the Helmet Bird from all other members of the family. It is also known as the Helmeted Vanga.

Communal groups of 5–10 birds are usually found in mixed feeding flocks in the middle layer of the forest, moving quickly through the foliage to glean insects from small branches. The Helmet Bird has also been known to eat frogs and small reptiles. Although this odd species is difficult to observe, its tremulous, prolonged whistle is easy to identify, particularly at dusk.

3/ CORAL-BILLED NUTHATCH
Hypositta corallirostris

RANGE: E Madagascar
HABITAT: evergreen forest from sea level to 6,000 ft (1,800 m)
SIZE: 5–6 in (13–15 cm)

Like its much bigger and very different-looking relative the Helmet Bird, this small vanga is usually found in mixed feeding flocks in the middle layer of the forest. Although it does not climb head downward as true nuthatches do (pp. 302–5), it clings with its feet to the upper parts of tree trunks to gather its insect food. The female and juvenile differ from the male in having dark slate-gray underparts and dark brown crowns. Although examination of female specimens has shown that the species breeds in August and September, little else is known of its reproductive habits.

FAMILY BOMBYCILLIDAE
Waxwings

Small to medium, rather starlinglike. Tree-dwelling, usually gregarious. Feed largely on insects in summer and fruits in winter. Plumage soft, dense and silky, mainly brown, pinkish, gray and black, sometimes with red and yellow. Sexes alike except in Phainopepla. Usually nomadic, strongly territorial. Nest chiefly of twigs, in trees. Eggs 2–7, blue or greenish-white. Incubation 12–16 days, nestling period 16–25 days. 8 species.

4/ BOHEMIAN WAXWING
Bombycilla garrulus

RANGE: breeds N Eurasia and North America; irregular winter migrant to temperate areas S to 35°N
HABITAT: breeds in dense coniferous or mixed forest; occasionally found in town parks and gardens in winter
SIZE: 8 in (20 cm)

The beautiful pinkish-buff plumage of the Bohemian Waxwing is offset by yellow tips to the tail feathers, and waxlike red blobs at the tips of the secondary wing feathers, from which the common name of this species is derived. During their courtship display, the male presents the female with a berry or ant pupa, which the birds then pass back and forth from beak to beak but never swallow.

5/ PHAINOPEPLA
Phainopepla nitens

RANGE: breeds SW USA, S to Baja California and C Mexico; winters in S
HABITAT: brushland, river banks and chaparral in wetter areas
SIZE: 8 in (20 cm)

The flight of this species is buoyant and fluttery, but direct and often very high. Its call note is a querulous whistled *warp*, and its brief warbling song is seldom heard. The Phainopepla is particularly fond of mistletoe berries and also takes winged insects in flycatcherlike style. The male builds the well-concealed, cuplike tree nest. The first, early spring nesting is usually followed by a second nesting in a cooler, wetter habitat.

6/ GRAY HYPOCOLIUS
Hypocolius ampelinus

RANGE: breeds SW Asia and Middle East; occasional migrant to Himalayan foothills, N India and Pakistan
HABITAT: fields, scrub and gardens in semiarid climates
SIZE: $8\frac{1}{2}$ in (22 cm)

These sociable birds communicate with squeaking calls. Outside the breeding season, small groups of them feed together on fruits, berries and the occasional insect. Both male and female build the bulky and untidy nest, generally well concealed among the leaves of a palm tree. If disturbed, the birds desert the nest and reputedly return and destroy it before building another.

FAMILY DULIDAE
Palmchat

There is only one species in this family.

7/ PALMCHAT
Dulus dominicus

RANGE: **Hispaniola, Gonave (West Indies)**
HABITAT: **open woodland, palms, pines**
SIZE: **7 in (18 cm)**

The Palmchat is sometimes included in the wax-wing family, but its plumage is much coarser and it has a heavier bill. Palmchats are sociable birds which live in large communal nests woven around the trunk and base of the fronds of a royal palm tree. Some nests have housed as many as 30 pairs, each with a separate entrance burrow in the side of the mass leading into its own compartment.

Palmchats characteristically perch very close together and are often noisy and aggressive, a whole group suddenly making raucous calls, then falling silent. They spend almost all their time in trees, where they feed on berries and flowers.

FAMILY CINCLIDAE
Dippers

Small, plump, short-tailed, with long, strong legs and feet. Sexes similar. Unique among passerines in being adapted to swim, dive and walk under water. Movable membrane over nostrils, closed when head submerged. Characteristically bob their whole bodies up and down (hence name). Soft, long, dense plumage; chiefly black, brown or gray, in some species with white cap, back or "bib." Nest large, globe-shaped, built over running water. Eggs 4–5, white. Incubation 12–18 days, nestling period 19–24 days. 5

8/ WHITE-THROATED DIPPER
Cinclus cinclus

RANGE: **Europe and C Asia**
HABITAT: **fast-flowing upland streams**
SIZE: **7–8¼ in (18–21 cm)**

The White-throated Dipper has a rich diet of insect larvae, fish fry and fish eggs, freshwater shrimp and mollusks. Male and female both build the dome-shaped nest of moss, grass and leaves, with an entrance directly over running water. The birds generally roost communally during the winter. The race illustrated is *C.c. gularis*, from western and northern Britain. By contrast, the race *C.c. cinclus*, from northern Europe, has a black belly, while the race *C.c. leucogaster* of central Asia has a white belly.

9/ NORTH AMERICAN DIPPER
Cinclus mexicanus

RANGE: **Alaska to S Mexico**
HABITAT: **fast-flowing upland streams from 2,000 ft (600 m) up to the tree line**
SIZE: **7–8¼ in (18–21 cm)**

The North American Dipper is territorial in the summer, and to a variable extent during the winter, unless frozen streams force it to move to lower altitudes. Like other dippers, it has a well-developed, whitish nictitating membrane which protects its eyes from spray and when it is submerged. A dipper uses this membrane, which appears dramatically white against its dark head plumage, in a blinking action to signal alarm, excitement or aggression, combining it with the bobbing, or "dipping," of its body.

FAMILY TROGLODYTIDAE
Wrens

Small, agile insect-eaters, with short wings and plump bodies; many species with cocked-up tails. Plumage generally brown, chestnut, gray or black, often barred or streaked, some species with white cap, back or "bib." Sexes similar. Nest in cavities, roofed, with side entrance, some with access tunnel. Eggs 2–10, white or white with reddish speckles. Incubation 12–20 days, nestling period 12–18 days. 69 species.

10/ BLACK-CAPPED DONACOBIUS
Donacobius atricapillus

RANGE: **E Panama to Bolivia, N Argentina**
HABITAT: **marsh vegetation, swampy river bank scrub, wet meadows**
SIZE: **9 in (23 cm)**

The Black-capped Donacobius is the largest of all species of wren. When disturbed from cover, this species typically flies to an open perch on marsh grasses where it scolds. During displays, pair members perch together and each bobs its head and wags its tail. Orange patches of skin on the neck are often exposed, and the pair calls antiphonally.

11/ BICOLORED WREN
Campylorhynchus griseus

RANGE: **Colombia, Venezuela, N Brazil, Guyana**
HABITAT: **semiarid to arid savanna, cactus scrub, open woods, some habitats near human habitations**
SIZE: **8½ in (22 cm)**

This large, bold and conspicuous wren is usually found on or close to the ground, poking and peering into crevices in search of insects and their eggs. Its song is less guttural and scratchy than those of its close relatives, though the Giant Wren *C. chiapensis* of southeastern Mexico has similar characteristics of song, plumage and behavior, and is sometimes considered to be merely a race of the Bicolored Wren.

12/ ROCK WREN
Salpinctes obsoletus

RANGE: **breeds W Canada and NW USA to Costa Rica; winters in N breeding areas**
HABITAT: **arid and semiarid rocky barrens**
SIZE: **6 in (15 cm)**

The Rock Wren is distinguished from other wrens by its cinnamon rump and the buff tips of its outer tail feathers. It survives in a harsh rock-strewn environment, with little or no vegetation, by eating a variety of small insects and worms.

Its harsh and gritty song is reminiscent of that of the Northern Mockingbird *Mimus polyglottos* or the Brown Thrasher *Toxostoma rufum*.

Both male and female build a cup nest of any available materials beneath overhanging rocks or in a rock crevice. Often they construct a path of rock chips, and occasionally small bones and other objects, leading to the entrance.

13/ SEDGE WREN
Cistothorus platensis

RANGE: **breeds S Canada to E and C USA, C Mexico S to W Panama; winters in SE USA, E Mexico**
HABITAT: **wet, grassy meadows, drier bogs and marshes dominated by sedges**
SIZE: **4¼ in (11 cm)**

The Sedge Wren is slightly smaller than its relative the Marsh Wren *C. palustris*, but its song is quite distinct – a weak, staccato, chattering trill, often delivered at night. Its call note, a robust *chip*, is often doubled. As with other wrens, the male constructs dummy nests, from which the female selects one for egg laying.

14/ ZAPATA WREN
Ferminia cerverai Ⓡ

RANGE: **Zapata Swamp (Cuba)**
HABITAT: **sawgrass and woody hummocks in drier parts of the swamp**
SIZE: **6¼ in (16 cm)**

The Zapata Wren is the only wren native to the Greater Antilles. Almost flightless, this species was only discovered in 1926, and by 1974 it had become extremely rare. Any draining of the swamp could further jeopardize this wren and 2 other Zapata Swamp endemics, the Zapata Rail *Cyanolimnas cerverai* and the Zapata Sparrow *Torreornis inexpectata*.

15/ WINTER WREN
Troglodytes troglodytes

RANGE: **breeds C and S Canada, Alaska, coastal W USA, parts of E USA, Europe, Asia E to Japan, N Africa; N populations winter to S**
HABITAT: **woodland, gardens, cultivated land, moors, heaths, rocky islands**
SIZE: **3 in (8 cm)**

The tiny, cock-tailed Winter Wren, the only wren that occurs in the Old World, is equally at home in a damp, broad-leaved wood, in the gorse and bracken of an upland moor, or on the cliffs of a windswept Atlantic or Pacific island.

There are nearly 40 races, including *T. t. indigenus* of the British mainland, *T. t. zetlandicus* of the Shetland Islands and *T. t. helleri* of Kodiak Island, off Alaska. Races are paler in hot, desert regions, darker in wetter places.

16/ FLUTIST WREN
Microcerculus ustulatus

RANGE: **S Venezuela, Guyana, N Brazil**
HABITAT: **humid mountain forest**
SIZE: **4¾ in (12 cm)**

As its name suggests, the song of this wren has a flutelike character. It can start with 3–4 single notes and end with a long ascending whistle, or consist of a descending series of high-pitched whistles and may last up to 30 seconds.

The Flutist Wren lives in dense and humid cloud forest at altitudes of 2,800–7,000 ft (850–2,100 m). It spends much of its time alone foraging for insects on the ground and in the forest understory.

MOCKINGBIRDS, ACCENTORS, THRUSHES

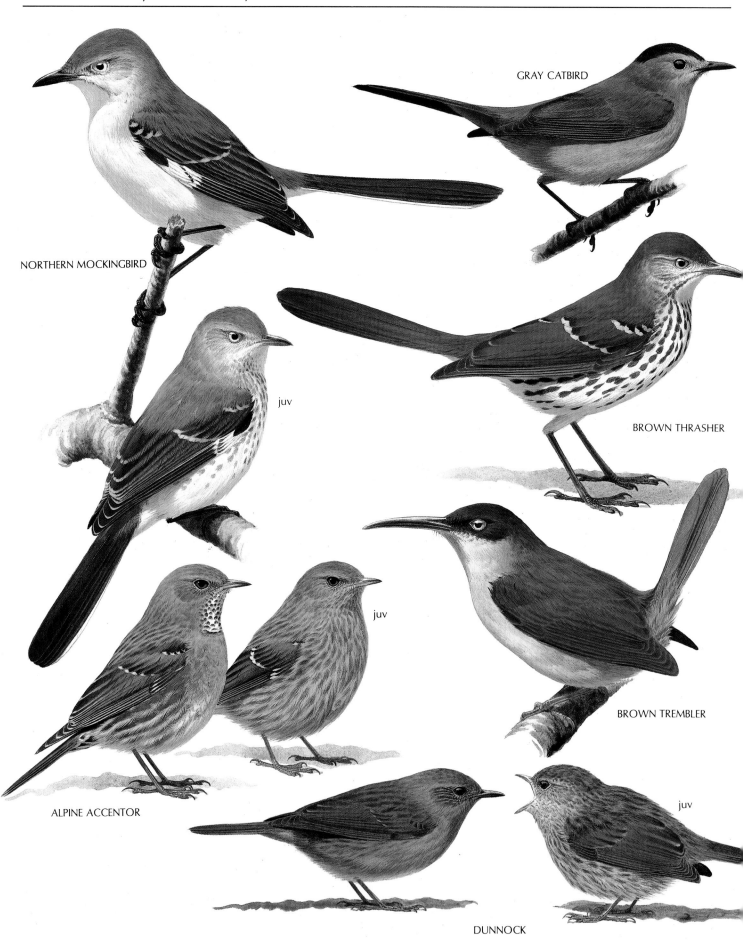

GRAY CATBIRD

NORTHERN MOCKINGBIRD

juv

BROWN THRASHER

juv

ALPINE ACCENTOR

BROWN TREMBLER

juv

DUNNOCK

BLUE SHORTWING

♂

race *cruralis*
♀

RUFOUS SCRUB-ROBIN

NIGHTINGALE

juv

EUROPEAN ROBIN

juv

race *svecica*
♂

race *cyanecula*
♂

BLUETHROAT

juv

RED-CAPPED ROBIN-CHAT

MOCKINGBIRDS, ACCENTORS, THRUSHES

FAMILY MIMIDAE
Mockingbirds

Small to medium, long-tailed birds. Plumage usually brown or gray above and paler but marked below; brighter in some. Sexes similar. Cup nest. Eggs 2–5, whitish to greenish-blue, often with dark markings. Incubation 12–13 days, nestling period 12–13 days. 30 species.

1/ GRAY CATBIRD
Dumetella carolinensis

RANGE: breeds S Canada, USA; winters Central America, West Indies
HABITAT: dense vegetation in woodland edge; readily adapts to human settlements
SIZE: 7¾ in (20 cm)

The Gray Catbird often forages on the ground and has a habit of flinging leaves about during its search for food. Its diet includes a variety of fruits and invertebrates. Since it can survive on fruit alone, it can winter occasionally in some northern areas. This bird is well known for the catlike cries that give it its name and is a versatile mimic.

A nocturnal migrant, the Gray Catbird often arrives in the southern USA in spring in large waves. Nesting activities begin soon after arrival. The female builds a low, well-concealed nest in dense thickets, bushes, small trees or tangles of vines. The male provides some help by bringing materials such as twigs, strips of bark, leaves, grasses and even paper and string. Usually 2 broods are raised in one season, the nestlings of the first brood being fed mostly with insects, while those of the second receive much fruit. Gray Catbirds are aggressive in defense of their nests and young.

2/ NORTHERN MOCKINGBIRD
Mimus polyglottos

RANGE: S Canada, USA, Mexico, Caribbean islands; introduced to Bermuda, Hawaiian islands
HABITAT: open areas in cities, suburbs, countryside, deserts
SIZE: 9–11 in (23–28 cm)

Despite its rather drab gray and white plumage, the Northern Mockingbird is a familiar and popular species, chosen as the state bird for 5 states of the USA. It is an accomplished mimic, usually repeating learned phrases in each song. It is sometimes called the American Nightingale because of its habit of singing on moonlit nights. Its diet includes fruit, berries and invertebrates, and good sources of food are often vigorously defended against all competing species.

This bird's habit of wing flashing – pausing as it runs along the ground and deliberately raising and partially opening its wings – is a common but, as yet, poorly explained form of behavior. Some ornithologists believe it may be a way of startling potential prey out of hiding.

Breeding begins as early as mid-February. The nests are open cups composed of sticks and lined with fine grasses, rootlets, leaves and plant down. Pieces of string, cotton, plastic and hair are often incorporated into the nest, which is usually well concealed in a bush or the lower branches of a tree, often near human dwellings.

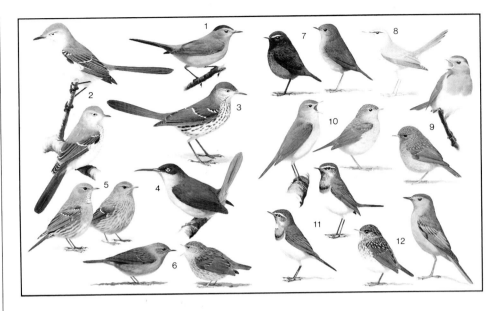

3/ BROWN THRASHER
Toxostoma rufum

RANGE: E USA and S Canada to the foothills of the Rocky Mountains
HABITAT: woodland, forest edge, hedgerows, scrubland, pastures, gardens
SIZE: 9¾ in (25 cm)

This well-known species is most commonly observed skulking along the ground in search of food, or singing on an exposed perch. It typically forages by poking through leaves and other ground cover with its bill, occasionally pausing to pick up leaves and toss them aside. It feeds mostly on insects, but also eats other invertebrates and some small vertebrates. Fruits and acorns also contribute to its diet, especially in winter.

Breeding begins as early as March in the southern part of the range and continues through July. The male sings from the top of a tree or tall shrub, head held high and long tail drooping. His song is a series of rapid, short, musical phrases, usually uttered in pairs; it resembles the song of the Northern Mockingbird, but is wilder. The nest is a bulky cup of sticks, lined with dead leaves, grasses and fine rootlets. It is often placed in thorny bushes to provide added protection.

4/ BROWN TREMBLER
Cinclocerthia ruficauda

RANGE: Lesser Antilles
HABITAT: rain forest; also secondary forest
SIZE: 9–9¾ in (23–25 cm)

This uncommon species – named for its strange and unexplained habit of violently shaking – has been driven from much of its former range by a combination of human predation, habitat destruction and the introduction of predators. The Brown Trembler feeds on seeds, fruit, large invertebrates and small vertebrates such as frogs and lizards.

It moves about chiefly by hopping on the ground and through vegetation and by making short, direct flights. It has also been observed flapping upward in trees, hanging upside-down and clinging vertically like a woodpecker. It nests in tree cavities, hollow tree-fern stumps and, less commonly, at the bases of palm fronds.

FAMILY PRUNELLIDAE
Accentors

Small. Plumage streaked rufous or brownish-gray above, grayish with rufous-brown markings below. Sexes similar. Nest on ground, in low vegetation or in rock crevices. Eggs 3–6, pale bluish-green to blue. Incubation 11–15 days, nestling period 12–14 days. 12 species.

5/ ALPINE ACCENTOR
Prunella collaris

RANGE: from Iberia and NW Africa E through S and E Asia to Japan
HABITAT: breeds in rocky areas and alpine meadows from about 5,000 ft (1,500 m) to at least 16,500 ft (3,300 m); usually winters lower down
SIZE: 7 in (18 cm)

The accentors have the distinction of being the only family of birds that is almost entirely restricted to the Palearctic region. The Alpine Accentor has a huge range within this region, but it normally occurs only at high altitudes, where it is well adapted to survive the harsh conditions.

The Alpine Accentor is a larger and stouter bird than any other accentor, with quite colorful plumage. It has rippling, larklike calls, and a larklike song, uttered from the ground, from a perch or often in a brief, larklike song-flight.

Alpine Accentors regularly breed as high as 16,500 ft (5,000 m) in central Asia, and in the Himalayas they have been seen even at an altitude of almost 26,250 ft (8,000 m) on Mount Everest. In winter, they usually move down to the lower slopes in family parties and small flocks, although they usually stay above 5,000 ft (1,500 m). They sometimes peck at crumbs in ski resorts and also visit bird tables. Isolation on various mountain ranges has resulted in the evolution of some 9 different races distinguished by generally slight details of plumage.

6/ DUNNOCK
Prunella modularis
RANGE: **Europe S to C Spain and Italy and E to the Urals, Lebanon, Turkey, N Iran, Caucasus**
HABITAT: **scrub, heathland, mixed woodland, young coniferous forest, farmland hedgerows, parks, gardens, vacant urban land, scrubby coastal cliffs and dunes**
SIZE: **5½ in (14 cm)**

This generally unobtrusive little bird spends much of its time in cover among shrubs and hedgerows, but also forages on the open ground for its food with a curious, shuffling, jerky, rather mouselike gait; it can also hop. In winter it feeds mainly on seeds and in summer eats chiefly insects and their larvae.

At one time it was known in the British Isles as the Hedge Sparrow, from the superficial similarity of its plumage to that of a female House Sparrow. Because of its typical accentor appearance, the name Hedge Accentor is perhaps the most satisfactory, but the bird is generally known in Britain by its old English name Dunnock, from its gray-brown, or dun, coloration.

The Dunnock has interesting breeding habits. The birds establish 3 different types of territory: those held by a solitary male, those held by a conventional male-female pair, and larger territories held by a male-female pair plus an additional male. The extra male in the last type of territory sometimes mates with the female, helps the other male defend the territory and helps feed the young. The situation is further complicated by the regular occurrence of associations between 1 male and 2 or even 3 females, and between 2 or 3 males and 2 to 4 females.

FAMILY TURDIDAE
Thrushes
Small to medium. Plumage variable, some mostly brown or gray, others brightly colored. Sexes alike or dissimilar. Nest sites variable. Eggs 1–10, pale, often speckled. Incubation 12–15 days, nestling period 12–15 days. 329 species.

7/ BLUE SHORTWING
Brachypteryx montana
RANGE: **E Nepal to W and S China, Taiwan, Philippines, Borneo, Sumatra, Java**
HABITAT: **upland forest thickets of rhododendron and oak**
SIZE: **6 in (15 cm)**

The 6 species of shortwing are insectivorous, wrenlike birds, with short tails and rounded wings. They breed mainly in Southeast Asia and the islands of Indonesia. The Blue, or White-browed, Shortwing is typical of the group in its preference for dense undergrowth in evergreen forests. In the mountain forests of northern Burma it ranges as high as 8,500 ft (2,600 m).

There are some 13 races, differing mainly in plumage details. In some, such as the race *B. m. cruralis* from the Himalayas, northern Burma and western China, the female is brown, while in others, such as *B. m. poliogyna* from north and central Luzon and Mindoro in the Philippines, she

is similar to the male but with a chestnut-brown head and neck. In some races, some males have the brown female plumage.

The female lays 3 white eggs inside a domed nest, built against clumps of moss on a tree trunk or on a rock. The side entrance runs parallel with the face of the trunk or rock and is hidden from view. Nevertheless, the nest is sometimes parasitized by the Small Cuckoo *Cuculus poliocephalus*, which lays its own eggs inside.

8/ RUFOUS SCRUB-ROBIN
Erythropygia galactotes
RANGE: **Mediterranean, SW Asia E to Pakistan, C Asia**
HABITAT: **open grassland, scrub, stony country, oases, parks, gardens**
SIZE: **6 in (15 cm)**

The Rufous Scrub-Robin is intermediate in form between the thrushes and the warblers. It stands high off the ground on its long pinkish-gray legs and it can cock its long rufous tail up over its back to create a *U* shape. Although it is sometimes rather skulking by nature, it is not a particularly shy bird. The male's song is rich and flutelike and is often uttered during the display flight.

The diet of this species includes worms, ants and beetles, as well as fruit. The nest is a loose structure of grasses and twigs placed in a shrub about 6 ft (2 m) above the ground. Its lining of wool and plant down sometimes includes fragments of snake skin. Populations of this bird that breed in sub-Saharan Africa are sedentary, while those of North Africa and Eurasia winter in the south of their range.

9/ EUROPEAN ROBIN
Erithacus rubecula
RANGE: **Europe and N Africa E to W Siberia and N Iran**
HABITAT: **woodland and forest; also gardens, parks in Britain**
SIZE: **5½ in (14 cm)**

The European Robin has an upright, bold stance on the ground, regularly flicking its wings and tail. It is commonly seen as it flits from one low perch to another, and the red breast figures prominently in the bird's display. Continental European races are shy, but in Britain, where this species is the national bird, many can be seen around human habitations. Most populations are resident, and their songs can be heard for much of the year. The European Robin is larely monogamous, and both sexes defend winter territories. Although they are very aggressive birds, they rarely make physical contact during fights. When they do, one may peck the other to death.

Invertebrates form the basic diet of European Robins, although the birds will eat seeds and fruit during cold, winter weather. Nesting takes place in hollows in banks, holes in trees and walls, and in an extraordinary variety of artificial items including discarded cans, kettles and even unmade beds. The nest is a cup of moss, feathers and sometimes plastic strips, built on a base of leaves.

10/ NIGHTINGALE
Luscinia megarhynchos
RANGE: **NW Africa, Eurasia S to Caucasus, E to Altai range; winters Nigeria E to Kenya, Tanzania**
HABITAT: **woodland, dense hedges, thickets near water, shrubland**
SIZE: **6½ in (16.5 cm)**

The somberly colored Nightingale has declined in numbers in Britain, France and some other parts of Europe. The Nightingale is richly praised for its fine song, which consists of deep, plaintive notes, trills and slurred *jug-jugs*. It sings both at night and in the daytime.

This species forages on the ground and in the dense vegetation under the shrub layer, searching for insects such as ants and beetles. In late summer it will also eat berries and soft fruits. The nest is well hidden among nettles or ivy in a dark spot usually on or close to the ground. The typical clutch contains 4–5 olive-green eggs.

11/ BLUETHROAT
Luscinia svecica
RANGE: **Eurasia, W Alaska**
HABITAT: **wooded tundra, alpine meadows, dry, stony slopes, shrubby wetlands**
SIZE: **5½ in (14 cm)**

There are some 10 races of this delightful little bird across its vast range. In some, such as *L. s. svecica* of the northernmost latitudes, the center of the blue throat patch is red, while in others, such as *L. s. cyanecula* of Spain, central Europe and parts of western USSR, the center spot is white.

The Bluethroat flies close to the ground with a flitting action, followed by a flat glide or swoop into low cover. It has a more upright stance on the ground than the European Robin, but, like that species, frequently flicks its tail. The song is more tinkling than that of the Nightingale. It may be uttered in the air or from a perch and often dominates the sounds of the Arctic tundra.

The Bluethroat's diet consists largely of insects, sometimes caught in the air, but usually found by turning over leaf litter. The cup-shaped nest is built on the ground in thick vegetation, in a clump of grass, under a shrub, or sometimes in a hollow in a bank.

12/ RED-CAPPED ROBIN-CHAT
Cossypha natalensis
RANGE: **South Africa N to Somalia, SW Ethiopia, W to Cameroon**
HABITAT: **dense evergreen forest and undergrowth**
SIZE: **7¾ in (20 cm)**

The genus *Cossypha* contains some of the most distinctively marked of the so-called African robins. Although its plumage is striking, the Red-capped, or Natal, Robin-Chat is a shy bird and could be overlooked were it not for its loud, warbling songs which often mimic other birds.

Nowhere very common, this species has extended its choice of habitat to include deciduous as well as evergreen forests. Its diet consists mostly of insects and fruit. Both sexes build the nest, placing it among branches, creepers or mossy boulders.

FIRE-CRESTED ALETHE

♀

♂

WHITE-THROATED ROBIN

♀

COMMON REDSTART

♂

♀

♂

ASIAN
MAGPIE-ROBIN

PHILIPPINE WATER REDSTART

HODGSON'S GRANDALA

♀

juv

♂

EASTERN BLUEBIRD

WHITE-CROWNED FORKTAIL

STONECHAT

race *hibernans*

GREEN COCHOA

ARNOT'S CHAT

ROCK THRUSH

DESERT WHEATEAR

race *homochroa*

1/ FIRE-CRESTED ALETHE
Alethe castanea

RANGE: C Africa
HABITAT: tropical forest
SIZE: $6\frac{1}{4}$–$6\frac{3}{4}$ in (16–17 cm)

One of 6 species of alethe or forest-robin, this bird is somewhat thrushlike, with long legs. It is active and pugnacious, erecting its tawny orange crest and spreading its tail when excited or threatened.

Fire-crested Alethes search for insects in the shaded undergrowth of tropical forests. They often associate with parties of safari ants that march across the ground. The advancing ants disturb insects in their path, which the birds wait to snap up.

This species' nest is a cup of moss and roots placed on a tree stump or on a heap of leaf litter on the forest floor. The clutch consists of 2–3 pinkish eggs blotched with lilac or maroon.

2/ ASIAN MAGPIE-ROBIN
Copsychus saularis

RANGE: India, S China, Southeast Asia, Indonesia, Philippines
HABITAT: up to 6,500 ft (2,000 m) in scrub, around cultivation, gardens; also coastal mangroves
SIZE: 8 in (20 cm)

The magpie-robins occur in Africa and tropical Asia. They are sometimes known as shamas and tend to range in color from bluish to black. They are fine singers, and the Asian Magpie-Robin is no exception. Its loud, varied and melodious song is interspersed with some discordant notes and imitations of other birds' calls. It often cocks its tail while perching.

Asian Magpie-Robins are regularly seen hunting for insects in gardens in Borneo, and they are common in many towns in Peninsular Malaysia. They nest in holes, often in buildings and under the eaves of houses. The clutch consists of 3–6 eggs which are pale blue-green, blotched and mottled with reddish brown. They are incubated by both parents for 12–13 days.

3/ WHITE-THROATED ROBIN
Irania gutturalis

RANGE: Turkey to Afghanistan; winters S through Arabia and Iran to Kenya, Tanzania, Zimbabwe
HABITAT: stony slopes with shrubs, oak steppes up to 9,500 ft (2,850 m); dense scrub along dry riverbeds in winter
SIZE: $6\frac{3}{4}$ in (17.5 cm)

The male White-throated Robin is easy to recognize in his breeding range but may be confused with the robin-chats in his winter quarters. This species resembles a Nightingale *Luscinia megarhynchos* in its gait, moving across the ground with hops and drooping wings. In flight it reveals its long wings and tail. It often perches on weed stems, as well as bushes and stones. The male has a loud, fluid and melodious song.

White-throated Robins are monogamous. The female builds the nest in the lower part of a shrub or tree some 6–50 in (15–125 cm) above the ground. The nest has a base of dry twigs, bark or leaves and is lined with wool, hair, feathers or

even pieces of rag. The 4–5 greenish-blue eggs are spotted with yellow or brown spots. The young hatch after 13 days.

4/ COMMON REDSTART
Phoenicurus phoenicurus

RANGE: Europe, Asia S to Iran and E to Lake Baikal; winters S to Arabia and W and E Africa
HABITAT: forests with clearings, heaths, moors with scattered trees, parks, orchards; winters on savanna and woodland
SIZE: $5\frac{1}{2}$ in (14 cm)

The Common Redstart is a small, elegant chat with rather long wings and an orange-chestnut tail that it characteristically quivers up and down. Its diet consists mainly of insects, and the male's aerial flycatching technique, as well as his prominent display flight, demand open spaces in its woodland habitat. The female feeds mainly on the ground. Both sexes supplement their diet with small snails, berries and fruit.

Common Redstarts often site their nests in tree holes, including those abandoned by woodpeckers. They may use cavities in stone walls in hilly country and will even nest in holes in the ground. The female lays and incubates 5–7 pale blue eggs, sometimes producing 2 broods in a single season.

5/ PHILIPPINE WATER REDSTART
Rhyacornis bicolor   ?

RANGE: Luzon Island (Philippines)
HABITAT: mountain streams
SIZE: $5\frac{1}{2}$ in (14 cm)

The Philippine Water Redstart lives along clear mountain streams and rivers. It often occurs in rocky gorges and other inaccessible terrain. It feeds mainly on insects which it gleans from boulders among the torrents, but little else is known of its lifestyle.

The breeding habits of this bird are probably similar to those of its close relative, the Plumbeous Water Redstart *Phoenicurus fuliginosus*, which is found in the mountains of central, east and Southeast Asia. This species nests in stream banks and lays eggs of a whitish hue thickly speckled with brown marks.

6/ HODGSON'S GRANDALA
Grandala coelicolor

RANGE: Himalayas, mountains of SE Tibet and W China
HABITAT: boulder-strewn alpine meadows, rocky slopes, scree and cliffs above scrub zone
SIZE: $8\frac{3}{4}$ in (22 cm)

Hodgson's Grandala is a bird of the high mountains of Asia, foraging in scrub and on the open slopes up to 14,800 ft (4,500 m) above sea level. It feeds on insects, especially caterpillars and other larvae, as well as on seeds and berries. Occasionally, it turns to cultivated fruit. The only member of its genus, it is a short-legged, long-winged bird. When perched, it looks rather like a rock thrush, but in flight it more closely resembles a starling. It spends much of the time in the air and usually occurs in flocks.

The nest is a cup of dry grass, covered with moss and lined with feathers. It is built on a rock ledge, often on a vertical cliff. The clutch contains 2 greenish-white eggs with brown markings.

7/ EASTERN BLUEBIRD
Sialia sialis

RANGE: **E North America and Central America**
HABITAT: **open woodland, roadsides, farms, orchards, gardens, parks**
SIZE: **$5\frac{1}{2}$–$7\frac{1}{2}$ in (14–19 cm)**

Eastern Bluebirds often form flocks in autumn and winter and several birds may roost together in the same cavity during winter. Typically they have a hunched appearance when perching. They often fly down from their perch to catch insects on the ground. In colder months, berries become an important part of their diet. Nesting usually takes place in natural tree cavities and old woodpecker holes. Although the eggs of this species are typically blue, some individual females lay clutches of white eggs. Multiple broods are common, with 2 chicks often produced in a single season in northern areas, and up to 4 in southeastern USA.

In many areas, the Eastern Bluebird has declined in numbers because of competition for nest sites with other birds. The provision of nest-boxes by conservation organizations and concerned individuals has helped the species, however, and it has consequently made something of a comeback in recent years.

8/ WHITE-CROWNED FORKTAIL
Enicurus leschenaulti

RANGE: **Himalayas, S to Malaysia, Indochina, Sumatra, Java and Borneo**
HABITAT: **rocky streams, forest rivers, swamps**
SIZE: **8–11 in (20–28 cm)**

This is the largest and darkest of the 7 species of forktail, all of which have black and white plumage. It lives close to mountain torrents, where it forages for insects on the surface of the water or along rocky banks. Its penetrating alarm call is a high-pitched screech.

The White-crowned Forktail nests in crevices in vertical banks covered with ferns or in hollows in trees or rocks, where the nest is often soaking wet. It is built of green moss mixed with rootlets, fibers and dead leaves. Both sexes incubate the 3–4 cream or rich buff eggs which are densely marked with brick-red or brownish speckles.

9/ GREEN COCHOA
Cochoa viridis   ?

RANGE: **Himalayas and mountains of N Southeast Asia**
HABITAT: **undergrowth, often near streams in dense evergreen forest**
SIZE: **11–$11\frac{3}{4}$ in (28–30 cm)**

One of 3 species of cochoa, this bird haunts forested mountain slopes, usually 3,300–5,000 ft (1,000–1,500 m) above sea level. It is a shy and retiring species and lives singly or in pairs. It searches through the undergrowth for insects and other invertebrates and berries.

The nest is a shallow cup of green moss, leaves and fibers built in a tree. A white, threadlike fungus is typically present and this seems to be a characteristic feature of the nests of this genus. The clutch varies from 2–4; the eggs are sea-green with reddish-brown blotches.

10/ STONECHAT
Saxicola torquata

RANGE: **much of Eurasia and Africa**
HABITAT: **grassland, heaths, plantations, coastal gorse**
SIZE: **5 in (12.5 cm)**

There are some 24 races of this widespread bird, including *S. t. hibernans* of the British Isles, western France and the west coast of the Iberian peninsula. The western races are residents or partial migrants, while the eastern ones are migratory, spending their winters in northeast Africa, Arabia, India and Southeast Asia. The species has declined in parts of western Europe after suffering hard winters and habitat changes.

The Stonechat uses low, exposed perches to spot its invertebrate prey, which it usually catches after a glide or hop to the ground. In spring the perch is usually about 3 ft (1 m) above the ground, but in summer, when the vegetation is taller, the preferred height is about 5 ft (1.6 m). The birds may also feed on small fish, lizards, seeds and berries and sometimes take fast-flying insects, such as flies, butterflies and moths, in flight or by hovering in front of foliage.

Stonechats are largely monogamous, each pair building its nest either on or very near the ground. The structure is a loose cup of unwoven grass stems or leaves with a lining of wool or hair. The female lays 4–6 pale bluish eggs with reddish-brown marks.

11/ ARNOT'S CHAT
Myrmecocichla arnoti

RANGE: **C, E and S Africa**
HABITAT: **open woodland, margins of cultivated land**
SIZE: **7 in (18 cm)**

Sometimes known as the White-headed Black Chat, this species is now only locally common because of destruction of its forest habitat. It is a conspicuous, thickset bird, rather like a thrush, and has a loud, whistled song, which first rises then falls in pitch. This is often combined with mimicry of other bird calls. In addition, its wings make a noise when it flies. It forages at low level for spiders and insects, particularly ants, which are gathered from the gnarled trunks of trees and from the ground.

Arnot's Chat is fairly easy to observe and is generally seen in pairs or family parties. The nest is made of coarse plant material and sited in a hole or a hollow. The clutch contains 2–4 bluish or greenish eggs which are speckled with rufous or mauve markings.

12/ DESERT WHEATEAR
Oenanthe deserti

RANGE: **N Africa, Middle East, C Asia, Mongolia**
HABITAT: **heaths, coasts, dunes, rocky mountain passes; N and high-altitude S breeders move to lower altitudes or migrate S in winter**
SIZE: **$5\frac{1}{2}$–6 in (14–15 cm)**

One of a score of wheatear species, this bird occurs in a variety of dry, open habitats where there are sandy or stony soils. Most of its populations are migratory, although some are only partial migrants. The illustration shows the north African race *O. d. homochroa*, which has been seen in Britain as a rare vagrant.

The Desert Wheatear perches freely on low shrubs, mounds and stones from which it can watch the ground for ants, beetles and their larvae, spiders, worms and small lizards. Seeds may also form part of the diet.

In the breeding season, the male Desert Wheatear performs a song-flight up to 25–30 ft (8–10 m) into the air and utters a few mournful notes. The female builds a rather bulky nest of grass and dead leaves among stones, in a hole in the ground or in a rabbit burrow. The 4–5 pale blue eggs with reddish-brown spots are incubated by the female for 13–14 days.

13/ ROCK THRUSH
Monticola saxatilis

RANGE: **breeds NW Africa, S and C Europe E to Lake Baikal and China; winters in W Africa**
HABITAT: **rocky, shrubby terrain, vineyards, savanna, stony gullies, gardens in winter**
SIZE: **$7\frac{1}{4}$ in (18.5 cm)**

This bird of rocky terrain has a rather long body and looks more like a short-tailed chat than a thrush. It is essentially a ground bird, although it may also perch on trees, buildings and overhead wires. The Rock Thrush is shy and solitary on its breeding grounds, shooting behind boulders or plummeting down crags when disturbed.

The male has a far-carrying, mellow, piping or warbling song. He begins singing from a perch, then climbs steeply into the air with slow, powerful wing beats. His song reaches a peak at the top of his ascent, then he soars, flutters his wings quickly and mimics song phrases of other birds before parachuting silently down to earth.

The large insects on which the Rock Thrush feeds are obtained by swooping from a perch down to the ground or, more rarely, during flight. Many kinds of berries are also eaten. The nest site is a horizontal crack in the rock face, crag or ruin, or under a boulder. The female builds the nest from grass and moss and incubates 4–5 pale blue eggs with some speckles at the broader end.

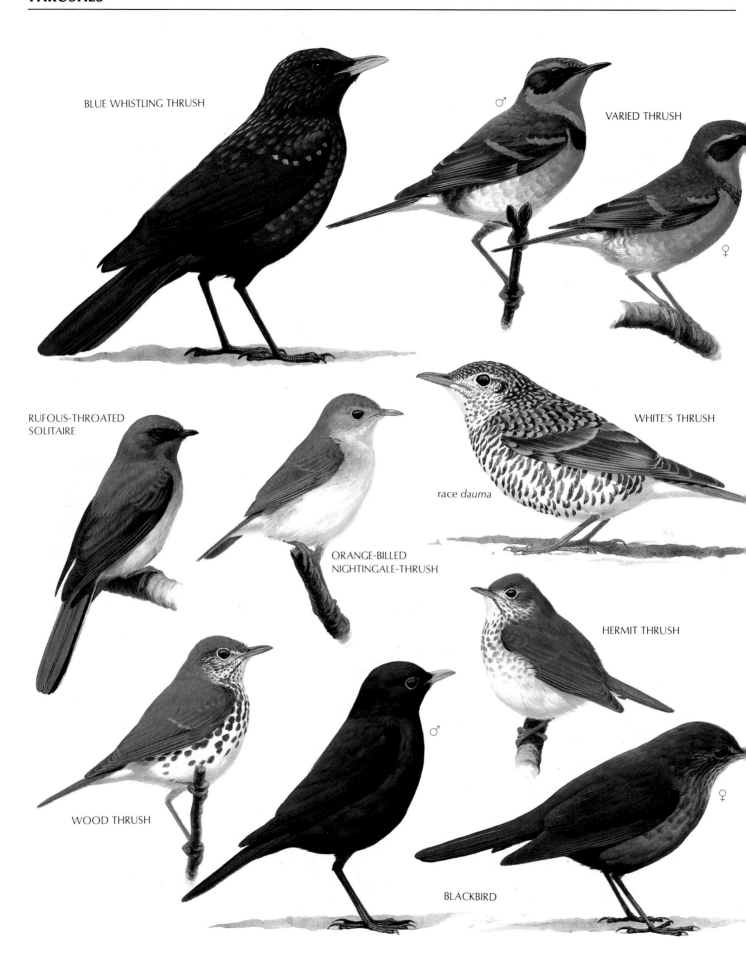

BLUE WHISTLING THRUSH

♂

VARIED THRUSH

♀

RUFOUS-THROATED
SOLITAIRE

WHITE'S THRUSH

race *dauma*

ORANGE-BILLED
NIGHTINGALE-THRUSH

HERMIT THRUSH

WOOD THRUSH

♂

♀

BLACKBIRD

ISLAND THRUSH

race *layardi*

race *papuensis*

race *niveiceps*

juv

FIELDFARE

RED-LEGGED THRUSH

AUSTRAL THRUSH

CLAY-COLORED ROBIN

juv

AMERICAN ROBIN

THRUSHES

1/ RUFOUS-THROATED SOLITAIRE
Myadestes genibarbis
RANGE: **West Indies**
HABITAT: **mountain forest**
SIZE: **7½ in (19 cm)**

The Rufous-throated Solitaire is a tropical forest bird, with a diet consisting mainly of fruit but also including insects and other invertebrates. It obtains much of its food from a perched position, although it will occasionally hover and regularly darts out from a prominent perch to catch flying beetles and moths on the wing. Its song is a series of flutelike, whistling notes.

The cup nest consists primarily of moss and other plant material. It is built in the side of a bank, in a tree cavity, in the fork of a branch or in the heart of a tree fern or bromeliad. Each pair usually rears 2 chicks, which emerge from the egg with a covering of blackish natal down. Both parents take part in feeding the young.

2/ BLUE WHISTLING THRUSH
Myiophoneus caeruleus
RANGE: **C Asia, India, W China, Southeast Asia, Java, Sumatra**
HABITAT: **edges of mountain and forest streams; also limestone rock faces**
SIZE: **11¾–12½ in (30–32 cm)**

Sometimes known as the Whistling Schoolboy, this dark blue songbird with glistening blue spots is one of about 6 semiaquatic species within the thrush family. Its rich songs can be heard ringing out over the roar of tumbling waters as it forages on and around the wet rocks, damp moss and water surface for insects, snails and crustaceans.

Male and female Blue Whistling Thrushes look alike and each pair generally lives alone. Both adults share nest-building, incubation and the care of the young. The nest is a mossy cup often placed on a ledge in a small cave. The female lays 3–5 gray-green eggs with brown spots.

3/ WHITE'S THRUSH
Zoothera dauma
RANGE: **E Europe E to China and Japan, Southeast Asia, Indonesia, New Guinea, E and S Australia; N populations migrate S**
HABITAT: **woodland and forest**
SIZE: **10¼–11 in (26–28 cm)**

Usually shy and secretive, this large thrush feeds on the forest floor, turning over the dead leaves with its bill in its search for earthworms, snails and insects. It suddenly opens its wings and tail to panic insects into movement, and apparently also raises itself up on its toes and vibrates its whole body rapidly for several seconds to bring worms to the surface.

White's Thrush is usually solitary outside the breeding season, but birds from migratory populations may form small flocks when traveling.

There is much regional variation in the song: indeed, the analysis of their songs using sonagraphs formed part of the evidence that led to the recent separation of 2 Australian races into full species – the Bassian Thrush *Z. lunulata* and the Russet-tailed Ground Thrush *Z. heinei*. Races living in Siberia, Manchuria and Japan have a

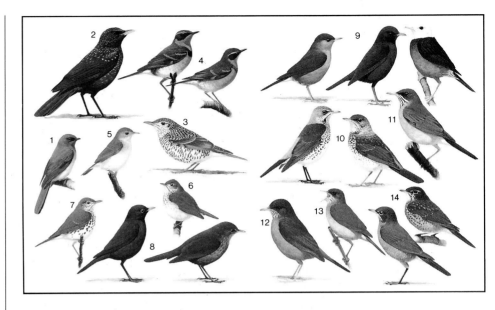

haunting, melancholy song, consisting of repeated loud, fluting whistles, which may continue for hours on end, while those found in southern Asia, including *Z. d. dauma* of the Himalayas, southwest China and parts of Burma and Southeast Asia, have a typically thrushlike song.

4/ VARIED THRUSH
Ixoreus naevius
RANGE: **W coast of North America, from NC Alaska S to N California**
HABITAT: **moist coniferous forest**
SIZE: **7¾–9¾ in (20–25 cm)**

The Varied Thrush often forages on the ground, taking a variety of insects, snails, earthworms, seeds and fruit. In winter it migrates from the mountains to the valleys in search of food. The song is a long, vibrating whistle, followed by a pause and then a series of rapidly trilled notes all at different pitches.

The nesting season begins in late April. The female builds a bulky cup nest of twigs, moss and mud, lined with fine grasses, on the horizontal branch of a small tree. The clutch of 2–5 pale blue eggs with a few brown speckles is incubated solely by the female for about 14 days, but both sexes feed the nestlings. Juvenile Varied Thrushes resemble the females, but they have an incomplete breast band and speckling on the breast.

5/ ORANGE-BILLED NIGHTINGALE-THRUSH
Catharus aurantiirostris
RANGE: **Mexico, Central America, Venezuela, Colombia**
HABITAT: **low rain forest and cloud forest, forest edge, dense thickets, coffee plantations**
SIZE: **6½ in (17 cm)**

The Orange-billed Nightingale-Thrush is a shy, secretive bird that forages for invertebrates on the ground, near the ground in dense thickets or at low levels in trees. It has a poor voice compared with most other nightingale-thrushes; its simple song consisting of short, jumbled

warbles with a rather squeaky tone. Although it often sings uninterrupted for long periods, it usually does so from a concealed perch where it is difficult to observe. This bird also has a nasal *waa-a-a-a* call.

The bulky cup nest of moss and grass is generally built low in a thicket or shrub, and the average clutch consists of 2 pale blue eggs with brown spots. This species is parasitized by the Bronze Cowbird *Molothrus aeneus*.

6/ HERMIT THRUSH
Catharus guttatus
RANGE: **North and Central America**
HABITAT: **coniferous, deciduous or mixed woodland, forest edge, thickets**
SIZE: **6–7¾ in (15–20 cm)**

The Hermit Thrush has one of the most beautiful of all bird songs. The song has a clear, flutelike introductory note followed by a series of rising and falling phrases of different pitches. This bird has a habit of slowly raising and dropping its tail several times a minute while perched; this is usually accompanied by a low *chuck* call.

Hermit Thrushes forage mainly on the ground for insects, spiders, snails, earthworms and also salamanders. In winter, fruits and seeds make up an important part of their diet. The nest is a cup of twigs, dried grass, moss and, sometimes, mud, constructed by the female. In the eastern part of the bird's range, the nest is commonly built on the ground in a natural depression. In the west, it is usually placed in a low tree.

7/ WOOD THRUSH
Hylocichla mustelina
RANGE: **E North and Central America, from S Canada to Panama**
HABITAT: **woodland, wooded slopes, parks, often near streams**
SIZE: **7½–8½ in (19–22 cm)**

The Wood Thrush is a migratory species which winters in the south of its range. It has a rapid *pit-pit-pit* alarm call and, in addition, raises its head feathers when alarmed. This bird generally forages at ground level but also catches insect food among tree foliage.

Male Wood Thrushes first appear in the southern USA in March or April. They then move north and begin singing when they arrive in their nesting territories. The song consists of loud, flutelike phrases with 3–5 notes, each differing in pitch and ending with a soft, guttural trill. The female builds a bulky cup nest of dead leaves, moss and rootlets, the lack of grass distinguishing it from the nest of an American Robin. Often, a piece of white paper or cloth is included in the base.

8/ BLACKBIRD
Turdus merula

RANGE: **breeds NW Africa, Europe E to India, S China; N and some E populations winter S to Egypt, SW Asia, Southeast Asia; introduced to Australia, New Zealand**
HABITAT: **diverse, including forest, farmland, moors, scrub, gardens, parks, inner city**
SIZE: **9½–9¾ in (24–25 cm)**

The Blackbird is a familiar species throughout western Europe, where its melodious, fluty song is a common sound over a wide range of habitats. From its original woodland haunts, the bird has spread into gardens and even into the centers of towns and cities. Today, gardens harbor the densest populations, followed by parks and farmland. Densities are lowest deep in woodland, where the birds are often much shyer.

Blackbirds prise earthworms from the soil all year round and, by avidly turning over leaf litter, they catch a variety of insects and other invertebrates. They have a mixed diet, and at certain times of the year the fruits of hawthorn, holly, elder and yew provide an important source of food. Their nest is a substantial cup of grasses or roots, cemented together with wet leaves or mud. The usual clutch contains 3–5 pale greenish eggs with red-brown speckles.

9/ ISLAND THRUSH
Turdus poliocephalus

RANGE: **Christmas Island, Taiwan, Indonesia through Melanesia to Samoa and Fiji**
HABITAT: **dense rain forest and clearings**
SIZE: **9½–9¾ in (24–25 cm)**

In size, habits and call-notes, the Island Thrush resembles the Blackbird and the American Robin. There are about 50 races of this species reflecting its wide geographical range. Many are restricted to single islands or groups of islands, including *T.p. niveiceps* of Taiwan and *T.p. layardi* of Viti Levu Island, in Fiji, and *T.p. papuensis* of southeastern New Guinea.

The altitude at which Island Thrushes live differs from one island to another. In New Guinea, the birds occur above the tree line from 7,500 ft–13,500 ft (2,300 m–4,100 m). In Viti Levu, they range from sea level over 3,300 ft (1,000 m) up to the tops of the highest mountains. Island Thrushes are also found on low coral islands. They are basically ground-feeding birds, with a diet that includes worms and snails. They build their nests on rocky ledges.

10/ FIELDFARE
Turdus pilaris

RANGE: **breeds N Eurasia E to C Siberia, Greenland; winters widely in Europe, SW Asia**
HABITAT: **subarctic scrub, light coniferous and birch woodland, parks, gardens, towns; winters in open country, woodland edges, fields**
SIZE: **10¼ in (26 cm)**

This is a gregarious, noisy species of thrush that has colonized parts of western Europe, including parts of the British Isles, in recent years. It is essentially a migratory species that breeds in northern latitudes and usually only winters in the southern part of its range.

The Fieldfare eats many kinds of invertebrates, as well as plant food such as seeds and fruit. Fruit is especially important in autumn and winter, and the bird is a specialist feeder on apples and haws. The nest is a bulky cup of grass reinforced with roots and mud, usually placed in the fork of a tree. The typical clutch consists of 5–6 pale blue eggs with brown markings. When defending their young, the adults will readily and accurately "bomb" predators with their droppings.

11/ RED-LEGGED THRUSH
Turdus plumbeus

RANGE: **West Indies**
HABITAT: **forest areas in mountains and lowlands, gardens, city lawns**
SIZE: **9¾–11 in (25–28 cm)**

This striking bird is the most widespread of the West Indian thrushes. Its plumage varies among the islands, the chin and throat ranging from white to black, and the belly from reddish yellow to gray and white. Its song is rather weak and melancholy and, when disturbed, the bird utters a loud *wet-wet* call, sometimes repeatedly.

The Red-legged Thrush frequents a variety of habitats. In some areas it is shy and difficult to observe, while in others it is quite bold and easy to watch. It commonly forages on the ground, making loud, rustling sounds as it searches under dead leaves for insects. It has an omnivorous diet, including insects, reptiles and fruit. The cup nest is built in a bush, in the fork of a branch or among the fronds of a palm.

12/ AUSTRAL THRUSH
Turdus falcklandii

RANGE: **Chile, Argentina, Falkland Islands, Juan Fernandez Islands**
HABITAT: **farmland with some trees, groves of willows, forest borders**
SIZE: **9¾–10½ in (25–27 cm)**

The Austral Thrush frequently feeds on the ground, hopping about on grassy areas and cocking its head from side to side to look for earthworm burrows. It takes insects and other arthropods from the ground or from plant debris and also feeds on fruit. The territorial song, which is made up of repeated whistled phrases such as *tee-yoo*, *churr* and *tee*, is delivered from a conspicuous perch. This species also utters an alarm call *kreep* in rapid succession.

The nesting season of the Austral Thrush runs

from September to January, with each pair producing up to 3 broods per season. The bulky nest of grasses often has a base of mud. The female carries out the incubation, but both adults are active in feeding the nestlings.

13/ CLAY-COLORED ROBIN
Turdus grayi

RANGE: **SE Mexico, Central America, coastal Colombia**
HABITAT: **open woodland, woodland edge and clearings, usually near streams**
SIZE: **9–9½ in (23–24 cm)**

The Clay-colored Robin is one of the best known tropical American songsters, with a musical, caroling song. A generalist in feeding habits, it spends much of its time on the ground searching for insects, earthworms, slugs and lizards. Fruit also forms part of its diet, and it has been known to come to feeding stations for bananas. Although somewhat secretive and solitary, it often lives close to human settlements.

The nesting season usually lasts from March to June, but it varies from region to region. In central Panama, for example, the birds nest mainly during the dry season from December to April. They build a bulky cup nest of mud, moss, twigs, leaves and other plant materials, the structure placed low in a small bush or in dense cover in a tree. Incubation of the 2–4 eggs takes 12–13 days, with the young hatching at different times.

14/ AMERICAN ROBIN
Turdus migratorius

RANGE: **North America**
HABITAT: **forest borders, woodland, parks, lawns, suburbs**
SIZE: **9–11 in (23–28 cm)**

Like the much smaller European Robin, this species is also known colloquially as the Robin Redbreast. It is the largest of the North American thrushes and is a very common and well-known bird. It is a habitat generalist, occurring in almost any environment with cover, from city suburbs to western mountainsides 12,000 ft (3,600 m) high.

American Robins usually feed on grassy ground, cocking their heads to search for earthworm burrows. Experiments have shown that the birds locate earthworms by sight rather than sound, as was previously believed. Their diet also includes insects, snails and much fruit, especially in winter.

In the southern portion of its range, the American Robin has both resident and migratory populations. Migration northward begins in February, with the males leaving first. The females arrive in the north in April, by which time the males have started singing. The song is a musical caroling of short rising and falling phrases, sometimes described as *cheerily cheer-up cheerio*. Both male and female build the bulky cup nest of protruding twigs, grass and mud. This is placed in any sheltered location, from the ground to the treetops. The birds may also nest on buildings and fences. Each year, 2, or sometimes 3, broods may be raised. The male will care for the young of the first brood while the female incubates the second clutch.

LOGRUNNERS, BABBLERS

EASTERN WHIPBIRD

race *pulcher*

MID-MOUNTAIN RAIL-BABBLER

race *castanonota*

PALE-BREASTED THRUSH-BABBLER

race *albicollis*

WHISKERED YUHINA

race *temporalis*

GRAY-CROWNED BABBLER

race *flavicollis*

LARGE WREN-BABBLER

race *rubeculus*

WREN-TIT

race *fasciata*

WHITE-NECKED TREE-BABBLER

race *leucolophus*

RED-BILLED LEIOTHRIX

WHITE-CRESTED LAUGHING-THRUSH

race *bicolor*

race *strigula*

CHESTNUT-TAILED MINLA

CHESTNUT-HEADED FULVETTA

race *malayana*

young in nest

race *caudatus*

COMMON BABBLER

WHITE-NECKED ROCKFOWL

LOGRUNNERS, BABBLERS

FAMILY ORTHONYCHIDAE
Logrunners

Small to medium, secretive birds. Plumage mainly brown, black or white; some brighter, with blue, chestnut and olive-green. Sexes alike or different. Cup or domed nest, usually in dense shrubs. Eggs 1–3, white or pale blue. Incubation 17–21 days, nestling period 12–14 days. 19 species.

1/ EASTERN WHIPBIRD
Psophodes olivaceus

RANGE: E coast of Australia from N Queensland to Victoria
HABITAT: thick shrubbery in wet forest, dense heath
SIZE: $9\frac{3}{4}$–$11\frac{3}{4}$ in (25–30 cm)

The Eastern Whipbird is a secretive species. It takes its name from the contact call uttered while pairs forage out of sight of each other in thick cover. The male gives a long whistle ending in a sharp whip-crack, and this is answered by 2 or 3 chirrups from the female.

Eastern Whipbirds make low, short flights on their short wings, with their long tails fanned. Usually, however, they bounce along the ground and through shrubs, sometimes raising their short crests. They feed on insects and larvae by raking through leaf litter with their bills and feet and by probing into crevices and low shrubbery. The nest is a cup of twigs built in the thick foliage of the understory layer. The young leave the nest before they can fly and are guarded by the adults while they hide in the undergrowth.

2/ MID-MOUNTAIN RAIL-BABBLER
Ptilorrhoa castanonota

RANGE: New Guinea, Batanta Island, Yapen Island
HABITAT: lower mountain forest
SIZE: 9 in (23 cm)

The 3 species of rail-babbler replace each other altitudinally in New Guinea. This species, which is also known as the Chestnut-backed Jewel-Babbler, is as handsome as its relatives and, like them, has several races that differ in plumage details. Those illustrated are *P. c. pulcher* of southeastern New Guinea and *P. c. castanonota* from the Vogelkop region of New Guinea.

The Mid-mountain Rail-Babbler has a beautiful song of clear, bell-like whistles, uttered from the ground or from a fallen log. Pairs or small groups of this species often occur together, walking on the ground and foraging in the leaf litter or probing in the earth on the forest floor.

FAMILY TIMALIIDAE
Babblers

Small to medium, thrushlike. Plumage diverse: many species brown and gray; many dense forest species brighter, with red, blue, yellow. Sexes similar, except in some colorful groups. Nest open or domed, usually in bushes or trees. Eggs 2–7, various colors. Incubation 13–16 days, nestling period 13–16 days (except for rockfowls: incubation 24 days, nestling period 26 days). 256 species.

3/ PALE-BREASTED THRUSH-BABBLER
Illadopsis rufipennis

RANGE: W Africa E to Kenya and Tanzania
HABITAT: forests
SIZE: $5\frac{1}{2}$ in (14 cm)

There are few groups of birds that conceal themselves more effectively or are more drab in plumage than this African babbler and its close relatives. A sedentary species of thick forest, the Pale-breasted Thrush-Babbler spends its life either on or close to the forest floor. It is quite possible to spend weeks in a forest where these birds are comparatively common without ever catching a glimpse of one.

There is some evidence that this species is most active at dawn and dusk, when it seems to forage more widely for insects and small mollusks. In the fading light, it can sometimes be seen on paths and in clearings. The call is thought to be a series of ascending whistled notes, since this sound is commonly heard when these birds are about. The breeding habits are apparently unknown.

4/ GRAY-CROWNED BABBLER
Pomatostomus temporalis

RANGE: N and E Australia
HABITAT: open woodland
SIZE: $9\frac{3}{4}$ in (25 cm)

The Gray-crowned Babbler is a perky, excitable bird with a slender, downcurved bill. It lives in family groups of up to 12 individuals, which defend communal territories. Each group usually consists of a pair or trio and their offspring from previous years. These all forage together, bounding along the ground or along branches, and making short, weak, fluttering and gliding flights. They feed on invertebrates and lizards by probing into leaf litter, soil, foliage and bark crevices, or by turning over rocks, sticks and cowpats.

Each group builds many nests, some of which are used only for roosting: these are bulky, globular stick nests, with a side entrance. The normal clutch consists of 2–3 pale brown, finely pencilled eggs. These are incubated by the female. More than one female may lay in the nest. The whole group cooperates to feed the sitting female and young. The 2 races of this species shown here are *P. t. temporalis* of southern Queensland and eastern New South Wales and *P. t. rubeculus* of northern and northwestern Australia.

5/ LARGE WREN-BABBLER
Napothera macrodactyla

RANGE: Malay Peninsula, Java, Sumatra
HABITAT: forests
SIZE: $7\frac{1}{2}$ in (19 cm)

The Large Wren-Babbler is a dumpy, short-tailed bird of dense forest undergrowth. It occurs in lowland rather than hill forest, and must therefore be under greater threat from logging operations than some of its highland relatives.

This bird's song is a series of repeated whistles. However, it is often very difficult to catch sight of the singing bird among the rotting debris and sun-dappled obscurity of the forest floor. The habits of this species are not well known, although nesting has been recorded in West Java in March and September. The nest is a large, cup-shaped construction sited in a thicket, and the female lays a clutch of 2 buff-colored eggs, speckled with red.

6/ WHITE-NECKED TREE-BABBLER
Stachyris leucotis

RANGE: S Thailand to Sumatra, Borneo
HABITAT: forests
SIZE: 6 in (15 cm)

The White-necked Tree-Babbler haunts tall, mature forest in the lowlands and foothills of its range. A sedentary bird, it keeps close to ground level and is one of a number of species with such habits about which extremely little is known. It is, however, not uncommon, particularly in the southern part of its range.

This species has a rather heavy bill and strong feet, and appears to feed on beetles and caterpillars. One nest found in dense scrub consisted of a compact cup of grass, roots and fibers and held 3 white eggs.

7/ WREN-TIT
Chamaea fasciata
RANGE: USA from W Oregon S to N Baja California
HABITAT: chaparral, coniferous brushland
SIZE: 6 in (15 cm)

The Wren-Tit, the only American member of the babbler family, is more closely related to the thrushes than to the wrens and titmice, for which it is named. At first sight, it may act and look like a wren, but its pale eyes, streaked breast and long, unbarred tail help to distinguish it. The plumage varies in color, from reddish-brown in northern races to grayish-brown in southern races such as *C.f. fasciata*.

The Wren-Tit dwells secretively in dense chaparral and low tangles, which it seldom leaves except to make short, weak, tail-pumping flights from bush to bush. There it gleans food from the bark surfaces of shrubs, taking ants, wasps, beetles, caterpillars, bugs, flies and spiders. It also eats various berries and is an irregular visitor to bird feeders, where it will eat breadcrumbs.

The voice of the Wren-Tit is its signature, likely to be heard before the bird is seen. The male sings year round. His loud song begins with a series of accelerating staccato notes and runs together in a descending trill at the end *pit-pit-pit-r-r-r*. The female sings a similar, but trill-less version.

Wren-Tits mate for the life of either member of the pair. The nest is placed low in a tree or shrub. Both sexes construct the compact cup of fibers, bark and grasses, bound with spiders' webs and ornamented by small lichens. Male and female alike incubate the 3–5, pale greenish-blue eggs and tend the young, which leave the nest when they are 15–16 days old.

8/ COMMON BABBLER
Turdoides caudatus
RANGE: S Iraq and Indian peninsula E to Bangladesh
HABITAT: dry scrub and bushes in open country
SIZE: 9 in (23 cm)

A gregarious, untidy-looking babbler, this species scuttles and hops below the bushes or along a hedgerow in an almost ratlike manner, jerking its long tail spasmodically. It is a reluctant flier and, when forced into the air, it will flap and glide rather feebly to the next patch of cover. It forages for insects, grain and berries and, when the bushes are in flower, it supplements its diet with nectar. There are 4 races: the one illustrated is *T. c. caudatus* from India and part of west Pakistan, which is darker and browner than the others.

The Common Babbler is a noisy bird, especially when alarmed. Flocks constantly utter musical whistling calls to keep in contact as they move through the undergrowth. The communal habits of this bird extend to cooperative breeding, with nonbreeding birds in the flock helping with the care of the young. The nest is a small, deep cup with noticeably thick walls. The typical clutch consists of 3–5 turquoise eggs.

9/ WHITE-CRESTED LAUGHING-THRUSH
Garrulax leucolophus
RANGE: Himalayas through Southeast Asia to Sumatra
HABITAT: undergrowth, scrub and bamboo thickets
SIZE: 11 in (28 cm)

As a flock of these gregarious birds forages through the grass and bushes, or in low foliage, there is a constant, subdued chuckling and chirruping. Every now and then, these sounds erupt into bursts of wild, cackling laughter, from which the birds take their name.

White-crested Laughing-Thrushes are active, strong-footed birds that typically bounce over the ground or follow one another in short glides over gulleys or ravines. They are primarily birds of the foothills, where they have sedentary habits. Those birds that nest at higher altitudes tend to move down to the lower slopes in winter. The illustration shows 2 races, *G. l. leucolophus* of the Himalayas and *G. l. bicolor* of Sumatra.

10/ RED-BILLED LEIOTHRIX
Leiothrix lutea
RANGE: Himalayas, Burma, S China
HABITAT: undergrowth in forests
SIZE: 5 in (13 cm)

A loud, melodious, warbling song, combined with attractive plumage, have long made this a favorite cage bird, especially in China. In the wild, the song is often uttered from the cover of dense undergrowth in a shady ravine, where the bird's bright colors are difficult to detect.

Outside the breeding season, the Red-billed Leiothrix often occurs in small parties that forage through bamboo, grass or scrub. They frequently feed in company with other small babblers, keeping in touch with a constant, low, piping note. This species is resident throughout its range but, like many other birds of the Himalayas, it tends to move to lower altitudes in winter. It becomes scarcer toward the western limits of its range.

11/ CHESTNUT-TAILED MINLA
Minla strigula
RANGE: Himalayas and Southeast Asia
HABITAT: deciduous or evergreen forest and rhododendron groves
SIZE: 6¼ in (16 cm)

This is a common and colorful little babbler, often seen in company with other species as it searches through the foliage. It is a bird of the middle story of the forest, where it moves quite acrobatically among the small twigs. Small parties of Chestnut-tailed Minlas keep up a constant chirruping as the flock moves onward, bird after bird flitting across clearings or from one treetop to the next. Insects provide the bulk of its food, but it also eats seeds and berries.

The Chestnut-tailed Minla, which is sometimes known as the Bar-throated Siva, is resident throughout its range. Of the 2 races illustrated, *M. s. strigula* occurs in the eastern Himalayas and *M. s. malayana* occurs in Malaysia. The latter is one of the most common small birds on top of the highest peaks in the Malay Peninsula.

12/ CHESTNUT-HEADED FULVETTA
Alcippe castaneceps
RANGE: Himalayas and Southeast Asia
HABITAT: thick undergrowth and scrub, forest edge and clearings
SIZE: 4 in (10 cm)

This tiny, titlike babbler is a bird of high altitudes, ranging up to 13,000 ft (4,000 m) above sea level. Although it often occurs in groups of up to 30 of its own species, it also joins mixed-species flocks to forage through hill forest. It builds a deep nest in low bamboo, rhododendron or juniper bushes.

Chestnut-headed Fulvettas are active, noisy birds. Every twig or branch, patch of moss or clump of fern is searched carefully as the birds swing on the slender stems or flutter upside-down. They will also launch briefly into the air after a passing insect. The contact note is a repeated cheeping, and the birds also have a rising, 3-note song.

13/ WHISKERED YUHINA
Yuhina flavicollis
RANGE: Himalayas E to Burma and Laos
HABITAT: secondary forest and scrub, clearings and forest edge
SIZE: 5 in (13 cm)

The erect crest (common to several closely related species) gives this familiar babbler a perky appearance as it swings through the twigs, or clings briefly to a tree trunk, like a tit, while inspecting the bark for insects or grubs. Its diet also includes many varieties of berry and seed. It is a gregarious species, often associating with other birds in mixed foraging parties, and is highly vocal, keeping up a continual "chipping" note.

The Whiskered Yuhina ascends the mountains to somewhat lower altitudes than some other Himalayan babblers. It is widely distributed in the foothills in winter. Of the 2 races illustrated, *Y. f. flavicollis* occurs in the eastern and *Y. f. albicollis* in the western Himalayas.

14/ WHITE-NECKED ROCKFOWL
Picathartes gymnocephalus [V]
RANGE: W Africa from Guinea and Sierra Leone to Togo
HABITAT: rock outcrops with caves in primary forest
SIZE: 15¾ in (40 cm)

The 2 species of rockfowl are mysterious birds of strange appearance and uncertain relationships. The function of the brightly colored bare skin on the rockfowls' heads is also unknown, since the birds spend much of their time in the darkness of caves and in the dim light of dense forest. They are ground-dwellers that move with long, springy hops as they search for insects, frogs or crustaceans. They forage among moss-covered rocks, often near forest streams.

The rockfowls' dependence on caves for nesting is unusual among birds. They construct mud nests on the smooth cave ceilings, possibly using existing wasps' nests as foundations. The White-necked Rockfowl is a sociable bird and breeds colonially. The alarm note is a repeated guttural call; it also utters a curious, low, muffled groan.

♂

♂

BEARDED REEDLING

♀

VINOUS-THROATED PARROTBILL

race *webbianus*

race *bulomachus*

HALF-COLLARED GNATWREN

♂

BLUE-GRAY GNATCATCHER

♀

race *cetti*

CETTI'S WARBLER

race *albiventris*

AFRICAN SEDGE-WARBLER

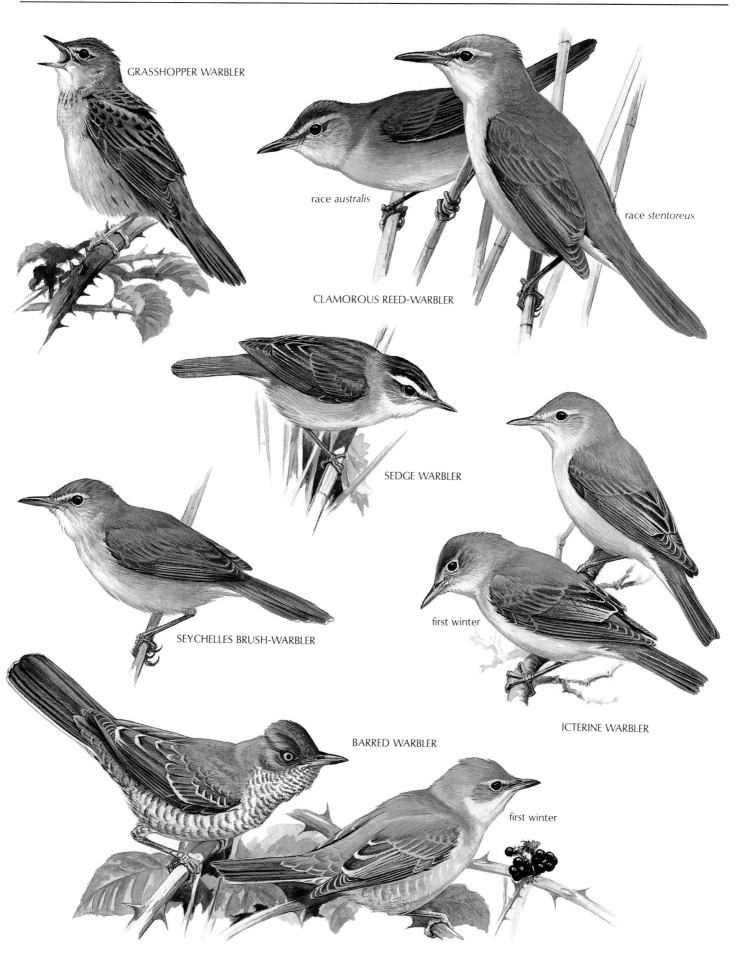

GRASSHOPPER WARBLER

race *australis*

race *stentoreus*

CLAMOROUS REED-WARBLER

SEDGE WARBLER

SEYCHELLES BRUSH-WARBLER

first winter

ICTERINE WARBLER

BARRED WARBLER

first winter

PARROTBILLS, OLD WORLD WARBLERS

FAMILY PARADOXORNITHIDAE
Parrotbills

Small to medium, titlike, mostly brown and gray. Plumage soft and loose. Most species with strongly arched bills. Sexes alike except in Bearded Reedling. Nest compact, cup-shaped, in bamboo, grass or reed. Eggs 2–7, whitish or blue with reddish speckling. Incubation 12–13 days, nestling period 9–12 days. 19 species.

1/ BEARDED REEDLING
Panurus biarmicus

RANGE: **W Europe, Turkey, Iran across Asia to E Manchuria**
HABITAT: **reedbeds**
SIZE: **6 in (15 cm)**

A metallic, pinging call and a glimpse of a tawny, long-tailed bird like a tiny pheasant whirring over the reedbeds on rounded wings is becoming an increasingly familiar experience throughout western Europe.

Although they are basically sedentary birds, confined to a restricted habitat, Bearded Reedlings tend to flock together in the fall and will undertake mass movements away from their breeding quarters. Over the last 30 years or so these movements have become annual events and the species has colonized many sites beyond its previous range.

Delightfully active and acrobatic, the Bearded Reedling is adept at straddling 2 reeds with its feet turned outward to grip each stem. In summer it feeds mainly on insects such as mayflies, but in winter it will eat seeds, particularly those of the common reed *Phragmites*. Pairs often roost together on reed stems, the male distinguished by his blue-gray head and jaunty black moustaches.

2/ VINOUS-THROATED PARROTBILL
Paradoxornis webbianus

RANGE: **Manchuria, S through China and Korea to Burma**
HABITAT: **bamboo groves, scrub, tea plantations and reedbeds**
SIZE: **4¾ in (12 cm)**

This is an abundant bird in parts of China. Outside the breeding season they often move through the undergrowth in large flocks in search of seeds and insects, keeping in touch with one another with a constant sharp, chirruping call.

The plumage varies with race: *P. w. webbianus* of parts of coastal eastern China has a chestnut crown and nape, whereas *P. w. bulomachus* of Taiwan has a rufous-pink crown and nape. All races have a strong bill which is used for tearing bamboo and reed stems to expose the insects within. The bills of some other members of the family are even more powerful, but the name "parrotbill" somewhat overemphasizes their massiveness and, strictly speaking, applies to only a couple of species.

FAMILY SYLVIIDAE
Old World warblers and relatives

Small, tree-dwelling or grassland birds. Plumage generally unobtrusive, although some tropical species brighter. Sexes usually similar, although males often brighter. Nests open, domed or purse-shaped in shrubs or on ground. Eggs usually 2–7, pale with fine speckles. Incubation 10–17 days, nestling period 9–20 days (40 days in some). 376 species.

3/ HALF-COLLARED GNATWREN
Microbates cinereiventris

RANGE: **Central and South America from Nicaragua to Colombia, Ecuador and Peru**
HABITAT: **lowland forest**
SIZE: **4½ in (11.5 cm)**

This slender, dainty little bird is one of a dozen or so gnatwrens and gnatcatchers found in the Americas. Classified in a subfamily of their own (the Polioptilinae), they are the only New World members of this family. They are very like the Old World warblers and are probably descended from warblers that found their way to the New World. Gnatwrens are predominantly brown birds, with long bills and wrenlike cocked tails. They are found in the lower levels of woodland and forest, in contrast to gnatcatchers, all but one of which live higher in the tree canopy.

The Half-collared, or Tawny-faced, Gnatwren is a lively bird with an engaging habit of bobbing or wagging its tail. It forages actively for insects, either making excursions from a perch down to the ground or flitting among the foliage. It will often hover to pick its prey off a twig or leaf.

Its nest is a tight cup of plant down, leaves or petals bound with spiders' webs and covered in lichen or moss. There are 2–3 whitish eggs with dark spots.

4/ BLUE-GRAY GNATCATCHER
Polioptila caerulea

RANGE: **North America from S Canada to Guatemala and Cuba; winters S of South Carolina along Atlantic coast, and S of S Mississippi and S Texas**
HABITAT: **forest, timbered swamps, thorny chaparral, wooded areas of towns**
SIZE: **4½–5 in (11.5–13 cm)**

The Blue-Gray Gnatcatcher is typical of the gnatcatcher group: bluish-gray, slender, with a long tail, which it often cocks like a wren, and a long, thin, pointed bill. It is a tiny, restless bird, often pugnacious, which forages among the leaves and twigs of trees for insects. It will sometimes catch these on the wing, or pick them off leaves while hovering like a kinglet (pp. 282–85). Its song is a wheezy whisper.

The nest is usually placed in a tree fork or on a branch. It is a beautifully constructed cup made of plant down, bound together with spider and insect silk and covered with pieces of lichen. Both adults build the nest, and they also share the incubation of the 4–5 tiny, pale blue, brown-spotted eggs.

5/ CETTI'S WARBLER
Cettia cetti

RANGE: **Mediterranean E to Iran and Turkestan; currently spreading N**
HABITAT: **swamps, scrub alongside reedbeds, dense bushes and hedges with brambles and tamarisks, edges of cornfields**
SIZE: **5½ in (14 cm)**

In 1900 Cetti's Warbler was largely confined to Mediterranean climates, but in recent years it has been advancing north and has been recorded as far north as Sweden. One of 11 species in its genus, it is a small, plumpish bird with a short, graduated tail; the males are heavier and longer-winged than the females. The central Asian race *C. c. albiventris* is larger and does not molt in spring like the western race *C. c. cetti*, and as a result is much paler.

Skulking and secretive, Cetti's Warbler spends most of its time in dense cover, but it occasionally shows itself on top of a bush or hedge. The position of the male is often given away by his brief, explosive song.

Males play little part in breeding and may mate with 2 or more females. The female builds the nest – usually among dense vegetation such as an overgrown hedge, a reedbed or bramble thicket – and incubates the 3–5 brick-red eggs alone.

6/ AFRICAN SEDGE-WARBLER
Bradypterus baboecalus

RANGE: **S Africa (except dry W) N to Chad and Ethiopia**
HABITAT: **reedbeds, swamps, sewage works**
SIZE: **6–7½ in (15–19 cm)**

The tropical and subtropical marshes and scrublands of Africa and Asia are home to 11 species of *Bradypterus* bush warbler.

The African Sedge-Warbler is one of the most common of these birds in some areas of Africa, particularly around lagoons and in swamps. If its accustomed haunts are badly affected by drought in the dry season, it will migrate to find areas where water is still plentiful.

Shy by nature, it rarely emerges from among the sedges and rushes where it forages close to the ground for insects, but it can be located by its call, a series of sharp, staccato notes. It builds a rather bulky nest of strips of sedge, lined with rootlets, and lays a clutch of 2–4 eggs.

7/ GRASSHOPPER WARBLER
Locustella naevia

RANGE: **Europe S to N Spain and Balkans, Baltic and W USSR, C Asia E to Tian Shan; winters NW Africa, Iran, India, Afghanistan**
HABITAT: **marshes, wet meadows with shrubs, moist woods, osiers, rough grassland, heaths, dunes, conifer plantations**
SIZE: **5 in (12.5 cm)**

Visually undistinguished, the Grasshopper Warbler is renowned for its extraordinary song: a vibrant, high-pitched mechanical trill, resembling the whirr of an angler's reel, formed from double or triple notes produced at a rate of up to 1,400 triplets a minute.

Tracking the source of the song can be difficult, for the bird is able to "throw its voice" like a ventriloquist and it only rarely emerges from cover to sing in the open. Although a restless, agile species, it is very retiring: it generally forages for its insect prey deep within the foliage and, when disturbed, it often prefers to creep away through the grass rather than take flight.

The nest is as hard to find as the bird itself, for it is usually well hidden in low vegetation, with a concealed entrance.

8/ SEDGE WARBLER
Acrocephalus schoenobaenus

RANGE: **Europe (except Spain, Portugal and some Mediterranean coasts) E to Siberia and SE to Iran; winters Africa S of Sahara and E of Nigeria**
HABITAT: **osiers, marsh ditches, lakes, sewage works, gravel pits, conifer plantations, cereal and rape fields**
SIZE: **5 in (12.5 cm)**

The reed warblers of the genus *Acrocephalus* are essentially marsh-dwelling birds that occur in many parts of the Old World. The Sedge Warbler is one of the best known, for although it tends to keep to dense cover like most of its family, the male can be quite conspicuous early in the breeding season. It often advertises its presence with a stuttering call that is interspersed with mimicry of other species.

Sedge Warblers feed mainly on slow-moving insects which they pick out of low vegetation; in Africa they take many lake flies. They nest in hedges, among osiers, reeds or coarse grass, or even among standing crops of beans, rape or cereals, binding the cup-shaped nest securely to the stems.

9/ CLAMOROUS REED-WARBLER
Acrocephalus stentoreus

RANGE: **NE Africa, across S Asia to Australia**
HABITAT: **swampy vegetation, especially reedbeds**
SIZE: **6¼ in (16 cm)**

Like other reed warblers, the Clamorous Reed-Warbler is a denizen of thick reedbeds, but it will often venture into other swampy habitats; during droughts it will move into scrubland and even into gardens. The birds in southern Australia appear to leave in the fall, although their destination is not known. There are numerous races, including the southeast Australian and Tasmanian race *A. s. australis* and the Middle Eastern race *A. s. stentoreus*.

The bird owes its name to its loud, varied song, which has harsh scratchy notes interspersed with melodious phrases. It feeds on insects gleaned from vegetation and, sometimes, by flycatching.

The nest is skilfully woven from reed sheaths and decayed water plants and is attached to several reed stems.

10/ SEYCHELLES BRUSH-WARBLER
Bebrornis sechellensis   Ⓡ

RANGE: **Cousin and Aride islands, Seychelles**
HABITAT: **dense scrub and swamp**
SIZE: **5 in (13 cm)**

There are 2 species of warbler in the genus *Bebrornis*: one on the island of Rodriguez and this species which occurs in very small numbers on Cousin Island. With a population of only 30 individuals in 1968, it faced extinction but was saved by the International Council for Bird Preservation (ICBP). As a result of habitat conservation and translocation of birds to Aride Island from their original home on Cousin Island,

numbers were increased to over 450 by 1987.

A distinctive warbler with a weak and fluttering flight, its favored haunts are the dense bushy growth alongside old coconut plantations, mangroves and coastal scrub. It pursues flying insects and forages for caterpillars among the branches of small trees and bushes.

The nest is an oval cup of grass and coconut fiber lined with fine material such as cotton and wood shavings; it is built among bamboos, mangroves and other shrubs up to 16 ft (5 m) above ground level.

11/ ICTERINE WARBLER
Hippolais icterina

RANGE: **N and E Europe S to Alps, Asia Minor and Caucasus, Asia E to Altai Mountains; winters E and tropical Africa**
HABITAT: **open broad-leaved woods, parks, riversides, farmland, orchards and large gardens**
SIZE: **5 in (13 cm)**

The tree warblers of the genus *Hippolais* are relatively large, heavily built birds with prominent legs and feet and a habit of flicking their tails. The Icterine Warbler is one of the more striking members of the group, with bright yellow underparts and a powerful mimetic song. In fall its plumage is duller.

It is a lively, active warbler, more conspicuous than many as it moves about the tree canopy in search of insects and their larvae. In fall it will also take fruits, especially berries.

The nest of the Icterine Warbler is a fine example of tree architecture. Built in the fork of a tree, it is made of stems or grasses held together with wool and spiders' silk; some nests incorporate bark, paper or even rags. The 4–5 eggs are variable in size.

12/ BARRED WARBLER
Sylvia nisoria

RANGE: **C and E Europe, Asia E to Tian Shan**
HABITAT: **thorny scrub, wet fields with trees, broad-leaved woods, parks, peat bogs; winters on thorn savanna**
SIZE: **6 in (15 cm)**

The Barred Warbler is a stout little bird with distinctive barred underparts and staring yellowish-white irises to its eyes. When excited it raises its crown feathers to form a small crest.

This is one of a genus of 17 or 18 species of active insect-eating warblers. It is shy and secretive with a preference for thick cover, where it searches through the foliage for ants, young locusts, beetles and a variety of bugs. When startled, it utters a harsh chattering alarm note, but its song is rich and melodious, resembling that of the Nightingale.

In Europe the Barred Warbler often builds its nest close to that of a Red-backed Shrike, down near the ground, possibly gaining protection from other predators in this way.

race *atricapilla*

♀

♂

BLACKCAP

♂

race *heineken*

♂
melanistic form

♂ CYPRUS WARBLER

♀

♂

DARTFORD WARBLER

♀

WILLOW WARBLER

race *proregulus*

race *chloronotus*

YELLOW-BREASTED
FLYCATCHER-WARBLER

PALLAS'S LEAF-WARBLER

RUBY-CROWNED KINGLET

♀

♂

♂

GOLDCREST

♀

♂

♀

SEVERTZOV'S TIT-WARBLER

♂

race *saharae*

race *buryi*

non-breeding

♂

TINK-TINK CISTICOLA

STREAKED SCRUB-WARBLER

song-flight

♂

KAROO PRINIA

ZITTING CISTICOLA

OLD WORLD WARBLERS

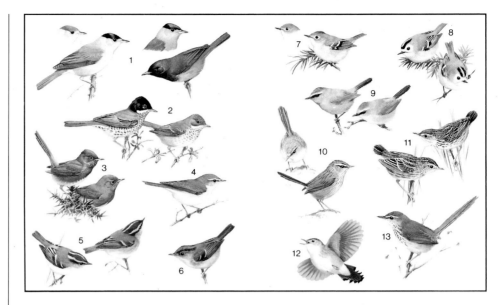

1/ BLACKCAP
Sylvia atricapilla

RANGE: **Eurasia E to River Irtysh in Siberia and N Iran, NW Africa and Atlantic islands; winters Mediterranean and Africa S to Tanzania**
HABITAT: **broad-leaved and conifer woods, overgrown hedges, scrub with tall trees**
SIZE: **$5\frac{1}{2}$ in (14 cm)**

This active, lively bird is often easy to observe in the trees as it combs the foliage for insects. The glossy black cap of the male and the reddish-brown cap of the female are distinctive. The male has a wavy or rippling song full of rich, pure notes; he is also an accomplished mimic.

Before the females arrive on the breeding grounds, the male often builds several rudimentary "cock's nests" of dry grass or roots, each slung between 2 twigs, up to 10 ft (3 m) from the ground. The female may reject them all and build one of her own – sometimes with the male's help – or she may accept one of his, finishing it off with a lining of down or wool. Both adults incubate the 4–6 eggs, which vary greatly in color and markings.

The race *S. a. heineken* found on Madeira and the Canary Islands is darker than the European race *S. a. atricapilla*. An even darker (melanistic) variety of *S. a. heineken* was once numerous, but now seems to be rarer.

2/ CYPRUS WARBLER
Sylvia melanothorax

RANGE: **Cyprus, but may wander to nearby coasts of E Mediterranean**
HABITAT: **hill scrub and orange groves up to 6,500 ft (2,000 m)**
SIZE: **$5\frac{1}{4}$ in (13.5 cm)**

Very similar to the Sardinian Warbler, and sometimes regarded as the same species, the Cyprus Warbler is usually heard rather than seen as it forages for food among the hillside orange groves or maquis scrub of its native island. It is distinguished from its close relative by its strongly barred underparts.

When glimpsed, it is a restless bird which tends to hold its tail up at right angles to its body. It usually keeps to cover, betraying its presence with a harsh single-note alarm call. On Cyprus its caution is well merited, since many are trapped each year (along with other warblers) to be pickled in jars and exported as a gastronomic delicacy.

The nest – a cup of leaves and grass with a hair lining and 3–5 eggs – is built in scrub.

3/ DARTFORD WARBLER
Sylvia undata

RANGE: **S England, W France, S Europe E to Italy and Sicily, N Africa E to Tunisia**
HABITAT: **in N, lowland heath with dense heather or gorse; in S, spiny maquis**
SIZE: **5 in (12.5 cm)**

In the north of its range this small, dark warbler suffers badly in cold winters for, despite its susceptibility to harsh weather, it does not migrate to warmer latitudes. It has also been a victim of habitat loss as the heathlands have been exploited for farming, forestry, housing and mineral extraction. Its declining habitat is also vulnerable to human disturbance and fire.

Dartford Warblers are generally skulking, furtive birds that keep to the bushes, but on sunny mornings the males will propel themselves some 7 ft (2 m) into the air in dancing song-flights. They feed almost exclusively on insects in summer but often eat small fruits during winter.

The nest is built of grass and moss with wool, down and spiders' cocoons, near the ground in a cistus, heather or gorse bush.

4/ WILLOW WARBLER
Phylloscopus trochilus

RANGE: **Scandinavia and NW Europe to E Siberia and Alaska; winters tropical and S Africa**
HABITAT: **open woods, scrub, conifer plantations, moorland with shrubs, hedges**
SIZE: **4 in (10.5 cm)**

The Willow Warbler is one of about 45 species of leaf warbler in the genus *Phylloscopus*: all small, slender, graceful birds with basically green, yellow or brown plumage. It is almost identical to the Chiffchaff *P. collybita* in appearance but its song is completely different: a descending series of liquid, silvery notes, in contrast to the chiffchaff's 2-note repetition of its name.

It is an adaptable bird which will thrive in any type of open woodland, and its song is a common sound in many regions. It feeds on insects taken on the wing or picked off the foliage with delicate precision. In winter, when the insect supply fails in the north, it flies south to Africa.

The nest is a domed structure with a side entrance, built on or near the ground by the female. If disturbed on the nest, she may feign injury, fluttering along the ground to lure the intruder away from the eggs or nestlings.

5/ PALLAS'S LEAF-WARBLER
Phylloscopus proregulus

RANGE: **Himalayas, mountains from Altai to Sakhalin; vagrants often reported to W; winters N India and S China**
HABITAT: **pine or birch forest; winters in light woodland, mixed forest or scrub**
SIZE: **$3\frac{1}{2}$ in (9 cm)**

This is a diminutive leaf warbler with a distinctive yellow crown stripe, double wing bar and rump. The western Chinese race *P. p. chloronotus* has a duller, ocher crown stripe and wing bar compared with other races, such as *P. p. proregulus* of central and northeast Asia.

It is a vivacious, highly active bird which often feeds by hovering among the leaves. It will also hawk after flying insects in the manner of a flycatcher. In its wintering grounds it spends most of its time in the forest canopy.

Its nest is domed, with a hair or feather lining, and is built on the branch of a moss-covered tree.

6/ YELLOW-BREASTED FLYCATCHER-WARBLER
Seicercus montis

RANGE: **Malaysia, Sumatra to Borneo, Palawan and Timor, usually above 6,500 ft (2,000 m)**
HABITAT: **mountain forest**
SIZE: **4 in (10 cm)**

There are several species of flycatcher-warbler in the genus *Seicercus* found from the Himalayas to Southeast Asia. The Yellow-breasted Flycatcher-Warbler is one of these; it is generally seen in mountain gullies and among the scrub and undergrowth in forest clearings – either alone, in pairs or in small parties. The male has an attractive trilling song.

Like all the flycatcher-warblers, it builds a dome-shaped nest, locating it in a crevice beneath an overhanging bank. It lays only 2 white eggs.

7/ RUBY-CROWNED KINGLET
Regulus calendula

RANGE: North America, from NW Alaska S to Arizona, also E Canada to Nova Scotia; winters S to N Mexico
HABITAT: mixed woods, spruce bogs, fir woods
SIZE: $3\frac{3}{4}$–$4\frac{1}{2}$ in (9.5–11.5 cm)

Similar to the Goldcrest of Eurasia, this tiny, short-tailed American species is an active, nervous bird which habitually flits its wings with sudden, jerking movements. This is a useful recognition point, since the characteristic scarlet patch on the crown is often concealed.

It hunts assiduously for insects among the twigs and leaves and may also dart after any that fly past. It will also feed on fruits and seeds. In contrast with that of the other Kinglets, such as the Goldcrest, the song of the male Ruby-crowned Kinglet is surprisingly rich.

The nest is a distinctive cup-shaped construction of plant down, slung beneath a pine branch and covered in lichens and lined with feathers.

8/ GOLDCREST
Regulus regulus

RANGE: discontinuous, from Azores and NW Europe and Scandinavia to E Asia
HABITAT: conifer woods to 14,700 ft (4,500 m), also some broad-leaved woods
SIZE: $3\frac{1}{2}$ in (9 cm)

This attractive little bird gets its name from its black-bordered erectile crest, which is orange in the male and yellow in the female.

Small groups of Goldcrests can often be seen flying from tree to tree in coniferous forest, drawing attention to themselves by their soft but extremely shrill, high-pitched *zee* calls. They feed mainly on small insects, which they obtain by diligent searching of the foliage or by hovering at the ends of branches, but they have also been seen sipping tree sap.

Goldcrests suffer badly in cold weather but after a succession of mild winters they may increase their numbers tenfold. They may lay up to 13 eggs, incubating them for the unusually long period (for passerines) of 14–17 days.

9/ SEVERTZOV'S TIT-WARBLER
Leptopoecile sophiae

RANGE: Pakistan, NW India, Nepal, Sikkim and China, from Tian Shan to Sichuan
HABITAT: rhododendron and juniper scrub above the tree line
SIZE: $4\frac{1}{4}$ in (11 cm)

Very like the Goldcrest in appearance, and often considered to be a close relation, Severtzov's Tit-Warbler is restricted to mountain habitats where it feeds on insects gathered in the scrub belt from 8,000–13,000 ft (2,500–4,000 m). The true relationships of these 2 species remain a matter of controversy. Indeed, at one time both they and the Goldcrest and its relatives were considered to be atypical members of the tit family Paridae.

A lively bird, it is difficult to observe, since it spends much of its time in dense undergrowth, hopping and flitting about restlessly. Occasion- ally it will perch on the top of a bush with its tail cocked, uttering loud, high-pitched calls, but soon flies down to the base of the nest bush to disappear from view again.

Its habits are not well known but it appears to migrate up and down the mountains with the seasons. Its nest is an oval dome of leaves with an entrance at the top, built some 6 ft (2 m) above the ground among dense rhododendron foliage. Outside the breeding season, it may live in small flocks sometimes with other small insect-eating birds.

10/ STREAKED SCRUB-WARBLER
Scotocerca inquieta

RANGE: N Africa from Morocco to Red Sea, Iran and Afghanistan
HABITAT: rocky desert and semidesert with sparse bushes, dry hillsides, wadis
SIZE: 4 in (10 cm)

This pale, excitable, nervous bird belongs to a somewhat amorphous group of birds known as the bush warblers, which includes the genera *Cisticola*, *Cettia* and *Prinia*.

In the eastern part of its range the Streaked Scrub-Warbler can be found in hills up to 9,800 ft (3,000 m) but it comes down to lower slopes for the winter. It feeds on insects, small snails and seeds, tending to stay in cover but rushing about like a frenzied mouse when upset by an intruder. It may hop about on the ground or among low vegetation with its long tail cocked up and waving up and down or from side to side. During spring and summer, the Streaked Scrub-Warbler is usually encountered in family groups.

There are several distinct races, including the pale *S. i. saharae*, found in southeast Morocco and Algeria, and the dark *S. i. buryi* of southern Arabia.

11/ TINK-TINK CISTICOLA
Cisticola textrix

RANGE: Zaire, S Angola, Zambia and South Africa in S and on highveld N to Transvaal
HABITAT: short grassland with bare patches between tufts; flat marshland in the Cape
SIZE: $3\frac{1}{2}$–4 in (9–10 cm)

The cisticolas are a large group of small, shy, brownish birds, many with dark streaks in their plumage. In general they fall into 3 categories: birds of grassland, savanna or swamp.

The Tink-tink Cisticola is a grassland species: a tiny, short-tailed, solitary bird which feeds on the ground on insects, especially grasshoppers. The nest is a ball of dry grass, built within or under a grass tussock. The normal clutch is of 4 eggs, which are pale pink, greenish or turquoise with brown spots.

Although normally inconspicuous, the male has a rattling song produced during a display flight that often takes the bird high in the air, well beyond the range of human vision. The Tink-tink Cisticola is also known as the Pinc-pinc, or Cloud, Cisticola.

12/ ZITTING CISTICOLA
Cisticola juncidis

RANGE: discontinuous around Mediterranean, W France, sub-Saharan Africa, India, Sri Lanka, Southeast Asia, Indonesia, N Australia
HABITAT: grassland, marshy savanna, paddy fields, brush in open areas
SIZE: 4 in (10 cm)

This is a diminutive brown bird which, when perched, frequently cocks its tail in a jaunty fashion. This short, rounded tail gives it its alternative name of Fan-tailed Warbler. It is restless and shy and best known for its song – a series of high, rasping *dzeep* notes separated by very short intervals uttered by the male during a jerky, high, aerial song-flight. He may climb to a height of 115 ft (35 m) or more and circle around over a wide area of territory, several hundred yards in breadth. Sometimes, however, a male will sing from a fence or other perch instead of or prior to making a song-flight.

Although essentially a lowland bird, the Zitting Cisticola can be found at altitudes of up to 4,400 ft (1,330 m) in Southeast Asia. It spends most of its time in the grass, foraging for adult and larval insects, particularly bush crickets, and rarely flies unless disturbed.

The nest is a delicate pear-shaped construction with the entrance at the top, made from spiders' webs woven around the living stems of grasses and club-rushes and lined with plant down. Many males are polygamous and build several "cock's nests" to attract breeding females.

13/ KAROO PRINIA
Prinia maculosa

RANGE: S Namibia, S and E South Africa
HABITAT: Karoo veld, valleys and mountain slopes, farmland and coastal scrub
SIZE: 5–6 in (13–15 cm)

There are about 26 species of prinia in Africa and Asia. Sometimes known as wren-warblers, they are generally short-billed birds with long tails; some are similar to the cisticolas. They favor grasslands and scrubby habitats and some prefer to remain on the ground or among low vegetation instead of taking to the wing. They are commonly found in small groups outside the breeding season.

The Karoo Prinia is common in some parts of southern Africa and is able to tolerate very dry conditions. It can be hard to spot as it hunts for insects through the bushes and tall grasses, but when alarmed it may perch on top of a tall plant, flicking its wings and uttering its harsh chirping calls. If approached closely, it often dives into thick vegetation and hides, but it can become quite tame in gardens.

The small pear-shaped nest is intricately woven into twigs or plant stems and is so well disguised that it is extremely difficult to find. The female lays 3–5 bright blue eggs, with dark reddish-brown spots.

OLD WORLD WARBLERS

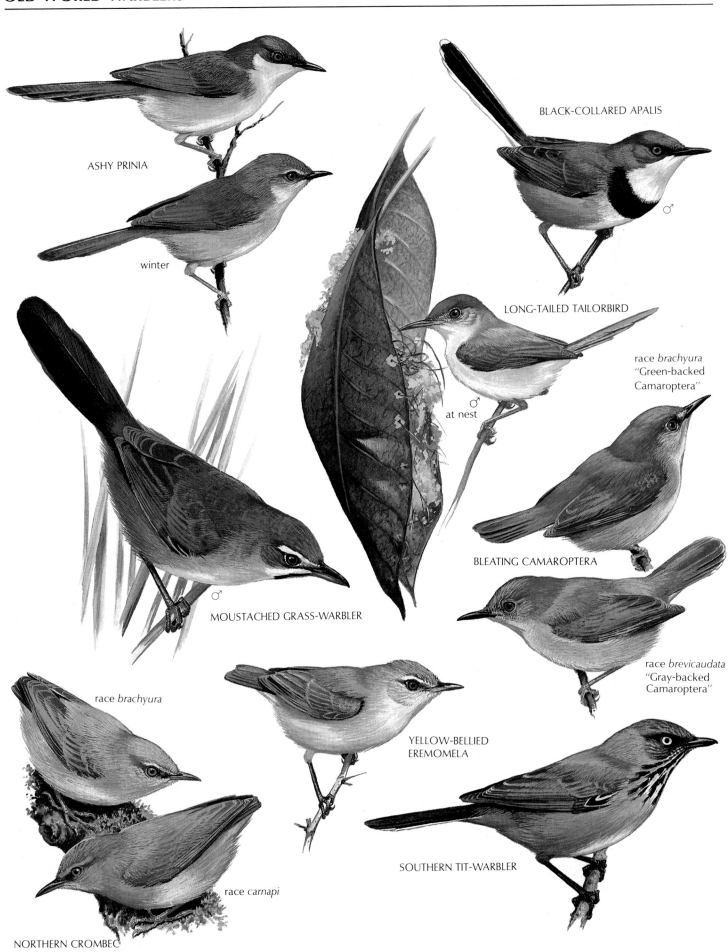

ASHY PRINIA

winter

BLACK-COLLARED APALIS

♂

LONG-TAILED TAILORBIRD

♂ at nest

race *brachyura*
"Green-backed
Camaroptera"

BLEATING CAMAROPTERA

race *brevicaudata*
"Gray-backed
Camaroptera"

MOUSTACHED GRASS-WARBLER

♂

race *brachyura*

race *carnapi*

NORTHERN CROMBEC

YELLOW-BELLIED
EREMOMELA

SOUTHERN TIT-WARBLER

GRAY LONGBILL

LITTLE MARSHBIRD

race *punctatus*

FERNBIRD

BROWN SONGLARK

♂

♀

SPINIFEXBIRD

race *badiceps*

FIJI WARBLER

race *ruficapilla*

GREEN HYLIA

OLD WORLD WARBLERS

1/ ASHY PRINIA
Prinia socialis
RANGE: **Indian subcontinent and W Burma**
HABITAT: **scrub, grassland, grain fields, open forest, reedbeds, stream banks, mangroves**
SIZE: **5 in (12.5 cm)**

This long-tailed bird is a common sight in the scrublands of southern Asia, where it can be found on hills up to 4,000 ft (1,200 m). Its range of habitats is typical of the tropical prinias.

It is a very nervous bird and, when seen, it is usually hopping restlessly through the foliage cocking its tail. It feeds on insects gleaned from low vegetation and also takes nectar from flowers.

In the northern race *P. s. stewarti*, there is a marked difference between summer and winter plumages, and the tail is longer in winter.

The purselike nest is built in a bush and the 3–5 eggs are incubated by both adults for 12 days.

2/ BLACK-COLLARED APALIS
Apalis pulchra
RANGE: **Africa, from Cameroon to Sudan and Kenya**
HABITAT: **undergrowth in highland forest**
SIZE: **5 in (12.5 cm)**

The *Apalis* warblers are mainly forest-dwellers of slender build with long, thin, graduated tails and gray, green or brown plumage.

The Black-collared Apalis is a noisy, lively resident of mountain and upland forests in central Africa. In areas where it is common, it can often be seen sidling up and down plant stems with its tail cocked up and wagging from side to side. It feeds mainly on insects picked out of the ground vegetation. The male has a brief, warbling song.

This species occasionally adopts the nests of other birds but, if it has to, it will build a purse-shaped nest of its own, using moss and lichens with a lining of soft feathers.

3/ MOUSTACHED GRASS-WARBLER
Melocichla mentalis
RANGE: **From W Africa to Ethiopia in the N, down to Angola and across to Zambezi River in the S**
HABITAT: **edges of mountain evergreen forest with coarse grass and scattered trees, marshy land along streams**
SIZE: **7–8 in (18–20 cm)**

This is a stoutly built species which looks more like a bulbul (pp. 250–53) than a warbler. Only the male sports the black cheek stripe that gives the species its name.

Its alarm note is a rasping call, but the male has an attractive, thrushlike song and will sometimes sing or sunbathe on top of a tuft of grass. In general, though, it is a solitary, stealthy species which often skulks behind vegetation. It feeds mainly on insects, especially grasshoppers and beetles. It lays 2 pinkish-white eggs, marbled with red, in a bowl-shaped nest built in a tussock.

4/ LONG-TAILED TAILORBIRD
Orthotomus sutorius
RANGE: **Indian subcontinent, Southeast Asia to Java, S China; up to 5,250 ft (1,600 m) in Southeast Asia**
HABITAT: **thickets, scrub, bamboo, gardens**
SIZE: **4¾ in (12 cm); breeding male 6 in (15.5 cm)**

Widespread and familiar throughout southern Asia, the Long-tailed Tailorbird is often seen hopping about in bushes and around verandas in search of insects and spiders. It has a habit of carrying its tail high over its back and jerking it up and down. The tail is usually longest in the breeding male.

Its name is derived from its astonishing nest-building technique. Taking 1 or 2 large leaves on a low bush or branch, it uses its bill as a needle to perforate the edges and sew them together using individual stitches of cottony plant material or the silk from spiders' webs or insect cocoons. The nest itself, made of soft plant fibers, is formed inside this pocket. The 2–3 eggs are incubated by both of the parents.

5/ BLEATING CAMAROPTERA
Camaroptera brachyura
RANGE: **sub-Saharan Africa**
HABITAT: **woodland thickets, forest edge, riverine bush, parks, gardens**
SIZE: **5 in (12.5 cm)**

Of the half dozen or so camaropteras found in Africa, this is the most common. There are 2 groups: a green-backed group of races, including *C. b. brachyura*, which occurs mostly down the eastern edge of Africa, from Kenya south to South Africa, and a gray-backed group, *C. b. brevicaudata*, which is widespread elsewhere. This is often regarded as a separate species, the Gray-backed Camaroptera *C. brevicaudata*. The green-backed birds prefer moist evergreen forests, whereas the gray-backed ones favor dry thorn-veld and open broad-leaved woodlands.

Skulking by habit, these birds are not always easy to see as they forage among the vegetation, but their alarm call is quite distinctive, like the bleating of a lamb. Another equally curious call sounds like stones being tapped together.

Its soft, downy nest is made within a frame formed from the broad leaves of a single twig or spray, with more leaves added to make a roof.

6/ YELLOW-BELLIED EREMOMELA
Eremomela icteropygialis
RANGE: **Africa from Sudan, Ethiopia and Somalia S through Kenya and Tanzania to Zimbabwe and Transvaal**
HABITAT: **woodland, bushveld, scrub**
SIZE: **4–4¼ in (10–11 cm)**

This pert, short-tailed warbler is common in many parts of its range, although in dry areas it tends to be nomadic. It is usually seen in pairs or family parties, busily seeking insects among the twigs and branches of trees, especially acacias.

Its nest is a thin-walled cup of dry grass, bound together with spiders' silk and sited in a bush. The hen bird usually lays a clutch of 2–3 white, chocolate-spotted eggs.

7/ NORTHERN CROMBEC
Sylvietta brachyura
RANGE: **widespread across the S Sahel zone from Senegal in the W to Somalia in the E; thence through Uganda and Kenya to Tanzania**
HABITAT: **acacia woodland, dry scrub, coastal bush**
SIZE: **3½ in (9 cm)**

The Northern Crombec is a plump little warbler with an extremely short tail. Its habit of running along branches and climbing through the foliage of thorn trees in search of insects has earned it the alternative name Nuthatch Warbler.

Usually seen in pairs, they are common birds in many parts of Africa. The Northern Crombec is one of 9 species of crombec, all African. There are about 6 races. In contrast to the others, such as *S. b. brachyura* of Senegal to Ethiopia, *S. b. carnapi* of Cameroon and Central African Republic has distinctive chestnut underparts.

8/ SOUTHERN TIT-WARBLER
Parisoma subcaeruleum
RANGE: **S Africa N to Angola and S Zambia**
HABITAT: **thornveld, semiarid scrub, dry hillsides, savanna thickets, riverine bush**
SIZE: **5½–6¼ in (14–16 cm)**

This is one of 5 warblers in the genus *Parisoma*, all found in Africa and Arabia. As its name suggests, the Southern Tit-Warbler is a titlike bird, commonly seen alone or in pairs hopping restlessly through the foliage in search of insects, spiders and fruit, or taking short, low flights from tree to tree. The male has a piping, bubbling song which often includes mimicry of other species.

The nest is a thin-walled cup of grass, roots and spiders' webs built in a tree. The 2–3 white eggs are adorned with greenish-brown spots.

9/ GRAY LONGBILL
Macrosphenus concolor
RANGE: **W and C Africa from Sierra Leone to Uganda**
HABITAT: **undergrowth, vines and creepers, canopy of dense forest**
SIZE: **5 in (13 cm)**

Variously known as longbills or bush-creepers, the 5 species of *Macrosphenus* are all found only in Africa. The Gray Longbill is typical of the genus: a secretive bird, with a long, thin, hook-tipped bill and loose-feathered flanks, which frequents dense vegetation and feeds largely on insects.

They are a poorly studied group, and the facts about their breeding are hazy; an undisputed Gray Longbill nest has yet to be described, so the size, color and number of eggs are not known.

10/ LITTLE MARSHBIRD
Megalurus gramineus
RANGE: **E and SW Australia, Tasmania**
HABITAT: **grassy swamps and marshes**
SIZE: **5 in (13 cm)**

The Little Marshbird, or Little Grassbird, is an inconspicuous, furtive denizen of swamp vegetation, where it feeds on a variety of small insects and spiders gleaned from the foliage. It rarely flies, but when it does, it flutters its wings continuously, moving slowly and keeping low down, with its tail trailing downward. This elusive little bird is best detected by its trisyllabic song, with the first syllable short and the second and third much longer. Sometimes, it misses out the first short syllable.

It is usually associated with coastal marshland, but in wet years it is often found far inland, suggesting that it is an opportunistic, nomadic species – despite its weak flight.

A pair of Little Marshbirds will often breed in an old Reed Warbler nest but, if they have to, they will build a deep, cup-shaped nest using grasses and other plant material. There are 3–5 eggs.

11/ FERNBIRD
Megalurus punctatus
RANGE: **New Zealand**
HABITAT: **reed mace swamps, marshy scrub with ferns, bracken**
SIZE: **7 in (18 cm)**

Once widespread and common throughout New Zealand, the Fernbird has been badly hit by habitat loss as more and more swamps and ferny areas have been reclaimed for agriculture. As a result, the population has become fragmented. The race illustrated, *M. p. punctatus*, occurs on the main (North and South) islands; other races, differing in plumage, occur on small offshore islands.

The Fernbird usually feeds on or near the ground. It is reluctant to take flight and will travel only short distances on the wing, flying clumsily with its tail hanging down. It has a mechanical 2-note call, consisting of a low note followed by a clicking one. As they travel through the dense vegetation, pairs maintain contact by calling to one another, the male uttering one note and the female the other. Occasionally, males may sing a simple warbling song.

Both adults build the nest: a deep cup of neatly woven dry rushes and grasses hidden deep among swamp plants.

12/ BROWN SONGLARK
Cinclorhamphus cruralis
RANGE: **C and S Australia (not Tasmania)**
HABITAT: **grasslands and saltbush plains**
SIZE: **male 9½ in (24 cm); female 7½ in (19 cm)**

The Brown Songlark takes its name from the male's loud, jangling, somewhat discordant song, which it utters in a song-flight that involves quivering wings and dangling legs. As he descends, with his wings held aloft, the male makes a clucking sound. If he lands on a perch rather than on the ground, he may carry on singing with his tail cocked like that of a wren.

Brown Songlarks live in open country and are among the most common birds on arable farmland. They feed on the ground, taking seeds and insects, although the male frequently perches on a post or telephone wire. They are migratory in the southern part of their range.

The male weighs twice as much as the female. This disparity suggests that the male is polygamous, because the males of species that have more than one mate face greater competition in acquiring mates than do those of monogamous species. Evolution favors larger, stronger males, which have more chance of ousting rivals.

13/ SPINIFEXBIRD
Eremiornis carteri
RANGE: **N and W inland Australia**
HABITAT: **arid grassland and semidesert with spinifex grass**
SIZE: **5½ in (14 cm)**

The aptly named Spinifexbird is a secretive species that rarely flies, spending most of its time hidden in dense thickets of spinifex grass (*Triodia* spp.), an abundant plant in the dry Australian grasslands. It feeds on beetles and a range of other insects, as well as seeds. If danger threatens, it may climb to the top of a clump of spinifex to gain a good view of its surroundings. When forced to fly, the Spinifexbird flutters along, low over the ground, its tail trailing behind it and pumping up and down.

It has a high-pitched call that appears to vary between individuals. The male's song is a high-pitched, whistling warble. Each pair nests near the ground in a clump of spinifex, laying only 2 eggs which are pinkish white, speckled with lilac and reddish-brown.

14/ FIJI WARBLER
Cettia ruficapilla
RANGE: **Fiji**
HABITAT: **mountain forests and scrub**
SIZE: **5–6¼ in (13–16 cm)**

This drab, long-legged warbler is a shy bird that hops and flits through dense undergrowth in an apparently ceaseless search for food, combing the branches of tree ferns and other plants for insects and their larvae, spiders, harvestmen and mites.

Now often placed with warblers such as Cetti's Warbler (pp. 278–81) in the genus *Cettia*, it is also sometimes classified in the genus *Vitia*. It is confined to the 4 larger islands in the Fiji group; on Taveuni it is restricted to wet forest but elsewhere it is common in dense scrub. Some of the islands have distinct races: *C. r. badiceps* of Viti Levu and *C. r. ruficapilla* of Kandavu are examples.

Fiji Warblers build untidy, roofed nests with side entrances and lay 2 chocolate-colored eggs. Many pairs are parasitized by cuckoos.

15/ GREEN HYLIA
Hylia prasina
RANGE: **W and C Africa from Guinea to W Kenya, S to N Angola**
HABITAT: **forest undergrowth**
SIZE: **4½ in (11.5 cm)**

This is a species of somewhat uncertain status which is often placed among the sunbirds. It has a more specialized diet than most warblers, using its short, slightly curved bill to gather sap-sucking scale insects and wax. Although quite common, the Green Hylia can be elusive; when seen, it is often feeding in a mixed party of birds high in the canopy.

It builds a flat-domed nest at the end of a branch, usually quite low down in a forest tree, and lays 1–2 eggs.

OLD WORLD FLYCATCHERS, MONARCH FLYCATCHERS

PIED FLYCATCHER

♂

♀

RUFOUS-BELLIED NILTAVA

♀

♂

juv

SPOTTED FLYCATCHER

BLUE-AND-WHITE
FLYCATCHER

♀

♂

JACKY WINTER

race *cyanomela*

FLAME ROBIN

♀

♂

imm

♀

♂

CHIN-SPOT PUFF-BACK FLYCATCHER

BROWN-THROATED WATTLE-EYE

BLUE FLYCATCHER

AFRICAN PARADISE FLYCATCHER

chestnut phase

♂ white phase

♀

♂

imm

BLACK-FACED
MONARCH

♂ race azurea

BLACK-NAPED
BLUE MONARCH

♂

race sclateri

♂

♀

race sandwichensis

YELLOW-BREASTED BOATBILL

ELEPAIO

291

OLD WORLD FLYCATCHERS, MONARCH FLYCATCHERS

FAMILY MUSCICAPIDAE
Old World flycatchers

Small to medium insect-eaters. Relatively broad, flat bills, with bristles around nostrils. Dull or brightly colored, some with ornamental wattles. Sexes often different. Nest either open cup, domed or in holes or deserted nests. Eggs 1–11, uniform green to bluish, reddish or whitish with mottling. Incubation 12–17 days, nestling period 13–19 days. 147 species.

1/ SPOTTED FLYCATCHER
Muscicapa striata

RANGE: **Eurasia N to N Russia and W Siberia, E to N Mongolia, S to NW Africa and Himalayas; winters C and S Africa, Arabia, NW India**
HABITAT: **open woods and scrub, parks, gardens; winters in acacia woods and thorn bush**
SIZE: **5½ in (14 cm)**

This rather undistinguished mouse-gray bird has a habit of sitting on a bare branch or other exposed perch, from which it makes short aerial sallies after insects, often returning to the same spot. Its flying style is erratic with many swerves and twists; it flicks its wings or tail when at rest. The Spotted Flycatcher feeds almost entirely on insects but may take berries in autumn.

The nest is placed against a wall in a creeper or shrub, on a beam or in a hole; it is a slight structure of moss, wool or hair, held together with spiders' webs. The clutch is usually 4–5 eggs (rarely 2–7). The eggs are pale blue or green with some brown spots, often around the broad end. Incubation, largely by the female, lasts 12–14 days and fledging takes 11–15 days.

2/ PIED FLYCATCHER
Ficedula hypoleuca

RANGE: **much of Europe, W Asia to River Yenisey, NW Africa; winters in tropical Africa S to Tanzania**
HABITAT: **ancient broad-leaved woodland (especially in uplands) coniferous forest, well-wooded parks, orchards, gardens**
SIZE: **5 in (13 cm)**

The Pied Flycatcher often flicks its wings and moves its tail up and down. It sallies out from a perch after insects and usually returns to a different one. Besides insects, birds will take earthworms and berries in the fall.

The strikingly black and white male sometimes mates with several females, but is often monogamous. Pied Flycatchers nest in holes in trees and walls up to a height of 23 ft (7 m) and widely use nest-boxes when these are available. The female builds a loose nest of moss, roots and strips of bark and lines it with feathers. Clutches of 1–11 eggs are known; they are pale blue in color with reddish speckles.

3/ BLUE-AND-WHITE FLYCATCHER
Cyanoptila cyanomelana

RANGE: **breeds in NE and E Asia, including Manchuria, W China and Japan; migrates through E and S China to winter in Southeast Asia, S to Greater Sundas**
HABITAT: **mountain forest and wooded regions**
SIZE: **7 in (18 cm)**

This flycatcher of the eastern Palearctic region lives in forested areas, and on migration and in its winter quarters it can be found up to heights of 6,500 ft (2,000 m).

The face, throat and breast of the Japanese race *C. c. cyanomelana* are black, while those of the race *C. c. cumatilis* are greenish-blue. The upperparts of *C. c. cumatilis* are greenish-blue with a shining blue crown. Immature males have an olive-brown head, back and breast, with a whitish throat patch and bluish wings and tail.

The nest, constructed from lichens, moss and roots, is sited in hollows in low bluffs, on cliff ledges or in holes in buildings. There are 4–5 white or pale brown eggs with pale markings at the large ends.

4/ RUFOUS-BELLIED NILTAVA
Niltava sundara

RANGE: **Himalayas to W China, Burma**
HABITAT: **forest undergrowth and scrub**
SIZE: **7 in (18 cm)**

There are 24 species of niltava. The male Rufous-bellied Niltava is distinguished from the males of his relatives by the (not always visible) shining blue neck patch and by the black throat (with only a hint of blue), with its straight lower edge. The female's distinctive feature is the white gorget on her lower throat. Immatures have brown upperparts with rusty buff spots, and buff-brown underparts with blackish scales.

In the Himalayas, the Rufous-bellied Niltava can be found breeding from 6,000–7,500 ft (1,800–2,300 m). It haunts low scrub and undergrowth, where it searches for insects such as ants and beetles. Birds have been seen on

migration in northern Laos and Thailand, but more specific details are not known.

Nests are built close to the ground, usually in holes in banks, roadside cuttings, dead tree stumps or in rock crevices. The nest is lined with moss and rootlets.

5/ JACKY WINTER
Microeca leucophaea

RANGE: **most of Australia, except the deserts, Tasmania and extreme NE; also S New Guinea**
HABITAT: **open forest, woodland and eucalyptus scrub**
SIZE: **5 in (13 cm)**

The Jacky Winter, or Australian Brown Flycatcher, is a dull gray-brown bird with white eyebrows and outer tail feathers. The sexes are similar; the juvenile is spotted brown and white.

Although a dull bird, the Jacky Winter is readily detected due to its active foraging. Typically it sits on a low perch, often a fencepost, and darts out after flying insects or pounces on prey on the ground. It is most often found in partly cleared country or on the edge of woodland and farmland. Its song is a loud *peter peter*, also sometimes described as *jacky winter*.

On a horizontal branch it builds a very small, shallow nest, made of grass and rootlets, with bark and lichen. The breeding season is from July to December and the usual clutch is 2–3 eggs.

6/ FLAME ROBIN
Petroica phoenicea

RANGE: **SE Australia and Tasmania**
HABITAT: **breeds in upland eucalyptus forest and woodland; winters in more open habitat**
SIZE: **5½ in (14 cm)**

The male Flame Robin is a striking bird compared with the much duller female and immatures. Like most members of their genus, Flame Robins usually pounce on their prey from a low branch, rock or stump, although they will sometimes hawk for flying insects.

Flame Robins are most common in open woodland near to the tree line in the Great Dividing Range. In autumn they migrate to lower altitudes and often westward into drier, more open country. Nests may be built on branches, but are often in large cavities in trunks, roots or posts.

FAMILY MONARCHIDAE
Monarch flycatchers and fantail flycatchers

Small to medium (monarch flycatchers) or small (fantail flycatchers) insect-eaters. Several monarch flycatchers with long tail feathers. Plumage often metallic black or gray, or chestnut with white underparts and sexes sometimes differing (monarch flycatchers); or black, gray, yellow, rufous or white and sexes similar (fantail flycatchers). Nest cup-shaped (goblet-shaped in some fantail flycatchers). Eggs 2–5, whitish (or cream in some fantail flycatchers) with brown spots or blotches. Incubation and nestling period unknown for most fantail flycatchers, (12–14 days and 13–15 days for *Rhipidura* species); 13–17 days and 12–18 days for monarch flycatchers. 164 species.

7/ CHIN-SPOT PUFF-BACK FLYCATCHER
Batis molitor
RANGE: **S Sudan, Kenya (except coast), SW Africa, Mozambique and E Cape Province**
HABITAT: **open acacia woodland, forests and their edges, cultivated areas, gardens**
SIZE: **$4\frac{1}{2}$ in (11.5 cm)**

The Chin-spot Puff-back Flycatcher is a restless bird, hawking after insects like a true flycatcher and hovering in the air while searching leaves. It will also forage in lower branches like a tit. The wings produce a rattle in flight.

The bird builds a small, cup-shaped nest of fibers and lichens, lashed together with spiders' webs. It is usually well concealed in the fork of a tree. The 2 eggs are grayish or greenish white with a girdle of dark spots.

8/ BROWN-THROATED WATTLE-EYE
Platysteira cyanea
RANGE: **W, C and E Africa, including Sudan, Uganda and Kenya**
HABITAT: **forest strips and secondary growth**
SIZE: **5 in (13 cm)**

The chief feature of the 10 species of wattle-eye, all of which are found only in Africa, is an ornamental wattle. This species is markedly black and white with bright scarlet eye-wattles. It occurs in pairs or noisy little flocks, and its habits are rather titlike or like those of a *Phylloscopus* warbler such as the Willow Warbler *P. trochilus* or Pallas's Leaf-Warbler *P. proregulus*. It feeds restlessly among the foliage and flicks its wings audibly in flight.

The nest is a small cup of fine grass, fiber and lichens, bound with spiders' webs and placed in the fork of a bush or tree. The normal clutch is of 2 cream or olive eggs with brown spots.

9/ BLUE FLYCATCHER
Elminia longicauda
RANGE: **W Africa, E to Kenya, S to Angola**
HABITAT: **woodland and forest, gardens, farmland**
SIZE: **$5\frac{1}{2}$ in (14 cm)**

Beautifully colored in pale cerulean blue and equally elegant in shape, this is one of the most attractive of African flycatchers. It is typically alert, upright and full of nervous energy, frequently fanning its rather long, graduated tail. At the same time, although always active and ready to chase some flying insect, it is very tame and confiding. It has a brief, twittering song, which is somewhat insignificant, but a little reminiscent of the songs of several of the sunbirds.

10/ BLACK-NAPED BLUE MONARCH
Hypothymis azurea
RANGE: **Indonesia, Philippines, China, W to India**
HABITAT: **mixed primary or secondary forest, farmland, plantations, bamboo**
SIZE: **$6\frac{1}{4}$ in (16 cm)**

Several races of this widespread species are known, including *H. a. ceylonensis*, which lacks a black bar across its throat, *H. a. styani* of mainland India, which is white below, and *H. a. tytleri* of the Andaman Islands, which is blue below. The race illustrated is *H. a. azurea* of the Philippines.

Black-naped Blue Monarchs are sociable birds. They are always active, with flicking wings and cocked, fanned tails. They catch insects in agile twisting and looping sallies from a perch. Insect prey is taken back to a perch and held under one foot as it is broken into pieces in a shrikelike manner. The species has no real song.

It lays 3–4 eggs in a nest of grass stems and bark shreds, placed in a fork of a tree or bush. The nest is often thickly plastered with white spiders' webs and spiders' egg cases and is secured to a branch by a binding of cobweb.

11/ AFRICAN PARADISE FLYCATCHER
Terpsiphone viridis
RANGE: **sub-Saharan Africa**
HABITAT: **forest and riverside woodland with mature trees**
SIZE: **$15\frac{3}{4}$ in (40 cm)**

In shady, mixed forest, or beside rivers and lakes where woodland glades and ornamental gardens provide relief from the dense canopy, this gorgeous bird flits out from a hidden perch to catch an insect in midair, giving a sudden flash of color and a glimpse of a long, trailing tail. Its call is a distinctive, sharp double or treble note.

Whereas the tails of males may be up to 8 in (20 cm) long, females usually have short tails. However, tail length, whether long or short, is not always a good guide to the sex of the bird.

The nest is a splendidly neat, surprisingly small construction of fibers and fine roots, bound and camouflaged with spiders' webs and lichens. It is always on a slender, open, bare twig in a shady spot, often over water, and the tail of the sitting bird trails elegantly over the side.

12/ ELEPAIO
Chasiempis sandwichensis
RANGE: **Hawaiian islands**
HABITAT: **high-altitude native and exotic forests and volcanic areas**
SIZE: **$5\frac{1}{2}$ in (14 cm)**

The 5 races of the Elepaio are found only on the Hawaiian islands. Three races – *C. s. sandwichensis*, *C. s. ridgwayi* and *C. s. bryani* – are confined to the island of Hawaii itself; *C. s. sclateri* occurs on the island of Kauai and *C. s. gayi* is scarce on the heavily populated island of Oahu. The surest way to identify this small flycatcher is by its behavior, stance and the plumage feathers common to all adults. All adults have 2 white wing bars, a white rump and a white-tipped tail. Hawaiian immatures are dull brown and those on Kauai and Oahu are rusty brown.

This active bird often perches with its tail cocked and is bold and curious by nature. It feeds on insects, gleaning them from foliage, picking them from trunks or hawking them in flight beneath the leaf canopy. In addition to various whistled and chattering calls, the song is a loudly whistled *chee-whee-o* or *e-le-pai-o*.

13/ BLACK-FACED MONARCH
Monarcha melanopsis
RANGE: **E Australia and New Guinea**
HABITAT: **rain forest and wet eucalyptus forest**
SIZE: **7 in (18 cm)**

The black face of this lovely bird gives it its usual Australian name; an alternative name is the Pearly-winged Monarch. Females are very similar to males, whereas immatures lack the black face.

Black-faced Monarchs feed on insects and spiders in a variety of ways. They generally glean them from leaves and bark by moving along a branch and then repeating the process after hopping up to a higher branch. They work their way methodically up to a height of 25 ft (8 m) before descending to repeat the process. Black-faced Monarchs also hawk for insects in midair or pick them off the ground. They have a loud, whistling song and various harsher notes. The nest is constructed from thin twigs, adorned with green moss.

14/ YELLOW-BREASTED BOATBILL
Machaerirhynchus flaviventer
RANGE: **NE Queensland, New Guinea**
HABITAT: **rain forest**
SIZE: **$4\frac{1}{4}$–$4\frac{3}{4}$ in (11–12 cm)**

The most unusual feature of the Yellow-breasted Boatbill, or Yellow-breasted Flatbill Flycatcher, is the broad, flat bill with its strongly hooked tip.

Boatbills feed by flycatching, or by gleaning from foliage, apparently only taking small, soft-bodied insects. They tend to keep to the canopy of rain forest. Sometimes, they join mixed feeding flocks of other species. As they move through the forest, they constantly utter soft, wheezing trills to maintain contact with one another.

The nest, built mostly by the male, is suspended from a small fork by vine tendrils. The 2 eggs are white with small reddish-brown spots.

FANTAIL FLYCATCHERS, FAIRY-WRENS, AUSTRALASIAN WARBLERS

race *rufifrons*

race *aureola*

WHITE-BROWED FANTAIL

RUFOUS FANTAIL

WILLIE WAGTAIL

SILKTAIL

♀ SUPERB FAIRY-WREN

♂

RUFOUS-CROWNED EMU-WREN

♀

♂

race *striatus*

STRIATED GRASSWREN

WHITE-THROATED GERYGONE

WEEBILL

RUFOUS BRISTLEBIRD

race *broadbenti*

INLAND THORNBILL

race *apicalis*

FERNWREN

race *maculatus*
"Spotted Scrubwren"
♂

♂
race *laevigaster*

ORIGMA

race *humilis* ♂

♂
race *frontalis*

NEW ZEALAND CREEPER

WHITE-BROWED SCRUBWREN

FANTAIL FLYCATCHERS, FAIRY-WRENS, AUSTRALASIAN WARBLERS

1/ SILKTAIL
Lamprolia victoriae

RANGE: **Fiji Islands**
HABITAT: **rain forest**
SIZE: **5 in (13 cm)**

The Silktail is named for its silky-white rump and tail and for the satinlike, velvet-black plumage of the rest of its body. The white rump and tail are conspicuous in the dim forest interior as the bird flits about on its large, rounded wings. The race *L. v. victoriae* is common on the island of Taveuni, while *L. v. kleinschmidti* is rare on Vanua Levu.

The Silktail is usually found in small groups below the tree canopy or on the forest floor. It forages for insects in leaf litter, flicking its tail prominently. Silktails also pick off insects from low branches and foliage, sometimes hovering to feed, and also catch them in midair.

The Silktail's courtship displays involve bowing and raising the tail, or flicking the wings and fanning the tail. Both postures produce a dramatic flash of white. The single, pale pink, spotted egg is laid in a cup nest that is suspended from a low branch and often overhung by large leaves.

2/ WHITE-BROWED FANTAIL
Rhipidura aureola

RANGE: **Sri Lanka, India, Pakistan, Bangladesh**
HABITAT: **forests, gardens, scrub**
SIZE: **6½ in (17 cm)**

There are 3 races of this flycatcher: *R. a. burmanica* in the east, with its crown and back of similar color, *R. a. aureola* across the bulk of India, with a darker cap, and *R. a. compressirostris* in the south and Sri Lanka, with less white in the tail. Sexes are similar, but females are generally a little paler on the head than the males.

Restless, alert birds, White-browed Fantails are usually seen in ones or twos, but sometimes join mixed parties of birds roving through low bushes and undergrowth. The tail is often fanned and held up high, with the wings drooped. The species is thought to use its flicking wings and tail to disturb insects from crevices in old bark. The insects are caught in midair in graceful, swooping flights from a perch.

The song is a thin, clear whistle, rising and descending in a short phrase. A compact nest of plant fiber and grass, covered with spiders' webs, is placed on a high branch; 3 eggs are laid.

3/ WILLIE WAGTAIL
Rhipidura leucophrys

RANGE: **throughout Australia; rare in Tasmania, New Guinea, Soloman Islands, Bismarck Archipelago and Moluccas**
HABITAT: **open woodland, scrub, grassland**
SIZE: **7¾ in (20 cm)**

The Willie Wagtail, or Black-and-white Fantail, is one of the most common and popular Australian birds. This is due to its striking black and white plumage, its tameness, its pugnacity toward other birds and its conspicuous feeding habits. Willie Wagtails spend about half of their time feeding on the ground, where they dart about after flies, beetles and ants. They wag and twist their tails from side-to-side, often rocking their bodies or

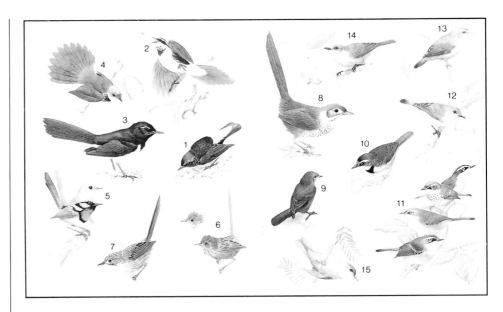

flicking their wings. At other times they fly out after insects from low branches, stumps or even from a sheep's back.

During the breeding season Willie Wagtails are very aggressive, attacking potential predators up to the size of an eagle, vigorously fluttering around the intruder's back and head with persistent chattering calls. The nest is often placed on a conspicuous horizontal branch but, despite this, and perhaps because the birds are so aggressive, young from 65 percent of nests survive.

4/ RUFOUS FANTAIL
Rhipidura rufifrons

RANGE: **New Guinea, Pacific and Indonesian islands, N and E Australia**
HABITAT: **eucalyptus forests, rain forests and mangroves**
SIZE: **6–6½ in (15–16.5 cm)**

The Rufous Fantail takes its name from its frequent habit of fanning out its boldly patterned tail. The species has several races which have differing shades of rufous and varying amounts of black on the throat. *R. r. mariae* on Guam is nearly extinct, but races elsewhere are quite common. The race illustrated, *R. r. rufifrons*, is from eastern Australia.

Bright orange flashes in the forest understory signal these birds as they dart in and out of the sunlight. They hop and flit among the vegetation, capturing insects in flight, mostly within 15 ft (5 m) of the ground. They are not as aerobatic as their duller relative, the Gray Fantail *R. fuliginosa*.

FAMILY MALURIDAE
Fairy-wrens

Small ground- and shrub-dwellers. Short bills; long, thick legs; long, usually cocked, tails. Plumage various combinations of bright blues, purples, chestnut, black, red and white in breeding male fairy-wrens; chestnut black and white in some grasswrens; brown in most others. Sexes differ, except for grasswrens. Nest usually domed with side entrance. Eggs 2–4, whitish with red-brown speckling. Incubation 12–15 days, nestling period 10–12 days. 24 species.

5/ SUPERB FAIRY-WREN
Malurus cyaneus

RANGE: **SE Australia, including Tasmania**
HABITAT: **eucalyptus woodland and forest with patches of dense cover**
SIZE: **5 in (13 cm)**

The Superb Fairy-Wren, or Blue Wren, is one of Australia's most familiar and best-studied birds. Superb Fairy-Wrens feed on centipedes and other arthropods on the ground, usually in open grassy areas, but are rarely far from dense cover to which they retreat if danger threatens.

Although many nest as a single pair, one or more helpers may assist to rear the nestlings and fledglings. The breeding male closely guards the female during her fertile periods. He occasionally uses a bright yellow flower petal in his display to a female. Helpers are usually males, often in drab plumage early in the breeding season, and are frequently related to one or more of the breeding birds. The nest is domed with an entrance near the top. Although a pair and its helpers may attempt to raise 3 or 4 broods a season, many eggs and young are taken by predators, especially snakes.

6/ RUFOUS-CROWNED EMU-WREN
Stipiturus ruficeps

RANGE: **C Australia**
HABITAT: **grassland, desert and scrubland**
SIZE: **5½ in (14 cm)**

Emu-Wrens are tiny birds with very long, central tail feathers. Not only are these feathers nearly twice as long as the body of the bird, but they are unusual in lacking barbicels – the tiny hooks that interlock with one another to keep a feather smooth and neat. This gives them the open and loose appearance of an Emu's feathers.

Rufous-crowned Emu-Wrens are poorly known as they inhabit remote areas of desert, which are usually covered with dense hummocks of porcupine grass (*Triodia*) or other grasses and low shrubs. They are inconspicuous birds, keeping in touch with weak, high-pitched, trilling contact calls. They also have shorter, churring alarm calls and males sometimes sing a brief, warbling song. They feed among vegetation on insects.

7/ STRIATED GRASSWREN
Amytornis striatus

RANGE: **inland Australia**
HABITAT: **sandy desert and scrub**
SIZE: **$5\frac{1}{2}$–$6\frac{1}{2}$ in (14–16.5 cm)**

The Striated, or Striped, Grasswren's favorite habitat is sand plains with prickly porcupine grass (*Triodia*). There are 3 races, distinguished by plumage color. The one illustrated is *A. s. striatus*, found in grassland among mallee scrub in central New South Wales, northwestern Victoria and southeastern Australia.

Striated Grasswrens feed on the ground, usually in dense cover. They eat centipedes and other invertebrates, as well as small seeds. They seldom fly, but run through the undergrowth like mice and hop vigorously. The partly domed nest, made of porcupine grass, sometimes mixed with shredded bark, and lined with seeds, plant down and fur, is placed in a clump of porcupine grass. The male helps to feed the young.

FAMILY ACANTHIZIDAE
Australasian warblers

Small to medium, with fine bills, short tails and wings. Plumage usually brown, olive or yellow. Sexes similar. Nest neat, domed, often with a hood. Eggs 2–3 (occasionally 4), white, sometimes with spots, or dark brown. Incubation 15–20 days, nestling period 15–20 days. 65 species.

8/ RUFOUS BRISTLEBIRD
Dasyornis broadbenti

RANGE: **restricted to a small area of SE Australia; probably extinct in SW Australia**
HABITAT: **dense scrub and thickets**
SIZE: **$10\frac{1}{2}$ in (27 cm)**

The 3 species of bristlebird are all inconspicuous birds that are sparsely distributed and not well known. Rufous Bristlebirds feed on the ground on seeds and on insects and other arthropods. They are very shy and are more easily heard than seen. The song has a squeaky and harsh quality.

They nest from September to December, close to the ground, building an oval nest with a side entrance. The 2 eggs are white, heavily freckled with red and a purplish color. There are 3 races: the southwestern race *D. b. littoralis* is probably extinct, but the other 2, *D. b. whitei* from South Australia and *D. b. broadbenti* from South Australia and Victoria, are still moderately abundant.

9/ ORIGMA
Origma solitaria

RANGE: **C coastal New South Wales**
HABITAT: **forest and heathland with rocky outcrops**
SIZE: **$5\frac{1}{2}$ in (14 cm)**

The Origma, or Rock Warbler, is an attractive bird with a shrill, repetitive song. It is confined to the sandstone and limestone areas around Sydney, which are characterized by a diverse, though rather stunted, vegetation.

Origmas feed mostly on bare rock surfaces and may climb almost vertically like a treecreeper.

They eat insects and spiders. Their nesting behavior is unusual, as the nest is almost invariably placed in the dark, in a cave, a deep cleft in the rock or even behind a waterfall. They sometimes take advantage of human structures, nesting in mineshafts and buildings. The nest is spherical and is usually suspended by spiders' webs from the ceiling of a cave or building.

10/ FERNWREN
Crateroscelis gutturalis

RANGE: **NE Australia**
HABITAT: **mountain rain forest above 2,000 ft (650 m)**
SIZE: **$4\frac{3}{4}$–$5\frac{1}{2}$ in (12–14 cm)**

The Fernwren is a quiet, unobtrusive bird and lives almost entirely on the ground. Moving alone or in pairs, they throw leaf litter into the air when searching for small invertebrates such as snails. They may also take insects disturbed by the foraging activities of larger birds.

Most breeding occurs between August and October. The bulky, rounded nest is made of green moss, fern fibers, rootlets and dry leaves. It is well concealed on the ground among dense vegetation, often among ferns on steep-sided banks.

11/ WHITE-BROWED SCRUBWREN
Sericornis frontalis

RANGE: **W, S and E Australia, Tasmania**
HABITAT: **understory of forest, heathland**
SIZE: **$4\frac{3}{4}$ in (12 cm)**

There are 9 or more races of the White-browed Scrubwren. They fall into 4 main groups, exemplified by *S. f. laevigaster* from eastern Queensland and northeastern New South Wales, *S. f. frontalis* from southeastern Queensland and New South Wales, *S. f. humilis* from Tasmania and *S. f. maculatus* (the Spotted Scrubwren) from eastern and southern Western Australia. Some of these well-differentiated races have at times been regarded as separate species.

White-browed Scrubwrens have a musical, though rather erratic song, and a variety of harsh call-notes. They feed on the ground in dense cover or in low bushes on insects and seeds. Birds in the far northwest of the range experience very high temperatures that restrict their feeding. They are able to drink weak salt solutions and can also concentrate their urine to conserve water.

12/ INLAND THORNBILL
Acanthiza apicalis

RANGE: **S and C Australia**
HABITAT: **arid woodland and eucalyptus scrub; forests, coastal scrub, heaths in SW; also mangroves**
SIZE: **4 in (10 cm)**

This is a bird to appeal to identification specialists. Known by a variety of names, the Inland Thornbill, or Broad-tailed Thornbill, is sometimes treated as a race of the Brown Thornbill *A. pusilla*. To confuse the issue, both species have more than 5 races each. To complicate matters further, it is a small, basically grayish-brown bird with a reddish rump and a baffling array of calls including mimicry.

The Inland Thornbill carries its tail cocked and is a perky, conspicuous bird. It forages within shrubs for insects and sometimes seeds, working through one bush and then flying jerkily to the next. It also feeds at flowers, inserting its bill into the flower head. The female builds a domed nest of bark and grass and incubates alone. The male is usually nearby defending the territory.

13/ WEEBILL
Smicrornis brevirostris

RANGE: **almost throughout Australia**
HABITAT: **eucalyptus woodland and forest; acacia woodland**
SIZE: **3–$3\frac{1}{2}$ in (8–9 cm)**

The Weebill is the smallest Australian bird typified by a pale iris and eyebrow and a very short, stubby beak. The song is quite loud for such a tiny bird and resembles *I'm a weebill*.

Weebills glean insects from the outer foliage of eucalyptus and other trees, often hovering on the edge of the canopy. They eat large numbers of scale insects. They have a long breeding season, from July to February. The nest is round or pear shaped, with a side entrance and sometimes a tail.

14/ WHITE-THROATED GERYGONE
Gerygone olivacea

RANGE: **N and E Australia; migrates as far as SE Australia; also SE New Guinea**
HABITAT: **eucalyptus woodland**
SIZE: **$4\frac{1}{4}$ in (11 cm)**

When feeding, these birds move rapidly through the canopy, snatching small insects from the foliage. They have a lively, high-pitched song which has earned them the name of bush-canary.

The White-throated Gerygone is a summer visitor to the southern part of its range, arriving in September and leaving in April. The pendant nest hangs from a low eucalyptus branch and has a long tail and a side entrance with a small veranda. It is constructed from bark, tied together with spiders' webs, and is lined with feathers. Nests may be infested with ants or wasps, which may protect them from predators.

15/ NEW ZEALAND CREEPER
Finschia novaeseelandiae

RANGE: **South Island, Stewart Island and neighboring islands (New Zealand)**
HABITAT: **mature forest and scrubland**
SIZE: **5 in (13 cm)**

The New Zealand Creeper, or Brown Creeper, lives in family groups throughout the year, sometimes forming larger flocks in winter. Non-breeders may remain with their natal group for several years. They are easily detected by song and calls, but remain in the canopy and are difficult to see. The Maori name for the bird, Pipipi, is imitative of its calls.

The New Zealand Creeper gleans insects from small branches, twigs and leaves. It is territorial while breeding in the spring, but less so at other times of the year. Some cooperative breeding has been recorded, although the breeding female performs all nest-building and incubation.

THICKHEADS, TRUE TITS, LONG-TAILED TITS, PENDULINE TITS

race *frontatus*
"Eastern Shrike-tit"

♀

♂

CRESTED SHRIKE-TIT

race *pectoralis*

♀

♂

GOLDEN WHISTLER

♂

race *littayei*

race *torquata*

VARIABLE PITOHUI

race *pallidus*

race *aruensis*

BLACK-CAPPED CHICKADEE

race *britannicus*

COAL TIT

CRESTED TIT

race *aemodius*

SOUTHERN BLACK TIT

race *major*

GREAT TIT

CHINESE YELLOW TIT

race *cinereus*

race *sultanea*

race *gayeti*

SULTAN TIT

BLUE TIT

race *pendulinus*

race *bicolor*

race *atricristatus*

race *macronyx*

TUFTED TITMOUSE

PENDULINE TIT

race *caudatus*

race *minimus*

race *rosaceus*

BUSHTIT

VERDIN

race *melanotis*
"Black-eared Bushtit"

LONG-TAILED TIT

THICKHEADS, TRUE TITS, LONG-TAILED TITS, PENDULINE TITS

FAMILY PACHYCEPHALIDAE
Thickheads and whistlers
Small to medium, robust birds with strong, often hooked bills. Mostly dull brown or gray, some brightly colored. Cup-shaped nests built in trees or crevices. Eggs 1–4, white to olive, spotted. Incubation 16–18 days, nestling period 13–16 days. 52 species.

1/ CRESTED SHRIKE-TIT
Falcunculus frontatus
RANGE: SE, SW and NW Australia
HABITAT: eucalyptus forests and woods
SIZE: 7 in (18 cm)

The Crested Shrike-Tit gains the second part of its name from the superficial resemblance of its plumage to the Great Tit and from its powerful, hooked, shrikelike beak, which, quite unlike a shrike, it uses to noisily pry and shred loose bark from eucalyptus trees in search of larvae and beetles. It also picks scale insects off twigs and rips open caterpillar cocoons and galls to prey on the animals within.

The race illustrated is the eastern *F.f. frontatus*. The male of the southwestern race *F.f. leucogaster* has a distinctive white abdomen, while the northern race *F.f. whitei* is smaller and yellower. The Crested Shrike-Tit's neat nest is made from shredded bark and spiders' webs, near the crown of a tree, and the birds nest in groups with non-breeding "helpers."

2/ GOLDEN WHISTLER
Pachycephala pectoralis
RANGE: E and S Australia, Tasmania, New Guinea, Indonesia and Pacific islands
HABITAT: rain forest, eucalyptus forest
SIZE: 6¼ in (16 cm)

The male Golden Whistler is one of the most colorful and melodious of Australian perching birds. It is also the most variable bird in the world, with at least 73 island races showing variations in plumage and bill pattern. Of the 3 races illustrated, *P.p. torquata* of Taveuni Island, for example, has a short bill, while *P.p. littayei* of the Loyalty Islands has an extra-long bill, as well as differences in plumage. The race *P.p. pectoralis*, which has a medium-length bill, occurs in New South Wales. The females of all races and males of some of the island races have dull olive plumage.

Golden Whistlers feed mainly on large insects, snatching or gleaning them from the foliage of wattles (*Acacia* spp.) or eucalyptus. Males tend to feed higher in the trees than females.

3/ VARIABLE PITOHUI
Pitohui kirhocephalus
RANGE: New Guinea, adjacent islands to W
HABITAT: lowland forest and forest edge
SIZE: 9 in (23 cm)

There are 7 species of pitohui, all restricted to the New Guinea area. The Variable Pitohui is remarkable for the striking geographic variation in its plumage: the largely black race *P.k. aruensis* of the Aru Islands and the gray-hooded race *P.k. pallidus* of the far western mainland and Waigeo and Batanta islands are extreme examples.

Small groups of Variable Pitohuis forage for insects among the bushes and trees, rarely visible but often advertising their presence with loud gurgling whistles and hoarse catlike sounds, as well as the musical fluttering of their wing beats.

FAMILY PARIDAE
True tits
Small, active, mostly brown or gray, some with brighter colors. Sexes similar. Hole-nesters. Eggs usually 4–12, white, red-brown spots. Incubation 13–14 days, nestling period 17–20 days. 50 species.

4/ BLACK-CAPPED CHICKADEE
Parus atricapillus
RANGE: Alaska, Canada, S to C USA
HABITAT: coniferous and broad-leaved forest
SIZE: 5 in (13 cm)

This is the most widely distributed tit in North America, and one of 6 species known as chickadees from their calls. It is a familiar garden visitor in winter, when small parties of 6 or so birds regularly descend on feeding stations, but in spring these parties split up into nesting pairs which spend the summer feeding in the forest.

The pair excavate their own nest-hole in the soft wood of a dead tree. They usually ignore any vacant holes, but will sometimes use a nest-box if it is previously stuffed with debris so that they have to dig their way in.

5/ COAL TIT
Parus ater
RANGE: Eurasia from Britain to Japan, N Africa
HABITAT: forests, mainly coniferous
SIZE: 4½ in (11.5 cm)

There are approximately 20 races of the widely distributed Coal Tit; most of them resemble *P.a. britannicus* of Great Britain, but the Himalayan race *P.a. aemodius* has a striking black crest.

In general, they favor conifer forests although some, such as those in Ireland, are found mainly in broad-leaved woodland. Outside the breeding season they often feed in mixed flocks, searching through the tree canopy for insects and seeds.

Coal Tits do not excavate their own nest-holes; they prefer to nest in vacant holes in trees, but will sometimes use abandoned rodent burrows in the ground.

6/ CRESTED TIT
Parus cristatus
RANGE: Europe and Scandinavia E to Urals
HABITAT: mature conifer forest
SIZE: 4¼ in (11.5 cm)

The Crested Tit lives almost exclusively among mature conifer trees, particularly spruce and pine, and as a result it is patchily distributed throughout its range. Easily recognized by its speckled crest, it feeds mainly on insects, which it picks out of crevices in the bark with its short bill, and pine seeds.

Crested Tits make their own nest-holes, usually in rotting tree stumps. The female does most of the work, excavating a new hole each year.

7/ SOUTHERN BLACK TIT
Parus niger
RANGE: SE Africa, N to Tanzania
HABITAT: woods, woodland edge, lightly wooded country
SIZE: 6¼ in (16 cm)

Found in a wide variety of woodland, ranging from dense evergreen forest to scattered trees, the Southern Black Tit breeds in family groups consisting of 3–4 birds; the "helpers" are generally the breeding pair's male offspring from the previous year's brood. But, despite this extra food-gathering capacity, each family raises only 3–4 chicks each season.

Although this species is restricted to the east of southern Africa, it is very similar to a bird known as Carp's Tit, found in some parts of the west and currently held to be a separate species, *P. carpi*.

8/ GREAT TIT
Parus major
RANGE: Eurasia, from Britain through USSR and S Asia to Japan
HABITAT: forests, mountain scrub, parks and gardens, mangroves
SIZE: $5\frac{1}{2}$ in (14 cm)

The Great Tit is a very widespread, adaptable bird, and there are about 30 distinct races. Many of these are yellow-bellied, green-backed birds like *P.m. major* of Europe and central Asia, but several eastern races, including *P.m. cinereus* of Java and the Lesser Sunda Islands, have a gray back and a whitish belly. Green/yellow forms and gray/whitish ones occur together in the eastern USSR, but do not seem to interbreed.

Acrobatic and vocal, the Great Tit has a wide vocabulary of metallic call notes. It is a common visitor to gardens, where it readily breeds in nest-boxes as well as in such unlikely sites as drain-pipes and mailboxes.

9/ CHINESE YELLOW TIT
Parus spilonotus
RANGE: Nepal, Burma, Thailand, S China
HABITAT: mountain forests
SIZE: $5\frac{1}{2}$ in (14 cm)

This species is often confused with the Yellow-cheeked Tit *P. xanthogenys*, for both of them have striking crests and heavily streaked backs.

The Chinese Yellow Tit lives in all types of forest, ranging from subtropical jungle to mountain pinewoods. It forages for food high in the trees and rarely descends to ground level. Like others in its family, it generally uses a hole in a tree as a nest site, but it will occasionally nest in a hole in a wall or a rocky bank.

10/ BLUE TIT
Parus caeruleus
RANGE: Europe E to Volga, Asia Minor, N Africa
HABITAT: woods, parks, gardens
SIZE: $4\frac{1}{4}$ in (11 cm)

These lively birds are popular visitors to suburban gardens in winter, giving virtuoso displays of agility as they cling to suspended coconuts or whisk tasty morsels away from beneath the bills of larger, slower birds. In their natural woodland habitat they often feed in loose mixed flocks with other tits such as the Great Tit and Coal Tit, working steadily from tree to tree.

An eager user of garden nest-boxes, the Blue Tit lays the largest clutch of any bird in the world (excluding some ducks and gamebirds, which do not feed their young). In good habitats, 11 eggs are common, while clutches of as many as 14–15 are by no means rare.

11/ TUFTED TITMOUSE
Parus bicolor
RANGE: E North America, S to Texas and currently extending N to Ontario
HABITAT: broad-leaved forest, open woods
SIZE: $6\frac{1}{2}$ in (17 cm)

Many tits owe their winter survival to bird lovers who put food out for them. The Tufted Titmouse is no exception, and it is likely that this is the reason why it is spreading farther north. Even without this help it is well equipped to gather winter food, for its stout bill enables it to hammer open nuts that would be too tough for most other tits to crack.

The race *P.b. bicolor* is from eastern, central and southeastern USA, and is typical of the species. At the other end of its range, in Texas, the bird has a longer, black crest. Once known as the Black-crested Titmouse, this is now generally thought to be a race, *P.b atricristatus*, of the Tufted Titmouse.

12/ SULTAN TIT
Melanochlora sultanea
RANGE: E Nepal to S China and Southeast Asia
HABITAT: chiefly in lowland forest
SIZE: $8\frac{1}{2}$ in (22 cm)

This giant among tits is so unlike the other members of its family that it has been classified in a genus of its own. Most races, such as *M.s. sultanea* of the eastern Himalayas, sport a flamboyant yellow crest, but an Indo-Chinese race *M.s. gayeti* has a black crest.

Sultan Tits live in many types of forests, where they usually hunt for food in the high branches with typical titlike resourcefulness and agility. They nest in holes in trees.

FAMILY AEGITHALIDAE
Long-tailed tits
Small, tail often longer than body. Mostly brown, black, white or gray. Sexes similar. Tree-nesters; nest woven, domed. Eggs 6–10, white, red-brown spots. Incubation 13–14 days, nestling period about 18 days. 7 species.

13/ LONG-TAILED TIT
Aegithalos caudatus
RANGE: continuous from Europe through C Asia to Japan
HABITAT: woods, woodland edge, scrub
SIZE: $5\frac{1}{2}$ in (14 cm)

These tiny birds, whose tails are more than half their body length, lose heat easily, and on winter nights they huddle together in family groups to keep warm. When day breaks, the groups set off to forage together through the treetops, often in mixed flocks with other small birds.

In spring they pair up to build beautifully woven, domed nests of lichens, spiders' silk and feathers. If a pair loses its brood they will often help to feed the broods of relatives.

There are some 20 races. The British race *A.c. rosaceus* has a distinctive broad black stripe above the eye, in contrast to the white-headed northern race *A.c. caudatus*.

14/ BUSHTIT
Psaltriparus minimus
RANGE: W North America, from British Columbia to Guatemala
HABITAT: open woods, chaparral scrub
SIZE: $4\frac{1}{4}$ in (11 cm)

This is the only North American long-tailed tit. At one time the Black-eared Bushtit of southern USA, Mexico and Guatemala was considered a separate species on the basis of the male's distinctive black mask, but it is now recognized as a local race, *P.m. melanotis*. *P.m. minimus* is one of several races found in western USA.

The Bushtit is a common and familiar bird which often feeds in gardens. Its finely woven nest is suspended from branches rather than attached at the bottom like that of the Long-tailed Tit.

FAMILY REMIZIDAE
Penduline tits
Small, bill finely pointed. Pale gray, white or yellow; some species with bright yellow, red, one with chestnut and black. Sexes similar. Domed, woven nest built in shrubs or thickets. Eggs 3–10, usually white, spotted red. Incubation 13–14 days, nestling period 18 days. 10 species.

15/ PENDULINE TIT
Remiz pendulinus
RANGE: S and E Europe, W Siberia, Asia Minor, C Asia, E to NW India, N China and Korea
HABITAT: reedbeds
SIZE: $4\frac{1}{4}$ in (11 cm)

The penduline tits are celebrated for their superbly made suspended purselike nests, which appear to be woven from woolly felt and have elaborate spoutlike entrances.

This species is the only penduline tit to occur outside Africa. There are several races: *R.p. pendulinus* of Europe, Asia Minor and western Siberia is the typical masked form, while *R.p. macronyx* of Iran has an all-black head. They are all restricted to reedbeds, where they feed on the seeds of reed mace (cat's-tail) and nest in marsh-edge trees such as willow and tamarisk.

16/ VERDIN
Auriparus flaviceps
RANGE: SW USA and N Mexico
HABITAT: semi-desert scrub
SIZE: $4\frac{1}{4}$ in (11 cm)

This common desert bird is the only member of its family found in America. It lives and nests among thorny bushes and cactus plants, weaving a rather untidy nest out of thorn twigs and siting it within the protection of the plant's spines. The result is such an effective fortress against predators that the nests are frequently used for roosting outside the breeding season.

race *caesia*
♂

race *europaea*
♂

EURASIAN NUTHATCH

♂
RED-BREASTED NUTHATCH

♂
KABYLIE NUTHATCH

♀
WALLCREEPER

♂

race *pileata*
♀
♂

race *striata*
♀

COMMON TREECREEPER

race *leucocephala*

VARIED SITTELLA

SPOTTED GRAY CREEPER

PLAIN-HEADED CREEPER

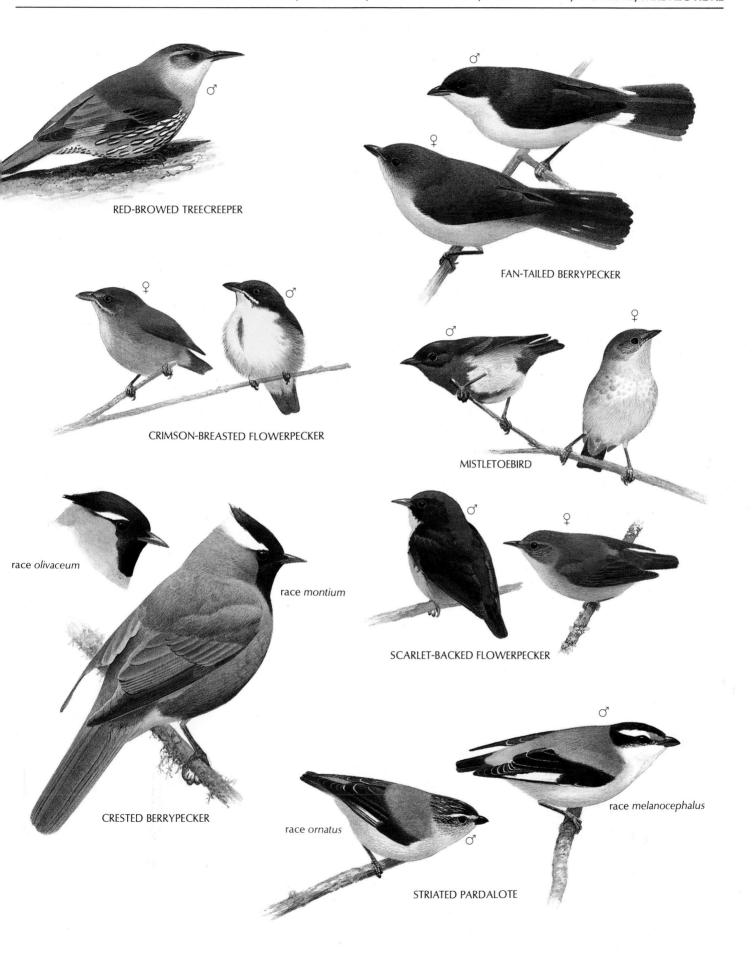

RED-BROWED TREECREEPER

♂

♀

FAN-TAILED BERRYPECKER

♀

♂

CRIMSON-BREASTED FLOWERPECKER

♂

♀

MISTLETOEBIRD

race *olivaceum*

race *montium*

♂

♀

SCARLET-BACKED FLOWERPECKER

CRESTED BERRYPECKER

♂

race *melanocephalus*

race *ornatus*

♂

STRIATED PARDALOTE

NUTHATCHES, TREECREEPERS, FLOWERPECKERS, PARDALOTES

FAMILY SITTIDAE
Nuthatches

Small, compact. Agile climbers, without stiffened tail as prop. Upperparts mostly blue-gray, underparts pale to rufous. Sexes similar. Nest in trees or rocks, mostly in holes. Eggs 4–10, white with reddish spots. Incubation 15–19 days, nestling period 23–29 days. 25 species.

1/ EURASIAN NUTHATCH
Sitta europaea

RANGE: **W Europe E to Japan and Kamchatka (USSR)**
HABITAT: **woodland with large trees**
SIZE: **4¼–5 in (11–13 cm)**

This widespread species depends on woodland trees, both for food and for the old tree holes that provide it with secure nest sites. It darts rapidly up and down trunks and branches, searching for invertebrates, seeds and nuts. It often wedges large items in crevices and hammers them vigorously with its sharp bill to break them open.

The race *S. e. europaea* from Scandinavia, eastern Europe and central Russia has very pale underparts, in contrast to races such as *S. e. caesia* of western Europe, including England and Wales. The 2 forms have met up after a long period of isolation and are intermingling.

The nest usually lies in an abandoned woodpecker hole toward the top of a tall tree and is freshly floored with flakes of pine bark and lichen. A "plaster" of dried clay and mud is used to reduce the size of the entrance hole.

2/ RED-BREASTED NUTHATCH
Sitta canadensis

RANGE: **S Canada to Mexico**
HABITAT: **coniferous forest**
SIZE: **4½–5 in (11–13 cm)**

The Red-breasted Nuthatch is closely dependent on conifers. It catches insects on their bark and hoards large quantities of their cone seeds as a food supply for the winter. Northerly birds may undertake large-scale migrations toward the south when the cone crop fails or when their population grows too large.

This species smears the rim of its tree hole with pine resin, usually the sticky "pitch" that oozes from balsam firs. The reason for this is unclear, although it may keep ants and larger creatures out of the nest. This means that the parents have to perform deft twists and turns in the air if they are to avoid becoming stuck fast themselves.

3/ KABYLIE NUTHATCH
Sitta ledanti　　　　　R

RANGE: **E Algeria**
HABITAT: **mixed woodland above 5,000 ft (1,500 m)**
SIZE: **4¾ in (12 cm)**

Discovered only as recently as 1975, the Kabylie, or Algerian, Nuthatch is one of the world's rarest birds. Until recently, it was thought to live only in the Babor Forest, an area of fir, cedar and oak woodland on a single mountain in the Atlas range. In 1989, a second population was located in the Taza National Park, but the total population is

still very small (only 80–100 pairs in the Babor Forest) and the species has an uncertain future.

The Kabylie Nuthatch excavates its own nest holes in soft and rotten wood. During the summer, it feeds mainly among oak trees, where insects are most abundant, but it will also feed its nestlings on hoarded conifer seeds. In winter, seeds form its staple diet.

4/ WALLCREEPER
Tichodroma muraria

RANGE: **N Spain E to the Himalayas**
HABITAT: **rocky gorges, cliffs, mountainsides**
SIZE: **6 in (15 cm)**

There has long been debate over the classification of this species, although today it is usually placed with the nuthatches. Whatever its ancestry, the Wallcreeper must have occupied its present habitat for a long time, for it is an excellent rock climber. It uses its wings for support when climbing up sheer walls and is nimble enough to walk beneath overhangs and jump across gaps.

It is a conspicuous bird in its lonely haunts up to 8,000 ft (2,500 m) high in the Alps and up to 16,500 ft (5,000 m) in the Himalayas. It frequently flicks open its bright red wings and often spreads them to bask in the sunshine. The colorful wings and its graceful, buoyant flight, have earned it the nickname "butterfly bird." In winter the male loses his black throat and thus resembles the female.

5/ VARIED SITTELLA
Neositta chrysoptera

RANGE: **Australia**
HABITAT: **eucalyptus woodland and forest; mallee scrub in more arid areas**
SIZE: **4¼ in (11 cm)**

The feeding behavior of sittellas is very similar to that of the true nuthatches: they comb the branches of large trees, prising into the rough bark for insects. Their breeding habits, however, are distinctly different. Instead of using a hole, they build a cup-shaped nest within a tree

fork. Like many Australian birds, they live in groups all year in which birds other than the breeding pair bring food to the young.

There are 5 races of the Varied Sittella: they include *N. c. pileata* from the west and south, *N. c. striata* from the north and northeast, and *N. c. leucocephala* from the central eastern region.

FAMILY CERTHIIDAE
Holarctic treecreepers

Small, tree-climbing birds with stiffened tails (*Certhia*). Thin, slightly downcurved bills. Plumage mainly brown, pale underparts. Sexes alike. Cup-shaped nest. Eggs 3–9, white with red-brown spots (*Certhia*); 2–3, pale blue-green with black and lilac markings (*Salpornis*). Incubation 14–15 days, nestling period 15–16 days. 7 species.

6/ COMMON TREECREEPER
Certhia familiaris

RANGE: **W Europe to Japan**
HABITAT: **woodland, especially coniferous**
SIZE: **5 in (12.5 cm)**

The feeding behavior of the treecreepers is superficially similar to that of the nuthatches, but there are important differences. A treecreeper cannot move down a tree trunk and must use its stiff tail as support during its spiral ascent. It takes generally smaller food items, including tiny insect eggs, and is exclusively insectivorous.

The Common Treecreeper normally roosts and nests behind a loose flap of bark, and the fledglings may cling to the surrounding bark for several days after leaving the nest.

7/ SPOTTED GRAY CREEPER
Salpornis spilonotus

RANGE: **sub-Saharan Africa, India**
HABITAT: **open bush and savanna**
SIZE: **5 in (13 cm)**

This species differs in many ways from the other members of its family and belongs to a separate genus. It runs rapidly over tree bark, its progress quite unlike the jerky movements of a treecreeper.

Its tail is not stiffened and, like a nuthatch, it can run down, as well as up, trees.

The nest is a cup-shaped structure of leaves, bark and cobwebs, often straddled across the fork of a branch, but never tucked behind loose wood like the nests of other treecreepers.

FAMILY RHABDORNITHIDAE
Philippine creepers

Small tree-climbers. Downcurved bill. Upperparts brown, underparts white with dark streaks. Female lighter brown. Nest in tree holes. Eggs, incubation and nestling period unknown. 2 species.

8/ PLAIN-HEADED CREEPER
Rhabdornis inornatus

RANGE: **Samar Island (Philippines)**
HABITAT: **deep forests, among large trees**
SIZE: **6 in (15 cm)**

Although the Plain-headed Creeper does forage on bark, exploiting the rich supply of insect eggs and pupae, it feeds mainly in the outer canopy of the trees, gleaning insects from leaves and twigs. It is not completely dependent on insects, however, for it uses its brush-tipped tongue to take advantage of the year-round supply of flower nectar in its tropical forest home and occasionally eats small fruits. Both species in this family are confined to islands in the Philippine archipelago.

FAMILY CLIMACTERIDAE
Australasian treecreepers

Small tree-climbers that also feed on ground. Downcurved bill. Plumage brown, gray or blackish above, striped or rufous below. Sexes differ slightly. Nest in tree holes. Eggs 2–3, white or pinkish, brown or gray markings. Incubation 16–23 days, nestling period 25–26 days. 7 species.

9/ RED-BROWED TREECREEPER
Climacteris erythrops

RANGE: **SE Australia**
HABITAT: **tall eucalyptus forests in mountains; less often near coast**
SIZE: **5½–6¼ in (14–16 cm)**

The Red-browed Treecreeper feeds largely on ants, foraging for them over the trunks and branches of smooth-barked trees, concentrating on places where the bark is peeling back. Small family groups maintain communal territories, with male birds from previous broods helping the breeding pair in nest-building and in feeding the young.

The female differs slightly from the male in that her upper breast is streaked with rufous. The immature bird has a gray rather than reddish face and few streaks on the underparts.

FAMILY DICAEIDAE
Flowerpeckers

Small, dumpy. Upperparts dark, glossy, underparts lighter. Sexes alike or males have bright patches. Nests open, cup-shaped, or hanging with side entrance. Eggs 1–3, white, some blotched. Incubation 12 days, nestling period about 15 days. 50 species.

10/ FAN-TAILED BERRYPECKER
Melanocharis versteri

RANGE: **New Guinea**
HABITAT: **understory shrubs and trees of upland rain forest over 4,000 ft (1,200 m)**
SIZE: **4 in (10 cm)**

The Fan-tailed Berrypecker is a common but timid and solitary bird. It feeds mainly on small fruit, taken from many different forest trees. Insects also form part of its diet, especially when it is breeding. At 4–5 in (10–12 cm) in diameter, the nest is large for the size of the bird and is constructed from stems, bark and spiders' webs placed astride a large branch. Unusually among passerines, the female is heavier than the male.

11/ CRIMSON-BREASTED FLOWERPECKER
Prionochilus percussus

RANGE: **Malay Peninsula, Sumatra, Java, Borneo, Philippines**
HABITAT: **lowland rain forest; also mangroves and overgrown plantations**
SIZE: **3–3½ in (8–9 cm)**

This is a lively, noisy bird, aggressive toward other birds even though it is one of the region's smallest species. Like many other members of its family, it spends much time among flowers, either catching spiders and insects or drinking nectar with its long, tubular tongue. However, the principal food of flowerpeckers is berries, especially those of mistletoes. These sugary fruits provide a rich source of energy for the birds. When they have passed through a flowerpecker's digestive system, the bird must remove their remains from around its vent by wiping its rear end against a branch. The wiping action deposits the seeds on the tree bark, where they can germinate.

12/ MISTLETOEBIRD
Dicaeum hirundinaceum

RANGE: **Australia, Aru Islands**
HABITAT: **varied, from dry scrub to wet forest**
SIZE: **4 in (10 cm)**

This bird has evolved an extremely close association with the 60 or so species of fruiting mistletoe in Australasia. Flowerpeckers generally have a reduced stomach, offset from the gut, but in the Mistletoebird the stomach has almost completely degenerated. The mistletoe berries pass very rapidly through the intestine, where most of the sweet flesh is stripped from the husk, but the seeds are left intact. Seeds may be defecated just 30 minutes after the berries are swallowed.

What remains of the bird's stomach is reserved for insects, food that requires a longer period of digestion. Nestlings are fed almost entirely on insects for the first week, before being weaned onto the staple diet of berries.

13/ SCARLET-BACKED FLOWERPECKER
Dicaeum cruentatum

RANGE: **India to S China, Southeast Asia, Indonesia**
HABITAT: **coastal lowland plains, open forest, scrub, gardens**
SIZE: **4 in (10 cm)**

This tiny, dumpy bird is a common inhabitant of the treetops of Southeast Asia. It is noticeable even at a distance because of its constant twittering while feeding, its frequent staccato calls and its erratic, dipping flight. It breeds from March to April, building a delicate, purse-shaped nest of cotton down and spiders' webs, suspended from a branch. The purse has a side entrance that is impossible for most predators to reach, although snakes may be able to penetrate the defences. The female incubates the eggs alone, but the male helps to feed the nestlings.

14/ CRESTED BERRYPECKER
Paramythia montium

RANGE: **C and SE New Guinea**
HABITAT: **moss forest from 6,500 ft (2,000 m) to tree line**
SIZE: **7¾ in (20 cm)**

The Crested Berrypecker is by far the largest member of its family. Common in the high-altitude forest in its range, it is a bold and engaging species. Its strange *swish* call is rather like the sound of dry twigs being scraped lightly together. It has the bizarre habit of plucking certain large flowers and rubbing its plumage with the crushed petals. It feeds on berries and insects. The larger-crested race *P. m. olivaceum*, with less white on its head, is found in the Snow Mountains, while the race *P. m. montium* occurs in central and southeastern New Guinea.

FAMILY PARDALOTIDAE
Pardalotes

Small, dumpy. Plumage gray to olive. Black, white, yellow or orange markings. Females duller in some species. Nest in tree holes or in burrows. Eggs 3–5, white. Incubation 14–16 days, nestling period about 25 days. 4 species.

15/ STRIATED PARDALOTE
Pardalotus striatus

RANGE: **Australia**
HABITAT: **forest, woodland, parks with eucalyptus**
SIZE: **4 in (10 cm)**

The pardalotes are small birds that comb the foliage for insects and other food. They feed heavily on "lerps" – sugary secretions exuded by the sap-sucking larvae of psyllid scale insects – and undertake nomadic movements in search of infested trees.

The Striated Pardalote is the most widespread species, with several races. There are 2 main groups: black-crowned races, such as the cinnamon-rumped *P. s. melanocephalus* from the northeast, and stripe-crowned races, such as the southeastern race *P. s. ornatus*.

PYGMY SUNBIRD

♂

♀

SAO THOMÉ
GIANT SUNBIRD

PURPLE SUNBIRD

♀

♂

race *asiatica*

♂

eclipse

♀

♀

♂

REGAL SUNBIRD

♀

♂

GOLDEN-WINGED SUNBIRD

♂

♂

NORTHERN ORANGE-TUFTED SUNBIRD

♀

race *dabryii*

♂

MRS GOULD'S SUNBIRD

SCARLET-CHESTED SUNBIRD
♂
♀

PURPLE-RUMPED SUNBIRD
♂
♀

YELLOW-BELLIED SUNBIRD
♂
♀

RED-TUFTED
MALACHITE SUNBIRD
♂
♀

SUPERB SUNBIRD
♂
♀

YELLOW-BACKED SUNBIRD
♀
♂

LONG-BILLED SPIDERHUNTER

SUNBIRDS

FAMILY NECTARINIIDAE
Sunbirds

Small, males with very colorful iridescent plumage (except some forest sunbirds and all spiderhunters); slim, often long, downcurved bills. Sexes differ markedly. Nest purse-shaped, suspended from twig; made of grass, lichens and other plant materials, often bound together with spiders' webs; entrance at side, often covered by "porch;" nests of spiderhunters cup-shaped. Eggs 2–3, white, spotted or streaked. Incubation 13–15 days, nestling period 14–19 days. 120 species.

1/ PYGMY SUNBIRD
Anthreptes platurus

RANGE: **Senegal to Egypt, Ethiopia, NW Kenya**
HABITAT: **savanna, parks, gardens**
SIZE: **$6\frac{1}{4}$–7 in (16–18 cm)**

A small, short-billed sunbird typical of thorny bush, the Pygmy Sunbird is also found in wooded suburbs planted with flowering acacia and mimosa trees. Its active behavior and tameness make it easy to find and watch as it perches acrobatically on twigs to probe inside small flowers for nectar and insects, behaving rather like a cross between a small tit and a warbler. It has a thin, penetrating call.

During summer the males have long tail spikes and metallic upper plumage, but in winter they have short tails and dull plumage, like the females. This rather dull, nonbreeding eclipse plumage is a characteristic of many sunbirds.

2/ SAO THOMÉ GIANT SUNBIRD
Nectarinia thomensis

RANGE: **Sao Thomé Island (W Africa)**
HABITAT: **thick forest on W slopes**
SIZE: **9 in (23 cm)**

The largest sunbird of all, this species behaves in an unusual way for a sunbird, frequently using its strong, hooked bill to probe into the bark of trees for insects, rather like a nuthatch (pp. 302–5). Its usual call is a single cheeping note, while its song is a strident repetition of 3 notes.

Its plumage looks black from a distance, for the steely-blue feather edges show up only at close range. Apart from being slightly smaller than the male, the female is otherwise similar. The nest, which is suspended from a branch, is made of moss, dead leaves and roots, lined with dry grass.

3/ SCARLET-CHESTED SUNBIRD
Nectarinia senegalensis

RANGE: **W and E Africa from Senegal to Kenya and S to Zimbabwe**
HABITAT: **woodland, parks, riverside scrub**
SIZE: **6 in (15 cm)**

This is a large species, with marked plumage variations depending on age, sex and time of year. An adult male in his breeding condition looks intensely black, except for the magnificent, eye-catching splash of red across his breast, but out of season his eclipse plumage is like that of the dull, mottled female or juvenile.

In many areas the Scarlet-chested Sunbird is a year-round resident, but at the limits of its range it

moves short distances according to the seasons, always searching for concentrations of showy, nectar-rich flowers such as those of *Leonotis*. It is fairly common in ornamental gardens, where it is often seen feeding in small groups. Its frequent call is a descending triple note, its song a loud, but undistinguished, warbling trill.

4/ PURPLE-RUMPED SUNBIRD
Nectarinia zeylonica

RANGE: **peninsular India, Bangladesh, Sri Lanka**
HABITAT: **jungle and dry cultivated plains with deciduous trees**
SIZE: **4 in (10 cm)**

Several sunbirds have evolved long bills which enable them to drink nectar from long, tubular flowers. Purple-rumped Sunbirds, with their short bills, cannot do this; instead they use their bills to pierce large flowers neatly at the base of the petals to reach the nectar.

Males and females differ in appearance; although young males look like rather yellow females, the adult males keep their metallic plumage all year round. They are usually found in pairs, actively flitting among thick foliage and flowers, perching acrobatically to reach into the flowers or – more rarely – hovering briefly to take a fly. The pair will defend their feeding tree and nesting area vigorously if other sunbirds appear. The song is a sharp twitter or a squeaky performance given with flicking wings and tail.

5/ YELLOW-BELLIED SUNBIRD
Nectarinia jugularis

RANGE: **Southeast Asia, from Indonesia to Solomon Islands, NE Australia**
HABITAT: **coastal rain forest, mangroves and gardens**
SIZE: **4–$4\frac{3}{4}$ in (10–12 cm)**

The Yellow-bellied, or Olive-backed, Sunbird is the only sunbird found in Australia, where it is a common, locally nomadic species in the forests and gardens of northeast Queensland.

It is an active bird, which searches a large variety of native and exotic plants for nectar and insects. It usually clings to foliage while feeding but may hover briefly to sip nectar from a flower or pluck a spider from its web. Like most sunbirds, it is incapable of the sustained hovering practiced by hummingbirds (pp. 190–97), which are the ecological equivalents of sunbirds in the New World.

Males and females are fairly similar, but the female's underparts are yellow throughout, whereas the male has a metallic purplish-blue throat and chest. The male defends the breeding territory, but the female builds the nest: this has a dangling "tail" of loose building material.

6/ PURPLE SUNBIRD
Nectarinia asiatica

RANGE: **Iran, India, Sri Lanka, Indochina**
HABITAT: **thorny riverbeds, forest edge, scrub**
SIZE: **4 in (10 cm)**

The Purple Sunbird is a summer visitor over much of its range: in many mountainous and hilly areas it moves uphill in summer and returns to the valleys as the days shorten. It is always found around flowering trees, which it raids for nectar, and it is an important pollinator of several kinds, especially *Loranthus* species.

Single birds often catch insects on the wing like flycatchers, using their extremely agile flight and excellent eyesight; large gatherings feeding on swarming gnats have also been reported. When the male sings and displays, he opens his wings slightly to display the pectoral tufts which, as on most sunbirds, are generally hidden. Outside the breeding season, the male has a much less dramatic eclipse plumage.

There are 3 races, of which *N. a. asiatica* (illustrated) occurs throughout much of India and Sri Lanka, north to Nepal. A shorter-billed race *N. a. brevirostris*, with a less green and more purple breeding male, is found in the west towards Iran, while a long-billed, purple race *N. a. intermedia* occurs in Bangladesh and to the east.

7/ REGAL SUNBIRD
Nectarinia regia

RANGE: **W Uganda, W Tanzania**
HABITAT: **mountain forest up to 12,000 ft (3,650 m)**
SIZE: **4¼ in (11 cm)**

The Regal Sunbird exhibits the sexual differences typical of sunbirds, with splendid, metallic males and rather dowdy females. It is one of many African species of sunbird with males patterned with green, yellow, purple, blue and red, all superficially very alike. Young birds are duller and somewhat darker than the adult female.

It is often associated with the Purple-breasted Sunbird *Nectarinia purpureiventris*, with which it seeks out flowering *Symphonia* trees in the remote mountain forests of the Ruwenzori range in Uganda. Here, in dense mist, amid dripping leaves, it is more often heard than seen. Like other sunbirds, it has a rapid trilling or warbling song with little precise pattern but with plenty of energy in the performance.

8/ NORTHERN ORANGE-TUFTED SUNBIRD
Nectarinia osea

RANGE: **Syria, Israel, W and S edge of Arabian peninsula**
HABITAT: **woods, orchards, gardens**
SIZE: **4¼ in (11 cm)**

Although it prefers bushy places or groves of planted eucalyptus, acacias or mimosas, the Northern Orange-tufted Sunbird is an adaptable species that will live anywhere, from quite bare rocky wadis to well-kept gardens – as long as they provide it with tiny insects or nectar-bearing flowers. In general it is resident throughout its range, but there is some winter dispersal.

Its song is a shrill, rapid, rambling trill, quite unlike that of any other bird in its range. The males may sing as they flit about in search of food, or while perched high in a tree, hidden in dense foliage. Sharp calls uttered in flight are equally characteristic of these birds.

From July to November the mature males look like dull females, but they often have a few traces of their breeding colors on the wings or throat. This is common among sunbirds in eclipse plumage. The small orange tufts flanking the breast are visible only in display.

9/ RED-TUFTED MALACHITE SUNBIRD
Nectarinia johnstoni

RANGE: **Kenya and Uganda, S to Tanzania**
HABITAT: **alpine moorlands with giant lobelia and proteaceous flowers**
SIZE: **9¾–11¾ in (25–30 cm)**

This large sunbird is remarkable for the long tail feathers of the male which, unusually, are retained even when the bird is in its dull eclipse plumage.

The Red-tufted Malachite Sunbird has a specialized way of life, being found only on high alpine slopes with distinctive vegetation types on remote, bleak uplands such as Mount Kenya, the Aberdare Range, the Ruwenzori Mountains and Mount Kilimanjaro. There it probes the strange and eye-catching flowers of giant lobelias for nectar. It also eats many insects.

10/ SUPERB SUNBIRD
Nectarinia superba

RANGE: **Sierra Leone E to Central African Republic, S to Congo**
HABITAT: **forest edge and clearings**
SIZE: **6 in (15 cm)**

In poor light the male Superb Sunbird looks almost black, but in full sunshine his metallic plumage dazzles the eye with its breathtakingly beautiful coloration. These birds are usually found in sunny places at the edges of forests, although they also visit savanna woods and thick bush as long as there is plenty of nectar-rich blossom for them to feed from.

These stocky, fairly large sunbirds are hard to follow as they fly swiftly from tree to tree, bounding and zigzagging. Although the species has an extensive range, it is nowhere common. Moreover, the birds' chirping calls and poor, jingling song are of little help in locating them.

11/ GOLDEN-WINGED SUNBIRD
Nectarinia reichenowi

RANGE: **Uganda, Kenya, W Tanzania**
HABITAT: **highland moors, scrub, forest edge above 5,000 ft (1,500 m)**
SIZE: **9 in (23 cm)**

The Golden-winged Sunbird is a highland specialist, found on bleak moorland and mountain scrub, apparently unlikely surroundings for a nectar-feeder. But as the sun warms the landscape each day, many of the upland plants such as the orange mint *Leonotis nepetifolia* unfurl large, showy flowers that are rich in nectar, which the Golden-winged Sunbird extracts with its powerful, strongly hooked bill. Like many other sunbirds, Golden-winged Sunbirds defend patches of flowers, but when they can obtain enough nectar from flowers shared with other sunbirds they do not need to defend a feeding territory. However, they do not invest energy in defense when nectar production within a patch of flowers is low – the cost to them would outweigh the advantage.

The nonbreeding males have largely black plumage, but a male in breeding condition is a gorgeous sight. In his strange display flight, slow for a sunbird, he zigzags between bushes with wings extended and tail flashing yellow, uttering clear, liquid calls and a warbling song.

12/ MRS GOULD'S SUNBIRD
Aethopyga gouldiae

RANGE: **Indochina W to Nepal**
HABITAT: **deciduous forest**
SIZE: **4 in (10 cm)**

For such a tiny creature, this sunbird inhabits some demanding places: in Nepal it breeds at altitudes of up to 12,000 ft (3,600 m) and may remain at 9,000 ft (2,700 m) even in winter, although most descend lower.

It is a particularly active, restless sunbird, searching for nectar among the blossoms of low bushes for a while, then turning its attention to the flowers of parasitic plants in the tall forest trees.

A scarlet-breasted race *A. g. dabryii* is found in the east of the species' range. Other races are yellow-breasted, including the deep-yellow-breasted *A. g. gouldiae*, which breeds high in the mountains of Nepal.

13/ YELLOW-BACKED SUNBIRD
Aethopyga siparaja

RANGE: **Sumatra, Borneo, Malaysia, W to India**
HABITAT: **gardens, orchards, pine forest**
SIZE: **4 in (10 cm)**

The Yellow-backed, or Crimson, Sunbird is a common resident throughout its range. In the Nepal region it moves higher up the mountains in summer and descends again in winter, when it often visits gardens. Unlike many sunbirds, the male Yellow-backed Sunbird retains his bright plumage throughout the year.

It often forages alone, taking nectar from a wide variety of trees and ornamental flowers and adapting its feeding technique to suit the flower. It will pierce larger blooms such as hibiscus to reach the nectar through the base of the petals, but will drink from tubular flowers by hovering before them, rather like a hummingbird, and inserting its tubular tongue. It seems to prefer bright red flowers to any others.

14/ LONG-BILLED SPIDERHUNTER
Arachnothera robusta

RANGE: **Malaysia, Sumatra, Borneo**
HABITAT: **moist, dense forest**
SIZE: **6 in (15 cm)**

Spiderhunters are long-billed relatives of the sunbirds, found singly or in pairs and often in mixed flocks with babblers and warblers high in the forest trees. This habit, combined with their swift flight and rapid movements, makes them extremely hard to locate and watch.

When seen, they resemble large, long-billed female sunbirds. The sexes are similar, although the male has a small orange-yellow tuft on each flank. They have fast, sharp, metallic calls. They take spiders from their webs while hovering on long, whirring wings, but they also drink nectar; like some of the sunbirds they are important pollinators of several species of tree.

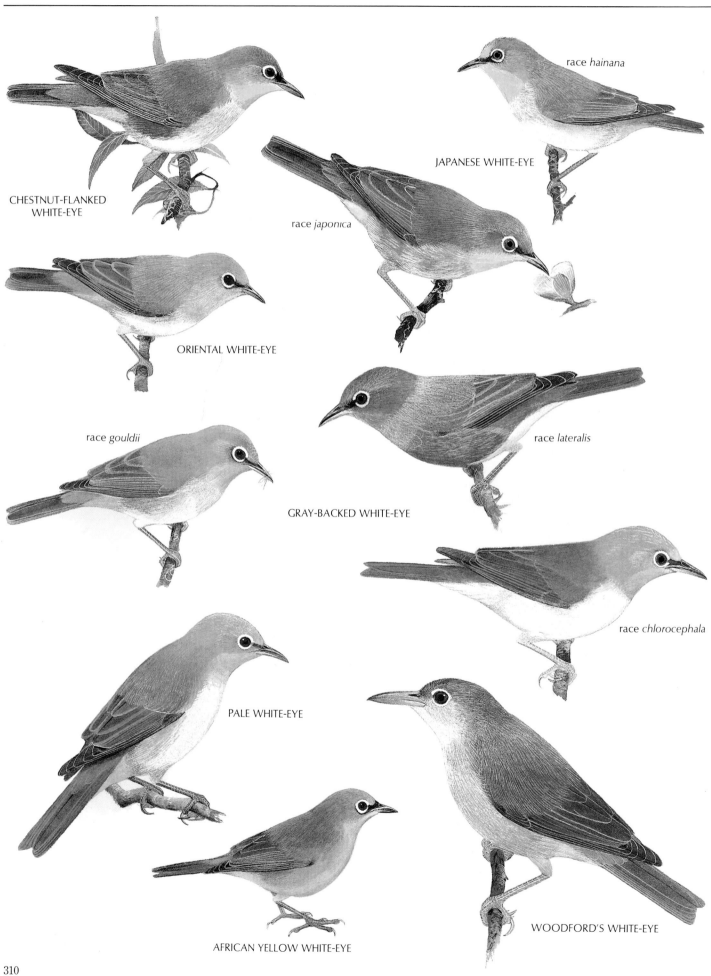

CHESTNUT-FLANKED
WHITE-EYE

race *hainana*

JAPANESE WHITE-EYE

race *japonica*

ORIENTAL WHITE-EYE

race *gouldii*

race *lateralis*

GRAY-BACKED WHITE-EYE

race *chlorocephala*

PALE WHITE-EYE

WOODFORD'S WHITE-EYE

AFRICAN YELLOW WHITE-EYE

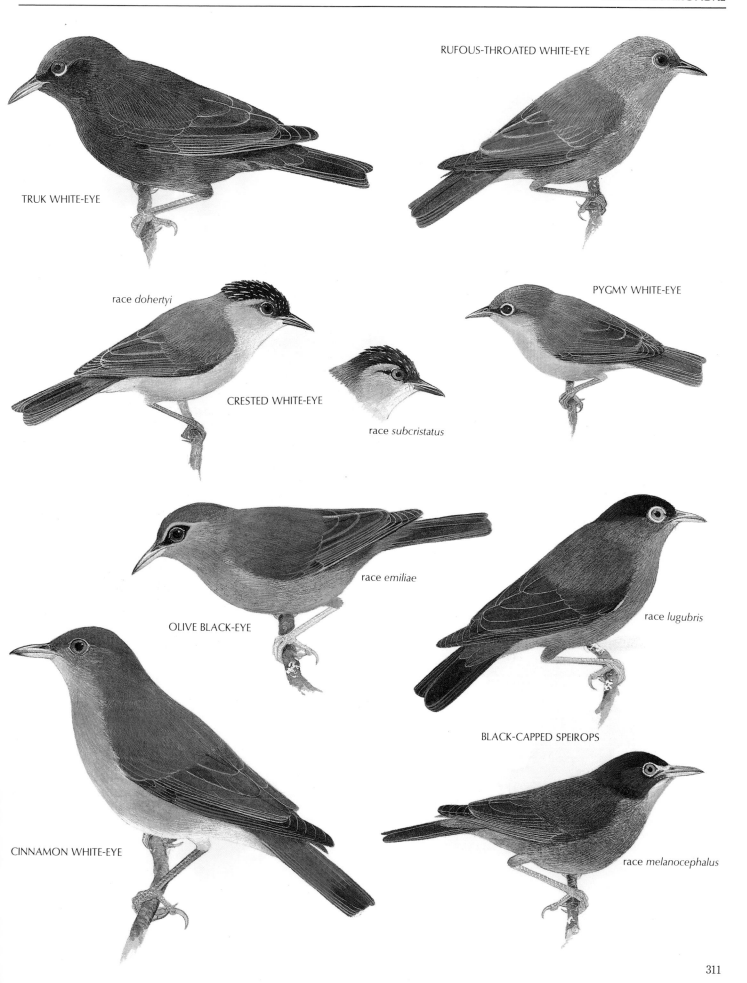

RUFOUS-THROATED WHITE-EYE

TRUK WHITE-EYE

race *dohertyi*

PYGMY WHITE-EYE

CRESTED WHITE-EYE

race *subcristatus*

OLIVE BLACK-EYE

race *emiliae*

race *lugubris*

BLACK-CAPPED SPEIROPS

CINNAMON WHITE-EYE

race *melanocephalus*

WHITE-EYES

FAMILY ZOSTEROPIDAE
White-eyes
Small perching birds with brush-tipped tongues, rounded wings and short legs. Plumage greenish with yellow, gray or brown underparts; most species with ring of white feathers around eye. Males sometimes brighter and bigger. Nests cup-shaped, built in trees. Eggs 2–4, whitish or pale blue. Incubation 10–12 days, nestling period 11–14 days. 85 species.

1/ CHESTNUT-FLANKED WHITE-EYE
Zosterops erythropleura
RANGE: **Manchuria, N Korea, China**
HABITAT: **forest, open woodland**
SIZE: **$4\frac{1}{4}$ in (11 cm)**

Most white-eyes are rather nondescript looking birds, with cryptic greenish plumage that blends well with the leaves among which they feed. With its reddish-brown flank patches and gray, white and yellow underparts, the Chestnut-flanked White-eye has a rather more striking appearance than most species, but in other respects it is typical of this versatile group of birds.

These birds are generally seen foraging in flocks, diligently searching through the foliage for insects and their larvae and occasionally feeding on fruit. Males and females form stable pairs, often for life, and build their nests in tree forks in well-protected positions.

White-eyes, including this species, are kept as cage birds in some Asian countries because of their attractive songs, but they do not breed successfully – the young generally die.

2/ JAPANESE WHITE-EYE
Zosterops japonica
RANGE: **China, Indochina, Japan**
HABITAT: **low hill forest, parks and gardens**
SIZE: **$4\frac{1}{4}$ in (11 cm)**

In the Far East the Japanese White-eye is a familiar winter visitor to gardens as it flies in to feast on seeds and soft fruit during the colder months. Small parties forage from tree to tree in the same way that winter flocks of tits move through European woods, advertising their presence with faint bell-like calls rather like those of the Spruce Siskin *Carduelis spinus* of northern Eurasia.

In summer, the Japanese White-eye uses its brush-tipped tongue to soak up nectar from large blooms, but its main diet consists of insects and spiders, which it gleans from tree foliage and picks out of bark crevices with its short, fine-pointed bill. Although these birds are regarded as pests by commercial fruit-growers, any damage they do in orchards is far outweighed by the number of insect pests they eat.

The race *Z. j. japonica* is found on Honshu Island, Japan. The distinctive *Z. j. hainana*, found on Hainan Island off southern China, is small, with brighter, more yellowish plumage.

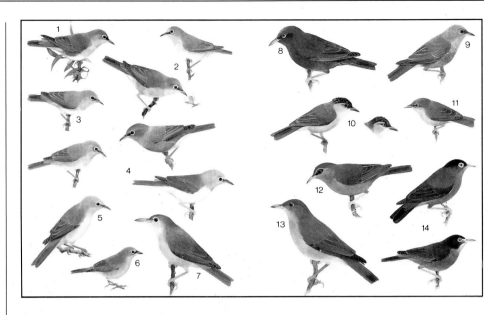

3/ ORIENTAL WHITE-EYE
Zosterops palpebrosa
RANGE: **Afghanistan E to China, Malaysia, Indonesia**
HABITAT: **hill forest, mangroves, gardens**
SIZE: **4 in (10 cm)**

Typically small, dumpy white-eyes, with a good deal of yellow, white and green in their plumage, Oriental White-eyes live in small groups which spend much of their time in the trees, searching for weevils, ants and other insects, as well as their eggs. The parties set up a high, querulous chorus of calls as they feed, repeating the song over and over again with no variation. In forests and cultivated areas they frequently forage in mixed-species flocks with other birds.

The male and female build the nest together, weaving a delicate cup of grass and spiders' webs suspended in the fork of a tree or shrub. The pale blue eggs are incubated for 12 days and the young leave the nest 12 days after hatching, freeing the parents to produce a second brood.

4/ GRAY-BACKED WHITE-EYE
Zosterops lateralis
RANGE: **Australia, Tasmania, SW Pacific islands**
HABITAT: **practically every type of vegetation, from rain forest, mangroves, woods and heaths, to urban parks and gardens**
SIZE: **$4\frac{1}{4}$–5 in (11–13 cm)**

Also known as the Gray-breasted Silvereye, the Gray-backed White-eye is a very variable species with 14 races distributed across the islands of the southwest Pacific. The races *Z. l. lateralis* of Tasmania, *Z. l. gouldii* of southwest Australia and *Z. l. chlorocephala* of the Great Barrier Reef islands illustrate the range of plumage variation. The female is usually paler than the male within a given pair, but may be brighter than other females.

Foraging Gray-backed White-eyes are constantly on the move through their habitat as they gather insects from low foliage, picking them off the leaves or snatching them as they attempt to escape. They also eat fruit and nectar. In winter they form flocks and in Australia some populations undertake long migrations.

Between August and January both sexes defend the breeding territory and help to build the tightly woven cup nest, which is suspended 3–39 ft (1–12 m) above the ground. Both parents share the duties of incubating the 3 eggs for 14 days and feeding the young. The latter fledge when they are 12–14 days old.

5/ PALE WHITE-EYE
Zosterops citrinella
RANGE: **islands of Lesser Sundas and Torres Strait; isolated islands off N Australia**
HABITAT: **forest, monsoon scrub, mangroves, grassland with low shrubs**
SIZE: **4–$4\frac{3}{4}$ in (10–12 cm)**

Although easily confused with the northern Australian race of the Gray-backed White-eye (but distinguished from the latter by its greenish yellow rather than gray back), the Pale White-eye is a distinct species restricted to remote, isolated islands in northern Australasia. Because of the relative inaccessibility of its habitat, little is known about its biology, but it is regularly seen foraging at all levels in the forest, gleaning insects from leaves and flowers and feeding on berries and nectar when these foods are available. The Pale White-eye is sometimes known as the Ashy-bellied White-eye.

The birds breed in the wet season (December to June), building a deep, cup-shaped nest of dried leaves and spiders' webs to contain the clutch of 2–4 eggs. It is probable that both the male and female brood the eggs and feed the young.

6/ AFRICAN YELLOW WHITE-EYE
Zosterops senegalensis
RANGE: **sub-Saharan Africa**
HABITAT: **open thornbush, dry woods, gardens**
SIZE: **4 in (10 cm)**

This is the typical, common white-eye of Africa. Widespread and frequently encountered in open woodland or among scattered trees, it is rarely seen in dense forest. Small parties often mix with sunbirds and other species, flitting through the canopy and down into lower bushes in a constant search for the insects that make up most of their diet. The birds maintain contact with one another by means of weak, twittering calls and piping notes as they fly from tree to tree.

The pair builds a nest of fine plant fiber decorated with lichens, either placed in a tree fork or suspended from a branch.

7/ WOODFORD'S WHITE-EYE
Woodfordia superciliosa
RANGE: **Rennell Island (Solomon Islands)**
HABITAT: **woodland, bushes**
SIZE: **5½ in (14 cm)**

Closely related to the true white-eyes of the genus *Zosterops*, this slightly larger bird has a very similar way of life, moving about in small parties that search the foliage and outer twigs of trees for small insects and seeds. It has a rather long bill for a white-eye, and its facial patch and eye ring are of bare skin, not small white or silver feathers as in most of the family. It lays its clutch of 2 eggs in a delicate nest.

Woodford's White-eye shares its tiny island with another white-eye, the Rennell Island White-eye *Zosterops rennelliana*, a smaller bird with a thin white eye ring.

8/ TRUK WHITE-EYE
Rukia ruki　　　　　　　　　E
RANGE: **Truk Islands (tropical Pacific Ocean)**
HABITAT: **dense mountain forest**
SIZE: **5½ in (14 cm)**

The tropical islands north of New Guinea have many species limited to a single island. The Truk White-eye is found at the summit of Tol Island and reputedly on some others in the group. It has always been very rare and was not seen between its discovery early this century and its rediscovery in 1975, in the 30 acres (12 hectares) of mountain forest that remain on the island. Here it keeps to the outer branches of the canopy, probing among the tangled vines and other creepers to find its insect prey.

Rather larger and more solidly built than the true white-eyes of the genus *Zosterops*, this species lacks their greenish plumage and has only a small white mark beneath its eye instead of a complete ring. It has a loud, whistled song with a musical, warbling pattern.

9/ RUFOUS-THROATED WHITE-EYE
Madanga ruficollis　　　　　　?
RANGE: **NW Buru Island (Indonesia)**
HABITAT: **forests**
SIZE: **5–5½ in (13–14 cm)**

The Rufous-throated White-eye was first described in 1923, from just 4 specimens which were collected from the mountain forests of Buru Island. It then promptly disappeared from the scientific record and has not been recorded again. It seems likely that it is now extinct.

It is (or was) a large species, not closely related to any other white-eye. Nothing is known of its habits, although the specimens described in 1923 were taken at 2,750 and 5,000 ft (840 and 1,550 m) above sea level.

10/ CRESTED WHITE-EYE
Lophozosterops dohertyi　　　　?
RANGE: **Sumbawa and Flores islands (Indonesia)**
HABITAT: **forests**
SIZE: **4¾ in (12 cm)**

There are 2 quite distinct races of the Crested White-eye. On Flores Island the race *L. d. subcristatus* is found in light rain forest, at altitudes of 1,000–3,500 ft (300–1,100 m); it has a pale grayish crown with a very slight crest. The race found on Sumbawa, *L. d. dohertyi*, has a darker, browner crown, with each feather sharply spotted white, and a much more obvious crest.

Their behavior is very like that of other white-eyes; sociable and energetic, yet rather unobtrusive, with a preference for feeding among the foliage and tangled creepers of the forest.

11/ PYGMY WHITE-EYE
Oculocincta squamifrons　　　　?
RANGE: **Borneo**
HABITAT: **damp moss forest, clearings**
SIZE: **4 in (10 cm)**

This tiny white-eye is found along the mountain chain that forms the backbone of Borneo, at altitudes of 600–4,000 ft (180–1,200 m). Basically a bird of warm, moist forest, it is often seen among secondary scrub growing in areas of felled jungle, and in clearings around villages.

It keeps low, even in mature forest, and is well known for its habit of approaching humans and cattle very closely in dense scrub – possibly to snap up the insects they disturb. Despite this, its main food appears to be berries and seeds. Its nest and eggs have never been positively identified.

12/ OLIVE BLACK-EYE
Chlorocharis emiliae
RANGE: **Borneo**
HABITAT: **low-growing mountain heath, mossy areas, rhododendron thickets**
SIZE: **4½ in (11.5 cm)**

Many isolated island white-eyes have developed distinctive plumage variations of their own, but most have retained at least part of the white eye ring characteristic of the family. The Olive Black-eye is a unique exception to the rule. There are 4 races: the race illustrated is *C. e. emiliae*, found only on Mount Kinabalu in northern Borneo.

On the high mountains of Borneo the Olive Black-eye is the commonest bird, ranging throughout the region above the tree line where conifers, rhododendrons and heathers gradually give way with increasing altitude to bare, slippery rock with stunted scrub. It nests in dense heath, building a flattened cup of dead grass and lichens, sometimes lined with bright orange moss.

Olive Black-eyes feed mainly on insects and seeds and as they forage they utter twittering, finchlike calls that may be heard all day, even into the wet, gloomy dusk when gray cloud envelops their mountain retreats.

13/ CINNAMON WHITE-EYE
Hypocryptadius cinnamomeus
RANGE: **Mindanao Island (Philippines)**
HABITAT: **mountain forest, at 3,000–6,000 ft (900–1,800 m)**
SIZE: **5 in (13 cm)**

The Cinnamon White-eye is a very local species, restricted to the mountain forests of Mount Apo on the island of Mindanao in the Philippines. Its plumage is markedly different from that of other white-eyes, and some ornithologists consider that it should be classified in a separate family.

It feeds mainly on insects, picking them off leaves and tangled vegetation with its sharp-pointed bill. Apart from this, very little is known about the Cinnamon White-eye's behavior, and its nesting habits are still a mystery.

14/ BLACK-CAPPED SPEIROPS
Speirops lugubris
RANGE: **Cameroon, Sao Thomé Island (Gulf of Guinea)**
HABITAT: **mountain forest clearings**
SIZE: **5 in (13 cm)**

In the uplands of Sao Thomé Island, the Black-capped Speirops is a common sight as it forages through the trees in small, restless feeding parties. The birds search nonstop for food, flicking their wings and flitting from tree to tree like stout, short-tailed warblers or tits and communicating with short, musical chirps.

On Sao Thomé the race *S. l. lugubris* feeds in trees, in typical white-eye fashion, but the white-throated race *S. l. melanocephalus*, found in the mountain forests of Cameroon, prefers bushy places and clearings. Little is known about the nesting behavior of either race.

HONEYEATERS, SUGARBIRDS, AUSTRALIAN CHATS

CARDINAL HONEYEATER

MIMIC MELIPHAGA

race *chloropsis*

race *lunatus*

juv

race *cyanotis*

WHITE-NAPED HONEYEATER

race *albipennis*

BLUE-FACED HONEYEATER

YELLOW WATTLEBIRD

imm

STITCHBIRD

NOISY FRIARBIRD

LONG-BEARDED
MELIDECTES

KAUAI O-O

NEW HOLLAND HONEYEATER

WESTERN SPINEBILL

♂

♀

NOISY MINER

imm

TUI

♂

♂

♂

♀

MSON CHAT

♀

CAPE SUGARBIRD

315

HONEYEATERS, SUGARBIRDS, AUSTRALIAN CHATS

FAMILY MELIPHAGIDAE
Honeyeaters

Small to medium mostly tree-dwelling perching birds with brushlike tongues for feeding on nectar. Plumage generally dull green or brown. Sexes typically similar, but males brighter in some species and usually larger. Nest cup-shaped, in bush or tree. Eggs 2–4, white to buff with brown spots. Incubation 13–17 days, nestling period 10–16 days. 170 species.

1/ CARDINAL HONEYEATER
Myzomela cardinalis

RANGE: **islands of Vanuatu, Samoa, Santa Cruz and Solomons**
HABITAT: **coastal scrub, secondary forest, woodland, gardens**
SIZE: **5 in (13 cm)**

In most honeyeaters the sexes are similar, but the Cardinal Honeyeater is an exception. Whereas the female is dull olive-gray with small red patches, the male has bright scarlet and black plumage. His flamboyant appearance is matched by his noisy, aggressive territorial behavior.

These dramatic-looking birds normally feed in the canopy but they venture lower down when near the forest edge, sipping nectar from flowers and gleaning insects from the foliage. They may breed at any time of year, suspending a fragile nest of plant fiber from a tree fork and laying 2–3 eggs which are incubated by both birds.

2/ MIMIC MELIPHAGA
Meliphaga analoga

RANGE: **New Guinea, Aru and Geelvink islands**
HABITAT: **rain forest, forest edge, scrub**
SIZE: **6–6½ in (15–17 cm)**

This is one of 6 very similar species which often occur together at the edges of rain forest on New Guinea and adjacent islands. It spends most of its time among the smaller trees, but often ventures out into nearby scrub or enters gardens to feed on fruit and insects and take advantage of nectar-bearing flowers. Like many honeyeaters, the Mimic Meliphaga bathes by flying into water and then returning to a perch to preen.

3/ WHITE-NAPED HONEYEATER
Melithreptus lunatus

RANGE: **E and SW Australia (not Tasmania)**
HABITAT: **eucalyptus forest and woodland**
SIZE: **5–6 in (13–15 cm)**

The White-naped Honeyeater is one of several short-beaked species with generally olive-green upper plumage and black heads. The small patch of skin, or wattle, above the eye is red in the eastern race *M. l. lunatus* and chalky white in the western *M. l. chloropsis*.

These birds forage in pairs or small groups, gleaning insects from foliage and bark and drinking nectar. Most birds are resident, but some will form flocks of 30–50 birds and migrate north for the winter.

White-naped Honeyeaters may breed as pairs or in small groups, cooperating to defend the nest

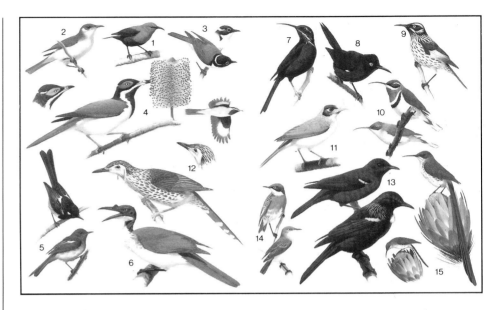

area. The nest is made of shredded bark and dry grasses bound with spiders' webs and is suspended from a fork high in the outer foliage of a tree or shrub.

4/ BLUE-FACED HONEYEATER
Entomyzon cyanotis

RANGE: **S New Guinea, N and E Australia**
HABITAT: **eucalyptus and paperbark woodland, plantations, parks, gardens; occasionally mangroves**
SIZE: **9½–11¾ in (24–30 cm)**

Well known for its pugnacious, inquisitive character, the Blue-faced Honeyeater has also earned a bad reputation as a pest of banana plantations, where it feeds on the ripe fruit. It usually forages in small groups, searching out fruit, nectar and insects in the upper foliage and branches.

Groups of 2–10 adults breed together, sharing the brooding and feeding of the 1–2 young. The nest is usually an untidy deep bowl of bark, but occasionally they will take over deserted nests of other birds. The northwestern race *E. c. albipennis* has white wing patches which are conspicuous in flight. The eastern race *E. c. cyanotis* has only a small buff patch on its wings.

5/ STITCHBIRD
Notiomystis cincta   [V]

RANGE: **Little Barrier Island (New Zealand); introduced to Hen and Kapiti islands**
HABITAT: **mature forest**
SIZE: **7–7½ in (18–19 cm)**

Once far more widespread across the northern islands of New Zealand, the Stitchbird is now reduced to three small islands off the northeast coast. Usually detected by its sharp, high-pitched call, it moves rapidly through the vegetation with its tail cocked, feeding on fruit, nectar and insects. Unlike most honeyeaters, it rarely congregates at rich feeding sites. The Stitchbird breeds in late spring and summer and, unusually for a honeyeater, nests in a hole in a tree trunk or branch, 10–60 ft (3–18 m) above the ground.

6/ NOISY FRIARBIRD
Philemon corniculatus

RANGE: **S New Guinea, E Australia**
HABITAT: **open forest, woodland and lowland savanna**
SIZE: **11¾–13¼ in (30–34 cm)**

This large honeyeater is also known as the Knobby-nosed Leatherhead because of the black, naked skin on its head and the small knob at the base of its upper mandible. It often gathers in groups at flowering trees, squabbling raucously over the spoils as it feeds on fruit and collects the nectar of banksia and eucalyptus trees. It also consumes insects, which provide valuable protein in an otherwise sugar-rich diet.

In the breeding season (July to January) the flocks break up, and the birds advertise their feeding and breeding territories with grating, discordant calls. The females incubate the 2–3 eggs alone, but both sexes feed the young.

7/ LONG-BEARDED MELIDECTES
Melidectes princeps

RANGE: **New Guinea, on E highlands of Central Range**
HABITAT: **mossy woodland, alpine scrub and grassland above tree line**
SIZE: **10½ in (27 cm)**

This species is fairly common within its confined range but, despite this, very little is known about its way of life. It seems that, like its better-known close relative the Short-bearded Melidectes *M. nouhuysi*, but unlike most other honeyeaters, the Long-bearded Melidectes spends much of its time on the ground, sifting through leaf litter to find fruit, berries, sedge seeds and insects. Its nesting behavior, too, is little known. The bulky cup-shaped nest is well concealed in an isolated shrub and on one occasion, in July, a pair of adults was seen feeding a single fledgling, suggesting, perhaps, that only one egg is laid.

After the 9 other members of the genus *Melidectes*, the closest relatives of the Long-bearded Melidectes appear to be the wattlebirds, such as the Yellow Wattlebird.

8/ KAUAI O-O
Moho braccatus [E]
RANGE: **island of Kauai (Hawaii)**
HABITAT: **dense rain forest**
SIZE: **7¾ in (20 cm)**

A century ago this was a common bird in forests all over its native island, but it became increasingly rare and was presumed extinct until it was rediscovered in 1960, in a small area of swamp forest. It was probably saved by its dull plumage, which made it unattractive to the Hawaiians who captured its brighter (and now extinct) relatives in great numbers.

An active, quick bird, it darts noisily from tree to tree searching for insects and spiders among the bark. Unfortunately it is now threatened by habitat destruction and introduced predators and is unlikely to survive. Indeed, it is thought that only a solitary male is still alive.

9/ NEW HOLLAND HONEYEATER
Phylidonyris novaehollandiae
RANGE: **SW and E Australia, Tasmania**
HABITAT: **heathland, mallee heath, woods and forests with shrubs**
SIZE: **6½–7½ in (17–19 cm)**

New Holland, or Yellow-winged, Honeyeaters are aggressive birds, but their aggression varies with the abundance of nectar and nesting resources. They catch insects for their protein content but rely on honeydew and nectar to supply energy. As they gather the nectar, they are dusted with pollen which is transferred to successive blossoms, and in this way they play an important role in the pollination of a wide range of Australian plants.

They may breed up to 3 times a year, depending on the availability of nectar. The males defend nest sites that are arranged in loose colonies, usually 3–6 ft (1–2 m) above the ground in shrubs. The females build the nests and incubate the 2–3 eggs, but the young are fed by both parents.

10/ WESTERN SPINEBILL
Acanthorhynchus superciliosus
RANGE: **SW corner of Australia**
HABITAT: **heathland, eucalyptus woodland with shrubs**
SIZE: **6 in (15 cm)**

The Western Spinebill is a small, active honeyeater with a long, downcurved bill. Being small, it is usually displaced from rich nectar sources by larger honeyeaters, but its very smallness enables it to forage efficiently at a wide range of less productive blooms that would not support bigger birds. It is a resourceful feeder, often hovering to sip nectar and hawking for insects.

When breeding, the male aggressively defends the nest site and engages in display flights. The nest is built by the female and she also incubates the 1–2 eggs. The nestlings are fed by both parents for 11 days.

11/ NOISY MINER
Manorina melanocephala
RANGE: **E Australia, Tasmania**
HABITAT: **open forest, woodland and partly cleared land**
SIZE: **9¾–11½ in (25–29 cm)**

Noisy Miners have a complex social system, with territorial groups of 6–30 birds gathering together into large colonies. The group members co-operate to mob predators and they will aggressively exclude most other bird species from the nesting area.

They breed communally, with as many as 12 males caring for the young of each polyandrous female. The nest, which is built by the female, is a loosely constructed bowl of twigs and grasses placed in the fork of a shrub or tree.

12/ YELLOW WATTLEBIRD
Anthochaera paradoxa
RANGE: **E Tasmania and King Island**
HABITAT: **dry eucalyptus forest and woodland, occasionally orchards and gardens**
SIZE: **17¼–18¾ in (44–48 cm)**

Named for the bright yellow wattles that hang from its cheeks, the Yellow Wattlebird is the largest of the honeyeaters and was once shot as a gamebird. Outside the breeding season it often lives in flocks of 10–12 birds; these may be sedentary or nomadic, foraging through the canopy for insects, gleaning them from the leaves, branches and bark. In addition, the birds eat nectar and fruit.

Yellow Wattlebirds breed as pairs, establishing territories in August and laying 2–3 eggs in an untidy nest built of thin twigs and grasses, placed in thick foliage.

13/ TUI
Prosthemadura novaeseelandiae
RANGE: **New Zealand**
HABITAT: **forests, suburban areas**
SIZE: **12¼ in (31 cm)**

This large, dark honeyeater is also known as the Parsonbird – a reference to the characteristic double tuft of curled white feathers at its throat, which bobs up and down during the bird's singing displays. The song is complex, involving both harsh and tuneful elements and even some notes inaudible to the human ear.

Tui often congregate in large numbers around rich food sources. They are wider-ranging than the other 2 New Zealand honeyeaters (the Stitchbird and the New Zealand Bellbird *Anthornis melanura*) and take more nectar in their diet, although some fruits and insects are also eaten.

They breed in late spring and summer, building bulky open nests of twigs in solid tree forks, well off the ground.

FAMILY EPHTHIANURIDAE
Australian chats
Small, open country, perching birds with red, yellow, or black and white plumage, males brighter than females. Nest on or near ground. Eggs 3–4, white or pinkish with brown spots. Incubation 12 days, nestling period 14 days. 5 species.

14/ CRIMSON CHAT
Ephthianura tricolor
RANGE: **inland and W Australia**
HABITAT: **acacia scrub, savanna, succulent shrub-steppe, often near salt lakes**
SIZE: **4¼–4¾ in (11–12 cm)**

Closely related to the honeyeaters, the Crimson Chat is a nomad of the arid zone. After the young fledge each year, Crimson Chats gather in flocks, sometimes with several hundred birds, and move across the country picking insects off the ground and sipping nectar from flowers.

In the breeding season the males defend females and a small area around the nest, which is a well-concealed cup of fine twigs and grasses placed close to the ground in a shrub or tussock. The nests are often clumped in loose colonies and both the male and the duller female share the incubation and feeding duties.

FAMILY PROMEROPIDAE
Sugarbirds
Long-billed perching birds resembling large honeyeaters. Males with greatly extended tails, sexes otherwise similar. Nest in bushes. Eggs 2, cream, buff or pinkish white, blotched, spotted and scrawled with gray, brown, chocolate or purplish-black. Incubation about 17 days, nestling period 17–21 days. 2 species.

15/ CAPE SUGARBIRD
Promerops cafer
RANGE: **S tip of South Africa**
HABITAT: **mountain slopes with protea blooms**
SIZE: **male 14½–17¼ in (37–44 cm); female 9½–11½ in (24–29 cm)**

Once considered close relatives of the Australian honeyeaters, the sugarbirds of South Africa are now often thought to be more closely related to the starlings. Nevertheless, these birds have many features in common with the honeyeaters: notably their diet.

Their chief food is insects, often caught in midair, but they also roam around in groups in search of the large flowers of protea plants, from which they drink nectar with their long bills.

In the breeding season the territorial males give loud metallic calls from bush tops and indulge in display flights, holding their extraordinarily long tails high and clapping their wings together. The tail of the male is 8½–12½ in (22–32 cm) long, whereas that of the female is only 4–6 in (11–15.5 cm) long.

OLD WORLD BUNTINGS AND NEW WORLD SPARROWS, PLUSH-CAPPED FINCH

♂ winter

♂

♀

REED BUNTING

race *schoeniclus*

♂ winter

LAPLAND LONGSPUR

♂

SNOW BUNTING

♀

♂

♂ winter

race *costaricensis*

race *maxima*

SONG SPARROW

race *saltonis*

RUFOUS-COLLARED SPARROW

race *hyemalis*
"Slate-colored Junco"
♂

race *thurberi*
"Oregon Junco"

♂

♂

DARK-EYED JUNCO

race *caniceps*
"Gray-headed Junco"

CHIPPING SPARROW

ZAPATA SPARROW

race *inexpectata*

race *americana*
"Wing-barred Seedeater"

♂

♀

VARIABLE SEEDEATER

race *corvina*
"Black Seedeater"

♂

♂

♀

YELLOW-FACED GRASSQUIT

♂

♀

LARGE GROUND FINCH

race *pallidus*

PLUSH-CAPPED FINCH

WOODPECKER FINCH

race
erythrophthalmus

♀

race *oregonus*

♂

♂

RUFOUS-SIDED TOWHEE

OLD WORLD BUNTINGS AND NEW WORLD SPARROWS, PLUSH-CAPPED FINCH

FAMILY EMBERIZIDAE/
SUBFAMILY EMBERIZINAE
Old World buntings and New World sparrows

Small, mainly ground-dwelling birds. Conical bills and strong feet for scratching. Chiefly seed-eaters, mostly in open habitats almost worldwide. Sexes often differ: plumage ranges from grays and dull browns in many species to yellow-red, blue-green, chestnut, black, white and black-and-white in some species. Nest cup-shaped, usually on ground or in low bush. Eggs 2–7 (usually 4–6), whitish, pale brown or pale blue, usually with reddish, brownish or blackish markings. Incubation 10–14 days, nestling period 8–15 days. 284 species.

1/ REED BUNTING
Emberiza schoeniclus

RANGE: Eurasia S to Iberia and S USSR and E to NE Asia and Manchuria; N and E populations winter S as far as N Africa, Iran and Japan
HABITAT: lowland marshes, reedbeds and, increasingly, drier habitats
SIZE: 6–6½ in (15.5–16.5 cm)

The Reed Bunting constantly flicks and half spreads its tail so that its bold white outer tail feathers serve as a conspicuous signal to others of its kind in the dense reedbeds and marshes. With the drainage of wetlands, this attractive bunting declined over much of its range, but during the past 50 years or so it has shown an increasing tendency to colonize drier habitats, such as scrubland, overgrown ditches and hedgerows.

The shape of the Reed Bunting's bill varies geographically to a striking extent, from very small, slight and pointed in races such as *E. s. parvirostris* of central Siberia, to thick and almost parrot-shaped in races such as *E. s. pyrrhuloides* of western and central Asia, western Mongolia and northwest China. The race *E. s. schoeniclus* from northwestern Europe and central Russia is one of the smaller-billed races, although its bill is stouter than that of *E. s. parvirostris*. The different sizes and shapes of the bills are related to the birds' habitat and winter diet.

2/ LAPLAND LONGSPUR
Calcarius lapponicus

RANGE: circumpolar in Arctic region; winters S to NE France and S USSR in Eurasia, and S to New Mexico and Texas in USA
HABITAT: Arctic tundra and high mountains; winters on moors, grassy fields, grain stubble and shores
SIZE: 6–6½ in (15.5–16.5 cm)

This bird prefers to breed in areas of tundra with some shrubs or dwarf trees. The male, in his handsome, bright, breeding plumage, utters a brief, tinkling, larklike song in a display flight or from a prominent perch on a rock or stunted tree. Lapland Longspurs often nest in small colonies.

Very small numbers of Lapland Longspurs established breeding sites in the late 1970s in northern Scotland, well to the south and west of the species' normal breeding range. However, by 1981 all the birds had disappeared.

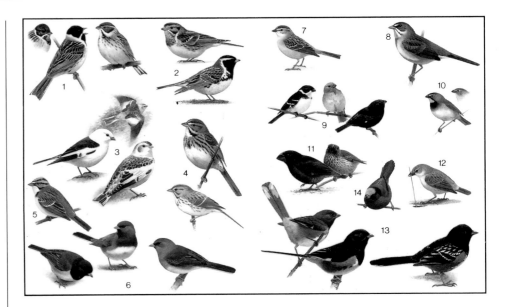

In winter, Lapland Longspurs are often seen in large mixed flocks with Horned Buntings, other buntings, finches and Horned Larks *Eremophila alpestris*, keeping a low crouching position as they walk, run or hop across a windswept stubble field or bleak, deserted beach.

3/ SNOW BUNTING
Plectrophenax nivalis

RANGE: circumpolar in Arctic region; winters S to N France and S USSR in Eurasia, and S to NW California, C Kansas and Virginia in the USA
HABITAT: Arctic stony tundra and rocky shores, rock outcrops in glaciers and snowfields, and on a few high mountains; winters on sandy shores, salt marshes, in fields and on grassy moorland
SIZE: 6¼ in (16.5 cm)

The Snow Bunting is the world's northernmost breeding land bird, nesting as far north as the northern tip of Greenland. To escape the intense cold, these plump little birds sometimes burrow in the snow. Their nests are hidden deep in a crack or beneath a large stone among fragmented rocks and boulders. Breeding birds utter a brief but musical song – loud for the bird's size – both on the wing and from a rock or other low perch. Snow Buntings also have a variety of musical, rippling, twittering calls.

These birds are gregarious outside the breeding season, occurring in small flocks and larger parties of several hundred birds. At this time of year they eat mainly seeds; in the breeding season they also eat insects, buds and grasses.

4/ SONG SPARROW
Melospiza melodia

RANGE: S Alaska, C Canada S to N Mexico
HABITAT: brushy, grassy areas, often near water; also hedgerows, thickets, gardens
SIZE: 5¼ in (14 cm)

This well-studied, widespread species has some resident and some migratory populations in North America. The breeding range of the species is

currently expanding in southeastern USA and is just now reaching the northern portions of the Gulf Coast states. Different races of this bird show great variation in size and color. Those illustrated are the largest race, *M. m. maxima* of the Aleutian Islands, and the pale desert race *M. m. saltonis* of southwestern USA. Songs also vary among populations, so much so that researchers can identify birds by their "dialect."

During the breeding season, males sing from dawn to dusk and sometimes even into the night. Each song begins with a rhythmic introduction, which is followed by a trill, and ends with a series of irregular notes. The male is highly territorial and defends an area of slightly less than 1 acre (0.4 hectares) in prime habitat. The Song Sparrow eats mainly seeds, but insects and other invertebrates comprise up to a third of its diet.

5/ RUFOUS-COLLARED SPARROW
Zonotrichia capensis

RANGE: S Mexico S to Tierra del Fuego, Hispaniola, Netherlands Antilles
HABITAT: open and semiopen natural and disturbed habitats, including cities
SIZE: 5½–6 in (14–15 cm)

This tame and conspicuous bird is the common "sparrow" of Latin America. Most populations are resident, but the southernmost apparently migrate. Although the song of this species varies considerably over the bird's wide range, the basic pattern is easily recognizable, consisting of 1–2 slurred whistles followed by a trill. The song perches are usually exposed, and include posts, poles and the corners of buildings. There are many races, which differ chiefly in the darkness and pattern on their heads: the one illustrated, *Z. c. costaricensis*, is from Costa Rica, Panama, Venezuela and Colombia.

The nest of the Rufous-collared Sparrow is a cup of grasses and roots. This is built near the ground and may be used for successive broods. The eggs are grayish to pale greenish-blue, blotched with gray and with a concentration of rusty spots around the larger end.

6/ DARK-EYED JUNCO
Junco hyemalis

RANGE: **breeds Canada, N and C USA; N populations migrate S as far as Mexico**
HABITAT: **forests of conifers, birch, aspen; various on migration and in winter**
SIZE: **6¼ in (16 cm)**

There are 5 recognizable forms of the Dark-eyed Junco, which used to be considered separate species. Although they vary considerably in plumage, they all have white outer tail feathers, a white belly and dark eyes. The different forms interbreed freely where their ranges meet. Of those illustrated, *J. h. hyemalis* is common in the boreal forests of northern Canada and northern central USA; *J. h. thurberi* breeds in coniferous forests of the far west; and *J. h. caniceps* occurs in the southern Rockies west to eastern California.

All forms of the Dark-eyed Junco sing a musical trill, and utter a rapid twitter in flight. Although primarily seed-eaters, they take many insects during the nesting season.

7/ CHIPPING SPARROW
Spizella passerina

RANGE: **Canada S to N Nicaragua**
HABITAT: **gardens, woodland, forest edge in E; open woodland and mountains in W**
SIZE: **5–5½ in (12.5–14 cm)**

The Chipping Sparrow is a tame, confiding species, well known to people who provide bird-feeding stations. It eats large quantities of grass and weed seeds, as well as weevils, leafhoppers and other insects. On occasion, it will dart out to catch flying insects. The song is a series of "chips" which at times runs together in a single-pitched, rapid trill. The Chipping Sparrow sometimes sings at night. In winter, the adult's bright chestnut crown becomes duller and streaked, its prominent white eyebrow is lost and it acquires a brown ear patch. The female carries out all the nest-building duties, although the male may accompany her while she is gathering material.

8/ ZAPATA SPARROW
Torreornis inexpectata

RANGE: **Cuba**
HABITAT: **selected open habitats with scattered trees and bushes**
SIZE: **6½ in (16.5 cm)**

This sparrow is enigmatic because its 3 different populations seem to be living in quite different environments. The western race, *T. i. inexpectata*, occurs in shrubbery near high ground in the Zapata Swamp. Another race, *T. i. sigmani*, lives in the arid scrublands of southeast Cuba, while the third, *T. i. varonai*, occurs on the island of Cayo Coco, off Cuba's north-central coast. Although these habitats differ greatly in their plant species and in the availability of water, they all consist of open terrain with a few trees and shrubs.

Although it has very short wings and seldom takes to the air, the Zapata Sparrow can fly well. The habitat of the Zapata Swamp population is now protected by the Cuban government. The population in the arid coastlands of the southeast also seems safe because the area is unsuitable for agriculture, but fire remains a serious hazard.

9/ VARIABLE SEEDEATER
Sporophila americana

RANGE: **Mexico S through Panama to parts of Colombia, Ecuador, Peru, Venezuela, Brazil and the Guianas**
HABITAT: **lowland grassy and shrubby areas, clearings, scrub, forest edge, plantations**
SIZE: **4¼–4½ in (11–11.5 cm)**

This species takes its name from the variability of its plumage among its 7 or so races. The 2 races illustrated here are *S. a. americana*, from eastern Venezuela to the lower Amazon, and *S. a. corvina*, from eastern Mexico to Panama. The birds are usually seen in small flocks in which females and immature birds predominate. As they forage, the birds cling to the stems of grasses and weeds to seize small seeds. At times, they may also feed on flowers and buds and nibble at fruit growing high in the trees.

The male Variable Seedeater's song is a fast, complex, musical twitter that it utters from an exposed perch. Both sexes also give a sweet *cheeeu* call note. Nesting seems to be timed according to the ripening of grass seeds.

10/ YELLOW-FACED GRASSQUIT
Tiaris olivacea

RANGE: **E Mexico to Colombia, Venezuela, Greater Antilles**
HABITAT: **grassy areas in clearings, pastures with scattered bushes, roadsides**
SIZE: **4 in (10 cm)**

This species is sometimes known in the cage-bird trade as the Olive Finch. Pairs and small flocks of these birds are often seen in the wild, picking small seeds from the ground or plucking them from seedheads by clinging to stems. The behavior of this species ranges from social and nonaggressive in Central America, to territorial and pugnacious in Jamaica. These differences have been attributed to the higher population density and more continuous habitat in Jamaica.

The bird's song is a thin, high-pitched, somewhat insectlike trill, which is delivered from a low perch. Its call note is a soft *tek*.

11/ LARGE GROUND FINCH
Geospiza magnirostris

RANGE: **Galapagos Islands**
HABITAT: **arid areas**
SIZE: **6½ in (16.5 cm)**

The Large Ground Finch is one of 13 species of "Darwin's finches" endemic to the Galapagos Islands. First collected by Charles Darwin, the finches provided one of the examples he used to develop his theory of evolution through natural selection. This species is the largest and also has the biggest bill, which can cope with hard seeds as well as the occasional large insect.

The bulky, dome-shaped nest with a side entrance is built of twigs, grasses and lichens and placed 3–30 ft (1–9 m) above the ground, often in a cactus. The male works on several nests and then displays to a female alongside one of them. Once the pair-bond is formed, the female either finishes one of the nests started by the male or builds a new one herself.

12/ WOODPECKER FINCH
Camarhynchus pallidus

RANGE: **Galapagos Islands (extinct on San Cristobal and Floreana)**
HABITAT: **humid highlands**
SIZE: **6 in (15 cm)**

The Woodpecker Finch is another of Darwin's finches endemic to the Galapagos Islands. When feeding, some individuals will use a cactus spine, leaf stalk or thin twig as a tool with which to extract invertebrate prey from cavities in dead branches. More commonly, the birds feed by probing their beaks into soft, decaying wood, behind bark or into crevices. They also eat some fruit. This bird has 2 types of song. A high descending whistle is usually sung near the nest, while the territorial song consists of 7–8 loud, rapid notes.

13/ RUFOUS-SIDED TOWHEE
Pipilo erythrophthalmus

RANGE: **SW Canada, USA S to Baja California**
HABITAT: **dense undergrowth, streamside thickets, open woodland forest edge**
SIZE: **8¾ in (22 cm)**

This showy, ground-dwelling bird has been split into many races, but these fall into one of 3 color forms. The eastern "red-eyed" race, *P. e. erythrophthalmus*, and the southeastern "white-eyed" races differ only in eye color; the western form, including such races as *P. e. oregonus*, differs in its white wing bars and white-spotted scapulars.

Rufous-sided Towhees enjoy a varied diet, from weed seeds and wild berries to insects. They commonly scratch through leaf litter with a raking motion and readily visit bird feeders for suet and seeds. Their stout cup nests are placed on the ground, hidden in dense undergrowth or brush, or low in dense thickets and vine tangles.

FAMILY EMBERIZIDAE/ SUBFAMILY CATAMBLYRHYNCHINAE
Plush-capped Finch

There is only one species in this subfamily.

14/ PLUSH-CAPPED FINCH
Catamblyrhynchus diadema

RANGE: **Andes from N Venezuela to N Argentina**
HABITAT: **open woodland and shrubby slopes of Andean highlands, usually near bamboo stands**
SIZE: **5½ in (14 cm)**

The Plush-capped Finch, or Plushcap, takes its name from the stiff, golden-brown feathers at the front of its crown. Very little is known about the habits of this species, and its relationships to the buntings and tanagers are equally enigmatic. It is usually seen in isolated pairs or in mixed foraging flocks with finches, conebills and tanagers. Limited information indicates that its diet includes bamboo leaves, other vegetable matter and insects. It feeds on bamboo stalks by pressing its bill into the bases of dense leaf whorls or by gleaning insects from the stems.

CARDINAL GROSBEAKS, TANAGERS

RED-CRESTED CARDINAL

ROSE-BREASTED GROSBEAK

♂

♀

NORTHERN CARDINAL

♂

♀

♂

SLATE-COLORED
GROSBEAK

♂

BLUE GROSBEAK

♀

♀

♂

PAINTED BUNTING

♂

WHITE-WINGED
SHRIKE-TANAGER

♀

race *auricularis*

BLACK-CAPPED HEMISPINGUS

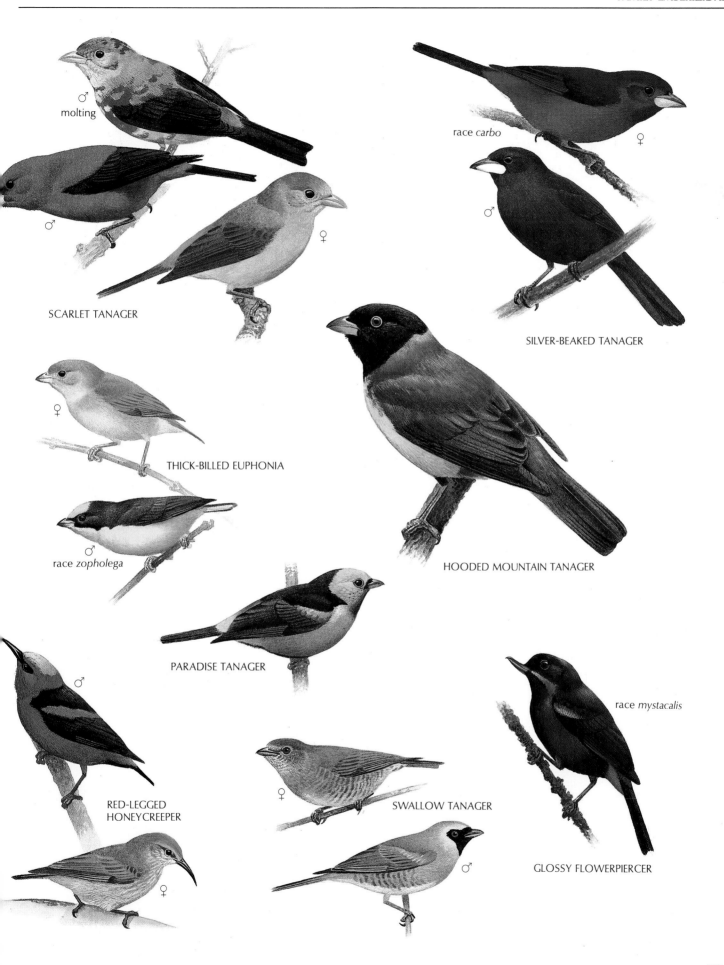

molting

♂

SCARLET TANAGER

♀

race *carbo*

♀

♂

SILVER-BEAKED TANAGER

♀

THICK-BILLED EUPHONIA

race *zopholega* ♂

PARADISE TANAGER

HOODED MOUNTAIN TANAGER

♂

RED-LEGGED HONEYCREEPER

♀

♀

SWALLOW TANAGER

♂

race *mystacalis*

GLOSSY FLOWERPIERCER

CARDINAL GROSBEAKS, TANAGERS

FAMILY EMBERIZIDAE/ SUBFAMILY CARDINALINAE
Cardinal grosbeaks

Small to medium birds with heavy bills. Plumage variable, often brightly colored. Sexes alike or different. Nests usually in trees and shrubs. Eggs 2–5, white, bluish, blue or greenish, unmarked or speckled or scrawled. Incubation 11–14 days, nestling period 9–15 days. 47 species.

1/ RED-CRESTED CARDINAL
Paroaria coronata

RANGE: E Bolivia, Paraguay, Uruguay, S Brazil, N Argentina; introduced to Hawaii
HABITAT: lowland humid scrub, semiopen terrain, especially near water
SIZE: $7\frac{1}{2}$ in (19 cm)

Red-crested Cardinals often feed on the ground in wet areas, and even walk on floating vegetation, where their large feet and long toes probably help to spread their weight. Although generally seen in pairs or small groups, they often form larger flocks outside the breeding season. Their diet includes both seeds and invertebrates.

Because of its beauty and rich, melodious song, this species has been widely trapped for the cage-bird trade, and its populations have declined in some areas. Introduced to Hawaii in 1928, it is now especially common on the island of Oahu.

2/ ROSE-BREASTED GROSBEAK
Pheucticus ludovicianus

RANGE: SC Canada, E USA; winters S to Mexico and N South America
HABITAT: secondary growth woodland, trees along watercourses
SIZE: $7\frac{3}{4}$ in (20 cm)

This thick-billed bird has a special fondness for blossoms and buds, although it also eats beetles, grasshoppers, cankerworms, seeds and some fruit and grain. It often visits feeding stations, especially during migration. The male often delivers his liquid melodies in flight, while pursuing a female. The drabber female also sings, producing a shorter, softer tune. Mates sometimes touch bills in courtship. Both share the nesting duties, the male later caring for the fledglings while the female re-nests. The male molts into a duller, brown-tipped winter plumage before migrating.

3/ NORTHERN CARDINAL
Cardinalis cardinalis

RANGE: SE Canada, E, C and SW USA; Mexico to Belize; introduced to Hawaii
HABITAT: woodland edges, swamps, thickets, suburban gardens
SIZE: $8\frac{1}{2}$ in (22 cm)

Among the most regular and popular of birds at feeding stations, Northern Cardinals often visit in pairs or family groups to take sunflower and safflower seeds. The wild food they eat depends upon availability, but includes insects, fruit, seeds, blossoms, buds and the residues that collect in holes drilled by sapsuckers. The loud, whistling song is uttered by both males and females almost all year round. A prolonged nesting season for this species may result in up to 4 broods.

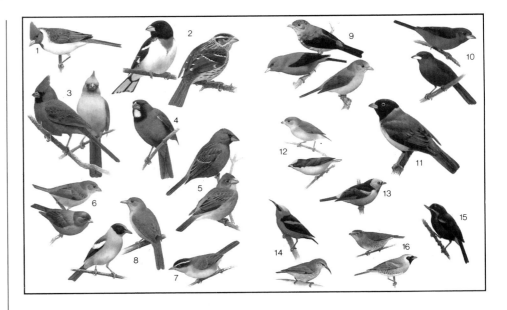

4/ SLATE-COLORED GROSBEAK
Pitylus grossus

RANGE: C and N South America S to N Bolivia
HABITAT: lowland humid forest
SIZE: $7\frac{3}{4}$ in (20 cm)

Slate-colored Grosbeaks are often found in pairs, the females being paler than the males, with no black on their neck and breast. Typically birds of the middle to upper forest, they occasionally descend to lower levels at the forest edge. Seeds and fruit make up the bulk of their diet, and they sometimes join mixed foraging flocks with other forest birds.

The call note of this bird is a sharp, metallic *speek* or *peek*, and its song is a loud, melodious series of deliberate whistles not unlike that of the Northern Cardinal. Little is known of the nesting habits of this deep forest species.

5/ BLUE GROSBEAK
Guiraca caerulea

RANGE: USA S to Costa Rica; winters in S part of range
HABITAT: fields, hedgerows, thickets, woodland edges, roadside brush
SIZE: $6–7\frac{1}{2}$ in (15–19 cm)

The Blue Grosbeak and the Indigo Bunting *Passerina cyanea* share much the same range and habitats. The plumage of the adult males is similar, but the Indigo Bunting is a deep, rich blue almost all over, while the Blue Grosbeak is a duller blue, with 2 broad, rusty-brown wing bars. Like other "blue" birds that take their color from feather structure rather than pigmentation, the Blue Grosbeak may appear gray or black in certain lights.

This species forages for insects, seeds and fruit at ground level and in trees. The female builds a neat cup nest of woven plant matter, sometimes adding cotton, paper or even cast snakeskins. This is placed among stems or in a twig fork up to 20 ft (6 m) from the ground.

6/ PAINTED BUNTING
Passerina ciris

RANGE: SE and S USA; winters from N Gulf Coast S to Panama, Cuba
HABITAT: shrubs, hedgerows, weed fields, woodland edges, moist thickets, gardens
SIZE: $5–5\frac{1}{2}$ in (12.5–14 cm)

No other North American bird is so generously daubed in paintpot colors as the adult male Painted Bunting. Nor does any other male North American bird share the green hues of the female and immature. All are suggestive of more tropical species. Although common in suitable habitats, this bunting is often difficult to see. The greens of the females and many males, and the disruptive pattern of the males, render them inconspicuous when eating seeds in brush fields or searching for insects. During the breeding season, however, the male sings his tinkling song from an exposed perch and is easy to locate.

FAMILY EMBERIZIDAE/ SUBFAMILY THRAUPINAE
Tanagers

Small to medium. Plumage variable, often bright. Sexes alike or different. Nests in most species usually open cups in trees and shrubs; Swallow Tanager nests in tunnels in banks and cliffs. Eggs usually 2, up to 4–5 in euphonias and the few North American species, blue, gray or white with lilac, brown or black markings. Incubation 12–18 days, nestling period 11–24 days. 246 species.

7/ BLACK-CAPPED HEMISPINGUS
Hemispingus atropileus

RANGE: Andes
HABITAT: wet high-altitude forests and scrub
SIZE: $5–5\frac{1}{2}$ in (13–14 cm)

When the forests are enveloped in mist clouds, small groups of these birds can be seen moving rapidly through the undergrowth, usually with other species. The Black-capped Hemispingus often feeds in bamboo, landing near the base of a diagonal stalk and then creeping upward. As it ascends, it peers into crevices and at the undersides of leaves, searching for caterpillars and other insect prey.

The Peruvian race *H. a. auricularis* has the blackish areas on the head deeper and more extensive, and the throat typically more orange-yellow than the other race *H. a. atropileus*, found from western Venezuela to Ecuador.

8/ WHITE-WINGED SHRIKE-TANAGER
Lanio versicolor
RANGE: **C South America, S of the Amazon**
HABITAT: **lowland tropical forest**
SIZE: **5–6 in (13–15 cm)**

The 4 species of shrike-tanager are adept at catching flying insects in midair. While large mixed flocks of birds work their way through the middle layers of vegetation, the shrike-tanagers sit quietly upright and often sally out briefly from their perches to snap up insects that are fleeing from the marauding band of birds. In this position, they are often the first to see an approaching predator, alerting other members of the flock by uttering a loud, downward pitched *tchew* call. At times, they will give false alarms that paralyse their flock mates and improve their own chances of snapping up particularly tasty morsels.

9/ SCARLET TANAGER
Piranga olivacea
RANGE: **E North America; winters mainly in N South America E of the Andes**
HABITAT: **forests**
SIZE: **6¼ in (16 cm)**

The Scarlet Tanager nests mainly in deciduous forests in eastern USA, where it eats bees, wasps, beetles, moths and their larvae, supplemented by a variety of fruits. After breeding, the male molts into olive plumage similar to that of the female. Family groups apparently break up at this time and individuals become solitary and quiet, often sitting motionless in dense foliage. This behavior continues when the birds migrate south to the tropics and is the reason that ornithologists have so little knowledge of exactly where most individuals spend the northern winter.

10/ SILVER-BEAKED TANAGER
Ramphocelus carbo
RANGE: **N South America E of the Andes**
HABITAT: **shrubbery and low trees at forest edge and on savannas**
SIZE: **6¼–6½ in (16–17 cm)**

The Silver-beaked Tanager haunts the tangle of vegetation at the edges of tropical forests, where different plant species produce a succession of fruit which tanagers devour eagerly. As the same fruits are eaten by many tanager species, ecological distinctions between them relate to their insect-eating behavior. When foraging for insects, the Silver-beaked Tanager hops rapidly through the foliage, peering at leaves and darting forward to capture any prey that tries to escape.

Silver-beaked Tanagers travel and forage in small bands, rarely tolerating other species or associating with mixed flocks. Members of each group call frequently, uttering a high-pitched *tseet* and a lower-pitched alarm note *chak*. The race illustrated, *R. c. carbo* from east Peru to Surinam, is one of the palest of the 8 races.

11/ HOODED MOUNTAIN TANAGER
Buthraupis montana
RANGE: **Andes**
HABITAT: **mountain forest, scrub near forest**
SIZE: **8¼ in (21 cm)**

Groups of 3–10 Hooded Mountain Tanagers are often seen flying from one feeding site to the next. After they land, they are surprisingly difficult to locate because they forage sluggishly and may remain immobile for long periods. As well as feeding on fruit, they search for insects hiding in mosses and other epiphytes or on the undersides of leaves and branches. At dawn, the mountain valleys echo to noisy choruses of *toot* and *weeck* calls, repeated individually or coupled in phrases by bands of Hooded Mountain Tanagers. Like the territorial calls of some monkeys, these outbursts may serve to advertise the presence of each group over long distances.

12/ THICK-BILLED EUPHONIA
Euphonia laniirostris
RANGE: **NW South America and Central America**
HABITAT: **open woodland, forest edge**
SIZE: **4 in (10 cm)**

The 25 species of euphonia are among the smallest of the tanagers. Although their digestive systems are specially adapted to cope with mistletoe berries, the balance of diet varies greatly from one species to another. Some eat a high proportion of insect food, while the Thick-billed Euphonia relies almost entirely on fruit. It does, however, feed spiders to its nestlings.

The Thick-billed Euphonia places its domed nest in a sheltered nook or cranny, sometimes choosing the flower baskets outside human dwellings. Unlike the 4 other races, such as *E. l. zopholega* from central Peru east of the Andes, the race *E. l. melanura* has an orange-yellow, buff-tinged throat and lacks the white tail spots.

13/ PARADISE TANAGER
Tangara chilensis
RANGE: **Amazonian South America**
HABITAT: **lowland forest, plantations nearby**
SIZE: **5 in (12.5 cm)**

This beautiful bird is but one of about 50 colorful species in the genus *Tangara*. Although up to 10 species may be found together, eating the same type of fruit, these birds tend to be highly specialized when foraging for insects. Paradise Tanagers are extremely gregarious birds, typically traveling through the upper layers of the forest in groups of 5–10. The groups often join up with other small birds: indeed, the Paradise Tanager is thought to be a core species around which large flocks form in the canopy layer of the Amazon forests.

14/ RED-LEGGED HONEYCREEPER
Cyanerpes cyaneus
RANGE: **Central America, N South America**
HABITAT: **edges of forest and woodland**
SIZE: **4¾ in (12 cm)**

The Red-legged Honeycreeper uses its long, curved bill not only to extract nectar from flowers, but also to snatch small insects from around the undersides of branches. It picks fleshy fruit out of slowly opening seed pods before other birds can reach inside, and it can extract orange pulp from holes drilled in the fruit by woodpeckers.

Highly gregarious when not breeding, the Red-legged Honeycreeper often occurs in flocks of 5–15 individuals. Groups of up to 100 sometimes gather at groves of flowering trees.

15/ GLOSSY FLOWERPIERCER
Diglossa lafresnayii
RANGE: **Andes S to Bolivia**
HABITAT: **stunted "elfin" forest and thickets above 8,000 ft (2,500 m)**
SIZE: **5½ in (14 cm)**

Flowerpiercers use their strange, upcurved bills to puncture the bases of tubular flowers so that they can extract the nectar and possibly also the small insects within. Where blooms abound, flowerpiercers are intensely competitive, not only among themselves but also with other nectar-sipping species such as hummingbirds. The Glossy Flowerpiercer is so competitive that, after breeding, males and females defend individual territories – unusual behavior for tropical tanagers.

Distinctive populations of the Glossy Flowerpiercer are separated from one another by low dips in the Andean chain and offer a fascinating portrait of evolution in progress. For example, the race illustrated, *D. l. mystacalis*, from the La Paz and Cochabanta regions of Bolivia, along with 3 other races in the same subspecies group from Bolivia and northern Peru, may already be better considered as a separate species, the Moustached Flowerpiercer. Another group of races, from western Colombia, has reddish-brown lower underparts, while another group is all black – these, too, may soon be split off as full species, known as the Chestnut-bellied Flowerpiercer and Glossy Flowerpiercer, respectively.

16/ SWALLOW TANAGER
Tersina viridis
RANGE: **E Panama, South America S to N Argentina**
HABITAT: **open woodland, forest edge, gallery forest, secondary forest**
SIZE: **5½ in (14 cm)**

The Swallow Tanager uses its large bill to pluck berries as well as to catch insects in aerial pursuits. It is a sociable bird, traveling in groups of about 12, although it discourages other species from joining the flocks. When not nesting, flocks appear to move about as different fruits ripen.

At the onset of the breeding season, males and females bow to one another as part of the courtship display. Unusually for a tanager, this species places its nest in holes, choosing tunnels and cavities in earth banks, cliffs and even bridges.

BLACK-AND-WHITE WARBLER

BACHMAN'S WARBLER

NORTHERN PARULA

YELLOW-RUMPED WARBLER

race *coronata*
"Myrtle Warbler"

race *memorabilis*
"Audubon's Warbler"

KIRTLAND'S WARBLER

AMERICAN REDSTART

OVENBIRD

PROTHONOTARY WARBLER

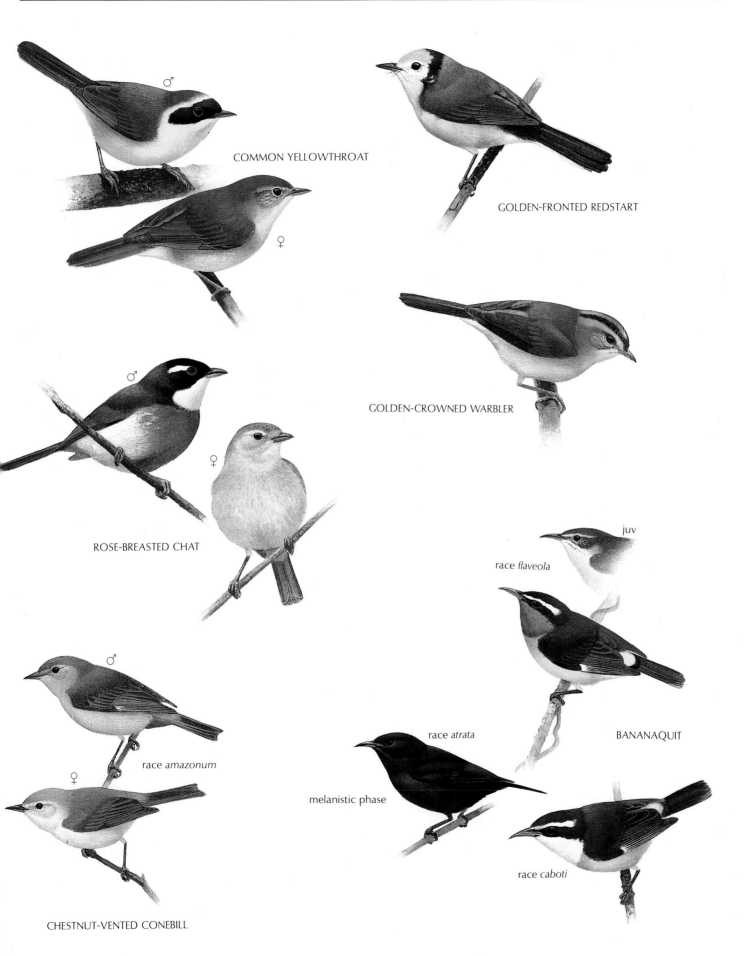

COMMON YELLOWTHROAT

GOLDEN-FRONTED REDSTART

GOLDEN-CROWNED WARBLER

ROSE-BREASTED CHAT

race *flaveola*

juv

race *atrata*

BANANAQUIT

melanistic phase

race *amazonum*

race *caboti*

CHESTNUT-VENTED CONEBILL

WOOD WARBLERS

FAMILY PARULIDAE
Wood warblers

Small, slender mostly foliage-gleaning insect-eaters. Some forage on the ground. Plumage often bright, with females duller. Nest well made, in tree or on ground; 2 species nest in holes. Eggs 2–8 (usually 4–5), white to green, often blotched or splashed with brown. Incubation 10–14 days, nestling period 8–12 days. 126 species.

1/ BLACK-AND-WHITE WARBLER
Mniotilta varia

RANGE: **breeds E North America, N to Northwest Territory, W to Montana, S to C Texas; winters extreme S USA to N South America**
HABITAT: **deciduous and mixed woodland**
SIZE: **$4\frac{1}{2}$–$5\frac{1}{2}$ in (11.5–14 cm)**

With its dramatic barred plumage, the Black-and-white Warbler is often easy to see as it forages for prey on tree trunks and bare branches. It hunts using a search and snatch technique, creeping along the trunks and larger, low limbs of deciduous trees, much like nuthatches or treecreepers (pp. 302–5), and probing with its unusually long bill for insects and spiders.

It flies north in spring earlier than most wood warblers, and its thin, wiry song may be heard well into northern Canada. It builds a cup-shaped nest in a hollow or crevice, usually on the ground under an overhang or among tree roots.

2/ BACHMAN'S WARBLER
Vermivora bachmanii   ⊡

RANGE: **breeds SE USA; winters in Cuba**
HABITAT: **swamps, low woods**
SIZE: **$4\frac{3}{4}$ in (12 cm)**

This endangered species once bred in many of the southern states of the USA, migrating to Cuba in winter via the Florida Keys and the Bahamas. By 1937 most of the breeding pairs were restricted to the I'On Swamp in South Carolina and since then no nests have been found. Adult birds were sighted in the 1970s, but since they resemble more common species such as the Hooded Warbler *Wilsonia citrina* and Wilson's Warbler *W. pusilla*, recent reports are naturally suspect.

Bachman's Warbler nests low down in thick cover, in mature hardwood forests, and the draining and cutting of its habitat may account for its decline or even extinction.

3/ NORTHERN PARULA
Parula americana

RANGE: **breeds E North America, with isolated nests in California, New Mexico, Mexico; winters Florida, West Indies, Central America**
HABITAT: **coniferous and mixed woods, swamps**
SIZE: **$4\frac{1}{2}$ in (11.5 cm)**

The Northern Parula is a widespread and adaptable bird, able to thrive in habitats ranging from northern spruce forests to the swamps of the southern states. Its song is a rising buzzy trill ending with an abrupt *zip* – almost identical to that of the very similar Tropical Parula *P.*

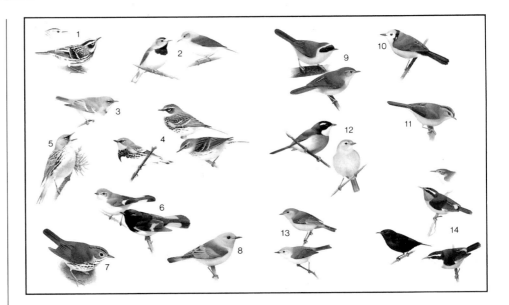

pitiayumi with which it is often confused. It feeds on insects, gathering them from the tree foliage.

Whenever possible, the Northern Parula builds its cup-shaped nest in a hanging tuft of tree lichen or Spanish moss, using the lichen or moss as nesting material. If neither is available it will nest in a more conventional site, such as a hanging cluster of twigs in a hemlock or spruce.

4/ YELLOW-RUMPED WARBLER
Dendroica coronata

RANGE: **breeds North America, S to C and S Mexico and Guatemala; winters S of breeding range, to Central America**
HABITAT: **coniferous and deciduous woods**
SIZE: **5–6 in (13–15 cm)**

This widespread and abundant species has 5 races. These fall into 2 groups, which were once thought to be separate species: the white-throated Myrtle Warbler, typified by *D. c. coronata* of Canada and central and eastern USA and the yellow-throated Audubon's Warbler, typified by *D. c. auduboni* of southwest Canada and western USA. The race illustrated, *D. c. memorabilis*, from southwest USA, is a particularly strongly marked form of the Audubon Warbler group.

Apart from their plumage differences, most noticeable in breeding males, their call notes are also distinct, that of Audubon's Warbler being softer than that of its eastern counterpart. Both nest in conifers and tall deciduous trees; they may interbreed where their ranges overlap.

In summer both races feed largely on insects, but in winter and during migration they take a much wider range of foods.

5/ KIRTLAND'S WARBLER
Dendroica kirtlandii   ⊡

RANGE: **breeds small area in C Michigan, USA; winters in the Bahamas**
HABITAT: **thickets of young jack pine**
SIZE: **6 in (15 cm)**

This large, tail-bobbing warbler is now considered endangered and is unlikely to be seen except on its nest sites in central Michigan, its wintering grounds in the Bahamas or, during migration, somewhere between the two.

Kirtland's Warbler nests on the ground, near the base of a jack pine tree. It requires a very special habitat for breeding, one that is found only at a particular stage in the succession of vegetation: it will breed only among stands of jack pines between 8 and 22 years old. This prime habitat can be maintained only by regular forest fires or clearing. Kirtland's Warbler is particularly prone to parasitism by the Brown-headed Cowbird *Molothrus ater*, which lays its eggs in the warbler's nest.

This natural hazard has probably accelerated a decline caused largely by the erosion of its very precise habitat, and it has been reduced to fewer than 200 nesting pairs. The strict protection, habitat maintenance and control of the cowbird population that are being undertaken may yet save Kirtland's Warbler. However, the mysterious loss of many young birds somewhere on their long migration between the breeding grounds and the Bahamas causes grave concern.

6/ AMERICAN REDSTART
Setophaga ruticilla

RANGE: **breeds SE Alaska, E through C Canada, S through Texas to E USA; winters extreme S USA to Brazil**
HABITAT: **deciduous and mixed woodland**
SIZE: **$4\frac{1}{4}$–$5\frac{1}{4}$ in (11–13.5 cm)**

Few warblers are as vividly patterned, as bold or as animated as the New World redstarts. In most of the 11 other species, placed in a different genus, *Myioborus*, the sexes are alike, but the female American Redstart is quite unlike her mate, with incandescent yellow where he has flaming orange.

The dazzling colors illuminate every flutter of wings and tail as the birds work through the foliage in search of caterpillars, or dart into the air like flycatchers to catch insects on the wing. Their songs feature shrill, sibilant, slurred notes, and they often utter sharp, staccato calls.

The female alone builds the cup nest, placing it in the fork of a tree or shrub and often decorating the lining with the gaudy feathers of brightly colored buntings or tanagers.

7/ OVENBIRD
Seiurus aurocapillus

RANGE: **breeds S Canada and E USA to Colorado and Georgia; winters SE USA to West Indies, Bahamas, Panama, N Venezuela and Colombia**
HABITAT: **forest, shrubby thickets**
SIZE: **5 in (13 cm)**

The largely brown Ovenbird might be easy to overlook were it not for its loud and unmistakable song – a clarion repetition of *teacher-teacher-teacher* that steadily increases in volume. It forages on the forest floor, poking through the leaf litter for insects, spiders and other small animals, and pausing every so often to fly to a low branch and sing.

Males are occasionally polygamous in spring, but usually the birds breed as pairs. They weave a curious domed nest out of dried grasses, pine needles, strips of bark and tiny twigs, lining it with hair. The nest is built on the ground, often at the base of a bush and sunk well into the leaf litter; it is shaped rather like a traditional bread-oven, which accounts for the bird's common name. The female alone does the incubation, often raising the young of the parasitic Brown-headed Cowbird *Molothrus ater* in place of her own.

8/ PROTHONOTARY WARBLER
Protonotaria citrea

RANGE: **breeds E USA, S Ontario; winters Mexico to N South America**
HABITAT: **moist woodland near water**
SIZE: **5½ in (14 cm)**

This golden beauty is named after the *protonotarias* – the saffron-robed clerks who serve the Pope. It feeds mainly on insects and a few small seeds, and with its bright plumage it is particularly easy to follow as it forages low down in damp woodlands. In winter it is often found in various swamp habitats, but it also occurs in drier places. It has a loud voice, calling with a series of 7–12 short tweets, or a longer, more fluid version sung while hovering on fanned wings.

Unusually for a wood warbler, the Prothonotary Warbler is a cavity nester, usually selecting a natural tree hollow or a woodpecker hole in forest habitat near water. The nest is built mainly by the female, using small twigs, bark, moss, lichens and grasses. In southern regions, many pairs raise 2 broods a season.

9/ COMMON YELLOWTHROAT
Geothlypis trichas

RANGE: **breeds North America S to Mexico; winters Bahamas, West Indies to N South America**
HABITAT: **young second growth, weedy areas, usually near water**
SIZE: **4–5 in (10–13 cm)**

The Common Yellowthroat is widespread and often abundant on river, lake and pond edges, fresh and saltwater marshes – indeed, almost anywhere that the weeds grow rank and ground is saturated with water. It feeds on insects, spiders and their eggs, snatching them from the ground or picking them off low vegetation.

The breeding pairs nest either on or very close to the ground, and sometimes over water. Each of the 3–6 white eggs is marked with brown, gray or black spots that often coalesce to form a ring around the broad end. There may be 2 broods each season, but, as with other wood warblers, many eggs fall victim to the parasitism of the Brown-headed Cowbird *Molothrus ater*.

10/ GOLDEN-FRONTED REDSTART
Myioborus ornatus

RANGE: **Andes in extreme W Venezuela and Colombia**
HABITAT: **subtropical and temperate mountain forest at 6,000–11,200 ft (1,800–3,400 m)**
SIZE: **5½ in (14 cm)**

This species is also known as the Golden-faced Redstart, and some have suggested that it would be more appropriately named a "whitestart" because of its conspicuous white outer tail feathers.

Common in temperate forests above 8,000 ft (2,400 m), it is usually seen in groups of up to 5 or 6 birds, sometimes on their own but often with other species. It forages high in the trees, either in the topmost branches or in the dense foliage at the periphery of the tree crown, searching for insects, spiders and similar prey. Its song is high-pitched and rambling, lasting for about 15 seconds, but it often gives short *tsip* contact notes while foraging or flying from tree to tree.

11/ GOLDEN-CROWNED WARBLER
Basileuterus culicivorus

RANGE: **C Mexico to E Bolivia, Paraguay, Uruguay, N Argentina**
HABITAT: **humid forest, forest edge, scrub, clearings, deciduous woods, plantations**
SIZE: **5 in (12.5 cm)**

The various populations of this wide-ranging wood warbler occur in 3 quite distinct habitats: tropical semideciduous forest, tropical evergreen forest and upland forest. They are sometimes regarded as 3 different, but closely related species. However, the races involved vary but little in plumage, chiefly in the grayness of their upperparts and the precise shade of their crown stripe.

Golden-crowned Warblers are usually seen in pairs or small groups, but they often join larger mixed-species flocks. They search for insects and spiders in the branches and vines of the low understory, moving quickly through the foliage or darting out to catch insects on the wing. The nest is a dome of grass placed low on a bank.

12/ ROSE-BREASTED CHAT
Granatellus pelzelni

RANGE: **S Venezuela and Guianas S through Amazonian Brazil to N Bolivia**
HABITAT: **lowland rain forest, older second growth near water**
SIZE: **5 in (13 cm)**

Often difficult to follow in the wild, the Rose-breasted Chat typically forages for insects amid tangled undergrowth, moving up into the canopy in the forest interior. It is most visible when it is feeding in scrub at the forest edge or near streams, and it will often stop to "pose" with raised, fanned tail.

Although included here with the wood warblers, the Rose-breasted Chat and its 2 close relatives, the Red-breasted Chat *G. venustus* and the Gray-throated Chat *G. sallaei*, are sometimes considered to be more closely allied to the tanagers. They are remarkable for their widely separated ranges, with one found in the Pacific lowlands of Mexico, one in Central America, and this one in South America.

13/ CHESTNUT-VENTED CONEBILL
Conirostrum speciosum

RANGE: **E of Andes from E Colombia W to the Guianas and S to N Argentina**
HABITAT: **open lowland deciduous forest, swampy forest, second growth, lake edges**
SIZE: **4–4½ in (10–11.5 cm)**

The Chestnut-vented Conebill and the 9 other conebills of the genus *Conirostrum* are sometimes considered to be aberrant wood warblers – as here – and sometimes included with the tanagers.

Whatever its affinities, this is a sociable species that forages in the treetops in pairs or small groups, often in mixed-species flocks. It frequently feeds in association with tanagers, probing blossoms for nectar, pollen and insects; at other times it gleans insects and spiders from the clustered foliage at branch tips, in typical wood warbler style. The race *C. s. amazonum* is found from the Guianas west to eastern Peru and is darker than other races.

14/ BANANAQUIT
Coereba flaveola

RANGE: **West Indies, Central and South America to N Argentina**
HABITAT: **arid to humid forest, swamp, parkland with flowering trees or shrubs**
SIZE: **4 in (10 cm)**

An active, adaptable little bird, the Bananaquit will thrive in a wide variety of habitats as long as it has some cover and a good food supply. It often feeds on nectar, using its downcurved bill to probe into small flowers or even puncture the bases of long tubular flowers to get at the nectaries. At other times it will pierce berries to suck the juice, or gather insects and spiders from the foliage.

The Bananaquit shows much geographical variation over its great range, including the many isolated Caribbean islands. Three island races are shown: *C. f. flaveola* from Jamaica; *C. f. atrata* from St. Vincent, in the melanistic phase most common in this race, as well as some others; and *C. f. caboti* from Cozumel Island and Holbox Island off the Yucatan Peninsula in southeast Mexico.

The true relationships of the Bananaquit are uncertain. Once it was classified with the honeycreepers, flowerpiercers and conebills in a family of their own, the Coerebidae. The honeycreepers and flowerpiercers are now considered to be specialized tanagers, while the conebills and Bananaquit are sometimes (as here) considered unusual members of the wood warbler family; sometimes regarded as aberrant tanagers; and sometimes placed in a reduced family Coerebidae.

VIREOS, AMERICAN BLACKBIRDS

race *virenticeps*

race *gujanensis*

YELLOW-THROATED VIREO

GREEN SHRIKE-VIREO

RUFOUS-BROWED PEPPERSHRIKE

RED-EYED VIREO

GRAY VIREO

COZUMEL VIREO

race *dariensis*

race *melanterus* ♂

LESSER GREENLET

♂ race *cela*

race *vitellinus* ♂

YELLOW-RUMPED CACIQUE

CRESTED OROPENDOLA

nest

race *galbula*
"Baltimore Oriole"
♂

race *bullocki*
"Bullock's Oriole"
♂

NORTHERN ORIOLE

RED-WINGED BLACKBIRD
♂

♀

race *abeillei*
"Black-backed Oriole"
♂

COMMON GRACKLE
♂

juv

EASTERN
MEADOWLARK
♂

BRONZED COWBIRD
♂

BOBOLINK
♂

♀

FAMILY VIREONIDAE
Vireos

Small, with mainly green upperparts, gray or brown on back, yellow or white underparts. Sexes similar. Cuplike or baglike nest, suspended by the rim from forked branches of trees or shrubs. Eggs 2–5, white with brown spots. Incubation 11–13 days, nestling period 11–13 days. 46 species.

1/ RUFOUS-BROWED PEPPERSHRIKE
Cyclarhis gujanensis
RANGE: Central and South America E of Andes to N C Argentina
HABITAT: tropical and subtropical forest edge, clearings, second growth, scrub forest, plantations
SIZE: 6¼–6½ in (16–17 cm)

The 2 distinctive species of peppershrike were once classified in a separate family but are now given subfamily rank within the vireo family. Both species use their heavy, strongly hooked bills to forage for insects and fruit in trees. They sit hidden, singing a monotonous litany of short but musical whistled phrases for hours, repeating one phrase for 5–10 minutes. They are weak fliers and do not migrate.

Many races of the Rufous-browed Peppershrike have been recognized. Two races are illustrated: *C. g. gujanensis* from east Colombia, south Venezuela, Guyana, Brazil, east Peru and northwestern Bolivia; and *C. g. virenticeps* from western Ecuador and northwestern Peru.

2/ GREEN SHRIKE-VIREO
Vireolanius pulchellus
RANGE: S Mexico to W Panama
HABITAT: rain and cloud forest up to 5,500 ft (1,700 m)
SIZE: 5½ in (14 cm)

Because of its sluggish nature and ability to blend with the foliage high in the forest canopy, relatively little is known about this vireo, with its heavy, almost shrikelike beak. It usually forages alone or in pairs, taking insects by probing leaf clusters and sallying out to catch them in midair. Outside the breeding season it may join mixed flocks of other insect-eating birds to feed lower in the forest foliage. Its song of 3–4 similar syllables resembles the *peter-peter-peter* of the Tufted Titmouse *Parus bicolor*.

The race *V. p. eximius*, illustrated, found in northern Colombia and western Venezuela, is often regarded as a separate species, the Yellow-browed Shrike-Vireo.

3/ COZUMEL VIREO
Vireo bairdi
RANGE: Cozumel Island, Mexico
HABITAT: open tropical forest, forest edge
SIZE: 4¼–4¾ in (11–12 cm)

The Cozumel Vireo is the only brown vireo; other species are green, yellow or gray above. It is a close relative of a local mainland species, the Mangrove Vireo *V. pallens*, and shares its white markings and chattering song. At least 5 song types, each of a different syllable, are recorded.

The wrenlike behavior of the Cozumel Vireo is similar to that of other scrub-foraging vireos: it takes insects and spiders from small branches and twigs, and some fruit. It is strongly territorial.

4/ GRAY VIREO
Vireo vicinior
RANGE: breeds SW USA to NW Mexico; winters from S Arizona and W Texas to Durango and N Sinaloa
HABITAT: dry brushy slopes, canyons, chaparral, dwarf oak woodland, winters in desert scrub
SIZE: 5½ in (14 cm)

A close relative of the forest-dwelling Solitary Vireo *V. solitarius*, the Gray Vireo occupies huge breeding and winter territories. It gleans insects from foliage and, occasionally, the ground and catches flying insects in midair.

The Gray Vireo is the only vireo to sing regularly in flight; the female also sings during nesting. The 3–5 syllables are loud and nonmusical, having a hoarse quality.

5/ YELLOW-THROATED VIREO
Vireo flavifrons
RANGE: breeds S and E C Canada, USA to Gulf States; winters from S Florida, S C Mexico and Greater Antilles to Colombia and N Venezuela
HABITAT: mixed broad-leaved coniferous forest and woodland in summer, tropical woodland and rain forest up to 6,000 ft (1,800 m) in winter
SIZE: 5½ in (14 cm)

This is one of the most clean-cut and brightly patterned of all vireos; it also has a prominent yellow eye ring. The Yellow-throated Vireo forages alone or with its mate for insects and spiders and the occasional berry in treetops. Its song, a sequence of brief, 2- or 3-note phrases, separated by long pauses, resembles that of the Solitary Vireo *V. solitarius*, but sounds huskier, and is given in its winter quarters as well as on its breeding grounds, along with chattering calls.

6/ RED-EYED VIREO
Vireo olivaceus
RANGE: breeds Canada S to the Gulf States; winters from NW South America to Amazonia
HABITAT: deciduous or mixed forest, river bank woodland
SIZE: 5½ in (14 cm)

The Red-eyed Vireo's melodious and fairly rapid song is composed of 2–3 syllables. It is highly vocal and strongly territorial in its summer breeding grounds, where it gleans treetop foliage for insects. By contrast, in its South American winter quarters the Red-eyed Vireo does not sing and eats fruit rather than insects. During the breeding season the male displays by swaying with body feathers fluffed and tail fanned, to which females may respond with a call.

7/ LESSER GREENLET
Hylophilus decurtatus
RANGE: SE Mexico to C Panama
HABITAT: tropical forest and second growth below 4,300 ft (1,300 m)
SIZE: 3½–4 in (9–10 cm)

Greenlets are small, warblerlike insect-eaters that often join mixed-species foraging flocks high in the forest canopy. Compared to other vireos, they have more pointed bills which lack the notch at the tip of the upper mandible. The constantly repeated call of the Lesser Greenlet is similar to a single phrase of the Red-eyed Vireo's song, though higher pitched and quieter. There are 3 races of the Lesser Greenlet. The race *H. d. dariensis* from eastern Panama and northern Colombia is illustrated.

FAMILY ICTERIDAE
American blackbirds (American orioles)

Small to medium. Most species black (often glossy) with patches of yellow, orange or red; brown common in females and in both sexes of many grassland species. Sexes differ markedly in plumage and size in temperate, migratory species and in polygynous species from all latitudes. Nests varied, from simple cups or domes on ground in terrestrial species to long, woven, purselike nests suspended from tree branches. Eggs very variable in color and markings, typically 4–6 in temperate species, 2–3 in tropical species. Incubation 12–15 days. Nestling periods from about 10 days in smallest species to about 10 weeks in largest ones. 96 species.

8/ CRESTED OROPENDOLA
Psarocolius decumanus
RANGE: **Panama to C South America**
HABITAT: **humid lowland and foothill forest, second growth forest, forest edge, clearings and plantations**
SIZE: **male 17–18¾ in (43–48 cm); female 15–16 in (38–41 cm)**

Female Crested Oropendolas have the same coloration as males but are smaller. The "crest" consists of a few hairlike feathers that protrude from the crown and are generally laid flat. There are 4 races: 3 of them are similar, including *P. d. melanterus* from Panama and northern Colombia, while the other, *P. d. maculosus*, from the Amazon southward, has pale yellow feathers scattered throughout its black body plumage.

The male Crested Oropendola performs a remarkable display, in which he raises his tail and flaps his wings noisily as he leans forward so far he almost falls from his perch, the whole time uttering loud gurgling and rasping calls that accelerate to a crescendo. Its food includes fruits, seeds and a variety of invertebrates.

Gregarious at all times, the birds breed in colonies, with 7–100 nests in a single tree. Each nest is an elaborate hanging structure of woven plant fiber over 3 ft (1 m) long, suspended from the tip of a flexible tree limb. No attempt is made to conceal the nest sites, which are the focus of constant coming and going by these large, vocal and conspicuous birds.

9/ YELLOW-RUMPED CACIQUE
Cacicus cela
RANGE: **Panama to C South America**
HABITAT: **humid lowland forest, forest edge, second growth woodland, clearings, plantations; also found in villages and even in towns**
SIZE: **male 11–12½ in (28–32 cm); female 9½–10¼ in (24–26 cm)**

The Yellow-rumped Cacique is a common bird in many parts of its range. Two of the 3 races are illustrated: *C. c. vitellinus* from Panama and northern Colombia and *C. c. cela* from northern Central America and Trinidad.

Yellow-rumped Caciques feed on berries, fruits and insects. They have a variety of calls, including loud cackles, squawks and more melodious notes. Birds of the race *C. c. cela* are frequent and excellent mimics of other birds, but those of the other 2 races seem to lack this ability.

These gregarious birds nest in conspicuous colonies, constructing hanging nests which are shorter and more oblong than those of the oropendolas, which may nest in the same tree. Cacique nests are often clumped close together, frequently near wasps' nests for protection.

10/ NORTHERN ORIOLE
Icterus galbula
RANGE: **breeds North America; winters in C and N South America**
HABITAT: **open and riverside woodland, forest edge, trees near human habitation**
SIZE: **6–6½ in (16–17 cm)**

Male Northern Orioles are conspicuous orange and black birds that show distinct plumage variations among races. Those illustrated are Bullock's Oriole *I. g. bullocki* from western North America to Nicaragua, the Baltimore Oriole *I. g. galbula* from eastern North America, and the Black-backed Oriole *I. g. abeillei* from south-central Mexico.

These birds weave nests of pliant plant material with top openings, where the female incubates 4–5 pale blue-gray eggs. Adults feed on insects, fruits, nectar and spring buds.

11/ RED-WINGED BLACKBIRD
Agelaius phoeniceus
RANGE: **North and Central America**
HABITAT: **marshes, watercourses, cultivated land**
SIZE: **male 7¾–9½ in (20–24 cm); female 7–7½ in (18–19 cm)**

The Red-winged Blackbird may be the most abundant North American land bird. Males sing from exposed perches and flash their brilliant yellow-tipped "epaulettes" to defend their breeding territories. At other times, the red is often concealed when the bird perches, and only the yellow tips show.

The female builds a cup-shaped grass nest 1–10 ft (0.5–3 m) above the ground, over or near water. Breeding males roost singly in their territories; after breeding, male birds gather into large flocks, joining other American blackbirds to form flocks of 1 million or more birds. The birds illustrated are typical of most races.

12/ EASTERN MEADOWLARK
Sturnella magna
RANGE: **S and E North America to N South America**
HABITAT: **savanna, pastures, cultivated land**
SIZE: **9–9¾ in (23–25 cm)**

This familiar American bird spends most of its time on the ground, where it walks about, frequently flicking its tail. When it does fly, it makes a series of rapid, shallow wing beats interspersed with brief glides during which its wings are held stiffly downward.

During the breeding season, the male displays his yellow breast to the female, points his bill skyward to expose his yellow throat and leaps into the air. He defends his territory by uttering his song – a sequence of clear, mellow whistling notes – from a fencepost or other prominent perch, from the ground, or in a fluttering song-flight. Typically monogamous, Eastern Meadowlarks lay 3–7 brown-spotted white eggs in a cuplike nest of woven grass and usually raise 2 broods in a season. North American birds migrate south in winter, but those from the West Indies and from Central and South America are sedentary.

13/ COMMON GRACKLE
Quiscalus quiscula
RANGE: **E USA; N populations winter S as far as Florida**
HABITAT: **open woodland, scattered trees, forest edge, areas near human habitation**
SIZE: **11–13 in (28–33 cm)**

The Common Grackle forms large, noisy roosts, often containing thousands of birds uttering loud *chuck* calls. The short, harsh, squeaky song sounds like the noise of a rusty-hinged gate. These birds nest in small colonies. The females build bulky nests of sticks and grasses 3–13 ft (1–4 m) above the ground. The nest is lined with dried grass and feathers and often with paper, string, rags and other debris.

Young birds eat insects and spiders; adults eat a wide range of animals, from earthworms and insects to fish, frogs, mice and the eggs and young of small birds. They also relish seeds and grain and large flocks of grackles can damage crops.

14/ BRONZED COWBIRD
Molothrus aeneus
RANGE: **S USA to Panama**
HABITAT: **savanna, pastures, cultivated land and human habitation in tropical and subtropical zones including arid land**
SIZE: **6½–8½ in (17–22 cm)**

This nest parasite feeds on insects and seeds, and regularly gathers in flocks of 25–30, which sometimes combine to form large groups of 500 or so birds. The male displays to the female, head thrown back and feathers ruffled, uttering a creaky whistle. After mating, the female lays one very pale bluish egg in the nest of another species, often puncturing host eggs already present. Young cowbirds, when they hatch in the host nest, are larger and more persistent than other young birds, and hence receive more food. The total number of eggs laid is unknown, but the closely related Brown-headed Cowbird *M. ater* lays up to 40 eggs over 2 months.

15/ BOBOLINK
Dolichonyx oryzivorus
RANGE: **breeds S Canada to C USA; winters S America, mostly in N Argentina**
HABITAT: **prairies, meadows; also marshes on migration and in winter**
SIZE: **6¼–7 in (16–18 cm)**

This bird is named for the male's loud, bubbling song, which sounds rather like *bob-o-link, bob-o-link, spink, spank, spink*, which he utters, often in a fluttering display flight over his territory, in spring and summer. The flight call, heard all year round, is also distinctive – a repeated, metallic, whistling *ink*. In his courtship display, the male erects his buff nape feathers, partly opens his wings to show off his white "shoulders," and points his bill downward. This is a polygynous species, each male mating with 2 or more females.

The Bobolink makes the longest migration of any member of its family. In summer, Bobolinks include many weed seeds and insect pests among their diet, but on their southward migration, they can be destructive to grain crops.

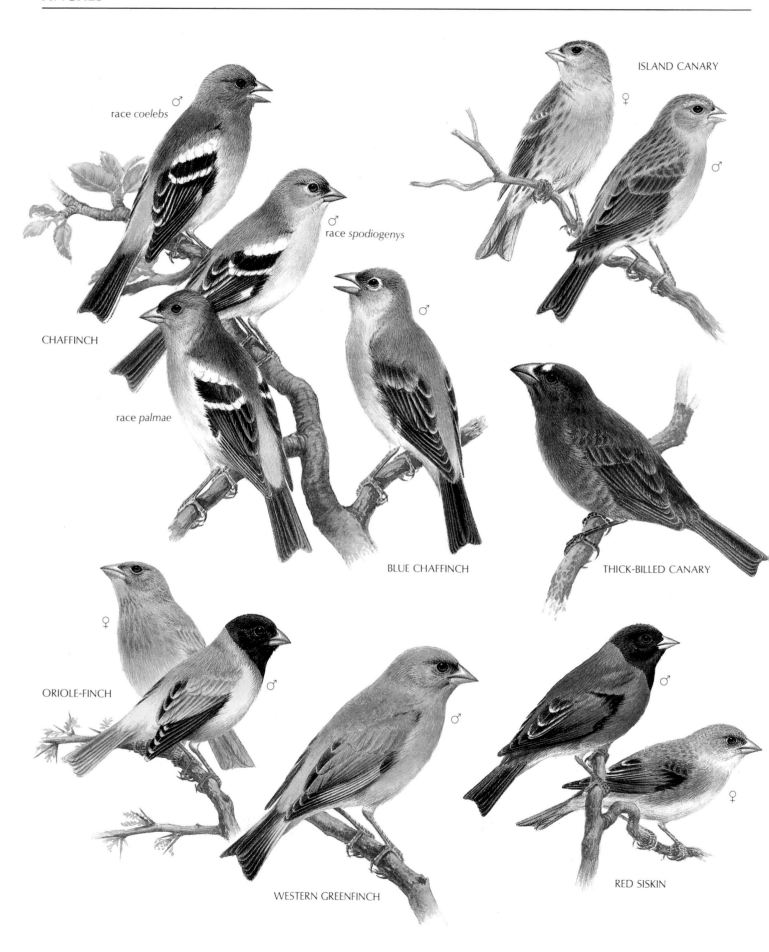

race *coelebs* ♂

race *spodiogenys* ♂

CHAFFINCH

race *palmae*

♂

ISLAND CANARY

♀

♂

BLUE CHAFFINCH

THICK-BILLED CANARY

♀

ORIOLE-FINCH

♂

♂

RED SISKIN

♂

♀

WESTERN GREENFINCH

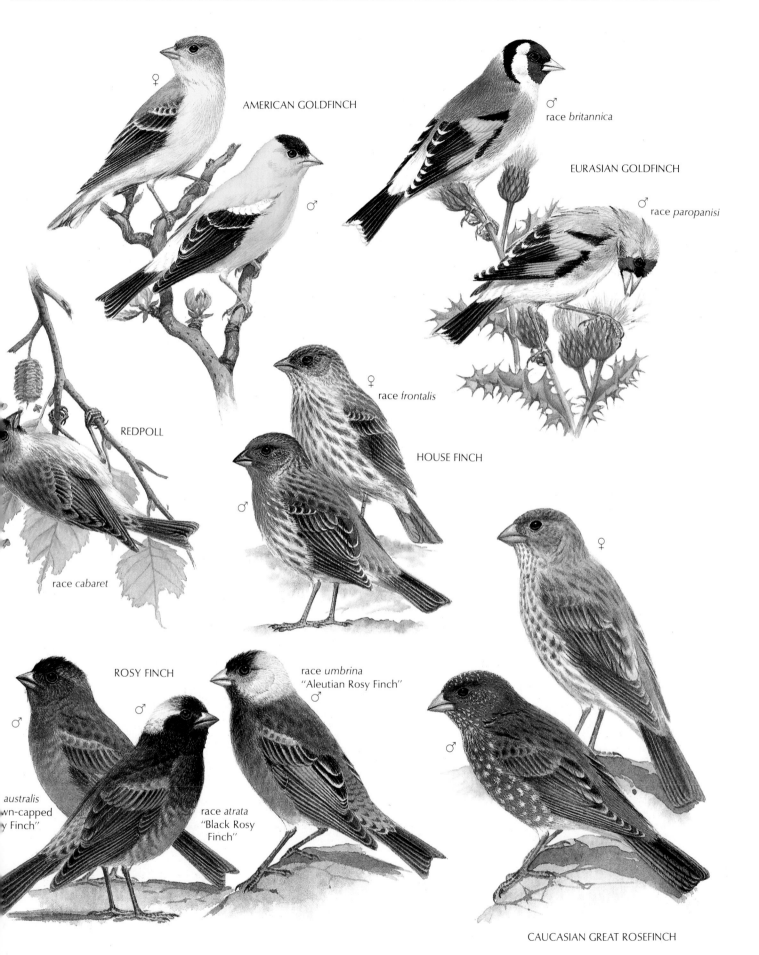

AMERICAN GOLDFINCH

♂ race *britannica*

EURASIAN GOLDFINCH

♂ race *paropanisi*

♀ race *frontalis*

REDPOLL

HOUSE FINCH

race *cabaret*

♂

♀

ROSY FINCH

race *umbrina*
"Aleutian Rosy Finch"
♂

australis
wn-capped
y Finch"

race *atrata*
"Black Rosy
Finch"

♂

♂

CAUCASIAN GREAT ROSEFINCH

FINCHES

FAMILY FRINGILLIDAE/ SUBFAMILY FRINGILLINAE
Fringilline finches

Small, with conical bills, fairly long tails and peaked head. Sexes differ. Males brightly colored, females duller; all species with prominent shoulder patches and wing and tail markings. Nest mainly of grass, moss and other vegetation, typically in a bush or tree. Eggs 3–5, dark blue-green with purple-brown streaks and spots. Incubation 12–14 days, nestling period 11–17 days. Young fed frequently on small amounts of insects directly from parents' bills. 3 species.

1/ CHAFFINCH
Fringilla coelebs

RANGE: **Europe to W Siberia, Middle East, N Africa, Atlantic islands**
HABITAT: **woodland, gardens and open country with scattered trees**
SIZE: **6 in (15 cm)**

Over most of its range, the Chaffinch is a very common and familiar bird, often living close to human dwellings. Its simple, far-carrying song varies subtly from one area to another, forming local dialects. There are many races, those in the north, including *F. c. coelebs*, from much of the European range, tending to have brightly colored males. Races from the drier southern regions, such as *F. c. spodiogenys* of Tunisia, are paler and the sexes are more alike. There are also several races on the Atlantic islands, including 3 in the Canaries which are all heavy-billed and have slate blue on the upperparts. The latter include *F. c. palmae* of Las Palmas Island.

Chaffinches form large flocks in winter, feeding on seeds in farmland and coming into gardens to forage. In the breeding season, however, they become highly territorial. The nest is placed in a tree or a bush and is finished on the outside with moss and lichen, often making it difficult to spot.

2/ BLUE CHAFFINCH
Fringilla teydea   Ⓡ

RANGE: **Canary Islands**
HABITAT: **forest scrub**
SIZE: **6½ in (16.5 cm)**

Along with the Chaffinch, which is widely distributed through the archipelago, the Canary Islands have a second, much rarer species of fringilline finch, the Blue Chaffinch. It is confined to the islands of Gran Canaria, where it is declining, and Tenerife.

The 2 species occupy quite different habitats, with the Chaffinch occurring in broad-leaved forest at low altitudes and the Blue Chaffinch living at high elevations (up to the tree line) in mountain pine and pine-laurel forests. Blue Chaffinches are resident in these forests throughout the year, seldom appearing elsewhere. They are late breeders, not starting to nest until the end of May or into June. The nest is usually placed in a pine or laurel tree, often high above the ground.

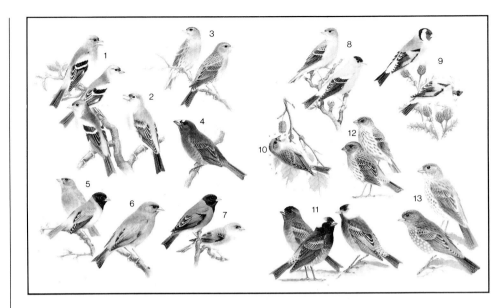

FAMILY FRINGILLIDAE/ SUBFAMILY CARDUELINAE
Cardueline finches

Small, with variably shaped conical bills, ranging from "tweezers" to deep, powerful bills (mandibles crossed in crossbills). Sexes differ, females duller. Very variable plumage, generally with distinctive wing and tail markings; many species streaked, particularly juveniles. Nest mainly of grass, moss and other vegetation, typically in a bush or tree. Eggs 3–5, whitish with brown spots. Incubation 12–14 days, nestling period 11–17 days. Young fed infrequently on large amounts of seeds by regurgitation (some species with special throat pouches for storing seeds). 121 species.

3/ ISLAND CANARY
Serinus canaria

RANGE: **Azores, Madeira, Canary Islands**
HABITAT: **open woodland, scrub and gardens**
SIZE: **5 in (12.5 cm)**

This close relative of the European Serin *S. serinus* was the ancestor of all domestic canaries. It was first brought into Europe in the early 16th century and was rapidly domesticated. The sexes are different in the wild form of the bird, but alike in the cage birds. The wild birds also have rather dull, streaky plumage, unlike the great majority of their domestic cousins.

Island Canaries are very common and found throughout the wooded parts of the islands on which they occur. They appear down at sea level, in gardens, vineyards, orchards and in all the cultivated areas, as well as up in the pine woods at 5,000 ft (1,500 m) or more. The male often utters his beautiful song in a showy song-flight, as he glides down from high above on quivering wings, landing on the crown of one of the tall trees in the native forests.

4/ THICK-BILLED CANARY
Serinus burtoni

RANGE: **W and E Africa**
HABITAT: **mountain forest**
SIZE: **7 in (18 cm)**

The Thick-billed Canary, or Thick-billed Seed-eater, is an unusual member of the serin group of finches, being very large with an especially heavy, robust bill. It inhabits forest edges at altitudes of 5,000–8,000 ft (1,500–2,500 m). It is notoriously difficult to locate because it remains high in the treetops and rarely calls.

Most Thick-billed Canaries occur in the mountains of Cameroon in west Africa, in the uplands on either side of Lake Victoria and in Angola. A distinct population, with white underparts streaked brown and with only a little green in the wings, occurs in the highlands of southern Tanzania. The sexes are similar in this species.

5/ ORIOLE-FINCH
Linurgus olivaceus

RANGE: **W and E Africa**
HABITAT: **upland and mountain forest**
SIZE: **5 in (13 cm)**

The striking Oriole-Finch takes its name from its similarity in color pattern to some of the orioles (pp. 354–57). It has an almost identical distribution to that of the Thick-billed Canary, being restricted to the equatorial mountain forests of Africa. Although it has been found at heights of around 9,000 ft (2,750 m), it generally lives at lower levels than the Thick-billed Canary, down to an altitude of about 1,800 ft (550 m). At these lower levels, this species is found at forest edges and in clearings.

Oriole-Finches are especially attracted to seeding nettles. Although usually rather silent birds, they utter soft, plaintive *twee* or wheezy *tzit tzit* calls from time to time and have a sweet, rather thin and high-pitched song. The nest is a shallow cup, generally placed low down, less than 3 ft (1 m) from the ground, in a bush at the forest edge.

6/ WESTERN GREENFINCH
Carduelis chloris
RANGE: **Europe, N Africa, Asia Minor, Middle East, C Asia**
HABITAT: **open woodland, bushes, gardens**
SIZE: **5¾ in (14.5 cm)**

This stocky finch is well known in gardens in winter, where it is especially fond of sunflower seeds and peanuts. An agile bird, it will readily take food from hanging dispensers. The more northerly populations migrate in winter, and, at this time, the birds turn up in many different habitats, including sea coasts.

During the breeding season, Western Greenfinches take up residence in parks, gardens and along hedgerows, as well as in larger areas of open woodland. The characteristic strident, nasal calls readily draw attention to the birds, as does the butterflylike courtship display flight, which is accompanied by a pleasant, twittering song, performed by the male. They build their nests in small trees and bushes, about 7–8 ft (2–2.5 m) above the ground.

7/ RED SISKIN
Carduelis cucullata   E
RANGE: **N Colombia, N Venezuela**
HABITAT: **dry scrub**
SIZE: **4 in (10 cm)**

This striking finch formerly roamed in semi-nomadic flocks over many parts of northern South America. It was also found on Trinidad and on 2 other Caribbean islands, Gasparee and Monos, from all of which it has since disappeared. Heavy trapping for the cage-bird trade has caused it to become very rare, and it is now regarded as endangered throughout its range.

As well as being trapped as a cage bird in its own right, the Red Siskin is caught because it hybridizes easily. Canary breeders have taken advantage of its red genes for improving the plumage color of their stock of birds. Despite legal protection, the trapping persists. In 1981, there were believed to be only 600–800 birds remaining in the wild.

8/ AMERICAN GOLDFINCH
Carduelis tristis
RANGE: **S Canada, USA; N populations migrate in winter**
HABITAT: **open woodland, weedy fields, roadsides**
SIZE: **4¼ in (11 cm)**

These sparkling little finches are commonly seen in flocks feeding on the seeds of roadside thistles and other weeds. When disturbed, the flocks fly up and swirl around, twittering all the time, before settling again. Their sweet, canarylike song, usually given during a circling song-flight, has earned them the popular, if ornithologically inaccurate, name of Wild Canary.

Although the male American Goldfinch's plumage is bright and distinctive in the breeding season, it becomes duller in color, much more like that of the female, through the rest of the year. This species' nest is a neat cup in a tree or shrub.

9/ EURASIAN GOLDFINCH
Carduelis carduelis
RANGE: **N Africa, Europe, Middle East to C Asia**
HABITAT: **open broad-leaved woodland, scrub with weedy areas, gardens**
SIZE: **4¾ in (12 cm)**

Throughout much of its range, the Eurasian Goldfinch has been heavily trapped as a cage bird because of its bright, delightful plumage and lovely, liquid, twittering song. Trapping has even been blamed for the extinction of some local populations. This species has many races, divided into 2 distinct groups. Western races, such as *C.c. britannica* of the British Isles, have black on the head, while eastern races, such as *C.c. paropanisi* of central Asia, have gray. The 2 forms interbreed where they come into contact in central Asia.

Like its cousin the American Goldfinch, the Eurasian Goldfinch feeds readily on the seeds of weeds. Flocks of the birds are often seen drifting along roadsides from one patch of thistles to another. The nests are built in bushes or trees, often high up and well out on side branches.

10/ REDPOLL
Acanthis flammea
RANGE: **circumpolar in N latitudes, Britain, central Europe**
HABITAT: **birch forest, shrub tundra, young conifer plantations**
SIZE: **5½ in (14 cm)**

Since the 1950s, one race of this bird, the Lesser Redpoll *A.f. cabaret*, has increased markedly in western Europe, taking advantage of the large areas of young conifer growth established by forestry interests. Just a few decades ago, there were only isolated populations of the race in upland Britain and the Alps. Its distribution now runs continuously from Britain, northeast France, and the Low Countries to the Alps and Czechoslovakia, and up into southern Scandinavia.

Elsewhere, races of the Redpoll breed across the northern latitudes of Eurasia and North America, wintering well to the south of their breeding ranges. In North America, the numbers of the birds in most wintering areas vary on a 2-year cycle, tied to the seeding of a variety of trees. Redpolls nest in the middle levels of trees and bushes, although the most northerly race, the very pale *A.f. hornemanni*, often called the Hoary Redpoll, nests on or near the ground above the Arctic tree line. Females lack the pinkish breast and rump of the males; juveniles also lack the black throat of the adults and their red forehead, or "poll," which gives the species its name.

11/ ROSY FINCH
Leucosticte arctoa
RANGE: **C and E Siberia, NW and W North America**
HABITAT: **mountains, above the tree line; winters at lower altitudes**
SIZE: **5¾–6½ in (14.5–17 cm)**

The widespread Rosy Finch is extremely variable in size and plumage. It has many races, some nearly as large as European Starlings *Sturnus vulgaris*, others as small as House Sparrows

Passer domesticus. Until recently, several of the races of the Rosy Finch were regarded as separate species. The North American races include the Black Rosy Finch *L.a. atrata* of the Great Basin and the Rockies, the Brown-capped Rosy Finch *L.a. australis* of southwestern USA, and the Aleutian Rosy Finch *L.a. umbrina* of the Pribilof Islands off Alaska.

Rosy Finches live on the bare hilltops, mountain sides and high plains of remote mountains and islands. They eat mainly seeds, but often supplement their diet with insects, especially those that are blown onto snowfields. Insects rapidly become torpid in the cold and fall easy prey to the birds. In winter, most populations of this bird migrate down to adjacent valleys, lowland plains and coastal areas. Rosy Finches nest in loose colonies in rock screes and on cliffs.

12/ HOUSE FINCH
Carpodacus mexicanus
RANGE: **North and Central America, S to Mexico**
HABITAT: **towns, open woodland, scrub, deserts**
SIZE: **6 in (15 cm)**

House Finches are common in dry, open habitats in western USA. They are major pests in California, where they feed on ripening fruit and buds. Formerly common as cage birds, some were released in New York State in about 1940, where they subsequently nested in 1943. After a slow start, they increased rapidly and are now widespread in eastern North America, from Florida to Canada. The race *C.m. frontalis* (illustrated) from southwestern Canada, western USA and northwest Mexico is typical. House Finches were also introduced to Hawaii in the last century, where they are now well established and widely regarded as pests.

By contrast, one race of the bird, McGregor's House Finch *C.m. mcgregori*, formerly confined to islands off Baja California, had become very rare by the turn of the century and dwindled to extinction by 1938.

13/ CAUCASIAN GREAT ROSEFINCH
Carpodacus rubicilla
RANGE: **Caucasus and C Asia**
HABITAT: **rocky alpine meadows and rocky slopes**
SIZE: **7¾ in (20 cm)**

The Caucasian Great Rosefinch is one of several closely related and very similar *Carpodacus* finches that occur in central Asia. One of the largest species, it is a denizen of windswept and barren high mountains, at altitudes of 6,500–16,500 ft (2,000–5,000 m). In winter, flocks descend to rocky ravines and overgrown thickets in mountain valleys, but even then the birds rarely appear below 3,300 ft (1,000 m).

The colorful male Caucasian Great Rosefinches have shiny, lustrous feathers which contrast markedly with those of the drably plumaged females. The birds breed in isolated pairs or in small colonies, siting their nests in cliff crevices or between boulders.

PINE GROSBEAK

♂

♀

RED CROSSBILL

race *curvirostra*

♂

♀

NORTHERN
BULLFINCH

♂

race *pileata*

♀

HAWFINCH

♂

EVENING GROSBEAK

♂

♀

AKIALOA

♀

AKIAPOLAAU

♂

race *procerus*

♂

MAUI PARROTBILL

♂

PALILA

AKOHEKOHE

imm

IIWI

FINCHES

1/ PINE GROSBEAK
Pinicola enucleator
RANGE: **N and W North America, N Scandinavia E to N Siberia**
HABITAT: **coniferous and scrub forest**
SIZE: **$7\frac{3}{4}$ in (20 cm)**

These large finches are often elusive and difficult to find in their northern forest homeland. They tend to be sparsely distributed, and their quiet, unobtrusive habits make them easy to overlook. Although the adult males are brightly colored, young males are somber-toned, like the females.

Pine Grosbeaks eat mainly berries and buds, hopping about heavily on the ground, or clambering around slowly in the treetops. While many birds are sedentary, others leave the breeding grounds and travel south and west in winter, sometimes in large numbers. The magnitude of these movements is related to the abundance of the Pine Grosbeak's natural food; in Europe, the size of the crop of mountain ash berries is especially important. Few birds are seen in years with poor crops. During winter, Pine Grosbeaks are often seen in small flocks, when they may be remarkably tame and approachable.

2/ RED CROSSBILL
Loxia curvirostra
RANGE: **America, from Alaska S to Guatemala, Eurasia, Algeria, Tunisia, Balearic Islands**
HABITAT: **coniferous forest**
SIZE: **$6\frac{1}{4}$ in (16 cm)**

The 4 species of crossbill and the Akepa *Loxops coccinea*, one of the Hawaiian finches, are the only birds in the world that have crossed bills. In the crossbills, the beak is used to open the scales of conifer cones, particularly those of pines, spruces and larches, to extract the seeds that make up almost all their diet. Their dependence on conifer seeds often gives rise to mass migrations (or irruptions); the birds sometimes sweep across entire continents during years of cone crop failure. Pines rarely suffer poor cone crops, however, and populations that feed on these are almost sedentary.

The race *L. c. curvirostra*, which occupies most of the species' range in Eurasia, including parts of the British Isles, feeds mainly on spruce; 11 isolated races are found in the Old World on mountains and islands outside the species' main range. These differ slightly in size and color from *L. c. curvirostra* and have different-sized bills, adapted for dealing with different cones. Some populations tend to have the bill crossed to the right and others crossed to the left. These differences may be related to clockwise and counter-clockwise spiraling of the scales of cones.

The Scottish Crossbill *L. scoticus*, which has a large bill for feeding on pine cones in northeast Scotland, is generally now regarded as a distinct species – Britain's only endemic species of bird. There is a similar variation in bill size and diet in the 8 New World races.

Red Crossbills can be very approachable if feeding at low levels, but they usually forage much higher, near the crowns of the tall forest trees. There, they are easily overlooked if their ringing calls are not recognized.

3/ NORTHERN BULLFINCH
Pyrrhula pyrrhula
RANGE: **Europe E across Asia to Japan**
HABITAT: **coniferous and broad-leaved forest, cultivated areas, gardens**
SIZE: **6 in (15 cm)**

The soft-plumaged and usually shy Northern Bullfinch is often a major agricultural pest in fruit-growing areas, where it can cause considerable damage by eating the buds of fruit trees, especially those of pears. During the breeding season, it carries food to the young in special pouches on the floor of its mouth, either side of the tongue. This is in contrast to most finches, which carry food in their throats.

The Azores Bullfinch *P. p. murina* has much duller plumage than its continental northern European relative *P. p. pileata*. The sexes are alike in the Azores Bullfinch, and both male and female lack the white on the rump characteristic of all other races, suggesting that it may in fact be a separate species. It occurs in upland forest and along the forest edge in the Azores. It is extremely rare and believed to be endangered. At the opposite end of the species range, in the Amur region of the extreme southeastern USSR, Manchuria and Japan, there is a race, *P. p. griseiventris*, with a gray breast and red face.

4/ HAWFINCH
Coccothraustes coccothraustes
RANGE: **Europe, North Africa, Asia**
HABITAT: **broad-leaved and mixed forest, parkland and orchards**
SIZE: **7 in (18 cm)**

A huge head and bill, stocky build and short tail give the Hawfinch its distinctive, heavy appearance. The bird feeds largely on tree seeds, such as those of hornbeam, elm and beech, which it takes directly from the trees or forages for on the ground. Like most finches, it takes some insects during the summer. The young are fed partly on insects and partly on regurgitated seeds.

However, it is the Hawfinch's ability to feed on the kernels of thick-walled seeds, such as cherry and olive stones, that is most well known. The head and massive bill are specialized for cracking these open. The skull is strengthened and modified to provide attachment for powerful muscles that bulge out and make the bird's cheeks look swollen. The inside of the bill contains special pads for gripping the stones. Experiments have revealed that the Hawfinch must be able to exert a force equivalent to more than 100 lb (45 kg) in order to crack open an olive stone. The bird itself weighs only 2 oz (55 g).

Hawfinches are very shy and usually disappear rapidly into the treetops long before they can be clearly seen. The middle flight feathers of the wing are curiously notched and curled at the tips, unlike those of any other finch. The reason for this feature is unclear, although it may have a role in courtship. Female Hawfinches are rather duller in plumage than the males.

5/ EVENING GROSBEAK
Coccothraustes vespertinus
RANGE: **W North America, S to Mexico, E across Canada**
HABITAT: **coniferous and mixed woodland**
SIZE: **$7\frac{3}{4}$ in (20 cm)**

This large, chunky finch was originally (and incorrectly) thought to sing only late in the day, hence its common name. Formerly a bird primarily of the western mountains of North America, the Evening Grosbeak has spread east across Canada as far as Nova Scotia during this century. This expansion of the bird's range is still continuing eastward.

During winter, the Evening Grosbeak migrates south and east, often coming to feeding stations, particularly if sunflower seeds are available. The numbers occurring each winter vary enormously, depending on the abundance of natural food. The bird's nest is a loose, shallow cup of twigs and roots placed in a woodland tree, sometimes up to 65 ft (20 m) above the ground.

FAMILY FRINGILLIDAE/
SUBFAMILY DREPANIDINAE
Hawaiian finches
Small, beaks highly variable in shape. Endemic to Hawaiian Island group. Generally simple plumage patterns, often yellow, red or black. Sexes different, or similar with males larger. Nests in trees, bushes or grass tussocks. Eggs 2–4, white, with lines or spots. Incubation 13–14 days, nestling period 15–22 days. 20 species; over half are considered endangered and many are now extremely rare.

6/ PALILA
Loxioides bailleui [E]
RANGE: **island of Hawaii**
HABITAT: **dry upper mountain forest**
SIZE: **6 in (15 cm)**

The Palila is found only in mamane and mamane/naio forest on the upper edges of the wooded zones of Mauna Kea, one of the 2 giant volcanoes on Hawaii. It now occurs only above 6,000 ft (1,800 m). Formerly it was quite common, and ranged down to lower altitudes of about 4,000 ft (1,200 m). The population is believed to number some 2,000–6,000 birds and the species is considered endangered.

Palilas are large, distinctive finches, the yellow plumage on the head being more pronounced in the males than in the females. The birds often roam about in small flocks, eating seeds, berries and insects (especially caterpillars). They hold the pods of mamane trees in their feet and crack or rip them open with their heavy bills. The call is rather bell-like, and the song is a collection of trills, whistles and warbles.

7/ MAUI PARROTBILL
Pseudonestor xanthophrys [V]
RANGE: **island of Maui**
HABITAT: **upper mountain rain forest**
SIZE: **5½ in (14 cm)**

The Maui Parrotbill is confined to forests on the upper slopes of Haleakala Mountain, an extinct volcano, on the island of Maui. Usually occurring at altitudes above 5,000 ft (1,500 m), it prefers forest with thick undergrowth and an open tree canopy. This species is very rare, as indeed it was when it was first discovered by western ornithologists in the 1890s. Today only about 500 individuals remain.

The Maui Parrotbill takes its name from its distinctive, thickset beak. A stocky bird, it moves along the trunks and branches of trees and low shrubs with slow, deliberate movements, rather like a little parrot. On occasion, it may even hang upside-down. Using its strong bill, it crushes or wrenches open small branches of koas and other trees to get at the larvae of wood-boring beetles. It also eats caterpillars and other insects. Its calls include a loud *kzeet* and a thin *queet*, and its song is a series of notes descending in pitch.

8/ AKIALOA
Hemignathus obscurus [E]
RANGE: **island of Kauai; extinct on Oahu, Lanai and Hawaii islands**
HABITAT: **upper mountain rain forest**
SIZE: **7½ in (19 cm)**

Of the 4 original races of the Akialoa, only one possibly still exists, the Kauai Akialoa *H. o. procerus*, which is sometimes regarded as a species in its own right. It was last seen for certain in 1967, although it had been numerous up to the 1890s. If any remain today, the population is undoubtedly very small and on the verge of extinction. Of the other races, the Lanai Akialoa *H. o. lanaiensis* has not been seen since 1894, when it probably became extinct due to habitat destruction; the Oahu Akialoa *H. o. ellisianus* was last seen in 1837; and the Hawaii Akialoa *H. o. obscurus* was last recorded in 1894–95, when it was still fairly common in the high rain forest.

The Akialoa feeds on invertebrates and nectar. It creeps up tree trunks and branches, probing in dense moss and bark in the manner of a treecreeper, searching for small insects and spiders. It also has a tubular tongue for drinking the nectar of flowers, particularly those of ohias and lobeliads. Its call is quite loud and deep and it utters a trilling song. Early descriptions referred to the song of the Kauai Akialoa as resembling that of a canary.

9/ AKIAPOLAAU
Hemignathus munroi [E]
RANGE: **island of Hawaii**
HABITAT: **upper mountain forest**
SIZE: **5½ in (14 cm)**

Like most of the Hawaiian finches, the Akiapolaau is found in forests on mountain slopes, in this case from 1,500–6,500 ft (450–2,000 m). It was formerly widespread, but is now confined to small patches of forest, where perhaps as few as 1,500 birds remain.

A stocky, short-tailed bird, the Akiapolaau has an extraordinary bill that is quite unique among birds. While the lower mandible is straight and stout, the upper mandible is long, slender and sickle-shaped. As a feeding tool, the bill combines the work of a woodpecker's bill together with that of a treecreeper.

The bird feeds on the trunks and branches of tall koa and mamane trees, hammering with the lower mandible in the soft bark in search of beetle larvae, other insects and spiders. When it finds prey, it uses the thin upper mandible to winkle the creature out of hiding.

The sound of hammering on bark is often a clue to the Akiapolaau's presence. Males also utter loud *chip* and *squeet* calls while foraging. The song is a bright series of whistled notes, with a rising then falling inflection in the last 2 notes.

10/ IIWI
Vestiaria coccinea
RANGE: **islands of Kaui, Oahu, Molokai, Maui, Hawaii; extinct Lanai**
HABITAT: **mountain forest**
SIZE: **6 in (15 cm)**

The Iiwi is one of the few species of Hawaiian finch that is not at present endangered. It is fairly common in some parts of Kaui and Hawaii, although rarer on Oahu and Maui. It is almost extinct on Molokai and has already disappeared from Lanai.

The Iiwi feeds mainly on flowering trees, especially ohia and mamane trees, probing into the flowers with its long, decurved bill to drink the nectar. It is slow and deliberate in its movements and usually hides in the interior of trees, only occasionally coming into the open. It makes daily movements, often of many miles, in search of the patchily distributed but locally abundant flowering trees. As well as uttering the creaking sounds for which it is named, the Iiwi produces a variety of gurgles, humanlike whistles and reedy notes, which have been likened to a child playing a rusty harmonica.

The Iiwi is one of about 6 Hawaiian finches whose plumage was traditionally used to make colorful cloaks and other ornamentation for Hawaiian nobility. Tufts of feathers from huge numbers of birds made garments of great beauty, some of which may still be seen in museums. Although hunting for this purpose stopped long ago, it has been blamed (perhaps unjustly) for the plight of many species.

A variety of other causes has brought about the Hawaiian finches' decline. Some of the most devastating of these have been habitat destruction, the introduction of livestock, cats, rats and non-native forest birds, and the spread of bird diseases transmitted by mosquitoes.

11/ AKOHEKOHE
Palmeria dolei [V]
RANGE: **island of Maui; extinct Molokai**
HABITAT: **upper mountain rain forest**
SIZE: **7 in (18 cm)**

With its spotted plumage, wing bars, reddish-orange nape and white tufted crest, the Akohekohe is unique among the otherwise simply patterned Hawaiian finches. Often known by its English name, Crested Honeycreeper, it is now very rare and confined to the higher northeastern slopes of Haleakala Mountain on Maui, from 5,800–6,500 ft (1,750–2,000 m) above sea level. It was formerly found on Molokai and once had a wider distribution on Maui. It was still locally abundant in the 1890s.

The Akohekohe is lively and active as it feeds in the tops of tall flowering trees, especially ohialehuas. It takes nectar as well as caterpillars and other insects. It is a noisy bird, with a variety of calls, including humanlike whistles. The sexes are similar in appearance.

WAXBILLS, PARASITIC VIDUINE WEAVERS AND WHYDAHS, BUFFALO WEAVERS

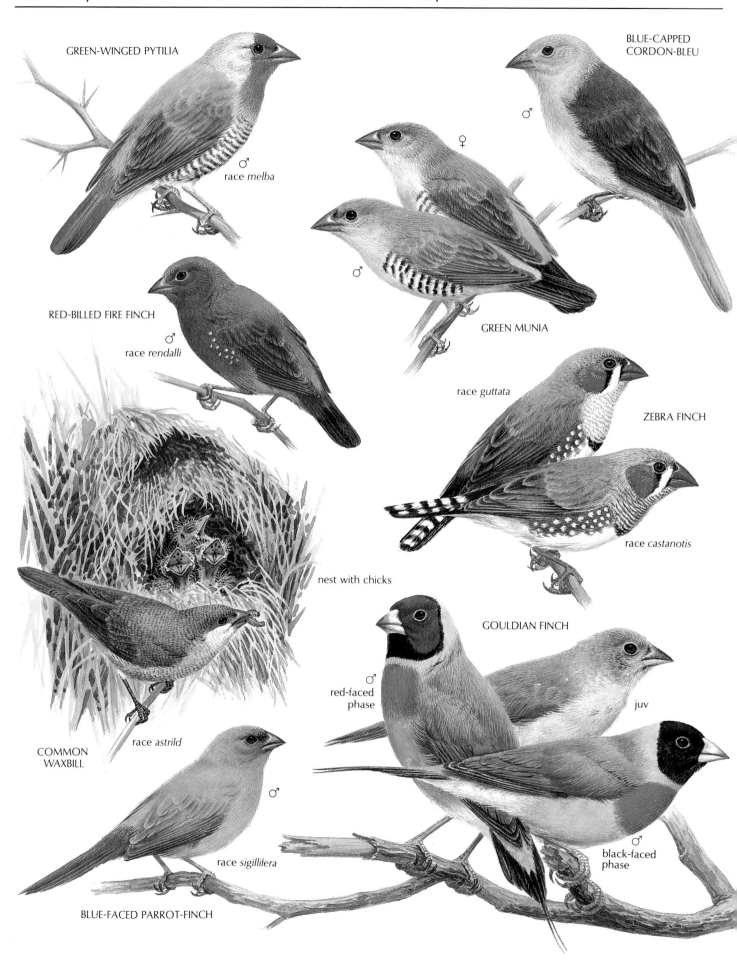

GREEN-WINGED PYTILIA

race *melba*

♂

BLUE-CAPPED
CORDON-BLEU

♂

♀

♂

GREEN MUNIA

race *guttata*

RED-BILLED FIRE FINCH

♂

race *rendalli*

ZEBRA FINCH

race *castanotis*

nest with chicks

GOULDIAN FINCH

♂
red-faced
phase

juv

COMMON
WAXBILL

race *astrild*

♂

race *sigillifera*

♂
black-faced
phase

BLUE-FACED PARROT-FINCH

WHITE-BACKED MUNIA

race *acuticauda*

race *striata*

juv

♂

♀

JAVA SPARROW

PIN-TAILED WHYDAH

♂

½ size in pro

PARADISE WHYDAH

♀

race *dinemelli*

WHITE-HEADED BUFFALO WEAVER

343

WAXBILLS, PARASITIC VIDUINE WEAVERS AND WHYDAHS, BUFFALO WEAVERS

FAMILY ESTRILDIDAE
Waxbills

Small birds. Diverse plumage: some brightly colored, some dull but with striking markings. Sexes usually similar, but pronounced differences in some species. Nests of most species domed, made of grass; some species nest in holes. Nestlings of many species have distinctive patterns of spots or lines and patches of color in their mouths that may help parents identify and see their young in the darkness of the nest and stimulate them to feed them. Eggs typically 4–8, white. Incubation 10–21 days, nestling period about 16 days. 133 species.

1/ GREEN-WINGED PYTILIA
Pytilia melba

RANGE: **sub-Saharan Africa**
HABITAT: **savanna and steppe**
SIZE: **5 in (13 cm)**

Most waxbills associate in flocks, but the Green-winged Pytilia, often called the Melba Finch, nearly always lives in pairs which occupy year-round territories in thorny thickets. It feeds on the ground, on grass seeds and insects – particularly termites – which it finds in leaf litter or by breaking into termite galleries. There are several races, including *P. m. melba* from Zaire and Tanzania to Namibia and northern Cape Province.

These birds sometimes gather together at drinking sites, but the red-faced males are usually very aggressive toward each other (or indeed to any other birds with red faces or bills). During the courtship display the male and female hop round each other while the male sings, holding a grass stem or feather in his bill. The nest is built in a thorn bush or small tree, and both sexes incubate the 4–6 eggs and feed the chicks.

As with those of other African waxbills, the nests of this species are often host to parasitic viduine weavers and whydahs – in this case the Paradise Whydah and the Broad-tailed Paradise Whydah *Vidua orientalis*.

2/ RED-BILLED FIRE FINCH
Lagonosticta senegalia

RANGE: **sub-Saharan Africa**
HABITAT: **dry areas, dense brush and near cultivated land**
SIZE: **3½ in (9 cm)**

This bird is one of the most common of all African birds, possibly because it has adapted well to the new environments created by human settlement. Outside the breeding season it travels in small flocks, foraging for seeds among dense scrub and in fields under cultivation, usually near water. It feeds mainly on the ground and often frequents villages to snatch spilled grain.

Red-billed Fire Finches breed during the latter half of the rainy season, when there are plenty of ripe seeds to feed to the nestlings. In wild country the monogamous pairs nest in shrubs, particularly acacias, but in settled areas they will nest in thatched roofs or wall cavities. The nests are often parasitized by a parasitic viduine weaver, the Village Indigobird *Vidua chalybeata*.

There are 6 or more races recognized, including *L. s. rendalli* from southern Angola to southern Tanzania and northern Cape province.

3/ BLUE-CAPPED CORDON-BLEU
Uraeginthus cyanocephala

RANGE: **Somalia to Kenya and Tanzania**
HABITAT: **dry steppe and semidesert with bushes or trees, especially acacia or thorn scrub**
SIZE: **5 in (13 cm)**

The male Blue-capped Cordon-bleu, or Blue-headed Cordon-bleu, is a startling sight in the breeding season when, with plumage fluffed out, he pursues the duller female like a flying ball of blue feathers. Having caught her, he will woo her by singing and bobbing up and down before her with a carefully selected grass stem held in his bill – a display typical of the waxbill family.

Cordon-bleus are typical of the dry country in East Africa, where they forage for grass seeds and insects in pairs or small parties. They often take termites by breaching the earth tunnels that these insects build up acacia saplings. The nestlings are fed exclusively on termites and other insects.

4/ COMMON WAXBILL
Estrilda astrild

RANGE: **sub-Saharan Africa; introduced to many tropical islands**
HABITAT: **grassland and cultivated areas**
SIZE: **4 in (10 cm)**

The Common Waxbill feeds mainly on grass seeds, either plucking them from the seed heads or picking them off the ground, and will also prey on swarming termites. Highly gregarious, these birds often forage in large flocks and return to communal roosts at night. They breed in the rainy season, when insects for feeding their young are most abundant.

The nest is often highly elaborate, with a small "roosting" nest built on top of the dome-shaped breeding nest. The brood is often parasitized by the Pin-tailed Whydah. In contrast to the chicks of some parasitic cuckoos, such as the Eurasian Cuckoo *Cuculus canorus*, those of the whydah do not destroy the rightful occupants of the nest, and the adult waxbills can often be seen feeding a mixed brood. There are some 8 races, including *E. a. astrild* from much of South Africa.

5/ GREEN MUNIA
Amandava formosa

RANGE: **C India**
HABITAT: **grassland and cultivated regions**
SIZE: **4 in (10 cm)**

Locally common throughout the northern half of peninsular India, this small waxbill, which is also known as the Green Avadavat, often associates in flocks of up to 50 birds, particularly in areas with tall grass, low scrub or crops that provide good cover. Green Munias feed on the ground, probably taking seeds and small insects, although the precise details of this species' feeding habits in the wild are unknown.

Green Munias are monogamous, but they often nest close together in the breeding season, building large, round nests of grasses and leaves among thick grass or sugar cane. The 4–7 eggs are incubated by both the male and female.

6/ ZEBRA FINCH
Poephila guttata

RANGE: **Australia, Lesser Sundas**
HABITAT: **dry grassland and other open habitats with scattered trees and shrubs, near water**
SIZE: **4 in (10 cm)**

The Zebra Finch is one of the most common birds in inland Australia. As a seed-eater, it needs water daily and provision of water for livestock has allowed it to increase over the last 100 years. There are 2 races: the Australian *P. g. castanotis* and *P. g. guttata* of the Sunda Islands.

Highly gregarious, Zebra Finches live in flocks of 10–100 birds throughout the year and will even breed colonially, with several pairs nesting in the same bush. The pairs mate for life, and in arid regions they may breed at any time of year in response to rain. In southern parts of the species' range, breeding is more regular and seasonal. Its exact timing depends not only on rainfall, but also on temperature, food supply and previous breeding. They feed on grass seeds and insects, usually in the morning, then move on to a pool or stock-watering point in the afternoon to drink, bathe and preen one another.

7/ BLUE-FACED PARROT-FINCH
Erythrura trichroa
RANGE: **NE Queensland, Indonesia, Pacific islands and New Guinea**
HABITAT: **rain forest**
SIZE: **4¾ in (12 cm)**

Like the other members of its family, the Blue-faced Parrot-Finch is a seed-eater, but instead of foraging on the ground in grassland, it feeds on the seeds of trees and shrubs at all levels in the rain forest. It has a preference for the seeds of bamboo, and small nomadic parties of these birds will wander all over their range in search of seeding bamboo thickets. It sometimes emerges into open forest to feed on casuarina and grass seeds, but in general it is elusive and rarely seen.

After a prolonged and elaborate courtship involving singing, tail-twisting and hopping up and down on the part of the male and tail-twisting and the uttering of a low, trilling identity call by the female, the birds mate and build a pear-shaped nest of moss and vines. Both birds incubate the 4 white eggs, sleeping together on the nest at night. The race illustrated is *E. t. sigillifera* from Australia and New Guinea.

8/ GOULDIAN FINCH
Chloebia gouldiae   ?
RANGE: **N Australia**
HABITAT: **grassland and open woodland**
SIZE: **5½ in (14 cm)**

This spectacularly plumaged bird occurs in 2 main color phases: most males have black faces, but about a quarter have red faces outlined with black, and there is a rare yellow phase. Its dazzling appearance has encouraged its capture for the cage-bird trade; this has contributed to a marked decline in recent years, but the seasonal burning of its grassland feeding grounds has probably been the main factor.

For much of the year it feeds on grass seeds, but instead of taking them from the ground it perches acrobatically on the seed heads, or picks out the seeds while clinging to a nearby twig. When the grasses in the Australian interior die back in the winter dry season, the finches move toward the coast, returning with the rains.

In the breeding season it feeds mainly on insects, often catching them in midair, and takes them to feed its brood of 4–8 chicks. The rudimentary nest is built in a tree hollow or termite mound. Several pairs may nest together in close association, sometimes in the same cavity.

9/ WHITE-BACKED MUNIA
Lonchura striata
RANGE: **India and Sri Lanka to Sumatra**
HABITAT: **grassland with scattered trees, cultivated land**
SIZE: **4 in (10 cm)**

This small, finchlike bird is generally found in large flocks throughout the year, foraging on the ground and amid growing vegetation for the seeds of wild grasses, particularly bamboo, as well as cultivated rice and insects. The nestlings are fed on green seeds, although according to some observers they will also take insects, like the young of many other waxbills.

The pairs breed during the rainy season, building a spherical or oval nest in a bush, tree, or sometimes among rank grass. The 3–8 eggs are brooded by both sexes, and both roost in the nest at night. There are several races, including *L. s. striata* of south India and Sri Lanka, and *L. s. acuticauda*, found from the Himalayas to Thailand. The domesticated form of this species is known as the Bengalese Finch.

10/ JAVA SPARROW
Padda oryzivora
RANGE: **Java and Bali; introduced to Africa, China, S Asia and Hawaii**
HABITAT: **scrub, grassland, bamboo thickets, mangroves, cultivated land**
SIZE: **5½ in (14 cm)**

The boldly marked Java Sparrow has become familiar well beyond its original range, owing to deliberate introductions and escapes from aviaries, for it is a popular cage bird. It feeds largely on seeds and has a strong predilection for rice. Its Latin name reflects this, *Padda* being a reference to the paddy fields and *oryzivora* meaning "rice-eating." During harvest time large flocks descend on the paddy fields to feast on the rice crop, often causing extensive damage.

Java Sparrows form monogamous pairs, breeding just after the rainy season. The nest is built among branches or in a cavity in a tree trunk, wall or roof. The juveniles begin to feed themselves soon after fledging, but are often fed by their parents for another 2–3 weeks.

FAMILY PLOCEIDAE/SUBFAMILY VIDUINAE
Parasitic viduine weavers and whydahs
Small seed-eaters. Sexes differ. Plumage of males black or steel blue, with white, yellow or chestnut in whydahs; females brown and sparrowlike in many species. Male parasitic whydahs have very long tails in breeding season. Eggs 3–4, white, laid in nests of waxbills; most species restricted to a single host. Incubation about 10 days (Village Indigobird), nestling period about 20 days (Pin-tailed Whydah). 10 species.

11/ PIN-TAILED WHYDAH
Vidua macroura
RANGE: **sub-Saharan Africa**
HABITAT: **savanna, cultivated land**
SIZE: **breeding male 13 in (33 cm); non-breeding male 6 in (15 cm); female 5 in (13 cm)**

Despite his spectacular breeding plumage, with a tail almost twice the length of his body, the male Pin-tailed Whydah is surprisingly inconspicuous when searching on the ground for seeds. Pin-tailed Whydahs often forage in small, lively flocks, with one long-tailed breeding male accompanying a group of short-tailed birds, both non-breeding young males and females.

During courtship the male chases other species and flies in looping, vertical circles above his mate in a whirring, dancing display. He will sing from a favored perch for several weeks, but the song is a hissing, rather wheezy performance. The female

lays her eggs one by one in the nests of the Common Waxbill and 3 other species of waxbill, and the chicks develop alongside those of their host. The whydah chicks mimic those of the hosts with remarkable accuracy, including the number and pattern of the spots on the waxbills' palates, the colors inside their mouths and the color of the highly reflective nodules at their gapes.

12/ PARADISE WHYDAH
Vidua paradisaea
RANGE: **C Africa S to Zimbabwe**
HABITAT: **dry bush and savanna woodland**
SIZE: **breeding male 16 in (41 cm); non-breeding male 6 in (15 cm); female 5 in (13 cm)**

In breeding plumage the male Paradise Whydah is a fantastic sight, with his immensely elongated, 11 in (28 cm) black tail feathers that play an important part in the territorial and courtship display. The male flies with the 2 short, broad tail feathers held upright above the long, pointed ones, circling at a height or hovering above a female, rising and falling in jerky undulations that make the tail plumes wave up and down.

These birds are often seen in small flocks searching bare ground or grassland for seeds. The eggs are laid in the nests of Green-winged Pytilias which then rear the young whydahs with their own brood. As with the other parasitic viduine weavers and whydahs, the chicks mimic the mouth patterns of the host chicks.

FAMILY PLOCEIDAE/SUBFAMILY BUBALORNITHINAE
Buffalo weavers
Medium, ground-dwelling seed- and insect-eaters of semiarid regions. Sexes alike. The 2 *Bubalornis* species are black, the 1 *Dinemellia* species is white, brown and red. Large, untidy domed nests of thorny twigs. Eggs 3–4, pale blue or grayish with olive markings. Incubation 11 days, nestling period 20–23 days. 3 species.

13/ WHITE-HEADED BUFFALO WEAVER
Dinemellia dinemelli
RANGE: **Ethiopia, Sudan S to Tanzania**
HABITAT: **dry thornbush, acacia woodland**
SIZE: **9 in (23 cm)**

When startled into flight from a dusty roadside, this large, thickset, almost parrotlike weaver shows its conspicuous red rump and tail coverts, which in combination with striking flashes of white make it unmistakable even at a brief glance. It is usually seen in pairs or small groups, often in company with Superb Starlings *Spreo superbus*, foraging on the ground beneath flat-topped acacia trees or perched low down in thorn bushes. It feeds mainly on seeds, cracking them open with its powerful bill.

These birds often breed in loose colonies, building large, ragged nests of twigs in the boughs of thorn trees which provide protection against nest-predators.

There are 2 races: the northern race *D. d. dinemelli* and the southern race *D. d. boehmi*, which has black mantle, wings and tail.

345

TRUE WEAVERS AND SPARROW-WEAVERS, PASSERINE FINCHES

GOLDEN PALM WEAVER

race *albifrons*

GROSBEAK WEAVER

nest

race *collaris*

race *scutatus*

nest

RED-VENTED MALIMBE

race *philippinus*

RED-BILLED QUELEA

race *lathan*

BAYA WEAVER

VILLAGE WEAVER

race *spilonotus*

MADAGASCAN RED FODY

♀

RED BISHOP

♂

race *orix*

♂

JACKSON'S
WIDOWBIRD

WHITE-BROWED
SPARROW-WEAVER

♂

♂

SOCIABLE WEAVER

colonial nest

STREAKED ROCK SPARROW

♀

♀

♂
race *domesticus*

HOUSE SPARROW

WHITE-WINGED SNOW FINCH

race *nivalis*

♂
race *luteus*
"Sudan Golden Sparrow"

GOLDEN SPARROW

TRUE WEAVERS AND SPARROW-WEAVERS, PASSERINE FINCHES

FAMILY PLOCEIDAE/SUBFAMILY PLOCEINAE
True weavers

Small, mainly tropical, mostly African, chiefly seed-eating birds. Mostly stout-billed and short-tailed (except for male widowbirds, with very long tails). Sexes often differ. Many species with bright yellow, red or glossy black plumage, especially in males; females of most *Ploceus* species with drab, sparrowlike plumage. Often breed in large colonies. Nests intricately woven, domed structures of grass, leaves and sometimes mud, suspended from branches. Eggs 2–4, white, pink, greenish or bluish with wide variety of markings. Incubation 11–17 days, nestling period 11–20 days. 105 species.

1/ GROSBEAK WEAVER
Amblyospiza albifrons
RANGE: **much of sub-Saharan Africa**
HABITAT: **swampy woodland, damp forest, reedbeds**
SIZE: 6½–7½ in (17–19 cm)

An alternative name for this large, gregarious species is Thick-billed Weaver. The striking male reveals white patches in the wings when he flies, with a rather undulating flight. The female shares the distinctive flight, but is a much drabber bird than the male, brown above and whitish with dark streaks below. There are several races, including *A. a. albifrons*, illustrated, from the Cape Province.

The male weaves the beautifully constructed sphere-shaped nest from thin grass strips, fixing it to 2 or 3 upright grass stems. The entrance is a small hole in the side, with or without a "porch," depending on the location, and nests are often in small colonies.

2/ GOLDEN PALM WEAVER
Ploceus bojeri
RANGE: **Somalia S to Tanzania**
HABITAT: **coconut palms, coastal scrub**
SIZE: 6 in (15 cm)

Although found locally over a wide area, this species is most common on the Kenya coast. The spectacular males are especially obvious; they are often found in small flocks, but ones and twos may also be seen in the bushes inland from the beach, or along the shoreline coconut palms, searching for fruits and berries.

Their calls are rather low pitched, sounding like a fizzing, hissing or jangling chatter. This species is very similar in appearance to the Golden Weaver *P. subaureus*, which has a similar range but is not found in Somalia and also occurs on the island of Zanzibar.

3/ VILLAGE WEAVER
Ploceus cucullatus
RANGE: **Sudan and Ethiopia S to Angola, Cape Province**
HABITAT: **forest, cultivated land, gardens**
SIZE: 6–7 in (15–18 cm)

The males of this widespread species have a strikingly patterned plumage in the breeding season, but females and nonbreeding males have greener, streaked plumage. There are some 7

races, including *P. c. collaris* of Zaire and N Angola and *P. c. spilonotus* of South Africa, which vary according to the pattern of black on the head and the strength of coloring below.

Village Weavers, which are also called Spotted-backed Weavers, breed in noisy, lively, dense colonies, with nests made of grass strips woven into kidney-shaped balls, with or without a "spout" at the opening. The nests are slung from the tips of spreading, drooping branches, often over water. The males build the nests and display at them. Each male hangs upside-down from the base of his nest with whirring wings. He takes little interest in the eggs or chicks.

4/ BAYA WEAVER
Ploceus philippinus
RANGE: **Pakistan E to Sri Lanka, Indochina, Sumatra**
HABITAT: **scrub, cultivated land, palms, grassland**
SIZE: 5½–6 in (14–15 cm)

The race illustrated, *P. p. philippinus*, is common all over India; there are several others, including *P. p. burmanicus* from Assam, Bangladesh, Bengal, eastern Nepal and Burma, which is more richly and darkly rufous beneath, with no yellow.

The Baya Weaver's wonderful nest is made of finely woven strips of grass, rice leaves or sugar cane, and is suspended from a drooping tree frond, telephone line or thatched roof. A male flutters noisily in excited display at the nest; once he has succeeded in attracting a female, he completes the nest lining, then, after the eggs are laid, builds another nest, and even a third or fourth, for other females.

5/ RED-VENTED MALIMBE
Malimbus scutatus
RANGE: **Sierra Leone E to Cameroon**
HABITAT: **coastal forest**
SIZE: 4¾ in (12 cm)

Small parties of Red-Vented Malimbes may be detected by the very harsh *zee-zee-zee* or *chit-it-zeer-zeer* calls they utter constantly as they move

through undergrowth, often near villages. They are chiefly insect-eaters but all feed on the husks of oil palm nuts.

The male of the race *M. s. scutopartitus* from Cameroon has a larger red breast patch than that of *M. s. scutatus* from farther west. Nests are constructed in small groups, in palm trees, each made of palm leaf ribs woven into a sphere with a very long entrance spout.

6/ RED-BILLED QUELEA
Quelea quelea
RANGE: **sub-Saharan Africa**
HABITAT: **damp woodland, swamps, cultivated land**
SIZE: 4¼–5 in (11–13 cm)

Huge, densely packed, perfectly synchronized flocks of a million or more Red-billed Queleas move across the land like clouds of smoke, sometimes breaking the branches of trees with their combined weight. These vast swarms still devastate grain crops despite determined efforts at pest control.

Colonies contain huge numbers of spherical nests of woven green grasses, usually attached to the branches of thorn trees. There may be as many as 500 nests in a single thorn tree. The male has a sweet song, but flocks make a confused roar of chirps and wing noise.

There are several races: *Q. q. lathamii*, from southern Africa, is paler and grayer above than the West African race *Q. q. quelea*; *Q. q. aethiopica* from the northeast is more rosy below, with less or no black on the forehead of breeding males.

7/ MADAGASCAN RED FODY
Foudia madagascariensis
RANGE: **Madagascar; introduced to Mauritius, Seychelles**
HABITAT: **forest edge, savanna, cultivated land, rice paddies**
SIZE: 5 in (13 cm)

On Madagascar this is one of the most common of birds, the red males strikingly obvious, the females browner, streaked above but unmarked below. Madagascan Red Fodies forage in groups or with mixed-bird flocks and do immense damage to the rice crop. They live in most places except the interior of the forest.

Madagascan Red Fodies have high-pitched, insectlike calls, and males sing with a very high, hissing and bubbling sound, like a tiny steam engine, displaying with wings and tail dropped and rump feathers fluffed out. These fodies live in and around villages, eating all kinds of seeds and also insects in the breeding season.

8/ RED BISHOP
Euplectes orix

RANGE: **sub-Saharan Africa**
HABITAT: **grassland**
SIZE: **$4\frac{3}{4}$–$5\frac{1}{2}$ in (12–14 cm)**

Of all the small African grassland birds, the male Red Bishop is perhaps the most eye-catching in his breeding colors. The race *E. o. orix*, illustrated, is the southern race. A male displays to a female with his rump feathers puffed out; he will also fly with his body plumage ruffled into a vivid ball, floating or bounding above the grass with a loud purring of vibrating wings.

Males have strict territories with 3–4 females. Nests are built in loose colonies. Made of grass and attached to reeds, tall grasses or palm fronds, the nests are oval in shape, with an entrance high in one side.

9/ JACKSON'S WIDOWBIRD
Euplectes jacksoni

RANGE: **Kenya, Tanzania**
HABITAT: **highland grassland, cultivated land**
SIZE: **$13\frac{1}{4}$ in (34 cm)**

The male is extraordinary and striking with his 8 in (20 cm) long tail; the female and nonbreeding male are streaky brown. Like other widowbirds, they are also often called whydahs. They are found in rather isolated areas of grassland above 5,000 ft (1,500 m) in western and central Kenya and northern Tanzania, forming flocks after breeding which move to cultivated land. Breeding males wear away special "rings" in the grass on which they display, springing into the air with heads thrown back, feet hanging and tail curved forward to touch the neck, except for 2 feathers pointing downward and outward. They have various brief, clicking and whistling songs and a softer, wheezy call note.

FAMILY PLOCEIDAE/SUBFAMILY PLOCEPASSERINAE
Sparrow-weavers

Small, ground-feeding, highly gregarious, stout-billed seed- and insect-eaters. Sexes almost alike, distinguished by head and wing markings. Plumage drab, with brown upperparts and white underparts. Roofed nests, thatched with (not woven from) grass stems, mostly with 2 openings, often communal and some used for roosting. Eggs 2–5, cream, white, pinkish or pale blue, with red, brown or gray speckles, scribbles or blotches. Incubation and nestling period (Sociable Weaver) 13–14 days and 21–24 days. 8 species.

10/ WHITE-BROWED SPARROW-WEAVER
Plocepasser mahali

RANGE: **Ethiopia to South Africa**
HABITAT: **light wooded savanna and semi-desert, coming into villages**
SIZE: **$6\frac{1}{4}$–7 in (16–18 cm)**

This common bird of acacia savanna is usually seen in noisy, chattering groups, either in the breeding trees or feeding on the ground on seeds and insects. The race *P. m. melanorhynchus*, from Sudan, Ethiopia, Uganda and Kenya, is illustrated. Some other races have brown markings on the breast that give the species an alternative name of Stripe-breasted Sparrow-Weaver.

White-browed Sparrow-Weavers build an untidy retort-shaped nest of dry grass at the ends of branches; there are often several nests to a tree. These nests are used for roosting by several birds; only one female in a group breeds, the remainder helping to feed the nestlings.

11/ SOCIABLE WEAVER
Philetirus socius

RANGE: **W and C southern Africa**
HABITAT: **dry acacia savanna**
SIZE: **$5\frac{1}{2}$ in (14 cm)**

This highly gregarious bird is most remarkable for its breeding behavior. Each colony, which may consist of anything from 6–300 birds, constructs a large communal nest in a tree or on the crosspiece of a bare utility pole. This extraordinary structure is the largest nest of any passerine. It measures up to 13 ft (4 m) deep and 25 ft (7.5 m) long and has a large roof, beneath which each individual pair has its own nest cavity. Grass stems are arranged pointing diagonally downward into the vertical entrance tunnel leading into each nest, forming a barrier against many predators. The communal nest is used by the group throughout the year, both for roosting and breeding, and may last for many years.

FAMILY PASSERIDAE
Passerine finches

Small, finchlike, chiefly seed-eating, typically social birds, mainly of open country. Sexes alike or differ. Plumage mainly brown, chestnut and gray, sometimes with black and, in snow finches, white; yellow in a few species. Usually breed in large colonies. Nests typically bulky, domed structures of dried grass. Eggs 2–7, whitish, cream or pinkish with delicate brown, gray or lilac markings. Incubation 12–15 days, nestling period 15–24 days. 32 species.

12/ HOUSE SPARROW
Passer domesticus

RANGE: **throughout Eurasia excluding Far East; introduced worldwide**
HABITAT: **farmland and built-up areas**
SIZE: **$5\frac{1}{2}$–7 in (14–18 cm)**

The familiar House Sparrow is a seed-eater, adapted to the large seeds of grasses and cultivated grains but also feeding on invertebrates and taking a variety of scraps from bread to meat fibers. The race illustrated is *P. d. domesticus* from

much of Eurasia; other races differ in plumage details and size. The House Sparrow is an extremely successful species, nesting in holes or openly in trees in loose colonies and capable of laying as many as 7 clutches of eggs in a single year in the tropics. In places it becomes an agricultural pest.

13/ GOLDEN SPARROW
Passer luteus

RANGE: **arid zone S of Sahara, from Senegal to Arabia**
HABITAT: **arid acacia savanna**
SIZE: **4–5 in (10–13 cm)**

There are 2 races of this attractive little sparrow which are sometimes regarded as separate species: *P. l. euchlorus* from Arabia, with striking canary-yellow males, and *P. l. luteus* from Africa, in which the males have a bright chestnut back. The females of both races have a more muted brown and pale yellow plumage. This is an intensely social species, occurring in flocks of up to 1 million birds, and can be an agricultural pest. The Golden Sparrow breeds opportunistically when rains produce suitable feeding conditions, nesting in large colonies in thorn trees.

14/ STREAKED ROCK SPARROW
Petronia petronia

RANGE: **Canary Islands, Mediterranean E to China**
HABITAT: **barren open country and rocky hillsides**
SIZE: **6 in (15 cm)**

The rock sparrows and bush sparrows of the genus *Petronia* replace the sparrows of the genus *Passer* in open barren country and light woodland, respectively. The Streaked Rock Sparrow, also known as the Chestnut-shouldered Petronia, is a typical rock sparrow, a streaky brown bird resembling a female House Sparrow, but characterized by an inconspicuous yellow throat patch.

The Streaked Rock Sparrow is usually found in open country, where it nests in holes in trees or rocks, although some individuals come into the more remote villages to breed in holes in buildings. It is a sedentary bird and is relatively common, although frequently overlooked as it feeds, often in large flocks, on the ground.

15/ WHITE-WINGED SNOW FINCH
Montifringilla nivalis

RANGE: **Spain to Mongolia**
HABITAT: **high, bare mountain country above the tree line**
SIZE: **$6\frac{3}{4}$ in (17.5 cm)**

The White-winged Snow Finch is one of 7 species of snow finch that all live in high mountain country. There are 4 races: the one illustrated is *M. n. nivalis* from southwest Europe.

It is one of the highest-dwelling of all birds, usually seen in small groups on rocks or on the ground near patches of melting snow. In winter it forms larger flocks that are often found near mountain huts. It builds its bulky nest in crevices or holes under rocks up to an altitude of 16,500 ft (5,000 m) or even higher.

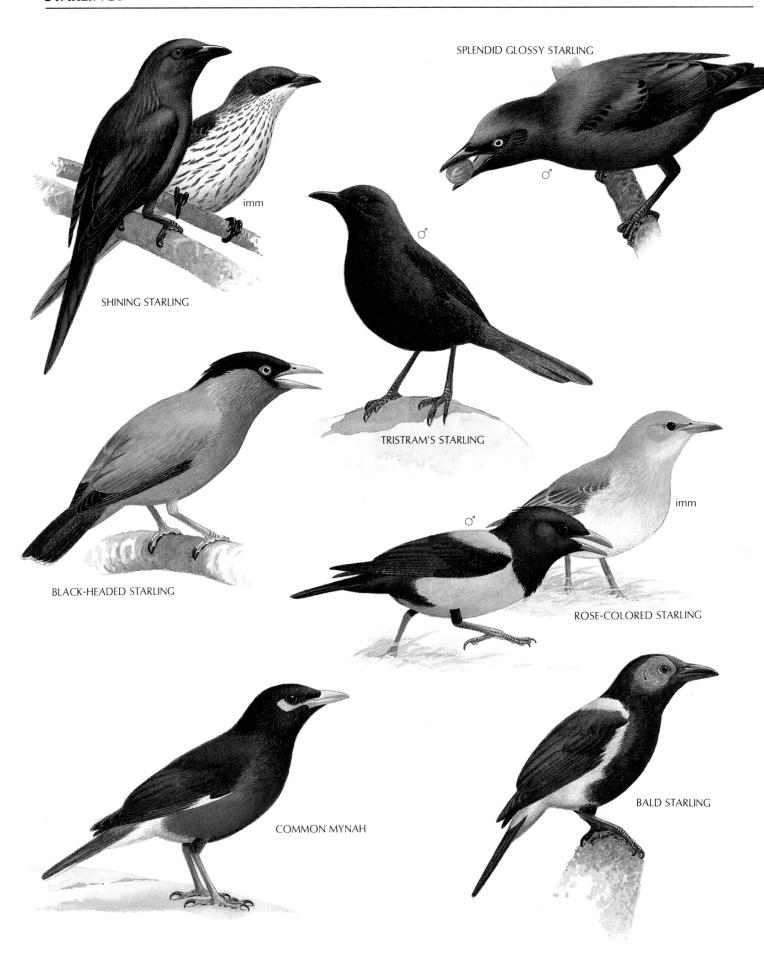

SPLENDID GLOSSY STARLING

imm

♂

SHINING STARLING

♂

TRISTRAM'S STARLING

imm

BLACK-HEADED STARLING

♂

ROSE-COLORED STARLING

COMMON MYNAH

BALD STARLING

AMETHYST STARLING

♀

♂

SUPERB STARLING

non-breeding ♂

WATTLED STARLING

♂

EUROPEAN STARLING

juv

♂

ROTHSCHILD'S MYNAH

GROSBEAK STARLING

HILL MYNAH

RED-BILLED OXPECKER

351

STARLINGS

FAMILY STURNIDAE
Starlings

Small to medium, active, sociable; with long straight bills and sturdy legs. Typically dark, iridescent; some brightly colored. Sexes similar. Mostly colonial, nesting in holes. Eggs 2–7, pale blue, spotted brown. Incubation 11–18 days, nestling period 18–30 days. 108 species.

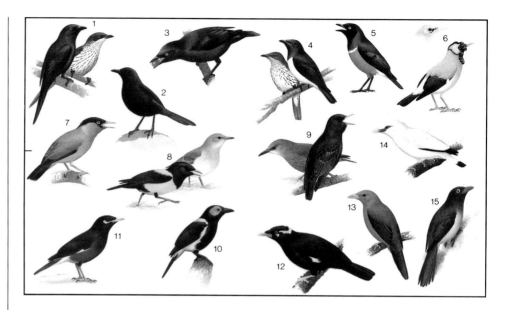

1/ SHINING STARLING
Aplonis metallica

RANGE: **Molucca Islands, Solomon Islands, New Guinea, NE Queensland**
HABITAT: **forest canopy, coastal woodlands, mangroves**
SIZE: **$8\frac{1}{4}$–$9\frac{1}{2}$ in (21–24 cm)**

Shining Starlings nest in trees, in colonies of up to 300 pairs. Each colony takes over a tree and drapes its branches with bulky, pendulous nests woven from plant stems, reminiscent of the nests of some weavers (pp. 346–49) and quite unlike the nests of other starlings. New colonies may be started by young birds which breed in immature plumage.

The Shining Starlings that breed in northern Australia migrate north after the breeding season to spend the winter (May–July) in the forests and mangrove swamps of New Guinea. There they feed alongside the resident birds, flying from tree to tree in great noisy flocks to feast on fruit, nectar and insects.

2/ TRISTRAM'S STARLING
Onychognathus tristramii

RANGE: **Israel, Jordan, Sinai Peninsula, W Arabia**
HABITAT: **rocky country, desolate ravines, spreading into towns**
SIZE: **$9\frac{3}{4}$ in (25 cm)**

In wild country, Tristram's Starling nests in rock crevices on cliffs and crags, lining the nest cavity with a sparse layer of hair, feathers, leaves and other soft material. Like many birds that are native to rocky areas, it is adapting to life on the artificial "cliffs" and "ledges" of urban areas. It is now beginning to colonize towns in Israel, where it builds its nests in tall, uninhabited buildings. Its song is sweet and wild, in keeping with its original habitat.

Tristram's Starlings feed in flocks, searching out insects and fruit in wadi beds and among low vegetation. The flocks are larger outside the breeding season and some consist entirely of newly fledged juveniles. Adult females and juveniles resemble mature males, but the head plumage is a duller gray.

3/ SPLENDID GLOSSY STARLING
Lamprotornis splendidus

RANGE: **Senegal W to Ethiopia, S to Angola and Tanzania; S populations winter N**
HABITAT: **tall woodland, secondary forest**
SIZE: **$11\frac{3}{4}$ in (30 cm)**

This large member of the glossy starling genus *Lamprotornis* is often encountered in the strips of gallery forest bordering river banks. Its wings make a distinctive swishing sound in flight, when its back shows a humped profile. Although it is a rather shy and elusive bird, spending much of its time in the treetops, it is frequently heard uttering a variety of guttural and nasal calls, especially a *quonk quonk* and a *chak*, as well as liquid whistles. It has a wide diet, including many tree fruits. This bird breeds in holes in trees, lining its nest with dried vegetation.

4/ AMETHYST STARLING
Cinnyricinclus leucogaster

RANGE: **SW Arabia, sub-Saharan Africa, South Africa, Gabon, Congo and Zaire**
HABITAT: **rain forest, wooded savanna, woodland edge, parks, gardens**
SIZE: **$6\frac{1}{4}$–7 in (16–18 cm)**

Unusually for starlings, male and female Amethyst Starlings are quite distinct in appearance: in contrast to the gaudy violet and white male, the female, like the juvenile, has mainly brown plumage. They are also less noisy than other species, despite being highly gregarious. They nest in tree holes, lining the cavity with feathers, soft plant material and even animal dung.

In some parts of their range these starlings are year-round residents. Elsewhere they are nomadic, or even migratory, although they do not travel far. They have a taste for fruit and flocks of these birds will arrive in an area when the fruit ripens, strip the trees and then disappear. They will also take insects, often hawking for termites on the wing.

5/ SUPERB STARLING
Spreo superbus

RANGE: **SE Sudan, E to Somalia and S to Tanzania**
HABITAT: **open acacia savanna, lawns, farmland**
SIZE: **7 in (18 cm)**

This spectacular-looking starling is a common East African bird. It feeds mainly on the ground, eating a range of seeds, fruits and insects. It will devour food scraps with relish and small flocks will often gather at campsites and hotels to beg for food, which makes it very popular with tourists.

While Superb Starlings will nest in holes like other starlings, they often build large, untidy, domed nests in low thorn bushes. Occasionally a breeding pair is assisted by one or more non-breeding birds which help to feed the chicks. Juveniles can be distinguished by their duller plumage and brown eyes.

6/ WATTLED STARLING
Creatophora cinerea

RANGE: **Ethiopia to Cape Province, Angola**
HABITAT: **open thornbush savanna**
SIZE: **$8\frac{1}{4}$ in (21 cm)**

This stocky, short-tailed bird undergoes dramatic changes in the breeding season: the male loses his head feathers, exposing bare yellow skin, and long black wattles develop on the forehead, crown and throat. The Wattled Starling has been used in medical research. Its ability to resorb its wattles has attracted the attention of cancer specialists, while the annual regrowth of its head feathers has prompted investigations by researchers attempting to find an antidote to human baldness.

Wattled Starlings feed on the ground, being particularly fond of locusts and grasshoppers. The birds are nomadic, huge flocks of them following locust swarms.

They build colonies of large, untidy domed nests in thorn trees. The eggs are pale blue, usually unmarked. This, together with the bird's habits and appearance, suggest a close affinity with the *Sturnus* starlings – indicating that this African species may have an Asian origin.

7/ BLACK-HEADED STARLING
Sturnus pagodarum

RANGE: **Afghanistan, India, Sri Lanka**
HABITAT: **woodland, scrub, farmland, gardens**
SIZE: **$8\frac{1}{2}$ in (22 cm)**

The Black-headed, or Brahminy, Starling has a varied diet. It is fond of feeding on nectar, which it extracts from flowers with its brush-tipped tongue. In the process its bill becomes dusted with pollen, which it carries to other flowers, and the bird is believed to have an important role as a pollinator of nectar-producing trees. It also eats fruit and seeds and may be an important agent in the dispersal of sandalwood (*Santalum album*) seeds. Adult birds are distinguished by their glossy black caps, crowned with elongated feathers that can be raised in a crest.

8/ ROSE-COLORED STARLING
Sturnus roseus

RANGE: **E Europe and WC Asia; migrates to India in winter**
HABITAT: **arid lowlands, steppes, hills; winters on grassland, farmland, thornbush**
SIZE: **9 in (23 cm)**

The locust-devouring habits of this bird have been appreciated for centuries. The starlings gather in large flocks wherever locusts are abundant and may settle to breed in the area. If the locusts fail to appear in subsequent years, the starlings stay away as well and may not return to breed for several seasons.

Despite this, they are not exclusively locust-eaters. They will prey on other insects and also eat fruits, seeds and nectar; occasionally a flock will cause extensive damage to a fruit crop.

Rose-colored Starlings have an unusual migration pattern: instead of flying north–south like most temperate birds, they migrate east–west. In some years, they undergo irruptions, moving in much larger numbers farther west than usual and reaching western Europe.

9/ EUROPEAN STARLING
Sturnus vulgaris

RANGE: **Europe and W Asia; introduced to North America, South Africa, S Australia, New Zealand**
HABITAT: **open woods, parks, gardens, towns**
SIZE: **8¼ in (21 cm)**

From a distance the adult has a dark, nondescript appearance, but a closer look reveals a beautiful iridescent adult plumage of blue, violet, green and bronze. The feathers have pale buff tips, giving the bird a spotted appearance, especially after the annual molt in fall. By the time the breeding season approaches, these pale tips have become worn away and the plumage is much glossier and, especially in the male, iridescent. Also, the legs change color from brown to reddish-pink and the bill changes from dark brown to yellow, with a creamy pink base in females and a steel-blue base in males.

The European Starling is an adaptable opportunist with a broad diet and a complex, variable breeding system which encompasses monogamy, polygamy, mate exchange and nest parasitism. This may account for its success as a colonist. In North America, for example, it is one of the most numerous birds, but these are all descendants of some 120 birds released in New York a century ago, which have since increased a millionfold.

10/ BALD STARLING
Sarcops calvus

RANGE: **Philippines, Sulu Islands**
HABITAT: **farmland, gardens**
SIZE: **8½ in (22 cm)**

The Bald Starling, or Coleto, has large areas of bare skin around its eyes, separated by a narrow line of short bristly feathers on the crown. This "baldness" is an extreme example of a trend found in several other Philippine and Sulawesi starlings in the genus *Basilornis*.

The Bald Starling breeds in tree holes, which are usually abandoned woodpecker nests, and feeds mainly on fruit. Its call is a metallic click, but in the Philippines, where it is kept as a cage bird, it is said to be capable of mimicking human speech.

11/ COMMON MYNAH
Acridotheres tristis

RANGE: **Afghanistan, India and Sri Lanka to Burma; currently extending its range to Malaysia and USSR; introduced to South Africa, New Zealand, Australia**
HABITAT: **farmland, parks, towns**
SIZE: **9 in (23 cm)**

The Common Mynah has learned how to profit from association with humans and as human habitation spreads, so does the range of the bird. It has a celebrated delectation for locusts and it has been introduced to many places, especially tropical islands, in the hope that it would control insect pests. Unfortunately, the bird has become a pest itself in most areas, by eating fruit.

This jaunty bird shows a conspicuous white wing patch in flight and often makes its presence felt through its loud fluty calls. Daytime flocks assemble in large communal roosts at night, and the large trees in which they sleep are the stage for a raucous musical chorus at dawn and dusk.

12/ HILL MYNAH
Gracula religiosa

RANGE: **India and Sri Lanka to Malaysia and Indonesia**
HABITAT: **mountain forests, especially in foothills**
SIZE: **11½ in (29 cm)**

Few birds can challenge the Hill Mynah's skill as a mimic and it is widely kept in captivity for its ability to learn phrases of human speech. Paradoxically, it never imitates the calls of other bird species in the wild, although it will mimic the songs of neighboring Hill Mynahs. It has a wide repertoire of calls and is generally noisy and gregarious, associating in small groups outside the breeding season.

Hill Mynahs normally feed in the trees on fruit – especially figs – as well as on nectar, insects and small lizards. They nest in tree holes, often using old woodpecker nests, and this habit has been exploited in Assam where bamboo nest-boxes are erected so that chicks can be gathered for the pet trade.

13/ GROSBEAK STARLING
Scissirostrum dubium

RANGE: **Sulawesi (Celebes)**
HABITAT: **open woodland**
SIZE: **8 in (20 cm)**

These starlings live in large flocks which forage through the treetops searching for fruit and nectar. They also form dense breeding colonies in dying trees, using their large bills to excavate pear-shaped nest-holes in the tree trunks. These wood-boring habits have given this species its alternative name of Woodpecker Starling. The protractor muscles in the skull are particularly well developed, serving as a shock absorber during the birds' tree-boring activities, as in the completely unrelated woodpeckers (pp. 214–21). There may be more than 50 nests per colony, each only 12–20 in (30–50 cm) apart; the nest trees are often so weakened by the holes that they collapse.

Grosbeak Starlings are handsome birds with red, waxy tail feathers on their rumps. They will breed in captivity and have recently attracted the interest of aviculturalists, but the trade in these birds will have to be closely controlled to ensure their survival in the wild.

14/ ROTHSCHILD'S MYNAH
Leucopsar rothschildi E

RANGE: **NW Bali**
HABITAT: **wooded grassland, woodland**
SIZE: **8½ in (22 cm)**

With a wild population of fewer than 200 birds, Rothschild's Mynah (also known as the Bali Starling) is the rarest member of the starling family. It had a limited range when it was first recorded in 1911, occurring only on the northern coast of Bali, but since then its habitat has been cut back even more by agricultural development.

This bird's striking appearance and its ability to erect the long crest on its head have always attracted collectors and trapping for the cage-bird trade may have contributed to its decline. Much of its diet consists of large insects taken from the ground but it also eats small reptiles and fruit.

15/ RED-BILLED OXPECKER
Buphagus erythrorhynchus

RANGE: **Eritrea to South Africa**
HABITAT: **savanna with grazing mammals**
SIZE: **7–7½ in (18–19 cm)**

The oxpeckers are placed in a different subfamily from the rest of the starlings. They feed chiefly on the ticks that infest the skins of cattle and other grazing mammals such as zebras, antelopes and rhinos. They have short legs and sharp claws which enable them to cling to the hide of the moving animals while they rid them of the parasitic ticks.

There are 2 species: the Red-billed Oxpecker and the more widely distributed Yellow-billed Oxpecker, also found in west Africa. Both are sociable birds that feed in flocks and retreat to communal roosts at night. They nest in tree holes.

In recent years the adoption of chemical tick control for domestic cattle in Africa has reduced the oxpeckers' food supply and they are fewer and less widespread than before. Ways of reversing this decline are currently under investigation.

ORIOLES AND FIGBIRDS, DRONGOS, NEW ZEALAND WATTLEBIRDS, MAGPIE-LARKS, AUSTRALIAN MUD-NESTERS, WOOD SWALLOWS, BELL MAGPIES

GOLDEN ORIOLE ♀

♂

MAROON ORIOLE

♀

BLACK ORIOLE

race *rufusater*

SADDLEBACK

race *carunculatus*
imm

race *carunculatus*
"Jack-bird"

WHITE-WINGED CHOUGH

♀

HUIA

♂

PIED CURRAWONG

♀ MAGPIE-LARK

♂

FAMILIES ORIOLIDAE, DICRURIDAE, CALLAEIDAE, GRALLINIDAE, CORCORACIDAE, ARTAMIDAE, CRACTICIDAE

race *vieilloti*
"Green Figbird"
♂

race *vieilloti*
♀

FIGBIRD

race *flaviventris*
"Yellow Figbird"
♂

GREATER
RACKET-TAILED
DRONGO

HAIR-CRESTED
DRONGO

MASKED WOODSWALLOW
♂
♀

race *hypoleuca*
"White-backed Magpie"
♂

race *tibicen*
"Black-backed Magpie" ♂

AUSTRALIAN MAGPIE

CRESTED DRONGO

355

ORIOLES AND FIGBIRDS, DRONGOS, NEW ZEALAND WATTLEBIRDS, MAGPIE-LARKS, AUSTRALIAN MUD-NESTERS, WOOD SWALLOWS, BELL MAGPIES

FAMILY ORIOLIDAE
Orioles and Figbird

Medium, starlinglike, tree-dwellers. Males usually black and yellow or other striking colors, females duller. Nest slung from branches high in tree, deep cup (orioles) or shallow, untidy cup (Figbird). Eggs 2–4, white, buff or pink with dark spots or blotches (orioles); usually 3, greenish, with purplish or brown markings (Figbird). Incubation and nestling periods 14–15 days for Golden Oriole; unknown for other species. 26 species.

1/ GOLDEN ORIOLE
Oriolus oriolus

RANGE: Europe, Asia, extreme NW Africa; Asian populations resident, others winter in tropical Africa
HABITAT: breeds in open deciduous woodland, parks, orchards and olive groves; winters in open forest
SIZE: 9¾ in (25 cm)

Despite the brilliant gold and black coloration of his plumage, the secretive male Golden Oriole is surprisingly well camouflaged in the strongly dappled shadows of the woodland canopy. However, he draws attention to himself with his melodious, fluting *weela-weeoo* call.

Golden Orioles use their sharp, stout beaks to feed on insects and fruit. They spend most of their time in the trees, either alone or in pairs, only rarely descending to ground level to feed on fallen fruit. The nest is a masterpiece – an intricately woven grass hammock slung by its rim between 2 twigs. The female carries out most of the nest-building, as well as the most of the incubation and feeding of the young.

2/ BLACK ORIOLE
Oriolus husii

RANGE: Borneo, Sulawesi (Celebes)
HABITAT: mountain forest
SIZE: 8½ in (22 cm)

The Black Oriole is a denizen of upland forests, reaching altitudes of some 3,300 ft (1,000 m). Above this limit, it appears to be replaced by its ecological counterpart, the Black-and-crimson Oriole O. cruentus.

Agile and active, Black Orioles move through the canopy in small bands, feeding on small fruits and insects, including foraging ants and termites. The bird's almost all-black plumage is offset by a rich chestnut patch beneath the tail which is surprisingly conspicuous when viewed from the forest floor. Because of its remote haunts, little is known of the nesting habits of this species.

3/ MAROON ORIOLE
Oriolus traillii

RANGE: Himalayan foothills, S China, much of Southeast Asia
HABITAT: forests up to 10,000 ft (3,000 m)
SIZE: 9¾ in (25 cm)

Although the Maroon Oriole sometimes descends into low bushes or onto the forest floor, it is essentially a canopy bird, feeding on small fruits, insects and, occasionally, flower nectar. It is

often solitary but birds sometimes gather in small groups.

The Maroon Oriole has a great variety of calls, including a simple warbling song, a mewing, catlike call and a rattling laugh. It is more often heard than seen and, in poor light, the distinctive maroon plumage of the male's body often appears as dark as his blue-black head, throat and wings. However, the paler maroon tail is usually visible, especially as the bird flares its tail when it comes to land on a branch. The nest is a deep, bulky cup of woven plant fibers, bound with spiders' webs, suspended in the horizontal fork of a branch.

4/ FIGBIRD
Sphecotheres viridis

RANGE: N and E Australia, New Guinea
HABITAT: rain forest, eucalyptus forest, parks, gardens
SIZE: 11 in (28 cm)

The plumage of the male Figbird varies across the bird's range. In the northern race *S. v. flaviventris*, the underparts are yellow, while the Green Figbird *S. v. vieilloti* from eastern Asutralia has a green belly and a gray throat. Hybridization occurs where these 2 forms meet, and birds with yellow, gray, green or white throats may be seen.

The natural habitat of the Figbird is forest, but it has become one of the most common urban birds in many parts of its range. It eats a wide variety of fruit, both wild and cultivated, as well as some insects. The shallow nest is composed of thin twigs, grass and plant tendrils, placed toward the end of a slender branch, and is often so flimsy that the eggs are visible inside against the light.

FAMILY DICRURIDAE
Drongos

Small to medium tree-dwellers. Short legs. Long, often forked tail. Many with crests. Plumage glossy black or gray. Sexes similar. Shallow, saucer-shaped nests in trees. Eggs 2–4, whitish, often speckled or blotched with brown. Incubation about 16 days for some species, unknown for most species. Nestling period unknown. 22 species.

5/ CRESTED DRONGO
Dicrurus forficatus

RANGE: Madagascar and part of Comoro archipelago
HABITAT: forests, woods, savanna, plantations, coastal scrubland
SIZE: 13 in (33 cm)

The local name for this species, "Drongo," has passed into general usage in English as the name for the whole family. This is a common bird in woodland on Madagascar, preferring the canopy and middle story. It perches in a conspicuous position, ready to dash out for a passing insect or chase away an enemy, for it is an aggressive species: these are traits typical of all drongos. Like many of its relatives, this species has a long, deeply forked tail, which enables it to perform impressive aerobatics in pursuit of its insect prey.

Although rather solitary, the Crested Drongo is a vocal bird, with a wide repertoire of calls and whistles. It is a year-round resident that occurs at all altitudes from sea level to 6,000 ft (1,800 m). Its breeding season is from September to December.

6/ HAIR-CRESTED DRONGO
Dicrurus hottentottus

RANGE: India, S China, Southeast Asia, Philippines, Indonesia
HABITAT: forest and secondary growth
SIZE: 13 in (33 cm)

The fine, curved feathers of this bird's crest are rarely visible in the wild, but the iridescence on the neck and breast gives a distinctive spangled effect. The color of these spangles is variable and is one of the characteristics that distinguishes this widespread species. A close relative, the Spangled Drongo *D. bracteatus* occurs in the Philippines, Moluccas, Australia, New Guinea, New Britain, Solomons and Lesser Sundas.

Noisy and often common birds, Hair-crested Drongos sometimes gather in parties, especially around fruiting and flowering trees, for they are nectar-feeders as well as predators of a wide range of insects. They utter an astonishing medley of musical and fluty calls, as well as some harsh and strident notes.

7/ GREATER RACKET-TAILED DRONGO
Dicrurus paradiseus

RANGE: **India, Sri Lanka, S China, Southeast Asia, Borneo**
HABITAT: **open forest, woodland edge, tea plantations**
SIZE: **13¾ in (35 cm)**

This is a spectacular drongo, with a full, curving crest and extraordinary, wirelike tail streamers, up to 13¾ in (35 cm) long, tipped with broad "rackets." In flight, the rackets give the appearance of 2 small birds or bees trailing bouncily along behind. In one of the 2 Sri Lankan races, *D.p. lophorinus*, however, the elongated tail feathers are shorter and broader without rackets, being fully vaned along their length.

The Greater Racket-tailed Drongo is primarily insectivorous, catching its prey in flight as well as taking it from the ground or among foliage. It often accompanies troupes of monkeys, feeding on the insects they disturb. It is noisy all year round, with a wide range of metallic and fluty notes and some bell-like calls. It is also a persistent and gifted mimic of other birds, squirrels and other animals.

FAMILY CALLAEIDAE
New Zealand wattlebirds

Medium, strong-legged. Colored, fleshy wattles. Plumage mainly black or gray. Sexes almost alike (wattles larger in males) except for Huia. Shallow, open nest among branches or in tree hollow. Eggs 2–4, whitish with purple-brown blotches and spots. Incubation 18–25 days. Nestling period known for Kokako *Callaeas cinerea*: 27–28 days. 3 species (1 probably extinct).

8/ SADDLEBACK
Philesturnus carunculatus

RANGE: **offshore islands of New Zealand**
HABITAT: **forests**
SIZE: **9¾ in (25 cm)**

This species was once widespread in New Zealand but now occurs only on about 10 offshore islands. It was reintroduced to most of these after non-native browsing and predatory mammals had been removed. The race *P.c. rufusater*, originally from North Island, has a gold band across the front of the red-brown "saddle," which the South Island race *P.c. carunculatus* lacks.

Saddlebacks have small wings and weak flight. However, their legs are strong and they run and hop through the trees rather than fly. They feed mainly on insects, probing for them under bark or tearing apart rotting wood. They also eat some fruit and nectar.

A close relative, the Huia *Heteralocha acutirostris*, is unique among birds for the remarkable difference in bill shape between the sexes. The male's straight bill is adapted for hammering open rotting wood to expose grubs, while the female's thin, curved bill is ideal for probing crevices. The Huia is almost certainly extinct, perhaps partly as a result of hunting: Maoris killed them for their tail feathers and settlers collected their skins, but habitat destruction was probably the main reason for their disappearance. The Huia was last seen alive in 1907.

FAMILY GRALLINIDAE
Magpie-larks

Small to medium. Plumage black and white. Sexes differ slightly. Mud nests. Eggs 3–5, white to pink, blotched red and brown. Incubation 17–18 days and nestling period 18–23 days (Magpie-Lark). 2 species.

9/ MAGPIE-LARK
Grallina cyanoleuca

RANGE: **Australia**
HABITAT: **open pasture and grassland**
SIZE: **10½ in (27 cm)**

The black and white Magpie-Lark is most abundant on farmland, where it feeds on the ground on insects, snails and other invertebrates. It also frequents the edges of lakes and ponds and has become common in towns, where it is often seen feeding alongside busy roads, seemingly oblivious to the traffic. It has a loud *pee-wee* call, which gives it one of its popular names; another is Mudlark, from its nest.

The clearance of forests and the provision of water in dry regions have probably encouraged this species. However, its population has declined in some areas, perhaps because the water has become too saline or because the snails have been poisoned in an effort to control liver flukes.

FAMILY CORCORACIDAE
Australian mud-nesters

Medium to large, strong-legged ground birds. Plumage sooty black with white wing patch, or gray, brown and black. Sexes alike. Mud nests. Eggs 2–5, cream or white, with brown, black and gray blotches. Incubation 18–19 days, nestling period 13–25 days. 2 species.

10/ WHITE-WINGED CHOUGH
Corcorax melanorhamphos

RANGE: **Australia**
HABITAT: **open woodland**
SIZE: **17¾ in (45 cm)**

These birds are black, with white "windows" in the center of the wings. The adults have brilliant red irises that become expanded when the birds are excited. They live in open, grassy eucalyptus woodland, feeding on the ground, turning over leaf litter and cowpats in search of large invertebrates, and sometimes eating grain.

White-winged Choughs are highly social and cooperative, living in groups of 3–12 birds. They may join even larger flocks in winter when they wander outside their breeding grounds. Several birds help to construct the mud nest, and when the young hatch, all group members help to feed them. Occasionally 2 females may lay a total of up to 10 eggs in the same nest.

FAMILY ARTAMIDAE
Woodswallows

Small to medium, aerial birds. Short legs, long wings. Plumage black, gray or brown, and white with chestnut in 1 species. Sexes differ in some species. Flimsy cup nest of sticks. Eggs 2–4, white or cream, spotted red-brown. Incubation 12–16 days, nestling period 16–20 days. 10 species.

11/ MASKED WOODSWALLOW
Artamus personatus

RANGE: **Australia**
HABITAT: **woodland and shrubland**
SIZE: **7½ in (19 cm)**

Woodswallows are related to bell magpies, but have taken to aerial feeding. They are long-winged, but short-tailed, and resemble bee-eaters (pp. 202–205) in their manner of feeding.

Masked Woodswallows occur throughout inland Australia. They tend to move south in spring, in some years extending well beyond their usual range. They feed mostly on aerial insects, but occasionally glean prey from the ground, taking small locusts and ants. They may even feed on the nectar from eucalyptus and mistletoes.

FAMILY CRACTICIDAE
Bell magpies

Medium to large, strong build. Heavy, hooked bill. Plumage gray, white and black. Sexes differ in some species. Nests in trees. Eggs 3–5, blue or green, brown blotches and streaks. Incubation 20 days, nestling period 28 days. 10 species.

12/ AUSTRALIAN MAGPIE
Gymnorhina tibicen

RANGE: **Australia, S New Guinea; introduced to New Zealand**
HABITAT: **woodland and grassland**
SIZE: **15¾ in (40 cm)**

The plumage on the back of the Australian Magpie varies according to race. For example, the race *G.t. tibicen*, often called the Black-backed Magpie, from central and northern Australia, differs markedly from the race *G.t. hypoleuca*, often called the White-backed Magpie, from southern Australia and Tasmania.

Australian Magpies eat scarab beetle larvae and other invertebrates, listening for them in the soil and then digging them up with their strong, pointed bills. These birds have a complex social organization, linked to habitat. Permanent groups, with a high breeding success, live in prime habitat with trees and grassland. More transitory groups live in poorer-quality sites, and nonbreeding flocks may occupy the areas of grassland with the fewest trees.

13/ PIED CURRAWONG
Strepera graculina

RANGE: **E Australia**
HABITAT: **forest and woodland**
SIZE: **18 in (46 cm)**

This species is primarily a tree-dweller. The name currawong comes from one of the bird's calls, but it utters a wide variety of other loud and often musical sounds. Pied Currawongs tend to inhabit forests in the breeding season, where they snatch stick insects and other large arthropods from the foliage. They are also nest-robbers, and may have a major impact on the breeding success of other birds. In winter, large numbers move into towns, where they feed on berries. Their numbers have increased with the introduction of many new berry-producing plants; by dispersing seeds, the birds have helped to spread these exotic plants.

BOWERBIRDS, BIRDS OF PARADISE

SPOTTED CATBIRD

VOGELKOP
GARDENER
BOWERBIRD

♂ SATIN BOWERBIRD

♀

♂ courtship
display

TRUMPET MANUCODE

♀

♂

♀

MAGNIFICENT RIFLEBIRD

TWELVE-WIRED BIRD OF PARADISE

♀

KING BIRD OF PARADISE

♂

♀

♂ race raggiana

♂

courtship display

SUPERB BIRD OF PARADISE

RAGGIANA BIRD OF PARAD

GREAT GRAY
BOWERBIRD

♀

courtship
display

♂

race *nuchalis*

♀

SICKLE-CRESTED BIRD OF PARADISE

♂

RIBBON-TAILED BIRD OF PARADISE

♂

♀

♂ courtship display

♀

KING OF SAXONY
BIRD OF PARADISE

♀

courtship display
♂

courtship display

BLUE BIRD OF PARADISE

359

BOWERBIRDS, BIRDS OF PARADISE

FAMILY PTILONORHYNCHIDAE
Bowerbirds

Medium, stout with strong bills. Males of 9 species brighter than females; otherwise drab brown, gray or green. Males of most species construct ornate "bowers" to which females are attracted for mating; the females build the bulky cup-shaped nests alone. Eggs 1–2, plain white to buff or blotched at larger end. Incubation 19–24 days, nestling period 18–21 days. 18 species.

1/ SPOTTED CATBIRD
Ailuroedus melanotis

RANGE: **New Guinea, 3,000–6,000 ft (900–1,800 m); Misool and Aru islands; NE Australia**
HABITAT: **rain forest**
SIZE: **11½ in (29 cm)**

Most male bowerbirds will attempt to mate with several females each season, attracting them to their elaborate bowers by their showy plumage and ritualized courtship. By contrast, the 3 species of catbird are monogamous, the males do not build bowers and the sexes look alike.

The Spotted Catbird is typical: each pair defends a breeding territory and, although the female builds the nest, both male and female share the job of feeding the young.

Named for their catlike, wailing calls, catbirds have a broad diet, ranging from fruit and leaves to insects, small reptiles and nestlings.

2/ VOGELKOP GARDENER BOWERBIRD
Amblyornis inornatus

RANGE: **W Irian Jaya (New Guinea), 3,300–6,600 ft (1,000–2,000 m)**
HABITAT: **lower mountain rain forest**
SIZE: **10 in (25 cm)**

Among bowerbirds, the species with the least ornate plumage generally build the most impressive bowers. The male Vogelkop Gardener Bowerbird is particularly drab, but his bower is the most spectacular of all: a miniature tepee of sticks built over a mat of moss which the bird collects and decorates with colorful fruits and flowers. He then attracts potential mates – and warns off other males – by mimicking bird calls and other sounds.

The nesting biology of this species is unknown, but the females of other gardener bowerbirds build their nests and raise their young alone.

3/ SATIN BOWERBIRD
Ptilonorhynchus violaceus

RANGE: **E Australia**
HABITAT: **rain forest, rain forest edge; adjacent open vegetation in winter**
SIZE: **12 in (30 cm)**

This is probably the best known of all the bowerbirds. The male builds an "avenue" with walls of sticks placed upright in a stick mat. He sometimes daubs the walls with a paste of chewed fruit or charcoal, often applying it with a wad of plant fiber held in his bill.

As a finishing touch he adorns the mat with trinkets, showing a marked preference for blue

flowers, blue feathers, blue bottle-tops, indeed anything blue. This taste reflects his own elegant bluish-black coloration, which takes 6–7 years to develop and provides a marked contrast to the female's sober grayish-green plumage, which helps camouflage her on her nest among the vegetation.

4/ GREAT GRAY BOWERBIRD
Chlamydera nuchalis

RANGE: **N Australia and adjacent islands**
HABITAT: **riverside and open savanna woods, eucalyptus and melaleuca woods, vine thickets, well-foliaged suburbia**
SIZE: **14 in (36 cm)**

This is the largest of the bowerbirds and is generally found in drier, more open habitats than the other species. The male sports a lilac nape crest which he erects during the courtship display. Some females have similar crests, but this is unusual. The race illustrated, *C.n. nuchalis* from northeast Western Australia to northwest Queensland, has more uniform, grayer upperparts than the other race.

Like many bowerbirds, Great Gray Bowerbirds are good mimics. Males imitate bird calls and other sounds, and both sexes mimic the calls of predatory birds near their bowers and nests. They feed mainly on fruit and insects, being particularly fond of figs and grasshoppers, but they will also eat small lizards.

FAMILY PARADISAEIDAE
Birds of paradise

Medium, stout, strong-legged with very varied bills. Most males have spectacular plumage; females drab. Nest usually cup- or dome-shaped. Eggs 1–2, pale, spotted, blotched or smudged mainly at larger end. Incubation 17–21 days, nestling period 17–30 days. 42 species.

5/ SICKLE-CRESTED BIRD OF PARADISE
Cnemophilus macgregorii

RANGE: **C, S and E highlands of New Guinea, 8,000–11,500 ft (2,400–3,500 m)**
HABITAT: **cloud forest**
SIZE: **10 in (25 cm)**

Whereas male bowerbirds use art to attract potential mates, many birds of paradise rely on the incomparable beauty of their plumage, which is often ornamented with long, decorative tail and crest feathers. The race illustrated, *C.m. sanguineus* from Mount Hagen, has orange-red upperparts; one of the 2 others has cinnamon-yellow upperparts.

The Sickle-crested Bird of Paradise is a fruit-eating species named for its unique crest of fine filaments. The male birds probably display to passing groups of females at solitary arenas, but this has never been described. The nest, built by the female, is a bulky dome of mosses and leaves on a stick foundation and is much more elaborate than the nests of other species.

6/ TRUMPET MANUCODE
Manucodia keraudrenii

RANGE: **New Guinea and islands to E and W, 650–6,600 ft (200–2,000 m); tip of Cape York Peninsula, NE Australia**
HABITAT: **rain forest canopy**
SIZE: **11 in (28 cm)**

The 5 species of manucode breed as stable pairs instead of mating polygamously in the family tradition. Accordingly, male and female birds are very similar, with uniform metallic blue-black plumage. They share the duties of incubating the eggs and feeding the young but, unusually, they do not defend their nesting territories.

They are primarily fruit-eaters and the Trumpet Manucode, or Trumpet Bird, feeds mainly on figs. The bird is named for the loud, mournful, trumpeting call produced by the male during his courtship display, after he has chased his prospective mate through the trees.

7/ MAGNIFICENT RIFLEBIRD
Ptiloris magnificus

RANGE: **New Guinea lowlands and hills to 2,300 ft (700 m), rarely higher; tip of Cape York Peninsula, NE Australia**
HABITAT: **rain forest, forest edge**
SIZE: **13 in (33 cm)**

There are 3 species of riflebird, of which this is the most impressive. The male is promiscuous, defending a territory from a visible perch which he uses for displaying. This involves raising his rounded wings and swaying his head from side to side while emitting a powerful whistle, which is said to sound like a passing bullet – hence the species' name.

Riflebirds have strong feet which they use for climbing and for clinging to tree trunks while they probe dead wood for insects. In addition, they often use their feet to hold food on the perch while tearing it apart.

8/ TWELVE-WIRED BIRD OF PARADISE
Seleucidis melanoleuca

RANGE: **New Guinea lowlands; Salawati Island**
HABITAT: **seasonally flooded rain forest dominated by sago and pandanus palm**
SIZE: **13½ in (34 cm)**

Adult males of this long-billed, short-tailed bird are spectacularly plumaged in iridescent purple-black and sulfur-yellow, with long "wires" curving up from the flank plumes. The females are drab by comparison, as with all the birds of paradise that breed polygamously.

The males are rarely observed except during the courtship season, when they display from bare branches high in the forest. A displaying male erects the feathers of his upper breast into a large black "shield", edged with iridescent emerald green feathers; at the same time, his elongated yellow flank plumes are expanded and the 12 wires extend forward. The few nests that have been found were built in the tops of trees and each contained a single egg.

9/ RIBBON-TAILED BIRD OF PARADISE
Astrapia mayeri [?]

RANGE: **New Guinea, W central highlands, 8,000–11,200 ft (2,400–3,400 m)**
HABITAT: **lower mountain rain forest**
SIZE: **53 in (135 cm)**

This was the last bird of paradise to be discovered by ornithologists, being initially described in 1939 on the basis of a pair of the male's long, ribbonlike central tail feathers found in a tribal headdress. Up to 39 in (1 m) long, these impressive plumes are twitched from side to side during a display which may attract several females to the male's perch high in the trees.

These birds have a broad diet, including fruits, insects, spiders, small mammals and reptiles.

10/ SUPERB BIRD OF PARADISE
Lophorina superba

RANGE: **mountains of New Guinea, 4,000–7,500 ft (1,200–2,300 m)**
HABITAT: **rain forest and forest edge**
SIZE: **10 in (25 cm)**

All the polygamous birds of paradise have intriguing courtship rituals, but few are as curious as the display of this fine-billed species. The male is equipped with highly modified breast plumage that flares into a "winged" display shield. This is mirrored behind the bird's head by a velvety cape of elongated nape feathers that fans around to meet the breast shield, giving a bizarre circular effect.

The males often display in the tops of trees but recent observations suggest that the birds also display and mate near the forest floor.

11/ KING OF SAXONY BIRD OF PARADISE
Pteridophora alberti

RANGE: **central ranges of New Guinea, 5,000–9,500 ft (1,500–2,850 m)**
HABITAT: **cloud forest**
SIZE: **8¾ in (22 cm)**

An adult male of this species presents an extraordinary appearance, having 2 head plumes up to 19¾ in (50 cm) long extending from behind his eyes. Each wirelike plume shaft is decorated along one side with small sky-blue lobes that look like little plastic flags.

During the courtship display the bird holds his plumes aloft while bounding up and down, hissing loudly. He greets a receptive female with a sweep of the plumes before mating.

12/ KING BIRD OF PARADISE
Cicinnurus regius

RANGE: **New Guinea, up to 1,000 ft (300 m), rarely to 2,800 ft (850 m)**
HABITAT: **rain forest and forest edge**
SIZE: **6¼ in (16 cm)**

Although basically a solitary species, like most of its family, the King Bird of Paradise often feeds with other bird species, gleaning insects and other small animals from foliage and bark beneath the canopy of the rain forest. It also eats fruit.

The female has inconspicuous olive-brown plumage, but males are mainly iridescent blood-red and white. This makes for a spectacular treetop display, but also renders the bird very vulnerable to attack by cruising predators. It is a risk shared by many of these flamboyant birds, but is evidently worthwhile in evolutionary terms. In one of the male's displays, he expands his breast fan and puffs up the feathers of his underparts so that he appears almost spherical. He then raises his long, wirelike tail shafts so that the green rackets at their tips are above his head, and raises and sways his head from side to side. In another display he hangs upside-down from a perch with wings spread and vibrating and his bill open, to display the bright yellow-green interior of his mouth.

13/ RAGGIANA BIRD OF PARADISE
Paradisaea raggiana

RANGE: **E New Guinea to 6,000 ft (1,800 m)**
HABITAT: **rain forest, forest edge, gardens**
SIZE: **13 in (33 cm)**

Instead of displaying alone, like most of their relatives, male Raggiana Birds of Paradise assemble in groups at traditional treetop arenas, or leks. In practice, 1 or 2 dominant males obtain nearly all the matings in any season and the other males on the lek display in vain.

When females appear at the lek, the males converge on them, calling excitedly and displaying by hopping, flapping their wings noisily and shaking their plumes. This initial frenzy is followed by a quieter but equally breathtaking display, in which each bird attempts to outdo his rivals in showing off his gaudy finery. At the height of their display, the males utter a rapid series of high-pitched nasal calls, rising and falling in pitch and intensity; during the quieter part, they give a single, ringing note. Other calls include a series of loud, raucous, bugling cries, all on one pitch, increasing in volume and slowing in tempo toward the end.

There are 5 races: the one illustrated is *P. r. raggiana* from southeast New Guinea.

14/ BLUE BIRD OF PARADISE
Paradisaea rudolphi [?]

RANGE: **New Guinea, E central highlands, 4,300–6,000 ft (1,300–1,800 m)**
HABITAT: **rain forest, forest edge, gardens**
SIZE: **12 in (30 cm)**

One of the most glorious birds of paradise, this is also one of the most endangered as a consequence of much of its habitat having been cleared for agriculture and housing.

The male displays alone, high in the trees. Uttering low mechanical-sounding cries, including one like radio static, he swings upside down from a branch with his long tail streamers sweeping over in a graceful arc, his magnificent plumes spread in a cascade of opalescent blue. The females probably go off to nest by themselves but the details are uncertain.

BLUE JAY

SCRUB JAY

race *coerulesc*

race *californica*

AZURE-WINGED MAGPIE

SILVERY-THROATED JAY

race *chinensis*

race *margaritae*

race *glandarius*

EURASIAN JAY

GREEN MAGPIE

race *atricapillus*

race *asirensis*

race *bispecularis*

race *pica*

PANDER'S GROUND JAY

BLACK-BILLED MAGPIE

CLARK'S NUTCRACKER

RED-BILLED CHOUGH

juv

WESTERN JACKDAW

juv

PIAPIAC

race *japonensis*

JUNGLE CROW

COMMON RAVEN

PIED CROW

AMERICAN CROW

FAMILY CORVIDAE
Crows

Medium to large, with powerful bills. Often black, but jays brightly colored. Sexes similar. Nests of twigs in trees or shrubs, some in holes. Eggs 2–8, whitish to pale green, blotched. Incubation 16–22 days, nestling period 20–45 days. 113 species.

1/ BLUE JAY
Cyanocitta cristata

RANGE: E North America, from S Canada to Mexican Gulf
HABITAT: deciduous forest, semiwoodland
SIZE: 12 in (30 cm)

Large noisy groups of food-gathering Blue Jays are a familiar sight in the gardens of North America. They hoard seeds and nuts for the winter, burying them in holes. Despite these precautions, Blue Jays in the far north normally migrate south in winter, whereas the southern birds usually stay near their nesting sites.

Although seeds and nuts make up most of its diet, the Blue Jay feeds avidly on insects – particularly the irregular outbreaks of tent moth caterpillars. It will also rob nests of eggs and chicks and take small mammals.

2/ SCRUB JAY
Aphelocoma coerulescens

RANGE: W USA and S to C Mexico; there is an isolated race in Florida
HABITAT: oak scrub in dry semidesert
SIZE: 13 in (33 cm)

Scrub Jays are communal breeders: instead of forming pairs, the birds live in year-round groups of up to a dozen individuals. Each group is based around a single breeding pair, which builds a bulky twig nest at the focus of a well-defined communal territory. The female incubates the eggs while the other birds stand guard or gather food. The young "helpers" – particularly the males – are usually earlier offspring of the breeding pair.

In contrast to western races such as *A. c. californica*, the isolated Florida race *A. c. coerulescens* has a whitish forehead.

3/ SILVERY-THROATED JAY
Cyanolyca argentigula

RANGE: Costa Rica
HABITAT: woodland, from cloud forest to oaks and firs
SIZE: 13 in (33 cm)

Of the 32 species of New World jay, 28 occur in Central America. The Silvery-throated Jay is one of these, and its similarity to many of the other species indicates that they evolved only recently from a common ancestor.

Less sociable than most jays, it is also less garrulous, having a limited repertoire of nasal clicks and squawks. Some reports suggest that it may follow columns of army ants to snap up the insects they disturb.

4/ EURASIAN JAY
Garrulus glandarius

RANGE: W Europe, across Asia to Japan and Southeast Asia
HABITAT: oakwoods, open country with oaks
SIZE: 13 in (33 cm)

The harsh screech of the Eurasian Jay is a familiar sound in European deciduous woodland. The first note is often followed by a second and a third as a family party scours the trees for insects, beech nuts and acorns.

This handsome bird has played a major part in shaping the landscape. The Eurasian Jay's habit of carrying acorns long distances (especially up-hill) and burying them has been an important factor in the dispersal of oak trees, and it is likely that the acorn has evolved to attract the Eurasian Jay. For their part, the birds rely heavily on stored acorns for winter food.

Of the many races, some have distinctive head plumage: those illustrated are *G. g. glandarius* of Europe, *G. g. atricapillus* of the Middle East and *G. g. bispecularis* of the western Himalayas.

5/ GREEN MAGPIE
Cissa chinensis

RANGE: N India to S China, Malaysia, Sumatra, Borneo
HABITAT: evergreen forest, bamboo jungle, forest clearings, gardens
SIZE: 13¾ in (35 cm)

This attractive and extremely active crow occurs in a wide variety of subtly different color phases, grading from brilliant green to a delicate blue. The 2 races illustrated are the widespread *C. c. chinensis*, and *C. c. margaritae*, found only in southern Annam (Vietnam).

The Green Magpie often feeds in mixed flocks with drongos (pp. 354–57) and laughing-thrushes (pp. 274–77), foraging for insects in the trees and on the ground. It will also scavenge for carrion, as well as eating small snakes and lizards, frogs and young birds.

6/ AZURE-WINGED MAGPIE
Cyanopica cyana

RANGE: E Asia, China, Mongolia, Korea, Japan; also S Spain and Portugal
HABITAT: open woodland, gardens, farmland
SIZE: 13 in (33 cm)

This magpie has a very odd distribution, with a virtually continuous series of races spread through eastern Asia and an isolated population in southern Spain and Portugal, some 3,000 mls (5,000 km) away. It is possible that the Iberian birds are descended from birds introduced to Spain or Portugal by early traders with the Far East, but much more likely that the species may have originally occurred throughout southern Eurasia, a range since fragmented by changes in climate (particularly glaciations) and habitat.

Azure-winged Magpies are sociable birds: they usually forage in small groups, roost together (especially in cold climates) and nest in loose colonies, each untidy nest being built in a separate tree or bush.

7/ BLACK-BILLED MAGPIE
Pica pica

RANGE: Eurasia, from W Europe to Japan; temperate North America
HABITAT: open woodland, scrub, farmland, towns
SIZE: 17¾ in (45 cm)

The Black-billed Magpie has a bad reputation for plundering the nests of other birds and it is often shot on sight on estates where there are game-birds. Elsewhere it flourishes, for it is an adaptable bird with a broad diet. It has adapted well to the man-made landscape and is now a familiar sight in suburban gardens. Most races are similar to the race *P. p. pica* of the British Isles, central and eastern Europe, although the race *P. p asirensis* of western Arabia is distinctive: very dark with less white, and a large bill.

Many pairs of Black-billed Magpies stay in their breeding territories throughout the year, but others form small winter flocks which gather at communal roosts for the night.

8/ PANDER'S GROUND JAY
Podoces panderi
RANGE: SW USSR
HABITAT: dry steppe and sandy, scrubby desert; breeds in saxaul bushes
SIZE: 13 in (33 cm)

The ground jays are a distinct group of open-country crows that normally travel by running over the ground instead of flying. Pander's Ground Jay is particularly well adapted to life in semidesert scrubland, for it can obtain all the moisture that it needs from its diet of insects and seeds.

It nests in low trees and bushes, probably using the same site each year. The 3–6 young are naked, blind and helpless when they hatch, but within 2 weeks they can run quite fast. Family parties of these birds wander widely over the plains in fall, calling to each other with loud cries and fluty whistles.

9/ CLARK'S NUTCRACKER
Nucifraga columbiana
RANGE: North America, from British Columbia to N Mexico
HABITAT: mountain conifer forest
SIZE: 13¾ in (35 cm)

Many crows hoard food for the winter but few species rely on the habit as heavily as Clark's Nutcracker. Found in some of the most inhospitable winter habitats endured by any of its family, the bird feeds almost exclusively on the seeds of conifers such as the Ponderosa Pine, extracting them with dexterous use of its powerful, slightly downcurved bill.

It may fly up to 12 mls (20 km) to gather food for its winter store, returning with up to 80 seeds carried in a pouch beneath its tongue. The hoarding sites, on steep, well-drained slopes, are often communal, but each bird makes its own cache and is able to remember its location beneath the winter snows.

10/ RED-BILLED CHOUGH
Pyrrhocorax pyrrhocorax
RANGE: W Europe, through S Asia to China
HABITAT: mountains to 11,500 ft (3,500 m), coastal cliffs, islands
SIZE: 15¾ in (40 cm)

Crows in general are opportunist feeders with broad tastes, but the Red-billed Chough is something of an expert at preying on small insects, particularly ants. It often feeds in small flocks, using its distinctive sharp, curved bill to probe for prey in very short rabbit- or sheep-cropped clifftop or mountain turf. The erosion of this type of habitat by changes in agriculture may be one reason why Red-billed Choughs have become scarce in northwestern Europe over the past 200 years.

Red-billed Choughs are spectacular performers on the wing, with a gloriously buoyant, easy flight. In spring the courting pair takes to the air in a mutual display flight before nesting in a crevice or cave.

11/ PIAPIAC
Ptilostomus afer
RANGE: Africa, from Senegal E to Uganda, Ethiopia, Sudan
HABITAT: open country with palm trees, farmland, towns
SIZE: 15¾ in (40 cm)

This bold, resourceful crow has learned to exploit the activities of other animals for its own ends. Flocks of 10 or more will often forage and scavenge in urban areas, showing little fear of man. In grassland they run after animals such as goats and cattle to catch the creatures disturbed by their grazing. The Piapiac will even pick parasitic mites and ticks from animals' skins and is one of the few bird species tolerated in this way by elephants.

These birds are most active in the morning, and the flocks generally roost in tall trees during the hottest hours of the day. Oil-palm trees are favored, for Piapiacs are very fond of the fruit.

12/ WESTERN JACKDAW
Corvus monedula
RANGE: W Europe, excluding extreme N, to C USSR
HABITAT: woods, parks, gardens, farmland, sea cliffs, towns
SIZE: 13 in (33 cm)

The Western Jackdaw is the smallest of the *Corvus* crows in Europe and one of the most familiar. This is partly because it is a hole-nesting bird that has learned to use the cavities in church towers, chimney stacks and other parts of tall buildings as artificial substitutes for tree holes and rock crevices. It is also common on ocean and inland cliffs and quarries, where it still breeds in more natural surroundings. In such places, its agility in the air can be seen to great advantage.

Western Jackdaws enjoy a broad diet which may include anything from caterpillars to crabs. They also scavenge for refuse and rob the nests of other birds. In spring they collect soft fiber for nesting material and are often seen plucking wool from the backs of sheep.

13/ AMERICAN CROW
Corvus brachyrhynchos
RANGE: North America, from S Canada to New Mexico
HABITAT: woods, parks, farmland
SIZE: 21¾ in (55 cm)

Crows have always been regarded as pests by farmers and the American Crow is no exception. Large flocks will descend on fields of corn, sorghum or peas and inflict serious damage; the farmers retaliate by trapping and poisoning them and, as a result, the birds have become increasingly wary and difficult to control.

The American Crow's caution extends to its nesting habits. The pairs nest singly, but the male often builds a whole series of "false nests" high in the treetops, which seem designed to decoy and confuse potential predators.

14/ JUNGLE CROW
Corvus macrorhynchos
RANGE: Asia, from Afghanistan to Japan, SE to Philippines
HABITAT: woods, semicultivated land, more rarely open country
SIZE: 19 in (48 cm)

The intelligence and cunning of the Jungle Crow are well known to travelers across central Asia, for their campsites are often raided by this powerful, large-billed scavenger. There are a number of races, of which *C. m. japonensis*, found in Japan and Sakhalin Island, is the largest and thickest billed.

Strongly territorial, it will steal scraps of meat and hoard them in caches dispersed around its home range, often making use of urban drainpipes, roofspaces and window ledges. These caches may also contain dead chicks, for the bird is a notorious nest-robber.

15/ PIED CROW
Corvus albus
RANGE: sub-Saharan Africa, Madagascar
HABITAT: open and semiopen country, forest clearings, urban areas
SIZE: 17¾ in (45 cm)

Although most of its diet consists of seeds and insects taken from the ground, the Pied Crow is most commonly seen congregating around carcasses or garbage dumps. It is a bold bird with little fear of humans or larger predators, and it is an eager mobber of African eagles and buzzards.

Its young stay in the nest a long time – they take 40 days to fledge – and the parents often fail to keep up the food supply. As a result, few pairs raise more than 3 young out of a clutch of up to 6 eggs. Many are also parasitized by Great Spotted Cuckoos. The cuckoo chicks hatch sooner, and are more vigorous and aggressive than the Pied Crow chicks, which may starve, although usually some are raised alongside the intruders.

16/ COMMON RAVEN
Corvus corax
RANGE: North America, except SE; Asia, except Southeast Asia and India; N Africa to S Sahara
HABITAT: sparsely inhabited landscapes: high mountains, sea coasts, tundra
SIZE: 25 in (64 cm)

The Common Raven is the largest, most powerful and most predatory of the crows. As big as a buzzard, it is quite capable of killing and eating a rabbit, but reports of Common Ravens attacking sheep and lambs are greatly exaggerated. Their main food is carrion, and many Common Ravens will gather around a large carcass to tear at the flesh with their heavy bills.

Like many other crows, they hoard food for the winter, but because there is usually plenty of carrion to be had, they are not greatly affected by harsh winters. If anything, they flourish, and they often nest in late winter when the mortality of local birds and mammals is at its peak.

This checklist includes all the world's bird species, arranged in taxonomic sequence by order, family and genus to indicate the relationships between them. English names reflect general usage as far as possible, but inevitably they are often a matter of choice and sometimes reflect the preferences of the editor. The letter "I" in an English name is an abbreviation for "Island" and "Is" for "Islands." The bold letters immediately following the names of the birds indicate their range (*see map and key*), while the symbols associated with some of the species refer to their conservation status as determined by the International Council for Bird Preservation (*for key, see page 41*).

KEY TO MAP
A NEARCTIC
B PALEARCTIC
C ETHIOPIAN (AFROTROPICAL)
D INDIAN OCEAN
E CENTRAL AMERICAN
F SOUTH AMERICAN
G GALAPAGOS
H INDO-PAKISTANI
I INDO-CHINESE
J MALAYAN
K INDONESIAN
L PAPUAN

M AUSTRALIAN
N NEW ZEALAND
O PACIFIC
P HAWAIIAN
Q ANTARCTIC

Shaded areas indicate where regions overlap.

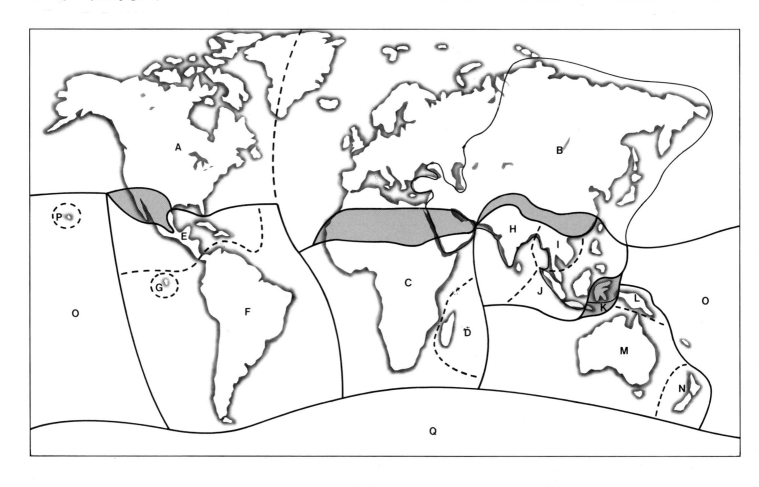

STRUTHIONIFORMES

1 STRUTHIONIDAE (OSTRICH)
STRUTHIO
S. camelus (Ostrich) **B,C**

RHEIFORMES

2 RHEIDAE (RHEAS)
RHEA
R. americana (Greater Rhea) **F**
PTEROCNEMIA
P. pennata (Lesser Rhea) **F**

CASUARIIFORMES

3 CASUARIIDAE (CASSOWARIES)
CASUARIUS
C. casuarius (Double-wattled Cassowary) **L,M**
C. bennetti (Dwarf Cassowary) **L**
C. unappendiculatus (One-wattled Cassowary) **K,L**
4 DROMAIIDAE (EMUS)
ROMAIUS
D. novaehollandiae (Emu) **M**

APTERYGIFORMES

5 APTERYGIDAE (KIWIS)
APTERYX
A. australis (Brown Kiwi) **N**
A. owenii (Little Spotted Kiwi) **N**   ?
A. haastii (Great Spotted Kiwi) **N**

TINAMIFORMES

6 TINAMIDAE (TINAMOUS)
TINAMUS
T. tao (Gray Tinamou) **F**
T. solitarius (Solitary Tinamou) **F**   ?
T. osgoodi (Black Tinamou) **F**   ?
T. major (Great Tinamou) **E,F**
T. guttatus (White-throated Tinamou) **F**
NOTHOCERCUS
N. bonapartei (Highland Tinamou) **E,F**
N. julius (Tawny-breasted Tinamou) **F**
N. nigrocapillus (Hooded Tinamou) **F**
CRYPTURELLUS
C. cinereus (Cinereous Tinamou) **F**

C. berlepschi (Berlepsch's Tinamou) **F**
C. soui (Little Tinamou) **E,F**
C. ptaritepui (Tepui Tinamou) **F**
C. obsoletus (Brown Tinamou) **F**
C. undulatus (Undulated Tinamou) **F**
C. transfasciatus (Pale-browed Tinamou) **F**
C. strigulosus (Brazilian Tinamou) **F**
C. duidae (Gray-legged Tinamou) **F**
C. erythropus (Red-footed Tinamou) **F**
C. noctivagus (Yellow-legged Tinamou) **F**   ?
C. atrocapillus (Black-capped Tinamou) **F**
C. cinnamomeus (Thicket Tinamou) **E**
C. boucardi (Slaty-breasted Tinamou) **E**
C. kerriae (Choco Tinamou) **F**
C. variegatus (Variegated Tinamou) **F**
C. brevirostris (Rusty Tinamou) **F**
C. bartletti (Bartlett's Tinamou) **F**
C. parvirostris (Small-billed Tinamou) **F**
C. casiquiare (Barred Tinamou) **F**
C. tataupa (Tataupa Tinamou) **F**

RHYNCHOTUS
R. rufescens (Red-winged Tinamou) **F**
NOTHOPROCTA
N. taczanowskii (Taczanowski's Tinamou) **F** [?]
N. kalinowskii (Kalinowski's Tinamou) **F** [?]
N. ornata (Ornate Tinamou) **F**
N. perdicaria (Chilean Tinamou) **F**
N. cinerascens (Brushland Tinamou) **F**
N. pentlandii (Andean Tinamou) **F**
N. curvirostris (Curve-billed Tinamou) **F**
NOTHURA
N. boraquira (White-bellied Nothura) **F**
N. minor (Lesser Nothura) **F** [?]
N. darwinii (Darwin's Nothura) **F**
N. maculosa (Spotted Nothura) **F**
TAONISCUS
T. nanus (Dwarf Tinamou) **F** [?]
EUDROMIA
E. elegans (Elegant Crested Tinamou) **F**
E. formosa (Quebracho Crested Tinamou) **F**
TINAMOTIS
T. pentlandii (Puna Tinamou) **F**
T. ingoufi (Patagonian Tinamou) **F**

SPHENISCIFORMES

7 SPHENISCIDAE (PENGUINS)
APTENODYTES
A. patagonicus (King Penguin) **F,M,Q**
A. forsteri (Emperor Penguin) **Q**
PYGOSCELIS
P. papua (Gentoo Penguin) **F,M,N,Q**
P. adeliae (Adélie Penguin) **Q**
P. antarctica (Chinstrap Penguin) **C,Q**
EUDYPTES
E. pachyrhynchus (Fjordland Crested Penguin) **N**
E. robustus (Snares I Penguin) **N**
E. sclateri (Big-crested Penguin) **N**
E. chrysocome (Rockhopper Penguin) **C,F,N,M,Q**
E. schlegeli (Royal Penguin) **M**
E. chrysolophus (Macaroni Penguin) **F,Q**
MEGADYPTES
M. antipodes (Yellow-eyed Penguin) **N** [?]
EUDYPTULA
E. minor (Little Penguin) **D,M,N**
E. albosignata (White-flippered Penguin) **N**
SPHENISCUS
S. demersus (Jackass Penguin) **C** [S]
S. humboldti (Humboldt Penguin) **F** [?]
S. magellanicus (Magellanic Penguin) **F**
S. mendiculus (Galapagos Penguin) **G**

GAVIFORMES

8 GAVIIDAE (LOONS)
GAVIA
G. stellata (Red-throated Loon) **A,B**
G. arctica (Arctic Loon) **A,B**
G. pacifica (Pacific Loon) **A**
G. immer (Common Loon) **A,B,E**
G. adamsii (Yellow-billed Loon) **A,B**

PODICIPEDIFORMES

9 PODICIPEDIDAE (GREBES)
TACHYBAPTUS
T. ruficollis (Little Grebe) **B,C,H,I,J,K,L**
T. novaehollandiae (Australian Dabchick) **L,M,O**
T. pelzelnii (Madagascar Little Grebe) **D** [?]
T. rufolavatus (Delacour's Little Grebe) **D** [E]
PODILYMBUS
P. podiceps (Pied-billed Grebe) **A,E,F**
P. gigas (Atitlan Grebe) **E** [X]
ROLLANDIA
R. rolland (White-tufted Grebe) **F**
R. micropterum (Short-winged Grebe) **F**
PODICEPS
P. major (Great Grebe) **F**
P. poliocephalus (Hoary-headed Grebe) **M**
P. rufopectus (New Zealand Dabchick) **N**
P. dominicus (Least Grebe) **A,E,F**
P. grisegena (Red-necked Grebe) **A,B**
P. cristatus (Great Crested Grebe) **B,C,H,M,N**
P. auritus (Horned Grebe) **A,B**
P. nigricollis (Eared Grebe) **A,B,C,E,F**
P. occipitalis (Silvery Grebe) **F**
P. taczanowskii (Puna Grebe) **F** [E]
P. gallardoi (Hooded Grebe) **F** [R]

AECHMOPHORUS
A. occidentalis (Western Grebe) **A,E**
A. clarkii (Clark's Grebe) **A,E**

PROCELLARIIFORMES

10 DIOMEDEIDAE (ALBATROSSES)
DIOMEDEA
D. exulans (Wandering Albatross) **C,D,H,M,Q**
D. epomophora (Royal Albatross) **F,M,N**
D. irrorata (Waved Albatross) **F,G**
D. albatrus (Short-tailed Albatross) **O,P** [E]
D. nigripes (Black-footed Albatross) **O,P**
D. immutabilis (Laysan Albatross) **P**
D. melanophris (Black-browed Albatross) **F,N**
D. bulleri (Buller's Albatross) **Q**
D. amsterdamensis (Amsterdam I Albatross) **M** [E]
D. cauta (Shy Albatross) **F,M,N**
D. chlororhynchos (Yellow-nosed Albatross) **C**
D. chrysostoma (Grey-headed Albatross) **Q**
PHOEBETRIA
P. fusca (Sooty Albatross) **C,M**
P. palpebrata (Light-mantled Sooty Albatross) **M,N,Q**
11 PROCELLARIIDAE (PETRELS, SHEARWATERS)
MACRONECTES
M. giganteus (Southern Giant Petrel) **Q**
M. halli (Northern Giant Petrel) **Q**
FULMARUS
F. glacialis (Northern Fulmar) **A,B**
F. glacialoides (Southern Fulmar) **N,Q**
THALASSOICA
T. antarctica (Antarctic Petrel) **Q**
DAPTION
D. capense (Pintado Petrel) **N,Q**
PAGODROMA
P. nivea (Snow Petrel) **Q**
LUGENSA
L. brevirostris (Kerguelen Petrel) **Q**
PTERODROMA
P. macroptera (Great-winged Petrel) **C,M,N,Q**
P. aterrima (Mascarene Black Petrel) **D** [E]
P. lessonii (White-headed Petrel) **N,Q**
P. hasitata (Black-capped Petrel) **E** [V]
P. cahow (Cahow) **E** [E]
P. incerta (Schlegel's Petrel) **C**
P. becki (Solomon Is Petrel) **O** [I]
P. alba (Phoenix Petrel) **O**
P. inexpectata (Mottled Petrel) **N**
P. solandri (Solander's Petrel) **M**
P. ultima (Murphy's Petrel) **M,O** [?]
P. neglecta (Kermadec Petrel) **F,M**
P. magentae (Taiko) **N** [E]
P. arminjoniana (Trinidade Petrel) **O,D**
P. heraldica (Tonga Petrel) **O**
P. mollis (Soft-plumaged Petrel) **C,M,Q**
P. feae (Cape Verde Petrel) **B** [R]
P. madeira (Madeira Petrel) **B** [E]
P. baraui (Barau's Petrel) **D**
P. phaeopygia (Hawaiian Petrel) **G,P**
P. externa (White-necked Petrel) **C,F**
P. cervicalis (Kermadec White-necked Petrel) **N**
P. cookii (Cook's Petrel) **F,N** [?]
P. defilippiana (Juan Fernandez Petrel) **F** [?]
P. leucoptera (White-winged Petrel) **F,M**
P. brevipes (Collared Petrel) **O**
P. hypoleuca (Bonin Petrel) **P**
P. nigripennis (Black-winged Petrel) **N**
P. axillaris (Chatham Is Petrel) **N** [E]
P. longirostris (Stejneger's Petrel) **F**
P. pycrofti (Pycroft's Petrel) **N** [?]
PSEUDOBULWERIA
P. macgillivrayi (Macgillivray's Petrel) **O**
P. rostrata (Tahiti Petrel) **O**
HALOBAENA
H. caerulea (Blue Petrel) **F,Q**
PACHYPTILA
P. vittata (Broad-billed Prion) **C,M,N,Q**
P. salvini (Salvin's Prion) **Q**
P. desolata (Dove Prion) **C,M,Q**
P. belcheri (Slender-billed Prion) **F,Q**
P. turtur (Fairy Prion) **F,M,N**
P. crassirostris (Thick-billed Prion) **N,Q**
BULWERIA
B. bulwerii (Bulwer's Petrel) **C,D,F,M,O**
B. fallax (Jouanin's Petrel) **N,Q**

PROCELLARIA
P. cinerea (Gray Shearwater) **C,M,Q**
P. aequinoctialis (White-chinned Petrel) **C,F,M, N,Q** [E]
P. parkinsoni (Black Petrel) **N**
P. westlandica (Westland Petrel) **N** [V]
CALONECTRIS
C. leucomelas (Streaked Shearwater) **O**
C. diomedea (Cory's Shearwater) **B,D,Q**
PUFFINUS
P. creatopus (Pink-footed Shearwater) **F,O** [?]
P. carneipes (Flesh-footed Shearwater) **M,N**
P. gravis (Greater Shearwater) **C,F**
P. pacificus (Wedge-tailed Shearwater) **M,N,P**
P. bulleri (Buller's Shearwater) **N**
P. griseus (Sooty Shearwater) **F,N**
P. tenuirostris (Short-tailed Shearwater) **M**
P. heinrothi (Heinroth's Shearwater) **L** [I]
P. nativitatis (Christmas I Shearwater) **O,P**
P. puffinus (Manx Shearwater) **B,P**
P. gavia (Fluttering Shearwater) **N**
P. huttoni (Hutton's Shearwater) **N**
P. opisthomelas (Black-vented Shearwater) **A** [?]
P. auricularis (Townsend's Shearwater) **E** [?]
P. assimilis (Little Shearwater) **B,C,M,N**
P. lherminieri (Audubon's Shearwater) **B,D,E,F,G, H,J,O,Q**
12 HYDROBATIDAE (STORM-PETRELS)
OCEANITES
O. oceanicus (Wilson's Storm-Petrel) **Q**
O. gracilis (Elliot's Storm-Petrel) **F,G**
GARRODIA
G. nereis (Grey-backed Storm-Petrel) **F,N,Q**
PELAGODROMA
P. marina (White-faced Storm-Petrel) **B,C,M,N**
FREGETTA
F. grallaria (White-bellied Storm-Petrel) **F,N**
F. tropica (Black-bellied Storm-Petrel) **C,O,Q**
NESOFREGETTA
N. fuliginosa (White-throated Storm-Petrel) **O**
HYDROBATES
H. pelagicus (British Storm-Petrel) **B**
HALOCYPTENA
H. microsoma (Least Storm-Petrel) **E,F** [?]
OCEANODROMA
O. tethys (Wedge-rumped Storm-Petrel) **F,G**
O. castro (Band-rumped Storm-Petrel) **A,B,C,E,G,O,P**
O. leucorhoa (Leach's Storm-Petrel) **A,B,E**
O. markhami (Sooty Storm-Petrel) **F,P** [?]
O. matsudairae (Matsudaira's Storm-Petrel) **J** [?]
O. tristrami (Tristram's Storm-Petrel) **B,J**
O. monorhis (Swinhoe's Storm-Petrel) **A,B,E**
O. homochroa (Ashy Storm-Petrel) **A**
O. hornbyi (Ringed Storm-Petrel) **F** [?]
O. furcata (Fork-tailed Storm-Petrel) **B,O**
O. melania (Black Storm-Petrel) **A,E** [?]
13 PELECANOIDIDAE (DIVING-PETRELS)
PELECANOIDES
P. garnotii (Peruvian Diving-Petrel) **F**
P. magellani (Magellan Diving-Petrel) **F**
P. georgicus (Georgian Diving-Petrel) **Q**
P. urinatrix (Common Diving-Petrel) **C,F,M,N,Q**

PELECANIFORMES

14 PHAETHONTIDAE (TROPICBIRDS)
PHAETHON
P. aethereus (Red-billed Tropicbird) **B,C,E,G**
P. rubricauda (Red-tailed Tropicbird) **D,J,M,N,O,P**
P. lepturus (White-tailed Tropicbird) **C,D,E,F,I,J,O**
15 PELECANIDAE (PELICANS)
PELECANUS
P. onocrotalus (Great White Pelican) **B,C**
P. rufescens (Pink-backed Pelican) **C**
P. philippensis (Gray Pelican) **B,H,I,J** [?]
P. crispus (Dalmatian Pelican) **B** [V]
P. conspicillatus (Australian Pelican) **L,M**
P. erythrorhynchos (American White Pelican) **A,E**
P. occidentalis (Brown Pelican) **A,E,F,G**
16 SULIDAE (GANNETS, BOOBIES)
SULA
S. bassana (Northern Gannet) **A,B**
S. capensis (Cape Gannet) **C**
S. serrator (Australian Gannet) **M,N**
S. nebouxii (Blue-footed Booby) **A,E,F,G**
S. variegata (Peruvian Booby) **F**
S. abbotti (Abbott's Booby) **J** [E]

CORMORANTS

S. dactylatra (Masked Booby) **C,D,E,G,J,K,L,M,O**
S. sula (Red-footed Booby) **D,E,F,G,H,J,K,O**
S. leucogaster (Brown Booby) **A,C,D,E,F,H,J,O**
17 PHALACROCORACIDAE (CORMORANTS)
PHALACROCORAX
P. auritus (Double-crested Cormorant) **A,E**
P. olivaceus (Olivaceous Cormorant) **A,E,F**
P. sulcirostris (Little Black Cormorant) **J,K,L,M,N**
P. carbo (Great Cormorant) **A,B,H,M,N**
P. lucidus (White-breasted Cormorant) **B,C**
P. fuscicollis (Indian Cormorant) **H,I**
P. capensis (Cape Cormorant) **C**
P. nigrogularis (Socotra Cormorant) **B,C**
P. neglectus (Bank Cormorant) **C**
P. capillatus (Japanese Cormorant) **B**
P. penicillatus (Brandt's Cormorant) **A**
P. aristotelis (Shag) **B**
P. pelagicus (Pelagic Cormorant) **A,B**
P. urile (Red-faced Cormorant) **A,J,O**
P. magellanicus (Magellan Cormorant) **F**
P. bougainvillei (Guanay Cormorant) **F**
P. featherstoni (Chatham Cormorant) **N**
P. varius (Pied Cormorant) **M,N**
P. fuscescens (Black-faced Cormorant) **M**
P. carunculatus (Rough-faced Cormorant) **N** [?]
P. campbelli (Campbell Is Cormorant) **N**
P. verrucosus (Kerguelen Cormorant) **Q**
P. gaimardi (Red-legged Cormorant) **F**
P. punctatus (Spotted Cormorant) **N**
P. atriceps (Imperial Shag) **F,Q**
P. georgianus (S Georgia Cormorant) **Q**
P. melanoleucos (Little Pied Cormorant) **J,K,L,M,N,O**
P. africanus (Reed Cormorant) **C,D**
P. coronatus (Crowned Cormorant) **C**
P. niger (Javanese Cormorant) **H,J**
P. pygmeus (Pygmy Cormorant) **B** [?]
NANNOPTERUM
N. harrisi (Flightless Cormorant) **G** [R]
18 ANHINGIDAE (DARTERS)
ANHINGA
A. rufa (African Darter) **B,C,D,L**
A. melanogaster (Indian Darter) **H,I,J,K**
A. novaehollandiae (Australian Darter) **L,M**
A. anhinga (Anhinga) **A,E,F**
19 FREGATIDAE (FRIGATEBIRDS)
FREGATA
F. aquila (Ascension Frigatebird) **C** [R]
F. andrewsi (Christmas I Frigatebird) **I,J** [V]
F. magnificens (Magnificent Frigatebird) **A,B,E,G**
F. minor (Great Frigatebird) **D,F,G,J,K,L,M,O,P**
F. ariel (Lesser Frigatebird) **D,F,J,K,L,M,O**

CICONIIFORMES

20 ARDEIDAE (HERONS, BITTERNS)
SYRIGMA
S. sibilatrix (Whistling Heron) **F**
PILHERODIUS
P. pileatus (Capped Heron) **F**
ARDEA
A. cinerea (Gray Heron) **B,C,D,J**
A. herodias (Great Blue Heron) **A,E,G**
A. cocoi (Cocoi Heron) **F**
A. pacifica (White-necked Heron) **M**
A. melanocephala (Black-headed Heron) **C**
A. humbloti (Malagasy Heron) **D** [?]
A. imperialis (Imperial Heron) **H,I** [?]
A. sumatrana (Dusky-gray Heron) **I,J,K,L,M**
A. goliath (Goliath Heron) **C**
A. purpurea (Purple Heron) **B,C,D,H,K**
EGRETTA
E. alba (Great Egret) **A,B,C,E,F,H,I,J,K,L,M**
E. rufescens (Reddish Egret) **A,E**
E. picata (Pied Heron) **K,L,M**
E. vinaceigula (Slaty Egret) **C** [I]
E. ardesiaca (Black Heron) **C**
E. tricolor (Tricolored Heron) **A,E,F**
E. intermedia (Intermediate Egret) **B,C,H,I,K,L,M**
E. novaehollandiae (White-faced Egret) **M,N**
E. caerulea (Little Blue Heron) **A,E,F**
E. thula (Snowy Egret) **A,E,F**
E. garzetta (Little Egret) **B,C,D,H,J,K,L,M**
E. eulophotes (Swinhoe's Egret) **B,I,J,K** [V]
E. sacra (Reef Heron) **J,K,M**
BUBULCUS
B. ibis (Cattle Egret) **A,B,C,D,F,H,I,J,K**

ARDEOLA
A. ralloides (Squacco Heron) **B,C**
A. grayii (Indian Pond Heron) **B,H,I**
A. bacchus (Chinese Pond Heron) **B,I,J**
A. speciosa (Javanese Pond Heron) **I,J,K**
A. idae (Malagasy Pond Heron) **C**
A. rufiventris (Rufous-bellied Heron) **C**
BUTORIDES
B. striatus (Green-backed Heron) **A,B,C,D,E,F,G, H,I,J,K,L,M,O**
AGAMIA
A. agami (Chestnut-bellied Heron) **E,F**
NYCTICORAX
N. violaceus (Yellow-crowned Night Heron) **A,E, F,G**
N. nycticorax (Black-crowned Night Heron) **A,B,C, E,F,K,P**
N. caledonicus (Nankeen Night Heron) **J,K,L,M,O**
N. leuconotus (White-backed Night Heron) **C**
GORSACHIUS
G. magnificus (Magnificent Night Heron) **B** [?]
G. goisagi (Japanese Night Heron) **B,J** [?]
G. melanolophus (Malaysian Night Heron) **B,H, I,J,K**
COCHLEARIUS
C. cochlearius (Boat-billed Heron) **E,F**
TIGRISOMA
T. mexicanum (Bare-throated Tiger Heron) **E,F**
T. fasciatum (Fasciated Tiger Heron) **F**
T. lineatum (Rufescent Tiger Heron) **E,F**
ZONERODIUS
Z. heliosylus (Forest Bittern) **L**
TIGRIORNIS
T. leucolophus (White-crested Tiger Heron) **C**
ZEBRILUS
Z. undulatus (Zigzag Heron) **F**
IXOBRYCHUS
I. involucris (Stripe-backed Bittern) **F**
I. exilis (Least Bittern) **A,E,F**
I. minutus (Little Bittern) **B,C,D,H,M,N**
I. sinensis (Chinese Little Bittern) **B,H,J,K**
I. eurhythmus (Schrenk's Bittern) **B,J,K**
I. cinnamomeus (Cinnamon Bittern) **B,H,J,K**
I. sturmii (African Dwarf Bittern) **C**
I. flavicollis (Black Bittern) **B,H,J,K,L,M,O**
BOTAURUS
B. pinnatus (Pinnated Bittern) **E,F**
B. lentiginosus (American Bittern) **A,E**
B. stellaris (Eurasian Bittern) **B,C**
B. poiciloptilus (Australian Bittern) **M,N**
21 SCOPIDAE (HAMMERKOP)
SCOPUS
S. umbretta (Hammerkop) **C**
22 BALAENICIPITIDAE (WHALE-HEADED STORK)
BALAENICEPS
B. rex (Whale-headed Stork) **C** [S]
23 CICONIIDAE (STORKS)
MYCTERIA
M. americana (Wood Stork) **A,E,F**
M. cinerea (Milky Stork) **J** [V]
M. ibis (Yellow-billed Stork) **C**
M. leucocephala (Painted Stork) **H,I,J**
ANASTOMUS
A. oscitans (Asian Open-bill Stork) **H,I**
A. lamelligerus (African Open-bill Stork) **C,D**
CICONIA
C. nigra (Black Stork) **B,C,H**
C. abdimii (Abdim's Stork) **C**
C. episcopus (Woolly-necked Stork) **C,H,I,J,K**
C. stormi (Storm's Stork) **J** [I]
C. maguari (Maguari Stork) **F**
C. ciconia (White Stork) **B,C,H** [?]
C. boyciana (Oriental White Stork) **B** [E]
EPIPPIORHYNCHUS
E. asiaticus (Black-necked Stork) **H,I,J,L,M**
E. senegalensis (Saddle-bill Stork) **C**
E. mycteria (Jabiru) **E,F**
LEPTOPTILOS
L. javanicus (Lesser Adjutant Stork) **B,H**
L. dubius (Greater Adjutant Stork) **H,I,K** [?]
L. crumeniferus (Marabou Stork) **C**

24 THRESKIORNITHIDAE (IBISES, SPOONBILLS)
THRESKIORNITHINAE
THRESKIORNIS
T. aethiopica (Sacred Ibis) **B,C,D**
T. melanocephala (Oriental Ibis) **B,H**
T. molucca (Australian White Ibis) **L,M**
T. spinicollis (Straw-necked Ibis) **M**
PSEUDIBIS
P. papillosa (Black Ibis) **H,I**
THAUMATIBIS
T. gigantea (Giant Ibis) **I**
GERONTICUS
G. eremita (Hermit Ibis) **B,C** [E]
G. calvus (Bald Ibis) **C** [R]
NIPPONIA
N. nippon (Japanese Crested Ibis) **B** [E]
LAMPRIBIS
L. olivacea (Olive Ibis) **C**
L. rara (Spot-breasted Ibis) **C**
HAGEDASHIA
H. hagedash (Hadada Ibis) **C**
BOSTRYCHIA
B. carunculata (Wattled Ibis) **C**
HARPIPRION
H. caerulescens (Plumbeous Ibis) **F**
THERISTICUS
T. caudatus (Buff-necked Ibis) **E,F**
T. melanopis (Black-faced Ibis) **F**
CERCIBIS
C. oxycerca (Sharp-tailed Ibis) **F**
MESEMBRINIBIS
M. cayennensis (Green Ibis) **E,F**
PHIMOSUS
P. infuscatus (Bare-faced Ibis) **F**
EUDOCIMUS
E. albus (White Ibis) **A,E,F**
E. ruber (Scarlet Ibis) **E,F**
PLEGADIS
P. falcinellus (Glossy Ibis) **B,C,E,H,I,J,K,M**
P. chihi (White-faced Ibis) **A,E,F**
P. ridgwayi (Puna Ibis) **F**
LOPHOTIBIS
L. cristata (Crested Wood Ibis) **D**
PLATALEINAE
PLATALEA
P. leucorodia (White Spoonbill) **B,C,H,J**
P. minor (Black-faced Spoonbill) **B,I,J** [?]
P. alba (African Spoonbill) **C**
P. regia (Royal Spoonbill) **K,L,M,N**
P. flavipes (Yellow-billed Spoonbill) **M**
AJAIA
A. ajaja (Roseate Spoonbill) **A,E,F**
25 PHOENICOPTERIDAE (FLAMINGOS)
PHOENICOPTERUS
P. ruber (Greater Flamingo) **B,C,E,F,H**
P. chilensis (Chilean Flamingo) **F**
PHOENICONAIAS
P. minor (Lesser Flamingo) **C,D,H**
PHOENICOPARRUS
P. andinus (Andean Flamingo) **F** [?]
P. jamesi (James' Flamingo) **F** [?]

ANSERIFORMES

26 ANHIMIDAE (SCREAMERS)
ANHIMA
A. cornuta (Horned Screamer) **F**
CHAUNA
C. torquata (Crested Screamer) **F**
C. chavaria (Northern Screamer) **F** [?]
27 ANATIDAE (DUCKS, GEESE, SWANS)
ANSERANATINAE
ANSERANAS
A. semipalmata (Magpie Goose) **L,M**
ANSERINAE
DENDROCYGNA
D. guttata (Spotted Whistling Duck) **J,K,L**
D. eytoni (Plumed Whistling Duck) **M**
D. bicolor (Fulvous Whistling Duck) **A,C,E,F,H**
D. arcuata (Wandering Whistling Duck) **J,K,L,M,O**
D. javanica (Indian Whistling Duck) **H,I,J**
D. viduata (White-faced Whistling Duck) **C,F**
D. arborea (Black-billed Whistling Duck) **E** [V]
D. autumnalis (Black-bellied Whistling Duck) **A,E,F**
CYGNUS
C. olor (Mute Swan) **B,C,H**

C. atratus (Black Swan) **M**
C. melanocoryphus (Black-necked Swan) **F**
C. cygnus (Whooper Swan) **A,B**
C. buccinator (Trumpeter Swan) **A**
C. columbianus (Tundra Swan) **A,B**
COSCOROBA
C. coscoroba (Coscoroba Swan) **F**
ANSER
A. cygnoides (Swan Goose) **B**
A. fabalis (Bean Goose) **B**
A. brachyrhynchus (Pink-footed Goose) **A,B**
A. albifrons (White-fronted Goose) **A,B,H**
A. erythropus (Lesser White-fronted Goose) **B**   ?
A. anser (Graylag Goose) **B,C,H**
A. indicus (Bar-headed Goose) **B,H,I**
A. caerulescens (Snow Goose) **A,B**
A. rossi (Ross's Goose) **A**
A. canagicus (Emperor Goose) **A,B**
BRANTA
B. sandvicensis (Hawaiian Goose) **P**   V
B. canadensis (Canada Goose) **A,B,E,N**
B. leucopsis (Barnacle Goose) **A,B**
B. bernicla (Brant Goose) **A,B**
B. ruficollis (Red-breasted Goose) **B**
CEREOPSIS
C. novaehollandiae (Cape Barren Goose) **M**
STICTONETTA
S. naevosa (Freckled Duck) **M**   ?
ANATINAE
CYANOCHEN
C. cyanopterus (Blue-winged Goose) **C**
CHLOEPHAGA
C. melanoptera (Andean Goose) **F**
C. picta (Magellan Goose) **F**
C. hybrida (Kelp Goose) **F**
C. poliocephala (Ashy-headed Goose) **F**
C. rubidiceps (Ruddy-headed Goose) **F**
NEOCHEN
N. jubatus (Orinoco Goose) **F**
ALOPOCHEN
A. aegyptiacus (Egyptian Goose) **B,C**
TADORNA
T. ferruginea (Ruddy Shelduck) **B,H**
T. cana (South African Shelduck) **C**
T. variegata (Paradise Shelduck) **N**
T. tadornoides (Australian Shelduck) **M**
T. tadorna (Northern Shelduck) **B,H**
T. radjah (Radjah Shelduck) **K,L,M**
T. cristata (Crested Shelduck) **B**   ?
TACHYERES
T. patachonicus (Flying Steamer Duck) **F**
T. pteneres (Flightless Steamer Duck) **F**
T. brachypterus (Falkland Is Flightless Steamer Duck) **F**
T. leucocephalus (White-headed Flightless Steamer Duck) **F**
PLECTROPTERUS
P. gambensis (Spur-winged Goose) **C**
CAIRINA
C. moschata (Muscovy Duck) **E,F**
C. scutulata (White-winged Wood Duck) **I,J**   V
SARKIDIORNIS
S. melanotos (Comb Duck) **B,C,F,H**
PTERONETTA
P. hartlaubii (Hartlaub's Duck) **C**
NETTAPUS
N. pulchellus (Green Pygmy Goose) **K,L,M**
N. coromandelianus (Cotton Pygmy Goose) **B,H, J,M**
N. auritus (African Pygmy Goose) **C**
CALLONETTA
C. leucophrys (Ringed Teal) **F**
AIX
A. sponsa (Wood Duck) **A,E**
A. galericulata (Mandarin Duck) **B**   ?
CHENONETTA
C. jubata (Maned Goose) **M**
AMAZONETTA
A. brasiliensis (Brazilian Teal) **F**
HYMENOLAIMUS
H. malacorhynchos (Blue Duck) **N**
MERGANETTA
M. armata (Torrent Duck) **F**
ANAS
A. waigiuensis (Salvadori's Duck) **K,L**
A. sparsa (African Black Duck) **C**

A. penelope (Eurasian Wigeon) **B,H**
A. americana (American Wigeon) **A,E**
A. sibilatrix (Chiloe Wigeon) **F**
A. falcata (Falcated Teal) **B**
A. strepera (Gadwall) **A,B,E,H,I**
A. formosa (Baikal Teal) **B**   ?
A. crecca (Green-winged Teal) **A,B,E,H**
A. flavirostris (Speckled Teal) **F**
A. capensis (Cape Teal) **C**
A. gibberifrons (Gray Teal) **I,J,K,L,M,N,O**
A. bernieri (Madagascar Teal) **D**   V
A. castanea (Chestnut-breasted Teal) **M**
A. aucklandica (New Zealand Teal) **N**   V
A. platyrhynchos (Mallard) **A,B,E,H,P**
A. rubripes (American Black Duck) **A**
A. melleri (Meller's Duck) **D**
A. undulata (African Yellow-billed Duck) **C**
A. poecilorhyncha (Spotbill Duck) **B,H,I,J,K,L,M, N,O**
A. luzonica (Philippine Duck) **J**
A. specularis (Bronze-winged Duck) **F**
A. specularioides (Crested Duck) **F**
A. acuta (Northern Pintail) **A,B,C,E,H,I,Q**
A. georgica (Yellow-billed Teal) **F,Q**
A. bahamensis (White-cheeked Pintail) **E,F,G**
A. erythrorhyncha (Red-billed Pintail) **C**
A. versicolor (Versicolor Teal) **F**
A. punctata (Hottentot Teal) **C,D**
A. querquedula (Garganey) **B,C,H,J,K,L**
A. discors (Blue-winged Teal) **A,E,F**
A. cyanoptera (Cinnamon Teal) **A,E,F**
A. platalea (Argentine Shoveller) **F**
A. smithii (Cape Shoveller) **C**
A. rhynchotis (Australian Shoveller) **M,N**
A. clypeata (Northern Shoveller) **A,B,C,E,H,I**
MALACORHYNCHUS
M. membranaceus (Pink-eared Duck) **M**
MARMARONETTA
M. angustirostris (Marbled Teal) **B,H**   ?
RHODONESSA
R. caryophyllacea (Pink-headed Duck) **H**   X
NETTA
N. rufina (Red-crested Pochard) **B,H**
N. erythrophthalma (Southern Pochard) **C,F**
N. peposaca (Rosybill) **F**
AYTHYA
A. valisineria (Canvasback) **A,E**
A. ferina (Common Pochard) **B,H**
A. americana (Redhead) **A,E**
A. collaris (Ring-necked Duck) **A,E**
A. australis (Hardhead) **L,M,N,O**
A. baeri (Baer's Pochard) **B,I**
A. nyroca (Ferruginous Duck) **B,C,I**
A. innotata (Madagascar Pochard) **D**   E
A. novaeseelandiae (New Zealand Scaup) **N**
A. fuligula (Tufted Duck) **B,H,J**
A. marila (Greater Scaup) **A,B,E,H**
A. affinis (Lesser Scaup) **A,E**
SOMATERIA
S. mollissima (Common Eider) **A,B**
S. spectabilis (King Eider) **A,B**
S. fischeri (Spectacled Eider) **A,B**
POLYSTICTA
P. stelleri (Steller's Eider) **A,B**
HISTRIONICUS
H. histrionicus (Harlequin Duck) **A,B**
CLANGULA
C. hyemalis (Oldsquaw) **A,B,H,I**
MELANITTA
M. nigra (Black Scoter) **A,B**
M. perspicillata (Surf Scoter) **A,B**
M. fusca (White-winged Scoter) **A,B**
BUCEPHALA
B. albeola (Bufflehead) **A**
B. islandica (Barrow's Goldeneye) **A,B**
B. clangula (Common Goldeneye) **A,B,H**
MERGUS
M. cucullatus (Hooded Merganser) **A**
M. albellus (Smew) **B,H**
M. octosetaceus (Brazilian Merganser) **F**   I
M. serrator (Red-breasted Merganser) **A,B,E,H,I**
M. squamatus (Chinese Merganser) **B**   I
M. merganser (Common Merganser) **A,B,H**
HETERONETTA
H. atricapilla (Black-headed Duck) **F**

OXYURA
O. dominica (Masked Duck) **E,F**
O. jamaicensis (Ruddy Duck) **A,E,F**
O. leucocephala (White-headed Duck) **B,C,H**   ?
O. maccoa (Maccoa Duck) **C**
O. vittata (Argentine Lake Duck) **F**
O. australis (Australian Blue-billed Duck) **M**
BIZIURA
B. lobata (Musk Duck) **M**
THALASSORNIS
T. leuconotos (White-backed Duck) **F,D**

FALCONIFORMES

28 CATHARTIDAE (NEW WORLD VULTURES)
CATHARTES
C. aura (Turkey Vulture) **A,E,F**
C. burrovianus (Lesser Yellow-headed Vulture) **E,F**
C. melambrotus (Greater Yellow-headed Vulture) **F**
CORAGYPS
C. atratus (Black Vulture) **A,E,F**
SARCORHAMPHUS
S. papa (King Vulture) **E,F**
GYMNOGYPS
G. californianus (Californian Condor) **A**   E
VULTUR
V. gryphus (Andean Condor) **F**
29 PANDIONIDAE (OSPREY)
PANDION
P. haliaetus (Osprey) **A,B,C,E,H,I,J,K,M,O**
30 ACCIPITRIDAE (KITES, VULTURES, HAWKS, EAGLES AND RELATIVES)
AVICEDA
A. cuculoides (African Cuckoo Hawk) **C**
A. madagascariensis (Madagascar Cuckoo Hawk) **D**
A. jerdoni (Jerdon's Baza) **H,J,K**
A. subcristata (Crested Baza) **J,K,L,M,O**
A. leuphotes (Black Baza) **B,H,I,J**
LEPTODON
L. cayanensis (Gray-headed Kite) **E,F**
CHONDROHIERAX
C. uncinatus (Hook-billed Kite) **E,F**
HENICOPERNIS
H. longicauda (Long-tailed Honey Buzzard) **K,L**
H. infuscata (Black Honey Buzzard) **O**   ?
PERNIS
P. apivorus (Western Honey Buzzard) **B,C**
P. ptilorhynchus (Oriental Honey Buzzard) **B,H,I,J**
P. celebensis (Barred Honey Buzzard) **J,K**
ELANOIDES
E. forficatus (American Swallow-tailed Kite) **A,E,F**
MACHAERHAMPHUS
M. alcinus (Bat Hawk) **C,J,L**
GAMPSONYX
G. swainsonii (Pearl Kite) **E,F**
ELANUS
E. leucurus (White-tailed Kite) **A,E,F**
E. caeruleus (Black-shouldered Kite) **C,J,K,L**
E. notatus (Australian Black-shouldered Kite) **M**
E. scriptus (Letter-winged Kite) **M**
CHELICTINIA
C. riocourii (Scissor-tailed Kite) **C**
ROSTRHAMUS
R. sociabilis (Snail Kite) **A,B,E,F**
R. hamatus (Slender-billed Kite) **E,F**
HARPAGUS
H. bidentatus (Double-toothed Kite) **E,F**
H. diodon (Rufous-thighed Kite) **F**
ICTINIA
I. plumbea (Plumbeous Kite) **E,F**
I. mississippiensis (Mississippi Kite) **A,E,F**
LOPHOICTINIA
L. isura (Square-tailed Kite) **M**
HAMIROSTRA
H. melanosternon (Black-breasted Buzzard Kite) **M**
MILVUS
M. migrans (Black Kite) **B,C,I,J,K,L,M**
M. milvus (Red Kite) **B**   ?
HALIASTUR
H. sphenurus (Whistling Kite) **L,M,O**
H. indus (Brahminy Kite) **H,I,J,K,L,M,O**
HALIAEETUS
H. leucogaster (White-bellied Sea Eagle) **B,H,M**
H. sanfordi (Sanford's Sea Eagle) **O**   ?
H. vocifer (African Fish Eagle) **C**
H. vociferoides (Madagascar Fish Eagle) **D**   E
H. leucoryphus (Pallas' Sea Eagle) **B,H,I**

H. leucocephalus (Bald Eagle) **A** [?]
H. albicilla (White-tailed Sea Eagle) **A,B,H** [V]
H. pelagicus (Steller's Sea Eagle) **B** [?]
ICHTHYOPHAGA
I. humilis (Lesser Fishing Eagle) **H,I,J,K**
I. ichthyaetus (Gray-headed Fishing Eagle) **H,J**
AEGYPIUS
A. monachus (European Black Vulture) **B,H** [?]
A. tracheliotus (Lappet-faced Vulture) **B,C**
A. occipitalis (White-headed Vulture) **C**
A. calvus (Red-headed Vulture) **H,I**
NECROSYRTES
N. monachus (Hooded Vulture) **C**
GYPS
G. fulvus (Griffon Vulture) **B,H**
G. indicus (Long-billed Griffon) **H,I**
G. himalayensis (Himalayan Griffon) **B,H**
G. rueppelli (Rüppell's Griffon) **C**
G. coprotheres (Cape Vulture) **C** [R]
G. bengalensis (Oriental White-backed Vulture) **H,I**
G. africanus (African White-backed Vulture) **C**
NEOPHRON
N. percnopterus (Egyptian Vulture) **B,C,H**
GYPAETUS
G. barbatus (Lammergeier) **B,C**
GYPOHIERAX
G. angolensis (Palm-nut Vulture) **C**
CIRCAETUS
C. gallicus (Short-toed Eagle) **B,C,H**
C. cinereus (Brown Snake Eagle) **C**
C. fasciolatus (Southern Banded Snake Eagle) **C**
C. cinerascens (Smaller Banded Snake Eagle) **C**
TERATHOPIUS
T. ecaudatus (Bateleur) **B,C**
SPILORNIS
S. cheela (Crested Serpent-Eagle) **B,H,I,J,K**
S. rufipectus (Sulawesi Serpent-Eagle) **K**
S. kinabaluensis (Kinabalu Serpent-Eagle) **C** [?]
S. minimus (Nicobar Serpent-Eagle) **I**
S. elgini (Andaman Serpent-Eagle) **I** [?]
DRYOTRIORCHIS
D. spectabilis (Congo Serpent-Eagle) **C**
EUTRIORCHIS
E. astur (Madagascar Serpent-Eagle) **D** [E]
POLYBOROIDES
P. typus (African Harrier-Hawk) **C**
P. radiatus (Madagascar Harrier-Hawk) **D**
GERANOSPIZA
G. caerulescens (Crane Hawk) **E,F**
CIRCUS
C. assimilis (Spotted Harrier) **K,L,M**
C. maurus (Black Harrier) **C**
C. cyaneus (Hen Harrier) **A,B,C**
C. cinereus (Cinereous Harrier) **F**
C. macrourus (Pallid Harrier) **B,C,H**
C. melanoleucos (Pied Harrier) **B,H,I**
C. pygargus (Montagu's Harrier) **B,C**
C. aeruginosus (Marsh Harrier) **B**
C. ranivorus (African Marsh Harrier) **C**
C. buffoni (Long-winged Harrier) **E,F**
MELIERAX
M. metabates (Dark Chanting-Goshawk) **B,C**
M. canorus (Pale Chanting-Goshawk) **C**
MICRONISUS
M. gabar (Gabar Goshawk) **C**
KAUPIFALCO
K. monogrammicus (Lizard Buzzard) **C**
ACCIPITER
A. poliogaster (Gray-bellied Goshawk) **F**
A. trivirgatus (Asian Crested Goshawk) **H.J.K**
A. griseiceps (Sulawesi Crested Goshawk) **J,K**
A. tachiro (African Goshawk) **C**
A. castanilius (Chestnut-bellied Sparrowhawk) **C**
A. brevipes (Levant Sparrowhawk) **B**
A. badius (Shikra) **B,C,H,I,J**
A. butleri (Nicobar Shikra) **I**
A. soloensis (Gray Frog Hawk) **B,I**
A. francesii (Frances' Sparrowhawk) **D**
A. trinotatus (Spot-tailed Sparrowhawk) **K**
A. fasciatus (Australian Goshawk) **J,K,L,M,O**
A. novaehollandiae (Variable Goshawk) **J,K,L,M,O**
A. melanochlamys (Black-mantled Goshawk) **L**
A. albogularis (Pied Goshawk) **O**
A. rufitorques (Fiji Goshawk) **O**
A. haplochrous (New Caledonia Sparrowhawk) **O**
A. henicogrammus (Gray's Goshawk) **K**

A. luteoschistaceus (Blue & Gray Sparrowhawk) **O**
A. imitator (Imitator Sparrowhawk) **O** [?]
A. poliocephalus (New Guinea Gray-headed Goshawk) **L**
A. princeps (New Britain Gray-headed Goshawk) **O**
A. superciliosus (Tiny Sparrowhawk) **F**
A. collaris (Semi-collared Sparrowhawk) **F** [?]
A. erythropus (Red-thighed Sparrowhawk) **C**
A. minullus (African Little Sparrowhawk) **C**
A. gularis (Japanese Sparrowhawk) **B,J**
A. virgatus (Besra Sparrowhawk) **B,H,I,J**
A. nanus (Dwarf Sparrowhawk) **K** [?]
A. cirrhocephalus (Australian Collared Sparrowhawk) **D,K,L,M**
A. brachyurus (New Britain Collared Sparrowhawk) **O** [?]
A. erythrauchen (Gray Moluccan Collared Sparrowhawk) **K**
A. rhodogaster (Vinous-breasted Sparrowhawk) **J,K**
A. madagascariensis (Madagascar Sparrowhawk) **D**
A. ovampensis (Ovampo Sparrowhawk) **C**
A. nisus (Northern Sparrowhawk) **B,H**
A. rufiventris (Rufous-breasted Sparrowhawk) **C**
A. striatus (Sharp-shinned Hawk) **A,E,F**
A. cooperii (Cooper's Hawk) **A**
A. gundlachii (Gundlach's Hawk) **E** [?]
A. bicolor (Bicoloured Sparrowhawk) **E,F**
A. melanoleucus (Great Sparrowhawk) **C**
A. henstii (Henst's Goshawk) **D**
A. gentilis (Northern Goshawk) **A,B,E**
A. meyerianus (Meyer's Goshawk) **K,O**
A. buergersi (Chestnut-shouldered Goshawk) **L**
ERYHROTRIORCHIS
E. radiatus (Red Goshawk) **M** [V]
MEGATRIORCHIS
M. doriae (Doria's Goshawk) **L**
UROTRIORCHIS
U. macrourus (African Long-tailed Hawk) **C**
BUTASTUR
B. rufipennis (Grasshopper Buzzard-Eagle) **C**
B. liventer (Rufous-winged Buzzard) **I,J,K**
B. teesa (White-eyed Buzzard) **H,I**
B. indicus (Gray-faced Buzzard-Eagle) **B,J**
LEUCOPTERNIS
L. schistacea (Slate-colored Hawk) **F**
L. plumbea (Plumbeous Hawk) **E,F** [?]
L. princeps (Barred Hawk) **E,F**
L. melanops (Black-faced Hawk) **F**
L. kuhli (White-browed Hawk) **F**
L. lacernulata (White-necked Hawk) **F** [?]
L. semiplumbea (Semi-plumbeous Hawk) **E,F**
L. albicollis (White Hawk) **E,F**
L. occidentalis (Gray-backed Hawk) **F** [I]
L. polionota (Mantled Hawk) **F** [I]
BUTEOGALLUS
B. anthracinus (Common Black Hawk) **A,E,F**
B. subtilis (Mangrove Black Hawk) **E,F**
B. aequinoctialis (Rufous Crab Hawk) **F**
B. urubitinga (Great Black Hawk) **E,F**
B. meridionalis (Savanna Hawk) **E,F**
HARPYHALIAETUS
H. solitarius (Black Solitary Eagle) **E,F** [?]
H. coronatus (Crowned Solitary Eagle) **F** [?]
BUSARELLUS
B. nigricollis (Black-collared Hawk) **E,F**
GERANOAETUS
G. melanoleucus (Black-chested Buzzard Eagle) **F**
PARABUTEO
P. unicinctus (Harris' Hawk) **A,E,F**
BUTEO
B. nitidus (Gray Hawk) **A,E,F**
B. magnirostris (Roadside Hawk) **E,F**
B. leucorrhous (White-rumped Hawk) **F**
B. ridgwayi (Ridgway's Hawk) **E** [?]
B. lineatus (Red-shouldered Hawk) **A,E**
B. platypterus (Broad-winged Hawk) **A,E,F**
B. brachyurus (Short-tailed Hawk) **A,E,F**
B. albigula (White-throated Hawk) **F**
B. swainsonii (Swainson's Hawk) **A,E,F**
B. galapagoensis (Galapagos Hawk) **G** [R]
B. albicaudatus (White-tailed Hawk) **A,E,F**
B. polyosoma (Red-backed Hawk) **F**
B. poecilochrous (Variable Hawk) **F**
B. albonotatus (Zone-tailed Hawk) **A,E,F**
B. solitarius (Hawaiian Hawk) **P** [R]
B. ventralis (Rufous-tailed Hawk) **F** [?]

B. jamaicensis (Red-tailed Hawk) **A,E,F**
B. buteo (Eurasian Buzzard) **B,C,I**
B. oreophilus (African Mountain Buzzard) **C**
B. brachypterus (Madagascar Buzzard) **D**
B. lagopus (Rough-legged Hawk) **A,B**
B. rufinus (Long-legged Buzzard) **B,C**
B. hemilasius (Upland Buzzard) **B**
B. regalis (Ferruginous Hawk) **A**
B. auguralis (African Red-tailed Buzzard) **C**
B. rufofuscus (Jackal Buzzard) **C**
MORPHNUS
M. guianensis (Guiana Crested Eagle) **E,F** [R]
HARPIA
H. harpyja (American Harpy Eagle) **E,F** [R]
HARPYOPSIS
H. novaeguineae (New Guinea Harpy Eagle) **L** [?]
PITHECOPHAGA
P. jefferyi (Philippine Eagle) **J** [E]
ICTINAETUS
I. malayensis (Indian Black Eagle) **H,I,J**
AQUILA
A. pomarina (Lesser Spotted Eagle) **B,H,I**
A. clanga (Greater Spotted Eagle) **B,C**
A. rapax (Tawny Eagle) **B,C,H,I**
A. heliaca (Imperial Eagle) **B,H** [?]
A. gurneyi (Gurney's Eagle) **K,L**
A. chrysaetos (Golden Eagle) **A,B**
A. audax (Wedge-tailed Eagle) **L,M**
A. verreauxii (Verreaux's Eagle) **C**
HIERAAETUS
H. wahlbergi (Wahlberg's Eagle) **C**
H. fasciatus (Bonelli's Eagle) **B,H,K**
H. spilogaster (African Hawk-Eagle) **C**
H. pennatus (Booted Eagle) **B**
H. morphnoides (Little Eagle) **L,M**
H. ayresii (Ayres' Hawk-Eagle) **C**
H. kienerii (Chestnut-bellied Hawk-Eagle) **H,I,J,K**
SPIZASTUR
S. melanoleucus (Black-&-White-Hawk-Eagle) **E,F**
SPIZAETUS
S. occipitalis (Long-crested Eagle) **C**
S. africanus (Cassin's Hawk-Eagle) **C**
S. cirrhatus (Changeable Hawk-Eagle) **H,I,J**
S. nipalensis (Hodgson's Hawk-Eagle) **B,H,I,J**
S. bartelsi (Java Hawk-Eagle) **J** [?]
S. lanceolatus (Sulawesi Hawk-Eagle) **K**
S. philippensis (Philippine Hawk-Eagle) **J** [?]
S. alboniger (Blyth's Hawk-Eagle) **I,J**
S. nanus (Wallace's Hawk-Eagle) **J,K**
S. tyrannus (Black Hawk-Eagle) **E,F**
S. ornatus (Ornate Hawk-Eagle) **E,F**
S. coronatus (Crowned Eagle) **C**
S. isidori (Black-&-Chestnut Eagle) **F**
POLEMAETUS
P. bellicosus (Martial Eagle) **C**
31 SAGITTARIIDAE (SECRETARY BIRD)
SAGITTARIUS
S. serpentarius (Secretary Bird) **C**
32 FALCONIDAE (CARACARAS, FALCONS)
DAPTRIUS
D. ater (Yellow-throated Caracara) **F**
D. americanus (Red-throated Caracara) **E,F**
PHALCOBOENUS
P. carunculatus (Carunculated Caracara) **F**
P. megalopterus (Mountain Caracara) **F**
P. albogularis (White-throated Caracara) **F**
P. australis (Forster's Caracara) **F**
POLYBORUS
P. plancus (Crested Caracara) **A,E,F**
MILVAGO
M. chimango (Chimango) **F**
M. chimachima (Yellow-headed Caracara) **E,F**
HERPETOTHERES
H. cachinnans (Laughing Falcon) **E,F**
MICRASTUR
M. ruficollis (Barred Forest-Falcon) **E,F**
M. gilvicollis (Lined Forest-Falcon) **F**
M. mirandollei (Slaty-backed Forest-Falcon) **E,F**
M. semitorquatus (Collared Forest-Falcon) **E,F**
M. buckleyi (Traylor's Forest-Falcon) **F** [?]
SPIZIAPTERYX
S. circumcinctus (Spot-winged Falconet) **F**
POLIHIERAX
P. semitorquatus (African Pygmy Falcon) **C**
P. insignis (White-rumped Pygmy Falcon) **I**

NEW WORLD QUAILS, PARTRIDGES, OLD WORLD QUAILS, PHEASANTS, PEAFOWL

MICROHIERAX
M. caerulescens (Collared Falconet) **H,I**
M. fringillarius (Black-thighed Falconet) **I,J**
M. latifrons (Bornean Falconet) **J**
M. erythrogenys (Philippine Falconet) **J**
M. melanoleucus (Pied Falconet) **I**
FALCO
F. naumanni (Lesser Kestrel) **B,C**
F. rupicoloides (Greater Kestrel) **C**
F. alopex (Fox Kestrel) **C**
F. sparverius (American Kestrel) **A,E,F**
F. tinnunculus (Eurasian Kestrel) **B,C,H,J**
F. newtoni (Madagascar Kestrel) **D**
F. punctatus (Mauritius Kestrel) **D**   E
F. araea (Seychelles Kestrel) **D**
F. moluccensis (Moluccan Kestrel) **K**
F. cenchroides (Australian Kestrel) **L,M**
F. ardosiaceus (Gray Kestrel) **C**
F. dickinsoni (Dickinson's Kestrel) **C**
F. zoniventris (Madagascar Banded Kestrel) **D**
F. vespertinus (Western Red-footed Falcon) **B,C**
F. amurensis (Eastern Red-footed Falcon) **B,C**
F. chicquera (Red-headed Falcon) **C,H**
F. columbarius (Merlin) **A,B,F,H,I**
F. berigora (Brown Falcon) **L,M**
F. novaezeelandiae (New Zealand Falcon) **N**
F. subbuteo (Northern Hobby) **B,C,H,I**
F. cuvieri (African Hobby) **C**
F. severus (Oriental Hobby) **I,J,L**
F. longipennis (Australian Hobby) **K,L,M**
F. eleonorae (Eleonora's Falcon) **B,C,D**
F. concolor (Sooty Falcon) **C,D**
F. rufigularis (Bat Falcon) **E,F**
F. femoralis (Aplomado Falcon) **A,E,F**
F. hypoleucos (Gray Falcon) **M**   ?
F. subniger (Black Falcon) **M**
F. biarmicus (Lanner Falcon) **B,C**
F. mexicanus (Prairie Falcon) **A,E**
F. jugger (Lagger Falcon) **H**
F. cherrug (Saker Falcon) **B,H**
F. rusticolus (Gyr Falcon) **A,B**
F. deiroleucus (Orange-breasted Falcon) **E,F**   ?
F. fasciinucha (Taita Falcon) **C**
F. peregrinus (Peregrine Falcon) **A,B,C,D,E,F,
H,I,J,K,L,M,O**   V
F. pelegrinoides (Barbary Falcon) **C**

GALLIFORMES

33 MEGAPODIIDAE (MEGAPODES)
MEGAPODIUS
M. nicobariensis (Nicobar Scrub Fowl) **I**   ?
M. cumingii (Philippine Scrub Fowl) **J,K**
M. bernsteinii (Sula Scrub Fowl) **K**   ?
M. affinis (New Guinea Scrub Fowl) **L**
M. reinwardt (Orange-footed Scrub Fowl) **K,L,M**
M. eremita (Bismarck Scrub Fowl) **L,O**
M. freycinet (Dusky Scrub Fowl) **K,L**
M. layardi (Banks Is Scrub Fowl) **O**
M. laperouse (Marianas Scrub Fowl) **J**   R
M. pritchardii (Polynesian Scrub Fowl) **O**   ?
M. wallacei (Moluccas Scrub Fowl) **K**   ?
LEIPOA
L. ocellata (Mallee Fowl) **M**   V
ALECTURA
A. lathami (Australian Brush-Turkey) **M**
TALEGALLA
T. cuvieri (Red-billed Brush-Turkey) **K,L**
T. fuscirostris (Black-billed Brush-Turkey) **L**
T. jobiensis (Brown-collared Brush-Turkey) **L**
AEPYPODIUS
A. arfakianus (Wattled Brush-Turkey) **K,L**
A. bruijnii (Bruijn's Brush-Turkey) **K**   ?
MACROCEPHALON
M. maleo (Maleo Fowl) **K**   V
34 CRACIDAE (GUANS, CURASSOWS)
ORTALIS
O. vetula (Plain Chachalaca) **A,E**
O. cinereiceps (Gray-headed Chachalaca) **E,F**
O. garrula (Chestnut-winged Chachalaca) **E,F**
O. ruficauda (Rufous-vented Chachalaca) **E,F**
O. erythroptera (Rufous-headed Chachalaca) **F**   ?
O. poliocephala (West Mexican Chachalaca) **E**
O. canicollis (Chaco Chachalaca) **F**
O. leucogastra (White-bellied Chachalaca) **E**
O. motmot (Variable Chachalaca) **F**

PENELOPE
P. argyrotis (Band-tailed Guan) **F**
P. barbata (Bearded Guan) **F**   ?
P. montagnii (Andean Guan) **F**
P. ortoni (Baudo Guan) **F**
P. marail (Marail Guan) **F**
P. superciliaris (Rusty-margined Guan) **F**
P. dabbenei (Red-faced Guan) **F**   ?
P. obscura (Dusky-legged Guan) **F**
P. jacquacu (Spix's Guan) **F**
P. albipennis (White-winged Guan) **F**   E
P. perspicax (Cauca Guan) **F**   E
P. purpurascens (Crested Guan) **E,F**
P. jacucaca (White-browed Guan) **F**   ?
P. ochrogaster (Chestnut-bellied Guan) **F**   ?
P. pileata (White-crested Guan) **F**
ABURRIA
A. pipile (Blue-throated Piping Guan) **E,F**
A. cujubi (Red-throated Piping Guan) **F**
A. jacutinga (Black-fronted Piping Guan) **F**
A. aburri (Wattled Guan) **F**
CHAMAEPETES
C. unicolor (Black Guan) **E**
C. goudotii (Sickle-winged Guan) **F**
PENELOPINA
P. nigra (Highland Guan) **E**   ?
OREOPHASIS
O. derbianus (Horned Guan) **E**   E
NOTHOCRAX
N. urumutum (Nocturnal Curassow) **F**
CRAX
C. tomentosa (Lesser Razor-billed Curassow) **F**
C. salvini (Salvin's Curassow) **F**
C. mitu (Razor-billed Curassow) **F**   E
C. pauxi (Helmeted Curassow) **F**
C. unicornis (Horned Curassow) **F**
C. rubra (Great Curassow) **E,F**
C. alberti (Blue-billed Curassow) **F**   V
C. daubentoni (Yellow-knobbed Curassow) **F**
C. alector (Black Curassow) **F**
C. globulosa (Wattled Curassow) **F**   ?
C. fasciolata (Bare-faced Curassow) **F**
C. blumenbachii (Red-billed Curassow) **F**   E
35 MELEAGRIDIDAE (TURKEYS)
MELEAGRIS
M. gallopavo (Wild Turkey) **A**
AGRIOCHARIS
A. ocellata (Ocellated Turkey) **E**   ?
36 TETRAONIDAE (GROUSE)
DENDRAGAPUS
D. falcipennis (Siberian Spruce Grouse) **B**
D. canadensis (Spruce Grouse) **A**
D. obscurus (Blue Grouse) **A**
LAGOPUS
L. lagopus (Willow Ptarmigan) **A,B**
L. mutus (Rock Ptarmigan) **A,B**
L. leucurus (White-tailed Ptarmigan) **A**
TETRAO
T. mlokosiewiczi (Caucasian Black Grouse) **B**   ?
T. tetrix (Black Grouse) **B**
T. parvirostris (Black-billed Capercaillie) **B**
T. urogallus (Western Capercaillie) **B**
BONASA
B. sewerzowi (Severtzov's Hazel Grouse) **B**
B. bonasia (Hazel Grouse) **B**
B. umbellus (Ruffed Grouse) **A**
CENTROCERCUS
C. urophasianus (Sage Grouse) **A**
TYMPANUCHUS
T. phasianellus (Sharp-tailed Grouse) **A**
T. cupido (Greater Prairie Chicken) **A**
T. pallidicinctus (Lesser Prairie Chicken) **A**
37 PHASIANIDAE (NEW WORLD QUAILS,
PARTRIDGES, OLD WORLD QUAILS,
PHEASANTS, PEAFOWL)
ODONTOPHORINAE
DENDRORTYX
D. barbatus (Bearded Tree Quail) **E**   ?
D. macroura (Long-tailed Tree Quail) **E**
D. leucophrys (Buffy-crowned Tree Quail) **E**
OREORTYX
O. picta (Mountain Quail) **A,E**
CALLIPEPLA
C. squamata (Scaled Quail) **A**
C. californica (California Quail) **A,E**

LOPHORTYX
L. gambelii (Gambel's Quail) **A,E**
L. douglasii (Elegant Quail) **E**
PHILORTYX
P. fasciatus (Banded Quail) **E**
COLINUS
C. virginianus (Northern Bobwhite) **A,E**
C. nigrogularis (Black-throated Quail) **E**
C. cristatus (Crested Bobwhite) **E,F**
ODONTOPHORUS
O. gujanensis (Marbled Wood Quail) **E,F**
O. capueira (Spot-winged Wood Quail) **F**
O. erythrops (Rufous-fronted Wood Quail) **E,F**
O. atrifrons (Black-fronted Wood Quail) **F**
O. melanonotus (Black-backed Wood Quail) **F**
O. hyperythrus (Chestnut Wood Quail) **F**   ?
O. speciosus (Rufous-breasted Wood Quail) **F**
O. strophium (Gorgeted Wood Quail) **F**   E
O. dialeucos (Tacarcuna Wood Quail) **F**
O. colombianus (Venezuela Wood Quail) **F**
O. leucolaemus (White-throated Wood Quail) **E**
O. balliviani (Stripe-faced Wood Quail) **F**
O. stellatus (Starred Wood Quail) **F**
O. guttatus (Spotted Wood Quail) **E**
DACTYLORTYX
D. thoracicus (Singing Quail) **E**
CYRTONYX
C. montezumae (Montezuma Quail) **A,E**
C. sallei (Salle's Quail) **E**
C. ocellatus (Ocellated Quail) **E**
RHYNCHORTYX
R. cinctus (Tawny-faced Quail) **E,F**
PHASIANINAE
LERWA
L. lerwa (Snow Partridge) **B**
AMMOPERDIX
A. griseogularis (See-See Partridge) **B,H**
A. heyi (Sand Partridge) **B,C**
TETRAOGALLUS
T. caucasicus (Caucasian Snowcock) **B**
T. caspius (Caspian Snowcock) **B**
T. tibetanus (Tibetan Snowcock) **B**
T. altaicus (Altai Snowcock) **B**   ?
T. himalayensis (Himalayan Snowcock) **B,H**
TETRAOPHASIS
T. obscurus (Verreaux's Monal Partridge) **B**
T. szechenyii (Szechenyi's Monal Partridge) **B**
ALECTORIS
A. graeca (Rock Partridge) **B,H**
A. chukar (Chukar Partridge) **B**
A. magna (Przewalski's Rock Partridge) **B**
A. philbyi (Philby's Rock Partridge) **C**
A. barbara (Barbary Partridge) **B**
A. rufa (Red-legged Partridge) **B**
A. melanocephala (Arabian Chukar) **C**
ANUROPHASIS
A. monorthonyx (Snow Mountain Quail) **L**
FRANCOLINUS
F. francolinus (Black Partridge) **B,H**
F. pictus (Painted Partridge) **H**
F. pintadeanus (Chinese Francolin) **B,H,I**
F. afer (Red-necked Francolin) **C**
F. swainsonii (Swainson's Francolin) **C**
F. rufopictus (Painted Francolin) **C**
F. leucoscepus (Yellow-necked Francolin) **C**
F. erckelii (Erckel's Francolin) **C**   E
F. ochropectus (Pale-bellied Francolin) **C**
F. castaneicollis (Chestnut-naped Francolin) **C**
F. jacksoni (Jackson's Francolin) **C**
F. nobilis (Handsome Francolin) **C**
F. camerunensis (Cameroun Mountain
Francolin) **C**   R
    I
F. swierstrai (Swierstra's Francolin) **C**
F. ahantensis (Ahanta Francolin) **C**
F. squamatus (Scaly Francolin) **C**
F. griseostriatus (Gray-striped Francolin) **C**
F. bicalcaratus (Double-spurred Francolin) **B,C**
F. icterorhynchus (Yellow-billed Francolin) **C**
F. clappertoni (Clapperton's Francolin) **C**
F. hildebrandti (Hildebrandt's Francolin) **C**
F. natalensis (Natal Francolin) **C**
F. hartlaubi (Hartlaub's Francolin) **C**
F. harwoodi (Harwood's Francolin) **C**
F. adspersus (Red-billed Francolin) **C**
F. capensis (Cape Francolin) **C**
F. sephaena (Crested Francolin) **C**

F. streptophorus (Ring-necked Francolin) **C**
F. psilolaemus (Montane Francolin) **C**
F. rovuma (Kirk's Francolin) **C**
F. shelleyi (Shelley's Francolin) **C**
F. africanus (Graywing Francolin) **C**
F. levalliantoides (Archer's Graywing Francolin) **C**
F. levaillantii (Red-winged Francolin) **C**
F. finschi (Finsch's Francolin) **C**
F. coqui (Coqui's Francolin) **C**
F. albogularis (White-throated Francolin) **C**
F. schlegelii (Schlegel's Francolin) **C**
F. lathami (Latham's Francolin) **C**
F. nahani (Nahan's Forest Francolin) **C**   R
F. pondicerianus (Indian Gray Francolin) **B,H**
F. gularis (Swamp Partridge) **H**   ?
PERDIX
P. perdix (Gray Partridge) **B**
P. dauuricae (Daurian Partridge) **B**
P. hodgsoniae (Tibetan Partridge) **B**
RHIZOTHERA
R. longirostris (Long-billed Wood Partridge) **J**
MARGAROPERDIX
M. madagarensis (Madagascar Partridge) **D**
MELANOPERDIX
M. nigra (Black Wood Partridge) **J**   ?
COTURNIX
C. coturnix (Common Quail) **B,C,D,H**
C. japonica (Japanese Quail) **B,I,J**
C. coromandelica (Rain Quail) **H,I**
C. delegorguei (Harlequin Quail) **C**
C. pectoralis (Pectoral Quail) **M**
C. australis (Brown Quail) **K,L,M**
C. ypsilophora (Tasmanian Brown Quail) **M**
C. chinensis (Asian Blue Quail) **C,H,I,J,K,L,M**
PERDICULA
P. asiatica (Jungle Bush Quail) **H**
P. argoondah (Rock Bush Quail) **H**
P. erythrorhyncha (Painted Bush Quail) **H**
P. manipurensis (Manipur Bush Quail) **H**   ?
ARBOROPHILA
A. torqueola (Common Hill-Partridge) **H,I**
A. rufogularis (Rufous-throated Hill-Partridge) **H,I**
A. atrogularis (White-cheeked Hill-Partridge) **H,I**   ?
A. crudigularis (White-throated Hill-Partridge) **J**
A. mandellii (Red-breasted Hill-Partridge) **H**
A. brunneopectus (Brown-breasted Hill-Partridge) **H,I**
A. rufipectus (Boulton's Hill-Partridge) **B**   ?
A. gingica (Rickett's Hill-Partridge) **B**   ?
A. davidi (David's Tree Partridge) **I**   ?
A. cambodiana (Chestnut-headed Tree Partridge) **I**   ?
A. orientalis (Sumatran Hill Partridge) **J**
A. javanica (Chestnut-bellied Tree Partridge) **J**
A. rubrirostris (Red-billed Tree Partridge) **J**
A. hyperythra (Red-breasted Tree Partridge) **J**
A. ardens (Hainan Hill-Partridge) **I**   ?
TROPICOPERDIX
T. charltonii (Chestnut-breasted Tree Partridge) **I,J**   ?
T. chloropus (Green-legged Hill Partridge) **I**
T. merlini (Annamese Hill Partridge) **I**
CALOPERDIX
C. oculea (Ferruginous Wood-Partridge) **I,J**
HAEMATORTYX
H. sanguiniceps (Crimson-headed Wood-Partridge) **J**
ROLLULUS
R. roulroul (Crested Wood-Partridge) **I,J**
PTILOPACHUS
P. petrosus (Stone Partridge) **C**
BAMBUSICOLA
B. fytchii (Bamboo Partridge) **B,H,I**
B. thoracica (Chinese Bamboo Partridge) **B,J**
GALLOPERDIX
G. spadicea (Red Spurfowl) **H**
G. lunulata (Painted Spurfowl) **H**
G. bicalcarata (Ceylon Spurfowl) **H**
OPHRYSIA
O. superciliosa (Himalayan Mountain Quail) **H**   X
ITHAGINIS
I. cruentus (Blood Pheasant) **B,H,I**
TRAGOPAN
T. melanocephalus (Western Tragopan) **H**   E
T. satyra (Satyr Tragopan) **H**
T. blythii (Blyth's Tragopan) **B,H,I**   R
T. temminckii (Temminck's Tragopan) **B,I**

T. caboti (Cabot's Tragopan) **B**   E
PUCRASIA
P. macrolopha (Koklass Pheasant) **B,H**
LOPHOPHORUS
L. impejanus (Himalayan Monal Pheasant) **H**
L. sclateri (Sclater's Monal Pheasant) **H,I**   R
L. lhuysii (Chinese Monal Pheasant) **B**   E
GALLUS
G. gallus (Red Junglefowl) **B,H,I,J**
G. lafayettii (Ceylon Junglefowl) **H**
G. sonneratii (Gray Junglefowl) **H**
G. varius (Green Junglefowl) **J,K**
LOPHURA
L. leucomelana (Kalij Pheasant) **H,I**
L. nycthemera (Silver Pheasant) **B,I**
L. imperialis (Imperial Pheasant) **I**   V
L. edwardsi (Edwards' Pheasant) **I**   V
L. haitiensis (Vo Quy's Pheasant) **I**   ?
L. swinhoii (Swinhoe's Pheasant) **J**   V
L. inornata (Salvadori's Pheasant) **J**
L. erythrophthalma (Crestless Fireback Pheasant) **I,J**
L. diardi (Siamese Fireback Pheasant) **I**   ?
L. bulweri (Bulwer's Pheasant) **J**   V
CROSSOPTILON
C. crossoptilon (White Eared-Pheasant) **B**   V
C. mantchuricum (Brown Eared-Pheasant) **B**   E
C. auritum (Blue Eared-Pheasant) **B**   ?
CATREUS
C. wallichii (Cheer Pheasant) **B**   E
SYRMATICUS
S. ellioti (Elliot's Pheasant) **B**   E
S. humiae (Mrs Hume's Pheasant) **B,I**   R
S. mikado (Mikado Pheasant) **J**   V
S. soemmerringi (Copper Pheasant) **B**
S. reevesii (Reeves' Pheasant) **B**   ?
PHASIANUS
P. colchicus (Common Pheasant) **B,I,J**
P. versicolor (Green Pheasant) **B**
CHRYSOLOPHUS
C. pictus (Golden Pheasant) **B**
C. amherstiae (Lady Amherst's Pheasant) **B,I**   ?
POLYPLECTRON
P. chalcurum (Sumatran Peacock-Pheasant) **J**
P. inopinatum (Rothschild's Peacock-Pheasant) **J**
P. germaini (Germain's Peacock-Pheasant) **I**   ?
P. bicalcaratum (Burmese Peacock-Pheasant) **H,I**
P. malacense (Malay Peacock-Pheasant) **I,J**   ?
P. emphanum (Palawan Peacock-Pheasant) **J**   V
RHEINARTIA
R. ocellata (Crested Argus Pheasant) **I,J**   R
ARGUSIANUS
A. argus (Great Argus Pheasant) **I,J**
PAVO
P. cristatus (Common Peafowl) **H**
P. muticus (Green Peafowl) **H,I,J**   V
AFROPAVO
A. congensis (Congo Peafowl) **C**   S
38 NUMIDIDAE (GUINEAFOWL)
PHASIDUS
P. niger (Black Guineafowl) **C**
AGELASTES
A. meleagrides (White-breasted Guineafowl) **C**   E
NUMIDA
N. meleagris (Helmeted Guineafowl) **B,C,D**
GUTTERA
G. plumifera (Plumed Guineafowl) **C**
G. edouardi (Crested Guineafowl) **C**
ACRYLLIUM
A. vulturinum (Vulturine Guineafowl) **C**

GRUIFORMES

39 MESITORNITHIDAE (MESITES)
MESITORNIS
M. variegata (White-breasted Mesite) **D**   R
M. unicolor (Brown Mesite) **D**   ?
MONIAS
M. benschi (Bensch's Monia) **D**   R
40 TURNICIDAE (BUTTONQUAILS)
TURNIX
T. sylvatica (Little Buttonquail) **B,C,H,I,J,K**
T. maculosa (Red-backed Buttonquail) **J,K,L,M,O**
T. everetti (Sumba Buttonquail) **K**   ?
T. worcesteri (Worcester's Buttonquail) **J**   ?
T. hottentotta (Hottentot Buttonquail) **C**
T. tanki (Yellow-legged Buttonquail) **B,H,I**

T. suscitator (Bustard Quail) **B,H,I,J,K**
T. nigricollis (Madagascar Buttonquail) **D**
T. ocellata (Spotted Buttonquail) **J**
T. melanogaster (Black-breasted Buttonquail) **M**   ?
T. varia (Painted Buttonquail) **M,O**
T. castanota (Chestnut-backed Buttonquail) **M**
T. pyrrhothorax (Red-chested Buttonquail) **M**
T. velox (Little Quail) **M**
ORTYXELOS
O. meiffrenii (Quail Plover) **C**
41 PEDIONOMIDAE (PLAINS-WANDERER)
PEDIONOMUS
P. torquatus (Plains-wanderer) **M**   ?
42 GRUIDAE (CRANES)
GRUINAE
GRUS
G. grus (Common Crane) **B,H**
G. nigricollis (Black-necked Crane) **B,H**   V
G. monacha (Hooded Crane) **B**   V
G. canadensis (Sandhill Crane) **A,B,E**
G. japonensis (Manchurian Crane) **B**   V
G. americana (Whooping Crane) **A**   E
G. vipio (Japanese White-naped Crane) **B**   V
G. antigone (Sarus Crane) **H,I**
G. rubicundus (Brolga) **L,M**
G. leucogeranus (Siberian White Crane) **B,H**   E
BUGERANUS
B. carunculatus (Wattled Crane) **C**   S
ANTHROPOIDES
A. virgo (Demoiselle Crane) **B,C**
A. paradisea (Stanley Crane) **C**
BALEARICINAE
BALEARICA
B. pavonina (Black Crowned Crane) **C**
B. regulorum (Gray Crowned Crane) **C**
43 ARAMIDAE (LIMPKIN)
ARAMUS
A. guarauna (Limpkin) **A,E,F**
44 PSOPHIIDAE (TRUMPETERS)
PSOPHIA
P. crepitans (Gray-winged Trumpeter) **F**
P. leucoptera (White-winged Trumpeter) **F**
P. viridis (Green-winged Trumpeter) **F**
45 RALLIDAE (RAILS, CRAKES, GALLINULES, COOTS)
HIMANTORNIS
H. haematopus (Nkulengu Rail) **C**
CANIRALLUS
C. oculeus (Gray-throated Rail) **C**
C. kioloides (Madagascar Gray-throated Rail) **D**
C. cuvieri (White-throated Rail) **D**
EULABEORNIS
E. castaneoventris (Chestnut-bellied Rail) **K,M**
E. plumbeiventris (Bare-eyed Rail) **K,L**
E. rosenbergii (Bald-faced Rail) **K**
E. calopterus (Red-winged Wood-Rail) **F**
E. saracura (Slaty-breasted Wood-Rail) **F**
E. ypecaha (Giant Wood-Rail) **F**
E. wolfi (Brown Wood-Rail) **F**
E. mangle (Little Wood-Rail) **F**
E. cajaneus (Gray-necked Wood-Rail) **E,F**
E. axillaris (Rufous-necked Wood-Rail) **E,F**
E. concolor (Uniform Crake) **E,F**
RALLUS
R. plateni (Platen's Rail) **K**
R. wallacii (Wallace's Rail) **K**
R. insignis (New Britain Rail) **O**
R. lafresnayanus (New Caledonian Wood-Rail) **O**
R. sylvestris (Lord Howe Wood-Rail) **M**
R. poecilopterus (Barred-wing Rail) **O**
R. sanguinolentus (Plumbeous Rail) **F**
R. nigricans (Blackish Rail) **F**
R. maculatus (Spotted Rail) **F**
R. philippensis (Buff-banded Rail) **J,K,L,M,N,O**
R. striatus (Blue-breasted Banded Rail) **B,H,I,J,K**
R. torquatus (Barred Rail) **J,K,L**
R. owstoni (Guam Rail) **O**   V
R. pectoralis (Slate-breasted Rail) **J,L,M,N**
R. caerulescens (Kaffir Rail) **C**
R. madagascariensis (Madagascar Rail) **D**
R. aquaticus (Water Rail) **B,C,H**
R. semiplumbeous (Bogota Rail) **F**   V
R. longirostris (Clapper Rail) **A,E,F**
R. wetmorei (Plain-flanked Rail) **F**   ?
R. limicola (Virginia Rail) **A,E,F**
R. antarcticus (Austral Rail) **F**   ?

R. okinawae (Okinawa Rail) **J** [?]
ATLANTISIA
A. rogersi (Inaccessible I Rail) **Q** [R]
GALLIRALLUS
G. australis (Weka) **N**
ROUGETIUS
R. rougetii (Rouget's Rail) **C**
CYANOLIMNAS
C. cerverai (Zapata Rail) **E** [R]
RALLINA
R. rubra (New Guinea Chestnut Rail) **L**
R. leucospila (White-striped Chestnut Rail) **L**
R. forbesi (Forbes' Chestnut Rail) **L**
R. mayri (Mayr's Chestnut Rail) **L**
R. castaneiceps (Chestnut-headed Crake) **E,F**
R. tricolor (Red-necked Crake) **J,L,M**
R. canningi (Andaman Banded Crake) **I**
R. fasciata (Red-legged Crake) **I,J,K**
R. eurizonoides (Banded Crake) **B,H,I,J**
R. paykullii (Band-bellied Crake) **B,J**
COTURNICOPS
C. rufa (Red-chested Crake) **C**
C. pulchra (White-spotted Crake) **C**
C. lugens (African Chestnut-headed Crake) **C**
C. boehmi (Streaky-breasted Crake) **C**
C. elegans (Buff-spotted Crake) **C**
C. affinis (Chestnut-tailed Crake) **C**
C. insularis (Madagascar Crake) **D**
C. watersi (Waters' Crake) **D**
C. ayresi (White-winged Crake) **C**
C. schomburgkii (Ocellated Crake) **F**
C. notata (Darwin's Rail) **F**
C. noveboracensis (Yellow Rail) **A,B,E**
LATERALLUS
L. fasciatus (Black-banded Crake) **F**
L. levraudi (Rusty-flanked Crake) **F** [?]
L. ruber (Ruddy Crake) **E**
L. viridis (Russet-crowned Crake) **F**
L. exilis (Gray-breasted Crake) **E,F**
L. spilonotus (Galapagos Rail) **G**
L. melanophaius (Rufous-sided Crake) **F**
L. albigularis (White-throated Crake) **E,F**
L. leucopyrrhus (Red & White Crake) **F**
L. jamaicensis (Black Rail) **A,E,F**
L. xenopterus (Rufous-faced Crake) **F** [?]
CREX
C. crex (Corn Crake) **B** [?]
PORZANA
P. egregia (African Crake) **C**
P. flavirostra (African Black Crake) **C**
P. olivieri (Olivier's Rail) **D**
P. flaviventer (Yellow-breasted Crake) **E,F**
P. cinerea (White-browed Rail) **J,K,L,M,O**
P. spiloptera (Dot-winged Crake) **F** [?]
P. albicollis (White-throated Crake) **F**
P. marginalis (Striped Crake) **C**
P. erythrops (Paint-billed Crake) **F**
P. columbiana (Colombian Crake) **E,F**
P. tabuensis (Sooty Crake) **L,M,N,O**
P. atra (Henderson Island Crake) **O**
P. parva (Little Crake) **B,H**
P. pusilla (Baillon's Crake) **B,C,H,J,L,M,N**
P. fluminea (Australian Spotted Crake) **M**
P. porzana (Spotted Crake) **B,H**
P. carolina (Sora) **A,E,F**
P. fusca (Ruddy-breasted Crake) **B,H,J,K**
AMAURORNIS
A. olivaceus (Rufous-tailed Moorhen) **J,K,L,M,O** [?]
A. isabellinus (Sulawesi Water Hen) **K**
A. ineptus (New Guinea Flightless Rail) **L**
A. akool (Brown Crake) **H,I**
A. bicolor (Elwes' Crake) **B,H,I**
A. phoenicurus (White-breasted Water Hen) **H,I,J,K**
GALLICREX
G. cinerea (Water Cock) **B,H,J,K**
GALLINULA
G. ventralis (Black-tailed Native Hen) **M**
G. mortierii (Tasmanian Native Hen) **M**
G. sylvestris (San Cristobal Mountain Rail) **O** [I]
G. pacifica (Samoan Wood Rail) **O** [X]
G. nesiotis (Gough I Coot) **C**
G. tenebrosa (Dusky Moorhen) **J,K,L,M**
G. chloropus (Common Moorhen) **B,C,D,E, F,H,I,J,P**
G. angulata (Lesser Moorhen) **C**
G. melanops (Spot-flanked Gallinule) **F**

G. flavirostris (Azure Gallinule) **F**
G. alleni (Allen's Gallinule) **C**
G. martinica (American Purple Gallinule) **A,E,F**
PORPHYRIO
P. porphyrio (Purple Swamphen) **B,C,D,H,I,J, K,L,M,N,O**
P. mantelli (Takahe) **N**
FULICA
F. armillata (Red-gartered Coot) **F**
F. leucoptera (White-winged Coot) **F**
F. rufifrons (Red-fronted Coot) **F**
F. gigantea (Giant Coot) **F**
F. cornuta (Horned Coot) **F** [R]
F. caribaea (Caribbean Coot) **E,F**
F. americana (American Coot) **A,E,F,P**
F. atra (Eurasian Coot) **B,J,K,L,M**
F. cristata (Red-knobbed Coot) **B,C,D**
46 HELIORNITHIDAE (SUNGREBES)
PODICA
P. senegalensis (Peters' Finfoot) **C**
HELIOPAIS
H. personata (Masked Finfoot) **H,J** [?]
HELIORNIS
H. fulica (Sungrebe) **E,F**
47 RHYNOCHETIDAE (KAGU)
RHYNOCHETOS
R. jubatus (Kagu) **O** [E]
48 EURYPYGIDAE (SUNBITTERN)
EURYPYGA
E. helias (Sunbittern) **E,F**
49 CARIAMIDAE (SERIEMAS)
CARIAMA
C. cristata (Red-legged Seriema) **F**
CHUNGA
C. burmeisteri (Black-legged Seriema) **F**
50 OTIDIDAE (BUSTARDS)
TETRAX
T. tetrax (Little Bustard) **B,H** [?]
NEOTIS
N. denhami (Denham's Bustard) **C**
N. ludwigii (Ludwig's Bustard) **C**
N. nuba (Nubian Bustard) **C**
N. heuglinii (Heuglin's Bustard) **C**
CHLAMYDOTIS
C. undulata (Houbara Bustard) **B,H** [?]
ARDEOTIS
A. arabs (Arabian Bustard) **B,C**
A. kori (Kori Bustard) **C**
CHORIOTIS
C. nigriceps (Great Indian Bustard) **H**
C. australis (Australian Bustard) **L,M**
OTIS
O. tarda (Great Bustard) **B** [?]
EUPODOTIS
E. ruficrista (Crested Bustard) **C**
E. afra (Black Bustard) **C**
E. vigorsii (Vigors' Bustard) **C**
E. rueppellii (Rüppell's Bustard) **C**
E. humilis (Little Brown Bustard) **C**
E. caerulescens (Blue Bustard) **C**
E. senegalensis (White-bellied Bustard) **C**
E. melanogaster (Black-bellied Bustard) **C**
E. hartlaubii (Hartlaub's Bustard) **C**
HOUBAROPSIS
H. bengalensis (Bengal Florican) **H,I** [?]
SYPHEOTIDES
S. indica (Lesser Florican) **H** [?]

CHARADRIIFORMES

51 JACANIDAE (JACANAS)
MICROPARRA
M. capensis (Smaller Jacana) **C**
ACTOPHILORNIS
A. africana (African Jacana) **C**
A. albinucha (Madagascar Jacana) **D**
IREDIPARRA
I. gallinacea (Comb-crested Jacana) **J,L,M**
HYDROPHASIANUS
H. chirurgus (Pheasant-tailed Jacana) **H,I,L**
METOPIDIUS
M. indicus (Bronze-winged Jacana) **H,I,J**
JACANA
J. spinosa (Northern Jacana) **E**
J. jacana (Wattled Jacana) **E,F**

52 ROSTRATULIDAE (PAINTED-SNIPE)
ROSTRATULA
R. benghalensis (Greater Painted-Snipe) **B,C,J,M**
NYCTICRYPHES
N. semicollaris (South American Painted-Snipe) **F**
53 DROMADIDAE (CRAB PLOVER)
DROMAS
D. ardeola (Crab Plover) **C,D,H,I**
54 HAEMATOPODIDAE (OYSTERCATCHERS)
HAEMATOPUS
H. ostralegus (Palearctic Oystercatcher) **B**
H. meadewaldoi (Canary Is Oystercatcher) **B** [X]
H. palliatus (American Oystercatcher) **A,E,F,G**
H. longirostris (Pied Oystercatcher) **K,L,M,N**
H. bachmani (American Black Oystercatcher) **A**
H. moquini (African Black Oystercatcher) **C**
H. unicolor (Variable Oystercatcher) **N**
H. chathamensis (Chatham Island Oystercatcher) **N** [E]
H. leucopodus (Magellanic Oystercatcher) **F**
H. ater (Blackish Oystercatcher) **F**
H. fuliginosus (Sooty Oystercatcher) **M**
55 IBIDORHYNCHIDAE (IBISBILL)
IBIDORHYNCHA
I. struthersii (Ibisbill) **B,H**
56 RECURVIROSTRIDAE (STILTS, AVOCETS)
HIMANTOPUS
H. himantopus (Black-winged Stilt) **B,C,H**
H. novaezelandiae (Black Stilt) **N** [E]
CLADORHYNCHUS
C. leucocephalus (Banded Stilt) **M**
RECURVIROSTRA
R. avosetta (Pied Avocet) **B,C,H**
R. americana (American Avocet) **A,E**
R. novaehollandiae (Red-necked Avocet) **M**
R. andina (Andean Avocet) **F**
57 BURHINIDAE (THICK-KNEES)
BURHINUS
B. oedicnemus (Stone-Curlew) **B,C,H,I**
B. senegalensis (Senegal Stone-Curlew) **C**
B. vermiculatus (Water Dikkop) **C**
B. capensis (Cape Dikkop) **C**
B. bistriatus (Double-striped Thick-knee) **E,F**
B. superciliaris (Peruvian Thick-knee) **F**
B. magnirostris (Bush Thick-knee) **M**
ESACUS
E. recurvirostris (Great Thick-knee) **H,I**
E. magnirostris (Beach Thick-knee) **J,K,L,M**
58 GLAREOLIDAE (COURSERS, PRATINCOLES)
CURSORIINAE
PLUVIANUS
Pluvianus aegyptius (Egyptian Plover) **C**
CURSORIUS
C. cursor (Cream-colored Courser) **B,H**
C. rufus (Burchell's Courser) **C**
C. coromandelicus (Indian Courser) **H**
C. temminckii (Temminck's Courser) **C**
RHINOPTILUS
R. africanus (Two-banded Courser) **C**
R. cinctus (Heuglin's Courser) **C**
R. chalcopterus (Bronze-winged Courser) **C**
R. bitorquatus (Jerdon's Courser) **H**
GLAREOLINAE
STILTIA
S. isabella (Australian Pratincole) **J,L,M**
GLAREOLA
G. pratincola (Common Pratincole) **B,C,H**
G. maldivarus (Eastern Collared Pratincole) **B,I,J**
G. nordmanni (Black-winged Pratincole) **B,C**
G. ocularis (Madagascar Pratincole) **C,D**
G. nuchalis (White-collared Pratincole) **C**
G. cinerea (Cream-coloured Pratincole) **C**
G. lactea (Little Pratincole) **H,I**
59 CHARADRIIDAE (PLOVERS)
VANELLUS
V. vanellus (Northern Lapwing) **B**
V. crassirostris (Long-toed Lapwing) **C**
V. spinosus (Spur-winged Plover) **B,C**
V. duvaucelii (River Lapwing) **H,I**
V. tectus (Black-headed Plover) **C**
V. malabaricus (Yellow-wattled Lapwing) **H**
V. albiceps (White-crowned Wattled Plover) **C**
V. lugubris (Senegal Plover) **C**
V. melanopterus (Black-winged Plover) **C**
V. coronatus (Crowned Plover) **C**
V. senegallus (Senegal Wattled Plover) **C**

V. melanocephalus (Spot-breasted Plover) **C**
V. superciliosus (Brown-chested Wattled Plover) **C**
V. gregarius (Sociable Plover) **C,H**
V. leucurus (White-tailed Plover) **B,C,H**
V. cayanus (Cayenne Plover) **F**
V. chilensis (Southern Lapwing) **F**
V. resplendens (Andean Lapwing) **F**
V. cinereus (Gray-headed Lapwing) **B,I,J**
V. indicus (Red-wattled Lapwing) **B,H,I,J**
V. macropterus (Javanese Wattled Lapwing) **J** ☐ I
V. tricolor (Banded Plover) **M**
V. miles (Masked Plover) **K,L,M**
ANITIBYX
A. armatus (Blacksmith Plover) **C**
PLUVIALIS
P. apricaria (European Golden Plover) **B,H**
P. dominica (American Golden Plover) **A,E,F**
P. fulva (Pacific Golden Plover) **A,B,I,J,M**
P. squatarola (Black-bellied Plover) **A,B,C,F,M**
P. obscura (New Zealand Dotterel) **N**
CHARADRIUS
C. hiaticula (Ringed Plover) **A,B,C**
C. semipalmatus (Semipalmated Plover) **A,E,F**
C. placidus (Long-billed Ringed Plover) **B,I**
C. dubius (Little Ringed Plover) **B,C,H,I,J,K,L,O**
C. wilsonia (Wilson's Plover) **A,E,F**
C. vociferus (Killdeer) **A,E,F**
C. melodus (Piping Plover) **E** ☐ ?
C. thoracicus (Black-banded Sand Plover) **D** ☐ R
C. pecuarius (Kittlitz's Sand Plover) **C,D**
C. sanctaehelenae (St Helena Sand Plover) **C** ☐ R
C. tricollaris (Three-banded Plover) **C,D**
C. alexandrinus (Snowy Plover) **A,B,C,E,F,H,I,J**
C. marginatus (White-fronted Sand Plover) **C,D**
C. ruficapillus (Red-capped Dotterel) **L,M**
C. peronii (Malaysian Sand Plover) **J,K**
C. venustus (Chestnut-banded Sand Plover) **C**
C. collaris (Collared Plover) **E,F**
C. bicinctus (Double-banded Plover) **M,N**
C. falklandicus (Two-banded Plover) **F**
C. alticola (Puna Plover) **F**
C. mongolus (Mongolian Plover) **B,C,H,J,K,M**
C. leschenaultii (Great Sand Plover) **B,C,H,J,M**
C. asiaticus (Caspian Plover) **B,C,H**
C. veredus (Eastern Sand Plover) **B,K,M**
C. modestus (Rufous-chested Dotterel) **F**
C. montanus (Mountain Plover) **A,E**
C. melanops (Black-fronted Plover) **M**
C. cinctus (Red-kneed Dotterel) **M**
C. rubricollis (Hooded Plover) **M** ☐ ?
C. novaeseelandiae (Long-billed Plover) **N** ☐ E
ANARHYNCHUS
A. frontalis (Wrybill) **N**
PHEGORNIS
P. mitchellii (Mitchell's Plover) **F**
PELTOHYAS
P. australis (Inland Dotterel) **M**
EUDROMIAS
E. morinellus (Eurasian Dotterel) **B**
E. ruficollis (Tawny-throated Dotterel) **F**
60 PLUVIANELLIDAE (MAGELLANIC PLOVER)
PLUVIANELLUS
P. socialis (Magellanic Plover) **F**
61 SCOLOPACIDAE (SANDPIPERS, SNIPES)
TRINGINAE
LIMOSA
L. limosa (Black-tailed Godwit) **B,H,J,K,M**
L. haemastica (Hudsonian Godwit) **A,E,F**
L. lapponica (Bar-tailed Godwit) **A,B,C,H,I,J,K, M,O**
L. fedoa (Marbled Godwit) **A,E,F**
NUMENIUS
N. minutus (Little Curlew) **B,H,I,J,K,M**
N. borealis (Eskimo Curlew) **A,E,F** ☐ E
N. phaeopus (Whimbrel) **A,B,C,D,H,J,K,M,O**
N. tahitiensis (Bristle-thighed Curlew) **A,O,P** ☐ ?
N. tenuirostris (Slender-billed Curlew) **B** ☐ ?
N. arquata (Western Curlew) **B,C,H,I**
N. madagascariensis (Far Eastern Curlew) **B,M**
N. americanus (Long-billed Curlew) **A,E**
BARTRAMIA
B. longicauda (Upland Sandpiper) **A,E,F**
TRINGA
T. erythropus (Spotted Redshank) **B,C**
T. totanus (Common Redshank) **B,C,H,I,J,K**
T. stagnatilis (Marsh Sandpiper) **B,C,M**

T. nebularia (Common Greenshank) **B,C,H,I,J,N**
T. guttifer (Spotted Greenshank) **B,H,J** ☐ I
T. melanoleuca (Greater Yellowlegs) **A,E,F**
T. flavipes (Lesser Yellowlegs) **A,E,F**
T. ochropus (Green Sandpiper) **B,C,H,I,J**
T. solitaria (Solitary Sandpiper) **A,E,F**
T. glareola (Wood Sandpiper) **B,C,I,J,M**
CATOPTROPHORUS
C. semipalmatus (Willet) **A,E,F**
XENUS
X. cinereus (Terek Sandpiper) **B,C,H,J,M**
ACTITIS
A. hypoleucos (Common Sandpiper) **B,C,I,J,K,L,M**
A. macularia (Spotted Sandpiper) **A,E,F**
HETEROSCELUS
H. brevipes (Gray-tailed Tattler) **B,M**
H. incanus (Wandering Tattler) **A,O**
PROSOBONIA
P. cancellata (Tuamotu Sandpiper) **O** ☐ V
ARENARIINAE
ARENARIA
A. interpres (Ruddy Turnstone) **A,B,C,E,F,I,J,K,M**
A. melanocephala (Black Turnstone) **A**
PHALAROPODINAE
PHALAROPUS
P. tricolor (Wilson's Phalarope) **A,E,F**
P. lobatus (Red-necked Phalarope) **A,B**
P. fulicarius (Red Phalarope) **A,B,C,F**
SCOLOPACINAE
SCOLOPAX
S. rusticola (Eurasian Woodcock) **B,H**
S. mira (Amami Woodcock) **B**
S. saturata (Rufous Woodcock) **J,L**
S. celebensis (Sulawesi Woodcock) **K** ☐ ?
S. rochussenii (Obi Woodcock) **K** ☐ ?
S. minor (American Woodcock) **A,E**
GALLINAGONINAE
COENOCORYPHA
C. aucklandica (Subantarctic Snipe) **N** ☐ R
GALLINAGO
G. solitaria (Solitary Snipe) **B,I**
G. hardwickii (Japanese Snipe) **B,M**
G. nemoricola (Wood Snipe) **H,I** ☐ ?
G. stenura (Pintail Snipe) **B,H,K**
G. megala (Swinhoe's Snipe) **B,I,J,M**
G. nigripennis (African Snipe) **C**
G. macrodactyla (Madagascar Snipe) **D**
G. media (Great Snipe) **B,C**
G. gallinago (Common Snipe) **A,B,C,E,H**
G. paraguaiae (Magellan Snipe) **F**
G. nobilis (Noble Snipe) **F**
G. undulata (Giant Snipe) **F**
G. stricklandii (Cordilleran Snipe) **F**
G. jamesoni (Andean Snipe) **F**
G. imperialis (Imperial Snipe) **F**
LYMNOCRYPTES
L. minima (Jack Snipe) **B,C,H**
LIMNODROMUS
L. griseus (Short-billed Dowitcher) **A,E,F**
L. scolopaceus (Long-billed Dowitcher) **A,E,F**
L. semipalmatus (Asiatic Dowitcher) **B,I** ☐ R
CALIDRIDINAE
APHRIZA
A. virgata (Surfbird) **A,E,F**
CALIDRIS
C. canutus (Red Knot) **A,B,C,E,F,I,J,K,L,M**
C. tenuirostris (Great Knot) **B,H,M**
C. alba (Sanderling) **A,B,F,H,M**
C. pusilla (Semipalmated Sandpiper) **A,E,F**
C. mauri (Western Sandpiper) **A,E,F**
C. ruficollis (Rufous-necked Stint) **A,B,I,J,K,L,M**
C. minuta (Little Stint) **B,C,H**
C. temminckii (Temminck's Stint) **B,C**
C. subminuta (Long-toed Stint) **A,B,H,J**
C. minutilla (Least Sandpiper) **A,E,F**
C. fuscicollis (White-rumped Sandpiper) **A,E,F**
C. bairdii (Baird's Sandpiper) **A,B,E,F**
C. melanotos (Pectoral Sandpiper) **A,B,E,F**
C. acuminata (Sharp-tailed Sandpiper) **B,I,J,K,L,M,O**
C. paramelanotus (Cox's Sandpiper) **M** ☐ ?
C. maritima (Purple Sandpiper) **A,B**
C. ptilocnemis (Rock Sandpiper) **A,B**
C. alpina (Dunlin) **A,B,C,H**
C. ferruginea (Curlew Sandpiper) **A,B,C,H,M**

EURYNORHYNCHUS
E. pygmeus (Spoon-billed Sandpiper) **B** ☐ ?
LIMICOLA
L. falcinellus (Broad-billed Sandpiper) **B,H,M**
MICROPALAMA
M. himantopus (Stilt Sandpiper) **A,E,F**
TRYNGITES
T. subruficollis (Buff-breasted Sandpiper) **A,E,F**
PHILOMACHUS
P. pugnax (Ruff) **B,C,H,I**
62 THINOCORIDAE (SEEDSNIPES)
ATTAGIS
A. gayi (Rufous-bellied Seedsnipe) **F**
A. malouinus (White-bellied Seedsnipe) **F**
THINOCORUS
T. orbignyianus (Grey-breasted Seedsnipe) **F**
T. rumicivorus (Least Seed-Snipe) **F**
63 CHIONIDIDAE (SHEATHBILLS)
CHIONIS
C. alba (Snowy Sheathbill) **F,Q**
C. minor (Black-faced Sheathbill) **Q**
64 STERCORARIIDAE (SKUAS, JAEGERS)
CATHARACTA
C. skua (Great Skua) **A,B,C,F**
C. chilensis (Chilean Skua) **F**
C. maccormicki (South Polar Skua) **A,O,Q**
C. antarctica (Antarctic Skua) **C,D,F,M,N,O**
STERCORARIUS
S. pomarinus (Pomarine Jaeger) **A,B,C,D,F,H,M**
S. parasiticus (Parasitic Jaeger) **A,B,C,F,H,M**
S. longicaudus (Long-tailed Jaeger) **A,B,C,F**
65 LARIDAE (GULLS)
LARINAE
GABIANUS
G. pacificus (Pacific Gull) **M**
G. scoresbii (Magellan Gull) **F**
PAGOPHILA
P. eburnea (Ivory Gull) **A,B**
LARUS
L. fuliginosus (Dusky Gull) **G** ☐ ?
L. modestus (Gray Gull) **F**
L. heermanni (Heermann's Gull) **A,E**
L. leucophthalmus (White-eyed Gull) **C** ☐ ?
L. hemprichii (Sooty Gull) **B,C**
L. belcheri (Band-tailed Gull) **B,C**
L. crassirostris (Japanese Gull) **B**
L. audouinii (Audouin's Gull) **B** ☐ R
L. delawarensis (Ring-billed Gull) **A,E**
L. canus (Mew Gull) **A,B**
L. kamtschatschensis (Eastern Mew Gull) **B**
L. argentatus (Herring Gull) **A,B,E,H**
L. armenicus (Armenian Gull) **B**
L. thayeri (Thayer's Gull) **A**
L. fuscus (Lesser Black-backed Gull) **B,C**
L. californicus (Californian Gull) **A,E**
L. occidentalis (Western Gull) **A,E**
L. livens (Yellow-footed Gull) **A,E**
L. dominicanus (Southern Black-backed Gull) **C,F,M**
L. schistisagus (Slaty-backed Gull) **B**
L. marinus (Great Black-backed Gull) **A,B,E**
L. glaucescens (Glaucous-winged Gull) **A,B**
L. hyperboreus (Glaucous Gull) **A,B**
L. glaucoides (Iceland Gull) **A,B**
L. ichthyaetus (Great Black-headed Gull) **B,C,H**
L. atricilla (Laughing Gull) **A,E,F**
L. brunnicephalus (Indian Black-headed Gull) **B,H,I,J,K,L**
L. cirrocephalus (Gray-headed Gull) **C,D,F**
L. serranus (Andean Gull) **F**
L. pipixcan (Franklin's Gull) **A,E,F**
L. novaehollandiae (Silver Gull) **C,M,N,O**
L. melanocephalus (Mediterranean Gull) **B**
L. relictus (Relict Gull) **B** ☐ R
L. bulleri (Buller's Gull) **N**
L. maculipennis (Brown-hooded Gull) **F**
L. ridibundus (Common Black-headed Gull) **B,C,H,J**
L. genei (Slender-billed Gull) **B**
L. philadelphia (Bonaparte's Gull) **A**
L. minutus (Little Gull) **B**
L. saundersi (Saunders' Gull) **B** ☐ ?
RHODOSTETHIA
R. rosea (Ross's Gull) **A,B**
RISSA
R. tridactyla (Black-legged Kittiwake) **A,B,C**
R. brevirostris (Red-legged Kittiwake) **A**

CREAGRUS
C. furcatus (Swallow-tailed Gull) **G**
XEMA
X. sabini (Sabine's Gull) **A,B,C**
66 STERNIDAE (TERNS)
CHLIDONIAS
C. hybrida (Whiskered Tern) **B,C,D,H,I,J,K,L,M**
C. leucoptera (White-winged Black Tern) **B,C,H,J,K,M**
C. nigra (Black Tern) **A,B,C,E,F**
PHAETUSA
P. simplex (Large-billed Tern) **F**
GELOCHELIDON
G. nilotica (Gull-billed Tern) **A,B,C,E,F,H,M**
HYDROPROGNE
H. caspia (Caspian Tern) **A,B,C,H,I,J,M,N**
STERNA
S. aurantia (Indian River Tern) **B,J,K**
S. hirundinacea (South American Tern) **F**
S. hirundo (Common Tern) **A,B,C,E,F,H,J,K**
S. paradisaea (Arctic Tern) **A,B,C,F,Q**
S. vittata (Antarctic Tern) **C,N,Q**
S. virgata (Kerguelen Tern) **D,H,M**   ?
S. forsteri (Forster's Tern) **A,E**
S. trudeaui (Trudeau's Tern) **F**
S. dougallii (Roseate Tern) **A,B,C,D,H,I,J,K,M,O**
S. striata (White-fronted Tern) **M,N**
S. repressa (White-cheeked Tern) **C**
S. sumatrana (Black-naped Tern) **E,H,I,M,O**
S. melanogaster (Black-bellied Tern) **H,I**
S. aleutica (Aleutian Tern) **B**
S. lunata (Spectacled Tern) **J,K,P**
S. anaethetus (Bridled Tern) **C,D,E,F,H,J,K,L,M**
S. fuscata (Sooty Tern) **B,C,E,H,I,J,L,M,O,P,Q**
S. nereis (Fairy Tern) **M,N,O**
S. albistriata (Black-fronted Tern) **N**   ?
S. superciliaris (Amazon Tern) **F**
S. balaenarum (Damara Tern) **C**   R
S. lorata (Chilean Tern) **F**
S. albifrons (Little Tern) **B,C,H,I,J,K,L,M**
S. antillarum (Least Tern) **A,E,F**
S. saundersii (Black-shafted Tern) **C,H**
THALASSEUS
T. bergii (Greater Crested Tern) **B,C,D,H,J,M**
T. maximus (Royal Tern) **A,C,E,F**
T. bengalensis (Lesser Crested Tern) **B,C,D,H,I,J,K,M**
T. bernsteini (Chinese Crested Tern) **B,J**
T. elegans (Elegant Tern) **A,E,F**
T. sandvicensis (Sandwich Tern) **A,B,C,E,F,H**
LAROSTERNA
L. inca (Inca Tern) **F**
PROCELSTERNA
P. cerulea (Blue-gray Noddy) **F,J,O,P**
ANOUS
A. stolidus (Brown Noddy) **C,D,E,F,G,H,I,J,O,P**
A. tenuirostris (Lesser Noddy) **D,M**
A. minutus (Black Noddy) **C,E,F,J,L,O,P**
GYGIS
G. alba (White Tern) **C,D,F,J,O,P**
67 RYNCHOPIDAE (SKIMMERS)
RYNCHOPS
R. niger (Black Skimmer) **A,E,F**
R. flavirostris (African Skimmer) **C**
R. albicollis (Indian Skimmer) **H,I**
68 ALCIDAE (AUKS)
ALLE
A. alle (Dovekie) **A,B**
ALCA
A. torda (Razorbill) **A,B**
URIA
U. lomvia (Thick-billed Murre) **A,B**
U. aalge (Common Murre) **A,B**
CEPPHUS
C. grylle (Black Guillemot) **A,B**
C. columba (Pigeon Guillemot) **A,B**
C. carbo (Spectacled Guillemot) **B**
BRACHYRAMPHUS
B. marmoratus (Marbled Murrelet) **A,B**
B. brevirostris (Kittlitz's Murrelet) **A,B**
B. hypoleucus (Xantus' Murrelet) **A**
B. craveri (Craveri's Murrelet) **A,E**
SYNTHLIBORAMPHUS
S. antiquus (Ancient Murrelet) **A,B**
S. wumizusume (Crested Murrelet) **B**   ?

PTYCHORAMPHUS
P. aleuticus (Cassin's Auklet) **A,B**
CYCLORRHYNCHUS
C. psittacula (Parakeet Auklet) **A,B**
AETHIA
A. cristatella (Crested Auklet) **A,B**
A. pusilla (Least Auklet) **A,B**
A. pygmaea (Whiskered Auklet) **B**
CERORHINCA
C. monocerata (Rhinoceros Auklet) **A,B**
FRATERCULA
F. arctica (Atlantic Puffin) **A,B**
F. corniculata (Horned Puffin) **A,B**
LUNDA
L. cirrhata (Tufted Puffin) **A,B**

PTEROCLIDIFORMES

69 PTEROCLIDIDAE (SANDGROUSE)
SYRRHAPTES
S. tibetanus (Tibetan Sandgrouse) **B,H**
S. paradoxus (Pallas's Sandgrouse) **B**
PTEROCLES
P. alchata (Pintailed Sandgrouse) **B,H**
P. namaqua (Namaqua Sandgrouse) **C**
P. exustus (Chestnut-bellied Sandgrouse) **B,C,H**
P. senegallus (Spotted Sandgrouse) **B,H**
P. orientalis (Black-bellied Sandgrouse) **B,H**
P. coronatus (Crowned Sandgrouse) **B,H**
P. gutturalis (Yellow-throated Sandgrouse) **C**
P. burchelli (Variegated Sandgrouse) **C**
P. personatus (Madagascar Sandgrouse) **D**
P. decoratus (Black-faced Sandgrouse) **C**
P. lichtensteinii (Lichtenstein's Sandgrouse) **C,H**
P. bicinctus (Double-banded Sandgrouse) **C**
P. indicus (Painted Sandgrouse) **H**
P. quadricinctus (Four-banded Sandgrouse) **C**

COLUMBIFORMES

70 COLUMBIDAE (DOVES, PIGEONS)
COLUMBA
C. livia (Rock Dove/Feral Pigeon) **B,C,H**
C. rupestris (Eastern Rock Dove) **B**
C. leuconota (Snow Pigeon) **B**
C. guinea (Speckled Pigeon) **C**
C. albitorques (White-collared Pigeon) **C**
C. oenas (Stock Dove) **B**
C. eversmanni (Yellow-eyed Stock Dove) **B,H**   ?
C. oliviae (Somali Pigeon) **C**   R
C. palumbus (Wood Pigeon) **B,H**
C. trocaz (Trocaz Pigeon) **B**   R
C. bollii (Bolle's Pigeon) **B**   R
C. unicincta (African Wood Pigeon) **C**
C. junoniae (Laurel Pigeon) **B**   R
C. sjostedti (Cameroun Olive Pigeon) **C**
C. arquatrix (Olive Pigeon) **C**
C. thomensis (Sao Thome Olive Pigeon) **C**   V
C. pollenii (Comoro Olive Pigeon) **D**
C. hodgsonii (Speckled Wood Pigeon) **B,H,I**
C. albinucha (White-naped Pigeon) **C**
C. pulchricollis (Ashy Wood Pigeon) **C,I**
C. elphinstonii (Nilgiri Wood Pigeon) **H**   ?
C. torringtoni (Sri Lanka Wood Pigeon) **H**   ?
C. punicea (Pale-capped Pigeon) **H,I,J**   ?
C. argentina (Silver Pigeon) **J**   ?
C. palumboides (Andaman Wood Pigeon) **I**
C. janthina (Black Wood Pigeon) **B,J**
C. vitiensis (White-throated Pigeon) **J,K,L,O**
C. leucomela (White-headed Pigeon) **M**
C. jouyi (Silver-banded Black Pigeon) **J**   X
C. pallidiceps (Yellow-legged Pigeon) **L,O**   ?
C. leucocephala (White-crowned Pigeon) **A,E**
C. squamosa (Red-necked Pigeon) **E**
C. speciosa (Scaled Pigeon) **E,F**
C. picazuro (Picazuro Pigeon) **E,F**
C. corensis (Bare-eyed Pigeon) **E,F**
C. maculosa (Spotted Pigeon) **F**
C. fasciata (Band-tailed Pigeon) **E,F**
C. araucana (Chilean Pigeon) **F**
C. caribaea (Jamaican Band-tailed Pigeon) **E**   ?
C. cayennensis (Rufous Pigeon) **E,F**
C. flavirostris (Red-billed Pigeon) **E,F**
C. oenops (Salvin's Pigeon) **F**
C. inornata (Plain Pigeon) **E**
C. plumbea (Plumbeous Pigeon) **F**
C. subvinacea (Ruddy Pigeon) **E,F**
C. nigrirostris (Short-billed Pigeon) **E**

C. goodsoni (Dusky Pigeon) **F**
C. delegorguei (Delegorgue's Pigeon) **C**
C. iriditorques (Bronze-naped Pigeon) **C**
C. malherbii (Sao Thome Bronze-naped Pigeon) **C**
C. mayeri (Pink Pigeon) **D**
STREPTOPELIA
S. turtur (Turtle Dove) **B,C**
S. lugens (Dusky Turtle Dove) **B,C**
S. hypopyrrha (Pink-bellied Turtle Dove) **C**
S. orientalis (Eastern Turtle Dove) **B,H,I**
S. bitorquata (Javanese Collared Dove) **J,K**
S. decaocto (Collared Dove) **B,I**
S. roseogrisea (African Collared Dove) **B,C**
S. reichenowi (White-winged Collared Dove) **C**
S. decipiens (Mourning Collared Dove) **C**
S. semitorquata (Red-eyed Dove) **C**
S. capicola (Ring-necked Dove) **C**
S. vinacea (Vinaceous Dove) **C**
S. tranquebarica (Red-collared Dove) **B,H,I,J**
S. picturata (Madagascar Turtle Dove) **D,H,I**
S. chinensis (Spotted-necked Dove) **B,H,I,J**
S. senegalensis (Laughing Dove) **B,C,H**
APLOPELIA
A. larvata (Lemon Dove) **C**
MACROPYGIA
M. unchall (Bar-tailed Cuckoo-Dove) **B,H,I,J**
M. amboinensis (Large Brown Cuckoo-Dove) **J,K,L,M**
M. cinnamomea (Enggano Cuckoo-Dove) **J**
M. emiliana (Indonesian Cuckoo-Dove) **J**
M. magna (Large Cuckoo-Dove) **J,K**
M. rufipennis (Andaman Cuckoo-Dove) **I**
M. nigrirostris (Lesser Bar-tailed Cuckoo-Dove) **L**
M. mackinlayi (Mackinlay's Cuckoo-Dove) **J,L,O**
M. ruficeps (Little Cuckoo-Dove) **B,I,J,K**
REINWARDTOENA
R. reinwardtsi (Reinwardt's Long-tailed Pigeon) **K,L**
R. browni (Brown's Long-tailed Pigeon) **O**
R. crassirostris (Crested Long-tailed Pigeon) **O**
TURACOENA
T. manadensis (White-faced Pigeon) **K**
T. modesta (Timor Black Pigeon) **K**
TURTUR
T. chalcospilos (Emerald-spotted Wood Dove) **C**
T. abyssinicus (Black-billed Wood Dove) **C**
T. afer (Blue-spotted Wood Dove) **C**
T. tympanistria (Tambourine Dove) **C**
T. brehmeri (Blue-headed Wood Dove) **C**
OENA
O. capensis (Namaqua Dove) **C,D**
CHALCOPHAPS
C. indica (Emerald Dove) **B,H,I,J,K,L,M,O**
C. stephani (Brown-backed Emerald Dove) **K,L,O**
HENICOPHAPS
H. albifrons (Black Bronzewing) **K,L**
H. foersteri (New Britain Bronzewing) **O**
PHAPS
P. chalcoptera (Common Bronzewing) **M**
P. elegans (Brush Bronzewing) **M**
P. histrionica (Flock Bronzewing) **M**
OCYPHAPS
O. lophotes (Crested Pigeon) **M**
PETROPHASSA
P. plumifera (Spinifex Pigeon) **M**
P. ferruginea (Red-plumed Pigeon) **M**
P. scripta (Partridge Bronzewing) **M**
P. smithii (Bare-eyed Partridge Bronzewing) **M**
P. rufipennis (Chestnut-quilled Rock Pigeon) **M**
P. albipennis (White-quilled Rock Pigeon) **M**
GEOPELIA
G. cuneata (Diamond Dove) **M**
G. striata (Zebra Dove) **I,J,L,M**
G. maugei (Timor Zebra Dove) **J,K,L**
G. placida (Gould's Zebra Dove) **M**
G. humeralis (Bar-shouldered Dove) **L,M**
LEUCOSARCIA
L. melanoleuca (Wonga Pigeon) **M**
ZENAIDA
Z. macroura (Mourning Dove) **A,E,F**
Z. auriculata (Eared Dove) **E,F**
Z. aurita (Zenaida Dove) **F**
Z. galapagoensis (Galapagos Dove) **G**
Z. asiatica (White-winged Dove) **A,E,F**
COLUMBINA
C. passerina (Common Ground-Dove) **A,E,F**
C. minuta (Plain-breasted Ground-Dove) **E**

C. buckleyi (Ecuadorean Ground-Dove) **F**
C. talpacoti (Ruddy Ground-Dove) **E,F**
C. picui (Picui Dove) **F**
C. cruziana (Gold-billed Ground-Dove) **F**
C. cyanopis (Blue-eyed Ground-Dove) **F**   ?
CLARAVIS
C. pretiosa (Blue Ground-Dove) **E,F**
C. godefrida (Purple-barred Ground-Dove) **F**   V
C. mondetoura (Purple-breasted Ground-Dove) **F**
METRIOPELIA
M. ceciliae (Bare-faced Ground-Dove) **F**
M. morenoi (Bare-eyed Ground-Dove) **F**
M. melanoptera (Black-winged Ground-Dove) **F**
M. aymara (Bronze-winged Ground-Dove) **F**
SCARDAFELLA
S. inca (Inca Dove) **A,E**
S. squammata (Scaly Dove) **A,E,F**
UROPELIA
U. campestris (Long-tailed Ground-Dove) **F**
LEPTOTILA
L. verreauxi (White-tipped Dove) **E,F**
L. megalura (White-faced Dove) **F**
L. rufaxilla (Gray-fronted Dove) **E,F**
L. plumbeiceps (Gray-headed Dove) **E**
L. pallida (Pallid Dove) **F**
L. wellsi (Grenada Dove) **E**   I
L. jamaicensis (White-bellied Dove) **E**
L. cassini (Cassin's Dove) **E,F**
L. ochraceiventris (Buff-bellied Dove) **F**   ?
L. conoveri (Tolima Dove) **F**   I
GEOTRYGON
G. lawrencii (Lawrence's Quail Dove) **E**
G. costaricensis (Costa Rican Quail Dove) **E**
G. goldmani (Russet-crowned Quail Dove) **E**
G. saphirina (Sapphire Quail Dove) **F**
G. caniceps (Gray-faced Quail Dove) **F**   ?
G. versicolor (Crested Quail Dove) **E**
G. veraguensis (Olive-backed Quail Dove) **E,F**
G. linearis (Lined Quail Dove) **E,F**
G. frenata (White-throated Quail Dove) **F**
G. chrysia (Key West Quail Dove) **E**
G. mystacea (Bridled Quail Dove) **E**
G. violacea (Violaceous Quail Dove) **E,F**
G. montana (Ruddy Quail Dove) **E,F**
STARNOENAS
S. cyanocephala (Blue-headed Quail Dove) **E**   ?
CALOENAS
C. nicobarica (Nicobar Pigeon) **I,J,L,O**
GALLICOLUMBA
G. luzonica (Luzon Bleeding Heart) **J**
G. criniger (Bartlett's Bleeding Heart) **J**
G. platenae (Mindoro Bleeding Heart) **J**   ?
G. keayi (Negros Bleeding Heart) **J**   ?
G. menagei (Tawitawi Bleeding Heart) **J**   ?
G. rufigula (Golden Heart) **K,L**
G. tristigmata (Sulawesi Quail Dove) **K**
G. jobiensis (White-breasted Ground Pigeon) **L,O**
G. kubaryi (Truk Is Ground Dove) **O**
G. erythroptera (Society Is Ground Dove) **O**   I
G. xanthonura (White-throated Dove) **J,O**
G. stairi (Friendly Quail Dove) **O**
G. sanctaecrucis (Santa Cruz Ground Dove) **J**   ?
G. salamonis (Thick-billed Ground Dove) **J**   ?
G. rubescens (Marquesas Ground Dove) **O**   I
G. beccarii (Gray-breasted Quail Dove) **L,O**
G. canifrons (Palau Ground Dove) **J**
G. hoedtii (Wetar Ground Dove) **K**   ?
TRUGON
T. terrestris (Thick-billed Ground Pigeon) **L**
MICROGOURA
M. meeki (Solomon Is Ground Pigeon) **O**   X
OTIDIPHAPS
O. nobilis (Pheasant Pigeon) **K,L**
GOURA
G. cristata (Blue Crowned Pigeon) **L**
G. scheepmakeri (Maroon-breasted Crowned Pigeon) **L**   ?
G. victoria (Victoria Crowned Pigeon) **L**   ?
DIDUNCULUS
D. strigirostris (Tooth-billed Pigeon) **O**   V
PHAPITRERON
P. leucotis (Lesser Brown Fruit Dove) **J**
P. amethystina (Greater Brown Fruit Dove) **J**
TRERON
T. fulvicollis (Cinnamon-headed Green Pigeon) **J,K**
T. olax (Little Green Pigeon) **J**

T. vernans (Pink-necked Green Pigeon) **I,J,K,L**
T. bicincta (Orange-breasted Green Pigeon) **H,I,J**
T. pompadora (Pompadour Green Pigeon) **H,I,J,K**
T. curvirostra (Thick-billed Green Pigeon) **H,I,J,K**
T. griseicauda (Gray-faced Thick-billed Green Pigeon) **J,K**
T. teysmanni (Sumba Is Green Pigeon) **K**   ?
T. floris (Flores Green Pigeon) **J,K**   ?
T. psittacea (Timor Green Pigeon) **K**   ?
T. capellei (Large Green Pigeon) **J**   ?
T. phoenicoptera (Yellow-legged Green Pigeon) **H,I**
T. waalia (Yellow-bellied Green Pigeon) **C**
T. australis (Madagascar Green Pigeon) **D**
T. calva (African Green Pigeon) **C**
T. pembaensis (Pemba Is Green Pigeon) **C**
T. sanctithomae (Sao Thome Green Pigeon) **C**
T. apicauda (Pin-tailed Green Pigeon) **H,I**
T. oxyura (Yellow-bellied Pin-tailed Green Pigeon) **J**
T. seimundi (Yellow-vented Pin-tailed Green Pigeon) **I,J**
T. sphenura (Wedge-tailed Green Pigeon) **B,H,I,J**
T. sieboldii (Japanese Green Pigeon) **B,I,J**
T. formosae (Formosan Green Pigeon) **B,E,J**
PTILINOPUS
P. cincta (Black-backed Fruit-Dove) **J.K**
P. alligator (Black-banded Pigeon) **M**
P. dohertyi (Red-naped Fruit-Dove) **K**   ?
P. porphyrea (Pink-necked Fruit-Dove) **J**
P. marchei (Marche's Fruit-Dove) **J**   ?
P. merrilli (Merrill's Fruit-Dove) **J**
P. occipitalis (Yellow-breasted Fruit-Dove) **J**
P. fischeri (Fischer's Fruit-Dove) **K**
P. jambu (Jambu Fruit-Dove) **J**
P. subgularis (Dark-chinned Fruit-Dove) **K**
P. leclancheri (Black-chinned Fruit-Dove) **J**
P. bernsteini (Scarlet-breasted Fruit-Dove) **K**
P. magnificus (Wompoo Fruit-Dove) **L,M**
P. perlatus (Pink-spotted Fruit-Dove) **L**
P. ornatus (Ornate Fruit-Dove) **L**
P. tannensis (Silver-shouldered Fruit-Dove) **O**
P. aurantiifrons (Orange-fronted Fruit-Dove) **L**
P. wallacii (Wallace's Fruit-Dove) **K,L**
P. superbus (Superb Fruit-Dove) **K,L,M**
P. perousii (Many-colored Fruit-Dove) **O**
P. porphyraceus (Purple-capped Fruit-Dove) **O**
P. pelewensis (Palau Fruit-Dove) **J**
P. rarotongensis (Rarotongan Fruit-Dove) **N**
P. roseicapilla (Marianas Fruit-Dove) **J**   V
P. regina (Pink-capped Fruit-Dove) **J,K,L,M**
P. richardsii (Silver-capped Fruit-Dove) **O**
P. purpuratus (Gray-green Fruit-Dove) **O**
P. greyii (Grey's Fruit-Dove) **O**
P. huttoni (Rapa I Fruit-Dove) **O**   R
P. dupetithouarsii (White-capped Fruit-Dove) **O**
P. mercierii (Red-moustached Fruit-Dove) **O**   X
P. insularis (Henderson I Fruit-Dove) **O**
P. coronulatus (Lilac-capped Fruit-Dove) **K,L**
P. pulchellus (Crimson-capped Fruit-Dove) **L**
P. monacha (Blue-capped Fruit-Dove) **K**
P. rivoli (White-bibbed Fruit-Dove) **K,L**
P. solomonensis (Yellow-bibbed Fruit-Dove) **L,O**
P. viridis (Red-bibbed Fruit-Dove) **K,L,M,O**
P. eugeniae (White-headed Fruit-Dove) **O**
P. iozonus (Orange-bellied Fruit-Dove) **K,L**
P. insolitus (Knob-billed Fruit-Dove) **L,O**
P. hyogaster (Gray-headed Fruit-Dove) **K**
P. granulifrons (Carunculated Fruit-Dove) **K**
P. melanospila (Black-naped Fruit-Dove) **J,K**
P. naina (Dwarf Fruit-Dove) **L**
P. arcanus (Ripley's Fruit-Dove) **J**   ?
P. victor (Orange Dove) **O**
P. luteovirens (Golden Dove) **O**
P. layardi (Yellow-headed Dove) **O**
DREPANOPTILA
D. holosericea (Cloven-feathered Dove) **O**   V
ALECTROENAS
A. madagascariensis (Madagascar Blue Pigeon) **D**
A. sganzini (Comoro Blue Pigeon) **D**
A. pulcherrima (Seychelles Blue Pigeon) **D**
DUCULA
D. poliocephala (Philippine Zone-tailed Pigeon) **J**
D. forsteni (Green & White Zone-tailed Pigeon) **K**
D. mindorensis (Mindoro Zone-tailed Pigeon) **J**   ?
D. radiata (Gray-headed Zone-tailed Pigeon) **K**
D. carola (Gray-necked Fruit Pigeon) **J**   ?
D. aenea (Green Imperial Pigeon) **H,I,J,K**

D. perspicillata (White-eyed Imperial Pigeon) **K**
D. concinna (Blue-tailed Imperial Pigeon) **K,L**
D. pacifica (Pacific Pigeon) **L,O**
D. oceanica (Micronesian Pigeon) **J,O**
D. aurorae (Society Is Pigeon) **O**   V
D. galeata (Marquesas Pigeon) **O**   E
D. rubricera (Red-knobbed Pigeon) **L,O**
D. myristicivora (Black-knobbed Pigeon) **L**
D. rufigaster (Rufous-bellied Fruit Pigeon) **L**
D. basilica (Moluccan Rufous-bellied Fruit Pigeon) **K**
D. finschii (Finsch's Rufous-bellied Fruit Pigeon) **L**
D. chalconota (Mountain Rufous-bellied Fruit Pigeon) **L**
D. pistrinaria (Island Imperial Pigeon) **L,O**   ?
D. rosacea (Pink-headed Imperial Pigeon) **K**
D. whartoni (Christmas I Imperial Pigeon) **J**   V
D. pickeringii (Gray Imperial Pigeon) **J,K**
D. latrans (Peale's Pigeon) **O**
D. brenchleyi (Chestnut-bellied Pigeon) **O**
D. bakeri (Baker's Pigeon) **O**
D. goliath (New Caledonian Pigeon) **O**   V
D. pinon (Pinon Imperial Pigeon) **L**
D. melanochroa (Black Imperial Pigeon) **L**
D. mullerii (Black-collared Fruit Pigeon) **K,L**
D. zoeae (Banded Imperial Pigeon) **L**
D. badia (Mountain Imperial Pigeon) **H,I,J**
D. lacernulata (Dark-backed Imperial Pigeon) **J**
D. cineracea (Timor Imperial Pigeon) **K**
D. bicolor (Pied Imperial Pigeon) **I,J,K**
D. luctuosa (Sulawesi Pied Imperial Pigeon) **J,K**
D. spilorrhoa (Australian Pied Imperial Pigeon) **K,L,M**
LOPHOLAIMUS
L. antarcticus (Top-knot Pigeon) **M**
HEMIPHAGA
H. novaeseelandiae (New Zealand Pigeon) **N**
CRYPTOPHAPS
C. poecilorrhoa (Sulawesi Dusky Pigeon) **K**
GYMNOPHAPS
G. albertisii (Bare-eyed Mountain Pigeon) **K,L**
G. mada (Long-tailed Mountain Pigeon) **K**
G. solomonensis (Pale Mountain Pigeon) **O**

PSITTACIFORMES

71 PSITTACIDAE (LORIES, COCKATOOS, PARROTS)
LORIINAE (LORIES)
CHALCOPSITTA
C. atra (Black Lory) **L**
C. duivenbodei (Duyvenbode's Lory) **L**
C. sintillata (Yellow-streaked Lory) **K,L**
C. cardinalis (Cardinal Lory) **O**
EOS
E. cyanogenia (Black-winged Lory) **M**   ?
E. squamata (Violet-necked Lory) **K,L**
E. reticulata (Blue-streaked Lory) **J,L**
E. histrio (Red & Blue Lory) **K**   ?
E. bornea (Red Lory) **K**
E. semilarvata (Blue-eared Lory) **K**
PSEUDEOS
P. fuscata (Dusky Lory) **L**
TRICHOGLOSSUS
T. ornatus (Ornate Lory) **K**
T. haematodus (Rainbow Lorikeet) **J,K,L,M,O**
T. rubiginosus (Ponape Lory) **O**
T. johnstoniae (Johnstone's Lorikeet) **J**
T. flaroviridis (Yellow & Green Lorikeet) **J,K**
T. chlorolepidotus (Scaly-breasted Lorikeet) **M**
T. euteles (Perfect Lorikeet) **K**
T. versicolor (Varied Lorikeet) **M**
T. iris (Iris Lorikeet) **K**
T. goldiei (Goldie's Lorikeet) **L**
LORIUS
L. hypoinochrous (Purple-bellied Lory) **L**
L. lory (Black-capped Lory) **L**
L. albidinuchus (White-naped Lory) **O**
L. amabilis (Stresemann's Lory) **O**
L. chlorocercus (Yellow-bibbed Lory) **O**
L. domicellus (Purple-naped Lory) **K**   ?
L. tibialis (Blue-thighed Lory) **(possibly K)**
L. garrulus (Chattering Lory) **K**
PHIGYS
P. solitarius (Collared Lory) **O**
VINI
V. australis (Blue-crowned Lory) **O**
V. kuhlii (Kuhl's Lory) **O**

V. stepheni (Stephen's Lory) **O**
V. peruviana (Tahitian Lory) **O** [R]
V. ultramarina (Ultramarine Lory) **O** [R]
GLOSSOPSITTA
G. concinna (Musk Lorikeet) **M**
G. pusilla (Little Lorikeet) **M**
G. porphyrocephala (Purple-crowned Lorikeet) **M**
CHARMOSYNA
C. palmarum (Palm Lorikeet) **O**
C. rubrigularis (Red-chinned Lorikeet) **L,O**
C. meeki (Meek's Lorikeet) **O**
C. toxopei (Blue-fronted Lorikeet) **K** [?]
C. multistriata (Striated Lorikeet) **L** [?]
C. wilhelminae (Wilhelmina's Lorikeet) **L**
C. rubronotata (Red-spotted Lorikeet) **L**
C. placentis (Red-flanked Lorikeet) **K,L,O**
C. diadema (New Caledonian Lorikeet) **O** [X]
C. amabilis (Red-throated Lorikeet) **O**
C. margarethae (Duchess Lorikeet) **O**
C. pulchella (Fairy Lorikeet) **L**
C. josefinae (Josephine's Lory) **L**
C. papou (Papuan Lory) **L**
OREOPSITTACUS
O. arfaki (Whiskered Lorikeet) **L**
NEOPSITTACUS
N. musschenbroekii (Musschenbroek's Lorikeet) **L**
N. pullicauda (Emerald Lorikeet) **L**
CACATUINAE (COCKATOOS)
PROBOSCIGER
P. aterrimus (Palm Cockatoo) **L,M**
CALYPTORHYNCHUS
C. funereus (Yellow-tailed Black Cockatoo) **M**
C. magnificus (Red-tailed Black Cockatoo) **M**
C. lathami (Glossy Black Cockatoo) **M**
C. baudinii (Long-billed Black Cockatoo) **M**
C. latirostris (White-tailed Black Cockatoo) **M**
CALLOCEPHALON
C. fimbriatum (Gang-gang Cockatoo) **M**
EOLOPHUS
E. roseicapillus (Galah) **M**
CACATUA
C. leadbeateri (Major Mitchell's Cockatoo) **M**
C. sulphurea (Lesser Sulfur-crested Cockatoo) **J,K** [?]
C. galerita (Sulfur-crested Cockatoo) **L,M**
C. ophthalmica (Blue-eyed Cockatoo) **O**
C. moluccensis (Salmon-crested Cockatoo) **K** [?]
C. alba (White Cockatoo) **K** [?]
C. haematuropygia (Red-vented Cockatoo) **J** [?]
C. goffini (Goffin's Cockatoo) **L**
C. sanguinea (Little Corella) **M**
C. tenuirostris (Long-billed Corella) **M**
C. pastinator (Eastern Long-billed Corella) **M**
C. ducorps (Ducorp's Cockatoo) **O**
NYMPHICINAE
NYMPHICUS
N. hollandicus (Cockatiel) **M**
NESTORINAE
NESTOR
N. notabilis (Kea) **N**
N. meridionalis (Kaka) **N**
MICROPSITTINAE
MICROPSITTA
M. pusio (Buff-faced Pygmy Parrot) **L**
M. keiensis (Yellow-capped Pygmy Parrot) **L**
M. geelvinkiana (Geelvink Pygmy Parrot) **L**
M. meeki (Meek's Pygmy Parrot) **L**
M. finschii (Finsch's Pygmy Parrot) **L,O**
M. bruijnii (Red-breasted Pygmy Parrot) **K,L,O**
PSITTACINAE
OPOPSITTA
O. gulielmitertii (Orange-breasted Fig Parrot) **L**
O. diophthalma (Double-eyed Fig Parrot) **L,M**
PSITTACULIROSTRIS
P. desmarestii (Desmarest's Fig Parrot) **L**
P. edwardsii (Edwards' Fig Parrot) **L**
P. salvadorii (Salvadori's Fig Parrot) **L**
BOLBOPSITTACUS
B. lunulatus (Guaiabero) **J**
PSITTINUS
P. cyanurus (Blue-rumped Parrot) **J**
PSITTACELLA
P. brehmii (Brehm's Parrot) **L**
P. picta (Painted Parrot) **L**
P. modesta (Modest Parrot) **L**
P. maderaszi (Maderasz's Parrot) **L**

GEOFFROYUS
G. geoffroyi (Red-cheeked Parrot) **J,K,L,M**
G. simplex (Blue-collared Parrot) **L**
G. heteroclitus (Singing Parrot) **L,O**
PRIONITURUS
P. luconensis (Green Racket-tailed Parrot) **J** [?]
P. discurus (Blue-crowned Racket-tailed Parrot) **J** [?]
P. platenae (Palawan Racket-tailed Parrot) **J**
P. verticalis (Sulu Racket-tailed Parrot) **J**
P. waterstradti (Mindanao Racket-tailed Parrot) **J**
P. montanus (Mountain Racket-tailed Parrot) **J** [?]
P. flavicans (Red-spotted Racket-tailed Parrot) **K**
P. platurus (Golden-mantled Racket-tailed Parrot) **K**
P. mada (Buru Racket-tailed Parrot) **K**
TANYGNATHUS
T. megalorhynchos (Great-billed Parrot) **J,K,L**
T. lucionensis (Blue-naped Parrot) **J**
T. sumatranus (Muller's Parrot) **J,K**
T. heterurus (Rufous-tailed Parrot) **K**
T. gramineus (Black-lored Parrot) **K**
ECLECTUS
E. roratus (Eclectus Parrot) **K,L,M,O**
PSITTRICHAS
P. fulgidus (Pesquet's Parrot) **L**
PROSOPEIA
P. tabuensis (Red Shining Parrot) **O**
P. splendens (Kandavu Shining Parrot) **O**
P. personata (Masked Shining Parrot) **O**
ALISTERUS
A. scapularis (Australian King Parrot) **M**
A. chloropterus (Green-winged King Parrot) **L**
A. amboinensis (Amboina King Parrot) **K,L**
APROSMICTUS
A. erythropterus (Red-winged Parrot) **L,M**
A. jonquillaceus (Timor Red-winged Parrot) **K**
POLYTELIS
P. swainsonii (Superb Parrot) **M**
P. anthopeplus (Regent Parrot) **M**
P. alexandrae (Princess Parrot) **M** [?]
PURPUREICEPHALUS
P. spurius (Red-capped Parrot) **M**
BARNARDIUS
B. barnardi (Mallee Ringneck Parrot) **M**
B. zonarius (Port Lincoln Parrot) **M**
PLATYCERCUS
P. caledonicus (Green Rosella) **M**
P. elegans (Crimson Rosella) **M**
P. flaveolus (Yellow Rosella) **M**
P. adelaidae (Adelaide Rosella) **M**
P. eximius (Eastern Rosella) **M**
P. adscitus (Pale-headed Rosella) **M**
P. venustus (Northern Rosella) **M**
P. icterotis (Western Rosella) **M**
PSEPHOTUS
P. haematonotus (Red-rumped Parrot) **M**
P. varius (Mulga Parrot) **M**
P. haematogaster (Blue Bonnet) **M**
P. chrysopterygius (Golden-shouldered Parrot) **M** [R]
P. pulcherrimus (Paradise Parrot) **M** [E]
CYANORAMPHUS
C. unicolor (Antipodes Green Parakeet) **N** [?]
C. novaezelandiae (Red-fronted Parakeet) **N,O**
C. auriceps (Yellow-fronted Parakeet) **N**
C. cornutus (Horned Parakeet) **N,O**
NEOPHEMA
N. bourkii (Bourke's Parrot) **M**
N. chrysostoma (Blue-winged Parrot) **M** [R]
N. elegans (Elegant Parrot) **M**
N. petrophila (Rock Parrot) **M**
N. chrysogaster (Orange-bellied Parrot) **M**
N. pulchella (Turquoise Parrot) **M**
N. splendida (Scarlet-chested Parrot) **M** [R]
LATHAMUS
L. discolor (Swift Parrot) **M**
MELOPSITTACUS
M. undulatus (Budgerigar) **M**
PEZOPORUS
P. wallicus (Ground Parrot) **M** [E]
GEOPSITTACUS
G. occidentalis (Night Parrot) **M** [I]
CORACOPSIS
C. vasa (Vasa Parrot) **D**
C. nigra (Black Parrot) **D**
PSITTACUS
P. erithacus (Gray Parrot) **C**

POICEPHALUS
P. robustus (Brown-necked Parrot) **C**
P. gulielmi (Red-fronted Parrot) **C**
P. cryptoxanthus (Brown-headed Parrot) **C**
P. crassus (Niam-Niam Parrot) **C**
P. senegalus (Senegal Parrot) **C**
P. rufiventris (Red-bellied Parrot) **C**
P. meyeri (Brown Parrot) **C**
P. rueppellii (Ruppell's Parrot) **C**
P. flavifrons (Yellow-faced Parrot) **C**
AGAPORNIS
A. cana (Gray-headed Lovebird) **D**
A. pullaria (Red-faced Lovebird) **C**
A. taranta (Black-winged Lovebird) **C**
A. swinderniana (Black-collared Lovebird) **C**
A. roseicollis (Peach-faced Lovebird) **C**
A. fischeri (Fischer's Lovebird) **C**
A. personata (Masked Lovebird) **C**
A. lilianae (Nyasa Lovebird) **C**
A. nigrigenis (Black-cheeked Lovebird) **C** [R]
LORICULUS
L. vernalis (Vernal Hanging Parrot) **H,I**
L. beryllinus (Ceylon Hanging Parrot) **H**
L. philippensis (Philippine Hanging Parrot) **J**
L. galgulus (Blue-crowned Hanging Parrot) **J**
L. stigmatus (Sulawesi Hanging Parrot) **K**
L. catamene (Sangihe Hanging Parrot) **K** [?]
L. amabilis (Moluccan Hanging Parrot) **K**
L. exilis (Green Hanging Parrot) **K**
L. flosculus (Wallace's Hanging Parrot) **K** [?]
L. pusillus (Yellow-throated Hanging Parrot) **J**
L. aurantiifrons (Orange-fronted Hanging Parrot) **K,L**
PSITTACULA
P. eupatria (Alexandrine Parakeet) **H,I**
P. krameri (Rose-ringed Parakeet) **C,H,I**
P. echo (Mauritius Parakeet) **D**
P. himalayana (Slaty-headed Parakeet) **H,I**
P. cyanocephala (Plum-headed Parakeet) **H**
P. roseata (Blossom-headed Parakeet) **H,I**
P. intermedia (Intermediate Parrot) **H** [?]
P. columboides (Malabar Parakeet) **H**
P. calthorpae (Emerald-collared Parakeet) **H**
P. derbiana (Lord Derby's Parakeet) **H,I**
P. alexandri (Moustached Parakeet) **H,I,J,K**
P. caniceps (Blyth's Parakeet) **I** [?]
P. longicauda (Long-tailed Parakeet) **I,J**
ANODORHYNCHUS
A. hyacinthus (Hyacinth Macaw) **F** [?]
A. glaucus (Glaucous Macaw) **F** [X]
A. leari (Indigo Macaw) **F** [E]
CYANOPSITTA
C. spixii (Spix's Macaw) **F** [E]
ARA
A. ararauna (Blue-&-Yellow Macaw) **E,F**
A. caninde (Wagler's Macaw) **F** [I]
A. militaris (Military Macaw) **E,F**
A. ambigua (Buffon's Macaw) **E,F**
A. macao (Scarlet Macaw) **E,F**
A. chloroptera (Green-winged Macaw) **E,F**
A. rubrogenys (Red-fronted Macaw) **F** [?]
A. auricollis (Yellow-collared Macaw) **F**
A. severa (Chestnut-fronted Macaw) **E,F**
A. manilata (Red-bellied Macaw) **F**
A. maracana (Illiger's Macaw) **F** [?]
A. couloni (Blue-headed Macaw) **F**
A. nobilis (Red-shouldered Macaw) **F**
ARATINGA
A. acuticaudata (Blue-crowned Conure) **F**
A. guarouba (Golden Conure) **F** [V]
A. holochlora (Green Parakeet) **F**
A. strenua (Pacific Parakeet) **E**
A. finschi (Finsch's Conure) **E**
A. wagleri (Red-fronted Conure) **E,F**
A. mitrata (Mitred Conure) **F**
A. erythrogenys (Red-masked Conure) **F**
A. leucophthalmus (White-eyed Conure) **F**
A. chloroptera (Hispaniolan Conure) **E**
A. euops (Cuban Conure) **F** [?]
A. auricapilla (Golden-capped Conure) **F** [?]
A. jandaya (Jandaya Conure) **F**
A. solstitialis (Sun Conure) **F**
A. weddellii (Dusky-headed Conure) **F**
A. nana (Olive-throated Conure) **E**
A. canicularis (Orange-fronted Conure) **E**
A. pertinax (Brown-throated Conure) **E,F,G**

A. cactorum (Cactus Conure) **F**
A. aurea (Peach-fronted Conure) **F**
NANDAYUS
N. nenday (Nanday Conure) **F**
LEPTOSITTACA
L. branickii (Golden-plumed Conure) **F** [?]
OGNORHYNCHUS
O. icterotis (Yellow-eared Conure) **F** [V]
RHYNCHOPSITTA
R. pachyrhyncha (Thick-billed Parrot) **E** [V]
R. terrisi (Maroon-fronted Parrot) **E** [E]
CYANOLISEUS
C. patagonus (Patagonian Conure) **F**
PYRRHURA
P. cruentata (Blue-throated Conure) **F** [R]
P. devillei (Blaze-winged Conure) **F**
P. frontalis (Maroon-bellied Conure) **F**
P. perlata (Pearly Conure) **F** [?]
P. rhodogaster (Crimson-bellied Conure) **F**
P. molinae (Green-cheeked Conure) **F**
P. leucotis (White-eared Conure) **F**
P. picta (Painted Conure) **E,F**
P. viridicata (Santa Marta Conure) **F**
P. egregia (Fiery-shouldered Conure) **F**
P. melanura (Maroon-tailed Conure) **F**
P. orcesi (El Oro Conure) **F**
P. rupicola (Black-capped Conure) **F**
P. albipectus (White-necked Conure) **F** [?]
P. calliptera (Brown-breasted Conure) **F** [?]
P. hoematotis (Red-eared Conure) **F**
P. rhodocephala (Rose-crowned Conure) **F**
P. hoffmanni (Hoffmann's Conure) **E**
ENICOGNATHUS
E. ferrugineus (Austral Conure) **F**
E. leptorhynchus (Slender-billed Conure) **F** [?]
MYIOPSITTA
M. monachus (Monk Parakeet) **F**
BOLBORHYNCHUS
B. aymara (Sierra Parakeet) **F**
B. aurifrons (Mountain Parakeet) **F**
B. lineola (Barred Parakeet) **E,F**
B. orbygnesius (Andean Parakeet) **F**
B. ferrugineifrons (Rufous-fronted Parakeet) **F** [I]
FORPUS
F. cyanopygius (Mexican Parrotlet) **E,F**
F. passerinus (Green-rumped Parrotlet) **F**
F. xanthopterygius (Blue-winged Parrotlet) **F**
F. conspicillatus (Spectacled Parrotlet) **F**
F. sclateri (Dusky-billed Parrotlet) **F**
F. coelestis (Pacific Parrotlet) **F**
F. xanthops (Yellow-faced Parrotlet) **F**
BROTOGERIS
B. tirica (Plain Parakeet) **F**
B. versicolurus (Canary-winged Parakeet) **F**
B. pyrrhopterus (Grey-cheeked Parakeet) **F** [?]
B. jugularis (Orange-chinned Parakeet) **F**
B. cyanoptera (Cobalt-winged Parakeet) **F**
B. chrysopterus (Golden-winged Parakeet) **F**
B. sanctithomae (Tui Parakeet) **F**
NANNOPSITTACA
N. panychlora (Tepui Parrotlet) **F**
TOUIT
T. batavica (Lilac-tailed Parrotlet) **F**
T. huetii (Scarlet-shouldered Parrotlet) **F**
T. dilectissima (Red-winged Parrotlet) **F**
T. purpurata (Sapphire-rumped Parrotlet) **F**
T. melanonota (Black-eared Parrotlet) **F** [R]
T. surda (Golden-tailed Parrotlet) **F** [I]
T. stictoptera (Spot-winged Parrotlet) **F** [?]
PIONITES
P. melanocephala (Black-headed Caique) **F**
P. leucogaster (White-bellied Caique) **F**
PIONOPSITTA
P. pileata (Red-capped Parrot) **F** [?]
P. haematotis (Brown-hooded Parrot) **E,F**
P. pulchra (Rose-faced Parrot) **F**
P. barrabandi (Orange-cheeked Parrot) **F**
P. pyrilia (Saffron-headed Parrot) **E,F**
P. caica (Caica Parrot) **F**
GYPOPSITTA
G. vulturina (Vulturine Parrot) **F**
HAPALOPSITTACA
H. melanotis (Black-winged Parrot) **F**
H. amazonina (Rusty-faced Parrot) **F** [?]
GRAYDIDASCALUS
G. brachyurus (Short-tailed Parrot) **F**

PIONUS
P. menstruus (Blue-headed Parrot) **F**
P. sordidus (Red-billed Parrot) **F**
P. maximiliani (Scaly-headed Parrot) **F**
P. tumultuosus (Plum-crowned Parrot) **F**
P. seniloides (White-headed Parrot) **F**
P. senilis (White-capped Parrot) **E**
P. chalcopterus (Bronze-winged Parrot) **F**
P. fuscus (Dusky Parrot) **F**
AMAZONA
A. collaria (Yellow-billed Amazon) **E**
A. leucocephala (Cuban Amazon) **E**
A. ventralis (Hispaniolan Amazon) **E**
A. albifrons (White-fronted Amazon) **E**
A. xantholora (Yellow-lored Amazon) **E**
A. agilis (Black-billed Amazon) **E**
A. vittata (Puerto Rican Amazon) **E** [E]
A. tucumana (Tucuman Amazon) **F**
A. pretrei (Red-spectacled Amazon) **F** [V]
A. viridigenalis (Red-crowned Amazon) **E** [?]
A. finschi (Lilac-crowned Amazon) **E**
A. autumnalis (Red-lored Amazon) **E,F**
A. brasiliensis (Red-tailed Amazon) **F** [E]
A. dufresniana (Blue-cheeked Amazon) **F**
A. festiva (Festive Amazon) **F**
A. xanthops (Yellow-faced Amazon) **F** [?]
A. barbadensis (Yellow-shouldered Amazon) **E,F**
A. aestiva (Blue-fronted Amazon) **F**
A. ochrocephala (Yellow-crowned Amazon) **E,F**
A. amazonica (Orange-winged Amazon) **E,F**
A. mercenaria (Scaly-naped Amazon) **F**
A. farinosa (Mealy Amazon) **E,F**
A. vinacea (Vinaceous Amazon) **F** [?]
A. versicolor (St Lucia Amazon) **E** [E]
A. arausiaca (Red-necked Amazon) **E** [E]
A. guildingii (St Vincent Amazon) **E** [E]
A. imperialis (Imperial Amazon) **E** [E]
DEROPTYUS
D. accipitrinus (Hawk-headed Parrot) **F**
TRICLARIA
T. malachitacea (Purple-bellied Parrot) **F** [?]
STRIGOPINAE
STRIGOPS
S. habroptilus (Kakapo) **N** [E]

CUCULIFORMES

72 MUSOPHAGIDAE (TURACOS)
CORYTHAEOLA
C. cristata (Great Blue Turaco) **C**
CRINIFER
C. piscator (Gray Plantain-eater) **C**
C. zonurus (Eastern Gray Plantain-eater) **C**
CORYTHAIXOIDES
C. concolor (Gray Go-away Bird) **C**
C. personata (Bare-faced Go-away Bird) **C**
CRINIFEROIDES
C. leucogaster (White-bellied Go-away Bird) **C**
MUSOPHAGA
M. porphyreolopha (Violet-crested Turaco) **C**
M. johnstoni (Ruwenzori Turaco) **C**
M. violacea (Violet Turaco) **C**
M. rossae (Lady Ross's Turaco) **C**
TAURACO
T. persa (Green Turaco) **C**
T. schuetti (Black-billed Turaco) **C**
T. fischeri (Fischer's Turaco) **C**
T. erythrolophus (Red-crested Turaco) **C**
T. bannermani (Bannerman's Turaco) **C** [E]
T. macrorhynchus (Crested Turaco) **C**
T. hartlaubi (Hartlaub's Turaco) **C**
T. leucotis (White-cheeked Turaco) **C**
T. ruspolii (Prince Ruspoli's Turaco) **C** [R]
T. leucolophus (White-crested Turaco) **C**
73 OPISTHOCOMIDAE (HOATZIN)
OPISTHOCOMUS
O. hoazin (Hoatzin) **C**
74 CUCULIDAE (CUCKOOS)
CUCULINAE
CLAMATOR
C. glandarius (Great Spotted Cuckoo) **B,C**
C. coromandus (Red-winged Crested Cuckoo) **B,H,J**
OXYLOPHUS
O. jacobinus (Black-&-White Cuckoo) **C,H,I**
O. levaillantii (Levaillant's Cuckoo) **C**
PACHYCOCCYX
P. audeberti (Thick-billed Cuckoo) **C,D**

CUCULUS
C. crassirostris (Sulawesi Hawk Cuckoo) **K**
C. sparverioides (Large Hawk Cuckoo) **H,I,J,K**
C. varius (Common Hawk Cuckoo) **H**
C. vagans (Small Hawk Cuckoo) **I,J**
C. fugax (Fugitive Hawk Cuckoo) **B,H,I,J**
C. solitarius (Red-chested Cuckoo) **C**
C. clamosus (Black Cuckoo) **C**
C. micropterus (Short-winged Cuckoo) **B,H,I,J**
C. canorus (Eurasian Cuckoo) **B,C,H,I,J,K,L**
C. gularis (African Cuckoo) **C**
C. saturatus (Oriental Cuckoo) **B,H,I,J,K**
C. poliocephalus (Small Cuckoo) **J,K**
C. rochii (Madagascar Cuckoo) **D**
C. pallidus (Pallid Cuckoo) **M**
CERCOCOCCYX
C. mechowi (Dusky Long-tailed Cuckoo) **C**
C. olivinus (Olive Long-tailed Cuckoo) **C**
C. montanus (Mountain Long-tailed Cuckoo) **C**
PENTHOCERYX
P. sonneratii (Banded Bay Cuckoo) **H,I,J**
CACOMANTIS
C. merulinus (Plaintive Cuckoo) **H,I,J,K**
C. variolosus (Brush Cuckoo) **K,L,M,O**
C. sepulcralis (Indonesian Cuckoo) **K**
C. castaneiventris (Chestnut-breasted Cuckoo) **L,M**
C. heinrichi (Heinrich's Brush Cuckoo) **K**
C. pyrrhophanus (Fan-tailed Cuckoo) **L,M,O**
RHAMPHOMANTIS
R. megarhynchus (Little Long-billed Cuckoo) **K,L**
MISOCALIUS
M. osculans (Black-eared Cuckoo) **K,L,M**
CHRYSOCOCCYX
C. cupreus (African Emerald Cuckoo) **C**
C. flavigularis (Yellow-throated Green Cuckoo) **C**
C. klaas (Klaas' Cuckoo) **C**
C. caprius (Didric Cuckoo) **C**
CHALCITES
C. maculatus (Asian Emerald Cuckoo) **B,H,I,J,K**
C. xanthorhynchus (Violet Cuckoo) **H,I,J**
C. basalis (Horsfield's Bronze Cuckoo) **K,M**
C. lucidus (Golden-Bronze Cuckoo) **K,L,M,N,O**
C. poecilurus (New Guinea Bronze Cuckoo) **L**
C. russatus (Gould's Bronze Cuckoo) **J,K,L,M**
C. rufomerus (Green-cheeked Bronze Cuckoo) **K** [?]
C. minutillus (Little Bronze Cuckoo) **J,K,M**
C. crassirostris (Pied Bronze Cuckoo) **K,L**
C. ruficollis (Reddish-throated Bronze Cuckoo) **L**
C. meyeri (Meyer's Bronze Cuckoo) **L**
CALIECHTHRUS
C. leucolophus (White-crowned Koel) **L**
SURNICULUS
S. lugubris (Drongo-Cuckoo) **B,H,I,J,K**
MICRODYNAMIS
M. parva (Black-capped Cuckoo) **L**
EUDYNAMYS
E. scolopacea (Common Koel) **B,H,I,J,K,L,O**
URODYNAMIS
U. taitensis (Long-tailed Koel) **N**
SCYTHROPS
S. novaehollandiae (Channel-billed Cuckoo) **K,L,M**
PHAENICOPHAEINAE
COCCYZUS
C. pumilus (Dwarf Cuckoo) **F**
C. cinereus (Ash-coloured Cuckoo) **F**
C. erythrophthalmus (Black-billed Cuckoo) **A,E,F**
C. americanus (Yellow-billed Cuckoo) **A,E,F**
C. euleri (Pearly-breasted Cuckoo) **F**
C. minor (Mangrove Cuckoo) **A,E,F**
C. ferrugineus (Cocos Cuckoo) **E** [?]
C. melacoryphus (Dark-billed Cuckoo) **F,G**
C. lansbergi (Gray-capped Cuckoo) **F**
HYETORNIS
H. rufigularis (Rufous-breasted Cuckoo) **E**
H. pluvialis (Chestnut-bellied Cuckoo) **E**
PIAYA
P. cayana (Squirrel Cuckoo) **E,F**
P. melanogaster (Black-bellied Cuckoo) **F**
P. minuta (Little Cuckoo) **E,F**
SAUROTHERA
S. merlini (Great Lizard Cuckoo) **E**
S. vetula (Jamaican Lizard Cuckoo) **E**
S. longirostris (Hispaniolan Lizard Cuckoo) **E**
S. vieilloti (Puerto Rican Lizard Cuckoo) **E**
CEUTHMOCHARES
C. aereus (Yellow-bill) **C**

RHOPODYTES
R. diardi (Lesser Green-billed Malcoha) **J**
R. sumatranus (Rufous-bellied Malcoha) **J**
R. tristis (Greater Green-billed Malcoha) **H,I,J**
R. viridirostris (Small Green-billed Malcoha) **H**
TACCOCUA
T. leschenaultii (Sirkeer Cuckoo) **H**
RHINORTHA
R. chlorophaea (Raffles' Malcoha) **I,J**
ZANCLOSTOMUS
Z. javanicus (Red-billed Malcoha) **I,J**
RHAMPHOCOCCYX
R. calyorhynchus (Fiery-billed Malcoha) **K**
R. curvirostris (Chestnut-breasted Malcoha) **I,J**
PHAENICOPHAEUS
P. pyrrhocephalus (Red-faced Malcoha) **H**   [?]
DASYLOPHUS
D. superciliosus (Rough-crested Cuckoo) **J**
LEPIDOGRAMMUS
L. cumingi (Scale-feathered Cuckoo) **J**
CROTOPHAGINAE
CROTOPHAGA
C. major (Greater Ani) **E,F**
C. ani (Smooth-billed Ani) **E,F**
C. sulcirostris (Groove-billed Ani) **E,F**
GUIRA
G. guira (Guira Cuckoo) **F**
NEOMORPHINAE
TAPERA
T. naevia (Striped Cuckoo) **F**
MOROCOCCYX
M. erythropygus (Lesser Ground Cuckoo) **E**
DROMOCOCCYX
D. phasianellus (Pheasant Cuckoo) **E,F**
D. pavoninus (Pavonine Cuckoo) **F**
GEOCOCCYX
G. californianus (Greater Roadrunner) **A,E**
G. velox (Lesser Roadrunner) **E**
NEOMORPHUS
N. geoffroyi (Rufous-vented Ground Cuckoo) **E,F**
N. squamiger (Scaled Ground Cuckoo) **F**
N. radiolosus (Banded Ground Cuckoo) **F**   [?]
N. rufipennis (Rufous-winged Ground Cuckoo) **F**
N. pucheranii (Red-billed Ground Cuckoo) **F**
CARPOCOCCYX
C. radiceus (Ground Cuckoo) **J**   [?]
C. renauldi (Coral-billed Ground Cuckoo) **I**
COUINAE
COUA
C. gigas (Giant Madagascar Coucal) **D**
C. coquereli (Coquerel's Madagascar Coucal) **D**
C. serriana (Rufous-breasted Madagascar Coucal) **D**
C. reynaudii (Red-footed Madagascar Coucal) **D**
C. cursor (Running Coucal) **D**
C. ruficeps (Red-capped Madagascar Coucal) **D**
C. cristata (Crested Madagascar Coucal) **D**
C. verreauxi (Southern Crested Madagascar Coucal) **D**
C. caerulea (Blue Madagascar Coucal) **D**
CENTROPODINAE
CENTROPUS
C. milo (Buff-headed Coucal) **A,O**
C. goliath (Large Coucal) **K**
C. violaceus (Violet Coucal) **O**
C. menbecki (Greater Coucal) **J,K,L**
C. ateralbus (New Britain Coucal) **O**
C. chalybeus (Biak Island Coucal) **L**
C. phasianinus (Pheasant Coucal) **K,L,M**
C. spilopterus (Kai Coucal) **L**
C. bernsteini (Bernstein's Coucal) **L**
C. chlororhynchus (Ceylon Coucal) **H**   [?]
C. rectunguis (Short-toed Coucal) **J**
C. steerii (Steere's Coucal) **J**   [?]
C. sinensis (Common Crow-Pheasant) **H,I,J**
C. nigrorufus (Sunda Coucal) **J**   [?]
C. viridis (Philippine Coucal) **J**
C. toulou (Black Coucal) **D**
C. bengalensis (Lesser Coucal) **H,I,J,K**
C. grillii (Black-chested Coucal) **C**
C. epomidis (Rufous-bellied Coucal) **C**
C. leucogaster (Black-throated Coucal) **C**
C. neumanni (Smaller Black-throated Coucal) **C**
C. anselli (Gabon Coucal) **C**
C. monachus (Blue-headed Coucal) **C**
C. cupreicaudus (Coppery-tailed Coucal) **C**
C. senegalensis (Senegal Coucal) **C**

C. superciliosus (White-browed Coucal) **C**
C. melanops (Black-faced Coucal) **J**
C. celebensis (Bay Coucal) **K**
C. unirufus (Rufous Coucal) **J**

STRIGIFORMES

75 TYTONIDAE (BARN OWLS)
TYTONINAE
TYTO
T. soumagnei (Madagascar Masked Owl) **D**   [I]
T. alba (Common Barn-Owl)
A,B,C,D,E,F,G,H,I,J,K,L,M,O
T. glaucops (Ashy-faced Barn Owl) **E**
T. rosenbergii (Sulawesi Masked Owl) **K**
T. nigrobrunnea (Sula Masked Owl) **J**   [?]
T. inexpectata (Minnahassa Masked Owl) **K**   [?]
T. sororcula (Lesser Masked Owl) **K,L**   [?]
T. noaehollandiae (Australian Masked Owl) **L,M**
T. aurantia (New Britain Barn Owl) **O**   [?]
T. tenebricosa (Greater Sooty Owl) **L,M**
T. multipunctata (Lesser Sooty Owl) **M**
T. capensis (Grass Owl) **B,C,H,I,J,K,L,M,O**
PHODILINAE
PHODILUS
P. badius (Bay Owl) **H,I,J**
P. prigoginei (Congo Bay Owl) **C**   [I]
76 STRIGIDAE (OWLS)
BUBONINAE
OTUS
O. sagittatus (White-fronted Scops Owl) **I,J**   [?]
O. rufescens (Rufous Scops Owl) **J**
O. icterorhynchus (Cinnamon Scops Owl) **C**
O. ireneae (Sokoke Scops Owl) **C**   [E]
O. spilocephalus (Spotted Scops Owl) **H,I,J**
O. balli (Andaman Scops Owl) **I**
O. longicornis (Luzon Scops Owl) **J**
O. mindorensis (Mindoro Scops Owl) **J**   [?]
O. mirus (Mindanao Scops Owl) **J**
O. manadensis (Sulawesi Scops Owl) **K**
O. alfredi (Flores Scops Owl) **J**   [?]
O. angelinae (Javan Scops Owl) **J**   [?]
O. umbra (Simalur Scops Owl) **J**
O. hartlaubi (Sao Thome Scops Owl) **C**   [R]
O. brucei (Pallid Scops Owl) **B,C,H**
O. flammeolus (Flammulated Owl) **A,E**
O. senegalensis (African Scops Owl) **C**
O. scops (Eurasian Scops Owl) **B,C,H,I,J**
O. sunia (Oriental Scops Owl) **H,I**
O. elegans (Riukiu Scops Owl) **B,E,J**
O. mantananensis (South Philippines Scops Owl) **J**
O. magicus (Moluccan Scops Owl) **J,K**
O. rutilus (Madagascar Scops Owl) **D**
O. pembaensis (Pemba Scops Owl) **C**
O. brookii (Rajah Scops Owl) **J**
O. bakkamoena (Indian Scops Owl) **B,C,H,I**
O. lempiji (Collared Scops Owl) **B,I,J**
O. megalotis (Philippine Scops Owl) **J**
O. fuliginosus (Palawan Scops Owl) **J**
O. mentawi (Sipora Scops Owl) **J,L**
O. silvicola (Wallace's Scops Owl) **J**
O. beccarii (Biak Island Scops Owl) **L**   [?]
O. insularis (Bare-legged Scops Owl) **J**   [R]
O. leucotis (White-faced Scops Owl) **C**
O. asio (Eastern Screech Owl) **A,E**
O. kennicotti (Western Screech Owl) **A,E**
O. seductus (Balsas Screech Owl) **E**
O. cooperii (Pacific Screech Owl) **E**
O. trichopsis (Whiskered Screech Owl) **E,F**
O. choliba (Tropical Screech Owl) **E,F**
O. sanctaecatarinae (Long-tufted Screech Owl) **F**
O. roboratus (Peruvian Screech Owl) **F**
O. koepckeae (Maria Koepcke's Screech Owl) **F**
O. clarkii (Bare-shanked Screech Owl) **E**
O. barbarus (Bearded Screech Owl) **E**
O. marshalli (Cloud-forest Screech Owl) **F**
O. ingens (Rufescent Screech Owl) **F**
O. colombianus (Colombian Screech Owl) **F**
O. petersoni (Cinnamon Screech Owl) **F**
O. watsonii (Tawny-bellied Screech Owl) **F**
O. atricapillus (Black-capped Screech Owl) **F**
O. guatemalae (Vermiculated Screech Owl) **E,F**
O. nudipes (Puerto Rico Screech Owl) **E**
O. lawrencii (Cuban Screech Owl) **E**
O. podarginus (Palau Scops Owl) **J**
O. albogularis (White-throated Screech Owl) **F**

MIMIZUKU
M. gurneyi (Giant Scops Owl) **J**
JUBULA
J. lettii (Maned Owl) **C**
LOPHOSTRIX
L. cristata (Crested Owl) **E,F**
PULSATRIX
P. perspicillata (Spectacled Owl) **E,F**
P. koeniswaldiana (Tawny-browed Owl) **F**
P. melanota (Band-tailed Owl) **F**
BUBO
B. virginianus (Great Horned Owl) **A,E,F**
B. bubo (Northern Eagle Owl) **B**
B. ascalaphus (Desert Eagle Owl) **B**
B. bengalensis (Indian Eagle Owl) **H**
B. capensis (Cape Eagle Owl) **C**
B. africanus (Spotted Eagle Owl) **E**
B. poensis (Fraser's Eagle Owl) **C**
B. nipalensis (Forest Eagle Owl) **H,I**
B. sumatrana (Malay Eagle Owl) **I,J**
B. shelleyi (Shelley's Eagle Owl) **C**
B. lacteus (Verreaux's Eagle Owl) **C**
B. coromandus (Dusky Eagle Owl) **H,I,J**
B. leucostictus (Akun Eagle Owl) **C**
B. philippensis (Philippine Eagle Owl) **J**   [?]
B. blakistoni (Blakiston's Fish Owl) **B**
B. zeylonensis (Brown Fish Owl) **B,H,I**
B. flavipes (Tawny Fish Owl) **B,H,I**
B. ketupu (Malay Fish Owl) **H,I,J**
SCOTOPELIA
S. peli (Pel's Fishing Owl) **C**
S. ussheri (Rufous Fishing Owl) **C**   [R]
S. bouvieri (Vermiculated Fishing Owl) **C**
NYCTEA
N. scandiaca (Snowy Owl) **A,B**
CICCABA
C. virgata (Mottled Owl) **E,F**
C. nigrolineata (Black & White Owl) **E,F**
C. huhula (Black-banded Owl) **F**
C. albitarsus (Rufous-banded Owl) **F**
STRIX
S. woodfordi (African Wood Owl) **C**
S. seloputo (Spotted Wood Owl) **I,J**
S. ocellata (Mottled Wood Owl) **H**
S. leptogrammica (Brown Wood Owl) **H,I,J,K**
S. aluco (Eurasian Tawny Owl) **B,I,J**
S. butleri (Hume's Owl) **B**
S. varia (Barred Owl) **A,E**
S. fulvescens (Fulvous Owl) **E**
S. occidentalis (Spotted Owl) **A,E**
S. uralensis (Ural Owl) **B**
S. nebulosa (Great Gray Owl) **A,B**
S. hylophila (Rusty Barred Owl) **F**
S. rufipes (Rufous-legged Owl) **F**
SURNIA
S. ulula (Hawk Owl) **A,B**
GLAUCIDIUM
G. brodiei (Collared Owlet) **H,I,J**
G. passerinum (Eurasian Pygmy Owl) **B**
G. perlatum (Pearl-spotted Owlet) **C**
G. gnoma (Northern Pygmy Owl) **A,E**
G. minutissimum (Least Pygmy Owl) **E,F**
G. brasilianum (Ferruginous Pygmy Owl) **A,E,F**
G. nanum (Austral Pygmy Owl) **F**
G. jardinii (Andean Pygmy Owl) **F**
G. siju (Cuban Pygmy Owl) **E,F**
G. tephronotum (Red-chested Owlet) **C**
G. sjostedti (Chestnut-backed Owlet) **C**
G. radiatum (Jungle Owlet) **H**
G. cuculoides (Cuckoo Owlet) **B,H,I**
G. castanopterum (Chestnut-winged Owlet) **J**
G. capense (African Barred Owlet) **C**
G. castaneum (Ituri Owlet) **C**
G. albertinum (Prigogine's Owlet) **C**   [R]
G. scheffleri (Eastern Barred Owlet) **C**
XENOGLAUX
X. loweryi (Long-whiskered Owlet) **F**
MICRATHENE
M. whitneyi (Elf Owl) **A,E**
ATHENE
A. noctua (Little Owl) **B,C,H**
A. brama (Spotted Owlet) **B,H,I**
A. blewitti (Forest Owlet) **H**   [I]
A. cunicularia (Burrowing Owl) **A,E,F**

AEGOLIUS
A. funereus (Tengmalm's Owl) **A,B**
A. acadicus (Northern Saw-whet Owl) **A**
A. ridgwayi (Unspotted Saw-whet Owl) **E**
A. harrisii (Buff-fronted Owl) **F**
UROGLAUX
U. dimorpha (Papuan Hawk-Owl) **L**
NINOX
N. rufa (Rufous Hawk-Owl) **K,L,M**
N. strenua (Powerful Owl) **M**
N. connivens (Barking Owl) **K,L,M**
N. novaeseelandiae (Boobook Owl) **J,K,L,M,N**
N. rudolfi (Sumba Boobook Owl) **K**
N. scutulata (Brown Hawk-Owl) **B,H,I,J,K**
N. affinis (Andaman Hawk-Owl) **J**
N. superciliaris (Madagascar Hawk-Owl) **D**
N. philippensis (Philippine Hawk-Owl) **J**
N. spilonota (Spotted Hawk-Owl) **J**
N. spilocephala (Tweedale's Hawk-Owl) **J**
N. ochracea (Ochre-bellied Hawk-Owl) **K**
N. squamipila (Moluccan Hawk-Owl) **J,K,L**
N. theomacha (Jungle Hawk-Owl) **K,L**
N. meeki (Admiralty Is Hawk-Owl) **L**
N. punctulata (Speckled Hawk-Owl) **K**
N. variegata (Bismarck Hawk-Owl) **O**
N. odiosa (New Britain Hawk-Owl) **O**
N. jacquinoti (Solomon Is Hawk-Owl) **A,O**
SCELOGLAUX
S. albifacies (White-faced Owl) **N**   ☒
ASIO
A. clamator (Striped Owl) **E,F**
A. otus (Long-eared Owl) **A,B**
A. stygius (Stygian Owl) **E,F**
A. abyssinicus (Abyssinian Long-eared Owl) **C**
A. madagascariensis (Madagascar Long-eared Owl) **D**
A. flammeus (Short-eared Owl) **A,B,F,G,P**
A. capensis (African Marsh Owl) **C,D**
PSEUDOSCOPS
P. grammacus (Jamaican Owl) **E**
NESASIO
N. solomonensis (Fearful Owl) **O**

CAPRIMULGIFORMES

77 STEATORNITHIDAE (OILBIRD)
STEATORNIS
S. caripensis (Oilbird) **F**
78 PODARGIDAE (FROGMOUTHS)
PODARGUS
P. strigoides (Tawny Frogmouth) **M**
P. papuensis (Papuan Frogmouth) **L,M**
P. ocellatus (Marbled Frogmouth) **L,M,O**
BATRACHOSTOMUS
B. auritus (Large Frogmouth) **J**
B. harterti (Dulit Frogmouth) **J**   ?
B. septimus (Philippine Frogmouth) **J**
B. stellatus (Gould's Frogmouth) **J**
B. moniliger (Ceylon Frogmouth) **H**
B. hodgsoni (Hodgson's Frogmouth) **H,I**
B. poliolophus (Pale-headed Frogmouth) **J**
B. mixtus (Sharpe's Frogmouth) **J**
B. javensis (Javan Frogmouth) **I,J**
B. cornutus (Bornean Frogmouth) **J**
79 NYCTIBIIDAE (POTOOS)
NYCTIBIUS
N. grandis (Great Potoo) **E,F**
N. aethereus (Long-tailed Potoo) **F**   ?
N. griseus (Common Potoo) **E,F**
N. leucopterus (White-winged Potoo) **F**   ?
N. bracteatus (Rufous Potoo) **F**   ?
80 AEGOTHELIDAE (OWLET-NIGHTJARS)
AEGOTHELES
A. crinifrons (Halmahera Owlet-Nightjar) **K**
A. insignis (Large Owlet-Nightjar) **L**
A. cristatus (Australian Owlet-Nightjar) **L,M**
A. savesi (New Caledonian Owlet-Nightjar) **O**   ☒
A. bennettii (Barred Owlet-Nightjar) **L**
A. wallacii (Wallace's Owlet-Nightjar) **L**
A. albertisi (Mountain Owlet-Nightjar) **L**
A. archboldi (Eastern Mountain Owlet-Nightjar) **L**
81 CAPRIMULGIDAE (NIGHTHAWKS, NIGHTJARS)
CHORDEILINAE
LUROCALIS
L. semitorquatus (Semi-collared Nighthawk) **E,F**

CHORDEILES
C. pusillus (Least Nighthawk) **F**
C. rupestris (Sand-coloured Nighthawk) **F**
C. acutipennis (Lesser Nighthawk) **A,E,F**
C. minor (Common Nighthawk) **A,E,F**
C. gundlachii (Antillean Nighthawk) **E**
NYCTIPROGNE
N. leucopyga (Band-tailed Nighthawk) **F**
PODAGER
P. nacunda (Nacunda Nighthawk) **F**
CAPRIMULGINAE
EUROSTOPODUS
E. argus (Spotted Nightjar) **K**
E. mystacalis (White-throated Nightjar) **L,M,O**
E. diabolicus (Satanic Nightjar) **K**   ?
E. papuensis (Papuan Nightjar) **L**
E. archboldi (Archbold's Nightjar) **L**
E. temminckii (Malaysian Eared Nightjar) **J**
E. macrotis (Great Eared Nightjar) **H,I,J,K**
VELES
V. binotatus (Brown Nightjar) **C**
NYCTIDROMUS
N. albicollis (Common Pauraque) **A,E,F**
PHALAENOPTILUS
P. nuttallii (Common Poorwill) **A,E**
SIPHONORHIS
S. brewsteri (Least Pauraque) **E**
OTOPHANES
O. mcleodii (Eared Poorwill) **E**
O. yucatanicus (Yucatan Poorwill) **E**
NYCTIPHRYNUS
N. ocellatus (Ocellated Poorwill) **E,F**
CAPRIMULGUS
C. carolinensis (Chuck Will's Widow) **A,E**
C. rufus (Rufus Nightjar) **F**
C. otiosus (St Lucian Nightjar) **E**
C. cubanensis (Greater Antillean Nightjar) **E**
C. sericocaudatus (Silky-tailed Nightjar) **F**
C. salvini (Tawny-collared Nightjar) **E**
C. badius (Yucatan Tawny-collared Nightjar) **E**
C. ridgwayi (Ridgway's Whip-poor-will) **E**
C. vociferus (Whip-poor-will) **A,E**
C. noctitherus (Puerto Rican Nightjar) **E**   Ⓡ
C. saturatus (Dusky Nightjar) **E**
C. longirostris (Band-winged Nightjar) **F**
C. cayennensis (White-tailed Nightjar) **E,F**
C. candicans (White-winged Nightjar) **F**   ?
C. maculicaudus (Spot-tailed Nightjar) **F**
C. parvulus (Little Nightjar) **F**
C. maculosus (Cayenne Nightjar) **F**
C. nigrescens (Blackish Nightjar) **F**
C. whitelyi (Roraiman Nightjar) **F**   ?
C. hirundinaceus (Pygmy Nightjar) **F**   ?
C. ruficollis (Red-necked Nightjar) **B,C**   ?
C. indicus (Jungle Nightjar) **B,H,I,J**
C. europaeus (European Nightjar) **B,C,H**
C. mahrattensis (Sykes' Nightjar) **B,H**
C. centralasicus (Vaurie's Nightjar) **B**   ?
C. nubicus (Nubian Nightjar) **C**
C. aegyptius (Egyptian Nightjar) **B,C**
C. eximius (Golden Nightjar) **C**
C. atripennis (Indian Long-tailed Nightjar) **H**
C. macrurus (Long-tailed Nightjar) **H,I,J,K,L,M,O**
C. pectoralis (African Dusky Nightjar) **C**
C. nigriscapularis (Black-shouldered Nightjar) **C**
C. rufigena (Rufous-cheeked Nightjar) **C**
C. fraenatus (Sombre Nightjar) **C**
C. donaldsoni (Donaldson Smith's Nightjar) **C**
C. poliocephalus (Abyssinian Nightjar) **C**
C. ruwenzorii (Ruwenzori Nightjar) **C**
C. asiaticus (Indian Nightjar) **D,H,I**
C. natalensis (African White-tailed Nightjar) **C**
C. inornatus (Plain Nightjar) **C**
C. stellatus (Star-spotted Nightjar) **C**
C. ludovicianus (Ludovic's Nightjar) **C**
C. monticolus (Franklin's Nightjar) **H,I,J**
C. affinis (Allied Nightjar) **J,K**
C. tristigma (Freckled Nightjar) **C**
C. concretus (Bonaparte's Nightjar) **J**
C. pulchellus (Salvadori's Nightjar) **J**
C. enarratus (Collared Nightjar) **D**
C. batesi (Bates' Nightjar) **C**
SCOTORNIS
S. fossii (Gabon Nightjar) **C**
S. climacurus (Long-tailed Nightjar) **C**
S. clarus (Slender-tailed Nightjar) **C**

MACRODIPTERYX
M. longipennis (Standard-winged Nightjar) **C**
M. vexillarius (Pennant-winged Nightjar) **C**
HYDROPSALIS
H. climacocerca (Ladder-tailed Nightjar) **F**
H. brasiliana (Scissor-tailed Nightjar) **F**
UROPSALIS
U. segmentata (Swallow-tailed Nightjar) **F**
U. lyra (Lyre-tailed Nightjar) **F**
MACROPSALIS
M. creagra (Long-trained Nightjar) **F**
ELEOTHREPTUS
E. anomalus (Sickle-winged Nightjar) **F**   ?

APODIFORMES

82 APODIDAE (SWIFTS)
CYPSELOIDINAE
CYPSELOIDES
C. fumigatus (Sooty Swift) **E,F**
C. cherriei (Spot-fronted Swift) **F**
C. cryptus (White-chinned Swift) **E,F**
C. lemosi (White-chested Swift) **F**   ?
C. major (Great Swift) **F**
C. phelpsi (Tepui Swift) **F**
C. rutilus (Chestnut-collared Swift) **E,F**
NEPHOECETES
N. niger (Black Swift) **A,E,F**
AERORNIS
A. senex (Great Dusky Swift) **F**
STREPTOPROCNE
S. zonaris (White-collared Swift) **E,F**
S. biscutatus (Biscutate Swift) **F**
S. semicollaris (White-naped Swift) **E**
APODINAE
HYDROCHOUS
H. gigas (Waterfall Swift) **J**   ?
AERODRAMUS
A. infuscatus (Moluccan Swiftlet) **K**
A. spodiopygius (White-rumped Swiftlet) **J,L,M,O**
A. hirundinaceus (Mountain Swiftlet) **J,M**
A. fuciphagus (Edible-nest Swiftlet) **I,K**
A. francica (Gray-rumped Swiftlet) **D**
A. germani (Oustalet's Swiftlet) **I,J**
A. amelis (Philippine Swiftlet) **J**
A. vanikorensis (Uniform Swiftlet) **J,K,L,M,O**
A. salangana (Mossy Swiftlet) **H,I,J**
A. inquietus (Caroline Swiftlet) **O**
A. bartschi (Mariana Swiftlet) **O,J**
A. mearnsi (Brown-rumped Swiftlet) **J**
A. orientalis (Guadalcanal Swiftlet) **O**
A. papuensis (Idenburg River Swiftlet) **L**
A. nuditarsus (Schrader Mountain Swiftlet) **L**
A. whiteheadi (Whitehead's Swiftlet) **J,L**
A. brevirostris (Himalayan Swiftlet) **B,H,I,J,K**
A. maximus (Lowe's Swiftlet) **J,K**
A. elaphra (Seychelles Cave Swiftlet) **D**
A. unicolor (Indian Edible-nest Swiftlet) **H**
A. leucophaeus (Tahitian Swiftlet) **O**   ?
A. ocista (Marquesan Swiftlet) **O**
A. sawtelli (Cook Islands Swiftlet) **O**
COLLOCALIA
C. esculenta (White-bellied Swiftlet) **I,J,K,L,O**
C. marginata (Philippine Swiftlet) **J**
C. troglodytes (Pygmy Swiftlet) **J**
C. linchi (Linchi Swiftlet) **J,K**
SCHOUTEDENAPUS
S. myioptilus (Scarce Swift) **C**
S. schoutedeni (Schouteden's Swift) **C**   Ⓘ
MEARNSIA
M. picina (Philippine Spinetailed Swift) **J**
M. novaeguineae (New Guinea Spinetailed Swift) **L**
ZOONAVENA
Z. grandidieri (Madagascar Spinetailed Swift) **D**
Z. thomensis (Sao Thomé Spinetailed Swift) **C**
Z. sylvatica (Indian White-rumped Spinetailed Swift) **H,I**
TELACANTHURA
T. ussheri (Mottle-throated Spinetailed Swift) **C**
T. melanopygia (Ituri Mottle-throated Spinetailed Swift) **C**
RAPHIDURA
R. leucopygialis (White-rumped Spinetailed Swift) **I,J**
R. sabini (Sabine's Spinetailed Swift) **C**

NEAFRAPUS
N. cassini (Cassin's Spinetailed Swift) **C**
N. boehmi (Boehm's Spinetailed Swift) **C**
HIRUNDAPUS
H. caudacuta (White-throated Spinetailed Swift) **B,H,I,J,K,M**
H. cochinchinensis (White-vented Spinetailed Swift) **H,I,J**
H. gigantea (Brown Spinetailed Swift) **H,I,J**
H. celebensis (Sulawesi Spinetailed Swift) **K**
CHAETURA
C. spinicauda (Band-rumped Swift) **E,F**
C. martinica (Lesser Antillean Swift) **E**
C. cinereiventris (Gray-rumped Swift) **E,F**
C. egregia (Pale-rumped Swift) **F**
C. pelagica (Chimney Swift) **A,E,F**
C. vauxi (Vaux's Swift) **A,E,F**
C. chapmani (Chapman's Swift) **F**
C. andrei (Ashy-tailed Swift) **F**
C. brachyura (Short-tailed Swift) **E,F**
AERONAUTES
A. saxatilis (White-throated Swift) **A,E**
A. montivagus (White-tipped Swift) **F**
A. andecolus (Andean Swift) **F**
TACHORNIS
T. phoenicobia (Antillean Palm Swift) **E**
T. furcata (Pygmy Swift) **F**
T. squamata (Fork-tailed Palm Swift) **F**
PANYPTILA
P. sanctihieronymi (Great Swallow-tailed Swift) **E**
P. cayennensis (Lesser Swallow-tailed Swift) **E,F**
CYPSIURUS
C. batasiensis (Asian Palm Swift) **H,I,J**
C. parvus (African Palm Swift) **C**
TACHYMARPTIS
T. melba (Alpine Swift) **B,C,D,H**
T. aequatorialis (Mottled Swift) **F**
APUS
A. alexandri (Alexander's Swift) **B**
A. barbatus (African Black Swift) **C,D**
A. berliozi (Berlioz' Swift) **C**
A. bradfieldi (Bradfield's Swift) **C**
A. niansae (Nyanza Swift) **C**
A. pallidus (Pallid Swift) **B,C,H**
A. apus (Eurasian Swift) **B,C,H**
A. unicolor (Plain Swift) **B**
A. acuticauda (Dark-backed Swift) **H**   ?
A. pacificus (Fork-tailed Swift) **B,H,I,J,K,L,M**
A. affinis (House) Swift) **B,C,H,I,J**
A. horus (Horus Swift) **C**
A. caffer (White-rumped Swift) **C**
A. batesi (Bates' Black Swift) **C**
83 HEMIPROCNIDAE (TREE SWIFTS)
HEMIPROCNE
H. longipennis (Crested Tree Swift) **H,I,J,K,L**
H. mystacea (Whiskered Tree Swift) **K,L,O**
H. comata (Lesser Tree Swift) **J,L**
84 TROCHILIDAE (HUMMINGBIRDS)
DORYFERA
D. johannae (Blue-fronted Lancebill) **F**
D. ludoviciae (Green-fronted Lancebill) **F**
ANDRODON
A. aequatorialis (Tooth-billed Hummingbird) **F**
RAMPHODON
R. naevius (Saw-billed Hermit) **F**
GLAUCIS
G. dohrnii (Hook-billed Hermit) **F**   E
G. aenea (Bronzy Hermit) **E,F**   E
G. hirsuta (Rufous-breasted Hermit) **E,F**   E
THRENETES
T. niger (Sooty Barbthroat) **F**   ?
T. grzimeki (Black Barbthroat) **F**
T. leucurus (Pale-tailed Barbthroat) **F**
T. ruckeri (Band-tailed Barbthroat) **F**
PHAETHORNIS
P. yaruqui (White-whiskered Hermit) **F**
P. guy (Green Hermit) **E,F**
P. syrmatophorus (Tawny-bellied Hermit) **F**
P. superciliosus (Long-tailed Hermit) **E,F**
P. malaris (Great-billed Hermit) **F**
P. margarettae (Klabin Farm Long-tailed Hermit) **F**
P. eurynome (Scale-throated Hermit) **F**
P. nigrirostris (Black-billed Hermit) **F**   R
P. hispidus (White-bearded Hermit) **F**
P. anthophilus (Pale-bellied Hermit) **E,F**
P. koepckeae (Koepcke's Hermit) **F**

P. bourcieri (Straight-billed Hermit) **F**
P. philippii (Needle-billed Hermit) **F**
P. squalidus (Dusky-throated Hermit) **F**
P. augusti (Sooty-capped Hermit) **F**
P. pretrei (Planalto Hermit) **F**
P. subochraceus (Buff-bellied Hermit) **F**
P. nattereri (Cinnamon-throated Hermit) **F**
P. gounellei (Broad-tipped Hermit) **F**
P. ruber (Reddish Hermit) **E,F**
P. stuarti (White-browed Hermit) **F**
P. griseogularis (Gray-chinned Hermit) **F**
P. longuemareus (Little Hermit) **E,F**
P. idaliae (Minute Hermit) **F**   ?
EUTOXERES
E. aquila (White-tipped Sicklebill) **E,F**
E. condamini (Buff-tailed Sicklebill) **F**
PHAEOCHROA
P. cuvierii (Scaly-breasted Hummingbird) **E,F**
CAMPYLOPTERUS
C. curvipennis (Wedge-tailed Sabrewing) **E**
C. excellens (Long-tailed Sabrewing) **E**
C. largipennis (Gray-breasted Sabrewing) **F**
C. rufus (Rufous Sabrewing) **E**
C. hyperythrus (Rufous-breasted Sabrewing) **F**
C. duidae (Buff-breasted Sabrewing) **F**
C. hemileucurus (Violet Sabrewing) **E**
C. ensipennis (White-tailed Sabrewing) **E**   ?
C. falcatus (Lazuline Sabrewing) **F**
C. phainopeplus (Santa Marta Sabrewing) **F**
C. villaviscensio (Napo Sabrewing) **F**   ?
EUPETOMENA
E. macroura (Swallow-tailed Hummingbird) **F**
FLORISUGA
F. mellivora (White-necked Jacobin) **E,F**
MELANOTROCHILUS
M. fuscus (Black Jacobin) **F**
COLIBRI
C. delphinae (Brown Violetear) **E,F**
C. thalassinus (Green Violetear) **E,F**
C. coruscans (Sparkling Violetear) **F**
C. serrirostris (White-vented Violetear) **F**
ANTHRACOTHORAX
A. viridigula (Green-throated Mango) **F**
A. prevostii (Green-breasted Mango) **E,F**
A. nigricollis (Black-throated Mango) **E,F**
A. veraguensis (Veraguas Mango) **E**
A. dominicus (Antillean Mango) **E**
A. viridis (Green Mango) **E**
A. mango (Jamaican Mango) **E**
AVOCETTULA
A. recurvirostris (Fiery-tailed Awlbill) **F**   ?
EULAMPIS
E. jugularis (Purple-throated Carib) **E**
SERICOTES
S. holosericeus (Green-throated Carib) **E**
CHRYSOLAMPIS
C. mosquitus (Ruby-Topaz Hummingbird) **F**
ORTHORHYNCUS
O. cristatus (Antillean Crested Hummingbird) **E**
KLAIS
K. guimeti (Violet-headed Hummingbird) **E,F**
ABEILLIA
A. abeillei (Emerald-chinned Hummingbird) **E**
STEPHANOXIS
S. lalandi (Black-breasted Plovercrest) **F**
LOPHORNIS
L. ornata (Tufted Coquette) **E,F**
L. gouldii (Dot-eared Coquette) **F**
L. magnifica (Frilled Coquette) **F**
L. delattrei (Rufous-crested Coquette) **E,F**
L. stictolopha (Spangled Coquette) **F**
L. chalybea (Festive Coquette) **F**
L. pavonina (Peacock Coquette) **F**
L. insignibarbis (Bearded Coquette) **F**
PAPHOSIA
P. helenae (Black-crested Coquette) **E**
P. adorabilis (White-crested Coquette) **E**
POPELAIRIA
P. popelairii (Wire-crested Thorntail) **F**
P. langsdorffi (Black-bellied Thorntail) **F**
P. letitiae (Coppery Thorntail) **F**   ?
P. conversii (Green Thorntail) **E,F**
DISCOSURA
D. longicauda (Racket-tailed Coquette) **F**
CHLORESTES
C. notatus (Blue-chinned Sapphire) **F**

CHLOROSTILBON
C. mellisugus (Blue-tailed Emerald) **E,F**
C. vitticeps (Simon's Emerald) **F**
C. aureoventris (Glittering-bellied Emerald) **F**
C. canivetii (Fork-tailed Emerald) **E,F**
C. assimilis (Garden Emerald) **E**
C. ricordii (Cuban Emerald) **E**
C. swainsonii (Hispaniolan Emerald) **E**
C. maugaeus (Puerto Rican Emerald) **E**
C. gibsoni (Red-billed Emerald) **F**
C. russatus (Coppery Emerald) **F**
C. stenura (Narrow-tailed Emerald) **F**
C. alice (Green-tailed Emerald) **F**
C. poortmani (Short-tailed Emerald) **F**
CYNANTHUS
C. sordidus (Dusky Hummingbird) **E**
C. latirostris (Broad-billed Hummingbird) **A,E**
CYANOPHAIA
C. bicolor (Blue-headed Hummingbird) **E**
THALURANIA
T. colombica (Crowned Woodnymph) **E,F**
T. furcata (Fork-tailed Woodnymph) **F**
T. watertonii (Long-tailed Woodnymph) **F**
T. glaucopis (Violet-capped Woodnymph) **F**
T. lerchi (Lerch's Woodnymph) **F**
NEOLESBIA
N. nehrkorni (Blue-tailed Sylph) **F**
PANTERPE
P. insignis (Fiery-throated Hummingbird) **E**
DAMOPHILA
D. julie (Violet-bellied Hummingbird) **E,F**
LEPIDOPYGA
L. coeruleogularis (Sapphire-throated Hummingbird) **E,F**
L. lilliae (Sapphire-bellied Hummingbird) **F**   ?
L. goudoti (Shining Green Hummingbird) **F**
HYLOCHARIS
H. xantusii (Black-fronted Hummingbird) **E**
H. leucotis (White-eared Hummingbird) **A,E**
H. eliciae (Blue-throated Goldentail) **E**
H. sapphirina (Rufous-throated Sapphire) **F**
H. cyanus (White-chinned Sapphire) **F**
H. pyropygia (Flame-rumped Sapphire) **F**
H. chrysura (Gilded Hummingbird) **F**
H. grayi (Blue-headed Sapphire) **F**
CHRYSURONIA
C. oenone (Golden-tailed Sapphire) **F**
GOLDMANIA
G. violiceps (Violet-capped Hummingbird) **E**
GOETHALSIA
G. bella (Pirre Hummingbird) **E**
TROCHILUS
T. polytmus (Streamertail) **E**
LEUCOCHLORIS
L. albicollis (White-throated Hummingbird) **F**
POLYTMUS
P. guainumbi (White-tailed Goldenthroat) **F**
P. milleri (Tepui Goldenthroat) **F**
P. theresiae (Green-tailed Goldenthroat) **F**
LEUCIPPUS
L. fallax (Buffy Hummingbird) **E,F**
L. baeri (Tumbes Hummingbird) **F**
L. taczanowskii (Spot-throated Hummingbird) **F**
L. chlorocercus (Olive-spotted Hummingbird) **F**
TAPHROSPILUS
T. hypostictus (Many-spotted Hummingbird) **F**
AMAZILIA
A. chionogaster (White-bellied Hummingbird) **F**
A. viridicauda (Green-&-White Hummingbird) **F**
A. candida (White-bellied Emerald) **E**
A. chionopectus (White-chested Emerald) **E**
A. versicolor (Versicolored Emerald) **F**
A. luciae (Honduras Emerald) **F**   ?
A. fimbriata (Glittering-throated Emerald) **F**
A. distans (Tachira Emerald) **F**   ?
A. lactea (Sapphire-spangled Emerald) **F**
A. decora (Charming Hummingbird) **E**
A. amabilis (Blue-chested Hummingbird) **E,F**
A. rosenbergi (Purple-chested Hummingbird) **F**
A. boucardi (Mangrove Hummingbird) **E**   ?
A. franciae (Andean Emerald) **F**
A. leucogaster (Plain-bellied Emerald) **F**
A. cyanocephala (Red-billed Azurecrown) **E**
A. microrhyncha (Small-billed Azurecrown) **E**
A. cyanifrons (Indigo-capped Hummingbird) **E,F**
A. beryllina (Berylline Hummingbird) **E**

A. cyanura (Blue-tailed Hummingbird) **E**
A. saucerrottei (Steely-vented Hummingbird) **E,F**
A. tobaci (Copper-rumped Hummingbird) **E,F**
A. virdigaster (Green-bellied Hummingbird) **F**
A. edward (Snowy-breasted Hummingbird) **E**
A. rutila (Cinnamon Hummingbird) **E**
A. yucatanensis (Buff-bellied Hummingbird) **E**
A. tzacatl (Rufous-tailed Hummingbird) **E,F**
A. castaneiventris (Chestnut-bellied Hummingbird) **F** [?]
A. amazilia (Amazilia Hummingbird) **F**
A. viridifrons (Green-fronted Hummingbird) **E**
A. violiceps (Violet-crowned Hummingbird) **E**
EUPHERUSA
E. poliocerca (White-tailed Hummingbird) **E**
E. eximia (Stripe-tailed Hummingbird) **E**
E. cyanophrys (Oaxaca Hummingbird) **E** [?]
E. nigriventris (Black-bellied Hummingbird) **E**
ELVIRA
E. chionura (White-tailed Emerald) **E**
E. cupreiceps (Coppery-headed Emerald) **E**
MICROCHERA
M. albocoronata (Snowcap) **E**
CHALYBURA
C. buffonii (White-vented Plumeleteer) **E,F**
C. urochrysia (Bronze-tailed Plumeleteer) **E**
APHANTOCHROA
A. cirrochloris (Sombre Hummingbird) **F**
LAMPORNIS
L. clemenciae (Blue-throated Hummingbird) **E**
L. amethystinus (Amethyst-throated Hummingbird) **E**
L. viridipallens (Green-throated Mountain Gem) **E**
L. sybillae (Green-breasted Mountain Gem) **E**
L. hemileucus (White-bellied Mountain Gem) **E**
L. castaneoventris (White-throated Mountain Gem) **E**
L. calolaema (Purple-throated Mountain Gem) **E**
L. cinereicauda (Gray-tailed Mountain Gem) **E**
LAMPROLAIMA
L. rhami (Garnet-throated Hummingbird) **E**
ADELOMYIA
A. melanogenys (Speckled Hummingbird) **F**
ANTHOCEPHALA
A. floriceps (Blossomcrown) **F** [?]
UROSTICTE
U. benjamini (Whitetip) **F**
PHLOGOPHILUS
P. hemileucurus (Ecuadorean Piedtail) **F** [?]
P. harterti (Peruvian Piedtail) **F** [?]
CLYTOLAEMA
C. rubricauda (Brazilian Ruby) **F**
POLYPLANCTA
P. aurescens (Gould's Jewel-front) **F**
HELIODOXA
H. rubinoides (Fawn-breasted Brilliant) **F**
H. leadbeateri (Violet-fronted Brilliant) **F**
H. jacula (Green-crowned Brilliant) **F**
H. xanthogonys (Velvet-browed Brilliant) **F**
H. schreibersii (Black-throated Brilliant) **F**
H. gularis (Pink-throated Brilliant) **F** [?]
H. branickii (Rufous-webbed Brilliant) **F**
H. imperatrix (Empress Brilliant) **F**
EUGENES
E. fulgens (Magnificent Hummingbird) **A,E**
HYLONYMPHA
H. macrocerca (Scissor-tailed Hummingbird) **F** [?]
STERNOCLYTA
S. cyanopectus (Violet-chested Hummingbird) **F**
TOPAZA
T. pella (Crimson Topaz) **F**
T. pyra (Fiery Topaz) **F**
OREOTROCHILUS
O. melanogaster (Black-breasted Hillstar) **F**
O. estella (Andean Hillstar) **F**
O. leucopleurus (White-sided Hillstar) **F**
O. adela (Wedgetailed Hillstar) **F**
UROCHROA
U. bougueri (White-tailed Hillstar) **F**
PATAGONA
P. gigas (Giant Hummingbird) **F**
AGLAEACTIS
A. cupripennis (Shining Sunbeam) **F**
A. aliciae (Purple-backed Sunbeam) **F** [?]
A. castelnaudii (White-tufted Sunbeam) **F**
A. pamela (Black-hooded Sunbeam) **F**

LAFRESNAYA
L. lafresnayi (Mountain Velvetbreast) **F**
PTEROPHANES
P. cyanopterus (Great Sapphirewing) **F**
COELIGENA
C. coeligena (Bronzy Inca) **F**
C. wilsoni (Brown Inca) **F**
C. prunellei (Black Inca) **F** [I]
C. torquata (Collared Inca) **F**
C. phalerata (White-tailed Starfrontlet) **F**
C. bonapartei (Golden-bellied Starfrontlet) **F**
C. orina (Dusky Starfrontlet) **F**
C. helianthea (Blue-throated Starfrontlet) **F**
C. lutetiae (Buff-winged Starfrontlet) **F**
C. violifer (Violet-throated Starfrontlet) **F**
C. iris (Rainbow Starfrontlet) **F**
ENSIFERA
E. ensifera (Sword-billed Hummingbird) **F**
SEPHANOIDES
S. sephanoides (Green-backed Firecrown) **F**
S. fernandensis (Fernandez Firecrown) **F** [?]
BOISSONNEAUA
B. flavescens (Buff-tailed Coronet) **F**
B. matthewsii (Chestnut-breasted Coronet) **F**
B. jardini (Velvet-Purple Coronet) **F**
HELIANGELUS
H. mavors (Orange-throated Sunangel) **F**
H. spencei (Merida Sunangel) **F**
H. amethysticollis (Amethyst-throated Sunangel) **F**
H. strophianus (Gorgeted Sunangel) **F**
H. regalis (Royal Sunangel) **F** [?]
H. exortis (Tourmaline Sunangel) **F**
H. viola (Purple-throated Sunangel) **F** [?]
H. micraster (Little Sunangel) **F**
H. squamigularis (Olive-throated Sunangel) **F**
ERIOCNEMIS
E. nigrivestris (Black-breasted Puffleg) **F** [?]
E. soederstroemi (Soderstrom's Puffleg) **F**
E. vestitus (Glowing Puffleg) **F**
E. godini (Turquoise-throated Puffleg) **F** [?]
E. cupreoventris (Coppery-bellied Puffleg) **F**
E. luciani (Sapphire-vented Puffleg) **F**
E. isaacsonii (Isaacson's Puffleg) **F**
E. mosquera (Golden-breasted Puffleg) **F**
E. glaucopoides (Blue-capped Puffleg) **F**
E. mirabilis (Colourful Puffleg) **F** [?]
E. alinae (Emerald-bellied Puffleg) **F**
E. derbyi (Black-thighed Puffleg) **F** [?]
HAPLOPHAEDIA
H. aureliae (Greenish Puffleg) **E,F**
H. lugens (Hoary Puffleg) **F** [?]
OCREATUS
O. underwoodii (Booted Racket-tail) **F**
LESBIA
L. victoriae (Black-tailed Trainbearer) **F**
L. nuna (Green-tailed Trainbearer) **F**
SAPPHO
S. sparganura (Red-tailed Comet) **F**
POLYONYMUS
P. caroli (Bronze-tailed Comet) **F**
ZODALIA
Z. glyceria (Purple-tailed Comet) **F**
RAMPHOMICRON
R. microrhynchum (Purple-backed Thornbill) **F**
R. dorsale (Black-backed Thornbill) **F**
METALLURA
M. phoebe (Black Metaltail) **F**
M. theresiae (Coppery Metaltail) **F**
M. purpureicauda (Purple-tailed Thornbill) **F**
M. aeneocauda (Scaled Metaltail) **F**
M. baroni (Violet-throated Metaltail) **F** [?]
M. eupogon (Fire-throated Metaltail) **F**
M. odomae (Neblina Metaltail) **F** [?]
M. williami (Viridian Metaltail) **F**
M. tyrianthina (Tyrian Metaltail) **F**
M. iracunda (Perija Metaltail) **F**
CHALCOSTIGMA
C. ruficeps (Rufous-capped Thornbill) **F**
C. olivaceum (Olivaceous Thornbill) **F**
C. stanleyi (Blue-mantled Thornbill) **F**
C. heteropogon (Bronze-tailed Thornbill) **F**
C. herrani (Rainbow-bearded Thornbill) **F**
OXYPOGON
O. guerinii (Bearded Helmetcrest) **F**
OPISTHOPRORA
O. euryptera (Mountain Avocetbill) **F**

TAPHROLESBIA
T. griseiventris (Gray-billed Comet) **F** [?]
AGLAIOCERCUS
A. kingi (Long-tailed Sylph) **F**
A. coelestis (Violet-tailed Sylph) **F**
OREONYMPHA
O. nobilis (Bearded Mountaineer) **F**
AUGASTES
A. scutatus (Hyacinth Visor-bearer) **F** [?]
A. lumachellus (Hooded Visor-bearer) **F** [?]
SCHISTES
S. geoffroyi (Wedge-billed Hummingbird) **F**
HELIOTHRYX
H. barroti (Purple-crowned Fairy) **E,F**
H. aurita (Black-eared Fairy) **F**
HELIACTIN
H. cornuta (Horned Sungem) **F**
LODDIGESIA
L. mirabilis (Marvelous Spatuletail) **F** [?]
HELIOMASTER
H. constantii (Plain-capped Starthroat) **E**
H. longirostris (Long-billed Starthroat) **E,F**
H. squamosus (Stripe-breasted Starthroat) **F**
H. furcifer (Blue-tufted Starthroat) **F**
RHODOPIS
R. vesper (Oasis Hummingbird) **F**
THAUMASTURA
T. cora (Peruvian Sheartail) **F**
PHILODICE
P. evelynae (Bahama Woodstar) **E**
P. bryantae (Magenta-throated Woodstar) **E**
P. mitchellii (Purple-throated Woodstar) **F**
DORICHA
D. enicura (Slender Sheartail) **E**
D. eliza (Mexican Sheartail) **E**
TILMATURA
T. dupontii (Sparkling-tailed Hummingbird) **E**
MICROSTILBON
M. burmeisteri (Slender-tailed Woodstar) **E**
CALOTHORAX
C. lucifer (Lucifer Hummingbird) **E**
C. pulcher (Beautiful Hummingbird) **E**
ARCHILOCHUS
A. colubris (Ruby-throated Hummingbird) **A,E**
A. alexandri (Black-chinned Hummingbird) **A,E**
CALLIPHLOX
C. amethystina (Amethyst Woodstar) **F**
MELLISUGA
M. minima (Vervain Hummingbird) **E**
CALYPTE
C. anna (Anna's Hummingbird) **A,E**
C. costae (Costa's Hummingbird) **A**
C. helenae (Bee Hummingbird) **E**
STELLULA
S. calliope (Calliope Hummingbird) **A,E**
ATTHIS
A. heloisa (Bumblebee Hummingbird) **E**
A. ellioti (Wine-throated Hummingbird) **E**
MYRTIS
M. fanny (Purple-collared Woodstar) **F**
EULIDIA
E. yarrellii (Chilean Woodstar) **F**
MYRMIA
M. micrura (Short-tailed Woodstar) **F**
ACESTRURA
A. mulsant (White-bellied Woodstar) **F**
A. bombus (Little Woodstar) **F**
A. heliodor (Gorgeted Woodstar) **F**
A. astreans (Colombian Woodstar) **F**
A. berlepschi (Esmeralda's Woodstar) **F**
A. harterti (Hartert's Woodstar) **F**
CHAETOCERCUS
C. jourdanii (Rufous-shafted Woodstar) **F**
SELASPHORUS
S. platycercus (Broad-tailed Hummingbird) **A,E**
S. rufus (Rufous Hummingbird) **A,E**
S. sasin (Allen's Hummingbird) **A**
S. flammula (Volcano Hummingbird) **E**
S. ardens (Glow-throated Hummingbird) **E**
S. scintilla (Scintillant Hummingbird) **E**

COLIIFORMES

85 COLIIDAE (MOUSEBIRDS)
COLIUS
C. striatus (Speckled Mousebird) **C**
C. castanotus (Red-backed Mousebird) **C**
C. colius (White-backed Mousebird) **C**

C. leucocephalus (White-headed Mousebird) **C**
UROCOLIUS
U. indicus (Red-faced Mousebird) **C**
U. macrourus (Blue-naped Mousebird) **C**
TROGONIFORMES
86 TROGONIDAE (TROGONS)
PHAROMACHRUS
P. mocinno (Resplendent Quetzal) **E**
P. antisianus (Crested Quetzal) **F**
P. fulgidus (White-tipped Quetzal) **F**
P. auriceps (Golden-headed Quetzal) **F**
P. pavoninus (Pavonine Quetzal) **F**
EUPTILOTIS
E. neoxenus (Eared Trogon) **E**
PRIOTELUS
P. temnurus (Cuban Trogon) **E**
TEMNOTROGON
T. roseigaster (Hispaniolan Trogon) **E**
TROGON
T. massena (Slaty-tailed Trogon) **E,F**
T. clathratus (Lattice-tailed Trogon) **E**
T. melanurus (Black-tailed Trogon) **E,F**
T. comptus (Blue-tailed Trogon) **F**
T. bairdii (Baird's Trogon) **E**
T. viridis (White-tailed Trogon) **E,F**
T. citreolus (Citreoline Trogon) **E**
T. melanocephalus (Black-headed Trogon) **E**
T. mexicanus (Mexican Trogon) **E**
T. elegans (Elegant Trogon) **E**
T. collaris (Collared Trogon) **E,F**
T. aurantiiventris (Orange-bellied Trogon) **E**
T. personatus (Masked Trogon) **F**
T. rufus (Black-throated Trogon) **F**
T. surrucura (Surucua Trogon) **F**
T. curucui (Blue-crowned Trogon) **F**
T. violaceus (Violaceous Trogon) **E,F**
APALODERMA
A. narina (Narina's Trogon) **C**
A. aequatoriale (Bare-cheeked Trogon) **C**
A. vittatum (Bar-tailed Trogon) **C**
HARPACTES
H. reinwardtii (Reinwardt's Blue-tailed Trogon) **J**
H. fasciatus (Malabar Trogon) **H**
H. kasumba (Red-naped Trogon) **J**
H. diardii (Diard's Trogon) **J**
H. ardens (Philippine Trogon) **J**
H. whiteheadi (Whitehead's Trogon) **J**
H. orrhophaeus (Cinnamon-rumped Trogon) **J**
H. duvaucelii (Scarlet-rumped Trogon) **J**
H. oreskios (Orange-breasted Trogon) **I,J**
H. erythrocephalus (Red-headed Trogon) **H,I,J**
H. wardi (Ward's Trogon) **I**

CORACIIFORMES
87 ALCEDINIDAE (KINGFISHERS)
CERYLINAE
MEGACERYLE
M. lugubris (Greater Pied Kingfisher) **B,H,I**
M. maxima (Giant Kingfisher) **C**
M. torquata (Ringed Kingfisher) **E,F**
M. alcyon (Belted Kingfisher) **A,E,F**
CERYLE
C. rudis (Lesser Pied Kingfisher) **B,C,H,I,J**
CHLOROCERYLE
C. amazona (Amazon Kingfisher) **E,F**
C. americana (Green Kingfisher) **A,E,F**
C. inda (Green & Rufous Kingfisher) **E,F**
C. aenea (Pygmy Kingfisher) **E**
ALCEDININAE
ALCEDO
A. hercules (Blyth's Kingfisher) **H,I**
A. atthis (River Kingfisher) **A,H,J,K,L,O**
A. semitorquata (Half-collared Kingfisher) **C**
A. meninting (Blue-eared Kingfisher) **H,I,J**
A. quadribrachys (Shining-blue Kingfisher) **C**
A. euryzona (Blue-banded Kingfisher) **J**
A. coerulescens (Small Blue Kingfisher) **J**
A. azurea (Azure Kingfisher) **K,L,M**
A. pusilla (Mangrove Kingfisher) **K,L,M,O**
A. cristata (Malachite Kingfisher) **C**
A. vintsioides (Madagascar Malachite Kingfisher) **D**
A. leucogaster (White-bellied Kingfisher) **C**
CEYX
C. lecontei (African Dwarf Kingfisher) **C**
C. picta (African Pygmy Kingfisher) **C**

C. madagascariensis (Madagascar Pygmy Kingfisher) **D**
C. cyanopectus (Dwarf River Kingfisher) **J**
C. argentatus (Silvery Kingfisher) **J**
C. goodfellowi (Goodfellow's Kingfisher) **J**
C. lepidus (Dwarf Kingfisher) **J,K,L,O**
C. websteri (Bismarck Pygmy Kingfisher) **L**
C. erithacus (Three-toed Kingfisher) **H,I,J,K**
C. melanurus (Philippine Forest Kingfisher) **J**
C. fallax (Sulawesi Pygmy Kingfisher) **K**
LACEDO
L. pulchella (Banded Kingfisher) **I,J**
DACELO
D. novaeguineae (Laughing Kookaburra) **M**
D. leachii (Blue-winged Kookaburra) **M**
D. tyro (Aru Giant Kingfisher) **L**
D. gaudichaud (Rufous-bellied Giant Kingfisher) **L**
CLYTOCEYX
C. rex (Shovel-billed Kingfisher) **L**
MELIDORA
M. macrorrhina (Hook-billed Kingfisher) **K,L**
CITTURA
C. cyanotis (Sulawesi Blue-eared Kingfisher) **K**
HALCYON
H. amauroptera (Brown-winged Kingfisher) **H,I,J**
H. capensis (Stork-billed Kingfisher) **H,I,J,K**
H. melanorhyncha (Great-billed Kingfisher) **K**
H. coromanda (Ruddy Kingfisher) **B,I,J,K**
H. badia (Chocolate-backed Kingfisher) **C**
H. smyrnensis (White-throated Kingfisher) **B,H,I,J**
H. pileata (Black-capped Kingfisher) **B,H,J,K**
H. cyanoventris (Java Kingfisher) **J**
H. leucocephala (Gray-headed Kingfisher) **B,C**
H. senegalensis (Woodland Kingfisher) **C**
H. senegaloides (African Mangrove Kingfisher) **C**
H. malimbica (Blue-breasted Kingfisher) **C**
H. albiventris (Brown-hooded Kingfisher) **C**
H. chelicuti (Striped Kingfisher) **C**
H. nigrocyanea (Blue-black Kingfisher) **J,L**
H. winchelli (Winchell's Kingfisher) **J**
H. diops (Moluccan Kingfisher) **K**
H. lazuli (South Moluccan Kingfisher) **K**
H. macleayii (Forest Kingfisher) **L,M**
H. albonotata (White-backed Kingfisher) **M**
H. leucopygia (Ultramarine Kingfisher) **O**
H. farquhari (Chestnut-bellied Kingfisher) **O**
H. pyrrhopygia (Red-backed Kingfisher) **M**
H. torotoro (Lesser Yellow-billed Kingfisher) **L,M**
H. megarhyncha (Mountain Yellow-billed Kingfisher) **L**
H. australasia (Timor Kingfisher) **J,K,L**
H. sancta (Sacred Kingfisher) **J,M,N,O**
H. cinnamomina (Micronesian Kingfisher) **J,O**
H. funebris (Sombre Kingfisher) **K**
H. chloris (White-collared Kingfisher) **C,H,I,J, K,L,O**
H. enigma (Obscure Kingfisher) **K**
H. saurophaga (White-headed Kingfisher) **K,L,O**
H. recurvirostris (Flat-billed Kingfisher) **O**
H. venerata (Tahitian Kingfisher) **O**
H. tuta (Borabora Kingfisher) **O**
H. ruficollaris (Mangaia Kingfisher) **O**
H. gambieri (Tuamotu Kingfisher) **O**
H. godeffroyi (Marquesas Kingfisher) **O**
CARIDONAX
C. fulgida (Glittering Kingfisher) **J**
ACTENOIDES
A. bougainvillei (Moustached Kingfisher) **O**
A. concreta (Chestnut-collared Kingfisher) **I,J**
A. lindsayi (Spotted Wood Kingfisher) **J**
A. monacha (Blue-headed Wood Kingfisher) **K**
A. princeps (Bar-headed Wood Kingfisher) **K**
TANYSIPTERA
T. hydrocharis (Aru Paradise Kingfisher) **L**
T. galatea (Common Paradise Kingfisher) **J,K,L**
T. riedelii (Biak Paradise Kingfisher) **L**
T. carolinae (Numfor Paradise Kingfisher) **L**
T. ellioti (Kofiau Paradise Kingfisher) **L**
T. nympha (Pink-breasted Paradise Kingfisher) **L**
T. danae (Brown-backed Paradise Kingfisher) **L**
T. sylvia (White-tailed Kingfisher) **L,M,O**
88 TODIDAE (TODIES)
TODUS
T. multicolor (Cuban Tody) **E**
T. angustirostris (Narrow-billed Tody) **E**
T. todus (Jamaican Tody) **E**

T. mexicanus (Puerto Rican Tody) **E**
T. subulatus (Broad-billed Tody) **E**
89 MOMOTIDAE (MOTMOTS)
HYLOMANES
H. momotula (Tody-Motmot) **E,F**
ASPATHA
A. gularis (Blue-throated Motmot) **E**
ELECTRON
E. platyrhynchum (Broad-billed Motmot) **E,F**
E. carinatum (Keel-billed Motmot) **E**
EUMOMOTA
E. superciliosa (Turquoise-browed Motmot) **E**
BARYPHTHENGUS
B. ruficapillus (Rufous-capped Motmot) **E,F**
B. martii (Rufous Motmot) **F**
MOMOTUS
M. mexicanus (Russet-crowned Motmot) **E**
M. momota (Blue-crowned Motmot) **E,F**
90 MEROPIDAE (BEE-EATERS)
NYCTYORNIS
N. amicta (Red-bearded Bee-eater) **J**
N. athertoni (Blue-bearded Bee-eater) **H,I**
MEROPOGON
M. forsteni (Sulawesi Bearded Bee-eater) **K**
MEROPS
M. gularis (Black Bee-eater) **C**
M. muelleri (Blue-headed Bee-eater) **C**
M. bulocki (Red-throated Bee-eater) **C**
M. bullockoides (White-fronted Bee-eater) **C**
M. pusillus (Little Bee-eater) **C**
M. variegatus (Blue-breasted Bee-eater) **C**
M. oreobates (Cinnamon-chested Bee-eater) **C**
M. hirundineus (Swallow-tailed Bee-eater) **C**
M. breweri (Black-headed Bee-eater) **C**
M. revoilii (Somali Bee-eater) **C**
M. albicollis (White-throated Bee-eater) **C**
M. orientalis (Little Green Bee-eater) **C,H,I**
M. boehmi (Boehm's Bee-eater) **C**
M. viridis (Chestnut-headed Bee-eater) **I,J**
M. superciliosus (Blue-cheeked Bee-eater) **B,C, H,J,K,L,O**
M. ornatus (Australian Bee-eater) **K,M**
M. apiaster (European Bee-eater) **B,C,H**
M. leschenaulti (Bay-headed Bee-eater) **H,I,J**
M. malimbicus (Rosy Bee-eater) **C**
M. nubicus (Carmine Bee-eater) **C**
91 CORACIIDAE (ROLLERS)
CORACIAS
C. garrulus (European Roller) **B,C,H**
C. abyssinica (Abyssinian Roller) **C**
C. caudata (Lilac-breasted Roller) **C**
C. spatulata (Racket-tailed Roller) **C**
C. naevia (Rufous-crowned Roller) **C**
C. benghalensis (Indian Roller) **C**
C. temminckii (Sulawesi Roller) **K**
C. cyanogaster (Blue-bellied Roller) **C**
EURYSTOMUS
E. glaucurus (African Broad-billed Roller) **C,D**
E. gularis (Blue-throated Roller) **C**
E. orientalis (Eastern Broad-billed Roller) **B,H,I, J,K,L,M,O**
E. azureus (Azure Roller) **K**
BRACHYPTERACIAS
B. leptosomus (Short-legged Ground-Roller) **D**
B. squamigera (Scaly Ground-Roller) **D**
ATELORNIS
A. pittoides (Pitta-like Ground-Roller) **D**
A. crossleyi (Crossley's Ground-Roller) **D**
URATELORNIS
U. chimaera (Long-tailed Ground-Roller) **D**
92 LEPTOSOMATIDAE (CUCKOO-ROLLER)
LEPTOSOMUS
L. discolor (Cuckoo-Roller) **D**
93 UPUPIDAE (HOOPOE)
UPUPA
U. epops (Hoopoe) **B,C,D,H,J**
94 PHOENICULIDAE (WOOD-HOOPOES)
PHOENICULUS
P. purpureus (Green Wood-Hoopoe) **C**
P. somaliensis (Black-billed Wood-Hoopoe) **C**
P. damarensis (Violet Wood-Hoopoe) **C**
P. bollei (White-headed Wood-Hoopoe) **C**
P. castaneiceps (Forest Wood-Hoopoe) **C**
P. aterrimus (Black Wood-Hoopoe) **C**

HORNBILLS

RHINOPOMASTUS
R. minor (Abyssinian Scimitar-bill) **C**
R. cyanomelas (Scimitar-bill) **C**
95 BUCEROTIDAE (HORNBILLS)
TOCKUS
T. birostris (Indian Gray Hornbill) **H**
T. fasciatus (Pied Hornbill) **C**
T. alboterminatus (Crowned Hornbill) **C**
T. bradfieldi (Bradfield's Hornbill) **C**
T. pallidirostris (Pale-billed Hornbill) **C**
T. nasutus (African Gray Hornbill) **C**
T. hemprichii (Hemprich's Hornbill) **C**
T. monteiri (Monteiro's Hornbill) **C**
T. griseus (Malabar Gray Hornbill) **H**
T. hartlaubi (Black Dwarf Hornbill) **C,D,H,J,K,L**
T. camurus (Red-billed Dwarf Hornbill) **C**
T. erythrorhynchus (Red-billed Hornbill) **C**
T. flavirostris (Eastern Yellow-billed Hornbill) **C**
T. leucomelas (Southern Yellow-billed Hornbill) **C**
T. deckeni (Von der Decken's Hornbill) **C**
T. jacksoni (Jackson's Hornbill) **C**
BERENICORNIS
B. comatus (Long-crested Hornbill) **I,J**
B. albocristatus (African White-crested Hornbill) **C**
PTILOLAEMUS
P. tickelli (Tickell's Hornbill) **H,I**   ?
ANORRHINUS
A. galeritus (Bushy-crested Hornbill) **I,J**
PENELOPIDES
P. panini (Rufous-tailed Hornbill) **J**
P. exarhatus (Temminck's Hornbill) **K**
ACEROS
A. nipalensis (Rufous-necked Hornbill) **H,I**   ?
A. corrugatus (Wrinkled Hornbill) **J**
A. leucocephalus (White-headed Hornbill) **J**
A. cassidix (Sulawesi Hornbill) **K**
A. undulatus (Wreathed Hornbill) **H,I,J**
A. plicatus (Blyth's Hornbill) **I,J,K,L,O**
A. everetti (Everett's Hornbill) **K**
A. narcondami (Narcondam Hornbill) **H**   ?
ANTHRACOCEROS
A. malayanus (Black Hornbill) **J**
A. albirostris (Oriental Pied Hornbill) **H,I,J**
A. coronatus (Malabar Pied Hornbill) **H**
A. montani (Sulu Hornbill) **J**   ?
A. marchei (Palawan Hornbill) **J**
CERATOGYMNA
C. fistulator (Piping Hornbill) **C**
C. bucinator (Trumpeter Hornbill) **C**
C. cylindricus (Brown-cheeked Hornbill) **C**
C. subcylindricus (Black-&-White Casqued Hornbill) **C**
C. brevis (Silvery-cheeked Hornbill) **C**
C. atrata (Black-casqued Hornbill) **C**
C. elata (Yellow-casqued Hornbill) **C**
BUCEROS
B. rhinoceros (Rhinoceros Hornbill) **J**
B. bicornis (Great Indian Hornbill) **H,I,J**
B. hydrocorax (Rufous Hornbill) **J**
RHINOPLAX
R. vigil (Helmeted Hornbill) **J**   I
BUCORVUS
B. abyssinicus (Abyssinian Ground Hornbill) **C**
B. cafer (Southern Ground Hornbill) **C**

PICIFORMES

96 GALBULIDAE (JACAMARS)
GALBALCYRHYNCHUS
G. leucotis (Chestnut Jacamar) **F**
G. purusianus (Purus Jacamar) **F**
BRACHYGALBA
B. albogularis (White-throated Jacamar) **F**
B. lugubris (Brown Jacamar) **F**
B. goeringi (Pale-headed Jacamar) **F**
B. salmoni (Dusky-backed Jacamar) **F**
JACAMARALCYON
J. tridactyla (Three-toed Jacamar) **F**   ?
GALBULA
G. albirostris (Yellow-billed Jacamar) **F**
G. cyanicollis (Blue-necked Jacamar) **F**
G. galbula (Green-tailed Jacamar) **F**
G. ruficauda (Rufous-tailed Jacamar) **F**
G. tombacea (White-chinned Jacamar) **F**
G. cyanescens (Bluish-fronted Jacamar) **F**
G. pastazae (Coppery-chested Jacamar) **F**
G. leucogastra (Bronzy Jacamar) **F**

G. dea (Paradise Jacamar) **F**
JACAMEROPS
J. aurea (Great Jacamar) **E,F**
97 BUCCONIDAE (PUFFBIRDS)
NOTHARCHUS
N. macrorhynchos (White-necked Puffbird) **E,F**
N. pectoralis (Black-breasted Puffbird) **E,F**
N. ordii (Brown-banded Puffbird) **F**
N. tectus (Pied Puffbird) **E,F**
BUCCO
B. macrodactylus (Chestnut-capped Puffbird) **F**
B. tamatia (Spotted Puffbird) **F**
B. noanamae (Sooty-capped Puffbird) **F**
B. capensis (Collared Puffbird) **F**
NYSTALUS
N. radiatus (Barred Puffbird) **E,F**
N. chacuru (White-eared Puffbird) **F**
N. striolatus (Striolated Puffbird) **F**
N. maculatus (Spot-backed Puffbird) **F**
HYPNELUS
H. ruficollis (Russet-throated Puffbird) **F**
MALACOPTILA
M. striata (Crescent-chested Puffbird) **F**
M. fusca (White-chested Puffbird) **F**
M. semicincta (Semicollared Puffbird) **F**
M. fulvogularis (Black-streaked Puffbird) **F**
M. rufa (Rufous-necked Puffbird) **F**
M. panamensis (White-whiskered Puffbird) **E,F**
M. mystacalis (Moustached Puffbird) **F**
MICROMONACHA
M. lanceolata (Lanceolated Monklet) **F**
NONNULA
N. rubecula (Rusty-breasted Nunlet) **F**
N. sclateri (Fulvous-chinned Nunlet) **F**
N. brunnea (Brown Nunlet) **F**
N. ruficapilla (Gray-cheeked Nunlet) **F**
N. amaurocephala (Chestnut-headed Nunlet) **F**
HAPALOPTILA
H. castanea (White-faced Nunbird) **F**
MONASA
M. atra ((Black Nunbird) **F**
M. nigrifrons (Black-fronted Nunbird) **F**
M. morphoeus (White-fronted Nunbird) **E,F**
M. flavirostris (Yellow-billed Nunbird) **F**
CHELIDOPTERA
C. tenebrosa (Swallow-wing Puffbird) **F**
98 CAPITONIDAE (BARBETS)
CAPITO
C. aurovirens (Scarlet-crowned Barbet) **E**
C. maculicoronatus (Spot-crowned Barbet) **E,F**
C. squamatus (Orange-fronted Barbet) **F**
C. hypoleucus (White-mantled Barbet) **F**   ?
C. dayi (Black-girdled Barbet) **F**
C. quinticolor (Five-colored Barbet) **F**
C. niger (Black-spotted Barbet) **F**
EUBUCCO
E. richardsoni (Lemon-throated Barbet) **F**
E. bourcierii (Red-headed Barbet) **E,F**
E. tucinkae (Scarlet-hooded Barbet) **F**
E. versicolor (Versicolored Barbet) **F**
SEMNORNIS
S. frantzii (Prong-billed Barbet) **E**   V
S. ramphastinus (Toucan Barbet) **F**   V
PSILOPOGON
P. pyrolophus (Fire-tufted Barbet) **J**
MEGALAIMA
M. virens (Great Barbet) **B,H,I,J**
M. lagrandieri (Red-vented Barbet) **I**
M. zeylanica (Oriental Green Barbet) **H**
M. lineata (Lineated Barbet) **H,J**
M. viridis (Small Green Barbet) **H**
M. faiostricta (Green-eared Barbet) **I**
M. corvina (Brown-throated Barbet) **J**
M. chrysopogon (Gold-whiskered Barbet) **I,J**
M. rafflesii (Many-colored Barbet) **I,J**
M. mystacophanos (Gaudy Barbet) **I,J**
M. javensis (Black-banded Barbet) **J**   ?
M. flavifrons (Yellow-fronted Barbet) **H**
M. franklinii (Golden-throated Barbet) **H,I,J**
M. oorti (Muller's Barbet) **I,J**
M. asiatica (Blue-throated Barbet) **H,I,J**
M. incognita (Hume's Blue-throated Barbet) **I,J**
M. henricii (Yellow-crowned Barbet) **I,J**
M. armillaris (Blue-crowned Barbet) **J**
M. pulcherrima (Golden-naped Barbet) **J**
M. australis (Blue-eared Barbet) **H,I,J**

M. eximia (Black-throated Barbet) **J**
M. rubricapilla (Crimson-throated Barbet) **H**
M. haemacephala (Crimson-breasted Barbet) **H,I,J**
CALORHAMPHUS
C. fuliginosus (Brown Barbet) **I,J**
GYMNOBUCCO
G. calvus (Naked-faced Barbet) **C**
G. peli (Bristle-nosed Barbet) **C**
G. sladeni (Sladen's Barbet) **C**
G. bonapartei (Gray-throated Barbet) **C**
SMILORHIS
S. leucotis (White-eared Barbet) **C**
CRYPTOLYBIA
C. olivacea (Green Barbet) **C**
STACTOLAEMA
S. anchietae (Anchieta's Barbet) **C**
S. whytii (Whyte's Barbet) **C**
BUCCANODON
B. duchaillui (Yellow-spotted Barbet) **C**
POGONIULUS
P. scolopaceus (Speckled Tinkerbird) **C**
P. leucomystax (Moustached Green Tinkerbird) **C**
P. simplex (Green Tinkerbird) **C**
P. coryphaeus (Western Green Tinkerbird) **C**
P. pusillus (Red-fronted Tinkerbird) **C**
P. chrysoconus (Yellow-fronted Tinkerbird) **C**
P. bilineatus (Yellow-rumped Tinkerbird) **C**
P. makawai (White-chested Tinkerbird) **C**   I
P. subsulphureus (Yellow-throated Tinkerbird) **C**
P. atroflavus (Red-rumped Tinkerbird) **C**
TRICHOLAEMA
T. lacrymosa (Spotted-flanked Barbet) **C**
T. leucomelaina (Pied Barbet) **C**
T. diademata (Red-fronted Barbet) **C**
T. frontata (Miombo Pied Barbet) **C**
T. melanocephala (African Black-throated Barbet) **C**
T. hirsuta (Hairy-breasted Barbet) **C**
LYBIUS
L. undatus (Banded Barbet) **C**
L. vieilloti (Vieillot's Barbet) **C**
L. torquatus (Black-collared Barbet) **C**
L. guifsobalito (Black-billed Barbet) **C**
L. rubrifacies (Red-faced Barbet) **C**
L. chaplini (Chaplin's Barbet) **C**
L. leucocephalus (White-headed Barbet) **C**
L. minor (Black-backed Barbet) **C**
L. melanopterus (Brown-breasted Barbet) **C**
L. bidentatus (Double-toothed Barbet) **C**
L. dubius (Bearded Barbet) **C**
L. rolleti (Black-breasted Barbet) **C**
TRACHYPHONUS
T. purpuratus (Yellow-billed Barbet) **C**
T. vaillantii (Levaillant's Barbet) **C**
T. erythrocephalus (Red & Yellow Barbet) **C**
T. darnaudii (d'Arnaud's Barbet) **C**
T. usambiro (Usambiro Barbet) **C**
T. margaritatus (Yellow-breasted Barbet) **C**
99 INDICATORIDAE (HONEYGUIDES)
PRODOTISCUS
P. insignis (Cassin's Honeybird) **C**
P. zambesiae (Green-backed Honeybird) **C**
P. regulus (Wahlberg's Honeybird) **C**
MELIGNOMON
M. zenkeri (Zenker's Honeyguide) **C**
M. eisentrauti (Yellow-footed Honeyguide) **C**   ?
INDICATOR
I. maculatus (Spotted Honeyguide) **C**
I. variegatus (Scaly-throated Honeyguide) **C**
I. indicator (Black-throated Honeyguide) **C**
I. minor (Lesser Honeyguide) **C**
I. conirostris (Thick-billed Honeyguide) **C**
I. exilis (Least Honeyguide) **C**
I. willcocksi (Willcocks' Honeyguide) **C**
I. meliphilus (Eastern Least Honeyguide) **C**
I. pumilio (Pygmy Honeyguide) **C**
I. xanthonotus (Indian Honeyguide) **C,H**
I. archipelagus (Malay Honeyguide) **J**
MELICHNEUTES
M. robustus (Lyre-tailed Honeyguide) **C**
100 RAMPHASTIDAE (TOUCANS)
AULACORHYNCHUS
A. prasinus (Emerald Toucanet) **E,F**
A. sulcatus (Groove-billed Toucanet) **F**
A. derbianus (Chestnut-tipped Toucanet) **F**
A. haematopygus (Crimson-rumped Toucanet) **F**
A. huallagae (Yellow-browed Toucanet) **F**   ?

A. coeruleicinctis (Blue-banded Toucanet) **F**
PTEROGLOSSUS
P. viridis (Green Aracari) **F**
P. inscriptus (Lettered Aracari) **F**
P. bitorquatus (Red-necked Aracari) **F**
P. flavirostris (Ivory-billed Aracari) **F**
P. aracari (Black-necked Aracari) **F**
P. castanotis (Chestnut-eared Aracari) **F**
P. pluricinctus (Many-banded Aracari) **F**
P. torquatus (Collared Aracari) **E,F**
P. frantzii (Fiery-billed Aracari) **F**
P. beauharnaesii (Curl-crested Aracari) **F**
SELENIDERA
S. maculirostris (Spot-billed Toucanet) **F**
S. gouldii (Gould's Toucanet) **F**
S. reinwardtii (Golden-collared Toucanet) **F**
S. nattereri (Tawny-tufted Toucanet) **F**
S. culik (Guianan Toucanet) **F**
S. spectabilis (Yellow-eared Toucanet) **F**
BAILLONIUS
B. bailloni (Saffron Toucanet) **F**
ANDIGENA
A. hypoglauca (Gray-breasted Mountain Toucan) **F**
A. laminirostris (Plate-billed Mountain Toucan) **F**
A. cucullata (Hooded Mountain Toucan) **F**
A. nigrirostris (Black-billed Mountain Toucan) **F**
RAMPHASTOS
R. dicolorus (Red-breasted Toucan) **F**
R. vitellinus (Channel-billed Toucan) **F**
R. brevis (Choco Toucan) **F**
R. sulfuratus (Keel-billed Toucan) **F**
R. toco (Toco Toucan) **F**
R. tucanus (Red-billed Toucan) **F**
R. swainsonii (Chestnut-mandibled Toucan) **F**
R. ambiguus (Black-mandibled Toucan) **F**
101 PICIDAE (WOODPECKERS)
JINGINAE
JYNX
J. torquilla (Northern Wryneck) **B,H**
J. ruficollis (Rufous-necked Wryneck) **C**
PICUMNINAE
PICUMNUS
P. innominatus (Speckled Piculet) **H,I,J**
P. aurifrons (Bar-breasted Piculet) **F**
P. lafresnayi (Lafresnaye's Piculet) **F**
P. exilis (Golden-spangled Piculet) **F**
P. sclateri (Ecuadorean Piculet) **F**
P. squamulatus (Scaled Piculet) **F**
P. spilogaster (White-bellied Piculet) **F**
P. minutissimus (Guianan Piculet) **F**
P. pygmaeus (Spotted Piculet) **F**
P. steindachneri (Speckle-chested Piculet) **F**   [?]
P. varzeae (Varzea Piculet) **F**
P. cirratus (White-barred Piculet) **E,F**
P. albosquamatus (White-wedged Piculet) **F**
P. fuscus (Rusty-necked Piculet) **F**
P. rufiventris (Rufous-breasted Piculet) **F**
P. fulvescens (Tawny Piculet) **F**
P. limae (Ochraceous Piculet) **F**
P. nebulosus (Mottled Piculet) **F**
P. castelnau (Plain-breasted Piculet) **F**
P. subtilis (Fine-barred Piculet) **F**
P. olivaceus (Olivaceous Piculet) **E,F**
P. granadensis (Grayish Piculet) **F**
P. cinnamomeus (Chestnut Piculet) **F**
SASIA
S. africana (African Piculet) **F**
S. abnormis (Rufous Piculet) **I,J**
S. ochracea (White-browed Piculet) **H,I**
PICINAE
NESOCTITES
N. micromegas (Antillean Piculet) **E**
MELANERPES
M. candidus (White Woodpecker) **F**
M. lewis (Lewis' Woodpecker) **A,E**
M. herminieri (Guadeloupe Woodpecker) **E**
M. portoricensis (Puerto Rican Woodpecker) **E**
M. erythrocephalus (Red-headed Woodpecker) **A**
M. formicivorus (Acorn Woodpecker) **A,E,F**
M. cruentatus (Red-fronted Woodpecker) **F**
M. flavifrons (Yellow-fronted Woodpecker) **F**
M. chrysauchen (Golden-naped Woodpecker) **E,F**
M. pucherani (Black-cheeked Woodpecker) **E,F**
M. cactorum (White-fronted Woodpecker) **F**
M. striatus (Hispaniolan Woodpecker) **E**
M. radiolatus (Jamaican Woodpecker) **E**

M. chrysogenys (Golden-cheeked Woodpecker) **E**
M. hypopolius (Gray-breasted Woodpecker) **E**
M. pygmaeus (Yucatan Woodpecker) **E**
M. rubricapillus (Red-crowned Woodpecker) **E**
M. hoffmanni (Hoffmann's Woodpecker) **E**
M. uropygialis (Gila Woodpecker) **A,E**
M. aurifrons (Golden-fronted Woodpecker) **E**
M. carolinus (Red-bellied Woodpecker) **A**
M. superciliaris (Great Red-bellied Woodpecker) **E**
SPHYRAPICUS
S. varius (Yellow-bellied Sapsucker) **A,E**
S. nuchalis (Red-naped Sapsucker) **A,E**
S. ruber (Red-breasted Sapsucker) **A**
S. thyroideus (Williamson's Sapsucker) **A,E**
XIPHIDIOPICUS
X. percussus (Cuban Green Woodpecker) **E**
CAMPETHERA
C. punctuligera (Fine-spotted Woodpecker) **C**
C. bennettii (Bennett's Woodpecker) **C**
C. nubica (Nubian Woodpecker) **C**
C. abingoni (Golden-tailed Woodpecker) **C**
C. notata (Knysna Woodpecker) **C**
C. cailliautii (Green-backed Woodpecker) **C**
C. maculosa (Little Green Woodpecker) **C**
C. tullbergi (Tullberg's Woodpecker) **C**
C. nivosa (Buff-spotted Woodpecker) **C**
C. caroli (Brown-eared Woodpecker) **C**
GEOCOLAPTES
G. olivaceus (Ground Woodpecker) **C**
DENDROPICOS
D. elachus (Little Gray Woodpecker) **C**
D. poecilolaemus (Speckle-breasted Woodpecker) **C**
D. abyssinicus (Gold-mantled Woodpecker) **C**
D. fuscescens (Cardinal Woodpecker) **C**
D. gabonensis (Gabon Woodpecker) **C**
D. stierlingi (Stierling's Woodpecker) **C**
D. namaquus (Bearded Woodpecker) **C**
D. xantholophus (Yellow-crested Woodpecker) **C**
D. pyrrhogaster (Fire-bellied Woodpecker) **C**
D. elliotii (Elliot's Woodpecker) **C**
D. goertae (Gray Woodpecker) **C**
D. griseocephalus (Olive Woodpecker) **C**
PICOIDES
P. temminckii (Temminck's Pygmy Woodpecker) **K**
P. maculatus (Philippine Pygmy Woodpecker) **J**
P. moluccensis (Brown-capped Woodpecker) **H,I,J**
P. obsoletus (Brown-backed Woodpecker) **C**
P. kizuki (Japanese Spotted Woodpecker) **B,J**
P. canicapillus (Gray-capped Woodpecker) **B,H,I,J**
P. minor (Lesser Spotted Woodpecker) **B**
P. macei (Streak-bellied Woodpecker) **H,I,J**
P. atratus (Stripe-breasted Woodpecker) **I**
P. auriceps (Brown-fronted Woodpecker) **H**
P. mahrattensis (Yellow-crowned Woodpecker) **H,I**
P. dorae (Arabian Woodpecker) **B**
P. hyperythrus (Rufous-bellied Woodpecker) **B,H,I**
P. cathpharius (Crimson-breasted Woodpecker) **H,I**
P. darjellensis (Brown-throated Woodpecker) **H,I**
P. medius (Middle-spotted Woodpecker) **B**
P. leucotos (White-backed Woodpecker) **B,I**
P. himalayensis (Himalayan Woodpecker) **H**
P. assimilis (Sind Woodpecker) **B,H**
P. syriacus (Syrian Woodpecker) **B**
P. leucopterus (White-winged Woodpecker) **B**
P. major (Great Spotted Woodpecker) **B,I**
P. mixtus (Checkered Woodpecker) **F**
P. lignarius (Striped Woodpecker) **F**
P. scalaris (Ladder-backed Woodpecker) **A,E**
P. nuttallii (Nuttall's Woodpecker) **A**
P. pubescens (Downy Woodpecker) **A**
P. borealis (Red-cockaded Woodpecker) **A**   [V]
P. stricklandii (Strickland's Woodpecker) **A,E**
P. villosus (Hairy Woodpecker) **A,E**
P. albolarvatus (White-headed Woodpecker) **A**
P. tridactylus (Three-toed Woodpecker) **A,B,E**
P. arcticus (Black-backed Woodpecker) **A**
VENILIORNIS
V. callonotus (Scarlet-backed Woodpecker) **F**
V. dignus (Yellow-vented Woodpecker) **F**
V. nigriceps (Bar-bellied Woodpecker) **F**
V. fumigatus (Smoky-brown Woodpecker) **E,F**
V. passerinus (Little Woodpecker) **F**
V. frontalis (Dot-fronted Woodpecker) **F**
V. spilogaster (White-spotted Woodpecker) **F**
V. sanguineus (Blood-colored Woodpecker) **F**
V. maculifrons (Yellow-eared Woodpecker) **F**

V. affinis (Red-stained Woodpecker) **F**
V. cassini (Golden-collared Woodpecker) **F**
V. kirkii (Red-rumped Woodpecker) **E,F**
PICULUS
P. leucolaemus (White-throated Woodpecker) **E,F**
P. flavigula (Yellow-throated Woodpecker) **F**
P. chrysochloros (Golden-green Woodpecker) **E,F**
P. aurulentus (White-browed Woodpecker) **F**
P. rubiginosus (Golden-olive Woodpecker) **E,F**
P. auricularis (Gray-crowned Woodpecker) **E**
P. rivolii (Crimson-mantled Woodpecker) **F**
COLAPTES
C. atricollis (Black-necked Flicker) **F**
C. punctigula (Spot-breasted Flicker) **E,F**
C. melanochloros (Green-barred Flicker) **F**
C. auratus (Northern Flicker) **A,E**
C. fernandinae (Fernandina's Flicker) **E**
C. pitius (Chilean Flicker) **F**
C. rupicola (Andean Flicker) **F**
C. campestris (Campo Flicker) **F**
CELEUS
C. brachyurus (Rufous Woodpecker) **H,I,J**
C. loricatus (Cinnamon Woodpecker) **E,F**
C. undatus (Waved Woodpecker) **F**
C. grammicus (Scale-breasted Woodpecker) **F**
C. castaneus (Chestnut-colored Woodpecker) **E**
C. elegans (Chestnut Woodpecker) **F**
C. lugubris (Pale-crested Woodpecker) **F**
C. flavescens (Blond-crested Woodpecker) **F**
C. flavus (Cream-colored Woodpecker) **F**
C. spectabilis (Rufous-headed Woodpecker) **F**
C. torquatus (Ringed Woodpecker) **F**
DRYOCOPUS
D. galeatus (Helmeted Woodpecker) **F**
D. schulzi (Black-bodied Woodpecker) **F**
D. lineatus (Lineated Woodpecker) **E,F**
D. pileatus (Pileated Woodpecker) **A**
D. javensis (White-bellied Woodpecker) **H,I,J**
D. martius (Black Woodpecker) **B**
CAMPEPHILUS
C. pollens (Powerful Woodpecker) **F**
C. haematogaster (Crimson-bellied Woodpecker) **E,F**
C. rubricollis (Red-necked Woodpecker) **F**
C. robustus (Robust Woodpecker) **F**
C. guatemalensis (Pale-billed Woodpecker) **E**
C. melanoleucos (Crimson-crested Woodpecker) **F**
C. gayaquilensis (Guayaquil Woodpecker) **F**
C. leucopogon (Cream-backed Woodpecker) **F**
C. magellanicus (Magellanic Woodpecker) **F**
C. principalis (Ivory-billed Woodpecker) **A,E**
C. imperialis (Imperial Woodpecker) **E**
PICUS
P. miniaceus (Banded Red Woodpecker) **I,J,K**
P. puniceus (Crimson-winged Woodpecker) **I,J,K**
P. chlorolophus (Lesser Yellow-naped Woodpecker) **H,I,J**
P. mentalis (Checker-throated Woodpecker) **I,J**
P. flavinucha (Greater Yellow-naped Woodpecker) **H,I,J**
P. vittatus (Laced Woodpecker) **I,J**
P. xanthopygaeus (Streak-throated Woodpecker) **H,I,J,K**
P. squamatus (Scaly-bellied Woodpecker) **B,H**
P. awokera (Wavy-bellied Woodpecker) **B**
P. viridis (Green Woodpecker) **B**
P. rabieri (Red-collared Woodpecker) **I**
P. erythropygius (Black-headed Woodpecker) **I**
P. canus (Gray-faced Woodpecker) **B,H,I,J**
DINOPIUM
D. rafflesii (Olive-backed Woodpecker) **I,J**
D. shorii (Himalayan Gold-backed Woodpecker) **H,I**
D. javanense (Common Gold-backed Woodpecker) **H,I,J,K**
D. benghalense (Lesser Flame-backed Woodpecker) **H**
CHRYSOCOLAPTES
C. lucidus (Greater Flame-backed Woodpecker) **H,I,J,K**
C. festivus (Black-rumped Woodpecker) **H**
GECINULUS
G. grantia (Bamboo Woodpecker) **H,I,J,K**
SAPHEOPIPO
S. noguchii (Okinawa Woodpecker) **J**

BLYTHIPICUS
B. rubiginosus (Maroon Woodpecker) **I,J**
B. pyrrhotis (Bay Woodpecker) **H,I,J**
REINWARDTIPICUS
R. validus (Orange-backed Woodpecker) **J**
MEIGLYPTES
M. tristis (Buff-rumped Woodpecker) **I,J**
M. jugularis (Black & Buff Woodpecker) **I**
M. tukki (Buff-necked Woodpecker) **J,K**
HEMICIRCUS
H. concretus (Gray & Buff Woodpecker) **I,J**
H. canente (Heart-spotted Woodpecker) **H,I**
MULLERIPICUS
M. fulvus (Fulvous Woodpecker) **J,K**
M. funebris (Sooty Woodpecker) **J**
M. pulverulentus (Great Slaty Woodpecker) **H,I,J,K**

PASSERIFORMES

102 EURYLAIMIDAE (BROADBILLS)
EURYLAIMINAE
SMITHORNIS
S. capensis (African Broadbill) **C**
S. rufolateralis (Red-sided Broadbill) **C**
S. sharpei (Gray-headed Broadbill) **C**
PSEUDOCALYPTOMENA
P. graueri (Grauer's Broadbill) **C**
CORYDON
C. sumatranus (Dusky Broadbill) **I,J,K**
CYMBIRHYNCHUS
C. macrorhynchos (Black & Red Broadbill) **I,J,K**
EURYLAIMUS
E. javanicus (Banded Broadbill) **I,J,K**
E. ochromalus (Black & Yellow Broadbill) **I,J,K**
E. steerii (Wattled Broadbill) **J**
SERILOPHUS
S. lunatus (Silver-breasted Broadbill) **H,I,J,K**
PSARISOMUS
P. dalhousiae (Long-tailed Broadbill) **H,I,J,K**
CALYPTOMENINAE
CALYPTOMENA
C. viridis (Lesser Green Broadbill) **I,J,K**
C. hosii (Magnificent Green Broadbill) **J**
C. whiteheadi (Black-throated Green Broadbill) **J**
103 DENDROCOLAPTIDAE (WOODCREEPERS)
DENDROCINCLA
D. tyrannina (Tyrannine Woodcreeper) **F**
D. macrorhyncha (Large Tyrannine Woodcreeper) **F**
D. fuliginosa (Plain-brown Woodcreeper) **E,F**
D. anabatina (Tawny-winged Woodcreeper) **E**
D. merula (White-chinned Woodcreeper) **F**
D. homochroa (Ruddy Woodcreeper) **E,F**
DECONYCHURA
D. longicauda (Long-tailed Woodcreeper) **E,F**
D. stictolaema (Spot-throated Woodcreeper) **F**
SITTASOMUS
S. griseicapillus (Olivaceous Woodcreeper) **E,F**
GLYPHORHYNCHUS
G. spirurus (Wedge-billed Woodcreeper) **E,F**
DRYMORNIS
D. bridgesii (Scimitar-billed Woodhewer) **F**
NASICA
N. longirostris (Long-billed Woodcreeper) **F**
DENDREXETASTES
D. rufigula (Cinnamon-throated Woodcreeper) **F**
HYLEXETASTES
H. perrotii (Red-billed Woodcreeper) **F**
H. stresemanni (Bar-bellied Woodcreeper) **F**
XIPHOCOLAPTES
X. promeropirhynchus (Strong-billed Woodcreeper) **E,F**
X. albicollis (White-throated Woodcreeper) **F**
X. villanovae (Vila Nova Woodcreeper) **F**
X. falcirostris (Moustached Woodcreeper) **F**
X. franciscanus (Snethlage's Woodcreeper) **F**
X. major (Great Rufous Woodcreeper) **F**
DENDROCOLAPTES
D. certhia (Barred Woodcreeper) **E,F**
D. concolor (Concolor Woodcreeper) **F**
D. hoffmannsi (Hoffmann's Woodcreeper) **F**
D. picumnus (Black-banded Woodcreeper) **E,F**
D. platyrostris (Planalto Woodcreeper) **F**
XIPHORHYNCHUS
X. picus (Straight-billed Woodcreeper) **E,F**
X. necopinus (Zimmer's Woodcreeper) **F**
X. obsoletus (Striped Woodcreeper) **F**
X. ocellatus (Ocellated Woodcreeper) **F**

X. spixii (Spix's Woodcreeper) **F**
X. elegans (Elegant Woodcreeper) **F**
X. pardalotus (Chestnut-rumped Woodcreeper) **F**
X. guttatus (Buff-throated Woodcreeper) **E,F**
X. eytoni (Dusky-billed Woodcreeper) **F**
X. flavigaster (Ivory-billed Woodcreeper) **E**
X. striatigularis (Stripe-throated Woodcreeper) **E**
X. lachrymosus (Black-striped Woodcreeper) **E,F**
X. erythropygius (Spotted Woodcreeper) **E,F**
X. triangularis (Olive-backed Woodcreeper) **E,F**
LEPIDOCOLAPTES
L. leucogaster (White-striped Woodcreeper) **E**
L. souleyetii (Streak-headed Woodcreeper) **E,F**
L. angustirostris (Narrow-billed Woodcreeper) **E,F**
L. affinis (Spot-crowned Woodcreeper) **E,F**
L. squamatus (Scaled Woodcreeper) **F**
L. fuscus (Lesser Woodcreeper) **F**
L. albolineatus (Lineated Woodcreeper) **F**
CAMPYLORHAMPHUS
C. pucheranii (Greater Scythebill) **F**
C. trochilirostris (Red-billed Scythebill) **E,F**
C. falcularius (Black-billed Scythebill) **F**
C. pusillus (Brown-billed Scythebill) **E,F**
C. procurvoides (Curve-billed Scythebill) **F**
104 FURNARIIDAE (OVENBIRDS)
FURNARIINAE
GEOSITTA
G. poeciloptera (Campo Miner) **F**
G. cunicularia (Common Miner) **F**
G. maritima (Grayish Miner) **F**
G. peruviana (Coastal Miner) **F**
G. punensis (Puna Miner) **F**
G. saxicolina (Dark-winged Miner) **F**
G. isabellina (Creamy-rumped Miner) **F**
G. antarctica (Short-billed Miner) **F**
G. rufipennis (Rufous-banded Miner) **F**
G. crassirostris (Thick-billed Miner) **F**
G. tenuirostris (Slender-billed Miner) **F**
UPUCERTHIA
U. certhioides (Chaco Earthcreeper) **F**
U. harterti (Bolivian Earthcreeper) **F**
U. ruficauda (Straight-billed Earthcreeper) **F**
U. andaecola (Rock Earthcreeper) **F**
U. albigula (White-throated Earthcreeper) **F**
U. serrana (Striated Earthcreeper) **F**
U. dumetaria (Scale-throated Earthcreeper) **F**
U. validirostris (Buff-breasted Earthcreeper) **F**
U. jelskii (Plain-breasted Earthcreeper) **F**
CINCLODES
C. fuscus (Bar-winged Cinclodes) **F**
C. excelsior (Stout-billed Cinclodes) **F**
C. olrogi (Olrog's Cinclodes) **F**
C. comechingonus (Comechingones Cinclodes) **F**
C. pabsti (Long-tailed Cinclodes) **F**
C. atacamensis (White-winged Cinclodes) **F**
C. palliatus (White-bellied Cinclodes) **F**
C. oustaleti (Gray-flanked Cinclodes) **F**
C. patagonicus (Dark-bellied Cinclodes) **F**
C. nigrofumosus (Seaside Cinclodes) **F**
C. taczanowskii (Taczanowski's Cinclodes) **F**
C. antarcticus (Blackish Cinclodes) **F**
CHILIA
C. melanura (Crag Chilia) **F**
FURNARIUS
F. minor (Lesser Hornero) **F**
F. figulus (White-banded Hornero) **F**
F. tricolor (Tricolor Hornero) **F**
F. leucopus (Pale-legged Hornero) **F**
F. torridus (Pale-billed Hornero) **F**
F. rufus (Rufous Hornero) **F**
F. cristatus (Crested Hornero) **F**
SYNALLAXINAE
SYLVIORTHORHYNCHUS
S. desmursii (Des Murs' Wiretail) **F**
APHRASTURA
A. spinicauda (Thorn-tailed Rayadito) **F**
A. masafuerae (Masafuera Rayadito) **F**
LEPTASTHENURA
L. fuliginiceps (Brown-capped Tit-Spinetail) **F**
L. yanacensis (Tawny Tit-Spinetail) **F**
L. platensis (Tufted Tit-Spinetail) **F**
L. aegithaloides (Plain-mantled Tit-Spinetail) **F**
L. setaria (Araucaria Tit-Spinetail) **F**
L. striata (Streaked Tit-Spinetail) **F**
L. striolata (Striolated Tit-Spinetail) **F**
L. pileata (Rusty-crowned Tit-Spinetail) **F**

L. xenothorax (White-browed Tit-Spinetail) **F**
L. andicola (Andean Tit-Spinetail) **F**
SCHIZOEACA
S. fuliginosa (White-chinned Spinetail) **F**
S. coryi (Ochre-browed Thistletail) **F**
S. griseomurina (Mouse-colored Thistletail) **F**
S. palpebralis (Eye-ringed Thistletail) **F**
S. moreirae (Itatiaia Spinetail) **F**
SCHOENIOPHYLAX
S. phryganophila (Chotoy Spinetail) **F**
SYNALLAXIS
S. ruficapilla (Rufous-capped Spinetail) **F**
S. superciliosa (Buff-browed Spinetail) **F**
S. frontalis (Sooty-fronted Spinetail) **F**
S. azarae (Azara's Spinetail) **F**
S. elegantior (Elegant Spinetail) **F**
S. albigularis (Dark-breasted Spinetail) **F**
S. albescens (Pale-breasted Spinetail) **E,F**
S. spixi (Chicli Spinetail) **F**
S. hypospodia (Cinereous-breasted Spinetail) **F**
S. infuscata (Plain Spinetail) **F**
S. brachyura (Slaty Spinetail) **E,F**
S. courseni (Apurimac Spinetail) **F**
S. moesta (Dusky Spinetail) **F**
S. macconnelli (McConnell's Spinetail) **F**
S. subpudica (Silvery-throated Spinetail) **F**
S. tithys (Blackish-headed Spinetail) **F**
S. cinerascens (Gray-bellied Spinetail) **F**
S. maranonica (Maranon Spinetail) **F**
S. propinqua (White-bellied Spinetail) **F**
S. hellmayri (Reiser's Spinetail) **F**
S. gujanensis (Plain-crowned Spinetail) **F**
S. albilora (Ochre-breasted Spinetail) **F**
S. rutilans (Ruddy Spinetail) **F**
S. cherriei (Chestnut-throated Spinetail) **F**
S. unirufa (Rufous Spinetail) **F**
S. castanea (Black-throated Spinetail) **F**
S. fuscorufa (Santa Marta Spinetail) **F**
S. zimmeri (Russet-bellied Spinetail) **F**
S. erythrothorax (Rufous-breasted Spinetail) **E**
S. cinnamomea (Stripe-breasted Spinetail) **E,F**
S. stictothorax (Necklaced Spinetail) **F**
S. candei (White-whiskered Spinetail) **F**
S. kollari (Hoary-throated Spinetail) **F**
S. scutatus (Ochre-cheeked Spinetail) **F**
HELLMAYREA
H. gularis (Lafresnaye's White-browed Spinetail) **F**
CERTHIAXIS
C. erythrops (Red-faced Spinetail) **F**
C. demissa (Tepui Spinetail) **F**
C. antisiensis (Line-cheeked Spinetail) **F**
C. pallida (Pallid Spinetail) **F**
C. curtata (Ash-browed Spinetail) **F**
C. obsoleta (Olive Spinetail) **F**
C. hellmayri (Streak-capped Spinetail) **F**
C. subcristata (Crested Spinetail) **F**
C. pyrrhophia (Stripe-crowned Spinetail) **F**
C. marcapatae (Marcapata Spinetail) **F**
C. albiceps (Light-crowned Spinetail) **F**
C. semicinerea (Gray-headed Spinetail) **F**
C. albicapilla (Creamy-chested Spinetail) **F**
C. vulpina (Rusty-backed Spinetail) **F**
C. muelleri (Scaled Spinetail) **F**
C. gutturata (Speckled Spinetail) **F**
C. sulphurifera (Sulfur-throated Spinetail) **F**
C. cinnamomea (Yellow-throated Spinetail) **F**
C. mustelina (Red & White Spinetail) **F**
THRIPOPHAGA
T. pyrrholeuca (Lesser Canastero) **F**
T. baeri (Short-billed Canastero) **F**
T. pudibunda (Canyon Canastero) **F**
T. ottonis (Rusty-fronted Canastero) **F**
T. heterura (Iquico Canastero) **F**
T. modesta (Cordillera Canastero) **F**
T. cactorum (Cactus Canastero) **F**
T. dorbignyi (Creamy-breasted Canastero) **F**
T. berlepschi (Berlepsch's Canastero) **F**
T. steinbachi (Chestnut Canastero) **F**
T. humicola (Dusky-tailed Canastero) **F**
T. patagonica (Patagonian Canastero) **F**
T. humilis (Streak-throated Canastero) **F**
T. usheri (White-tailed Canastero) **F**
T. anthoides (Austral Canastero) **F**
T. wyatti (Streak-backed Canastero) **F**
T. sclateri (Cordoba Canastero) **F**
T. urubambensis (Line-fronted Canastero) **F**

T. virgata (Junin Canastero) **F**
T. maculicauda (Scribble-tailed Canastero) **F**
T. flammulata (Many-striped Canastero) **F**
T. cherriei (Orinoco Softtail) **F**
T. macroura (Striated Softtail) **F**
T. hudsoni (Hudson's Canastero) **F**
T. hypochondriacus (Great Spinetail) **F**
PHACELLODOMUS
P. rufifrons (Rufous-fronted Thornbird) **F**
P. sibilatrix (Little Thornbird) **F**
P. striaticeps (Streak-fronted Thornbird) **F**
P. erythrophthalmus (Red-eyed Thornbird) **F**
P. striaticollis (Freckle-breasted Thornbird) **F**
P. dorsalis (Chestnut-backed Thornbird) **F**
P. ruber (Greater Thornbird) **F**
P. fusciceps (Plain Softtail) **F**
P. berlepschi (Russet-mantled Softtail) **F**
P. dendrocolaptoides (Canebrake Groundcreeper) **F**
SPARTONOICA
S. maluroides (Bay-capped Wren Spinetail) **F**
PHLEOCRYPTES
P. melanops (Wren-like Rushbird) **F**
LIMNORNIS
L. curvirostris (Curve-billed Reedhaunter) **F**
L. rectirostris (Straight-billed Reedhaunter) **F**
ANUMBIUS
A. annumbi (Firewood-Gatherer) **F**
CORYPHISTERA
C. alaudina (Lark-like Brushrunner) **F**
EREMOBIUS
E. phoenicurus (Band-tailed Earthcreeper) **F**
SIPTORNIS
S. striaticollis (Spectacled Prickletail) **F**
METOPOTHRIX
M. aurantiacus (Orange-fronted Plushcrown) **F**
XENERPESTES
X. minlosi (Double-banded Graytail) **E,F**
X. singularis (Equatorial Graytail) **F**
PHILYDORINAE
MARGARORNIS
M. adustus (Roraima Barbtail) **F**
M. guttuligera (Rusty-winged Barbtail) **F**
M. brunnescens (Spotted Barbtail) **E,F**
M. tatei (White-throated Barbtail) **F**
M. rubiginosus (Ruddy Treerunner) **E**
M. stellatus (Fulvous-dotted Treerunner) **F**
M. bellulus (Beautiful Treerunner) **E**
M. squamiger (Pearled Treerunner) **F**
LOCHMIAS
L. nematura (Sharp-tailed Streamcreeper) **E,F**
PSEUDOSEISURA
P. cristata (Rufous Cachalote) **F**
P. lophotes (Brown Cachalote) **F**
P. gutturalis (White-throated Cachalote) **F**
PSEUDOCOLAPTES
P. lawrencii (Buffy Tuftedcheek) **E,F**
P. boissonneautii (Streaked Tuftedcheek) **F**
BERLEPSCHIA
B. rikeri (Point-tailed Palmcreeper) **F**
PHILYDOR
P. strigilatus (Chestnut-winged Hookbill) **F**
P. subulatus (Striped Woodhaunter) **E,F**
P. guttulatus (Guttulated Foliage-gleaner) **F**
P. subalaris (Lineated Foliage-gleaner) **E,F**
P. rufosuperciliatus (Buff-browed Foliage-gleaner) **F**
P. striaticollis (Montane Foliage-gleaner) **F**
P. amaurotis (White-browed Foliage-gleaner) **F** [?]
P. variegaticeps (Scaly-throated Foliage-gleaner) **E,F**
P. ruficaudatus (Rufous-tailed Foliage-gleaner) **F**
P. erythrocercus (Rufous-rumped Foliage-gleaner) **E,F**
P. erythropterus (Chestnut-winged Foliage-gleaner) **F**
P. lichtensteini (Lichtenstein's Foliage-gleaner) **F**
P. erythronotus (Rufous-backed Foliage-gleaner) **E,F**
P. novaesi (Novaes' Foliage-gleaner) **F** [?]
P. atricapillus (Black-capped Foliage-gleaner) **F**
P. rufus (Buff-fronted Foliage-gleaner) **E,F**
P. pyrrhodes (Cinnamon-rumped Foliage-gleaner) **F**
P. dimidiatus (Russet-mantled Foliage-gleaner) **F** [?]
P. fuscus (White-collared Foliage-gleaner) **F**
P. ucayalae (Peruvian Recurvebill) **F**
P. striatus (Bolivian Recurvebill) **F**
CICHLOCOLAPTES
C. leucophrus (Pale-browed Treehunter) **F**

THRIPADECTES
T. ignobilis (Uniform Treehunter) **F**
T. rufobrunneus (Streak-breasted Treehunter) **E**
T. melanorhynchus (Black-billed Treehunter) **F**
T. holostictus (Striped Treehunter) **F**
T. virgaticeps (Streak-capped Treehunter) **F**
T. scrutator (Buff-throated Treehunter) **F**
T. flammulatus (Flammulated Treehunter) **F**
AUTOMOLUS
A. ruficollis (Rufous-necked Foliage-gleaner) **F** [?]
A. ochrolaemus (Buff-throated Foliage-gleaner) **E,F**
A. infuscatus (Olive-backed Foliage-gleaner) **F**
A. dorsalis (Crested Foliage-gleaner) **F**
A. leucophthalmus (White-eyed Foliage-gleaner) **F**
A. melanopezus (Brown-rumped Foliage-gleaner) **F**
A. albigularis (White-throated Foliage-gleaner) **F**
A. rubiginosus (Ruddy Foliage-gleaner) **E,F**
A. rufipileatus (Chestnut-crowned Foliage-gleaner) **F**
A. rectirostris (Chestnut-capped Foliage-gleaner) **F** [?]
A. erythrocephalus (Henna-hooded Foliage-gleaner) **F** [?]
SCLERURUS
S. mexicanus (Tawny-throated Leafscraper) **E,F**
S. rufigularis (Short-billed Leafscraper) **F**
S. albigularis (Gray-throated Leafscraper) **E,F**
S. caudacutus (Black-tailed Leafscraper) **F**
S. scansor (Rufous-breasted Leafscraper) **F**
S. guatemalensis (Scaly-throated Leafscraper) **F**
XENOPS
X. contaminatus (Sharp-billed Treehunter) **F**
X. milleri (Rufous-tailed Xenops) **F**
X. tenuirostris (Slender-billed Xenops) **F**
X. minutus (Plain Xenops) **E,F**
X. rutilans (Streaked Xenops) **E,F**
MEGAXENOPS
M. parnaguae (Great Xenops) **F** [?]
PYGARRHICHAS
P. albogularis (White-throated Treerunner) **F**
105 FORMICARIIDAE (ANTBIRDS)
CYMBILAIMUS
C. lineatus (Fasciated Antshrike) **E,F**
HYPOEDALEUS
H. guttatus (Spot-backed Antshrike) **F**
BATARA
B. cinerea (Giant Antshrike) **F**
MACKENZIAENA
M. leachii (Large-tailed Antshrike) **F**
M. severa (Tufted Antshrike) **F**
FREDERICKENA
F. viridis (Black-throated Antshrike) **F**
F. unduligera (Undulated Antshrike) **F**
TARABA
T. major (Great Antshrike) **E,F**
SAKESPHORUS
S. canadensis (Black-crested Antshrike) **F**
S. cristatus (Silvery-cheeked Antshrike) **F**
S. bernardi (Collared Antshrike) **F**
S. melanonotus (Black-backed Antshrike) **F**
S. melanothorax (Band-tailed Antshrike) **F**
S. luctuosus (Glossy Antshrike) **F**
BIATAS
B. nigropectus (White-bearded Antshrike) **F**
THAMNOPHILUS
T. doliatus (Barred Antshrike) **E,F**
T. multistriatus (Bar-crested Antshrike) **F**
T. palliatus (Lined Antshrike) **F**
T. bridgesi (Black-hooded Antshrike) **E**
T. nigriceps (Black Antshrike) **F**
T. praecox (Cocha Antshrike) **F** [?]
T. nigrocinereus (Blackish-gray Antshrike) **F**
T. cryptoleucus (Castelnau's Antshrike) **F**
T. aethiops (White-shouldered Antshrike) **F**
T. unicolor (Uniform Antshrike) **F**
T. schistaceus (Black-capped Antshrike) **F**
T. murinus (Mouse-colored Antshrike) **F**
T. aroyae (Upland Antshrike) **F**
T. punctatus (Slaty Antshrike) **E,F**
T. amazonicus (Amazonian Antshrike) **F**
T. insignis (Streak-backed Antshrike) **F**
T. caerulescens (Variable Antshrike) **F**
T. torquatus (Rufous-winged Antshrike) **F**
T. ruficapillus (Rufous-capped Antshrike) **F**
PYGIPTILA
P. stellaris (Spot-winged Antshrike) **F**

MEGASTICTUS
M. margaritatus (Pearly Antshrike) **F**
NEOCTANTES
N. niger (Black Bushbird) **F**
CLYTOCTANTES
C. alixii (Recurvebill Bushbird) **F** [?]
XENORNIS
X. setifrons (Speckle-breasted Antshrike) **E,F**
THAMNISTES
T. anabatinus (Russet Antshrike) **E,F**
DYSITHAMNUS
D. stictothorax (Spot-breasted Antvireo) **F**
D. mentalis (Plain Antvireo) **E,F**
D. striaticeps (Streak-crowned Antvireo) **E**
D. puncticeps (Spot-crowned Antvireo) **E,F**
D. xanthopterus (Rufous-backed Antvireo) **F**
D. ardesiacus (Gray-throated Antvireo) **F**
THAMNOMANES
T. saturninus (Saturnine Antshrike) **F**
T. occidentalis (Western Antshrike) **F**
T. plumbeus (Plumbeous Antshrike) **F** [?]
T. caesius (Cinereous Antshrike) **F**
T. schistogynus (Bluish-slate Antshrike) **F**
MYRMOTHERULA
M. brachyura (Pygmy Antwren) **E,F**
M. obscura (Short-billed Antwren) **F**
M. sclateri (Sclater's Antwren) **F**
M. klagesi (Klages' Antwren) **F** [?]
M. surinamensis (Streaked Antwren) **E,F**
M. ambigua (Yellow-throated Antwren) **F**
M. cherriei (Cherrie's Antwren) **F**
M. guttata (Rufous-bellied Antwren) **F**
M. longicauda (Stripe-chested Antwren) **F**
M. hauxwelli (Plain-throated Antwren) **F**
M. gularis (Star-throated Antwren) **F**
M. gutturalis (Brown-bellied Antwren) **F**
M. fulviventris (Checker-throated Antwren) **E,F**
M. leucophthalma (White-eyed Antwren) **F**
M. haematonota (Stipple-throated Antwren) **F**
M. ornata (Ornate Antwren) **F**
M. erythrura (Rufous-tailed Antwren) **F**
M. erythronotos (Black-hooded Antwren) **F** [E]
M. axillaris (White-flanked Antwren) **E,F**
M. schisticolor (Slaty Antwren) **E,F**
M. sunensis (Rio Suno Antwren) **F**
M. longipennis (Long-winged Antwren) **F**
M. minor (Salvadori's Antwren) **F** [?]
M. iheringi (Ihering's Antwren) **F**
M. fluminensis (Rio de Janeiro Antwren) **F**
M. grisea (Ashy Antwren) **F** [?]
M. unicolor (Unicolored Antwren) **F**
M. behni (Plain-winged Antwren) **F**
M. urosticta (Band-tailed Antwren) **F**
M. menetriesii (Gray Antwren) **F**
M. assimilis (Leaden Antwren) **F**
DICHROZONA
D. cincta (Banded Antcatcher) **F**
MYRMORCHILUS
M. strigilatus (Stripe-backed Antbird) **F**
HERPSILOCHMUS
H. pileatus (Black-capped Antwren) **F** [?]
H. sticturus (Spot-tailed Antwren) **F**
H. stictocephalus (Todd's Antwren) **F**
H. dorsimaculatus (Spot-backed Antwren) **F**
H. roraimae (Roraiman Antwren) **F**
H. pectoralis (Pectoral Antwren) **F**
H. longirostris (Large-billed Antwren) **F**
H. parkeri (Ash-throated Antwren) **F** [?]
H. axillaris (Yellow-breasted Antwren) **F**
H. rufimarginatus (Rufous-winged Antwren) **E,F**
MICRORHOPIAS
M. quixensis (Dot-winged Antwren) **E,F**
FORMICIVORA
F. iheringi (Narrow-billed Antwren) **F** [V]
F. grisea (White-fringed Antwren) **E,F**
F. serrana (Serra Antwren) **F**
F. melanogaster (Black-bellied Antwren) **F**
F. rufa (Rusty-backed Antwren) **F**
DRYMOPHILA
D. ferruginea (Ferruginous Antbird) **F**
D. rubricollis (Bertoni's Antbird) **F**
D. genei (Rufous-tailed Antbird) **F** [?]
D. ochropyga (Ochre-rumped Antbird) **F**
D. devillei (Striated Antbird) **F**
D. caudata (Long-tailed Antbird) **F**
D. malura (Dusky-tailed Antbird) **F**

D. squamata (Scaled Antbird) **F**
TERENURA
T. maculata (Streak-capped Antwren) **F**
T. sicki (Orange-bellied Antwren) **F** [?]
T. callinota (Rufous-rumped Antwren) **F**
T. humeralis (Chestnut-shouldered Antwren) **F**
T. sharpei (Yellow-rumped Antwren) **F** [?]
T. spodioptila (Ash-winged Antwren) **F**
CERCOMACRA
C. cinerascens (Gray Antbird) **F**
C. brasiliana (Rio de Janeiro Antbird) **F** [?]
C. tyrannina (Dusky Antbird) **E,F**
C. nigrescens (Blackish Antbird) **F**
C. serva (Black Antbird) **F**
C. nigricans (Jet Antbird) **E,F**
C. carbonaria (Rio Branco Antbird) **F** [?]
C. melanaria (Matto Grosso Antbird) **F**
C. ferdinandi (Bananal Antbird) **F**
SIPIA
S. berlepschi (Stub-tailed Antbird) **F**
S. rosenbergi (Esmeralda's Antbird) **F**
PYRIGLENA
P. leuconota (White-backed Fire-eye) **F**
P. atra (Swainson's Fire-eye) **F** [E]
P. leucoptera (White-shouldered Fire-eye) **F**
RHOPORNIS
R. ardesiaca (Slender Antbird) **F** [V]
MYRMOBORUS
M. leucophrys (White-browed Antcreeper) **F**
M. lugubris (Ash-breasted Antcreeper) **F**
M. myotherinus (Black-faced Antcreeper) **F**
M. melanurus (Black-tailed Antcreeper) **F**
HYPOCNEMIS
H. cantator (Warbling Antbird) **F**
H. hypoxantha (Yellow-browed Antbird) **F**
HYPOCNEMOIDES
H. melanopogon (Black-chinned Antcreeper) **F**
H. maculicauda (Band-tailed Antcreeper) **F**
MYRMOCHANES
M. hemileucus (Black & White Antcatcher) **F**
GYMNOCICHLA
G. nudiceps (Bare-crowned Antcatcher) **E,F**
SCLATERIA
S. naevia (Silvered Antbird) **F**
PERCNOSTOLA
P. rufifrons (Black-headed Antbird) **F**
P. macrolopha (White-lined Antbird) **F**
P. schistacea (Slate-colored Antbird) **F**
P. leucostigma (Spot-winged Antbird) **F**
P. caurensis (Caura Antbird) **F**
P. lophotes (Rufous-crested Antbird) **F**
MYRMECIZA
M. longipes (Swainson's Antcatcher) **E,F**
M. exsul (Chestnut-backed Antbird) **E,F**
M. ferruginea (Ferruginous-backed Antbird) **F**
M. ruficauda (Scalloped Antbird) **F** [?]
M. loricata (White-bibbed Antbird) **F**
M. squamosa (Squamate Antbird) **F**
M. laemosticta (Dull-mantled Antbird) **E,F**
M. disjuncta (Yapacana Antbird) **F**
M. pelzelni (Gray-bellied Antbird) **F**
M. hemimelaena (Chestnut-tailed Antbird) **F**
M. hyperythra (Plumbeous Antbird) **F**
M. goeldii (Goeldi's Antbird) **F**
M. melanoceps (White-shouldered Antbird) **F**
M. fortis (Sooty Antbird) **F**
M. immaculata (Immaculate Antbird) **F**
M. griseiceps (Gray-headed Antbird) **F** [?]
M. atrothorax (Black-throated Antbird) **F**
M. stictothorax (Spot-breasted Antbird) **F** [?]
PITHYS
P. albifrons (White-plumed Antbird) **F**
P. castanea (White-masked Antbird) **F**
GYMNOPITHYS
G. rufigula (Rufous-throated Antcatcher) **F**
G. salvini (White-throated Antcatcher) **F**
G. lunulata (Lunulated Antcatcher) **F**
G. leucaspis (Bicolored Antcatcher) **E,F**
RHEGMATORHINA
R. gymnops (Bare-eyed Antcatcher) **F** [?]
R. berlepschi (Harlequin Antcatcher) **F**
R. cristata (Chestnut-crested Antcatcher) **F**
R. hoffmannsi (White-breasted Antcatcher) **F**
R. melanosticta (Hairy-crested Antcatcher) **F**
HYLOPHYLAX
H. naevioides (Spotted Antbird) **E,F**

H. naevia (Spot-backed Antbird) **F**
H. punctulata (Dot-backed Antbird) **F**
H. poecilonota (Scale-backed Antbird) **F**
PHLEGOPSIS
P. nigromaculata (Black-spotted Bare-eye) **F**
P. barringeri (Argus Bare-eye) **F**
P. erythroptera (Reddish-winged Bare-eye) **F**
SKUTCHIA
S. borbae (Pale-faced Bare-eye) **F**
PHAENOSTICTUS
P. mcleannani (Ocellated Antbird) **E,F**
FORMICARIUS
F. colma (Rufous-capped Ant-Thrush) **F**
F. analis (Black-faced Ant-Thrush) **E,F**
F. rufifrons (Rufous-fronted Ant-Thrush) **F** [?]
F. nigricapillus (Black-headed Ant-Thrush) **E,F**
F. rufipectus (Rufous-breasted Ant-Thrush) **E,F**
CHAMAEZA
C. campanisona (Short-tailed Ant-Thrush) **F**
C. nobilis (Striated Ant-Thrush) **F**
C. ruficauda (Rufous-tailed Ant-Thrush) **F**
C. mollissima (Barred Ant-Thrush) **F**
MYRMORNIS
M. torquata (Wing-banded Ant-Thrush) **E,F**
PITTASOMA
P. michleri (Black-crowned Antpitta) **E,F**
P. rufopileatum (Rufous-crowned Antpitta) **F**
GRALLARIA
G. squamigera (Undulated Antpitta) **F**
G. gigantea (Giant Antpitta) **F** [?]
G. excelsa (Great Antpitta) **F** [?]
G. varia (Variegated Antpitta) **F**
G. alleni (Moustached Antpitta) **F** [I]
G. carrikeri (Pale-billed Antpitta) **F**
G. guatimalensis (Scaled Antpitta) **E,F**
G. chthonia (Tachira Antpitta) **F** [?]
G. haplonota (Plain-backed Antpitta) **F**
G. dignissima (Ochre-striped Antpitta) **F**
G. eludens (Elusive Antpitta) **F**
G. ruficapilla (Chestnut-crowned Antpitta) **F**
G. watkinsi (Watkins' Antpitta) **F**
G. bangsi (Santa Marta Antpitta) **F**
G. andicola (Stripe-headed Antpitta) **F**
G. punensis (Puna Antpitta) **F**
G. rufocinerea (Bicolored Antpitta) **F** [?]
G. nuchalis (Chestnut-naped Antpitta) **F**
G. blakei (Chestnut Antpitta) **F**
G. albigula (White-throated Antpitta) **F**
G. erythroleuca (Chestnut-brown Antpitta) **F**
G. hypoleuca (Bay-backed Antpitta) **F**
G. griseonucha (Gray-naped Antpitta) **F**
G. rufula (Rufous Antpitta) **F**
G. erythrotis (Rufous-faced Antpitta) **F**
G. quitensis (Tawny Antpitta) **F**
G. milleri (Brown-banded Antpitta) **F** [I]
HYLOPEZUS
H. perspicillatus (Streak-chested Antpitta) **E,F**
H. macularius (Spotted Antpitta) **F**
H. fulviventris (Fulvous-bellied Antpitta) **F**
H. berlepschi (Amazonian Antpitta) **F**
H. ochroleucus (Speckle-breasted Antpitta) **F**
MYRMOTHERA
M. campanisona (Thrush-like Antpitta) **F**
M. simplex (Brown-breasted Antpitta) **F**
GRALLARICULA
G. flavirostris (Ocher-breasted Antpitta) **E,F**
G. ferrugineipectus (Rusty-breasted Antpitta) **F**
G. nana (Slate-crowned Antpitta) **F**
G. loricata (Scallop-breasted Antpitta) **F** [?]
G. peruviana (Peruvian Antpitta) **F**
G. lineifrons (Crescent-faced Antpitta) **F**
G. ochraceifrons (Ocher-fronted Antpitta) **F**
G. cucullata (Hooded Antpitta) **F** [?]
CONOPOPHAGA
C. lineata (Rufous Gnateater) **F**
C. aurita (Chestnut-belted Gnateater) **F**
C. roberti (Hooded Gnateater) **F** [?]
C. peruviana (Ash-throated Gnateater) **F**
C. ardesiaca (Slaty Gnateater) **F**
C. castaneiceps (Chestnut-crowned Gnateater) **F**
C. melanops (Black-cheeked Gnateater) **F**
C. melanogaster (Black-bellied Gnateater) **F**
106 RHINOCRYPTIDAE (TAPACULOS)
PTEROPTOCHOS
P. castaneus (Chestnut-throated Huet-huet) **F**
P. tarnii (Black-throated Huet-huet) **F**

P. megapodius (Moustached Turka) **F**
SCELORCHILUS
S. albicollis (White-throated Tapaculo) **F**
S. rubecula (Chucao Tapaculo) **F**
RHINOCRYPTA
R. lanceolata (Crested Gallito) **F**
TELEDROMAS
T. fuscus (Sandy Gallito) **F**
LIOSCELES
L. thoracicus (Rusty-belted Tapaculo) **F**
MELANOPAREIA
M. torquata (Collared Crescentchest) **F**
M. maximiliani (Olive-crowned Crescentchest) **F**
M. maranonica (Maranon Crescentchest) **F**
M. elegans (Elegant Crescentchest) **F**
PSILORHAMPHUS
P. guttatus (Spotted Bamboowren) **F**
MERULAXIS
M. ater (Slaty Bristlefront) **F**
M. stresemanni (Stresemann's Bristlefront) **F** [I]
EUGRALLA
E. paradoxa (Ocher-flanked Tapaculo) **F**
MYORNIS
M. senilis (Ash-coloured Tapaculo) **F**
SCYTALOPUS
S. unicolor (Unicolored Tapaculo) **F**
S. speluncae (Mouse-colored Tapaculo) **F**
S. macropus (Large-footed Tapaculo) **F**
S. femoralis (Rufous-vented Tapaculo) **F**
S. argentifrons (Silvery-fronted Tapaculo) **E**
S. panamensis (Pale-throated Tapaculo) **E,F**
S. vicinior (Narino Tapaculo) **F**
S. latebricola (Brown-rumped Tapaculo) **F**
S. novacapitalis (Brasilia Tapaculo) **F** [I]
S. indigoticus (White-breasted Tapaculo) **F**
S. magellanicus (Andean Tapaculo) **F**
S. superciliaris (White-browed Tapaculo) **F**
ACROPTERNIS
A. orthonyx (Ocellated Tapaculo) **F**
107 COTINGIDAE (COTINGAS)
PHOENICERCUS
P. carnifex (Guianian Red Cotinga) **F**
P. nigricollis (Black-necked Red Cotinga) **F**
LANIISOMA
L. elegans (Shrike-like Cotinga) **F**
PHIBALURA
P. flavirostris (Swallow-tailed Cotinga) **F**
TIJUCA
T. atra (Black & Gold Cotinga) **F**
T. condita (Gray-winged Cotinga) **F**
CARPORNIS
C. cucullatus (Hooded Berryeater) **F**
C. melanocephalus (Black-headed Berryeater) **F**
AMPELION
A. rubrocristata (Red-crested Cotinga) **F**
A. rufaxilla (Chestnut-crested Cotinga) **F**
A. sclateri (Bay-vented Cotinga) **F**
A. stresemanni (White-cheeked Cotinga) **F**
PIPREOLA
P. riefferii (Green & Black Fruiteater) **F**
P. intermedia (Band-tailed Fruiteater) **F**
P. arcuata (Barred Fruiteater) **F**
P. aureopectus (Golden-breasted Fruiteater) **F**
P. frontalis (Scarlet-breasted Fruiteater) **F**
P. chlorolepidota (Fiery-throated Fruiteater) **F**
P. formosa (Handsome Fruiteater) **F**
P. whitelyi (Red-banded Fruiteater) **F**
AMPELIOIDES
A. tschudii (Scaled Fruiteater) **F**
IODOPLEURA
I. pipra (Buff-throated Purpletuft) **F**
I. fusca (Dusky Purpletuft) **F**
I. isabellae (White-browed Purpletuft) **F**
CALYPTURA
C. cristata (Kinglet Calyptura) **F** [I]
LIPAUGUS
L. subalaris (Gray-tailed Piha) **F**
L. cryptolophus (Olivaceus Piha) **F**
L. fuscocinereus (Dusky Piha) **F**
L. vociferans (Screaming Piha) **F**
L. unirufus (Rufous Piha) **E,F**
L. lanioides (Cinnamon-vented Piha) **F**
L. streptophorus (Rose-colored Piha) **F**
CHIROCYLLA
C. uropygialis (Scimitar-winged Piha) **F**

PORPHYROLAEMA
P. porphyrolaema (Purple-throated Cotinga) **F**
COTINGA
C. amabilis (Lovely Cotinga) **E**
C. ridgwayi (Ridgway's Cotinga) **E**
C. nattererii (Blue Cotinga) **F**
C. maynana (Plum-throated Cotinga) **F**
C. cotinga (Purple-breasted Cotinga) **F**
C. maculata (Banded Cotinga) **F**
C. cayana (Spangled Cotinga) **F**
XIPHOLENA
X. punicea (Pompadour Cotinga) **F**
X. lamellipennis (White-tailed Cotinga) **F**
X. atropurpurea (White-winged Cotinga) **F**
CARPODECTES
C. hopkei (Black-tipped Cotinga) **F**
C. nitidus (Snowy Cotinga) **E**
C. antoniae (Yellow-billed Cotinga) **E**
CONIOPTILON
C. mcilhennyi (Black-faced Cotinga) **F**
GYMNODERUS
G. foetidus (Bare-necked Fruitcrow) **F**
HAEMATODERUS
H. militaris (Crimson Fruitcrow) **F**
QUERULA
Q. purpurata (Purple-throated Fruitcrow) **E,F**
PYRODERUS
P. scutatus (Red-ruffed Fruitcrow) **F**
CEPHALOPTERUS
C. glabricollis (Bare-necked Umbrellabird) **E**
C. ornatus (Amazonian Umbrellabird) **F**
C. penduliger (Long-wattled Umbrellabird) **F**
PERISSOCEPHALUS
P. tricolor (Capuchin Bird) **F**
PROCNIAS
P. averano (Bearded Bellbird) **F**
P. nudicollis (Bare-throated Bellbird) **F**
P. tricarunculata (Three-wattled Bellbird) **F**
P. alba (White Bellbird) **F**
RUPICOLA
R. rupicola (Guianan Cock of the Rock) **F**
R. peruviana (Andean Cock of the Rock) **F**
108 PIPRIDAE (MANAKINS)
SCHIFFORNIS
S. major (Greater Manakin) **F**
S. virescens (Greenish Manakin) **F**
S. turdinus (Thrushlike Manakin) **E,F**
SAPAYOA
S. aenigma (Broad-billed Manakin) **E,F**
PIPRITES
P. griseiceps (Gray-hooded Manakin) **E**
P. chloris (Wing-barred Manakin) **F**
P. pileatus (Black-capped Manakin) **F**
NEOPIPO
N. cinnamomea (Cinnamon Manakin) **F**
CHLOROPIPO
C. flavicapilla (Yellow-headed Manakin) **F**
C. holochlora (Green Manakin) **E,F**
C. uniformis (Olive Manakin) **F**
C. unicolor (Jet Manakin) **F**
XENOPIPO
X. atronitens (Black Manakin) **F**
ANTILOPHIA
A. galeata (Helmeted Manakin) **F**
TYRANNEUTES
T. stolzmanni (Dwarf Tyrant Manakin) **F**
T. virescens (Tiny Tyrant Manakin) **F**
NEOPELMA
N. pallescens (Pale-bellied Tyrant Manakin) **F**
N. chrysocephalum (Saffron-crested Tyrant Manakin) **F**
N. aurifrons (Wied's Tyrant Manakin) **F**
N. sulphureiventer (Sulfur-bellied Tyrant Manakin) **F**
HETEROCERCUS
H. aurantiivertex (Orange-crowned Manakin) **F**
H. flavivertex (Yellow-crowned Manakin) **F**
H. linteatus (Flame-crowned Manakin) **F**
MACHAEROPTERUS
M. regulus (Striped Manakin) **F**
M. pyrocephalus (Fiery-capped Manakin) **F**
M. deliciosus (Club-winged Manakin) **F**
MANACUS
M. manacus (White-bearded Manakin) **E,F**
CORAPIPO
C. leucorrhoa (White-ruffed Manakin) **E,F**

C. gutturalis (White-throated Manakin) **F**
ILICURA
I. militaris (Pin-tailed Manakin) **F**
MASIUS
M. chrysopterus (Golden-winged Manakin) **F**
CHIROXIPHIA
C. linearis (Long-tailed Manakin) **E,F**
C. lanceolata (Lance-tailed Manakin) **E,F**
C. pareola (Blue-backed Manakin) **E,F**
C. caudata (Swallow-tailed Manakin) **F**
PIPRA
P. pipra (White-crowned Manakin) **E,F**
P. coronata (Blue-crowned Manakin) **E,F**
P. isidorei (Blue-rumped Manakin) **F**
P. caeruleocapilla (Caerulean-capped Manakin) **F**
P. nattereri (Snow-capped Manakin) **F**
P. vilasboasi (Golden-crowned Manakin) **F**
P. iris (Opal-crowned Manakin) **F**
P. serena (White-fronted Manakin) **F**
P. aureola (Crimson-hooded Manakin) **F**
P. fasciicauda (Band-tailed Manakin) **F**
P. filicauda (Wire-tailed Manakin) **F**
P. mentalis (Red-capped Manakin) **E,F**
P. erythrocephala (Golden-headed Manakin) **E,F**
P. rubrocapilla (Red-headed Manakin) **F**
P. chloromeros (Round-tailed Manakin) **F**
P. cornuta (Scarlet-horned Manakin) **F**
109 TYRANNIDAE (TYRANT FLYCATCHERS)
PHYLLOMYIAS
P. fasciatus (Planalto Tyrannulet) **F**
P. burmeisteri (Rough-legged Tyrannulet) **E,F**
P. virescens (Greenish Tyrannulet) **F**
P. sclateri (Sclater's Tyrannulet) **F**
P. griseocapilla (Gray-capped Tyrannulet) **F**
P. griseiceps (Sooty-headed Tyrannulet) **E,F**
P. plumbeiceps (Plumbeous-crowned Tyrannulet) **F**
P. nigrocapillus (Black-capped Tyrannulet) **F**
P. cinereiceps (Ashy-headed Tyrannulet) **F**
P. uropygialis (Tawny-rumped Tyrannulet) **F**
ZIMMERIUS
Z. vilissimus (Paltry Tyrannulet) **E,F**
Z. bolivianus (Bolivian Tyrannulet) **F**
Z. cinereicapillus (Red-billed Tyrannulet) **F**
Z. gracilipes (Slender-footed Tyrannulet) **F**
Z. viridiflavus (Golden-faced Tyrannulet) **F**
ORNITHION
O. inerme (White-lored Tyrannulet) **F**
O. semiflavum (Yellow-bellied Tyrannulet) **E**
O. brunneicapillum (Brown-capped Tyrannulet) **E,F**
CAMPTOSTOMA
C. obsoletum (Southern Beardless Tyrannulet) **E,F**
C. imberbe (Northern Beardless Tyrannulet) **A,E**
PHAEOMYIAS
P. murina (Mouse-colored Tyrannulet) **E,F**
SUBLEGATUS
S. modestus (Scrub Flycatcher) **E,F,G**
S. obscurior (Dusky Flycatcher) **F**
SUIRIRI
S. suiriri (Suiriri Flycatcher) **F**
TYRANNULUS
T. elatus (Yellow-crowned Tyrannulet) **E,F**
MYIOPAGIS
M. gaimardii (Forest Elaenia) **E,F**
M. caniceps (Gray Elaenia) **E,F**
M. subplacens (Pacific Elaenia) **F**
M. flavivertex (Yellow-crowned Elaenia) **F**
M. viridicata (Greenish Elaenia) **E,F**
M. cotta (Yellow Elaenia) **E**
PSEUDELAENIA
P. leucospodia (Gray & White Tyrannulet) **E**
ELAENIA
E. flavogaster (Yellow-bellied Elaenia) **E,F**
E. martinica (Caribbean Elaenia) **E**
E. spectabilis (Large Elaenia) **F**
E. albiceps (White-crested Elaenia) **F**
E. parvirostris (Small-billed Elaenia) **F**
E. mesoleuca (Olivaceous Elaenia) **F**
E. strepera (Slaty Elaenia) **F**
E. gigas (Mottle-backed Elaenia) **F**
E. pelzelni (Brownish Elaenia) **F**
E. cristata (Plain-crested Elaenia) **F**
E. chiriquensis (Lesser Elaenia) **E,F**
E. ruficeps (Rufous-crowned Elaenia) **F**
E. frantzii (Mountain Elaenia) **E,F**
E. obscura (Highland Elaenia) **F**
E. dayi (Great Elaenia) **F**

E. pallatangae (Sierran Elaenia) **F**
E. fallax (Greater Antillean Elaenia) **E**
MECOCERCULUS
M. leucophrys (White-throated Tyrannulet) **F**
M. poecilocercus (White-tailed Tyrannulet) **F**
M. hellmayri (Buff-banded Tyrannulet) **F**
M. calopterus (Rufous-winged Tyrannulet) **F**
M. minor (Sulfur-bellied Tyrannulet) **F**
M. stictopterus (White-banded Tyrannulet) **F**
SERPOPHAGA
S. cinerea (Torrent Tyrannulet) **E,F**
S. hypoleuca (River Tyrannulet) **F**
S. nigricans (Sooty Tyrannulet) **F**
S. araguayae (Bananal Tyrannulet) **F**
S. subcristata (White-crested Tyrannulet) **F**
INEZIA
I. tenuirostris (Slender-billed Tyrannulet) **F**
I. inornata (Plain Tyrannulet) **F**
I. subflava (Pale-tipped Tyrannulet) **F**
STIGMATURA
S. napensis (Lesser Wagtail Tyrant) **F**
S. budytoides (Greater Wagtail Tyrant) **F**
ANAIRETES
A. alpinus (Ash-breasted Tit Tyrant) **F**
A. agraphia (Unstreaked Tit Tyrant) **F**
A. agilis (Agile Tit Tyrant) **F**
A. reguloides (Pied-crested Tit Tyrant) **F**
A. flavirostris (Yellow-billed Tit Tyrant) **F**
A. parulus (Tufted Tit Tyrant) **F**
A. fernandezianus (Juan Fernandez Tit Tyrant) **F**
TACHURIS
T. rubrigastra (Many-colored Rush Tyrant) **F**
CULICIVORA
C. caudacuta (Sharp-tailed Tyrant) **F**
POLYSTICTUS
P. superciliaris (Gray-backed Tachuri) **F**
P. pectoralis (Bearded Tachuri) **F**
PSEUDOCOLOPTERYX
P. dinellianus (Dinelli's Doradito) **F**
P. sclateri (Crested Doradito) **F**
P. acutipennis (Subtropical Doradito) **F**
P. flaviventris (Warbling Doradito) **F**
EUSCARTHMUS
E. meloryphus (Tawny-crowned Pygmy Tyrant) **F**
E. rufomarginatus (Rufous-sided Pygmy Tyrant) **F**
MIONECTES
M. striaticollis (Streak-necked Flycatcher) **F**
M. olivaceus (Olive-striped Flycatcher) **F**
M. oleagineus (Ocher-bellied Flycatcher) **E,F**
M. macconnelli (MacConnell's Flycatcher) **F**
M. rufiventris (Gray-hooded Flycatcher) **F**
LEPTOPOGON
L. rufipectus (Rufous-breasted Leptopogon) **F**
L. taczanowskii (Inca Leptopogon) **F**
L. amaurocephalus (Sepia-capped Leptopogon) **E,F**
L. superciliaris (White-bellied Leptopogon) **E,F**
PHYLLOSCARTES
P. nigrifrons (Black-fronted Tyrannulet) **F**
P. poecilotis (Variegated Bristle Tyrant) **F**
P. chapmani (Chapman's Tyrannulet) **F**
P. ophthalmicus (Marble-faced Bristle Tyrant) **F**
P. eximius (Southern Bristle Tyrant) **F**
P. gualaquizae (Ecuadorean Bristle Tyrant) **F**
P. flaviventris (Yellow-bellied Bristle Tyrant) **F**
P. venezuelanus (Venezuelan Bristle Tyrant) **F**
P. orbitalis (Spectacled Bristle Tyrant) **F**
P. lanyoni (Antioquia Bristle Tyrant) **F**
P. flaveolus (Yellow Tyrannulet) **E,F**
P. roquettei (Minas Geraes Tyrannulet) **F** [?]
P. ventralis (Mottle-cheeked Tyrannulet) **F**
P. paulistus (Sao Paulo Tyrannulet) **F** [?]
P. oustaleti (Oustalet's Tyrannulet) **F**
P. difficilis (Ihering's Tyrannulet) **F**
P. ceciliae (Long-tailed Tyrannulet) **F** [?]
P. flavovirens (Yellow-green Tyrannulet) **E**
P. virescens (Olive-green Tyrannulet) **F**
P. superciliaris (Rufous-browed Tyrannulet) **E,F**
P. sylviolus (Bay-ringed Tyrannulet) **F**
PSEUDOTRICCUS
P. pelzelni (Bronze-olive Pygmy Tyrant) **E,F**
P. simplex (Hazel-fronted Pygmy Tyrant) **F**
P. ruficeps (Rufous-headed Pygmy Tyrant) **F**
CORYTHOPIS
C. delalandi (Delalande's Antpipit) **F**
C. torquata (Ringed Antpipit) **F**

TYRANT FLYCATCHERS

MYIORNIS
M. auricularis (Eared Pygmy Tyrant) **F**
M. ecaudatus (Short-tailed Pygmy Tyrant) **F**
M. atricapillus (Black-capped Pygmy Tyrant) **E,F**
M. albiventris (White-breasted Pygmy Tyrant) **F**
LOPHOTRICCUS
L. pileatus (Scale-crested Pygmy Tyrant) **E,F**
L. eulophotes (Long-crested Pygmy Tyrant) **F**
L. vitiosus (Double-banded Pygmy Tyrant) **F**
L. galeatus (Helmeted Pygmy Tyrant) **F**
ATALOTRICCUS
A. pilaris (Pale-eyed Pygmy Tyrant) **E,F**
POECILOTRICCUS
P. ruficeps (Rufous-crowned Tody Tyrant) **F**
P. capitale (Black & White Tody Flycatcher) **F**
P. tricolor (Tricolored Tody Flycatcher) **F**
P. andrei (Black-chested Tyrant) **F**
ONCOSTOMA
O. olivaceum (Southern Bentbill) **E,F**
O. cinereigulare (Northern Bentbill) **E**
HEMITRICCUS
H. minor (Snethlage's Tody Tyrant) **F**
H. josephinae (Boat-billed Tody Tyrant) **F**
H. diops (Drab-breasted Pygmy Tyrant) **F**
H. obsoletus (Brown-breasted Pygmy Tyrant) **F**
H. flammulatus (Flammulated Pygmy Tyrant) **F**
H. zosterops (White-eyed Tody Tyrant) **F**
H. aenigma (Zimmer's Tody Tyrant) **F**
H. orbitatus (Olivaceous Tody Tyrant) **F**
H. iohannis (Johanne's Pygmy Tyrant) **F**
H. striaticollis (Stripe-necked Tody Tyrant) **F**
H. nidipendulus (Hangnest Tody Tyrant) **F**
H. spodiops (Yungas Tody Tyrant) **F**
H. margaritaceiventer (Pearly-vented Tody Tyrant) **F**
H. inornatus (Pelzeln's Tody Tyrant) **F**
H. granadensis (Black-throated Tody Tyrant) **F**
H. mirandae (Buff-breasted Tody Tyrant) **F**
H. kaempferi (Kaempfer's Tody Tyrant) **F**
H. rufigularis (Buff-throated Tody Tyrant) **F**
H. furcatus (Fork-tailed Pygmy Tyrant) **F**
TODIROSTRUM
T. senex (Plumbeous-crowned Tody Flycatcher) **F**
T. russatum (Ruddy Tody Flycatcher) **F**
T. plumbeiceps (Ocher-faced Tody Flycatcher) **F**
T. fumifrons (Smoky-fronted Tody Flycatcher) **F**
T. latirostre (Rusty-fronted Tody Flycatcher) **F**
T. sylvia (Slate-headed Tody Flycatcher) **F**
T. maculatum (Spotted Tody Flycatcher) **F**
T. poliocephalum (Gray-headed Tody Flycatcher) **F**
T. cinereum (Common Tody Flycatcher) **E,F**
T. viridanum (Short-tailed Tody Flycatcher) **F** [?]
T. pictum (Painted Tody Flycatcher) **F**
T. chrysocrotaphum (Yellow-browed Tody Flycatcher) **F**
T. nigriceps (Black-headed Tody Flycatcher) **E,F**
T. calopterum (Golden-winged Tody Flycatcher) **F**
CNIPODECTES
C. subbrunneus (Brownish Flycatcher) **F**
RAMPHOTRIGON
R. megacephala (Large-headed Flatbill) **F**
R. ruficauda (Rufous-tailed Flatbill) **F**
R. fuscicauda (Dusky-tailed Flatbill) **F**
RHYNCHOCYCLUS
R. brevirostris (Eye-ringed Flatbill) **E,F**
R. olivaceus (Olivaceous Flatbill) **E,F**
R. fulvipectus (Fulvous-breasted Flatbill) **F**
TOLMOMYIAS
T. sulphurescens (Yellow-olive Flycatcher) **E,F**
T. assimilis (Yellow-margined Flycatcher) **E,F**
T. poliocephalus (Gray-crowned Flycatcher) **F**
T. flaviventris (Yellow-breasted Flycatcher) **F**
PLATYRINCHUS
P. saturatus (Cinnamon-crested Spadebill) **F**
P. cancrominus (Stub-tailed Spadebill) **E**
P. mystaceus (White-throated Spadebill) **E,F**
P. coronatus (Golden-crowned Spadebill) **E,F**
P. flavigularis (Yellow-throated Spadebill) **F**
P. platyrhynchos (White-crested Spadebill) **F**
P. leucoryphus (Russet-winged Spadebill) **F** [?]
ONYCHORHYNCHUS
O. coronatus (Royal Flycatcher) **E,F**
MYIOTRICCUS
M. ornatus (Ornate Flycatcher) **F**
TERENOTRICCUS
T. erythrurus (Ruddy-tailed Flycatcher) **E,F**

MYIOBIUS
M. villosus (Tawny-breasted Flycatcher) **F**
M. barbatus (Sulphur-rumped Flycatcher) **E,F**
M. atricaudus (Black-tailed Flycatcher) **E,F**
MYIOPHOBUS
M. flavicans (Flavescent Flycatcher) **F**
M. phoenicomitra (Orange-crested Flycatcher) **F**
M. inornatus (Unadorned Flycatcher) **F**
M. roraimae (Roraiman Flycatcher) **F**
M. lintoni (Orange-banded Flycatcher) **F**
M. pulcher (Handsome Flycatcher) **F**
M. cryptoxanthus (Olive-crested Flycatcher) **F**
M. ochraceiventris (Ochraceous-breasted Flycatcher) **F**
M. fasciatus (Bran-colored Flycatcher) **E,F**
LATHROTRICCUS
L. euleri (Euler's Flycatcher) **E,F**
APHANOTRICCUS
A. capitalis (Tawny-chested Flycatcher) **E** [?]
A. audax (Black-billed Flycatcher) **E,F**
XENOTRICCUS
X. callizonus (Belted Flycatcher) **F** [?]
X. mexicanus (Pileated Flycatcher) **F**
PYRRHOMYIAS
P. cinnamomea (Cinnamon Flycatcher) **F**
MITREPHANES
M. phaeocercus (Tufted Flycatcher) **E,F**
M. olivaceus (Olive Flycatcher) **F**
CONTOPUS
C. borealis (Olive-sided Flycatcher) **A,E,F**
C. fumigatus (Smoke-colored Pewee) **A,E,F**
C. ochraceus (Ochraceous Pewee) **F**
C. sordidulus (Western Wood Pewee) **A,E,F**
C. virens (Eastern Wood Pewee) **A,E,F**
C. cinereus (Tropical Pewee) **E,F**
C. albogularis (White-throated Pewee) **F**
C. nigrescens (Blackish Pewee) **F**
C. caribaeus (Greater Antillean Pewee) **E**
C. latirostris (Lesser Antillean Pewee) **E**
EMPIDONAX
E. flaviventris (Yellow-bellied Flycatcher) **A,E**
E. virescens (Acadian Flycatcher) **A,E,F**
E. traillii (Willow Flycatcher) **A,E,F**
E. alnorum (Alder Flycatcher) **A,E,F**
E. griseipectus (Gray-breasted Flycatcher) **F**
E. albigularis (White-throated Flycatcher) **E**
E. minimus (Least Flycatcher) **A,E,F**
E. hammondii (Hammond's Flycatcher) **A,E**
E. oberholseri (Dusky Flycatcher) **A,E**
E. wrightii (Gray Flycatcher) **A,E**
E. affinis (Pine Flycatcher) **E**
E. difficilis (Western Flycatcher) **A,E**
E. flavescens (Yellowish Flycatcher) **E**
E. fulvifrons (Buff-breasted Flycatcher) **A,E**
E. atriceps (Black-capped Flycatcher) **E**
NESOTRICCUS
N. ridgwayi (Cocos I Flycatcher) **E**
CNEMOTRICCUS
C. fuscatus (Fuscous Flycatcher) **E,F**
SAYORNIS
S. phoebe (Eastern Phoebe) **A,E**
S. nigricans (Black Phoebe) **A,E,F**
S. saya (Say's Phoebe) **A,E**
PYROCEPHALUS
P. rubinus (Vermilion Flycatcher) **A,E,F,G**
OCHTHOECA
O. cinnamomeiventris (Slaty-backed Chat Tyrant) **F**
O. diadema (Yellow-bellied Chat Tyrant) **F**
O. frontalis (Crowned Chat Tyrant) **F**
O. jelskii (Jelski's Chat Tyrant) **F**
O. pulchella (Golden-browed Chat Tyrant) **F**
O. rufipectoralis (Rufous-breasted Chat Tyrant) **F**
O. fumicolor (Brown-backed Chat Tyrant) **F**
O. oenanthoides (D'Orbigny's Chat Tyrant) **F**
O. parvirostris (Patagonian Chat Tyrant) **F**
O. leucophrys (White-browed Chat Tyrant) **F**
O. piurae (Piura Chat Tyrant) **F**
O. littoralis (Drab Water Tyrant) **F**
MYIOTHERETES
M. striaticollis (Streak-throated Bush Tyrant) **F**
M. erythropygius (Red-rumped Bush Tyrant) **F**
M. pernix (Santa Marta Bush Tyrant) **F**
M. fumigatus (Smoky Bush Tyrant) **F**
M. fuscorufus (Rufous-bellied Bush Tyrant) **F**
POLIOXOLMIS
P. rufipennis (Rufous-webbed Bush Tyrant) **F**

XOLMIS
X. pyrope (Fire-eyed Diucon) **F**
X. cinerea (Gray Monjita) **F**
X. coronata (Black-crowned Monjita) **F**
X. velata (White-rumped Monjita) **F**
X. dominicana (Black & White Monjita) **F**
X. irupero (White Monjita) **F**
NEOXOLMIS
N. rubetra (Rusty-backed Monjita) **F**
N. rufiventris (Chocolate-vented Tyrant) **F**
AGRIORNIS
A. montana (Black-billed Shrike Tyrant) **F**
A. andicola (White-tailed Shrike Tyrant) **F**
A. livida (Great Shrike Tyrant) **F**
A. microptera (Gray-bellied Shrike Tyrant) **F**
A. murina (Mouse-brown Shrike Tyrant) **F**
MUSCISAXICOLA
M. maculirostris (Spot-billed Ground Tyrant) **F**
M. macloviana (Dark-faced Ground Tyrant) **F**
M. fluviatilis (Little Ground Tyrant) **F**
M. capistrata (Cinnamon-bellied Ground Tyrant) **F**
M. rufivertex (Rufous-naped Ground Tyrant) **F**
M. albilora (White-browed Ground Tyrant) **F**
M. juninensis (Puna Ground Tyrant) **F**
M. alpina (Plain-capped Ground Tyrant) **F**
M. cinerea (Cinereous Ground Tyrant) **F**
M. albifrons (White-fronted Ground Tyrant) **F**
M. flavinucha (Ocher-naped Ground Tyrant) **F**
M. frontalis (Black-fronted Ground Tyrant) **F**
LESSONIA
L. rufa (Rufous-backed Negrito) **F**
L. oreas (Salvin's Negrito) **F**
KNIPOLEGUS
K. striaticeps (Cinereous Tyrant) **F**
K. hudsoni (Hudson's Black Tyrant) **F**
K. poecilocercus (Amazonian Black Tyrant) **F**
K. signatus (Jelski's Bush Tyrant) **F**
K. cyanirostris (Blue-billed Black Tyrant) **F**
K. poecilurus (Rufous-tailed Tyrant) **F**
K. orenocensis (Riverside Tyrant) **F**
K. aterrimus (White-winged Black Tyrant) **F**
K. lophotes (Crested Black Tyrant) **F**
K. nigerrimus (Velvety Black Tyrant) **F**
HYMENOPS
H. perspicillata (Spectacled Tyrant) **F**
FLUVICOLA
F. pica (Pied Water Tyrant) **E,F**
F. nengeta (Masked Water Tyrant) **F**
F. leucocephala (White-headed Marsh Tyrant) **F**
COLONIA
C. colonus (Long-tailed Tyrant) **E,F**
ALECTRURUS
A. tricolor (Cock-tailed Tyrant) **F**
A. risora (Strange-tailed Tyrant) **F**
GUBERNETES
G. yetapa (Streamer-tailed Tyrant) **F**
SATRAPA
S. icterophrys (Yellow-browed Tyrant) **F**
TUMBEZIA
T. salvini (Tumbes Tyrant) **F**
MUSCIGRALLA
M. brevicauda (Short-tailed Field Tyrant) **F**
HIRUNDINEA
H. ferruginea (Cliff Flycatcher) **F**
MACHETORNIS
M. rixosus (Cattle Tyrant) **F**
MUSCIPIPRA
M. vetula (Shear-tailed Gray Tyrant) **F**
ATTILA
A. phoenicurus (Rufous-tailed Attila) **F**
A. cinnamomeus (Cinnamon Attila) **F**
A. torridus (Ochraceous Attila) **F**
A. citriniventris (Citron-bellied Attila) **F**
A. bolivianus (Dull-capped Attila) **F**
A. rufus (Gray-hooded Attila) **F**
A. spadiceus (Bright-rumped Attila) **E,F**
CASIORNIS
C. rufa (Rufous Casiornis) **F**
C. fusca (Ash-throated Casiornis) **F**
RHYTIPTERNA
R. simplex (Grayish Mourner) **F**
R. immunda (Pale-bellied Mourner) **F**
R. holerythra (Rufous Mourner) **E,F**
LANIOCERA
L. hypopyrra (Cinereous Mourner) **F**
L. rufescens (Speckled Mourner) **E,F**

SIRYSTES
S. sibilator (Sirystes) **E,F**
MYIARCHUS
M. semirufus (Rufous Flycatcher) **F**
M. yucatanensis (Yucatan Flycatcher) **E**
M. barbirostris (Sad Flycatcher) **E**
M. tuberculifer (Dusky-capped Flycatcher) **A,E,F**
M. swainsoni (Swainson's Flycatcher) **F**
M. venezuelensis (Venezuelan Flycatcher) **E,F**
M. panamensis (Panama Flycatcher) **E,F**
M. ferox (Short-crested Flycatcher) **F**
M. apicalis (Apical Flycatcher) **F**
M. cephalotes (Pale-edged Flycatcher) **F**
M. phaeocephalus (Sooty-crowned Flycatcher) **F**
M. cinerascens (Ash-throated Flycatcher) **A,E**
M. nuttingi (Pale-throated Flycatcher) **E**
M. crinitus (Great Crested Flycatcher) **A,E**
M. tyrannulus (Brown Crested Flycatcher) **A,E,F**
M. magnirostris (Galapagos Flycatcher) **G**
M. nugator (Grenada Flycatcher) **E**
M. validus (Rufous-tailed Flycatcher) **E**
M. antillarum (Puerto Rican Flycatcher) **E**
M. sagrae (La Sagra's Flycatcher) **E**
M. stolidus (Stolid Flycatcher) **E**
M. oberi (Wied's Crested Flycatcher) **E**
DELTARHYNCHUS
D. flammulatus (Flammulated Flycatcher) **E**
PITANGUS
P. sulphuratus (Great Kiskadee) **E,F**
PHILOHYDOR
P. lictor (Lesser Kiskadee) **E,F**
MEGARHYNCHUS
M. pitangua (Boat-billed Flycatcher) **E,F**
MYIOZETETES
M. cayanensis (Rusty-margined Flycatcher) **E,F**
M. similis (Social Flycatcher) **E,F**
M. granadensis (Gray-capped Flycatcher) **E,F**
M. luteiventris (Dusky-chested Flycatcher) **F**
PHELPSIA
P. inornatus (White-bearded Flycatcher) **F**
CONOPIAS
C. parva (White-ringed Flycatcher) **E,F**
C. trivirgata (Three-striped Flycatcher) **F**
C. cinchoneti (Lemon-browed Flycatcher) **F**
MYIODYNASTES
M. hemichrysus (Golden-bellied Flycatcher) **E**
M. maculatus (Streaked Flycatcher) **E,F**
M. luteiventris (Sulfur-bellied Flycatcher) **A,E,F**
M. bairdi (Baird's Flycatcher) **F**
M. chrysocephalus (Golden-crowned Flycatcher) **F**
LEGATUS
L. leucophaius (Piratic Flycatcher) **E,F**
EMPIDONOMUS
E. varius (Variegated Flycatcher) **F**
GRISEOTYRANNUS
G. aurantioatrocristatus (Crowned Slaty Flycatcher) **F**
TYRANNOPSIS
T. sulphurea (Sulfury Flycatcher) **F**
TYRANNUS
T. niveigularis (Snowy-throated Kingbird) **F**
T. albogularis (White-throated Kingbird) **F**
T. melancholicus (Tropical Kingbird) **A,E,F**
T. couchii (Couch's Kingbird) **A,E**
T. vociferans (Cassin's Kingbird) **A,E**
T. crassirostris (Thick-billed Kingbird) **A,E**
T. verticalis (Western Kingbird) **A,E**
T. forficata (Scissor-tailed Flycatcher) **A,E**
T. savana (Fork-tailed Flycatcher) **E,F**
T. tyrannus (Eastern Kingbird) **A,E,F**
T. dominicensis (Gray Kingbird) **A,E,F**
T. caudifasciatus (Loggerhead Kingbird) **E**
T. cubensis (Giant Kingbird) **E**
XENOPSARIS
X. albinucha (White-naped Xenopsaris) **F**
PACHYRAMPHUS
P. viridis (Green-backed Becard) **F**
P. versicolor (Barred Becard) **E,F**
P. spodiurus (Slaty Becard) **F**
P. rufus (Cinereous Becard) **F**
P. castaneus (Chestnut-crowned Becard) **F**
P. cinnamomeus (Cinnamon Becard) **F**
P. polychopterus (White-winged Becard) **E,F**
P. marginatus (Black-capped Becard) **F**
P. albogriseus (Black & White Becard) **E,F**
P. major (Gray-collared Becard) **E**

P. surinamus (Glossy-backed Becard) **F**
P. aglaiae (Rose-throated Becard) **E**
P. homochrous (One-colored Becard) **E**
P. minor (Pink-throated Becard) **F**
P. validus (Plain Becard) **F**
P. niger (Jamaican Becard) **E**
TITYRA
T. cayana (Black-tailed Tityra) **F**
T. semifasciata (Masked Tityra) **E,F**
T. inquisitor (Black-crowned Tityra) **E,F**
110 OXYRUNCIDAE (SHARPBILL)
OXYRUNCUS
O. cristatus (Sharpbill) **E,F**
111 PHYTOTOMIDAE (PLANTCUTTERS)
PHYTOTOMA
P. rara (Rufous-tailed Plantcutter) **F**
P. rutila (Red-breasted Plantcutter) **F**
P. raimondii (Peruvian Plantcutter) **F**
112 PITTIDAE (PITTAS)
PITTA
P. phayrei (Phayre's Pitta) **I**
P. nipalensis (Blue-naped Pitta) **H,I**
P. soror (Blue-backed Pitta) **I**
P. oatesi (Fulvous Pitta) **I,J**
P. schneideri (Schneider's Pitta) **J**
P. caerulea (Giant Pitta) **I,J**
P. kochi (Koch's Pitta) **J**
P. erythrogaster (Red-breasted Pitta) **J,K,L,O**
P. arcuata (Blue-banded Pitta) **J**
P. granatina (Garnet Pitta) **J**
P. venusta (Black-crowned Garnet Pitta) **J**
P. cyanea (Blue Pitta) **H,I**
P. elliotii (Elliot's Pitta) **I**   [?]
P. guajana (Blue-tailed Pitta) **I,J**
P. gurneyi (Gurney's Pitta) **I**   [E]
P. baudi (Blue-headed Pitta) **J**   [?]
P. sordida (Hooded Pitta) **H,I,J,K,L**
P. brachyura (Blue-winged Pitta) **H**
P. nympha (Fairy Pitta) **B,I,J**   [?]
P. angolensis (African Pitta) **C**
P. reichenowi (Green-breasted Pitta) **C**
P. superba (Superb Pitta) **L**   [?]
P. maxima (Great Pitta) **K**
P. steerei (Steere's Pitta) **J**
P. moluccensis (Moluccan Pitta) **I,J,K**
P. versicolor (Noisy Pitta) **M**
P. elegans (Elegant Pitta) **J,K**
P. iris (Rainbow Pitta) **M**
P. anerythra (Black-faced Pitta) **O**   [?]
113 XENICIDAE (NEW ZEALAND WRENS)
ACANTHISITTA
A. chloris (Rifleman) **N**
XENICUS
X. longipes (Bush Wren) **N**   [E]
X. gilviventris (Rock Wren) **N**
114 PHILEPITTIDAE (ASITIES)
PHILEPITTA
P. castanea (Velvet Asity) **D**
P. schlegeli (Schlegel's Asity) **D**
NEODREPANIS
N. coruscans (Wattled False Sunbird) **D**
N. hypoxantha (Small-billed False Sunbird) **D**   [I]
115 MENURIDAE (LYREBIRDS)
MENURA
M. novaehollandiae (Superb Lyrebird) **M**
M. alberti (Prince Albert's Lyrebird) **M**
116 ATRICHORNITHIDAE (SCRUB-BIRDS)
ATRICHORNIS
A. clamosus (Western Scrub-bird) **M**   [E]
A. rufescens (Rufous Scrub-bird) **M**   [R]
117 ALAUDIDAE (LARKS)
MIRAFRA
M. javanica (Singing Bush Lark) **C,H,I,J,K,L,M**
M. hova (Hova Lark) **D**
M. cordofanica (Kordofan Bush Lark) **C**
M. williamsi (Marsabit Lark) **C**
M. cheniana (Southern Singing Bush Lark) **C**
M. albicauda (Northern White-tailed Bush Lark) **C**
M. passerina (Monotonous Lark) **C**
M. candida (Nyiro Bush Lark) **C**
M. pulpa (Friedmann's Bush Lark) **C**
M. ashi (Ash's Lark) **C**   [?]
M. hypermetra (Red-winged Bush Lark) **C**
M. somalica (Somali Long-billed Lark) **C**
M. africana (Rufous-naped Bush Lark) **C**
M. angolensis (Angolan Lark) **C**

M. rufocinnamomea (Flappet Lark) **C**
M. apiata (Clapper Lark) **C**
M. africanoides (Fawn-colored Bush Lark) **C**
M. ruddi (Long-clawed Lark) **C**
M. collaris (Collared Lark) **C**
M. assamica (Rufous-winged Bush Lark) **H,I**
M. rufa (Rusty Bush Lark) **C**
M. sidamoensis (Sidamo Bush Lark) **C**
M. gilletti (Gillett's Bush Lark) **C**
M. poecilosterna (Pink-breasted Lark) **C**
M. sabota (Sabota Lark) **C**
M. erythroptera (Red-winged Bush Lark) **H**
PINAROCORYS
P. nigricans (Dusky Bush Lark) **C**
P. erythropygia (Red-tailed Bush Lark) **C**
CERTHILAUDA
C. curvirostris (Long-billed Lark) **C**
C. chuana (Short-clawed Lark) **C**
C. erythrochlamys (Red Lark) **C**
C. albescens (Karoo Lark) **C**
C. albofasciata (Spike-heeled Lark) **C**
EREMOPTERIX
E. australis (Black-eared Finch Lark) **C**
E. leucotis (Chestnut-backed Finch Lark) **C**
E. signata (Chestnut-headed Finch Lark) **C**
E. verticalis (Gray-headed Finch Lark) **C**
E. nigriceps (Black-crowned Finch Lark) **C,H**
E. grisea (Ashy-crowned Finch Lark) **H**
E. leucopareia (Fischer's Finch Lark) **C**
AMMOMANES
A. cincturus (Bar-tailed Desert Lark) **C,H**
A. phoenicurus (Rufous-tailed Desert Lark) **H**
A. deserti (Desert Lark) **B,C,H**
A. dunni (Dunn's Lark) **C**
A. grayi (Gray's Lark) **C**
A. burra (Ferruginous Lark) **C**
ALAEMON
A. alaudipes (Hoopoe Lark) **B,C,H**
A. hamertoni (Lesser Hoopoe Lark) **C**
RAMPHOCORIS
R. clotbey (Thick-billed Lark) **B**
MELANOCORYPHA
M. calandra (Calandra Lark) **B**
M. bimaculata (Bimaculated Lark) **B,H**
M. mongolica (Mongolian Lark) **B**
M. maxima (Long-billed Calandra Lark) **B,H**
M. leucoptera (White-winged Lark) **B**
M. yeltoniensis (Black Lark) **B**
CALANDRELLA
C. razae (Raza Island Lark) **B**
C. cinerea (Short-toed Lark) **B,C,H,I**
C. blanfordi (Blanford's Lark) **C**
C. acutirostris (Hume's Short-toed Lark) **B,H**
C. raytal (Indian Sand Lark) **H,I**
C. rufescens (Lesser Short-toed Lark) **B,C**
C. cheleensis (Mongolian Short-toed Lark) **B**
SPIZOCORYS
S. conirostris (Pink-billed Lark) **C**
S. starki (Stark's Short-toed Lark) **C**
S. sclateri (Sclater's Short-toed Lark) **C**
S. obbiensis (Obbia Lark) **C**
S. personata (Masked Lark) **C**
BOTHA
B. fringillaris (Botha's Lark) **C**   [I]
CHERSOPHILUS
C. duponti (DuPont's Lark) **B**
PSEUDALAEMON
P. fremantlii (Short-tailed Lark) **C**
GALERIDA
G. cristata (Crested Lark) **B,C,H**
G. theklae (Thekla Lark) **B,C**
G. malabarica (Malabar Crested Lark) **H**
G. deva (Sykes' Crested Lark) **H**
G. modesta (Sun Lark) **C**
CALENDULA
C. magnirostris (Thick-billed Lark) **C**
LULLULA
L. arborea (Wood Lark) **B**
ALAUDA
A. arvensis (Sky Lark) **B,H**
A. gulgula (Oriental Sky Lark) **B,H,I,J**
EREMOPHILA
E. alpestris (Horned Lark) **A,B,E,F,H**
E. bilopha (Temminck's Horned Lark) **B**

118 HIRUNDINIDAE (SWALLOWS, MARTINS)
PSEUDOCHELIDONINAE
PSEUDOCHELIDON
P. eurystomina (African River Martin) **C**
P. sirintarae (White-eyed River Martin) **I**   I
HIRUNDININAE
TACHYCINETA
T. bicolor (Tree Swallow) **A,E**
T. albilinea (Mangrove Swallow) **E,F**
T. albiventer (White-winged Swallow) **F**
T. leucorrhoa (White-rumped Swallow) **F**
T. leucopyga (Chilean Swallow) **F**
T. thalassina (Violet-green Swallow) **A,E**
T. cyaneoviridis (Bahama Swallow) **E**
T. euchrysea (Golden Swallow) **E**
PHAEOPROGNE
P. tapera (Brown-chested Martin) **F**
PROGNE
P. subis (Purple Martin) **A,E,F**
P. cryptoleuca (Cuban Martin) **E**
P. dominicensis (Caribbean Martin) **E**
P. sinaloae (Sinaloa Martin) **E**
P. chalybea (Gray-breasted Martin) **A,E,F**
P. modesta (Southern Martin) **F,G**
NOTIOCHELIDON
N. murina (Brown-bellied Swallow) **F**
N. cyanoleuca (Blue & White Swallow) **E,F**
N. flavipes (Pale-footed Swallow) **F**
N. pileata (Black-capped Swallow) **E**
ATTICORA
A. fasciata (White-banded Swallow) **F**
A. melanoleuca (Black-collared Swallow) **F**
NEOCHELIDON
N. tibialis (White-thighed Swallow) **E,F**
ALOPOCHELIDON
A. fucata (Tawny-headed Swallow) **F**
STELGIDOPTERYX
S. serripennis (Northern Rough-winged Swallow)
A,E,F
S. ruficollis (Southern Rough-winged Swallow) **E,F**
CHERAMOECA
C. leucosterna (White-backed Swallow) **M**
RIPARIA
R. paludicola (African Sand Martin) **C,H,J**
R. congica (Congo Sand Martin) **C**
R. riparia (Bank Swallow) **A,B,C,F,H,I,J**
R. cincta (Banded Sand Martin) **C**
PHEDINA
P. borbonica (Mascarene Martin) **C,D**
PHEDINOPSIS
P. brazzae (Brazza's Martin) **C**
HIRUNDO
H. griseopyga (Gray-rumped Swallow) **C**
H. rupestris (Crag Martin) **B,H**
H. obsoleta (Pale Crag Martin) **B,C,H**
H. fuligula (African Rock Martin) **C**
H. concolor (Dusky Crag Martin) **H,I**
H. rustica (Barn Swallow) **A,B,C,E,F,H**
H. lucida (Red-chested Swallow) **C**
H. angolensis (Angola Swallow) **C**
H. tahitica (Pacific Swallow) **B,C,J,K,L,M,O**
H. albigularis (White-throated Swallow) **C**
H. aethiopica (Ethiopian Swallow) **C**
H. smithii (Wire-tailed Swallow) **C,H,I**
H. atrocaerulea (Blue Swallow) **C**
H. nigrita (White-throated Swallow) **C**
H. leucosoma (Pied-winged Swallow) **C**
H. megaensis (White-tailed Swallow) **C**   R
H. nigrorufa (Black & Rufous Swallow) **C**
H. dimidiata (Pearl-breasted Swallow) **C**
H. cucullata (Greater Striped Swallow) **C**
H. abyssinica (Lesser Striped Swallow) **C**
H. semirufa (Red-breasted Swallow) **C**
H. senegalensis (Mosque Swallow) **C**
H. daurica (Red-rumped Swallow) **B,C,H,I**
H. striolata (Greater Striated Swallow) **I,J,K,L**
H. rufigula (Red-throated Cliff Swallow) **C**
H. preussi (Preuss' Cliff Swallow) **C**
H. andecola (Andean Swallow) **F**
H. nigricans (Tree Martin) **K,M,O**
H. perdita (Red Sea Cliff Swallow) **C**   ?
H. spilodera (South African Cliff Swallow) **C**
H. pyrrhonota (American Cliff Swallow) **A,E,F**
H. fulva (Cave Swallow) **A,E**
H. fluvicola (Indian Cliff Swallow) **B,H**
H. ariel (Fairy Martin) **M**

H. fuliginosa (Dusky Cliff Swallow) **C**
DELICHON
D. urbica (House Martin) **B,C,H,I**
D. dasypus (Asian House Martin) **B,H,J**
D. nipalensis (Nepal House Martin) **H,I**
PSALIDOPROCNE
P. nitens (Square-tailed Saw-wing) **C**
P. fuliginosa (Cameroun Saw-wing) **C**
P. albiceps (White-headed Saw-wing) **C**
P. pristoptera (Black Saw-wing) **C**
P. oleaginea (Kaffa Saw-wing) **C**
P. antinorii (Brown Saw-wing) **C**
P. petiti (Petit's Saw-wing) **C**
P. orientalis (Eastern Saw-wing) **C**
P. obscura (Fantee Saw-wing) **C**
119 MOTACILLIDAE (WAGTAILS, PIPITS)
DENDRONANTHUS
D. indicus (Forest Wagtail) **B,H,I,J**
MOTACILLA
M. flava (Yellow Wagtail) **B,C,H,I,J,K**
M. citreola (Citrine Wagtail) **B,H,I**
M. cinerea (Gray Wagtail) **B,H,J**
M. alba (Pied Wagtail) **B,H,I,J**
M. grandis (Japanese Pied Wagtail) **B**
M. maderaspatensis (Large Pied Wagtail) **H**
M. aguimp (African Pied Wagtail) **C**
M. clara (Mountain Wagtail) **C**
M. capensis (Cape Wagtail) **C**
M. flaviventris (Madagascar Wagtail) **D**
TMETOTHYLACUS
T. tenellus (Golden Pipit) **C**
MACRONYX
M. capensis (Cape Longclaw) **C**
M. croceus (Yellow-throated Longclaw) **C**
M. fuelleborni (Fulleborn's Longclaw) **C**
M. flavicollis (Abyssinian Longclaw) **C**
M. aurantiigula (Pangani Longclaw) **C**
M. ameliae (Rosy-breasted Longclaw) **C**
M. grimwoodi (Grimwood's Longclaw) **C**
HEMIMACRONYX
H. sharpei (Sharpe's Longclaw) **C**
H. chloris (Yellow-breasted Pipit) **C**
ANTHUS
A. novaeseelandiae (Richard's Pipit) **B,C,H,I,J,K,**
l,M,N,O
A. godlewskii (Blyth's Pipit) **B,H,I**
A. campestris (Tawny Pipit) **B,H**
A. similis (Long-billed Pipit) **B,C,H,I**
A. nyassae (Woodland Pipit) **C**
A. vaalensis (Sandy Plain-backed Pipit) **C**
A. leucophrys (Dark Plain-backed Pipit) **C**
A. pallidiventris (Long-legged Pipit) **C**
A. pratensis (Meadow Pipit) **B**
A. trivialis (Tree Pipit) **B,C,H**
A. hodgsoni (Olive Tree Pipit) **B,H,J**
A. roseatus (Hodgson's Pipit) **B,H**
A. cervinus (Red-throated Pipit) **B,C,H**
A. gustavi (Pechora Pipit) **B,J,K**
A. rubescens (Buff-bellied Pipit) **A,B,E,H,I**
A. spinoletta (Water Pipit) **B**
A. petrosus (Rock Pipit) **B**
A. nilghiriensis (Nilgiri Pipit) **H**
A. sylvanus (Upland Pipit) **B,H**
A. berthelotii (Canarian Pipit) **B**
A. lineiventris (Striped Pipit) **C**
A. brachyurus (Short-tailed Pipit) **C**
A. caffer (Bushveld Pipit) **C**
A. latistriatus (Jackson's Pipit) **C**
A. sokokensis (Sokoke Pipit) **C**   V
A. melindae (Malindi Pipit) **C**
A. crenatus (Large Yellow-tufted Pipit) **C**
A. gutturalis (New Guinea Pipit) **L**
A. spragueii (Sprague's Pipit) **A,E**
A. furcatus (Short-billed Pipit) **F**
A. lutescens (Yellowish Pipit) **E,F**
A. chacoensis (Chaco Pipit) **F**   ?
A. correndera (Correndera Pipit) **F**
A. antarcticus (South Georgia Pipit) **Q**
A. nattereri (Ocher-breasted Pipit) **F**   ?
A. hellmayri (Hellmayr's Pipit) **F**
A. bogotensis (Paramo Pipit) **F**
120 CAMPEPHAGIDAE (CUCKOO-SHRIKES)
PTERODOCYS
P. maxima (Ground Cuckoo-Shrike) **M**

CORACINA
C. novaehollandiae (Black-faced Cuckoo-Shrike)
H,I,J,K,L,M
C. personata (Wallacean Cuckoo-Shrike) **J,K**
C. fortis (Buru Is Cuckoo-Shrike) **K**
C. atriceps (Moluccan Cuckoo-Shrike) **K**
C. schistacea (Slaty Cuckoo-Shrike) **K**
C. caledonica (Melanesian Cuckoo-Shrike) **O**
C. caeruleogrisea (Stout-billed Graybird) **K,L**
C. temminckii (Caerulean Cuckoo-Shrike) **K**
C. larvata (Black-faced Graybird) **J**
C. striata (Barred Cuckoo-Shrike) **I,J,K**
C. bicolor (Pied Cuckoo-Shrike) **K**
C. lineata (Lineated Cuckoo-Shrike) **K,L,M,O**
C. boyeri (White-lored Cuckoo-Shrike) **J,L**
C. leucopygia (White-rumped Cuckoo-Shrike) **K**
C. papuensis (Papuan Cuckoo-Shrike) **K,L,M,O**
C. robusta (Little Cuckoo-Shrike) **M**
C. longicauda (Black-hooded Graybird) **L**
C. parvula (Halmahera Cuckoo-Shrike) **K**
C. abbotti (Pygmy Cuckoo-Shrike) **K**
C. analis (Caledonian Graybird) **O**   ?
C. caesia (African Gray Cuckoo-Shrike) **C**
C. pectoralis (White-breasted Cuckoo-Shrike) **C**
C. graueri (Grauer's Cuckoo-Shrike) **C**
C. cinerea (Madagascar Cuckoo-Shrike) **D**
C. azurea (Blue Cuckoo-Shrike) **C**
C. typica (Mauritius Graybird) **D**   V
C. newtoni (Reunion Graybird) **D**   V
C. coerulescens (Philippine Black Graybird) **J**   ?
C. dohertyi (Sumba Cicadabird) **J,K**
C. dispar (Kei Cicadabird) **L**
C. tenuirostris (Common Cicadabird) **J,K,L,M,O**
C. sula (Sula Cicadabird) **J**
C. morio (Sulawesi Cicadabird) **K**
C. ceramensis (Pale Cicadabird) **K**
C. incerta (Philippine Cicadabird) **J,K,L**
C. ostentata (White-winged Cuckoo-Shrike) **J**
C. schisticeps (New Guinea Graybird) **L**
C. melaena (Black Graybird) **K,L**
C. montana (Black-bellied Graybird) **L**
C. holopolia (Black-bellied Cuckoo-Shrike) **O**
C. mcgregori (Sharp-tailed Graybird) **J**
C. panayensis (Philippines Graybird) **J**
C. polioptera (Indochinese Cuckoo-Shrike) **I**
C. melaschistos (Dark-gray Cuckoo-Shrike) **H,I**
C. fimbriata (Lesser Cuckoo-Shrike) **I,J**
C. melanoptera (Black-headed Cuckoo-Shrike) **H**
CAMPOCHAERA
C. sloetii (Orange Cuckoo-Shrike) **L**
CHLAMYDOCHAERA
C. jefferyi (Black-breasted Triller) **J**
LALAGE
L. melanoleuca (Black & White Triller) **J**
L. nigra (Pied Triller) **I,J,K**
L. sueurii (White-winged Triller) **J,K,L**
L. aurea (Red-bellied Triller) **K**
L. atrovirens (Black-browed Triller) **K,L**
L. leucomela (White-browed Triller) **J,K,L,M,O**
L. maculosa (Spotted Triller) **O**
L. sharpei (Samoan Triller) **O**
L. leucopyga (Long-tailed Triller) **O**
CAMPEPHAGA
C. sulphurata (African Black Cuckoo Shrike) **C**
C. phoenicea (Red-shouldered Cuckoo Shrike) **C**
C. petiti (Petit's Cuckoo Shrike) **C**
C. quiscalina (Purple-throated Cuckoo Shrike) **C**
C. lobata (Wattled Cuckoo Shrike) **C**   V
PERICROCOTUS
P. roseus (Rosy Minivet) **B,H,I**
P. divaricatus (Ashy Minivet) **B,J**
P. cinnamomeus (Small Minivet) **H,I,J,K**
P. lansbergei (Flores Minivet) **J**
P. erythropygius (Jerdon's Minivet) **H,I**
P. solaris (Yellow-throated Minivet) **I,J**
P. ethologus (Long-tailed Minivet) **B,H,I**
P. brevirostris (Short-billed Minivet) **H,I**
P. miniatus (Sunda Minivet) **J**
P. flammeus (Scarlet Minivet) **H,I,J**
HEMIPUS
H. picatus (Bar-winged Flycatcher Shrike) **H,I,J**
H. hirundinaceus (Black-winged Flycatcher Shrike)
J,K
TEPHRODORNIS
T. gularis (Brown-tailed Wood Shrike) **H,I,J**
T. pondicerianus (Common Wood Shrike) **H,I**

121 PYCNONOTIDAE (BULBULS)
SPIZIXOS
S. canifrons (Crested Finchbill) **H,I**
S. semitorques (Collared Finchbill) **J**
PYCNONOTUS
P. zeylanicus (Straw-crowned Bulbul) **J**
P. striatus (Striated Green Bulbul) **H,I**
P. leucogrammicus (Striated Bulbul) **J**
P. tympanistrigus (Olive-crowned Bulbul) **J**
P. melanoleucos (Black & White Bulbul) **J**
P. priocephalus (Gray-headed Bulbul) **H**
P. atriceps (Black-headed Bulbul) **H,I,J**
P. melanicterus (Black-crested Bulbul) **H,I,J**
P. squamatus (Scaly-breasted Bulbul) **J**
P. cyaniventris (Gray-bellied Bulbul) **J**
P. jocosus (Red-whiskered Bulbul) **H,I,J**
P. xanthorrhous (Anderson's Bulbul) **I**
P. sinensis (Chinese Bulbul) **B,I**
P. taivanus (Formosan Bulbul) **J**
P. leucogenys (White-cheeked Bulbul) **B,H**
P. cafer (Red-vented Bulbul) **H**
P. aurigaster (White-eared Bulbul) **B,I,J**
P. xanthopygos (Black-capped Bulbul) **B**
P. nigricans (Red-eyed Bulbul) **C**
P. capensis (Cape Bulbul) **C**
P. barbatus (Garden Bulbul) **C**
P. eutilotus (Puff-backed Bulbul) **J**
P. nieuwenhuisii (Blue-wattled Bulbul) **J** [?]
P. urostictus (Yellow-wattled Bulbul) **J**
P. bimaculatus (Orange-spotted Bulbul) **J**
P. finlaysoni (Stripe-throated Bulbul) **I,J**
P. xantholaemus (Yellow-throated Bulbul) **H**
P. penicillatus (Yellow-tufted Bulbul) **H**
P. flavescens (Flavescent Bulbul) **H,I,J**
P. goiavier (Yellow-vented Bulbul) **I,J,K**
P. luteolus (White-browed Bulbul) **H**
P. plumosus (Olive-brown Bulbul) **J,K**
P. blanfordi (Blanford's Olive Bulbul) **I,J**
P. simplex (White-eyed Brown Bulbul) **I,J**
P. brunneus (Red-eyed Brown Bulbul) **J**
P. erythrophthalmus (Lesser Brown Bulbul) **J**
P. masukuensis (Shelley's Greenbul) **C**
P. montanus (Mountain Little Greenbul) **C**
P. virens (Little Greenbul) **C**
P. hallae (Hall's Greenbul) **C**
P. gracilis (Little Gray Greenbul) **C**
P. ansorgei (Ansorge's Greenbul) **C**
P. curvirostris (Cameroun Somber Greenbul) **C**
P. importunus (Zanzibar Somber Greenbul) **C**
P. latirostris (Yellow-whiskered Greenbul) **C**
P. gracilirostris (Slender-billed Greenbul) **C**
P. tephrolaemus (Olive-breasted Mountain Greenbul)
C
P. milanjensis (Stripe-cheeked Greenbul) **C**
CALYPTOCICHLA
C. serina (Serine Greenbul) **C**
BAEOPOGON
B. indicator (Honeyguide Greenbul) **C**
B. clamans (Sjostedt's Honeyguide Greenbul) **C**
IXONOTUS
I. guttatus (Spotted Greenbul) **C**
CHLOROCICHLA
C. falkensteini (Yellow-necked Greenbul) **C**
C. simplex (Simple Greenbul) **C**
C. flavicollis (Yellow-throated Leaflove) **C**
C. flaviventris (Yellow-bellied Greenbul) **C**
C. laetissima (Joyful Greenbul) **C**
C. prigoginei (Prigogine's Greenbul) **C** [V]
THESCELOCICHLA
T. leucopleura (Swamp Bulbul) **C**
PHYLLASTREPHUS
P. scandens (Leaflove) **C**
P. terrestris (Bristle-necked Brownbul) **C**
P. strepitans (Northern Brownbul) **C**
P. cerviniventris (Gray Olive Greenbul) **C**
P. fulviventris (Pale Olive Greenbul) **C**
P. poensis (Cameroun Olive Greenbul) **C**
P. baumanni (Toro Olive Greenbul) **C**
P. poliocephalus (Gray-headed Greenbul) **C**
P. flavostriatus (Yellow-streaked Greenbul) **C**
P. debilis (Slender Greenbul) **C**
P. lorenzi (Sassi's Olive Greenbul) **C**
P. albigularis (White-throated Greenbul) **C**
P. fischeri (Fischer's Greenbul) **C**
P. cabanisi (Cabanis' Greenbul) **C**
P. placidus (Olive Mountain Greenbul) **C**

P. icterinus (Icterine Greenbul) **C**
P. xavieri (Xavier's Greenbul) **C**
P. leucolepis (Spot-winged Greenbul) **C**
P. madagascariensis (Madagascar Tetraka) **D**
P. zosterops (Short-billed Tetraka) **D**
P. apperti (Appert's Tetraka) **D** [R]
P. tenebrosus (Dusky Tetraka) **D** [R]
P. cinereiceps (Gray-crowned Greenbul) **C**
BLEDA
B. syndactyla (Common Bristle-Bill) **C**
B. eximia (Green-tailed Bristle-Bill) **C**
B. canicapilla (Gray-headed Bristle-Bill) **C**
NICATOR
N. chloris (Western Nicator) **C**
N. gularis (Eastern Nicator) **C**
N. vireo (Yellow-throated Nicator) **C**
CRINIGER
C. barbatus (Bearded Greenbul) **C**
C. calurus (Red-tailed Greenbul) **C**
C. ndussumensis (White-bearded Bulbul) **C**
C. olivaceus (Yellow-throated Olive Bulbul) **C** [V]
C. finschii (Finsch's Bearded Bulbul) **J**
C. flaveolus (Ashy-fronted Bearded Bulbul) **H,I**
C. pallidus (Olivaceous Bearded Bulbul) **I**
C. ochraceus (Ochraceous Bearded Bulbul) **I,J**
C. bres (Gray-cheeked Bearded Bulbul) **J**
C. phaeocephalus (Gray-headed Bearded Bulbul) **J**
SETORNIS
S. criniger (Long-billed Bulbul) **J**
HYPSIPETES
H. viridescens (Blyth's Olive Bulbul) **H,I**
H. propinquus (Gray-eyed Bulbul) **I,J**
H. charlottae (Crested Olive Bulbul) **J**
H. palawanensis (Golden-eyed Bulbul) **J**
H. criniger (Hairy-backed Bulbul) **J**
H. philippinus (Rufous-breasted Bulbul) **J**
H. siquijorensis (Slaty-crowned Bulbul) **J** [?]
H. everetti (Yellow-washed Bulbul) **J**
H. affinis (Golden Bulbul) **J,K**
H. indicus (Golden-browed Bulbul) **H**
H. mcclellandii (Mountain Streaked Bulbul) **H,I,J**
H. malaccensis (Green-backed Bulbul) **I,J**
H. virescens (Sumatran Bulbul) **J**
H. flavalus (Ashy Bulbul) **I,J**
H. amaurotis (Chestnut-eared Bulbul) **B,J**
H. crassirostris (Thick-billed Bulbul) **D**
H. borbonicus (Reunion Bulbul) **D**
H. madagascariensis (Black Bulbul) **D,H,I**
H. nicobariensis (Nicobar Bulbul) **I**
H. thompsoni (Bingham's Bulbul) **I**
MALIA
M. grata (Malia) **K**
NEOLESTES
N. torquatus (Black-collared Bulbul) **C**
TYLAS
T. eduardi (Kinkimavo) **D**
122 CHLOROPSEIDAE (LEAFBIRDS)
AEGITHINA
A. tiphia (Common Iora) **H,I,J**
A. nigrolutea (Marshall's Iora) **H**
A. viridissima (Green Iora) **I,J**
A. lafresnayei (Great Iora) **I,J**
CHLOROPSIS
C. flavipennis (Yellow-quilled Leafbird) **J**
C. palawanensis (Palawan Leafbird) **J**
C. sonnerati (Greater Green Leafbird) **I,J**
C. cyanopogon (Lesser Green Leafbird) **I,J**
C. cochinchinensis (Blue-winged Leafbird) **H,I,J**
C. aurifrons (Golden-fronted Leafbird) **H,I,J**
C. hardwickei (Orange-bellied Leafbird) **H,I,J**
C. venusta (Blue-mantled Leafbird) **J**
123 IRENIDAE (FAIRY BLUEBIRDS)
IRENA
I. puella (Blue-backed Fairy Bluebird) **H,I,J**
I. cyanogaster (Black-mantled Fairy Bluebird) **J**
124 LANIIDAE (SHRIKES)
MALACONOTINAE
LANIOTURDUS
L. torquatus (Chat-Shrike) **C**
NILAUS
N. afer (Brubru Shrike) **C**
DRYOSCOPUS
D. pringlii (Pringle's Puffback) **C**
D. gambensis (Puffback) **C**
D. cubla (Black-backed Puffback) **C**
D. senegalensis (Red-eyed Puffback) **C**

D. angolensis (Pink-footed Puffback) **C**
D. sabini (Sabine's Puffback) **C**
TCHAGRA
T. minuta (Lesser Tchagra) **C**
T. senegala (Black-headed Tchagra) **B,C**
T. tchagra (Levaillant's Tchagra) **C**
T. australis (Brown-headed Tchagra) **C**
T. jamesi (Three-streaked Tchagra) **C**
T. cruenta (Rosy-patched Shrike) **C**
LANIARIUS
L. ruficeps (Red-crowned Bush Shrike) **C**
L. luhderi (Luhder's Bush Shrike) **C**
L. turatii (Turati's Boubou) **C**
L. aethiopicus (Tropical Boubou) **C**
L. bicolor (Gabon Boubou) **C**
L. ferrugineus (Southern Boubou) **C**
L. barbarus (Common Gonolek) **C**
L. erythrogaster (Black-headed Gonolek) **C**
L. mufumbiri (Mufumbiri Shrike) **C**
L. atrococcineus (Burchell's Gonolek) **C**
L. atroflavus (Yellow-breasted Boubou) **C**
L. fuelleborni (Fulleborn's Black Boubou) **C**
L. funebris (Slate-colored Boubou) **C**
L. leucorhynchus (Sooty Boubou) **C**
TELOPHORUS
T. bocagei (Gray-green Bush Shrike) **C**
T. sulfureopectus (Sulfur-breasted Bush Shrike) **C**
T. olivaceus (Olive Bush Shrike) **C**
T. nigrifrons (Black-fronted Bush Shrike) **C**
T. multicolor (Many-colored Bush Shrike) **C**
T. kupeensis (Serle's Bush Shrike) **C**
T. zeylonus (Bokmakierie Shrike) **C**
T. viridis (Perrin's Bush Shrike) **C**
T. quadricolor (Four-colored Bush Shrike) **C**
T. dohertyi (Doherty's Bush Shrike) **C**
MALACONOTUS
M. cruentus (Fiery-breasted Bush Shrike) **C**
M. lagdeni (Lagden's Bush Shrike) **C**
M. gladiator (Green-breasted Bush Shrike) **C** [R]
M. blanchoti (Gray-headed Bush Shrike) **C**
M. monteiri (Monteiro's Bush Shrike) **C** [I]
M. alius (Black-cap Bush Shrike) **C** [R]
LANIINAE
CORVINELLA
C. corvina (Yellow-billed Shrike) **C**
C. melanoleuca (Magpie Shrike) **C**
LANIUS
L. tigrinus (Tiger Shrike) **B,J,K**
L. souzae (Souza's Shrike) **C**
L. bucephalus (Bull-headed Shrike) **B**
L. cristatus (Brown Shrike) **B,H,I,J,K**
L. collurio (Red-backed Shrike) **B,C,H**
L. collurioides (Burmese Shrike) **H,I**
L. gubernator (Emin's Shrike) **C**
L. vittatus (Bay-backed Shrike) **B,H**
L. schach (Long-tailed Shrike) **H,J,K,L**
L. validirostris (Strong-billed Shrike) **J**
L. mackinnoni (Mackinnon's Shrike) **C**
L. minor (Lesser Gray Shrike) **B,C**
L. ludovicianus (Loggerhead Shrike) **A,E**
L. excubitor (Northern Shrike) **A,B,C,H**
L. excubitoroides (Gray-backed Fiscal) **C**
L. sphenocercus (Chinese Great Gray Shrike) **B**
L. cabanisi (Long-tailed Fiscal) **C**
L. dorsalis (Taita Fiscal) **C**
L. somalicus (Somali Fiscal) **C**
L. collaris (Fiscal Shrike) **C**
L. newtoni (Newton's Fiscal) **C** [I]
L. senator (Woodchat Shrike) **C**
L. nubicus (Masked Shrike) **B**
125 PITYRIASIDAE (BORNEAN BRISTLEHEAD)
PITYRIASIS
P. gymnocephala (Bornean Bristlehead) **J**
126 PRIONOPIDAE (HELMET SHRIKES)
EUROCEPHALUS
E. ruppelli (Ruppell's White-crowned Shrike) **C**
E. anguitimens (White-crowned Shrike) **C**
PRIONOPS
P. plumata (Long-crested Helmet Shrike) **C**
P. poliolopha (Gray-crested Helmet Shrike) **C**
P. caniceps (Red-billed Helmet Shrike) **C**
P. alberti (Yellow-crested Helmet Shrike) **C**
P. retzii (Retz's Red-billed Helmet Shrike) **C**
P. gabela (Rand's Red-billed Helmet Shrike) **C** [I]
P. scopifrons (Chestnut-fronted Helmet Shrike) **C**

127 VANGIDAE (VANGA SHRIKES)
CALICALICUS
C. madagascariensis (Red-tailed Vanga) **D**
SCHETBA
S. rufa (Rufous Vanga) **D**
VANGA
V. curvirostris (Hook-billed Vanga) **D**
XENOPIROSTRIS
X. xenopirostris (Lafresnaye's Vanga) **D**
X. damii (Van Dam's Vanga) **D**   R
X. polleni (Pollen's Vanga) **D**   R
FALCULEA
F. palliata (Sicklebill) **D**
ARTAMELLA
A. viridis (White-headed Vanga) **D**
LEPTOPTERUS
L. chabert (Chabert Vanga) **D**
L. madagascarinus (Blue Vanga) **D**
ORIOLIA
O. bernieri (Bernier's Vanga) **D**
EURYCEROS
E. prevostii (Helmet Bird) **D**
HYPOSITTA
H. corallirostris (Coral-billed Nuthatch) **D**
128 BOMBYCILLIDAE (WAXWINGS)
BOMBYCILLINAE
BOMBYCILLA
B. garrulus (Bohemian Waxwing) **A,B**
B. japonica (Japanese Waxwing) **B**
B. cedrorum (Cedar Waxwing) **A,E,F**
PTILOGONATINAE
PTILOGONYS
P. cinereus (Gray Silky Flycatcher) **E**
P. caudatus (Long-tailed Silky Flycatcher) **E**
PHAINOPEPLA
P. nitens (Phainopepla) **A,E**
PHAINOPTILA
P. melanoxantha (Black & Yellow Silky Flycatcher) **E**
HYPOCOLIINAE
HYPOCOLIUS
H. ampelinus (Gray Hypocolius) **B**
129 DULIDAE (PALMCHAT)
DULUS
D. dominicus (Palmchat) **E**
130 CINCLIDAE (DIPPERS)
CINCLUS
C. cinclus (White-throated (Dipper)) **B,H**
C. pallasii (Brown Dipper) **C,H,I**
C. mexicanus (North American Dipper) **A,E**
C. leucocephalus (White-capped Dipper) **F**
C. schulzi (Rufous-throated Dipper) **F**   I
131 TROGLODYTIDAE (WRENS)
DONACOBIUS
D. atricapillus (Black-capped Donacobius) **F**
CAMPYLORHYNCHUS
C. jocosus (Boucard's Wren) **E**
C. gularis (Spotted Wren) **E**
C. yucatanicus (Yucatan Cactus-Wren) **E**
C. brunneicapillus (Cactus-Wren) **A,E**
C. chiapensis (Giant Wren) **E**
C. griseus (Bicolored Wren) **F**
C. rufinucha (Rufous-naped Wren) **E**
C. turdinus (Thrush-like Wren) **F**
C. albobrunneus (White-headed Wren) **E,F**
C. nuchalis (Stripe-backed Wren) **F**
C. fasciatus (Fasciated Wren) **F**
C. zonatus (Banded-backed Wren) **E,F**
C. megalopterus (Gray-barred Wren) **E**
ODONTORCHILUS
O. cinereus (Tooth-billed Wren) **F**
O. branickii (Gray-mantled Wren) **F**
SALPINCTES
S. obsoletus (Rock Wren) **A,E**
CATHERPES
C. mexicanus (Canyon Wren) **A**
HYLORCHILUS
H. sumichrasti (Slender-billed Wren) **E**   ?
CINNYCERTHIA
C. unirufa (Rufous Wren) **F**
C. peruana (Sepia-brown Wren) **F**
CISTOTHORUS
C. platensis (Sedge Wren) **A,E,F**
C. meridae (Paramo Wren) **F**
C. apolinari (Apolinar's Wren) **F**   V
C. palustris (Marsh Wren) **A,E**

THRYOMANES
T. bewickii (Bewick's Wren) **A,E**
T. sissonii (Revillagigedo Wren) **E**
FERMINIA
F. cerverai (Zapata Wren) **E**   R
THRYOTHORUS
T. atrogularis (Black-throated Wren) **E**
T. spadix (Sooty-headed Wren) **E,F**
T. fasciatoventris (Black-bellied Wren) **E,F**
T. euophrys (Plain-tailed Wren) **F**
T. eisenmanni (Inca Wren) **F**
T. genibarbis (Moustached Wren) **F**
T. coraya (Coraya Wren) **F**
T. felix (Happy Wren) **E**
T. maculipectus (Spot-breasted Wren) **E**
T. rutilus (Rufous-breasted Wren) **E,F**
T. semibadius (Riverside Wren) **E**
T. nigricapillus (Bay Wren) **E,F**
T. thoracicus (Stripe-breasted Wren) **E**
T. leucopogon (Stripe-throated Wren) **E,F**
T. pleurostictus (Banded Wren) **E**
T. ludovicianus (Carolina Wren) **A,E**
T. rufalbus (Rufous & White Wren) **E,F**
T. nicefori (Niceforo's Wren) **F**
T. sinaloa (Bar-vented Wren) **E**
T. modestus (Plain Wren) **E**
T. leucotis (Buff-breasted Wren) **E,F**
T. superciliaris (Superciliated Wren) **F**
T. guarayanus (Fawn-breasted Wren) **F**
T. longirostris (Long-billed Wren) **F**
T. griseus (Gray Wren) **F**
TROGLODYTES
T. troglodytes (Winter Wren) **A,B,H,I**
T. tanneri (Clarion Wren) **E**
T. aedon (House Wren) **A,E,F**
T. solstitialis (Mountain Wren) **E,F**
T. rufulus (Tepui Wren) **F**
THRYORCHILUS
T. browni (Timberline Wren) **E**
UROPSILA
U. leucogastra (White-bellied Wren) **E**
HENICORHINA
H. leucosticta (White-breasted Wood Wren) **E,F**
H. leucophrys (Gray-breasted Wood Wren) **E,F**
H. leucoptera (Bar-winged Wood Wren) **F**
MICROCERCULUS
M. philomela (Nightingale Wren) **F**
M. marginatus (Scaly-breasted Wren) **F**
M. ustulatus (Flutist Wren) **F**
M. bambla (Wing-banded Wren) **F**
CYPHORINUS
C. thoracicus (Chestnut-breasted Wren) **F**
C. aradus (Musician Wren) **E,F**
132 MIMIDAE (MOCKINGBIRDS, THRASHERS)
DUMETELLA
D. carolinensis (Gray Catbird) **A,E**
MELANOPTILA
M. glabrirostris (Black Catbird) **E**
MELANOTIS
M. caerulescens (Blue Mockingbird) **E**
M. hypoleucus (Blue & White Mockingbird) **E**
MIMUS
M. polyglottos (Northern Mockingbird) **A,E**
M. gilvus (Tropical Mockingbird) **E,F**
M. gundlachii (Bahama Mockingbird) **E**
M. thenca (Chilean Mockingbird) **F**
M. longicaudatus (Long-tailed Mockingbird) **F**
M. saturninus (Chalk-browed Mockingbird) **F**
M. patagonicus (Patagonian Mockingbird) **F**
M. triurus (White-banded Mockingbird) **F**
M. dorsalis (Brown-backed Mockingbird) **F**
NESOMIMUS
N. trifasciatus (Galapagos Mockingbird) **G**
MIMODES
M. graysoni (Socorro Thrasher) **E**   ?
OREOSCOPTES
O. montanus (Sage Thrasher) **A,E**
TOXOSTOMA
T. rufum (Brown Thrasher) **A**
T. longirostre (Long-billed Thrasher) **E**
T. guttatum (Cozumel Thrasher) **E**
T. cinereum (Gray Thrasher) **E**
T. bendirei (Bendire Thrasher) **A,E**
T. ocellatum (Ocellated Thrasher) **E**
T. curvirostre (Curve-billed Thrasher) **A,E**
T. lecontei (Le Conte Thrasher) **A,E**

T. redivivum (California Thrasher) **A,E**
T. dorsale (Crissal Thrasher) **A,E**
CINCLOCERTHIA
C. ruficauda (Brown Trembler) **E**
RAMPHOCINCLUS
R. brachyurus (White-breasted Trembler) **E**   E
ALLENIA
A. fusca (Scaly-breasted Thrasher) **E**
MARGAROPS
M. fuscatus (Pearly-eyed Thrasher) **E**
133 PRUNELLIDAE (ACCENTORS)
PRUNELLA
P. collaris (Alpine Accentor) **B,H**
P. himalayana (Himalayan Accentor) **B,H**
P. rubeculoides (Robin Accentor) **B,H**
P. strophiata (Rufous-breasted Accentor) **H,I**
P. montanella (Siberian Accentor) **B**
P. fulvescens (Brown Accentor) **B,H**
P. ocularis (Radde's Accentor) **B**
P. atrogularis (Black-throated Accentor) **B,H**
P. koslowi (Koslov's Accentor) **B**
P. modularis (Dunnock) (Hedge Accentor) **B**
P. rubida (Japanese Hedge Sparrow) **B**
P. immaculata (Maroon-backed Accentor) **B,I**
134 TURDIDAE (THRUSHES, CHATS)
BRACHYPTERYX
B. stellata (Gould's Shortwing) **I**
B. hyperythra (Rusty-bellied Shortwing) **H,I**   ?
B. major (White-bellied Shortwing) **H**
B. leucophrys (Lesser Shortwing) **I,J,K**
B. montana (Blue Shortwing) **B,I,J**
HEINRICHIA
H. calligyna (Sulawesi Shortwing) **K**
ERYTHROPYGIA
E. coryphaea (Karoo Scrub-Robin) **C**
E. leucoptera (White-winged Scrub-Robin) **C**
E. leucophrys (White-browed Scrub-Robin) **C**
E. zambesiana (Red-backed Scrub-Robin) **C**
E. hartlaubi (Brown-backed Scrub-Robin) **C**
E. galactotes (Rufous Scrub-Robin) **B,C,H**
E. paena (Kalahari Sandy Scrub-Robin) **C**
E. leucosticta (Western Bearded Scrub-Robin) **C**
E. quadrivirgata (Eastern Bearded Scrub-Robin) **C**
E. barbata (Central Bearded Scrub-Robin) **C**
E. signata (Brown Scrub-Robin) **C**
NAMIBORNIS
N. herero (Herero Chat) **C**
CERCOTRICHAS
C. podobe (Black Scrub-Robin) **C**
PINARORNIS
P. plumosus (Boulder Chat) **C**
CHAETOPS
C. frenatus (Cape Rockjumper) **C**
C. aurantius (Orange-breasted Rockjumper) **C**
DRYMODES
D. brunneopygia (Southern Scrub-Robin) **M**
D. superciliaris (Northern Scrub-Robin) **J,L,M**
POGONOCICHLA
P. stellata (Starred Robin) **C**
P. swynnertoni (Swynnerton's Bush-Robin) **C**
SHEPPARDIA
S. gabela (Gabela Akelat) **C**
S. cyornithopsis (Common Akelat) **C**
S. aequatorialis (Jackson's Akelat) **C**
S. erythrothorax (Forest Robin) **C**
S. sharpei (Sharpe's Akelat) **C**
S. gunningi (East Coast Akelat) **C**
ERITHACUS
E. rubecula (European Robin) **B**
E. akahige (Japanese Robin) **B**
E. komadori (Riukiu Robin) **B**
LUSCINIA
L. sibilans (Swinhoe's Robin) **B**
L. luscinia (Thrush Nightingale) **B,C**
L. megarhynchos (Nightingale) **B,C**
L. calliope (Siberian Rubythroat) **B,H**
L. svecica (Bluethroat) **B,H**
L. pectoralis (Himalayan Rubythroat) **B,H,I**
L. ruficeps (Rufous-headed Robin) **B**   ?
L. obscura (Black-throated Blue Robin) **B**   ?
L. pectardens (David's Rubythroat) **B**
L. brunnea (Indian Bluechat) **H,I**
L. cyane (Siberian Blue Robin) **B,I,J**
TARSIGER
T. cyanurus (Red-flanked Bluetail) **B,H,I**
T. chrysaeus (Golden Bush Robin) **B,H,I**

T. indicus (White-browed Bush Robin) **H,I**
T. hyperythrus (Rufous-breasted Bush Robin) **H,I**
T. johnstoniae (Collared Bush Robin) **J**
COSSYPHA
C. roberti (White-bellied Robin Chat) **C**
C. natalensis (Red-capped Robin Chat) **C**
C. dichroa (Chorister Robin Chat) **C**
C. semirufa (Black-tailed Robin Chat) **C**
C. heuglini (White-browed Robin Chat) **C**
C. cyanocampter (Blue-shouldered Robin Chat) **C**
C. caffra (Cape Robin Chat) **C**
C. humeralis (White-throated Robin Chat) **C**
C. ansorgei (Ansorge's Robin Chat) **C**
C. niveicapilla (Snowy-headed Robin Chat) **C**
C. heinrichi (Rand's Robin Chat) **C**   ☐ I
C. albicapilla (White-crowned Robin Chat) **C**
DRYOCICHLOIDES
D. anomala (Olive-flanked Robin Chat) **C**
D. bocagei (Gray-headed Robin Chat) **C**
D. insulana (Rufous-cheeked Robin Chat) **C**
D. polioptera (Gray-winged Robin Chat) **C**
D. archeri (Archer's Robin Chat) **C**
D. isabellae (Mountain Robin Chat) **C**
D. montana (Usambara Robin Chat) **C**   ☐ R
D. lowei (Iringa Robin Chat) **C**   ☐ R
MODULATRIX
M. stictigula (Spot Throat) **C**
ARCANATOR
A. orostruthus (Dappled Mountain Robin) **C**
CICHLADUSA
C. guttata (Spotted Morning Warbler) **C**
C. arquata (Collared Morning Warbler) **C**
C. ruficauda (Red-tailed Morning Warbler) **C**
ALETHE
A. diademata (White-tailed Alethe) **C**
A. castanea (Fire-crested Alethe) **C**
A. poliophrys (Red-throated Alethe) **C**
A. fuelleborni (White-chested Alethe) **C**
A. poliocephala (Brown-chested Alethe) **C**
A. choloensis (Cholo Mountain Alethe) **C**   ☐ E
COPSYCHUS
C. saularis (Asian Magpie-Robin) **H,I,J,K**
C. sechellarum (Seychelles Magpie Robin) **D**   ☐ E
C. albospecularis (Madagascar Magpie Robin) **D**
C. malabaricus (White-rumped Shama) **H,I,J**
C. stricklandii (Strickland's Shama) **J**
C. luzoniensis (White-browed Shama) **J**
C. niger (Black Shama) **J**
C. pyrrhopygus (Orange-tailed Shama) **J**
IRANIA
I. gutturalis (White-throated Robin) **B,C**
PHOENICURUS
P. alaschanicus (Przewalski's Redstart) **B**
P. erythronotus (Eversmann's Redstart) **B,H**
P. caeruleocephalus (Blue-headed Redstart) **B**
P. ochruros (Black Redstart) **B,H,I**
P. phoenicurus (Common Redstart) **B,C**
P. hodgsoni (Hodgson's Redstart) **B,H,I**
P. frontalis (Blue-fronted Redstart) **H,I**
P. fuliginosus (Plumbeous Water Redstart) **B,H,I**
P. leucocephalus (White-capped Redstart) **B,H,I**
P. schisticeps (White-throated Redstart) **B,H,I**
P. auroreus (Daurian Redstart) **B,H,I**
P. moussieri (Moussier's Redstart) **B**
P. erythrogaster (Guldenstadt's Redstart) **B,H**
RHYACORNIS
R. bicolor (Philippine Water Redstart) **J**   ☐ ?
HODGSONIUS
H. phaenicuroides (White-bellied Redstart) **H,I**
CINCLIDIUM
C. leucurum (White-tailed Blue Robin) **H,I,J**
C. diana (Sunda Blue Robin) **J**
C. frontale (Blue-fronted Callene) **H,I**   ☐ ?
GRANDALA
G. coelicolor (Hodgson's Grandala) **B,H,I**
SIALIA
S. sialis (Eastern Bluebird) **A,E**
S. mexicana (Western Bluebird) **A,E**
S. currucoides (Mountain Bluebird) **A,E**
ENICURUS
E. scouleri (Little Forktail) **B,H,J**
E. velatus (Lesser Forktail) **J**
E. ruficapillus (Chestnut-backed Forktail) **I,J**
E. immaculatus (Black-backed Forktail) **I,J**
E. schistaceus (Slaty-backed Forktail) **I,J**
E. leschenaulti (White-crowned Forktail) **H,I,J**

E. maculatus (Spotted Forktail) **H,I**
COCHOA
C. purpurea (Purple Cochoa) **H,I**
C. viridis (Green Cochoa) **H,I**   ☐ ?
C. azurea (Malaysian Cochoa) **J**   ☐ ?
C. beccarii (Sumatra Cochoa) **J**
MYADESTES
M. obscurus (Hawaiian Thrush) **P**
M. myadestinus (Large Kauai Thrush) **P**   ☐ ?
M. palmeri (Small Kauai Thrush) **P**   ☐ E
M. lanaiensis (Lanai Thrush) **P**   ☐ ?
M. townsendi (Townsend's Solitaire) **A,E**
M. occidentalis (Brown-backed Solitaire) **E**
M. elisabeth (Cuban Solitaire) **E**
M. genibarbis (Rufous-throated Solitaire) **E**
M. melanops (Black-faced Solitaire) **E**
M. coloratus (Varied Solitaire) **E**
M. ralloides (Andean Solitaire) **F**
M. unicolor (Slate-colored Solitaire) **E**
M. leucogenys (Rufous-brown Solitaire) **F**   ☐ ?
ENTOMODESTES
E. leucotis (White-eared Solitaire) **F**
E. coracinus (Black Solitaire) **F**
STIZORHINA
S. fraseri (Rufous Broad-billed Ant-thrush) **C**
S. finschii (Finsch's Broad-billed Ant-thrush) **C**
NEOCOSSYPHUS
N. rufus (Red-tailed Ant-thrush) **C**
N. poensis (White-tailed Ant-thrush) **C**
CERCOMELA
C. sinuata (Sicklewing Chat) **C**
C. familiaris (Familiar Chat) **C**
C. tractrac (Layard's Chat) **C**
C. schlegelii (Karoo Chat) **C**
C. fusca (Brown Rockchat) **H**
C. dubia (Somber Rockchat) **C**
C. melanura (Blackstart) **B,C**
C. scotocerca (Brown-tailed Rockchat) **C**
C. sordida (Hill Chat) **C**
SAXICOLA
S. rubetra (Whinchat) **B,C**
S. macrorhyncha (Stoliczka's Bushchat) **B,H**   ☐ ?
S. insignis (Hodgson's Bushchat) **B,H**   ☐ ?
S. dacotiae (Canary Islands Chat) **B**   ☐ R
S. torquata (Stonechat) **B,C,D,H,I**
S. leucura (White-tailed Stonechat) **H**
S. caprata (Pied Stonechat) **B,H,I,J,K,L,O**
S. jerdoni (Jerdon's Bushchat) **H,I**
S. ferrea (Gray Bushchat) **H,I**
S. gutturalis (White-bellied Bushchat) **J**
MYRMECOCICHLA
M. tholloni (Congo Moorchat) **C**
M. aethiops (Anteater Chat) **C**
M. formicivora (Southern Anteater Chat) **C**
M. nigra (Sooty Chat) **C**
M. arnoti (Arnot's Chat) **C**
M. albifrons (White-fronted Black Chat) **C**
M. melaena (Rüppell's Chat) **C**
THAMNOLAEA
T. cinnamomeiventris (Cliffchat) **C**
T. coronata (White-crowned Cliffchat) **C**
T. semirufa (White-winged Cliffchat) **C**
OENANTHE
O. bifasciata (Buff-streaked Chat) **C**
O. isabellina (Isabelline Wheatear) **B,C,H**
O. bottae (Red-breasted Wheatear) **C**
O. xanthoprymna (Red-tailed Wheatear) **B,H**
O. oenanthe (Northern Wheatear) **A,B,C**
O. phillipsi (Somali Wheatear) **C**
O. deserti (Desert Wheatear) **B,C,H**
O. hispanica (Black-eared Wheatear) **B,C**
O. finschii (Finsch's Wheatear) **B,H**
O. picata (Variable Wheatear) **B,H**
O. lugens (Mourning Wheatear) **B,C**
O. monacha (Hooded Wheatear) **B,H**
O. alboniger (Hume's Wheatear) **B,H**
O. pleschanka (Pied Wheatear) **B,C**
O. cypriaca (Cyprus Wheatear) **B,C**
O. leucopyga (White-tailed Black Wheatear) **C**
O. leucura (Black Wheatear) **B,C**
O. monticola (Mountain Chat) **C**
O. moesta (Red-rumped Wheatear) **B**
O. pileata (Capped Wheatear) **C**
SAXICOLOIDES
S. fulicata (Black-backed Robin) **H**

PSEUDOCOSSYPHUS
P. imerinus (Madagascar Robin Chat) **D**
P. bensoni (Farkas' Robin Chat) **D**
MONTICOLA
M. rupestris (Cape Rock Thrush) **C**
M. explorator (Sentinel Rock Thrush) **C**
M. brevipes (Short-toed Rock Thrush) **C**
M. rufocinereus (Little Rock Thrush) **C**
M. angolensis (Miombo Rock Thrush) **C**
M. saxatilis (Rock Thrush) **B,H**
M. cinclorhynchus (Blue-capped Rock Thrush) **H,I**
M. gularis (White-throated Rock Thrush) **B,I**
M. rufiventris (Chestnut-bellied Rock Thrush) **B,I**
M. solitarius (Blue Rock Thrush) **B,C,H,J,K,L**
MYIOPHONEUS
M. blighi (Ceylon Whistling Thrush) **H**   ☐ ?
M. melanurus (Shiny Whistling Thrush) **J**
M. glaucinus (Sunda Whistling Thrush) **J**
M. robinsoni (Malayan Whistling Thrush) **J**
M. horsfieldii (Malabar Whistling Thrush) **H**
M. insularis (Formosan Whistling Thrush) **I**
M. caeruleus (Blue Whistling Thrush) **B,H,I,J**
GEOMALIA
G. heinrichi (Sulawesi Mountain Thrush) **K**   ☐ ?
ZOOTHERA
Z. schistacea (Slaty-backed Ground Thrush) **L**   ☐ ?
Z. dumasi (Moluccan Ground Thrush) **K**
Z. interpres (Chestnut-capped Ground Thrush) **I,J**
Z. erythronota (Red-backed Ground Thrush) **K**   ☐ ?
Z. dohertyi (Chestnut-backed Ground Thrush) **J**
Z. wardii (Pied Ground Thrush) **H**
Z. cinerea (Ashy Ground Thrush) **J**
Z. peronii (Orange-banded Ground Thrush) **J,K**   ☐ ?
Z. citrina (Orange-headed Ground Thrush) **H,I,J**
Z. everetti (Everett's Ground Thrush) **J**   ☐ ?
Z. sibirica (Siberian Ground Thrush) **B,I,J**
Z. piaggiae (Abyssinian Ground Thrush) **C**
Z. tanganjicae (Western Orange Ground Thrush) **C**
Z. oberlaenderi (Forest Ground Thrush) **C**
Z. gurneyi (Orange Ground Thrush) **C**
Z. kibalensis (Prigogine's Ground Thrush) **C**
Z. cameronensis (Black-eared Ground Thrush) **C**
Z. princei (Gray Ground Thrush) **C**
Z. crossleyi (Crossley's Ground Thrush) **C**
Z. guttata (Spotted Ground Thrush) **C**
Z. spiloptera (Spotted-winged Thrush) **H**   ☐ ?
Z. andromedae (Sunda Ground Thrush) **J**
Z. mollissima (Plain-backed Mountain Thrush) **H,I**
Z. dixoni (Long-tailed Mountain Thrush) **I**
Z. dauma (White's Thrush) **B,H,I,J,O**
Z. machiki (Fawn-breasted Thrush) **L**   ☐ ?
Z. heinei (Russet-tailed Ground Thrush) **M**
Z. lunulata (Bassian Thrush) **M**
Z. talaseae (Melanesian Ground Thrush) **O**
Z. monticola (Greater Long-billed Thrush) **H,I**
Z. marginata (Lesser Long-billed Thrush) **H,I**
IXOREUS
I. naevius (Varied Thrush) **A**
RIDGWAYIA
R. pinicola (Aztec Thrush) **E**
AMALOCICHLA
A. sclateriana (Greater New Guinea Thrush) **L**
A. incerta (Lesser New Guinea Thrush) **L**
CATAPONERA
C. turdoides (Cataponera Thrush) **K**
NESOCICHLA
N. eremita (Tristan Thrush) **C**
CICHLHERMINIA
C. lherminieri (Forest Thrush) **E**
CATHARUS
C. gracilirostris (Slender-billed Nightingale Thrush) **E**
C. aurantiirostris (Orange-billed Nightingale Thrush) **E,F**
C. fuscater (Slaty-backed Nightingale Thrush) **E,F**
C. occidentalis (Russet Nightingale Thrush) **E**
C. frantzii (Frantzius' Nightingale Thrush) **E**
C. mexicanus (Black-headed Nightingale Thrush) **E**
C. dryas (Spotted Nightingale Thrush) **E,F**
C. fuscescens (Veery) **A,E**
C. minimus (Gray-cheeked Thrush) **A,E**
C. ustulatus (Swainson's Thrush) **A,E**
C. guttatus (Hermit Thrush) **A,E**
HYLOCICHLA
H. mustelina (Wood Thrush) **A,E**

PLATYCICHLA
P. flavipes (Yellow-legged Thrush) **F**
P. leucops (Pale-eyed Thrush) **F**
TURDUS
T. bewsheri (Comoro Thrush) **D**
T. olivaceofuscus (Sao Thomé Thrush) **C**
T. olivaceus (Olive Thrush) **C**
T. abyssinicus (Northern Olive Thrush) **C**
T. helleri (Taita Olive Thrush) **C**   **E**
T. libonyanus (Kurrichane Thrush) **C**
T. tephronotus (African Bare-eyed Thrush) **C**
T. menachensis (Yemen Thrush) **C**   ?
T. ludoviciae (Somali Blackbird) **C**
T. litsipsirupa (Groundscraper Thrush) **C**
T. dissimilis (Black-breasted Thrush) **B,H,I**
T. unicolor (Tickell's Thrush) **H**
T. cardis (Japanese Gray Thrush) **B,I**
T. albocinctus (White-collared Blackbird) **I**
T. torquatus (Ring Ouzel) **B**
T. boulboul (Gray-winged Blackbird) **H,I**
T. merula (Blackbird) **B,H**
T. poliocephalus (Island Thrush) **J,K,L,O**
T. chrysolaus (Red-billed Thrush) **B,J**
T. celaenops (Seven Islands Thrush) **B**
T. rubrocanus (Gray-headed Thrush) **H,I**
T. kessleri (Kessler's Thrush) **B**
T. feae (Fea's Thrush) **B,I**   ?
T. pallidus (Pale Thrush) **B,I**
T. obscurus (Eye-browed Thrush) **B,I**
T. ruficollis (Black-throated Thrush) **B,H,I**
T. naumanni (Dusky Thrush) **B,I**
T. pilaris (Fieldfare) **B**
T. iliacus (Redwing) **B**
T. philomelos (Song Thrush) **B**
T. mupinensis (Mongolian Song Thrush) **B**
T. viscivorus (Mistle Thrush) **B,H**
T. aurantius (White-chinned Thrush) **E**
T. ravidus (Grand Cayman Thrush) **E**
T. plumbeus (Red-legged Thrush) **E**
T. chiguanco (Chiguanco Thrush) **F**
T. nigrescens (Sooty Robin) **E**
T. fuscater (Great Thrush) **F**
T. infuscatus (Black Robin) **E**
T. serranus (Glossy-black Thrush) **E,F**
T. nigriceps (Slaty Thrush) **F**
T. reevei (Plumbeous-backed Thrush) **F**
T. olivater (Black-hooded Thrush) **F**
T. maranonicus (Maranon Thrush) **F**
T. fulviventris (Chestnut-bellied Thrush) **F**
T. rufiventris (Rufous-bellied Thrush) **F**
T. falcklandii (Austral Thrush) **F**
T. leucomelas (Pale-breasted Thrush) **F**
T. amaurochalinus (Creamy-bellied Thrush) **F**
T. plebejus (Mountain Robin) **F**
T. ignobilis (Black-billed Thrush) **F**
T. lawrencii (Lawrence's Thrush) **F**
T. fumigatus (Cocoa Thrush) **F**
T. personus (Lesser Antillean Thrush) **E**
T. obsoletus (Pale-vented Thrush) **F**
T. haplochrous (Unicolored Thrush) **F**
T. grayi (Clay-colored Thrush) **E,F**
T. nudigenis (Bare-eyed Thrush) **E,F**
T. jamaicensis (White-eyed Thrush) **E**
T. albicollis (White-necked Thrush) **E,F**
T. rufopalliatus (Rufous-backed Robin) **E**
T. swalesi (La Selle Thrush) **E**
T. rufitorques (Rufous-collared Robin) **E**
T. migratorius (American Robin) **A,E**
135 ORTHONYCHIDAE (LOGRUNNERS)
ORTHONYX
O. temminckii (Spine-tailed Logrunner) **L,M**
O. spaldingii (Spalding's Logrunner) **M**
ANDROPHOBUS
A. viridis (Green-backed Babbler) **L**
PSOPHODES
P. olivaceus (Eastern Whipbird) **M**
P. nigrogularis (Western Whipbird) **M**
SPHENOSTOMA
S. cristatum (Wedgebill) **M**
CINCLOSOMA
C. punctatum (Spotted Quail-Thrush) **M**
C. castanotum (Chestnut Quail-Thrush) **M**
C. alisteri (Nullarbor Quail-Thrush) **M**
C. cinnamomeum (Cinnamon Quail-Thrush) **M**
C. castaneothorax (Chestnut-breasted Quail-Thrush) **M**

C. ajax (Ajax Quail-Thrush) **L**
PTILORRHOA
P. leucosticta (High-mountain Rail-Babbler) **L**
P. caerulescens (Lowland Rail-Babbler) **L**
P. castanonota (Mid-mountain Rail-Babbler) **K,L**
EUPETES
E. macrocerus (Malay Rail-Babbler) **J**
MELAMPITTA
M. lugubris (Lesser Melampitta) **L**
M. gigantea (Greater Melampitta) **L**
IFRITA
I. kowaldi (Blue-capped Babbler) **L**
136 TIMALIIDAE (BABBLERS)
TIMALIINAE
TRICHASTOMA
T. rostratum (White-chested Jungle Babbler) **J**
T. celebense (Sulawesi Jungle Babbler) **J,K**
T. bicolor (Ferruginous Jungle Babbler) **J**
T. woodi (Bagobo Babbler) **J**
MALACOCINCLA
M. abbotti (Abbott's Jungle Babbler) **H,I,J**
M. sepiaria (Horsfield's Jungle Babbler) **J**
M. perspicillata (Black-browed Jungle Babbler) **J**
M. malaccensis (Short-tailed Jungle Babbler) **J**
M. cinereiceps (Ashy-headed Jungle Babbler) **J**
PELLORNEUM
P. tickelli (Tickell's Jungle Babbler) **H,I,J**
P. albiventre (Plain Brown Babbler) **H,I**
P. palustre (Marsh Spotted Babbler) **H**   ?
P. ruficeps (Spotted Babbler) **H,I,J**
P. fuscocapillum (Brown-capped Jungle Babbler) **H**
P. pyrrogenys (Temminck's Jungle Babbler) **J**
P. capistratum (Black-capped Babbler) **J**
MALACOPTERON
M. magnirostre (Moustached Tree Babbler) **I,J**
M. affine (Sooty-capped Babbler) **I,J**
M. cinereum (Scaly-crowned Babbler) **I,J**
M. magnum (Rufous-crowned Tree Babbler) **I,J**
M. palawanense (Palawan Tree Babbler) **J**
M. albogulare (Gray-breasted Babbler) **J**
ILLADOPSIS
I. cleaveri (Blackcap Thrush-Babbler) **C**
I. albipectus (Scaly-breasted Thrush-Babbler) **C**
I. rufescens (Rufous-winged Thrush-Babbler) **C**
I. puveli (Puvel's Thrush-Babbler) **C**
I. rufipennis (Pale-breasted Thrush-Babbler) **C**
I. fulvescens (Brown Thrush-Babbler) **C**
I. pyrrhopterus (Mountain Thrush-Babbler) **C**
I. abyssinicus (African Hill Babbler) **C**
KAKAMEGA
K. poliothorax (Gray-chested Thrush-Babbler) **C**
PTYRTICUS
P. turdinus (African Thrush-Babbler) **C**
POMATORHINUS
P. hypoleucos (Long-billed Scimitar Babbler) **H,I,J**
P. erythrogenys (Rusty-cheeked Scimitar Babbler) **H,I**
P. horsfieldii (Travancore Scimitar Babbler) **H**
P. schisticeps (Slaty-headed Scimitar Babbler) **H,I,J**
P. montanus (Chestnut-backed Scimitar Babbler) **J**
P. ruficollis (Streak-breasted Scimitar Babbler) **H,I**
P. ochraceiceps (Red-billed Scimitar Babbler) **H,I**
P. ferruginosus (Coral-billed Scimitar Babbler) **H,I**
GARRITORNIS
G. isidorei (Isidor's Rufous Babbler) **L**
POMATOSTOMUS
P. temporalis (Gray-crowned Babbler) **M**
P. superciliosus (White-browed Babbler) **M**
P. halli (Hall Babbler) **M**
P. ruficeps (Chestnut-crowned Babbler) **M**
XIPHIRHYNCHUS
X. superciliaris (Slender-billed Scimitar Babbler) **H,I**
JABOUILLEIA
J. danjoui (Danjou's Babbler) **I**   ?
RIMATOR
R. malacoptilus (Long-billed Wren-Babbler) **H,I,J**
PTILOCICHLA
P. leucogrammica (Bornean Wren-Babbler) **J**   ?
P. mindanensis (Streaked Ground Babbler) **J**   ?
P. falcata (Palawan Wren-Babbler) **J**
KENOPIA
K. striata (Striped Wren-Babbler) **J**
NAPOTHERA
N. rufipectus (Sumatran Wren-Babbler) **J**
N. atrigularis (Black-throated Wren-Babbler) **J**
N. macrodactyla (Large Wren-Babbler) **J**

N. marmorata (Marbled Wren-Babbler) **J**   ?
N. crispifrons (Limestone Wren-Babbler) **I**
N. brevicaudata (Streaked Wren-Babbler) **H,I,J**
N. crassa (Mountain Wren-Babbler) **J**
N. rabori (Luzon Wren-Babbler) **J**   ?
N. epilepidota (Lesser Wren-Babbler) **H,I,J**
PNOEPYGA
P. albiventer (Scaly-breasted Wren-Babbler) **H,I**
P. pusilla (Pygmy Wren-Babbler) **H,I,J**
SPELAEORNIS
S. caudatus (Short-tailed Wren-Babbler) **H**
S. badeigularis (Mishmi Wren-Babbler) **H**   ?
S. troglodytoides (Bar-winged Wren-Babbler) **H,I**
S. formosus (Spotted Wren-Babbler) **H**
S. chocolatinus (Godwin-Austin's Wren-Babbler) **H,I**
S. longicaudatus (Long-tailed Wren-Babbler) **H**
SPHENOCICLA
S. humei (Wedge-billed Wren-Babbler) **H,I**
NEOMIXIS
N. tenella (Northern Jery) **D**
N. viridis (Southern Green Jery) **D**
N. striatigula (Stripe-throated Jery) **D**
N. flavoviridis (Wedge-tailed Jery) **D**
STACHYRIS
S. rodolphei (Deignan's Babbler) **I**   ?
S. rufifrons (Red-fronted Tree-Babbler) **I,J**
S. ambigua (Buff-chested Babbler) **H,I**
S. ruficeps (Red-headed Tree-Babbler) **H,I**
S. pyrrhops (Red-billed Tree-Babbler) **H**
S. chrysaea (Golden-headed Tree-Babbler) **H,I,J**
S. plateni (Pygmy Tree-Babbler) **J**
S. capitalis (Rufous-crowned Tree-Babbler) **J**
S. speciosa (Rough-templed Tree-Babbler) **J**
S. whiteheadi (Whitehead's Tree-Babbler) **J**
S. striata (Striped Tree-Babbler) **J**   ?
S. nigrorum (Negros Tree-Babbler) **J**
S. hypogrammica (Palawan Tree-Babbler) **J**
S. grammiceps (White-breasted Tree-Babbler) **J**   ?
S. herberti (Sooty Tree-Babbler) **J**   ?
S. nigriceps (Black-throated Tree-Babbler) **H,I,J**
S. poliocephala (Gray-headed Tree-Babbler) **J**
S. striolata (Spot-necked Tree-Babbler) **I,J**
S. oglei (Austen's Spotted Tree-Babbler) **H**
S. maculata (Chestnut-rumped Tree-Babbler) **J**
S. leucotis (White-necked Tree-Babbler) **J**
S. nigricollis (Black-throated Tree-Babbler) **J**
S. thoracica (White-collared Tree-Babbler) **J**
S. erythroptera (Chestnut-winged Tree-Babbler) **J**
S. melanothorax (Pearl-cheeked Tree-Babbler) **J**
S. zantholeuca (White-bellied Tree-Babbler) **I,J**
DUMETIA
D. hyperythra (Rufous-bellied Babbler) **H**
RHOPOCICHLA
R. atriceps (Black-headed Babbler) **H**
MACRONOUS
M. gularis (Striped Tit-Babbler) **H,I,J**
M. kelleyi (Gray-faced Tit-Babbler) **I**
M. striaticeps (Brown Tit-Babbler) **J**
M. ptilosus (Fluffy-backed Tit-Babbler) **J**
MICROMACRONUS
M. leytensis (Leyte Tit-Babbler) **J**   ?
TIMALIA
T. pileata (Chestnut-capped Babbler) **H,I,J**
CHRYSOMMA
C. sinense (Oriental Yellow-eyed Babbler) **H,I**
MOUPINIA
M. altirostris (Jerdon's Babbler) **H,I**   ?
M. poecilotis (Rufous-crowned Babbler) **B**
CHAMAEA
C. fasciata (Wren-Tit) **A**
TURDOIDES
T. nipalensis (Spiny Babbler) **H**
T. altirostris (Iraq Babbler) **B**   ?
T. caudatus (Common Babbler) **B,H**
T. earlei (Striated Babbler) **H**
T. gularis (White-throated Babbler) **I**
T. longirostris (Slender-billed Babbler) **H**
T. malcolmi (Large Gray Babbler) **H**
T. squamiceps (Arabian Babbler) **C**
T. fulvus (Fulvous Babbler) **C**
T. aylmeri (Scaly Chatterer) **C**
T. rubiginosus (Rufous Chatterer) **C**
T. subrufus (Rufous Babbler) **H**
T. striatus (White-headed Jungle Babbler) **H**
T. rufescens (Ceylon Jungle Babbler) **H**
T. affinis (White-headed Babbler) **H**

T. melanops (Black-lored Babbler) **C**
T. tenebrosus (Dusky Babbler) **C**
T. reinwardtii (Blackcap Babbler) **C**
T. plebejus (Brown Babbler) **C**
T. jardineii (Arrow-marked Babbler) **C**
T. squamulatus (Scaly Babbler) **C**
T. leucopygius (White-rumped Babbler) **C**
T. hindei (Hinde's Pied Babbler) **C**   V
T. hypoleucus (Northern Pied Babbler) **C**
T. bicolor (Pied Babbler) **C**
T. gymnogenys (Bare-cheeked Babbler) **C**
BABAX
B. lanceolatus (Chinese Babax) **I**
B. waddelli (Giant Babax) **I**
B. koslowi (Koslow's Babax) **I**
GARRULAX
G. cinereifrons (Ashy-headed Laughing-Thrush) **H**
G. palliatus (Gray & Brown Laughing-Thrush) **J**
G. rufifrons (Red-fronted Laughing-Thrush) **J**
G. perspicillatus (Spectacled Laughing-Thrush) **I**
G. albogularis (White-throated Laughing-Thrush) **H,I**
G. leucolophus (White-crested Laughing-Thrush) **H,I,J**
G. monileger (Lesser Necklaced Laughing-Thrush) **H,I**
G. pectoralis (Greater Necklaced Laughing-Thrush) **H,I**
G. lugubris (Black Laughing-Thrush) **J**
G. striatus (Striated Laughing-Thrush) **H,I**
G. strepitans (Tickell's Laughing-Thrush) **I**
G. milleti (Black-hooded Laughing-Thrush) **I**   ?
G. maesi (Maes' Laughing-Thrush) **B,I**   ?
G. nuchalis (Chestnut-backed Laughing-Thrush) **H,I**
G. chinensis (Black-throated Laughing-Thrush) **H,I**
G. vassali (White-cheeked Laughing-Thrush) **I**   ?
G. galbanus (Austen's Laughing-Thrush) **H,I**   ?
G. delesserti (Rufous-vented Laughing-Thrush) **H,I**
G. variegatus (Variegated Laughing-Thrush) **H**
G. davidi (David's Laughing-Thrush) **B**
G. sukatschewi (Black-fronted Laughing-Thrush) **B**
G. cineraceus (Ashy Laughing-Thrush) **H,I**
G. rufogularis (Rufous-chinned Laughing-Thrush) **H,I**
G. lunulatus (Bar-backed Laughing-Thrush) **B**
G. bieti (Biet's Laughing-Thrush) **B**   ?
G. maximus (Giant Laughing-Thrush) **B**
G. ocellatus (White-spotted Laughing-Thrush) **H,I**
G. caerulatus (Gray-sided Laughing-Thrush) **H,I**
G. poecilorhynchus (Rufous Laughing-Thrush) **I**
G. mitratus (Chestnut-capped Laughing-Thrush) **J**
G. ruficollis (Rufous-necked Laughing-Thrush) **I**
G. merulinus (Spot-breasted Laughing-Thrush) **H,I**
G. canorus (Melodious Laughing-Thrush) **I**
G. sannio (White-browed Laughing-Thrush) **B, H,I**
G. cachinnans (Nilgiri White-breasted Laughing-Thrush) **H**   ?
G. jerdoni (White-breasted Laughing-Thrush) **H**
G. lineatus (Himalayan Streaked Laughing-Thrush) **H**
G. virgatus (Striped Laughing-Thrush) **H,I**
G. austeni (Brown-capped Laughing-Thrush) **H,I**
G. squamatus (Blue-winged Laughing-Thrush) **I**
G. subunicolor (Plain-colored Laughing-Thrush) **I**
G. elliotii (Elliot's Laughing-Thrush) **B**
G. henrici (Prince Henry's Laughing-Thrush) **B**
G. affinis (Black-faced Laughing-Thrush) **H,I**
G. erythrocephalus (Red-headed Laughing-Thrush) **H,I,J**
G. yersini (Yersin's Laughing-Thrush) **I**   ?
G. formosus (Crimson-winged Laughing-Thrush) **I**   ?
G. milnei (Red-tailed Laughing-Thrush) **I**
LIOCICHLA
L. phoenicea (Red-faced Liocichla) **H**
L. omeiensis (Mount Omei Liocichla) **B**   ?
L. steerii (Steere's Liocichla) **I**
LEIOTHRIX
L. argentauris (Silver-eared Mesia) **H,I,J**
L. lutea (Red-billed Leiothrix) **H,I**
CUTIA
C. nipalensis (Nepal Cutia) **I,J**
PTERUTHIUS
P. rufiventer (Rufous-bellied Shrike Babbler) **I**
P. flaviscapis (Red-winged Shrike Babbler) **I,J**

P. xanthochlorus (Green Shrike Babbler) **H,I**
P. melanotis (Black-eared Shrike Babbler) **H,I,J**
P. aenobarbus (Chestnut-fronted Shrike Babbler) **H,I,J**
GAMPSORHYNCHUS
G. rufulus (White-headed Shrike Babbler) **H,I,J**
ACTINODURA
A. egertoni (Rusty-fronted Barwing) **H,I**
A. ramsayi (Spectacled Barwing) **I**
A. nipalensis (Hoary Barwing) **H,I**
A. waldeni (Austen's Barwing) **H,I**
A. souliei (Streaked Barwing) **I**
A. morrisoniana (Formosan Barwing) **J**
MINLA
M. cyanouroptera (Blue-winged Minla) **H,I,J**
M. strigula (Chestnut-tailed Minla) **H,I,J**
M. ignotincta (Red-tailed Minla) **B,H,I**
M. annectens (Chestnut-backed Minla) **I**
ALCIPPE
A. chrysotis (Golden-breasted Fulvetta) **B,H,I**
A. variegaticeps (Variegated Fulvetta) **B**   ?
A. cinerea (Yellow-throated Fulvetta) **I**
A. castaneceps (Chestnut-headed Fulvetta) **I,J**
A. vinipectus (White-browed Fulvetta) **H,I**
A. striaticollis (Chinese Mountain Fulvetta) **B**
A. ruficapilla (Spectacled Fulvetta) **B,I**
A. cinereiceps (Streak-throated Fulvetta) **H,I**
A. rufogularis (Rufous-throated Fulvetta) **H,I**
A. brunnea (Gould's Fulvetta) **H,I**
A. brunneicauda (Brown Fulvetta) **J**
A. poioicephala (Brown-cheeked Fulvetta) **H,I**
A. pyrrhoptera (Javanese Fulvetta) **J**
A. peracensis (Mountain Fulvetta) **I,J**
A. morrisonia (Gray-cheeked Fulvetta) **B,I,J**
A. nipalensis (Nepal Fulvetta) **H,I**
LIOPTILUS
L. nigricapillus (Bush Blackcap) **C**
KUPEORNIS
K. gilberti (White-throated Mountain Babbler) **C**
K. rufocinctus (Red-collared Flycatcher Babbler) **C**
K. chapini (Chapin's Flycatcher Babbler) **C**
PAROPHASMA
P. galinieri (Abyssinian Catbird) **C**
PHYLLANTHUS
P. atripennis (Capuchin Babbler) **C**
CROCIAS
C. langbianis (Mt Langbian Sibia) **I**   ?
C. albonotatus (Spotted Sibia) **J**
HETEROPHASIA
H. capistrata (Black-capped Sibia) **H,I**
H. gracilis (Gray Sibia) **H,I**
H. melanoleuca (Black-headed Sibia) **I**
H. auricularis (White-eared Sibia) **J**
H. pulchella (Beautiful Sibia) **H,I**
H. picaoides (Long-tailed Sibia) **I,J**
YUHINA
Y. castaniceps (Striated Yuhina) **H,I**
Y. bakeri (White-naped Yuhina) **H,I**
Y. flavicollis (Whiskered Yuhina) **H,I**
Y. gularis (Striped-throated Yuhina) **H,I**
Y. diademata (White-collared Yuhina) **I**
Y. occipitalis (Rufous-vented Yuhina) **H,I**
Y. brunneiceps (Formosan Yuhina) **I**
Y. nigrimenta (Black-chinned Yuhina) **H,I**
MYZORNIS
M. pyrrhoura (Fire-tailed Myzornis) **I**
HORIZORHINUS
H. dohrni (Dohrn's Thrush-Babbler) **C**
OXYLABES
O. cinereiceps (Gray-crowned Oxylabes) **D**
O. madagascariensis (White-throated Oxylabes) **D**
O. xanthophrys (Yellow-browed Oxylabes) **D**
MYSTACORNIS
M. crossleyi (Crossley's Babbler) **D**
PICATHARTINAE
PICATHARTES
P. gymnocephalus (White-necked Rockfowl) **C**   V
P. oreas (Gray-necked Rockfowl) **C**   R
137 PARADOXORNITHIDAE (PARROTBILLS)
PANURUS
P. biarmicus (Bearded Reedling) **B**
CONOSTOMA
C. oemodium (Great Parrotbill) **H,I**
PARADOXORNIS
P. paradoxus (Three-toed Parrotbill) **B**
P. unicolor (Brown Parrotbill) **H,I**

P. flavirostris (Gould's Parrotbill) **H,I**   ?
P. guttaticollis (Spot-breasted Parrotbill) **H,I**
P. conspicillatus (Spectacled Parrotbill) **B**
P. ricketti (Yunnan Parrotbill) **B**
P. webbianus (Vinous-throated Parrotbill) **B,I**
P. alphonsianus (Ashy-throated Parrotbill) **B,I**
P. zappeyi (Zappey's Parrotbill) **B**
P. przewalskii (Gray-crowned Parrotbill) **B**
P. fulvifrons (Fulvous-fronted Parrotbill) **B,H**
P. nipalensis (Blyth's Parrotbill) **B,H,I**
P. davidianus (David's Parrotbill) **I**
P. atrosuperciliaris (Lesser Red-headed Parrotbill) **H,I**
P. ruficeps (Greater Red-headed Parrotbill) **I**   ?
P. gularis (Gray-headed Parrotbill) **I**
P. heudei (Heude's Parrotbill) **B**   I
138 SYLVIIDAE (OLD WORLD WARBLERS)
POLIOPTILINAE
MICROBATES
M. collaris (Collared Gnatwren) **F**
M. cinereiventris (Half-collared Gnatwren) **E,F**
RAMPHOCAENUS
R. melanurus (Long-billed Gnatwren) **E,F**
POLIOPTILA
P. caerulea (Blue-gray Gnatcatcher) **A,E**
P. melanura (Black-tailed Gnatcatcher) **A,E**
P. lembeyei (Cuban Gnatcatcher) **E**   ?
P. albiloris (White-lored Gnatcatcher) **E**
P. nigriceps (Black-capped Gnatcatcher) **E**
P. plumbea (Tropical Gnatcatcher) **E,F**
P. lactea (Cream-bellied Gnatcatcher) **F**
P. guianensis (Guianan Gnatcatcher) **F**
P. schistaceigula (Slate-throated Gnatcatcher) **F**
P. dumicola (Masked Gnatcatcher) **F**
SYLVIINAE
OLIGURA
O. castaneocoronata (Chestnut-headed Ground Warbler) **H,I**
TESIA
T. superciliaris (Java Ground Warbler) **J**
T. olivea (Slaty-bellied Ground Warbler) **I**
T. cyaniventer (Gray-bellied Ground Warbler) **H,I**
T. everetti (Russet-capped Stubtail) **J**
UROSPHENA
U. subulata (Timor Stubtail) **J**
U. whiteheadi (Bornean Stubtail) **J**
U. squameiceps (Scaly-headed Stubtail) **B,I**
CETTIA
C. pallidipes (Pale-footed Stubtail) **H,I**
C. diphone (Japanese Bush Warbler) **B,J**
C. annae (Palau Bush Warbler) **J**
C. fortipes (Strong-footed Bush Warbler) **H**
C. parens (Shade Warbler) **O**
C. ruficapilla (Fiji Warbler) **O**
C. vulcania (Muller's Bush Warbler) **J,K**
C. major (Large Bush Warbler) **I**
C. carolinae (Yamdena Warbler) **L**
C. flavolivacea (Aberrant Bush Warbler) **H,I**
C. robustipes (Swinhoe's Bush Warbler) **H,J**
C. brunnifrons (Rufous-capped Bush Warbler) **H,I**
C. cetti (Cetti's Warbler) **B,H**
BRADYPTERUS
B. baboecala (African Sedge Warbler) **C**
B. graueri (Grauer's Warbler) **C**   V
B. grandis (Ja River Warbler) **C**   ?
B. carpalis (White-winged Warbler) **C**
B. alfredi (Bamboo Warbler) **C**
B. sylvaticus (Knysna Scrub Warbler) **C**
B. lopezi (Lopez' Warbler) **C**
B. mariae (Evergreen Forest Warbler) **C**
B. barratti (Scrub Warbler) **C**
B. victorini (Victorin's Scrub Warbler) **C**
B. cinnamomeus (Cinnamon Bracken Warbler) **C**
B. brunneus (Brown Feather-tailed Warbler) **D**
B. thoracicus (Spotted Bush Warbler) **B,I**
B. major (Large-billed Bush Warbler) **B,H**   ?
B. tacsanowskius (Chinese Bush Warbler) **B,I**
B. luteoventris (Brown Bush Warbler) **H,I**
B. palliseri (Palliser's Warbler) **H**   ?
B. seebohmi (Mountain Scrub Warbler) **I,J**
B. caudatus (Long-tailed Ground Warbler) **J**
B. accentor (Kinabalu Scrub Warbler) **J**
B. castaneus (Chestnut-backed Bush Warbler) **K**
BATHMOCERCUS
B. cerviniventris (Black-capped Rufous Warbler) **C**
B. rufus (Black-faced Rufous Warbler) **C**

OLD WORLD WARBLERS

B. winifredae (Mrs Moreau's Warbler) **C**
AMPHILAIS
A. seebohmi (Seebohm's Feather-tailed Warbler) **D**
NESILLAS
N. typica (Tsikirity Warbler) **D**
N. mariae (Comoro Warbler) **D**
N. aldabranus (Aldabra Warbler) **D**   [E]
THAMNORNIS
T. chloropetoides (Kiritika Warbler) **D**
MELOCICHLA
M. mentalis (Moustached Grass Warbler) **C**
ACHAETOPS
A. pycnopygius (Damaraland Rock Jumper) **C**
SPHENOEACUS
S. afer (Cape Grassbird) **C**
MEGALURUS
M. pryeri (Japanese Marsh Warbler) **B**
M. timoriensis (Tawny Marshbird) **J,K,L,M**
M. palustris (Striated Canegrass Warbler) **H,I**
M. albolimbatus (Fly River Grass Warbler) **L**
M. gramineus (Little Marshbird) **L,M**
M. punctatus (Fernbird) **N**
CINCLORHAMPHUS
C. mathewsi (Rufous Songlark) **M**
C. cruralis (Brown Songlark) **M**
EREMIORNIS
E. carteri (Spinifexbird) **M**
MEGALURULUS
M. bivittatus (Buff-banded Bushbird) **J**
M. mariei (New Caledonian Grass Warbler) **O**
CICHLORNIS
C. whitneyi (Thicket Warbler) **O**
C. grosvenori (Whiteman Mountains Warbler) **O**
C. llaneae (Bougainville Thicket Warbler) **O**
ORTYGOCICHLA
O. rubiginosa (Rufous-faced Thicket Warbler) **O**
O. rufa (Long-legged Warbler) **O**
CHAETORNIS
C. striatus (Bristled Grass Warbler) **H**
GRAMINICOLA
G. bengalensis (Large Grass Warbler) **H,I**
SCHOENICOLA
S. platyura (Broad-tailed Warbler) **C,H**
LOCUSTELLA
L. lanceolata (Lanceolated Warbler) **B,J,K,L**
L. naevia (Grasshopper Warbler) **B,H,I**
L. certhiola (Pallas's Grasshopper Warbler) **B,H,I**
L. ochotensis (Middendorff's Grasshopper Warbler)
B,I,J,K
L. pleskei (Styan's Grasshopper Warbler) **B,I,J**
L. fluviatilis (River Warbler) **B,C**
L. luscinioides (Savi's Warbler) **E**
L. fasciolata (Gray's Grasshopper Warbler) **B,J,K,L**
L. amnicola (Stepanyan's Grasshopper Warbler) **B**
ACROCEPHALUS
A. melanopogon (Moustached Warbler) **B**
A. paludicola (Aquatic Warbler) **B**   [?]
A. schoenobaenus (Sedge Warbler) **B,C**
A. sorghophilus (Speckled Reed Warbler) **B,I,J**   [?]
A. bistrigiceps (Schrenk's Reed Warbler) **B,I**
A. agricola (Paddyfield Warbler) **B,H**
A. concinens (Blunt-winged Paddyfield Warbler)
B,H,I
A. scirpaceus (Reed Warbler) **B,C**
A. cinnamomeus (Reichenow's Reed Warbler) **C**
A. baeticatus (African Reed Warbler) **C**
A. palustris (Marsh Warbler) **B,C**
A. dumetorum (Blyth's Reed Warbler) **B,H**
A. arundinaceus (Great Reed Warbler) **B,C**
A. stentoreus (Clamorous Reed Warbler) **B,C,H,I,J, K,M**
A. orinus (Large-billed Reed Warbler) **H**
A. orientalis (Oriental Great Reed Warbler) **B,J**
A. luscinia (Nightingale Reed Warbler) **O**
A. kingii (Hawaiian Reed Warbler) **P**
A. aequinoctialis (Polynesian Reed Warbler) **O**
A. caffer (Long-billed Reed Warbler) **O**
A. atyphus (Tuamotu Warbler) **O**
A. vaughanii (Pitcairn Warbler) **O**
A. rufescens (Rufous Swamp Warbler) **C**
A. brevipennis (Cape Verde Swamp Warbler) **C**
A. gracilirostris (Swamp Warbler) **C**
A. newtoni (Madagascar Swamp Warbler) **D**
A. aedon (Thick-billed Warbler) **B,H,I**
BEBRORNIS
B. rodericanus (Rodriguez Brush Warbler) **I**

B. sechellensis (Seychelles Brush Warbler) **D**
HIPPOLAIS
H. caligata (Booted Warbler) **B,H**
H. pallida (Olivaceous Warbler) **B,C**
H. languida (Upcher's Warbler) **B,C**
H. olivetorum (Olive-tree Warbler) **B**
H. polyglotta (Melodious Warbler) **B,C**
H. icterina (Icterine Warbler) **B,C**
CHLOROPETA
C. natalensis (Yellow Warbler) **C**
C. similis (Mountain Yellow Warbler) **C**
C. gracilirostris (Yellow Swamp Warbler) **C**   [R]
CISTICOLA
C. erythrops (Red-faced Cisticola) **C**
C. lepe (Angolan Cisticola) **C**
C. cantans (Singing Cisticola) **C**
C. lateralis (Whistling Cisticola) **C**
C. woosnami (Trilling Cisticola) **C**
C. anonyma (Chattering Cisticola) **C**
C. bulliens (Bubbling Cisticola) **C**
C. chubbi (Chubb's Cisticola) **C**
C. hunteri (Hunter's Cisticola) **C**
C. nigriloris (Black-browed Cisticola) **C**
C. aberrans (Lazy Cisticola) **C**
C. bodessa (Boran Cisticola) **C**
C. chiniana (Rattling Cisticola) **C**
C. cinereola (Ashy Cisticola) **C**
C. ruficeps (Red-pate Cisticola) **C**
C. rufilata (Gray Cisticola) **C**
C. subruficapilla (Red-headed Cisticola) **C**
C. lais (Wailing Cisticola) **C**
C. restricta (Tana River Cisticola) **C**   [?]
C. njombe (Churring Cisticola) **C**
C. galactotes (Winding Cisticola) **C**
C. carruthersi (Carruthers' Cisticola) **C**
C. pipiens (Chirping Cisticola) **C**
C. tinniens (Levaillant's Cisticola) **C**
C. robusta (Stout Cisticola) **C**
C. aberdare (Aberdare Mountain Cisticola) **C**
C. natalensis (Croaking Cisticola) **C**
C. fulvicapilla (Piping Cisticola) **C**
C. angusticauda (Tabora Cisticola) **C**
C. melanura (Slender-tailed Cisticola) **C**
C. brachyptera (Siffling Cisticola) **C**
C. rufa (Rufous Cisticola) **C**
C. troglodytes (Foxy Cisticola) **C**
C. nana (Tiny Cisticola) **C**
C. incana (Incana) **V**
C. juncidis (Zitting Cisticola) **B,C,H,I,J,K,M**
C. haesitata (Socotra Cisticola) **C**   [?]
C. cherina (Madagascar Cisticola) **D**
C. aridula (Desert Cisticola) **C**
C. textrix (Tink-tink Cisticola) **C**
C. eximia (Black-necked Cisticola) **C**
C. dambo (Cloud-scraping Cisticola) **C**
C. brunnescens (Pectoral-patch Cisticola) **C**
C. ayresii (Wing-snapping Cisticola) **C**
C. exilis (Gold-capped Cisticola) **B,H,J,K,L,M,O**
SCOTOCERCA
S. inquieta (Streaked Scrub-Warbler) **C,H**
RHOPOPHILUS
R. pekinensis (White-browed Chinese Warbler) **B**
PRINIA
P. burnesii (Long-tailed Prinia) **H**   [?]
P. criniger (Hill Prinia) **B,H,J**
P. polychroa (Brown Hill Prinia) **I,J**
P. atrogularis (White-browed Prinia) **H,I,J**
P. cinereocapilla (Hodgson's Long-tailed Warbler) **H**
P. buchanani (Rufous-fronted Prinia) **H**
P. rufescens (Lesser Brown Prinia) **H,I,J**
P. hodgsonii (Franklin's Prinia) **H,I**
P. gracilis (Graceful Warbler) **B,C,H**
P. sylvatica (Jungle Prinia) **H**
P. familiaris (Bar-winged Prinia) **J**
P. flaviventris (Yellow-bellied Prinia) **H,I,J**
P. socialis (Ashy Prinia) **H**
P. subflava (Tawny-flanked Prinia) **C,H,I**
P. somalica (Pale Prinia) **C**
P. fluviatilis (Lake Chad Prinia) **C**   [?]
P. maculosa (Karoo Prinia) **C**
P. flavicans (Black-chested Prinia) **C**
P. substriata (White-breasted Prinia) **C**
P. molleri (Sao Thome Prinia) **C**
P. robertsi (Roberts' Prinia) **C**
P. leucopogon (White-chinned Prinia) **C**
P. leontica (Sierra Leone Prinia) **C**

P. bairdii (Banded Prinia) **C**
P. erythroptera (Red-winged Warbler) **C**
P. pectoralis (Rufous-eared Prinia) **C**
DRYMOCICHLA
D. incana (Red-winged Gray Warbler) **C**
UROLAIS
U. epichlora (Green Longtail) **C**
SPILOPTILA
S. clamans (Cricket Warbler) **C**
APALIS
A. thoracica (Bar-throated Apalis) **C**
A. pulchra (Black-collared Apalis) **C**
A. ruwenzorii (Collared Apalis) **C**
A. nigriceps (Black-capped Apalis) **C**
A. jacksoni (Black-throated Apalis) **C**
A. chariessa (White-winged Apalis) **C**   [?]
A. binotata (Masked Apalis) **C**
A. personata (Mountain Masked Apalis) **C**
A. flavida (Yellow-chested Apalis) **C**
A. ruddi (Rudd's Apalis) **C**
A. rufogularis (Buff-throated Apalis) **C**
A. sharpii (Sharpe's Apalis) **C**
A. goslingi (Gosling's Apalis) **C**
A. bamendae (Bamenda Apalis) **C**
A. porphyrolaema (Chestnut-throated Apalis) **C**
A. melanocephala (Black-headed Apalis) **C**
A. chirindensis (Chirinda Apalis) **C**
A. cinerea (Gray Apalis) **C**
A. alticola (Brown-headed Apalis) **C**
A. karamojae (Karamoja Apalis) **C**
A. rufifrons (Red-faced Warbler) **C**
STENOSTIRA
S. scita (Fairy Flycatcher) **C**
PHYLLOLAIS
P. pulchella (Buff-bellied Warbler) **C**
ORTHOTOMUS
O. metopias (Red-capped Forest Warbler) **C**
O. moreaui (Long-billed Forest Warbler) **C**   [R]
O. cucullatus (Mountain Tailorbird) **H,I,J,K**
O. sutorius (Long-tailed Tailorbird) **H,I,J**
O. atrogularis (Black-necked Tailorbird) **H,I,J**
O. derbianus (Luzon Tailorbird) **J**
O. sericeus (Red-headed Tailorbird) **I,J**
O. ruficeps (Gray Tailorbird) **I,J,K**
O. sepium (Ashy Tailorbird) **J**
O. cinereiceps (White-eared Tailorbird) **J**
O. nigriceps (Black-headed Tailorbird) **J**
O. samarensis (Samar Tailorbird) **J**
CAMAROPTERA
C. brachyura (Bleating Camaroptera) **C**
C. harterti (Hartert's Cameroptera) **C**
C. superciliaris (Yellow-browed Camaroptera) **C**
C. chloronota (Olive-green Camaroptera) **C**
CALAMONASTES
C. simplex (Gray Wren Warbler) **C**
C. stierlingi (Stierling's Wren Warbler) **C**
C. fasciolata (Barred Camaroptera) **C**
EURYPTILA
E. subcinnamomea (Kopje Warbler) **C**
POLIOLAIS
P. lopezi (White-tailed Warbler) **C**
GRAUERIA
G. vittata (Grauer's Warbler) **C**
EREMOMELA
E. icteropygialis (Yellow-bellied Eremomela) **C**
E. flavicrissalis (Yellow-vented Eremomela) **C**
E. scotops (Green-cap Eremomela) **C**
E. pusilla (Smaller Green-backed Eremomela) **C**
E. canescens (Green-backed Eremomela) **C**
E. gregalis (Yellow-rumped Eremomela) **C**
E. badiceps (Brown-crowned Eremomela) **C**
E. turneri (Turner's Eremomela) **C**   [R]
E. atricollis (Black-necked Eremomela) **C**
E. usticollis (Burnt-neck Eremomela) **C**
RANDIA
R. pseudozosterops (Marvantsetra Warbler) **D**
NEWTONIA
N. amphichroa (Tulear Newtonia) **D**
N. brunneicauda (Common Newtonia) **D**
N. archboldi (Tabity Newtonia) **D**
N. fanovanae (Fanovana Newtonia) **D**   [I]
SYLVIETTA
S. virens (Green Crombec) **C**
S. denti (Lemon-bellied Crombec) **C**
S. leucophrys (White-browed Crombec) **C**
S. brachyura (Northern Crombec) **C**

S. philippae (Somali Short-billed Crombec) **C**
S. whytii (Red-faced Crombec) **C**
S. ruficapilla (Red-capped Crombec) **C**
S. rufescens (Long-billed Crombec) **C**
S. isabellina (Somali Long-billed Crombec) **C**
HEMITESIA
H. neumanni (Neumann's Short-tailed Warbler) **C**
MACROSPHENUS
M. kempi (Kemp's Longbill) **C**
M. flavicans (Yellow Longbill) **C**
M. concolor (Gray Longbill) **C**
M. pulitzeri (Pulitzer's Longbill) **C** I
M. kretschmeri (Kretschmer's Longbill) **C**
AMAUROCICHLA
A. bocagei (Bocage's Longbill) **C**
HYPERGERUS
H. atriceps (Oriole Warbler) **C**
H. lepida (Gray-capped Warbler) **C**
HYLIOTA
H. flavigaster (Yellow-bellied Flycatcher) **C**
H. australis (Southern Yellow-bellied Flycatcher) **C**
H. violacea (Violet-backed Flycatcher) **C**
HYLIA
H. prasina (Green Hylia) **C**
PHYLLOSCOPUS
P. ruficapilla (Yellow-throated Woodland Warbler) **C**
P. laurae (Mrs Boulton's Woodland Warbler) **C**
P. laetus (Red-faced Woodland Warbler) **C**
P. budongoensis (Uganda Woodland Warbler) **C**
P. herberti (Black-capped Woodland Warbler) **C**
P. umbrovirens (Brown Woodland Warbler) **C**
P. trochilus (Willow Warbler) **B,C**
P. collybita (Chiffchaff) **B,H**
P. sindianus (Eastern Chiffchaff) **B,H**
P. neglectus (Plain Willow Warbler) **B,H**
P. bonelli (Bonelli's Warbler) **B**
P. sibilatrix (Wood Warbler) **B,C**
P. fuscatus (Dusky Warbler) **B,H,I**
P. fulgiventer (Smoky Warbler) **B,H**
P. affinis (Tickell's Willow Warbler) **B,H,I**
P. griseolus (Sulfur-bellied Willow Warbler) **B,H**
P. armandii (Milne-Edwards' Willow Warbler) **B,I**
P. schwarzi (Radde's Bush Warbler) **B,I**
P. pulcher (Orange-barred Willow Warbler) **B,H,I**
P. maculipennis (Gray-faced Willow Warbler) **H,I**
P. proregulus (Pallas's Leaf Warbler) **B,H,I,J**
P. subviridis (Brooks's Willow Warbler) **B,H**
P. inornatus (Yellow-browed Warbler) **B,H,I**
P. borealis (Arctic Warbler) **A,B,H,I,J,K**
P. trochiloides (Greenish Warbler) **B,H,I**
P. nitidus (Green Willow Warbler) **B,H**
P. plumbeitarsus (Two-barred Greenish Warbler) **B,I**
P. tenellipes (Pale-legged Willow Warbler) **B**
P. borealoides (Japanese Pale-legged Willow Warbler) **B**
P. magnirostris (Large-billed Willow Warbler) **B,H**
P. tytleri (Tytler's Willow Warbler) **H**
P. occipitalis (Large Crowned Willow Warbler) **B,H**
P. coronatus (Temminck's Crowned Willow Warbler) **B,I,J**
P. ijimae (Ijima's Willow Warbler) **B,J**
P. reguloides (Blyth's Crowned Willow Warbler) **B,H,I**
P. davisoni (White-tailed Willow Warbler) **B,I**
P. cantator (Yellow-faced Leaf Warbler) **H,I**
P. ricketti (Black-browed Leaf Warbler) **I**
P. olivaceus (Philippine Leaf Warbler) **J**
P. cebuensis (Dubois' Leaf Warbler) **J**
P. trivirgatus (Mountain Leaf Warbler) **J**
P. sarasinorum (Sulawesi Leaf Warbler) **K**
P. presbytes (Timor Leaf Warbler) **J**
P. poliocephalus (Island Leaf Warbler) **J,K,L,O**
P. makirensis (San Cristobal Leaf Warbler) **O**
P. amoenus (Kulambangra Warbler) **O**
SEICERCUS
S. burkii (Yellow-eyed Flycatcher-Warbler) **H,I**
S. xanthoschistos (Gray-headed Flycatcher-Warbler) **H**
S. affinis (Allied Flycatcher-Warbler) **I**
S. poliogenys (Gray-cheeked Flycatcher-Warbler) **H,I**
S. castaniceps (Chestnut-headed Flycatcher-Warbler) **H,I,J**
S. montis (Yellow-breasted Flycatcher-Warbler) **J**
S. grammiceps (Sunda Flycatcher-Warbler) **J**

TICKELLIA
T. hodgsoni (Broad-billed Flycatcher-Warbler) **H,I**
ABROSCOPUS
A. albogularis (White-throated Flycatcher-Warbler) **H,I**
A. schisticeps (Black-faced Flycatcher-Warbler) **H,I**
A. superciliaris (Yellow-bellied Flycatcher-Warbler) **H,I,J**
PARISOMA
P. buryi (Yemen Tit-Warbler) **C**
P. lugens (Brown Tit-Warbler) **C**
P. boehmi (Banded Tit-Warbler) **C**
P. layardi (Layard's Tit-Warbler) **C**
P. subcaeruleum (Southern Tit-Warbler) **C**
SYLVIA
S. atricapilla (Blackcap) **B,C**
S. borin (Garden Warbler) **B,C**
S. communis (Whitethroat) **B,C**
S. curruca (Lesser Whitethroat) **B,C,H**
S. nana (Desert Whitethroat) **B,H**
S. nisoria (Barred Warbler) **B,C**
S. hortensis (Orphean Warbler) **B,C,H**
S. leucomelaena (Red Sea Warbler) **B,C**
S. rueppelli (Rüppell's Warbler) **B,C**
S. melanocephala (Sardinian Warbler) **B**
S. melanothorax (Cyprus Warbler) **B**
S. mystacea (Menetries' Warbler) **B**
S. cantillans (Subalpine Warbler) **B,C**
S. conspicillata (Spectacled Warbler) **B,C**
S. deserticola (Tristram's Warbler) **B**
S. undata (Dartford Warbler) **B**
S. sarda (Marmora's Warbler) **B**
REGULUS
R. ignicapillus (Firecrest) **B**
R. goodfellowi (Taiwan Firecrest) **J**
R. regulus (Goldcrest) **B**
R. satrapa (Golden-crowned Kinglet) **A,E**
R. calendula (Ruby-crowned Kinglet) **A,E**
LEPTOPOECILE
L. sophiae (Severtzov's Tit Warbler) **B,H**
L. elegans (Crested Tit Warbler) **B**
139 MUSCICAPIDAE (OLD WORLD FLYCATCHERS)
MUSCICAPINAE
MELAENORNIS
M. semipartitus (Silverbird) **C**
M. pallidus (Pale Flycatcher) **C**
M. infuscatus (African Brown Flycatcher) **C**
M. mariquensis (Mariqua Flycatcher) **C**
M. microrhynchus (Gray Flycatcher) **C**
M. chocolatinus (Abyssinian Slaty Flycatcher) **C**
M. fischeri (White-eyed Slaty Flycatcher) **C**
M. brunneus (Angolan Flycatcher) **C**
M. edolioides (Black Flycatcher) **C**
M. pammelaina (South African Black Flycatcher) **C**
M. ardesiaca (Berlioz' Black Flycatcher) **C**
M. annamarulae (Liberian Black Flycatcher) **C**
M. ocreata (Forest Flycatcher) **C**
M. cinerascens (White-browed Forest Flycatcher) **C**
M. silens (Fiscal Flycatcher) **C**
RHINOMYIAS
R. addita (Buru Jungle Flycatcher) **K** ?
R. oscillans (Flores Jungle Flycatcher) **J**
R. brunneata (White-gorgetted Jungle Flycatcher) **I,J** ?
R. olivacea (Olive-backed Jungle Flycatcher) **I,J**
R. umbratilis (White-throated Jungle Flycatcher) **J**
R. ruficauda (Rufous-tailed Jungle Flycatcher) **J**
R. colonus (Sula Jungle Flycatcher) **J,K** ?
R. gularis (White-browed Jungle Flycatcher) **J** ?
R. insignis (Lepanto Jungle Flycatcher) **J** ?
R. goodfellowi (Mindanao Jungle Flycatcher) **J**
MUSCICAPA
M. striata (Spotted Flycatcher) **B,C**
M. gambagae (Gambaga Spotted Flycatcher) **C**
M. griseisticta (Gray-spotted Flycatcher) **B,J,K,L**
M. sibirica (Siberian Flycatcher) **H,I,J**
M. dauurica (Brown Flycatcher) **H,I,J**
M. muttui (Brown-breasted Flycatcher) **H**
M. ruficauda (Rufous-tailed Flycatcher) **H**
M. ferruginea (Ferruginous Flycatcher) **H,I,J,K**
M. sordida (Sri Lankan Dusky Blue Flycatcher) **H**
M. thalassina (Indian Verditer Flycatcher) **H,I,J**
M. panayensis (Philippine Verditer Flycatcher) **J,K**
M. albicaudata (Nilgiri Verditer Flycatcher) **H**
M. indigo (Indigo Flycatcher) **J**

M. infuscata (African Sooty Flycatcher) **C**
M. ussheri (Ussher's Dusky Flycatcher) **C**
M. boehmi (Bohm's Flycatcher) **C**
M. aquatica (Swamp Flycatcher) **C**
M. olivascens (Olivaceous Flycatcher) **C**
M. lendu (Chapin's Flycatcher) **C** R
M. adusta (Dusky Flycatcher) **C**
M. epulata (Little Gray Flycatcher) **C**
M. sethsmithi (Yellow-footed Flycatcher) **C**
M. comitata (Dusky Blue Flycatcher) **C**
M. tessmanni (Tessman's Flycatcher) **C**
M. cassini (Cassin's Gray Flycatcher) **C**
M. coerulescens (Ashy Flycatcher) **C**
M. griseigularis (Gray-throated Flycatcher) **C**
MYIOPARUS
M. plumbeus (Gray Tit Flycatcher) **C**
HUMBLOTIA
H. flavirostris (Humblot's Flycatcher) **D** R
FICEDULA
F. hypoleuca (Pied Flycatcher) **B,C**
F. albicollis (Collared Flycatcher) **B,C**
F. zanthopygia (Yellow-rumped Flycatcher) **B,J**
F. narcissina (Narcissus Flycatcher) **B,J,K**
F. mugimaki (Mugimaki Flycatcher) **B,J**
F. hodgsonii (Rusty-breasted Blue Flycatcher) **B,H**
F. dumetoria (Orange-breasted Flycatcher) **J**
F. strophiata (Orange-gorgetted Flycatcher) **H,I**
F. parva (Red-breasted Flycatcher) **B,H,I**
F. subrubra (Kashmir Flycatcher) **H**
F. monileger (White-gorgetted Flycatcher) **H,I**
F. solitaris (Rufous-browed Flycatcher) **I,J**
F. hyperythra (Thicket Flycatcher) **H,I,J,K**
F. rufigula (White-vented Flycatcher) **K**
F. basilanica (Little Slaty Flycatcher) **J**
F. buruensis (Cinnamon-chested Flycatcher) **J,K**
F. henrici (Damar Flycatcher) **J** ?
F. harterti (Hartert's Flycatcher) **J** ?
F. platenae (Palawan Flycatcher) **J**
F. crypta (Vaurie's Flycatcher) **J** ?
F. bonthaina (Lompobattang Flycatcher) **K** ?
F. westermanni (Little Pied Flycatcher) **H,I,J,K**
F. superciliaris (White-browed Blue Flycatcher) **B,H**
F. tricolor (Slaty Blue Flycatcher) **H,I**
F. sapphira (Sapphire-headed Flycatcher) **B,I**
F. nigrorufa (Black & Orange Flycatcher) **H**
F. timorensis (Black-banded Flycatcher) **J** ?
CYANOPTILA
C. cyanomelana (Blue & White Flycatcher) **B,I,J**
NILTAVA
N. grandis (Large Niltava) **I,J,K**
N. macgregoriae (Small Niltava) **H,I**
N. davidi (Fukien Niltava) **I**
N. sundara (Rufous-bellied Niltava) **H,I**
N. sumatrana (Sumatran Niltava) **J**
N. vivida (Vivid Niltava) **H,J**
N. hyacinthina (Blue-backed Niltava) **J,K**
N. hoevelli (Blue-fronted Niltava) **K**
N. sanfordi (Matinan Niltava) **K**
N. concreta (White-tailed Niltava) **H,I,J**
N. ruecki (Rueck's Niltava) **J,K**
N. herioti (Blue-breasted Niltava) **J**
N. hainana (Grant's Niltava) **I**
N. pallipes (White-bellied Niltava) **H**
N. poliogenys (Brooks' Niltava) **H,I**
N. unicolor (Pale Niltava) **H,I,J**
N. rubeculoides (Blue-throated Niltava) **H,I,J**
N. banyumas (Hill Blue Niltava) **H,I,J**
N. superba (Bornean Niltava) **J**
N. caerulata (Large-billed Niltava) **J**
N. turcosa (Malaysian Niltava) **J**
N. tickelliae (Tickell's Niltava) **H,I,J,K**
N. rufigastra (Mangrove Niltava) **J,K**
N. hodgsoni (Pygmy Blue Niltava) **H,I,J**
CULICICAPA
C. ceylonensis (Gray-headed Canary Flycatcher) **H,I,J**
C. helianthea (Citrine Canary Flycatcher) **J,K**
EOPSALTRINAE
MONACHELLA
M. muelleriana (River Flycatcher) **L,O**
MICROECA
M. leucophaea (Jacky Winter) **L,M**
M. flavigaster (Lemon-breasted Flycatcher) **L,M**
M. hemixantha (Tanimbar Microeca Flycatcher) **L**
M. griseoceps (Yellow-footed Flycatcher) **L,M**
M. flavovirescens (Olive Microeca Flycatcher) **K,L**

MONARCH FLYCATCHERS, FANTAIL FLYCATCHERS

M. papuana (Papuan Microeca Flycatcher) **L**
EUGERYGONE
E. rubra (Red-backed Warbler) **L**
PETROICA
P. bivittata (Forest Robin) **L**
P. archboldi (Rock Robin) **L**
P. multicolor (Scarlet Robin) **M,O**
P. goodenovii (Red-capped Robin) **M**
P. phoenicea (Flame Robin) **M**
P. rodinogaster (Pink Robin) **M**
P. rosea (Rose Robin) **M**
P. cucullata (Hooded Robin) **M**
P. macrocephala (New Zealand Tit) **N**
P. vittata (Dusky Robin) **M**
P. australis (New Zealand Robin) **N**
P. traversi (Chatham I Robin) **N**   [E]
TREGELLASIA
T. leucops (White-faced Robin) **L,M**
T. capito (Pale Yellow Robin) **M**
EOPSALTRIA
E. australis (Yellow Robin) **M**
E. georgiana (White-breasted Robin) **M**
E. flaviventris (Yellow-bellied Robin) **O**
PENEOENANTHE
P. pulverulenta (Mangrove Robin) **K,L,M**
POECILODRYAS
P. brachyura (White-breasted Robin) **L**
P. hypoleuca (Black & White Robin) **L**
P. placens (Olive-yellow Robin) **L**
P. albonotata (Black-throated Robin) **L**
P. superciliosa (White-browed Robin) **M**
PENEOTHELLO
P. sigillatus (White-winged Thicket Flycatcher) **L**
P. cryptoleucus (Gray Thicket Flycatcher) **L**
P. cyanus (Slaty Thicket Flycatcher) **L**
P. bimaculatus (White-rumped Thicket Flycatcher) **L**
HETEROMYIAS
H. albispecularis (Ground Thicket Robin) **L**
H. cinereifrons (Gray-headed Thicket Robin) **L**
PACHYCEPHALOPSIS
P. hattamensis (Green Thicket Flycatcher) **L**
P. poliosoma (White-throated Thicket Flycatcher) **L**
140 MONARCHIDAE (MONARCH FLYCATCHERS, FANTAIL FLYCATCHERS)
PLATYSTEIRINAE
BIAS
B. flammulatus (African Shrike Flycatcher) **C**
B. musicus (Black & White Flycatcher) **C**
PSEUDOBIAS
P. wardi (Ward's Flycatcher) **D**
BATIS
B. diops (Ruwenzori Puff-back Flycatcher) **C**
B. margaritae (Boulton's Puff-back Flycatcher) **C**
B. mixta (Short-tailed Puff-back Flycatcher) **C**
B. dimorpha (Malawi Puff-back Flycatcher) **C**
B. capensis (Cape Puff-back Flycatcher) **C**
B. fratrum (Zululand Puff-back Flycatcher) **C**
B. molitor (Chin-spot Puff-back Flycatcher) **C**
B. soror (Paler Chin-spot Puff-back Flycatcher) **C**
B. pirit (Pirit Puff-back Flycatcher) **C**
B. senegalensis (Senegal Puff-back Flycatcher) **C**
B. orientalis (Gray-headed Puff-back Flycatcher) **C**
B. minor (Black-headed Puff-back Flycatcher) **C**
B. perkeo (Pygmy Puff-back Flycatcher) **C**
B. minulla (Angola Puff-back Flycatcher) **C**
B. minima (Verreaux's Puff-back Flycatcher) **C**
B. ituriensis (Chapin's Puff-back Flycatcher) **C**
B. poensis (Fernando Po Puff-back Flycatcher) **C**
B. occultus (Lawson's Puff-back Flycatcher) **C**
MONARCHINAE
ERYTHROCERCUS
E. holochlorus (Little Yellow Flycatcher) **C**
E. mccallii (Chestnut-capped Flycatcher) **C**
E. livingstonei (Livingstone's Flycatcher) **C**
ELMINIA
E. longicauda (Blue Flycatcher) **C**
E. albicauda (White-tailed Blue Flycatcher) **C**
TROCHOCERCUS
T. nigromitratus (Dusky Crested Flycatcher) **C**
T. albiventris (White-bellied Crested Flycatcher) **C**
T. albonotatus (White-tailed Crested Flycatcher) **C**
T. nitens (Blue-headed Crested Flycatcher) **C**
PHILENTOMA
P. pyrrhopterum (Chestnut-winged Monarch) **I,J**
P. velatum (Maroon-breasted Monarch) **J**

HYPOTHYMIS
H. azurea (Black-naped Blue Monarch) **H,I,J,K**
H. helenae (Short-crested Blue Monarch) **J**   [?]
H. coelestis (Celestial Blue Monarch) **J**   [?]
EUTRICHOMYIAS
E. rowleyi (Rowley's Flycatcher) **K**   [?]
TERPSIPHONE
T. rufiventer (Red-bellied Paradise Flycatcher) **C**
T. bedfordi (Bedford's Paradise Flycatcher) **C**
R. malaitae (Malaita Rufous Fantail) **O**
R. rufifrons (Rufous Fantail) **K,L,M,O**
T. cyanomelas (Cape Crested Flycatcher) **C**
T. rufocinerea (Rufous-vented Paradise Flycatcher) **C**
T. viridis (African Paradise Flycatcher) **C**
T. paradisi (Asiatic Paradise Flycatcher) **B,H,I,J,K**
T. atrocaudata (Black Paradise Flycatcher) **B,J**
T. cyanescens (Blue Paradise Flycatcher) **J**
T. cinnamomea (Rufous Paradise Flycatcher) **J**
T. atrochalybea (Sao Thome Paradise Flycatcher) **C**
T. mutata (Madagascar Paradise Flycatcher) **D**
T. corvina (Seychelles Paradise Flycatcher) **D**   [R]
T. bourbonnensis (Mascarene Paradise Flycatcher) **D**
CHASIEMPIS
C. sandwichensis (Elepaio) **P**
POMAREA
P. dimidiata (Rarotonga Flycatcher) **O**   [V]
P. nigra (Society Is Flycatcher) **O**   [E]
P. mendozae (Marquesas Flycatcher) **O**   [?]
P. iphis (Allied Flycatcher) **O**
P. whitneyi (Large Flycatcher) **O**
MAYRORNIS
M. schistaceus (Small Slaty Flycatcher) **O**
M. versicolor (Ogea Flycatcher) **O**   [?]
M. lessoni (Slaty Flycatcher) **O**
NEOLALAGE
N. banksiana (Buff-bellied Flycatcher) **O**
CLYTORHYNCHUS
C. pachycephaloides (Southern Shrikebill) **O**
C. vitiensis (Fiji Shrikebill) **O**
C. nigrogularis (Black-throated Shrikebill) **O**
C. hamlini (Rennell Shrikebill) **O**   [?]
METABOLUS
M. rugiensis (Truk Monarch) **O**   [R]
MONARCHA
M. axillaris (Black Monarch) **L**
M. rubiensis (Rufous Monarch) **L**
M. cinerascens (Island Gray-headed Monarch) **J,K,L**
M. melanopsis (Black-faced Monarch) **L,M**
M. frater (Black-winged Monarch) **L,M**
M. erythrosticta (Bougainville Monarch) **O**
M. castaneiventris (Chestnut-bellied Monarch) **O**
M. richardsii (Richard's Monarch) **O**
M. leucotis (White-eared Monarch) **K,L,M**
M. guttula (Spot-winged Monarch) **K,L**
M. mundus (Tanimbar Monarch) **K**
M. sacerdotum (Mees' Monarch) **J**   [?]
M. boanensis (Black-chinned Monarch) **K**   [?]
M. trivirgatus (Spectacled Monarch) **J,K,L,M**
M. leucurus (Kei Monarch) **L**   [?]
M. everetti (White-tipped Monarch) **L**   [?]
M. loricatus (Black-tipped Monarch) **K**
M. julienae (Kofiau Monarch) **K,L**   [?]
M. brehmii (Biak Monarch) **L**
M. manadensis (Black & White Monarch) **L**
M. infelix (Unhappy Monarch) **L**
M. menckei (St Matthias Monarch) **O**
M. verticalis (Bismarck Monarch) **L**
M. barbatus (Pied Monarch) **O**
M. browni (Kulambangra Monarch) **O**
M. viduus (San Cristobal Monarch) **O**
M. godeffroyi (Yap Monarch) **O**
M. takatsukasae (Tinian Monarch) **O**
M. chrysomela (Black & Yellow Monarch) **L**
ARSES
A. kaupi (Australian Pied Monarch) **M**
A. telescophthalmus (Frilled Monarch) **K,L,M**
MYIAGRA
M. oceanica (Micronesian Myiagra Flycatcher) **J,O**
M. galeata (Helmet Flycatcher) **K**
M. atra (Black Myiagra Flycatcher) **L**   [?]
M. rubecula (Leaden Flycatcher) **L,M**
M. ferrocyanea (Steel-blue Flycatcher) **O**
M. cervinicauda (San Cristobal Myiagra Flycatcher) **O**

M. caledonica (New Caledonian Myiagra Flycatcher) **O**
M. vanikorensis (Red-bellied Flycatcher) **O**
M. albiventris (White-vented Flycatcher) **J**
M. azureocapilla (Blue-headed Flycatcher) **O**
M. ruficollis (Broad-billed Flycatcher) **L,M,O**
M. cyanoleuca (Satin Flycatcher) **L,M**
M. alecto (Shining Flycatcher) **K,L,M**
M. hebetior (Dull Flycatcher) **L**
M. inquieta (Restless Flycatcher) **M**
LAMPROLIA
L. victoriae (Silktail) **O**
MACHAERIRHYNCHUS
M. flaviventer (Yellow-breasted Boatbill) **K,L,M**
M. nigripectus (Black-breasted Boatbill) **L**
PELTOPS
P. blainvillii (Lowland Peltops Flycatcher) **L**
P. montanus (Mountain Peltops Flycatcher) **L**
RHIPIDURINAE
RHIPIDURA
R. hypoxantha (Yellow-bellied Fantail) **B,H,I**
R. superciliaris (Blue Fantail) **J**
R. cyaniceps (Blue-headed Fantail) **J**
R. phoenicura (Red-tailed Fantail) **J**
R. nigrocinnamomea (Black & Cinnamon Fantail) **J**
R. albicollis (White-throated Fantail) **H,I,J**
R. euryura (White-bellied Fantail) **J**
R. aureola (White-browed Fantail) **H,I**
R. javanica (Pied Fantail) **J**
R. perlata (Pearlated Fantail) **J**
R. leucophrys (Willie Wagtail) **K,L,M**
R. rufiventris (Northern Fantail) **J,K,L,M,O**
R. cockerelli (Cockerell's Fantail) **O**
R. albolimbata (Friendly Fantail) **L**
R. threnothorax (Sooty Thicket Fantail) **K,L**
R. hyperythra (Chestnut-bellied Fantail) **K,L**
R. maculipectus (Black Thicket Fantail) **K,L**
R. leucothorax (White-breasted Fantail) **L**
R. atra (Black Fantail) **L**
R. fuliginosa (Collared Gray Fantail) **L,M,N,O**
R. drownei (Mountain Fantail) **O**
R. tenebrosa (Dusky Fantail) **O**
R. rennelliana (Rennell Fantail) **O**
R. spilodera (Spotted Fantail) **O**
R. nebulosa (Samoan Fantail) **O**
R. brachyrhyncha (Dimorphic Rufous Fantail) **L**
R. personata (Kandavu Fantail) **O**
R. dedemi (Seram Rufous Fantail) **K**
R. superflua (Moluccan Fantail) **K**   [?]
R. teysmanni (Sulawesi Rufous Fantail) **K**
R. fuscorufa (Cinnamon-tailed Fantail) **K**
R. diluta (Brown-capped Fantail) **J**
R. opistherythra (Long-tailed Fantail) **L**
R. lepida (Palau Fantail) **J**
R. rufidorsa (Gray-breasted Rufous Fantail) **L**
R. dahli (Island Rufous Fantail) **O**
R. matthiae (St Matthias Rufous Fantail) **O**   [?]
R. malaitae (Malaita Rufous Fantail) **O**
R. rufifrons (Rufous Fantail) **K,L,M,O**
PLATYSTEIRA
P. cyanea (Brown-throated Wattle-eye) **C**
P. albifrons (White-fronted Wattle-eye) **C**
P. peltata (Black-throated Wattle-eye) **C**
P. laticincta (Bamenda Wattle-eye) **C**
P. tonsa (White-spotted Wattle-eye) **C**
P. castanea (Chestnut Wattle-eye) **C**
P. blissetti (Red-cheeked Wattle-eye) **C**
P. chalybea (Reichenow's Wattle-eye) **C**
P. jamesoni (Jameson's Wattle-eye) **C**
P. concreta (Yellow-bellied Wattle-eye) **C**
141 MALURIDAE (FAIRY-WRENS)
CLYTOMIAS
C. insignis (Orange-crowned Fairy-Wren) **L**
MALURUS
M. wallacii (Wallace's Fairy-Wren) **K,L**
M. grayi (Broad-billed Fairy-Wren) **L**
M. alboscapulatus (Black-and-white Fairy-Wren) **M**
M. melanocephalus (Red-backed Fairy-Wren) **M**
M. leucopterus (White-winged Fairy-Wren) **M**
M. cyaneus (Superb Fairy-Wren) **M**
M. splendens (Splendid Fairy-Wren) **M**
M. lamberti (Variegated Fairy-Wren) **M**
M. pulcherrimus (Blue-breasted Fairy-Wren) **M**
M. elegans (Red-winged Fairy-Wren) **M**
M. coronatus (Purple-crowned Fairy-Wren) **M**   [?]
M. cyanocephalus (Emperor Fairy-Wren) **K,L**

STIPITURUS
S. malachurus (Southern Emu-Wren) **M**
S. mallee (Mallee Emu-Wren) **M**
S. ruficeps (Rufous-crowned Emu-Wren) **M**
AMYTORNIS
A. textilis (Thick-billed Grasswren) **M** [?]
A. purnelli (Dusky Grasswren) **M**
A. housei (Black Grasswren) **M**
A. woodwardi (White-throated Grasswren) **M**
A. dorotheae (Red-winged Grasswren) **M** [?]
A. striatus (Striated Grasswren) **M**
A. barbatus (Gray Grasswren) **M** [?]
A. goyderi (Eyrean Grasswren) **M** [I]
142 ACANTHIZIDAE (AUSTRALASIAN WARBLERS)
DASYORNIS
D. brachypterus (Eastern Bristlebird) **M**
D. longirostris (Western Bristlebird) **M**
D. broadbenti (Rufous Bristlebird) **M**
PYCNOPTILUS
P. floccosus (Pilot Bird) **M**
ORIGMA
O. solitaria (Origma) **M**
CRATEROSCELIS
C. gutturalis (Fernwren) **M**
C. murina (Lowland Mouse Warbler) **K,L**
C. nigrorufa (Mid-mountain Mouse Warbler) **L**
C. robusta (Mountain Mouse Warbler) **L**
SERICORNIS
S. citreogularis (Yellow-throated Scrubwren) **M**
S. frontalis (White-browed Scrubwren) **M**
S. beccarii (Little Scrubwren) **K,L,M**
S. nouhuysi (Large Mountain Scrubwren) **L**
S. magnirostris (Large-billed Scrubwren) **M**
S. keri (Atherton Scrubwren) **M**
S. spilodera (Pale-billed Scrubwren) **K,L**
S. parspicillatus (Buff-faced Scrubwren) **L**
S. rufescens (Vogelkop Scrubwren) **L**
S. papuensis (Papuan Scrubwren) **L**
S. arfakianus (Gray-green Scrubwren) **L**
S. magnus (Scrub-Tit) **M**
PYRRHOLAEMUS
P. brunneus (Redthroat) **M**
CHTHONICOLA
C. sagittata (Little Fieldwren) **M**
CALAMANTHUS
C. fuliginosus (Striated Fieldwren) **M**
C. campestris (Rufous Fieldwren) **M**
HYLACOLA
H. pyrrhopygius (Chestnut-rumped Heathwren) **M**
H. cautus (Shy Heathwren) **M**
ACANTHIZA
A. murina (De Vis' Tree Warbler) **L**
A. inornata (Western Thornbill) **M**
A. reguloides (Buff-tailed Thornbill) **K,L,M**
A. iredalei (Samphire Thornbill) **M**
A. katharina (Mountain Thornbill) **M**
A. pusilla (Brown Thornbill) **M**
A. apicalis (Inland Thornbill) **M**
A. ewingi (Tasmanian Thornbill) **M**
A. chrysorrhoa (Yellow-tailed Thornbill) **M**
A. uropygialis (Chestnut-tailed Thornbill) **M**
A. robustirostris (Robust Thornbill) **M**
A. nana (Little Thornbill) **M**
A. lineata (Striated Thornbill) **M**
SMICRORNIS
S. brevirostris (Weebill) **M**
GERYGONE
G. cinerea (Gray Gerygone) **L**
G. chloronota (Green-backed Gerygone) **K,L,M**
G. palpebrosa (Black-headed Gerygone) **K,L,M**
G. olivacea (White-throated Gerygone) **L,M**
G. dorsalis (Rufous-sided Gerygone) **K,L**
G. chrysogaster (Yellow-bellied Gerygone) **K,L**
G. ruficauda (Rufous-tailed Gerygone) **M**
G. magnirostris (Large-billed Gerygone) **K,L,M**
G. sulphurea (Golden-bellied Gerygone) **J,K**
G. inornata (Plain Gerygone) **K**
G. ruficollis (Treefern Gerygone) **L**
G. fusca (White-tailed Gerygone) **M**
G. tenebrosa (Dusky Gerygone) **M**
G. laevigaster (Mangrove Gerygone) **L,M**
G. flavolateralis (Fan-tailed Gerygone) **O**
G. mouki (Brown Gerygone) **M**
G. modesta (Norfolk Island Gerygone) **M**
G. igata (New Zealand Gray Gerygone) **N**

G. albofrontata (Chatham Is Gerygone) **N**
APHELOCEPHALA
A. leucopsis (Southern Whiteface) **M**
A. pectoralis (Chestnut-breasted Whiteface) **M**
A. nigricincta (Banded Whiteface) **M**
MOHOUA
M. ochrocephala (Yellowhead) **N**
FINSCHIA
F. novaeseelandiae (New Zealand Creeper) **N**
143 PACHYCEPHALIDAE (THICKHEADS)
EULACESTOMA
E. nigropectus (Wattled Shrike-Tit) **L**
FALCUNCULUS
F. frontatus (Crested Shrike-Tit) **M**
OREOICA
O. gutturalis (Crested Bellbird) **M**
PACHYCARE
P. flavogrisea (Golden-faced Pachycare) **L**
RHAGOLOGUS
R. leucostigma (Mottled Whistler) **L**
HYLOCITREA
H. bonensis (Buff-throated Thickhead) **K**
CORACORNIS
C. raveni (Maroon-backed Whistler) **K**
ALEADRYAS
A. rufinucha (Rufous-naped Whistler) **L**
PACHYCEPHALA
P. tenebrosa (Sooty Whistler) **L**
P. olivacea (Olive Whistler) **M**
P. rufogularis (Red-lored Whistler) **M**
P. inornata (Gilbert Whistler) **M**
P. grisola (Mangrove Whistler) **H,I,J**
P. plateni (Palawan Whistler) **J**
P. phaionota (Island Whistler) **K,L**
P. hyperythra (Rufous-breasted Whistler) **L**
P. modesta (Brown-backed Whistler) **L**
P. philippinensis (Yellow-bellied Whistler) **J**
P. sulfuriventer (Sulfur-vented Whistler) **K**
P. hypoxantha (Bornean Mountain Whistler) **J**
P. meyeri (Vogelkop Whistler) **L** [?]
P. soror (Sclater's Whistler) **L**
P. simplex (Gray Whistler) **K,L,M**
P. orpheus (Fawn-breasted Whistler) **K**
P. pectoralis (Golden Whistler) **J,K,L,M,O**
P. melanops (Tonga Whistler) **O**
P. melanura (Mangrove Golden Whistler) **L,M**
P. flavifrons (Yellow-fronted Whistler) **O**
P. caledonica (New Caledonian Whistler) **O**
P. implicata (Mountain Whistler) **O**
P. nudigula (Bare-throated Whistler) **J**
P. lorentzi (Lorentz's Whistler) **L**
P. schlegelii (Schlegel's Whistler) **L**
P. aurea (Yellow-backed Whistler) **L**
P. rufiventris (Rufous Whistler) **M,O**
P. monacha (Aru Whistler) **K**
P. leucogastra (White-bellied Whistler) **L**
P. arctitorquis (Wallacean Whistler) **K**
P. griseonota (Drab Whistler) **K**
P. lanioides (White-breasted Whistler) **M**
COLLURICINCLA
C. megarhyncha (Rufous Shrike-Thrush) **K,L,M**
C. boweri (Stripe-breasted Shrike-Thrush) **M**
C. harmonica (Gray Shrike-Thrush) **M**
C. woodwardi (Sandstone Shrike-Thrush) **M**
PITOHUI
P. kirhocephalus (Variable Pitohui) **K,L**
P. dichrous (Black-headed Pitohui) **L**
P. incertus (Mottle-breasted Pitohui) **L**
P. ferrugineus (Rusty Pitohui) **K,L**
P. cristatus (Crested Pitohui) **L**
P. nigrescens (Black Pitohui) **L**
P. tenebrosus (Morning Bird) **J**
TURNAGRA
T. capensis (New Zealand Thrush) **N**
144 AEGITHALIDAE (LONG-TAILED TITS)
AEGITHALOS
A. caudatus (Long-tailed Tit) **B**
A. leucogenys (White-cheeked Tit) **H**
A. concinnus (Red-headed Tit) **H,I**
A. iouschistos (Blyth's Long-tailed Tit) **H,I**
A. fuliginosus (Sooty Long-tailed Tit) **B**
PSALTRIA
P. exilis (Pygmy Tit) **J**
PSALTRIPARUS
P. minimus (Bushtit) **A,E**

145 REMIZIDAE (PENDULINE TITS)
REMIZ
R. pendulinus (Penduline Tit) **B,H**
ANTHOSCOPUS
A. punctifrons (Sennar Kapok Tit) **C**
A. parvulus (Yellow Penduline Tit) **C**
A. musculus (Mouse-colored Tit) **C**
A. flavifrons (Yellow-fronted Tit) **C**
A. caroli (African Penduline Tit) **C**
A. sylviella (Rungwe Penduline Tit) **C**
A. minutus (Southern Kapok Tit) **C**
AURIPARUS
A. flaviceps (Verdin) **A,E**
CEPHALOPYRUS
C. flammiceps (Fire-capped Tit Warbler) **B,H**
146 PARIDAE (TRUE TITS)
PARUS
P. palustris (Marsh Tit) **B,I**
P. lugubris (Sombre Tit) **B**
P. hyrcanus (Iranian Sombre Tit) **B**
P. montanus (Willow Tit) **B**
P. atricapillus (Black-capped Chickadee) **A**
P. carolinensis (Carolina Chickadee) **A**
P. sclateri (Mexican Chickadee) **A,E**
P. gambeli (Mountain Chickadee) **A**
P. superciliosus (White-browed Tit) **B**
P. davidi (Père David's Tit) **B**
P. cinctus (Siberian Tit) **A,B**
P. hudsonicus (Boreal Chickadee) **A**
P. rufescens (Chestnut-backed Chickadee) **A**
P. wollweberi (Bridled Titmouse) **E**
P. rubidiventris (Black-crested Tit) **H,I**
P. rufonuchalis (Rufous-naped Tit) **B,H**
P. melanolophus (Vigors' Crested Tit) **H**
P. ater (Coal Tit) **B,H,I,J**
P. venustulus (Yellow-bellied Tit) **B**
P. elegans (Elegant Tit) **J**
P. amabilis (Palawan Tit) **J**
P. cristatus (Crested Tit) **B**
P. dichrous (Brown Crested Tit) **B,H,I**
P. afer (Southern Gray Tit) **C**
P. cinerascens (Acacia Gray Tit) **C**
P. griseiventris (Miombo Gray Tit) **C**
P. niger (Southern Black Tit) **C**
P. leucomelas (White-winged Black Tit) **C**
P. carpi (Carp's Tit) **C**
P. albiventris (White-breasted Tit) **C**
P. leuconotus (White-backed Black Tit) **C**
P. funereus (Dusky Tit) **C**
P. fasciiventer (Stripe-breasted Tit) **C**
P. fringillinus (Red-throated Tit) **C**
P. rufiventris (Rufous-bellied Tit) **C**
P. major (Great Tit) **B,H,I,J,K**
P. bokharensis (Turkestan Tit) **B**
P. monticolus (Green-backed Tit) **B,H,I,J**
P. nuchalis (White-naped Tit) **H** [?]
P. xanthogenys (Yellow-cheeked Yellow Tit) **H**
P. spilonotus (Chinese Yellow Tit) **H,I**
P. holsti (Formosan Yellow Tit) **J** [?]
P. caeruleus (Blue Tit) **B**
P. cyanus (Azure Tit) **B**
P. varius (Varied Tit) **B,J**
P. semilarvatus (White-fronted Tit) **J**
P. inornatus (Plain Titmouse) **A,E**
P. bicolor (Tufted Titmouse) **A,E**
MELANOCHLORA
M. sultanea (Sultan Tit) **H,I,J**
SYLVIPARUS
S. modestus (Yellow-browed Tit) **H,I**
147 SITTIDAE (NUTHATCHES)
SITTINAE
SITTA
S. europaea (Eurasian Nuthatch) **B,H,I**
S. castanea (Chestnut-bellied Nuthatch) **H,I**
S. himalayensis (White-tailed Nuthatch) **H,I**
S. victoriae (White-browed Nuthatch) **I** [?]
S. pygmaea (Pygmy Nuthatch) **A,E**
S. pusilla (Brown-headed Nuthatch) **A,E**
S. whiteheadi (Corsican Nuthatch) **B** [?]
S. yunnanensis (Yunnan Nuthatch) **B** [?]
S. canadensis (Red-breasted Nuthatch) **A**
S. villosa (Chinese Nuthatch) **B**
S. leucopsis (White-cheeked Nuthatch) **H**
S. carolinensis (White-breasted Nuthatch) **A,E**
S. krueperi (Krüper's Nuthatch) **B**
S. ledanti (Kabylie Nuthatch) **B** [R]

S. neumayer (Rock Nuthatch) **B**
S. tephronota (Eastern Rock Nuthatch) **B,H**
S. frontalis (Velvet-fronted Nuthatch) **H,I,J**
S. solangiae (Lilac Nuthatch) **I** ?
S. azurea (Azure Nuthatch) **J**
S. magna (Giant Nuthatch) **B,I** ?
S. formosa (Beautiful Nuthatch) **I** ?
TICHODROMADINAE
TICHODROMA
T. muraria (Wallcreeper) **B,H**
DAPHOENOSITTINAE
NEOSITTA
N. chrysoptera (Varied Sittella) **M**
N. papuensis (Papuan Sittella) **L**
DAPHOENOSITTA
D. miranda (Pink-faced Nuthatch) **L**
148 CERTHIIDAE (HOLARCTIC
TREECREEPERS)
CERTHIINAE
CERTHIA
C. familiaris (Common Treecreeper) **B,I**
C. americana (Brown Creeper) **A,E**
C. brachydactyla (Short-toed Treecreeper) **B**
C. himalayana (Himalayan Treecreeper) **B,H,I**
C. nipalensis (Stoliczka's Treecreeper) **B,H,I**
C. discolor (Brown-throated Treecreeper) **H,I**
SALPORNITHINAE
SALPORNIS
S. spilonotus (Spotted Gray Creeper) **C,H**
149 RHABDORNITHIDAE (PHILIPPINE
CREEPERS)
RHABDORNIS
R. mystacalis (Stripe-headed Creeper) **J**
R. inornatus (Plain-headed Creeper) **J**
150 CLIMACTERIDAE (AUSTRALIAN
TREECREEPERS)
CLIMACTERIS
C. erythrops (Red-browed Treecreeper) **M**
C. affinis (White-browed Treecreeper) **M**
C. picumnus (Brown Treecreeper) **M**
C. rufa (Rufous Treecreeper) **M**
C. melanura (Black-tailed Treecreeper) **M**
C. leucophaea (White-throated Treecreeper) **M**
C. placens (Papuan Treecreeper) **L**
151 DICAEIDAE (FLOWERPECKERS)
MELANOCHARIS
M. arfakiana (Obscure Berrypecker) **L**
M. nigra (Black Berrypecker) **K,L**
M. longicauda (Mid-mountain Berrypecker) **L**
M. versteri (Fan-tailed Berrypecker) **L**
M. striativentris (Streaked Berrypecker) **L**
RHAMPHOCHARIS
R. crassirostris (Spotted Berrypecker) **L**
PRIONOCHILUS
P. olivaceus (Olive-backed Flowerpecker) **J**
P. maculatus (Yellow-throated Flowerpecker) **I,J**
P. percussus (Crimson-breasted Flowerpecker) **I,J**
P. plateni (Palawan Yellow-rumped Flowerpecker) **J**
P. xanthopygius (Borneo Yellow-rumped
Flowerpecker) **J**
P. thoracicus (Scarlet-breasted Flowerpecker) **J**
DICAEUM
D. annae (Sunda Flowerpecker) **J**
D. agile (Thick-billed Flowerpecker) **H,I,J**
D. everetti (Brown-backed Flowerpecker) **J** ?
D. proprium (Gray-breasted Flowerpecker) **J**
D. chrysorrheum (Yellow-vented Flowerpecker)
H,I,J
D. melanoxanthum (Yellow-bellied Flowerpecker)
H,I
D. vincens (Legge's Flowerpecker) **H** ?
D. aureolimbatum (Yellow-sided Flowerpecker) **J,K**
D. nigrilore (Olive-capped Flowerpecker) **J**
D. anthonyi (Yellow-crowned Flowerpecker) **J**
D. bicolor (Bicolored Flowerpecker) **J**
D. australe (Philippine Flowerpecker) **J**
D. retrocinctum (Mindoro Flowerpecker) **J**
D. trigonostigma (Orange-bellied Flowerpecker)
H,I,J,K
D. hypoleucum (White-bellied Flowerpecker) **J**
D. erythrorhynchos (Tickell's Flowerpecker) **H,I**
D. concolor (Plain Flowerpecker) **H,I,J,K**
D. pygmaeum (Palawan Flowerpecker) **J**
D. nehrkorni (Red-headed Flowerpecker) **K**
D. vulneratum (Ashy-fronted Flowerpecker) **K**
D. erythrothorax (White-throated Flowerpecker) **K**

D. pectorale (Olive-crowned Flowerpecker) **K,L**
D. geelvinkianum (Red-capped Flowerpecker) **L**
D. nitidum (Louisiade Flowerpecker) **L**
D. eximium (New Ireland Flowerpecker) **O**
D. aeneum (Solomon Is Flowerpecker) **O**
D. tristrami (San Cristobal Flowerpecker) **O**
D. igniferum (Black-banded Flowerpecker) **J,K**
D. maugei (Blue-cheeked Flowerpecker) **J**
D. hirundinaceum (Mistletoebird) **K,L,M**
D. celebicum (Black-sided Flowerpecker) **K**
D. monticolum (Bornean Fire-breasted
Flowerpecker) **J**
D. ignipectus (Green-backed Flowerpecker) **H,J,K**
D. sanguinolentum (Blood-breasted Flowerpecker) **J**
D. cruentatum (Scarlet-backed Flowerpecker) **H,J**
D. trochileum (Scarlet-headed Flowerpecker) **J**
OREOCHARIS
O. arfaki (Tit Berrypecker) **L**
PARAMYTHIA
P. montium (Crested Berrypecker) **L**
152 PARDALOTIDAE (PARDALOTES)
PARDALOTUS
P. quadragintus (Forty-spotted Pardalote) **M** ?
P. punctatus (Spotted Pardalote) **M**
P. rubricatus (Red-browed Pardalote) **M**
P. striatus (Striated Pardalote) **M**
153 NECTARINIIDAE (SUNBIRDS)
ANTHREPTES
A. gabonicus (Brown Sunbird) **C**
A. fraseri (Scarlet-tufted Sunbird) **C**
A. reichenowi (Plain-backed Sunbird) **C**
A. anchietae (Anchieta's Sunbird) **C**
A. simplex (Plain-colored Sunbird) **I,J**
A. malacensis (Plain-throated Sunbird) **I,J,K**
A. rhodolaema (Shelley's Sunbird) **I,J**
A. singalensis (Ruby-cheeked Sunbird) **H,I,J**
A. longuemarei (Violet-backed Sunbird) **C**
A. orientalis (Kenya Violet-backed Sunbird) **C**
A. neglectus (Uluguru Violet-backed Sunbird) **C**
A. aurantium (Violet-tailed Sunbird) **C**
A. pallidigaster (Amani Sunbird) **C** R
A. rectirostris (Green Sunbird) **C**
A. rubritorques (Banded Green Sunbird) **C** R
A. collaris (Collared Sunbird) **C**
A. platurus (Pygmy Sunbird) **C**
HYPOGRAMMA
H. hypogrammicum (Blue-naped Sunbird) **I,J**
NECTARINIA
N. seimundi (Little Green Sunbird) **C**
N. batesi (Bates's Olive Sunbird) **C**
N. olivacea (Olive Sunbird) **C**
N. ursulae (Fernando Po Sunbird) **C**
N. veroxii (Mouse-colored Sunbird) **C**
N. balfouri (Socotra Sunbird) **C**
N. reichenbachii (Reichenbach's Sunbird) **C**
N. hartlaubii (Principe Sunbird) **C**
N. newtonii (Newton's Yellow-breasted Sunbird) **C**
N. thomensis (Sao Thomé Giant Sunbird) **C**
N. oritis (Cameroun Blue-headed Sunbird) **C**
N. alinae (Blue-headed Sunbird) **C**
N. bannermani (Bannerman's Sunbird) **C**
N. verticalis (Green-headed Sunbird) **C**
N. cyanolaema (Blue-throated Sunbird) **C**
N. fuliginosa (Carmelite Sunbird) **C**
N. rubescens (Green-throated Sunbird) **C**
N. amethystina (Amethyst Sunbird) **C**
N. senegalensis (Scarlet-chested Sunbird) **C**
N. hunteri (Hunter's Sunbird) **C**
N. adelberti (Buff-throated Sunbird) **C**
N. zeylonica (Purple-rumped Sunbird) **H**
N. minima (Small Sunbird) **H**
N. sperata (Van Hasselt's Sunbird) **H,I,J**
N. sericea (Black Sunbird) **J,K,L,O**
N. calcostetha (Macklot's Sunbird) **I,J**
N. dussumieri (Seychelles Sunbird) **D**
N. lotenia (Loten's Sunbird) **H**
N. jugularis (Yellow-bellied Sunbird) **I,J,K,L,M**
N. buettikoferi (Sumba I Sunbird) **K** ?
N. solaris (Timor Sunbird) **J**
N. asiatica (Purple Sunbird) **B,H,I**
N. souimanga (Souimanga Sunbird) **D**
N. humbloti (Humblot's Sunbird) **D**
N. comorensis (Anjouan Sunbird) **D**
N. coquerellii (Mayotte Sunbird) **D**
N. venusta (Variable Sunbird) **C**
N. talatala (Southern White-bellied Sunbird) **C**

N. oustaleti (Oustalet's White-bellied Sunbird) **C**
N. fusca (Dusky Sunbird) **C**
N. chalybea (Lesser Double-collared Sunbird) **C**
N. manoensis (Miombo Double-collared Sunbird) **C**
N. afra (Greater Double-collared Sunbird) **C**
N. prigoginei (Double-breasted Sunbird) **C** E
N. preussi (Northern Double-collared Sunbird) **C**
N. mediocris (Eastern Double-collared Sunbird) **C**
N. neergaardi (Neergaard's Sunbird) **C**
N. chloropygia (Olive-bellied Sunbird) **C**
N. minulla (Tiny Sunbird) **C**
N. regia (Regal Sunbird) **C**
N. loveridgei (Loveridge's Sunbird) **C**
N. moreaui (Moreau's Sunbird) **C**
N. rockefelleri (Rockefeller's Sunbird) **C** R
N. violacea (Orange-breasted Sunbird) **C**
N. habessinica (Shining Sunbird) **B,C**
N. bouvieri (Southern Orange-tufted Sunbird) **C**
N. osea (Northern Orange-tufted Sunbird) **B,C**
N. cuprea (Coppery Sunbird) **C**
N. tacazze (Tacazze Sunbird) **C**
N. bocagii (Bocage's Sunbird) **C**
N. purpureiventris (Purple-breasted Sunbird) **C**
N. shelleyi (Shelley's Sunbird) **C**
N. mariquensis (Mariqua Sunbird) **C**
N. pembae (Violet-breasted Sunbird) **C**
N. bifasciata (Purple-banded Sunbird) **C**
N. coccinigastra (Splendid Sunbird) **C**
N. erythrocerca (Red-chested Sunbird) **C**
N. congensis (Congo Black-bellied Sunbird) **C**
N. pulchella (Beautiful Sunbird) **C**
N. nectarinioides (Smaller Black-bellied Sunbird) **C**
N. famosa (Yellow-tufted Malachite Sunbird) **C**
N. johnstoni (Red-tufted Malachite Sunbird) **C**
N. notata (Noted Sunbird) **D**
N. rufipennis (Rufous-winged Sunbird) **C** R
N. johannae (Madame Verreaux's Sunbird) **C**
N. superba (Superb Sunbird) **C**
N. kilimensis (Bronze Sunbird) **C**
N. reichenowi (Golden-winged Sunbird) **C**
AETHOPYGA
A. primigenius (Hachisuka's Sunbird) **J**
A. boltoni (Apo Sunbird) **J**
A. flagrans (Flaming Sunbird) **J**
A. pulcherrima (Mountain Sunbird) **J**
A. duyvenbodei (Sanghir Yellow-backed
Sunbird) **K** ?
A. shelleyi (Palawan Sunbird) **J**
A. gouldiae (Mrs Gould's Sunbird) **H,I**
A. nipalensis (Green-tailed Sunbird) **H,I**
A. eximia (Kuhl's Sunbird) **J**
A. christinae (Fork-tailed Sunbird) **I**
A. saturata (Black-throated Sunbird) **B,H,I,J**
A. siparaja (Yellow-backed Sunbird) **H,I,J,K**
A. mystacalis (Scarlet Sunbird) **J**
A. ignicauda (Fire-tailed Sunbird) **H,I**
ARACHNOTHERA
A. longirostra (Little Spiderhunter) **H,I,J**
A. crassirostris (Thick-billed Spiderhunter) **I,J**
A. robusta (Long-billed Spiderhunter) **J**
A. flavigaster (Greater Yellow-eared Spiderhunter)
I,J
A. chrysogenys (Lesser Yellow-eared Spiderhunter)
I,J
A. clarae (Naked-faced Spiderhunter) **J**
A. affinis (Gray-breasted Spiderhunter) **I,J**
A. magna (Streaked Spiderhunter) **H,I**
A. everetti (Everett's Spiderhunter) **J**
A. juliae (Whitehead's Spiderhunter) **J**
154 ZOSTEROPIDAE (WHITE-EYES)
ZOSTEROPS
Z. erythropleura (Chestnut-flanked White-eye) **B**
Z. japonica (Japanese White-eye) **B,J**
Z. meyeni (Philippine White-eye) **J**
Z. palpebrosa (Oriental White-eye) **H,I,J,K**
Z. ceylonensis (Large Sri Lanka White-eye) **H**
Z. conspicillata (Bridled White-eye) **O**
Z. salvadorii (Enggano White-eye) **J**
Z. atricapilla (Black-capped White-eye) **J**
Z. everetti (Everett's White-eye) **J,K**
Z. nigrorum (Philippine Yellow White-eye) **J**
Z. montanus (Mountain White-eye) **J,K**
Z. wallacei (Yellow-spectacled White-eye) **J**
Z. flava (Javan White-eye) **J** ?
Z. chloris (Lemon-bellied White-eye) **J,K**
Z. citrinella (Pale White-eye) **K**

Z. consobrinorum (Pale-bellied White-eye) **K**
Z. grayi (Pearl-bellied White-eye) **K**
Z. uropygialis (Golden-bellied White-eye) **K**
Z. anomala (Lemon-throated White-eye) **K**
Z. atriceps (Creamy-throated White-eye) **K**
Z. atrifrons (Moluccan Black-fronted White-eye) **K**
Z. minor (New Guinea Black-fronted White-eye) **L**
Z. meeki (White-throated White-eye) **O** ?
Z. mysorensis (Biak White-eye) **L** ?
Z. fuscicapilla (Yellow-bellied Mountain White-eye)
L
Z. buruensis (Buru I White-eye) **K**
Z. kuehni (Ambon White-eye) **K** ?
Z. novaeguineae (New Guinea Mountain White-eye)
K,L
Z. metcalfii (Yellow-throated White-eye) **O**
Z. natalis (Christmas Island White-eye) **O**
Z. lutea (Yellow Silver-eye) **M**
Z. griseotincta (Louisiades White-eye) **L,O**
Z. rennelliana (Rennell I White-eye) **O**
Z. rendovae (Solomon Is White-eye) **O**
Z. murphyi (Kulambangra Mountain White-eye) **O**
Z. ugiensis (Gray-throated White-eye) **O**
Z. stresemanni (Malaita White-eye) **O**
Z. sanctaecrucis (Santa Cruz White-eye) **O** ?
Z. samoensis (Savaii White-eye) **O**
Z. explorator (Layard's White-eye) **O**
Z. flavifrons (Yellow-fronted White-eye) **O**
Z. minuta (Small Lifu White-eye) **O** ?
Z. xanthochroa (New Caledonia White-eye) **O**
Z. gouldi (Western Silver-eye) **M**
Z. lateralis (Gray-backed White-eye) **M,N,O**
Z. tenuirostris (Slender-billed White-eye) **O**
Z. albogularis (White-chested White-eye) **O** E
Z. inornata (Large Lifu White-eye) **O** ?
Z. cinerea (Gray-brown White-eye) **J**
Z. abyssinica (White-breasted White-eye) **C**
Z. pallida (Cape White-eye) **C**
Z. senegalensis (African Yellow White-eye) **C**
Z. borbonica (Bourbon White-eye) **D**
Z. ficedulina (Principe White-eye) **C**
Z. griseovirescens (Annobon White-eye) **C**
Z. hovarum (Hova Gray-backed White-eye) **D**
Z. maderaspatana (Madagascar White-eye) **D**
Z. mayottensis (Chestnut-sided White-eye) **D**
Z. modesta (Seychelles Brown White-eye) **D** E
Z. mouroniensis (Grand Comoro White-eye) **D** R
Z. olivacea (Olive White-eye) **D**
Z. chloronothos (Mauritius Olive White-eye) **D** V
Z. vaughani (Pemba White-eye) **C**
WOODFORDIA
W. superciliosa (Woodford's White-eye) **O**
W. lacertosa (Sanford's White-eye) **O** ?
RUKIA
R. palauensis (Palau White-eye) **J**
R. oleaginea (Yap White-eye) **O**
R. ruki (Truk White-eye) **O** E
R. longirostra (Ponape White-eye) **O** R
TEPHROZOSTEROPS
T. stalkeri (Bicolored White-eye) **K**
MADANGA
M. ruficollis (Rufous-throated White-eye) **K** ?
LOPHOZOSTEROPS
L. pinaiae (Gray-hooded White-eye) **K**
L. goodfellowi (Goodfellow's White-eye) **J,K**
L. squamiceps (Streaky-headed White-eye) **K**
L. javanicus (Javan Gray-throated White-eye) **J**
L. superciliaris (White-browed White-eye) **J**
L. dohertyi (Crested White-eye) **J** ?
OCULOCINCTA
O. squamifrons (Pygmy White-eye) **J** ?
HELEIA
H. muelleri (Timor White-eye) **J** ?
H. crassirostris (Stripe-headed White-eye) **J**
CHLOROCHARIS
C. emiliae (Olive Black-eye) **J**
HYPOCRYPTADIUS
H. cinnamomeus (Cinnamon White-eye) **J**
SPEIROPS
S. brunnea (Fernando Po Speirops) **C** R
S. leucophaea (Prince's I Speirops) **C** ?
S. lugubris (Black-capped Speirops) **C**
155 MELIPHAGIDAE (HONEYEATERS)
TIMELIOPSIS
T. fulvigula (Mountain Straight-billed Honeyeater) **L**
T. griseigula (Lowland Straight-billed Honeyeater) **L**

MELILESTES
M. megarhynchus (Long-billed Honeyeater) **K,L**
M. bougainvillei (Bougainville Honeyeater) **O**
TOXORHAMPHUS
T. novaeguineae (Yellow-bellied Longbill) **K,L**
T. poliopterus (Slaty-chinned Longbill) **L**
OEDISTOMA
O. iliolophum (Gray-bellied Honeyeater) **L**
O. pygmaeum (Pygmy Honeyeater) **L**
GLYCICHAERA
G. fallax (White-eyed Honeyeater) **L,M**
LICHMERA
L. lombokia (Lombok Honeyeater) **J**
L. argentauris (Plain Olive Honeyeater) **K,L**
L. indistincta (Brown Honeyeater) **J,K,L,M**
L. incana (Silver-eared Honeyeater) **O**
L. alboauricularis (White-eared Honeyeater) **L**
L. squamata (White-tufted Honeyeater) **L**
L. deningeri (Buru Honeyeater) **K**
L. monticola (Spectacled Honeyeater) **K**
L. flavicans (Timor Honeyeater) **J**
L. notabilis (Black-chested Honeyeater) **K**
L. cockerelli (White-streaked Honeyeater) **M**
MYZOMELA
M. blasii (Ambon Honeyeater) **K**
M. albigula (White-chinned Honeyeater) **L**
M. cineracea (Bismarck Honeyeater) **L,O**
M. eques (Red-spot Honeyeater) **L**
M. obscura (Dusky Honeyeater) **K,L,M**
M. cruentata (Red Honeyeater) **L,O**
M. nigrita (Black Honeyeater) **K,L**
M. pulchella (New Ireland Honeyeater) **O**
M. kuehni (Crimson-hooded Honeyeater) **K** ?
M. erythrocephala (Mangrove Red-headed
Honeyeater) **L,M**
M. adolphinae (Mountain Red-headed Honeyeater) **L**
M. sanguinolenta (Scarlet Honeyeater) **K,L,M**
M. cardinalis (Cardinal Honeyeater) **O**
M. sclateri (Scarlet-throated Honeyeater) **L,O**
M. lafargei (Small Bougainville Honeyeater) **O**
M. melanocephala (Black-headed Honeyeater) **O**
M. eichhorni (Yellow-vented Honeyeater) **O**
M. malaitae (Malaita Honeyeater) **O**
M. tristrami (Tristram's Honeyeater) **O**
M. jugularis (Orange-breasted Honeyeater) **O**
M. erythromelas (Black-bellied Honeyeater) **O**
M. vulnerata (Sunda Honeyeater) **J**
M. rosenbergii (Black & Red Honeyeater) **L**
CERTHIONYX
C. niger (Black Honeyeater) **M**
C. variegatus (Pied Honeyeater) **M**
MELIPHAGA
M. mimikae (Large Spot-breasted Honeyeater) **L**
M. montana (White-eared Mountain Honeyeater) **L**
M. orientalis (Small Spot-breasted Honeyeater) **L**
M. albonotata (White-marked Honeyeater) **L**
M. aruensis (Puff-backed Honeyeater) **K,L**
M. analoga (Mimic Meliphaga) **K,L**
M. vicina (Louisiades Honeyeater) **L** ?
M. gracilis (Graceful Honeyeater) **L,M**
M. notata (Lesser Lewin Honeyeater) **M**
M. flavirictus (Yellow-gaped Honeyeater) **L**
M. lewinii (Lewin Honeyeater) **M**
M. flava (Yellow Honeyeater) **M**
M. albilineata (White-striped Honeyeater) **M**
M. virescens (Singing Honeyeater) **M**
M. versicolor (Varied Honeyeater) **L,M**
M. fasciogularis (Mangrove Honeyeater) **M**
M. inexpectata (Guadalcanal Honeyeater) **O**
M. fusca (Fuscous Honeyeater) **L,M**
M. plumula (Yellow-fronted Honeyeater) **M**
M. chrysops (Yellow-faced Honeyeater) **M**
M. cratitia (Purple-gaped Honeyeater) **M**
M. keartlandi (Gray-headed Honeyeater) **M**
M. penicillata (White-plumed Honeyeater) **M**
M. hindwoodi (Eungella Honeyeater) **M**
M. ornata (Mallee Honeyeater) **M**
M. reticulata (Reticulated Honeyeater) **J**
M. leucotis (White-eared Honeyeater) **M**
M. flavicollis (Yellow-throated Honeyeater) **M**
M. melanops (Yellow-tufted Honeyeater) **M**
M. unicolor (White-gaped Honeyeater) **M**
M. flaviventer (Tawny-breasted Honeyeater) **K,L,M**
M. polygramma (Spotted Honeyeater) **K,L**
M. macleayana (Yellow-streaked Honeyeater) **M**
M. frenata (Bridled Honeyeater) **M**

M. subfrenata (Black-throated Honeyeater) **L**
M. obscura (Obscure Honeyeater) **L**
OREORNIS
O. chrysogenys (Orange-cheeked Honeyeater) **L**
FOULEHAIO
F. carunculata (Carunculated Honeyeater) **O**
F. provocator (Yellow-faced Honeyeater) **O**
CLEPTORNIS
C. marchei (Golden Honeyeater) **O**
APALOPTERON
A. familiare (Bonin Island Honeyeater) **B**
MELITHREPTUS
M. brevirostris (Brown-headed Honeyeater) **M**
M. lunatus (White-naped Honeyeater) **M**
M. albogularis (White-throated Honeyeater) **M**
M. affinis (Black-headed Honeyeater) **M**
M. gularis (Black-chinned Honeyeater) **M**
M. laetior (Golden-backed Honeyeater) **M**
M. validirostris (Strong-billed Honeyeater) **M**
ENTOMYZON
E. cyanotis (Blue-faced Honeyeater) **L,M**
NOTIOMYSTIS
N. cincta (Stitchbird) **N** V
PYCNOPYGIUS
P. ixoides (New Guinea Brown Honeyeater) **L**
P. cinereus (Gray-fronted Honeyeater) **L**
P. stictocephalus (Streak-capped Honeyeater) **K,L**
PHILEMON
P. meyeri (Meyer's Friarbird) **L** ?
P. brassi (Brass's Friarbird) **L** ?
P. citreogularis (Little Friarbird) **L,M**
P. inornatus (Plain Friarbird) **J**
P. gilolensis (Striated Friarbird) **K**
P. fuscicapillus (Dusky Friarbird) **K** ?
P. subcorniculatus (Gray-necked Friarbird) **K**
P. moluccensis (Moluccas Friarbird) **K,L** ?
P. buceroides (Timor Helmeted Friarbird) **J,K,M**
P. gordoni (Melville I Friarbird) **M**
P. novaeguineae (New Guinea Friarbird) **L,M**
P. cockerelli (New Britain Friarbird) **O**
P. eichhorni (New Ireland Friarbird) **O**
P. albitorques (White-naped Friarbird) **L**
P. argenticeps (Silver-crowned Friarbird) **M**
P. corniculatus (Noisy Friarbird) **M**
P. diemenensis (New Caledonian Friarbird) **O**
PTILOPRORA
P. plumbea (Leaden Honeyeater) **L**
P. meekiana (Meek's Streaked Honeyeater) **L**
P. erythropleura (Red-sided streaked Honeyeater) **L**
P. guisei (Red-backed Honeyeater) **L**
P. mayri (Mayr's Streaked Honeyeater) **L**
P. perstriata (Black-backed Streaked Honeyeater) **L**
MELIDECTES
M. fuscus (Sooty Honeyeater) **L**
M. whitemanensis (Gilliard's Honeyeater) **O**
M. princeps (Long-bearded Melidectes) **L**
M. nouhuysi (Short-bearded Melidectes) **L**
M. ochromelas (Mid-mountain Honeyeater) **L**
M. leucostephes (White-fronted Melidectes) **L**
M. belfordi (Belford's Melidectes) **L**
M. rufocrissalis (Reichenow's Melidectes) **L**
M. foersteri (Foerster's Melidectes) **L** ?
M. torquatus (Cinnamon-breasted Wattlebird) **L**
MELIPOTES
M. gymnops (Arfak Melipotes) **L**
M. ater (Huon Melipotes) **L** ?
M. fumigatus (Common Melipotes) **L**
MYZA
M. celebensis (Brown Honeysucker) **K**
M. sarasinorum (Spot-headed Honeysucker) **K**
MELIARCHUS
M. sclateri (San Cristobal Honeyeater) **O**
GYMNOMYZA
G. viridis (Green Honeyeater) **O**
G. samoensis (Black-breasted Honeyeater) **O**
G. aubryana (Red-faced Honeyeater) **O** ?
MOHO
M. braccatus (Kauai O-o) **P** E
GLYCIPHILUS
G. melanops (Tawny-crowned Honeyeater) **M**
PHYLIDONYRIS
P. pyrrhoptera (Crescent Honeyeater) **M**
P. novaehollandiae (New Holland Honeyeater) **M**
P. nigra (White-cheeked Honeyeater) **M**
P. albifrons (White-fronted Honeyeater) **M**
P. undulata (Barred Honeyeater) **O**

AUSTRALIAN CHATS

P. notabilis (White-bellied Honeyeater) **O**
RAMSAYORNIS
R. fasciatus (Bar-breasted Honeyeater) **M**
R. modestus (Brown-backed Honeyeater) **L,M**
PLECTORHYNCHA
P. lanceolata (Striped Honeyeater) **M**
CONOPOPHILA
C. whitei (Gray Honeyeater) **M**
C. albogularis (Rufous-banded Honeyeater) **K,L,M**
C. rufogularis (Red-throated Honeyeater) **M**
C. picta (Painted Honeyeater) **M**
XANTHOMYZA
X. phrygia (Regent Honeyeater) **M**   ?
CISSOMELA
C. pectoralis (Banded Honeyeater) **M**
ACANTHORHYNCHUS
A. tenuirostris (Eastern Spinebill) **M**
A. superciliosus (Western Spinebill) **M**
MANORINA
M. melanophrys (Bell Miner) **M**
M. melanocephala (Noisy Miner) **M**
M. obscura (Dusky Miner) **M**
M. flavigula (Yellow-throated Miner) **M**
M. melanotis (Black-eared Miner) **M**   ?
ANTHORNIS
A. melanura (New Zealand Bellbird) **N**
ACANTHAGENYS
A. rufogularis (Spiny-cheeked Honeyeater) **L,M**
ANTHOCHAERA
A. chrysoptera (Little Wattlebird) **M**
A. carunculata (Red Wattlebird) **M**
A. paradoxa (Yellow Wattlebird) **M**
PROSTHEMADURA
P. novaeseelandiae (Tui) **N**
156 EPHTHIANURIDAE (AUSTRALIAN CHATS)
EPHTHIANURA
E. albifrons (White-faced Chat) **M**
E. tricolor (Crimson Chat) **M**
E. aurifrons (Orange Chat) **M**
E. crocea (Yellow Chat) **M**
ASHBYIA
A. lovensis (Desert Chat) **M**
157 PROMEROPIDAE (SUGARBIRDS)
PROMEROPS
P. cafer (Cape Sugarbird) **C**
P. gurneyi (Gurney's Sugarbird) **C**
158 EMBERIZIDAE (BUNTINGS, TANAGERS
AND RELATIVES
EMBERIZINAE (OLD WORLD BUNTINGS, NEW WORLD
SPARROWS)
MELOPHUS
M. lathami (Crested Bunting) **H**
LATOUCHEORNIS
L. siemsseni (Fokien Blue Bunting) **B**
EMBERIZA
E. calandra (Corn Bunting) **B**
E. citrinella (Yellowhammer) **B**
E. leucocephala (Pine Bunting) **B**
E. cia (Rock Bunting) **B,H**
E. cioides (Siberian Meadow Bunting) **B**
E. jankowskii (Jankowski's Bunting) **B**   ?
E. buchanani (Gray-necked Bunting) **B,H**
E. stewarti (White-capped Bunting) **B,H**
E. cineracea (Cinereous Bunting) **B**
E. hortulana (Ortolan Bunting) **B,C**
E. caesia (Cretzschmar's Bunting) **B**
E. cirlus (Cirl Bunting) **B**
E. striolata (House Bunting) **C,H**
E. impetuani (Larklike Bunting) **C**
E. tahapisi (Cinnamon-breasted Rock Bunting) **B,C**
E. socotrana (Socotra Mountain Bunting) **C**
E. capensis (Cape Bunting) **C**
E. yessoensis (Marsh Bunting) **B**
E. tristrami (Tristram's Bunting) **B,H,I**
E. fucata (Gray-hooded Bunting) **B,H,I**
E. pusilla (Little Bunting) **B,H,I**
E. chrysophrys (Yellow-browed Bunting) **B**
E. rustica (Rustic Bunting) **B**
E. elegans (Yellow-headed Bunting) **B**
E. aureola (Yellow-breasted Bunting) **B,H,I,J**
E. poliopleura (Somali Golden-breasted Bunting) **C**
E. flaviventris (Golden-breasted Bunting) **C**
E. affinis (Brown-rumped Bunting) **C**
E. cabanisi (Cabanis's Yellow Bunting) **C**
E. rutila (Chestnut Bunting) **B,I**
E. koslowi (Koslow's Bunting) **I**

E. melanocephala (Black-headed Bunting) **B,H**
E. bruniceps (Red-headed Bunting) **B,H**
E. sulphurata (Japanese Yellow Bunting) **B,J**   ?
E. spodocephala (Black-faced Bunting) **B,H,I,J**
E. variabilis (Japanese Gray Bunting) **B**
E. pallasi (Pallas's Bunting) **B**
E. schoeniclus (Reed Bunting) **B,H**
CALCARIUS
C. mccownii (McCown's Longspur) **A**
C. lapponicus (Lapland Longspur) **A,B**
C. pictus (Smith's Longspur) **A**
C. ornatus (Chestnut-collared Longspur) **A**
PLECTROPHENAX
P. nivalis (Snow Bunting) **A,B**
P. hyperboreus (McKay's Bunting) **A,B**
CALAMOSPIZA
C. melanocorys (Lark Bunting) **A**
PASSERELLA
P. iliaca (Fox Sparrow) **A**
MELOSPIZA
M. melodia (Song Sparrow) **A,E**
M. lincolnii (Lincoln's Sparrow) **A,E**
M. georgiana (Swamp Sparrow) **A**
ZONOTRICHIA
Z. capensis (Rufous-collared Sparrow) **E,F**
Z. querula (Harris' Sparrow) **A**
Z. leucophrys (White-crowned Sparrow) **A,E**
Z. albicollis (White-throated Sparrow) **A,E**
Z. atricapilla (Golden-crowned Sparrow) **A**
JUNCO
J. vulcani (Volcano Junco) **E**
J. hyemalis (Dark-eyed Junco) **A,E**
J. phaeonotus (Yellow-eyed Junco) **A,E**
PASSERCULUS
P. sandwichensis (Savanna Sparrow) **A,E**
AMMODRAMUS
A. maritimus (Seaside Sparrow) **A**
A. caudacutus (Sharp-tailed Sparrow) **A**
A. leconteii (Le Conte's Sparrow) **A**
A. bairdii (Baird's Sparrow) **A**
A. henslowii (Henslow's Sparrow) **A**
A. savannarum (Grasshopper Sparrow) **A,E,F**
XENOSPIZA
X. baileyi (Sierra Madre Sparrow) **E**
MYOSPIZA
M. humeralis (Grassland Sparrow) **F**
M. aurifrons (Yellow-browed Sparrow) **F**
SPIZELLA
S. arborea (American Tree Sparrow) **A**
S. passerina (Chipping Sparrow) **A,E**
S. pusilla (Field Sparrow) **A**
S. wortheni (Worthen's Sparrow) **E**
S. atrogularis (Black-chinned Sparrow) **A**
S. pallida (Clay-colored Sparrow) **A,E**
S. breweri (Brewer's Sparrow) **A**
POOECETES
P. gramineus (Vesper Sparrow) **A**
CHONDESTES
C. grammacus (Lark Sparrow) **A,E**
AMPHISPIZA
A. bilineata (Black-throated Sparrow) **A,E**
A. belli (Sage Sparrow) **A**
AIMOPHILA
A. mystacalis (Bridled Sparrow) **E**
A. humeralis (Black-chested Sparrow) **E**
A. ruficauda (Stripe-headed Sparrow) **E**
A. sumichrasti (Cinnamon-tailed Sparrow) **E**
A. strigiceps (Stripe-capped Sparrow) **F**
A. aestivalis (Bachman's Sparrow) **A**
A. botterii (Botteri's Sparrow) **A,E**
A. cassinii (Cassin's Sparrow) **A,E**
A. quinquestriata (Five-striped Sparrow) **E**
A. carpalis (Rufous-winged Sparrow) **A**
A. ruficeps (Rufous-crowned Sparrow) **A,E**
A. notosticta (Oaxaca Sparrow) **E**
A. rufescens (Rusty Sparrow) **E**
RHYNCHOSPIZA
R. stolzmanni (Tumbes Sparrow) **F**
TORREORNIS
T. inexpectata (Zapata Sparrow) **E**   R
ORITURUS
O. superciliosus (Striped Sparrow) **E**
PHRYGILUS
P. atriceps (Black-hooded Sierra Finch) **F**
P. gayi (Gray-hooded Sierra Finch) **F**
P. patagonicus (Patagonian Sierra Finch) **F**

P. fruticeti (Mourning Sierra Finch) **F**
P. unicolor (Plumbeous Sierra Finch) **F**
P. dorsalis (Red-backed Sierra Finch) **F**
P. erythronotus (White-throated Sierra Finch) **F**
P. plebejus (Ash-breasted Sierra Finch) **F**
P. carbonarius (Carbonated Sierra Finch) **F**
P. alaudinus (Band-tailed Sierra Finch) **F**
MELANODERA
M. melanodera (Black-throated Finch) **F**   ?
M. xanthogramma (Yellow-bridled Finch) **F**
HAPLOSPIZA
H. rustica (Slaty Finch) **E,F**
H. unicolor (Uniform Finch) **F**
ACANTHIDOPS
A. bairdii (Peg-billed Sparrow) **E**
LOPHOSPINGUS
L. pusillus (Black-crested Finch) **F**
L. griseocristatus (Gray-crested Finch) **F**
DONACOSPIZA
D. albifrons (Long-tailed Reed Finch) **F**
ROWETTIA
R. goughensis (Gough I Finch) **C**   R
NESOSPIZA
N. acunhae (Nightingale I Finch) **O**   R
N. wilkinsi (Wilkins's Finch) **O**   R
DIUCA
D. speculifera (White-winged Diuca Finch) **F**
D. diuca (Common Diuca Finch) **F**
IDIOPSAR
I. brachyurus (Short-tailed Finch) **F**
PIEZORHINA
P. cinerea (Cinereous Finch) **F**
XENOSPINGUS
X. concolor (Slender-billed Finch) **F**   ?
INCASPIZA
I. pulchra (Great Inca Finch) **F**
I. personata (Rufous-backed Inca Finch) **F**
I. ortizi (Gray-winged Inca Finch) **F**   ?
I. laeta (Buff-bridled Inca Finch) **F**
I. watkinsi (Little Inca Finch) **F**
POOSPIZA
P. thoracica (Bay-chested Warbling Finch) **F**
P. boliviana (Bolivian Warbling Finch) **F**
P. alticola (Plain-tailed Warbling Finch) **F**
P. hypochondria (Rufous-sided Warbling Finch) **F**
P. erythrophrys (Rusty-browed Warbling Finch) **F**
P. ornata (Cinnamon Warbling Finch) **F**
P. nigrorufa (Black & Rufous Warbling Finch) **F**
P. lateralis (Red-rumped Warbling Finch) **F**
P. rubecula (Rufous-breasted Warbling Finch) **F**   ?
P. caesar (Chestnut-breasted Mountain Finch) **F**
P. hispaniolensis (Collared Warbling Finch) **F**
P. torquata (Ringed Warbling Finch) **F**
P. cinerea (Gray & White Warbling Finch) **F**
SICALIS
S. citrina (Stripe-tailed Yellow Finch) **F**
S. lutea (Puna Yellow Finch) **F**
S. uropygialis (Bright-rumped Yellow Finch) **F**
S. luteocephala (Citron-headed Yellow Finch) **F**
S. auriventris (Greater Yellow Finch) **F**
S. olivascens (Greenish Yellow Finch) **F**
S. lebruni (Patagonian Yellow Finch) **F**
S. colombiana (Orange-fronted Yellow Finch) **F**
S. flaveola (Saffron Finch) **F**
S. luteola (Grassland Yellow Finch) **E,F**
S. raimondii (Raimondi's Yellow Finch) **F**
S. taczanowskii (Sulfur-breasted Finch) **F**
COMPOSPIZA
C. garleppi (Cochabamba Mountain Finch) **F**
C. baeri (Tucuman Mountain Finch) **F**
EMBERIZOIDES
E. herbicola (Wedge-tailed Grass Finch) **E,F**
E. ypiranganus (Lesser Grass Finch) **F**
E. duidae (Mt Duida Grass Finch) **F**
EMBERNAGRA
E. platensis (Great Pampa Finch) **F**
E. longicauda (Buff-throated Pampa Finch) **F**
VOLATINIA
V. jacarina (Blue-black Grassquit) **E,F**
SPOROPHILA
S. frontalis (Buffy-throated Seedeater) **F**   ?
S. falcirostris (Temminck's Seedeater) **F**   ?
S. schistacea (Slate-colored Seedeater) **E,F**
S. intermedia (Gray Seedeater) **F**
S. plumbea (Plumbeous Seedeater) **F**
S. americana (Variable Seedeater) **E,F**

S. torqueola (White-collared Seedeater) **E**
S. collaris (Rusty-collared Seedeater) **F**
S. lineola (Lined Seedeater) **E,F**
S. luctuosa (Black & White Seedeater) **F**
S. nigricollis (Yellow-bellied Seedeater) **E,F**
S. ardesiaca (Dubois' Seedeater) **F**
S. melanops (Hooded Seedeater) **F**
S. obscura (Dull-colored Seedeater) **F**
S. caerulescens (Double-collared Seedeater) **F**
S. albogularis (White-throated Seedeater) **F**
S. leucoptera (White-bellied Seedeater) **F**
S. peruviana (Parrot-billed Seedeater) **F**
S. simplex (Drab Seedeater) **F**
S. nigrorufa (Black & Tawny Seedeater) **F**
S. bouvreuil (Capped Seedeater) **F**
S. insulata (Tumaco Seedeater) **F**   I
S. minuta (Ruddy-breasted Seedeater) **E,F**
S. hypoxantha (Tawny-bellied Seedeater) **F**
S. hypochroma (Rufous-naped Seedeater) **F**   ?
S. ruficollis (Dark-throated Seedeater) **F**   ?
S. palustris (Marsh Seedeater) **F**
S. castaneiventris (Chestnut-bellied Seedeater) **F**
S. cinnamomea (Chestnut Seedeater) **F**   ?
S. melanogaster (Black-bellied Seedeater) **F**   ?
S. telasco (Chestnut-throated Seedeater) **F**
ORYZOBORUS
O. nuttingi (Nicaraguan Seed Finch) **E**
O. crassirostris (Large-billed Seed Finch) **F**
O. maximiliani (Great-billed Seed Finch) **F**
O. atrirostris (Black-billed Seed Finch) **F**
O. angolensis (Lesser Seed Finch) **E,F**
AMAUROSPIZA
A. concolor (Blue Seedeater) **E,F**
A. moesta (Blackish-blue Seedeater) **F**   ?
MELOPYRRHA
M. nigra (Cuban Bullfinch) **E**
DOLOSPINGUS
D. fringilloides (White-naped Seedeater) **F**
CATAMENIA
C. analis (Band-tailed Seedeater) **F**
C. inornata (Plain-colored Seedeater) **F**
C. homochroa (Paramo Seedeater) **F**
C. oreophila (Colombian Seedeater) **F**
TIARIS
T. canora (Cuban Grassquit) **E**
T. olivacea (Yellow-faced Grassquit) **E,F**
T. bicolor (Black-faced Grassquit) **E,F**
T. fuliginosa (Sooty Grassquit) **F**
LOXIPASSER
L. anoxanthus (Yellow-shouldered Grassquit) **E**
LOXIGILLA
L. portoricensis (Puerto Rican Bullfinch) **E**
L. violacea (Greater Antillean Bullfinch) **E**
L. noctis (Lesser Antillean Bullfinch) **E**
MELANOSPIZA
M. richardsoni (St Lucia Black Finch) **E**
GEOSPIZA
G. magnirostris (Large Ground Finch) **G**
G. fortis (Medium Ground Finch) **G**
G. fuliginosa (Small Ground Finch) **G**
G. difficilis (Sharp-beaked Ground Finch) **G**
G. scandens (Cactus Ground Finch) **G**
G. conirostris (Large Cactus Ground Finch) **G**
CAMARHYNCHUS
C. crassirostris (Vegetarian Tree Finch) **G**
C. psittacula (Large Insectivorous Tree Finch) **G**
C. pauper (Charles Insectivorous Tree Finch) **G**   ?
C. parvulus (Small Insectivorous Tree Finch) **G**
C. pallidus (Woodpecker Finch) **G**
C. heliobates (Mangrove Finch) **G**   R
CERTHIDEA
C. olivacea (Warbler Finch) **G**
PINAROLOXIAS
P. inornata (Cocos Finch) **E**
PIPILO
P. ocai (Collared Towhee) **E**
P. erythrophthalmus (Rufous-sided Towhee) **A,E**
P. fuscus (Brown Towhee) **A,E**
P. aberti (Abert's Towhee) **A**
P. albicollis (White-throated Towhee) **E**
CHLORURUS
C. chlorurus (Green-tailed Towhee) **A,E**
MELOZONE
M. kieneri (Rusty-crowned Ground Sparrow) **E**
M. biarcuatum (Prevost's Ground Sparrow) **E**
M. leucotis (White-eared Ground Sparrow) **E**

ARREMON
A. taciturnus (Pectoral Sparrow) **F**
A. flavirostris (Saffron-billed Sparrow) **F**
A. aurantiirostris (Orange-billed Sparrow) **F**
A. schlegeli (Golden-winged Sparrow) **F**
A. abeillei (Black-capped Sparrow) **F**
ARREMONOPS
A. rufivirgatus (Olive Sparrow) **A,E**
A. tocuyensis (Tocuyo Sparrow) **F**
A. chloronotus (Green-backed Sparrow) **E**
A. conirostris (Black-striped Sparrow) **E,F**
ATLAPETES
A. albinucha (White-naped Brush Finch) **E**
A. gutturalis (Yellow-throated Brush Finch) **E,F**
A. pallidinucha (Pale-naped Brush Finch) **F**
A. rufinucha (Rufous-naped Brush Finch) **F**
A. leucopis (White-rimmed Brush Finch) **F**
A. melanocephalus (Santa Marta Brush Finch) **F**
A. pileatus (Rufous-capped Brush Finch) **E**
A. flaviceps (Olive-headed Brush Finch) **F**   I
A. fuscoolivaceus (Dusky-headed Brush Finch) **F**
A. tricolor (Tricolored Brush Finch) **F**
A. albofrenatus (Moustached Brush Finch) **F**
A. schistaceus (Slaty Brush Finch) **F**
A. nationi (Rusty-bellied Brush Finch) **F**
A. leucopterus (White-winged Brush Finch) **F**
A. albiceps (White-headed Brush Finch) **F**
A. pallidiceps (Pale-headed Brush Finch) **F**   ?
A. maximiliani (Bolivian Brush Finch) **F**
A. rufigenis (Rufous-eared Brush Finch) **F**
A. semirufus (Ocher-breasted Brush Finch) **F**
A. personatus (Tepui Brush Finch) **F**
A. fulviceps (Fulvous-headed Brush Finch) **F**
A. citrinellus (Yellow-striped Brush Finch) **F**
A. apertus (Plain-breasted Brush Finch) **E**
A. brunneinucha (Chestnut-capped Brush Finch) **E,F**
A. virenticeps (Green-striped Brush Finch) **E**
A. torquatus (Stripe-headed Brush Finch) **F**
A. atricapillus (Black-headed Brush Finch) **E,F**
PEZOPETES
P. capitalis (Big-footed Sparrow) **E**
OREOTHRAUPIS
O. arremonops (Tanager Finch) **F**
PSELLIOPHORUS
P. tibialis (Yellow-thighed Sparrow) **E**
P. luteoviridis (Yellow-green Sparrow) **E**
LYSURUS
L. castaneiceps (Olive Finch) **E**
L. crassirostris (Sooty-faced Finch) **E**
UROTHRAUPIS
U. stolzmanni (Black-backed Bush Tanager) **F**
CHARITOSPIZA
C. eucosma (Coal-crested Finch) **F**
SALTATRICULA
S. multicolor (Many-colored Chaco Finch) **F**
CORYPHASPIZA
C. melanotis (Black-masked Finch) **F**   ?
CORYPHOSPINGUS
C. pileatus (Pileated Finch) **F**
C. cucullatus (Red-crested Finch) **F**
RHODOSPINGUS
R. cruentus (Crimson Finch) **F**
CATAMBLYRHYNCHINAE (PLUSH-CAPPED FINCH)
CATAMBLYRHYNCHUS
C. diadema (Plush-capped Finch) **F**
CARDINALINAE (CARDINAL GROSBEAKS)
GUBERNATRIX
G. cristata (Yellow Cardinal) **F**   ?
PAROARIA
P. coronata (Red-crested Cardinal) **F**
P. dominicana (Red-cowled Cardinal) **F**
P. gularis (Red-capped Cardinal) **F**
P. baeri (Crimson-fronted Cardinal) **F**
P. capitata (Yellow-billed Cardinal) **F**
SPIZA
S. americana (Dickcissel) **A,E,F**
PHEUCTICUS
P. chrysopeplus (Yellow Grosbeak) **E,F**
P. tibialis (Black-thighed Grosbeak) **E**
P. chrysogaster (Yellow-bellied Grosbeak) **F**
P. aureoventris (Black-backed Grosbeak) **F**
P. ludovicianus (Rose-breasted Grosbeak) **A,E,F**
P. melanocephalus (Black-headed Grosbeak) **A,E**
CARDINALIS
C. cardinalis (Northern Cardinal) **A,E**

PYRRHULOXIA
P. phoeniceus (Vermilion Cardinal) **F**
P. sinuatus (Pyrrhuloxia) **E**
CARYOTHRAUSTES
C. canadensis (Yellow-green Grosbeak) **F**
C. poliogaster (Black-faced Grosbeak) **E**
C. humeralis (Yellow-shouldered Grosbeak) **F**
RHODOTHRAUPIS
R. celaeno (Crimson-collared Grosbeak) **E**
PERIPORPHYRUS
P. erythromelas (Red & Black Grosbeak) **F**
PITYLUS
P. grossus (Slate-colored Grosbeak) **E,F**
P. fuliginosus (Black-throated Grosbeak) **F**
SALTATOR
S. atriceps (Black-headed Saltator) **E**
S. maximus (Buff-throated Saltator) **E,F**
S. atripennis (Black-winged Saltator) **F**
S. similis (Green-winged Saltator) **F**
S. coerulescens (Grayish Saltator) **E,F**
S. orenocensis (Orinocan Saltator) **F**
S. maxillosus (Thick-billed Saltator) **F**
S. aurantiirostris (Golden-billed Saltator) **F**
S. cinctus (Masked Saltator) **F**   ?
S. atricollis (Black-throated Saltator) **F**
S. rufiventris (Rufous-bellied Saltator) **F**
S. albicollis (Streaked Saltator) **E,F**
CYANOLOXIA
C. glaucocaerulea (Indigo Grosbeak) **F**
CYANOCOMPSA
C. cyanoides (Blue-black Grosbeak) **E,F**
C. brissonii (Ultramarine Grosbeak) **F**
C. parellina (Blue Bunting) **E**
GUIRACA
G. caerulea (Blue Grosbeak) **A,E**
PASSERINA
P. cyanea (Indigo Bunting) **A,E,F**
P. amoena (Lazuli Bunting) **A,E**
P. versicolor (Varied Bunting) **A,E**
P. ciris (Painted Bunting) **A,E**
P. rositae (Rose-bellied Bunting) **E**
P. leclancherii (Orange-breasted Bunting) **E**
PORPHYROSPIZA
P. caerulescens (Blue Finch) **F**
THRAUPINAE (TANAGERS)
ORCHESTICUS
O. abeillei (Brown Tanager) **F**
SCHISTOCLAMYS
S. ruficapillus (Cinnamon Tanager) **F**
S. melanopis (Black-faced Tanager) **F**
NEOTHRAUPIS
N. fasciata (White-banded Tanager) **F**
CYPSNAGRA
C. hirundinacea (White-rumped Tanager) **F**
CONOTHRAUPIS
C. speculigera (Black & White Tanager) **F**
C. mesoleuca (Cone-billed Tanager) **F**   ?
LAMPROSPIZA
L. melanoleuca (Red-billed Pied Tanager) **F**
CISSOPIS
C. leveriana (Magpie Tanager) **F**
CHLORORNIS
C. riefferii (Grass-green Tanager) **F**
COMPSOTHRAUPIS
C. loricata (Scarlet-throated Tanager) **F**
SERICOSSYPHA
S. albocristata (White-capped Tanager) **F**
NESOSPINGUS
N. speculiferus (Puerto Rican Tanager) **E**
CHLOROSPINGUS
C. ophthalmicus (Common Bush Tanager) **E,F**
C. tacarcunae (Tacarcuna Bush Tanager) **E**
C. inornatus (Pirre Bush Tanager) **E**
C. semifuscus (Dusky-bellied Bush Tanager) **F**
C. pileatus (Pileated Bush Tanager) **E**
C. parvirostris (Short-billed Bush Tanager) **F**
C. flavigularis (Yellow-throated Bush Tanager) **F**
C. flavovirens (Yellow-green Bush Tanager) **F**
C. canigularis (Ash-throated Bush Tanager) **E,F**
CNEMOSCOPUS
C. rubrirostris (Gray-hooded Bush Tanager) **F**
HEMISPINGUS
H. atropileus (Black-capped Hemispingus) **F**
H. parodii (Parodi's Tanager) **F**
H. superciliaris (Superciliaried Hemispingus) **F**
H. reyi (Gray-capped Hemispingus) **F**

BUNTINGS, TANAGERS AND RELATIVES

H. frontalis (Oleaginous Hemispingus) **F**
H. melanotis (Black-eared Hemispingus) **F**
H. goeringi (Slaty-backed Hemispingus) **F**
H. rufosuperciliaris (Rufous-browed Hemispingus) **F**
H. verticalis (Black-headed Hemispingus) **F**
H. xanthophthalmus (Drab Hemispingus) **F**
H. trifasciatus (Three-striped Hemispingus) **F**
PYRRHOCOMA
P. ruficeps (Chestnut-headed Tanager) **F**
THLYPOPSIS
T. fulviceps (Fulvous-headed Tanager) **F**
T. ornata (Rufous-chested Tanager) **F**
T. pectoralis (Brown-flanked Tanager) **F**
T. sordida (Orange-headed Tanager) **F**
T. inornata (Buff-bellied Tanager) **F**
T. ruficeps (Rust & Yellow Tanager) **F**
HEMITHRAUPIS
H. guira (Guira Tanager) **F**
H. ruficapilla (Rufous-headed Tanager) **F**
H. flavicollis (Yellow-backed Tanager) **F**
CHRYSOTHLYPIS
C. chrysomelas (Black & Yellow Tanager) **E**
C. salmoni (Scarlet & White Tanager) **F**
NEMOSIA
N. pileata (Hooded Tanager) **F**
N. rourei (Cherry-throated Tanager) **F**   **E**
PHAENICOPHILUS
P. palmarum (Black-crowned Palm Tanager) **E**
P. poliocephalus (Gray-crowned Palm Tanager) **E**
CALYPTOPHILUS
C. frugivorus (Chat-Tanager) **E**
RHODINOCICHLA
R. rosea (Rose-breasted Thrush-Tanager) **E,F**
MITROSPINGUS
M. cassinii (Dusky-faced Tanager) **E,F**
M. oleagineus (Olive-backed Tanager) **F**
CHLOROTHRAUPIS
C. carmioli (Carmiol's Tanager) **E,F**
C. olivacea (Lemon-browed Tanager) **E,F**
C. stolzmanni (Ocher-breasted Tanager) **F**
ORTHOGONYS
O. chloricterus (Olive-green Tanager) **F**
EUCOMETIS
E. penicillata (Gray-headed Tanager) **E,F**
LANIO
L. fulvus (Fulvous Shrike-Tanager) **F**
L. versicolor (White-winged Shrike-Tanager) **F**
L. aurantius (Black-throated Shrike-Tanager) **E**
L. leucothorax (White-throated Shrike-Tanager) **E**
CREURGOPS
C. verticalis (Rufous-crested Tanager) **F**
C. dentata (Slaty Tanager) **F**
HETEROSPINGUS
H. xanthopygius (Scarlet-browed Tanager) **E,F**
TACHYPHONUS
T. cristatus (Flame-crested Tanager) **F**
T. nattereri (Natterer's Tanager) **F**
T. rufiventer (Yellow-crested Tanager) **F**
T. surinamus (Fulvous-crested Tanager) **F**
T. luctuosus (White-shouldered Tanager) **E,F**
T. delatrii (Tawny-crested Tanager) **E,F**
T. coronatus (Ruby-crowned Tanager) **F**
T. rufus (White-lined Tanager) **E,F**
T. phoenicius (Red-shouldered Tanager) **F**
TRICHOTHRAUPIS
T. melanops (Black-goggled Tanager) **F**
HABIA
H. rubica (Red-crowned Ant-Tanager) **E,F**
H. fuscicauda (Red-throated Ant-Tanager) **E,F**
H. atrimaxillaris (Black-cheeked Ant-Tanager) **E**   **?**
H. gutturalis (Sooty Ant-Tanager) **F**   **?**
H. cristata (Crested Ant-Tanager) **F**
PIRANGA
P. bidentata (Flame-colored Tanager) **E**
P. flava (Hepatic Tanager) **A,E,F**
P. rubra (Summer Tanager) **A,E,F**
P. roseogularis (Rose-throated Tanager) **E**
P. olivacea (Scarlet Tanager) **A,E,F**
P. ludoviciana (Western Tanager) **A,E**
P. leucoptera (White-winged Tanager) **E,F**
P. erythrocephala (Red-headed Tanager) **E**
P. rubriceps (Red-hooded Tanager) **F**
CALOCHAETES
C. coccineus (Vermilion Tanager) **F**
RAMPHOCELUS
R. sanguinolentus (Crimson-collared Tanager) **E**
R. nigrogularis (Masked Crimson Tanager) **F**

R. dimidiatus (Crimson-backed Tanager) **E,F**
R. melanogaster (Black-bellied Tanager) **F**
R. carbo (Silver-beaked Tanager) **F**
R. bresilius (Brazilian Tanager) **F**
R. passerinii (Scarlet-rumped Tanager) **E**
R. flammigerus (Flame-rumped Tanager) **F**
R. icteronotus (Yellow-rumped Tanager) **E,F**
SPINDALIS
S. zena (Stripe-headed Tanager) **E**
THRAUPIS
T. episcopus (Blue-gray Tanager) **E,F**
T. sayaca (Sayaca Tanager) **F**
T. glaucocolpa (Glaucous Tanager) **F**
T. cyanoptera (Azure-shouldered Tanager) **F**
T. ornata (Golden-chevroned Tanager) **F**
T. abbas (Yellow-winged Tanager) **E**
T. palmarum (Palm Tanager) **E,F**
T. cyanocephala (Blue-capped Tanager) **F**
T. bonariensis (Blue & Yellow Tanager) **F**
CYANICTERUS
C. cyanicterus (Blue-backed Tanager) **F**
BUTHRAUPIS
B. arcaei (Blue & Gold Tanager) **E**
B. melanochlamys (Black & Gold Tanager) **F**   **?**
B. rothschildi (Golden-chested Tanager) **F**
B. edwardsi (Moss-backed Tanager) **F**
B. aureocincta (Gold-ringed Tanager) **F**   **?**
B. montana (Hooded Mountain Tanager) **F**
B. eximia (Black-chested Mountain Tanager) **F**
B. aureodorsalis (Golden-backed Mountain
Tanager) **F**   **?**
B. wetmorei (Masked Mountain Tanager) **F**
WETMORETHRAUPIS
W. sterrhopteron (Orange-throated Tanager) **F**
ANISOGNATUS
A. melanogenys (Black-cheeked Mountain Tanager)
F
A. lacrymosus (Lacrimose Mountain Tanager) **F**
A. igniventris (Scarlet-bellied Mountain Tanager) **F**
A. flavinuchus (Blue-winged Mountain Tanager) **F**
A. notabilis (Black-chinned Mountain Tanager) **F**
STEPHANOPHORUS
S. diadematus (Diademed Tanager) **F**
IRIDOSORNIS
I. porphyrocephala (Purplish-mantled Tanager) **F**
I. analis (Yellow-throated Tanager) **F**
I. jelskii (Golden-collared Tanager) **F**
I. rufivertex (Golden-crowned Tanager) **F**
I. reinwardti (Yellow-scarfed Tanager) **F**
DUBUSIA
D. taeniata (Buff-breasted Mountain Tanager) **F**
DELOTHRAUPIS
D. castaneoventris (Chestnut-bellied Mountain
Tanager) **F**
PIPRAEIDEA
P. melanonota (Fawn-breasted Tanager) **F**
EUPHONIA
E. jamaica (Jamaican Euphonia) **E**
E. plumbea (Plumbeous Euphonia) **F**
E. affinis (Scrub Euphonia) **E**
E. luteicapilla (Yellow-crowned Euphonia) **E**
E. chlorotica (Purple-throated Euphonia) **F**
E. trinitatis (Trinidad Euphonia) **E,F**
E. concinna (Velvet-fronted Euphonia) **F**
E. saturata (Orange-crowned Euphonia) **F**
E. finschi (Finsch's Euphonia) **F**
E. violacea (Violaceous Euphonia) **F**
E. laniirostris (Thick-billed Euphonia) **E,F**
E. hirundinacea (Yellow-throated Euphonia) **E**
E. chalybea (Green-throated Euphonia) **F**   **?**
E. musica (Antillean Euphonia) **E**
E. fulvicrissa (Fulvous-vented Euphonia) **E,F**
E. imitans (Spot-crowned Euphonia) **E**
E. gouldi (Olive-backed Euphonia) **F**
E. chrysopasta (Golden-bellied Euphonia) **F**
E. mesochrysa (Bronze-green Euphonia) **F**
E. minuta (White-vented Euphonia) **E,F**
E. anneae (Tawny-capped Euphonia) **E,F**
E. xanthogaster (Orange-bellied Euphonia) **E,F**
E. rufiventris (Rufous-bellied Euphonia) **F**
E. pectoralis (Chestnut-bellied Euphonia) **F**
E. cayennensis (Golden-sided Euphonia) **F**
CHLOROPHONIA
C. flavirostris (Yellow-collared Chlorophonia) **F**
C. cyanea (Blue-naped Chlorophonia) **F**
C. pyrrhophrys (Chestnut-breasted Chlorophonia) **F**

C. occipitalis (Blue-crowned Chlorophonia) **E**
C. callophrys (Golden-browed Chlorophonia) **E**
CHLOROCHRYSA
C. phoenicotis (Glistening-green Tanager) **F**
C. calliparaea (Orange-eared Tanager) **F**
C. nitidissima (Multicolored Tanager) **F**   **?**
TANGARA
T. phillipsi (Sira Tanager) **F**
T. inornata (Plain-colored Tanager) **E,F**
T. cabanisi (Azure-rumped Tanager) **E**   **I**
T. palmeri (Gray & Gold Tanager) **E,F**
T. mexicana (Turquoise Tanager) **F**
T. chilensis (Paradise Tanager) **F**
T. fastuosa (Seven-colored Tanager) **F**   **V**
T. seledon (Green-headed Tanager) **F**
T. cyanocephala (Red-necked Tanager) **F**
T. desmaresti (Brassy-breasted Tanager) **F**
T. cyanoventris (Gilt-edged Tanager) **F**
T. johannae (Blue-whiskered Tanager) **F**
T. schrankii (Green & Gold Tanager) **F**
T. florida (Emerald Tanager) **E,F**
T. arthus (Golden Tanager) **F**
T. icterocephala (Silver-throated Tanager) **E,F**
T. xanthocephala (Saffron-crowned Tanager) **F**
T. chrysotis (Golden-eared Tanager) **F**
T. parzudakii (Flame-faced Tanager) **F**
T. xanthogastra (Yellow-bellied Tanager) **F**
T. punctata (Spotted Tanager) **F**
T. guttata (Speckled Tanager) **E,F**
T. varia (Dotted Tanager) **F**
T. rufigula (Rufous-throated Tanager) **F**
T. gyrola (Bay-headed Tanager) **E,F**
T. lavinia (Rufous-winged Tanager) **E**
T. cayana (Burnished-buff Tanager) **F**
T. cucullata (Lesser Antillean Tanager) **E**
T. peruviana (Black-backed Tanager) **F**
T. preciosa (Chestnut-backed Tanager) **F**
T. vitriolina (Scrub Tanager) **F**
T. meyerdeschauenseei (Green-capped Tanager) **F**
T. rufigenis (Rufous-cheeked Tanager) **F**
T. ruficervix (Golden-naped Tanager) **F**
T. labradorides (Metallic-green Tanager) **F**
T. cyanotis (Blue-browed Tanager) **F**
T. cyanicollis (Blue-necked Tanager) **F**
T. larvata (Golden-masked Tanager) **E,F**
T. nigrocincta (Masked Tanager) **F**
T. dowii (Spangle-cheeked Tanager) **E**
T. fucosa (Green-naped Tanager) **E**
T. nigroviridis (Beryl-spangled Tanager) **F**
T. vassorii (Blue & Black Tanager) **F**
T. heinei (Black-capped Tanager) **F**
T. viridicollis (Silvery Tanager) **F**
T. argyrofenges (Green-throated Tanager) **F**
T. cyanoptera (Black-headed Tanager) **F**
T. pulcherrima (Yellow-collared Tanager) **F**
T. velia (Opal-rumped Tanager) **F**
T. callophrys (Opal-crowned Tanager) **F**
DACNIS
D. albiventris (White-bellied Dacnis) **F**
D. lineata (Black-faced Dacnis) **F**
D. flaviventer (Yellow-bellied Dacnis) **F**
D. hartlaubi (Turquoise Dacnis) **F**
D. nigripes (Black-legged Dacnis) **F**
D. venusta (Scarlet-thighed Dacnis) **E,F**
D. cayana (Blue Dacnis) **E,F**
D. viguieri (Viridian Dacnis) **E,F**
D. berlepschi (Scarlet-breasted Dacnis) **F**
CHLOROPHANES
C. spiza (Green Honeycreeper) **E,F**
CYANERPES
C. nitidus (Short-billed Honeycreeper) **F**
C. lucidus (Shining Honeycreeper) **E,F**
C. caeruleus (Purple Honeycreeper) **F**
C. cyaneus (Red-legged Honeycreeper) **E,F**
XENODACNIS
X. parina (Tit-like Dacnis) **F**
OREOMANES
O. fraseri (Giant Conebill) **F**
DIGLOSSA
D. baritula (Slaty Flowerpiercer) **E,F**
D. lafresnayii (Glossy Flowerpiercer) **F**
D. carbonaria (Coal-black Flowerpiercer) **F**
D. venezuelensis (Venezuelan Flowerpiercer) **F**
D. albilatera (White-sided Flowerpiercer) **F**
D. duidae (Scaled Flowerpiercer) **F**
D. major (Greater Flowerpiercer) **F**
D. indigotica (Indigo Flowerpiercer) **F**

DIGLOSSOPIS
D. glauca (Deep-blue Flowerpiercer) **F**
D. caerulescens (Bluish Flowerpiercer) **F**
D. cyanea (Masked Flowerpiercer) **F**
EUNEORNIS
E. campestris (Orangequit) **E**
TERSINA
T. viridis (Swallow Tanager) **E,F**
159 PARULIDAE (WOOD WARBLERS)
MNIOTILTA
M. varia (Black & White Warbler) **A,E,F**
VERMIVORA
V. bachmanii (Bachman's Warbler) **A,E**
V. chrysoptera (Golden-winged Warbler) **A,E,F**
V. pinus (Blue-winged Warbler) **A,E**
V. peregrina (Tennessee Warbler) **A,E,F**
V. celata (Orange-crowned Warbler) **A,E**
V. ruficapilla (Nashville Warbler) **A,E**
V. virginiae (Virginia's Warbler) **A,E**
V. crissalis (Colima Warbler) **A,E**
V. luciae (Lucy's Warbler) **A,E**
V. gutteralis (Flame-throated Warbler) **E**
V. superciliosa (Crescent-chested Warbler) **E**
PARULA
P. americana (Northern Parula) **A,E**
P. pitiayumi (Tropical Parula) **E,F**
DENDROICA
D. petechia (Yellow Warbler) **A,E,F,G**
D. pensylvanica (Chestnut-sided Warbler) **A,E**
D. cerulea (Cerulean Warbler) **E,F**
D. caerulescens (Black-throated Blue Warbler) **A,E**
D. plumbea (Plumbeous Warbler) **E**
D. pharetra (Arrow-headed Warbler) **E**
D. angelae (Elfin Woods Warbler) **E**
D. pinus (Pine Warbler) **A,E**
D. graciae (Grace's Warbler) **A,E**
D. adelaidae (Adelaide's Warbler) **E**
D. pityophila (Olive-capped Warbler) **E**
D. dominica (Yellow-throated Warbler) **A,E**
D. nigrescens (Black-throated Gray Warbler) **A,E**
D. townsendi (Townsend's Warbler) **A,E**
D. occidentalis (Hermit Warbler) **A,E**
D. chrysoparia (Golden-cheeked Warbler) **A,E**
D. virens (Black-throated Green Warbler) **A,E**
D. discolor (Prairie Warbler) **A,E**
D. vitellina (Vitelline Warbler) **E**
D. tigrina (Cape May Warbler) **A,E**
D. fusca (Blackburnian Warbler) **A,E,F**
D. magnolia (Magnolia Warbler) **A,E**
D. coronata (Yellow-rumped Warbler) **A,E**
D. palmarum (Palm Warbler) **A,E**
D. kirtlandii (Kirtland's Warbler) **A,E**
D. striata (Blackpoll Warbler) **A,E**
D. castanea (Bay-breasted Warbler) **A,E,F**
CATHAROPEZA
C. bishopi (Whistling Warbler) **E**
SETOPHAGA
S. ruticilla (American Redstart) **A,E,F**
SEIURUS
S. aurocapillus (Ovenbird) **A,E,F**
S. noveboracensis (Northern Waterthrush) **A,E**
S. motacilla (Louisiana Waterthrush) **A,E,F**
LIMNOTHLYPIS
L. swainsonii (Swainson's Warbler) **A,E**
HELMITHEROS
H. vermivorus (Worm-eating Warbler) **A,E**
PROTONOTARIA
P. citrea (Prothonotary Warbler) **A,E,F**
GEOTHLYPIS
G. trichas (Common Yellowthroat) **A,E**
G. beldingi (Peninsular Yellowthroat) **E**
G. flavovelata (Yellow-crowned Yellowthroat) **E**
G. rostrata (Bahama Yellowthroat) **E**
G. semiflava (Olive-crowned Yellowthroat) **E,F**
G. speciosa (Black-polled Yellowthroat) **E**
G. nelsoni (Hooded Yellowthroat) **E**
G. chiriquensis (Chiriqui Yellowthroat) **E**
G. aequinoctialis (Masked Yellowthroat) **F**
G. poliocephala (Gray-crowned Yellowthroat) **E**
G. formosa (Kentucky Warbler) **A,E,F**
G. agilis (Connecticut Warbler) **A,E,F**
G. philadelphia (Mourning Warbler) **A,E,F**
G. tolmiei (MacGillivray's Warbler) **A,E**
MICROLIGEA
M. palustris (Green-tailed Ground Warbler) **E**

XENOLIGEA
X. montana (White-winged Ground Warbler) **E**
TERETISTRIS
T. fernandinae (Yellow-headed Warbler) **E**
T. fornsi (Oriente Warbler) **E**
LEUCOPEZA
L. semperi (Semper's Warbler) **E**
WILSONIA
W. citrina (Hooded Warbler) **A,E**
W. pusilla (Wilson's Warbler) **A,E**
W. canadensis (Canada Warbler) **A,E,F**
CARDELLINA
C. rubifrons (Red-faced Warbler) **A,E**
ERGATICUS
E. ruber (Red Warbler) **E**
E. versicolor (Pink-headed Warbler) **E**
MYIOBORUS
M. pictus (Painted Redstart) **E**
M. miniatus (Slate-throated Redstart) **E,F**
M. brunniceps (Brown-capped Redstart) **F**
M. pariae (Yellow-faced Redstart) **F**
M. cardonai (Saffron-breasted Redstart) **F**
M. torquatus (Collared Redstart) **E**
M. ornatus (Golden-fronted Redstart) **F**
M. melanocephalus (Spectacled Redstart) **F**
M. albifrons (White-fronted Redstart) **F**
M. flavivertex (Yellow-crowned Redstart) **F**
M. albifacies (White-faced Redstart) **F**
EUTHLYPIS
E. lachrymosa (Neotropic Fan-tailed Warbler) **E**
BASILEUTERUS
B. fraseri (Gray & Gold Warbler) **F**
B. bivittatus (Two-banded Warbler) **F**
B. chrysogaster (Golden-bellied Warbler) **F**
B. flaveolus (Flavescent Warbler) **F**
B. luteoviridis (Citrine Warbler) **F**
B. signatus (Pale-legged Warbler) **F**
B. nigrocristatus (Black-crested Warbler) **F**
B. griseiceps (Gray-headed Warbler) **F**
B. basilicus (Santa Marta Warbler) **F**
B. cinereicollis (Gray-throated Warbler) **F**
B. coronatus (Russet-crowned Warbler) **F**
B. culicivorus (Golden-crowned Warbler) **E,F**
B. rufifrons (Rufous-capped Warbler) **E,F**
B. belli (Golden-browed Warbler) **E**
B. melanogenys (Black-cheeked Warbler) **E**
B. ignotus (Pirre Warbler) **E**
B. tristriatus (Three-striped Warbler) **E,F**
B. trifasciatus (Three-banded Warbler) **F**
B. hypoleucus (White-bellied Warbler) **F**
B. leucoblepharus (White-browed Warbler) **F**
B. leucophrys (White-striped Warbler) **F**
B. rivularis (River Warbler) **E,F**
NEPHELORNIS
N. oneilli (Pardusco) **F**
ZELEDONIA
Z. coronata (Wren Thrush) **F**
PEUCEDRAMUS
P. taeniatus (Olive Warbler) **A,E**
GRANATELLUS
G. venustus (Red-breasted Chat) **E**
G. sallaei (Gray-throated Chat) **E**
G. pelzelni (Rose-breasted Chat) **F**
ICTERIA
I. virens (Yellow-breasted Chat) **A,E**
CONIROSTRUM
C. speciosum (Chestnut-vented Conebill) **F**
C. leucogenys (White-eared Conebill) **F**
C. bicolor (Bicolored Conebill) **F**
C. margaritae (Pearly-breasted Conebill) **F** [?]
C. cinereum (Cinereous Conebill) **F**
C. tamarugensis (Tamarugo Conebill) **F**
C. ferrugineiventre (White-browed Conebill) **F**
C. rufum (Rufous-browed Conebill) **F**
C. sitticolor (Blue-backed Conebill) **F**
C. albifrons (Capped Conebill) **F**
COEREBA
C. flaveola (Bananaquit) **E,F**
160 VIREONIDAE (VIREOS)
CYCLARHINAE
CYCLARHIS
C. gujanensis (Rufous-browed Peppershrike) **E,F**
C. nigrirostris (Black-billed Peppershrike) **F**
VIREOLANIINAE
VIREOLANIUS
V. melitophrys (Chestnut-sided Shrike-Vireo) **E**

V. pulchellus (Green Shrike-Vireo) **E**
V. leucotis (Slaty-capped Shrike-Vireo) **F**
VIREONINAE
V. brevipennis (Slaty Vireo) **E**
V. huttoni (Hutton's Vireo) **A,E**
V. atricapillus (Black-capped Vireo) **A,E** [?]
V. griseus (White-eyed Vireo) **A,E**
V. pallens (Mangrove Vireo) **E**
V. caribaeus (St Andrew Vireo) **E** [?]
V. bairdi (Cozumel Vireo) **E**
V. gundlachii (Cuban Vireo) **E**
V. crassirostris (Thick-billed Vireo) **E**
V. vicinior (Gray Vireo) **A,E**
V. bellii (Bell's Vireo) **A,E**
V. nelsoni (Dwarf Vireo) **E**
V. hypochryseus (Golden Vireo) **E**
V. modestus (Jamaican White-eyed Vireo) **E**
V. nanus (Flat-billed Vireo) **E**
V. latimeri (Puerto Rican Vireo) **E**
V. osburni (Blue Mountain Vireo) **E**
V. carmioli (Carmiol's Vireo) **E**
V. solitarius (Solitary Vireo) **A,E**
V. flavifrons (Yellow-throated Vireo) **A,E,F**
V. philadelphicus (Philadelphia Vireo) **A,E,F**
V. olivaceus (Red-eyed Vireo) **A,E,F**
V. flavoviridis (Yellow-green Vireo) **E,F**
V. magister (Yucatan Vireo) **E**
V. altiloquus (Black-whiskered Vireo) **A,E,F**
V. gilvus (Warbling Vireo) **A,E,F**
V. leucophrys (Brown-capped Vireo) **F**
HYLOPHILUS
H. poicilotis (Rufous-crowned Greenlet) **F**
H. thoracicus (Lemon-chested Greenlet) **F**
H. semicinereus (Gray-chested Greenlet) **F**
H. pectoralis (Ashy-headed Greenlet) **F**
H. sclateri (Tepui Greenlet) **F**
H. muscicapinus (Buff-chested Greenlet) **F**
H. brunneiceps (Brown-headed Greenlet) **F**
H. semibrunneus (Rufous-naped Greenlet) **F**
H. aurantiifrons (Golden-fronted Greenlet) **E,F**
H. hypoxanthus (Dusky-capped Greenlet) **F**
H. flavipes (Scrub Greenlet) **E,F**
H. olivaceus (Olivaceous Greenlet) **F**
H. ochraceiceps (Tawny-crowned Greenlet) **E,F**
H. decurtatus (Lesser Greenlet) **E,F**
161 ICTERIDAE (NEW WORLD BLACKBIRDS)
ICTERINAE
PSAROCOLIUS
P. oseryi (Casqued Oropendola) **F**
P. latirostris (Band-tailed Oropendola) **F**
P. decumanus (Crested Oropendola) **E,F**
P. viridis (Green Oropendola) **F**
P. atrovirens (Dusky-green Oropendola) **F**
P. angustifrons (Russet-backed Oropendola) **F**
P. wagleri (Chestnut-headed Oropendola) **E**
P. montezuma (Montezuma Oropendola) **E**
P. cassini (Chestnut-mantled Oropendola) **F** [?]
P. bifasciatus (Para Oropendola) **F**
P. guatimozinus (Black Oropendola) **E,F**
P. yuracares (Olive Oropendola) **F**
CACICUS
C. cela (Yellow-rumped Cacique) **E,F**
C. haemorrhous (Red-rumped Cacique) **E,F**
C. uropygialis (Scarlet-rumped Cacique) **E,F**
C. chrysopterus (Golden-winged Cacique) **F**
C. koepckeae (Selva Cacique) **F** [?]
C. leucoramphus (Mountain Cacique) **F**
C. sclateri (Ecuadorian Black Cacique) **F**
C. solitarius (Solitary Cacique) **F**
C. melanicterus (Yellow-winged Cacique) **E**
C. holosericeus (Yellow-billed Cacique) **E,F**
ICTERUS
I. chrysocephalus (Moriche Oriole) **F**
I. cayanensis (Epaulet Oriole) **F**
I. chrysater (Yellow-backed Oriole) **E,F**
I. nigrogularis (Yellow Oriole) **E,F**
I. leucopteryx (Jamaican Oriole) **E**
I. auratus (Orange Oriole) **E**
I. mesomelas (Yellow-tailed Oriole) **E,F**
I. auricapillus (Orange-crowned Oriole) **E,F**
I. graceannae (White-edged Oriole) **F**
I. xantholaemus (Yellow-throated Oriole) **F**
I. pectoralis (Spot-breasted Oriole) **E**
I. gularis (Altamira Oriole) **A,E**
I. pustulatus (Streak-backed Oriole) **E**
I. cucullatus (Hooded Oriole) **A,E**

FINCHES

I. icterus (Troupial) **E,F**
I. galbula (Northern Oriole) **A,E,F**
I. spurius (Orchard Oriole) **A,E**
I. dominicensis (Black-cowled Oriole) **E**
I. wagleri (Black-vented Oriole) **E**
I. laudabilis (St Lucia Oriole) **E**
I. bonana (Martinique Oriole) **E** ?
I. oberi (Montserrat Oriole) **E** ?
I. graduacauda (Audubon's Oriole) **E**
I. maculialatus (Bar-winged Oriole) **E**
I. parisorum (Scott's Oriole) **A,E**
NESOPSAR
N. nigerrimus (Jamaican Blackbird) **E**
XANTHOPSAR
X. flavus (Saffron-cowled Blackbird) **E**
GYMNOMYSTAX
G. mexicanus (Oriole Blackbird) **F**
XANTHOCEPHALUS
X. xanthocephalus (Yellow-headed Blackbird) **A,E**
AGELAIUS
A. xanthophthalmus (Yellow-eyed Blackbird) **F**
A. thilius (Yellow-winged Blackbird) **F**
A. phoeniceus (Red-winged Blackbird) **A,E**
A. tricolor (Tricolored Blackbird) **A**
A. icterocephalus (Yellow-hooded Blackbird) **F**
A. humeralis (Tawny-shouldered Blackbird) **E**
A. xanthomus (Yellow-shouldered Blackbird) **E** V
A. cyanopus (Unicolored Blackbird) **F**
A. ruficapillus (Chestnut-capped Blackbird) **F**
STURNELLA
S. superciliaris (Bonaparte's Blackbird) **F**
S. militaris (Red-breasted Blackbird) **F**
S. bellicosa (Peruvian Red-breasted Meadowlark) **F**
S. defilippi (Lesser Red-breasted Meadowlark) **F** ?
S. loyca (Long-tailed Meadowlark) **F**
S. magna (Eastern Meadowlark) **A,E,F**
S. neglecta (Western Meadowlark) **A,E**
PSEUDOLEISTES
P. guirahuro (Yellow-rumped Marshbird) **F**
P. virescens (Brown-yellow Marshbird) **F**
AMBLYRAMPHUS
A. holosericeus (Scarlet-headed Blackbird) **F**
HYPOPYRRHUS
H. pyrohypogaster (Red-bellied Grackle) **F** ?
CURAEUS
C. curaeus (Austral Blackbird) **F**
C. forbesi (Forbes's Blackbird) **F** ?
GNORIMOPSAR
G. chopi (Chopi Blackbird) **F**
OREOPSAR
O. bolivianus (Bolivian Blackbird) **F**
LAMPROPSAR
L. tanagrinus (Velvet-fronted Grackle) **F**
MACROAGELAIUS
M. subalaris (Mountain Grackle) **F**
M. imthurni (Golden-tufted Grackle) **F**
DIVES
D. atroviolacea (Cuban Blackbird) **E**
D. dives (Melodious Blackbird) **E**
D. warszewiczi (Scrub Blackbird) **E**
QUISCALUS
Q. mexicanus (Great-tailed Grackle) **A,E,F**
Q. major (Boat-tailed Grackle) **A**
Q. nicaraguensis (Nicaraguan Grackle) **E**
Q. quiscula (Common Grackle) **A**
Q. niger (Antillean Grackle) **E**
Q. lugubris (Carib Grackle) **E,F**
EUPHAGUS
E. carolinus (Rusty Blackbird) **A**
E. cyanocephalus (Brewer's Blackbird) **A,E**
MOLOTHRUS
M. badius (Bay-winged Cowbird) **F**
M. rufoaxillaris (Screaming Cowbird) **F**
M. bonariensis (Shiny Cowbird) **E,F**
M. aeneus (Bronzed Cowbird) **A,E,F**
M. ater (Brown-headed Cowbird) **A,E**
SCAPHIDURA
S. oryzivora (Giant Cowbird) **E,F**
DOLICHONYCHINAE
DOLICHONYX
D. oryzivorus (Bobolink) **A,E,F**
162 FRINGILLIDAE (FINCHES)
FRINGILLINAE (FRINGILLINE FINCHES)
FRINGILLA
F. coelebs (Chaffinch) **B**
F. teydea (Blue Chaffinch) **B**

F. montifringilla (Brambling) **B,H** R
CARDUELINAE (CARDUELINE FINCHES)
SERINUS
S. pusillus (Red-fronted Serin) **B**
S. serinus (European Serin) **B**
S. syriacus (Syrian Serin) **B**
S. canaria (Island Canary) **B**
S. citrinella (Citril Finch) **B**
S. thibetanus (Tibetan Siskin) **B,H,I**
S. canicollis (Yellow-crowned Canary) **C**
S. nigriceps (Black-headed Siskin) **C**
S. citrinelloides (African Citril Finch) **C**
S. capistratus (Black-faced Canary) **C**
S. koliensis (Papyrus Canary) **C**
S. scotops (Forest Canary) **C**
S. leucopygius (White-rumped Seedeater) **C**
S. atrogularis (Yellow-rumped Seedeater) **C**
S. citrinipectus (Lemon-breasted Seedeater) **C**
S. mozambicus (Yellow-fronted Canary) **C**
S. donaldsoni (Grosbeak Canary) **C**
S. flaviventris (Yellow Canary) **C**
S. dorsostriatus (White-bellied Canary) **C**
S. sulphuratus (Brimstone Canary) **C**
S. albogularis (White-throated Seedeater) **C**
S. reichardi (Stripe-breasted Seedeater) **C**
S. gularis (Streaky-headed Seedeater) **C**
S. mennelli (Black-eared Seedeater) **C**
S. tristriatus (Brown-rumped Seedeater) **C**
S. ankoberensis (Ankober Serin) **C** R
S. menachensis (Yemen Serin) **C**
S. striolatus (Streaky Seedeater) **C**
S. burtoni (Thick-billed Canary) **C**
S. rufobrunneus (Principe Seedeater) **C**
S. leucopterus (White-winged Seedeater) **C**
S. tottus (Cape Siskin) **C**
S. symonsi (Drakensberg Siskin) **C**
S. alario (Black-headed Canary) **C**
S. estherae (Malay Goldfinch) **J,K**
NEOSPIZA
N. concolor (Sao Thomé Grosbeak-Weaver) **C** I
LINURGUS
L. olivaceus (Oriole-Finch) **C**
RHYNCHOSTRUTHUS
R. socotranus (Golden-winged Grosbeak) **C**
CARDUELIS
C. chloris (Western Greenfinch) **B**
C. sinica (Oriental Greenfinch) **B**
C. spinoides (Black-headed Greenfinch) **H,I**
C. ambigua (Yunnan Greenfinch) **B,H,I**
C. spinus (Spruce Siskin) **B**
C. pinus (Pine Siskin) **A,E,F**
C. atriceps (Black-capped Siskin) **E**
C. spinescens (Andean Siskin) **F**
C. yarrellii (Yellow-faced Siskin) **F** ?
C. cucullata (Red Siskin) **F** E
C. crassirostris (Thick-billed Siskin) **F**
C. magellanica (Hooded Siskin) **F**
C. dominicensis (Antillean Siskin) **E**
C. siemiradzkii (Saffron Siskin) **F** ?
C. olivacea (Olivaceous Siskin) **F**
C. notata (Black-headed Siskin) **E**
C. xanthogastra (Yellow-bellied Siskin) **F**
C. atrata (Black Siskin) **F**
C. uropygialis (Yellow-rumped Siskin) **F**
C. barbata (Black-chinned Siskin) **F**
C. tristis (American Goldfinch) **A,E**
C. psaltria (Lesser Goldfinch) **A,E,F**
C. lawrencei (Lawrence's Goldfinch) **A,E**
C. carduelis (Eurasian Goldfinch) **B,H**
ACANTHIS
A. flammea (Redpoll) **A,B**
A. flavirostris (Twite) **B,H**
A. cannabina (Linnet) **B,H**
A. yemenis (Yemeni Linnet) **C**
A. johannis (Warsangli Linnet) **C**
LEUCOSTICTE
L. nemoricola (Hodgson's Rosy Finch) **H,I**
L. brandti (Brandt's Rosy Finch) **B,H,I**
L. arctoa (Rosy Finch) **A,B**
CALLACANTHIS
C. burtoni (Red-browed Rosefinch) **H**
RHODOPECHYS
R. sanguinea (Crimson-winged Finch) **B**
R. githaginea (Trumpeter Finch) **B,H**
R. mongolica (Mongolian Trumpeter Finch) **B,H**
R. obsoleta (Lichtenstein's Desert Finch) **B,H**

URAGUS
U. sibiricus (Long-tailed Rosefinch) **B**
UROCYNCHRAMUS
U. pylzowi (Przewalski's Rosefinch) **B**
CARPODACUS
C. rubescens (Blanford's Rosefinch) **B,H**
C. nipalensis (Dark Rosefinch) **H,I**
C. erythrinus (Common Rosefinch) **B,H,I**
C. purpureus (Purple Finch) **A**
C. cassinii (Cassin's Finch) **A,E**
C. mexicanus (House Finch) **A,E**
C. pulcherrimus (Beautiful Rosefinch) **H**
C. eos (Stresemann's Rosefinch) **B**
C. rhodochrous (Pink-browed Rosefinch) **H**
C. vinaceus (Vinaceous Rosefinch) **B,J**
C. edwardsii (Large Rosefinch) **B,H,I**
C. synoicus (Sinai Rosefinch) **B**
C. roseus (Pallas's Rosefinch) **B**
C. trifasciatus (Three-banded Rosefinch) **B**
C. rhodopeplus (Spot-winged Rosefinch) **H,I**
C. thura (White-browed Rosefinch) **B,H,I**
C. rhodochlamys (Red-mantled Rosefinch) **B,H,I**
C. rubicilloides (Eastern Great Rosefinch) **B,H**
C. rubicilla (Caucasian Great Rosefinch) **B,H**
C. puniceus (Rose-breasted Rosefinch) **B,H**
C. roborowskii (Roborovski's Rosefinch) **B**
PINICOLA
P. enucleator (Pine Grosbeak) **A,B**
P. subhimachalus (Red-headed Finch) **H**
HAEMATOSPIZA
H. sipahi (Scarlet Finch) **H,I**
LOXIA
L. pytyopsittacus (Parrot Crossbill) **B**
L. scotica (Scottish Crossbill) **B**
L. curvirostra (Red Crossbill) **A,B,E,H,I,J**
L. leucoptera (White-winged Crossbill) **A,B,E**
PYRRHULA
P. nipalensis (Brown Bullfinch) **H,I,J**
P. leucogenys (Philippine Bullfinch) **J**
P. aurantiaca (Orange Bullfinch) **H**
P. erythrocephala (Red-headed Bullfinch) **H**
P. erythaca (Beavan's Bullfinch) **B,H,J**
P. pyrrhula (Northern Bullfinch) **B**
COCCOTHRAUSTES
C. coccothraustes (Hawfinch) **B,H**
C. migratorius (Black-tailed Hawfinch) **B**
C. personatus (Masked Hawfinch) **B**
C. icterioides (Black & Yellow Grosbeak) **B,H**
C. affinis (Allied Grosbeak) **B,H**
C. melanozanthos (Spotted-wing Grosbeak) **B,H,I**
C. carnipes (White-winged Grosbeak) **B,H**
C. vespertinus (Evening Grosbeak) **A,E**
C. abeillei (Hooded Grosbeak) **E**
PYRRHOPLECTES
P. epauletta (Gold-headed Finch) **H,I**
DREPANIDINAE (HAWAIIAN FINCHES)
TELESPYZA
T. cantans (Laysan Finch) **P** ?
T. ultima (Nihoa Finch) **P** ?
PSITTIROSTRA
P. psittacea (Ou) **P** E
LOXIOIDES
L. bailleui (Palila) **P** E
PSEUDONESTOR
P. xanthophrys (Maui Parrotbill) **P** V
HEMIGNATHUS
H. virens (Amakihi) **P**
H. parvus (Anianiau) **P**
H. obscurus (Akialoa) **P**
H. lucidus (Nukupuu) **P** E
H. munroi (Akiapolaau) **P** E
OREOMYSTIS
O. bairdi (Kauai Creeper) **P** ?
O. mana (Hawaii Creeper) **P** ?
PAROREOMYZA
P. montana (Maui Creeper) **P** ?
P. flammea (Molokai Creeper) **P**
P. maculata (Oahu Creeper) **P** ?
LOXOPS
L. coccineus (Akepa) **P** ?
VESTIARIA
V. coccinea (Iiwi) **P**
PALMERIA
P. dolei (Akohekohe) **P**
HIMATIONE
H. sanguinea (Apapane) **P**

MELAMPROSOPS
M. phaeosoma (Po'ouli) **p**
163 ESTRILDIDAE (WAXBILLS)
PARMOPTILA
P. woodhousei (Flowerpecker Weaver Finch) **C**
P. jamesoni (Red-fronted Flowerpecker Weaver Finch) **C**
NIGRITA
N. fusconota (White-breasted Negro Finch) **C**
N. bicolor (Chestnut-breasted Negro Finch) **C**
N. luteifrons (Pale-fronted Negro Finch) **C**
N. canicapilla (Gray-crowned Negro Finch) **C**
NESOCHARIS
N. shelleyi (Fernando Po Olive-back) **C**
N. ansorgei (White-collared Olive-back) **C**
N. capistrata (Gray-headed Olive-back) **C**
PYTILIA
P. phoenicoptera (Crimson-winged Pytilia) **C**
P. hypogrammica (Red-faced Pytilia) **C**
P. afra (Orange-winged Pytilia) **C**
P. melba (Green-winged Pytilia) **C**
MANDINGOA
M. nitidula (Green-backed Twin-spot) **C**
CRYPTOSPIZA
C. reichenovii (Red-faced Crimson-wing) **C**
C. salvadorii (Ethiopian Crimson-wing) **C**
C. jacksoni (Dusky Crimson-wing) **C**
C. shelleyi (Shelley's Crimson-wing) **C**
PYRENESTES
P. sanguineus (Crimson Seedcracker) **C**
P. ostrinus (Black-bellied Seedcracker) **C**
P. minor (Lesser Seedcracker) **C**
SPERMOPHAGA
S. poliogenys (Grant's Bluebill) **C**
S. haematina (Western Bluebill) **C**
S. ruficapilla (Red-headed Bluebill) **C**
CLYTOSPIZA
C. monteiri (Brown Twin-spot) **C**
HYPARGOS
H. margaritatus (Rosy Twin-spot) **C**
H. niveoguttatus (Peter's Twin-spot) **C**
EUSCHISTOSPIZA
E. dybowskii (Dybowski's Dusky Twin-spot) **C**
E. cinereovinacea (Dusky Twin-spot) **C**
LAGONOSTICTA
L. rara (Black-bellied Fire Finch) **C**
L. rufopicta (Bar-breasted Fire Finch) **C**
L. nitidula (Brown Fire Finch) **C**
L. senegala (Red-billed Fire Finch) **C**
L. virata (Kuli Koro Fire Finch) **C**
L. rubricata (African Fire Finch) **C**
L. landanae (Pale-billed Fire Finch) **C**
L. rhodopareia (Jameson's Fire Finch) **C**
L. larvata (Masked Fire Finch) **C**
L. vinacea (Vinaceous Fire Finch) **C**
URAEGINTHUS
U. angolensis (Cordon-bleu) **C**
U. bengalus (Red-cheeked Cordon-bleu) **C**
U. cyanocephala (Blue-capped Cordon-bleu) **C**
U. granatina (Common Grenadier) **C**
U. ianthinogaster (Purple Grenadier) **C**
ESTRILDA
E. caerulescens (Lavender Waxbill) **C**
E. perreini (Black-tailed Waxbill) **C**
E. thomensis (Cinderella Waxbill) **C**
E. melanotis (Swee Waxbill) **C**
E. quartinia (East African Swee Waxbill) **C**
E. poliopareia (Anambra Waxbill) **C**   ?
E. paludicola (Fawn-breasted Waxbill) **C**
E. melpoda (Orange-cheeked Waxbill) **C**
E. rhodopyga (Crimson-rumped Waxbill) **C**
E. rufibarba (Arabian Waxbill) **C**
E. troglodytes (Black-rumped Waxbill) **C**
E. astrild (Common Waxbill) **C**
E. nigriloris (Black-faced Waxbill) **C**   ?
E. nonnula (Black-crowned Waxbill) **C**
E. atricapilla (Black-headed Waxbill) **C**
E. erythronotos (Black-cheeked Waxbill) **C**
E. charmosyna (Red-rumped Waxbill) **C**
AMANDAVA
A. amandava (Red Munia) **H,I,J**
A. formosa (Green Munia) **H**
A. subflava (Zebra Waxbill) **C**
ORTYGOSPIZA
O. atricollis (African Quailfinch) **C**
O. gabonensis (Red-billed Quailfinch) **C**

O. locustella (Locust Finch) **C**
AEGINTHA
A. temporalis (Red-browed Waxbill) **M**
EMBLEMA
E. picta (Painted Finch) **M**
E. bella (Beautiful Firetail Finch) **M**
E. oculata (Red-eared Firetail Finch) **M**
E. guttata (Diamond Firetail Finch) **M**
OREOSTRUTHUS
O. fuliginosus (Crimson-sided Mountain Finch) **L**
NEOCHMIA
N. phaeton (Crimson Finch) **L,M**
N. ruficauda (Star Finch) **M**
POEPHILA
P. guttata (Zebra Finch) **K,M**
P. bichenovii (Double-barred Finch) **M**
P. personata (Masked Finch) **M**
P. acuticauda (Long-tailed Finch) **M**
P. cincta (Black-throated Finch) **M**
ERYTHRURA
E. hyperythra (Bamboo Parrot-Finch) **J,K,L**
E. prasina (Pin-tailed Parrot-Finch) **I,J**
E. viridifacies (Green-faced Parrot-Finch) **J**   ?
E. tricolor (Three-colored Parrot-Finch) **L**
E. coloria (Mount Katanglad Parrot-Finch) **J**   ?
E. trichroa (Blue-faced Parrot-Finch) **K,L,M,O**
E. papuana (Papuan Parrot-Finch) **L**
E. psittacea (Red-throated Parrot-Finch) **O**
E. pealii (Fiji Parrot-Finch) **O**
E. cyaneovirens (Red-headed Parrot-Finch) **O**
E. kleinschmidti (Pink-billed Parrot-Finch) **O**   R
CHLOEBIA
C. gouldiae (Gouldian Finch) **M**
AIDEMOSYNE
A. modesta (Plum-headed Finch) **M**
LEPIDOPYGIA
L. nana (Bib-Finch) **D**
LONCHURA
L. cantans (African Silverbill) **C**
L. malabarica (Indian Silverbill) **C,H**
L. griseicapilla (Gray-headed Silverbill) **C**
L. cucullata (Bronze Mannikin) **C**
L. bicolor (Black & White Mannikin) **C**
L. fringilloides (Magpie Mannikin) **C**
L. striata (White-backed Munia) **H,I,J,K**
L. leucogastroides (Javanese Mannikin) **J**
L. fuscans (Dusky Mannikin) **J**
L. molucca (Moluccan Mannikin) **K**
L. punctulata (Nutmeg Mannikin) **B,H,I,J,K**
L. kelaarti (Rufous-bellied Mannikin) **H**
L. leucogastra (White-headed Munia) **I,J**
L. tristissima (Streak-headed Mannikin) **L**
L. leucosticta (White-spotted Mannikin) **L**
L. quinticolor (Colored Finch) **J,K**
L. malacca (Chestnut Mannikin) **H,I,J,K**
L. maja (Pale-headed Mannikin) **I,J**
L. pallida (Pallid Finch) **K**
L. grandis (Great-billed Mannikin) **L**
L. vana (Arfak Mannikin) **L**
L. caniceps (Gray-headed Mannikin) **L**
L. nevermanni (White-crowned Mannikin) **L**
L. spectabilis (New Britain Mannikin) **L,O**
L. forbesi (New Ireland Finch) **O**
L. hunsteini (White-headed Finch) **O**
L. flaviprymna (Yellow-tailed Mannikin) **M**
L. castaneothorax (Chestnut-breasted Mannikin) **L,M**
L. stygia (Black Mannikin) **L**
L. teerinki (Grand Valley Mannikin) **L**
L. monticola (Alpine Mannikin) **L**
L. montana (Snow Mountain Mannikin) **L**
L. melaena (New Britain Finch) **O**
L. pectoralis (Pictorella Finch) **M**
PADDA
P. fuscata (Timor Dusky Sparrow) **K**   ?
P. oryzivora (Java Sparrow) **J,K**
AMADINA
A. erythrocephala (Paradise Sparrow) **C**
A. fasciata (Cut-throat Weaver) **C**
PHOLIDORNIS
P. rushiae (Tit-Hylia) **C**
164 PLOCEIDAE (WEAVERS AND RELATIVES)
VIDUINAE (PARASITIC VIDUINE WEAVERS, WYDAHS)
VIDUA
V. chalybeata (Village Indigobird) **C**
V. purpurascens (Dusky Indigobird) **C**

V. funerea (Variable Indigobird) **C**
V. wilsoni (Pale-winged Indigobird) **C**
V. hypocherina (Steel-blue Whydah) **C**
V. fischeri (Fischer's Whydah) **C**
V. regia (Shaft-tailed Whydah) **C**
V. macroura (Pin-tailed Whydah) **C**
V. paradisaea (Paradise Whydah) **C**
V. orientalis (Broad-tailed Paradise Whydah) **C**
BUBALORNITHINAE (BUFFALO WEAVERS)
BUBALORNIS
B. albirostris (White-billed Buffalo Weaver) **C**
B. niger (Red-billed Buffalo Weaver) **C**
DINEMELLIA
D. dinemelli (White-headed Buffalo Weaver) **C**
PLOCEINAE (TRUE WEAVERS)
AMBLYOSPIZA
A. albifrons (Grosbeak Weaver) **C**
PLOCEUS
P. baglafecht (Baglafecht Weaver) **C**
P. bannermani (Bannerman's Weaver) **C**   V
P. batesi (Bates's Weaver) **C**   R
P. nigrimentum (Black-chinned Weaver) **C**   R
P. bertrandi (Bertrand's Weaver) **C**
P. pelzelni (Slender-billed Weaver) **C**
P. subpersonatus (Loanga Slender-billed Weaver) **C** R
P. luteolus (Little Masked Weaver) **C**
P. ocularis (Spectacled Weaver) **C**
P. nigricollis (Black-necked Weaver) **C**
P. alienus (Strange Weaver) **C**
P. melanogaster (Black-billed Weaver) **C**
P. capensis (Cape Weaver) **C**
P. temporalis (Bocage's Weaver) **C**
P. subaureus (Golden Weaver) **C**
P. burnieri (Kilombero Weaver) **C**
P. xanthops (Holub's Golden Weaver) **C**
P. aurantius (Orange Weaver) **C**
P. heuglini (Heuglin's Masked Weaver) **C**
P. bojeri (Golden Palm Weaver) **C**
P. castaneiceps (Taveta Golden Weaver) **C**
P. princeps (Principe Golden Weaver) **C**
P. xanthopterus (Brown-throated Golden Weaver) **C**
P. castanops (Northern Brown-throated Weaver) **C**
P. galbula (Rüppell's Weaver) **C**
P. victoriae (Lake Victoria Weaver) **C**   R
P. taeniopterus (Northern Masked Weaver) **C**
P. intermedius (Lesser Masked Weaver) **C**
P. velatus (African Masked Weaver) **C**
P. ruweti (Lufira Masked Weaver) **C**   R
P. katangae (Katanga Masked Weaver) **C**
P. reichardi (Tanzanian Masked Weaver) **C**
P. vitellinus (Vitelline Masked Weaver) **C**
P. spekei (Speke's Weaver) **C**
P. spekeoides (Fox's Weaver) **C**
P. cucullatus (Village Weaver) **C**
P. nigriceps (Layard's Black-headed Weaver) **C**
P. grandis (Giant Weaver) **C**
P. nigrerrimus (Vieillot's Black Weaver) **C**
P. weynsi (Weyns's Weaver) **C**
P. golandi (Clarke's Weaver) **C**   E
P. dicrocephalus (Salvadori's Weaver) **C**
P. melanocephalus (Black-headed Weaver) **C**
P. jacksoni (Eastern Golden-backed Weaver) **C**
P. badius (Cinnamon Weaver) **C**
P. rubiginosus (Chestnut Weaver) **C**
P. aureonucha (Gold-naped Weaver) **C**   R
P. tricolor (Yellow-mantled Weaver) **C**
P. albinucha (Maxwell's Black Weaver) **C**
P. nelicourvi (Nelicourvi Weaver) **D**
P. hypoxanthus (Asian Golden Weaver) **I,J**
P. superciliosus (Compact Weaver) **C**
P. benghalensis (Bengal Weaver) **H,I**
P. manyar (Streaked Weaver) **H,I,J**
P. philippinus (Baya Weaver) **H,I,J**
P. megarhynchus (Finn's Weaver) **H**   ?
P. bicolor (Forest Weaver) **C**
P. preussi (Western Golden-backed Weaver) **C**
P. dorsomaculatus (Yellow-capped Weaver) **C**
P. olivaceiceps (Olive-headed Golden Weaver) **C**
P. nicolli (Usambara Weaver) **C**   R
P. insignis (Brown-capped Weaver) **C**
P. angolensis (Bar-winged Weaver) **C**
P. sanctaethomae (Sao Thomé Weaver) **C**
MALIMBUS
M. flavipes (Yellow-legged Malimbe) **C**   R
M. coronatus (Red-crowned Malimbe) **C**

M. cassini (Black-throated Malimbe) **C**
M. racheliae (Rachel's Malimbe) **C**
M. ballmani (Tai Malimbe) **C**   [I]
M. scutatus (Red-vented Malimbe) **C**
M. ibadanensis (Ibadan Malimbe) **C**   [E]
M. nitens (Gray's Malimbe) **C**
M. rubricollis (Red-headed Malimbe) **C**
M. erythrogaster (Red-bellied Malimbe) **C**
M. malimbicus (Crested Malimbe) **C**
ANAPLECTES
A. melanotis (Red-headed Weaver) **C**
QUELEA
Q. cardinalis (Cardinal Quelea) **C**
Q. erythrops (Red-headed Quelea) **C**
Q. quelea (Red-billed Quelea) **C**
FOUDIA
F. madagascariensis (Madagascan Red Fody) **D**
F. eminentissima (Mascarene Fody) **D**
F. omissa (Red Forest Fody) **D**
F. rubra (Mauritius Fody) **D**   [E]
F. sechellarum (Seychelles Fody) **D**   [E]
F. flavicans (Rodriguez Fody) **D**   [E]
F. sakalava (Sakalava Fody) **D**
BRACHYCOPE
B. anomala (Bob-tailed Weaver) **C**
EUPLECTES
E. afer (Golden Bishop) **C**
E. diademata (Fire-fronted Bishop) **C**
E. gierowii (Gierow's Bishop) **C**
E. nigroventris (Zanzibar Red Bishop) **C**
E. hordeacea (Red-crowned Bishop) **C**
E. orix (Red Bishop) **C**
E. aurea (Golden-backed Bishop) **C**
E. capensis (Yellow-rumped Bishop) **C**
E. axillaris (Fan-tailed Widowbird) **C**
E. macrourus (Yellow-mantled Widowbird) **C**
E. hartlaubi (Marsh Widowbird) **C**
E. psammocromius (Mountain Marsh Widowbird) **C**
E. albonotatus (White-winged Widowbird) **C**
E. ardens (Red-collared Widowbird) **C**
E. progne (Long-tailed Widowbird) **C**
E. jacksoni (Jackson's Widowbird) **C**
ANOMALOSPIZA
A. imberbis (Parasitic Weaver) **C**
PLOCEPASSERINAE (SPARROW-WEAVERS)
PLOCEPASSER
P. mahali (White-browed Sparrow-Weaver) **C**
P. superciliosus (Chestnut-crowned Sparrow-Weaver) **C**
P. donaldsoni (Donaldson-Smith's Sparrow-Weaver) **C**
P. rufoscapulatus (Chestnut-mantled Sparrow-Weaver) **C**
HISTURGOPS
H. ruficauda (Rufous-tailed Weaver) **C**
PSEUDONIGRITA
P. arnaudi (Gray-headed Social Weaver) **C**
P. cabanisi (Black-capped Social Weaver) **C**
PHILETAIRUS
P. socius (Sociable Weaver) **C**
SPOROPIPINAE (SCALY WEAVERS)
SPOROPIPES
S. squamifrons (Scaly Weaver) **C**
S. frontalis (Speckle-fronted Weaver) **C**
165 PASSERIDAE (PASSERINE FINCHES)
PASSER
P. ammodendri (Saxaul Sparrow) **B**
P. domesticus (House Sparrow) **A,B,C,H,I,M**
P. hispaniolensis (Spanish Sparrow) **B,H**
P. pyrrhonotus (Sind Jungle Sparrow) **B,H**
P. castanopterus (Somali Sparrow) **C**
P. rutilans (Cinnamon Sparrow) **B,H,I,J**
P. flaveolus (Pegu House Sparrow) **I**
P. moabiticus (Dead Sea Sparrow) **B**
P. motitensis (Great Sparrow) **C**
P. melanurus (Cape Sparrow) **C**
P. insularis (Socotra Sparrow) **C**
P. rufocinctus (Kenya Rufous Sparrow) **C**
P. griseus (Gray-headed Sparrow) **C**
P. swainsonii (Swainson's Sparrow) **C**
P. gongonensis (Parrot-billed Sparrow) **C**
P. suahelicus (Swahili Sparrow) **C**
P. simplex (Desert Sparrow) **B,C**
P. montanus (Eurasian Tree Sparrow) **B,H,I,J,K**
AURIPASSER
A. luteus (Golden Sparrow) **C**

SORELLA
S. eminibey (Chestnut Sparrow) **C**
PETRONIA
P. brachydactyla (Pale Rock Sparrow) **C**
P. xanthosterna (Yellow-spotted Rock Sparrow) **C,H**
P. petronia (Streaked Rock Sparrow) **B,H**
P. superciliaris (South African Rock Sparrow) **C**
P. dentata (Lesser Rock Sparrow) **C**
MONTIFRINGILLA
M. nivalis (White-winged Snow Finch) **B**
M. adamsi (Adams' Snow Finch) **B,H**
M. taczanowskii (Mandelli's Snow Finch) **H**
M. davidiana (Père David's Snow Finch) **B**
M. ruficollis (Red-necked Snow Finch) **B**
M. blanfordi (Blanford's Snow Finch) **B,H**
M. theresae (Meinertzhagen's Snow Finch) **B**
166 STURNIDAE (STARLINGS)
STURNINAE
APLONIS
A. zelandica (New Hebrides Starling) **O**
A. santovestris (Mountain Starling) **O**   [R]
A. pelzelni (Ponape Starling) **O**
A. atrifusca (Samoan Starling) **O**
A. cinerascens (Rarotonga Starling) **O**   [?]
A. tabuensis (Striped Starling) **O**
A. striata (Striated Starling) **O**
A. fusca (Norfolk I Starling) **O**
A. opaca (Micronesian Starling) **O**
A. cantoroides (Singing Starling) **L**
A. crassa (Tanimbar Starling) **L**
A. feadensis (Fead Is Starling) **L,O**
A. insularis (Rennell I Starling) **O**
A. dichroa (San Cristobal Starling) **O**
A. grandis (Large Glossy Starling) **O**
A. mysolensis (Moluccan Starling) **K,L**
A. magna (Long-tailed Starling) **L**
A. minor (Short-tailed Starling) **J,K**
A. panayensis (Philippine Glossy Starling) **H,I,J,K**
A. metallica (Shining Starling) **K,L,M**
A. mystacea (Grant's Starling) **L**
A. brunneicapilla (White-eyed Starling) **O**
POEOPTERA
P. kenricki (Kenrick's Starling) **C**
P. stuhlmanni (Stuhlmann's Starling) **C**
P. lugubris (Narrow-tailed Starling) **C**
GRAFISIA
G. torquata (White-collared Starling) **C**
ONYCHOGNATHUS
O. walleri (Waller's Red-winged Starling) **C**
O. nabouroup (Pale-winged Starling) **C**
O. morio (African Red-winged Starling) **C**
O. blythii (Somali Chestnut-winged Starling) **C**
O. frater (Socotra Chestnut-winged Starling) **C**
O. tristramii (Tristram's Starling) **B**
O. fulgidus (Chestnut-winged Starling) **C**
O. tenuirostris (Slender-billed Red-winged Starling) **C**
O. albirostris (White-billed Starling) **C**
O. salvadorii (Bristle-crowned Starling) **C**
LAMPROTORNIS
L. iris (Iris Glossy Starling) **C**
L. cupreocauda (Copper-tailed Glossy Starling) **C**
L. purpureiceps (Purple-headed Glossy Starling) **C**
L. corruscus (Black-bellied Glossy Starling) **C**
L. purpureus (Purple Glossy Starling) **C**
L. nitens (Red-shouldered Glossy Starling) **C**
L. chalcurus (Bronze-tailed Glossy Starling) **C**
L. chalybaeus (Greater Blue-eared Glossy Starling) **C**
L. chloropterus (Lesser Blue-eared Glossy Starling) **C**
L. acuticaudus (Sharp-tailed Glossy Starling) **C**
L. splendidus (Splendid Glossy Starling) **C**
L. ornatus (Principe Glossy Starling) **C**
L. australis (Burchell's Starling) **C**
L. mevesii (Meve's Starling) **C**
L. purpuropterus (Rüppell's Long-tailed Glossy Starling) **C**
L. caudatus (Long-tailed Glossy Starling) **C**
CINNYRICINCLUS
C. femoralis (Abbott's Starling) **C**   [?]
C. sharpii (Sharpe's Starling) **C**
C. leucogaster (Amethyst Starling) **C**
SPECULIPASTOR
S. bicolor (Magpie Starling) **C**
NEOCICHLA
N. gutturalis (White-winged Starling) **C**

SPREO
S. fischeri (Fischer's Starling) **C**
S. bicolor (Pied Starling) **C**
S. albicapillus (White-crowned Starling) **C**
S. superbus (Superb Starling) **C**
S. pulcher (Chestnut-bellied Starling) **C**
S. hildebrandti (Hildebrandt's Starling) **C**
S. shelleyi (Shelley's Starling) **C**
COSMOPSARUS
C. regius (Golden-breasted Starling) **C**
C. unicolor (Ashy Starling) **C**
SAROGLOSSA
S. aurata (Madagascar Starling) **D**
S. spiloptera (Spot-winged Starling) **H,I**
CREATOPHORA
C. cinerea (Wattled Starling) **C**
STURNUS
S. senex (Ceylon White-headed Starling) **H**   [?]
S. malabaricus (Ashy-headed Starling) **H,I**
S. erythropygius (White-headed Starling) **I**
S. pagodarum (Black-headed Starling) **B,H**
S. sericeus (Silky Starling) **B**
S. philippensis (Violet-backed Starling) **B,J,K**
S. sturninus (Daurian Starling) **I,J,K,L**
S. roseus (Rose-colored Starling) **B,H**
S. vulgaris (European Starling) **B,H**
S. unicolor (Spotless Starling) **B**
S. cineraceus (Gray Starling) **B**
S. contra (Asian Pied Starling) **H,I,J**
S. nigricollis (Black-collared Starling) **I,J**
S. burmannicus (Jerdon's Starling) **I**
S. melanopterus (Black-winged Starling) **J**
S. sinensis (Chinese Starling) **I,J**
LEUCOPSAR
L. rothschildi (Rothschild's Mynah) **J**   [E]
ACRIDOTHERES
A. tristis (Common Mynah) **B,C,H,I,J,K**
A. ginginianus (Bank Mynah) **H**
A. fuscus (Indian Jungle Mynah) **H,I,J,K**
A. grandis (Great Mynah) **H,I**
A. albocinctus (White-collared Mynah) **B,H**
A. cristatellus (Chinese Jungle Mynah) **B,I,J**
AMPELICEPS
A. coronatus (Gold-crested Mynah) **H,I**
MINO
M. anais (Golden-breasted Mynah) **L**
M. dumontii (Yellow-faced Mynah) **K,L,O**
BASILORNIS
B. celebensis (Sulawesi King Starling) **K**
B. galeatus (Greater King Starling) **K**
B. corythaix (Seram King Starling) **K**
B. miranda (Mount Apo King Starling) **J**
STREPTOCITTA
S. albicollis (White-necked Mynah) **K**
S. albertinae (Bare-eyed Mynah) **K**
SARCOPS
S. calvus (Bald Starling) **J**
GRACULA
G. ptilogenys (Ceylon Grackle) **H**
G. religiosa (Hill Mynah) **H,I,J,K**
ENODES
E. erythrophris (Fiery-browed Enodes Starling) **K**
SCISSIROSTRUM
S. dubium (Grosbeak Starling) **K**
BUPHAGINAE
BUPHAGUS
B. africanus (Yellow-billed Oxpecker) **C**
B. erythrorhynchus (Red-billed Oxpecker) **C**
167 ORIOLIDAE (ORIOLES AND FIGBIRD)
ORIOLUS
O. szalayi (Brown Oriole) **L**
O. phaeochromus (Dusky Brown Oriole) **K**
O. forsteni (Gray-collared Oriole) **K**
O. bouroensis (Black-eared Oriole) **L**
O. melanotis (Olive Brown Oriole) **K**
O. sagittatus (Olive-backed Oriole) **L,M**
O. flavocinctus (Australian Yellow Oriole) **K,L,M**
O. xanthonotus (Dark-throated Oriole) **J**
O. albiloris (White-lored Oriole) **J**
O. isabellae (Isabella Oriole) **J**   [?]
O. oriolus (Golden Oriole) **B,H**
O. auratus (African Golden Oriole) **C**
O. chinensis (Black-naped Oriole) **H,I,J,K**
O. chlorocephalus (Green-headed Oriole) **C**
O. crassirostris (Sao Thomé Oriole) **C**
O. brachyrhynchus (Western Black-headed Oriole) **C**

O. monacha (Dark-headed Oriole) **C**
O. percivali (Montane Oriole) **C**
O. larvatus (African Black-headed Oriole) **C**
O. nigripennis (Black-winged Oriole) **C**
O. xanthornus (Asian Black-headed Oriole) **H,I,J**
O. hosii (Black Oriole) **J**
O. cruentus (Black & Crimson Oriole) **J**
O. traillii (Maroon Oriole) **H,I,J**
O. mellianus (Stresemann's Maroon Oriole) **B**   [?]
SPHECOTHERES
S. viridis (Figbird) **M,O**
168 DICRURIDAE (DRONGOS)
CHAETORHYNCHUS
C. papuensis (Papuan Mountain Drongo) **L**
DICRURUS
D. ludwigii (Square-tailed Drongo) **C**
D. atripennis (Shining Drongo) **C**
D. adsimilis (Fork-tailed Drongo) **C**
D. fuscipennis (Comoro Drongo) **D**   [R]
D. aldabranus (Aldabra Drongo) **D**
D. forficatus (Crested Drongo) **D**
D. waldenii (Mayotte Drongo) **D**   [R]
D. macrocercus (Black Drongo) **B,H,I,J**
D. leucophaeus (Ashy Drongo) **B,H,I,J**
D. caerulescens (White-bellied Drongo) **H**
D. annectans (Crow-billed Drongo) **H,I**
D. aeneus (Bronzed Drongo) **H,I,J**
D. remifer (Lesser Racket-tailed Drongo) **H,I,J**
D. balicassius (Balicassio Drongo) **J**
D. bracteatus (Spangled Drongo) **J,K,L,O**
D. megarhynchus (New Ireland Drongo) **O**
D. densus (Wallacean Drongo) **J,K,L**
D. sumatranus (Sumatran Drongo) **J**
D. hottentottus (Hair-crested Drongo) **H,I,J,K**
D. andamanensis (Andaman Drongo) **I**
D. paradiseus (Greater Racket-tailed Drongo) **H,I,J**
169 CALLAEIDAE (NEW WATTLEBIRDS)
CALLAEAS
C. cinerea (Kokako) **N**   [E]
CREADION
C. carunculatus (Saddleback) **N**   [?]
170 GRALLINIDAE (MAGPIE-LARKS)
GRALLININAE
GRALLINA
G. cyanoleuca (Magpie-Lark) **M**
G. bruijni (Torrent-Lark) **L**
171 CORCORACIDAE (AUSTRALIAN MUD-NESTERS)
CORCORAX
C. melanorhamphos (White-winged Chough) **M**
STRUTHIDEA
S. cinerea (Apostlebird) **M**
172 ARTAMIDAE (WOODSWALLOWS)
ARTAMUS
A. fuscus (Ashy Woodswallow) **H**
A. leucorhynchus (White-breasted Woodswallow) **J,K,L,M**
A. monachus (White-backed Woodswallow) **K**
A. maximus (Papuan Woodswallow) **L**
A. insignis (Bismarck Woodswallow) **O**
A. personatus (Masked Woodswallow) **M**
A. superciliosus (White-browed Woodswallow) **M**
A. cinereus (Black-faced Woodswallow) **K,M**
A. cyanopterus (Dusky Woodswallow) **M**
A. minor (Little Woodswallow) **M**
173 CRACTICIDAE (BELL MAGPIES)
CRACTICUS
C. mentalis (Black-backed Butcherbird) **L,M**
C. torquatus (Gray Butcherbird) **M**
C. nigrogularis (Black-throated Butcherbird) **M**
C. cassicus (Black-headed Butcherbird) **L**
C. louisiadensis (White-rumped Butcherbird) **L**   [?]
C. quoyi (Black Butcherbird) **K,L,M**
GYMNORHINA
G. tibicen (Australian Magpie) **L,M**
STREPERA
S. graculina (Pied Currawong) **M**
S. fuliginosa (Black Currawong) **M**
S. versicolor (Gray Currawong) **M**
174 PTILONORHYNCHIDAE (BOWERBIRDS)
AILUROEDUS
A. buccoides (White-eared Catbird) **L**
A. crassirostris (Green Catbird) **M**
A. melanotis (Spotted Catbird) **L,M**
SCENOPOEETES
S. dentirostris (Tooth-billed Catbird) **M**

ARCHBOLDIA
A. papuensis (Archbold's Bowerbird) **L**
AMBLYORNIS
A. inornatus (Vogelkop Gardener Bowerbird) **L**
A. macgregoriae (Macgregor's Gardener Bowerbird) **L**
A. subularis (Striped Gardener Bowerbird) **L**
A. flavifrons (Yellow-fronted Gardener Bowerbird) **L**
PRIONODURA
P. newtoniana (Golden Bowerbird) **M**
SERICULUS
S. aureus (Flamed Bowerbird) **L**
S. bakeri (Adelbert Bowerbird) **L**   [?]
S. chrysocephalus (Regent Bowerbird) **M**
PTILONORHYNCHUS
P. violaceus (Satin Bowerbird) **M**
CHLAMYDERA
C. maculata (Spotted Bowerbird) **M**
C. nuchalis (Great Gray Bowerbird) **M**
C. lauterbachi (Lauterbach's Bowerbird) **L**
C. cerviniventris (Fawn-breasted Bowerbird) **L,M**
175 PARADISAEIDAE (BIRDS OF PARADISE)
CNEMOPHILINAE
LORIA
L. loriae (Loria's Bird of Paradise) **L**
LOBOPARADISEA
L. sericea (Wattle-billed Bird of Paradise) **L**
CNEMOPHILUS
C. macgregorii (Sickle-crested Bird of Paradise) **L**
PARADISAEINAE
MACGREGORIA
M. pulchra (Macgregor's Bird of Paradise) **L**   [?]
LYCOCORAX
L. pyrrhopterus (Paradise Crow) **L**
MANUCODIA
M. ater (Glossy-mantled Manucode) **L**
M. jobiensis (Jobi Manucode) **L**
M. chalybatus (Crinkle-collared Manucode) **L**
M. comrii (Curl-crested Manucode) **L**
M. keraudrenii (Trumpet Manucode) **K,L,M**
PTILORIS
P. paradiseus (Paradise Riflebird) **M**
P. victoriae (Victoria's Riflebird) **M**
P. magnificus (Magnificent Riflebird) **L,M**
SEMIOPTERA
S. wallacei (Wallace's Standardwing) **K**   [?]
SELEUCIDIS
S. melanoleuca (Twelve-wired Bird of Paradise) **L**
PARADIGALLA
P. carunculata (Long-tailed Paradigalla) **L**   [?]
P. brevicauda (Short-tailed Paradigalla) **L**
DREPANORNIS
D. albertisii (Black-billed Sicklebill) **L**
D. bruijnii (Pale-billed Sicklebill) **L**
EPIMACHUS
E. fastosus (Black Sicklebill) **L**   [?]
E. meyeri (Brown Sicklebill) **L**   [?]
ASTRAPIA
A. nigra (Arfak Bird of Paradise) **L**
A. splendidissima (Splendid Bird of Paradise) **L**
A. mayeri (Ribbon-tailed Bird of Paradise) **L**   [?]
A. stephaniae (Princess Stephanie's Bird of Paradise) **L**
A. rothschildi (Huon Bird of Paradise) **L**   [?]
LOPHORINA
L. superba (Superb Bird of Paradise) **L**
PAROTIA
P. sefilata (Arfak Parotia) **L**
P. carolae (Queen Carola's Parotia) **L**
P. lawesii (Lawes' Parotia) **L**
P. wahnesi (Wahnes' Parotia) **L**   [?]
PTERIDOPHORA
P. alberti (King of Saxony Bird of Paradise) **L**
CICINNURUS
C. regius (King Bird of Paradise) **K,L**
DIPHYLLODES
D. magnificus (Magnificent Bird of Paradise) **L**
D. respublica (Wilson's Bird of Paradise) **K,L**
PARADISAEA
P. apoda (Greater Bird of Paradise) **K,L**
P. raggiana (Raggiana Bird of Paradise) **L**
P. minor (Lesser Bird of Paradise) **L**
P. decora (Goldie's Bird of Paradise) **L**   [?]
P. rubra (Red Bird of Paradise) **K,L**
P. guilielmi (Emperor of Germany Bird of Paradise) **L**   [?]

P. rudolphi (Blue Bird of Paradise) **L**   [?]
176 CORVIDAE (CROWS, JAYS)
PLATYLOPHUS
P. galericulatus (Crested Shrike-Jay) **I,J**
PLATYSMURUS
P. leucopterus (White-winged Magpie) **J**
GYMNORHINUS
G. cyanocephala (Pinyon Jay) **A**
CYANOCITTA
C. cristata (Blue Jay) **A**
C. stelleri (Steller's Jay) **A,E**
APHELOCOMA
A. coerulescens (Scrub Jay) **A,E**
A. ultramarina (Gray-breasted Jay) **A,E**
A. unicolor (Unicolored Jay) **E**
CYANOLYCA
C. viridicyana (White-collared Jay) **F**
C. armillata (Collared Jay) **F**
C. turcosa (Turquoise Jay) **F**
C. pulchra (Beautiful Jay) **F**   [?]
C. cucullata (Azure-hooded Jay) **E**
C. pumilo (Black-throated Jay) **E**
C. nana (Dwarf Jay) **E**   [?]
C. mirabilis (White-throated Jay) **E**   [?]
C. argentigula (Silvery-throated Jay) **E**
CISSILOPHA
C. melanocyanea (Bushy-crested Jay) **E**
C. sanblasiana (San Blas Jay) **E**
C. yucatanica (Yucatan Jay) **E**
C. beecheii (Purplish-backed Jay) **E**
CYANOCORAX
C. caeruleus (Azure Jay) **F**   [?]
C. cyanomelas (Purplish Jay) **F**
C. violaceus (Violaceous Jay) **F**
C. cristatellus (Curl-crested Jay) **F**
C. heilprini (Azure-naped Jay) **F**
C. cayanus (Cayenne Jay) **F**
C. affinis (Black-chested Jay) **E,F**
C. chrysops (Plush-crested Jay) **F**
C. cyanopogon (White-naped Jay) **F**
C. mystacalis (White-tailed Jay) **F**
C. dickeyi (Tufted Jay) **E**
C. yncas (Green Jay) **E,F**
PSILORHINUS
P. morio (Brown Jay) **E**
CALOCITTA
C. formosa (White-throated Magpie-Jay) **E**
C. colliei (Collie's Magpie-Jay) **E**
GARRULUS
G. glandarius (Eurasian Jay) **B,H,I,J**
G. lanceolatus (Lanceolated Jay) **H**
G. lidthi (Purple Jay) **B**
PERISOREUS
P. canadensis (Gray Jay) **A**
P. infaustus (Siberian Jay) **B**
P. internigrans (Szechwan Gray Jay) **B**   [?]
UROCISSA
U. ornata (Ceylon Blue Magpie) **H**   [?]
U. caerulea (Formosan Blue Magpie) **J**
U. flavirostris (Yellow-billed Blue Magpie) **H,I**
U. erythrorhyncha (Red-billed Blue Magpie) **B,H,I**
U. whiteheadi (White-winged Magpie) **I**
CISSA
C. chinensis (Green Magpie) **H,I,J**
C. hypoleuca (Eastern Green Magpie) **I**
C. thalassina (Short-tailed Green Magpie) **J**
CYANOPICA
C. cyana (Azure-winged Magpie) **B**
DENDROCITTA
D. vagabunda (Indian Tree Pie) **H,I**
D. occipitalis (Malaysian Tree Pie) **J**
D. formosae (Himalayan Tree Pie) **H,I,J**
D. leucogastra (Southern Tree Pie) **H**
D. frontalis (Black-browed Tree Pie) **H,I**
D. bayleyi (Andaman Tree Pie) **I**
CRYPSIRINA
C. temia (Black Racket-tailed Tree Pie) **I,J**
C. cucullata (Hooded Racket-tailed Tree Pie) **I**   [?]
TEMNURUS
T. temnurus (Notch-tailed Tree Pie) **I**
PICA
P. pica (Black-billed Magpie) **A,B,H,I**
P. nuttalli (Yellow-billed Magpie) **A**
ZAVATTARIORNIS
Z. stresemanni (Stresemann's Bush Crow) **C**   [R]

LIST OF CONTRIBUTORS

PODOCES
P. hendersoni (Henderson's Ground Jay) **B**
P. biddulphi (Biddulph's Ground Jay) **B**
P. panderi (Pander's Ground Jay) **B**
P. pleskei (Pleske's Ground Jay) **B**
PSEUDOPODOCES
P. humilis (Hume's Ground Chough) **B**
NUCIFRAGA
N. columbiana (Clark's Nutcracker) **A**
N. caryocatactes (Spotted Nutcracker) **B,H,I,J**
PYRRHOCORAX
P. pyrrhocorax (Red-billed Chough) **B,H,I**
P. graculus (Alpine Chough) **B**
PTILOSTOMUS
P. afer (Piapiac) **C**
CORVUS
C. monedula (Western Jackdaw) **B,H**
C. dauuricus (Daurian Jackdaw) **B**
C. splendens (House Crow) **H,I,J**
C. moneduloides (New Caledonian Crow) **O**
C. unicolor (Banggai Crow) **K**   ?
C. enca (Slender-billed Crow) **J,K**
C. typicus (Piping Crow) **K**
C. florensis (Flores Crow) **J**   ?
C. kubaryi (Marianas Crow) **O**   E
C. validus (Moluccan Crow) **K**
C. woodfordi (White-billed Crow) **O**
C. fuscicapillus (Brown-headed Crow) **K,L**
C. tristis (Gray Crow) **K**
C. capensis (Black Crow) **C**
C. frugilegus (Rook) **B,H**
C. brachyrhynchos (American Crow) **A**
C. caurinus (Northwestern Crow) **A**
C. imparatus (Mexican Crow) **E**
C. sinaloae (Sinaloa Crow) **E**
C. ossifragus (Fish Crow) **A**
C. palmarum (Palm Crow) **E**
C. jamaicensis (Jamaican Crow) **E**
C. nasicus (Cuban Crow) **E**
C. leucognaphalus (White-necked Crow) **E**
C. corone (Carrion Crow) **B,H**
C. macrorhynchos (Jungle Crow) **B,H,I,J,K**
C. orru (Torresian Crow) **L,M,O**
C. bennetti (Little Crow) **M**
C. coronoides (Torresian Raven) **M**
C. tasmanicus (Forest Raven) **M**
C. mellori (Little Raven) **M**
C. torquatus (Collared Crow) **I**
C. albus (Pied Crow) **D**
C. hawaiiensis (Hawaiian Crow) **P**
C. cryptoleucus (Chihuahuan Raven) **A**
C. ruficollis (Brown-necked Raven) **B,C,H**
C. corax (Common Raven) **A,B,H**
C. rhipidurus (Fan-tailed Raven) **B**
C. albicollis (African White-necked Raven) **C**
C. crassirostris (Thick-billed Raven) **C**

ARTISTS
Norman Arlott: pages 1, 2–3, 162–63, 166–67, 170–71, 174–75, 198–99, 206–7, 210–11, 214–15, 218–19, 250–51, 306–7, 350–51, 354–55, 358–59, 362–63.
Dianne Breeze: pages 134–35, 138–39, 142–43.
Hilary Burn: pages 26–27, 226–27, 278–79, 282–83, 286–87.
Chris Christoforou: pages 86–87, 90–91, 94–95.
Robert Gillmor: pages 58–59, 62–63, 66–67, 70–71, 122–23, 150–51.
Tony Graham: page 18.
Peter Hayman: pages 46–47, 54–55, 126–27, 130–31, 186–87, 190–91, 194–95, 310–11.
Vana Haggerty: pages 24, 27, 29.
John Hutchinson: page 32.
Colin Newman: pages 10–11, 14–15.
Denys Ovenden: pages 2, 6–7, 42–43, 50–51, 110–11, 114–15, 118–19, 234–35, 238–39, 330–31, 334–35, 338–39, 342–43, 346–47.
David Quinn: pages 146–47, 202–3, 298–99, 302–3, 318–19, 322–23, 326–27.
Andrew Robinson: pages 154–55, 158–59.
Chris Rose: pages 4–5, 242–43, 246–47, 262–63, 266–67, 270–71, 314–15.
Ed Stuart: maps on pages 17, 22–23, 24–25, 26–27, 29, 30–31, 366.
David Thelwell: pages 222–23, 230–31, 254–55, 274–75.
Owen Williams: pages 74–75, 78–79, 82–83.
Ken Wood: pages 98–99, 102–3, 106–7.
Michael Woods: pages 8–9, 12–13, 17, 33, 178–79, 182–83, 258–59, 290–91, 294–95.

AUTHORS
Dr Jon C. Barlow, Curator of Ornithology, Royal Ontario Museum, Toronto, Canada.
Robert Burton, MA, MI Biol, natural history writer, Eltisley, Cambridgeshire, UK.
Mark Cocker, writer and conservationist, Norwich, Norfolk, UK.
Dr William E. Davis, Jr., Chairman and Professor, Division of Science and Mathematics, Boston University, Boston, Mass., USA.
Stephen Debus, Research Fellow in Zoology, University of New England, Armidale, NSW, Australia.
Jonathan Elphick, ornithological/natural history editor, author and consultant, Clapham, Exeter, Devon, UK.
Mike Everett, RSPB Press Officer, author, RSPB, Sandy, Bedfordshire, UK.
Dr Chris Feare, Head of Bird Pests & Farmland Conservation Branch, ADAS Central Science Laboratories, Worplesdon, Surrey, UK.
Dr Jim Flegg, Deputy Director, Institute of Horticultural Research, East Malling, Kent, UK.
Dr Hugh Ford, Australasian Consultant.
Clifford Frith, author, photographer and wildlife consultant, Townsville, Queensland, Australia.
Dr C. Hilary Fry, Professor of Biology, Sultan Qaboos University, Muscat, Oman.
Rosemarie Gnam, ornithologist, American Museum of Natural History, New York, USA.
Dr Llewellyn Grimes, Warwick, UK.
Dr David Hill, Director of Development, British Trust for Ornithology, Tring, Hertfordshire, UK.
Dr John Horsfall, formerly demonstrator at the Edward Grey Institute of Field Ornithology, Oxford, UK.

Anne Houtman, research student, Edward Grey Institute of Field Ornithology, Oxford, UK.
Rob Hume, ornithological editor, author, tour leader, artist, RSPB, Sandy, Bedfordshire, UK.
Dr George A. Hurst, Professor of Wildlife & Fisheries, Mississippi State University, Miss., USA.
Morton and Phyllis Isler, research associates, Smithsonian Institution, Washington, DC, and Museum of Natural Science, Louisiana State University, Baton Rouge, La., USA.
Dr Bette J. S. Jackson, Associate Professor of Biology, Mary Holmes College, West Point, Miss., USA.
Dr Jerome A. Jackson, US Consultant.
Dr Alan Kemp, Head Curator, Department of Birds, Transvaal Museum, Pretoria, Republic of South Africa, Chairman IUCN/ICBP Hornbill Specialist Group.
Dr Alan Knox, avian taxonomist, Buckinghamshire County Museum, Halton, Buckinghamshire, UK.
Dr John C. Kricher, author, Professor of Biology, Wheaton College, Norton, Mass., USA.
Dr David McFarland, ecologist, bird artist, Queensland National Parks & Wildlife Service, Brisbane, Queensland, Australia.
Dr Robert W. McFarlane, ornithological consultant and author, Houston, Tex., USA.
Dr Ian McLean, Senior Lecturer in Zoology, University of Canterbury, Christchurch, New Zealand.
Dr Carl D. Marti, Professor of Zoology, Weber State College, Ogden, Utah, USA.
Chris Mead, C Biol, MI Biol, author and broadcaster, Head of Bird Ringing Scheme, British Trust for Ornithology, Tring, Hertfordshire, UK.
Rick Morris, natural history editor, author, Twickenham, London, UK.
Dr Bryan Nelson, Hon Reader in Zoology, University of Aberdeen, Aberdeen, UK.
Nancy L. Newfield, ornithological consultant, author, lecturer and tour guide, Metairie, La., USA.
Dr Malcolm Ogilvie, author and wildlife consultant, Bruichladdich, Isle of Islay, UK.
Dr John P. O'Neill, ornithological author and artist, Museum of Zoology, Louisiana State University, Baton Rouge, La., USA.
Dr Christopher M. Perrins, Consultant-in-Chief.
Dr Richard O. Prum, Post-doctoral Fellow, Ornithology, American Museum of Natural History, New York, USA.
Eric Simms, DFC, MA, MBOU, ornithologist, broadcaster, wildlife sound recordist, author, South Witham, Lincolnshire, UK.
Dr Denis Summers-Smith, mechanical engineer and obsessional sparrow enthusiast, Guisborough, Cleveland, UK.
Judith A. Toups, ornithological consultant and author, Gulfport, Miss., USA.
Dr Juliet Vickery, Senior Research Associate, School of Biological Sciences, University of East Anglia, Norwich, UK.
Lori Willimont, wildlife biologist, US Fish & Wildlife Service, Charleston, S.C., USA.
Martin W. Woodcock, ornithological artist and author, Staplehurst, Kent, UK.
John Woodward, natural history editor and author, Brighton, East Sussex, UK.